American
Jewish
Year Book

The American Jewish Committee acknowledges with appreciation the foresight and wisdom of the founders of the Jewish Publication Society (of America) in the creation of the AMERICAN JEWISH YEAR BOOK in 1899, a work committed to providing a continuous record of developments in the U.S. and world Jewish communities. For over a century JPS has occupied a special place in American Jewish life, publishing and disseminating important, enduring works of scholarship and general interest on Jewish subjects.

The American Jewish Committee assumed responsibility for the compilation and editing of the YEAR BOOK in 1908. The Society served as its publisher until 1949; from 1950 through 1993, the Committee and the Society were co-publishers. In 1994 the Committee became the sole publisher of the YEAR BOOK.

American

Jewish

Year Book 2001

VOLUME 101

Editors
DAVID SINGER
LAWRENCE GROSSMAN

THE AMERICAN JEWISH COMMITTEE
NEW YORK

COPYRIGHT © 2001 BY THE AMERICAN JEWISH COMMITTEE

All rights reserved. No part of this book may be reproduced in any form without permission in writing from the publisher, except by a reviewer who may quote brief passages in a review to be printed in a magazine or newspaper.

ISBN 0-87495-116-x

Library of Congress Catalogue Number: 99-4040

PRINTED IN THE UNITED STATES OF AMERICA
BY MAPLE-VAIL BOOK MANUFACTURING GROUP, BINGHAMTON, N.Y.

Preface

With volume 101, which covers the events of the year 2000, the AMERICAN JEWISH YEAR BOOK begins its second century of publication. The first of three specially commissioned articles, Alvin H. Rosenfeld's "The Assault on Holocaust Memory" assesses the recent trend calling for an end to public focus on the Nazi destruction of European Jewry. Professor Rosenfeld shows that this school of thought has serious negative implications for world Jewry and the State of Israel. Dana Evan Kaplan's "The Jews of Cuba since the Castro Revolution" picks up the story of a Jewish community that has been absent from the pages of the YEAR BOOK since 1962, tracing the vicissitudes of the Cuban Jewish community since the revolution of 1959 and describing its current rebirth. "Contemporary Jewish Music in America," by Mark Kligman, is the first article on Jewish music ever to appear in the YEAR BOOK. Professor Kligman analyzes the recent fascination with new forms of Jewish music and shows its connection to the broader issue of the search for Jewish identity in contemporary America.

For Jews, 2000 was a year of momentous events, and all of them are covered in the YEAR BOOK's regular articles about Jewish life in the United States and other countries. Two were of particular importance. The breakdown of the Middle East peace talks and the Palestinian resort to violence are treated, in the YEAR BOOK, from the perspectives of Israel, American foreign policy, the American Jewish community, and other Jewish communities. A far happier event—the first major-party nomination of a Jew for vice president of the United States—receives coverage both for what it says about the role of Jews in American national politics and for what it demonstrates about Jewish perceptions of how "Jewish" a Jew in the public eye should be.

Updated estimates of Jewish population are provided for the United States and for the world. Carefully compiled directories of national Jewish organizations, periodicals, and federations and welfare funds, as well as obituaries and religious calendars, round out the 2001 AMERICAN JEWISH YEAR BOOK.

We gratefully acknowledge the indispensable role played by Denise Rowe, our administrative assistant, in preparing the directories and the index, and the assistance of our colleagues, Cyma M. Horowitz and Michele Anish, of the American Jewish Committee's Blaustein Library.

THE EDITORS

Contributors

HENRIETTE BOAS: Journalist; Amsterdam, Holland; deceased June 23, 2001.

SERGIO DELLAPERGOLA: Professor and head, Division of Jewish Demography and Statistics, Avraham Harman Institute of Contemporary Jewry, Hebrew University of Jerusalem, Israel.

RICHARD T. FOLTIN: Legislative director and counsel, Office of Government and International Affairs, American Jewish Committee.

ZVI GITELMAN: Professor, political science, and Preston R. Tisch Professor of Judaic Studies, University of Michigan.

MURRAY GORDON: Adjunct professor, Austrian Diplomatic Academy, Vienna, Austria.

LAWRENCE GROSSMAN: Editor, AMERICAN JEWISH YEAR BOOK; associate director of research, American Jewish Committee.

RUTH ELLEN GRUBER: European-based American journalist and author, specialist in contemporary Jewish affairs; Morre, Italy.

GEORGE E. GRUEN: Adjunct professor, international affairs, Middle East Institute and School of International and Public Affairs, Columbia University.

DANA EVAN KAPLAN: Oppenstein Brothers Assistant Professor of Judaic and Religious Studies, University of Missouri-Kansas City.

MARK KLIGMAN: Associate professor, Jewish musicology, Hebrew Union College-Jewish Institute of Religion, New York.

WENDY KLOKE: M.A. candidate, Humboldt University, Berlin.

LIONEL E. KOCHAN: Historian; Wolfson College, Oxford, England.

MIRIAM L. KOCHAN: Free-lance journalist and translator; Oxford, England.

ALVIN H. ROSENFELD: Professor, English, and director, Robert A. and Sandra S. Borns Jewish Studies Program, Indiana University.

COLIN L. RUBENSTEIN: Executive director, Australia/Israel and Jewish Affairs Council; honorary associate, Monash University, Melbourne, Australia.

JEFFREY SCHECKNER: Research consultant, United Jewish Communities; administrator, North American Jewish Data Bank, City University of New York.

JIM SCHWARTZ: Research director, United Jewish Communities; director, North American Jewish Data Bank, City University of New York.

MILTON SHAIN: Professor, Hebrew and Jewish studies, and director, Kaplan Centre for Jewish Studies and Research, University of Cape Town, South Africa.

HANAN SHER: Senior editor, *The Jerusalem Report;* Jerusalem, Israel.

BRIGITTE SION: Secretary general, CICAD, the Committee against anti-Semitism and Defamation; Geneva, Switzerland.

MEIR WAINTRATER: Editor in chief, *L'Arche,* the French Jewish monthly, Paris, France.

HAROLD M. WALLER: Professor, political science, McGill University; director, Canadian Centre for Jewish Community Studies, Montreal, Canada.

Contents

OTHER COUNTRIES

DIRECTORIES, LISTS, AND OBITUARIES

Special
Articles

The Assault on Holocaust Memory

By Alvin H. Rosenfeld

Jewish literature of the Holocaust is animated by the imperative to remember. Through the innumerable pages of the testimonial writings of those who endured the ghettos and camps of occupied Europe runs a passionate determination to record the Nazi crimes and transmit knowledge of them to others. These authors, for all the differences in their backgrounds and the diverse nature of their Jewish identification, issue one common appeal: know what has happened to us in these infernal places, and keep the memory of our fate alive.

To be sure, the inscription, transmission, and reception of historical memory are not simple matters. The work of the Holocaust deniers, whose manifest malevolence and dishonesty — as proven in Deborah Lipstadt's legal victory over David Irving in a British courtroom in 2000 — put them beyond the pale, should be less a cause for concern than the work of the critics of what is coming to be called, pejoratively, "Holocaust consciousness." These are writers who question not the facts but the prominence of the Holocaust in public consciousness and the motives of those who seek to perpetuate its memory.

Norman Finkelstein is a case in point. His book, *The Holocaust Industry,* published in 2000, indicts "The Holocaust" as an ideological representation of history that has been fraudulently devised and "sold" to the American public in order to revive a faltering Jewish identity and to "justify criminal policies of the Israeli state and U.S. support for these policies." Beyond these motives, Finkelstein charges, those who run the so-called "Holocaust industry" are embarked on a multibillion dollar scheme of extortion, and the major share of these funds goes not to the survivors but to those who exploit their suffering for personal and communal gain.[1] Finkelstein's book caused a stir in Europe, largely because of its harsh and inflammatory language. Yet for all its extremism, it represents little more than a new stage of a polemical engagement with the Holocaust that has been building over the years in the work of other writers, many of whom employ terms that resemble Finkelstein's. As a result,

---

[1]Norman G. Finkelstein, *The Holocaust Industry: Reflections on the Exploitation of Jewish Suffering* (London and New York, 2000), pp. 7–8.

Holocaust memory at the outset of the 21st century finds itself under mounting attack.

Like all traumatic memories, the memory of the Holocaust has long evoked ambivalent and even antithetical reactions. These reactions have often been intense, compounded, as they frequently are, by complex issues of national identity, political ideology, economic interests, religious passions, cultural loyalties, and more. Two prime examples, strange as the implied comparison may seem, are Germany and Israel.

Since 1945, contrary pulls within German culture have given rise to periodic, heated, and public debate among intellectuals and politicians about responsibility for the Nazi crimes against the Jews. As Jane Kramer has put it, the Germans are looking for ways to resolve "a duty to remember and a longing to forget,"[2] a goal that so far has eluded them. As long as this radical ambivalence persists, sharply divided debates about Germany's Nazi past are likely to continue. The most recent manifestation of this division came to the fore in the Walser-Bubis dispute. In October 1998, in his acceptance speech upon receiving the Frankfurt Peace Prize, author Martin Walser declared his doubts about the construction of a central Holocaust memorial in Berlin. Arguing that "public acts of conscience run the risk of becoming mere symbols," Walser called for an end to the "incessant presentation of our disgrace." In response, Ignatz Bubis, president of the Central Council of Jews in Germany, accused Walser of "spiritual arson." The debate took off from there and revealed some strong differences in German public opinion regarding memory of the Holocaust.[3]

A similar ambivalence, though from an altogether different historical perspective, can be observed in Israel. Israeli culture is marked, on the one hand, by highly ritualized forms of public memorialization of the victims and, on the other, by a desire to be relieved of the burdensome legacy of the European catastrophe. Thus Tom Segev, who has chronicled this emotionally charged story in *The Seventh Million: The Israelis and the Holocaust,* calls the Israelis' confrontation with the Holocaust a "great human drama of repression and recognition." And Segev is hardly alone in noting the deeply conflicted role that Holocaust memory plays in Israeli society.[4]

---

[2]Jane Kramer, *Politics of Memory: Looking for Germany in the New Germany* (New York, 1996), p. 258.

[3]For an incisive analysis of the Walser-Bubis controversy, see Amir Eshel, "Vom eigenen Gewissen: Die Walser-Bubis-Debatte und der Ort des Nationalsozialismus im Selbstbild der Bundesrepublik," *Deutsche Vierteljahrsschrift für Literaturwissenschaft und Geschichte* 74, June 2000, pp. 333–60.

[4]Tom Segev, *The Seventh Million: The Israelis and the Holocaust* (New York, 1993), p. 11.

Because the Shoah is such a significant fact of Israeli life and is also subject to manipulation and misuse, many have voiced disquiet over the prominence of the Holocaust in the public sphere and, on occasion, have even advocated something like suppression. In a controversial essay published in the Israeli daily *Ha'aretz* in 1988, Yehuda Elkana, at the time a prominent scholar at Tel Aviv University and himself a child survivor of the Holocaust, argued that his countrymen suffered from a surplus of memory and would do well to unburden themselves of the symbols, ceremonies, and purported lessons of their traumatic past. While it "may be important for the world at large to remember," Elkana wrote, "for our part, we must forget!" Indeed, Elkana was so convinced of the pernicious effects of Holocaust memory that he saw "no greater danger to the future of Israel" than the perpetuation of such memory, and he exhorted his country's leaders to uproot "the rule of historical remembrance . . . from our lives."[5]

Elkana wrote his article during the time of the first intifada, in protest against the "abnormal" behavior of Israeli soldiers towards Palestinians. Searching for ways to understand this behavior, he attributed the soldiers' actions to the negative effects of a Holocaust consciousness that pervaded Israeli society and perverted the morality of the young. In his view, Israelis harbored an exaggerated sense of themselves as victims, and this fearful self-image, itself the result of "wrong" lessons learned from the Holocaust, prevented them from seeing the Palestinians in a more realistic light and thus impeded a reasonable political solution to the Arab-Israeli conflict. Elkana's position was not representative of majority sentiment within Israel and provoked a good deal of criticism, but his "plea for forgetting" was endorsed by some prominent figures. As Amos Elon put it in an article of his own that ran along parallel lines, "our hope lies in the possibility that the vision of Yehuda Elkana will prevail" since, Elon believed, "a little forgetfulness might finally be in order."[6]

Elon entitled his article "The Politics of Memory," and he was surely right in pointing out the role politics play in the memorialization of the Holocaust. But if there is a politics of memory, so, too, is there a politics of forgetting, evading, suppressing, and denying. Both—memory and forgetting—are in contention whenever the Holocaust is prominently invoked, and both are affected by contemporary social realities and political concerns as much as they are shaped by serious reflection on the past. In Germany and Israel, many yearn for normalization, which argues for

---

[5]*Ha'aretz,* Mar. 16, 1988, quoted in Segev, *Seventh Million,* pp. 503–04.
[6]Amos Elon, "The Politics of Memory," *New York Review of Books,* Oct. 7, 1993, pp. 3–5.

one kind of response to the Nazi era, while others respond that the time is not yet ripe, a view that entails a very different response. When prominent German figures such as Martin Walser publicly declare that the time has come to begin to "look away" from the shaming images of the Nazi era, they strike a sympathetic chord among many Germans, just as they bring on protests from others, who insist that it is too early to draw a final line under the worst chapter of their nation's history. A similarly strong yearning for normalization exists within Israel as well, particularly among those who are convinced that an end to the conflict with the Arabs is being frustrated by the weight of the past.

In an essay published several years before Elkana's piece, Boas Evron argued that Holocaust memory was responsible for creating a "paranoid reaction" among Israelis and even a "moral blindness," which posed a real "danger to the nation" and could lead to an occurrence of "racist Nazi attitudes" within Israel itself.[7] In line with this view, Elkana worried that a Holocaust-induced image of the Jews as eternal victims might encourage Israelis to justify the cruelest behavior toward the Palestinians. Drawing parallels between the "excesses" committed by soldiers in the territories and "what happened in Germany," Elkana was concerned that his countrymen could end up mimicking the behavior of the worst of their enemies and thereby grant Hitler a "paradoxical and tragic victory."[8]

The evocation of Hitler in this context recalls some famous words of the philosopher Emil Fackenheim, but with a notable twist. Fackenheim exhorted Jews to remember the victims of Auschwitz, and thereby *not* hand Hitler a posthumous victory, while Elkana's exhortation to forget is based on the conviction that Hitler will prevail precisely if Jews continue to hold fast to the memory of the victims. What Fackenheim took to be the historical and moral imperatives of Holocaust memory, Elkana, Evron, and others have taken to be its dangers. There is simply no way to reconcile these two positions philosophically or to harmonize the different political understandings of present-day Jewish and Israeli life that derive from them.

In contrast to Germany and Israel, Holocaust memory in America had not been so passionately contested until recently. Indeed, since the 1960s, the Holocaust has come to public attention in ways that most people considered more salutary than not. But this consensus now finds itself em-

---

[7]Boas Evron, "The Holocaust: Learning the Wrong Lessons," *Journal of Palestine Studies* 10, Spring 1981, pp. 17, 19, 21. See also Evron, "Holocaust: The Uses of Disaster," *Radical America* 17, July/Aug. 1983, pp. 7–21; Evron, *Jewish State or Israeli Nation?* (Bloomington, 1995), pp. 250–53; and Israel Shahak, "The 'Historical Right' and the Other Holocaust," *Journal of Palestine Studies* 10, Spring 1981, pp. 27–34.

[8] Quoted in Segev, *Seventh Million*, p. 503.

battled and, in some instances, under outright attack. The issues on which the arguments typically turn have less to do with the Holocaust as a historical event than with accusations about the manipulative use of the Holocaust as an exaggerated element of contemporary Jewish identity. What is at stake in these increasingly bitter debates, in other words, is yet another version of the politics of memory, according to which American Jews allegedly use the moral advantages that are theirs as privileged "victims" to advance parochial aims and partisan political agendas. The "centering" of the Holocaust in Jewish consciousness and general public awareness, it is charged, not only distorts Jewish identity and deforms Jewish life, but also seriously injures others, whose own histories of persecution and suffering have been marginalized and all but forgotten as a consequence of the overwhelming emphasis that has been placed on Jewish suffering. As it has been advanced in America by a "substantial cadre of Holocaust-memory professionals"—the term is Peter Novick's[9]—Holocaust consciousness serves the purposes of Jewish self-aggrandizement and prevents other victimized peoples from receiving a proper share of public attention and sympathy. For these and related reasons, critics see it as their proper function to expose the "Holocaust industry" for what it is and thereby loosen the hold that Holocaust memory has had on the Jewish and general American imagination for too many years.

While these charges have become more overt and impassioned over the last decade or so, versions of them, in milder form, appeared in American Jewish journals as far back as the late 1970s and picked up steam in the 1980s. The complaints then had to do with what some thought was the disproportionate amount of money and attention being devoted to Holocaust-related matters, at the expense of other priorities. Rabbi Arnold Jacob Wolf was among the first to maintain that the Holocaust had become the very "center of Jewish self-consciousness" and "is being sold—it is not being taught." Wolf charged that the "Holocaust now overshadows all else." He complained that in New Haven, Connecticut, the Jewish community was spending "about ten times as much money on the Holocaust memorial as it does on all the college students" in the city.[10] Robert Alter, writing in *Commentary,* charged that a proliferation of college courses on the Holocaust was drawing on scarce academic resources that might better be spent helping students "find out what the Haskalah was, how a page of Talmud reads, or who Judah Hanasi might have

---

[9]Peter Novick, *The Holocaust in American Life* (Boston, 1999), p. 6.
[10]Arnold Jacob Wolf, "The Holocaust as Temptation," *Sh'ma,* Nov. 2, 1979, p. 162; Wolf, "The Centrality of the Holocaust is a Mistake," *National Jewish Monthly,* Oct. 1980, p. 8.

been."[11] Jacob Neusner bemoaned the fact that, as a result of their being so decidedly focused on the destruction of the Jews of Europe and the rebirth of Jewish life in Israel, Jews in this country were being kept from discovering America as their true Promised Land.[12] Others argued that an overemphasis on the Holocaust has returned Jews to a lachrymose sense of Jewish history, submerging more positive aspects of Jewish identity; that it has distanced Jews theologically from the promises inherent in the biblical Covenant and left them too little room for hope; or that it has provoked anger and resentment among other minority groups and impeded constructive dialogue and useful political alliances with them. These and other criticisms demonstrate that there never has been an absence of voices within the American Jewish community to oppose what some have called the Jewish "fixation" on the Holocaust.

Of late, though, these criticisms have become more expansive and have taken on a tone of disparagement and derision that seldom appeared in earlier years. Michael Goldberg, in his 1995 book, *Why Should Jews Survive?* decried the emergence of Holocaust consciousness as something that "mutilates Jewish self-understanding" and insisted that "the challenge to Jews today is not outliving Hitler and the Nazis but overcoming the life-threatening story created in their aftermath." The Holocaust, according to Goldberg, had become a "cult," with its own "tenets of faith, rites, and shrines," presided over by a "High Priest," Elie Wiesel. Goldberg criticized Wiesel for the cultic powers he allegedly wields, the lecture fees he demands, and his supposed failure to sensitize his followers to the sufferings of others, most especially the Palestinians, who were "beaten, tortured, and worse" during the intifada. So convinced was Goldberg of the pernicious effects of Holocaust consciousness that he concluded his book by stating that "Jews cannot long remain Jews while holding a Holocaust-shaped story" and "neither can humankind stay human. . . ."[13]

Goldberg, like Wolf, a rabbi, opposes the "Holocaust story" also on theological grounds. He believes that its negative impact subverts religious faith and, with it, the very ground of Jewish existence. Philip Lopate, a prominent essayist who refers to himself as a "secular, fallen Jew," has other reasons to oppose what he sees as an excessive Jewish preoccupation with the Holocaust. Writing in 1989, he declared the very term

---

[11]Robert Alter, "Deformations of the Holocaust," *Commentary,* Feb. 1981, p. 49.
[12]Jacob Neusner, "The Real Promised Land is America," *Washington Post,* Mar. 8, 1987, p. B1. See also Neusner's "Beyond Catastrophe, Before Redemption," *Reconstructionist,* Apr. 1980, pp. 7–12; *Stranger at Home: "The Holocaust," Zionism, and American Judaism* (Chicago, 1981); and elsewhere.
[13]Michael Goldberg, *Why Should Jews Survive? Looking Past the Holocaust toward a Jewish Future* (New York, 1995), pp. 5, 41, 59, 175.

"Holocaust" objectionable because it has a "self-important, strutting air." As a rhetorical figure, "the Holocaust is a bully," used by the "Holocaustians" as a "club to smash back their opponents." Those who insist on the term's exclusivity "diminish, if not demean, the mass slaughter of other people": "Is it not possible for us to have a little more compassion for the other victimized peoples of this century and not insist quite so much that our wounds bleed more fiercely?" Like Goldberg, Lopate is not shy in singling out Elie Wiesel as the one most responsible for this Jewish chauvinism. Wiesel, he says, heads up the Holocaust as if it were "a corporation." Lopate acknowledges that millions of Jews were murdered by the Nazis, but he knows that multitudes of Bengalis, East Timorese, and Ibos have also been murdered, and "when it comes to mass murder, I can see no difference between their casualties and ours." Finding no justification in Jewish "extermination pride," and having no taste for "tribal smugness," Lopate argues that the most authentic stance toward the Holocaust today is one of resistance. As he puts it, "just because someone has suffered a lot doesn't mean you have to like them [sic]."[14]

These critical voices must be understood against the development of Holocaust consciousness in America over time. For years after the end of World War II, Jews in America were unable or unwilling to face up to the horrors of what was not yet even called the "Holocaust." It was only in the 1960s, beginning with Israel's abduction and 1961 trial of Adolf Eichmann, and intensifying in June 1967, when the State of Israel seemed, like European Jewry a generation earlier, to be on the verge of destruction, that American Jews came to grips with the full significance of the Holocaust. Following Israel's victory in the Six-Day War of 1967 and continuing after the perilous situation that Israel faced in the 1973 Yom Kippur War, there was an outpouring of writing about the Holocaust, an exceptional effort by Jews to educate themselves and the public at large about the Nazi crimes. This was an important and legitimate goal, and it succeeded in bringing the Holocaust into the mainstream culture. That success, however, perhaps made it inevitable that Holocaust consciousness would become subjected to the compromises and abuses that come along with the popularization, commercialization, and politicization of history. Inevitable, though, does not mean desirable, and it is salutary that critical attention has been drawn to some of the more dubious ways in which the stories and images of the Holocaust have circulated in the public sphere.

Quite different, though, are the glib, caustic, and often mean-spirited

---

[14]Philip Lopate, "Resistance to the Holocaust," in David Rosenberg, ed., *Testimony: Contemporary Writers Make the Holocaust Personal* (New York, 1989), pp. 307, 287, 289, 300, 293, 299, 286. An earlier version of this essay appeared in *Tikkun* 4, May/June 1989, pp. 55–65, with critical replies from Yehuda Bauer and Deborah Lipstadt, pp. 65–70.

attitudes that some of these critics show towards those they accuse of "selling" the Holocaust or otherwise promoting it for pecuniary or parochial ends. Attacks against the "purveyors" of Holocaust consciousness often carry exaggerated claims about a Jewish "obsession" with the Holocaust, Jewish "hegemony" over news about mass suffering, the elevation of the Holocaust as American Jewry's substitute "religion," and the like.[15] Peter Novick, who has written the most comprehensive study of the development of Holocaust consciousness in America, names the United States Holocaust Memorial Museum as "the principal 'address' of American Jewry" and states that the Holocaust is now regarded by American Jews as "the emblematic Jewish experience."[16] Propelled by the power of American Jewish organizational skill, money, and media power, he charges, a virtual Holocaust juggernaut is sweeping away all other claims to Jewish identity, morality, and political sensitivity.

What is behind these charges is often a range of complaints about perceived failings in American Jewish life and in the broader American culture, for which the Holocaust is said to be responsible. Long before *Schindler's List* and the United States Holocaust Memorial Museum drew the attention of millions, Rabbi Wolf lamented that "one does not learn about God or the Midrash or Zionism nearly as carefully as one learns about the Holocaust," and that while Jews found the money to erect memorials to the victims of the Nazis, there were no memorials in America "to the pioneers of Israel or to the rabbis of the Talmud, or even to the patriarchs and matriarchs."[17] Similarly, Michael Goldberg charged that "virtually every Jewish community of any size is assured a turnout at its annual Holocaust observance that easily dwarfs synagogue attendance on Passover."[18]

Surely, however, Holocaust consciousness is here taken to be the cause of developments that have their origins elsewhere. Well before the Holocaust had overwhelmed the Jews of Europe, for instance, most American Jews had stopped going to the synagogue on Passover, stopped engaging in substantial religious study, and stopped caring about the rabbis of the Talmud, let alone the biblical patriarchs and matriarchs. It was not attendance at public gatherings commemorating the Holocaust that distanced American Jews from traditions of Jewish piety and learning but rather the transforming influences of Americanization and secularization.

Interestingly, just as the rabbis lament that attention to the Holocaust

---

[15]Tim Cole, *Selling the Holocaust: From Auschwitz to Schindler, How History Is Bought, Packaged, and Sold* (New York, 1999), p. 1.

[16]Novick, *Holocaust in American Life,* pp. 11, 10.

[17]Wolf, "The Centrality of the Holocaust is a Mistake," pp. 15–16.

[18]Goldberg, *Why Should Jews Survive?* p. 4.

is distracting American Jews from their religious duties, so avowed secularists like Peter Novick and Philip Lopate charge that too much Holocaust on the brain is eroding the social consciousness of American Jews and hardening their hearts to the sufferings of others. If, as Novick claims, American Jewry has turned "inward and rightward in recent decades," it is surely not owing to the "centering of the Holocaust in the minds of American Jews,"[19] a claim that Novick does not, indeed cannot, prove. Taking this line of thinking to another level of crudeness, Lopate contends that "the Jewish preoccupation with the Holocaust" has made American Jews "uncharitable, self-absorbed, self-righteous—and pushy."[20] Had he seen fit to add "venal," he would have rounded out the profile of the Ugly Jew in classic anti-Semitic fashion (Norman Finkelstein, in fact, has done exactly that through his brutal sketches of the opportunistic, money-grubbing Jew).

The Holocaust, in short, is supposed to be to blame for much of what ails American Jews. Traditionalists hold it responsible for distorting Judaism and replacing religious observance with a new civil religion that enshrines Jewish victimization, instead of God, at its core. And liberal-minded thinkers call it to account for narrowing the Jewish political vision and replacing an older, broader-based universalism with a chauvinistic particularism. The result, then, is that almost every deviation from what is held to be normative or desirable—the growing assimilation of American Jews, an alleged indifference to the pain and sufferings of other people, an apologetic attitude to what some regard to be Israeli "atrocities"—all of this, and more, is placed at the doorstep of those who have worked to perpetuate Holocaust memory.

To make matters even worse, one now commonly hears that Jewish Holocaust advocates are responsible, in no small measure, for what ails other groups as well. As proponents of a so-called radically ethnocentric view of history, "certain Jewish scholars and their acolytes" insist that the Holocaust is an unprecedented crime that bestows upon the Jews a preeminence of suffering.[21] This "cult" of "zealots" with "powerful friends in high places" has managed to win broad sympathy for the Jews through a "self-serving masquerade of Jewish genocide uniqueness," and anyone who raises questions about this "deception" is "immediately in danger of being labeled an anti-Semite." Nevertheless, writes one author unintimidated by this Jewish strategy, "not only is the essence of their argument demonstrably erroneous, the larger thesis that it fraudulently advances is

---

[19]Novick, *Holocaust in American Life,* p. 10.
[20]Lopate, "Resistance to the Holocaust," p. 307.
[21]David Stannard, "Preface," to Ward Churchill, *A Little Matter of Genocide: Holocaust and Denial in the Americas, 1492 to the Present* (San Francisco, 1997), p. xvii.

fundamentally racist and violence-provoking. At the same time, moreover, it willingly provides a screen behind which opportunistic governments today attempt to conceal their own past and ongoing genocidal actions." Among these governments, the worst is Israel, which has used the Holocaust as "justification for [its] territorial expansionism and suppression of the Palestinian people," a crime that for too long has gone unacknowledged, thanks to the "hegemonic product of many years of strenuous intellectual labor by a handful of Jewish scholars and writers. . . ."[22]

I have been quoting from David Stannard, a scholar of Native American history. His work, and that of others like him, raises the argument against Holocaust consciousness to a new polemical level, introducing a rhetoric of aggression against Jews that, until now, has rarely been encountered outside of anti-Semitic literature. This same note is forcefully sounded in Ward Churchill's *A Little Matter of Genocide: Holocaust and Denial in the Americas, 1492 to the Present.* A scholar of Native American history like Stannard, Churchill is convinced that too little attention has been paid to the fate of indigenous peoples in the "American Holocaust" because too much attention has been paid to the Jewish victims of the Nazi Holocaust. He charges that victims of other genocides have been virtually erased from history because a "substantial component of Zionism . . . contends . . . that no 'true' genocide has ever occurred other than the Holocaust suffered by the Jews. . . ." The politics of this militant chauvinism are clear for all to see: Jewish "exclusivism" serves to "compel permanent maintenance of the privileged political status of Israel, the Jewish state established on Arab land in 1947 as an act of international atonement for the Holocaust." It also seeks to "construct a conceptual screen behind which to hide the realities of Israel's ongoing genocide against the Palestinian population whose rights and property were usurped in its very creation."[23]

Both Stannard and Churchill accuse Jewish scholars of the Nazi Holocaust of "denying" other "holocausts." Stannard charges the "Jewish uniqueness advocates" with being the equivalent of Holocaust deniers, even claiming that they "almost invariably mimic exactly the same assertions laid out by the anti-Semitic historical revisionists."[24] Churchill denounces these scholars in similar terms: "The techniques used by pro-

---

[22]David Stannard, "Uniqueness as Denial: The Politics of Genocide Scholarship," in Alan S. Rosenbaum, ed., *Is the Holocaust Unique? Perspectives on Comparative Genocide* (Boulder, 1996), pp. 192, 198, 168, 167, 194, 167. On this question see Gavriel D. Rosenfeld, "The Politics of Uniqueness: Reflections on the Recent Polemical Turn in Holocaust and Genocide Scholarship," *Holocaust and Genocide Studies* 13, Spring 1999, pp. 28–61.

[23]Churchill, *Little Matter of Genocide,* pp. 7, 73–74.

[24]Stannard, "Uniqueness as Denial," p. 198.

ponents of Jewish exclusivism in presenting their doctrine of 'uniqueness' [are comparable] to those of the neo-Nazi revisionists." And he carries the accusation one step further: "The proponents of 'Jewish exclusivism' represent a proportionately greater and more insidious threat to understanding than do the Holocaust deniers," for in denying that other peoples have been the target of genocidal crimes, they have marginalized the sufferings of countless others and rendered them inconsequential. They have, he says, peddled a "mythology" about history that "dovetails perfectly with the institutionalized denials of genocide" put forth by numerous governments intent on seeing to it that their own "hidden holocausts" remain hidden. For the sheer invidiousness of their work, therefore, the Jewish scholars—Churchill names Steven Katz, Yehuda Bauer, Elie Wiesel, Lucy Dawidowicz, Leni Yahil, Yisrael Gutman, Michael Marrus, Deborah Lipstadt, and Martin Gilbert—are in a class by themselves: "Those who would deny the Holocaust, after all, focus their distortions upon one target. Those who deny all holocausts other than that of the Jews have the same effect upon many."[25]

Stannard and Churchill are clearly guilty of the same fallacy that mars the work of some of the Jewish critics referred to above. While it is true that the history of Native American peoples has been neglected over the years, the fault lies not with scholars of the European Holocaust but with generations of American historians and political leaders who, for their own reasons, have not focused on some shameful chapters of their own country's past. The omission is a serious one, but, chronologically, it long predates the Holocaust and therefore cannot reasonably be explained by pinning the blame on proponents of "Zionism" or "Jewish exclusivism." Castigating scholars of the Nazi Holocaust for neglecting the history of Native American suffering would be equivalent to charging scholars of Native American history of diverting attention from the immense sufferings of African slavery, the massacres of Armenians, or the murder of millions of Cambodians. Each of these histories has unique features, and those who write about them are justified in saying so. Nevertheless, Stannard and Churchill place blame specifically on the work of those scholars who have understood the Holocaust to have unique historical dimensions. In their view, "uniqueness" equals "denial" of others, and the "Jewish uniqueness advocates," in consciously aiding and abetting "the willful maintenance of public ignorance regarding the genocidal and racist horrors . . . that have been and are being perpetrated by many nations," are in "murderous complicity with both past and present genocidal regimes."[26]

---

[25]Churchill, *Little Matter of Genocide,* pp. 9, 50, 36.
[26]Stannard, "Uniqueness as Denial," pp. 198–99.

These are serious accusations, and they have moved well beyond the sphere of academic Native American studies. The charge is now commonly made that Jews use their own past history of suffering as a pretext to inflict suffering on others or to divert attention from the oppression of other peoples. The State of Israel is often singled out, an Israel whose image has been transformed into that of an aggressor state shielded by the protective cover of Holocaust memory. No less an establishment media figure than *New York Times* columnist Thomas Friedman wrote, during the first intifada, that "Israel today is becoming Yad Vashem with an air force."[27] At the same time, but in less colorful language, sociologist Zygmunt Bauman reiterated the notion of an aggressive Israel that manipulates Holocaust memory for self-serving ends: "The Jewish state [has] tried to employ the tragic memories [of the Holocaust] as the certificate of its political legitimacy, a safe conduct pass for its past and future policies, and above all as the advance payment for the injustices it might itself commit."[28] Bauman's words are favorably cited by Stannard, Churchill, Novick, Finkelstein, and others, for whom it is now a given that the Holocaust has been cynically used by the Jews, and especially by the Jewish state, as a matchless resource against its foes.

As it defines Holocaust memory as little more than a tool of Jewish empowerment, the political logic of this thinking is evident. In the name of Auschwitz, the Jewish state is said to be brutally oppressing another people. What is required to restore the Holocaust to its proper historical perspective and the Jews to their authentic ethical vocation is an "end to Auschwitz." This critique of Holocaust consciousness, in other words, links an appeal to disengage from the Holocaust with an appeal for Jews to disengage from the exercise of political power by disconnecting from the State of Israel.

No one has stated this as clearly as Marc Ellis, a Jewish theologian and professor of religion with strong pro-Palestinian sympathies. From his standpoint, "Jews are essentially a diaspora people" that does not require a state organization anyway. For them to live freely and ethically among the peoples of the world, the Jews should recognize the need for the "de-absolutization of Israel," which, he reasons, entails at the same time "de-absolutizing the Holocaust"[29]:

> *Auschwitz has become a burden to the Jewish future.* . . . To continue Auschwitz as a central overriding memory is in a sense to postpone . . . the explosive realities within our community as they relate to power and injustice. . . . Thus,

---

[27]Thomas Friedman, *From Beirut to Jerusalem* (New York, 1989), p. 281.

[28]Zygmunt Bauman, *Modernity and the Holocaust* (Ithaca, 1989), p. ix.

[29]Marc H. Ellis, *Beyond Innocence and Redemption: Confronting the Holocaust and Israeli Power* (San Francisco, 1990), p. 187.

to end Auschwitz is to admit that we are no longer innocent and that Israel is not our redemption. . . . "Ending Auschwitz" would also allow us, or perhaps even compel us, to think the unthinkable—that our future is bound up in an essential solidarity with those whom we have displaced, a solidarity with the Palestinian people. . . . The only way for the renewal of Palestine in the Jewish imagination to take hold is through ending Auschwitz; or, put another way, ending Auschwitz and the renewal of Palestine are bound together.[30]

The theological/political argument Ellis makes is predicated on the belief that "Auschwitz was in fact killing us as a people long after the crematoria were destroyed,"[31] and that in the name of Auschwitz, Jews have felt at liberty to humiliate, oppress, and kill another people. Avishai Margalit describes the same connection even more cynically: "Against the weapon of the Holocaust, the Palestinians are amateurs. . . . As soon as operation 'Holocaust Memory' is put into high gear, . . . the Palestinians cannot compete."[32] It is no doubt due to this perceived linkage of the Holocaust and the State of Israel that Palestinian schoolbooks and newspapers, as well as the media in Arab countries, are so intent on exposing the Holocaust as a "myth," and that the most passionate critics of Israel are so intent on deriding the "Holocaust industry" and putting an "end to Auschwitz."

Although the notion of a "Holocaust industry" has been popularized by Norman Finkelstein, Peter Novick—a much more serious scholar— employs roughly similar terms in *The Holocaust in American Life,* which appeared in 1999.[33] Through his repeated references to the work of well-placed Jewish influentials—including a "substantial cadre of Holocaust professionals," a "growing cadre of Holocaust professionals," Jews who "occupy strategic positions in the mass media" and who project images of the Holocaust "through the culture at large"—Novick comes close to positing a "Holocaust industry" in all but name. His book, which one reviewer has called "sharp, brusque, and sometimes nearly Swiftian in its acerbities,"[34] is a combination of carefully researched historical analysis and harsh political complaint. It provides a valuable exposition of the evolution of Holocaust consciousness in America, but also puts forward

---

[30]Marc H. Ellis, *Ending Auschwitz: The Future of Jewish and Christian Life* (Louisville, 1994), pp. 40, 42, 43.

[31]Ibid., p. 39.

[32]Avishai Margalit, "The Kitsch of Israel," *New York Review of Books,* Mar. 9, 2000, p. 19.

[33]Novick is on record as a critic of Finkelstein's work and has written a sharply negative review of *The Holocaust Industry;* see "A charge into darkness that sheds no light," *Jewish Chronicle* (London), July 28, 2000, p. 28. For Finkelstein on Novick, see *London Review of Books,* Jan. 6, 2000, p. 33.

[34]Eva Hoffman, "The Uses of Hell," *New York Review of Books,* Mar. 9, 2000, p. 19.

a polemical, quarrelsome, and cynical treatment of "American Jewish leaders," whom the author holds responsible for shaping the history of Jewish suffering to further parochial Jewish aims. Novick's book, in fact, is a determined critique of the politics of Holocaust memory, stresses many of the same themes found in the writings of Stannard, Churchill, and others, and foreshadows the later full-blown attack of Norman Finkelstein.[35]

Novick, who undervalues the Jewish historical tradition of memorializing national tragedies,[36] aims to expose Holocaust consciousness as a deliberate construct of American Jewish organizations and institutions. The leaders of these organizations, he says, recognized that Jewish identity in America was weakening. They focused on the Holocaust as "the one item in stock with consumer appeal" and set about shoring up flagging Jewish commitment by creating "a Holocaust-centered Jewish identity." In addition, they worked to spread Holocaust awareness to "mobilize support for a beleaguered Israel, pictured as being in a kind of pre-Holocaust danger." They were aided in these efforts, claims Novick, by a powerful Jewish presence among the "media and opinion-making elites"—the Jews who "play an important and influential role in Hollywood, the television industry, and the newspaper, magazine, and book publishing world." Through the dedicated work of these people—and Jews are "not just 'the people of the book,' but the people of the Hollywood film and the television mini-series, of the magazine article and the newspaper column, of the comic book and the academic symposium"—the Holocaust was repositioned from the margins to the very forefront of American consciousness. In addition, thanks to the efforts of certain powerful individuals of a traditionalist persuasion, such as Elie Wiesel and Irving Greenberg, the Holocaust underwent a "perverse sacralization" and emerged, for many American Jews, as something of a "mystery religion." In a culture that has come to valorize victims, Jews established primacy of place for the Holocaust and have reaped the benefits that come with such success. Not to be outdone in the high-stakes arena of "comparative atrocitology," the Jews now "possess the gold medal in the Victimization Olympics."[37]

Novick much prefers an earlier generation of American Jews with whom he more closely identifies, Jews who were integrationist and universalistic. He claims that it was "Holocaust consciousness" that "contributed to the erosion of that larger social consciousness" that was the

---

[35]Novick, *Holocaust in American Life*, pp. 6, 168, 208, 12.

[36]This has led one reviewer to the conclusion that Novick is "a stranger to the inner life of the Jews." David Roskies, "Group Memory," *Commentary*, Sept. 1999, p. 64.

[37]Novick, *Holocaust in American Life*, pp. 186–88, 269, 207, 12, 201, 110, 195.

"hallmark of the American Jewry of [his] youth—post-Holocaust but pre-Holocaust fixation."[38]

This negative note brings us, finally, to Norman Finkelstein. Drawing on the work of earlier critics of Holocaust consciousness—Novick, Arnold Jacob Wolf, Jacob Neusner, David Stannard, Boas Evron, and others—Finkelstein, in an earlier work, had already indicted "The Holocaust" as little more than "the Zionist account of the Nazi holocaust."[39] In *The Holocaust Industry,* he appreciates what he calls the "muckraking" quality of Novick's book and affirms Novick's view of Holocaust memory as "an ideological construct of vested interests," but argues that Novick does not carry his argument nearly far enough. Finkelstein deplores the "soft" categories that Novick employs—"'memory' is surely the most impoverished concept to come down the academic pike in a long time"—and prefers to think in terms of "power," "interests," and "ideology." In making the shift from the "bland" categories of cultural analysis to the more "robust" categories of political analysis, Finkelstein is convinced that he has discovered the real culprits—not just the Holocaust memory manipulators, but the Holocaust racketeers and extortionists. He has nothing but contempt for these people, whom he denounces as shakedown artists whose corrupt practices are "the main fomentor of anti-Semitism in Europe." It is they who run the Holocaust industry, and it is they whom Norman Finkelstein is determined to run out of business so that "those who perished . . . [can] finally rest in peace."[40]

In a gesture that is calculated to win him special sympathy, Finkelstein adopts the persona of the indignant son of Holocaust survivors. Though a fierce opponent of the "exploitation of Jewish suffering," Finkelstein exploits the fact that his father and mother had been in Hitler's camps and were the sole members of their family to survive. His book, he avers, is an attempt to "represent my parents' legacy," but whatever that legacy might be, the book is, more than anything else, a tirade against a nonexistent Judeo-Zionist conspiracy. But armed with the credentials of the son of his suffering parents, Finkelstein feels entitled to wage war on anyone and everyone who has dealt with the Holocaust in ways that he dislikes. With few exceptions, the works of other Holocaust scholars are dismissed as "worthless"—no more than "shelves upon shelves of shlock." The resources contributed to memorializing the Nazi genocide are also "worthless, a tribute not to Jewish suffering but to Jewish aggrandize-

---

[38]Ibid., p. 10.
[39]Norman G. Finkelstein and Ruth Bettina Birn, *A Nation on Trial: The Goldhagen Thesis and Historical Truth* (New York, 1998), p. 94.
[40]Finkelstein, *Holocaust Industry,* pp. 4, 5, 130, 150.

ment." As for Israel, "one of the world's most formidable military powers, with a horrendous human rights record," it has used the Holocaust as an "indispensable ideological weapon" to "cast itself as a 'victim' state," even as it continues its unconscionable abuse of the Palestinians. Finkelstein charges the "American ruling elites" who support the "criminal policies" of the Zionist state with complicity in Zionist crimes. Avaricious lawyers intent on bilking Swiss banks and German industrial corporations in the name of Holocaust survivors are excoriated for running a "restitution racket." In his view, many people who pass themselves off as Holocaust survivors often are not survivors at all, but masquerade as such to get money. Furthermore, the testimony of the true survivors is often suspect, and Elie Wiesel is contemptuously derided as the biggest fraud of all, guilty of a "shameful record of apologetics on behalf of Israel," and a "charlatan."[41]

These people—bogus Holocaust scholars, Zionist ideologues, Israeli aggressors, Jewish influence peddlers, phony survivors, and other assorted Jewish politicos and mercenaries—make up Finkelstein's "Holocaust industry," a corrupt, ruthlessly exploitative bunch that has used the Holocaust to acquire personal wealth and political power, and to gain immunity for those in the Zionist and American Jewish camps who are busy "lording it over those least able to defend themselves." Rising above the machinations of this morally bankrupt crowd is the figure of the author's mother, whom he cites more than once for her moral probity and worldly wisdom. Instead of exploiting Jewish suffering for selfish ends, Finkelstein writes, "the time is long past to open our hearts to the rest of humanity's sufferings. This was the main lesson my mother imparted. . . . In the face of the sufferings of African-Americans, Vietnamese and Palestinians, my mother's credo always was: We are all Holocaust victims." Or again: "If everyone who claims to be a survivor actually is one," my mother used to exclaim, "who[m] did Hitler kill?"[42]

One is tempted to set aside this book as so much sentimental drivel or bullying rant, but that would be a mistake. To be sure, while Finkelstein has not been taken seriously in the United States—the reviewer for the *New York Times Book Review*, for example, called his book "sad," "indecent," "juvenile, self-contradictory, arrogant and stupid," "irrational and insidious," among other things[43]—he has found an attentive audience in England, Germany, and elsewhere. His book, even before its translation into European languages, was widely discussed and, in some circles,

---

[41]Ibid., pp. 7, 55, 32, 8, 3, 7, 94, 82, 45, 4, 56.

[42]Ibid., pp. 38, 8, 81.

[43]Omer Bartov, "A Tale of Two Holocausts," *New York Times Book Review*, Aug. 6, 2000, p. 8.

lauded.[44] The notion that "we are all Holocaust victims" appeals to people who have had enough of the Jews and their sorrows. They do not like it that the Jews, and they alone, are singled out for special sympathy. In addition, Finkelstein's argument that crafty "Holocaust hucksters" are pumping up the numbers of survivors in order to cash in on Jewish suffering wins sympathy among those already inclined to see a predatory hand in the much-publicized Holocaust-related litigation.

Inevitably, the notion of an enterprising and manipulative "Holocaust industry" has found a willing audience among the worst of the Holocaust deniers. Though these people may not be his natural allies, Finkelstein, like them, has vilified Israel and "organized American Jewry" in relentless fashion and held "The Holocaust" up for scorn. Not surprisingly, extreme right-wing circles in Europe and the U.S. have been touting his book. Thoughtful people in Germany, in particular, worry that Finkelstein's fantasies will encourage the most dangerous elements in that country, who will find in the book ample confirmation of a Jewish conspiracy to exploit German historical guilt for selfish ends. In fact, as the alert reader will see, Finkelstein's "Holocaust industry" is as much an ideological construct as neo-Nazi constructions of a Holocaust-that-never-was. But for people who are weary of hearing about Hitler and the Jews, Finkelstein's impassioned "exposé" of an elaborate Holocaust extortion racket will be a welcome development long overdue. As one of his German reviewers has commented, reading *The Holocaust Industry* "is like opening a window for a sudden gust of fresh air."[45] The German translation's initial print run of 50,000 quickly sold out, and, for a time, the book topped the German best-seller list for nonfiction. In a poll taken by the prestigious Emnid Institute soon after the German translation appeared, 65 percent of Germans questioned agreed, either fully or partially, that Jewish organizations exaggerate Holocaust-related compensation claims in order to enrich themselves.[46]

Even under the best of conditions, Holocaust memory, like all historical memories, is bound to attenuate over time. Indeed, the very enormity of the Nazi crimes against the Jews makes it notoriously difficult for the mind to assimilate the horror, let alone to make any sense of it. One can hardly be confident, then, that public awareness of the Holocaust will be widely and responsibly maintained. It is no wonder that writers like Primo Levi, Jean Améry, and others, who reflected most deeply about the Nazi assault against the Jews, often came close to despair when they contem-

---

[44]Finkelstein has posted the laudatory reviews, and replies to the negative ones, on his Web site.

[45]Lorenz Jäger, "Necessary Hyperbole," *Frankfurter Allgemeine Zeitung,* Aug. 14, 2000.

[46]*Der Spiegel,* July 2000, p. 224.

plated the future of Holocaust memory, for they recognized how tenuous a thing such memory is.

However, even the best of these writers could not have foreseen the invidiousness that has come to accompany attacks on Holocaust consciousness, often delivered in a tone that amounts almost to mocking the dead. The popularization of the flippant expression, "There is no business like Shoah business," is symptomatic of the derisive attitude that is now so common, one that calls into question the value of *any* ongoing engagement with the Holocaust. Add to this belittling tendency an inclination to reduce the catastrophe to an ideological construct of vested interests, and the story of Jewish fate under Hitler suffers further devaluation. And the integrity of Holocaust memory is weakened still more by those who link their critique of Holocaust consciousness to a critique of Jewish "power," especially as such power is exercised in Israel. One would never know, from the work of Finkelstein and some other critics of Holocaust consciousness, that people might feel compelled to think about the Jewish catastrophe under Hitler for other, less cynical reasons. One would never suspect that there might be historical, religious, moral, or ethical claims on consciousness as legitimate prods to remember the Nazi crimes.

The accumulated force of the tendencies encouraging forgetting may, over time, bring about the "end of Auschwitz." But the result will be neither the return of the Jewish people to traditional religious practice nor to a higher ethical calling, but their return to the kind of vulnerability that preceded Auschwitz and helped bring it about.

The Jews of Cuba since the Castro Revolution

BY DANA EVAN KAPLAN

CUBA HAS BEEN ATTRACTING a great deal of attention recently. While the protracted custody battle over Elián González received the most publicity,[1] there have also been two cases of alleged spying, several high-level cultural exchanges, American trade missions, trials of Cuban dissidents, and even a series of baseball games between the Baltimore Orioles and a Cuban team.

From the Jewish standpoint as well, Cuba has become more important, as various American Jewish organizations send missions to visit the Cuban Jewish community, participate in religious and cultural activities, and provide essential food and medicine. Till soon after the revolution, the *American Jewish Year Book* published regular reports on the Jews of the country written by Abraham J. Dubelman. Dubelman's last report appeared in the 1962 volume, and, with the exception of a report on the Cuban Jews of Miami,[2] this is the first AJYB article on the topic since.

The Jewish community in Cuba today is but a small percentage of what it was before the revolution of 1959.[3] Then, among the more than six million Cubans, there were 10,000–16,500 Jews, with communities not only in Havana but also in Santa Clara, Camagüey, Santiago de Cuba, and

---

Note: The author thanks Jacob Kovadloff of the American Jewish Committee for his encouragement and assistance in the preparation of this article, and Dr. Margalit Bejarano, Dr. Moisés Asís, and Mr. Arturo López Levy for carefully reading and commenting on an early draft. He also thanks the many individuals in Cuba, the United States, Israel, Canada, and throughout the world who graciously answered questions, provided information, and gave constructive criticism.

[1] For a Jewish view on the case, see Dana Evan Kaplan, "The Aftermath of the Elián González Affair: A Jewish Perspective," *Congress Monthly* 67, Sept./Oct. 2000, pp. 12–15.

[2] Seymour B. Liebman, "Cuban Jewish Community In South Florida," AJYB 1969, vol. 70, pp 238–246. Caroline Bettinger-López has recently discussed this subject in *Cuban-Jewish Journeys: Searching for Identity, Home, and History in Miami* (Knoxville, Tenn., 2000).

[3] Robert M. Levine has written the standard work on the history of the Cuban Jewish community, *Tropical Diaspora: The Jewish Experience In Cuba* (Gainesville, Fla., 1993). Another important source is Margalit Bejarano, ed., *La Comunidad Hebrea De Cuba: La Memoria y la Historia* (Jerusalem, 1996), a collection of oral histories.

many other locations. The Jews of Havana[4] had five synagogues: Unión Hebrea Chevet Ahim,[5] the United Hebrew Congregation,[6] Adath Israel, Centro Sefaradi, and the Patronato, the largest, which had been built as a Jewish center in 1953 (its full name was Patronato de la Casa de la Comunidad Hebrea de Cuba). About 75 percent of the Jews in the country were Ashkenazi, the rest Sephardi.

Unlike the Catholics, the mainline Protestants, and the smaller religious groups such as the Jehovah's Witnesses, Gideon's Band, and Pentecostals, substantial numbers of whom remained in the country after the revolution, most of the Jewish community emigrated.[7] Those who remained, like the Christian religious groups, went into a "dormant state" enabling their community to survive in skeletal form under unfavorable political circumstances. Finally, with the fall of socialism in Eastern Europe, the catastrophic decline of the Cuban economy in the early 1990s, and the resulting government reforms, religious groups were able to come out of hibernation and rebuild their organizations. After years of using a combination of confrontation, defiance, silence, cooperation, and subterfuge, the various religious groups are now in a position to play a leading role in Cuban society and perhaps assist the country in moving away from socialism.[8]

Because of their small numbers, the Jews have been exceptionally careful to avoid antagonizing the government, and the government, for its own reasons, has been equally keen to avoid any action that might be perceived as anti-Jewish. Thus the Jewish community escaped the worst of the antireligious policies of the regime, particularly in the early decades of Communist rule. Nevertheless, in another respect the tiny Jewish community operated at a distinct disadvantage: Unlike the Christian groups, establishment or fringe, the Jews could not recruit freely from the general population. Nevertheless, a remarkable Jewish renaissance is under-

---

[4]On the Jews of Havana see Reinaldo Sanchez Porro, "Tradición y Modernidad: Los Judíos en La Habana," *Cuadernos de Historia Contemporánea* 18, 1996, pp. 175–189; and Maritza Corrales Capestany, "Comportamiento economico y espacial de los comercios e industrias judíos en La Habana: 1902–1959," in Judit Bokser de Liwerant and Alicia Gojman de Backal, eds., *Encuentro y Alteridad, Vida y cultura judía en America Latina* (Mexico City, 1999), pp. 500–527.

[5]Chevet Ahim is also spelled Chevet Achim, Shevet Ajim, or Shevet Ahim. The congregation was at Calle Inquisidor (Inquisitor Street!) número 407 in Old Havana. On the High Holy Days it met at Calle Prado número 557, a location also used for social functions.

[6]In Spanish, Congregación Hebrea Unida.

[7]Jehovah's Witnesses actively resisted the authority of the regime. As a consequence, many were jailed and the 1976 constitution specifically forbade their religious practices.

[8]Teresita Pedraza, " 'This Too Shall Pass': The Resistance and Endurance of Religion in Cuba," *Cuban Studies* (annual published by the University of Pittsburgh) 28, 1999, pp. 16–39.

way in Cuba.[9] To understand this phenomenon requires some background on Jewish life in the country during the Castro years.

The Cuban Revolution and The Jews

It is difficult for Americans to conceive of a Cuba without its charismatic and idiosyncratic leader Fidel Castro. He has held power for more than 40 years, after leading a revolutionary movement that overthrew the corrupt government of Fulgencio Batista y Zaldívar. Despite their small numbers and the enormous amount of military aid that the United States gave Batista, the revolutionary forces of Ché Guevara and Camilo Cienfuegos took control of Havana on New Year's Day, 1959. Most Cubans— including many Cuban Jews—greeted Castro's victory with tremendous enthusiasm. Cubans of all economic classes had suffered under Batista's rule and were disgusted by his excesses and corruption. Not only Batista, but the entire political system had been discredited; Castro and the other rebels had tremendous moral authority.

The majority of Jewish men were owners of small businesses, with about 15 percent owning large stores and wholesale enterprises. Others were professionals—engineers, physicians, managers, and so forth. Although many Jews, particularly among the Ashkenazim, had originally intended to pass through "Hotel Cuba" on their way to the United States, by the late 1950s nearly all who remained in Cuba had developed strong economic roots in the country. There was a small group of dedicated Jewish Communists, but since so much of the community owned businesses, Jews were identified as "capitalists." Their businesses were potential targets for confiscation, putting their middle-class lifestyle in jeopardy. But at that point nothing was for certain.

1959 was a time of both hope and uncertainty as Cubans waited to see how the new government would deal with many pressing issues. In July 1959, President Carlos Manuel Urrutia Lleo resigned, and over the next several months Castro, then the premier, appointed Communists to head most of the ministries. Communists also took control of the trade unions. While few Jews emigrated during 1959, they watched the unfolding political events with great trepidation, worried less about anti-Semitism than about the political and economic policies that the government might adopt.

In fact the revolutionaries displayed no signs of anti-Semitic sentiments; if anything, they seemed well-disposed toward Jews. Three of the

---

[9]Dana Evan Kaplan, "A Jewish Renaissance in Castro's Cuba," *Judaism* 49, Spring 2000, pp. 218–36.

ten original members of the Cuban Communist Party came from Jewish backgrounds. Fabio Grobart, who had arrived in Cuba with the name Abraham Simchowitz, remained an important Communist leader until his death many years later.[10] Among the younger generation, Manuel (Stolik) Novigrod, whose parents had been long-time Jewish Communists, fought with the revolutionaries in the Sierra Maestra Mountains and became a career diplomat under the Castro regime. A number of other Jews also served in the revolutionary government, most prominently Enrique Oltuski, the son of Jewish immigrants from Poland who arrived in Cuba after World War I. While studying in Miami, he watched the unfolding of the revolutionary struggle with a growing sense of guilt. "My conscience pricked me . . . my comrades were dying and fighting in Cuba, while I was living well in the United States. Every day, I used to say I had to go back to Cuba, so one day I got up and went."[11] Oltuski joined the struggle in 1955 and organized the 26th of July movement in the province of Las Villas. In 1959, at the age of 27, he was made minister of communications, staying in the cabinet even after the fall of President Urrutia, in itself a remarkable political accomplishment. Originally at odds with Ché Guevara, the two soon became quite close.[12] Despite a number of political setbacks he continued in government service, and today is deputy minister of fisheries. Other Jews became prominent as well, such as Dr. José Altschuler, president of the Comisión de Intercosmos de Cuba, responsible for overseeing the Cuban space program.[13]

Castro did not apply the same political pressure on the Jewish community that he did on the Catholic Church and most other Christian denominations. Unlike the Catholic Church, which had a vast organizational network that could conceivably have been used to develop an opposition movement, and unlike the other Christian groups, which had the potential to organize mass resistance among the populace, the tiny Jewish community was no threat whatsoever.

After the Revolution

During the course of 1959 it became increasingly clear that Castro's economic policies would ruin the middle class, but still, very few Jews emigrated. As late as December 1960, the leadership of the Patronato—the most important Jewish communal institution—was essentially the same

---

[10]Fabio Grobart, *Un Forjador Eternamente Joven* (Havana, 1985); Luis Suardíaz, "Tributo a Fabio Grobart," *Granma*, Oct. 23, 1991, p. 2.

[11]Paco Ignacio Taibo, *Guevara Also Known as Ché*, trans. Martin Michael Roberts (New York, 1997), p. 610. Taibo interviewed Oltuski in January 1995.

[12]Enrique Oltuski, "Que Puedo Decir?" *Recuerdos*, Jan./Feb. 1968, pp. 41–45.

[13]*Vuelo Especial Conjunto Urss-Cuba Victoria del Socialismo* (Havana, 1981), p. 45.

as before the revolution.[14] Herman Heisler remained president, Morris Konski, Dr. Enrique Eiber, and Herman Lipstein remained the three vice presidents, Isaac Gurwitz was the general secretary, and Abraham Marcus Matterín and Jaime Bloch were the vice secretaries. Dr. Bernardo Benes, later to become well known as emissary to Fidel Castro for Presidents Jimmy Carter and Ronald Reagan,[15] was the congregation's attorney. Moisés Baldás, who would take over as president the following year, was not yet on the board.

According to the teachings of the revolution, those who had developed businesses were guilty of profiting at the expense of the masses, and were therefore "enemies of the revolution." As businesses were confiscated during 1960 and 1961, more Jews left. In 1961, Israel and Cuba reached an agreement permitting Cuban Jews to go to Israel in return for shipments of goats and eggs; a good number of these Jews soon left Israel and went elsewhere. Many more Cuban Jews left directly for Miami, the center of Cuban exile life. Others stayed, hoping that the situation would stabilize or improve. By 1962 all such hopes were dashed, and many more Jews left as part of a massive exodus of hundreds of thousands of other middle- and upper-class Cubans. Those who remained were disproportionately elderly or ill.

The emigration process could be traumatic. Once a family applied for an exit visa, a Cuban governmental official would come and make an inventory of everything in the house. If the family was suspected of removing things from the home prior to the inspection, emigration could be delayed. A representative of the Hebrew Immigrant Aid Society (HIAS) reported on the situation in July 1961:

> It is disastrous—the rich have left, some having foreseen the situation, but these are few. . . . all assets [have been] taken over by the government, the militia, or other bandits who have simply taken over everything which our brothers have left behind after having worked for many years, sacrificing themselves to make their way. . . . Those who remain can do nothing; business is dying for lack of merchandise, and the large industries, as well as the small ones, are being nationalized. Owners are being watched strictly.[16]

By December 1961 at least 3,800 Jews had already left the country, with another thousand in the process of leaving. The previous month Castro

---

[14]*Comunitarias: Organo Oficial de la Casa de la Comunidad Hebrea de Cuba*, 1, Dec. 1960, p. 4.

[15]On Benes's negotiations with Castro in the late 1970s and 1980s, see the new work by Robert M. Levine, *Secret Missions to Cuba* (New York and London, 2001); Benes, "Perder la Revolucion," in Bejarano, ed., *La Comunidad Hebrea de Cuba*, pp. 242–44; and Meg Laughlin, "Bernardo's List," *Miami Herald*, Nov. 6, 1994, p. 2. For a Cuban governmental perspective, see Jesus Arboleya, *La Contrarrevolucion Cubana* (Havana, 1997), p. 175.

[16]Marek Schindelman to [James] Rice, United HIAS Service, July 1961, trans. Carmen Roman, RG AR3344, JDC Archive, as cited in Levine, *Tropical Diaspora*, p. 243.

had declared: " I am a Marxist-Leninist and I shall be one until the last day of my life." This put an end to any remaining hopes for a return to the life that Jews had known before the revolution. By early 1963 a much larger number of Jews had left. At that time Congregation Adath Israel and the Unión Sionista de Cuba (Zionist Union of Cuba) conducted a census of those registering to receive Passover supplies. They found that there were only 1,022 Jewish families in the country, composed of 2,586 individuals, most living in Havana.

Israeli ambassador Haim Yaari estimated that 45 percent of the Jews who remained in the country during the 1960s were unemployed.[17] Most of these people survived by gradually selling off their more valuable possessions, such as washing machines, dryers, ovens, family heirlooms, and jewelry. Once again, there is little evidence to suggest that Jews were singled out for negative treatment. A number of American Jewish organizations that were monitoring the situation stressed that Jews were fleeing Cuba because of political and economic difficulties, not anti-Semitism.

Charles Shapiro, an important businessman in Havana and an American citizen, appears to have been a specific target of violence. A leader of the United Hebrew Congregation, Shapiro had been living in Cuba for about 35 years. In August 1960 Shapiro and his wife, Wilma, along with ten other relatives and several servants, were beaten, tied up, and robbed in their elegant home by five armed Cubans, who ransacked the house and took all the money and jewelry they found. Almost simultaneously, the family's department store, Los Precios Fijos, one of the largest in Havana, went up in flames, and government authorities detained the Shapiros' son, the store manager, for a short time. While there was no evidence that the Shapiros were targeted because they were Jewish, the incident increased Jewish trepidation about staying in the country.[18]

Another spur to emigration was fear that the government might at some point decide to restrict the freedom of Cubans to leave the country. Indeed, a law went into effect on July 26, 1963, stating that all males between the ages of 15 and 50 were obligated to perform military service, and from then on emigration became more difficult for men in that age bracket and their families.

---

[17]Margalit Bejarano, "Antisemitism in Cuba Under Democratic, Military, and Revolutionary Regimes, 1944–1963," *Patterns of Prejudice* 24, Summer 1990, p. 40. The entire article is on pp. 32–46.

[18]See Wilma Shapiro's reminiscences, "Llegan los Milicianos," in Bejarano, ed., *La Comunidad Hebrea de Cuba,* pp. 244–46.

The Castro Government and the Jews

The revolutionary forces had portrayed themselves as reformers whose goal was to redress the injustices committed by the former government, and specifically to reverse the arrangements that had been allowed to develop through sweetheart deals signed by corrupt senior officials. The groups that faced retribution were those that had been part of the Batista regime, and virtually no Jews had been high-ranking government officials or military officers under Batista. It is true that some American Jewish gangsters, such as Meyer Lansky, were involved with Batista in the development of casino gambling, but none of them were arrested or tried. When Lansky's Havana Riviera Hotel was officially confiscated on October 24, 1960, no one suggested that the Communists had anti-Semitic motives; after all, 165 other American enterprises, including the Cuban subsidiaries and franchises of Canada Dry, Goodyear, Kodak, Westinghouse, and Woolworth's, were also seized.[19]

Although Castro's foreign policy towards the State of Israel has had its ups and downs, he has pursued a consistently benign policy towards the local Cuban Jewish community. There are a number of theories about why Castro did not adopt the kind of anti-Jewish policies instituted by the Communists in the Soviet Union and its East European satellites. Castro had a number of Jewish friends and supporters, and his relations with one or more of them may have predisposed him not to attack the Jewish community. It is also possible that Castro wanted to avoid anti-Semitism precisely in order to differentiate his regime from that of the Soviet Union, an explanation that would also cover his decision to maintain diplomatic relations with Israel after the 1967 Six-Day War, when the entire Communist bloc broke relations with the exception of Cuba. Some have argued that the Castro regime did not want to generate additional hostility by persecuting a small and vulnerable religious minority, but it is hard to believe that the same government that was willing to antagonize the superpower to the north would fear the fallout from its treatment of local Jews. Havana historian Maritza Corrales Capestany suggests that, in the early years, many Cubans, and perhaps Castro as well, felt that Cuba and Israel were both small, struggling, socialist states beset by much larger and stronger enemies. Many Cubans also felt great sympathy for the tremendous suffering that the Jews had endured in the Holocaust.[20]

Another theory is that Castro believes he is of Marrano ancestry. Certainly the name Castro was a common last name of Marranos (*anusim*

---

[19]Robert Lacey, *Little Man: Meyer Lansky and the Gangster Life* (Boston, 1991), p. 324.
[20]Interview with Maritza Corrales Capestany, Feb. 2000.

in Hebrew, sometimes called *conversos* in Spanish), Jews who converted to Christianity—either willingly or unwillingly—before or at the time of the expulsion of the Jews from Spain in 1492. Maurice Halperin writes that in 1960 Castro told Ricardo Wolf, Cuba's ambassador to Israel, that he had Marrano ancestors.[21] Lavy Becker, who visited Cuba for the Canadian Jewish Congress, recalls hearing the same thing from Wolf.[22] This account has also been confirmed by Dr. Bernardo Benes, who told reporter Ann Louise Bardach that "He [Castro] said to me in passing, 'As you know, I have Jewish ancestors.' He said he wanted Cuba to be a second Israel."[23] In a recent conversation, Benes added a few details: "I had heard that he [Castro] was from Jewish ancestry. . . . I told him, 'The next time you go to a mirror, look at your nose, and look what you have done with this little island here in front of the powerful United States. Only a Jew could have done that.' Castro asked me, 'So there is no problem with being a Jew?' and I said 'Of course not, I'm one.' " Benes recalled a time in 1984, when he, Benes, was negotiating with Castro on behalf of President Reagan: "I remember the exact date. It was May 18, 1984. . . . In the middle of an unrelated conversation, he said to me, 'You know, my Jewish ancestors. . . .' I remember the words exactly." Benes told me, "I gave him to read the autobiography of Golda Meir, *My Life*. He was very impressed after he read it. He told me that she was one of the most distinguished women of the 20th century." "This is just my personal opinion," concluded Benes, "but I think he wanted to do in Cuba what the Israelis had done in the Middle East."[24]

Castro's daughter, Alina, has written that Castro's maternal grandfather was a Turkish Jew from Istanbul named Francisco Ruz. She described her great-grandfather as "a boy in Istanbul, who had ancestral memories of a greater empire, when his family of Jewish renegades probably dropped a letter from their last name, shortening it [from Ruiz] to Ruz."[25] This would be a startling revelation if true, but it is not, since Alina Fernández told her mother Naty (Natalia) Revuelta that this was "the only lie in the book."[26] What apparently is true is that many of Cas-

---

[21]Halperin himself did not interview Wolf, but rather heard this from Shlomo Lavav, Israel's ambassador to Cuba between 1965 and 1968, who said he heard it from Wolf. Maurice Halperin, *The Taming of Fidel Castro* (Berkeley, Cal., 1981), pp. 241–242, n. 10.

[22]Lavy Becker, "Report on Jewish Community of Cuba, May 29–June 4, 1975," p. 1, Records of Alan Rose, Canadian Jewish Congress National Archives, Montreal.

[23]Ann Louise Bardach, "Fidel! Fidel!" *Talk*, Aug. 2001, p. 122.

[24]Interview with Bernardo Benes, July, 2001.

[25]Alina Fernández, *Castro's Daughter: An Exile's Memoir of Cuba* (New York, 1998), p. 1. In addition, Francisco's ancestry is clearly labeled on the genealogical tree that appears on an unnumbered page at the beginning of the book.

[26]Interview with Jaime Sarusky, June 2000. Sarusky, a noted Cuban journalist and author, spoke directly with Revuelta.

tro's classmates called him *judío*, "Jew," because he had not been baptized by the age of seven. In popular Cuban usage, the word *judío* was used to refer to a child who had not yet been baptized.[27] It is certainly possible that this and other experiences made him sympathize with the plight of the Jews. In his discussions with Frei Betto, Castro talks about his memories of Holy Week:

> Holy Week in the countryside—I remember them from when I was very young—were days of solemnity; there was great solemnity. What was said? That Christ died on Good Friday. You couldn't talk or joke or be happy, because Christ was dead and the Jews killed him every year. This is another case in which accusations or popular beliefs have caused tragedies and historic prejudices. I tell you, I didn't know what that term meant, and I thought, at first, that those birds called *judíos* had killed Christ.[28]

Whatever his motivations, Castro's attitude toward the Jews of Cuba after the revolution was remarkably positive. Instead of tarring the emigrating Jews with the taint of disloyalty, he expressed regret that so many Jews, who might have contributed much to the new Cuba, were leaving. James Rice, executive director of HIAS from 1956 to 1966, recalled that Castro asked the Israeli ambassador in Havana why Cuban Jews felt it necessary to emigrate, since he had nothing whatsoever against them and would have been happy to use their talents to develop the new socialist regime.[29] Furthermore, David Kopilow has noted that the revolutionary government classified Cuban Jews going to Israel as *repatriados,* repatriated ones, rather than *gusanos,* worms, which is what other emigrants were called.[30]

Despite the small number of Jews left in the country, Judaism continued to be a subject of great interest in Castro's Cuba. The regime found numerous ways to use Jewish subjects in creative ways consistent with its ideological program. The government-controlled media lavished attention on Jewish holidays and cultural events: Passover was portrayed as a celebration of the "national liberation" of the Jews, and other holidays were likewise given a "Fidelistic" interpretation.

Of course the country had many problems, and Cuban Jews suffered along with the rest of the population. On the most basic level, living in Communist Cuba meant adapting to a lower standard of living than before. Nevertheless, those affiliated with the Jewish community enjoyed

---

[27]Robert E. Quirk, *Fidel Castro* (New York and London, 1993), p. 3; Frei Betto, ed., *Fidel y la Religion: Conversaciones con Frei Betto*, (Havana, 1985), pp. 101, 107–108, available in English translation, *Fidel and Religion: Talks with Frei Betto,* (Havana, 1987).

[28]Betto, ed., *Fidel y la Religion*, p. 123.

[29]James Rice, "A Retrospective View: 1960s Cuba Exodus Brought Jews to U.S.," *Intermountain Jewish News*, May 30, 1980, p. 23.

[30]David Kopilow, *Castro, Israel, and the PLO* (Washington, D.C., 1984), p 17.

certain benefits. Kosher butchers were among the few private businesses not nationalized by the government. There was a widely held perception that Jews were allowed additional meat and poultry to compensate for the fact that they did not eat pork. Moisés Baldás, head of the community from 1961 through 1978, believed that the Cuban authorities thought that Jews had to have kosher meat in order to comply with the Jewish religion; that is, that Judaism required the eating of meat.[31] The government allowed a kosher restaurant to stay open in Havana, and Radio Havana continued to broadcast Communist propaganda in Yiddish even after other foreign-language radio programs were banned.[32]

Aiding the Emigrants

When Cubans started fleeing Cuba, the U.S. Department of Health, Education, and Welfare (HEW)—the government department with authority over resettlement assistance—asked the Hebrew Immigrant Aid Society (HIAS) to establish an office in the Miami area. The government hoped that HIAS, along with other refugee agencies, could help provide assistance to the large number of Cubans streaming into the country. And since, at the beginning of the exodus, many Cubans fled by small boats not only to the United States but also to islands in the Caribbean, HIAS set up a network of offices there as well to help Jewish communities deal with the influx.

Not all families left Cuba together: in the early 1960s, 14,048 children were sent out of Cuba without their parents. In December 1960 the American government held discussions about how to handle the possible arrival of large numbers of minors with no chaperones, and, on January 9, 1961, the U.S. Department of State granted Father Bryan O. Walsh the authority to grant a visa waiver to any child aged 6–16 entering the country under the guardianship of the Catholic Diocese of Miami.[33] Reporter Gene Miller later dubbed the program Operation Pedro Pan, and the name stuck. Because the diocese coordinated the program, the perception developed that only Catholic children were taken care of in this manner. Actually the same provisions were also made with Protestant and Jewish agencies.[34] In fact there were two separate operations. One, Oper-

---

[31]Correspondence with Margalit Bejarano, Apr. 2001. Bejarano conducted 20 hours of interviews with Baldás shortly after he left Cuba. Tapes of the interviews, in Hebrew, are in the Oral History Division, Institute of Contemporary Jewry, The Hebrew University of Jerusalem.

[32]Interview with Moisés Asís, Feb. 2001.

[33]Joan Didion, *Miami* (New York, 1987), p. 122.

[34]Bryan O. Walsh, "Cuban Refugee Children," *Journal of Inter-American Studies and World Affairs* 12, July/Oct. 1971, p. 391.

ation Pedro Pan, was a semi-clandestine program to help children leave Cuba for the United States.[35] The other was the Cuban Children's Program, which was a social service designed primarily to care for Cuban children who were in the United States without parents or other close relatives. HIAS was involved in Operation Pedro Pan, helping 28 Jewish children get out of Cuba, and the Jewish Family and Children Services participated in the Cuban Children's Program, assisting 117 children whose parents were not with them (the Catholic Welfare Bureau assisted 7,041 such children).

Marcos Kerbel, a former president of Miami's Cuban Hebrew Congregation, was one of the children who got out of Cuba through HIAS. Kerbel's family had a clothing store in Guanabacoa, which they had developed into a thriving business over 30 years. Understandably reluctant to emigrate and leave behind all they had worked for, the Kerbels did not think the revolution would last, assuming, as did many others, that the United States would invade and overthrow Castro. Marcos Kerbel recalled:

> In the summer of 1960 things began to get a little bit tight in Cuba, and some of my friends started leaving. We used to meet on Sundays at the Patronato and we had what was known as a bar mitzvah club. There was concern at the time that the laws would be changed, what was known as the *patria potestas,* which means that the state would have total control over the kids. And there were rumors that anybody between the ages of 14 and 27 wouldn't be able to leave Cuba after that, even if they went into the service. They were in the process of drafting; meanwhile they wanted the kids, right after the first day of the school year, to go into the mountains to teach the peasants there how to read and write. That scared a lot of the parents, especially of the girls, because they felt that once the girls started going up into the mountains there that they were going to be coming back pregnant.

At first Kerbel found even his relatives unwilling to talk about their contacts with HIAS, but eventually they put him in touch with the local representative:

> So the whole [emigration] movement started. I was not aware of the Catholic group [Operation Pedro Pan] until I arrived here, but there was a contact of HIAS in Havana, and I started checking how to get out. I did not have a passport at the time or a visa. I had found out at one of the Sundays that some

---

[35]Yvonne M. Conde, a Pedro Pan child who left Cuba at the age of ten and now lives in New York, has written a sympathetic account, *Operation Pedro Pan: The Untold Exodus of 14,048 Cuban Children* (New York and London, 1999). In contrast, two Cuban writers have published a book that portrays the operation as part of an American "psychological war" against Cuba. See Ramón Torreira Crespo and José Buajasán Marrawi, *Operación Peter Pan: Un Caso de Guerra Psicológica Contra Cuba* (Havana, 2000). Conde's book uses the name "Pedro" Pan to signify that this was an operation done to save Cubans, while Crespo and Marrawi use "Peter" Pan to show that this was an anti-Cuban American operation.

cousins of mine were leaving, and I said, "how are you leaving? I know you don't have a passport and you don't have a visa." So at first there was such a hush-hush thing that even the kids' grandmother, who was my father's sister-in-law, said, "I don't know anything." Finally I went to my godfather, and I said, "What's going on here? Why are they leaving, how are they leaving?" So he put me in touch with somebody who was the contact from HIAS, telling him that I wanted to go.[36]

Fourteen-year-old Marcos was sent to Los Angeles, where he was placed under the supervision of Vista del Mar Child Care, a Jewish orphanage. He was then sent to live with a strictly Orthodox family, but he found the adjustment difficult. In June 1962 his uncles arrived in Miami from Cuba, and Marcos went to live with them. His parents came on October 19, 1962, on the next-to-the-last Pan Am flight before the Cuban missile crisis stopped all flights until 1965. In January 1963, the entire family moved to Atlanta, Georgia. Marcos lived in Atlanta through his college years, after which he settled in Miami.

Communal Impact

As Jewish emigration rose over the course of the early 1960s, the impact was felt even more strongly in the provinces than in Havana. Even though a lower percentage of those from outside Havana emigrated, many of those who remained in the country gravitated to the capital, destroying the smaller communities. By December 1965 more than 90 percent of the Cuban Jewish community had left, and of the roughly 2,300 who remained, 1,900 lived in Havana.

For almost 30 years, religious matters in Castro's Cuba have been largely in the hands of Dr. José Felipe Carneado, director of the Department of Religious Affairs of the Central Committee of the Cuban Communist Party. Carneado, a strong supporter of the revolution and at the same time possessing a "deep respect" for popular Cuban tradition and beliefs, operated on the principle that religious groups that cooperated with the government should be protected by the regime, and Jews considered him a friend.[37]

Religious activities continued. All five synagogues in Havana held weekly Sabbath services and most held services during the week as well. Because of the difficulty of achieving a minyan (the quorum of ten required for group prayer) in Havana, it became customary to count Torahs scrolls as part of a minyan—if there were only eight people, two Torahs

---

[36]Interview with Marcos Kerbel, July 2000.

[37]Margalit Bejarano, "The Jewish Community of Cuba: Between Continuity and Extinction," *Jewish Political Studies Review* 3, Spring 1991, p. 129.

would be counted. The number of Torahs needed tended to increase, until a minyan might have as few as five breathing people. Jacob Kovadloff, the American Jewish Committee's consultant on Latin America, reports that the expression "having a Cuban-style minyan" has become common in several other Latin American countries as well. In 1961 there were 19 bar mitzvahs and 50 Jewish weddings in Havana up until Rosh Hashanah.[38] But as emigration swelled thereafter, such occasions became few and far between. Until the revival of the early 1990s, the last bar mitzvah was celebrated in Havana in 1973, and the last Jewish wedding in 1976.[39]

The congregation that suffered the smallest short-term decline in members was Adath Israel. This Orthodox Ashkenazi synagogue had approximately 800 members and, at least in the early 1960s, seemed to have survived the emigration rush. Adath Israel was the most traditional of all the congregations. Rabbi Everett Gendler, who visited in 1969, gave a description:

> Maintaining a daily minyan morning and evening, it has curtained sections at either side of the main floor for the women worshipers. Yom Kippur morning there were some 250 people present, and before the Torah reading the devout *davening* [prayer service] was led by two older members of the congregation whose mastery of both the traditional *nusach* [melody] and the "oy vey" was quite moving.[40]

The community *shohet* (ritual slaughterer), a man in his eighties, executed the Torah reading with great accuracy. Although many of the congregants were elderly, there were also eight to ten congregants in their late teens and early twenties, as well as a number of young children. Of course, Adath Israel too would eventually suffer the same diminution of numbers that the other congregations faced.

The congregation that suffered the most precipitous loss of members was the United Hebrew Congregation, which was Reform. The revolution caught United Hebrew in the midst of plans to build a new, larger temple on Fifth Avenue in Miramar. But most of the members, American Jews living in Cuba, left the country within a year of the revolution, and plans for the building were scrapped. Rose Granison, the widow of Rabbi Abram Granison, who served the congregation during the early 1950s, said, "When Castro came into power, everybody ran. He was not inviting people to stay. It was a very scary scene."[41]

[38]Abraham J. Dubelman, "Cuba," AJYB 1962, vol. 63, pp. 483–84.
[39]Moisés Asís, "Judaism in Cuba 1959–99, A Personal Account," Web site www.jewishcuba.org.
[40]Everett Gendler, "Holy Days in Habana," *Conservative Judaism* 23, Winter 1969, p. 17.
[41]Interview with Rose Granison, May 2000.

With the loss of the American Jews, who were the founders and still constituted the bulk of the membership, there was every reason to believe that the congregation would fold. However a number of dedicated Cuban Jewish families, led by Isidoro Stettner, managed to keep the services going. Rabbi Everett Gendler also visited this congregation in 1969:

> Temple Beth Israel, situated in a fine old converted mansion on a broad palm-lined boulevard of Vedado, is often referred to as the American congregation, even though the majority of its present members are not from the United States. They attend because it offers the only liberal service in Habana today. Established some sixty years ago through the merger of two groups, it uses the *Union Prayer Book,* gives page announcements in Spanish, carries on the services in Hebrew and English, and has a full Torah reading following the annual cycle. Men and women sit together, *kippot* [skullcaps] are used, and services are held Shabbat mornings and both days of the Festivals.

Gendler reported that the congregation had about 30 members, most of them in their fifties and sixties, and, he noted, "one senses both present dignity and sad recollections of a more vigorous and numerous community life in days past."[42]

In 1981, after Stettner's death, the congregation ceased operating, but it survived as a legal entity. This was because the United Hebrew Congregation was the official proprietor of the Jewish cemetery, and, as Margalit Bejarano of The Hebrew University of Jerusalem explains, "in Cuba, as in other Communist countries, you exist if you exist on paper—not necessarily in real life."[43] Adath Israel took over the cemetery book and the congregational records.

The Patronato remained the most important Jewish institution in Havana. Herman Heisler, an immigrant from Lithuania, is credited with the original idea of building a community center in the thriving seaside suburb of Vedado. He was president of the Patronato Association, saw the project through to completion in the 1950s, and then served as president of the community center and synagogue until his emigration in the early 1960s. Once Heisler left, though, the Patronato went through a period of uncertainty, with several presidents serving for very brief periods. Finally, the election of Moisés Baldás as president brought stability, and Baldás became the undisputed chief of the Havana Jewish community: "Everyone knew that if you needed to talk with the Jewish community, you went to Baldás."[44] By the mid-1960s, though, most of the members had emigrated. Everett Gendler described what he saw in 1969:

---

[42]Gendler, "Holy Days in Habana," p. 16.
[43]Correspondence with Margalit Bejarano, Apr. 2001.
[44]Interview with Adela Dworin, June 2000.

[The congregation] has a large building some fifteen years old, with synagogue, auditorium, dining hall, kosher kitchen, library, music room, game rooms. Ashkenazic-traditional in orientation, it had perhaps 250 worshipers occupying its one thousand seats on Rosh Hashanah, with the Consul of Israel also in attendance and seated on the *bimah* [platform]. The service is led by knowledgeable laymen, and certain of the old stratifications persist: one man, for example, introduces himself to me as the "gabbai sheni"![45]

Over the course of the next few decades, the Patronato's roof began leaking and the building became riddled with termites. Skeletal remains of dead birds that had fallen from nests in the rafters lay on the floor of the main sanctuary. According to one estimate made in the late 1980s, the building needed $50,000 just for basic repairs.[46] The congregational leadership felt it would be prudent to remove the Torah scrolls from the ark to prevent damage to them. The Patronato, suffering severe budgetary problems, sold a part of the community-center section of the building to the government in 1981.

The Sephardi Jews of Havana also suffered a dramatic depletion of numbers. Chevet Achim, now defunct, was still an active congregation when Gendler visited:

A large converted house serves as the setting for an energetic, vigorous and highly vocal Sephardic service quite winning in its wild way. Women were seated separately, above and behind the men, with a total attendance of perhaps seventy-five people, including some youths. Various male members of the congregation ascended the *bimah* to shout out verses from the Yom Kippur *piyuttim* [liturgical poems], the rest of the congregation responding with resounding counter-shouts. One old member of the congregation was in general charge of the *davening* and led the *duchaning* [priestly benediction] as well, and here as elsewhere one saw an entirely lay-directed service of some power and conviction.[47]

The congregation was located in old Havana, and Sephardim who had moved to the suburbs generally preferred to attend the Centro Sefaradi, where about 150 worshipers came to services on Rosh Hashanah. As the two Sephardi congregations lost more and more members, there was talk of merging Chevet Achim and the Centro Sefaradi, and this was slowly accomplished over several years. Eventually one service was held, alternating between the two buildings.

Of the five Jewish elementary schools and one high school that had existed when the community was at its peak, by the time the government took control of the country's entire educational system, in June 1961, only

---

[45]Gendler, "Holy Days in Habana," p. 16. "Gabbai sheni" is Hebrew for assistant sexton.

[46]Mimi Whitefield, "Jews in Cuba: The Fragile Flame, *Miami Herald,* Dec. 9, 1990, p. H4.

[47]Gendler, "Holy Days in Habana," pp. 17–18.

the Colegio Hebreo, an elementary school, was still in operation. But it was on the verge of collapse since many Cuban Jewish parents had begun sending their children to the United States through HIAS. After discussions with the authorities, an arrangement was reached whereby the school would be taken over by the government and function as a quasi-Jewish public school. Its student body would be mostly Jewish, and while Judaic subjects would not be part of the curriculum, the Jewish community was allowed to operate a religious school in the building for 90 minutes every afternoon, after the completion of the regular school day. Thus students attending the school could remain in the building after school for religious studies without having to be transported elsewhere, and Jewish children attending other public schools in the city could join them after school.

In 1965, Ben G. Kayfetz of Toronto, a Canadian Jewish Congress staff member, visited Cuba. Having paid an earlier visit in 1962, Kayfetz was in a position to make comparisons. The title of his report, "Cuban Jewry—A Community in Dissolution," told it all. The remnants of Cuban Jewry, Kayfetz noted, was a "community of ex-'s." They included ex-*comereiantes,* ex-*fabricantes,* "ex-this, and ex-that." Kayfetz reported that in the old city of Havana, where "hundreds upon hundreds of small shops were huddled next to each other, strung together for miles along narrow sixteenth-century streets," there were now "far more metal graded shutters covering closed up shops than there are open places of business." Kayfetz observed, "The traveler, even when he does not speak to Cubans, can feel soon enough that he is in a Revolutionary state of the Marxist stripe." Kayfetz wrote that "propaganda messages are to be found on all placards and billboards—commercial messages of sales appeal are now obsolete." Freedom of speech "in the North American and West European sense" was unknown, and the newspapers featured a constant supply of Fidel's speeches. Signs on every city block announced the existence of the local unit of the Committee for the Defense of the Revolution (CDR).[48]

And yet Cuba was the only country in the Communist orbit that continued to permit the existence of a Zionist organization, the Unión Sionista. Kayfetz noticed that right next door to it was the Sociedad Club Arabe (Arab Social Club), which had a large poster of Egyptian president Nasser on the door. Local Jews assured the Canadian visitor that Jews and Arabs got along "quite cordially" in Cuba. Kayfetz noted the termination of large-scale Jewish fund-raising "because of currency reg-

---

[48]B. G. Kayfetz, "Cuban Jewry—A Community in Dissolution," *Congress Bulletin* (published by the Canadian Jewish Congress), Dec. 1965, pp. 3, 8.

ulations." Previously, the Cuban Jewish community had raised generous sums of money for Histadrut, Youth Aliyah, the Hebrew University, and, in particular, Keren Hayesod. There was such a shortage of money that rumors circulated in Mexico that the Patronato had to sell some of its synagogue benches in order to pay its bills. Vehemently denying this, Patronato board members said that the benches were sold because the decline in members made them unnecessary. Kayfetz wrote that the Jewish community had "been destroyed" but it was "destroyed without any prior or deliberate intention, for no person I spoke to had any complaints as Jews against the Revolutionary government, all acknowledging its fairness and objectivity in dealing with Jewish communal and religious affairs."[49]

There was only one advantage to the community's drastic reduction in numbers: it was more unified than before. A coordinating committee of all five Havana congregations met every other week, the sites of the meetings alternating between the different synagogues.

Communal Leaders Who Remained

Although most of the Cuban Jewish community's leaders emigrated in the years immediately following the revolution, there were those who stayed to guarantee that the community would at least survive, if not flourish. The key figure was Moisés Baldás, mentioned earlier in connection with his leadership of the Patronato. Baldás, who had a Polish yeshivah background as well as a good secular education and spoke a fluent Hebrew, had came to Cuba in the 1920s as a young man. By 1959 he was a successful businessman and the owner of a seven-story building in the center of Havana that housed a supermarket as well as apartments and his own private penthouse. A 60-year-old widower when the revolution took place, he was known as "Mr. Zionism" of Cuba. The Castro regime nationalized his building but compensated him with a pension and permitted him to retain his penthouse.

Baldás turned his energies to the community, taking a personal interest in every aspect of its affairs, particularly education. Lavy Becker of the Canadian Jewish Congress, reporting on the situation in 1975, identified Baldás as the force behind the Hebrew school, all Zionist activities in the community, the youth choir, the training of new ritual slaughterers and the *mohel,* and the encouragement of young people to assume leadership roles. Many others have confirmed this perception. Since the government gave him clearance to attend a World Jewish Congress (WJC)

---

[49]Ibid., p. 3.

conference in Brussels and a World Zionist Organization (WZO) conference in Jerusalem, Baldás could simply have declined to return, and settled abroad. It was his strong commitment to, and sense of responsibility for, the Cuban Jewish community that kept him from doing this for many years. Becker wrote of Baldás, "because of his good judgment and able leadership, he has achieved the respect of his community and has been a major factor in maintaining a unified, well-balanced and hopeful Jewish community."[50]

After the government's decision to break diplomatic relations with Israel in 1973 (see below, p. 52), Baldás's strong identification with Zionism placed him in an uncomfortable position, and by the late 1970s he felt ready to leave Cuba and retire to Israel. Having made this decision, Baldás began grooming Dr. José Miller Fredman to succeed him as leader.

Miller was a successful maxillofacial surgeon who was born and raised in Yaguajay, then part of Las Villas province and now part of Sancti Spíritus province. There were three Jewish families there when Miller was growing up, two Ashkenazi and one Sephardi. He told me that "there were some Presbyterians [and] some Baptists in my town, but the majority were Catholic. My family kept the tradition. We were Jews not only because we knew we were Jews but also because the goyim knew we were Jews. We had celebrations of the Jewish festivals among the three families that were there. There were seders every year." Miller came to Havana in order to attend dental school, and stayed. His second wife, Dalia Gomez, converted to Judaism and become active in the community, serving on the Patronato board and working in the Patronato office. Miller told me that he was surprised when Baldás asked him to consider becoming the next president: "I became the leader of the Jewish community because they had no one else. I had no experience in community leadership—I was a doctor. But I learned."[51] As part of his preparation to assume the presidency, Miller attended German classes so that he would be able to understand the Yiddish spoken by many of the old-timers on the board of the Patronato.

Miller was unusual in that he was a highly trained professional who nevertheless stayed after the revolution. "I stayed in the country because I enjoyed living here. Don't remind me how much money I could have earned in America. I enjoyed living in Cuba very much, and for that reason I'm glad I stayed here. But we all make choices and we have to live with the good and the bad consequences of those choices." Miller took over the presidency in 1978, and Baldás stayed for about a year and a half

---

[50]Becker, "Report on the Jewish Community of Cuba," p. 8
[51]Interview with José Miller Fredman, June 2000.

to help with the transition. He then flew to Canada and the United States before settling in Givatayim, Israel. The transition was carried out smoothly and Miller's leadership was accepted virtually unanimously. Miller has provided the Jewish community with strong and visionary leadership during a very difficult period. Margalit Bejarano explains that "the most important point in Miller's leadership is his good relationship with the authorities. He is a good diplomat, who knows how to move among the Cuban leaders, and thanks to his good contacts the community can survive."[52] He was among the first to suggest programs and funding possibilities that have resulted in the remarkable regeneration of the Havana Jewish community.

Abraham Marcus Matterín, director of the Patronato library from its founding in 1953 until his death in 1983, was another important Jewish community leader. He was born in Lithuania in 1916 and arrived in Havana as a teenager. A self-educated journalist, Matterín wrote for *Periodico: El Mundo,* an influential Cuban newspaper, and was writer and editor for the Jewish periodicals *Hebraica* and *Reflejos,* both of which were published in the 1950s. He befriended Cuban writers, painters, intellectuals, and poets, founded the Cuban-American Cultural Association of Havana — an intellectual group that sponsored cultural activities and issued publications — and was regarded as a key bridge between the Jewish community and the broader Cuban society. Among his many friends were Juan Marinello, writer, intellectual, and prominent leader of the Communist Party; Luis Gómez Wangüemert, the editor of *El Mundo;* Fernando Ortiz, the most respected Cuban historian and anthropologist of his generation; and Nicolas Guillén, the Cuban national poet. Matterín stayed in Cuba because of the intellectually satisfying role he was able to play, even though he was not a member of the Communist Party.[53]

José Dworin left his native Pinsk for Cuba in 1924 with the intention of going from there to the United States and then raising money to bring over his mother and siblings. But he never got to the United States, and in 1930 his mother and two brothers came to Cuba. After the revolution Dworin's clothing factory was nationalized and he made plans to leave the country, but his daughter Adela talked him out of it. He stayed and took a job working for the government. Dworin was one of the founders of the Anti-Tuberculosis Committee, which later expanded into the field of mental health, providing economic aid for Jews who were hospitalized in mental institutions; every Sunday, Dworin and his committee went to

---

[52]Correspondence with Margalit Bejarano, Apr. 2001.
[53]The Matterín papers, including most of the Patronato records, are in the archives of the Office of History of the City of Havana.

visit the patients. He was a member of the board of the Patronato until his death in 1971.

His daughter, Adela, was raised as a traditional Jew, and would come to be known as one of the most observant members of the Jewish community. She attended two Jewish day schools that existed in prerevolutionary Havana, the Tarbut School and the Yavneh Institute. At the same time she was active in Hashomer Hatzair, a left-socialist Zionist youth movement, and participated in the youth organization of the Patronato. At the outbreak of the revolution Adela Dworin was a law student, but the University of Havana closed down for three years, and when it reopened the new revolutionary government wanted to decrease the number of law students. As a result, she did not return to the university and never completed her degree. In 1970, she began a long career in the Patronato library. Her responsibilities gradually expanded, especially after Abraham Matterín died.

"Petering Out" in the 1970s

Adela Dworin recalls that even after 1965 there was still a substantial amount of activity in the Jewish community. But from about 1970 onward, "there were really only elderly people coming in, and not very many of those."[54] Lavy Becker, the Canadian Jewish Congress representative who visited Cuba a number of times during the decade, referred to "this once-flourishing community . . . now petering out." In 1975 Becker noted that "all five synagogues in Havana and one in Santiago still function, with regular services and social interaction before and after services." He did point out, however, that on any given Shabbat a total of only 70–80 people attended all of the Havana synagogues, and that these Jews were mostly elderly, almost all over the age of 70. The synagogues supported themselves through a combination of monthly membership dues, rental money they received from the government for the use of their auditoriums, and the sale of Passover products brought in with the help of the Canadian Jewish Congress.[55]

The Havana community had an afternoon Hebrew school with an enrollment of 37 children between the ages of five and eleven, which, as noted above, operated in the "Jewish" public school five days a week for an hour-and-a-half a day. Those 37 students represented slightly more than 40 percent of the 90 children estimated to be in that age bracket in the Jewish community at the time. Not only did the government allow those children who had to come from other public schools to leave early so that they could get to Hebrew school on time, but it also granted the

---

[54]Dworin interview.
[55]Becker, "Report on the Jewish Community of Cuba," pp. 1, 3.

Jewish community the use of two small buses, as well as the necessary gas ration, to transport the children. This was a deviation from the norm in Cuba, where children typically went to the grade school nearest their homes, and therefore would not require bus transportation. Furthermore, Cuban schoolchildren would normally go home for lunch, but the Jewish children attending the "Jewish" school—who were in many cases much farther from home than other students—were provided a lunch by the government in the school building. Becker explained that "since the government nationalized this building [the former Jewish day school] . . . it may well be that the government considers these concessions a quid pro quo."[56] Becker visited the school shortly before it closed. Just prior to the opening of the 1975–76 school year, the government sent Moisés Baldás a letter instructing him that Jewish children should now attend their neighborhood public schools.

Before the revolution, the Havana community had had very active Maccabi and Betar youth organizations. During the first years of the revolution both disappeared, due mainly to the emigration of their leaders and members. But in 1969, the Unión Sionista sponsored a new youth organization.

An important source of inspiration for the Havana Jewish community in the 1970s was its young-adult choral group, where, as Moisés Asís explained, "young people learned a lot of Israeli popular songs in Hebrew, patriotic marches in Hebrew and Yiddish, and traditional Jewish songs in Hebrew." These activities inspired many young Cuban Jews, said Asís, "despite the strong anti-Israel, anti-Zionism, and anti-religion stand by the Cuban government in those critical years in which any religious believers were banned from universities and from many jobs."[57] Becker commented that "the level of their music may be low, the repertoire limited, but their joy is unbounded." The group served an important social function. "This is a program without which these more than 20 young people would have hardly any contact with anything Jewish," Becker noted.[58] Led by a violinist who was employed in a restaurant orchestra, the choral group performed on holidays such as Hanukkah, Purim, and Israeli Independence Day, as well as at more solemn occasions, such as a program to commemorate the fall of the Warsaw Ghetto.

It was through this choir that the community found a schoolteacher for its afternoon school—Miss Mercedes Villapol, a Catholic from Spain who would eventually convert to Judaism in Havana. Moisés Baldás encouraged her to join the choral group, where she learned Hebrew and Yid-

---

[56]Ibid, p. 9.
[57]Correspondence with Moisés Asís, Mar. 2001.
[58]Becker, "Report on the Jewish Community of Cuba," p. 9.

dish melodies by rote. She later began to study in the adult Hebrew classes, and was then persuaded to take over the teaching of the children. Becker commented, "her whole life these last four to five years is related to Jews and Judaism. It will surprise no one to learn that she now has a strong desire to become a Jewess."[59]

The government was very generous to the Jewish community in the allocation of meat. In 1975 each Cuban was entitled to three-fourths of a pound of meat every nine days. The government regulated the slaughter of animals and the packaging of meat for sale in government butcher shops so as to maintain equal rationing for all. But the government made special arrangements to enable the Jewish community to prepare kosher meat: the two *shohetim* were permitted the use of one of the abattoirs, and the two kosher butchers were authorized to package the kosher meat.

Before the 1959 revolution, the Cuban Jewish community, like most others in South America, was strongly Zionist, but the interest in Israel and commitment to it gradually lessened over the following decades. The three most important reasons were that the vast majority of the most committed Zionists had left the country; the relationship between Cuba and the State of Israel had deteriorated; and the acceleration of intermarriage meant that even in cases where the intermarried couple affiliated with the Jewish community, the non-Jewish partner had only a weak sense of Jewish peoplehood, and no historical or familial ties with Israel. Interestingly, even though Castro suddenly broke diplomatic relations with Israel in September 1973, his government allowed the Unión Sionista to continue to function, and granted formal permission to hold large public celebrations of Israeli Independence Day in 1974 and 1975. Unión Sionista even remained in operation for three years after the 1975 United Nations "Zionism is Racism" resolution, which Cuba supported. Baldás believed that the authorities were simply unaware that such an organization was still functioning, and when the continued existence of the Unión Sionista came to their attention, they ordered it closed.[60]

B'nai B'rith Maimonides Lodge also continued to function even though the American Jews who had created the organization had long since left the country. Becker was encouraged by the fact that a relatively young man had succeeded Miller as president of B'nai B'rith. He was a 37-year-old accountant named Luis Szklarz, the head of the department of ferrous and non-ferrous metals and oil in the government foreign-trade office. Another sign that younger people sought identification with the Jewish community was that, in addition to the choral group, about 30

---

[59]Ibid., p. 3.
[60]Correspondence with Margalit Bejarano, July 2001.

young married people and singles met regularly under the auspices of the Juventud Hebrea de Cuba. The handful of ordained rabbis in Cuba had all left the community years earlier. One of them, Nissim Gambach, lives in Miami Beach to this day.[61] There were a number of non-ordained ritual functionaries in the Sephardi community who continued to serve into the early 1980s. These included José Pinto, who was born in Jerusalem and died in Havana in 1984. According to his son, who still lives in Havana, he ministered to the Sephardi community at both Chevet Achim and Centro Sefaradi until 1982.[62] Solomon Sussi, born in Turkey, also served the Cuban community until his death in 1986. In the mid-1970s, Baldás hired Isaac Chammah, a learned Jew born in Syria, to teach Torah reading and synagogue skills to Moisés Asís and Jacobo Epelbaum. Epelbaum served as community *mohel* for a number of years until his emigration in 1979. Asís led services at the Patronato on Friday nights from the mid-1980s until his emigration in 1993. A number of elderly congregants also played key roles in keeping the services running. Of particular note was Jacobo Peretz, who was important for the survival of Chevet Ahim: he ran a bar on the first floor of the synagogue building, the revenues helping maintain the congregation.

Shrinkage of the community meant a shortage of Jewish marriage partners, and the intermarriage rate rose. Since Jewish families had to register for the purchase of Passover products, there are data on intermarriage for March and April 1975. In Havana, there were 430 families containing at least one Jewish member. Of this total, 308 had both spouses Jewish and 122 were composed of intermarried couples. In 26 other locations in Cuba there were a total of 113 Jewish families, of which 53 had two Jewish partners and 60 were intermarried. Thus, of the total of 543 families recorded in this census, 361 consisted of two Jewish partners and 192 were intermarried. The intermarriage rate was much higher—over 50 percent—outside of Havana than in the city, where it was below 30 percent.[63]

Many of those who identified as Jews were only partly Jewish by parentage. Of the 1,041 individuals affiliated with the Havana Jewish commu-

[61]See his comments, "Un Refugiado de la Guerra Civil Española," in Bejarano, ed., *La Comunidad Hebrea De Cuba,* pp. 123–124.

[62]Interview with Alberto Pinto, June 2000.

[63]The numbers of intermarried individuals varied not only between Havana and the rest of the country, but also between males and females. In Havana, 362 males were of two Jewish parents, whereas 309 females were; 132 men were of mixed parentage whereas 94 were; 46 men were non-Jewish whereas 98 females were. This last number indicates that twice as many Jewish men were married to non-Jewish women as Jewish women were married to non-Jewish men. In the 26 other locations the percentages were even more skewed, with more than three times as many Jewish men married to non-Jewish women as the reverse.

nity, 671 had two Jewish parents, 226 were born of mixed marriages, and 144 were of non-Jewish parentage. The total number of Jews for the rest of the country was 352, 173 of whom had two Jewish parents, 113 were of mixed parentage, and 66 were of non-Jewish parentage. Thus of the total number of 1,393 individuals counted in the census, 844 had two Jewish parents, 339 were of mixed parentage, and 210 had no Jewish parents.

Virtually all of those categorized as without Jewish parentage were married to Jews; since they were part of a family that was receiving Passover supplies, they were seen as being affiliated with the community. Likewise, those of mixed parentage reported in this census were either married to Jews or felt a sufficient degree of Jewish identity to register for the Passover supplies. By 1975, community leaders were well aware of the substantial presence in the Jewish community of people of non-Jewish and mixed origins, many of whom had "shifting identities." They might at one point identify as Jews—such as during the Passover distribution of food—and at other times, such as visits to the non-Jewish side of their families on Christian holidays, identify as Cubans of Catholic background. A number of Jewish leaders suggested that a rabbi or a panel of rabbis visit Cuba to regularize their status, a step that would not be taken till the early 1990s. Meanwhile, these individuals were accepted on their own terms into the community, if they chose to participate. The Jewish population was so small that tolerance and acceptance had become central values. This marked a dramatic change from the more exclusionary attitudes of the 1950s and earlier, when the community had been much larger.

By the late 1970s the community had hit its low point. Bernardo Benes, the prominent Cuban Jew residing in the U.S. who functioned as President Carter's unofficial emissary to Castro, had begun visiting regularly, and he did what he could to assist the local Jewish community. He recalls: "I was the first Cuban Jew to go back from Miami and meet with the leadership of the Cuban Jewish community, in 1978." The next year, when Benes had to fly in for a one-day meeting with Cuban authorities, he brought with him Rabbi Mayer Abramowitz, the rabbi of the Miami Cuban Jewish community. The first rabbi to set foot in the country in almost two decades, Abramowitz visited three of the Havana synagogues and performed a memorial service at the Jewish cemetery.[64]

That same year, 1979, Rabbi Isidoro Aizenberg visited the country on behalf of the Canadian Jewish Congress (CJC). Born in Argentina and having served a congregation in Caracas, Venezuela, Aizenberg went to each of the Havana synagogues and later described their low level of ac-

---

[64]Benes interview.

tivity. Though all five congregations held Sabbath services, and two—
Adath Israel and Chevet Ahim—tried to keep up a daily minyan, "a
minyan is [a] precious commodity." The Patronato, which had the largest
Sabbath service, could muster "over a dozen men and some women." In
the Centro Hebreo Sefaradi, Aizenberg and his wife encountered "several non-Jewish men and women, who, we were told, regularly and faithfully participate in the weekly Shabbat services." The United Hebrew
Congregation survived "thanks to the unshakable devotion of its elder
statesman, Isidoro Stettner," who "brings together a few people who pray
for half an hour from the *Union Prayer Book.*"

All the congregations were dominated by the elderly, for three reasons.
First, no one could be excused from work on religious grounds, and since
Saturday morning was part of the workweek, only retired people could
attend services without penalty. Second, as was the case elsewhere in
Latin America, most Cuban Jews had never been inclined to attend services regularly, and "today's conditions certainly do not encourage greater
attendance." Finally, there were few Jews who knew how to lead services
or read the Torah, and those who could tended to be the very elderly. Sabbath services in all the synagogues were followed by a kiddush, which
played a role "far beyond that of any such kiddush in Canada or the
U.S.A." For many of the 50–70 people attending services at the five synagogues, the food served—a roll with a slice of kosher canned meat, a
hard-boiled egg, and a piece of pound cake—"represents a daily meal."
Services in Chevet Ahim and the United Hebrew Congregation were held
in the main sanctuaries, which were relatively small and provided the only
available spaces for prayer. The other three congregations conducted
their services in their chapels, since "in reality, there is never—even during the High Holidays—a need to use the sanctuaries."[65]

Indeed, the congregations were all in the process of deciding how best
to utilize their facilities. The Patronato arranged for a government-
sponsored theater group to rent its central hall, and, in 1981, the government purchased this part of the building. At the time of Aizenberg's
visit, the Patronato's officers were in the middle of a debate over whether
to rent out the fully equipped kitchen and large "mirror hall," which had
served kosher meals. By 1979, this meal service was no longer operating
and the government's restaurant administration was interested in renting
out the space. The officers faced a dilemma. On one hand, they did not
use the space and did not need it. On the other hand, they had already
rented out a large portion of the building, and turning over an additional

---

[65]Isidoro Aizenberg, "Confidential Report to Alan Rose, Canadian Jewish Congress,
July 23, 1979," pp. 3–4, Rose Records.

segment appeared to signify a further step toward the community's demise.

Aizenberg's visit came shortly before the Sixth Conference of Non-aligned Nations, which Cuba was hosting in Havana, and the city was already plastered with slogans, one of which was "contra el sionismo," against Zionism. When the government ordered the closing of the Jewish community's Unión Sionista in June 1978—the only Jewish institution ever confiscated by the authorities, in marked contrast to the government's willingness to allow dwindling congregations to retain large synagogue buildings—the structure was turned over to the Palestine Liberation Organization (PLO), in an obvious attempt to demonstrate Cuban hostility to Zionism and the State of Israel.[66]

Aizenberg concluded, "During our two-week stay in Havana we witnessed the slow death of a Jewish community. Given the Jewish experience under other Communist regimes, there is little or no hope of reversing this process. Jewish destiny has always been *havrutah o mitutah,* fellowship or death, and there cannot be such fellowship in today's Havana."[67]

Many Cuban Jews apparently agreed, for when an opportunity came to leave the country—the Mariel boatlift—a substantial number seized it. In 1980 a group of 12 Cubans charged into the Peruvian embassy in Havana seeking asylum and safe exit from the country. A Cuban guard was killed in the course of the incident. In response to the Peruvian government's refusal to eject the occupants, Castro withdrew the Cuban military guards from outside the embassy. Word spread quickly that the Peruvian embassy was now unguarded, and within 24 hours more than 10,000 Cubans rushed into the embassy. Concerned about the widespread media coverage of the event and anxious to defuse what could be a catastrophic situation, Castro announced that any Cuban who would like to leave the country was free to do so. This caused great excitement in Florida's Cuban community, where plans were immediately made to bring relatives and loved ones from Cuba. American boats sped to pick up the thousands of Cubans who chose to emigrate. About 125,000 eventually left, most from the port of Mariel west of Havana, among them some 400 Jews. Those Cubans who reached the United States between April 1980 and September 1981 as part of this boatlift were called *marielitos.* Castro also used the Mariel boatlift as an opportunity to free himself of some of the most disaffected citizens of the country, releasing criminals from prison, as well as letting out psychiatric cases and other "antisocial" elements, and allowing them to emigrate to the U.S.

---

[66]Ibid, p. 12.
[67]Ibid, p. 14.

Some stigma attached to all the *marielitos,* and not only because of the association with Cuban misfits. Rosa Levy, a Jew who left Cuba at this time, forbade her children to tell people how and when they got out of Cuba. Levy believed—not without reason—that *marielito* was a label to be avoided at all costs, explaining: "I have been mentioned [in the community as a possible Communist]. While I was arriving here, the moment that I arrived, they, the first ones [1960 emigrants], mentioned that. . . . It's like you came late because you were a Communist.[68]

But the boatlift was an overwhelmingly positive experience for most participants. Whatever the underlying tensions, Jewish arrivals were greeted by Jewish Cuban Americans and assisted by the Greater Miami Jewish Federation's Resettlement Task Force and HIAS. With the emigration of the Jewish *marielitos* it was believed that the Jewish population of Cuba (not counting part-Jews or those who had disaffiliated) was now below 800, consisting mostly of the elderly and the hard-core supporters of the regime.

Attempts at Revitalization in the 1980s

Jacob Kovadloff, the American Jewish Committee's specialist on Latin American affairs, visited Cuba in 1981, 1983, and 1985.[69] On his first visit he found that about 300 Havana Jews were affiliated with one or another of the four synagogues left in the city. However, 831 people registered for kosher-for-Passover meals, which were sent into the country free of charge by the CJC and sold for a small fee by the local Jewish communities. Kovadloff agreed with earlier visitors that "Cuban Jews actually enjoy certain special privileges, such as being able to obtain the special Passover meals, year-round kosher meat and chicken, and fish for Rosh Hashanah and Passover, as well as additional potatoes. Religious services are permitted; but for cultural meetings the community must receive authorization, and this is frequently denied."[70]

Cuban Jews, fearful of spies, would only talk to Kovadloff in private. Nevertheless, one Cuban Jewish leader who preferred to remain anonymous told him, "twenty years after the revolution, we cannot say we are disappearing because of anti-Semitism. Rather, we are disappearing because of attrition." This attrition was particularly severe in the interior of the country. Three months before Kovadloff's arrival in 1981, the synagogue in Santiago de Cuba closed due to lack of attendance. Its four

---

[68]Bettinger-López, *Cuban-Jewish Journeys,* pp. 88–90.

[69]Interview with Jacob Kovadloff, June 2000.

[70]Memo from Jacob Kovadloff to Abraham Karlikow, Apr. 17, 1981, p. 1, American Jewish Committee Archives.

Torah scrolls had been brought to Havana, and community leaders asked Kovadloff to take them to the United States. Government approval was arranged and two of the scrolls were sent to congregations in Miami, one went to Puerto Rico, and one to Israel. The government "is anxious to prove that Cuba is not anti-Semitic, which is true," Kovadloff reported. However, he noted, Jews felt enormous pressure because of the government's anti-Zionism.

José Miller made a number of attempts to interest individual Jews and Jewish organizations outside the country in the Cuban Jewish community. As early as 1985 he proposed that a religious leader be sent from abroad to encourage young Jews to involve themselves in the Jewish community. He told Edgar Strauss, a visiting Canadian, that the community in Cuba was dying for lack of young leaders to replace the older people. The time was right for outside help, since the Cuban government was in the process of changing its religious policies, and Catholic and Protestant groups were rebuilding their communities. Strauss, the Canadian visitor, suggested, "in view of the make up of the Jewish community in Cuba, the rabbi or religious leader going there should not be Orthodox. Too many of the young people are from mixed marriages and uncertain background."[71] Alan Rose of the CJC was skeptical, responding, "it will be difficult indeed to find a religious leader to spend time in Cuba, although such a person would be performing a mitzvah."[72] (Two years earlier, when Jacob Luski, a Conservative rabbi in St. Petersburg, Florida, who had been born in Havana and lived there with his family until leaving for the United States in 1960, sought to volunteer his services to the Cuban Jewish community, Rose had advised that "it would be a great mitzvah to visit Cuba as a tourist" and do some religious visitations on an unofficial basis. Luski never made it to Cuba, but still hopes to do so.[73])

Another impediment to assisting the Cuban Jews was political sentiment in the United States, especially in the Miami area, that entailed "labeling Cubans who have remained in revolutionary Cuba as Communists, Castro-lovers, and traitors to the 'real' Cuba, the Cuba of the past."[74] Eddie Levy, the director of Jewish Solidarity, a Miami-based assistance program that helps Cuban Jews, explained, "the people who normally would have been in charge of helping the community there would have

---

[71]Edgar Strauss to Allan [sic] Rose, Mar. 14, 1985, Rose Records.

[72]Alan Rose to Edgar Strauss, Mar. 26, 1985, ibid.

[73]Jacob Luski to Alan Rose, Dec. 2, 1983; Rose to Luski, Dec. 20, 1983, ibid.; interview with Luski, May 2001.

[74]Bettinger-López, *Cuban-Jewish Journeys,* p. xl.

been the Cuban Jews that lived in the United States, and for political reasons they have kept apart from doing that, because they were afraid of the reaction that they would have had from the more reactionary elements in South Florida." One woman, a prominent Cuban Jew in the Miami area, told Levy, "Those Jews had a chance to go when I went, and they chose to stay behind. As far as I care they could all die of hunger."[75]

Marcus Kerbel served in a number of capacities for both of the "Cuban" congregations in Miami. During his time as president of the Cuban Hebrew Congregation in Miami Beach, Kerbel, too, found great reluctance on the part of the Jewish Cubans in Miami to help those still in Cuba live more comfortably there or to come to the United States. While one reason was the fear of bomb threats from the militants, another concern was that new waves of immigrants would place financial pressures on the existing congregations. "None of the congregations received the Cubans too warmly," recalled Kerbel. "Part of it was they couldn't figure out why there were Jews in Cuba, and, number two, they put a budget strain on those congregations. I was treasurer of Temple Beth Moshe [in North Miami], an American congregation, and they look to the budget."[76]

Despite the many obstacles, there were some promising developments in the 1980s. After years of discouraging tourism, the government shifted policy and began welcoming tourists. Many Jews came to visit, mostly from elsewhere in Latin America, and they frequently made contact with the local Jewish community. A number of foreign Jewish communities made specific donations that helped to set the stage for the revitalization of the community, such as the gift of *la gauguita,* a minibus, from the Jewish community of Venezuela. Chabad-Lubavitch started to work in Cuba in the late 1980s, bringing over educators and helping create new educational and social programs.

Cuban-Israeli Relations and the Cuban Jewish Community

Cuba adopted an aggressive anti-Israel policy after the Six-Day War of 1967 and especially after the 1973 Yom Kippur War. This position gradually softened over the years till the outbreak of sustained conflict between the Palestinians and Israelis in 2000 undermined much of the quiet progress that had been made.

The State of Israel began assisting the Cuban Communist government

---

[75]Interview with Eddie Levy, June 2000.
[76]Kerbel interview.

in the early 1960s, with Israeli scientists and engineers providing technical help in a number of areas. For example, farming specialists from kibbutzim affiliated with the left-wing socialist Hashomer Hatzair movement helped Cuba develop its agricultural sector. In addition, several private Israeli companies conducted business in Cuba. Even after the break in diplomatic relations an unofficial relationship between some Israeli business concerns and the Cuban government has continued and even intensified, in marked contrast to the official hostility between the two governments.

In 1966, Cuba invited members of the PLO and other Palestinian military organizations to come to Cuba for advanced training. This set the stage for Yasir Arafat, George Habash, and other Palestinian leaders to pay official visits to Havana. Castro was eager to extend Cuba's military and political influence in the Arab world beyond the Palestinians to Libya, Algeria, Syria, South Yemen, and elsewhere. There have been numerous reliable reports that Cuban military advisors helped train Spanish Basque fighters on Libyan soil, Polisario guerillas fighting against the Moroccan government in Algerian territory, and Communist government troops in South Yemen.

The outbreak of the Six-Day War in June 1967 came as the culmination of several weeks of growing political tension; Israel's Arab neighbors threatened to destroy the Jewish state, and Israel's preemptive strike in response to those threats was as remarkable as it was decisive. For Fidel Castro, the war offered an opportunity to fulfill his aspiration of playing a leading role among the nonaligned nations by supporting the Arab countries, which were part of the so-called third world. Furthermore, Israel was closely allied with the United States, and supporting the Arab cause would be another way of opposing American interests. Nevertheless, Castro hesitated. He had always maintained good relations with the Cuban Jewish community, and up until this point Cuban foreign policy had been generally sympathetic toward the State of Israel. The Soviet Union had broken diplomatic relations with the Jewish state in the aftermath of the war, which further complicated matters. Had Cuba done the same, it would have appeared as if Castro was mimicking the Soviet line. Therefore, he avoided taking these steps immediately, but instead, while condemning what the Arab side referred to as "Israeli aggression," he placed the bulk of the blame on "American imperialism." Castro did not break diplomatic relations with Israel, and he criticized the Arab countries for their political and military failures.

To be sure, on June 23, 1967, Ricardo Alarcón Quesada, the Cuban ambassador to the UN, gave an incendiary speech criticizing the State of Israel in very strong terms. Alarcón argued that Israel had committed "armed aggression against the Arab peoples."[77] Even more upsetting from a Jewish point of view, Alarcón described the Israeli preemptive strike as a "surprise attack, in the Nazi manner." Further, he opposed Israel's seeming ambition to annex the West Bank, Golan Heights, and Sinai Desert, "occupied by force of arms." This was the first time that any Cuban ambassador to the UN had condemned Israel in such unequivocal terms.

Alarcón, however, began his speech by declaring Cuba's opposition to any form of prejudice and stating that the Jews as well as the Palestinians deserved peace and justice. The diplomat argued that Cuba "as a matter of principle, [is] opposed to every manifestation of religious, national, or racial prejudice, from whatever source, and also objects to any political proclamation which advocates the destruction of any people or State. This principle is applicable to the Palestinian people . . . unjustly deprived of its territory, as well as the Jewish people, which for two thousand years has suffered racial prejudice and persecution, and during the recent Nazi period, one of the most cruel attempts at mass extermination."[78]

Consistent with Castro's own determination, Alarcón put the lion's share of the responsibility on "North American imperialism." "Our position with respect to the State of Israel is determined by [its] aggressive conduct . . . as an instrument of imperialism against the Arab world . . . it is in the context of the global strategy of imperialism that the true meaning . . . of the aggression . . . is revealed. . . . The criminal war unleashed by the imperialist government of the United States against the people of Vietnam, with absolute impunity, demonstrates this affirmation, if the experience of Korea, the Congo, and Santo Domingo . . . are not sufficient proof."[79]

The Soviet Union had broken diplomatic relations with Israel; all of the Eastern European Communist countries, except for Romania, had done likewise. But Castro's foreign policy priorities were different from those of the Soviet Union: while the Soviet Union felt it was essential to maintain a dialogue with the United States, Castro wanted to stress what he believed to be the American role in the development of conflict throughout the world.[80] Castro had a complex relationship with the Soviet Union. On one hand, he was a close ally, while on the other, he at-

---

[77] *Granma*, June 24, 1967, p. 7.
[78] Ibid.
[79] Ibid.
[80] Cuban diplomats sarcastically called the Soviets "big tailors" because they were "taking measures," trying to look like they were doing things when they actually were doing nothing. In contrast, the revolutionary Cubans prided themselves on being doers.

tempted to maintain as much independence from the USSR as possible. As Susan Eckstein puts it, "Shaped by the Cold War, Castro never became a complete pawn of Moscow . . . he on occasion implemented policies at odds with Moscow's and he manipulated Cold War politics to his country's advantage."[81]

In the years following the Six-Day War, Castro consistently refused to break diplomatic relations with Israel. But a few days before the Yom Kippur War in 1973, he succumbed to pressure. At this point, Castro was the leader of the pro-Soviet element among the third-world countries. In Algeria to participate in a conference of nonaligned nations, Castro was looking forward to refuting the idea, supported by the Chinese, that there were two imperialisms threatening the world, one from the United States and the other from the Soviet Union. Castro spoke for only half an hour, and his speech drew tremendous criticism. The exiled Prince Norodom Sihanouk of Cambodia, for one, cited the recent history of his own country as a classic example of how the two imperialistic powers had colluded to destroy countries and nations.

More seriously, Colonel Muammar Qaddafi, the Libyan leader, went so far as to state that Cuba had no business belonging to an organization of nonaligned states because Cuba was, like Uzbekistan or Czechoslovakia, allied with the Soviet Union. Qaddafi's verbal attack nearly caused the conference to break up in chaos. Castro needed to make a dramatic gesture to save his reputation as a third-world leader, and so he announced that he had been persuaded to sever diplomatic relations with the State of Israel. Qaddafi rushed over to Castro and gave him a big hug. *Granma,* the official Cuban Communist Party newspaper, reported that Castro's announcement was greeted with a standing ovation that "seemed to last forever."[82]

There is no doubt that breaking diplomatic relations with Israel was Castro's spur-of-the-moment personal decision, and it caught the Cuban government bureaucracy completely by surprise. But the country's officials and its media quickly fell into line. During the Yom Kippur War that broke out soon thereafter, a contingent of Cuban soldiers actually participated in tank battles on the Syrian side. Cuba portrayed Israel not only as the aggressor but also as having committed atrocities against civilians, particularly Syrians. Cuba became one of the most extreme anti-Israel voices on the international scene, even lobbying against the Egyptian-Israeli peace process and lining up as one of the sponsors of the "Zion-

---

[81]Susan Eva Eckstein, *Back from the Future: Cuba Under Castro* (Princeton, N.J., 1994), p. 5.

[82]*Granma,* Sept. 16, 1973, p. 6.

THE JEWS OF CUBA

Memories of the past . . .

Collection of Arturo López Levy

The Jewish cemetery, Havana.

Building of the once thriving United Hebrew Congregation,
closed in 1981.

Services at the Patronato, center of the Jewish revival.

The social hall.

The main sanctuary.

Collection of Arturo López Levy

The Centro Sefaradi, interior and exterior views.

Collection of Arturo López Levy

Collection of Arturo López Levy

Women's organization of Adath Israel.

**Adath Israel,
the Orthodox
synagogue.**

Collection of Arturo López Levy

Signs of renewal . . .

Collection of Arturo López Levy

The recently revived Jewish community of Santa Clara, in Central Cuba.

Alberto Behar of Havana, first native-born Torah reader since the revolution.

FACES OF CUBAN

José Miller Fredman, president of the Jewish community since 1978.

Isaac Gelen, president, B'nai B'rith Maimonides Lodge.

Maritza Corrales Capestany, historian.

JEWISH LIFE TODAY

José Levy Tur, interfaith activist.

Prof. Lourdes Albo, leader of the
Jewish seniors club.

Ivan Glait, JDC director.

A new generation . . .

Young Cuban Jews celebrate
Purim at the Patronato.

ism is Racism" resolution adopted by the UN General Assembly on November 10, 1975. The government newspaper called this resolution a "forward step by the peoples of the world" which "left no doubt about the identical imperialist origins and racist structure of the Israeli Zionist regime that is occupying Palestine and the one that is exploiting the black masses of Zimbabwe and South Africa."[83]

In November 1974, PLO leader Yasir Arafat visited Cuba, where the government gave him a high-level reception and Cuba's highest decoration, the Order of Playa Girón. In 1975, in his opening report to the Congress of the Cuban Communist Party, Castro strongly attacked Israel as a tool of "U.S. imperialism," which the American government was using to threaten the territorial integrity of the Soviet Union along its southern flank.[84] The congress adopted a strong statement in support of Palestinian national rights. In December 1975, Castro confirmed reports that Cuban troops had been sent to Syria before the 1973 war, a public demonstration that his anti-Zionism had moved from the realm of polemics into actual military involvement on the Arab side.

On October 12, 1979, in a speech at the UN, Castro claimed that the State of Israel was committing genocide against the Palestinian people, similar to the "genocide that the Nazis once visited on the Jews."[85] Castro stated that the Palestinians were "living symbols of the most terrible crime of our era," thus inferring that Israeli crimes against the Palestinians were worse than anything that had been done in Uganda, Vietnam, or Cambodia.[86]

This was certainly a dramatic change in Cuban policy, but Allan Metz has argued that it did not cause Castro any sleepless nights: "Principle may have had nothing to do with the abrupt change in Cuban policy toward Israel. In this respect, he was no different from others who wielded arbitrary power. At any rate, the main reason for Castro's shift in his policy toward Israel was pure and simple opportunism. And once he embarked on this new policy, he sought to gain as much benefit as possible. Castro proved to be very successful because he bolstered his ambition of portraying himself as a third-world leader while simultaneously gaining the appreciation of the Soviet Union."[87]

Castro's new Israel policy made things difficult for Cuban Jews, espe-

---

[83]Ibid., Jan. 18, 1976.

[84]*Granma Weekly Review*, Jan. 4, 1976, p. 10.

[85]Allan Metz, "Cuban-Israeli Relations: From the Cuban Revolution to the New World Order," *Cuban Studies* 23, 1993, p. 123, quotes from the official UN proceedings.

[86]*Granma Weekly Review*, Oct. 21, 1979, quoted in Halperin, *Taming of Fidel Castro*, p. 254, n. 16.

[87]Metz, "Cuban-Israeli Relations," p. 123.

cially as the turn against the Jewish state coincided with a period of deterioration within the Cuban Jewish community that had nothing to do with the Middle East. In 1975, the Patronato's kosher restaurant closed down, and the "Jewish" public school with its afternoon Hebrew school came to an end. Hebrew classes, instead of being conducted daily, were reduced to once a week, and came close to being stopped entirely. It appeared that the community no longer had the critical mass necessary to sustain a viable Jewish life. Moisés Baldás, the leader of the Jewish community, had worked hard to cultivate good relations between Cuba and Israel, and the turn toward virulent anti-Zionism, coinciding with other danger signals for the Jewish community, made it impossible for him to function effectively as the representative of Cuban Jewry. In 1981, as noted above, Baldás settled in Israel. José Miller Fredman, his protégé and successor, long a supporter of the revolution, had to be particularly careful in presenting his views on Israel and Zionism, since, while the Jewish community looked to the Jewish state as a treasured homeland, the government portrayed it as a tool of Yankee imperialism.

By the late 1980s, there were signs that Cuban-Israeli relations were warming up again. In 1988, Castro was reported to have told Venezuelan Jewish leaders traveling in Cuba that "Cuba has a lot to learn from Israel."[88] That same year, an official economic delegation from Cuba visited Israel to study irrigation methods; Israel had pioneered a number of innovative techniques, and this was of great importance to Cuban agricultural specialists who were trying to improve citrus production. Since 1988, Israeli experts have continued to provide technical assistance in this area, in methods of growing other agricultural products, and even in fishing.

These contacts preceded, if only by a short period, the crisis that engulfed Cuba after the fall of Communism in Eastern Europe. By June 1990, Cuba had opened unofficial lines of communication with Israel, using the left-wing socialist party Mapam, whose ideology seemed congenial to Cuban socialist principles, as the conduit. Castro's primary concern after the fall of Soviet Communism was the survival of his regime, all other factors taking a back seat. Despite Cuba's acute need for oil in the aftermath of the Soviets' withdrawal of subsidies, Cuba had little to gain politically from a virulent anti-Israel position at a time when Arab countries were beginning to sign peace treaties with Israel.

But Israeli support for the American embargo against Cuba remained a source of tension. In November 1999, the State of Israel was the only country to join with the United States against a UN vote to end the em-

---

[88]"Around the Hemisphere: Cuba," *Latin American Report,* Dec. 1988, p. 5.

bargo. *Granma,* the Communist Party newspaper, featured the vote on its front page, noting that 157 nations had voted to end the economic embargo. The headline read "The World Against the Blockade," with a subheading: "Two countries NO: United States, Israel."[89] Conversely, because of its alignment with the Arab countries, the Cuban government voted against Israel on various issues at the UN.

The question of Cuba's policy toward Israel was addressed by a delegation from the American Jewish Congress, led by its president, Jack Rosen, in July 1998. The delegation, which said it was ready to "look seriously" into calling for an end to the U.S. economic boycott of Cuba, met with President Castro for a six-hour dinner at the presidential palace. Delegates expressed their disappointment that Cuba was the only country in the Western Hemisphere to vote against rescinding the UN's "Zionism is Racism" resolution, and Castro responded that he was actually unaware of the position taken by the Cuban delegation at the UN. As it happened, Ricardo Alarcón, the Cuban UN representative who actually cast the vote, was present at the dinner, and, not surprisingly, he did not offer to field the question. Other Cuban officials informally told Rosen that the vote was to be expected, given the fact that Israel voted against Cuba on virtually every matter.

In June 2001, the Cuban government expressed strong support for the Palestinians at a two-day UN-organized regional forum on the Middle East conflict held in Havana and attended by representatives from 45 countries. Cuban foreign minister Felipe Pérez Roque told the forum: "There will be no fair and lasting peace in the region until an independent Palestinian state is proclaimed, with eastern Jerusalem recognized as its capital." Farouk Kaddoumi, the head of the PLO's political department, exclaimed, "Cuba has been the Palestinian people's best friend in our fight for the peace and stability of the Middle East." Pérez Roque went on to connect Israel's alleged "crimes" with the political support it received from the United States. "Israel's killing machinery has been developed and perfected for years thanks to the financial, military and technological aid of the United States, its unconditional ally which shares responsibility for the grave violations of the Palestinian people's basic human rights."[90]

Following the forum, President Castro personally led a demonstration of solidarity with the Palestinian people held in the "anti-imperialist" plaza built during the Elián González controversy, directly across from the United States Interests Section on the Malecón (seaside promenade)

---

[89] *Granma,* Nov. 10, 1999, p. 1.
[90] "Cuba backs Palestinians at U.N. forum in Havana," Reuters report, June 12, 2001.

in Havana. A student addressed the approximately 10,000 people with the words: "We want to demand the end of the genocide against our brother Arab nation. Long live the heroic Palestinian people! Long live the Arab people who fight against Imperialism! Socialism or death!"[91] Speakers alternated with poets, singers, and even pantomime artists acting out scenes of violence from the Middle East. Yasir Arafat wrote to thank Castro for his enthusiastic support: "It was with great emotion that we have seen your excellency with the Palestinian flag on your shoulders leading a massive show of solidarity with our heroic people. I consider this show of unbreakable friendship and firmness in Havana as a strong and effective message on the part of a loved international leader who enjoys great world prestige."[92]

It deserves emphasis that anti-Zionist or anti-Israel policies pursued by the Cuban government in the 1970s, 1980s, and later did not result in any increased local anti-Jewish activity. There remains a great deal of sympathy for Jews among the Cuban people and among government officials, and this carries the seeds for improved relations with the State of Israel in the future.

The Fall of Communism and the New Religious Environment

Soon after Mikhail Gorbachev came to power in the Soviet Union in 1985 he embarked on a course of reform, and the fallout was immediate. Within a year, virtually all of the Eastern European states had started the long and difficult process of transformation into democracies with free-market capitalism. The final, dramatic conclusion occurred on November 9, 1989, with the fall of the Berlin Wall, followed soon thereafter by the unification of Germany.

With European Communism dying, Castro had to face the loss of his few remaining allies in 1989 and 1990. On December 20, 1989, U.S. forces invaded Panama, and Manuel Noriega's cocaine-financed government toppled almost immediately. On February 25, 1990, the Nicaraguan Sandinistas called an election and were defeated by Violeta Barrios de Chamorro. Castro took the loss hard, since he had considered Sandinista leader Daniel Ortega not only a political ally but also his "revolutionary son." Ortega's defeat left the Cuban government with no close ideological allies in the entire region.

---

[91]"Castro leads pro-Palestinian rally in Cuba," *Ha'aretz,* June 15, 2001, p. 1.

[92]"Arafat agradece el apoyo de Castro," *El Nuevo Herald,* June 22, 2001. Thanks to Prof. Jaime Suchlicki for faxing me a copy of this article.

There were those who expected the Communist Cuban government to fall just as quickly as those in Eastern Europe. *Miami Herald* journalist Andres Oppenheimer named his 1992 book *Castro's Final Hour: An Eyewitness Account of the Disintegration of Castro's Cuba*. The book described the withdrawal of Soviet support, the apparent dissatisfaction even among the highest-ranking politicians and military leaders, the loss of Cuba's regional allies, and the terrible shortages of almost all consumer goods—a situation of economic stringency that Cubans came to call, euphemistically, the "special period." Oppenheimer can be forgiven for feeling confident that Cuba had indeed reached "Castro's final hour," and he was not alone. *Time* magazine crowed, "Castro's Cuba—The End of the Dream"; *U.S. News and World Report* wrote about "Fidel Castro's Last Battle"; while the *New York Times* titled one article, "The Last Days of Castro's Cuba." *Newsweek* more accurately described what was going on in the country as "Cuba's Living Death," and *Life* magazine titled one report, "Waiting for the end in Cuba."[93] *Life* magazine has since ceased publication for the second time, but Fidel Castro, in 2001, goes on.

With Communism in retreat throughout the world, Cuba has successfully redefined itself and avoided radical political change. One tactic has been the co-optation of previously excluded groups, such as religious believers, a policy that has yielded the added benefit of helping develop relationships with foreign-based programs of a religious nature that provide economic aid.

For more than two decades, the government has gradually increased religious freedom, though the rapprochement between religion and state is both complex and ambivalent.[94] At the same time that the government has been easing the old restrictions on religious activities, Cubans have demonstrated an increased level of interest in religious participation, but there may not be a simple cause-and-effect relationship between the two trends. Jorge Ramirez Calzadilla of the Center of Psychological and Sociological Research in Havana argues that the resurgence of religion in Cuba has little to do with government policy but is in large measure a response to the spiritual and economic crisis brought on by the collapse of the Soviet Union and the economic rigors of the "special period."[95] This is a widely held view. Today few Cubans take Communism seri-

[93]The headlines are cited in Tom Miller, *Trading with the Enemy: A Yankee Travels Through Castro's Cuba* (New York, 1992), p. xxii.

[94]John M. Kirk, *Between God and the Party: Religion and Politics in Revolutionary Cuba* (Tampa, 1989).

[95]Eloy O. Aguilar, "Religion Grows in Cuba," Associated Press report, Aug. 18, 1997.

ously, and they are looking for something to believe in. When Rabbi Jeffrey Salkin of the Community Synagogue of Port Washington, New York, visited Cuba during Passover in 1997, he asked some of the university students he met why there was so much interest in religion. "They had one answer," reported Salkin: " 'Communism is a spiritual failure.' "[96] Aside from the spiritual vacuum, there are other needs that religion fills. In Cuba, money is scarce; there are no multiplex cinemas, no Disney theme parks, and no shopping malls. Churches and synagogues provide a place to meet, mingle, and be entertained. They offer classes, services, and even festive dinners.[97]

The Communist government had never banned religious affiliation or activity for the general public, although it was forbidden for members of the Communist Party. Still, since the authorities viewed it with disfavor, many Cubans believed that involvement with a church or synagogue could stigmatize them and stunt their career opportunities. Thus the Cuban Communist Party's repeal of the prohibition on religious involvement for members in October 1991 came as a great surprise. The Cuban constitution was then revised to state that education would henceforth be "secular," rather than "atheistic," as set forth in the previous version. The old Marxist-Leninist philosophical definition of the Cuban state was also excised from the constitution.

In the decades following the 1959 revolution, most congregations of all religions had become accustomed to seeing a steady decline in membership. Many of the most devoted church members, fearful of religious intolerance, left the country in the early years, and those who remained often distanced themselves from religious activity. That is no longer the case. Today, Christian churches are growing exponentially, the number of baptisms jumping from 25,258 in 1979, to 50,979 in 1990, and 62,664 in 1992.[98] Although some of the "new faithful" are returning to the churches they were raised in, many are former atheists with no previous history of religious involvement.

The rising fortunes of Judaism have been directly tied to the successes of other Cuban religious groups.

Pope John Paul II's visit to Cuba on January 25, 1998, had a profound impact on the whole country. Enrique López Oliva, a professor of the history of religion at the University of Havana for many years and now a

---

[96]Rabbi Jeffery K. Salkin, "Cuba: A Preparation for Liberation," sermon delivered on Shabbat Chol Ha-Mo'ed Pesach, Apr. 19, 1997, at the Community Synagogue, Port Washington, New York.
[97]Tom Masland, "Learning To Keep The Faith," *Newsweek,* Mar. 13. 1995, p. 30.
[98]These statistics were culled from the *Amario Pontifica Vaticano.*

freelance journalist, emphasized its significance: "Do you remember that John Reed book about the Bolshevik Revolution, *Ten Days That Shook the World?* Well, we can call this 'Five Days that Shook Cuba.' "[99] Speaking to hundreds of thousands of Cubans gathered in Plaza de la Revolución for the final Mass of his historic visit, the pope argued that atheism could not be the official ideology of a modern state. Rather, he said, personal freedom was the only way to achieve true justice: "This is the time to start out on the new paths called for by the times of renewal that we are experiencing."[100]

On Sunday, January 25, the pope met with two Cuban Jewish representatives, Dr. José Miller, the community's head, and Abraham Berezniak, president of Adath Israel. After Berezniak and the pope chatted about their Polish backgrounds, the three men discussed Christian-Jewish relations.[101]

In the aftermath of the pope's visit the government set up a committee to decide whether to make December 25 an official holiday, and Castro named Miller and Adela Dworin as members The fact that two prominent Jews were placed on a panel to decide on the recognition of a Christian holiday, a matter unrelated to the Jewish community, showed how seriously Castro took the opinion of the tiny Jewish minority. Furthermore, it was through participation in these meetings that Miller began to develop a personal relationship with Castro that he would use for the benefit of the Cuban Jewish community.[102]

Then, as part of the new openness to religion resulting from the papal visit, Miller and Dworin invited Fidel Castro to celebrate Hanukkah, in December 1998, at the Patronato. Castro came with Carlos Lage Dávila, one of Cuba's five vice presidents, and Felipe Pérez Roque, considered by many to be Castro's closest confidant outside of his family, who then served as his personal assistant and who today is minister of foreign affairs. Also in attendance were two members of the Central Committee, Eusebio Leal Spengler, the official historian of the city of Havana, and Caridad Diego Bello, head of the Department of Religious Affairs. Castro spoke extemporaneously and at great length on a variety of subjects

---

[99]Interview with Enrique López Oliva, June 2000.

[100]"Pontiff calls for 'New Paths' in Cuba," *Miami Herald*, Jan. 26, 1998, p. 1.

[101]A photograph of the pope and Berezniak, taken at that meeting, is displayed today at Adath Israel. Berezniak died in April 1998, three months after the papal visit, at the age of 50.

[102]Miller interview. In November 1998, at one of the committee meetings, Castro turned to Miller and asked, "What do you think?" Miller responded, "How could I possibly object to a holiday celebrating the birth of a nice Jewish boy?"

related to Jews and Judaism in a warm and informal style. He also asked the audience questions, and paid rapt attention to the answers.[103]

There had been very little formal contact between Jewish and Christian organizations in Cuba until 1980, when Dr. Kenneth Schulman, a professor of social work at Boston University, introduced Moisés Asís to Adolfo Ham, a Presbyterian minister serving as president of the Ecumenical Council of Cuba. Ham had a special interest in the philosophy of Martin Buber and was very keen on developing a relationship with Asís and with the Jewish community. When the Patronato held a commemoration of the 850th birthday of Maimonides, Ham was invited as one of the speakers. Subsequently, Asís was appointed to be the first Jewish representative on CEHILA, a center for religious ecumenism, and began contributing articles to the Ecumenical Council's *Mensaje* magazine. Today, the Jewish community is a special member of the Ecumenical Council, and its representative on CEHILA is José Levy Tur. There have also been contacts with the National Council of Churches in Cuba. When the Jewish community has a special event, Christian visitors often come as invited guests.

Such interfaith involvement has helped the Jewish community achieve greater recognition in the broader society, especially since the government sometimes calls on representatives of religious groups, including Jews, to help it achieve political objectives. For example, Dr. José Miller traveled to the United States as part of a delegation that included prominent Cuban church leaders to explain why he believed the embargo against Cuba should be lifted.

The relationship between the Cuban Jewish community and the Catholic Church has been growing. The Vatican embassy in Cuba invited the leaders of the Jewish community to attend an event there on the occasion of Pope John Paul's visit, and around the same time the Catholic magazine *Espacios* published an article by Arturo López Levy about Catholic-Jewish relationships, "Tenemos Tanto que Hacer Juntos" (We have so many things to do together). This was the first time that any Cuban Catholic publication had included an article by a Jew. Shortly thereafter, the Dominican Order included the Jewish community—represented by Arturo López Levy—in a roundtable discussion for leaders of different religious bodies to discuss the meaning of the papal visit for religion in Cuba. During Catholic Social Week the next year, in June 1999, Levy was invited to

---

[103]José Miller, "La Visita del Presidente Fidel Castro a la Comunidad Judía de Cuba," *Menorah*, Nov./Dec. 1998, p. 3. The description of Castro's behavior is based on a privately taken video of the event. The visit was reported in the party newspaper, which also published a positive editorial, "Asiste el Comandante en Jefe a actividad de la Comunidad Judía," *Granma*, Dec. 22, 1998, p. 8.

make a presentation on globalization and how the religious communities in Cuba might help the country integrate into the world economy. In September 1999, Cardinal Jaime Ortega of Havana visited Adath Israel to hear the blowing of the shofar for Rosh Hashanah 5760. In a pastoral letter, Ortega recounted his visit to the synagogue, referring to the Jews as "his older brothers." Ortega wrote: "When I say 'our future' I am not invoking the Catholic God, rather the only God—Father, creator of all. If we are sons of the same father, then it opens in us these wonderful and complementary truths: all men are my brothers."[104]

Outside Aid

THE CANADIAN JEWISH CONGRESS ASSISTANCE PROGRAM

After the revolution, the Jews remaining in Cuba came to feel increasingly isolated. Since, for many Cuban Jews, the distribution of Passover foods was the sole Jewish activity they remembered from their childhood, providing those foods became the primary way of reasserting the Jewish world's link with Cuban Jewry.

Before the revolution the Jewish community of Cuba had obtained Passover supplies from the American Jewish Joint Distribution Committee (JDC), in the United States, but once the two countries severed diplomatic relations this was no longer feasible. In 1961 representatives of the community issued an urgent appeal for help. Since the JDC in New York was unable to provide direct assistance, Moses Leavitt, the JDC executive vice chairman, routed the request to the Canadian Jewish Congress (CJC). Canada had never broken diplomatic relations with Cuba, and Canadians were not restricted from visiting or conducting business with Cuba. Jack Silverstone of the CJC stated, "Canada has a rather good relationship . . . compared to the Americans. We give quite a bit of foreign aid down there, so we have very good access without difficulty."[105]

The Canadians needed to obtain a permit from Cuba for permission to import food products for Passover use, and another permit in Ottawa to export the food from Canada. They had difficulty finding shipping space, and at one point it seemed certain that the only way they would be able to send in any goods would be by air. Finally, space was obtained on a boat leaving from St. John, New Brunswick, on March 13, 1961, with a scheduled arrival date in Havana of March 23. Since this arrangement

---

[104]Cardinal Jaime Ortega, "Un Solo Díos Padre de Todos," *Palabra Nueva,* Dec. 1999, section 28.
[105]Interview with Jack Silverstone, Dec. 1999.

was made at the last minute, the CJC feared it would not be able to get the matzo and kosher Passover wine to port in time for loading.[106] But it did, and on April 5 Congregation Adath Israel sent a cable to Sigmund Unterberg of the CJC in Montreal to acknowledge that the shipment had arrived.[107]

The CJC has continued to send the Passover products annually. Over the years, Edmond Lipsitz, the executive director of the Ontario CJC, was concerned that there might have been difficulties in receiving or distributing the Passover supplies in Cuba.[108] When he visited in 1987, Lipsitz found that while the Cuban Jewish community had often been uncertain about the arrival dates of the ships, the community had indeed received the food, and, he remarked, "The fact is [that] we are sending more matzo than they need."[109]

To give an example of the quantity of food shipped and the cost involved, the CJC's Josh Rotblatt calculated the exact expense for 1992. Three thousand pounds of matzo sent at $1.53 Canadian per pound worked out to $4,590. Two thousand pounds of matzo meal were sent at $1.50 per pound, and 3,600 liters of oil at $2.375 per liter. With a thousand cans of tuna at $1.00 a can, 1,500 cans of sardines at $1.82 a can, 240 boxes of tea at $2.95 a box, and 504 jars of horseradish at $2.10 a jar, the total came to $21,636 Canadian. (Not included in the estimate were 840 bottles of kosher wine, 2,500 packages of kosher soup, 600 pounds of powdered milk, and $22,000 for airfreight expenses via Mexico—the food was assembled too late that year to send by boat).[110] The Jewish communities of Mexico, Venezuela, and Panama have also provided some assistance, as have individual American Jews. Jack Rosen of New Jersey, for example, who owned a private plane, made a number of trips to Havana to deliver Passover supplies.

In 2000, the Cuban government agreed for the first time to cooperate actively in the CJC's annual shipment of Passover goods. Pedro Garcia Roque, Cuba's consul general in Montreal, helped arrange for Cubana, the country's national airline, to ship 4,000 kilograms of kosher supplies

---

[106]"CJC Rushes Passover Supplies to Cuba," *Congress Bulletin,* Apr. 1961, p. 1.

[107]Cominidad Religiosa Hebrea Adath Israel to Sigmund Unterberg, Apr. 5, 1961, Anglo-American collection 493, Western Union International Communications. The telegram read: "Received matzoth wine good order twenty-eighth paid five thousand five hundred custom tax stop fully satisfied and much obliged your excellent attention stop after Passover will send letters."

[108]Interview with Edmond Lipsitz, Nov. 2000.

[109]Ben Kayfetz, "Cuban Jews in Need of Rabbis, Visitor Finds," *Ottawa Jewish Bulletin and Review,* Sept. 11, 1987, p. 22.

[110]Josh Rotblatt to Yehuda Lipsitz, Feb. 27, 1992; and "Passover Products for Cuban Jewry," both in Canadian Jewish Congress National Archives.

free of charge, and another 6,000 kilograms at a greatly reduced rate. In previous years the CJC had shipped about 40 percent of the supplies via Cubana at regular airfreight rates, with the rest being sent by ship; in 2000 the Cubana offer made it possible to send the entire shipment by air. The goods left Montreal on March 31, and arrived in Havana the same day, the first time a shipment was received so far ahead of the Passover holiday, which began that year on the evening of April 19. Furthermore, businessman Walter Arbib of Toronto-based Skylink Aviation underwrote the cost of sending the supplies from Havana to the Jewish communities in the provinces by air rather than overland.[111]

Over the years, the food has not only served the ritual requirements and nutritional needs of Cuban Jews, but has also been of great symbolic significance. Jack Silverstone of the CJC said, "I can't overestimate the importance of the Passover food order to these folks. For a long time, it was their only connection to Judaism; they just couldn't get what they needed. They are extremely appreciative of it, and rely on it." He added, "I almost didn't realize how important it was until I got down there and they spoke so emotionally about the Canadian connection. It was very touching. When the community got together for seders, that was basically *the* major Jewish event across the island, and it was important."[112]

UJA (UJC) MISSIONS

From spiritual retreats to Internet study groups, American Jewish organizations are harnessing progressively more sophisticated and creative techniques for grabbing and holding the interest of their actual or potential clientele. Missions abroad have become a popular part of an increasingly complex network of informal American Jewish educational projects. Such missions, generally restricted to those who give substantial contributions to the UJA, reinforce the most viscerally felt values of civil Judaism, especially the classical rabbinic injunction that "all Jews are responsible for one another."[113]

During the 1990s, Cuba became a popular destination for these missions, as the American government quietly eased certain restrictions on contact with that country. On January 5, 1999, the U.S. announced its first public change of policy, allowing the institution of direct charter flights to Cuba to help facilitate family reunions, reestablishing direct mail con-

---

[111]Ron Csillag, "Cuba to help CJC bring in food for Pesach," *Canadian Jewish News,* Apr. 13, 2000, p. 7.
[112]Silverstone interview.
[113]On Jewish civil religion in the U.S., see Jonathan S. Woocher, *Sacred Survival: The Civil Religion of American Jews* (Bloomington and Indianapolis, 1986).

tact, and legalizing educational, cultural, journalistic, athletic, and religious exchanges. Direct charter flights between New York and Havana began in the fall of 1999, offering travelers an option in addition to the Miami-Havana route. A Los Angeles-Havana flight was inaugurated shortly thereafter.

The new regulations gave added impetus to the work of nonprofit organizations, religious and secular, interested in bringing groups to Cuba, and the flow of United Jewish Appeal (UJA) missions to Cuba intensified. UJA, since reorganized and merged with the Council of Jewish Federations and the United Israel Appeal, is today known as the United Jewish Communities (UJC). Its missions now arrive at the rate of about one a month from many American Jewish communities, including Detroit, San Francisco, Houston, Boston, New York, and, of course, South Florida.[114]

When UJA began sponsoring missions abroad, almost all were to Israel, the Jewish spiritual homeland, or to Eastern Europe, where the majority of American Jews trace their roots. Cuba is neither of these things. Amir Shaviv, assistant executive vice president of the JDC, explained, "The reason they go to Cuba is because it's a nearby destination that gives you, in a nutshell, the entire scope of Jewish revival of a community that was barred from Jewish life. If you have three days and you want to go somewhere and see what your money is doing, Cuba is the place to go."[115] Furthermore, Cuban Jewry seems tailor-made to fulfill the psychological needs of the mission participants: Cuban Jews are well educated and many speak English. They are in the midst of an extraordinary process of Jewish return, which cannot help but inspire American Jews who are deeply concerned about perpetuating their own religious identity. And finally, the economic deprivation that is so evident in Cuba inspires mission participants and convinces them that there is a real need they can help fill. So popular have missions to Cuba become, in fact, that in 1998 the JDC, which has professionals in the country working to revive Cuban Jewish life, felt compelled to ask American Jewish groups "to cut back on the number of visits, which have been somewhat overwhelming for the community."[116]

---

[114]In truth, the South Florida embarkation point is less obvious than it might appear, since Cuban Americans residing there are subjected to considerable pressure not to visit Cuba so long as Fidel Castro is president.

[115]Melissa Radler, "Cuba Emerges as Destination Much Favored by Federations," *Forward*, Apr. 28, 2000, p. 5.

[116]Kenneth Bandler, "Jewish organization considers call for end to embargo of Cuba," *Jewish Telegraphic Agency Daily News Bulletin*, June 25, 1998, p. 3.

Stephanie Simon participated on one of these missions.[117] The mother of three young children, Simon had to pass up a number of missions that were offered by the UJA's Young Leadership Cabinet, of which she is a member, because the trips to Poland, Czechoslovakia, and Israel ran from ten days to two weeks, far too long for her to be away from her children. But when a four-day mission to Cuba was announced, she jumped at the chance. A reporter interviewed her in her Marblehead, Massachusetts, home shortly after her return from Havana. Simon spoke enthusiastically of the "amazing trip, which changed my life," relating that when she was halfway home from the airport, she suddenly burst into tears from all that she had seen and experienced in Cuba. Simon told of meeting people who walked an hour and a half to get their children to the Sunday morning Hebrew school, and remarked on the joy she felt when watching a performance that the Hebrew school gave. These children sang the same Hebrew songs her own children sing, bringing home the conviction that these could be her children.

She described the poverty of the community, and was immensely excited about the important work that the UJA was doing to alleviate it, saying, "I saw where our Federation dollars go. People here [in the United States] complain about the Jewish Community Center (JCC), or this or that. In Cuba, those dollars are buying milk for children. The funds are purchasing a breakfast and a lunch. This is 60 [sic] miles from the U.S.! These are kids who don't have enough food to eat." Participating in Friday night services at the Patronato, Sephanie Simon's mission saw the congregation make the blessing over bread using matzo that was left over from Passover, and then eat a small chicken dinner. The UJA group decided to pool their contributions to provide the congregation with real hallah (Sabbath loaves), as well as chicken, wine, candles, and other products so that the congregation could celebrate Shabbat comfortably. Almost on the spot, the group raised $18,000, enough to sponsor Shabbat dinner for the entire congregation for a year.

Not everyone in the Jewish community supports these Cuban missions. The weekly *Forward* newspaper, for one, criticized the missions in a front-page editorial in 2000. Directly under the by-now-infamous photo of Elián González being taken at gunpoint from the home of his Miami relatives, the *Forward* questioned why there were 30 Jewish missions planned for the near future, asking whether the aim was "to help the 600 [sic] Jews trapped in the communist country," or whether "the backers of the

---

[117]Bette Wineblatt Keva, "Young Mother's UJA Mission to Cuba," *Jewish Journal* (Boston), Mar. 16–20, 1998.

biggest American Jewish charitable structure emerge with those pressing for a soft line on the communist regime during the twilight years of its dictator, Fidel Castro" instead of "the hard line for which so many have sacrificed so much."[118]

The "biggest American Jewish charitable structure" meant the United Jewish Communities (UJC), the umbrella organization for local Jewish federations, which, among them, raise approximately $790 million annually for Jewish charitable needs, and the *Forward* was virtually accusing it of being soft on Castro-style Communism. While the missions were ostensibly apolitical, the *Forward* believed that they served a political agenda by creating goodwill for the Castro regime and pumping tourist dollars into the Cuban economy. In contrast to many in the Jewish community, the *Forward* continued to support the economic embargo of Cuba: "This embargo may not have toppled Mr. Castro's dictatorship, but it has helped stymie his efforts to export his revolution to Latin America. And it has curbed the ability of communist sympathizers, or rank opportunists, to exploit properties the communists seized in Cuba."[119]

In an accompanying front-page news story, the *Forward* quoted both defenders of the missions as well as other critics, who contended that the amount of Jewish money spent in Cuba was way out of proportion to the needs of other sectors of world Jewry, such as the large numbers of poverty-stricken Jews living in the former Soviet Union and elsewhere in Eastern Europe. While the *Forward,* in its editorial, questioned the missions from a politically conservative perspective, the divisions on this issue did not break down along simple liberal/conservative lines.

One important leader of a liberal Jewish organization expressing uneasiness about the amount of Jewish attention and money lavished on Cuba was Rabbi Eric Yoffie, president of the Union of American Hebrew Congregations (UAHC), the national body of Reform synagogues. He said, "Realistically, I think we need to acknowledge that this is a small and mostly elderly community, so a sense of proportion might dictate that it might not merit an extensive mission program from the United States." Conversely, a political conservative, Joshua Muravchik, resident scholar at the American Enterprise Institute, favored the missions, claiming that letting citizens of the free world interact with Cubans has the effect of exposing the latter to democratic ideals, thereby increasing popular pressure on Castro to liberalize his regime. Jewish professionals who sponsored and led the missions Cuba defended them on the practical ground that people increased the size of their donations when they saw where

---

[118]"Elian and Us," *Forward,* Apr. 28, 2000, pp. 1, 8.
[119]Ibid., p. 8.

their money was going. For example, John Ruskay, executive vice president of the UJA-Federation of New York, said that his organization raised over $75,000 specifically for the Cuban Jewish community as a direct result of a mission to Cuba in 1999.[120]

THE PROFESSIONAL MEDICAL EDUCATIONAL PROJECT

The JDC originated during World War I to provide material relief to Jews living in the war zones, and it has a long history of assisting Jewish communities around the world. The JDC played a major role in the revitalization of Jewish life in Cuba in the 1990s; it is universally praised for sending representatives to run services, teach classes, and organize activities. These representatives are JDC community workers from Argentina, who have been granted government permission to enter Cuba and work as resident directors for the program. Based in Havana, they work with Jews throughout the country.

The JDC is funded by the UJC (previously the UJA), as well as by grants from individuals and foundations. There is also a nonsectarian JDC program operating in more than 30 countries, that provides humanitarian aid, particularly for disaster relief. One initiative in Cuba funded in this manner is the Professional Medical Educational Project, which came into being in a roundabout way. In 1992, Dr. José Miller told the JDC that the Havana Jewish community needed a rabbi—they hadn't had one since the early 1960s. The JDC sent Alberto Senderey, a community-development worker, from its Paris office. Seeing the condition of the community, Senderey reported that not only were Cuban Jews desperately in need of spiritual help, but that they were short of food and medicine.

To deal with the medical problem, the JDC sent Dr. Ted Myers, one of its senior medical consultants, to assess the needs of the community in 1994.[121] Although the Cuban government provides free medical care to all citizens, there was a severe shortage of drugs during the "special period" of economic stringency, and many Cubans could not get the prescriptions they needed. Working together with the JDC, Dr. Rosa Behar and the local Hadassah organization decided to open a private pharmacy in the Patronato that would provide medicines, vitamins, and other medical supplies to anyone needing them.

Jewish Solidarity, run by Eddie Levy in Miami, has been instrumental in supplying the pharmacy. Levy, who left Cuba in the mid-1950s, before

---

[120]Radler, "Cuba Emerges as Destination Much Favored by Federations," pp. 1, 5.
[121]Correspondence with Ted Myers, Apr. 2000.

the revolution, founded Jewish Solidarity in 1993, during the worst part of the "special period." Since then, his Miami-based organization has imported into Cuba a large amount of food and medicines. He explained the importance of the medical donations not only as vitally needed material assistance, but also as a way of expressing Jewish values and engendering political good will:

> They [the Patronato pharmacy] get the credit for it, you know, they're recognized for doing that, plus anybody that needs any medicine in that pharmacy, regardless if they're Jewish or not, and they've got a prescription, it's given to them. It is not only what Judaism is all about, which is to help each other and help in general, but it's also good strategy, because nobody can say in Cuba that the Jews have privilege over all the Cubans, because after all, the Jews of Cuba are *Cuban*—with a capital letter—Jews. They're not a separate entity, like happened in the Eastern Bloc, in which people were looked at as somewhat different from the rest of the people. In Cuba Jewish people are Cuban, with a religious preference of Judaism."[122]

According to Laina Richter, coordinator of the nonsectarian medical program in Cuba, the JDC also found that Cuban doctors were "really out of touch with what was going on in the Western industrialized world in terms of the most recent techniques and methods; they didn't know anything about the newest medications and drugs."[123] Myers therefore established the Professional Medical Educational Project, which sent Jewish doctors from the United States at a rate of about one every two months. The JDC covered the cost of the doctors' travel to Cuba as well as their accommodations, and the individual doctor picked up all other expenses. The approximate total cost per doctor was $2,000. Many of the doctors established ties with the local medical community that they have maintained on their own since the initial visits.

Doctors sent to Havana on the Professional Medical Educational Project work intensively with Cuban counterparts for one week, going on rounds with their Cuban colleagues, helping train local medical students, and giving lectures. As Richter explained the preparation for each doctor's visit, "There would be a dialogue before the doctor went down, to get an idea of what was needed as well as to bring in medical literature that they didn't really have access to. In addition to kind of bringing down their expertise and knowledge, they also brought down literature, and medical equipment and supplies." Although the program was nonsectarian, it did have a specifically Jewish communal component as well: "While they were there, they would spend Shabbat with the Jewish com-

---

[122]Levy interview.
[123]Interview with Laina Richter, Mar. 2000.

munity and make connections within the Cuban medical community . . . and the Jewish community."[124]

B'NAI B'RITH

In February 1997, B'nai B'rith announced the formation of a Committee on Cuban Affairs, chaired by Elizabeth (Betty) Baer, wife of Tommy P. Baer, B'nai B'rith International's president. This committee grew out of a B'nai B'rith humanitarian mission in which 32 members of the organization brought medicine, food, and clothes into Cuba. Six of the 32 were Cuban-born, including Michael Mandel, a cantorial student who performed concerts of Jewish songs for the Cuban Jewish community. Richard D. Heideman, then chairing the B'nai B'rith Center for Public Policy, stated,

> In keeping with B'nai B'rith's 153-year tradition of providing aid to Jews throughout the world, we have created this special committee to assist in improving the lives of this isolated community who are in desperate need of even the basic necessities of life. . . . We plan to obtain and send educational and religious materials written in Spanish and sponsor more humanitarian missions. The needs are immense.[125]

In the winter of 1999, B'nai B'rith sent 23 members from its Tri-state, Allegheny/Ohio Valley, and Golden Pacific regions to Havana and Santiago de Cuba. In addition to 2,000 pounds of supplies shipped to Cuba in advance of their arrival, the mission personally delivered 700 pounds of food, Hanukkah toys, Judaica, clothing, and medicine. The group celebrated Hanukkah with the local Jewish community in the city of Santiago de Cuba. One participant reported: "A touching moment occurred when small necklaces containing Moginai David [Stars of David] were distributed to the adults and children of the congregation. Many of us, adults and children alike, wept as we helped them adorn their necks with this precious reminder of their faith. It was an extremely emotional experience and one that we will cherish when we remember our visit."[126]

Thus began B'nai B'rith's Cuban Jewish Relief Project, coordinated by Stanley Cohen and carried out in conjunction with the Brother's Brother Foundation of Pittsburgh and with Eddie Levy's Jewish Solidarity. It collects clothing, pharmaceuticals, and food products in the U.S., which are then shipped to Cuba via Jewish Solidarity in Miami. The goods are

---

[124]Richter interview.

[125]B'nai B'rith press release, Feb. 12, 1997.

[126]Stuart Cooper, "B'nai B'rith goes back to Cuba: Humanitarian mission delivers two thousand-seven hundred pounds of supplies," *B'nai B'rith Today,* Jan./Feb. 2000, pp. 1, 3.

consigned to the Department of Religious Affairs in Havana to be given to the Jewish community. In mid-February 2000, for example, the project shipped over 1,600 pounds of antibiotics, vitamins, antacids, children's medicine, hygienic supplies, high-protein canned goods such as tuna and salmon, and powdered milk.[127]

The Renaissance of the 1990s

In the early 1990s there was a visible revitalization of Jewish life in Cuba. As the regime's loosening of restrictions on religion encouraged Cubans of all types to discover or rediscover religion, a steady stream of people began to acknowledge Jewish antecedents and seek affiliation with the community.

Primary credit for the revival of Jewish life in Cuba goes to the JDC, whose representatives, sent from Buenos Aires, have educated a new generation of Cuban Jews. Jorge Diener was the first resident JDC director. He was followed by Roberto Senderovitch, who was in turn succeeded by Diego and Laura Mendelbaum. The current directors, Ivan and Cynthia Glait, took over in May 2000.

RABBI SZTEINHENDLER

During the early years of the revival, the JDC brought in numerous other educators as well—rabbis, community workers, volunteers—for short periods of time. Many were from the United States and Canada and spoke English; others were Spanish-speaking Jews from Central and South America.

One of the most influential was Rabbi Shmuel (Samuel) Szteinhendler, a native of Argentina and a Conservative rabbi. During the 1990s, he made several trips a year to Cuba from his congregational base in Guadalajara, Mexico. (About 20 percent of that congregation had emigrated from Cuba after the revolution.) Before his first trip, Szteinhendler had been led to believe that the only Jews left in Cuba were a few old people. But when he arrived in January 1992, sent by the JDC, he witnessed first-hand the incipient revival of interest in Judaism and the potential for communal growth. Szteinhendler conducted services in the Havana synagogues and around the country, and officiated at ritual circumcisions and weddings. He instituted programs of "education, training for religious services, youth activities, cultural activities, holiday services and celebrations," as well as Judaica lending libraries, Israeli dancing and the-

---

[127]Interview with Stanley Cohen, Apr. 2000.

atrical groups, and distributed prayer books with Spanish translation and transliteration. Szteinhendler also worked with the communities to clean up the Jewish cemeteries and the abandoned sanctuaries and make them usable.[128] He influenced and inspired many. "Rabbi Szteinhendler is our spiritual father. We only see him two or three times a year, but he is always in our minds," José Levy Tur told a visiting journalist in 1996.[129] Szteinhendler has recently taken a pulpit in Santiago, Chile, and is no longer able to visit as often as he would like.

THE RENOVATED PATRONATO

While the various JDC representatives have worked with Jewish communities throughout Cuba, their primary focus has been the Patronato, and it has emerged as the center of Jewish life in Havana. Not only do Jews come there for services on Friday night and Saturday morning, but they also come to use the computers in the library, to get vitamins and drugs from the pharmacy, and to participate in organizations, clubs, and activities sponsored directly or indirectly by the Patronato. Renovation of the Patronato was initiated by a challenge grant from the Harry & Jeanette Weinberg Foundation of Baltimore, Maryland, after members of the Weinberg family visited Cuba. The Scheck family donated money to renovate the community center, and the Zelcer family paid to fix up the prestigious and heavily used Patronato library. A number of Cuban Jews living in Miami made donations through the Greater Miami Jewish Federation, but such aid remains controversial. When the building was dedicated in May 2000—with the Elián González controversy still unresolved—some of the donors declined to attend out of fear that their presence would hurt their communal standing in Miami.

Although the Patronato is constitutionally required to have a 24-member board, the responsibility for decisions falls primarily on a very small group led by the president, José Miller. Adela Dworin, vice president of the Patronato and its librarian, is very active in running the institution, taking many of the American tour groups around to show them the newly renovated sanctuary and relate the history of the congregation. In 1995 the Patronato launched *Menorah,* a newsletter for the Havana Jewish community. The congregation also sponsors social and cultural groups geared to different age levels. Mácabi Cuba, the youth group for ages 13–30, has helped stimulate and promote the renaissance of Jewish life

---

[128]Interview with Shmuel (Samuel) Szteinhendler, July 2000.

[129]Kenneth Bandler, "Argentine rabbi ignites fervor in dormant Cuban communities," *Jewish Telegraphic Agency Daily News Bulletin,* Jan. 11, 1996, p. 4.

throughout the country. Guesher (bridge), led by Tatiana Asís, a physician, is for 30–55-year-olds. Simcha, for the over-55 group, is led by University of Havana English professor Lourdes Albo. Each group meets once a month, alternating locations between the Centro and the Patronato, after the kiddush that follows services on Shabbat morning. The groups also go on trips, sometimes outside Havana. The Simcha group runs an exercise program that meets on Mondays and Tuesdays at Adath Israel.

"Collective birthday celebrations" are held every three months, giving special recognition to those whose birthdays fall out during that time span. Lourdes Albo explains: "In its beginnings the meetings were held with only a few participants. Today more than 60 members come to each meeting. It is very meaningful for them to have the opportunity to socialize, share their vivid memories, interests, celebrate their birthdays, go on excursions—in other words, to have a good time with their brothers and sisters of the Cuban Jewish community."[130] In July 1999, the first national camping experience for the Simcha seniors group was held in Aguas Claras, where some 80 Jewish seniors from all over the country gathered for two days. After experiencing Shabbat together, the program continued on Saturday night with a havdalah ceremony, and was followed by an exercise program and an outing to La Cueva del Indio the next day. There were also group discussions on psychological, social, and religious issues.

A number of other Jewish cultural events take place regularly at the Patronato. About eight times a year the Asociación Femenina Hebrea de Cuba (Jewish Women's Association of Cuba) brings together more than 100 women from the three Havana synagogues for dialogues on Jewish issues. The program is led by Rosa Behar, who also heads Hadassah in Cuba. The Patronato recently held an exhibition of paintings by Israeli and Palestinian children that had been created under the auspices of Givat Haviva, an Israeli organization dedicated to furthering Arab-Israeli understanding; the president of the Cuban Arab Federation, Alfredo Deriche, attended the opening ceremonies. There have also been several dance presentations by the Mexican Jewish group Anajnu Ve Atem (We and You), one of which was held at the National Theater as part of Cuba's International Ballet Festival.

A milestone in the resurrection of Jewish life in Cuba took place at the Patronato on Rosh Hashanah 1999, when Alberto Behar chanted from the Torah, becoming Cuba's first native-born Torah reader since the revolution. Diego Mendelbaum, then JDC's representative in Cuba, trained

---

[130]Interview with Lourdes Albo, Mar. 2000.

Behar. Mendelbaum recalled, "When we started, he could scarcely read Hebrew. But he had the desire. We decided on a two-month course of study. In the process, he learned much more than the musical symbols he would need. He studied commentaries and reflections on the Torah. He moved beyond the technique of reading the Torah and investigated the spiritual and emotional meaning contained in each portion. When you hear him read, you can sense his fulfillment." Behar commented, "While following the text with my eyes, I can see in the scrolls the reflection of my father's and grandfather's faces. They are happy that I am maintaining the Jewish tradition."[131]

ADATH ISRAEL

Adath Israel is located in the middle of Old Havana, the area of original settlement in colonial times. This neighborhood is the country's primary tourist attraction, and with the economy in bad shape, it made sense for Cuba to invest in it. In 1978, a year after UNESCO declared it a world heritage site, the government adopted a plan to renovate the entire area. As part of this project, the Havana Restoration Commission sent architecture student Jorge Herrera to Germany, on scholarship, to study the architecture of German synagogues so that he might develop a plan for Adath Israel. Upon Herrera's return, he worked with leaders of the congregation on a proposed full restoration of the sanctuary, and also suggested a number of innovative features, such as a frame attached to the roof of the building that could be used for the erection of a sukkah. The government contributed part of the cost for the renovation, with the rest donated by a number of wealthy Orthodox businessmen from Panama, Venezuela, and elsewhere.[132]

The president of the Adath Israel Congregation today is Alberto Zilberstein Toruncha, an engineer, whose father was Ashkenazi and whose mother was of Turkish Sephardic descent. He attended a Jewish day school as a child and his mother was active in the Chevet Achim Sephardic synagogue, but by 1970 she decided to end the family's public involvement in Jewish activities in order to shield her children from the possible stigma of being identified as "religious." She nevertheless tried to maintain some degree of Jewish tradition in their home. When Alberto's own children reached school age, his mother encouraged him to send them to the Patronato's Sunday school, and the parents became in-

---

[131]"The Torah Finds its Cuban Voice: JDC-trained Cuban *Baal Kore* is Welcomed by his Community," on JDC's Web site, www.jdc.org.

[132]Laura Gooch, "Cuba's Jews Struggle to Renovate their Crumbling Synagogues," *Cleveland Jewish News*, Feb. 16, 1999.

volved through the children. In 1994, leaders of Adath Israel sought him out to become active in their congregation.[133]

Adath Israel consists of about 120 people who travel there from all over the greater Havana metropolitan area, including Santos Suarez, Alamar, San Francisco de Paula, Santiago de las Vegas, and many other suburbs and towns. Even though it is nominally Orthodox, it differs little from the non-Orthodox congregations in its high rate of intermarriage.[134] The congregation has a system for awarding extra rations to those who commit to coming to the minyan at Adath Israel, and no other synagogue, a certain number of times per week. Thus Adath Israel is the only synagogue that even attempts to have a daily minyan both morning and evening, and it succeeds about 85 percent of the time—a feat made more difficult by the Orthodox rule that only males can be counted. Friday night attendance is between 65 and 70, with about 35–40 on Saturday morning and 30–35 on Saturday night.

One of the most emotional moments in the revival of Cuban Jewry occurred at Adath Israel in December 1994—its first bar mitzvah in over 30 years. The bar mitzvah boy was Jacobo Berezniak, the son of Abraham Berezniak, Havana's kosher butcher and one of the leaders of the congregation. Beside the regulars, relatives, and friends, the congregation that morning included a 20-person group visiting from the United States and a camera crew that was filming a documentary on Jewish life in Cuba. (The crew was permitted to film because the service was held on a Thursday rather than a Saturday.) The bar mitzvah boy was escorted up to the Torah by his father and the president of the congregation, and he read his portion in what one of the American visitors described as a "steady and competent manner."[135]

SOCIAL, EDUCATIONAL, AND YOUTH PROGRAMS

It was mostly affluent American Jewish businessmen who founded the local branch of B'nai B'rith in Cuba in 1943, which, till the revolution, combated anti-Semitism and did philanthropic work. The organization never disbanded after the revolution, but it did little till the early 1990s, when the organization was revitalized as part of the broader Jewish renaissance. A key player in that revitalization was Isaac Gelen, now president of the B'nai B'rith Maimonides Lodge in Havana. As Gelen explained to me, the revived organization had to change its original mission,

---

[133]Interview with Alberto Zilberstein Toruncha, June 2000.
[134]Interview with Salim Tache Jalak, Adath Israel's executive director, Nov. 1999.
[135]Paul Margolis, "A Young Man's Coming of Age Mirrors the Rebirth of Judaism in Cuba," *Jewish Standard*, Feb. 18, 1996.

since there was now very little anti-Semitism to fight and the members were not in a position to donate the large sums of money necessary for meaningful philanthropy. Instead, B'nai B'rith has expanded its educational activities, meeting monthly with approximately 20 people (out of the 41 official members) in attendance.[136]

Moisés Asís, now living in Miami, founded the community's current one-day-a-week educational program in 1985. Two years later, Rabbi Marshall Meyer, dean of the Seminario Rabínico Latinoamericano, the rabbinical school in Buenos Aires, personally recruited Asís for an intensive six-month program to train him for communal religious leadership, and the JDC gave Asís a scholarship for this purpose. He studied not only academic subjects, but also practical techniques such as circumcision. Today, Alberto Meshulam Cohen, a pediatric neurologist, directs the Hebrew school, which is cooperatively sponsored by all three Havana congregations and taught by dedicated volunteers. Approximately 40 children up to the age of 15 attend classes at the Patronato every Sunday morning for three hours. Simultaneously, some 30 people over the age of 15 attend sessions at the Centro Hebreo Sefaradi. The JDC provides two buses that shuttle the participants from their neighborhoods to the programs and back. Over the past two years at least 112 Cuban Jews involved with the Sunday school, teachers and students, have settled in Israel, but new people get involved each year and the school continues to thrive.[137]

Mácabi Cuba has the responsibility for running the Friday night service at the Patronato, and this is one reason that the service is so popular with young people. On Saturdays the Mácabi has meetings devoted to the study of Judaism that stress practical, hands-on activities and the use of creative techniques to communicate the spiritual dimension of Jewish life. Mácabi also sponsors a volleyball team that conducts training on weekday evenings, and each Tuesday night there is a meeting of the Israeli dance group.

Mácabi sponsors two camping experiences during the year, one in March and the other in July, bringing together about 150 young Jews from all over the country. The camp, which lasts for four days, is the only opportunity young Cuban Jews have to experience intensive Jewish living 24 hours a day, including a full Shabbat. Most of these children — up until a few years ago, almost all of them — were from homes where there was no Jewish expression whatsoever; all they knew was that their parents had told them they were Jewish. In August 1999 Cuba hosted a "Pan-

---

[136]Interview with Isaac Gelen, June 2000.
[137]Interview with Alberto Cohen, Mar. 2000.

American Camp" in Aguas Claras, Pinar del Rio, with assistance from the Jewish communities of the United States, Venezuela, Panama, Mexico, Brazil, and Nicaragua. Not only was there a strong Jewish educational component to the camp, but the young Cuban Jews had the opportunity to meet and interact with Jews from other countries and to feel that they are part of world Jewry.

Mácabi Cuba, however, is beginning to pay a price for its success: during 1999 it lost two of the most active members of its executive committee. Liver Humaran Maya, a dynamic young leader, received a gala public send-off when he left to study Jewish education for a year at the seminary in Buenos Aires, with the intention of returning to teach in Cuba. As part of his studies, though, he went to Israel to study Hebrew, and decided to settle there; not only would he not complete his training in Buenos Aires, but he would not be returning to Cuba to bolster Jewish education in the community. Dania Martínez Nissenbaum, another member of the executive committee, also left the country, settling in the United States. Both losses came as heavy blows to Mácabi Cuba.

Conversion and Other Denominational Issues

Shortly after the revival of Jewish life began in the 1990s, communal leaders in Havana reached an understanding to promote conversion as the way to formalize Jewish status for those who were of Jewish origin or married to Jews, but who were not Jews according to Jewish law. However individuals who approached the community on their own without either Jewish ancestry or a Jewish partner were not generally encouraged to convert, a reflection of the dominant national/ethnic conception of Jewishness. About 150 conversions have taken place over the last several years, with Conservative rabbis from other Latin American communities performing them. Among the earliest converts were José Miller's wife and children.

Rabbi Szteinhendler explained how he approached the issue of conversion. "First, we regularized the Jewish status of people who belonged to mixed-marriage families and are active in some way, or at least related, to the community. Secondly, we will go to the mixed marriages and their families who are there but are not related to the community. Third, we regularized the Jewish status of those people who are third generation of some Jewish grandparent. Last, we attended [to] people who had not had any Jewish former relatives." The process involved intensive consultation with Miller and other communal representatives.

All the cases were accepted first by the local leadership, and then we established a study program that took almost a whole year. People had to participate weekly in study sessions, in the communal activities, in the Shabbat and holiday services, and meet with me each time I was in the island to have intensive study sessions. The ritual of accepting them as fully Jewish followed the rules of the Committee on Law and Standards of the Conservative/Masorti Movement, which means: men needed to go through Brit Milah [circumcision] and all the people went through *mikveh* [ritual immersion]. We had, each year, a bet din [religious court] of three Conservative rabbis. The *mohel* was brought from Mexico to perform the Brit Milah of each one according to Jewish law.[138]

According to Rabbi Szteinhendler, when Rabbi Yisrael Meir Lau, the Ashkenazi chief rabbi of Israel, visited Cuba in 1994, he made known his acceptance of these conversions.[139]

In light of the fact that conversions in Cuba were performed under the auspices of Conservative Judaism, it is hardly surprising to find that much of the community has developed formal or informal ties with the Conservative movement. Rabbi Jerome Epstein, executive director of the United Synagogue of Conservative Judaism, has been the point man for the development of the Conservative movement in Cuba. While this would normally be the responsibility of the World Council of Synagogues, which is the umbrella organization for the Conservative movement around the world, it was decided that the U.S.-based United Synagogue would take responsibility for Cuba and Barbados, because of their proximity to the United States. Also, the United Synagogue's budget could accommodate the extra expenditures involved.

Even though the Patronato and other Cuban congregations are affiliated with the Conservative movement, the form of Judaism that the congregations practice is not completely consistent with Conservative Judaism elsewhere. Epstein explained: "They are Conservative in large part because they are not Orthodox and they want to maintain some tradition. They are not what you could say committed to an ideology that is similar to Conservative Judaism here in North America, and because of what they went through in the Castro regime, they really don't have a lot of knowledge of Judaism at all."[140]

Epstein first visited Cuba in 1997, when he and a number of other Conservative leaders met with representatives of the different Cuban congregations and began a dialogue on how the United Synagogue could help strengthen Judaism in Cuba. The United Synagogue provided Spanish-Hebrew prayer books, and translated and distributed selections from its popular tract series, short essays on aspects of Jewish law, holidays, and

---

[138]Szteinhendler interview.
[139]Kenneth Bandler, "Jewish youth lead the way in a long-isolated community," *Jewish Telegraphic Agency Daily News Bulletin,* Jan. 8, 1996, p. 2.
[140]Interview with Jerome Epstein, Apr. 2000.

prayer. Epstein explains, "We tried to develop a strategy that would make it possible for us to do something constructive without being perceived as 'the Ugly Yankee.' " Epstein recalls, "Most of the people felt badly that they had let their memories fade, in terms of Judaism, and a lot of them were very hungry to get something back again. It was almost as if they felt deprived. Not necessarily of all the ritual elements—they just wanted a connection with God." In particular, Epstein was struck by the interest the young people showed.[141]

Originally, the Patronato synagogue had been officially Orthodox, although the congregants were not very observant. It was only at the beginning of the 1990s—when the JDC became involved in the Havana Jewish community—that the nominal Orthodox label was dropped. Jorge Diener, the first JDC representative in Cuba, encouraged all three Havana congregations to affiliate with the Conservative movement. The Patronato was the first to do so, and the Centro Sefaradi followed suit several years later. Nevertheless, the two congregations retain certain religious differences: the Patronato has men and women sitting together and allows women to lead services and read the Torah, while the Centro Sefaradi retains separate seating (without a physical barrier) and does not allow women any leading role in the service.

Adath Israel, still nominally Orthodox, has consistently resisted JDC suggestions to join the Conservative movement. Yet it is not a member of any international Orthodox Jewish organization, perhaps because its membership includes many people who are not Jewish according to Halakhah. Zeiling Mooris, a retired Romanian-born Jew living in England, has made several trips to Havana to help lead services, but his involvement has created tensions. When he first came he expressed a willingness to accept the congregational situation and deal leniently with the questionable Jewish identity of members, but as time went on—and possibly as a result of a felt need to conform to Lubavitch standards—Mooris began to balk at calling up to the Torah congregants who had non-Jewish mothers and who had converted through the Conservative movement. Alberto Zilberstein, the president, had to insist that Mooris either allow these people to participate or "get off the *bimah* [platform] and let us continue with our service."[142]

When Chevet Achim closed down, some of the members joined the Centro Sefaradi in Vedado, but many of those living in Old Havana preferred to remain with a synagogue that was close by and so they joined the ostensibly Eastern European Adath Israel. As a consequence of the influx of Sephardim from Chevet Achim, as well as the presence of many

---

[141]Ibid.
[142]Zilberstein interview.

spouses from non-Jewish backgrounds, the Eastern European flavor of Adath Israel is far less pronounced today than it was at the time of the revolution. Despite its Orthodoxy, Adath Israel is fully involved with the rest of the community. It participates together with the other two Havana congregations in the joint Sunday programs, the one for children held at the Patronato, and the one for adults held at the Centro Sefaradi. Whenever an issue of concern to the broader Jewish community arises, representatives of the three congregations meet together.

However Adath Israel, like the other congregations, has had to face certain boundary issues. Early in 2000, one congregant who had been raised with virtually no Judaism in his home and had begun to attend services was asked not to come any longer because he was also a regular attendee at a Protestant church. Such syncretistic religious activity is widespread among segments of the Cuban population—many Catholics are also involved in Afro-Cuban religious activities, specifically Santeria—but syncretism has made no inroads in the Jewish community.

As of July 2000, Chabad-Lubavitch had sent a total of 56 missions to Cuba under the auspices of Chabad Friends of Cuban Jewry, headquartered originally in Brooklyn and now in Toronto, and directed by Rabbi Shimon Aisenbach.[143] Each mission is staffed by two emissaries, usually young, unmarried rabbis. For the holiday of Shavuot 2000, Aisenbach sent a young, married couple. Aisenbach commented, "Periodically I have this idea to send a couple as well [as two single rabbis], the reason being simply that the Jewish community should see religious family life."

Chabad-Lubavitch is dedicated to seeing that the Cuban Jews be led down the proper halakhic path, and it is especially alarmed by the high incidence of intermarriage and what it considers halakhically incorrect conversions. Rabbi Aisenbach explained: " 'Who is a Jew' is definitely a problem that we must take into consideration. Many people identify themselves as Jews who really are not. . . . Who are these people and what are they going to claim that they are? They immigrate to Israel and then they are dating your daughter, for example. It brings a lot of confusion. It brings such confusion. People think that it's just a game, but it's not a game. It eventually brings confusion and eventually even disaster."

Aisenbach is especially puzzled about Adath Israel, since it is officially Orthodox and at the same time contains a majority of intermarried couples. "Everything is wishy washy there," he says:

> For example, that shul itself was built as an Orthodox shul. Even when I came six-and-a-half years ago it wasn't running like an Orthodox shul. Seventy-five-to-eighty percent were non-Jews, men and women sitting to-

---

[143]All the information about the role of Lubavitch in Cuba is based on an interview with Rabbi Aisenbach, June 2000.

gether. I spoke to a couple of people there and I said, "Listen, at least respect the way the shul was built. It was built as an Orthodox shul." Is it 100 percent Orthodox, are the meals kosher yet? Not yet. For example, there is no kosher meat coming out of the kosher butcher. To make a piece of meat kosher is not a simple thing. Even though I am an official rabbi, I took the exams on becoming a rabbi, I'm not a *shohet*. . . . In Cuba there are even [halakhically] non-Jews doing *shehitah* [ritual slaughtering]. Even if they're doing a perfect job, the animal is not kosher. And also the knives are from before the revolution, and obviously almost inevitably there is a problem with them.

Aisenbach wanted to arrange for a *shohet* to visit Cuba every few weeks, have the meat stored in special freezers, and distribute it to community members. As for the meat people were eating, he said, "its not 20 percent kosher, its not 50 percent kosher, its not kosher meat at all."

Chabad in Cuba also operates a summer day camp where, in addition to sports, the children pray and are taught about Jewish practice. Says Aisenbach, "We feed them and their parents a meal and we go on night trips with them. We printed a 96-page booklet in Spanish with illustrations all about the basic mitzvahs and an entire Yiddishkeit guide." Chabad insists that "every single child in our camp is born to a Jewish mother, and therefore "we don't have many children. There were years it was 20, and there were years it was 17. But as the focus of the camp was Jewish education, a Jewish education belongs to a Jewish child." Seven of the children who have attended Chabad camps over the years have gone on to study at yeshivot in other countries.

Communal Renaissance Outside of Havana

CAMAGÜEY

JDC representatives and other Jewish visitors have had a profound impact on this community. Sarah Albojaire, a former president of the Jewish community now living in Miami, states, "They taught us how to sing the prayers; they brought books, gefilte fish—and, most importantly, they taught what we couldn't to our children." Albojaire explains what happened to the Jews of Camagüey. "Years without formally practicing and without any organized services really removed us from Judaism. Most of us, like me, had to marry out of the religion. There were no Jews."[144]

Since most of the Camagüey Jews were intermarried, many of those

---

[144]David Abel, "Cuba's Jews Take Heart from First New Synagogue since Revolution," *Newark Star Ledger,* July 24, 1998.

expressing interest in Judaism were themselves only partly Jewish. In 1995 Rabbi Szteinhendler came to Camagüey to officiate at the conversion ceremonies of 21 people, mostly spouses of Jews and children of Jewish fathers and non-Jewish mothers, just as was being done elsewhere in the country under similar circumstances. But since then visits from rabbis have been infrequent. In 1999, two boys, ages 10 and 12, were medically circumcised at a hospital in the city. As there was no *mohel* or rabbi available, a member of the community read the prayers.[145]

The original Sephardi synagogue in Camagüey, built in the 1920s, closed down after the revolution. On Rosh Hashanah 1998 the 37-family community dedicated a new synagogue building in a whitewashed turn-of-the-century house, connected to a row of homes in the center of the city. It was named Tiferet Israel, the same name as the prerevolutionary synagogue, and was bought for the congregation by Ruben Beraja, who was then serving as leader of the Jewish community of Argentina.[146]

Merle Salkin, director of education at the Society Hill Synagogue in Philadelphia, made several trips to Camagüey to teach Hebrew to the Jewish community. Salkin's congregation donated $3,000 for the Camagüey synagogue, as well as for prayer books and other ritual items. She explains that after the religious revival began, "people started coming out of the woodwork, asking questions and signing up for conversion classes." As is the case in many small communities, there is one member who has taken the lead and inspired others. In Camagüey, according to Salkin, that individual is Reina Roffe, "the spiritual heart and driving force of Jewish education in the city." Roffe started the first conversion class and developed the curriculum for the synagogue school. She was brought to Kol Ami in Philadelphia in 1999 to learn Hebrew and received intensified training for her work in Cuba. She celebrated her own bat mitzvah at Kol Ami and then celebrated her son Daniel's bar mitzvah in Camagüey shortly after her return to Cuba. Working with Salkin, she has taught adult education classes, including Hebrew, holiday observance, and Jewish symbols.[147]

CIENFUEGOS

The 29-member Jewish community of Cienfuegos, even smaller than the one in Camagüey, is held together by a strong-minded, energetic

---

[145]Correspondence with Merle Salkin, February 2001.
[146]Correspondence with Merle Salkin, March 2001.
[147]Ibid.

woman, Rebeca Langos Rodriguez, a Spanish teacher in a local middle school, who is the community president. Raising her two small sons as Jews although her husband is not Jewish, Rodriguez told a reporter that she would like them to marry Jews but realizes that in Cienfuegos this is unlikely to happen. Since there was only one girl in the community, she asked, "What are we going to do?"[148] She has considered moving with her family to Israel, but her husband doesn't want to leave his ailing mother. The continued presence of Rodriguez is of crucial importance for the local Jewish community; were she to leave, Jewish communal life would probably fall apart. About once a month Shabbat services are held in Rodriguez's home, although never with a minyan. Every Saturday the community's seven children come to her second-floor apartment for Hebrew school. Sometimes the parents stay with the children till the end of the Sabbath for havdalah.

SANTA CLARA

David Tacher, the president of the Jewish community in Santa Clara, explains that until 1995 the community was virtually inactive. That year, a visitor donated *The Jewish Book of Why.* A number of local Jews started reading it, and thus began the process of revival. "Families got together to reencounter their roots. There was a revival of interest about being Jewish. At the end, we realized we were lacking; we weren't practicing our religion. Then, all the community began to celebrate *Kabbalat Shabbat* services, the blessing of the wine, the bread, then step by step, havdalah, then the first Passover, then learning Hebrew."[149] In 1996 the Jews of Santa Clara celebrated Purim together for the first time, and, later in the year, commemorated Holocaust Memorial Day.

Tacher explains that the Jews in Santa Clara always knew each other. They had visited the Jewish cemetery and were familiar with the names on the tombstones; they knew which people in town were related to those deceased ancestors, and so there had never been a complete loss of Jewish memory. But there had been no religious activities for years. Now, though, there are seven active families consisting of about 30 individuals. Tacher is not planning to move to Israel. "I have my mother here and she's sick. She can't start over; she's an old woman," he says. Tacher believes that he can be a faithful Jew in Santa Clara. "If you are Jewish, you

---

[148]Lisa J. Huriash, "Judaism: Alive in Castro's Cuba," *Young Israel Viewpoint,* Spring 2000, p. 74. The article appears on pp. 71–78.
[149]Ibid., p. 75.

are Jewish. My mind and heart are in Israel. As long as there is a Jew in Cuba, Judaism will never die in Cuba."[150]

SANTIAGO DE CUBA

Santiago de Cuba, the second largest city in the country, is regarded as the most Caribbean of all Cuban cities. Local residents are proud of the role that the city played in the revolution. Most of the early Jewish settlers came from the Ottoman Empire, though a number of Ashkenazi families from Poland also came before World War II. The Sociedad Unión Israelita del Oriente de Cuba, the Jewish Society of Eastern Cuba, was founded here in October 1924. The community held services in rented quarters until 1939, when a synagogue building was erected. From that time on it was referred to as the Sinogoga de Santiago de Cuba. Two spiritual leaders served the community, one from 1924 until 1943 and the other from 1946 through 1967. The revolution brought a dramatic decline in community activity. Most of the local Jews emigrated, and by 1978 the community had ceased functioning. As the synagogue building was not being used, the remaining Jews gave it to the government.[151]

Yet, a small number of Jews in the Santiago area, most of them intermarried, retained some interest in their ancestral faith. At Passover each year the Santiago Jews would gather to receive their Passover packages from the CJC, which were routed through the Havana Jewish community. The regular annual receipt of this aid made a deep impression on the local Jews, showing them that there was a Jewish presence outside of their area and giving them a sense of global Jewish solidarity.

After 15 year of inactivity, the Santiago community revived in October 1993 when Jewish communal activities began to be held on a regular basis in the home of Rebeca Botton Behar. Talks with the government resulted in the return of the original synagogue building to the Jewish community, and a joyous rededication ceremony took place, Rabbi Shmuel Szteinhendler officiating, on July 25, 1995—a date coinciding with the 480th anniversary of the founding of the city.[152]

The congregation now has regular Sabbath services and, after the Saturday morning prayers, a kiddush lunch is served for the entire congregation, followed by a class on the Torah portion of the week in Spanish. The community has two Jewish dance groups, one for children and the

---

[150]Ibid.
[151]Margalit Bejarano, interview with Rebeca Botton Behar, as related in correspondence with the author, Apr. 2001.
[152]Interview with Evely Laser Schelnsky, Apr. 2000.

other for adults. In 1996, a double bar mitzvah was held for two cousins, Robertito Novoa Bonne and Andresito Novoa Castiel, attended by the entire Jewish community. These were the first bar mitzvahs held in the city in almost 20 years.[153]

Rabbi Stuart Kelman of Congregation Netivot Shalom of Berkeley, California, has brought several missions from Northern California to work with the Jewish community of Santiago. "There's a certain laxness about kashrut rules," he notes, "about Shabbat, and that is all very understandable, given the fact that they are situated on the edge of the island, and have had no leadership in God knows how many years in that sense. They are a struggling community, and in a way, the Judaism that they practice is the best that they can do."[154]

Operation Cigar, Aliyah, and the Future of the Community

"Operation Cigar," the clandestine emigration of 400 Cuban Jews, made headlines in October 1999 after the Israeli government confirmed a report that appeared in the *Jewish Chronicle* of London. President Castro apparently gave his approval for it in 1994, allegedly soon after meeting with Israeli chief rabbi Lau. Through this operation, the Jewish Agency for Israel, with the help of the Canadian government, arranged for the departure of mostly younger Cuban Jews from Havana through Paris to Tel Aviv beginning in 1995.

Once "Operation Cigar" became public knowledge, a number of theories developed as to why Castro had agreed to it and why it had been kept secret. Some believed that Castro saw the operation as a way to win favor with the U.S. government and bring an end to the economic boycott, or, if that were not possible, at least to induce Israel to drop its support of the boycott. There were also allegations that Israel had paid Cuba between $3,000 and $5,000 per Jew as "compensation" for Cuba's investment in their education. As for the secrecy, Israeli sources claimed that Castro insisted on a news blackout for fear that publicity would cause civil unrest in his country among the many other Cubans who were denied the ability to emigrate. Arturo López Levy, however, has argued that Cuba's reason for maintaining a low profile had less to do with domestic considerations than with a reluctance to offend Arab nations.[155]

---

[153]Lesley Pearl, "Bay Area Jews Visit Cuban Shul for First Bar Mitzvah in Twenty Years," *Jewish Bulletin of Northern California,* June 13, 1997.

[154]Interview with Stuart Kelman, Apr. 2000.

[155]" 'Operation Cigar': A not-so-secret Cuban aliyah gets world attention," *Jewish Telegraphic Agency Daily News Bulletin,* Oct. 13, 1999, pp. 1–2. For a Cuban perspective see Aldo Madruga, "No hay tal pacto secreto," *Granma,* Oct. 31, 1999, p. 4.

Whatever strategies lay behind "Operation Cigar," many Cuban Jewish leaders were quite upset by press descriptions of the emigration as "top secret." José Miller, for example, was appalled at the implication that this was a Jewish Agency rescue mission similar to Operation Solomon in Ethiopia, in which thousands of Ethiopian Jews were quite literally saved from famine and civil war. Miller stated that, in contrast to that type of dramatic evacuation, the emigration of Jews from Cuba was a voluntary process that occurred over a prolonged period. The individuals involved chose to relocate for economic or social reasons. They were not escaping from cataclysmic events or the imminent threat of violent death.[156]

All the publicity served to shed light on the actual process of Cuban Jewish emigration to Israel, which had been going on, albeit on a smaller scale, even before 1995, and has continued since. As Israel and Cuba do not have diplomatic relations, the Canadian embassy in Havana represents the interests of the State of Israel. Cuban Jews wishing to emigration must ask for permission from the Cuban government and also fill out a request for immigration to Israel with the consular section of the Canadian embassy. These applications are then sent from the embassy in Havana to Ottawa, and from there the Canadian government turns them over the Israeli embassy, which forwards them to the appropriate government department in Tel Aviv.

Prospective emigrants then have to wait for their exit permits from the Cuban government. While this can take months, there have been no reported cases of any Cuban Jew being turned down (for Cubans seeking to emigrate to other countries, the process can take years). The emigrants leave Cuba in groups, using Cuban exit visas and passports. They travel from Havana to Paris, where they disembark from the plane and go to the Israeli embassy to receive documentation to enter Israel as *olim,* immigrants. They complete the final leg of their journey on Canadian travel documents.

Recent public attention to the organized aliyah of Cuban Jews has also stimulated interest in their reception in Israel and their feelings about living in the Jewish state. Aside from the usual problems that immigrants face — learning a new language, finding a job — the major complaint is that the aid package available to them, they believe, is the same as that provided to new immigrants from other Western countries, and considerably less than what is given to Jews coming from countries defined as "distressed," such as Ethiopia, Yemen, Syria, and Iran. The Cuban Jews believe that this is unfair since the government of Cuba, unlike those of

---

[156]Interviews with Dr. José Miller Fredman, Nov. 1999 and Feb. 2000.

other Western states, takes away the job of anyone applying for an exit visa, Jewish or not, and confiscates all of the property of those who leave except for 20 kilograms of clothing.[157]

Another source of dissatisfaction stems from unrealistic expectations. Some Cuban Jews immigrate to Israel because, as Jews, it is the simplest way of escaping from the poverty and lack of job opportunities in Cuba. Their ultimate aim, however, is to reach the U.S. They have found, however, that it is extremely difficult to get to the U.S., and many feel trapped in Israel. There is a unique psychological aspect to this frustration as well: Cuban *olim* know that many of their friends and neighbors who settled in Miami have been very successful, and they compare their own situation with those Cubans, not with other Israeli immigrant groups, and they tend to feel shortchanged.

A few among the *olim* have returned to Cuba, and the dissatisfaction of Cubans in Israel may cause other Cuban Jews to think twice about aliyah. However, younger *olim*, especially those with technical skills and proficiency in Hebrew, have integrated successfully into the Israeli economy and are very happy in their adopted country.[158]

Whatever the short-term problems, the slow but steady emigration of many of the younger Cuban Jews seems destined to siphon off much of the Jewish energy that was generated over the course of the 1990s. Barring dramatic improvement in the Cuban economy, emigration will continue, and since the Jewish community in Cuba will only convert those who have some Jewish ancestry or are married to Jews—virtually all of whom, if they were interested, have already converted—the Cuban Jewish community will shrink in size.

The fate of this tiny community largely depends on what happens to the country. Life in Cuba remains a struggle: the few stores that exist are poorly stocked; almost everything is rationed; very few people have cars, and most of the vehicles on the road are old and in constant need of repair. As for the political situation, Fidel Castro recently fainted in the middle of a speech, underscoring the potential for a sudden change in leadership.[159] Castro has repeatedly insisted that his brother Raúl, currently the defense minister, is his heir, adding that, "There is not only

---

[157]Erik Schechter, "Out of Castro's Frying Pan," *Jerusalem Report,* Oct. 25, 1999, pp. 20–22. In fact the notion that the Cubans are treated as Westerners is a misperception. Since July 1992 Cuban immigrants have received benefits at the level of Soviet immigrants, which is higher than that for Westerners. Correspondence with Margalit Bejarano, Apr. 2001.

[158]Avi Machlis, "Despite grievances, Cuban *olim* feel lucky to be in Jewish state," *Jewish Telegraphic Agency Daily News Bulletin,* Oct. 21, 1999, pp. 1–2.

[159]Anita Snow, "Castro Fainting Underscores Mortality," Associated Press report, July 2, 2001.

Raúl, but a plethora of young people with talent." Raúl has the loyalty of the military, but is seen as lacking charisma and popular appeal. Other potential leaders include Carlos Lage Dávila, the secretary of the Council of Ministers; Ricardo Alarcón Quesada, president of Cuba's parliament; and Felipe Pérez Roque, the foreign minister. Jaime Suchlicki, director of the University of Miami's Institute for Cuban and Cuban-American Studies, argues that without Fidel, Raúl will have to establish a joint leadership, but that a swift shift to democracy was unlikely: "They want a smooth passing of power, not another revolution." The Cuban leadership, Suchliki notes, has carefully studied the Chinese model that would allow for gradual economic change while maintaining tight political control, and this might be the basis for an evolving governmental structure in a post-Fidel Cuba.[160]

Despite the demographic challenge symbolized by aliyah and the uncertainty surrounding the political and economic future, the Jewish renaissance in Cuba is real. Jewish leaders no longer speak with sadness about the "death of a community"; instead, locals and visitors alike talk with excitement about a miraculous rebirth, a testament to the endurance of Jewish identity and faith.

---

[160]Interview with Jaime Suchlicki, July 2001.

Contemporary Jewish Music in America

By Mark Kligman

Jewish music in America has become a growth industry over the past few decades. Over 2,000 recordings of Jewish music are currently available, with close to 250 new releases produced each year. And although most listeners and consumers are aware of only a few performers, more than 400 artists and groups are engaged in creating and performing this music.[1]

Beyond the impressive numbers, the Jewish music being created, performed, preserved, and disseminated today in America not only reflects the vast changes that have taken place in American Jewish life, but represents a quintessentially American Jewish phenomenon.

The scope of contemporary Jewish music encompasses a wide range of genres and styles, including music for the synagogue, folk and popular music on religious themes, Yiddish songs, klezmer music, Israeli music, and art music by serious composers. Every sector of the Jewish community—from the most right-wing Orthodox to the most secular—participates in the Jewish music endeavor, creating, performing, and listening to the particular music that meets its taste and needs. Jewish music is sung and performed in synagogues of all sizes and types, in schools, community centers, and summer camps, at organizational conclaves, and in college campus auditoriums or in concert halls as august as Carnegie Hall. Ironically, at a time when Jewish commitment is declining,[2] Jewish musical self-expression is on the upswing.

Note: The author gratefully acknowledges the following musicians and producers for giving of their time and sharing their knowledge and experiences: Sam Adler, Merri Arian, Judy Bressler, Marsha Bryant Edelman, Rabbi Daniel Freelander, Avraham Fried, Randee Friedman, Rabbi Ya'akov Gabriel, Rabbi Shefa Gold, Jordon Gorfinkel, Yossi Green, Jim Guttman, Linda Hirschorn, Joshua Jacobson, Arthur Kiron, Jeff Klepper, Matthew Lazar, Frank London, Sheya Mendlowitz, Alan Nelson, Mayer Pasternak, Velvel Pasternak, Bruce Phillips, Seth Rosner, Nachum Segal, Lenny Solomon, Robbie Solomon, Andy Statman, Craig Taubman, Izzy Taubenfeld, and Josh Zweiback. Thanks also to Judah Cohen, Marion Jacobson, Arthur Kiron, Barbara Kirshenblatt-Gimblett, Bruce Phillips, and Jeffrey Shandler for reading earlier drafts of this study and offering insightful comments.

[1]This number is based on data in the *Mostly Music Catalogue* (1996–1997) and interviews with Izzy Taubenfeld of Sameach Music, July 27, 1998, and Velvel Pasternak of Tara Publications, Sept. 14, 1998.

[2]Jack Werthheimer, *A People Divided: Judaism in Contemporary America* (New York, 1993), pp. 43–65.

To be sure, the creation of Jewish music in America is not a new phenomenon. The period between 1880 and 1940—the golden age of the cantors and the heyday of Yiddish theater and cinema—was a fertile period for Jewish music. But as the children of the last immigrant generation came of age during and after World War II, and Yiddish no longer served as their primary language, a distinctively new Jewish music gradually evolved, a process significantly accelerated by changes in the community after the Six-Day War of 1967.[3] Contemporary Jewish music—which developed at about the same time across the entire spectrum of American Judaism—makes use primarily of English and Hebrew (especially liturgical texts for life-cycle events), not Yiddish. And while Eastern European motifs have not totally disappeared, today's Jewish music employs many elements of popular American music. Thus, members of the postwar generation have developed an American Jewish music, a vehicle that distinguishes themselves from their parents, a new, positive expression of their Jewishness.

Since Jewish music is so diverse, and there is no producer, distributor, or retailer who services the musical needs of the entire community, it is not easy to assess the Jewish musical tastes of American Jewry as a whole. One effort to do so was a poll of listeners' favorite Jewish music artists, conducted in the fall of 1997 by Tara Publications and *Moment* magazine. The poll came up with the following top ten artists, in order of their popularity: Debbie Friedman, Safam, Itzhak Perlman, Klezmer Conservatory Band, Klezmatics, Judy Frankel, Shlomo Carlebach, Kol B'Seder, Craig Taubman, Rebbesoul.[4] This listing certainly reflected the diversity of the Jewish community. Debbie Friedman and Kol B'Seder are active in the Reform movement; Safam and Craig Taubman in the Conservative movement; Shlomo Carlebach—an Orthodox rabbi—is known in a wide variety of settings; Klezmer Conservatory Band and Klezmatics play in concert or community settings, and usually not in a religious context; Itzhak Perlman has been prominent in classical and now klezmer concerts; and Judy Frankel performs Sephardic music.[5] Yet even the broad spectrum represented in this poll is misleading since *Moment* has very few

---

[3]Ibid., pp. 30–31; see also J. J. Goldberg, *Jewish Power: Inside the American Jewish Establishment* (Reading, Mass., 1996), pp. 133–40.

[4]"Readers Choice: Jewish Music Poll Results," *Moment,* Feb. 1998, p. 78. While popularity of artists may not necessarily reflect sales figures, there is no question that, in the non-Orthodox market, the top five artists in this poll sell more recordings than do the others.

[5]All artists believe that their music is for the entire Jewish community, not just for a specific group. Nevertheless, as will be discussed in detail below, different groups expect a particular type of musical style, texts, and other qualities in the music they listen to. The association of artists or groups with a community is based upon the type of setting where they most commonly perform.

Orthodox readers, and thus solo performers such as Mordechai Ben David and Avraham Fried, and groups such as D'veykus and the Miami Boys Choir, all popular in the Orthodox community, are not represented. Nevertheless, the music of the ten artists and groups at the top of the *Moment* poll, plus several from the Orthodox community, do represent, more or less, the core of contemporary Jewish music.[6] While there are many other noteworthy up-and-coming performers, the present article focuses on the major established artists and groups.

Pertinent concerns for the investigation of contemporary Jewish music that this essay addresses are: the nature of the music; the degree to which older European styles are retained and innovations made; how traditional motifs are made into something "new"; the identity of the new music's creators; the function it plays in Jewish life; and the reasons why it has become a growth industry.

DEFINITIONS

No attempt is made here to define Jewish music. Jewish music is, always has been, and will be, in many different styles, reflecting particular historic periods and geographic locations. Music written by and for Jews in Central or Eastern Europe during the 19th century differs from that of American or Israeli Jews in the 20th century, each being influenced by the music of its environs. Musical style is informed by aesthetic taste, and since this never remains constant, "Jewish" music continually changes and develops. While there may be a set of descriptive musical traits (modes, forms, and styles) that define Hassidic, cantorial, or klezmer music, this applies only for a particular period of time. Today, a wealth of Jewish musical styles allows American Jews to choose the music that expresses a particular dimension of Judaism—be it religious or secular or a combination of both.

The term "community" will often be used in this study to denote a segment of American Jewry that has one or another taste in Jewish music. While there is considerable documentation on the nuances and concerns of each of the main religious streams,[7] there is no comparable literature on those who do not affiliate religiously, that is secular or cultural Jews, Yiddishists, and so on. Furthermore, since Jewish identity is complex, the

---

[6]This study focuses primarily on music in Ashkenazi communities. For a recent study on Sephardi music, see Edwin Seroussi, "New Directions in the Music of the Sephardic Jews," in Ezra Mendelsohn, ed., *Modern Jews and Their Musical Agendas,* Studies in Contemporary Jewry 9 (London and New York, 1993), pp. 61–77.

[7]Wertheimer, *A People Divided,* pp. 95–169.

boundaries between these segments are by no means clear-cut. People who listen to Yiddish and klezmer music, for example, may be religious or secular, while the performers and artists of this music generally do not identify religiously. The characterization of communities throughout this study, then, should not be viewed as mutually exclusive, but rather as expressing the traits most commonly found in the music and the artists of a particular group.

HISTORICAL BACKGROUND

Several genres of Jewish music were brought over from Europe in the 1880–1920 period, when over two million East European Jews migrated to the United States:[8]

1. Cantorial music[9] is based on *nusach*, a Hebrew term denoting melodic phrases traditionally used for leading synagogue worship, in which specific prayers in the liturgy are sung in a particular mode or scale.[10] A cantorial virtuoso not only performs the *nusach* accurately, but is also capable of improvisation and of vocal embellishments that have specific vocal "effects," such as a *drei* (turn) or *kvetch* (cry).

2. Yiddish music might derive from either a religious or secular context, with much of the latter coming from the Yiddish theater. Such music reflected the desire of many American Jews to hold on to the Yiddish culture of their birthplaces without any sort of religious commitment.

---

[8]Studies focusing broadly on pre-1950s Jewish music are few. Two useful treatments are Irene Heskes, "Three Hundred Years of Jewish Music in America," in her book *Passport to Jewish Music: Its History, Traditions, and Culture* (Wesport, Conn., 1994), pp. 177–226; and Joseph Levine, *Synagogue Song in America* (Crown Point, Ind., 1989). Valuable studies that focus on specific areas are Mark Slobin, *Tenement Songs: The Popular Music of the Jewish Immigrants* (Urbana, Ill., 1982); *Chosen Voices: The Story of the American Cantorate* (Urbana, Ill., 1989); and Jeffrey A. Summit, *The Lord's Song in a Strange Land: Music and Identity in Contemporary Jewish Worship* (London and New York, 2000). For comparison with the Christian experience see Lawrence Hoffman and Janet Walton, eds., *Sacred Sound and Social Change: Liturgical Music in Jewish and Christian Experience* (South Bend, Ind., 1992).

[9]See Irene Heskes's introduction to Velvel Pasternak and Noah Schall, *The Golden Age of Cantors: Musical Masterpieces of the Synagogue* (Cedarhurst, N.Y., 1991), which also appears under the title "The Golden Age of the Cantorial Art," in Heskes, *Passport to Jewish Music*, pp. 56–68.

[10]The Jewish prayer mode system uses three primary modes: *Adoshem Malach*, a major scale with a lowered seventh and flatted tenth; *Magen Avot*, equivalent to the Western minor scale; and *Ahavah Rabbah*, a scale with a lowered second and a raised third producing an augmented-second interval typically avoided in Western classical music. For a further discussion see Baruch J. Cohon, "Structure of the Synagogue Prayer Chant," *Journal of the American Musicological Society* 3 (1950), pp. 17–32; and Hanoch Avenary, "The Concept of Mode in European Synagogue Chant: Studies of the Jewish Music Research Centre," *Yuval* 2 (1971), pp. 11–21.

3. Klezmer (derived from *k'lei zemer,* literally "vessels of song," the Hebrew term for musical instruments) denotes the music heard at Jewish weddings, bar mitzvahs, and other life-cycle events, as well as the instrumental accompaniment to Yiddish songs in the theater. Much of it was derived from non-Jewish folk traditions of Eastern Europe.

4. Hassidic music, both vocal and instrumental, was produced in the courts of the dynasties of rebbes (charismatic leaders) of the Hassidic movement, which originated in the Ukraine in the late 18th century and subsequently spread throughout Eastern Europe. Joyous and fervent singing characterize the *niggun,* the wordless song sung in the synagogue and at a *tisch* (literally "table," referring to a gathering with the rebbe).

5. Art music is that which is heard in the concert hall, such as, in Europe, the works produced by the members of the Society for Jewish Folk Music in St. Petersburg. Composers such as Joel Engel (1868–1927), Joseph Achron (1886–1943), and Moses Milner (1886–1953) wrote symphonies, chamber works, and art songs based upon folk melodies and incorporating aspects of the traditional Jewish modal system.[11]

Obviously, sharp lines cannot be drawn between these five genres. Cantors not only sang for the synagogue, they also performed Yiddish songs. Conversely, some of the Yiddish songs depict a *hazzan* (cantor), and may even parody the emotional nature of his singing. In a klezmer performance, the aesthetic of the clarinet player often mimics the *geshray* (wail) of the cantor. The very fabric of the music itself proves the interrelationship: cantorial *nusach* is incorporated into Yiddish songs, klezmer, Hassidic tunes, and art music. When new songs were composed for each genre, more often than not they were written in the traditional modes of Jewish prayer. The clearest way to distinguish these genres, then, is through their use or context: cantorial music—the synagogue; Yiddish songs—folk or theater; klezmer—life-cycle events; Hassidic music—liturgical and paraliturgical occasions; art music—the concert hall.

Yet a sixth musical genre evolved over the first half of the 20th century—Zionist songs in Hebrew, English, and a variety of other languages that focused on the dream of a Jewish homeland in Palestine. Popularized in schools, synagogues, summer camps, and at social events, such music took on much greater significance with the establishment of the State of Israel in 1948, and even more so after the Six-Day War of 1967.

---

[11]For further discussion see Albert Weisser, *The Modern Renaissance of Jewish Music* (New York, 1954). A noted composer for the concert hall who based some works on Jewish melodies was Ravel; he wrote a setting of the kaddish for voice and orchestra, *Deux Mélodies Hébraïques* (1915).

The Immigrant Generation

The cultural conflict between Jews of Central European origin, who came to the United States in the middle of the 19th century, and the Eastern Europeans, who started coming in large numbers in the 1880s, was expressed in music as well. Beginning in early-19th-century Germany, Central European cantors sought to incorporate a more orderly style of worship modeled on the Protestant church. When Jews from this area came to America, they brought with them the liturgical innovations of composers Solomon Sulzer (1804–1890), Louis Lewandowski (1821–1894), and Samuel Naumbourg (1815–1880).[12] As the Central European immigrants Americanized and became largely identified with the Reform movement, new hymnals and new compositions provided a rich array of music for their synagogues.[13] Abraham W. Binder (1895–1966), along with Isadore Freed (1900–1960) and Herbert Fromm (1905–1995), formulated an American Reform style of music for cantor, choir, and organ in which the choir took a prominent role. In addition, the music of the cantorial line was written out in musical notation[14] and did not consist solely of the traditional *nusach* passages or rely on the cantor's expertise in *nusach*.[15] Thus a trained cantor was no longer needed in a Reform temple, only a musician who could read the music.

The newcomers, Eastern European Jews, tended to perpetuate the more emotional sound of their synagogue music, and in their traditional synagogues—all the Orthodox and many of the Conservative—the organ was not employed. Nevertheless, traditional congregations that sought to innovate used the choral music of David Nowakowsky (1848–1921), Eliezer Gerovitsch (1844–1914), and others, which was influenced by the German synagogue composers. The many recordings and surviving radio broadcasts of the great cantors made during the early part of the 20th century have frozen the sound of this musical style in time.

---

[12]The music of these three composers defined the bulk of the repertoire for many Ashkenazi Jews during the second half of the 19th century and the early 20th century both in Europe and America. For a clear understanding of their contributions see Geoffrey Goldberg, "Jewish Liturgical Music in the Wake of Nineteenth Century Reform," in Hoffman and Walton, eds., *Sacred Sound and Social Change*, pp. 59–83.

[13]Benjie Ellen Schiller, "The Hymnal as an Index of Musical Change in Reform Synagogues," ibid., pp. 187–212.

[14]In some synagogue contexts, including traditional synagogues where musical instruments were used without restriction, the cantor would improvise based on *nusach;* in most instances the accompaniment was also improvised.

[15]Some synagogue composers who immigrated to America and based their music on the European tradition were Heinrich Schalit (1886–1976), Frederick Piket (1903–1974), Max Janowski (1912–1991), and Max Helfman (1901–1963).

For the immigrants from Eastern Europe, the synagogue and its class-rooms could also be the place to hear Yiddish songs and Zionist songs. At home, families sang all of these as well as *zemirot* (Sabbath table songs) and holiday songs, such as those for the Passover seder. Yiddish songs and klezmer music were a vital part of Jewish life for these immigrants. New music created for the Yiddish theater, which was at its height in the 1930s, and for Yiddish cinema, which began in 1930, was the basis of an industry that included recorded music on 78-rpm records, live concerts, and the publication of sheet music. Yiddish theater music could be heard not only on the Lower East Side of Manhattan but also in neighborhood theaters in Brooklyn and the Bronx, and in cities across the United States.[16]

Yiddish theater and its music expressed the struggles of adjusting to American life combined with a hopeful message. The music provided a way to cope, and singing the songs made one feel part of a community of people all undergoing the same ordeal of acculturation. In cinema and theater, the songs expressed the full range of Jewish life. Tragedies such as the sinking of the Titanic and the Triangle Fire of 1913 were the topics of popular Yiddish songs. Song texts portrayed life in "the old country" in romanticized and idyllic form, while also conveying the horror and pain of pogroms and hunger.[17] Musically, composers for the Yiddish theater employed the wide range of styles available to them. Composers such as Sholom Secunda (1894–1974) and Abraham Ellstein (1907–1963), both of whom grew up singing in synagogue choirs, incorporated the music of the synagogue together with popular American styles.

Ultimately, the lure of writing or performing for mainstream audiences led to the decline of the Yiddish theater and its music, relegating klezmer musicians to performing at *simchas* (happy occasions such as weddings and bar mitzvahs), banquets, and social and political functions. During their early years as immigrants, klezmer musicians formed unions; these unions, however, dissolved when the desire to work in mainstream settings became more attractive.[18] In the 1920s klezmer ensembles adapted to American ways with the introduction of American rhythms and with changes in instrumentation: the clarinet became the lead instrument, and the *tsimble* (hammer dulcimer) and *harmonica* (small accordion) fell out of use. By the 1930s klezmer music began to decline, and the very term

---

[16]Nahma Sandrow, *Vagabond Stars: A World History of Yiddish Theater* (Syracuse, 1977; reprint 1996), p. 251.

[17]Slobin, *Tenement Songs*, pp. 6–7.

[18]James Loeffler, "Di Rusishe Progresiv Muzikal Yunyon No. 1 Fun Amerike: The First Klezmer Union in America," *Judaism* 47, Winter 1998, p. 35.

"klezmer" came to have a derogatory connotation, referring to musicians who could not adapt to the American music scene.[19] Those who did adapt assimilated into the musical mainstream, paralleling the assimilation of the immigrant generation in other areas. Parents, now, sought to educate their children in classical music rather than klezmer music. Musicians sought out formal music education, many at elite institutions; thereafter they joined symphonies, played for Broadway theater, and joined American musicians' unions, not Jewish unions.[20]

After World War II

The vacuum left by the decline of Yiddish and klezmer music in the 1940s was filled, first, by music from Israel. In the 1940s and 1950s there were songs of the *Yishuv,* the prestate Jewish community in Palestine, such as "V'ulai," and songs of the War of Independence of 1948, such as "Hafinjan" and "Shir Hapalmach." The repertoire later came to include army-troupe songs, the music of professional performers, and the songs of Naomi Shemer and other composers.[21] The practice of singing Israeli songs in American synagogues, camps, and at social gatherings, which spread in the 1950s, accelerated in the 1960s and 1970s as young American Jews looked to Israel as a positive model for Jewish identity, and the songs' popularity also served as a Jewishly unifying factor.[22] Israeli songs popular in the United States—such as "Bashana Haba'a," "Erev Shel Shoshanim," and Naomi Shemer's "Yerushalayim Shel Zahav" and "Al Kol Ayleh"—exuded yearning for the land and commitment to it, appreciation for the beauty of life in Israel, and the longing for peace.[23] Several song festivals and performing troupes aided in the spread of Israeli folk music. The flow of new musical repertoire from Israel slowed consider-

---

[19]Hankus Netsky, "An Overview of Klezmer Music and Its Development in the U. S.," ibid., pp. 6, 8.

[20]For a portrayal of an immigrant family whose members joined a variety of musical institutions see Andy Logan, "Profiles: Five Generations," *New Yorker,* Oct 29, 1949, pp. 32 51. On the desire of Jews to become part of the musical mainstream see Heskes, *Passport to Jewish Music,* pp. 220–21; and on actors in the Yiddish theater, Sandrow, *Vagabond Stars,* p. 292.

[21]These categories are based on the work of Moshe Shokeid, who studied Israelis living in New York City and attended sessions of group singing in the borough of Queens. See Shokeid, *Children of Circumstances: Israeli Emigrants in New York* (Ithaca, N.Y., 1988), pp. 104–25.

[22]New Israeli songs particularly influenced summer camps. The Conservative movement's Ramah camps typically sang only Hebrew songs (interview with Marsha Edelman, July 29, 1998), and the Reform camps started doing so in the 1970s (interview with Dan Freelander, Mar. 27, 1998). This is discussed in more detail below.

[23]Shokeid, *Children of Circumstances,* pp. 107–09.

ably in the late 1970s and thereafter, undoubtedly reflecting the process of distancing between Israel and American Jewry that was taking place.[24]

The vibrant folk-song revival of the 1950s had a major impact on American culture and subsequently on American Jewish culture. In discussing this period, folklorist Barbara Kirshenblatt-Gimblett describes the efforts of entertainer Theodore Bikel and other Jews involved in folk music: "Bikel quickly became a part of the revival scene. While Jewish repertoire may not have been central to the folk song revival, Jews certainly were. They owned and managed clubs and record companies. They were composers, performers, agents, and managers. They were writers and critics."[25] Bikel produced his first recording devoted to Jewish songs, *Folksongs of Israel,* in 1955. On the record he sang Jewish melodies to Hebrew and Yiddish texts, in a performance style that was polished and professional.[26] (Shlomo Carlebach, who began his career under folk-music influence around this time but whose focus was on a spiritual Jewish message, is discussed in more detail below.) The polish of Bikel stands in marked contrast to the insider Yiddish humor of Mickey Katz's clever musical parodies, which grew out of the frenetic dance music of wedding bands and were widely disseminated in radio broadcasts, recordings, and performances.[27] Kirshenblatt-Gimblett views these musical parodies as the forerunners of the witty "shtick" of klezmer performers of the '80s and '90s.[28] Other entertainers, like Allan Sherman, whose popular *My Son, the Folk Singer* (1962) sold over one million recordings, were able to appeal more broadly to popular American culture.[29] The musical *Fiddler on the Roof* (1964), based on a story by the great Yiddish writer Sholem Aleichem (Shalom Rabinovitz, 1859–1916), was enormously popular and its music appeared on many recordings thereafter.[30]

Music of the concert hall was also prominent in American Jewish life from the 1940s on. To Jews who valued high culture, the musical expres-

---

[24]Steven T. Rosenthal, *Irreconcilable Differences? The Waning of the American Jewish Love Affair With Israel* (Hanover and London, 2001), pp. 42–60.

[25]Barbara Kirshenblatt-Gimblett, "Sounds of Sensibility," *Judaism* 47, Winter 1998, p. 66.

[26]Ibid., p. 67.

[27]Ibid., pp. 69–71.

[28]Ibid., p. 68.

[29]Sherman's more general appeal was due to his limited use of Yiddish and his avoidance of insider vocabulary or detailed Jewish references, though the names of characters in the songs, Zelda, for example, are typically Jewish, and the dialect rhymes retain a Jewish flavor. Jeffrey Shandler, who has analyzed Sherman's work, kindly allowed me to use his unpublished paper, "'My Son the Folksinger': The Folkloristics of Allan Sherman's Antifolklore," which he delivered at the American Folklore Society, Philadelphia, 1989.

[30]Kirshenblatt-Gimblett, "Sounds of Sensibility," p. 71.

sion of Jewishness in this form was more praiseworthy than the traditional forms of Jewish music, which they deemed second-rate. In fact, the acceptance of Jewish composers and noted performers in the concert hall paralleled the Jews' own growing sense of being comfortably at home in America. The compositions of Ernest Bloch (1880–1959), such as *Schelomo* (1916) and *Avodath Hakodesh* (1933), were regularly performed by American orchestras. Wide critical acclaim greeted symphonic works by Leonard Bernstein (1918–1990)—*Jeremiah Symphony* (1943) and *Symphony No. 3 "Kaddish"* (1963)—which consciously made use of Jewish musical themes taken from the traditional Jewish biblical chant, as well as his *Chichester Psalms* (1965), which used the Hebrew text of biblical psalms.[31] Opera singers Jan Peerce and Richard Tucker, both cantors, achieved worldwide recognition. Against a background of the growing cultural assimilation of American Jewry, Jews prominent in artistic settings, even if they did not focus on specifically "Jewish" music, were embraced as exemplary Jews and role models.

Changes in the institutions of Jewish life had a direct affect on the development of contemporary Jewish music. In the synagogue sphere, the 1950s accelerated the decline of the cantor as musical virtuoso, a trend that had begun earlier in the Reform movement.[32] The era of star performing cantors, such as Yosele Rosenblatt, Samuel Vigoda, and Moshe and David Koussevitzky, came to an end, as the cantor was increasingly seen as a synagogue "professional," with responsibilities as prayer leader, musical expert, music teacher, educator, pastoral counselor, and administrator.[33] In the 1940s and 1950s cantorial schools and professional societies were established for each denomination; these aided the growth of music in synagogues.[34] Jewish music was disseminated more widely with

[31]For a discussion of Jewish elements in Bernstein see Jack Gottlieb, "Symbols of Faith in the Music of Leonard Bernstein," *Musical Quarterly* 66, 1980, pp. 287–95; and Geoffrey Fine, "The Vocal Music of Leonard Bernstein: Jewish Applications and Interpretations," Master's thesis, Hebrew Union College-Jewish Institute of Religion (hereafter HUC-JIR), 1998.

[32]Max Wohlberg, "Some Thoughts on the Hazzanic Recitative," *Journal of Synagogue Music* 9, 1979, pp. 82–86.

[33]Slobin, *Chosen Voices,* pp. 135–91.

[34]The first American cantorial school was the School of Sacred Music at HUC-JIR, founded in 1948; its graduates primarily serve the Reform movement. The Cantor's Institute at the Jewish Theological Seminary, established in 1952, provides cantors for Conservative congregations, and Yeshiva University's Cantorial Training Institute, opened in 1964, trains cantors for Orthodox synagogues. Each denomination also has its own professional cantorial organization (Reform: American Conference of Cantors; Conservative: Cantors Assembly; Orthodox: Cantorial Council of America), but some cantors belong to more than one organization. The Reform movement invested women as cantors in 1976 and the Conservative movement followed suit in 1987.

the publication of volumes of melodies traditionally sung in synagogues, schools, and at home.[35]

Thus varieties of Jewish music with roots in European traditions, modified by accommodations to American tastes, were well established by the mid-1960s. But a movement of new Jewish music was about to transform the scene.

Hassidic Goes Mainstream

A pivotal development in the 1950s and early 1960s was the recording of noncantorial Jewish music. This began with Benzion Shenker's recording of the music of the Modzitz Hassidic sect, *Modzitzer Melaveh Malka Melodies,* in 1950. Born in 1925 and raised in Williamsburg, Brooklyn, Shenker was a talented singer who, from an early age, performed with some of the great cantors—in 1937, at the age of 12, he appeared in concert with David Roitman, Adolph Katchko, and Eliahu Kretchman.[36] In 1940 the Modzitzer Rebbe, Shaul Taub, came to America. Shenker developed a personal relationship with the rabbi, one that had a deep impact on him and that lasted a lifetime. Twelve other recordings followed the first, and they included many original songs by Shenker, as well as traditional Modzitz melodies. Two of Shenker's 450 original compositions are regularly sung in many homes on the Sabbath: "Mizmor Le-David" (Psalm 23) and "Aishes Chayil" ("A Woman of Valor"—Proverbs 31:10–31). Both appeared on his *Joy of the Shabbath* album of 1960. In the early 1960s and through the 1970s, David Werdyger, a cantor, also recorded Hassidic melodies. His recordings through the 1970s featured the music of the Gerer, Melitzer, Skulener, Bobover, Boyaner, and Rodomsker dynasties.[37] Recordings of the music of other dynasties, such as Lubavitch and Munkacs, by a variety of other artists, followed.

The original Hassidic melodies that Shenker and Werdyger recorded exemplify the two styles of Hassidic song: a *stam niggun,* a melody with a

---

[35]Two important liturgical publications are the *Out of Print Classics* series, published by HUC-JIR in the 1950s, which includes the works of Baer, Birnbaum, Dunajewsky, Gerovitsch, Lewandowski, Naumbourg, Nowakowsky, Sulzer, Weintraub, and others; and Gershon Ephros, *The Cantorial Anthology: Traditional and Modern Synagogue Music,* 6 vols. (New York, 1929–1975), which also includes works by various composers. Harry Coopersmith, *Favorite Songs of the Jewish People* (New York, 1939) is primarily for home use.

[36]Rochelle Maruch Miller, "Benzion Shenker: An Exclusive Interview with the Master of Jewish Music," *Country Yossi Family Magazine,* Jan./Feb. 1995, p. 51.

[37]Werdyger states that he knew the rebbes of each of these dynasties, was impressed by all of them, and considered it a high honor to lead prayers at their synagogues. David Werdyger as told to Avraham Yaakov Finkel, *Songs of Hope, the Holocaust Diaries* (New York, 1993), pp. 308–14.

regular rhythm used for group singing; and a *deveykus niggun*, a melody that is rhythmically free, most typically sung by one individual, with the goal of achieving a state of spiritual ecstasy.[38] In traditional contexts— such as *seudah shelishit* (the third Sabbath meal, late on Saturday afternoon), *yahrtzeit* (yearly commemoration of a death), or *tisch* (gathering at the rabbi's table)—both musical styles are used: first a *deveykus niggun* to express feelings of longing, followed by a *stam niggun* to express joy. The Hassidic recordings of Shenker and the others, like the recordings of other types of folk music, generally presented the music in appropriate, unsophisticated folk-style arrangements, but sometimes the orchestral accompaniment and choral arrangements followed a more "classical" musical style.[39]

Another development was the inception of the Hassidic Song Festival in Israel in 1969, a phenomenon that lasted more than a decade. Devoted to the creation of new Jewish music based on liturgical texts, it was actually a contest, consisting of an evening presentation of newly created Hassidic-style songs performed by well-known singers who were not Hassidim. Entries were judged and prizes were awarded. Memorable songs among the winners include: Nurit Hirsh's "Ose Shalom," Tsvika Pick's "Sh'ma Yisrael," Shlomo Carlebach's "Od Yishama" and "V'haer Enenu," and David Weinkranz's "Y'varech'cha." Annual recordings and multiple performances by the Hassidic Song Festival troupe in the U.S. helped popularize these songs.[40] Although the music performed was certainly not Hassidic in the traditional sense, the fact that the festival gave prominence to new Jewish music based on liturgy demonstrated that music in popular and folk styles based on Jewish sources could convey an authentic Jewish message.

Carlebach

Jewish musical artists of today consider Shlomo Carlebach (1925–1994) the father of contemporary Jewish music. Combining the participatory ease of folk music, the energy of the newly created music from Israel, and the religious fervor of the Hassidic *niggun*, he succeeded in moving liturgical music out of the synagogue and into a wide range of

---

[38] A. Z. Idelsohn, *Jewish Music in Its Historical Development* (New York, 1929), pp. 411–34; Velvel Pasternak, *Songs of the Chassidim* (Cedarhurst, N.Y., 1968); Ellen Koskoff, "Contemporary Nigun Composition in an American Hasidic Community," *Selected Reports in Ethnomusicology* 3, 1978, pp. 153–74.

[39] Velvel Pasternak interview.

[40] Velvel Pasternak's unpaginated foreword to *The Best of the Chassidic Song Festivals* (Cedarhurst, N.Y., 1989). This book has the sheet music for these and other songs.

other settings, including concert halls and night clubs, and used his music to educate and inspire Jews to renew their Jewish identity and discover the beauty of Jewish life. A charismatic and controversial figure, he remained active for over 30 years, until his passing in 1994.[41]

Shlomo Carlebach was born in Berlin, the son of Rabbi Naftali Hartwig Carlebach (1889–1968), a well-known rabbi. The family moved to Vienna and, when the Nazis took over Austria in 1938, they fled to Lithuania and then the United States, settling in the Williamsburg section of Brooklyn. He studied in a number of yeshivahs and received rabbinical ordination in 1953. During his student years he developed ties with a number of Hassidic groups and came under the influence of Rabbi Menachem Mendel Schneerson (1902–1994), who succeeded his father-in-law as Lubavitcher Rebbe in 1951. Carlebach, in fact, at Schneerson's behest, spent two years spreading the message of Judaism on college campuses (Carlebach subsequently severed his ties with Lubavitch, and rarely spoke about this part of his life). In the mid-1950s, feeling unfulfilled as a yeshivah teacher and part-time congregational rabbi in New Jersey, Carlebach began his musical career. Although he had always loved music, Carlebach's yeshivah teachers, considering it a waste of time, discouraged him from pursuing it. He could not read music and had no formal technical training.[42] In his own words:

> I saw someone playing guitar, and I started learning. I got a teacher, and one day while she was on the phone I started making up a melody and she heard it, said it sounded beautiful, and she wrote it down. Then she said, "Whenever you have a new song, call me and I'll write it down." So a few days later I had a new melody for the wedding song "Od Yishama" and I called her up and she wrote it down. And that's how my career began.[43]

His first record album, in 1959, *Haneshomoh Loch*—known in English as *Songs of My Soul*—was followed in 1960 by *Borchi Nafshi*. The lyrics were liturgical texts, psalms, and other passages from the Bible, and the melodies were folk-like in their straightforward and easy-to-sing stepwise design. Carlebach, in fact, explained that the melodies came to him first, and only then did he scan the prayer book or the Bible to find the words

---

[41]Ari L. Goldman, "Shlomo Carlebach, 69, a Rabbi and Songwriter," *New York Times,* Oct. 22, 1994) p. 11; "Obituaries: Shlomo Carlebach," *Jewish Chronicle* (London), Oct. 28, 1994; "The Pied Piper of Judaism," *Jerusalem Report,* Nov. 1994, p. 45. All appear in M. Brandwine, *Reb Shlomele: The Life and World of Shlomo Carlebach,* trans. Gabriel A. Sivan (Efrat, Israel, 1997). Besides obituaries this book includes biographical material about Carlebach—not all of which is reliable—newspaper articles about him, and memorial tributes.

[42]Eric Offenbacher, "Interview with a Jewish Minstrel," *Jewish Life,* Aug. 1959, pp. 53–57.

[43]Michael Lerner, "Practical Wisdom from Shlomo Carlebach," *Tikkun* 12, Sept./Oct. 1997, p. 54.

to fit them. "Some call me a balladeer, some call me a revivalist—maybe I'm both," he told an interviewer after his first album appeared. The songs were immediately popular and were adopted by Jews of all denominations. Carlebach himself estimated that 90 percent of those who came to hear him perform were not Orthodox.[44] Other recordings followed, including some on the well-known Vanguard folk-music label: *Shlomo Carlebach at the Village Gate,* recorded live, in 1963, and *Shlomo Carlebach in the Palace of the King* in 1965. About his own sudden popularity, Carlebach explained: "After the Second World War, nothing happened in [the] Jewish religious music market. So every *niggun* [melody] I made up, right away hundreds of people were singing it, because nothing else was happening. It was a major breakthrough."[45] Over the course of his career Carlebach recorded over 25 albums. Some estimate that he wrote close to 1,000 melodies, many of which other singers have performed on hundreds of recordings.[46]

In 1967, together with his twin brother Eli Chaim, Shlomo Carlebach took over the direction of his deceased father's congregation, Kehillath Jacob, on Manhattan's West Side, popularly known as the Carlebach Shul. But he seemed to be forever on the move, performing at folk festivals around the country and appearing on stage with Bob Dylan and Joan Baez, setting up a House of Love and Prayer in the San Francisco area in the late-1960s to reach out to "hippies," and traveling around the world. His first trip to the Soviet Union was in 1970, and there too he inspired many Jews to seek out their heritage. Carlebach performed for many Jewish organizations and before a broad spectrum of Jewish audiences, equally at home in all settings. He was well known in Israel, where he frequently performed for the Israel Defense Force, notably during the wars of 1967 and 1973. Because he lived so much of his life on the road, the image many people have of Carlebach is that of the rabbi with a suitcase of books in one hand and a guitar in the other.[47]

From the standpoint of the development of Jewish music in America, Carlebach's most striking innovation was the blending of Hassidic song

---

[44]Offenbacher, "Interview with a Jewish Minstrel," p. 53.

[45]Brandwine, *Reb Shlomele,* p. 9.

[46]Ibid., p. 37. Others estimate that he wrote some 5,000 melodies, only a relatively small number of which were recorded. See Gitta Schreiber, "Shlomo Carlebach: An Exclusive Interview," *Country Yossi Family Magazine,* Nov. 1989, p. 30. The last recording released during his lifetime was *Shabbos with Shlomo,* recorded in 1993; the recording previous to this was ten years earlier. Shortly after he died a recording entitled *Shabbos in Shomayim* was released. Collections of songs were published prior to his death and after. A recent collection, *The Best of Shlomo Carlebach 1960–1990,* includes 90 songs and 24 stories. These and other recent Carlebach recordings are produced by Jerusalem Star Productions.

[47]Brandwine, *Reb Shlomele,* p. 29.

with folk music. As noted above, Hassidic music is typically written either to a religious text or is wordless—a *niggun*. In Hassidic music, individual sections are repeated one or more times. Also, sometimes the musical modes of different sections of the same song, and their respective rhythms, too, may be quite distinct from each other, thus giving a unique character to each.[48] The major characteristics of folk songs, on the other hand, are easy-to-sing lyrics, regular rhythms, and simple harmonies. Carlebach's music encompasses both genres. A typical Carlebach song has two related sections, each having a different character, with the lyrics coming from a religious text. The songs are easy to sing and to remember—the melody is instantly familiar, as if the listener has heard it before. Carlebach frequently began a song by quietly whistling the melody. Whistling is not part of any Jewish musical style, but Carlebach made it work.[49] The accompaniment would grow stronger, and then he sang the text. The consistent, steady beat—perhaps reminiscent of the march-like Modzitz melodies that he had absorbed growing up in Williamsburg—along with the warmth and a certain pathos, inevitably induced the audience to join in the singing. In concert, Carlebach's appeal came not only from the music but also from his charm and magnetic personality. He would intersperse the music with stories, Jewish legends, accounts of his experiences with people, and insights into the Jewish tradition. Communal involvement was essential for him, he said:

> I'm never satisfied with my singing. I don't think I have a good voice. I think my voice is just good enough to inspire people to sing with me. If I would have a *gevald* [incredible] voice like, let's say, Moshe Koussevitzky, then nobody would want to sing with me, because then they'll think they don't want to miss my voice, but my voice is just good enough to make them sing.[50]

Many of Carlebach's songs have become standard fare in synagogues, at weddings, and at other Jewish gatherings. So quickly and completely did his music penetrate the Jewish world that many who hear or sing the tunes assume that they are traditional melodies; they have no idea that Carlebach created them. Among the best known are "Am Yisrael Hai," "Yerushalayim," "Esa Einai," "Od Yishama," "Va Ha'er Eyneynu," "Ki Mi-Tsiyon," "U-va'u Ha-Ovdim," and "Le-Ma'an Ahai Ve-Re'ai."

Shlomo Carlebach's legacy was profound. As noted above, though he was an Orthodox rabbi he was among the top ten musical artists in the *Moment* magazine poll, a great majority of whose respondents were un-

---

[48]On form in Hassidic music see Andre Hajdu and Yaakov Mazur, "Hasidism: The Musical Tradition of Hasidism," *Encyclopædia Judaica* 7, 1972, pp. 1421–32; and Uri Sharvit, *Chassidic Tunes from Galicia* (Jerusalem, 1995), pp. xxxi–xxxiii.

[49]Interview with Nachum Segal, July 19, 1998.

[50]Brandwine, *Reb Shlomele,* p. 9.

doubtedly not Orthodox Jews. Considering that his main contributions were in the 1960s and 1970s, his continuing popularity in the late 1990s is noteworthy. Within the Orthodox world, he was viewed with some skepticism during his lifetime because of his apparent affinity with the "hippie" lifestyle. But Carlebach's popularity among the Orthodox rose considerably after his passing in 1994. The Carlebach Shul in Manhattan, which used to have trouble getting a minyan (prayer quorum), is now packed every Shabbat, and many "Carlebach minyanim" or Carlebach-style synagogues have sprung up in Jewish communities throughout the United States and in Israel.[51]

According to Velvel Pasternak, a publisher and scholar of Jewish music, the key to the Carlebach mystique was his unconventional persona. Although Carlebach was a rabbi, notes Pasternak, had he worn traditional East European rabbinical hat and long black coat, no one would have been interested. "People responded to his melodies and his personality, he had charisma. Melodies as simple as they were became hypnotic. . . . People wanted something different, people didn't want Eastern European music."[52] Jewish radio-show personality Nachum Segal, in contrast, stresses Carlebach's message, remarking that what made him unique was that "Carlebach was there to infuse Jews with Jewish pride."[53]

Carlebach's music and message provided a model for younger artists, particularly those in the religious denominations—Orthodox, Conservative, and Reform. Robbie Solomon, cantor, songwriter, and performer in the group Safam; Jeff Klepper, cantor and performer in Kol B'Seder; and Avraham Fried, performer in the Orthodox and Hassidic communities, all sang his music in the 1960s and 1970s and then went on to create their own. Today it is taken for granted that Jewish music is an effective vehicle to connect Jews to Judaism, but it is all-too-often forgotten that Carlebach was the first to envision the concept and carry it out. For those who are critical of the commercialized aspects of the Jewish music industry today, another positive Carlebach legacy was that he seemed less interested in making money—he was slipshod about copyrighting his tunes and they were often "stolen"—than in seeking to touch and change

---

[51]The term "Carlebach minyan" or "happy minyan" refers to a prayer group or synagogue that uses Carlebach melodies and a spirited prayer style for Sabbath services. See Gary Rosenblatt, "The Sound of Prayer," *New York Jewish Week,* July 17, 1998, p. 7, which sees attempts to incorporate Carlebach melodies as an expression of the quest for spirituality in the 1990s. Cantor Sherwood Goffin, commenting on Rosenblatt's column, pointed out that though Carlebach was innovative, he always kept to the *nusach.* "Not Just Tunes," ibid., July 31, 1998, p. 7.
[52]Pasternak interview.
[53]Segal interview.

the lives of people, a quality ever more in demand today as American Jewry worries about Jewish continuity. In these ways, the Carlebach legacy lives on.

THE "NEW" JEWISH MUSIC

The Jewish music that came into being in the 1960s and 1970s consciously moved away from Eastern European musical modes, styles, and aesthetics to appeal to the tastes of the younger generation. But the shift was gradual and hardly clear-cut. A comment by folklorist Barbara Kirshenblatt-Gimblett about the klezmer revival of the 1970s applies to all forms of the new music: "There is no smooth continuity from yesterday's *klezmorim* to today's klezmers. There is no dramatic rupture, no simple sequence of life, death, and rebirth, as the term revival would imply. Instead, old and new are in a perpetually equivocal relationship."[54]

As already noted in relation to Shlomo Carlebach, one distinguishing feature of the new music is its new purpose—performance. Previously, American Jewish music was sung or played for particular occasions as part of the fabric of Jewish life in synagogues or for other liturgical and life-cycle events. Even the music that was recorded—cantorial, Yiddish, klezmer, Hassidic—was produced as created for its particular context. The new Jewish music, in contrast, provided performances and recordings in a variety of concert venues. These contexts shaped a type of music that was complex and diverse, and which contributed to the formation of a new kind of American Jewish culture.

Developments in Jewish music, as in other areas of Jewish life, responded to political events as well as changes in American culture. The Israeli military victory in the Six-Day War of 1967 engendered great Jewish pride, inspiring many young Jews to look more closely into the Jewish tradition. America, at the time, was a hospitable place for the recovery of one's cultural roots since the older melting-pot model of acculturation had been replaced by emphasis on ethnic pride, largely as a result of the black-power movement and the rising consciousness of white ethnic groups.

It was in the religious sphere—in all three of the major streams of American Judaism—that a new generation of artists began to introduce new styles and contexts, with the aim, modeled on Carlebach, of cultivating a connection with Judaism through music. The most evident in-

---

[54]Kirshenblatt-Gimblett, "Sounds of Sensibility," p. 55.

novation across the board was the use of English lyrics, either alone or together with Hebrew texts. The new Orthodox music grew out of weddings and other quasi-religious contexts such as the *melave malke* (Saturday night post-Sabbath gathering); Reform and Conservative music grew out of camp and synagogue use. Each context had its own imperatives that shaped the creation and development of its music.

Orthodox

The Orthodox world in the 1960s faced a significant challenge: a post-World-War-II generation of Jews — many of them, refugees from Hitler's Europe, relative newcomers — sought to maintain an Orthodox Jewish life but also wanted to be "modern" and not live in the past. These people were caught between two cultures, and, from a musical standpoint, there was a vacuum. In his memoirs, cantor and Hassidic singer David Werdyger describes the situation at the time from the perspective of Hassidic Jews:

> Until the advent of recorded *hassidic* music and popular *frum* [Orthodox] singers, the only records available to the Jewish public were those of the great *chazzanim* [cantors]. Popular entertainment was provided by recordings of the syrupy songs of the Yiddish theater, which flourished on Second Avenue at that time. Often these songs were sung by female ensembles, and in some instances, there was even a women *"chazzante."* At *frum* weddings, "Here Comes the Bride" was invariably played instead of the traditional *chasunah niggunim* [wedding melodies]. Through music, the spirit of looseness and laxity that was prevalent among the assimilated Jewish youngsters in America was worming its way into the most observant homes.[55]

Note the disdain for and fear of Yiddish theater, perceived as antireligious, and of American wedding practices, such as the use of "Here Comes the Bride." There was, then, a strong motivation to create music that would strengthen a commitment to the Orthodox way of life. Werdyger explains how new Jewish music accomplished this aim:

> An entirely new panorama of Jewish song was opening up. Yeshivah students and young *hassidim* eagerly picked up the new tunes, singing them at home and at bar mitzvahs, engagements and weddings. The Wagnerian wedding march was left by the wayside and replaced by meaningful Jewish songs that were chosen by the *chossan* [groom] and *kallah* [bride].[56]

---

[55]Werdyger, *Songs of Hope,* p. 278.

[56]Ibid. The two most popular melodies played at traditional weddings today are tunes to "Od Yishama," one of them by Carlebach; both can be found in Velvel Pasternak, *The International Jewish Songbook* (Owings Mills, Md., 1994), pp. 232–33.

This new Orthodox Jewish music was never intended for use in the synagogue, where traditional liturgical melodies have continued to hold sway. But, as singer Avraham Fried pointed out, there is no longer a market for recordings of cantorial music—what people want are good dance songs and ballads.[57]

The sheer quantity of contemporary Orthodox Jewish music is staggering, representing at least half of all the Jewish music that is available. The Orthodox music industry, based predominantly in Brooklyn, New York, encompassing performers, songwriters, arrangers, and distributors, has grown significantly over the past 25 years. While few Reform and klezmer, and no Conservative, popular artists are able to make a living from their music, about ten Orthodox musicians support themselves entirely through the creation and performance of new music.[58]

The simple explanation for this growth is the rising number of right-wing yeshivah and Hassidic Jews who do not listen to popular American music.[59] And since activities such as watching television or attending the theater or a movie are also discouraged, their own music is virtually the sole means of entertainment. They listen to it at home, in the car, in the buses and vans that transport groups to school or work, and, for women, while tending the children and preparing meals. Live performances of this music are social events (men and women sitting separately). In short, Orthodox popular music is to Orthodox Jewish life as popular music is to American life, and one has the sense that as American popular music has become increasingly influenced by the drug culture, the counter-message of Orthodoxy's traditional values has become ever more pointed in Orthodox music.

The growing popularity of the new music has not been accepted without reservation, as the entire phenomenon raises serious issues for the Orthodox community, and there are no historical precedents. Should limits be placed on the use of "non-Jewish" musical styles? Should the goal of the artist be to make money or to inspire people in their Jewish commitment? What can music do for those who are searching to connect to Judaism? Do rabbis have any responsibility to monitor this music? Might

---

[57]Interview with Avraham Fried, July 6, 1998.

[58]This estimate refers to popular artists, not to professionals employed as cantors, song leaders, and wedding-band musicians. While Orthodox synagogues in America support fewer than 25 full-time cantors, there are well over 500 professionally employed cantors working at Reform and Conservative synagogues. See Slobin, *Chosen Voices,* p. xxiii.

[59]Mark Kligman, "On the Creators and Consumers of Orthodox Popular Music in Brooklyn, New York," *YIVO Annual* 23, 1996, pp. 259–93. The term "yeshivah" refers to non-Hassidic, strictly Orthodox Jews. Of course the decision to listen to a particular form of music is ultimately an individual matter, and thus the characterizations in the text are no more than useful generalizations.

there not be dangers in allowing performers who are not rabbis to serve as charismatic role models for Orthodox youth?[60] Clearly, a new dimension has been added to Orthodox Jewish life.

In terms of musical style, the new Orthodox music, while rooted in the past, has modernized way beyond Carlebach to incorporate pop, rock, easy listening, blues, country, and other musical styles. Historian Haym Soloveitchik described the situation:

> Rock music sung with "kosher" lyrics was heard at the weddings of the most religious. There had been no "kosher" jazz or "kosher" swing, for music is evocative, and what was elicited by the contemporary beat was felt by the previous generation to be alien to a "Jewish rejoicing" (*yiddishe simche*). This was no longer the case. The body syncopated to the beat of rock, and the emotional receptivities that the contemporary rhythm engendered were now felt to be consonant with the spirit of "Jewish rejoicing." Indeed, "Hassidic" rock concerts, though decried, were not unheard of.[61]

The rejection of Eastern European musical elements was deliberate, reflecting a broader rejection of what was perceived as outmoded Jewish nostalgia. Here is Yossi Green, composer of over 320 songs recorded on 40 albums by the most successful Orthodox performers, on the subject of klezmer music:

> Klezmer music is more of a caricature of what Jewish music used to be. Of course it's very effective, apparently. An instrumentalist can then go ahead and show off his instrument, show off his ability to play. And that really has nothing to do with where Jewish music is today. That's my opinion. I'm in the center—I'm writing most of this music for years. . . . New Hassidic music [his term for new Orthodox music] has definitely replaced klezmer. If klezmer was the downtrodden, stepped-on poor little shtetl Jew's music then this is the music of today for the young, wealthier, more educated, forward thinking Jewish mind. . . . Klezmer is totally Jewish when ours is influenced by Elton John. You listen to "Tanyeh" or "Didoh Bei"[62] and you tell me how beautiful these songs are. It is fresh, it is new. It is the young Jewish person saying, "I'm here, it's the '90s, I'm proud of my Judaism, I'm learning a lot but I'm also having fun—it's allowed and its okay, my kids are having fun, we're relaxing and enjoying ourselves, we're Jewish and we're proud of it."[63]

And, commenting on the use of the *Ahavah Rabbah* prayer mode, which is based on a scale not used in Western music:

---

[60]See, for example, Dovid Sears, "Who Took the 'Jewish' Out of Jewish Music?" *Jewish Observer*, Jan. 1997, pp. 12–16.

[61]Haym Soloveitchik, "Rupture and Reconstruction: The Transformation of Contemporary Orthodoxy," *Tradition* 28, Summer 1994, p. 75.

[62]The lyrics of these two songs, among the most popular composed by Yossi Green and performed by Avraham Fried, are from the Babylonian Talmud. "Tanya" appears on *Avraham Fried: We Are Ready!* (1988), the text taken from Tractate B'rachot, p. 7a. "Didoh Bei" appears on *Avraham Fried: Chazak!* (1997), the text taken from Tractate Nedarim, p. 41a.

[63]Interview with Yossi Green, July 1, 1998.

[This] is a mode where you have to be very careful while using it in the modern music. It's a throwback to a time where people don't want to be. People don't want to live on the East Side with the pickle jars and the tenement buildings. That's what they associated with the old Art Raymond, 20–40 years ago. They don't associate with that, it is not a pleasant memory, it's a memory when things were very bad, when people were very poor and they didn't have things. Music today is about the new, a new spirit.[64]

The heavy reliance of the Orthodox on rock and pop music for entertainment—forms different from the Eastern European musical traditions conventionally regarded as "Jewish"—is clearly rooted in sociological factors. Barred by ever-intensifying religious inhibitions from participating in the world of non-Jewish culture, the Orthodox Jew appropriates and makes Jewish the music of that culture as a way to feel "modern" without going outside the community.

INFLUENTIAL ORTHODOX FIGURES

Young Orthodox musical groups began to appear in the early 1960s, among them The Rabbi's Sons, Mark III, Ruach, and Simchatone. Over time, members of these and other groups moved to new groups or became solo artists. Perhaps the most popular was The Rabbi's Sons (each member of the group in fact was the son of a rabbi), which recorded its first album in 1967 and three others thereafter. Clearly influenced by the music of Shlomo Carlebach, the group was noted for its lyric vocal lines in a late-1960s folk idiom, accompanied by mostly acoustic instruments, often in a fast tempo. The group was described as "the Peter, Paul, and Mary of Jewish music in the type of songs they sang and the harmonies."[65] Although The Rabbi's Sons did not last through the 1970s, their influence continued. The group's leader, Rabbi Baruch Chait, formed a new group called Kol Solonika, which incorporated a similar folk style but added a Greek sound and the use of the stringed Greek bouzouki.[66]

This period also saw the rise of several boys' choirs, such as Pirchei and London Pirchei—now known as the London School of Jewish Song. A performer who began singing in the 1960s and is still active today is Jo Amar. His music encompasses a variety of Sephardic styles, Moroccan and Arabic, including both folk songs and cantorial melodies. Amar has produced numerous recordings that remain popular, and he performs frequently in concerts all over the world.

---

[64]Ibid. Art Raymond was the well-known host of New York radio station WEVD.
[65]Interview with Sheya Mendlowitz, July 22, 1998.
[66]Its first recording, *Kol Solonika: The New Greek Hassidic Sound* (1972), was followed by five others.

In the 1970s a group called D'veykus ("clinging" [to God]) had a significant influence. Its composer, Abie Rotenberg, following Carlebach, wrote songs with liturgical texts that were easy to sing, memorable, and pleasant.[67] Many admirers describe the music as soulful and contemplative. The group's melodious tunes secured a place in Orthodox life at weddings, in the synagogue, and as *zemirot* sung at home. Some of the best-known D'veykus melodies are "Lev Tahor" and "Hiney Yomim" (vol. 1), "Kol Dodi" and "Gam Kee Aylech" (vol. 2), "V'Lee Yerushalayim" and "Na'ar Hayiti" (vol. 3), and "Hamalach" (vol. 4).[68] This group did not perform live concerts, but only recorded its music in the studio, marking an important transition whereby recording music became an end in itself, rather than just a means of preserving and disseminating music written for live performance.

Another group that had a significant impact beginning in the late 1970s and through the early 1980s was the Diaspora Yeshiva Band, the name taken from the yeshivah in Jerusalem where members of the group studied. Their contribution was using American folk styles such as rock and blue grass as settings for religious texts. Most members of the band, like the other students at the Diaspora Yeshiva, were *ba'alei teshuvah,* newly observant Jews, who were steeped in secular American culture and had received their musical training in the United States before adopting Orthodoxy. Their music provided a gateway for other *ba'alei teshuvah,* as well as for those raised as Orthodox, to experience a contemporary Jewish American music. The melodies were often complex, and the arrangements included virtuoso instrumental playing.

If one person had to be chosen as the most influential figure in contemporary Orthodox music, it would be Mordechai Ben David. The son of David Werdyger (hence the name, Mordechai the son of David), Mordechai began singing at an early age in his father's concerts and on recordings.[69] With 25 recordings of his own to date, Ben David is one of the most successful solo performers in the field. His first solo album, released in 1974, entitled *Hineni,* had two important innovations, both of which became precedents for his later albums as well. First, the music was arranged professionally and performed by a full orchestra. Second, the title song had an English text, though it centered upon the Hebrew word *hineni,* meaning, "I am here" ready to serve God, the response that the

---

[67]Another example of the recycling of personnel is D'veykus singer Label Sharfman, who was also a member of The Rabbi's Sons.

[68]The longevity of this group is remarkable. The first three volumes were recorded in the 1970s, volume four in 1990, and volume five in 1995.

[69]Werdyger, *Songs of Hope,* p. 297

patriarch Abraham gave when God called on him.[70] A quick review of the English-language Jewish spiritual messages embedded at the start of three albums by Ben David follows:

Hineni (1974)
So my brother, put your faith in the Above, say *"hineni,"* I am ready, to serve you with love.

I'd Rather Pray and Sing (1977)
I don't want a thing, I'd rather pray and sing. I'd rather tell the story of your holiness and glory.

Just One Shabbos (1981)
Just one Shabbos and we'll all be free, just one Shabbos come and join with me. Let's sing and dance to the sky, with our spirits so high, we'll show them all it's true, let them come and join us too.

The music of these albums is in a 1970s soft-rock ballad style in which the chorus is more energetic than the verses; when they first appeared, the upgraded arranging standards gave the songs a fresh sound, and many other artists and groups continued these innovations. Just as Carlebach forged a link between folk music and Jewish music, Ben David appropriated an American musical style and a secular idiom and adapted them to fit a Jewish message. Despite the English texts of the title numbers, the majority of the songs appearing on Ben David's albums are in Hebrew. Most of them are original songs written either by Ben David or other songwriters; the rest are songs of Carlebach, Benzion Shenker, and Hassidic dynasties, or are well-known Israeli songs.[71] Ben David performs for a wide variety of Orthodox audiences, but his music is geared mainly to its right-wing segment, popularly known as the "Borough Park community," after the name of a heavily Orthodox Brooklyn neighborhood.

Another popular Orthodox singer who began performing in the early 1980s is Avraham Fried. The English title song of his first album, in 1981, *No Jew Will Be Left Behind,* was written by songwriter Yossi Green. Its words, which Fried explains he composed after hearing a discourse by the Lubavitcher Rebbe, state that when the Messiah comes all Jews will go to Israel and no one will be left behind. Fried is indeed a Lubavitcher Hassid living in Crown Heights, Brooklyn, and many of his songs incor-

---

[70]For a more detailed discussion of the text of this song see Kligman, "Creators and Consumers of Orthodox Popular Music," pp. 268–71.

[71]The *Hineni* album includes an "Od Yishama" of Carlebach and "Shema Yisroel" of Tzvika Pick. Many of Ben David's albums combine folk, popular, and Hassidic music together with original songs. Some from the late 1980s and 1990s focus on a particular theme, such as holidays or weddings.

porate the messianic message of redemption.[72] Some of the best known are "The Time Is Now" (1982), "We Are Ready" (1988), "Goodbye Golus" (1989), "On Giants' Shoulders" (1993), and "Don't Hide from Me" (1995).[73] In much the same way as Ben David, Fried sees the English songs as "a chance to say how I'm feeling at that moment, in my own words, not based on a verse or taken out of psalms."[74]

Although Fried and Ben David also sing and record songs based on liturgical texts, their English-message songs may well be the most favored by their listeners. At the end of the 1980s Fried introduced songs with a message rather than a traditional text in languages other than English — Aramaic, Yiddish, and Hebrew. The song "Tanyeh," appearing on *We Are Ready* (1988), is taken from a passage in the Talmud (B'rachot 7a) relating how Rabbi Yishmael entered the holiest area of the Temple and saw a vision of God. "Aderaba" ("on the contrary"), from a 1991 album by the same name, is based on a prayer written by Rabbi Elimelech, who says, "Let's see the good points of our neighbors and overlook their shortcomings." "Shtar Hatnoim," recorded in 1993 on an album by the same name, compares the wedding contract of the title to the contract between God and the Jewish people. The composer of these three songs, Yossi Green, has taken the format of the English-language message songs and applied it to non-English texts, creating deeply expressive stories or images. The music combines cantorial *nusach,* Hassidic *niggun,* and passages with a soothing melodic line, all tied together by an orchestral accompaniment. "Tiher," on the album *Chazak!* (1997), recorded by Fried, has been called the most developed example of this song type.[75]

An indicator that Orthodox popular music had entered the mainstream was a concert in January 1988 at Lincoln Center's Avery Fisher Hall, a benefit for the Hebrew Academy for Special Children (HASC), featuring Mordechai Ben David, Avraham Fried, and the Sephardi singer Yoel Sharabi. While similar performances had been held at Brooklyn College and Queens College, this was the first concert of Orthodox popular music to take place in Manhattan.[76] Since then, similar benefits featuring Orthodox popular music, for this and other causes, have taken place at

---

[72]Fried interview. See also Calev Ben-David, "Music with a Soul," *Jerusalem Report,* Feb. 23, 1995, p. 42.

[73]The first three songs come from recordings of the same name; the last two are from *Shtar Hatnoim* (1993) and *Brocha V'Hatzlocha* (1995).

[74]Fried interview.

[75]Green interview.

[76]Of course there had been many previous performances of cantorial and Yiddish music in New York City and elsewhere, but they had not been specifically identified with the Orthodox community.

Carnegie Hall, Radio City Music Hall, the Paramount Theater of Madison Square Garden, Nassau Coliseum, Westbury Music Fair, and the Metropolitan Opera House. Outside of New York, such music is performed throughout North America as well as in Europe and Israel, at synagogues, schools, and other locations large enough to hold an audience of several hundred people. Top performers play between 30 and 50 concerts a year. According to producer Sheya Mendlowitz, "There are masses out there that are interested now and it is growing. The younger generation is very much into Jewish music, the market is growing. I don't even think we've touched the tip of the iceberg yet."[77]

While Orthodox Jews in their 30s and older have grown up with the music of Mordechai Ben David and Avraham Fried, a younger generation is being reached by new performers in their mid-to-late 20s: Shloime Dachs, Sandy Shmuely, Mendy Wald, Yisroel Williger, and Yehuda. Two other performers whose popularity has grown over the last decade are Michoel Streicher, with more than ten recordings since 1989, and Dedi, who has recorded four albums since 1993. Kol Solonika and D'veykus remain popular, their music recently transferred to the CD format. Other popular groups include Regesh, which began performing in 1983 and has issued ten albums;[78] the Miami Boys Choir, with close to 20 recordings, active since 1979;[79] and Journeys, a group that has recorded three albums since 1984 — a majority of the songs, written in English, are by Abie Rotenberg, who was the composer for D'veykus.[80] Instrumental music has become more common, especially recordings of wedding music such as

---

[77]Mendlowitz interview.

[78]Regesh's "Shalom Aleichem" from *Shabbos,* vol. 3 (1985), is well known and frequently sung on Friday nights before the Sabbath meal. For a further discussion of Regesh and this song see Kligman, "Creators and Consumers of Orthodox Popular Music," pp. 277–79.

[79]A well-known English song, "Besiyta Dishamaya" ("with the help of heaven"), was recorded by the group in 1984. Emulating Mordechai Ben David's "Hineni," "Besiyta Dishamaya" is the only non-English phrase in the song, but that Hebrew title encapsulates its message. Another English song, "We Need You" (1988), addresses the problem of talking during synagogue services. "Meherah," a frequently heard original song in Hebrew composed by choir director Yerachmiel Begun, appears on the album *Klal Yisroel Together* (1987).

[80]Many of the 28 songs that appear on the three albums are well known, such as "The Place Where I Belong," vol. 1 (1984), about a Torah scroll that travels from Europe to America; "Teardrop," vol. 2 (1989), the story of an old woman who lights candles on the Sabbath in grief and despair but is transformed by the magic of the experience; and "Who Am I," vol. 3 (1992), written for the Hebrew Academy for Special Children's annual concert, which conveys the message that children with special needs are like everyone else. The acceptance of this song, by the way, marked a milestone in American Orthodoxy's public acknowledgement of the phenomenon of children with handicaps. Abie Rotenberg also made two recordings with the group Lev V'Nefesh, the first in 1990 and the second in 1998, both consisting primarily of original songs by Rotenberg to Hebrew texts.

Dance with Neginah, Neshoma Orchestra, and *What a Wedding.* Groups that record instrumental versions of well-known songs are Teva and Project X. Children's music is also popular, and there are numerous groups that record stories and songs with Jewish messages and themes: Uncle Moishy, Country Yossi, 613 Torah Avenue, Mitzvah Tree, Rabbi Shmuel Kunda, and Torah Tots, to name a few.

Modern Orthodox Jews, who do not avoid secular culture and attend concerts and other forms of general American entertainment, do not have the same need to listen only to Jewish music. They are not frequent buyers of Jewish music and there are no groups or artists specifically catering to them.[81] Nevertheless, the group called Shlock Rock would seem to be closer to modern Orthodoxy than to any other group, and its performers come from that community. It has been successful in reaching modern Orthodox audiences—mostly Jewish day schools and National Conference of Synagogue Youth (NCSY) conventions—but it also performs in Reform and Conservative venues as well as at Jewish community centers. The writer and director of the group, Lenny Solomon, has completed 20 recordings since 1986.

Shlock Rock is best known for songs that educate and entertain through parody. As anthropologist Elliott Oring has noted, modern Orthodoxy, which more than any other Jewish subgroup seeks seriously to balance the world of strict halakhic tradition with that of secular modernity, is apt to cope with the tension by creating parodies of it.[82] Some examples of Shlock Rock are "Old Time Torah Scroll," which parodies "Old Time Rock and Roll," from the album *Learning Is Good* (1986); "Under the Huppah," which parodies "Under the Boardwalk," from the album *Purim Torah* (1987); "Every Bite You Take," reminding one to say a blessing after a meal, which parodies "Every Breath You Take," from the album *To Unite All Jews* (1989); "All Night Long," which is about staying up the night of the Shavuot holiday to study Torah and parodies Lionel Richie's "All Night Long," also from *To Unite All Jews;* and "We've Got a Strong Desire," which recounts all of Jewish history in 42 lines and parodies Billy Joel's "We Didn't Start the Fire," from the album *Sgt. Shlocker's Magical History Tour* (1991). Lenny Solomon has also written original songs based upon recent events in Israel and New York, such

---

[81]For further discussion of the distinction between modern Orthodoxy and the yeshivah community see Kligman, "Creators and Consumers of Orthodox Popular Music"; and Mark Kligman, "The Media and the Message: The Recorded Music of Orthodox Jews in Brooklyn, N.Y.," *Jewish Folklore and Ethnology Review: Special Issue on Media* 16, 1994, pp. 9–11.

[82]Elliott Oring, "Rechnitzer Rejects: A Humor of Modern Orthodoxy," in Jack Kugelmass, ed., *Between Two Worlds: Ethnographic Essays on American Jewry* (Ithaca and London, 1988), pp. 148–61.

as "Keep on Giving," which focuses on charity and helping the homeless and was written for a joint African American-Jewish rally after the 1991 Crown Heights riots. It appears on the album *Manual for the Moral Minded* (1994). Shlock Rock's primary audience was originally children and teenagers, but this has changed. According to Solomon, "My age group is more of a family audience now. The listeners are still varied, from unaffiliated to Haredi, but the age group is 3 to 13 and their parents and grandparents."[83]

Other modern Orthodox groups have appeared more recently with distinctive musical styles. Kol Achai ("voice of my brothers"), which has recorded three albums since 1990, consists of three Israeli brothers whose music combines folk and popular styles. Beat'achon (a play on the English "beat" and the Hebrew word for "faith")—three recordings since 1993—is an all-male a cappella group whose music ranges from 1950s doo-wop to jazz and rhythm and blues. Jordan Gorfinkel, a singer for the six-man Beat'achon and its manager, notes that the group does not adhere to any specific Jewish style; rather, it strives for "the same quality music as heard on the radio, but with Jewish values."[84]

A noteworthy feature of the new Orthodox music is that it is created and performed chiefly by men—but listened to by both men and women. This is because Halakhah considers the voice of a woman singing to be sexually arousing to men, and therefore prohibits men from hearing it (the reverse is not the case). As a kind of musical subculture, however, the Orthodox world has produced female singers who perform their own original songs, as well as songs written by male performers, at concerts exclusively for women, and make recordings as well. Some of the established female performers are Ruthi Navon, Ashira, Kineret, Rochel Miller, Susan Kates, Dana Mase, and Julia Blum. Groups or ensembles of women include A Taste of Music, in Brooklyn, and Tofa'ah, in Israel. Since modern Orthodox Jews tend to be more lenient on the issue of hearing female singers, there are some performers—Shlomo Carlebach's daughter, Neshama, is a good example—who will perform either for all-female audiences or for mixed audiences.[85]

Ironically, even in Orthodox circles where women's singing voices are not supposed to be heard, the women play an important role in popularizing the music, and it is they who often determine which songs or singers are "in." This is because a primary function of much of the new

---

[83]E-mail message from Lenny Solomon to the author, Sept. 18, 1998.

[84]Interview with Jordan Gorfinkel, July 20, 1998.

[85]For a discussion of women's popular music in general, including both Orthodox and non-Orthodox, see Rahel Musleah, "An Explosion of Jewish Women's Popular Music," *Lilith*, Winter 1995, pp. 18–26, 28–29.

Orthodox music is to accompany dancing at weddings, known as *simcha* dancing (men and women dance in separate circles, often separated by a partition). Examples of such music are Mordechai Ben David's Yiddish songs "Yidden" (1986) and "Moshiach, Moshiach, Moshiach" (1992), and Avraham Fried's "Dido Bei" (1997). Women, who seem especially to enjoy the dancing, practice on their own time and choreograph group dances to new songs. Many in the Orthodox music industry say that getting a song onto the dance floor at an Orthodox wedding can significantly increase the sales of recordings.[86]

Finally, despite the proliferation of new music in the Orthodox community and its broad acceptance, there remains an undertone of criticism that the whole enterprise—especially as its musical sophistication takes it ever farther from its simple roots—neglects true spirituality and cares only about making money.[87] Some performers are sensitive to this criticism. Avraham Fried, for example, who had a close personal relationship with the late Lubavitcher Rebbe, is careful to balance his popular recordings with more traditional works, such as his recordings of the Yiddish songs of Yom Tov Ehrlich as well as Lubavitch and other traditional Hassidic melodies.[88] However Lenny Solomon of Shlock Rock believes the criticism is misguided:

> Jewish music is going in the right direction. Music is the language of the people. If they are listening to your music then you are speaking their language and both the performer and the listener can help bring *moshiach* [the Messiah]—the performer by writing inspired music that helps people get closer to God, and the listener by getting inspired and moving in the right direction. I expect to see Jewish music expand into television, perhaps, at first, music videos here and there, until a station geared to the purpose of reinforcing Jewish identity is established.[89]

Reform

Music in the Reform community, like that among the Orthodox, emerges from the confluence of Judaism and American life, but the response is different. The synagogue is the primary setting for Jewish ex-

---

[86]Jill Gellerman, "Sources of Jewish Dance: A Select Bibliography," *Jewish Folklore and Ethnology Newsletter* 5, 1981, pp. 1–2; Gellerman, *"Simchas Bais Hasho'eva* in Crown Heights: Rehearsing for the Ultimate *Simcha* Among the Lubavitcher Hasidim," *Jewish Folklore and Ethnology Review: Jewish Dance* 20, 2000, pp. 110–22.

[87]Mendlowitz and Segal interviews.

[88]Fried interview. The Yiddish songs appear in two volumes, both under the title *Yiddish Gems* (1992 and 1994), and the Lubavitch and other Hassidic melodies are on *Hupp Cossack* (1996) and *Niggun Habesht* (1998), both of which are updated versions of recordings made by others in the 1950s.

[89]Solomon e-mail.

pression among most Reform Jews, and it is there that musicians have directed their efforts to revitalize older Reform music, which, they felt, was too formal and out of date. Today, Reform popular music has significantly displaced the traditional repertoire, despite ongoing resistance, particularly among Reform cantors.

Before the 1960s music in Reform synagogues consisted chiefly of hymns sung by the congregation and compositions sung by cantor and choir with organ accompaniment, using artistic settings of the liturgy by Binder, Freed, Fromm, and others, discussed above.[90] The dominant language was English—the *Union Hymnal* contains 284 hymns, 280 in English and four in Hebrew. In Reform summer camps sponsored by the National Federation of Temple Youth (NFTY) and the Union of American Hebrew Congregations (UAHC) communal singing at meals and services consisted of a few Israeli and Carlebach songs and lots of American folk tunes, such as "Puff the Magic Dragon," "Blowin in the Wind," and "Leaving on a Jet Plane," and black spirituals like "Follow the Drinking Gourd," "This Train Bound for Glory," and "Go Down Moses." These English songs had a message that resonated with the political, ethical, and humanitarian issues of the 1960s.

Cantor Jeff Klepper, who first attended summer camp in 1968, describes the lack of a tradition of music for Reform youth:

> But what was our Jewish music heritage? Well in shul [synagogue] it was Freed and Binder . . . it was nothing to come away with. That was artistic and professional music. . . . There was nothing for us in the synagogues in the late '60s, nothing. Because to be 13, or 14, or 15, to walk into a shul with long hair and to have a choir and, you know, have a cantor singing quasi-operatic music, that frankly wasn't very good, a style that was totally foreign to us. If there were Jewish melodies in that music we didn't hear them.[91]

For Klepper and other young Reform Jews in the 1960s and early 1970s, folk singers Pete Seeger, Bob Dylan, Tom Paxton, and James Taylor were important influences:

---

[90]Schiller, "The Hymnal as an Index of Musical Change in Reform Synagogues," looks at the breadth of change in Reform liturgical music during the 20th century. Lawrence Hoffman includes comments about music in his work on changes in liturgy: "Musical Traditions and Tension in the American Synagogue," in *Music and the Experience of God: Concilium 222* (Edinburgh, 1989), pp. 30–38; and *The Art of Public Prayer: Not for Clergy Only* (Washington, D.C., 1988; 2nd ed. Woodstock, Ver., 1999), pp. 171–200. A study focusing on Reform camps is Wally Schachet-Briskin, "The Music of Reform Youth," Master's thesis, HUC-JIR, 1996.

[91]Interview with Jeff Klepper, June 16, 1998. The introduction (unpaged) to Jeff Klepper and Dan Freelander, *The Kol B'Seder Songbook* (Owings Mills, Md., 1996), describes the lack of congregational involvement in synagogue music and the perceived need to encourage participation.

MUSIC of the YIDDISH THEATER

AP/Wide World Photos

Leonard Bernstein

Into the Musical Mainstream

Akira Kinoshita/IMG Artists

Itzhak Perlman

Debbie Friedman

Pioneers of
Religious
Renewal

Shlomo Carlebach

The Klezmatics

The Klezmer Revival

Klezmer Conservatory Band

Pete Seeger's music had an ethos to it, and the ethos was everybody sings and that makes it democratic, and it's anticommercial because you could sit in your living room with a guitar and enjoy the evening in front of the fire singing folk songs. You don't need to buy the music that Capital Records is trying to get you to buy. You don't need to buy the teenybopper bubble-gum music. So it's free, you just sit around with your guitar or your banjo. It was Communist. But it's great, it worked for us, it totally worked.[92]

Although generally disdainful of European Jewish music, such as Hassidic *niggunim*, these young Reform Jews recognized Shlomo Carlebach as an authentic Jewish folk singer. The fact that he, an Orthodox rabbi, was an innovator may have given them license to create a new Jewish music of their own in a folk style.

By the late 1960s, when ethnic pride was intensifying, American Jews embraced Israeli culture as a vehicle for expressing their Jewish identity. According to Rabbi Daniel Freelander, "This ethnic, pro-ethnic, and pro-Israel stuff, combined with the anti-authority stuff of the late '60s, created the stage for radical change." [93] Camp songbooks underwent major revisions. There was an increase in the use of Hebrew, more Israeli songs—including some composed by Naomi Shemer and others from the Hassidic Song Festival—and Shlomo Carlebach tunes. According to Freelander, "Our people wanted to hear Hebrew and they wanted to sing Hebrew, so Hebrew becomes a real crucial piece. This is the change from the 1965 songbook, which is almost entirely in English, only a few Yiddish pieces. Yiddish goes out of fashion in 1967."[94] And beginning in the 1970s the English repertoire—the American folk tunes and black spirituals—shrunk dramatically.

It was in the summer camps that Reform young people, Jewishly invigorated by their camp experience, set off a revolution in liturgical music that would eventually transform Reform synagogue services across America. Jeff Klepper relates what happened:

And then we took Reform war-horse melodies and played them on guitar. That was part of the revolution. Which means we stripped them of their choral music, for instance the [Isadore] Freed Hassidic "Mi Chamocha,"[95] which was a Hassidic melody, or quasi-Hassidic. . . . We didn't have an organ in the woods, there was no place to plug it in and you couldn't have a piano because a piano was too big to shlep, and you didn't have Casio keyboards. Since services were in the woods, in a little clearing in the woods a guitar was used. It was portable, it was mellifluous, it was rhythmic. Guitar in my mind is the perfect instrument to accompany worship because it can do everything.

---

[92]Klepper interview.
[93]Freelander interview.
[94]Ibid.
[95]Isadore Freed, *Hassidic Service for Sabbath Eve* (New York, 1962). The piece was written in 1954.

> So there was a certain percentage of music that was taken and everyone brought their pet tunes. . . . People started writing tunes to fill in the gaps for prayers that we wanted. . . .[96]

Thus, the creation of new liturgy was based on need and on the desire for an aesthetically satisfying musical style that was participatory and playable on guitar. Three new musical services reflecting the camp influence were composed in this period: Ray Smolover's *Edge of Freedom* (1967) and *Gates of Freedom* (1970) services, and Michael Isaacson's *Songs NFTY Sings* (1972), later published as *Avodah Amamit*. Debbie Friedman's first recording was a youth service she wrote for high-school students entitled *Sing Unto God* (1972). [97]

The campers, returning home after the summer, wanted their local cantors to sing the new melodies, but the cantors did not know them. The need to preserve and disseminate the camp melodies became evident. According to Freelander,

> In 1972 [the music is] released on albums — record albums. That's a great way of disseminating information because you could mail it all over the country. Notice, it's not written for keyboard; keyboard falls out of favor because organs are the symbols of the Reform they are running away from, the pre-ethnic Reform. Guitar becomes the instrument of choice. . . .[98]

The recordings he refers to are the annual NFTY compilations of melodies popular at camp during a given summer, beginning in 1972. In 1979 Ray Smolover arranged *Songs and Hymns for Gates of Prayer,* and in the late 1970s and early 1980s sheet music helped to spread the popular melodies. In 1987 *Sha'are Shirah* was published, providing at least three versions of liturgical selections for Sabbath services, with the keyboard scoring and chords reflecting the move away from organ-and-choir accompaniment.[99]

Astonishingly, within one decade after Israel's Six-Day War, Hebrew-infused camp music had begun to influence the synagogue liturgy. Choral singing went into decline, and a new Reform prayer book, *Gates*

---

[96]Klepper interview.

[97]Jeffrey K. Salkin, "The New Trend in Synagogue Music," *Reform Judaism* 9 (Winter 1980), p. 4. The folk-rock service has become popular in the liturgies of other American religions as well. See Virgil C. Funk, *Sung Liturgy: Toward 2000 A.D.* (Washington, D.C., 1991).

[98]Freelander interview.

[99]Two UAHC surveys of Reform synagogues, one in 1987 and the other in 1993, indicated a decline in the use of organ music and greater reliance on electronic keyboard, piano, guitar, and a cappella song. Daniel Freelander, Robin Hirsch, and Sanford Seltzer *Emerging Worship and Music Trends in UAHC Congregations* (New York, 1994), p. 18.

of Prayer, published in 1975, reflected the growing desire of Reform congregations throughout the country to sing more of the service in Hebrew. By the 1980s the folk-rock style had become commonplace in Reform worship, except in the oldest, most Classical Reform congregations.

Reaction have ranged from enthusiastic endorsement to disdain. One proponent, Rabbi Freelander, director of programs for the UAHC, argues for the folk-rock style on the basis of its positive effect on the communal experience:

> I'm forced to contrast that "high art" [composed synagogue music of the 19th and 20th centuries] with the "popular art" [folk-rock style music] we experience in the large communal song sessions at the conventions of the UAHC, CAJE [Coalition for the Advancement of Jewish Education], and now even the GA [the United Jewish Communities' General Assembly]. They remind us baby boomers of our youth, singing together at summer camp, on the college campus or at the protest rally. Those were special and spiritual moments these adult communal singing sessions recreate for us. Our souls open up, and we sing familiar sounding melodies and words, and feel comfortably connected once again to our community and our God.[100]

Samuel Adler, however, a noted composer and teacher at the Eastman School of Music and Juilliard, is critical of the new synagogue music, which he refers to as "spiritual entertainment." In his view, supporters of communal singing are eager to blame low synagogue attendance on the traditional music rather than seeing that the fault lies in the decline in familiarity with, and affinity to, synagogue ritual life.

> The status of liturgical music in the American Reform synagogue today (and I include here also the handful of large Conservative congregations that emphasize composed music as part of the worship experience) is best described as confused, even chaotic, fueled by ignorance, misinformation, and simple neglect. . . . Synagogue music today has thus fallen largely into the hands of the "new traditional composers" who write in a popular style that is pseudo-Jewish, pseudo-pop-American, and pseudo-Israeli. These composers are believed because their style offends no one, challenges no one, and is easy to perform. If this state of affairs continues, the more challenging musical works composed for the synagogue since the 19th century—already rarely heard today—will become museum pieces to be resurrected only for special occasions.[101]

---

[100]Daniel H. Freelander, "The Role of Jewish Communal Singing," *Sh'ma,* Oct. 4, 1996, p. 6.

[101]Adler, "Sacred Music in a Secular Age," in Hoffman and Walton, eds., *Sacred Sound and Social Change,* pp. 294, 296–97. Michael Isaacson takes a similarly negative approach, as quoted in David Mermelstein, "Is Popular Culture Defining Synagogue Music?" *Reform Judaism* 24 (Spring 1996), pp. 44, 50.

After noting parallels to conflicts over liturgical music in various Christian denominations, Adler sharply attacks the Hassidic-style or Israeli tunes as "the trademark of the Jewish commercial sacred music norm."[102] Many cantors in the Reform movement share Adler's views, as do some Conservative cantors.

In a number of articles and books, Hebrew Union College liturgist Lawrence Hoffman has explored the conflict in historic depth. Here is how he frames the debate:

> Worship is seen more and more as belonging to the people, and demanding, therefore, an engaging musical style that evokes their active participation. By contrast, both cantorial music and art music are incomprehensible to all but very sophisticated worshipers. From the perspective of the cantor, the demand for musical "accessibility" threatens both the age-old internally authentic tradition and the relatively new externally authentic art-music tradition too, since the newest sing-along tunes may lack roots in the synagogue's history and fail the test of refined taste as well.[103]

Since it is the laity that makes decisions in the synagogue, most Reform cantors and composers of music for the synagogue have learned to synthesize the folk and artistic styles and combine them with traditional chants.[104] Reform cantor and composer Benjie-Ellen Schiller describes the situation in the 1980s:

> Composers . . . fuse musical aesthetics with the need for effective congregational worship, sometimes by stressing traditional modes, other times by leaning more or less heavily toward the classical Reform choral genre, or by weaving a simple congregational refrain into a richly textured setting for cantor and choir. Diversity of voice is a concern, too, especially given the rising number of female cantors who require music written in a vocal style appropriate for women.[105]

Schiller notes that while Reform synagogues run the gamut from large temples that use organ and choir to small congregations that do not even employ professional clergy, one common feature is the increasing desire of congregants to participate in worship. Those involved in the training of cantors have developed new techniques and publications to help advance this goal.[106] Music educator Merri Arian, for example, teaches can-

---

[102]Adler, "Sacred Music in a Secular Age," p. 297.

[103]Hoffman, "Musical Traditions and Tension," p. 35.

[104]Adler, "Sacred Music in a Secular Age," p. 298; Hoffman, "Musical Traditions and Tension," p. 37; Schiller, "The Hymnal as an Index of Musical Change in Reform Synagogues," pp. 210–11; Mermelstein, "Is Popular Culture Defining Synagogue Music?" p. 44.

[105]Schiller, "The Hymnal as an Index of Musical Change in Reform Synagogues," p. 209.

[106]Some Reform camps have programs to train song leaders, such as one called Hava Nashira, which disseminates repertoire and teaches techniques in leading group singing.

torial students and song leaders that music needs to be sung with clarity, in a comfortable key, and at a reasonable tempo in order for congregants to join in.[107]

INFLUENTIAL REFORM FIGURES

Debbie Friedman is by far the most influential performer and creator of contemporary Reform liturgical music, with congregants frequently asking for her songs to be included in Reform services. In her two-and-a-half decades on the scene Friedman has made a lasting impact on contemporary Jewish music. Alone among the performers of Jewish "religious" music, her recordings are included in the inventory of national retail chains — Tower, HMV, and Virgin — and on Web sites like those of Amazon and CDNOW. Her recordings are among the most widely sold in the Jewish market — even beyond the Reform movement — and her songs are commonly included in song sessions for youth and adults at camps and conventions.

Friedman, who grew up in a Reform family, says that her interest in inspiring others to gain a closer connection to Judaism stems from her own need to reconnect to Jewish practices she lost in childhood. After moving from Utica, New York, to St. Paul, Minnesota, her family dropped various Jewish traditions it had observed when living close to her grandparents. "I missed them," Friedman explains, "as I did my grandparents, who lived upstairs from us. I know now that some of what I'm doing is to reclaim what was taken away from me."[108] Friedman got her start as a song leader at Reform summer camps and at educators' conferences and other adult programs run by the Reform and Conservative movements. Although lacking a cantorial diploma, Friedman served as a cantor in Los Angeles for several years, working extensively with young people in the creation of new prayer services. As her reputation grew, she began performing at concerts around the country.

Like the creators of contemporary music in the Orthodox community, Friedman composes Hebrew songs to traditional liturgical or biblical texts, as well as original English songs. She uses the social-action songs in the folk genre of the 1960s and 1970s as models for her creation of new Jewish songs that communicate a message of engagement with Jewish tradition. Her musical influences are Peter, Paul, and Mary,[109] Joan Baez, Judy Collins, and Melissa Manchester.

---

[107]Interview with Merri Arian, July 22, 1998.

[108]Irv Lichtman, "Singer Makes Jewish Music Her Own," *Billboard,* Mar. 1, 1997, p. 39.

[109]Peter Yarrow, who has known Friedman for years, says, "Hers is the music of jubilation and confirmation. It is a call to community and commonality that rages against total

Her first album, *Sing Unto God* (1972), was a youth service, which she described as an effort to make prayer accessible. The album, in her words as quoted on the liner notes, "is a new experience in worship that emphasizes through song the importance of community involvement in worship. This music carries a solid message in a simple, easily understood form. It enables those who are willing to join together as a community in contemporary songs of prayer." The album's title song is entirely in English, and the other ten songs are either set to Hebrew liturgical texts or to a combination of Hebrew and English. The melodies are easy to sing and to understand, partly because they are repetitive—characteristics that would continue to mark her style in later years.

Friedman is concerned with making Judaism relevant to modern life. Her third recording, *Ani Ma-Amin* (1976), uses the same type of songs and language as her first, but here the songs focus on the concept of Messiah, one that poses serious theological questions that Reform Judaism has struggled with since its inception almost two centuries ago. For Friedman, the Jewish Messiah is not an individual who emerges as a leader of the Jewish people, and does not connote the resurrection of the dead. Rather, it is through the messianic belief that Judaism offers hope for the future and challenges Jews to struggle to make the dreams and visions of a messianic age come true. Friedman's message and approach in this recording—as in all her work—are notably optimistic.

Like other musical innovators in the Reform movement and their counterparts in Orthodoxy, Friedman has had to respond to critics who claim that her music is not based on Jewish musical tradition:

> Who is my music hurting? I don't want to compete with anybody. I'm not a great lover of organ music, but I am a great lover of *nusach*. How is writing in our own musical vernacular not an acceptable or legitimate expression of our culture? My music may be uniquely American, but it is rooted in a tradition that is Russian and Hungarian, and influenced by Israel.[110]

Since—her disclaimer notwithstanding—the style of Friedman's music is clearly the American folk tradition, her reference to its European "roots" perhaps refers to the sentiments it conveys.

Friedman has a remarkable stage presence, and many of her admirers consider her three performances at Carnegie Hall in 1996, 1997, and 1998 as marking the pinnacle of her career. Always encouraging the audience to participate, she also shares stories and relates her own experiences, skillfully drawing the listeners in. The manner in which she seeks

---

darkness and spreads light." Susan Josephs, "Queen of Souls," *Baltimore Jewish Times,* Jan. 19, 1996, p. 47.

[110]Ibid., p. 48.

to educate her audiences and engage them in a positive Jewish life has led some to compare her to Shlomo Carlebach. Like him, as well, Friedman's music blurs the boundary between prayer and song by making prayers singable and songs prayerful. A comment she made on stage at Carnegie Hall is revealing: she told the audience, "Thank you for creating *Beth Carnegie*." For Friedman, praying in a synagogue or singing on stage both have the goal of connecting with and uplifting the audience.

Many of her songs have entered the core repertoire of Reform, Conservative, and other Jewish camps. They include the title English songs of the albums *Sing Unto God* (1972), *Not By Might* (1974), and *And the Youth Shall See Visions* (1981), as well as "L'chi Lakh," "Miriam's Song," and "T'filat Haderech,"—a prayer for traveling—all on *And You Shall Be a Blessing* (1989). A number of her Hebrew songs have achieved similar status: "L'Dor Vador" from *Not by Might,* "Im Tirtzu" from *Ani Ma-Amin* (1976), "Im Ein Ani Li" from *If Not Now, When?* (1980), and "Oseh Shalom" from *And the Youth Shall See Visions.* Friedman has also recorded children's albums, and often performs her compositions "The Alef Bet Song" and "The Latke Song" at her concerts.[111]

Friedman has acquired a large and devoted audience and has achieved a rare status in contemporary Jewish life. Aside from her undeniable musical gifts, there are two special factors that have helped propel her career. One is her association with the phenomenon of the "healing service," a liturgical attempt to afford spiritual help to the sick that has become popular both within and outside the Reform movement. Many of the songs on Friedman's album *Renewal of Spirit* (1995), which includes new songs as well as some from her earlier albums, are taken from her healing service. "Mi Shebeirach," based on the traditional prayer for the healing of the sick and first recorded on *And You Shall Be a Blessing,* is probably her song that is most often requested in Reform congregations. The other factor is Friedman's appeal to women, not only as a woman herself but also as a writer and performer of songs that mirror their feelings and concerns. "Miriam's Song," for example, has become a staple at special women's seders at Passover, and not only in the Reform movement.

Daniel Freelander and Jeffrey Klepper have also made important contributions to the revival of Jewish music in the Reform movement. After performing together for several years, the pair began appearing under the name Kol B'Seder in 1975. The influences on their music should by now be familiar—Reform summer camps, Shlomo Carlebach, the Hassidic Song Festival, and Israeli folk music. Their folk influences were Bob

---

[111]Television character "Barney" recorded "The Alef Bet Song," and used "The Latke Song" in one of his programs.

Dylan, Joni Mitchell, and James Taylor, and the harmonies of the Beatles, Simon and Garfunkel, and Peter, Paul, and Mary. In the conviction that "singing empowers the worshiper to own the prayers, to use the melody as a bridge to the sacred,"[112] Kol B'Seder has specialized in songs that are Hebrew settings of liturgical passages. Some of their best-known works are: "Shalom Rav," "Lo Alecha," and "Modeh Ani" on the album *Shalom Rav* (1981); "Oseh Shalom" on *The Bridge* (1985); and "Mah Tovu" on *Sparks of Torah* (1989). They have also written several English songs. Once described as the "Lennon and McCartney" of Jewish music,[113] they perform, at most, 25 concerts a year and have completed four recordings that are notable for their high production standards.

There are several other well-known performers in the Reform community. Doug Cotler has recorded five albums—the most influential are *Listen* and *It's So Amazing!*—and performs extensively on the concert circuit. Winner of a 1984 Grammy award, he has also served as a cantorial soloist in California. Another is Steve Dropkin, who previously headed Ketzev, a group whose Hebrew and English songs are being increasingly adopted for synagogue use. Julie Silver, like Cotler a cantorial soloist in California, is a relatively new solo performer who writes many English songs. Beged Kefet, a popular group widely praised for its lush vocal harmonies, is composed of eight men and women, most of whom are Reform cantors and rabbis.

Very recently Jeffrey Klepper of Kol B'Seder, in solo recordings such as *In This Place: Jewish Songs of Time and Space* (1997), has sought to incorporate the free style of Hassidic melodies (*niggunim*) into his music, arguing that it is a more authentic expression of Jewish spirituality than "using musical idioms from the Beatles or from folk music or blues or whatever."[114] Nevertheless the predominant trend in contemporary Reform music remains the folk-pop style that grew out of experimentation in Reform summer camps in the 1970s, matured with the music of Debbie Friedman and Kol B'Seder in the 1980s, and, despite initial cantorial resistance, became the norm for synagogue services.

Conservative

Contemporary Jewish music in the Conservative movement presents yet a different picture. While no particular groups create specifically "Con-

[112]"Introduction," *Kol B'Seder Songbook,* p. [6].
[113]Interview with singer-songwriter Josh Zweiback, May 7, 1998.
[114]Klepper interview.

servative" music, certain performers do perform in predominantly Conservative settings. Safam, an all-male group, has been doing so since 1974, and Craig Taubman, a solo artist, almost as long. Unlike the Reform movement, where the camps constituted the seedbed for new music, the Conservative movement's network of Ramah summer camps have not had anywhere near the same musical impact. One reason may have been Ramah's emphasis on the Hebrew language. Music educator Marsha Bryan Edelman describes the 1970s repertoire at Ramah camps as consisting primarily of Israeli and Carlebach Hebrew songs; English songs were not permitted, and thus the creation of new Jewish music in English was virtually ruled out.[115]

Music for worship in Conservative congregations ranges from solo cantorial artistry to the folk-style singing of a *havurah,* the small, informal fellowship group that developed out of the Jewish youth culture of the 1960s. The traditional style of the golden age of the cantorate is more common in Conservative congregations than it is in Orthodox or Reform, though it is waning there as well. Most Conservative congregations sing "traditional" melodies each Sabbath, the repertoire dating to the first half of the 20th century and composed by Israel Goldfarb (1879–1967), Max Wohlberg (1906–96), and Zavel Zilberts (1881–1949).[116] Samuel Rosenbaum has noted that in most Conservative synagogues congregants expect to hear the same old prayers sung with the same old melodies, a familiarity that provides comfort. Inclusion of new music, therefore, is minimal.[117]

The most significant change in Conservative congregations since the 1960s has been the inclusion of Israeli songs at public gatherings and occasionally during the *kedushah* section of the service—melodies such as "Erev Shel Shoshanim" and "Yerushalayim Shel Zahav" are the most common. Generally, though, as in the case of the Orthodox, new music functions for Conservative Jews as a means of entertainment rather than worship.

According to the *Moment* magazine poll, Safam was the second most popular singing group among American Jews—at least those who read that magazine. Its members—Robbie Solomon, Joel Sussman, Daniel Funk, and Alan Nelson—were inspired by the singing of the Zamir

---

[115]Edelman interview.

[116]Two publications of synagogue melodies are Moshe Nathanson, *Zamru Lo* (New York, 1955–1960; reprint 1974), published by the Cantors Assembly; and Velvel Pasternak, *Siddur in Song: 100 Prayerbook Melodies* (Cedarhurst, N.Y., 1986).

[117]Samuel Rosenbaum, "Another New Tune?" in the Cantors Assembly publication, *Words About Music* (New York, 1982), p. 11.

Chorale in Boston, the home of all four of them (see below, pp. 135–36). Like their hero, Shlomo Carlebach, Safam sings liturgical songs in Hebrew; unlike him, they use electric guitars and sing in rock-and-roll rather than folk style.[118] In their earliest performances, which took place at Jewish organizational functions and youth gatherings, they sang music of Carlebach and the Hassidic Song Festival. After successfully performing some original songs—Solomon and Sussman are the group's songwriters—they went on to record their first album, *Dreams of Safam,* in 1976. Safam then released nine other recordings at fairly regular intervals: *Safam Encore* (1978), *Sons of Safam* (1980), *Bittersweet* (1982), *Peace by Piece* (1984), *A Brighter Day* (1986), *The Greater Scheme of Things* (1989), *On Track* (1993), *After All These Years* (1995), and *In Spite of It All* (1999), plus four "Greatest Hits" volumes. One component of Safam's success is the variety of songs they perform and their mix of styles— Jewish elements such as cantorial and Hassidic music stylized in rock, pop, Latin, and reggae rhythms. Today Safam performs some 25 concerts a year in Jewish community centers and synagogues around the country and at events sponsored by federations and by the Conservative movement's United Synagogue Youth.

Although its repertoire includes both Hebrew liturgical settings and English ballads, Safam is best known for its English songs. The most famous of these is "Leaving Mother Russia," a song about refuseniks, Russian Jews not allowed to leave for Israel, that appeared on *Safam Encore.* Written at the height of the repression of Soviet Jews, this song became the anthem for the cause (and, as such, was recorded by other artists as well). For three years in a row in the early 1980s Safam sang "Leaving Mother Russia" at mass protest rallies at the United Nations, and since then the group has often sung the song as an encore at its concerts. Other Safam songs with a Jewish political message, geared to issues in Israel and elsewhere, are "Just Another Foreigner" and "Yamit" from *Bittersweet;* "Falasha Nevermore," from *A Brighter Day;* and "Maranno" from *On Track.* Their song "We Are One," from *Peace by Piece,* was used on the soundtrack for UJA's 1991–92 fund-raising video. Safam's original wedding songs—"My Beloved" from *Bittersweet* and "Dodi Li" from *A Brighter Day*—are widely used for wedding processions and for the newlyweds' first dance. Their liturgical songs incorporate *nusach,* as in "Yismechu" from *Bittersweet* and "Birkat Hallel" from *Sons of Safam,* while they employ a novel use of barbershop style in "Vene'emar" from *Safam Encore.*

Robbie Solomon, who is critical of contemporary Jewish music that tries to be immediately accessible, describes Safam's music as "intelligent

---

[118]Interview with Robbie Solomon, July 8, 1998.

music for modern intelligent Jews." The group's songs and music communicate a synthesis of Jewish and modern values. Musically, there is an affinity to the traditional sounds of *nusach,* which undoubtedly stems from Solomon's traditional upbringing, but it is framed in a modern style. As his modern songwriting influences Robbie Solomon names Paul Simon, Billy Joel, and Elton John, and the lush harmonies of Crosby, Stills, and Nash. He also admires the Beatles—like Safam, a four-member male group.[119]

Craig Taubman, who grew up in the Conservative movement and found his first audiences there, now performs in Reform synagogues and other venues as well. A prolific recording artist, he has released 13 albums of Jewish music—two of them for children—as well as ten commercial children's albums, not on Jewish themes, on the Disney and Rhino labels. He also writes children's songs for television and manages to give up to 70 concerts a year. Taubman's songs—often written as responses to events in his life, from the birth of a child to the death of a relative—are in Hebrew, English, or a mixture of both. [120] Frequently, the English portion of the song it not a translation of the Hebrew but stands alone; examples are "Anim Zmirot" and "Shema B'ni" from *Journey* (1991). Other well-known songs, such as "Shir Chadash" from *Encore* (1989), combine biblical and rabbinic texts, and English-language ballads such as "Where Heaven and Earth Touch"—from a 1993 album of the same name—articulate his thoughts about liturgical and biblical passages. The musical style ranges from rock-and-roll and pop to adult contemporary music. Taubman sees his music strictly as artistic statements intended for performance, not as songs to be incorporated into synagogue services, with the exceptions of two special services he composed and recorded: *Yad B'Yad* (1986) and *Friday Night Live* (1999). Taubman's recordings for Jewish children, *My Jewish Discovery* (1995) and *My Newish Jewish Discovery* (1997), have sold up to five times better than his adult albums. He somewhat sadly explains this stark contrast as a reflection of the non-Orthodox attitude to Judaism: it's something you go out of your way to teach your children, but it's not for you.[121] As further proof of the same point, Paul Zim, a noted cantor and singer in Conservative circles who has released many albums for adults, has recently turned his attention to recording children's songs.

Clearly, contemporary Jewish music in the Conservative setting is less developed than it is in either Orthodoxy or Reform, in a sense parallel-

---

[119]Ibid.
[120]Interview with Craig Taubman, July 23, 1998.
[121]Ibid.

ing Conservatism's middle position on the denominational spectrum. While Reform Jews, to the left, seek to incorporate new music within the liturgy, Conservative worship—like the Orthodox—is more-or-less fixed and can accommodate only minimal change. And while Orthodox Jews, on the right, who avoid American popular music, need their new Jewish music as a cultural outlet, Conservative Jews, who seek out all types of entertainment, do not have the same need. Performers like Safam and Craig Taubman appeal to a desire among Conservative Jews to listen to Jewish music that inspires and entertains—but these Jews are satisfied with the occasional listening opportunities they get at religious services and those organizational functions that include concerts. The only other viable market for Conservative Jewish music is children, and so it is widely marketed to schools and young families.

Jewish Renwal

The Jewish Renewal movement is an organized effort to experience a "renewed encounter with God" based on meditation and spiritual awareness. The movement seeks "through prayer, study, and action" to "nurture the rebbe-spark in everyone without fearing its emergence in different ways and degrees at different moments in different people; to nurture communities that dance and wrestle with God, that are intimate, participatory, and egalitarian, and that create a 'field of rebbetude'; and to assist the spiritual growth and healing of individuals, communities, whole societies, and the planet."[122] Rabbi Ya'akov Gabriel has described it as a non-Orthodox Hassidism.[123]

Renewal has generated a new form of Jewish music. All the participants repeat over and over, in a meditative fashion, simple, easily learned musical phrases. In worship or at concerts, hand-held drums are often beaten to keep the rhythm constant, and the music is coordinated with the bodily movements of dance.

Rabbi Shefa Gold, a Renewal leader, synthesizes a variety of Jewish and non-Jewish elements in her music. While in Israel in 1990 she developed a chanting service that has influenced others—including Debbie Friedman and Jeffrey Klepper—to incorporate melodic and meditative chants in worship.[124] Among Gold's best-known recordings are *Chants Encounters*

---

[122]"A-Definition-in-Process" by ALEPH: Alliance for Jewish Renewal, Web site www.aleph.org, accessed June 22, 1999. ALEPH supports a journal, the Elat Chayyim retreat center, a biennial Kallah (conference), and a network of 40 local affiliates throughout the United States and abroad.

[123]Conversation with Rabbi Ya'akov Gabriel, June 30, 1999. In 1997 Gabriel began writing a regular column, "Sounds of Renewal," in *Tikkun* magazine.

[124]Interview with Shefa Gold, Apr. 19, 1999.

(1994) and *Chanscendence* (1997). Two of her most popular melodies are "Elohai N'shama" from *Tzuri* (1993) and "Mah Gadlu" from *Chants Encounters*. Other renewal artists are Linda Hirschorn,[125] Aryeh Hirschfield, Yitz Husbands-Hankin, Michael Shapiro, and Ya'akov Gabriel.

Nonreligious Contexts

Yiddish, klezmer, and Israeli music still provide a rich source of musical pleasure both for Jews affiliated with religious life and for those whose connection to Judaism is primarily cultural.

THE KLEZMER REVIVAL

The klezmer revival began in the late 1970s and spread quickly in the 1980s and thereafter.[126] Henry Sapoznik, a writer and producer of klezmer, one of the revival's first proponents, and founder of the group Kapelye, has described his personal journey:

> I guess I first thought about it as its own entity around 1975. I had been playing in a bluegrass band, traditional American old-time stuff—everyone in the band was Jewish, of course—and I just had this feeling, why is it that everyone else had their own fiddle music and Jews didn't?[127]

He also recalls old-time fiddler Tommy Jarrell saying to him, "Don't your people got none of your own music?" When Sapoznik was introduced to YIVO's collection of klezmer music on 78-rpm records, he realized that he, the son of a cantor who sang at Catskills hotels, had heard similar music in the Borsht Belt as a youngster, but that by the 1950s and 1960s the music had become "diluted with self-conscious Israeli and Fiddler on the Roof medleys."[128] For Sapoznik, then, the discovery of klezmer was a rediscovery.

---

[125]Linda Hirschorn has recorded three solo albums as well as three with the six-voice female Vocolot.

[126]Compared to the other forms of contemporary Jewish music, klezmer is well documented. See, for example, Mark Slobin, *Fiddler on the Move: Exploring the Klezmer World* (Oxford, 2000); Seth Rogovoy, *The Essential Klezmer* (Chapel Hill, 2000); Susan Bauer, *Von Der Khupe Zum Klezkamp: Klezmer-Musik in New York* (Berlin, 1999; in German); Henry Sapoznik, *Klezmer!: Jewish Music from Old World to Our World* (New York, 1999); Shulamis Lynn Dion, "Klezmer Music in America: Revival and Beyond," *Jewish Folklore and Ethnology Newsletter* 8, 1986, pp. 2–14; Walter Zev Feldman, "Bulgareasca/ Bulgarish/ Bulgar: The Transformation of a Klezmer Dance Genre," *Ethnomusicology* 38, 1994, pp. 1–35; Kirshenblatt-Gimblett, "Sounds of Sensibility"; Netsky, "Overview of Klezmer Music"; Henry Sapoznik with Pete Sokolow, *The Compleat Klezmer* (Cedarhurst, N.Y., 1987); and Mark Slobin, "Klezmer Music: An American Ethnic Genre," *Yearbook for Traditional Music* 16, 1984, pp. 34–41.

[127]Quoted in Dion, "Klezmer Music in America," p. 4.

[128]Sapoznik, *The Compleat Klezmer*, p. 15.

For others, it was completely new. Frank London was a trumpet player studying in the Third Stream Music Department at the New England Conservatory during the mid-1970s. Klezmer, he recalls, was simply an interesting musical style to learn: "I was already playing Salsa, Balkan, Haitian, and other musics. Why not Jewish?"[129] He and a few fellow students, picking up klezmer from recordings and by imitation, formed the Klezmer Conservatory Band (he now leads the group The Klezmatics). The band began by playing three songs at a concert; then came other concerts, parties, and eventually recordings and more concerts. London recalls:

> I believe that for myself, and many of my peers that I've spoke to, our focus was on trying to play the music, trying to play it well, trying to get better on the nuances, and others were saying, "Oh, that's not why you were trying to do it; you're carrying on your ancestors' legacy, you're reigniting this torch that went out"—they were getting very heavy about this. But no; we were trying to play some music, make some money, and have some fun. Many of the musicians who were doing klezmer music weren't Jewish, so they weren't discovering their roots . . . . People ask, "why klezmer?" What many miss is that when I listen to this music, I get aesthetically interested. It cuts through all the shlock, all the shmaltz, all the things about Jewish music that never interested me, all the Israeli music, all the Yiddish theater music, about all that sentimentality. Why klezmer music? Because it's good, just on it's own terms.[130]

Since the klezmer tradition had largely faded away, some revival musicians sought out veteran klezmer performers to study with. The recordings of legendary clarinetists Naftule Brandwein (1884–1963) and Dave Tarras (1897–1989) were models for the musicians of the klezmer revival. Andy Statman, for example, klezmer clarinetist and mandolinist, studied with Tarras.[131] In addition, in an effort to preserve and make available the klezmer style of the early 20th century, Henry Sapoznik undertook a project of reissuing the old 78-rpm recordings of the pre-1920 repertoire, which had become the staple of the klezmer revival.[132]

The four revival bands of the 1970s were Klezmorim, Kapelye, Klezmer Conservatory Band, and Andy Statman Klezmer Orchestra. The Klezmorim, cofounded by Lev Liberman and David Skuse in Berkeley, California, in 1975, recorded its first album, *East Side Wedding,* in 1977 and stopped performing in 1988. Liberman has described the music of the

---

[129]Frank London, "An Insider's View: How We Traveled from Obscurity to the Klezmer Establishment in Twenty Years," *Judaism* 47, Winter 1998, p. 40.

[130]Ibid., pp. 41, 43.

[131]Interview with Andy Statman, Aug. 5, 1998.

[132]*Klezmer Music, 1910–1942* (Smithsonian-Folkways, 1980), *The Compleat Klezmer* (Global Music Village, 1987), *Klezmer Pioneers: 1905–1952* (Rounder, 1993), *Dave Tarras: Yiddish-American Klezmer Music* (Yazoo, 1992), *Naftule Brandwein: King of the Klezmer Clarinet* (Rounder, 1997).

Klezmorim as originating "in our early experiments with tight ensemble playing, improvisation, klezmer/jazz fusions, neo-klezmer composition, street music, world beat, and New Vaudeville."[133] Kapelye, formed in 1979, combined klezmer with a variety of Yiddish vocal styles. Starting with a folk sound, the group eventually evolved into an eclectic ragtime-tinged ensemble. Four recordings have been issued: *Future and Past* (1981), *Levine and His Flying Machine* (1985), *Kapelye's Chicken* (1987), and *Kapelye On the Air* (1995). The group performs infrequently today, but its original members have gone on to work with other bands. The Klezmer Conservatory Band "uses a full Yiddish theater orchestra instrumentation to showcase a sound that ranges from big-band hybrid to chamber-orchestral."[134] It has released eight albums and performs frequently in synagogues, Jewish community centers, colleges, and concert halls.

By the late-1980s klezmer music had moved into the commercial mainstream, with groups employing professional managers and recording on major labels in the United States (such as Rounder and Sony) and Germany. Klezmer was "in," and music periodicals and major newspapers featured articles about performers and reviews of recordings and performances.[135] Musically, klezmer changed in the late 1980s as groups moved away from the "revival" approach of mainly performing the traditional repertoire and began creating new music, combining klezmer with pop, jazz, and other styles.[136]

Andy Statman, who has performed and recorded frequently since the mid-1970s, describes his music now not as klezmer but as "an exploration of spiritual music . . . informed by klezmer."[137] Statman, a newly observant Jew who is part of the Hassidic world, goes so far as to claim that his teacher Dave Tarras also viewed klezmer as a spiritual form of music, albeit one performed outside of the synagogue. Two of Statman's

---

[133]Lev Liberman, KlezShack, www.well.com. Last revised Oct. 25, 1998.

[134]Netsky, "Overview of Klezmer Music," p. 11.

[135]In a textbook on multicultural music in America, the editors single out klezmer as having succeeded in revitalizing a musical genre with "overwhelming enthusiasm," as compared to other, less successful revival efforts. Kip Lornell and Anne K. Rasmussen, eds., *Musics of Multicultural America: A Study of Twelve Musical Communities* (New York, 1997), p. 9.

[136]Other groups formed in the U.S. and Europe have adapted klezmer to avant garde, world beat, and roots-music styles. Kirshenblatt-Gimblett, "Sounds of Sensibility," pp. 51, 57, sees klezmer as a form of music that was ripe for transformation since it had not been picked up previously, and suggests that the variety of its incorporated styles proves its acceptance.

[137]Statman interview. The use of the word "klezmer" is itself an issue, since some performers are more comfortable describing what they perform as "klezmer music" rather than "Jewish music." For a discussion of this issue, see Kirshenblatt-Gimblett, "Sounds of Sensibility," pp. 50–54. Pete Sokolow and others discuss "klezmer" as a derogatory label for musicians in Dion, "Klezmer Music in America: Revival and Beyond," p. 3. Slobin, "Klezmer Music: An American Ethnic Genre," emphasizes klezmer's American aspect.

most successful recordings—*Songs of Our Fathers* with Dave Grisman (1994) and *The Andy Statman Quartet: Between Heaven and Earth* (1997)—consist of Hassidic *niggunim* "filtered through the impression of jazz," or "the meeting of Hassidic music and late Coltrane," a reference to the leading jazz musician who also saw his music as a spiritual pursuit. Statman, in fact, has criticized the popular and rock music that is commonplace in the Orthodox and Hassidic communities because it has replaced and marginalized traditional klezmer. Among his many other musical activities, Statman performs for small Hassidic gatherings in an effort to restore the kelzmer tradition to that community.

In the mid-1980s, two new klezmer bands became prominent—Brave Old World and Klezmatics. Michael Alpert, vocalist and violinist of Brave Old World, came from Kapelye, while Frank London, the leader and trumpet player of the Klezmatics, had previously played with the Klezmer Conservatory Band.

The founders of Brave Old World felt that klezmer had become too conventional: "concerts were not to be too 'serious,' audiences were encouraged to clap along or dance, and easily accessible musical values such as virtuosity, energy, and individual charisma dominated over stylistic authenticity and ensemble musicianship."[138] Therefore Brave Old World chose to create "new Yiddish music, whose language and forms would be consciously created for the concert stage and a listening audience, but still deeply rooted in Yiddish folk materials."[139] The group did this through the use of mainly European classical aesthetics. Its three recordings—*Klezmer Music* (1990), *Beyond the Pale* (1993), and *Blood Oranges* (1997)—include both traditional melodies and new Yiddish songs. The latter address contemporary issues: "Chernobyl" on *Klezmer Music;* "Berlin 1990" (about the fall of the Berlin Wall) on *Beyond the Pale;* and "Welcome" on *Blood Oranges.* The group frequently performs in Germany, where it has been able to develop its European style further.

The Klezmatics, who do frequent nightclub performances and reach a broad audience, aim primarily to entertain, but move beyond the playing of nostalgic melodies, weaving together popular and world-music styles, with lyrics on a variety of contemporary social issues.[140] Early recordings—*The Klezmatics: Shvaygn=Toyt* (1988), *Rhythm and Jews* (1992), and *Jews with Horns* (1994)—include their interpretations of the classical klezmer repertoire. An example is their version of Brandwein's "Der Heyser Bulgar." While Brandwein's own recording, on *Naftule*

---

[138]"From Klezmer to New Jewish Music: The Musical Evolution of Brave Old World," p. 2, included in the press kit distributed by the group's manager.
[139]Ibid., p. 3.
[140]Interview with Frank London, Jan. 14, 1998.

Brandwein: King of the Klezmer Clarinet, includes several accompanying instruments, the Klezmatics' rendition, on *Rhythm and Jews,* has the clarinetist accompanied only by percussion.[141] The group has more recently branched out into a variety of other ventures such as *Possessed* (1997), which is a score for Tony Kushner's adaptation of S. An-ski's *The Dybbuk,* and *The Well* (1998), musical settings for Yiddish poems composed and sung by Israeli singer Chava Alberstein.

Klezmer, which the large commercial stores carry under the "world music" category, is extremely popular among young Jews on the political left who do not identify religiously and do not desire to listen to the music produced by the Hebrew-speaking world of Israel and Zionism. Often part of a broader interest in Yiddish culture, it has given rise to such ongoing music festivals as KlezKamp, Buffalo Gap, Ashkenaz, and others, which attract participants of all ages. Klezmer is the musical embodiment of a Jewishness that enables musicians and listeners to be "cultural Jews . . . being Jewish while still being themselves."[142] Klezmatics violinist Alicia Svigals explains:

> So identifying with Israel was a way for American Jews to assimilate and remain Jewish at the same time. In the same way, fashioning a new Jewish culture in the '70s, '80s, and '90s, which is in harmony with hip and progressive young America, can perhaps be seen as yet another Jewish way to be American, complete with a traditional music scene—klezmer—to mirror its American folk music counterpart.[143]

ISRAELI MUSIC

Immigrants to Israel in the first half of the 20th century brought with them the music of their countries of origin while at the same time aspiring to discover or create a uniquely Jewish music in the Jewish homeland. The first model for such an "authentic" Jewish music was that of the Yemenite Jews, which was regarded as having ancient roots. In the 1930s Bracha Zephira, a Yemenite performer, gained wide popularity, collaborating with European-born composers and arrangers in Palestine such as Nachum Nardi (from Russia) and Paul Ben Haim (from Germany) in adapting Yemenite music to folk and artistic styles and then performing and recording these new songs. Other immigrant composers in Palestine, such as Oedoen Partos (Hungary) and Marc Lavry (Latvia), continued

---

[141]The Klezmer Conservatory Band includes a more faithful rendition of the piece on *In the Fiddler's House* (1995).

[142]Alicia Svigals, "Why We Do This Anyway: Klezmer As Jewish Youth Subculture," *Judaism* 47, Winter 1998, p. 44.

[143]Ibid., p. 47.

to work in this direction, creating what came to be known as a Mediterranean style of Jewish music.[144] This Westernization of Middle Eastern musical features crowded out and marginalized indigenous Middle Eastern music.

Even the huge influx of Middle Eastern and North African immigrants into the new State of Israel after 1948 did not reverse the trend because the dominant Ashkenazi-Labor establishment retained cultural dominance. Things only began to change in the late 1960s with growing Sephardi participation in the political system, culminating in the rise to power in 1977 of the Likud Party, which was heavily supported by Jews of Sephardi background. The legitimacy and encouragement given to Sephardi culture led to a new, integrated musical style, called at first *Musika Mizrachit,* Eastern Music, or *Musikat Ha-Tachana Ha-Merkazit,* Central-Bus-Station Music, referring to its primary location of purchase. It later came to be known as *Musika Yam Tikhonit Yisraelit,* Israeli Mediterranean Music, and indeed it is popular not only in Israel but throughout the Middle East. The core repertoire uses Hebrew texts, but the music integrates a variety of styles: "Hebrew lyrics commingle with Arabic, Persian, Kurdish and Turkish texts, and Eastern European, Greek, Turkish or Arabic tunes feature local aesthetic markers drawing in Egyptian, Jordanian, Lebanese, Syrian and Palestinian listeners."[145] A mix of Western and Middle Eastern instruments and musical styles add to this rich hybrid of creative expression. Performers of note include Daklon, Shiri Ben-Moshe, Zohar Argov, and Haim Moshe.[146] Ofra Haza, who came from a Yemenite family and achieved international renown with songs in this genre beginning in the late 1980s, died tragically young in 2000.

American Jews developed an early interest in the music of the Jews in Palestine. A.W. Binder, for example, promoted the singing of folk songs from Palestine in the 1930s, and as Yiddish waned as an active language for Jewish musical expression, Hebrew took its place. A significant repertoire of songs from the 1948 War of Independence and from the subsequent years of building the state became a part of the American Jewish music repertoire. After the Six-Day War of 1967 interest in Israeli music increased, and artists such as Shlomo Artzi, Mati Caspi, Tzvika Pick,

---

[144]Jehoash Hirshberg, *Music in the Jewish Community of Palestine, 1880–1948: A Social History* (London and New York, 1995).

[145]Amy Horowitz, "Performance in Disputed Territory," *Musical Performance* 1, issue title "The Performance of Jewish and Arab Music in Israel Today," 1997, p. 50.

[146]See Amnon Shiloah and Erik Cohen, "The Dynamics of Change in Jewish Oriental Music in Israel," *Ethnomusicology* 27, 1983, pp. 222–51; and Jeff Halper, Edwin Seroussi, and Pamela Squires-Kidron, "*Musica Mizrakhit:* Ethnicity and Class Culture in Israel," *Popular Music* 8, 1989, pp. 131–41.

Yehudit Ravitz, and the group Poogy became well known to American Jews in the 1970s. However since Israeli music of this era moved out of the realm of folk music and was difficult to perform, few new songs were added to the American "Israeli song canon."[147] By the late 1970s American Jews were creating their own music and relying less on Israel for new music, perhaps also reflecting a more general distancing from Israel. One sector of American Jewry where interest has remained constant is the Israeli folk-dancing circuit, which often features new music from Israel.

Musika Yam Tikhonit Yisraelit is not widely known among American Jews, and few American Jewish bookstores carry it except for those located in neighborhoods with high concentrations of Israelis. American Jews are much more likely to know the Israeli music of performing troupes like the Hassidic Song Festival and of the veteran popular artists like Shoshana Damari, Yaffa Yarkoni, Yehoram Gaon, and Naomi Shemer, all of whom, even the Sephardim Damari and Gaon, sing in the older style. Chava Alberstein, a performer for over 30 years, with 45 albums recorded by CBS Israel, is well known internationally for her Yiddish and children's songs in addition to her Hebrew repertoire. Dudu Fisher performed the role of Jean Valjean in the musical *Les Miserables* in London and on Broadway, as well as in Tel Aviv, and performs frequently in a range of musical styles throughout the world. David Broza has released four albums in America with English titles since 1989, and in 1995 he was the opening act for Sting. Noa (Achinoam Nini), who was born in Israel and raised in New York, studied music in Israel. She performs internationally and records an eclectic repertoire.

Other Trends

Jewish choral music has been growing in importance. The pioneer in this area is the Zamir Chorale. Zamir (the Hebrew word for nightingale) began in New York in 1960 with a group of enthusiastic young people who had attended Massad, a Zionist and Hebrew-speaking summer camp. The original director was Stanley Sperber. Zamir's repertoire in the 1960s consisted of great synagogue choral works of the 19th century as

---

[147]This determination is based, in part, on an investigation of Israeli songs that appear in Reform (*Shireinu: Our Songs,* 1997), Conservative (*Kol Be Ramah,* 1996), Orthodox (*Shiron Hashulchan,* 1993), and Jewish communal (*United Jewish Appeal Book of Songs and Blessings,* 1993) songbooks, and sheet music publications (Pasternak, *The International Jewish Songbook,* 1994; *The Jewish Fake Book,* 1997). Of a total of 140 songs, 41, 30 percent, were common to all. Some of these are settings of the liturgy and are among the best-known Israeli songs. Further research on the transmission and dissemination of Israeli music in America is clearly needed.

well as Zionist and folk songs. Over time its scope expanded to include the liturgical music of the Italian Jewish composer Salomone Rossi (ca.1570–ca.1630), biblical oratorios by George Friedrich Handel (1685–1759), and works by Israeli composer Yehezkiel Braun (b. 1922) and other composers such as Darius Milhaud (1892–1974) and Stefan Wolpe (1902–1972). Choral arrangements of folk, Israeli, and Jewish holiday songs were also featured. Matthew Lazar, who has directed Zamir since the 1970s, recalls that the group's performances in Israel in 1967 and 1970 had a profound effect on his life and on those of many of the singers, inspiring them to devote their lives to Hebrew music.[148]

Zamir has had a broad impact. Members of important singing groups mentioned above—Safam, Kol B'Seder, and Beged Kefet—started out as members of Zamir. A number of Zamir spin-offs in communities outside New York perform regular concerts that have helped train and influence a generation of musicians. The best known is the Zamir Chorale of Boston, which began in 1969 under the direction of Joshua Jacobson. The group gives some 15 concerts each year in concert halls and schools, has 15 recordings to its credit, and has received numerous awards.[149] Zamir, together with the Union of American Hebrew Congregations, runs the Jewish Choral Festival each summer, as well as youth programs and a variety of educational and outreach events. The example of Zamir has led to the establishment of Jewish a cappella groups in colleges around the country that perform in a variety of musical styles.[150] Synagogues and Jewish community centers have also started choral groups.

The concert hall continues to be a venue for musical contact between established Western art forms and Jewish music. As noted above, works on Jewish themes by Ernest Bloch and Leonard Bernstein long ago found their place in the serious music repertoire. Since the 1970s, a number of composers—including Sam Adler, Bruce Adolphe, Michael Isaacson, Louis Karchin, David Lefkowitz, Michael Rose, Morris Rosenzweig, and

---

[148]Interview with Matthew Lazar, May 6, 1999. In addition to his work for Zamir, Lazar directs other ensembles and guest-conducts choirs and orchestras throughout the United States. Among his most highly regarded recordings is *Chants Mystiques: Hidden Treasures of a Living Tradition* (1995), featuring Alberto Mizrahi and Chorale Mystique singing Jewish choral music.

[149]See www.zamir.org, accessed June 22, 1999. Information also provided by Joshua Jacobson, e-mail communication, June 25, 1999.

[150]Judah Cohen, in an e-mail message to the author dated June 24, 1999, lists the most influential Jewish college a cappella groups as: Pizmon (Columbia/JTS); Magevet (Yale University); Shir Appeal (Tufts University); Manginah (Brandeis); Kol HaKavod (University of Michigan); and Kol HaLayla, (Rutgers, New Brunswick campus). The first group listed, Pizmon, was the first, beginning in 1984. Cohen estimates that there are over 25 such groups in existence.

Bruce Roter—have turned to biblical and other Hebrew texts for inspiration, at times using melodic devices such as cantillation (the traditional melody for chanting the Torah in the synagogue) in their music. Steve Reich's *Tehillim* (1981) is based on the Book of Psalms, and Mario Davidovsky's *Scenes from Shir Ha-Shirim* is based on the Song of Songs. Aaron Jay Kernis, who received the Pulitzer Prize for music in 1998 at the age of 38, composed *Death Fugue* for bass-baritone with double bass and percussion (1981) based on Paul Célan's classic poem about the Holocaust, and the piece is frequently performed at concerts. Composer Sam Adler notes the irony that composers for the synagogue have eliminated traditional Jewish musical elements from their compositions at the same time that young composers writing for the concert hall are more willing to make use of them.[151]

Recognized artists of mainstream classical and popular music have also recorded Jewish music; the name recognition of the artists plus the fact that the albums are sold at commercial chain retail stores generally ensure high sales. Jazz saxophonist Kenny G, together with Cantor Bruce Benson, recorded *The Jazz Service* in 1986. Violinist Itzhak Perlman's 1995 recording, *In the Fiddler's House,* which features him with the four leading klezmer groups—Brave Old World, the Klezmatics, the Andy Statman Klezmer Orchestra, and the Klezmer Conservatory Band—sold over 200,000 copies. Mandy Patinkin recorded *Mamaloshen,* his interpretation of Yiddish songs, in 1997. That same year Barbra Streisand's *Higher Ground* included Max Janowski's well-known liturgical setting for "Avinu Malkeinu."

Sephardic music also has its audience. Performers and groups such as Judy Frankel, Judith Cohen, Voice of the Turtle, and Alhambra perform and record songs in Judeo-Spanish.[152] And just as klezmer revival bands achieved a distinct personality through an amalgam of styles, so too Sephardic artists incorporate a variety of European and Middle Eastern elements to create their own musical identity.[153]

Then there are "crossover" musicians who are hard to categorize. One is Yossi Piamenta, a rock guitarist called the "Sephardic Santana" by *Time* magazine and the "Jewish Hendrix" by the *New York Times.*[154] He plays a blend of rock and Middle Eastern music in a variety of New York

---

[151]Personal conversation with Adler, Feb. 19, 1999.

[152]See Seroussi, "New Directions in the Music of the Sephardic Jews."

[153]Gerard Edery and Michael Ian Elias incorporate Sephardic elements in their music, as do new Israeli bands popular in America, such as Ethnix and Esta.

[154]See "Jammin with the Sephardic Santana," *Time,* Aug. 3, 1998, p. 28; and "Rocking All Night, in Hebrew: Hasidic Guitarist Mixes Religion and Heavy Metal," *New York Times,* Aug. 10, 1998, p. B4.

clubs and has also issued recordings. For some, his success raises the question of whether music intended for Jewish spiritual purposes loses its power and authenticity if it travels outside the Jewish community. Another example is the Jewish music corner of Avant-Garde Jazz. Primarily a New York phenomenon, the popularity of this music has been growing steadily, perhaps more outside the Jewish community than within it. Klezmatics trumpeter Frank London and saxophonist Greg Wall have released three albums with the Hassidic New Wave group: *Jews and the Abstract Truth* (1997), *Psycho-Semitic* (1998), and *Kabalogy* (1999). In this music Hassidic and klezmer tunes are stylized and put within the new jazz framework, incorporating pop, rock, jazz, blues, and contemporary classical styles within a single piece. Recordings of Hassidic New Wave, which became known initially through its performances at the Knitting Factory in Lower Manhattan, have sold well.[155] John Zorn has moved into this arena as well with his Massada project. The eclectic tastes of such musicians, though, certainly push the limits of Jewish music.

TENDENCIES AND ISSUES

Looking to the future, several emerging trends are worth noting. One is the growing influence of Hassidic *niggunim* and Hassidic lore. This is true among the Orthodox, where the traditional Hassidic goal of cleaving to God through music can now be achieved by listening to a recording without being physically present at a Hassidic *tisch*. In the Reform world, Debbie Friedman has incorporated texts and stories from Hassidic masters in recent songs—"You Are the One," on her *Renewal of Spirit* (1995) recording, is based on a prayer by Rebbe Nachman of Bratslav—and Jeff Klepper includes *niggunim* in his solo album *In This Place* (1997). Recent Klezmer also owes much to the Hassidic tradition. The Klezmer Conservatory Band includes Hassidic melodies such as "Meron Nign" on the album *Dancing in the Aisles* (1997);[156] Andy Statman's *Between Heaven and Earth* is exclusively devoted to Hassidic melodies, as is Frank London's 1998 release, *Niggunim*.

Another significant trend in all the religious streams is the push for participatory prayer, in contrast to the older cantor-listener (or cantor/choir-listener) model of worship. Debbie Friedman, once again, is the prime

---

[155]Interview with Seth Rosner, Aug. 7, 1998. The Knitting Factory started a sub-label of its record line called "JAM," Jewish Alternative Music; the first release, *A Guide for the Perplexed* (1998), is a sampler of several groups, including Hassidic New Wave.

[156]This melody was taken from Andre Hajdu, "Le Niggun Meron," in *Yuval: Studies of the Jewish Music Research Centre* 2, 1971, pp. 109–11 (in French, with recording).

example in the Reform community. The growth of B'nai Jeshurun—a synagogue in New York City with spirited Sabbath services attended by over 1,500 people, most of them young, where full participation by everyone is the norm—has become a model for many other congregations in America. And the proliferation of Carlebach-style prayer services indicates that a similar need exists among the Orthodox. Rabbi Sam Intrator, till recently the rabbi of the Carlebach Shul in New York City, explains:

> Our individual voices when offered in an authentic, meaningful and free, spiritual prayer provide us with a far greater hope in keeping our people unified than the voices of our leaders with their proclamations and negotiations. . . . Clearly there is a great hunger for energetic leadership in participatory-based prayer. I mean this literally, in terms of the traditional *chazan* [cantor], but I also offer it as a wake-up call to our policy makers to look more closely at reviving and unifying Judaism.[157]

The Jewish establishment has already responded. Synagogue 2000, created jointly by the Reform and Conservative movements in 1999, has been experimenting with new forms of worship services that might attract more Jews to the synagogue. And in 2000, alarmed that many Jews were finding their synagogues spiritually uninviting, three wealthy philanthropists founded STAR (Synagogue Transformation and Renewal) to develop and disseminate innovative ideas to make the synagogue an exciting and inspiring place (see below, p. 229).

The efflorescence of new Jewish music has also generated a number of questions, some practical and others substantive.

Whatever else it is, music is also a business—musicians want to perform and sell their music. Both young and veteran artists worry that they are reaching only that limited portion of the Jewish community that goes into Jewish bookstores, or that sees ads placed by distributors and producers in Jewish periodicals. Commercial outlets, after all, carry Jewish music only by nationally known musicians, some klezmer, and Debbie Friedman. The Reform and Conservative communities have the fewest retail-selling venues and the Orthodox the most, which is why Orthodox music is the largest segment of the Jewish music industry in terms of both production and sales.[158] Since the mid-1990s the Jewish music industry has sought to reach consumers directly through the Internet. Mayer Pasternak, former marketing director for Tara Publications, says that he can provide over 1,600 titles of Jewish music on the Tara Web site, as com-

---

[157]Sam Intrator, "Letters: Power of Prayer," *New York Jewish Week,* Aug. 7, 1998, p. 7.
[158]Samuel Heilman, "Jews and Judaica: Who Owns and Buys What?" in Walter P. Zenner, ed., *Persistence and Flexibility: Anthropological Perspectives on the American Jewish Experience* (Albany, N.Y., 1988), pp. 260–79.

pared to the several hundred titles carried by the average Jewish bookstore. Besides making recordings available, Tara also plays a significant role in the spread of Jewish music through the sale of sheet music, now numbering over 300 items, and books.[159]

Nevertheless, Jewish musicians all across the spectrum fear that they will soon reach the limit of their popularity, under current means of distribution. That is why leading performers—Avraham Fried, Mordechai Ben David, and Miami Boys Choir (Orthodox), Debbie Friedman (Reform), the Klezmatics and Brave Old World (klezmer)—have been actively pursuing new markets, hoping to cross over to other parts of the Jewish community and even beyond.

In terms of substance, the new Jewish music, as noted several times above, has not lacked for critics. In the Reform world, where so-called "camp music" has become the norm, questions are being asked about the appropriateness of "pleasant, catchy tunes," as Cantor Richard Botton calls them, for conducting solemn prayer.[160] Similarly among the Orthodox, as Dovid Sears has suggested, "rock-and-roll tunes, sutured together with Jewish lyrics, and promoted with a vengeance" might not be the best music the Jewish tradition has to offer.[161] Such criticism, however, has so far not limited the growth and popularity of the new music in either denomination.

Contemporary Jewish music reflects American Jewry's religious and cultural diversity and also shapes it by staking a claim to a synthesized contemporary Jewish identity. The baby-boomer creators of the music accept, reject, and reshape the Eastern European heritage, showing a younger generation different ways of accommodating Jewish life and ideals to current challenges. Through this music the present looks to the past and the past in reinvented in the present, providing guidance and inspiration as young Jews create their own Jewish destiny in America.

---

[159]The following books, edited by Tara Publications founder Velvel Pasternak, include many of the musical selections mentioned in this study: *The International Jewish Songbook* (1994), *The World's Most Popular Jewish Songs*, 2 vols. (1997), and *The Jewish Fake Book* (1997).

[160]Richard Botton, "Letters: Musical Banality," *Reform Judaism* 9, Jan. 1981, p. 44. Also see Debbie Friedman's letter, "Not Camp Music," ibid; Mermelstein, "Is Popular Culture Defining Synagogue Music?" p. 44; Lawrence Hoffman, "How to Cure the Synagogue & Satisfy the Soul," *Reform Judaism* 22, Summer 1994, p. 34; Hoffman, *Art of Public Prayer,* p. 181; and the comments on Hoffman's views in *CCAR Journal* 38, Summer 1991, pp. 1–22.

[161]Sears, "Who Took the 'Jewish' Out of Jewish Music?" p. 14. In a supportive response to this article, David Altschuler describes a performance on a Los Angeles Chabad telethon in 1995 that "showed a rocking Chassid shoving a microphone down his throat. Several chubby men in yeshiva garb nearby had sweat rolling down their *peyos* [side curls], their hands and hips gyrating in all-too-perfect synchronization." "A Call for Civilized Enthusiasm at Simchos," *Jewish Observer,* Apr. 1997, p. 59.

Clearly, more research is needed in a number of areas. Of particular importance is contextualization—relating contemporary Jewish music to popular and folk music trends, to the musical traditions of other ethnic groups, and to the music of other religions in America. Investigations focused internally should assess the musical repertoire found in songbooks for camps, schools, and various Jewish organizations, and analyze the attitudes of the consumers to find out what the experience of listening to the music and seeing it performed means to them. A clear understanding of the relationship between Jewish music and Jewish identity would constitute a major contribution to the current debate over the future of Jewish life in America.

Review
of
the
Year

UNITED STATES

United States

National Affairs

IF THE DAWNING OF THE new millennium brought with it neither the catastrophe which some had feared nor the redemption for which others had hoped, it was, for all of that, a remarkable year. On the national scene, while Jewish organizations and activists continued their long-standing efforts to counter anti-Semitism, improve relations with other ethnic and religious groups, bolster American support for Israel, and promote public-policy positions that served the interests of Jews and all Americans, an exciting new ingredient was added to the mix in 2000.

This was a year when, for the first time, a Jew was nominated to the national ticket of a major American political party, bringing an unprecedented message of acceptance by a great nation of its tiny Jewish minority. For some, it also brought visions of a kosher kitchen at the Naval Observatory, home of the vice president, only to have the achingly close race decided, as much as any other single factor, by a badly designed Florida ballot that led a crucial number of Jewish votes to be cast, inadvertently, for the candidate on the ballot most Jews found most appalling. Nevertheless, the nomination had broken a barrier, and Jewish life in America had entered a new era.

THE POLITICAL ARENA

The Presidential Election

PRIMARY SEASON

Since Jews tended overwhelmingly to vote Democratic, the contest between Vice President Al Gore and former New Jersey senator Bill Bradley for the Democratic nomination attracted great interest in the Jewish community. New York, the state with the largest concentration of Jews, had its primary scheduled for "Super Tuesday," March 7. Even though Gore could boast a long pro-Israel record, and had, over the years, nurtured more extensive connections with the Jewish com-

145

munity than Bradley, he did not take the New York Jewish vote for granted. Both men spoke before Jewish audiences, Gore telling the Conference of Presidents of Major American Jewish Organizations the day before the primary of his strong commitment to Israel and warning that it would be "unwise" for the Palestinians to declare statehood unilaterally. Gore won New York easily, capturing 62 percent of the Jewish Democratic vote as against 38 percent for Bradley.

The New York primary raised fears among Jews about the deference both Democratic candidates accorded the Rev. Al Sharpton, the black leader widely regarded in the Jewish community as a promoter of anti-Semitism and racial divisiveness. Gore met with Sharpton privately in 1999 and Bradley did so in a more public setting in January 2000. Defending his visit, Bradley said, "I don't agree with Al Sharpton on everything, but I think that he's got to be given respect, and people have to be allowed to grow." Gore, for his part, commented simply that he "was not hesitant" to meet with Sharpton. Jewish concerns were aggravated in February, when Sharpton was accorded the honor of asking the first question at a nationally televised Democratic presidential debate held at the Apollo Theater in Harlem.

Among Jewish Republicans in New York, Senator John McCain of Arizona scored an even more decisive win than Gore had among Democrats, besting Governor George W. Bush of Texas 64 percent to 23 percent. Earlier, in the course of a debate moderated by CNN host Larry King in February before the South Carolina primary, the two Republicans had both confirmed their commitment to American recognition of Jerusalem as the capital of Israel. Bush said, "I think we ought to recognize it, yes," and McCain suggested that recognizing Jerusalem's status would make the peace process "simpler" because "as soon as the Palestinians and others know exactly where that capital is, then it'll be off the table."

In late May both Gore and Bush, having each locked up the delegates necessary for their respective party nominations, appeared at the annual policy conference of the American Israel Public Affairs Committee (AIPAC), the preeminent lobby for Israel, to promote their pro-Israel bona fides. The Jewish Telegraphic Agency pronounced their messages "indistinguishable," as "both candidates reiterated a strong relationship—and commitment—to Israel, condemned Iran for its trial of 13 Jews accused of espionage and expressed support for the Middle East peace process." In one important difference in tone, at least, Governor Bush stressed that the United States should avoid interfering in Israel's democratic process, thereby suggesting that the Clinton administration had pushed Israel too hard on the peace process. Vice President Gore defended the administration's role in what he described as facilitating, but not forcing, the movement toward a peaceful resolution of Israel's conflicts with its neighbors.

As had been the case throughout the primary season, the Republicans made clear at their national convention that they would contend for the Jewish vote in the fall despite the marked Democratic leanings of American Jews. This outreach was tempered, however, by the recognition that Republican positions on social issues—with which candidate Bush was solidly identified—were not likely to appeal to most Jews.

The unusual prominence of issues relating to religion and politics in the campaign, already apparent in the closing weeks of 1999, became more pronounced as the race gathered steam in 2000. At a January debate in Iowa, the Republican presidential candidates—with the exception of McCain, who did not speak directly to the issue—all announced their support for posting the Ten Commandments in public schools. Bush said, "No matter what a person's religion is, there's some inherent values in those great commandments," while fellow candidate Gary Bauer, formerly head of the Family Research Council and a one-time Reagan administration official, went him one better by announcing that he would post the commandments not only in schools, but also in the Oval Office. In the run-up to the convention, the American Jewish Congress and other Jewish groups criticized Governor Bush for having signed a proclamation declaring June 10, 2000, to be Jesus Day in Texas. While the proclamation did not have the force of law, AJCongress pronounced it a violation of the separation of church and state.

At events held by Jewish groups during the Philadelphia convention in July, the Republican leadership tended to downplay the social issues and concentrate on the commitment of their candidate and their platform to the security of Israel. Expanding on a theme they had used during the primaries, they criticized the Clinton administration for allegedly pressing Israel at the Camp David summit to make unilateral concessions to the Palestinians. This emphasis on the Middle East was also intended to counter the common Jewish perception that the candidate's father, President George H. W. Bush, and, in particular, his secretary of state, James Baker, had been hostile to Israel. Striking a bipartisan tone in her address to the convention, Condoleezza Rice, the likely national security adviser in a Bush administration, declared that Bush would join with past presidents of both parties in supporting "Israel's quest for enduring peace with its neighbors."

Governor Bush's vice-presidential selection—Richard Cheney, his father's secretary of defense—raised once again the question of just how different a second Bush presidency would be. Cheney himself contributed to Jewish misgivings when he suggested, soon after Bush announced his choice, that unilateral sanctions against Iran and Libya should be lifted because "they don't work." Nevertheless, the Jewish community greeted Cheney's selection with almost uniform expressions of respect for his foreign policy expertise and experience, and appreciation for the close working relationship he had developed with Israel during and after the Gulf War, even if with misgivings about policies he had previously espoused—on the sale of AWACs to Saudi Arabia, for example, and positions he had taken as a congressman on a range of domestic issues. Typifying this guarded but on-the-whole favorable response to the Cheney nomination was the observation of Jess Hordes, director of the Anti-Defamation League's Washington office, that while Cheney was "not automatically supportive of every action that Israel took," his overall record "is generally viewed as positive."

THE LIEBERMAN NOMINATION

Al Gore had set himself a deadline of the week prior to the opening of the Democratic convention, set for Sunday, August 13, to announce his choice of a running mate. On Saturday, August 5, Ed Rendell, the chairman of the Democratic National Committee, who was himself Jewish, offhandedly told reporters that Senator Joseph I. Lieberman of Connecticut was "maybe the finest person in politics" and that if "Lieberman was Episcopalian I think he'd almost be a slam dunk." However, he added, "I don't think anyone can calculate the effect of having a Jew on the ticket."

But by Monday morning, August 7, word had gotten out that the Connecticut senator was indeed to be Gore's pick. That day, Senator Lieberman advised the press of the telephone call he had received from Gore, and noted that, in the course of the call, they had "said a short prayer together." The next day Lieberman joined Al Gore in Nashville, where, in praising his running mate, Gore noted proudly that the Democratic Party would "tear down an old wall of division" in nominating Lieberman for vice president. Lieberman's own remarks were infused with religion, as he said to those assembled: "I ask you to allow me to let the spirit move me as it does to remember the words from Chronicles, which are to give thanks to God, to give thanks to God and declare his name and make his acts known to the people, to be glad of spirit, to sing to God and to make music to God and most of all, to give glory and gratitude to God from whom all blessings do truly fall. Dear Lord, maker of all miracles, I thank you for bringing me to this extraordinary moment in my life." His wife, Hadassah Lieberman, spoke of her parents, who had survived the Holocaust, and of the role of American soldiers in liberating her mother from a concentration camp.

Lieberman's name had been on Gore's "short list" since the spring, though many had assumed, like Rendell, that placing a Jew on a national ticket was too great a risk. A political centrist — and therefore often a distinctly minority voice within the liberal-leaning Democratic caucus on such issues as vouchers and foreign policy, though well within the Democratic mainstream on issues like abortion and gun control — Lieberman was expected to attract support for the ticket from moderate voters. But many political observers suggested that the most important factor in Gore's calculations was that Lieberman had been an early Democratic critic of President Bill Clinton during the Monica Lewinsky scandal, and this would help provide Vice President Gore some credible separation between himself and the outgoing administration.

By all accounts, it was difficult to find many outside the Jewish community who found the notion of a Jewish vice president problematic. Those of a certain age could well recall the burden of doubt presidential candidate John F. Kennedy had to overcome in 1960 over whether, as a Roman Catholic, he would be independent of the Vatican. But attitudes had changed. While Gallup surveys taken in 1932 found that only 46 percent of Americans were willing to vote for a Jew for president, in 1999, 92 percent said they would. Alan Lichtman, chairman of the history department at American University, observed, "those who would not be likely to vote for Joe Lieberman on religious grounds would not be likely to vote for Al Gore anyway." In fact, observers suggested, an Orthodox Jew on the Democratic ticket—a person with strong religious commitments and deeply pro-Israel—might even prove an asset for the Democrats with Christian fundamentalist voters. But some with positive feelings about the Jewish nominee for vice president also demonstrated confusion about the nature of Jewish religious practice: On the day Lieberman's nomination was announced, the influential Senator John Breaux (D., La.) remarked, "I think people don't care so much about where he goes to church on Sunday, but just that he has the morals and principles to lead the country."

The fascination among the general public with things Jewish that followed Gore's announcement resulted in a national education on the tenets and practices of Judaism that was without parallel in American history. At least initially this interest reflected the need of some Americans to be assured that the obligations of Senator Lieberman's observance would not be inconsistent with his duties as vice president or, if circumstances demanded, president. But there was also a good deal of innocent curiosity about a minority religion that was based on what Christians called the Old Testament and that was nevertheless distinct from the majority Christian faith.

For the Jewish community, the nomination was a sensation: This was the first time a Jew had been named to a major party's national ticket—and he was not just a nominal Jew, but observant, indeed Orthodox. American Jews of every political and religious stripe were quick to hail Senator Lieberman's nomination not only as a source of pride for the community but also as confirmation that the United States was an open society where minorities could aspire to the highest levels of national leadership. "We're seeing another barrier come down," said Malcolm Hoenlein, executive vice chairman of the Conference of President of Major American Jewish Organizations. "This is an important message to all young Americans, that anyone of hard work and integrity can answer the call to public service, regardless of religion, ethnicity or race." But Jewish leaders sought to make it clear that there was no automatic "Jewish" vote. Dr. Mandell Ganchrow, president of the Union of Orthodox Jewish Congregations (OU), noted that even though all Jews took pride in Lieberman's nomination, they would not vote for him based simply on his religious identity: "People will judge him on the issues. And that's the way it should be." Republican Jewish Coalition executive director Matthew Brooks noted that Jewish Republicans joined in the expressions of pride in the Lieberman pick, "but that doesn't necessarily mean that you're going to vote for him."

Yet there was an undercurrent of concern in some Jewish circles—rarely stated openly—that Lieberman's Jewish identity, given the high profile he seemed determined to give it, might prove problematic if the ticket were victorious. Would

Vice President Lieberman feel a need to show "even-handedness" on Middle East policy? If things went wrong in a Gore-Lieberman administration, would America blame "the Jews?" Rabbi Laura Geller, a Reform rabbi from Los Angeles, suggested that there was a generational divide in the community: some older Jews, who recalled the days when Jews in public life felt compelled to bend over backward so as not to appear "too Jewish," felt uncomfortable with the nomination, but as for younger Jews, she said, "we've seen a profound change in attitude, so that we can be both Jews at home and Jews in the street." Abraham Foxman, national director of the Anti-Defamation League, an organization whose mission it was to monitor anti-Semitism, expressed surprise at the concerns over anti-Semitism should Lieberman be elected. Foxman pointed out that the level of anti-Semitism was "the lowest it's ever been," and that "at the end of the day, Joe Lieberman will be judged as an individual and not by the fact that he goes to shul or doesn't go to shul." And as for lingering Jewish discomfort with the Senator's explicit references to his faith and his level of observance, no less an expert on politics than President Clinton reassured Jews that Lieberman's "God-talk" was a mark of his character and sincerity. At an event hosted by Jewish groups in Los Angeles on the Sunday the Democratic convention opened, the president declared: "More and more people will respect the fact that Senator Lieberman gives up all work and politics on the Sabbath."

This millennial tone reached its crescendo on the third night of the convention, as Senator Lieberman came to the podium to deliver his address. He was preceded by remarks delivered by his wife, Hadassah Lieberman, who was herself greeted by a sea of "Hadassah" signs. Mrs. Lieberman spoke of her "Joey's" bedrock values of "family, faith, congregation, and neighborhood." Senator Lieberman's speech, marked by humor and expressions of gratitude to a nation that had allowed one of its Jewish sons to progress so far (as well as by some old-fashioned digs at the Republicans), was greeted by raucous applause and standing ovations. He began by asking, "Is America a great country or what?" and finished by saying, "Only in America." Lieberman contrasted the persecution his immigrant grandmother had endured in her native Europe and the acceptance by Christian neighbors that she found in America, and noted the similar experience of his wife's parents, Holocaust survivors saved by American GIs who liberated the concentration camps.

However, for some in the Jewish community, the euphoria of seeing a Jewish nominee on a national ticket was quickly dissipated by what they felt were Lieberman's too-frequent invocations of God and the Bible in the course of his campaign. Nobody seemed terribly concerned that the senator delivered remarks that were, in effect, an English version of the traditional *shehehiyanu* prayer at the announcement that Gore had chosen him to run, and even the repeated references to God in his acceptance speech in Los Angeles brought few complaints. But in late August, speaking at an African American church in Detroit, Lieberman called on Americans to renew the "dedication of our nation and ourselves to God and God's purpose," and cited George Washington's warning not to assume that "morality can be maintained without religion."

The Anti-Defamation League immediately responded, sending him a letter similar to the one it had sent Republican and Democratic candidates the year before after several of them had made statements invoking their faiths. The ADL letter said, "Appealing along religious lines, or belief in God, is contrary to the American ideal," and that "to even suggest that one cannot be a moral person without being a religious person is an affront to many highly ethical citizens." Americans United for Separation of Church and State also wrote Lieberman, calling on him to cease using religion as part of his "campaign rhetoric." Lieberman, who had previously asserted the view that the public declaration of religious faith was not inconsistent with church-state separation, had a spokesman assert that the senator "respectfully disagrees" with the ADL. Lieberman, said the spokesman, was committed to "the importance of the separation of church and state" even as he had "great respect for the role faith has played in the lives of so many Americans."

It quickly became evident that the ADL critique of Lieberman did not express the sentiments of the entire Jewish community. David Zwiebel, executive vice president for government and public affairs of the (Orthodox) Agudath Israel of America, commented: "At a time when perhaps the greatest crisis America faces is a crisis of values, a candidate for national office who speaks unashamedly of his own religious faith and of the positive role religion can play in strengthening our society is to be commended, not condemned." The National Jewish Democratic Council made the point that Lieberman had never used his references to faith to exclude others or to justify public policies. Rabbi David Saperstein, director of the Religion Action Center of Reform Judaism, suggested that Lieberman, whose religious background was so unfamiliar to the general public, was in a sense compelled to do what the other candidates did not have to do, namely educate the public about his religious beliefs.

A Reuters/Zogby poll released in early September demonstrated that only a minority of the general population was concerned that Senator Lieberman's remarks about faith had gone too far. Some 48 percent of Americans felt that Senator Lieberman was not talking too much about religion, 24 percent believed that he was, and 24 percent were not sure. Indeed, a survey carried out by the Philadelphia-based Center for Jewish Community Studies, issued in the concluding days of the campaign but reflecting data gathered in September, indicated that non-Jews were twice as likely as Jews to approve of Senator Lieberman's references to God and Scripture. Furthermore, while 84 percent of Jews were pleased that the Jewish senator had been nominated for vice president, a lower number — 55 percent — were happy that he was a "religious Jew."

In an address at Notre Dame University on October 24, Lieberman called for a national "conversation" on the place of religious values in "the public square." Challenging the notion that the Founding Fathers wanted a strict separation of church and state, Lieberman suggested that they "knew that our experience in self-government was contingent on our faith and trust in the Creator who endowed us with the inalienable rights to life, liberty and the pursuit of happiness." Thus, he asserted, while the line of separation between church and state "is an important one and has always been hard to draw, . . . in recent years we have gone far beyond what the framers ever imagined in separating the two. So much so that we have practically banished religious values and religious institutions from the public square." Lieberman also defended his use of religious speech in the course of the campaign, arguing that one could discuss faith in politics without excluding those with differing viewpoints.

ADL national director Foxman characterized Lieberman's remarks at Notre Dame as "softer" and "more inclusive" than his earlier remarks at the black church that the ADL had criticized. But Foxman demurred nonetheless, arguing that "this is a debate that belongs in American society, not on the campaign trail," and that "the issue remains that if you're a person who's an atheist or a Muslim or a Buddhist, you felt excluded." Other criticisms were also heard. Matthew Brooks, executive director of the Republican Jewish Coalition, characterized the senator's speech as "hypocritical" in light of past Democratic responses to Republicans who invoked God in policy debates. And Robert Boston, assistant communications director for Americans United for Separation of Church and State, termed Lieberman's earlier reference to the commandment "honor thy mother and father" as a basis for Medicare reform as "turning religion into just another political football."

After arousing some consternation in traditionalist Jewish circles with remarks in August and September asserting that Judaism opposed neither freedom of choice on abortion nor intermarriage (see below, p. 234), in late September Lieberman dropped another bombshell. During an interview on a black-oriented radio station, he said that he had respect for Nation of Islam leader Louis Farrakhan "and for the Muslim community generally," and that he would be prepared to meet with Farrakhan and seek to work together with him on racial and religious reconciliation. His comments, seen by many as a continuation of the outreach to the black community that he had begun at the Democratic convention, brought sharp reactions from Jewish leaders, who saw Farrakhan and the group he headed as anti-Semitic and racist, notwithstanding Lieberman's suggestion in his radio remarks that the views Farrakhan had expressed were simply "not informed."

In remarks that were echoed by the Republican Jewish Coalition, Richard Foltin, legislative director of the American Jewish Committee, said that Farrakhan "is far outside of the mainstream of American politics" and that "by virtue of his statements and his extremist positions, . . . he has not earned a place at the table in terms of discussions of race relations or public policy." And even Ira Forman, executive director of the National Jewish Democratic Council—while defending Lieberman's commitment to the well-being of the Jewish community—acknowledged that he would not have suggested a meeting with Farrakhan and asserted that the NJDC would continue to work from "within the Democratic Party to exclude Farrakhan from the political process."

Farrakhan, ironically, had been quick after Lieberman's nomination to question whether the candidate would be capable of placing loyalty to the United State ahead of loyalty to Israel—a theme that he reiterated in mid-October, along with other anti-Semitic calumnies. A few days after these latter comments, Senator Lieberman said that he would not meet with Farrakhan after all because such a meeting would not be constructive and would be "too loaded with political controversy."

As a centrist Democrat whose views were sometimes at odds with those of his party's core constituency, Senator Lieberman's nomination initially raised some concerns unrelated to his religion: His record presented some ambiguity on issues such as vouchers and affirmative action. Lieberman's record of commitment to civil rights was not in question. As a college student he had traveled to Mississippi during the 1960s to register black voters, and as senator he had compiled a solid voting record on civil rights, including votes in 1995 and 1998 to preserve affirmative-action programs. Nevertheless, he had expressed some degree of support for a failed 1996 California referendum directed at that state's affirmative-action programs. And he had supported pilot projects involving vouchers when they came up for a vote in the Senate.

Early in the campaign Lieberman moved to clarify his positions on these and similar issues and to affirm that, in any event, he would carry out the policies of a President Gore and not seek to implement his own views where they differed. Upon his arrival in Los Angeles for the Democratic convention, Lieberman met with members of the Congressional Black Caucus and assured them that "I have supported affirmative action, I do support affirmative action and I will support affirmative action," a point he reinforced in his acceptance speech, which endorsed President Clinton's "mend it, don't end it" approach to affirmative action. Representative Maxine Waters (D., Cal.), a caucus member who had expressed some initial concern, pronounced herself satisfied with Lieberman's assurances. Other civil rights leaders took advantage of speaking opportunities at the convention to enunciate their support. The Rev. Jesse Jackson, who already the week before had hailed the Lieberman pick as an indication that "the tent is getting bigger and bigger," told the convention, "Gore ended the quota of zero of Jewish Americans on the national ticket last month. This was a bold act of affirmative action." And his fellow civil rights veteran Rep. John Lewis (D., Ga.), invoking his and Lieberman's common history as part of the 1960s civil-rights movement, asserted, "We need a man like Joseph Lieberman to walk with us."

ELECTION ISSUES

Though at times it may have seemed that way, the Lieberman candidacy was not the only matter of Jewish interest during the election campaign.

After a first debate that focused entirely on domestic affairs — including vouchers and other education issues as well as abortion — Vice President Gore and Governor Bush turned to foreign policy in their second meeting. There was little if any distance between them on the Middle East, as each man restated his support for Israel and urged PLO chairman Yasir Arafat to take steps to end the violence. In an area of concern to many in the Jewish community, Gore stressed his support for the enactment of federal hate-crimes legislation, while Bush suggested that state legislative action and aggressive prosecution, as he said was typical of Texas, would be adequate to deal with these crimes. The third and final presidential debate reprised the first in its primary focus on domestic matters, but both candidates took the opportunity to reemphasize their strong support for Israel.

The sole vice-presidential debate, held on the evening of October 5, played out with even less discussion of Israel. Senator Lieberman asserted that his running mate had had "a critical role in advancing [the peace] process" and, reflecting on the violence that had broken out over the preceding week, said: "I hope I might, through my friendships in Israel and throughout the Middle East, play a unique role in bringing peace to this sacred region of the world." Republican candidate Dick Cheney, following the same strategy as George W. Bush, avoided criticizing the Clinton administration's handling of the peace process, and instead spoke broadly of the need to "reassure both Arabs and Israelis that the United States would play a major role" in the Middle East. While Lieberman made references to God, prayer, and his faith during the debate — as had been his wont throughout the campaign — the topic of the role of religion in politics did not come up.

The campaign also brought to the fore certain views of Green Party presidential candidate Ralph Nader on Israel and the peace process that had not previously been generally known. In October, Nader termed Al Gore "cowardly" for supporting Israel as it confronted rising Palestinian violence. Nader maintained that Israel was responsible for the violence and asserted that the Middle East would not see peace "without justice for the Palestinians." As the election came down to the wire the Gore campaign came increasingly to fear that Nader might siphon off enough Democratic votes in a few close states to elect Bush. One tactic it used to stave off this possibility was to focus the attention of Jewish voters on Nader's seemingly pro-Palestinian views.

In the last week of what would clearly be a very close election race, both Democrats and Republicans contended for Jewish votes with a flurry of charges and counter-charges that the other side's candidate had backed away from support for moving the U.S. embassy in Israel from Tel Aviv to Jerusalem. Gore supporters pointed to assurances by former Republican congressman Paul Findley of Illinois to Arab and Muslim Americans, carried on the Web site of the American Muslim Alliance, that Bush would be more amenable than Gore to changing his position on this and other issues, while Bush supporters circulated reports appearing in the *Wall Street Journal* and several Michigan newspapers that Gore had told Arab Americans during a closed-door meeting in Dearborn that he supported keeping the embassy in Tel Aviv. The Bush campaign denied the report aimed at their man, reiterating his commitment to move the embassy, while Gore's campaign contended that the vice president had said that he supports relocation of the embassy but that it should take place in the context of the peace process. This version was confirmed by Gore campaign adviser and American Arab Institute president James Zogby, a participant in the Michigan meeting.

Although the winner of the presidential election would not be decided for some five weeks after Election Day, exit polls available the next day confirmed that Jewish Americans, following their historic tradition, still heavily favored the Democrats. In contrast to the uncannily even split between Bush and Gore nationwide—with 2 percent of the vote going to Green Party candidate Ralph Nader and 1 percent to Reform Party candidate Pat Buchanan—Jews, making up 4 percent of the electorate, preferred Gore over Bush by 79 percent to 19 percent, with 1 percent for Nader. Other than self-described Democrats and liberals, the only demographic group more favorable to Gore than the Jews were African Americans.

The great imponderable, one that political observers would surely debate for many years to come, was the impact of Joseph Lieberman on the ticket. Gore succeeded in states with significant Jewish populations, but these states—California, New York, New Jersey, Illinois, and Pennsylvania—had gone Democratic in recent presidential elections anyway. Some suggested that Gore's near-success in Florida, the state on which the election ultimately turned, was in part attributable to a Jewish running mate with tremendous appeal among a key constituency. But an analysis published by the Jewish Telegraphic Agency the day after the election suggested that there was little evidence that Lieberman's presence on the ticket had made a material difference in the already Democratic-leaning Jewish vote. And it remained a possibility—though there was no evidence one way or the other—that in Florida and elsewhere some voters turned away from the ticket because of Lieberman's religion. Weighing these factors, a post-election analysis prepared by the Washington office of the American Jewish Committee concluded:

> [S]urely Senator Lieberman proved to be a formidable asset to the campaign, a warm and energetic counterpoint to the sometimes fusty presidential nominee, and early polls found him appealing to voters across the religious, ethnic and even ideological spectrum. . . . [T]he consensus of political analysts immediately after the vice president made his selection . . . held that potential voters turned off by a Jewish candidate were probably unwinnable by Gore anyway, and that the few marginal voters Lieberman might cost the ticket would probably be more than offset by those voters, of various ethnic and religious backgrounds, he would likely attract. As Lieberman waged his spirited, almost successful, fight, the analysts' consensus held.

A FIVE-WEEK ELECTION NIGHT

In the early morning hours after Election Day it became apparent that the contest would be decided by the vote in Florida. Even though the Gore-Lieberman ticket seemed to have won the national popular vote, the Electoral College was so close that the victor in Florida would win a majority of the electoral vote, and therefore the presidency. But the result in Florida was too close to call, and as soon as that reality began to sink in a stunned American public realized that it would have to wait days, and perhaps longer, to learn the identity of the next president of the United States. As it became evident that rounds of recounts and challenges—possibly even an election decided by the United States Congress—could be in store, reports began to emerge of mammoth problems in the way votes were cast and counted in Florida.

Of all the irregularities alleged about the Florida vote, one particular development presented a striking irony for the Jewish community. While a Jewish candidate appeared on a major party's national ticket for the first time in U.S. history, there was a very real possibility that Jewish voters inadvertently voted for the wrong candidate—one who was, in fact, anathema to them—and that by doing so they had innocently sent the Jewish candidate and his running mate down to defeat.

In an effort to provide a ballot with type large enough to be readable by its sizable elderly population, the Palm Beach County Elections Canvassing Commission created a "butterfly ballot" on which it was not clear to many voters which punch hole corresponded to which candidate's name. The confusing ballot apparently led as many as thousands of the elderly, overwhelmingly Democratic, Jewish voters in the county to vote for Reform Party presidential candidate Patrick Buchanan—the conservative journalist and commentator whose animus toward Israel and differences with the Jewish community on a host of other issues aroused fear and loathing among many Jews—instead of the man they intended to back, Al Gore. Other voters, realizing in the voting booth that they had mistakenly punched a hole for the wrong candidate, sought to cure the problem by punching an additional hole for their choice, leading to a ballot that was discarded as an "overvote." More than 19,000 votes were discarded by Palm Beach County in the course of the vote count. The margin of miscast votes could conceivably have tipped the vote in Florida, and the election, away from Gore-Lieberman. As Jan Lederman, executive director of the Sarasota-Manatee Jewish Federation, observed as the story broke, "This entire election is now focused on a retired little old lady in Century Village in Boca Raton who cast the wrong ballot."

Long before the polls closed, angry Palm Beach County voters who had deposited their ballots, some already confused when they voted and others realizing only after the fact that they might have voted for the wrong candidate or spoiled their ballots, demanded to be allowed to correct their votes, a request that election supervisors had no choice but to deny. Other voters called Florida's election offices demanding recounts or a chance to recast their votes. There were reports of Jewish voters reduced to tears, crying out as they left the polling place, "I voted for Buchanan!" Buchanan won a remarkable 4,000 votes in Palm Beach County, well in excess of the votes he received in any other Florida county, a circumstance which, given the nature of the county's electorate, led even Buchanan himself to observe that many of the votes he received could hardly have been intended for him. In the aftermath of this debacle, an additional indignity was the portrayal of these long-time voters in the news media and on late-night comedy shows as too dim-witted to understand how to cast a ballot.

A lawsuit was brought in Florida state court calling for a revote before the winner of Florida's primary was finally determined, citing other cases in which courts had directed revotes. But the special circumstances of a presidential election led many legal experts to conclude that no court was likely to grant this relief — and, in fact, the suit was ultimately dismissed.

For some, Election Day's bizarre Palm Beach County events proved a catalyst for seeking to strengthen the historic black-Jewish civil-rights partnership. In the days and weeks after the vote, civil-rights leaders found a link between the distraught Jewish voters and the tens of thousands of blacks who, they believed, had been disenfranchised in various ways — the purging of individuals from the election rolls on the basis of nonexistent felony records, the intimidating presence of police officials at or near polling places, and the disqualification of votes of blacks and other minorities at far higher rates than whites because of the less advanced voting methods utilized in minority districts.

Thus the Rev. Jesse Jackson, a leading figure in the election protest, came together with local Jewish leaders at rallies throughout Florida in the weeks after Election Day, often joined by Rabbi Steven Jacobs, spiritual leader of Kol Tikvah in Woodland Hills, California, who argued that the recount dispute was a fundamental issue of civil rights. On November 29, Rev. Jackson came to the Stephen Wise Free Synagogue in New York City where he joined with area rabbis and Jewish and black politicians in a call to some 1,000 attending Jews and blacks to "keep your eyes on the prize" and to demand an "accurate count" of the Florida vote. Rabbi Balfour Brickner, rabbi emeritus at the Reform synagogue, echoed remarks that Rabbi Jacobs had made earlier, criticizing Florida rabbis and national Jewish organizations for treating the recount dispute as a partisan matter in which they did not want to be involved.

Senator Lieberman was widely credited with a leading role in urging Vice President Gore to continue the fight for a vote recount in Florida, and this led hundreds of Bush supporters to hold a demonstration outside of his Connecticut home. The timing of the protest — the Jewish Sabbath — caused some Democrats to charge the demonstration's organizers with anti-Semitism. In any event, Senator Lieberman was in Washington, D.C., on that particular Sabbath.

The historic fight for the presidency finally ended on the night of December 12 when the Supreme Court rendered its five-to-four decision effectively handing the presidency to Governor Bush. Some 24 hours later, Al Gore delivered his concession speech in the course of which he praised his running mate, saying that Lieberman had brought "passion and high purpose to our partnership, and opened new doors, not just for our campaign, but for our country."

The next day, Senator Lieberman came to the Senate floor to deliver his own coda to the race's remarkable denouement, complete with—in what was by now his accustomed fashion—a biblical flourish. In addition to calling for bipartisan investigation and reform of an election system that had left the close race so unsettled, Lieberman expressed his appreciation to Vice President Gore for having named a Jewish American, for the first time, to a place on the national ticket of a major party. He noted that, "while my faith was the focus of much of the early media reaction to my candidacy, it was not even mentioned at the end of the campaign, and that is the way we had all hoped it would be." Lieberman closed by invoking a theme from the 30th Psalm that seemed appropriate for what had, in the end, turned out to be an unsuccessful campaign: "So today, as some of us weep for what could have been, we look to the future with faith that on another morning, joy will surely come." As Lieberman finished his remarks, the presiding Republican senator commented, "We are all very proud of the Senator from Connecticut." Although he was speaking for his fellow lawmakers, the presiding senator could just as easily have been expressing the sentiment of the great bulk of American Jewry.

Congressional Elections

SENATOR CLINTON

First Lady and prospective New York senatorial candidate Hillary Rodham Clinton was faced, early in 2000, with a contretemps over her appearance at a program at the headquarters of the Rev. Al Sharpton marking Martin Luther King's birthday. Another speaker, appearing on the program before Mrs. Clinton's arrival, delivered remarks offensive to Jews, an offense made all the more egregious by Sharpton's reputation in much of the Jewish community as, at best, a borderline anti-Semite. In contrast to her delayed response the previous year to blood libels uttered by Palestinian Authority first lady Suha Arafat, Mrs. Clinton, alerted to the comments that had preceded her arrival, asserted in her speech that "we know that anti-Semitism still stalks our land." And she later told reporters, "I heard that one of the speakers made some divisive comments, which I soundly reject." Her participation in the event was criticized nevertheless—by Republicans, unsurprisingly, but also by Dr. Mandell Ganchrow, president of the Union of Orthodox Jewish Congregations (OU), who wondered why Mrs. Clinton would choose to commemorate Martin Luther King Day with such a "divisive" figure as Al Sharpton.

As Hillary Clinton continued her quest for the Jewish vote throughout the election year, her attendance at an event with Sharpton receded in importance as doubts over the depth of her support for Israel became the primary source of contention. When Mrs. Clinton officially announced her candidacy in February, she stressed that she would support a Middle East peace accord that "guarantees Israel's security." Since Jews made up as much as 14 percent of the electorate in New York, and they usually but not always tended to vote Democratic, appeals to the state's substantial Jewish community to vote either for or against her remained aggressive and relentless throughout the campaign.

Following New York City mayor Rudolph Giuliani's withdrawal from the Senate race in May in the wake of a diagnosis of prostate cancer, Rick Lazio, a Long Island congressman, assumed the role of Republican standard bearer. At times, the contest in the Jewish community seemed to boil down to whether Lazio or Mrs. Clinton would earn the title of Israel's best friend. Mrs. Clinton took exception to her husband's cautious stance on moving the U.S. embassy to Jerusalem, and distanced herself from her earlier comments expressing support for Palestinian statehood. Representative Lazio emphasized his votes for aid to Israel and for moving the embassy to Jerusalem.

Mrs. Clinton's cause was not helped when, in July, a report emerged that, following Bill Clinton's loss in a 1974 race for Congress, she had called her husband's campaign manager an anti-Semitic epithet. Mrs. Clinton quickly moved to deny the report as an "outrageous lie," with supportive remarks delivered as well by her husband and by Jewish congresswoman Nita Lowey (D., N.Y.). Some Jewish critics of Mrs. Clinton, distrusting her on other grounds, jumped on the report, while acknowledging that they had no way of knowing whether it was true. But at least one of her leading critics, State Assemblyman Dov Hikind, a Brooklyn Democrat, stressed to reporters that his differences with Mrs. Clinton were "about her record" and that he did not consider her to be an anti-Semite.

Mrs. Clinton received a bit of an assist when, in September — following Lazio's criticism of her for receiving the now notorious Suha Arafat kiss — the White House released a 1998 photo of the Republican candidate shaking hands with Yasir Arafat. In late October, Mrs. Clinton returned $50,000 in campaign contributions raised at a June event after the *New York Daily News* reported that the fund-raiser had been organized by the American Muslim Alliance, a group whose leader was quoted as saying that he supported the Palestinians' use of armed force against Israel. Earlier, Mrs. Clinton's returned $1,000 to Abudrahman Alamoudi of the American Muslim Council because of statements he had made supporting Hamas. But these actions, in response to criticism from some parts of the Jewish community that was quickly picked up by the Lazio camp, led to a predictable backlash in the Muslim and Arab communities. James Zogby, a Gore campaign adviser and president of the Arab American Institute, said that he wished the Clinton campaign would return the $500 contribution that he had made, even as he also disparaged Lazio's criticism of Mrs. Clinton for having taken the contentious contributions in the first place.

In the final week of what was surely the most scrutinized congressional race in the nation, one poll gave Mrs. Clinton some 63 percent of the Jewish vote, a figure considered low enough among that heavily Democratic constituency to place Lazio within striking distance of victory. In the end, Mrs. Clinton defeated Lazio by a decisive 55-43 percent. While the positions of the two candidates on Israel were hard to differentiate, other issues in this generally Democratic state seemed to break in Mrs. Clinton's favor among Jewish voters: She allied herself with the Gore-Lieberman messages on the economy, abortion rights, health-care costs, gun control, and future Supreme Court appointments. Nevertheless, according to Election Day exit polls, Mrs. Clinton defeated Lazio among Jewish voters by a slightly smaller percentage than the vote in the overall electorate, 53-45. This margin was less than even the latest polls had shown, and it was certainly lower than the percentage of Jewish voters traditionally won by Democratic candidates for statewide office in New York.

THE NEW CONGRESS

Even as election night stretched out into several weeks for the candidates at the top of the tickets, several congressional races also proved too close to call when the polls closed. In the end, two of those races, both involving Jewish challengers to sitting members, were resolved in favor of the incumbents. Democrat Elaine Bloom was defeated in her bid to unseat Rep. Clay Shaw (R., Fla.), while former New Jersey Republican representative Dick Zimmer, who had relinquished his seat to make an unsuccessful bid for the Senate back in 1996, failed to regain it from Rush Holt, the incumbent Democrat.

As the smoke cleared in the weeks after Election Day, it became clear that the Republican Senate majority had lost five seats and defeated one sitting Democrat, creating a 50-50 parity. A Gore victory would have left Republicans with a one-seat majority since the Republican governor of Connecticut was poised to appoint a Republican replacement as soon as returning Senator Joseph Lieberman resigned his Senate seat to assume the position of vice president. Lieberman, in fact, had come under criticism from fellow Democrats for running for reelection to his Senate seat simultaneously with his run for national office, setting up this possibility of tipping control of the Senate into Republican hands. Having lost the national election, however, Lieberman kept that Senate seat—and his day job. Republicans would control the upper chamber only by virtue of the tie-breaking vote of the incoming vice president, Dick Cheney.

Lieberman's return to the Senate meant that that body would retain an egalitarian minyan (quorum) of ten Jews, one less than in the 106th Congress. The reduction was attributable to the retirement of three-term Democrat Frank Lautenberg of New Jersey, a longtime champion of Israel and Soviet Jewry, among other causes important to American Jews. In addition to Lieberman, two other Jewish senators sought and easily won reelection—Democrats Dianne Feinstein in California and Herb Kohl in Wisconsin. Also remaining in the 107th Congress were the Senate's lone Jewish Republican, Arlen Specter of Pennsylvania, and Democrats Barbara Boxer of California, Russell Feingold of Wisconsin, Carl Levin of Michigan, Charles Schumer of New York, Paul Wellstone of Minnesota, and Ron Wyden of Oregon.

On the House side, Democrats failed in their effort to overcome the Republicans' 13-seat advantage and win back the control of that body. They made gains in a few contests but suffered losses in others, and ended up with a net gain of two seats, thereby narrowing the Republican margin to 9. The chamber would have 221 Republicans, 212 Democrats, and two independents.

Unlike the relatively steady situation in the Senate, the House's Jewish contingent went up considerably as a result of the 2000 election, from 23 members in the 106th Congress to 27 in the 107th. That number would include two Republicans—veteran New York representative and chairman of the House International Relations Committee Benjamin Gilman, and freshman Eric Cantor of Virginia. Except for Bernard Sanders, the Vermont independent who typically voted Democratic but did not identify with the party, all other Jewish House members in the incoming Congress were Democrats. The new additions to the group were Jane Harman of California, a former representative who returned to a seat she relinquished after three terms to make an unsuccessful bid for the gubernatorial nomination in 1998; Susan Davis and Adam Schiff, also of California; and Steve Israel of New York, a former area director for the American Jewish Congress. Rounding out the Jewish "caucus" in the House for the 107th Congress were Democrats Gary Ackerman of New York, Shelley Berkley of Nevada, Howard Berman of California, Benjamin Cardin of Maryland, Peter Deutsch of Florida, Eliot Engel of New York, Bob Filner of California, Barney Frank of Massachusetts, Martin Frost of Texas, Tom Lantos of California, Sander Levin of Michigan, Nita Lowey of New York, Jerrold Nadler of New York, Steve Rothman of New Jersey, Jan Schakowsky of Illinois, Brad Sherman of California, Norman Sisisky of Virginia, Henry Waxman of California, Anthony Weiner of New York, and Robert Wexler of Florida. The senior Jewish Democrat in the incoming House was Rep. Waxman, who easily won his 14th term.

Democrat Sam Gejdenson of Connecticut, a son of Holocaust survivors who was born in a displaced persons camp, was one of only a few sitting members to be defeated in a bid for reelection. Gejdenson's hold on the seat had been insecure for years; he won by just 21 votes in 1994. Nevertheless, he had risen to the important position of ranking Democrat on the International Relations Committee, where he worked closely with Benjamin Gilman, the committee's Republican chairman. It was quickly confirmed after the election that the ranking post would be taken over by Rep. Tom Lantos of California, himself a Holocaust survivor. It was less certain at election time who would wield the chairman's gavel on that committee. A Republican caucus rule, instituted when the Republicans assumed the majority in 1995, barred representatives from holding a particular chairmanship for more than three terms. Although he was lobbying for a waiver of this rule, as the year closed it appeared likely that Gilman, who was known for his advocacy of a close U.S.-Israel relationship and his support for direct, bilateral negotiations between Israel and its Arab neighbors, would have to relinquish his post. But credible reports had it that Gilman was to take over a newly created subcommittee on the Middle East in the new Congress, and so Gilman seemed likely to retain a prominent role in foreign policy issues of profound concern to the Jewish community.

The Bush Administration Takes Shape

With his election finally confirmed by the Supreme Court, George W. Bush moved quickly, in the short time left before his inauguration, to name the members of his cabinet—subject to Senate confirmation—and other high-ranking officials of the incoming administration. Bush's inner circle included at least two Jews—press secretary Ari Fleischer and former Indianapolis mayor Stephen Goldsmith, a key adviser on the faith-based-action initiative the new president was eager to promote. But despite its strikingly diverse makeup, and in stark contrast to the outgoing administration, there were no Jewish members in the new Bush cabinet.

As the names of Bush's high-level appointments emerged, the Jewish community greeted them with mixed reviews. The designation of Donald Rumsfeld as secretary of defense received high marks (notwithstanding his consistent opposition to clemency for convicted spy Jonathan Pollard), based primarily on his substantial experience, including a previous turn in the position under President Ford, and his role in highlighting the national-security threat posed by ballistic missiles. General Colin Powell, designated to head the State Department, was well regarded as a former head of the Joint Chiefs of Staff, but his views on Israel and the Middle East were unclear and some observers worried about his perceived reluctance to utilize American military power in international conflicts. At the announcement of his nomination on December 16, Powell spoke reassuringly of the need for American Middle East policy to be "based on the principle that we must always ensure that Israel lives in freedom and in security and peace." Powell echoed the Bush campaign theme that the United States could not impose a timetable on the Middle East for resolution of its conflicts. For his part, Bush himself named only one nation in his remarks announcing Powell's appointment, and it was Israel. Bush asserted, "We will defend America's interest in the Persian Gulf and advance peace in the Middle East, based, as any lasting peace must be, on a secure Israel." Condoleeza Rice, named as Bush's national security adviser at the same event, was given high marks by Jewish leaders for her work on Soviet Jewry issues when she served as a Russian specialist for the National Security Council during the administration of the first President Bush.

In contrast, the naming of outgoing Missouri senator John Ashcroft as attorney general quickly drew fire from the National Council of Jewish Women, which pledged to oppose his confirmation because of his history as a "champion for right-wing causes," in particular his positions on abortion, church-state issues, affirmative action, and gun control.

Terrorism

In March, a federal trial court upheld as constitutional a portion of the 1996 antiterrorism law that banned donations to foreign groups named by the State Department as supporters of terrorism, even where the contributions were designated for use for humanitarian purposes. Enactment of the law had been supported by a number of Jewish groups, and the court's opinion cited arguments made in a friend-of-the-court brief by the Anti-Defamation League.

Also in March, a $250-million lawsuit was filed in a Rhode Island federal court against the Palestinian Authority, Yasir Arafat, the PLO, and Hamas seeking to hold them responsible for the 1996 drive-by shooting of Yaron and Efrat Ungar, a Jewish American couple residing in the West Bank. Other defendants in the lawsuit were four Hamas members serving prison time in Israel following their convictions for the murders, and another member of the terrorist group who had evaded capture. Unlike the Flatow case, discussed below, this action was premised on a law enacted in 1985, after relatives of a man killed in the PLO's 1985 hijacking of the Achille Lauro faced difficulties in proceeding with their own suit. The 1985 law afforded federal courts jurisdiction over claims brought by American citizens injured by terrorist acts while in foreign countries. But, like the Flatow case, even if this suit were to result in a judgment, the collection of that judgment was likely to face obstacles because of U.S. foreign-policy concerns.

If the judicial odyssey of the Ungar family was just beginning, that of the Flatows seemed near its end. Earlier, Stephen Flatow had obtained a $247.5-million judgment against Iran under provisions of the 1996 antiterrorism law, based on Iran's complicity in an April 1995 bus bombing in Israel that killed Flatow's daughter, Alisa. The administration supported enactment of those provisions in 1996 but, after Flatow obtained the judgment, the government asserted that allowing enforcement of liens against Iran would endanger American diplomatic property abroad and prevent the U.S. from using blocked Iranian assets as a tool of foreign policy. Before 2000, the Clinton administration used presidential waiver authority to prevent Stephen Flatow or anyone else from going after Iranian assets in the United States. Others seeking to enforce or obtain judgments against state sponsors of terrorism were faced with similar barriers.

In October 1999, Senators Frank Lautenberg (D., N.J.) and Connie Mack (R., Fla.) introduced the Justice for Victims of Terrorism Act (S.1796) to assist American victims of terrorism in enforcing judgments obtained pursuant to the 1996 antiterrorism law. A companion bill was introduced by Rep. Bill McCollum (R., Fla.) in the House in April 2000. The Justice for Victims Act sought to address administration concerns by permitting the president to waive enforcement of a judgment pursuant to the 1996 antiterrorism act against frozen foreign diplomatic assets on an asset-by-asset basis, while enabling successful plaintiffs to satisfy judgments against assets of a nondiplomatic nature, such as rental property and commercial proceeds from sales of property. With passage of the House bill on a unanimous voice vote in July 2000, and little if any apparent opposition in the Senate, the bill seemed very close to landing on the president's desk. Nevertheless, the administration continued to resist the bill's enactment.

Finally, as the end of the session neared, the administration and sponsors of the bill negotiated a compromise and incorporated it into another bill moving toward passage. As signed into law in October 2000, the revised measure provided a procedure under which survivors of terrorist attacks who held judgments or brought actions filed on a set of specified dates would be allowed to collect, up to a set amount, against frozen assets on compensatory (but not punitive) judgments they obtained against state sponsors of terrorism under the 1996 law. Judgments for compensatory damages already obtained would not to be subject to blockage by the president, and any subsequent presidential waiver to prevent collection on the basis of national-security interests could only be invoked on a case-by-case basis. Among those eligible to proceed under the new law in addition to the Flatows were the families of Matthew Eisenfeld and Sara Duker, two students killed by a 1996 suicide bus bombing in Jerusalem. In July 2000, they obtained a $300 million judgment against Iran for that nation's role in the attack.

Steve Perles, attorney for the Flatows and for several other survivors of terrorism victims, hailed the legislation as a "historic precedent, since no administration has ever agreed to using blocked assets to satisfy judgments of federal courts." Stephen Flatow indicated that he would use money from the judgment to create an Alisa Flatow Memorial Fund that would provide scholarships for American students to study in Israel. The American Jewish Committee, which had supported enactment of legislation allowing victims of terrorism to collect judgments against terrorist states, applauded the law's enactment, while also noting that the law might have to be revisited in the 107th Congress "to assure that the benefits afforded to certain victims of terrorism, or their families, [were] available on an equitable basis," that is, to those survivors of victims of terrorism who did not fit within the defined class.

In March, President Clinton signed the Iran Nonproliferation Act (H.R.1833) into law. The measure required the president to impose sanctions on any nation that shared with Iran technology related to missiles or weapons of mass destruction, or else to report to Congress on his reasons for not doing so. The president had opposed an earlier version of the bill, passed by the House 419-0 in September 1999, because he said that it did not afford him adequate latitude in the conduct of foreign policy. The Senate (in February) and the House (in March) unanimously passed an amended version, clarifying that the sanctions were discretionary and not mandatory. This shift led President Clinton to pronounce, at the bill signing, that H.R.1833 was "less problematic" and in line with the administration's desire to combat Iran's efforts to acquire weapons of mass destruction. At a Senate Foreign Relations Committee hearing in October, the American Jewish Committee presented a report demonstrating that Russia was continuing to help Iran develop and acquire biological, chemical, and nuclear weapons.

Perhaps the most vexing issue for the Jewish community in the area of domestic responses to terrorism was presented by the Immigration and Naturalization Service's practice of using classified information in deportation proceedings directed at aliens accused of involvement in terrorist activities. Arab-American and Muslim-American groups, joined by the American Civil Liberties Union, mounted an intense campaign to end the practice. The House Judiciary Committee held hearings on, and ultimately conducted a committee mark-up of, the Secret Evidence Repeal Act (SERA), a bill intended to prohibit categorically the use of classified information in a deportation proceeding unless that information were made subject to discovery and examination on the same basis as any other evidence. Pointing up the sharp rift between Arab and Muslim Americans and the Jewish community, the American Jewish Committee and the Anti-Defamation League—both organizations with long histories of support for fair and generous immigration policies, as well as a commitment to due process and civil rights—opposed SERA. In hearings before the House Judiciary Committee that took place in May, AJC president Bruce Ramer called the bill "a hatchet taken to difficult issues that require a scalpel." While both AJC and ADL acknowledged that modification of INS practices might be in order, they argued that SERA's approach made no accommodation whatsoever to national security concerns.

Responding to the bill's critics at the House Judiciary Committee's mark-up of SERA in September, the sponsors proposed a substitute bill that, instead of completely barring the use of classified information in immigration proceedings, allowed authorities to utilize such classified information in a sharply limited set of circumstances. The new version was adopted 26-2 in committee, and then a voice vote moved it to the House floor. A bill similar to the House substitute was introduced in the Senate later in September. While AJC and ADL questioned whether even the revised bill appropriately balanced national security and due process concerns, the Religious Action Center of Reform Judaism pronounced itself satisfied with it, and endorsed the new version of SERA. An amendment proposed while the full House was considering an appropriations measure in August allowed a majority of House members to cast votes that symbolically expressed concern about the way INS was handling these cases, but SERA itself did not come up for a vote on final passage in 2000.

Much of the momentum for SERA was generated by its advocates' success in drawing attention to cases of individuals—virtually all of them Arab or Muslim Americans—held in detention for extended periods of time on the basis of classified information. While deportation proceedings plodded along, in two cases decided late in 1999, detainees were ordered released when courts found due process violations in the INS's reliance on classified information. As 2000 drew to a close, developments in the case of Mazen Al-Najjar, a major focus of the SERA campaign, provided further ammunition for the cause. Al-Najjar, a Palestinian who had not been formally charged with a crime but had been held in jail for three years while attempts were made to deport him for being in the country illegally, was ordered released by an immigration judge and an immigration appeals panel, only to have his release blocked by Attorney General Janet Reno on the grounds that he was a threat to national security. But, on December 15, 2000, Reno declined to further stay an immigration court's ruling that Al-Najjar be released from prison while the deportation case against him continued. The court refused to consider classified information that, the INS maintained, linked Al-Najjar to Middle East terrorist groups, and found that the other evidence before it afforded inadequate justification for continuing to hold him in detention.

Soviet Jewry, Refugees, and Immigration

In an expression of continuing concern about an apparent increase of anti-Semitism in Russia, more than 90 U.S. representatives wrote to the new Russian president, Vladimir Putin, in May, urging him "to make fighting anti-Semitism one of the priorities of your new administration."

In October, as Congress recessed for the election, a number of measures affecting immigrants were left hanging, to be resolved by an unusual postelection lame-duck session. These were supported by the Jewish community and other pro-immigrant groups and — in some cases — by the Clinton administration as well. Among these initiatives were a bill to restore eligibility for Medicaid, food stamps, and other public benefits to legal immigrants that had been stripped away by the welfare reform legislation of 1996, and the Latino and Immigrant Fairness Act (LIFA), intended to ease the process of obtaining legal immigrant status for certain refugees and undocumented immigrants present in the United States, including some Jews from the former Soviet Union. Weeks later, as the Congress wrapped up its business after the extended presidential election was resolved, most of the pending immigration initiatives were shelved. Only a drastically reduced version of LIFA, that applied a short-term bandage to some of the issues that bill would have addressed, was made part of the outgoing Congress's omnibus enactment.

There was, however, some good news. Congress provided funds enabling the Immigration and Naturalization Service to begin reduction of its backlog of 1.3 million immigrants awaiting naturalization, a matter of no small importance to the system of Jewish federations at a time when many government-assistance programs were available for citizens only. And, with Senator Frank Lautenberg (D., N.J.) about to retire, Congress extended for one more year the eponymous Lautenberg Amendment, a provision that expedited the extension of refugee status to

Jews, evangelical Christians, and others in the former Soviet Union. Senator Arlen Specter (R., Pa.), who in 2000, as in previous years, played a key role in getting the Lautenberg Amendment into the closing appropriations measures, was expected to carry chief responsibility for this initiative — newly dubbed the Lautenberg/Specter Amendment — in future years. Finally, right before it adjourned, Congress enacted the Syrian Asylee Adjustment Act, sponsored by Representative Rick Lazio (R., N.Y.) and Senator Charles Schumer (D., N.Y.), which enabled almost 2,400 Jews released from Syria to have their status adjusted to permanent residents by the INS.

Communal Priorities for Domestic Policy

The Washington Action Office of the United Jewish Communities observed that the failure of the 107th Congress—in particular, the Senate—to wrap up its appropriations work in a timely fashion (before the fiscal year expired on September 30) enabled President Clinton, a master negotiator even as a lame duck, to succeed "in stripping the bills of most of the riders that he deeply opposed and secur[ing] bipartisan agreement to ignore the budget caps and fund many of the White House's priority programs." As a result, "programs of greatest interest to the Federation system [administered by United Jewish Communities] avoided any serious funding set-backs . . . and programs that had been funded at last year's levels without any adjustment for inflation, typically received modest increases. . . ." However, this level of funding was made possible not only by the president's negotiating skills but also through the unexpectedly large budget surplus recorded for the completed fiscal year 2000, and the large surpluses projected for future years.

So-called "return to home" legislation emerged as a United Jewish Communities priority during 2000, in response to the exclusion of many Jewish homes for the elderly from the lists of approved providers maintained by long-term managed-care programs. This exclusion prevented many elderly Jews from returning, after hospitalization, to nursing homes that complied with religious dietary restrictions and Sabbath and holiday observances. In a successful conclusion to the campaign, "return to home" provisions were included in the omnibus bill with which Congress concluded its work for the year. Among other matters affecting the Jewish elderly, Congress reauthorized the Older Americans Act, a bill that provided support for such community-based services for the elderly as kosher meals-on-wheels and adult day care, and approved new legislation promoting housing for the low-income elderly.

Foreign Aid and U.S.-Israel Relations

U.S. aid to Israel appeared threatened as American concerns over a planned Israeli sale to China of the Phalcon airborne early-warning system began to metastasize into a full-fledged confrontation between two allies. Israel, for its part, argued that the deal fulfilled a long-standing contract that the American government had known about for years. In April, Rep. Sonny Callahan (R., Ala.), chairman of the crucial House Appropriations Subcommittee on Foreign Operations, threatened to cut $250 million from Israel's aid package, the amount of the contemplated sale, and prevent the customary early disbursal of U.S. aid. This was followed by hearings on the issue and two efforts in Congress to carry out these cuts. Though these efforts were eventually forestalled, they contributed to delays in moving the overall foreign-aid package, Israel included. While the Clinton administration sought to delink aid to Israel from the dispute, it also strongly pressed its concerns over the Phalcon sale. On July 12—with, in the phrase of an AIPAC analyst, an "unprecedented level of criticism aimed at Israel over the sale"and a looming Camp David summit that might result in a call for the U.S. to make substantial financial and military commitments—Israel announced its cancellation of the sale (see below, pp. 505–06). Rep. Callahan hailed Israel's action as important to "U.S. national security interests and, in fact, the national security interests of all our allies, such as Israel."

Whatever the tensions over the Phalcon sale, the voice of the U.S. Congress continued virtually always to be heard—as far as the Israel-Arab conflict was concerned—in support of the Jewish state. This remained true both early in the year, when Middle East peace negotiations appeared to move forward, and later, when the situation deteriorated sharply. Thus in February, while discussions between Israel and Syria were still under way, a bipartisan group of 37 members of Congress wrote to President Clinton calling on Syrian officials to distance themselves publicly from an article that had appeared in the Syrian press minimizing the Holocaust and terming Zionism worse than racism.

Similarly, just one day after the peace talks at Camp David collapsed in July, bipartisan legislation was introduced in the House of Representatives, followed shortly by a similar bill in the Senate, intended to block all U.S. aid to the Palestinian Authority in the event that the PA followed through with its announced intention to declare statehood on September 13, and also providing for other measures to forestall American or international recognition of such a Palestinian move. This congressional action was hailed by both AIPAC and the more dovish Israel Policy Forum, with IPF's Washington director, Tom Smerling, saying that it "couldn't hurt" for Arafat to be faced with these consequences were he to take a step that would be "anathema" to the peace process.

In stark contrast to the prevailing view elsewhere in the world, continuing American sentiment in support of Israel in its conflict with the Palestinians following Camp David was evident not only in Congress but also in the editorial pages of American newspapers. An ADL survey released in late October showed overwhelming support for Israel in editorials run by 67 newspapers between September 30 and October 15. Although the Clinton administration attempted to maintain its role as "honest broker" in the face of the spiraling violence, members of Congress were quick to make clear that they held Yasir Arafat and the Palestinians responsible. On October 12, 94 members of the Senate sent a letter to President Clinton expressing solidarity with Israel and saying that Arafat was engaged in a "deliberate campaign of violence." In September, the House of Representatives overwhelmingly passed the bill imposing substantial penalties on the Palestinian Authority should a Palestinian state be unilaterally declared, a far tougher measure than the resolutions passed by Congress on this subject the year before. In October, Representatives Benjamin Gilman (R., N.Y.) and Sam Gejdenson (D., Conn.), chairman and ranking member on the House International Relations Committee, respectively, introduced a resolution condemning Arafat for his role in promoting the violence, and the House passed it before month's end by 365-30. In mid-October the American Jewish Congress and the Zionist Organization of America formed an unusual alliance, both urging strong consideration for pulling some $100 million in aid to the Palestinians included in the pending foreign-operations appropriations bill.

On October 25, following delays unrelated to aid to Israel, Congress passed its $14.9-billion foreign-operations bill for fiscal year 2001. The vote was 307-101 in the House and 65-27 in the Senate. The package included $3 billion in aid for Israel — including $1.98 billion in military aid and $840 million in economic assistance — as well as nearly $2 billion in aid for Egypt, $225 million for Jordan, and some $100 million for the Palestinians. In accordance with an understanding reached earlier with Israel to phase out economic assistance by 2009, the package reflected a reduction of economic aid by $120 million from the previous year and an increase of $60 million in military aid. Although the level of aid to the Palestinians was not reduced pending concrete steps by the Palestinian leadership to halt the violence, Congress's passage of the foreign-aid package was seen by AIPAC and others as an expression of continuing U.S. support for Israel in the face of the ongoing violence initiated by the Palestinians after Camp David. Congressional support for Israel was underlined by the House's almost simultaneous passage, by a vote of 365-50, of the resolution that condemned the Palestinian leadership for its role in encouraging violence and urged that steps be taken to curb the uprising and end incitement against Israel.

Even before the 2001 aid package was finalized, there were reports that Israel was seeking, and that the administration would request, additional military aid, as well as funds to help defray the costs of withdrawing from Lebanon. But it was not until mid-November, with Congress still adjourned awaiting the results of the presidential election, that the administration requested a supplemental appropriation of $450 million for those purposes. The administration also sought an additional $225 million in military funds for Egypt and $75 million in military and economic aid for Jordan. The supplemental request made no additional provision, however, for the Palestinians.

Coming as it did during a volatile period in the Middle East — not to mention a contentious time in the United States when the presidential election had not yet been resolved—what might otherwise have been treated as a routine supplemental request seemed destined for uncertain treatment. Indeed, Rep. Sonny Callahan (R., Ala.), chairman of the House Appropriations Subcommittee on Foreign Operations, evinced skepticism when Congress returned for its lame-duck session, and no action was taken before Congress concluded its business for the year.

Jonathan Pollard

As the year neared its end, to be followed soon by the completion of President Clinton's term, advocates of clemency for convicted spy Jonathan Pollard accelerated their efforts, believing that the Christmas season, with its tradition of grants of pardon by the chief executive, provided the best opportunity for what would clearly be a controversial action. Starting in November with communications from B'nai B'rith International and a number of members of Congress, dozens of elected officials and Jewish organizational representatives weighed in for Pollard. First Lady Hillary Rodham Clinton, just elected to the Senate—who had not endorsed clemency for Pollard during her run for office—acknowledged that there were legitimate questions about the way that Pollard's case had been handled.

In the end, however, the White House announced that Pollard would not receive a Christmas pardon. Presidential press secretary Jake Siewert noted, however, that review of Pollard's plea for clemency had not been completed and that additional actions might be taken through the end of Clinton's term. In the meantime, Pollard's attorneys continued to argue in court that his life sentence should be dismissed on the grounds that he had not had adequate legal representation and that the government had failed to adhere to the terms of Pollard's plea agreement.

ANTI-SEMITISM AND EXTREMISM

Assessing Anti-Semitism

In April, the Anti-Defamation League issued its annual audit of anti-Semitic incidents, which indicated that 1,547 such incidents had been reported to the ADL during 1999, a 4-percent decrease from 1998. This decline maintained a general downward trend (with a small upturn in 1998) over the past five years. The reported anti-Semitic incidents, not all of them sufficiently serious to be considered crimes, consisted of 868 acts of harassment (intimidation, threats, assaults) and 679 of vandalism (property damage, as well as arson and cemetery desecrations). A report issued by California's attorney general in late July, asserting that hate crimes had increased by 12 percent in the state in 1999 as compared to the prior year, painted a grimmer picture. Of 1,962 reported hate crimes, some 17 percent were said to have been based on religion, of which anti-Semitic offenses were far and away the most common. But state authorities cautioned that the increase might be due to a higher rate of reporting.

In October, the FBI released its national hate-crime statistics report for 1999. Based on information collected pursuant to the 1990 Hate Crime Statistics Act, the report documented 7,876 hate crimes registered by 12,122 law-enforcement agencies across the country. In 1998, the FBI had reported 7,755 hate crimes from 10,461 agencies. While the FBI figures indicated a slight increase not only in the number of all incidents but also in the number of reported religion-based crimes over 1998, it was again difficult to draw broad conclusions, given the increase in the number of reporting agencies. Nevertheless, with nearly 80 percent of religion-based crimes being perpetrated against Jews and Jewish institutions, the Anti-Defamation League, calling the report "a disturbing snapshot of hate in America," noted that "this high level of violence and vandalism directed against Jews is another reminder that violent anti-Semitism remains a significant problem in America."

Acts of Violence

In February, U.S. prosecutors indicated that they would seek the death penalty against Buford Furrow, Jr., the white supremacist accused of murdering a Filipino-American mailman in August 1999 shortly after Furrow wounded five people at a Jewish community center in Los Angeles. When he surrendered to FBI agents one day after the shootings, Furrow reportedly told them that he wanted to send "a wake-up call to America to kill Jews." Differing views were heard in the Jewish community about the prosecution's decision to go for the death penalty. Jeff Rouss, executive director of the Jewish Community Centers of Los Angeles, pronounced capital punishment to be an appropriate penalty for a "man who killed an innocent individual who was a public servant. He terrorized children and hurt them at day care. His was an act of terrorism and it was an act of murder." But Stephen Rohde, an anti-death-penalty activist and a member of the board of the Progressive Jewish Alliance, asserted that his across-the-board opposition to capital punishment was as applicable to this case as to any other. He said that the state should not "model its conduct after the worst moment of a person's life, namely the moment that a person commits murder." Although the trial was originally set for 2000, in November the trial court accepted an agreement between attorneys for the prosecution and the defense attorneys that cited the complexity of the case as the reason for putting the trial over to April 2001.

The Jewish community in Pittsburgh and throughout the country was shocked by a shooting spree in late April in a Pittsburgh suburb that resulted in five deaths, including one Jewish woman. This followed by just weeks the alleged killing of three whites by a black man in another Pittsburgh suburb. Beside the

Jewish woman, also killed in the April shootings were three immigrants—two men of Pacific Asian origin and an Indian man—and an African American man. One Richard Scott Baumhammers was arrested and charged in the rampage, and he was charged as well with shooting through the windows of two synagogues and spray-painting anti-Semitic graffiti inside one of them. In searching Baumhammers's home, police found evidence to support hate-crimes charges, including anti-immigrant and far-right literature and links to "white rights" groups on a Web site that Baumhammers had created for his own "party." But it was soon discovered that Baumhammers had a history of mental disorder, and authorities had to confront the possibility that the accused might never stand trial. Indeed, in May a Pennsylvania judge found Richard Scott Baumhammers incompetent to stand trial and ordered him transferred to a state hospital for treatment and further evaluation.

In early December, five skinheads aged 19–26 received sentences in federal court of up-to-15 years in prison for their role in attempting to firebomb a synagogue in Reno, Nevada, more than a year earlier, on November 30, 1999. This followed a plea bargain in which one of the defendants admitted throwing a Molotov cocktail through the synagogue window and the federal prosecutor provided evidence tying the defendants' actions to their racist and anti-Semitic beliefs. An assistant U.S. attorney said that the sentence would send "a very strong message that this kind of hatred is not going to be tolerated, at least not in this community."

Also in December, more than six years after a machine-gun attack by an Arab American on a van full of yeshivah students that resulted in the death of one student, Ari Halberstam, and the wounding of another, Nachum Sosonkin, the U.S. Department of Justice announced that it had classified the shooting incident as an act of terrorism. Jewish groups, a number of which had pressed for this determination, hailed the department's action. One month earlier, the American Jewish Committee had issued a report calling for just such a reassessment, in part because of the context provided by the "marked increase in [recent weeks in] attacks against Jewish institutions as well as individuals as a result of tensions in the Middle East" that "appear to be inspired by recent fatwas—Islamic religious rulings—calling for holy war, or jihad, against Jews by the leaders of Islamic extremist movements."

Indeed, in the wake of the escalation of tension between Israel and the Arab world after the breakdown of the Camp David talks in July and the Palestinian attacks against Israelis that began in late September, many Jewish communities around the world faced attacks on their persons and property toward the end of 2000. American Jewish communities were no exception. In New York City, with its large Jewish population, there were at least ten attacks against Jews in Brooklyn reported in one week during the High Holy Days season—although it was by no means clear, as Jewish leaders were quick to say, that all these incidents were hate crimes. Nevertheless, concerns were heightened by reports of one case in which a 50-year-old Orthodox man was stabbed as he left services on Rosh Hashanah by a man believed to be a Palestinian American.

Incidents took place around or during the High Holy Days elsewhere in the country as well. An arson fire at Temple Ohev Sholom in Harrisburg, Pennsylvania, on Yom Kippur morning destroyed facilities used for Hebrew school classes as well as other portions of the premises. That same morning, congregants at Congregation Emanu-El–B'nei Jeshurun of Milwaukee arrived for services to find a burned Israeli flag on the steps of their synagogue—one of a number of flag-burning incidents during that season. Also during the holiday period, a bomb threat was called in to the Arizona State University Hillel.

Police cautioned local communities not to jump to the conclusion that any given act of violence was necessarily linked to events in the Middle East. But it was hard for many to avoid the suspicion that this was the case, and the assumption seemed borne out as investigations led to arrests in particular incidents. Thus, in addition to the Brooklyn incident described above, hate-crimes charges were filed against three Arab Americans in the October 8 vandalism of a synagogue in the Bronx, New York. On the night of October 12 there were three separate attacks on identifiably Jewish people in the Chicago neighborhood of West Rogers Park (all, happily, without injury to the victims), and three Palestinian teenagers were arrested in connection with two of the attacks. Based in part on statements made during one of the attacks, this matter, too, was treated as a hate crime. The very next night, Friday, October 13, a fire later labeled as arson caused substantial damage to Temple Beth El in Syracuse, New York, although the sanctuary and the chapel were not damaged.

Holocaust Denial, Hate Speech, and Defamation of Israel

The year began with the opening of an FBI investigation into the receipt of hate mail at 17 of the American Jewish Committee's 32 U.S. offices. Postmarked in Fayetteville, North Carolina, the letters denied the Holocaust had ever happened and added, "if there was [a Holocaust], Hitler didn't do a very good job." They also took a threatening tone, asserting, "We want to be ready to take this war to the next level on you kikes." Kenneth Stern, AJC's program specialist on anti-Semitism and extremism, noted that while AJC had received its share of "crazy mail" over the years, he could recall no other instance of "the same letter being sent to the majority of our offices."

Early 2000 also saw the Jewish community dealing with the circulation of a 19th-century anti-Semitic forgery purporting to demonstrate an international Jewish conspiracy to rule the world. Responding to complaints from the Anti-Defamation League, which was itself responding to what the ADL termed "an e-mail frenzy" of complaints, on-line booksellers Amazon and Barnes and Noble agreed to post disclaimers when offering the *Protocols of the Elders of Zion* for sale, as well as an ADL "rebuttal" identifying the publication as "plainly and simply a plagiarized forgery [that] . . . has been a major weapon in the arsenals of anti-Semites around the world." While ADL national director Abraham Foxman defended the disclaimer and the explanatory posting as simply providing appropriate information to potential customers, the Electronic Frontier Foundation, a civil-liberties organization, warned of "the beginning of a slippery slope" toward infringements on free speech. The American Jewish Committee, charting a different strategy than the ADL, issued a statement urging booksellers not to sell the *Protocols* at all. This case, however, was far from the only challenge posed by the presence of hate speech on the Internet. Earlier in 2000, Yahoo! announced that it would no longer host racist on-line clubs, and eBay indicated that it would act to bar the sale of hate materials on its Web site.

Another form of hate speech, Holocaust denial, also demanded substantial attention from the Jewish community. In November, Emory University, with assistance from the American Jewish Committee, established a Web site to combat Holocaust denial, www.holocaustdenialontrial.org, relying in large part on the research that had been conducted in preparing Emory professor Deborah Lipstadt's successful defense against the libel suit brought by Holocaust denier David Irving (see below, p. 310).

As Israel-Palestinian peace talks collapsed and their conflict gave rise to a new cycle of violence toward the end of the year, Jewish officials found themselves responding to what they viewed as biased presentations of events in the Middle East. In one instance, Jewish leaders responded with outrage when the December edition of the *ABA Journal,* a magazine published by the American Bar Association, ran a cover story asserting that international law was on the side of Palestinian refugees and their descendents who claimed a "right of return" to villages within Israel's pre-1967 borders. In a letter to the *Journal*—one of many similar letters that the periodical received—American Jewish Committee president Bruce Ramer protested that the article's "appearance at a time of Palestinian violence against Israelis meshes disturbingly with an aggressive campaign against the very legitimacy of the state of Israel," and argued that it was "a scandal that the *ABA Journal* ha[d] lent support to these efforts."

The intensification of the conflict in the Middle East made cyberspace a new front in Israel-Palestinian hostilities, as Jewish groups were compelled to adopt security measures to protect their Web sites and other computer facilities from attack. On November 1, Pakistani hackers—ostensibly in protest of alleged "atrocities in Palestine by the barbarian Israeli soldiers"—broke into the Web site of the American Israel Public Affairs Committee (AIPAC) and accessed databases containing supporters' e-mail addresses and credit card information. The FBI was immediately brought in to investigate the matter. Earlier, Israeli government Web sites had also been compromised, resulting in disruptions of service and crashes of entire systems.

On April 28, a Denver jury handed down a $10.5-million verdict against the Anti-Defamation League, finding that the venerable Jewish defense organization's

Mountain States chapter had violated the Federal Wiretap Act, and had invaded the privacy of and defamed a Colorado couple that it had publicly accused of anti-Semitism. Pronouncing itself "shocked and dismayed by the jury's decision," the ADL indicated that it would appeal what it believed to be a mistaken ruling, and that it would, in any event, "keep on representing Jews who feel threatened or harassed."

Discrimination

The CIA continued to be faced with allegations that observant Jews were subject to particular scrutiny as potential spies because of their religion. Adam Ciralsky, a former employee of the CIA, appeared on the CBS news program "60 Minutes" in February to press his claim that he had been fired from the agency because he was an observant Jew (see AJYB 2000, p. 168). The CIA, for its part, asserted that anti-Semitism had no place in the agency, and a CIA memo indicated that Ciralsky had failed two lie-detector tests when asked whether he had made U.S. secrets available to Israel. Following the broadcast, David Zwiebel, executive vice president for government and public affairs of Agudath Israel of America, wrote to CIA director George Tenet calling on the CIA to disassociate itself from charges made on the show by an unidentified CIA official that Israel had established a program of recruiting religious American Jews to spy on the United States. Zwiebel maintained that the remarks fostered the "canard of 'dual loyalty' and stereotyped Jews as the untrustworthy outsider."

Legislative Activity

Enactment of the Hate Crimes Prevention Act (HCPA) remained a priority of the Jewish community throughout 2000. Aimed at strengthening a law enacted in the late 1960s, it would facilitate the prosecution of hate crimes committed on the basis of race, color, religion, or national origin, and expand federal jurisdiction so as to include crimes motivated by a victim's sexual orientation, gender, or disability. Advocates argued that the measure would be utilized only as a safety net, when state and local law-enforcement agencies were unwilling or unable to investigate and prosecute hate crimes or when they sought federal assistance.

Although the Senate, spurred by a series of brutal hate crimes, passed the bill in July 1999 as part of an appropriations bill, Congress closed out its 1999 session without enacting the measure. Throughout 2000, President Clinton, supported by a broad civil-rights coalition that included many Jewish groups, reiterated on many occasions — beginning with his State of the Union address on January 27 — the necessity for the HCPA, and it also had strong bipartisan support in both houses of Congress. In July, the coalition announced the creation of a Web site, www.unitedagainsthate.org, to help press its campaign.

Supporters of the HCPA counted several victories during the year, but, in the end, fell short. On June 20, the Senate passed a revised version of the hate-crimes proposal by a bipartisan majority of 57-42 as an amendment to the Department of Defense authorization bill. Although a similar provision was not included in the House version of that bill, the House in September indicated its support for retaining the measure by approving it by a large bipartisan margin, 232-192, on a nonbinding procedural vote. But with the majority Republican leadership in both houses still resisting the measure, House and Senate conferees removed the hate-crimes provisions from the final conference report. As Congress went into recess before the election in anticipation of a rare, postelection lame-duck session, it was anticipated that the election returns would do much to clarify the likely disposition of HCPA.

Election Day made it clear that both the House and the Senate would still be controlled by the Republicans, but left unresolved the crucial question of who would occupy the White House. After delaying resumption of business for several weeks as the Gore-Bush contest played out, the leadership finally decided that Congress would reconvene on December 5. By this point even one of the bill's chief point persons, Anti-Defamation League Washington counsel Michael Lieberman, conceded to the Jewish Telegraphic Agency that inclusion of the measure in the final omnibus appropriations measure was "an uphill battle." And so it was. The final package, enacted by Congress after the results of the election were confirmed on December 12, did not include the HCPA, leaving the measure with an uncertain future in the 107th Congress.

It was unclear, however, whether a federal hate-crimes law, even if ultimately enacted, would survive constitutional challenge. In May, the U.S. Supreme Court struck down as unconstitutional provisions of the 1994 Violence Against Women Act (VAWA) allowing victims of sexual violence to sue their attackers in federal court. The decision found that the crimes did not have the impact on business that would have justified Congress in relying on its authority to regulate interstate commerce as a basis for the law. Although some advocates of the hate-crimes law thought it was distinguishable from VAWA, there was little doubt that the decision would provide the basis for a challenge. Another Supreme Court decision, handed down in June, ruled that any new hate-crimes law would have to require a jury, and not a judge, to determine whether the alleged "hate" element justifying the increased penalty was present in a particular crime. The HCPA, which already assigned this role to a jury, was unlikely to be affected.

In the wake of the Supreme Court's VAWA decision, a United States federal appeals court sitting in New York directed parties, in a case of great interest to the Jewish community, to brief the question of whether a 1968 federal law providing criminal penalties for certain civil rights violations was constitutional. Hanging in the balance was the viability of the convictions under that law of Lemrick Nelson, Jr., and Nelson Price in the killing of Jewish scholar Yankel Rosenbaum in the course of the 1991 Crown Heights riots. An array of Jewish groups, headed by the American Jewish Congress, joined with the NAACP in filing a friend-of-the-court brief arguing that the law in question should be upheld.

There was at least one piece of good news in 2000 for proponents of hate-crimes legislation. Governor George Pataki of New York signed such a law for his state in July, some ten years after the New York State Assembly first passed an earlier version of the bill.

INTERGROUP RELATIONS

African Americans

The virulently anti-Semitic Nation of Islam received a seeming accolade from an unexpected source in late January. On a Sunday morning news program, Republican presidential candidate George W. Bush, discussing religious groups that would be eligible to participate in the "charitable choice" initiative that he was supporting (see below, p. 186), described the Nation of Islam as "based upon some universal principles," including "love your neighbor like you'd like to be loved yourself." Ira Forman, executive director of the National Jewish Democratic Council, retorted, "If the principles that he's speaking about are hatred, anti-Semitism and fear and loathing of others, then he's right. But if he means anything else, he clearly does not understand the first thing about the Nation of Islam." A Bush spokesperson declined specifically to address the Texas governor's views of the organization, but asserted that his plan to fund faith-based programs was "to help people in need, not for the purpose of supporting any religion," and that "there is no place for racism or anti-Semitism anywhere" in the program.

During 2000, Louis Farrakhan, head of the Nation of Islam, continued the effort begun the previous year to "reach out" to the Jewish community by building a relationship with the extreme, anti-Zionist Neturei Karta sect. A Neturei Karta representative spoke to 20,000 members of the nation at a late-February Nation of Islam meeting in Chicago, and, at a press conference following the meeting, representatives of the two organizations joined together in praising each other's communities and attacking the State of Israel. Michael Kotzin, executive vice president of the Jewish Federation/Jewish United Fund of Metropolitan Chicago, commented, "what Farrakhan really seeks is the appearance of reconciliation [with the Jewish community] but not the real thing. In any event, he's not going to get very far so long as he continues to promote . . . anti-Zionist positions and fails to revoke his own long-standing attacks on the Jewish people as the enemies of black Americans."

There were far more positive aspects of black-Jewish relations to be found in 2000. The Project People Foundation, an African American organization dedicated to interfaith projects, continued its work with the North American Conference on Ethiopian Jewry in distributing black-skinned dolls to Ethiopian Jewish children in Israel. In March, Orthodox, Conservative, and Reform rabbis joined with 150 other religious leaders at a White House meeting that President Clinton convened as part of his "initiative on race." The group formally labeled racism a sin and pledged to work together toward racial reconciliation. In a follow-up to that meeting, a coalition of faith-based organizations—including a number of Jewish denominational and nondenominational bodies—signed on to a statement spearheaded by the National Conference for Community and Justice (formerly the National Conference of Christians and Jews) declaring racism "an evil that must be eradicated," and accompanied by guidelines for interfaith forums on racial justice and reconciliation.

The selection of Senator Joseph I. Lieberman as Al Gore's running mate presented the opportunity for some reflection on black-Jewish relations at the turn of the 21st century. After a brief flurry of concern, quickly mollified, about Lieberman's position on affirmative action, the mainstream civil rights leadership was quick to hail the selection as a breaking of barriers on behalf of all minorities. In response to a query from the Jewish Telegraphic Agency (August 23), NAACP board chairman Julian Bond observed that American Jews had historically been more supportive of civil rights "than other non-minority Americans"— although many American Jews might well have been puzzled at the reference to their community as "non-minority." Julius Lester, University of Massachusetts professor of Judaic and Near Eastern Studies and an African American covert to Judaism, told the JTA that "tension between blacks and Jews is at its lowest in quite some time." Lester pointed to the speed with which the NAACP had moved to censure and then fire the organization's Dallas chapter head for anti-Semitic remarks he made about Lieberman's nomination.

Lester's positive view of the state of black-Jewish relations was shared by Rabbi Marc Schneier, president of the Foundation for Ethnic Understanding, whose organization had found evidence in a 1998 poll of growing cooperation between the two groups. But the JTA cited, as well, the contrary findings of an ADL survey, also done in 1998, which concluded that blacks were three times more likely to hold anti-Semitic views than whites. And if nobody was surprised that Nation of Islam head Louis Farrakhan would join with some elements of the extreme right in making racist comments when Lieberman's selection was announced, it was disturbing to many that, soon after the announcement, the *Amsterdam News,* New York City's major black newspaper, editorialized that Gore had chosen Lieberman because, "It's the money, stupid," and that "Jews from all over the world . . . will be sending bundles of money" to the Democrats. The paper went on, "If this scenario is the correct one—and we believe it is—America is being sold to the highest bidder." Jewish organizations were quick to issue statements condemning Wilbert Tatum, the paper's chairman of the board and author of the piece, as an anti-Semite.

In September, the American Jewish Committee announced that it was ending its financial support for *CommonQuest,* a magazine on black-Jewish relations that it had published for five years in partnership with Howard University. This effectively put an end to the magazine. AJC indicated that it would be looking for other ways to address black-Jewish issues.

Asian Americans

The American Jewish Committee, which had a long history of support for American reparations to Japanese Americans who had been interned during World War II, endorsed the Clinton administration's proposal, introduced in February, to include in its fiscal year 2001 budget a $4.8-million fund to preserve the internment camps. This action, the AJC said, would help keep alive the "lesson of a tragic story of intolerance and betrayal."

Arab Americans

The year would ultimately see only further strains between America's Jewish and Arab communities over events in the Middle East. But it began with something of a grace note when Arab American Institute president James Zogby indicated that he was "perfectly willing" to protest the placement of an anti-Semitic caricature next to a column of his that appeared in a late-1999 edition of the Palestinian Authority's official newspaper. The cartoon portrayed a short man with a hooked nose, skullcap, and Star of David, bearing the label, "The Disease of the Century."

As incidents of hate-based violence directed at Jews accelerated during the fall in the wake of the deteriorating situation in the Middle East (see above, pp. 172–73), New York City's Arab and Jewish community leaders came together at a meeting convened by Mayor Rudolph Giuliani and pledged to work in harmony to calm tensions. Michael Miller, executive vice president of the Jewish Community Relations Council of New York, commented, "Never before have we sat together to minimize the potential for illegal activity connected with the situation in the Middle East."

Arab-Jewish tensions found expression in the vote of Arab Americans in the 2000 elections. A number of Arab-American groups endorsed Governor Bush for president, and the Jewish Telegraphic Agency quoted some members of the Arab American Political Action Committee as saying that they were "concerned" because Joseph Lieberman, the Democratic candidate for vice president, was an Orthodox Jew. Although a slight majority of Arab-American voters were registered as Democrats, exit polls indicated that 45 percent voted for Bush and 38 percent for Gore, with a high 13-percent vote (compared to 2 percent nationally) for Green Party candidate Ralph Nader, himself of Lebanese descent. James Zogby attributed the voting pattern to a perceived tilt by the Clinton-Gore administration toward Israel; about 80 percent of Arab Americans dissatisfied with the administration's Middle East policies voted for Bush or Nader. Concern about the "positions" of Gore's Orthodox Jewish running-mate were cited by 69 percent of those polled, although there was no indication of which of Lieberman's positions—as distinct from those of Gore himself—were responsible for this concern.

Whatever the reasons for its voting pattern, the Arab-American community was becoming increasingly important on the political scene. Both major-party candidates met with community leaders, and the level of financial contributions to candidates and volunteer campaign activity showed a marked increase over previous elections. In the final month of the campaign, the Gore-Lieberman operation brought James Zogby on board as an adviser on ethnic affairs, an action that was protested by the Zionist Organization of America and the Republican Jewish Coalition. The latter asserted that Zogby was "the lead American spokesman for the worst forms of Middle East Arab propaganda." But the Israel Policy Forum defended him as "courageously outspoken in his support for the peace process."

Catholics

On March 7, the Vatican issued a document titled *Memory and Reconciliation: The Church and the Errors of the Past,* that set forth several major areas in which the Roman Catholic Church had failed, including the forced conversion and other mistreatment of Jews during the Inquisition. It did not, however, apologize for the Church's actions and omissions during World War II, even as the document acknowledged that many Christians had not done enough to help Jews during the Holocaust. The tone of this document was reinforced by the pope's remarks on Sunday, March 12, less than one week later, in which he broadly acknowledged, and apologized for, sins committed by the Church against Jews through the ages, while making no specific mention of the Holocaust (see below, pp. 360–61). Rabbi A. James Rudin, interreligious-affairs director of the American Jewish Committee, reflected the ambivalence of many in the Jewish community when he hailed these statements as "unprecedented" even as he also noted that "we expected more than what came. . . ." Anti-Defamation League national director Abraham Foxman expressed satisfaction that these new pronouncements, unlike a 1998 Vatican document that drew strong criticism from the Jewish community, avoided defending the policies of Pope Pius XII during World War II.

A similar inclination to find the positive rather than accentuate the negative also emerged from the responses of many Jewish leaders to the pope's epoch-making trip to Israel. While visiting the Yad Vashem Holocaust memorial on March 23, the pope stated that he was "deeply saddened by the hatred, acts of persecution and displays of anti-Semitism directed against the Jews by Christians at any time and in any place." Rabbi Eric Yoffie, president of the Union of American Hebrew Congregations, asserted that it "was more important to stress what was included"—acknowledgment of the Church's history of anti-Semitism— than the specifics that the pontiff omitted. Seymour Reich, though, chairman of the International Jewish Committee on Interreligious Consultations (IJCIC), expressed disappointment that the pope did not use the occasion to "address the silence of the Church during the Holocaust."

Even fewer negative words could be heard after Pope John Paul II came to the

Western Wall to pray, and, in accordance with Jewish tradition, placed a note in the wall that sought God's forgiveness for Jewish suffering at the hands of Christians during "the course of history." As important as the visit, observed Rabbi David Rosen, director of the Anti-Defamation League's Israel office, was the precedent that had been set for succeeding popes who might not be as committed to reconciliation with the Jewish people. "He has set down solid foundations for a very healthy relationship between the Catholic Church and the Jewish people," said Rosen. "It is impossible today to have a serious position in the Catholic Church and to express an anti-Judaic opinion."

But the rest of the year was rife with other sources of tension between Jews and the Vatican. September 3 was the date set for the beatification—the last step before sainthood—of two popes, Pius IX and John XXIII. The latter was the mid-20th-century pontiff revered for building ecumenical bridges to the Jewish people. The former, in contrast, was infamous in the Jewish world for being the last pope to ghettoize the Jews of Rome and for ordering the 1858 kidnapping of Edgardo Mortara, a Jewish boy who had been baptized as a baby without his parents' knowledge, and who was never returned. IJCIC, in the name of the Anti-Defamation League, B'nai B'rith, the World Jewish Congress, the Israel Jewish Council on Interreligious Relations, and the Jewish denominational organizations, sent a letter of criticism to the Vatican in August, terming Pius IX "the pope who perpetuated centuries-old church contempt and hatred for Jews" and whose actions were an "assault on Judaism and parenthood."

The ink on the beatification was barely dry when, on September 5, the Vatican issued the document *Dominus Iesus,* which declared that followers of faiths other than Catholicism were "in a gravely deficient situation in comparison with those who, in the Church, have the fullness of the means of salvation." Many Jews wondered how the statement could be squared with the messages of repentance and outreach that Pope John Paul II had brought to Israel earlier in the year. In his weekly Sunday message delivered on October 1, the pope sought to reassure members of other faiths that the document was not intended to express "arrogance that shows contempt for other religions."

Perhaps the most sensitive area of tension between the Vatican and the Jewish community was the projected beatification of Pope Pius XII, notwithstanding questions that had been raised about his apparent passivity in the face of the destruction of European Jewry in the Holocaust. In October, a panel of six scholars—three Catholics and three Jews—established by the Vatican and IJCIC in 1999 to review already published Vatican documents on the Holocaust period, issued a report listing numerous open questions about Vatican policy and asking the Holy See to open its archives so that answers might be found. IJCIC chairman Seymour Reich noted, "The archives are being opened everywhere. The Swiss are accounting for gold, the Dutch are returning art that was confiscated from Jews who were sent to camps. It's a reckoning, a need for the world to understand what happened during this dreadful period of history."

In November, the National Conference of Catholic Bishops adopted a resolution on the Israel-Palestinian conflict that called for the creation of a Palestinian state, urged the Palestinians to accept Israel's right to exist within secure borders, and pressed the United States to persevere in its efforts to revive the peace process. The resolution elicited a reaction of "deep disappointment" from the American Jewish Committee for what the AJC saw as its one-sided approach to the accelerating pattern of violence between Israel and the Palestinians. The AJC statement pointedly noted that the resolution failed to call upon the Palestinians to "fully respect the religious liberties" of Jews, even though Jewish holy sites had been desecrated by Palestinians and some Muslim religious leaders were calling for "attacks on Jews worldwide."

Evangelical Christians

In November 1999, soon after the Southern Baptist Convention issued prayer guides targeted at converting Jews, Hindus, and Muslims (see AJYB 2000, p. 174), the convention announced a plan to bring 100,000 Christians to Chicago for a weekend of evangelizing in July, 2000. But the project was scaled back in February in the face of protests by local Jewish leaders. Moreover, Southern Baptist leaders assured the Jewish community that it was "the entire city of Chicago," not specific groups, that was being targeted. "In all honesty," said the Rev. Phil Miglioratti, a convention official, "we really don't have a Jewish strategy." Nevertheless, Jay Tcath, director of the Jewish Community Relations Council of Chicago, set up a task force to hold workshops and prepare pamphlets for Jewish educators and the public about the "arguments they [missionaries] cite, their tricks . . . in shaping the discussion down their path."

Notwithstanding Jewish mistrust of Southern Baptist missionary zeal, evangelical Christian support for Israel remained solid. As the conflict between Israel and the Palestinians intensified toward the end of the year, the International Fellowship of Christians and Jews, an organization dedicated to strengthening relations between Jews and evangelical Christians, demonstrated its solidarity with the Jewish state by presenting $3 million to the United Jewish Appeal for immigration, absorption, and welfare programs. The fellowship pledged to raise an additional $12 million for these purposes in 2001.

Jews and Christianity

Following decades of evolution in Christian attitudes toward Judaism—to a great extent the product of ongoing dialogue between Christian and Jewish communities—a document billed as the first statement of a Jewish view on Christianity was released in mid-September. It appeared under the title "Dabru Emet" (Hebrew for "speak the truth," from a phrase in the prophet Zechariah) as an advertisement in the *New York Times,* the *Baltimore Sun,* and other publications. Rabbi Michael Signer, professor of theology at the University of Notre

Dame and one of four chief drafters, said of the document that carried more than 150 Jewish signatories, "This is the first major statement by a group of Jewish scholars, congregational rabbis, and leaders of national organizations, which acknowledges the changes that have come about in Christian theology of Jews and the Jewish people." Rabbi David Novak of the University of Toronto, another of the drafters, stated: "Christians are not necessarily our enemies. . . . They can be very good friends to Jews and Judaism . . . not just out of good will, but out of Christian belief. That being the case, a Jewish response is called for."

But, while the statement drew a notable array of Conservative, Reform, and Reconstructionist leaders, as well as several Orthodox rabbis—who, in signing, departed from a general Orthodox disinclination to engage in interfaith theological discourse—there were several significant abstentions. Rabbi A. James Rudin, recently retired as director of interreligious affairs for the American Jewish Committee and now a consultant to the organization, was among those who declined to sign, in his case because of a section of the document stating that while "too many Christians participated in, or were sympathetic to Nazi atrocities against Jews . . . Nazism itself was not an inevitable outcome of Christianity." Rudin praised the overall statement as "a pioneering effort," but could not accept the omission of the "direct correlation between modern anti-Semitism and what I call the seedbed that created the poisonous weeds of anti-Semitism." Others objected to a reference to "Jesus Christ" in the document, and suggested that another term, such as "Jesus of Nazareth," would have been more appropriate in a Jewish document, since "Christ" means "Messiah."

CHURCH AND STATE

Church-State Separation

In late February, the Jewish Council for Public Affairs (JCPA), the Jewish umbrella organization dealing with public policy, adopted a "strict-separationist" resolution against any use of public funding to support religious schools. This move marked an about-face, since only two years earlier, in 1998, the JCPA had enunciated support for public funding of the so-called "three Ts"—transportation (school busing), technology (computers), and textbooks for parochial schools, to the extent allowed by the courts. David Gad-Harf, executive director of the Jewish Community Council of Metropolitan Detroit—the group that had led the campaign for the 1998 resolution now overruled—expressed disappointment, saying that funding bus transportation and other benefits was "not a real diversion of funds [to religious uses]." But others, such as Catherine Schwartz, associate director of the Jewish Federation of Greater Springfield, Mass., pointed out the difficulty in policing the use of funded items to ensure that they "would only be used for secular studies," and in any event, she argued, funding these services would free up money for religious schools to use for other purposes, and "in effect, that's funding religious education."

On June 28, a few months after the JCPA retreated from condoning public funding of instructional materials at religious schools, the U.S. Supreme Court rendered a split decision that allowed the government to make computers available to religious schools. A plurality of four justices ruled that there was no constitutional problem even were it to be shown that the publicly financed computers were being diverted for religious instruction, so long as the state was acting to further a secular purpose. The three dissenting justices, in contrast, wanted to strike down the challenged program since there was no way the state could ensure that such a diversion was not taking place. The two swing justices reasoned that providing the computers in this case was not constitutionally problematic so long as there was no evidence that they were being diverted for religious instruction.

The decision was greeted with the divided response that had by now become customary in the Jewish community. The Orthodox bodies, such as the Union of Orthodox Jewish Congregations (OU) and Agudath Israel of America, considered the ruling as simply allowing parochial-school children to benefit from government aid on the same basis as those in public school, and therefore an appropriate application of the principle of government neutrality toward religion. Other Jewish groups, such as the Anti-Defamation League and the American Jewish Congress, criticized the decision as opening the door to the use of materials paid for with public funds for religious purposes. What was clear to all, whatever side they had taken in briefs filed with the Supreme Court, was that the crucial swing opinion signed by Justices Sandra Day O'Connor and Stephen Breyer provided no clear indication of whether the current Supreme Court would uphold the constitutionality of school vouchers.

In a decision that seemed to prime that issue for Supreme Court review, on December 11 the U.S. Court of Appeals for the Sixth Circuit ruled two-to-one that Cleveland's school-vouchers program violated the separation of church and state. Noting that almost all of the aid under the program went to religious schools— some 96 percent of the 3,700 students utilizing the vouchers (worth up to $2,500) attended parochial, mostly Catholic, schools—Judge Eric Clay's decision for the majority found that the initiative "has the primary effect of advancing religion, and . . . constitutes an endorsement of religious and sectarian education." Once again, the Jewish community divided along familiar lines, with the bulk of the communal organizations, such as the American Jewish Congress and the American Jewish Committee, hailing the result. Orthodox groups expressed disappointment. David Zwiebel, Agudath Israel of America's executive vice president for government and public affairs, said, "Those who are committed to do all in their power to preserve the public school monopoly and to prevent parents from having meaningful educational options will surely have reason to be pleased with the outcome of this case."

The traditional separationist response of groups representing the larger Jewish community notwithstanding, many observers claimed to see a changing attitude toward vouchers in the Jewish community, for two reasons. First, an increasing number of Conservative and Reform Jews were sending their children to Jewish day schools, something that had historically been an overwhelmingly Orthodox phenomenon. Second, growing concerns about the viability of the public-school system made American Jews more open to a vouchers option. Thus Garver Keller, a lobbyist for Ohio Jewish Communities, commented that while in the past "[t]here was a feeling it wasn't appropriate for public tax dollars to be spent to promote religion," more Jews had begun to feel that vouchers would "allow Jews to go to Jewish schools." No Jewish children or Jewish day schools participated in the Cleveland voucher program, but in 1999 some 77 of the 168 students at Yeshiva Elementary School in Milwaukee paid part of their tuition with vouchers issued by the state of Wisconsin.

Opponents of vouchers scored another victory earlier in the year when, in March, a Florida state judge held a Florida vouchers program that allowed children in failing public schools to attend private schools to be in violation of the state constitution. The court order did allow the 53 children then attending private schools under the program to complete the school year, but state officials were directed to take no further action to implement the law. But in October, a Florida appellate court reversed the lower court's decision, finding that the vouchers program did not violate the state constitution.

Even though the 2000 election preserved Republican control of Congress and (eventually) returned control of the White House to the GOP, there was no evident groundswell of support for vouchers even though Republicans were generally identified with the idea. Voters in California turned back a referendum initiative that would have instituted a sweeping program providing a $4,000 voucher to any student in kindergarten through 12th grade who attended a private school, with no means testing. And a more modest proposal presented for consideration to Michigan voters, which would have provided a $3,300 "opportunity scholarship" to enable students to leave failing public schools for private institutions, was also defeated.

The year's other major issue related to government funding of religious institutions was charitable choice. Two different bills signed into law by President Clinton, one in October and the other in December, applied charitable choice to programs operated under the Substance Abuse and Mental Health Services Administration (SAMHSA). These allowed faith-based groups to receive funds for their substance-abuse programs without church-state and antidiscrimination safeguards of the type that many Jewish organizations had long championed. While Republican support for charitable choice was no surprise, its presence in one of these bills grew out of negotiations between President Clinton and Speaker of the House Dennis Hastert (R., Ill.), indicating that if charitable choice was not enthusiastically received by the administration, it was, at least, a price Democrats were willing to pay to further legislation they otherwise desired.

Enactment of these charitable choice provisions took place against the background of the first lawsuits brought by opponents of the approach. In July, the American Jewish Congress and the Texas Civil Rights Project filed an action challenging the constitutionality of a jobs program funded by the state of Texas. The challengers argued that taxpayers' money had been used to proselytize and buy Bibles, and that the program was premised on convincing beneficiaries to "change from the inside out, rather than from the outside in, . . . through a relationship with Jesus Christ." The Texas Department of Human Services, however, asserted that funding was being provided only for social services.

President-elect Bush wasted no time after resolution of the election to begin working toward expansion of charitable choice, confirming his long-standing pledge to make this a priority of his administration. On December 20 Bush met with some 30 Christian, Jewish, and Muslim leaders whom he had invited to Austin to discuss plans for the creation of a White House office dedicated to "faith-based action." In choosing the Jewish participants, the president-elect, not surprisingly, invited individuals who were generally supportive of his initiative—Murray Friedman, the director of the American Jewish Committee's Philadelphia chapter, and Rabbi Daniel Lapin, president of the politically conservative Toward Tradition organization. Also at the meeting was the Jewish former mayor of Indianapolis, Stephen Goldsmith, a chief domestic adviser to Bush during his campaign and widely rumored to be the likely head of the new office, an appointment that Rabbi Lapin predicted would help allay fears that the office was part of an effort to "Christianize" America.

Friedman, for his part, reminded Bush at the meeting that many in the Jewish community (including Friedman's employer, the American Jewish Committee, which had views on charitable choice at odds with Friedman's own) were greatly concerned by the religious intrusion in the public arena represented by charitable choice. Despite this disclaimer, after the meeting Abraham Foxman, the national director of the Anti-Defamation League, who was not in attendance, asserted that the American Jewish community and its views had not been represented in Austin. Orthodox organizations, supportive of charitable choice, expressed confidence that there would be future opportunities to meet with the new president.

If church-state separationists found themselves in a holding action in the Supreme Court and Congress on funding issues, they were more successful in pressing for the maintenance of constitutional barriers against officially sanctioned prayer at public-school events—notwithstanding a nonbinding House of Representatives resolution early in the year in support of prayer at school sporting events. On June 20, the Supreme Court ruled six-to-three that a school district in Santa Fe, Texas, had to end the practice of allowing a student representative selected by a majority vote of the student body to read prayers over the school's public address system before football games. This practice, Justice John Paul Stevens said for the majority, "establishes an improper majoritarian election on religion, and unquestionably has the purpose and creates the perception of encouraging the delivery of prayer at a series of important school events." The decision was hailed by a broad range of Jewish organizations that had filed briefs in the case, with Leonard Cole, national chair of the Jewish Council for Public Affairs (JCPA) noting, "Whatever the intention of such religious exercises, the net effect is to make children of minority faiths or no religious faith at all feel marginalized." Although expressing concern that the principles enunciated in the Santa Fe decision might be extended to the point that schools become "religion-free zones," the OU—often on the opposite side of its sister Jewish organizations on church-state separation issues—filed no brief in this case and, after the decision was handed down, stated its satisfaction with the ruling.

The sharp negative reaction to the Supreme Court decision in the Santa Fe case reminded some veteran observers of the uproar that followed the school-prayer decisions of the 1960s. By August, communities in the South and West, especially Texas, began to organize "spontaneous" prayer to precede football games. A group calling itself No Pray, No Play offered to assist communities around the country in organizing to recite the Lord's Prayer before football games. A West Virginia radio station made plans to broadcast prayers during local games, and some 25,000 people gathered at a rally in Asheville, North Carolina, supporting recital of the prayers. Legal analysts representing Jewish communal organizations noted that prayer at sporting events would not run afoul of the principles enunciated in the Santa Fe case so long as there was no use of school facilities (such as a public address system) and no involvement of school officials. But legal issues aside, the Jewish groups saw the prayer movement as a community-relations problem. In the words of Mark Pelavin, associate director of the Religious Action Center of Reform Judaism, "it begins to divide communities along religious lines." As the football season began, however, the issue seemed to generate far less heat than had been feared. At one high-school football game in Texas on the first weekend of September, only about 200 people engaged in a "spontaneous" prayer recital.

As the Supreme Court returned for business on the first Monday of October, one of its first actions was—in light of its decision in the Texas football case—to send back for further consideration the action of a federal appellate court upholding as constitutional a Florida county practice of allowing public-school students to elect a classmate to deliver a prayer or some other message of his or her choosing at high-school graduation. This suggested to some observers that whatever the Supreme Court might ultimately do on vouchers and other funding issues, it seemed to be moving in a separationist direction on the question of prayer at public-school events.

There were a number of other church-state developments during the year. In July, a federal trial judge in New York struck down that state's decades-old kosher food laws as unconstitutional. Following earlier decisions rendered by courts in New Jersey (1993) and the city of Baltimore (1995) striking down similar laws, this ruling cast in doubt the viability of state and local ordinances intended to protect consumers from fraudulent labeling of food as kosher.

The issue of whether and under what circumstances the Ten Commandments might be displayed in public places continued to roil the courts. In May, a U.S. district court directed that the Ten Commandments be removed from Kentucky courtrooms and public-school classrooms, and, in December, the U.S. Court of Appeals for the Seventh Circuit similarly ruled that the display of the Ten Commandments in front of a government building in Elkhart, Indiana, was an unconstitutional government endorsement of a particular religious perspective.

"Free Exercise"

A case dealing directly with the limits of religious accommodation in the workplace was decided in favor of the employer when, in February, a Florida jury ruled that a drugstore chain was entitled to fire an Orthodox Jewish employee for refusing to sell condoms to customers because of his religious beliefs. The jury found that accommodation of the employee in this instance would unduly hurt customer service. That same month, a Cincinnati-area school district announced that it would cease its two-year-old practice of closing for the Jewish holidays of Rosh Hashanah and Yom Kippur, which had ostensibly been adopted to take into account teacher absences on those days. The district denied that its decision had anything to do with a threatened lawsuit by the American Civil Liberties Union, which argued that the old policy gave special privileges to one religion. In another development, Sears settled a case brought against it by the attorney general of New York State under that state's religious accommodation laws when Sears refused to hire an Orthodox Jew who would not work on Saturdays. In defending against the case, Sears had claimed that it could not accommodate the would-be employee's religious practice because Saturday was its busiest business day. Sears capitulated, however, when a review of the department-store chain's records by New York authorities found that the busiest day of the week was in fact Tuesday. In the settlement, Sears agreed that it would henceforth adjust its schedule to accommodate Sabbath observers.

The Jewish community and the U.S. Congress continued to wrestle with the fallout from a pair of Supreme Court decisions rendered in 1990 and 1997. The first weakened constitutional protections of the free exercise of religion, and the second struck down a 1993 federal law intended to restore those protections. That law, the Religious Freedom Restoration Act (RFRA), required government at all levels—federal, state, and local—to demonstrate a "compelling state interest" if it passed any law or regulation that substantially burdened an individual's free exercise of religion. In its 1997 decision, however, the high court voided this law on the grounds that it infringed on states' prerogatives, thus leaving in place the rule that the state can require individuals to violate their religious beliefs so long as there is a "reasonable" basis for the regulation in question.

Immediately following the Supreme Court's 1997 decision, the politically and religiously broad coalition that had come together in the early 1990s to push for passage of that law reconvened to draft and promote passage of new legislation that might survive the high court's scrutiny. The difficult drafting process stretched out over several months, finally resulting in the introduction, in 1998, of the Religious Liberty Protection Act (RLPA), a bill drawn more narrowly than RFRA so as to meet the constitutional concerns raised by the Supreme Court and still afford religious liberty some protection against government action.

RLPA was introduced in the House again early in 1999, and was passed in that body in July by 306-118. But the House debate on RLPA split along party lines, with Republicans generally supporting a bill without exceptions and most Democrats favoring a failed substitute, introduced by Representative Jerrold Nadler (D., N.Y.), that would have largely excluded state and local civil-rights laws from RLPA's purview. Representative Nadler, who had been an original sponsor of RLPA, proposed this substitute because of claims by various civil-rights and gay-rights groups that the religious freedoms enshrined in RLPA might be used to undermine antidiscrimination laws. All of the Jewish members of the House voted for the amendment, although they split on this last vote, with a majority voting "no" because the concerns about civil rights had not been resolved.

This division was reflected among Jewish groups too, as it was in the broad coalition of religious and civil-rights organizations that had, until the summer of 1999, been united in support of RLPA. As 2000 began, the National Council of Jewish Women, the Anti-Defamation League, and the Religious Action Center of Reform Judaism no longer supported RLPA's enactment as passed by the House, while the American Jewish Congress, B'nai B'rith, Agudath Israel, and the OU continued to work in support of the bill. The American Jewish Committee struck its own course, continuing to advocate for RLPA, but insisting upon the inclusion of an amendment clarifying the limited extent to which it could be asserted as a defense to a civil-rights claim.

The prospects for a Senate bill stalled when, responding to the concerns of the civil-rights community, Senate Democrats began to voice their own hesitation about the initiative. In the closing days of the 1999 session, Trent Lott (R., Miss.), the majority leader of the Senate, promised to bring the House bill up for a Senate floor vote, but Congress adjourned before this could take place. On February 22, 2000, Senator Orrin Hatch (R., Utah) introduced a revised version of RLPA (S.2081), but one that did not address the civil rights concerns. The Senate Republican leadership signaled its willingness to bypass the committee process and bring that new bill directly to the Senate floor, a prospect that would likely have brought on a cloture battle.

Rather than ignite a struggle that might do more harm than good for religious liberty, the contending forces agreed, instead, to craft a more limited vehicle, the Religious Land Use and Institutionalized Persons Act, a bill directed specifically at protecting houses of worship and other religious institutions from zoning and other land-use regulations that imposed unreasonable or discriminatory burdens. RLUIPA also provided a remedy for persons confined to state residential facilities—such as homes for the disabled and chronically ill, or prisons—who were denied the right to practice their faith. RLUIPA's more limited scope avoided the civil-rights concerns raised by RLPA.

Relying on a record of religious discrimination earlier established in congressional hearings on RLPA, RLUIPA moved through Congress with near-record speed. Introduced in the Senate as S.2869 on July 13, 2000, by Senators Edward Kennedy (D., Mass.) and Orrin Hatch (R., Utah), and with the support of the House leadership and Representatives Charles Canady (R., Fla.) and Jerrold Nadler (D., N.Y.), RLUIPA passed the Senate by unanimous consent on July 27. The Senate bill was then raced over to the House within the hour, where it also passed by unanimous consent. On September 22, in an Oval Office ceremony attended by representatives of religious and civil-rights groups that had so recently been in heated contention, President Clinton signed the bill into law.

A bill with wide support in the Jewish community, the Workplace Religious Freedom Act, which was intended to assure religiously observant employees reasonable accommodation of their religious practices, once again failed to become law. The major development in 2000 was the bill's introduction in the House of Representatives on April 11 by Representatives Jerrold Nadler (D., N.Y.) and Asa Hutchinson (R., Ark.), who were joined as sponsors by a bipartisan group of 11 other representatives. The bill was identical to one that had been introduced in the Senate the prior year by Senators John Kerry (D., Mass.) and Sam Brownback (R., Kan.).

Though WRFA did not move forward, Alan Reinach, president of the Seventh-day Adventist Church-State Council for the Pacific Union Conference of Seventh-day Adventists, took advantage of the Lieberman candidacy for vice president to make a poignant argument for the bill's enactment. In August, soon after announcement of Lieberman's selection, Reinach wrote of the Sabbath-observant senator:

> Joe's lucky. He has a boss who knew he wanted Sabbath off, and agreed to "hire" him anyway. Thousands of Americans are not so lucky. When they tell a prospective employer they can't work on the Sabbath, they don't get hired. Thousands more lose their jobs each year when schedules are changed to require them to work in conflict with their faith. . . . America rightly celebrates the breaking down of barriers, and the spirit of inclusiveness symbolized by Senator Lieberman's nomination. But this symbolic gesture needs to be supported with concrete action. Both parties need to act now to pass the WRFA and insure that Americans of all faiths will not be forced to choose between their religion and their job.

In July, the U.S. Department of Education held a two-day conference commemorating the U.S. Supreme Court's 1925 decision in *Pierce v. Society of the Sisters of Holy Names of Jesus and Mary,* which, striking down a Ku-Klux-Klaninspired Oregon law requiring attendance at public schools, upheld the right of parents to send their children to private schools. The American Jewish Committee, the only Jewish organization to have filed a friend-of-the-court brief in support of the Catholic school that brought the action, received a commendation for its role in that case. AJC's brief back then was written by the noted jurist Louis Marshall, one of the founders of the organization and its longtime president.

HOLOCAUST-RELATED MATTERS

Reparations

The drawn-out efforts of Holocaust victims and their heirs to collect on insurance policies issued prior to World War II registered a victory when, on November 16, Assicurazioni Generali—Italy's largest insurance company and one of the largest insurers of Jews in Eastern Europe in the years between the world wars—signed an agreement to pay $100 million in settlement of Holocaust-era claims. The agreement, which contemplated that the funds would first go to insurance claimants, with any remaining funds to be utilized for humanitarian assistance for survivors, was also signed by Lawrence Eagleburger, chairman of the International Commission for Holocaust Era Insurance Claims (ICHEIC), and various Jewish organizations involved in restitution issues. That same week the commission also announced that it had located 20,000 wartime insurance policies in German archives and that the information would be posted on a Web site.

ICHEIC, created in 1998 as a central address for dealing with the billions of dollars in outstanding claims against Holocaust-era insurers, included representatives of five major European insurers, the U.S. National Association of Insurance Commissioners, European officials responsible for insurance regulation, an Israeli official, and the World Jewish Congress (WJC). Elan Steinberg, executive director of the WJC, indicated that the Generali agreement might bring pressure on the other participating European insurers to complete their own negotiations on a final settlement. But even so, there remained German and Austrian insurance companies that had refused to join ICHEIC or follow its guidelines, and claims against them were expected to remain outstanding.

Beginning in May, when the *New York Times* published a report purportedly based on internal ICHEIC documents, concern rose about the fact that some three out of every four claims filed with ICHEIC-member insurance companies were being rejected, generally on the grounds of insufficient proof or suspected postwar settlement. On September 29, 46 members of Congress, headed by Rep. Henry Waxman (D., Cal.), wrote to ICHEIC chairman Eagleburger about these reports. Eagleburger wrote back in October, assuring the legislators that these responses were not the "last word on these claims" and that there would soon be a process in place to provide an opportunity for filing appeals. Another issue raised in the Waxman letter was a provision of a June 12 agreement settling Nazi-era slave labor claims that capped at $150 million the amount that German insurance companies would have to pay for survivor claims, leading the members of Congress to observe, "These companies should not be immunized without full accountability for paying what they owe." Elan Steinberg, the WJC executive director, cautioned that while he sympathized with this concern, seeking to raise the insurance cap could delay payments to aging Holocaust survivors, if not "scuttle the entire German fund."

In November, the National Gallery of Art, part of the Smithsonian complex of museums in Washington, D.C., agreed to return to a Jewish family a painting believed to have been confiscated by the Nazis in Paris in 1941. This brought to 11 the number of paintings looted by the Nazis that the museum had identified in its collection. An agreement was reached later that month between American art museums and the Presidential Advisory Commission on Holocaust Assets whereby the museums would disclose on their Web sites the provenance of all art works they had acquired between 1939 and 1945. This would help determine whether the Nazis had stolen any of these works, and, if so, the property would be returned to its rightful owners.

On June 12, the United States joined with various European governments and industries to create the German Foundation Fund, which would pay individuals who had been pressed into service as slaves and forced laborers during World War II. The money would come from a $5.2-billion settlement fund established by the German government and various German businesses. Germany signed the agreement on July 17, presumably clearing the way for the survivors to begin receiving payments by December when, pursuant to the terms of the agreement, a U.S. court dismissed 49 class-action lawsuits against German firms for their use of slave labor. However legal obstacles delayed the start of payments into 2001 (see below, pp. 385–86).

In December, a federal judge appointed Paul Volcker, the former chairman of the Federal Reserve, to oversee the distribution of $800 million to Holocaust victims and their heirs that had been set aside to cover claims for money deposited with Swiss banks during World War II and never returned. This fund constituted part of a settlement agreement approved by a New York federal judge according to which $1.3 billion would be paid to resolve Holocaust-era claims against the banks. Efforts continued to year's end, as well, to press Poland to make restitution for property looted from Polish Jews during the Holocaust era, as H. Carl McCall and Alan Hevesi—the controllers, respectively, of New York State and New York City—called on Warsaw to cease efforts to block a lawsuit against Poland for billions of dollars in property stolen during those years.

Throughout the year concerns were increasingly heard about the perception that the drive for reparations could make it seem that the payment of money resolved the profound moral issues presented by the Holocaust. There were also allegations by survivor organizations and others that much of the money was not reaching the elderly survivors for whom it was intended. The Conference on Material Claims Against Germany vigorously denied the charge, pointing out that in 1999 alone it had distributed some $220 million to individual survivors and $85 million to programs intended to benefit Holocaust survivors. An even more damning accusation was made by City University of New York instructor Norman Finkelstein in his book *The Holocaust Industry: Reflections on the Exploitation of Jewish Suffering.* Finkelstein condemned Jewish organizations that, he charged, were extracting money from the German government and German businesses, as well as from the Swiss banks and others, to line their own pockets and aggrandize their own power. Finkelstein, whose long-standing left-wing political views and animosity toward Israel were well known, had a negligible impact on American opinion, in contrast to the situation in Europe, where he was taken much more seriously (see above, pp. 18–20).

It could not be denied, however—as illustrated in the Waxman letter in October—that Jewish groups, political leaders, and state governments were not of one mind about appropriate terms for the settlement of Holocaust-era claims. Some protested caps and bars to lawsuits that were often part of settlements, and, in the particular case of ICHEIC, others worried that not enough had been done to prod member insurance companies to release information on unclaimed policies purchased before the Holocaust. In the meantime, several state insurance commissioners—some members of ICHEIC, some not—continued their own efforts, to some extent in cooperation with ICHEIC, to obtain relief for Holocaust-era insurance-policy claimants.

As the year closed, Stuart Eizenstat, the U.S. deputy treasury secretary who had for several years led the Clinton administration's efforts to promote Holocaust restitution, expressed concern about how this issue would be handled under the incoming president. "It's not an issue, so far as I know, on the radar screen," he said.

OSI Actions

The Justice Department's Office of Special Investigations (OSI) continued to seek the deportation of the ever-declining number of Nazi war criminals who had found their way to the United States after World War II. In late February, a U.S. immigration appeals board upheld an immigration judge's determination that Chicago resident Juozas Naujalis be deported to Lithuania because of his role in a Nazi-affiliated unit that was responsible for the deaths of thousands of Jews. That same week, the U.S. Supreme Court let stand a court order calling for the deportation of Ferdinand Hammer, a Michigan resident said to have committed atrocities while serving as a guard at two concentration camps.

A U.S. District Court sitting in Philadelphia acted in July to revoke the citizenship of Ukrainian-born Theodor Szehinskj, a 76-year-old Philadelphia resident, based on evidence that he had served as a concentration-camp guard in

Poland and Germany during World War II. Although the government did not provide evidence of specific acts committed by Szehinskj, the court observed, "The heavy presumption from this incontrovertible historical record is that guards were, at a minimum, complicit in this closed culture of murder even if there may not be hard evidence of actual homicide at a particular guard's hands." Szehinskj, who maintained that he had been a slave laborer on a farm during the period he was said to have served at the camps, indicated his intention to appeal.

On September 28, Aleksandras Lileikis died of a heart attack at age 93 in Vilnius, the capital of his native Lithuania, some four years after he had left the United States upon being stripped of U.S. citizenship because of his role, as head of the Nazi-sponsored Lithanian secret police, in handing over at least 75 Jews to Nazi death squads. Lileikis died without a verdict ever being reached in his ongoing trial before a Lithuanian court for his wartime actions. The judge presiding over the case had allowed postponement of the trial, ostensibly due to Lileikis's poor health, but many Jewish critics saw the court's failure to move the case forward as emblematic of the lack of political will among Lithuanian authorities to bring war criminals to justice (see below, p. 441).

RICHARD T. FOLTIN

The United States, Israel, and the Middle East

AT THE START OF THE YEAR, prospects for significant progress in finally resolving the Arab-Israel conflict appeared bright. Israeli prime minister Ehud Barak, who swept into power by a landslide in May 1999, pledged to withdraw all Israeli troops from Lebanon by July 2000, expressed eagerness to continue the peace talks with the Syrians that had resumed in Washington in December 1999, and declared his intention to work for a final-status agreement with the Palestinian National Authority.

Palestinian Authority chairman Yasir Arafat seemed to share this sense of urgency. Having yielded to U.S. and international pressure not to declare a Palestinian state unilaterally in 1999, Arafat was demanding that this be achieved by September 13, 2000, the seventh anniversary of the signing of the original Oslo Accord on the White House lawn in 1993.

For his part, U.S. president Bill Clinton was prepared to continue to invest an enormous amount of time and energy to broker a major Arab-Israeli peace agreement before the end of his term on January 20, 2001. Many of the president's opponents charged that this was an ego-driven attempt to redeem his scandal-ridden presidential legacy. His supporters, though, saw the president's activist role as a manifestation of his deep personal commitment to end the suffering that continued conflict in the Middle East was bringing to Israelis and Arabs. Moreover, resolving the Arab-Israel conflict would promote regional peace and stability by removing a source of anti-American sentiment that was being effectively exploited by Saddam Hussein in Iraq and by radical, militant Islamic elements in Iran and elsewhere that continued to threaten vital American interests. Successful peace efforts would also help the presidential campaign of Vice President Al Gore and the senatorial campaign of First Lady Hillary Rodham Clinton, who was running for the New York seat being vacated by retiring Democrat Daniel Patrick Moynihan.

By the time the year ended, however, not only Clinton but also Barak was about to leave office; the Syrian talks had collapsed; and the breakdown of Israeli-Palestinian negotiations had brought a new wave of Palestinian violence that rocked the territories. In the end, Barak achieved only one of his campaign promises: Israeli forces completed their withdrawal from southern Lebanon to the recognized international border ahead of schedule, in May 2000.

Breakdown of the Syrian Negotiations

After a hiatus of nearly four years, Syrian president Hafez al-Assad had agreed in December 1999 to the resumption of high-level direct talks with Israel under

195

American auspices. Reportedly, it was President Clinton who played the crucial role in inducing him to do so. In direct phone calls to Assad and in written messages, the president reportedly assured the Syrian leader that the U.S. would back an Israeli withdrawal from the Golan, would help monitor security arrangements, and would give both countries generous aid as part of a peace treaty. "But," in the words of journalist Peter Hirschberg, "Clinton had added a rider: If Assad failed to bite, he would be left empty-handed: No Golan—no aid" (AJYB 2000, p. 462).

When Premier Barak and Syrian foreign minister Farouq a-Shara met for two days of talks in Washington in December 1999 with the participation of President Clinton, they did little more than crack the ice of their frozen relations. Shara refused Clinton's appeal to shake Barak's hand in public and the Syrian sharply criticized Israel's allegedly aggressive policies, while the government-controlled Syrian media not only attacked Israel but also sought to downplay the significance of the Holocaust. However, both sides agreed to return to the United States at the beginning of January 2000 and closet themselves together with American mediators for intensive talks at a modest conference center in Shepherdstown, West Virginia, a site far from the eyes of the media but close enough to Washington for President Clinton to shuttle by helicopter from the White House (see AJYB 2000, pp. 461–62).

On January 2 Secretary of State Madeleine Albright described the renewed negotiations as "a huge historic opportunity" but declined to predict how many more rounds of talks it might take to reach an agreement. In his parting words to reporters as he left Ben-Gurion Airport for the Shepherdstown talks, Barak similarly characterized the trip as a historic moment, noting that from the same runway "Menachem Begin took off to Camp David" to begin the talks leading to the peace agreement with Egypt, and "here from this runway Yitzhak Rabin took off to bring peace with Jordan, and thereafter with the Palestinians." The wishful thinking evident in the reference to Rabin bringing peace with the Palestinians was ironically prophetic—Barak was not to enjoy any success in his talks with the Syrians or the Palestinians.

On January 4 President Clinton succeeded in convening a face-to-face meeting between Barak and Shara and also helped overcome a procedural impasse. The Syrian delegation wanted the first item on the agenda to be the return of the Golan Heights, while the Israelis wanted first to discuss security guarantees. After hours of wrangling, Clinton got the two sides to agree to discuss land and security at the same time. Meanwhile, at a nearby location, four joint working committees began discussions on specific aspects of a proposed agreement.

American officials also began separate talks with the Israelis on the amount of U.S. aid that would be needed to upgrade the Israel Defense Force (IDF) and thus strengthen its deterrent capabilities if it could no longer rely on the strategic buffer zone provided by control of the Golan Heights. Reports out of Israel had it that Barak had presented Clinton with a $17-billion shopping list—

everything from AWAC radar planes to Tomahawk cruise missiles. State Department spokesman James P. Rubin called those reports "wildly premature" but did not dispute the numbers. In Israel, former foreign minister Moshe Arens, a leader in the opposition Likud, said that Barak's discussion with the Americans of Israel's "need for $20 billion" was proof that he was contemplating withdrawal from the Golan Heights. Arens and other opposition leaders warned that accepting such massive American aid would undercut Israel's autonomy and make the country more dependent than ever on Washington.

The issue of new American aid quickly became moot as the Shepherdstown talks broke down in mid-January when Israel refused to meet Syria's precondition of promising, in writing, a full withdrawal from the Golan Heights. Barak had insisted that such a promise could not be made without commitments from Syria on Israel's demands concerning security against attack, continued control of Israel's vital water supplies, and the normalization of relations. Barak agreed in principle to full withdrawal to the international border between the two countries as determined in 1923 by Britain and France, the League of Nations mandatory powers in Palestine and Syria at the time. However, the Syrians insisted that Israeli forces withdraw to the lines of June 4, 1967, the day before the start of the Six-Day War, during which the IDF had captured the Golan Heights.

While the actual amount of territory in dispute between the two lines was small, the potential significance was great. In drawing up the international frontier the British had made sure that the border extended a few meters to the east of the Sea of Galilee (actually a lake, also known as Lake Kinneret and Lake Tiberias), thus placing it entirely within the territorial waters of Palestine. After Israel declared its independence in May 1948, Syria and Israel's other Arab neighbors attacked the new state. At the end of the war Syrian troops had managed to establish a foothold along the southeastern shore of the lake, and under the United Nations Armistice Agreement concluded between Israel and Syria in 1949, that territory became a demilitarized zone under Syrian control. Although the armistice agreement had explicitly stated, at Arab insistence, that the demarcation lines neither constituted a political border nor implied recognition of the State of Israel, President Assad adamantly insisted in 2000 that Israel withdraw to the line of June 4, 1967, which was essentially that of the 1949 armistice. This would turn the Sea of Galilee into an international lake to which the Syrians could assert riparian rights.

But Israelis recalled how, as part of the Arab League's campaign to cripple Israel's economy in the early 1960s, the Syrians had made elaborate plans to divert the headwaters of the Jordan River to prevent their natural flow from the Golan Heights into the Sea of Galilee, Israel's primary storage reservoir. (The water from the Golan provided more than one-third of Israel's renewable water resources.) The Syrian diversion scheme resulted in Israeli-Syrian military clashes and rising Arab-Israeli tensions, culminating in the June 1967 Six-Day War. Consequently Prime Minister Barak, who had campaigned on his distinguished military record, had no intention of once again placing Israel's water resources at risk. Complicating the situation were declarations from Damascus that, following Israeli withdrawal, Syria planned to settle as many as 400,000 persons—mostly farmers and cattle herders, survivors of the region's roughly 100,000 inhabitants before the Six-Day War and their descendants—in the Golan. This number would far exceed the estimated population of just 35,000 in 2000 and make heavy additional demands on the region's water supply.

According to a draft Israeli-Syrian peace treaty that the United States had prepared summarizing the positions of the parties in the Shepherdstown talks, the Syrian delegation did make some specific concessions regarding security arrangements and normalization that Israel had demanded. But the Syrians reportedly rejected Israel's principal demand "to establish arrangements that will ensure the continuation of Israel's current use in quantity and quality of all the surface and underground waters in the areas from which Israeli forces will relocate."

In support of his insistence that Israel withdraw to the 1967 lines, Assad invoked the so-called "Rabin deposit," a message that the late Yitzhak Rabin, Israel's prime minister at the time, had left for Assad with Warren Christopher, the U.S. secretary of state, during the previous American-sponsored Syrian-Israeli talks in 1994–95. The Syrian leader interpreted this as an Israeli agreement to withdraw completely to the June 4 lines. In an interview with *U.S./Israel Security Watch* (published by the Israel Policy Forum) in February 2000, Professor Itamar Rabinovich was asked about Rabin's message. Rabinovich, a Tel Aviv University scholar who had written several books on Syrian affairs and had served as Israel's ambassador to the United States during 1992–1996 and as chief negotiator in the earlier round of talks with the Syrians, replied that "Rabin authorized Christopher to engage on Israel's behalf in a hypothetical exercise with Syria: If Assad were willing to make a deal on the same terms as Sadat, then he, Rabin, would agree to get off the Golan Heights." But, he noted, "the conditions set by Rabin were never met, so there was no agreement or commitment." The U.S. State Department backed the Israeli interpretation of the Rabin-Christopher exchange.

The second round of talks at Shepherdstown in mid-January 2000 failed to resolve the impasse. When the Syrians refused to return for a scheduled third round at the end of the month—ostensibly because Assad was embarrassed by a leak to the press of the American draft paper—the Israeli delegation stayed home as well. Barak, however, remained hopeful about the prospects of unfreezing the deadlock and completing an agreement during the year. In a clear signal to Damascus, Barak's office issued a statement on January 25 saying that, during a recent closed-door meeting with his security advisers, "the prime minister repeated his view that President Assad is a strong leader, who is serious and trustworthy and honors his word." Rabinovich, too, regarded the pause in Syrian-Israeli talks as only "a technical crisis."

There was much speculation in both Israel and the United States as to whether

Assad was serious about seeking a permanent agreement with Israel or just wanted to appear conciliatory in the eyes of the Americans. Those favoring the latter explanation pointed out that the anemic state of its economy made Syria eager to have its name removed from the State Department's list of states that sponsor terror so that it might become eligible for American aid and investment. But those who took Assad's overtures at face value pointed out that the pending Israeli withdrawal from southern Lebanon, which would remove a major point of pressure against the Israelis from Damascus's arsenal, might well have convinced Assad that it was time to settle. Another factor believed to be motivating the enigmatic and ailing Syrian leader was a sense of his own mortality: perhaps he was intent on leaving a more secure and stable situation for his son, Bashar, to inherit.

According to Rabinovich, during 2000 the United States was much more heavily involved in the Syrian negotiations than had been the case earlier; President Clinton was "playing a major personal role, much more intensively than before." Although Rabinovich himself would have preferred more direct and exclusive Israeli-Syrian contacts, the former Israeli ambassador to Washington acknowledged that the U.S. had an important and legitimate role. "This is a three-way negotiation because Assad wants a deal with Washington and economic aid from the West at least as much as he wants a deal with Jerusalem." Moreover, the U.S. was the facilitator of the talks and any security arrangements would need American participation.

Had the Syrian leadership been genuinely interested in a deal with Israel, one would have expected Damascus to court Israeli public opinion, since the Israeli Knesset had passed a law requiring an absolute majority of 61 votes in the 120-member body to approve withdrawal from the Golan Heights, and Barak had promised to submit any agreement to a popular referendum. Egyptian president Anwar Sadat had addressed Israeli public opinion, beginning with his dramatic visit to Israel and his speech to the Knesset in November 1977. Assad, however, not only rejected Barak's invitation to come to Israel, but also refused to meet directly with the Israeli leader either in Damascus or on neutral ground. Moreover, as soon as it was clear that the Shepherdstown talks had not broken the impasse, the government-controlled Syrian media returned to its traditional anti-Zionist and anti-Semitic diatribes. A January 31 editorial in *Tishreen*, an official Damascus paper, charged that "Zionists created the Holocaust myth to blackmail the world and terrorize its intellectuals and politicians." Similarly, Syria's delegate to the UN Economic and Social Council (UNESCO) declared on January 26 that "Zionism is based on the concept of ethnic superiority, of occupation and exclusion of others."

Furthermore, the Syrians not only questioned the good faith and impartiality of the American negotiating team, but also impugned its loyalty to the United States. In an interview with the Lebanese paper *Al-Safir* (January 20), Foreign Minister Shara was quoted as saying that "due to their loyalties and ties" most of the members of the American delegation held views that were close to "the Likud." Ignoring the key role of President Clinton, Shara went on to charge: "The entire delegation consists of Jews . . . I do not exaggerate when I say that some of them were unofficial members of the Israeli delegation." (Ironically, some right-wing Jews in Israel and the U.S. castigated those same career State Department officials as "court Jews" ready to sell out Israel's vital interests to promote President Clinton's misguided peace policies.)

Hopes for resuming the Syrian-Israeli talks were raised when President Assad agreed to a summit meeting with President Clinton on March 26. They met in Geneva, the neutral Swiss venue favored by the Syrian leader, where, in an earlier summit in January 1994, Assad had assured the American president that Syria had made a "strategic choice" for peace. Clinton now agreed to another meeting because of some positive signals from Damascus. Especially notable were Foreign Minister Shara's realistic comments on January 27 to the Arab Writers Association candidly conceding Israel's overwhelming military superiority and arguing that achieving a state of peace would give the Syrians a better chance of competing with Israel in "political, ideological, economic, commercial," and other ways.

In Geneva, however, it was clear within a half-hour that the Assad-Clinton summit had failed. The Syrian leader seemed to have assumed that Clinton would bring with him Barak's commitment to total withdrawal on Syrian terms, especially since Barak had explicitly declared on February 27 that he would not "erase the past" and was prepared to abide by the commitments that Rabin had made in 1995. Assad was furious that Clinton had not convinced Barak to meet all the Syrian demands, particularly regarding Syrian access to the shoreline of the Sea of Galilee. The rest of the three-hour meeting deteriorated into a lengthy and rambling historical lecture by Assad, which left the participants wondering whether the shrewd Lion of Damascus had finally lost his cunning. When Clinton attributed some conciliatory bridging proposals to Shara, Assad berated his hapless foreign minister, and it became apparent to the American negotiating team that Assad's sharply deteriorating health had emboldened the foreign minister, for the first time, to take some initiatives on his own.

According to British journalist Patrick Seale, Assad's authorized biographer and confidant, Clinton endorsed Barak's demand for continued Israeli control not only of the Sea of Galilee "but of the upper Jordan River and all the other tributaries" flowing into it from the Golan. In response, Assad repeated a story he liked to tell of how prior to 1967 he would often swim in the lake and cook fish on its shore. All he wanted were the riparian rights Syria had enjoyed before the war. "Clinton rejoined that Barak would no doubt be happy to let Assad swim in the lake, a jest Assad evidently did not appreciate." Seale wrote: "He grasped at once that, wittingly or not, Clinton had been mobilized in the Israeli cause." Assad returned home "in a sour mood," and, privately, "the Syrians were harshly critical of [U.S. Middle East peace coordinator] Dennis Ross who, they felt, had orchestrated the summit and allowed Barak to believe that Assad could be made to yield to pressure from Clinton."

Following the collapse of the Geneva summit, Clinton gave a frank assessment implying that Syrian intransigence was the reason for the failure. Barak "would like to [bring peace] as quickly as he can" and has "made very, very serious efforts on all tracks," Clinton said, so "the ball's in [Assad's] court now." In a statement on April 8, Foreign Minister Shara confirmed that Assad, at the Geneva summit with Clinton, had not only reiterated his demand for a return to the June 4, 1967, line, but also had explicitly asserted a Syrian claim to sovereignty over part of Lake Tiberias. (Syrian nationalists had never been happy with the international border drawn up by the British and French "imperialist" powers in 1923. They argued that international law supported the initial Syrian negotiating position of 1922, under which the border between Syria and Palestine would have been drawn through the middle of the lake.)

Patrick Seale's account of the summit, first published in Arabic in *Al-Hayat,* was reprinted in English in *Middle East International* on May 19, 2000, under the heading: "Obituary of the Syrian Track." Less than a month later Seale was writing the obituary of Hafez al-Assad himself, who died in Damascus on June 10 at the age of 69. Assad had seized power in a bloodless coup in 1970. In contrast to the internal instability of the pre-Assad era that had seen 14 presidents come and go in the space of 23 years, Assad succeeded in maintaining his rule in Syria with an iron hand for three decades. At the time of his death, the Syrian dictator no longer had many friends in the outside world; in contrast to the funeral of King Hussein of Jordan, which had been attended by many world leaders, only one Western head of state, President Jacques Chirac of France, came to Damascus. President Clinton sent Secretary of State Albright to head the American delegation. Some Syrians said they felt hurt by the obvious snub from the American president, and there were those who attributed it to the political clout of American Jews in an election year.

Despite predictions of instability, the transition of power was in fact swift and smooth. Bashar al-Assad, the 34-year-old son of the late president, the only candidate nominated, was quickly elected to succeed his father. The Syrian constitution was instantly and conveniently amended to lower the minimum age for president from 40 to 34. The new president was a British-trained ophthalmologist who had been called back home by his father after his older brother Basil, the heir apparent, had died in a car crash in 1994. Before his own death, Hafez al-Assad had begun preparing Bashar for his new responsibilities, giving him the important "Lebanon file" and sending him on missions to Saudi Arabia, Jordan, Amman, and Paris. The senior Assad had also purged the military of potential rivals to his son, and on March 13 named a new cabinet, composed mostly of technocrats. The outgoing cabinet had failed to enforce reforms that Assad had called for the previous year, and its replacement was widely seen as an attempt to rejuvenate Syria's ailing economy. In an interview with *Al-Hayat* at the time, Bashar al-Assad, with his father still alive, said that the first task of the new government would be "to modernize the administration and reduce the level of corruption" and that the new appointees were chosen for their "efficiency, honesty and administrative skills."

Both Syrian and foreign observers were hopeful that the new young president, despite his relative inexperience, would be a modernizing reformer who would bring more openness and freedom to Syrian society. One positive sign was that he served as director of the Syrian Scientific Society for Information Technology, which offered computer courses. And he had told the *Washington Post* that he personally favored lifting all of the onerous restrictions long imposed on what Syrians could read, watch on television, or discover on the Internet. His father's security-obsessed regime had severely restricted ordinary citizens' access even to fax machines and satellite dishes.

Secretary Albright, who met briefly with the new Syrian president on June 13, said that he had assured her that he was prepared to "continue discussions about the peace process" at an "appropriate time," presumably after the 40-day period of mourning. Senator Arlen Specter (R., Pa.), a prominent Jewish senator, was part of the American delegation to the funeral. Specter, who had met with the senior Assad on various issues about a dozen times over the years, including the ultimately successful effort to obtain permission for Syrian Jews to leave the country, reported that Bashar told him, "I'm going to carry on peace just like my father did." While that remark seemed equivocal, Specter and Secretary of State Albright interpreted it not as a reflection of the late father's intransigent attitude, but rather as expressing a more flexible approach of the son.

But there was to be no further progress in Syrian-Israeli talks during the remainder of the year. One reason given for the continuing stalemate was Bashar's need to focus first on domestic issues so as to consolidate his power. Bashar, after all, had no personal memories of swimming in the Sea of Galilee—he was only two years old when his father was defense minister in the government that lost control of the area in the 1967 war. In any case, Bashar could not be expected to modify his father's policy without assurances of significant economic and diplomatic benefits for Syria. Another factor in the new president's cautious approach was the Syrian assessment of Ehud Barak's increasingly precarious political position. Patrick Seale had already concluded in May that "the Syrian track is dead" because the Israeli leader could not secure the approval of his own cabinet, let alone the Knesset or the country as a whole, for a deal with Syria on the basis of the 1967 lines. As Palestinian violence escalated in the last quarter of the year and the Arab world joined in condemnation of Israel, prospects for meaningful talks with Syria became even more remote.

Withdrawal from Lebanon

Originally, the Israeli government had hoped to carry out the withdrawal from Lebanon within the framework of comprehensive peace agreements with both

Syria and Lebanon. But when it became clear in March that President Clinton's efforts to engage President Assad in peace talks with Israel had failed, Prime Minister Barak—who was, significantly, also minister of defense—reluctantly decided to go ahead with the withdrawal anyway.

Israel completed its withdrawal from southern Lebanon on May 24 (see below, pp. 479–83). In doing so unilaterally Israel retreated from its position in earlier years that had linked withdrawal to the removal of the estimated 35,000–40,000 Syrian "peacekeepers" from Lebanon and the cessation of all Syrian military and logistical support for Hezballah and various Palestinian rejectionist groups that were using bases in Syrian-controlled Lebanon to harass the Israelis. Damascus airport also served as a major conduit for the supply of weapons from Iran to the militant groups in Lebanon.

Indeed, UN Security Council Resolution 425, adopted in March 1978, which had called on Israel to "withdraw forthwith its forces from all Lebanese territory," had also, at Lebanon's request, established the United Nations Interim Force in Lebanon (UNIFIL), and called for "strict respect for the territorial integrity, sovereignty and political independence of Lebanon within its internationally recognized boundaries." The UN did nothing in 2000 to reduce Syria's hegemonic role in the affairs of the country. But increasingly bold comments began to be heard in Lebanon—voiced primarily by members of the Christian community—calling for a reassessment of Lebanese-Syrian relations now that the Israeli occupation, which was the ostensible justification for the continued large Syrian military presence, had come to an end.

Since Israeli withdrawal from Lebanon and restoration of calm on the Lebanese-Israeli frontier would remove an important bargaining chip for Syria in pressuring Israel, the government-controlled Syrian media had at first called the planned Israeli pullout a devious "plot" to deceive the world about Israel's expansionist tendencies. Yet it soon became clear that Syria was alone in opposing the Israeli pullout. Not only the United States but many other countries and high-ranking UN officials also supported the move. In May the United States Congress passed a resolution commending Israel for the withdrawal from Lebanon and "for taking risks for peace in the Middle East." It also recognized Israel's right to defend itself against future attacks. The bipartisan resolution, adopted unanimously in the Senate and by an overwhelming 403-3 vote in the House, called upon the international community to "ensure that southern Lebanon does not once again become a staging ground for attacks against Israel."

When Syrian foreign minister Shara visited Paris in April to dissuade the French from participating in an expanded role for UNIFIL, his French hosts warned him that Syria faced "international isolation" if it failed to support efforts to bring calm to Lebanon. Even in the Arab world, Egypt and Saudi Arabia were among the countries that called the Israeli action a positive development. Particularly embarrassing for Syria was a statement by Lebanese prime minister Selim al-Hoss warmly welcoming the pullout. Reversing Syria's earlier position opposing any Israeli withdrawal unless it were part of an Israeli-Syrian agreement,

Shara now said that Damascus would welcome an Israeli withdrawal from Lebanon, even if it were unilateral. The Syrians reportedly also assured the UN that they were prepared to cooperate with UNIFIL.

But the respective roles of UNIFIL and the Lebanese government in maintaining order in southern Lebanon was to become an issue of continuing concern to the United States, Israel, and the UN. In testimony before the U.S. Senate on June 14, Edward Walker, assistant secretary of state for Near Eastern affairs, noted that one of the primary objectives of UNIFIL, as spelled out in Security Council Resolution 425, was to assist the government of Lebanon in "ensuring the return of its effective authority in the area." He pointed out that while things were calm there for the time being, the fact that "Hezballah fighters are in close proximity with the Israeli forces on the border" was clearly "not desirable now or in the future." He said the United States actively supported the efforts of UNIFIL and the Lebanese government to work together, along with military observers from the UN Truce Supervisory Organization. In a veiled criticism of Syria, Walker declared: "We in the international community believe a strong . . . Lebanese military presence is crucial to the government's reestablishment of its sovereignty and order," adding that "Secretary Albright has been in direct contact with Lebanese president [Émile] Lahoud and [UN] secretary-general [Kofi] Annan to stress this point."

Walker called the Israeli withdrawal from Lebanon "a momentous development in the Middle East and a very positive one." The United States would continue to exert every effort to ensure that the border remained calm, he said, first, by supporting the implementation of Resolution 425 "in a peaceful and orderly manner, second, by garnering international support to assist in reconstructing the south, and, third, by keeping the door open for a comprehensive peace settlement between Israel and Syria and between Israel and Lebanon."

Prime Minister Barak's hope that full IDF withdrawal would lead to peace with Lebanon was not realized. In practice, the hasty IDF withdrawal fell far short of the disciplined and well-planned redeployment that Barak had envisioned. Moreover, the withdrawal was marred by the disintegration of the Israeli-supported South Lebanon Army (SLA), with television providing images, for all to see, of SLA members and their families fleeing in disarray before the onslaught of Hezballah forces (see below, pp. 481–82).

Some political analysts had expected that once Hezballah succeeded in ending the Israeli occupation in southern Lebanon the militant Shi'ite group would moderate its anti-Israel position and instead turn its efforts inward and seek to play a greater role within the Lebanese political system. In a dispatch from Beirut on February 27, *New York Times* correspondent John F. Burns quoted an interview given by Hezballah secretary-general Sheikh Hassan Nasrallah to the Pakistani newspaper *Dawn* in June 1998, saying that Hezballah could not be more Palestinian than the PLO. "If their leaders compromise, there is little we can do," he had said. "We cannot substitute for their leadership."

These optimistic hopes were soon dashed. Already in a February 2 interview with *Middle East Insight* Nasrallah declared that he was "against any reconciliation with Israel. I do not even recognize the presence of a state that is called 'Israel.' I consider its presence both unjust and unlawful." If the Lebanese government were to conclude a peace agreement with Israel and bring it to parliament for ratification, Nasrallah said, the Hezballah deputies would vote against it. But, he added, in a tone of moderation, "we would not make any turmoil out of it." He also said that the Hezballah high command had decided "for the time being" not to respond to questions as to whether or not its military resistance would stop if Israel withdrew its forces totally from southern Lebanon and the international frontier were reestablished.

Sheikh Nasrallah was adamant on the refugee question. Hezballah, he said, would ask not only for the 400,000 Palestinian refugees in the country "to leave Lebanon, but for their return to Palestine." Moreover, while acknowledging that international efforts to resettle the Palestinians from Lebanon in other countries around the world might solve the specifically Lebanese aspect of the problem, Nasrallah emphasized, in the *Middle East Insight* interview, that "the Palestinian issue should be considered a regional problem of greater importance than any other."

The United Nations Relief and Works Agency for Palestine Refugees (UNRWA) estimated that there were approximately 350,000 Palestinians in Lebanon—200,000 still living in refugee camps and 150,000 elsewhere in the country. With rare exceptions, the government in Beirut was unwilling to grant the Palestinians Lebanese citizenship. (Jordan was the only one of the Arab host countries to grant the refugees virtually automatic citizenship.) The refugee camps served as a fertile ground for recruiting terrorists against Israel.

Reportedly encouraged by some of the more radical leaders in the Islamic Republic of Iran, whom he met in Tehran following the Israeli withdrawal from Lebanon, Nasrallah proclaimed that his group would continue its jihad (holy struggle) until Israel withdrew from all Palestinian territories and the Jewish state in fact ceased to exist.

On July 24 UN secretary-general Annan confirmed that Israel had fully complied with the terms of Resolution 425, which paved the way for UNIFIL and Lebanese forces to move into the area. President Clinton, for his part, promised to increase American aid to Israel so that it might upgrade its security in light of the withdrawal from Lebanon. And he added: "We also want to help the government of Lebanon to strengthen its ability to control southern Lebanon." But it soon became clear that the Lebanese army, presumably under pressure from Syria, was unwilling to remove the Hezballah from the border region. Beirut indicated that it would not deploy its own troops along the border until there was a comprehensive peace agreement, including the return of the Golan Heights to Syria. Timur Göksel, the UNIFIL spokesman, criticized the Lebanese position. In an interview with the Associated Press at the end of August, he pointed out that "the UN is not responsible for guarding the border." UNIFIL's function was only "border monitoring," while "border security is essentially a national responsibility." As a result, there were hundred of reported incidents of Lebanese, Palestinian, and other individuals, notoriously including visiting Columbia University professor Edward Said, who approached the border fence to hurl not only verbal insults, but a barrage of stones and even firebombs at the Israeli soldiers on the other side.

The most serious incident occurred in October when a Hezballah band crossed the border into Israel and kidnapped three Israeli soldiers. International efforts for their release included a meeting between Ehud Barak and Kofi Annan, who told Barak that the soldiers were alive and receiving "fair treatment." The International Committee of the Red Cross asked for its representative to meet with the prisoners. On October 9 President Clinton called Bashar al-Assad, who had recently succeeded his father as president of Syria, urging him to curtail the activities of Hezballah in Lebanon and to assist in the timely release of the three captive soldiers. In addition, Secretary of State Madeleine Albright asked Syrian foreign minister Shara to do his utmost to prevent deterioration in the situation. The number of incidents declined in the latter part of the year, but by the end of the Clinton presidency the Israeli soldiers had still not been released. Reportedly, Hezballah was keeping them hostage, hoping to trade them for Hezballah supporters being held in Israeli prisons.

Israel and the Palestinians

The Israeli-Palestinian diplomatic track began the year on a favorable note when, on January 4, negotiators for the two sides agreed on a map detailing what specific additional territories Israel would hand over to the Palestinian Authority under the terms of the Sharm el-Sheikh agreement that had been reached previous September.

The second of three withdrawals had been scheduled for November 1999, but the Palestinians had balked at Israel's offer of 5 percent of the West Bank consisting largely of unpopulated areas in the Judean Desert. They wanted a say in determining which territory Israel was relinquishing, and specifically asked for additional populated territory near Jerusalem. According to the Israelis, however, this was a final-status issue to be discussed only after a framework was reached, hopefully by February 13. The Palestinians had also insisted that the third withdrawal of 6.1 percent be completed without reference to the final-status framework. Barak sought to skip the third withdrawal altogether and combine it with a final withdrawal, the extent of which would be determined by the degree to which the Palestinian negotiators would be forthcoming on other crucial final-status issues such as Jewish settlements, Jerusalem, refugees, and control over shared water resources.

Speaking together to reporters on January 4, the Israeli and Palestinian lead negotiators suggested that there had been a positive change in their relationship.

"Every moment we act as partners, we find solutions," Saeb Erakat said. "This is the key," responded Oded Eran, his Israeli counterpart, "both sides understood that the issues of 5 percent and 6.1 percent are important but that there are more important issues—that is, the future and the permanent relationships between the two of us. We found a way of removing these issues from the agenda that is satisfactory to both sides and enabled us to move forward."

But it soon became apparent that the two sides were still far from an agreement. A meeting between Arafat and Barak on February 3 at the Erez Junction ended badly. Barak reportedly told Arafat that he wanted to delay the framework agreement until September and postpone the final peace deal, planned for September, for another nine months. Arafat reportedly replied that the PA did not mind postponing the framework agreement beyond the planned mid-February deadline, but adamantly opposed delaying the final agreement beyond September 13, which was not only the seventh anniversary of the first Oslo agreement, but also the explicit date specified in the September 1999 Sharm el-Sheik agreement by which the parties "will conclude a permanent status agreement."

Arafat was apparently concerned that after mid-September the United States would be fully preoccupied with the presidential election campaign. Precious time would be lost, he felt, especially if a new Republican administration came to power. Arafat was also reportedly upset that Barak had reneged on his promise to include Abu Dis and other villages around Jerusalem in the next planned withdrawal. According to Palestinian sources, however, what most worried Arafat was his suspicion that Barak wanted to delay negotiations with the Palestinians until after he had finalized an agreement with Syria and Lebanon. If the Israeli leader managed to secure Israel's borders with all its immediate neighbors, the Palestinians would be in a far weaker bargaining position.

On February 7 the Palestinians signaled their displeasure by freezing the talks with Israel and releasing from prison Abdel-Aziz Rantisi, a charismatic fundamentalist leader from Gaza who outspokenly opposed the peace process and criticized the Palestinian Authority. American and Israeli officials interpreted the release as a provocative act intentionally done to coincide with the suspension of the peace negotiations. Sheik Ahmed Yassin, the spiritual leader of Hamas, greeted the released Rantisi at Hamas headquarters. A Palestinian political scientist in Gaza told a *New York Times* reporter, "It seems that the Palestinian Authority is sending a green light to Hamas, just as Assad is sending a green light to Hezballah to hit Israeli soldiers."

U.S. ambassador to Israel Martin Indyk called the senior Palestinian and Israeli negotiators to his home in Herzliya on February 12 to try to reconcile the differences over the interim agreement. They were joined by Middle East envoy Dennis Ross. Nabil Shaath, the Palestinian Authority planning minister, warned: "Time is related to substance. . . . there will be an explosion if we can't reach some sort of framework agreement by March," which was when the U.S. presidential primaries would end.

State Department officials closely involved in the negotiations shared this concern. As one official who asked not to be named told the author on May 10, in Syrian-Israeli relations there was a sustainable status quo because there was a physical separation between the Syrian and Israeli armed forces; therefore both sides could continue to live without a deal. This was not the case with regard to Israel and the Palestinian Authority. Because of the close physical proximity of the Israeli and Palestinian communities and their daily interaction, an agreement was "a strategic imperative." Lack of movement in the peace process, he warned— accurately—would lead to violence. Later in May rioting in the West Bank and Gaza escalated when Palestinian Authority police fired on Israeli soldiers. After a bomb wounded a Jewish child near Jericho, Barak suspended the negotiations with the Palestinians that had been proceeding in Stockholm.

PRESIDENTIAL POLITICS

The role the United States should play became an issue in the presidential campaign. In a *New York Times* op-ed piece on May 24, Milton Viorst called on President Clinton to exert pressure on Israel as a means of compensating for the superior bargaining power the Jewish state's overwhelming military and economic strength gave it over the Palestinians. Viorst wrote: "Only the United States can hope to curb Israel's advantage. Jimmy Carter was willing to exercise some muscle, at Camp David in 1977. So was George Bush, in convoking the Madrid conference of 1991." Noting that Washington's present doctrine, that "territorial differences must be resolved by the parties themselves," assured Israel, "as the stronger party, of prevailing," he criticized Governor George W. Bush for promising Israel support that is "not conditioned on the outcome of the peace process." This promise, Viorst contended, was at odds not only with President Clinton's position, "but with that of Governor Bush's father."

Republican presidential candidate Bush had made the comment Viorst objected to in a speech to the policy conference of the American Israel Public Affairs Committee (AIPAC) in Washington on May 22. Beginning with the acknowledgement that "America and Israel share a special friendship," Bush went on:

> I recognize the importance of the peace process and the key role the United States can play. But my support for Israel is not conditional on the outcome of the peace process. America's special relationship with Israel precedes the peace process. And Israel's adversaries should know that in my administration, the special relationship will continue, even if they cannot bring themselves to make true peace with the Jewish state.

Bush then noted examples of Israel's desire for peace, including "sacrificing land and oil" for peace with Egypt and Israel's achievement of a settlement with Jordan. The United States, the candidate continued, should encourage similar progress with other Arab states. He praised Israel for reaching out "toward the Palestinians, sacrificing land in hopes for a better future for both peoples." He said that the United States was "proud and respectful of the sacrifices Israel is making, sacrifices that few nations are called upon to make." In an obvious criticism of Clinton's prodding of the parties to reach a final agreement before the end of his term, Bush noted, "In recent times, Washington has tried to make Israel conform to its own plans and timetables: But this is not the path to peace." Governor Bush then pledged that he would "begin the process" of moving the U.S. embassy from Tel Aviv to Jerusalem as soon as he took office.

Vice President Al Gore, the Democratic presidential candidate, addressed the AIPAC conference the next day. He noted that when he and President Clinton entered office in 1993 they decided that the United States "needed to chart a new course with regard to the Middle East peace process. Unlike our immediate predecessors, we chose to get intimately involved." But, he reassured his pro-Israel audience, "we also established a firm new rule—and we followed this rule faithfully—that we must not and would not in any way try to pressure Israel to agree to measures that they themselves did not see were in their own best interests." Gore called on the Palestinians to recognize that they would not get all they wanted, and urged Arafat and the Palestinian leadership "to prevent those who would resort to violence from disrupting the peace process at this extraordinarily difficult and delicate time." He expressed his disappointment that "Syria, at least for now, has turned down offers made in good faith in Geneva." Noting that Israel was in the process of withdrawing its forces from Lebanon, he warned that "President Assad will bear a heavy responsibility before the entire world" if he continued to allow Hezballah to harass Israel and prevented peace from coming to the area.

(Of the unsuccessful candidates for president in the primaries and the general election, all were also vigorously supportive of American aid to Israel with the exception of Patrick Buchanan, candidate of one faction of the divided Reform Party, who espoused an essentially isolationist position, and Ralph Nader, candidate of the Green Party, who was harshly critical of Israel's actions against its Arab neighbors in general and the Palestinians in particular. It was not clear to what extent Nader's stance was rooted in his generally anti-establishment position and to what extent it reflected his Lebanese Christian origins.)

Speaking to the same AIPAC audience, Ambassador Dennis Ross commented on the limits on the American role in the peace process. "A go-between can help get things to the point where the two parties themselves resolve their differences, but only the two parties dealing directly will overcome the gaps that remain and produce an agreement, if it's possible." He stressed that the United States had always played a crucial supporting role: "There has never been an agreement in the history of this process, whether with Egypt or Jordan or with the Palestinians, where American support and assistance wasn't required to reach an agreement and, in the aftermath of the agreement, to provide assistance, including economic assistance." Predicting that "we will be called on to do that again," Ross explained why the United States would respond positively to future aid requests: "It's in our interest. It's not simply that it is right, it's in our interest."

Speaking to the AIPAC conference by satellite television, Prime Minister Barak said that "we are pleased and reassured that both presidential candidates reiterated their commitment to helping Israel make peace and to minimize these risks that we are taking in order to achieve peace. We are grateful for the unparalleled friendship of the American Congress, the bedrock of military and economic support for the state and people of Israel." Turning to the situation in the region, Barak said that Israel was entering "the crucial stage of our pullout from Lebanon," and declared that "we hold the Lebanese government and the Syrian government responsible to make sure that it will be quiet" along the border. Barak expressed deep concern over the escalating violence in the territories, especially the fact that for the first time "Palestinian policemen and security agents in uniform" were seen "shooting into our people." While Israeli forces had shown restraint in order to avoid more bloodshed, Barak said that he had called Arafat "and made it clear to him that we cannot continue serious steps toward him when his people in uniform are shooting Israelis."

During the following months Barak was to come under increasingly heavy domestic criticism, not only from the opposition but also from within his own One Israel bloc, for ignoring his own advice and pursuing negotiations with the Palestinians even in the face of continuing violence.

CAMP DAVID II

Barak and Arafat agreed to go to a mid-July summit meeting convened by President Clinton at Camp David, the same presidential retreat in Maryland where President Jimmy Carter had hosted Israeli prime minister Menachem Begin and Egyptian president Anwar Sadat in 1978. That earlier summit had laid the groundwork for peace between Egypt and Israel. This time, however, despite 15 days of intensive around-the-clock negotiations in which Clinton played a key role, the talks collapsed when Arafat sent a brief handwritten note, in Arabic, to Clinton, saying in effect that he could "not go further than I have gone" and declaring that "the suggestions I have heard do not take us in the direction I find acceptable."

According to a long analysis by *New York Times* reporters Jane Perlez and Elaine Sciolino (July 28), Clinton had been eager to convene the summit for a month before it actually took place, and Barak had reportedly badgered him to do so, "arguing during repeated phone calls that only what he called 'the pressure cooker' of such a meeting would force through excruciating decisions." Chairman Arafat, though, had been very reluctant to go. At a meeting with Secretary Albright in late June, Arafat had said, "The time is not right." But he had also reportedly told her that he had the highest respect for the president and would do as he was asked. According to some Palestinian sources, Arafat said that he feared for his life if he agreed to end the conflict with Israel without achieving complete acceptance of the major Palestinian demands. These included withdrawal of Israeli forces from Gaza and the West Bank to the lines of June 4, 1967—with the possibility of only minor mutual border adjustments—removal of Israeli settlements, the establishment of a Palestinian state with East Jerusalem as its capital—including exclusive Palestinian control of the Haram al-Sharif (Temple Mount)—and recognition of the Palestinian refugees' right of return.

Abu Ala, one of Arafat's key negotiators, had issued a stern warning on July 6: "If the Israelis think that by giving parts of the land in which to declare the Palestinian state, then I don't think this would bring peace to the area. Rather, it would be the flame that would explode the situation." This is in fact what would happen (for details of the failed negotiations, see below, pp. 490–94). In retrospect, Likud opposition leader Ariel Sharon was correct in arguing at the time that the gap between the parties was too wide to overcome. It would be wiser for Israel, Sharon claimed, to seek the modest goal of nonbelligerence and another long-term interim agreement, including Israeli-Palestinian cooperation, with international funding, in joint infrastructure projects such as large-scale desalination plants that would relieve the chronic and increasingly severe water shortage in the region. Yet proponents of Barak's more ambitious negotiating approach would later retort that seeking a more limited agreement would have enraged the Palestinians even more.

Had Clinton succeeded in hammering out a peace agreement between Israel and the Palestinians—and/or, for that matter, between Israel and Syria—he would have helped calm the region by reducing the sources of potential conflict. This, in turn, would have placed the United States and Israel in a far more favorable position to confront dangers from the more distant hostile states, such as Iraq and Iran, which were developing longer-range missiles and were suspected of seeking to acquire weapons of mass destruction. But Clinton failed, wrongly assuming that he could set the pace for negotiations and that his charisma and powers of persuasion, together with offers of generous American aid, would be sufficient to soften the positions of the parties.

As it turned out, two issues were deal breakers: recognition of the Palestinians' so-called right of return, and Jerusalem.

The right of all Palestinians who left the territory of the new Jewish state in 1948 and those who fled the territories in the Six-Day War of 1967—as well as their descendants—to "return" to their homes in what was now Israel had always been a key demand of Yasir Arafat, not least because various militant Palestinian groups living outside Palestine had provided his primary base of support in the early days of his Palestine Liberation Organization (PLO), and those Palestinians in exile remained a crucial constituency he dared not abandon. Palestinian estimates of the number of potential returnees ran as high as four million. Israel, however, not only disputed the accuracy of that estimate, but also insisted that relatively few could be admitted to Israel, and those only on grounds of family reunion. The vast majority of the refugees, according to the Israelis, would settle on the territory of the new Palestinian state, or else be resettled in neighboring host countries, other states in the region, or countries abroad that were prepared to welcome immigrants, such as Canada and Australia.

Even before Camp David II the United States had been engaged in exploratory talks with other potential donors to establish a multibillion-dollar compensation-and-resettlement fund for the refugees, to which Israel said it was also prepared to contribute. This was to be combined with generous development aid for countries in the region that would support the peace process and absorb some of the refugees. While Palestinian officials involved in the negotiations on the refugee issue indicated a willingness to be pragmatic and realistic in implementing any agreed-upon solution, Arafat himself adamantly insisted that the Israelis would first have to agree to the principle of the refugees' right of return. Despite intensive efforts, President Clinton was unable to get Arafat and Barak to agree on a formula for addressing the refugee problem.

On Jerusalem, Clinton appealed to Arafat at Camp David "to make a principled compromise." If he did so, the president promised that, at the Tokyo meeting of the G-8 leading industrial nations the following week, he would advocate generous economic aid to the new Palestinian state. Clinton provided a variety of options for dealing with the issue of sovereignty in the Old City. One was giving the Palestinians sovereignty over the Muslim and Christian quarters, while Israel retained sovereignty over the Jewish and Armenian quarters. Another would have given the Palestinians sovereignty over several neighborhoods surrounding the Old City and administrative autonomy within its walls. A third reported suggestion was to divide the Old City vertically: the Palestinians would have sovereignty, or at least formal control, over the Temple Mount, while Israel was to retain residual rights to the area underneath, as well as to the Western Wall and the adjoining Jewish Quarter. Yet a fourth possibility was placing the Temple Mount under "Divine" sovereignty, in effect deferring the issue to the indefinite future.

Arafat reportedly rejected all these suggestions and insisted that East Jerusalem be part of the Palestinian state and that the Haram al-Sharif be under exclusive Palestinian sovereignty. He contended that none of the Muslim Arab leaders whom he had consulted offered support for surrendering sovereignty over any part of Jerusalem. At one point in the negotiations, Arafat even refused to concede that the ancient Jewish temples had stood on the Temple Mount.

Ehud Barak's willingness to reach some accommodation with Arafat on the issue of Jerusalem, though rebuffed by the Palestinian leader, hurt Barak badly on the domestic front. From the moment he came home to Israel after the collapse of the talks and through the balance of the year, the prime minister was subjected to increasingly sharp criticism for reneging on his campaign promise never to divide Jerusalem. The charge would play a major role in the collapse of the government coalition and the call for new prime ministerial elections.

Clinton made no secret of his disappointment at the failure of Camp David II, and he let it be known that he regarded Arafat's intransigence as the primary reason. Trying to put the best possible face on the result, the president asserted, in an extraordinary interview on July 28 with Ehud Ya'ari on Israel TV, that the Israelis and Palestinians had broken seven years of silence to conduct "unprecedented" discussions of emotional issues like Jerusalem, and had made significant progress on every other core issue. As an example of a breakthrough in the negotiations, the president mentioned refugee compensation. He told Ya'ari that when the question of compensating Palestinian refugees came up the Israelis raised similar claims for the hundreds of thousands of Jews who fled or were evicted from Arab lands. There was, he said, "some interest, interestingly enough on both sides" in setting up an international fund to pay the claims of the two sets of refugees.

When Ya'ari asked whether Barak had been willing to divide Jerusalem, President Clinton responded that the prime minister "in no way ever compromised the vital interests of the security of the State of Israel." He added that the most progress at the summit had been made in the area of security, with Israelis and Palestinians reaching a consensus that "neither side would be secure after a peace agreement unless both were secure and unless both worked together." President Clinton assured the Israeli audience that he would immediately begin a "comprehensive review to improve our strategic relationship" and to ensure that "Israel maintains its qualitative edge, modernizes the IDF, and meets the new threats that Israel and the other countries will face in the 21st century."

Clinton was asked whether he supported a move in Congress, backed by his wife, senatorial candidate Hillary Rodham Clinton, to cut off aid to the Palestinian Authority if Arafat unilaterally declared a Palestinian state. He responded that it would be a "big mistake" for Arafat "to take a unilateral action and walk away from the peace process," and if that happened, "I would review our entire relationship" with the Palestinian Authority and there would be serious consequences, "not just here, but throughout the world." On September 27 the House of Representatives, by an overwhelming 385-27 margin, approved a bill prohibiting any funding for the Palestinian National Authority if there were a unilateral declaration of independence; a similar measure passed the Senate several days later.

RENEWED VIOLENCE

Frustration in the Palestinian community mounted as the stalemate in political negotiations delayed hoped-for additional Israeli withdrawals, while the seemingly inexorable Israeli expansion of existing settlements and the concomitant increase in the number of Israeli settlers continued. Moreover, in response to sporadic terrorist attacks, Israeli troops continued to subject Palestinians to burdensome travel restrictions and other security controls, and this, in turn, brought a marked deterioration in the economic situation in the territories.

The lesson of Hezballah's proclaimed success in routing the seemingly invincible Israel Defense Force (IDF) from Lebanon had not been lost upon the Palestinians in the territories. Militant elements among them—not only fundamentalist supporters of Islamic Jihad and Hamas, but also secular nationalist supporters of the PLO—sought to capitalize on the perceived Israeli war-weariness. They urged an escalation of violent confrontations in the hope that increasing casualties would hasten Israeli military withdrawal from the territories, leading to the abandonment of Jewish settlements and to other concessions to Palestinian demands.

Toward the end of the year, Palestinian rage and violence were directed with increasing ferocity not only at Israeli soldiers but also at Israeli civilians living in the territories. The Palestinian attacks, which began after President Clinton blamed Arafat for the failure of the Camp David peace talks in July, intensified into an organized revolt at the end of September following the highly publicized visit of Israeli Likud opposition leader Ariel Sharon, accompanied by a large complement of Israeli soldiers, to the Temple Mount. Although Sharon had been careful not to enter either the Dome of the Rock or the al-Aqsa mosque, the two Muslim shrines on the mount, Palestinians saw the visit as a demonstrative assertion of Israeli sovereignty over the Temple Mount, the site of both the first temple built by King Solomon and the second temple that had been enlarged by Herod.

The Palestinian uprising, soon termed the al-Aqsa intifada, began with groups of Palestinian teenagers throwing rocks and Molotov cocktails at Israeli soldiers manning checkpoints at border crossings, but it quickly escalated (see below, pp. 494–501). There were increasingly fierce clashes between armed security forces of the Palestinian Authority and the IDF. Palestinian snipers directed fire against Israeli civilian neighborhoods on the outskirts of Jerusalem.

There were reliable reports that Arafat had released dozens of Hamas and Islamic Jihad members from jail and had placed some of their leaders on a joint committee to help coordinate attacks on Israelis. Much of the most serious armed violence in the West Bank was carried out by the Tanzim, the paramilitary wing of Arafat's own Fatah faction of the PLO. Initially created to assert Arafat's leadership against the Islamic fundamentalist militias, it was acting increasingly as a major instigator of anti-Israeli actions. Marwan Barghouti, the secretary general of Fatah on the West Bank and the acknowledged head of the Tanzim, espoused some of the most hard-line Palestinian positions, particularly on the issues of Jerusalem and the Palestinian refugees' right of return. There was some question as to what extent Arafat fully controlled his operations, even though the PA continued to be the major funder of the group.

The cumulative impact upon the Israeli public was the opposite of what Arafat's militant supporters had intended. Evidence that the violence was neither spontaneous nor limited to Islamic rejectionist elements, but was condoned if not actively instigated by Arafat and carried out by units like the Tanzim, brought a profound hardening of Israeli attitudes. Disappointment, disillusionment, anger, and frustration replaced the optimism that had come in the wake of Barak's election. Even in the ranks of Peace Now and other dovish groups there was a sense of betrayal, dismay, and disgust at Arafat's behavior: Arafat not only did little to quell the violence, but viciously attacked Israel in his speeches, especially those given in Arabic to his own people. Furthermore, rather than seeking to calm the situation, the media controlled by the Palestinian Authority incited the masses to escalate the violence. Palestinian textbooks continued to deny Israel's legitimacy. Palestinian clerics delivered sermons in mosques denying any Jewish connection to the Temple Mount, and Palestinians began systematically to attack other Jewish historic holy places, notably Rachel's tomb near Bethlehem and Joseph's tomb in Shechem (Nablus).

Israelis across the political spectrum now seriously questioned whether the basic bargain of Palestinian-Israeli mutual recognition hammered out in Oslo still held or, indeed, whether Arafat had ever intended to carry out the various agreements in good faith. If Arafat rejected the generous peace proposals made not only by Barak but even the more far-reaching concessions suggested by President Clinton, then, Israelis asked themselves, what point was there in continuing to negotiate with him?

Not only did the upsurge of violence not elicit any Israeli concessions, it also made life considerably more difficult for the Palestinians. According to a report by Terje Rod-Larsen, the UN special coordinator for the Middle East peace process, by the end of 2000 the Palestinian economy was losing $8.6 million a day, unemployment—which had averaged 11 percent for the first nine months of the year—went up to 38 percent, and the number of Palestinians living in poverty doubled to nearly one-third of the population. As a result, "anger and uncertainty" had replaced many Palestinians' hopes for peace, he reported. Some of the popular Palestinian disappointment at the lack of economic progress and frustration over the failure to achieve political gains were directed at the Palestinian Authority, whose widespread corruption and arbitrary rule were widely resented.

AMERICAN REACTION

Televised pictures of Palestinian children being killed in clashes with Israeli soldiers aroused initial sympathy in the U.S. for the demonstrators and criticism of the Israelis for their use of what seemed to be excessive force. But as it became clear that Arafat was encouraging the violent clashes and cynically placing children in harm's way to score points in his propaganda campaign against Israel, public opinion and media columnists turned increasingly critical of Arafat's intransigence and supportive of Israel's peace efforts.

Sympathy for Israel's position was also evident in Congress. All through the spring and summer members of Congress from both parties decried the pressures being placed on Israel for concessions without reciprocity from the Palestinian side, with Republicans, naturally, more skeptical than Democrats about what they perceived as the administration's courting of Arafat. When the new surge of violence began in the fall, several members of Congress criticized the Clinton administration for its failure to veto a one-sided UN Security Council resolution on October 7 that censured Israel for using what the resolution described as "excessive force" against the Palestinians. The resolution did not criticize the Palestinian violence that had provoked the Israeli response.

The crisis in Israel caused by the mounting violence was addressed during the second presidential debate, on October 11, between Vice President Al Gore and Governor George W. Bush. According to the vice president: "We need to insist that Arafat send out instructions to halt some of the provocative acts of violence that have been going on." In a statesmanlike display of bipartisanship, Governor Bush responded that "particularly now during this difficult period, we ought to be speaking with one voice, and I appreciate the way the administration has worked hard to calm the tensions. Like the vice president, I call on Chairman Arafat to have his people pull back to make the peace."

Both candidates affirmed their strong support for U.S. ties with Israel. Bush said unequivocally, "should I be the president, Israel's going to be our friend. I'm going to stand by Israel." Gore agreed, declaring: "Our bonds with Israel are larger than agreements or disagreements on some details of diplomatic initiatives. They are historic, they are strong and they are enduring." But the vice president's high-profile position in the Clinton administration required him to justify current American policy even when it went against Israel's wishes, as it had four days earlier in abstaining on the Security Council resolution. Gore stressed, "we stand with Israel, but we have maintained the ability to serve as an honest broker." That was important, he said, especially in times of tension, when there were adversaries with whom Israel could not have direct dialogue: "And if we throw away that ability to serve as an honest broker, then we will have thrown away a strategic asset that's important not only to us but also to Israel."

In the third presidential debate, on October 17, Bush criticized the Clinton administration for attempting to force the pace of negotiations, remarking: "When it comes to timetables, it can't be the United States' timetable as to how discussions take place." He acknowledged that "this current administration's worked hard to keep the parties at the table," adding, "I will try to do the same thing. But it won't be on my timetable, it will be on the timetable that people are comfortable with in the Middle East."

Congress also expressed bipartisan support for Israel at this time of crisis and urged the United States to stand by Israel in the international arena. On October 12 in the Senate, Majority Leader Trent Lott (R., Miss.) and Minority Leader Thomas Daschle (D., S.D.) cosponsored a letter to the president expressing support for Israel and "profound disappointment and frustration" with PA chairman Arafat. A total of 96 of the 100 senators signed the letter, which declared: "One can only conclude that Arafat either seeks to use violence as a negotiating tool to extort further concessions from the government of Israel, or that he intends to end the peace process in its entirety as a prelude to a unilateral declaration of Palestinian statehood."

The House of Representatives passed a similar statement. Concurrent Resolution 426, sponsored by Reps. Benjamin Gilman (R., N.Y.), Sam Gejdenson (D., Conn.), Richard Armey (R., Tex.), and Richard Gephardt (D., Mo.), passed overwhelmingly, 365-30. Introducing the resolution, Gilman blamed Arafat directly for allowing the situation to spiral out of control, and charged that the "unbridled use of violence" was a cynical tactic by the Palestinian Authority chairman to attempt "to dictate Israeli concessions at the negotiating table." Gilman, who had long been critical of the way the negotiations were being handled and had worked to restrict funding for the PLO, stressed that Arafat's use of violence was a "fundamental" violation of the Oslo accords. The House resolution also urged the Clinton administration to use its veto power in the UN Security Council to block passage of additional one-sided resolutions against Israel and called on all parties to reinvigorate the peace process.

In a renewed effort to end the escalating cycle of violence, President Clinton managed to bring Prime Minister Barak and Chairman Arafat together again for a meeting at Sharm el-Sheikh on October 16–17. The two antagonists came with quite different objectives. According to Robert Satloff, executive director of the Washington Institute for Near East Policy, Barak's primary goals were securing a clear call from Arafat for an end to violence, avoiding an international commission of inquiry, and achieving a pathway back to negotiations. For Arafat the objectives were getting Israel to pull back from sites in Zone B (areas under Palestinian civilian control but with a continuing Israeli security presence) that abutted Palestinian urban centers and that had been the scenes of clashes; to lift the Israeli-imposed closure on the territories; to reopen the Gaza airport and the safe-passage route linking Gaza and the West Bank; and to obtain a full internationalization of the conflict, including a formal international inquiry.

No joint declaration emerged from this meeting, only a statement by Clinton, which, he claimed, had the support of both sides. It said that the parties had agreed not only to call for an end to violence, but to "take immediate concrete measures" to end the current confrontation and eliminate points of friction, including "enhancing security cooperation and ending the closure and opening the Gaza airport." He pledged that "the United States will facilitate security cooperation as needed." This referred to procedures that CIA director George Tenet worked out with the parties at a meeting in Paris, which included the creation of situation rooms jointly manned by Israelis and Palestinians to nip incipient incidents in the bud before they escalated. (This direct involvement of the CIA, which had been agreed upon in principle back in December 1998 as part of the Clinton-brokered Wye accord of December 1998, lasted all of one day before being overtaken by new acts of violence on the ground.)

Clinton also announced that a compromise had been reached on the issue of investigating the causes of the violence. The United States, together with the Israelis and Palestinians and in consultation with the UN secretary general, would establish a fact-finding committee — less powerful than a quasi-judicial commission of inquiry — that would be chaired by an American. The committee's report would be presented to the president, but also shared with the parties and the UN before publication. Names of the committee members were announced in November. The chairman was George Mitchell, the former U.S. senator who had played a key role in bringing about the 1998 Good Friday accord that led to the easing of the Protestant-Catholic conflict in Northern Ireland. Other members were former U.S. senator Warren Rudman, former Turkish president Suleyman Demirel, EU security representative Javier Solana, and Norway's foreign minister, Thorbjörn Jagland.

The presidential statement went on to say that the parties had agreed that the United States would consult with them over the next two weeks on seeking "a pathway back to negotiations and a resumption of efforts to reach a permanent-status agreement based on UN Security Council Resolutions 242 and 338 and subsequent understandings."

In Israel, meanwhile, the failure of the peace process led to the unraveling of Barak's coalition, his resignation in December, and a call for new elections for prime minister in early 2001 (see below, pp. 511–12). Arafat expressed a desire to resume negotiations with Israel after the elections at the point they had broken off. Clinton made it clear, however, that the specific bridging proposals he had personally made to the parties, including far-reaching concessions by Israel on Jerusalem and other crucial issues, were off the table once he left the White House on January 20, 2001, and did not bind the new American administration.

Other U.S.-Israel Matters

STRATEGIC COOPERATION

Despite the failure of U.S. peace initiatives in the Middle East, both Congress and the executive branch took important steps throughout the year to strengthen America's strategic cooperation with Israel.

One important area of cooperation was missile defense. Three major systems under joint development were further advanced during 2000: the Arrow missile interceptor program, the Boost Phase Intercept (BPI), and the Tactical High Energy Laser (THEL). Congress funded these programs not only because they aided an ally, Israel, but also because the American military would benefit from their success and American defense manufacturers shared in the contracts.

The successful test of the THEL in June at the White Sands Missile Range in New Mexico marked a key advance in Israel's efforts to develop an effective weapon to shoot down short-range missiles, such as the Katyushas that Hezbollah had been using to harass Israeli civilians living in the north of the country.

In a second test, in August, the THEL, which employs a high-energy laser beam fired at the speed of light, succeeded in shooting down two short-range rockets that had been launched only seconds apart. The U.S. Army hailed this as an unprecedented accomplishment and a tribute to the THEL's revolutionary new technology.

In September the Arrow missile system successfully downed a simulated Scud missile that had been launched by an Israeli F-15 fighter flying over the Mediterranean. The U.S. and Israel were working to enhance the Arrow's capabilities so that it could also confront long-distance ballistic missiles such as the Shahab-3 being developed by Iran.

In August Congress passed the defense spending bill for fiscal 2001, which included $240 million for Israeli projects. The Arrow program received $95 million and the THEL $11 million for further testing. Also included were funds for the Pentagon to purchase various Israeli high-tech systems. The Marine Corps received $90 million to purchase the Litening II pod, a system developed by the Israeli defense firm Rafael, that enhanced both navigation and target detection for fighter aircraft. The U.S. Army was given $20 million to buy the Reactive Armor Tile system, designed by Rafael and produced in the U.S., for the protection of armored vehicles from enemy fire. And the U.S. Navy received $15 million to purchase the ITALD, an unmanned fighter aircraft decoy designed by Israel Military Industries.

Despite continuing Palestinian violence and State Department warnings toward the end of the year advising Americans not to travel to the area, the Joint Political Military Group (JPMG), established by the United States and Israel in 1983, convened as scheduled in Eilat for its semiannual meetings. The JPMG was the principal forum for coordination of the strategic relationship, including joint U.S.-Israeli contingency planning, positioning of U.S. military hardware in Israel, and combined military exercises. As the level of cooperation had expanded in recent years, other formal bodies had been set up to oversee specific joint activities. The most important ones meeting during 2000 were the Defense Policy Advisory Group and the senior-level Strategic Policy Planning Group. In addition, the Joint Security Assistance Planning Group met to review and coordinate management of the U.S. funds used by Israel to modernize the IDF.

THE PHALCON AFFAIR

Despite the close cooperation between the defense establishments of the United States and Israel, a serious cloud appeared on the horizon in June over American opposition to Israel's planned $250-million sale of the first of four Phalcon AWAC-type planes to China (see also below, pp. 505–06). Although Secretary of State Albright had earlier said that the administration did not support linking the Phalcon dispute to U.S. aid to Israel, AIPAC and other American friends of Israel had been warning the Israelis for weeks of the storm brewing in Washington. William Cohen, the U.S. secretary of defense, bluntly told a press conference in Jerusalem on April 3 that the U.S. opposed sale of this type of technology to China "because of the potential of changing the strategic balance in that region, with the tensions running high as they are between China and Taiwan." Barak responded that he was aware of American sensitivity with regard to China, but insisted that Israel had to fulfill "our commitment in the contracts we have signed." Barak, who appeared deaf to the messages coming from Washington, told visiting Chinese president Jiang Zemin, at an April 13 press conference, that Israel hoped to proceed with the sale, adding, "we will keep discussing it with the Americans." This occurred just a few days after President Clinton, in a meeting with Barak, had reiterated American objections.

The U.S. House Appropriations Committee adopted a statement in June saying it was "very disturbed by reports that Israel is preparing to provide China with an airborne radar system that would threaten both the forces of democratic Taiwan and the United States in the region surrounding the Taiwan Straits." The statement was actually a milder replacement for the original proposal by Rep. Sonny Callahan (R., Ala.), chairman of the powerful House Subcommittee on Foreign Operations, to cut an equivalent $250 million from U.S. aid to Israel. Israel came under intense pressure to cancel the deal. Representative David Obey of Wisconsin, the ranking Democrat on the Appropriations Committee, was blunt: "If that sale goes forward, I have no intention of supporting further aid to Israel, period. That ought to be pretty damn clear."

On July 12, on the eve of his departure to the United States to participate in Camp David II, Barak finally ordered the Phalcon sale canceled. With this cloud removed from the discussion of Israel's share of the foreign-aid package, both houses of Congress approved $3 billion in assistance for Israel in fiscal year 2001. This included $1.98 billion in military assistance and $840 million in economic assistance. The proportion of economic aid was gradually being decreased under an Israeli proposal to phase it out over a ten-year period, in view of the vibrant growth of the Israeli economy. The military share of the aid, however, was going up due to Israel's growing defense needs. The aid package included all the traditional pro-Israel provisions—early disbursal of the money, offshore procurement allowing Israel to spend a portion of its military aid within Israel, and continued funding for refugee resettlement, primarily for the immigrants continuing to come from the former Soviet Union.

MOVING THE EMBASSY

According to the Israeli daily *Ha'aretz,* after the failed Arafat-Barak summit at Camp David, Barak urged Clinton to give some tangible signs of American support to help the prime minister shore up his shaky political base in the face of an impending no-confidence move in the Knesset and the defection of three coalition parties angered over Israel's proposed concessions at Camp David. In his interview with Israel Television on July 28, Clinton outlined some ways to "review and strengthen" American-Israeli ties and reward Israel for "the courageous actions the prime minister and the Israeli team took at the summit and in view of the withdrawal from Lebanon." In this connection he broached the subject of Jerusalem:

> You know, I have always wanted to move our embassy to West Jerusalem. We have a designated site there. I have not done so because I didn't want to do anything to undermine our ability to help to broker a secure and fair and lasting peace for Israelis and the Palestinians. But in light of what has happened, I've taken that decision under review and I'll make a decision sometime between now and the end of the year on that.

Later in the year, President Clinton indeed proposed, as part of the final-status agreement between Israel and the Palestinians, the establishment of two American embassies in Jerusalem, one in the western part of the city to serve Israel, and the other, in East Jerusalem, to serve the new Palestinian state. But no agreement was reached.

Twice during the year, in June and December, Clinton issued executive orders citing "national security interests" for delaying the move of the U.S. embassy from Tel Aviv to Jerusalem for another six months. This presidential authority to issue temporary waivers every six months postponing the embassy move had been included in the Jerusalem Embassy Act of 1995. In that law, Congress had declared it U.S. policy that Jerusalem "should remain an undivided city," that it "should be recognized as the capital of the State of Israel," and that the embassy "should be established in Jerusalem no later than May 31, 1999." As a sanction for noncompliance, the law specified that 50 percent of the State Department's 1999 budget for "acquisition and maintenance of buildings abroad" would be withheld until the opening of the embassy in Jerusalem. During her 2000 New York Senate campaign, First Lady Hillary Rodham Clinton declared that Jerusalem should be "the eternal and indivisible capital of Israel."

WEOG

Persistent American efforts, spearheaded by UN ambassador Richard Holbrooke, succeeded in getting Israel admitted as a provisional member of the Western European and Others Group (WEOG), comprised of the Western European states, the United States, Canada, Australia, and New Zealand. Since candidates for temporary seats on the Security Council and other UN bodies had to be nominated by the various regional groups, Israel's membership in WEOG would, at least theoretically, enable it to compete on equal terms with other UN members. In fact Israel had agreed, as the price for provisional membership, that it would hold off seeking nominations from the group. The Arabs and their nonaligned allies had for years barred Israel from joining the Asian regional group, which was Israel's logical place geographically.

Other Middle-East States

IRAN

On February 2 CIA Director George Tenet testified before the Senate Intelligence Committee about the growing threat posed by the continuing efforts of Iran and Iraq to develop Intercontinental Ballistic Missiles (ICBMs). While both these countries were currently benefiting from arms and weapons technology imports from Russia, China, and North Korea, he estimated that within a few years not only Iran and Iraq, but also Syria would have their own domestic weapons capabilities and even become exporters of missiles. "Iran, in the next few years, may be able to supply, not only complete Scuds, but also Shahab-3s and related technology" that could threaten its neighbors. Assessing the just-completed parliamentary election in Iran, Tenet concluded that although the overwhelming popular support for President Khatami, a relative moderate, reflected a desire among young people for change, Islamic hard-liners who controlled key positions would still be able to block movement toward a more open policy toward the United States. Tehran, he said, continued to reject the Middle East peace process, and Iran "remains the most active state sponsor [of terrorism]." Regrettably, he concluded, "the use of terrorism as a political tool by official Iranian organs has not changed since President Khatami took office in August of 1997."

In an effort to induce Russia to stop providing missile and nuclear technology to Iran, the Senate in March unanimously (98-0) passed the Iran Nonproliferation Act, which, among other provisions, would bar American aid to the Russian Space Agency unless the president certified that Moscow was taking the necessary measures to prevent the transfer of weapons of mass destruction to Iran. The House had passed a nearly identical measure the previous year.

An ominous sign that powerful elements in Iran sought to continue efforts to demonize Israel was the trial of 13 Iranian Jews arrested in May 1999 on charges of spying for Israel and aiding the United States. The long trial ended on July 1, 2000, with the conviction and sentencing to long prison terms of ten of the accused. The United States led the international protests against their unjust imprisonment and the manifestly unfair character of their secret trial, and pressed for their release. Independent scholars of Iranian affairs concluded that since none of the accused were ever in a position to obtain any official secrets or information of military significance, the Jews had been imprisoned on trumped-up charges as part of the policy of the hard-liners to embarrass the Khatami government and derail any plans it might have to normalize relations with the United States. On September 21, the prison terms of the ten were reduced on appeal.

IRAQ

In 2000, with no UN arms inspectors in Iraq for two years, persistent rumors circulated that Saddam Hussein was managing to evade the sanctions imposed on him and was continuing his efforts to acquire missiles and secretly rebuild his capacity to produce nuclear, chemical, and biological weapons. This quickly became a campaign issue. The Republican platform criticized the Clinton administration for failure to take effective action against Iraq, or even to release more than a token amount of the funds that Congress had appropriated for Iraqi opposition groups committed to toppling the regime. The Democrats countered that it was the miscalculations of President George Bush and his administration that had permitted the Iraqi dictator to remain in power after the American-led coalition defeated him in Operation Desert Storm in 1991.

American policy toward Iraq came up during the second presidential debate, with both candidates offering rather vague and general responses. Vice President Gore said that "we also have to keep a weather eye toward Saddam Hussein because he's taking advantage [of the current unrest in the region] to once again make threats and he needs to understand that he's not only dealing with Israel, he is dealing with us, if he is making the kinds of threats that he's talking about there." Governor Bush responded: "The coalition against Saddam has fallen apart or it's unraveling. . . . The sanctions are being violated. . . . We don't know whether he's developing weapons of mass destruction. He better not be or there's going to be a consequence, should I be the president."

JORDAN

On October 23 President Clinton and King Abdullah II of Jordan signed a free-trade agreement in Washington. When approved by Congress, Jordan would become the second country in the Middle East, after Israel, to enjoy these special tariff and other economic benefits. Clinton administration officials said they hoped the trade agreement would lift Jordan's stagnant economy. Although the United States sold Jordan only about $300 million in goods annually and Jordan exported even less to the United States, the deal was meant to send a positive signal to other countries in the region about the benefits of peace. Jordan had concluded a peace treaty with Israel in 1994, and a majority of its population was Palestinian, many of them refugees. But as the peace process unraveled at the end of the year, plans for other substantial new American assistance programs for the Palestinians and other potential Arab partners for peace with Israel were shelved.

GEORGE E. GRUEN

Jewish Communal Affairs

Privatizing Jewish Identity

T HE EMPHASIS ON INDIVIDUAL self-fulfillment that pervaded American society and that had affected American Jewish life through the 1990s continued unabated in 2000. One of the year's most important books on American Jewry, *The Jew Within: Self, Family, and Community in America,* by Steven M. Cohen and Arnold M. Eisen, made that abundantly clear. Interviewing 50 young-adult Jews around the country who were "moderately affiliated" — neither deeply committed nor totally alienated — and placing their responses in the framework of the findings of survey research, Cohen and Eisen concluded that such Jews were quite open to Jewish identification so long as they maintained the right to define what being Jewish meant to them. Two of the book's chapter titles told the story: "The Sovereign Self" and "The Retreat of Public Judaism."

Indicating just how pervasive such individualistic Judaism had become, former *New York Times* reporter Ari Goldman, in his new book *Being Jewish: The Spiritual and Cultural Practice of Judaism Today,* presented an "Orthodox" case for such individualism. The book sympathetically described the idiosyncratic practices of Jews who decided for themselves how to express their Jewishness, not as part of an integrated system of religious discipline, but as what felt right for them. For Goldman, a self-identified Orthodox Jew, the vast corpus of Jewish learning and practice provided a kind of smorgasbord of Judaism, from which the individual Jew was free to take and sample what was personally meaningful.

In religious terms, such individualistic Judaism was often characterized as "spirituality," a term with no simple definition. As Gary Rosenblatt, editor of the *New York Jewish Week,* put it in a headline (January 14), "Spirituality (Whatever That Means) Is On The Rise." According to Rabbi Shmuel Boteach, guru of the new Jewish revival and author of *Kosher Sex* and *Dating Secrets of the Ten Commandments,* "Judaism is the perfect spiritual model for 'Generation X,' the 'X' representing the confluence of the spiritual and material modalities" (*New York Jewish Week,* February 25). Michael Lerner, the controversial editor of *Tikkun* magazine, published a book, *Spirit Matters,* which argued for a Jewish spirituality that seeks to change the world through social action. "I'm speaking out of the prophetic tradition," Lerner told a reporter. "What 9-Letter Word Has Been Deleted from Reform Teachings?" asked Lawrence Kushner in the fall issue of *Reform Judaism.* His answer was, "Mysticism — and it's time to correct that mistake." Arguing against the assumption that Reform was by definition rational in its religious approach, Kushner insisted that Reform Jews could, in principle, be just as immersed in spiritual experience as "Black Hat Orthodoxy."

Inevitably, the personalization of Jewish identity brought a reevaluation of the entire question of Jewish continuity. Rabbi Irwin Kula, for example, president of CLAL (Center for Jewish Learning and Leadership), argued that what others saw as the erosion of Jewish practice was actually "a sign of the ongoing and healthy transformation of Jewish identity," since such identity was ultimately a personal matter not subject to objective criteria. Thus there was no Jewish continuity problem, only a reluctance to abandon outmoded definitions of what made a Jew (*New York Jewish Week,* March 17).

June saw the release of a long-awaited study of the New York Jewish community, *Connections and Journeys: Assessing Critical Opportunities for Enhancing Jewish Identity,* which also utilized the new, more subjective, approach. Directed by Bethamie Horowitz and sponsored by the UJA-Federation of New York, the survey was based on interviews and focus groups with over 1,500 Jews aged 22–52. Eschewing the standard questions asked on previous similar surveys that measured attitudes and practices associated with Judaism, *Connections and Journeys* sought to get the respondents to tell the stories of their personal "journeys," that is, to relate their earlier Jewish experiences and their Jewish expectations for the future. This approach provided a sense of how Jewish identification evolved over a person's lifetime. Horowitz found that feelings of attachment to Jewishness grew over time, even though Jewish practice tended to decline. Horowitz therefore concluded that Jewish identity "isn't necessarily declining." Hailing the study, Jewish communal leaders said they would design programs to assist Jews in their personal Jewish journeys. The 2000 National Jewish Population Survey—not expected to release its results till 2002 (see below, pp. 257–58)—was also said to be using more subjective measurements of Jewishness than had its 1990 predecessor.

Social scientist Charles Liebman launched a blistering attack on the subjective emphasis at the annual meeting of the Association for Jewish Studies in December. Acknowledging the fact that what constitutes Jewishness does evolve over time, Liebman nevertheless charged that the growing tendency to downplay any objective criteria for determining Jewish identity was an unscientific surrender to the assimilationist forces in American Jewish life, and he virtually accused certain unnamed researchers of dishonestly tailoring their findings to fit the optimistic wishful thinking of the bodies that funded them.

Acceptance of Intermarriage

So pervasive was the loss of any objective criteria for defining Jewishness that even marriage to a non-Jew was no longer taken as an act of separation from the Jewish community. On September 23, the front page of *New York Times* "arts and ideas" section ran a story headlined, "A Little Bad News, a Little Good News."

There was a big photo of the marriage of Rabbi Roger Ross to the Rev. Deborah Steen, "with rabbis, ministers and priests participating." Under it was a much smaller picture of a band performing music. The caption noted: "A high rate of intermarriage has led Jews to worry about assimilation. At the same time, Jewish culture is undergoing a renaissance, as seen in the popularity of klezmer music." That the marriage of a Jew to a Christian carried no more significance on the negative side than did klezmer's popularity on the positive side was not simply the idiosyncratic take of the reporter: Intermarriage had become a non-issue for most of American Jewry, and, as Cohen and Eisen demonstrated in *The Jew Within,* Jews saw no contradiction between being Jewish and having a non-Jewish spouse.

The year 2000 saw the publication of *What to Do When You're Dating a Jew,* a book by two Jewish women telling non-Jews enough about Jewish foods, holidays, and folkways so they would not embarrass themselves while courting Jews ("If you can hold your own at a Jewish dinner table, you've won half the battle"). Dovetail Institute, an organization for Jewish-Christian families, held a convention in June to talk about the "interfaith" Sunday schools that were sprouting up in many communities. A group called Jewish Family and Life, which had a Web site devoted to the needs of intermarried families, publicly urged the Jewish community to drop the goal of conversion from its outreach programs, and simply to encourage the Jewish involvement of two-religion families. Some mainstream Jewish leaders apparently agreed. Barry Shrage, president of the Combined Jewish Philanthropies of Greater Boston, one of the largest federations in the country, told a reporter that every case of intermarriage was an "opportunity." Shrage wanted the community to send a message to the non-Jewish spouse: "We have a gorgeous tradition. Come learn with us" (*New York Times,* September 23). New York UJA-Federation funded one program for engaged interfaith couples and another to train counselors to work with such couples. In September, Hillel at New York University announced a Rosh Hashanah workshop for interfaith couples, and Hillel's national headquarters explained that local branches had the leeway to decide such matters on their own.

Clear evidence of the breakdown of the old intermarriage taboo was provided by the American Jewish Committee's annual survey of American Jewish opinion, which was released in the fall. Eighty percent of the sample said that, "intermarriage is inevitable in an open society." Asked if "it would pain me if my child married a gentile," 39 percent agreed and 56 percent disagreed. While 25 percent felt that converting the non-Jewish spouse to Judaism was the "best response" to intermarriage, 68 percent did not think so. And, in a question that had particular resonance in a year when a Jewish vice-presidential candidate would be challenged on this issue — "Is it racist to oppose Jewish-gentile marriages?" — half of the Jews said "yes" and 47 percent "no." Fully 57 percent of one half-sample and 42 percent of the other half believed that rabbis should officiate at mixed marriages even if non-Jewish clergy was also involved in the ceremony. And yet, reflecting a lingering sense that intermarriage was somehow not good for the Jewish people, over two-thirds of the sample agreed that, "the Jewish community has an obligation to urge Jews to marry Jews."

Keeping Young Jews in the Fold

The fact that Jewish identity had come detached from its old moorings and was now very much a matter of individual preference made the community's search for ways of attracting and keeping young Jews' allegiance all the more difficult. Rabbis, educators, communal professionals, and philanthropists did what they could to light the spark of Jewishness—however defined—in as many souls as they could reach.

THE ISRAEL EXPERIENCE

The much-heralded Birthright Israel program, first announced by philanthropists Michael Steinhardt and Charles Bronfman in 1998, sought to give every young Jew, as a "birthright," a free ten-day trip to Israel, in the expectation that contact with the Jewish state would strengthen the participants' Jewish consciousness and lead to increased involvement in other areas of Jewish life. By the end of 1999, with other philanthropists and the Israeli government also committed to help fund the initiative, the first group of 6,000 college students prepared to leave for Israel on their winter break.

If the press reports were to be believed, Birthright Israel was a huge success. Interviews with the participants in Israel and, after their return, in the U.S., indicated a surge of Jewish pride, a determination to marry within the fold and create a Jewish home, and even some interest in eventual aliyah. Columnist Leonard Fein captured the widespread euphoria in the title of his piece on the project, "Blown Away by the Power of 10 Days" (*Forward*, January 21). The Jewish media continued to track some of the students after their return to see if the trip had an enduring impact, and the results were generally positive. As more than 1,750 other Jewish students registered for Birthright Israel trips set to depart during spring break or the summer, some observers who had been skeptical about the project in its planning stages admitted their mistake. "Birthright's Surprises are Convincing Some Skeptics," was the headline in the *Forward* (January 21), and one repentant critic wrote a detailed mea culpa, "Birthright Israel: Why I Was Wrong" (*Moment*, August).

In July, the positive impressionistic evidence was buttressed by the findings of a survey, carried out by the Cohen Center for Modern Jewish Studies at Brandeis University, of the short-term impact of the trip. Conducted on-line and over the phone, the survey found that the percentage of participants feeling a strong connection to the Jewish people rose from 40 percent to 60 percent as a result of the trip, and the percentage feeling a strong connection to Israel jumped from 25 percent to 55 percent. A control group, made up of students who had wanted to go on Birthright Israel but were turned away due to lack of space, scored lower than the returnees on both items.

Success bred success. In February, UJA-Federation of New York became the first federation to pledge its support for Birthright Israel, contributing $500,000. Other federations followed suit, and by the end of the year local federations had contributed a total of $18 million. In addition, United Jewish Communities, the umbrella organization of the federations, pledged $52.5 million over five years plus $90,000 for follow-up programs, and Hadassah gave $5 million. Hillel, the Jewish campus organization that handled the actual recruiting and selection of participants, had to hire eight new staff members to work on the project. Richard Joel, Hillel's president, declared: "Birthright Israel has become the strongest arrow in our quiver of engagement." But the unforeseen outbreak of violence in Israel at the end of the year endangered the program, as thousands of students canceled their plans to visit Israel on winter break after the U.S. State Department, on October 24, issued a warning to American citizens to "defer all travel" to Israel and the territories.

IS THE SYNAGOGUE THE ANSWER?

In recent years, those who worried about the erosion of Jewish identity had come increasingly to blame the American synagogue, and in 2000 this sentiment received unprecedented public expression. "The real truth," wrote Rabbi Sidney Schwartz, "is that most Jews can't pray. Nor does the contemporary American synagogue offer much help in this regard" (*Forward,* April 21). Schwartz contended that an exit poll of Jews leaving services would find few affirmative answers to the question, "Have you had a meaningful prayer experience?" Journalist David Margolick admitted: "Going to a synagogue—any synagogue, it seems—is pure torture for me. I literally loathe the experience" (*Forward,* September 22). Giving voice to the feelings of many young Jews, Margolick complained about the length of the prayers, their unintelligibility, their "excruciatingly repetitious" and "ossified" nature, and the rabbi's "pretentious and banal" sermon. Even the rabbinical students at the Jewish Theological Seminary seemed to agree: the regular Friday evening service there collapsed as everyone flocked to a "happy, clappy" Carlebach-style minyan. According to *Connections and Journeys,* Bethamie Horowitz's report on Jewish identity, while 34 percent of Jews in New York City between the ages of 22 and 52 said that their parents helped them develop a positive Jewish identification, only 5 percent could say that about their congregational rabbis, and 10 percent felt that rabbis had influenced them negatively.

Given the historic centrality of the synagogue in Jewish life, criticism of the institution was greeted with alarm, especially in the Conservative movement, where the problem seemed most acute. Unlike the situation in Reform Judaism, Conservative synagogues retained the long traditional service in Hebrew, but, unlike the Orthodox, relatively few Conservative congregants understood the words or felt that regular prayer was a religious obligation. Rabbi Jerome Epstein, executive vice president of the United Synagogue of Conservative Judaism, threw the ball into the court of the federations, arguing that the quality of synagogue life could only be upgraded with increased staffing, and that required more communal funding (*Forward,* May 19). Chancellor Ismar Schorsch of the Jewish Theological Seminary agreed, and, noting that fewer than half of American Jews belonged to a synagogue, urged a public campaign "to aim at defining citizenship in the American Jewish polity by membership in a synagogue" (*New York Jewish Week,* September 22).

In fact, Synagogue 2000, a joint Reform-Conservative project to revitalize congregational worship, was already receiving federation funding. And Rabbi Sidney Schwartz's new book, *Finding a Spiritual Home: How a New Generation of Jews Can Transform the American Synagogue,* provided four case studies of synagogues that, each in its own way, succeeded, he felt, in inspiring Jews through intimacy, warmth, and inclusiveness. In September 2000, three philanthropists—Charles Schusterman, Michael Steinhardt, and Edgar Bronfman—launched a new initiative, STAR (Synagogue Transformation and Renewal). These men invited some 150 rabbis and educators from around the country to Chicago for a two-day meeting about the project. Many of those who came were dismayed at what they saw as the philanthropists' dismissive attitude toward the contemporary synagogue and at Steinhardt's assertion that non-Orthodox forms of Judaism were "historical accidents," but critics were reluctant to speak for the record. The philanthropists together pledged at least $18 million over five years in the form of challenge grants for new programs, the hiring of outside consultants, and training programs for rabbis in pastoral skills and business management.

For some, the apparent crisis of synagogue Judaism raised the possibility of promoting secular Judaism as an organized, coherent alternative. To be sure, the International Federation of Secular Humanistic Jews had existed for some time, but its eighth biennial conference, held in New York in September with some 250 people in attendance, received unprecedented coverage, largely due to the participation of several eminent speakers, including Robert Pinsky, poet laureate of the United States. Secular Judaism was a potent reality in Israel, the Jewish state, and high hopes were expressed at the conference that unaffiliated American Jews who were interested in their cultural heritage but turned off by religion could be convinced to join the movement. With that in mind, the U.S. branch of secular humanist Jews moved its national office from a suburb of Detroit to New York, and hired a new executive director with a strong background in public relations. There was even talk of setting up an institute of secular Jewish learning. Several observers noted, however, that very few of the people at the New York conference were under the age of 50.

DAY SCHOOLS

For some time, as concern mounted over Jewish continuity, Jewish day-school education—which had been virtually an Orthodox preserve—had become increasingly popular outside the Orthodox community as well. Early in 2000, the Avi Chai Foundation released a national study showing an increase of some 25,000 students in Jewish day schools during the 1990s, with the largest growth in enrollment coming in the non-Orthodox sector. Fifteen new non-Orthodox Jewish high schools were planning to open around the country within the next three years, three of them Conservative and the other 12 nondenominational community schools. The proliferation of day schools worsened an already severe shortage of qualified teachers and administrators at all levels. Eliot Spack, executive director of CAJE (Coalition for the Advancement of Jewish Education), warned, in August, "Hundreds of Jewish classes will open in September without a teacher."

In light of the communal focus on day-school education as a potent means for the transfer of Jewish culture to the next generation and the heavy financial burden such schools entailed, many were shocked to hear that the JCPA (Jewish Council for Public Affairs), at its annual plenum in February, voted to oppose, on church-state grounds, government aid to private schools even where approved by the courts, such as for the costs of transportation, textbooks, and special education (see above, pp. 183–84). The motion to oppose such aid—actually a reversal of previous JCPA policy—was proposed by the National Council of Jewish Women and passed 318-259.

The question of how to fund Jewish education was the subject of two conferences later in the year. The American Jewish Committee, which had gone on record, in December 1999, in favor of more communal funding for Jewish education including day schools, hosted a meeting in June. One presenter, Chicago businessman George Hanus, explained his plan for all Jews to leave 5 percent of their estates to Jewish education. However Dr. Jack Wertheimer, provost of the Jewish Theological Seminary, insisted that the huge sums necessary were not available from Jewish sources and would have to come from government, and John Ruskay, executive vice president of New York UJA-Federation, agreed that "it is time to seriously reconsider" the traditional Jewish antipathy to government aid for private education. In September, the Partnership for Excellence in Jewish Education, made up of major donors to day schools, heard from several experts that no less than $1 billion would be needed for the day schools. Since many of the federations and family foundations were burdened with other responsibilities, several of the speakers suggested that the community would do well to reconsider its opposition to government vouchers.

Liebermania

None of the ideas and projects to promote Jewish identity had anything near the impact on American Jews in 2000 as the nomination of a Jew for vice president. As early as March rumor had Senator Joseph I. Lieberman of Connecticut on Al Gore's "short list" for the Democratic vice-presidential nomination. The possibility that the first Jew to be named to a national ticket would observe the kashrut and Sabbath laws and be publicly identified with Orthodox Judaism served to project internal Jewish debates over Jewish identity into the national arena, and this, in turn, made American Jews even more conscious of them and more anxious about their implications.

All spring and into the summer the media discussed how Lieberman's Orthodoxy would affect his possible candidacy. Few doubted that Lieberman's eloquent denunciation, on the Senate floor, of President Bill Clinton's conduct in the Monica Lewinsky affair, rooted as it was in his Orthodox Jewish worldview, strengthened his moral authority with the voters (though he had, in the end, voted against impeachment), and that his traditional religiosity, criticism of the values of Hollywood, and openness to school vouchers might attract evangelical Protestants and traditional Catholics to support the ticket. But could a Sabbath observer function as vice president, and, potentially, president? Lieberman did not ride in cars, answer telephones, or use electrical appliances on Saturdays. Reporters familiar with his career downplayed the issue, noting that his religious scruples had not interfered with the effective discharge of his Senate responsibilities: He had walked to the Capitol on the Sabbath and cast voice votes, and, where national security or the "needs of the community" were at stake, Orthodox rabbis had granted him leeway to fulfill his public duties.

Far more challenging was the question raised by journalist Philip Weiss, a Jew married to a non-Jew, in a *New York Observer* column (May 1), entitled: "What Would a Jewish Veep Say about Intermarriage?" Weiss noted that the Orthodox Judaism espoused by Lieberman was not only officially and adamantly opposed to intermarriage, but actually called it a threat to Judaism, barred such couples from its institutions, and treated them as pariahs. In Weiss's eyes this was no different from the racism exhibited by Bob Jones University, which till recently had prohibited interracial dating, and which George W. Bush, the likely Republican presidential candidate, had been criticized for visiting. Weiss's comments received little attention at the time, since a Lieberman candidacy still seemed like a long shot.

On August 7, when Gore indeed named Lieberman as his running mate, the questions previously raised hypothetically suddenly became quite real, and the American people got a quick education in the arcana of Halakhah, Jewish law. The *New York Times,* in its lead editorial the next day, put the Sabbath issue front and center:

> As an Orthodox Jew who does not customarily work on the Jewish Sabbath, Mr. Lieberman may be called upon to explain how he will handle a job that demands full attention 24 hours a day, seven days a week. Mr. Lieberman has already provided an answer. He states that, while he does not carry out political or campaign activities on the sabbath, Jewish law obligates him to perform official government duties demanded of his job. He makes the analogy that Jewish law also obligates a doctor to help a sick patient in such circumstances.

As Lieberman hit the campaign trail after his nomination, the media regularly reported his Sabbath breaks from campaigning and his reliance on fish dinners where kosher meat was unavailable. Meanwhile Barry Freundel, rabbi of the Kesher Israel Synagogue in Washington, where Lieberman and his family were members, became a popular guest on television news shows where he elucidated the intricacies of Jewish law to bemused interviewers and national audiences, repeating over and over, to questioners who still recalled suspicions about clerical authority raised about John F. Kennedy, a Catholic, in 1960, that Lieberman had never requested his guidance, or that of Jewish law, about how to vote on issues of public policy. Virtually lost in the positive media coverage was another attack by Philip Weiss in the *New York Observer* (August 21), charging that Lieberman "wants to lead the people, he just doesn't want his children to marry any of them."

Within the Jewish community, Lieberman's nomination reshaped denominational politics; over the course of the campaign no less than three movements sought to appropriate him.

Many in the modern Orthodox camp saw the nomination not only as a victory for their view of how to preserve Jewish tradition in contemporary America, but also as a long-sought elixir for a movement that had been placed on the defensive by more insular forms of Orthodoxy. Dr. Norman Lamm, president of the modern Orthodox bastion, Yeshiva University, said that "vindication would not be a bad word" to describe the effect of the nomination. "He's about as modern Orthodox as you can get," enthused Haskel Lookstein, a prominent modern Orthodox rabbi in New York City. Historian Jonathan D. Sarna agreed, pointing out that Lieberman "is clean-shaven, does not wear a yarmulke full-time, and his wife does not cover her hair. . . . Modern Orthodoxy," he wrote, "may well be poised for a come-back" (*Forward,* August 11).

Orthodox elements more hostile to modernity reacted with some confusion. There were Orthodox Jews who—anonymously—told the media (most notably the Internet "Drudge Report") that Lieberman was not really Orthodox because he was pro-choice and supported gay rights, kissed women other than his wife, and was seen drinking water, wearing leather shoes, and campaigning to the sound of live music on the Tish'ah B'Av fast day, when strictly Orthodox Jews refrain from such acts. Agudath Israel, the most important sectarian Orthodox organization, found itself in a quandary. It had worked with the senator in advancing legislation of interest to the Orthodox community, and would surely need his help in the future. Yet the group had drawn severe criticism from those to its right for honoring him at its annual dinner in 1997, and Lieberman's engagement with the modern world hardly made him a poster boy for Agudath Israel's sectarian ideology. Agudath Israel nevertheless issued an op-ed claiming that Lieberman's commitment to Jewish law as immutable marked him as one of theirs. David Zwiebel, the organization's executive vice president for government and public affairs, denied that Lieberman was modern Orthodox—an ideology he compared to "a rather slippery fish." "We would do well to get beyond misleading labels," wrote Zwiebel, since the senator espoused "the decidedly old-fashioned values that lie at the heart of traditional Judaism" (*Forward,* August 18). That same day, however, in the *New York Times,* Agudath Israel's public-relations director, taking a different tack, was quoted as saying: "He's running for vice president, not chief rabbi. Therefore, there might be some things we would consider not thought out from a religious perspective, but we're not here to critique his religious life."

In fact Lieberman's staff, during the Democratic convention, had sought to head off just such nit-picking by telling reporters that their man considered himself "observant" in his Jewishness rather than Orthodox, and the week after the convention Lieberman had a press aide issue the following statement: "He refers to himself as observant because he doesn't follow the strict Orthodox code and doesn't want to offend the Orthodox, and his wife feels the same way." The candidate himself explained, "Well, I like to think of myself as an observant Jew, because it is broader and it's inclusive." This position was warmly greeted by Conservative Jews who observed the Sabbath while not adhering to Orthodox Halakhah, since they could now see the candidate as a kindred spirit. They also proudly pointed out that Mrs. Lieberman's son from her first marriage was studying for the Conservative rabbinate.

Across the denominational spectrum, Jews speculated about the impact an observant vice president might have as a role model on the Jewish identity of young Jews. Articles appeared in both the Jewish and the general press about the possible positive health benefits of a kosher diet and of complete rest—no driving, no telephone, no television—one day a week. In just one *New York Times* Sunday issue—September 24—there were three prominent articles, with photographs, about Orthodox Jewish life: the metro section told of the courting habits of young Orthodox Jewish couples who got to know each other by taking walks through the Brooklyn Botanical Gardens, the Long Island section described "simcha dancing" classes for Orthodox women, and the entertainment section enlightened readers about the popular daily "unapologetically Orthodox" Jewish radio program, "JM in the AM." Visions of an American vice president and his family attending High Holy Day services, eating in a sukkah, and lighting Hanukkah candles excited the imaginations of rabbis and Jewish educators while at the same time worrying many nonobservant Jews—few of whom, however, went public with their misgivings. The Lieberman candidacy was an irresistible topic for sermons, as rabbis held up the senator's principled adherence to religion as a standard for their congregants to emulate. "Lieberman is not campaigning on Shabbat," Rabbi Marc Gellman told his Long Island Reform congregation on Rosh Hashanah, in an obvious attempt to shame them into changing their ways. "He is turning down the pork ribs in Alabama, and if he is elected he is going to walk to the inauguration on Saturday afternoon. Lieberman is a new thing and he marks a new time" (*First Things,* December).

Matters became far more complicated for Lieberman as the campaign wore on. In the area of public policy, he frightened liberals—including many Jews for whom separation of church and state had an almost religious significance—with a speech on August 27 calling for a greater role for religion in public life. But he was also accused of backtracking on some of the earlier positions that had made him popular with Orthodox Jews and conservative Christians, such as support for school vouchers, doubts about affirmative action, and harsh criticism of Hollywood.

He also got into hot water with his own traditional Jewish community. Lieberman, whose personal pro-choice views were well known, went much further on "Larry King Live" in August, averring that abortion was "a matter of personal judgment. And like everything else in Judaism, ultimately it's up to each of us to decide what we think is right." In addition, he changed his mind about supporting a bill backed by Orthodox organizations that sought to prevent assisted suicide by restricting the use of morphine and encouraging aggressive treatment of pain; Lieberman apparently feared losing votes in Oregon, which had approved assisted suicide in a referendum. And on September 15, appearing on the "Imus in the Morning" radio show, Lieberman acknowledged that he skipped the daily benediction in the Orthodox prayer book thanking God for not having made him a woman. Then the host, "shock-jock" Don Imus, sprung on Lieberman the question Philip Weiss had been hammering away at for months: Didn't Jewish law prohibit intermarriage? Not at all, the candidate replied, "there's no ban whatsoever," only the natural desire to "marry within to keep the faith going." The *Jerusalem Post* broke the story the next week under the headline, "Lieberman: Intermarriage is Kosher."

It was unclear whether Lieberman was indeed ignorant of the halakhic taboo on intermarriage and to what extent his response was prompted by the fear of offending non-Jews and intermarried families less than two months before what was sure to be a close election. Whatever the case, the intermarriage remark aroused disappointment and concern in the Jewish community, coming as it did from a man who had become the symbol of a principled traditional Judaism that was at home in contemporary America—the very antithesis of the blurred Jewish identity often associated with the decision to intermarry. Agudath Israel urged the senator to disavow the impression that he was speaking in the name of Orthodox Judaism, and Mandell Ganchrow, president of the Union of Orthodox Jewish Congregations (OU), commented, "Given that intermarriage is probably the number one problem affecting the Jews today, I don't know what went through Lieberman's mind when he said that." A campaign aide told Rabbi Freundel that the senator had simply made a factual error, and the rabbi commented to the *New York Jewish Week* (September 29): "Politicians shouldn't discuss theology, and especially not on Imus." Lieberman himself said that he would no longer answer questions about Jewish law since he was not an expert. Ironically, Lieberman's "liberal" statement on intermarriage came out just as Zev Chafets broke the news, in the *Jerusalem Report* (October 10), that the candidate had praised Shaare

Zedek hospital in Jerusalem, which was guilty, Chafets said, of "religious bigotry" for refusing in-vitro fertilization treatment for intermarried couples—and to make matters worse, Mrs. Lieberman had served as a paid consultant to the hospital till her husband's nomination.

Lieberman's ill-advised remarks on intermarriage made it open season for attacks by fringe Orthodox groups that considered him far too liberal on many issues. On October 5 the Union of Orthodox Rabbis of the United States and Canada—the body that had declared non-Orthodox forms of Judaism to be "not Judaism" in 1997—publicly denounced Lieberman's support for gay rights, and specifically mentioned his appearance at a gay-rights event "on the very eve of Yom Kippur." Another group, calling itself Jews for Morality, claimed to have convened a rabbinical panel to excommunicate Lieberman for allegedly falsifying Jewish teachings on homosexuality, abortion, and intermarriage. Yet all of this was soon overshadowed in the headlines by another controversial remark by the candidate on an African-American radio station stating his willingness to meet with Nation of Islam leader Louis Farrakhan, who had a long history of engaging in anti-Semitic rhetoric.

By Election Day, the original Jewish euphoria over the Lieberman nomination was a distant memory, though appreciation for the historic meaning of his candidacy and respect for the man survived more or less intact. The senator's seeming inconsistencies, explained Rabbi Freundel, were due to Lieberman's understanding that he had to subordinate his personal opinions to the views of the presidential candidate. After all, said his rabbi, Lieberman "is not a representative of the Jewish people. He's a senator" (*Forward,* November 10). The nation quickly became caught up in the vortex of the disputed election returns in Florida, the state with a pivotal Jewish electorate where Lieberman had spent many days campaigning, and it was not till December 12 that the Supreme Court finally gave the state—and the election—to the Republicans. Previous speculation about what would happen if the Gore-Lieberman team lost now moved to a new plane of reality: With no Orthodox Jewish vice president in the offing, would Lieberman, in 2004, be the first serious Jewish presidential candidate?

Denominational Life

In his book *Jew vs. Jew: The Struggle for the Soul of American Jewry,* Samuel G. Freedman depicted battles in several Jewish communities around the country that pitted "secularist against believer, denomination against denomination, gender against gender, liberal against conservative, traditionalist against modernist." By sheer serendipity, the Lieberman nomination happened just when Freedman's book came out, and it appeared to confirm his key finding, "the triumph of the Orthodox model" of American Judaism, meaning that "against a backdrop of ever-more complete assimilation," the Orthodox were correct in their insistence "that religion binds Jewish identity."

For the first time in many years, however, interdenominational relations were virtually absent from the American Jewish agenda in 2000. One reason was that the struggle over religious pluralism in Israel, which had long been the focus of denominational battles in the U.S., was far overshadowed by political and military events; even Prime Minister Barak's "civil reform plan," announced in August, which would have gone a long way toward ending the Orthodox monopoly on Israeli Judaism, turned out to be a short-lived political gambit. And there even seemed to be some progress toward religious pluralism in Israel, as the special interdenominational conversion institutes set up in 1998 graduated their first candidates. Another, more ominous reason for quiet on the denominational battle-front in the U.S. may have been that Orthodox and non-Orthodox forms of American Judaism had drifted so far apart that they no longer shared enough in common to fight about.

REFORM JUDAISM

A case in point was the muted, almost pro forma, reaction within Orthodoxy to Reform's acceptance of gay marriage.

At its 1996 convention, the Central Conference of American Rabbis (CCAR), the Reform rabbinic body, had gone on record in favor of civil marriage for homosexuals. Also, in accordance with the Reform principle of rabbinic autonomy, an unknown number of rabbis were performing Jewish weddings, often called commitment ceremonies, for them. But a proposal at the 1998 convention for the CCAR to recognize the "sanctity" of same-sex unions aroused opposition from members who pointed out that homosexuality was explicitly prohibited by the Bible and warned that the resolution would hurt the efforts of Reform to gain acceptance in Israel. The issue proved so divisive that the CCAR postponed its consideration (see AJYB 1999, pp. 189–90).

In early 2000, with the CCAR convention coming up in March, the Women's Rabbinic Network, a caucus of female rabbis within the organization, circulated a proposed resolution stating that same-sex unions were "worthy of affirmation" since "committed same-sex relationships between two Jews" could have holy status and "serve as the foundation of stable Jewish families, thus adding strength to the Jewish community." Those supporting the proposal viewed it as a simple matter of human rights. But a group of 12 other rabbis, feeling that such language would violate rabbinic autonomy by making it virtually impossible for any Reform rabbi to refuse to officiate at a same-sex union, suggested an alternative formulation, calling on rabbis "to create welcoming atmospheres for gays and lesbians, doing so in ways they deem ritually most appropriate," but also acknowledging the "diversity of views" in the CCAR about rabbinic officiation.

The resolution that finally passed on March 29 was a compromise, stating explicitly that the CCAR supported its members who "affirmed" the relationship of a "same-gender couple" through "appropriate Jewish ritual," while also supporting those members who did not. After the resolution passed overwhelmingly by voice vote, many of the rabbis stood and pronounced the *shehehiyanu* benediction, praising God "for bringing us to this moment." Supporters of rabbinic officiation predicted that the new Reform stand would lead to an outpouring of new, creative liturgies for the solemnization of same-sex unions, while those opposing officiation expressed statisfaction that the words "marriage," "commitment ceremony," and "sanctity" were absent from the document. The Reform rabbinate now became the largest group of American clergy to allow officiation at gay unions.

The reaction from the Orthodox was predictable. The Rabbinical Council of America, the organization of modern Orthodox rabbis, asserted that "Judaism's laws cannot be abrogated by fiat or majority vote," and Agudath Israel placed an ad in the *New York Times* emphasizing that "Judaism is not a mirror of society's shifting mores." Yet such statements seemed more like standard boilerplate than a call to denominational combat, and the issue faded away quickly. Indeed, despite the fears of some Reform rabbis, the Orthodox establishment in Israel did not use the resolution against Reform in the Jewish state. Rabbi Charles Kroloff, president of the CCAR, noted, "We do not seem to have appeared on their radar screen. I believe the fear was really overemphasized."

Reform Judaism had to endure a severe embarrassment in 2000. Early in December, the president of Hebrew Union College (HUC), the rabbinical seminary for the Reform movement, abruptly announced his resignation. Earlier that day he had been slapped with a two-year suspension from the CCAR for sexual misconduct that had taken place years earlier, while he served as a congregational rabbi; he did not contest the findings or the penalty. The CCAR had conducted a yearlong, secret investigation before issuing the suspension.

CONSERVATIVE JUDAISM

2000 was a year of serious introspection for the Conservative movement, with two books appearing that analyzed, in depth, its current state and future potential: *Jews in the Center: Conservative Synagogues and their Members,* a collection of essays edited by Jack Wertheimer, and *The Conservative Movement in Judaism,* by the late Daniel J. Elazar and Rela Mintz Geffen. Sociologist Steven M. Cohen, author of the lead article in the Wertheimer volume, warned that the movement was likely to shrink over time because its membership was skewed toward the elderly: almost a quarter of Conservative synagogue members were over age 65. Noting that younger Jews belonging to Conservative synagogues were more observant and more educated Jewishly than their parents, Cohen recommended that the movement target such intensively committed Jews rather than seek to swell its numbers through outreach to the less observant and to the intermarried.

Although Chancellor Ismar Schorsch of the Jewish Theological Seminary announced his disagreement with Cohen's "small tent" strategy—he believed that Conservative Judaism might well prove attractive to Reform and unaffiliated

Jews thirsting for greater spiritual sustenance—the movement had already taken steps to set minimum religious standards and define clear boundaries. In 1998 it had barred intermarried Jews from holding positions where they might be seen as Jewish role models for young Conservative Jews, and in 1999 it had circulated a set of "behavioral expectations" for the movement's lay leaders.

During 2000, Conservative Judaism focused on its educational and camping programs. Chancellor Schorsch unveiled an ambitious plan for the development of a new early-childhood curriculum that would "saturate the youngsters in Jewish vocabulary, music, and ritual." And the network of Ramah summer camps, which encompassed seven overnight and four day camps, for the first time included with its application form a notice that only Jews according to Halakhah would be accepted as campers and hired as staff. Ramah officials noted that this had always been the policy, but that the Reform movement's acceptance of Jewish status through patrilineal descent, as well as the fact that many romances that began at Ramah led to marriage, made it necessary to introduce a formal rule ensuring that only those who were Jewish by the standards of the Conservative movement would be at these camps. One outraged intermarried parent, speaking at the United Jewish Communities (UJC) General Assembly in November, compared Ramah's ban on patrilineal Jews to the American government's decision in 1939 to turn away the ship *St. Louis,* which was carrying Jewish refugees from Germany, dooming the passengers.

This insistence on maintaining the patrilineality barrier separating it from Reform was evident, as well, in the expulsion of Congregation Ner Tamid of Bloomfield, New Jersey, from the United Synagogue of Conservative Judaism. The congregation had been formed in 1980 through a merger between a Reform and a Conservative synagogue, and had maintained affiliation with the synagogue bodies of both denominations. Its current rabbi was ordained by the Reform movement, many members were intermarried, and patrilineal children were recognized as Jews. Explaining that the situation of this synagogue had only recently come to his attention, Rabbi Jerome Epstein, executive vice president of the United Synagogue, asserted: "The congregation must determine whether it wishes to remain a Conservative congregation and figure out a strategy to bring itself into line with the standards of the Conservative movement." Ner Tamid's rabbi, however, wanted to maintain its dual Reform and Conservative affiliations in such a manner "that the standards of the Conservative movement would not apply to us in the same way," and he went on to predict that unless it, too, adopted the patrilineal standard, Conservative Judaism was "going to be driving people out of their synagogues."

The increasing self-assertion of West-Coast Jewry and the strains this created in the management of national Jewish organizations had been evident for a number of years, and they affected the Conservative movement in 2000. In January, the United Synagogue fired the officers of its Pacific Southwest regional board, sent two representatives to close the region's office in Encino, California, and had its lawyers try to freeze the region's bank accounts. One regional executive committee member called this "a Gestapo tactic, like storm troopers came in and tried to seize everything." Unlike the United Synagogue's other regions, whose synagogues paid dues directly to the national organization, which in turn allocated funds to the regional offices for programming costs, the Southwest region had retained significant financial autonomy, receiving dues payments directly from the local synagogues. The national body claimed that Southwest owed it $85,000, but a California judge ruled against the national office. The Rabbinical Assembly, the denomination's rabbinic organization, intervened with a resolution calling on both sides to resolve the issue peacefully.

RECONSTRUCTIONIST JUDAISM

Reconstructionism, the movement founded on the basis of Mordecai M. Kaplan's vision of Judaism as an all-encompassing civilization, continued to be the most liturgically innovative denomination, releasing a new Passover Haggadah that included an Arab Palestinian woman's description of her family's displacement from its home by the State of Israel. In response to criticism from other Jewish quarters, Rabbi Joy Levitt, one of the editors, explained that the Haggadah sought to convey the truth that Israel had achieved its freedom in a morally "complicated" way.

Institutionally, the movement faced a dilemma brought on by its success. What drew many Jews to Reconstructionism was the democratic, egalitarian structure of the small-group congregations. However membership was growing rapidly, and more space was needed — more than a quarter of the approximately 100 Reconstructionist congregations were in the process of purchasing or constructing a building, or had launched building campaigns. But Reconstructionists were eager to avoid the temptation of "selling" honor to the highest bidder by naming rooms after the biggest givers and putting up plaques inscribed with their names, a practice that they felt had hurt the moral standing of the other movements. At a series of two-day workshops for rabbis and lay leaders on the "Torah of Money," participants shared ideas on how congregations might raise adequate funds without creating a hierarchy of prestige linked to wealth.

ORTHODOX JUDAISM

In a talk he delivered early in the year, Rabbi Norman Lamm, president of Yeshiva University, criticized the tendency within his own modern Orthodox community to cave in to the demands of more sectarian groups. "We've become very, very nervous about doing exactly what I think is right," he said. "It's, to my mind, crazy." There was evidence of such nervousness quite close to home. The Jewish Center, a synagogue in Manhattan where Lamm himself had served as rabbi for many years, elevated its associate rabbi to the senior position in 2000, and he immediately announced an end to social dancing at the annual synagogue dinner and to bat mitzvah girls reading from the Torah on the synagogue premises (the practice had never been allowed in the sanctuary itself). At Lamm's own Yeshiva University, the first student in the institution's history to win a Rhodes Scholarship reported pressure from students and faculty members to turn down the opportunity to study at Oxford since the secular environment and lack of time for serious Talmud study might have a negative effect on his spiritual life. And Touro College, which competed with Yeshiva for Orthodox male students seeking a rigorous program of religious studies together with a college degree, announced the establishment of a new branch, Lander College, in Queens, New York, and hired for its faculty some former Yeshiva professors. Touro's president said that there would be no tension between the religious and secular faculties at the new college — implying that such tension existed at Yeshiva and that the new college was therefore more authentically Orthodox.

The single most controversial issue, by far, for modern Orthodoxy was the religious role of women: Those on the Orthodox right charged that feminism had gone too far, and those on the left argued that much more had to be done. This pattern played itself out in 2000 in the area of women's Talmud study, something considered off limits in Orthodox circles a generation earlier. Responding to student demand to emulate the Drisha Institute in New York and several institutions in Israel, Yeshiva University announced a two-year full-time graduate program in Talmud for women, with $18,000 annual stipends, leading to a certificate. More traditionalist Orthodox elements, including some rabbis on the Yeshiva faculty, denounced the move as a step toward the ordination of female rabbis.

The strides already made by Orthodox women made the front page of the *New York Times* (December 21). The article traced "the small but steady revolution that is redefining the role of women in Orthodox Judaism." Women were having bat mitzvah ceremonies, participating in women's prayer groups, reading from the Torah, becoming Talmud scholars, and, quite possibly — the facts were unclear — receiving private rabbinic ordination. In fact, the two young women hired as "rabbinic interns" by Orthodox synagogues in New York in 1997 both left their jobs in 2000 and were not immediately replaced. Nevertheless, the two rabbis who had hired them declared the experiment a success and said that they were on the lookout for other qualified women to fill these positions.

The third International Conference on Feminism and Orthodoxy was held in February in New York, drawing some 1,800 people. Those who had been to the earlier conferences noted that the tone at this one seemed calmer and less strident, perhaps reflecting the findings on Orthodox women and feminism reported at the conference by Brandeis University sociologist Sylvia Barack Fishman from a study she carried out for the American Jewish Committee. The report spelled out the changes that feminism had already made in Orthodox life, and noted that improving the breadth and depth of Jewish education for women remained a high priority for many modern Orthodox women. Yet the younger women were far more cautious than their mothers' generation about any change in the status quo that might go beyond the bounds of Halakhah, and had relatively little interest in participating in women's prayer groups, let alone in becoming rabbis. More surprisingly, the young women showed little enthusiasm for activism on behalf of *agunot,* women whose husbands refused to give them a Jewish divorce and thus kept them from remarrying. (The day after the conference, a number of rabbis on the faculty of Yeshiva University issued a statement urging the use of a prenuptial agreement to head off the problem.)

Modern Orthodoxy was badly tarnished by scandal in 2000. In an investigative report entitled "Stolen Innocence" that appeared in its June 23 issue, the *New York Jewish Week* charged that a charismatic rabbi employed for almost 30 years by the National Conference of Synagogue Youth (NCSY), the outreach arm of the Union of Orthodox Jewish Congregations (OU), had physically and emotionally abused several young men and women under his charge. Once the article appeared, others came forward claiming that they too had been victims, and the newspaper printed several more articles on the subject. Though the rabbi maintained his innocence, the OU announced that he had voluntarily resigned, and in early July the organization named a special eight-member commission, made up of prominent people outside the OU, to investigate how the organization could have allowed the alleged abuse to go on for so long, and to recommend steps to make sure that nothing like it would happen again. Completion of the commission report was announced on December 26. A 54-page "short" version, made available to the public, confirmed many of the charges against the rabbi and recommended radical changes in the organization's management. It also noted that the rabbi was allowed to continue his harassment for years because of "the failure of certain members of the OU and NCSY leadership to take action." The details, presumably including names of those who had turned a blind eye to the problem, were contained in a larger, 331-page report, which was seen only by top OU officers.

In the world of sectarian Orthodoxy, the big news in 2000 was a rabbinic ban, issued in Israel, on the use of the Internet, which the rabbis termed a "terrible threat" to Judaism. Those who needed to use the Internet for work could get special permission from the authorities. Of course, there was no way to monitor what went on in people's homes, so that the ban was really little more than moral exhortation, and Orthodox organizations that utilized the Internet for religious outreach, such as Chabad-Lubavitch and a number of yeshivahs, were unlikely to comply. In the United States, Agudath Israel announced its support for the ban — it did not have a Web site of its own — as did the National Council of Young Israel, which did have a Web site.

The sectarian Orthodox community had been repeatedly embarrassed in recent years by the involvement of people associated with it, if only by the way they dressed, in various criminal activities. In the year 2000, for example, several Hassidic young men (one judge referred to them as "young yeshivah boy after young yeshivah boy") were convicted of smuggling the drug Ecstasy (*New York Times,*

March 29). Both keynote addresses at the annual convention of Agudath Israel, in November, hammered away at the "desecration of God's name" such behavior generated.

American Jews and Israel

Already on January 4, the internal American Jewish split over Israel's peace policies was evident to all. About 40 Lubavitch Hassidim arrived that day in Shepherdstown, West Virginia, where they were joined by a delegation from Americans for a Safe Israel and by students from a Jewish school near Washington. They assembled to protest the talks taking place there between President Clinton, Israeli prime minister Ehud Barak, and Syrian foreign minister Farouq a-Shara that were thought to be leading to a virtually full Israeli withdrawal from the Golan Heights that had been captured from Syria in the 1967 Six-Day War. The protesters shouted, "We will not move from the Golan," explaining to reporters that abandonment of the heights would leave Israel's northern border vulnerable. Some, addressing Barak, chanted, "Traitor, go home!"

The primary battleground for American Jewish activists was not Shepherdstown but Congress, which would have to appropriate the money to pay for any deal—including a large military-aid package for Israel to help offset its strategic sacrifice in the north. Estimates ran as high as $17 billion, and AIPAC (the American Israel Public Affairs Committee), the primary pro-Israel lobby, was already at work trying to convince lawmakers that such a huge outlay was a good investment for ultimate Middle East peace. Americans for a Safe Israel, on the other hand, which took upon itself the task of convincing Congress not to vote the money, told legislators that the real cost could go as high as $100 billion, that the funds would come out of the social security payments of senior citizens, and, since the Syrians could not be trusted to keep their word—they were, after all, on the State Department list of states sponsoring terrorism—the money would be wasted.

Although the talks at Shepherdstown broke up without reaching agreement, the controversial issues remained on the table. The Conference of Presidents of Major American Jewish Organizations, the umbrella group that spoke for the Jewish community on Israel issues and that generally arrived at its positions on the basis of a consensus of its members, decided to include a "fact-finding" visit to the Golan as part of its annual program in Israel, scheduled for the third week in February. Even though some of the more dovish constituents of the conference feared that a tour of the Golan, which would surely include conversations with the Jewish residents, might be interpreted as support for Israel's continued control, the fact that the prime minister's staff helped arrange the itinerary convinced the conference leadership that the Golan visit would have no negative repercussions.

By March Congress was again the focus of the internal Jewish debate over

Syria, as the Zionist Organization of America (ZOA) sought the signatures of senators and representatives on a letter opposing all aid to Syria so long as the regime supported terrorism and spread anti-Semitism. The letter was designed to forestall any plans to appropriate money for Israeli withdrawal from the Golan, some portion of which would go to Syria. AIPAC, the powerful pro-Israel lobby, urged lawmakers not to sign a statement that could become an obstacle to a settlement. But as it became evident that Syria would not budge from its maximalist position on a Golan withdrawal and that no deal was in sight, the funding question became academic.

The Israeli government, rebuffed on the Syrian front, resumed negotiations with the Palestinians, and American Jewish attention turned to what would surely prove the most difficult issue, Jerusalem. On January 19 some 300 Conservative, Reform, and Reconstructionist rabbis signed a statement drafted by the Jewish Peace Lobby declaring that "the pursuit of both peace and justice requires that, in some form, Jerusalem be shared with the Palestinian people." Jerome Segal, who had founded the lobby in 1989 to advocate Israel-PLO talks, acknowledged that more than 800 rabbis who had been asked to sign had refused. Segal explained that the purpose of the statement was to remove the taboo from discussions of sharing the city. "Jerusalem," he noted, "is still kind of viewed as the third rail of Israeli politics, with the right claiming that the left will redivide Jerusalem and the left saying that is a lie" (*New York Times,* January 20). A week later the Rabbinical Council of America and the Rabbinical Assembly—the Orthodox and Conservative rabbinical bodies—responded with a rare joint statement, asserting that Jerusalem was "the united and indivisible capital solely of the State of Israel" and that only Israel, in negotiations with the Palestinians, "should determine conditions for peace." Even though other dovish organizations declined to endorse the Peace Lobby's statement on the grounds that prematurely stating a willingness to divide Jerusalem might undercut Israel's bargaining position, the Charles R. Bronfman Foundation and the Nathan Cummings Foundation, two leading Jewish family foundations, helped fund a study by the Harvard University Program on International Conflict Analysis and Resolution that called for two states, with Jerusalem the shared capital of both.

If the idea of sharing Jerusalem was still not open to public discussion in the American Jewish mainstream in February, Jewish leaders were surprised to find mixed signals from Israel about Jerusalem's status. During its visit to Israel that month, a Conference of Presidents delegation was subjected to criticism from Jerusalem mayor Ehud Olmert for not more forcefully pressing the U.S. government to move its embassy from Tel Aviv to Jerusalem, a step that would go a long way toward defining Jerusalem "as an undivided capital." Prime Minister Barak told the Americans: "Jerusalem, undivided, under our sovereignty, the capital of Israel, period. That is our position." However, as members of the delegation pointed out, the Barak government, following in the footsteps of its predecessors, had instructed American Jewish leaders not to oppose the regular waivers of congressional legislation that President Clinton had used to avoid moving the embassy. Furthermore, at the very time that the Conference of Presidents was in Israel, cabinet members from Barak's own party were publicly stating that moving the embassy would endanger the peace talks.

On May 22 Barak visited the U.S. to attend AIPAC's annual policy conference. He also fit in an appearance at a dinner for Israel Bonds and meetings with the Conference of Presidents and the strongly pro-Barak Israel Policy Forum. His government had just decided to turn over Abu Dis and two other Jerusalem neighborhoods to the Palestinian Authority, to the dismay of those in Israel and the U.S. who feared that this was a precedent for the division of the city (Barak would later block the transfer in response to Palestinian violence). On May 15, the week before his arrival, Americans for a Safe Israel and local rabbis organized an anti-Barak rally in Brooklyn that drew about 100 people, and protesters also picketed Barak's appearance at the Israel Bonds dinner.

Meanwhile, Morton Klein, president of the ZOA, demanded the resignation of National Security Adviser Samuel (Sandy) Berger. In a speech on May 21 at Tel Aviv University Berger said that violence on both sides "is both the curse and the blessing of the Israeli-Palestinian conflict, for the tragedy that awaits in the event of inaction also constitutes the greatest incentive for immediate action." Klein claimed that Berger had called Palestinian violence against Israelis a "blessing." Berger explained that the quote was taken out of context and that he was actually calling for a solution to the conflict so as to end the violence. When the administration backed Berger, the ZOA placed ads in Jewish newspapers the week of June 9 featuring the picture of an Israeli killed by Palestinians and asking how this could be called "a blessing." The ad urged readers to contact the White House and their congressmen to call for Berger's ouster. But the mainstream Jewish groups refused to follow the ZOA's lead, with Anti-Defamation League (ADL) national director Abraham Foxman and the leaders of Reform Judaism chiding Klein.

In late May, Natan Sharansky, Israel's interior minister, publicly called on Prime Minister Barak not to make contemplated concessions to obtain a peace agreement, and, receiving no satisfaction, Sharansky leaked details about the Israeli-Palestinian talks to the media. The information, which was indeed an accurate blueprint of the American initiative that would bring Barak and Arafat to Camp David, called for Israeli annexation of settlement blocs in the territories with compensation from Israeli land for the Palestinians; the dismantling of Israeli settlements outside those blocs; acceptance of the right, in principle, of Palestinian refugees to return to their homes, even though few would actually be allowed to return; and Palestinian sovereignty over the Arab neighborhoods in Jerusalem. In return, the Palestinian Authority was to announce a final end to the conflict.

Sharing Sharansky's fears about the magnitude of the concessions, 30 American Jewish leaders signed an open letter to the prime minister that appeared in

American Jewish and Israeli papers at the end of June. Quoting extensively from Sharansky himself, the letter focused on the alarming possibility of "redividing" Jerusalem with no provisions for the security of its Jewish residents, "surrendering crucial territory" — including "92–95% of Judea, Samaria, and Gaza," "uprooting" thousands of Jews from their homes in the territories, and permitting "an unspecified number of Arabs from abroad to settle within Israel." Among the signers were not only leaders of Orthodox organizations and anti-peace-process groups, but also the chairman and four members of the AIPAC executive committee (the chairman's AIPAC affiliation was not mentioned in the letter), a past executive director of AIPAC, two past chairmen of the Conference of Presidents, and the national campaign chair of Israel Bonds. Publication of the letter caused something of a sensation since it appeared to break the long-standing rule that American Jewish leaders — especially those associated with mainstream organizations — did not publicly criticize the policies of the Israeli government.

The names of the AIPAC leaders on the letter indicated how seriously Barak's peace initiatives had alienated many in the American Jewish mainstream. AIPAC's constitution required support for whatever government was in power in Israel, but Gerald Charnoff, the executive committee chairman who signed the letter, explained, in an interview with the *Forward* (June 23), that it appeared to him — as it did to Sharansky — that Prime Minister Barak was running his own foreign policy without even consulting his colleagues: "I was very concerned that a consensus was not being built within the duly elected government to support these initiatives." AIPAC was quick to distance itself from the letter, a spokesman commenting, "This letter is totally outside the bounds of AIPAC policy. It was never officially presented to either the executive committee or the board." AIPAC also called for, and received, Charnoff's resignation as chairman of the executive committee. AIPAC explained that this was not because he signed the letter, but because his interview with the *Forward* violated the lobby's rule that only AIPAC's designated spokesman might speak to the press. A week later, Neal Sher, the former AIPAC executive director who had signed the letter, asked that his name be removed from it on the grounds that "people will use this to lobby against Israel and against the peace process."

The Jewish world and American political circles were still abuzz about the letter when, in early July, the administration announced that Barak and Yasir Arafat were coming to Camp David for a summit with the American president. The Israel Policy Forum quickly collected over 350 signatures on an open letter to the arriving Prime Minister Barak with the message: "The Overwhelming Majority of American Jews Support This Peace Initiative." A note at the bottom pointed out that among the signatories were "six former chairpersons of the Conference of Presidents of Major American Jewish Organizations, over two dozen executive committee members and officers of AIPAC, as well as numerous current and past presidents, chairpersons and high-level officials of almost every other leading American Jewish organization" (*Forward,* July 14). On the other side, American for a Safe Israel, accompanied by four opposition member of the Israeli Knesset, continued to lobby Congress—focusing especially on the Republican members—to oppose funding any deal that entailed what it saw as unilateral Israeli concessions.

The breakup of Camp David on July 25 did not heal the fissures within the American Jewish community. While the prospect of substantial Israeli concessions as part of a peace treaty was no longer imminent, reports, vague as they were, of just how much Barak had been willing to concede on the issue of Jerusalem confused and upset many Jewish leaders, who for years had taken the Israeli government at its word that an undivided Israeli Jerusalem was not open to compromise. To be sure, the ideological left and right of American Jewry reiterated their standard positions, Americans for Peace Now applauding the "paradigm shift" toward power-sharing in the city, and the Zionist Organization of America aghast that Barak "would betray his solemn commitment." But since the Israeli government had not announced any official change in its Jerusalem policy, neither did the Conference of Presidents, whose executive vice president, Malcolm Hoenlein, declared, "The position of the Jewish community remains the same as it always has been—a unified Jerusalem, the capital of Israel," though he added: "Ultimately, it's up to the government and people of Israel to make decisions about their sovereignty and future." This incontrovertible point—that only Israel's elected government had the authority to conduct its affairs—convinced other American Jewish leaders not to protest Barak's generous offers on Jerusalem. Abraham Foxman, the ADL national director, commented, "if this is what it would take to bring a final settlement, I think most Israelis and the American Jewish community would swallow and say, okay." That American Jews seemed satisfied to leave things up to the Israelis was evident in early September, when not only Barak but also Natan Sharansky, who had resigned from the government in protest, received enthusiastic receptions in separate appearances before the Conference of Presidents in New York.

On September 14, however, the Jerusalem issue heated up once more when Martin Indyk, the U.S. ambassador to Israel, stated in a public speech that, "there is no solution but to share the Holy City. It is not, and cannot be, the exclusive preserve of one religion, and the solution cannot come from one side challenging or denying another side's beliefs." Likud leaders in Israel, seconded by the ZOA in the United States, asked for Indyk's recall. One week later, on September 21, Secretary of State Madeleine Albright indeed took action against him, suspending Indyk and canceling his security clearance because he had allegedly mishandled classified information. Several theories circulated regarding the Indyk affair: his ouster was orchestrated by pro-Likud forces in America and their Republican allies in Congress; he was the victim of security paranoia in the wake of several embarrassing cases of leaks; or it was anti-Semitism (Indyk was Jewish). In any case, the ambassador was soon reinstated, his security clearance intact.

Around the same time back in the U.S., an American Jewish leader also got himself into trouble for injudicious remarks about Jerusalem. In what he thought was an off-the-record talk to a Jewish audience in New Jersey, Malcolm Hoenlein called on American Jews to oppose any attempt to compromise Jewish sovereignty over Jerusalem. As the top professional at the Conference of Presidents, Hoenlein was supposed to back the policies of Israel's government, which clearly had accepted the principle of compromise. When his words became public, Hoenlein explained that he had presented the anti-compromise position as his own personal point of view, and that, in any case, this still happened to be Israel's public position. Some member organizations of the conference wanted to question Hoenlein about his behavior, but the matter was soon overshadowed by the outbreak of new violence in Israel and the territories at the end of September.

The new situation in Israel (see below, pp. 494–501) affected American Jews in different ways. For those who had been skeptical of Barak's diplomacy, Arab violence following soon after Yasir Arafat's refusal to accept generous Israeli concessions at Camp David confirmed their suspicions that the Palestinians had no intention of making peace and would not rest until Israel was destroyed. In fact, some even voiced relief at the developments, in the expectation that Israel would reverse its conciliatory negotiating position or that a major shift in Israeli public opinion would bring a right-wing government to power. The pro-peace groups, in contrast, were heartbroken by the bloodshed and kept hoping—with gradually diminishing confidence—that somehow the peace process could be gotten back on track. Some on the left blamed Likud leader Ariel Sharon, whose walk on the Temple Mount seemed to have been the irritant that set off Arab violence.

The mainstream Jewish organizations concentrated on interpreting Israel's side of the story to the U.S. government, the American public, and especially the media, which showed pictures of seemingly helpless young Palestinians being confronted, and in some cases gunned down, by heavily armed Israelis—the most dramatic example of which was the videotape of 12-year-old Muhammad al-Dura being shot in a crossfire in Gaza. Another alarming development was the quick mobilization of Arab American groups in many cities in support of the uprising. On October 3 the Jewish Council for Public Affairs (JCPA) arranged a conference call for leaders of Jewish communities around the country to try to coordinate a response.

As it became clear that the violence was not likely to end soon, American Jewish opinion turned sharply against the Oslo peace process, and the *New York Times* (October 11) ran a story headlined, "Among U.S. Jews, a Deep Pessimism Takes Hold." The ADL, which had previously supported Israel's peace diplomacy, ran ads saying "Chairman Arafat has made it clear to the world—he prefers violence to peace. Prime Minister Barak: unfortunately today you still have no partner for peace." The American Jewish Congress, which had been even more dovish than the ADL, took out a full-page ad in the *New York Times* (November 12) reversing its stand, stating: "It takes a big organization to admit it was wrong." Attacks on Jews outside of Israel led some American Jewish leaders to speak of a religious war: Stephen Solender, president of the United Jewish Communities (UJC), told reporters that the violence in Israel was just one part of a global anti-Jewish onslaught, and Ronald Lauder, chairman of the Conference of Presidents, called for an international "Jewish summit" (it was never held).

Underlying the brave rhetoric, however, was a widespread sense that American Jewry was failing to fulfill its historic role as defender of the Jewish state. People still remembered the outpouring of Jewish support for Israel at the time of the 1967 Six-Day War and thereafter, and the contrast to the present situation was profound.

It took two full weeks from the start of the violence for the Jewish community of New York to organize a mass rally for Israel, a delay reportedly due to differences between Jewish groups over whether the message should include opposition to the peace process. The rally, cosponsored by the Conference of Presidents and the Jewish Community Relations Council of New York and held on October 12, drew mostly opponents of Oslo, a total of some 15,000 people, according to the *New York Times* (the crowd booed one speaker, Hillary Rodham Clinton). Many of the demonstrators were day-school students bused in for the occasion. A pro-Palestinian rally the next day drew about the same number of people. Other signs of American Jewish weakness included cancellations of tens of thousands of scheduled trips to Israel and the apparent inability or unwillingness of Jewish college students to defend Israel on campus against the verbal attacks of highly motivated Arab American student groups.

Some observers attributed this distancing from Israel to the perception that the Jewish state in 2000, unlike the case a generation earlier, was a regional power whose continued existence was not in danger. Others considered it just one example of a broader phenomenon, the erosion of Jewish identity among younger American Jews. Yet a third view, one voiced by many Jewish leaders who insisted on anonymity, was that the community could not be effectively mobilized in the absence of clear signals from Prime Minister Barak.

American Jewry hoped it would finally get such signals at the UJC's annual General Assembly, held this year in Chicago in November. Due in large part to the crisis in Israel and the opportunity to hear about it from Prime Minister Barak in person, a sell-out crowd of 6,000 registered. Those expecting to get simple marching orders, however, were disappointed. Despite the minimal consultation with American Jewish organizations that characterized his administration, Barak declared: "We derive great strength from knowing that we in Israel are not alone"; while saying several times that there was no alternative to peace, he placed blame for the violence solely on the Palestinians; and in the face of the concessions he was known to be offering on Jerusalem, he insisted on a "Jerusalem broader than it has ever been in history." Barak was warmly applauded. The day after his speech, opposition leader Ariel Sharon and Natan Sharansky addressed the General Assembly and attacked the Barak government's strategy.

The year ended with more manifestations of American Jewish demoralization, confusion, and division. Seeking to counter the precipitous decline in tourism to Israel, the Conference of Presidents planned an ad urging Jews to travel to Israel. Four member organizations of the conference—American for Peace Now, the Labor Zionist Alliance, the National Committee for Labor Israel, and the Jewish Labor Committee refused to endorse the ad because its reference to Jerusalem as the "eternal and undivided capital" of Israel might undercut Barak's ability to negotiate a compromise on Jerusalem. Malcolm Hoenlein, responding for the conference, said, "this is standard language used all the time that does not preempt anyone's negotiations." Meanwhile, an ad opposing Israeli renunciation of sovereignty over the Temple Mount, sponsored by the ZOA—an organization that the American Jewish mainstream had viewed as extremist till the breakdown of Camp David—managed to get the endorsement of five former chairs of the Conference of Presidents as well as the top leaders of the Orthodox and Conservative movements.

Organizations and Institutions

JEWISH PHILANTHROPY

United Jewish Communities, the merged entity encompassing the Council of Jewish Federations, the United Jewish Appeal, and the United Israel Appeal that officially came into existence in 1999, was still a work in progress a year later. One controversial issue was financial. The primary reason for the merger was to cut costs, and yet the administrative expenses of the merger process itself came to $11 million, far more than anticipated. In the spring, leaders of local federations complained about UJC's proposed $41.7-million budget for operating expenses, a sum that the large-city federations were being asked to pay.

Furthermore, the merger seemed to have no positive impact on federation campaigns. According to a study released in May and published in the *Chronicle of Philanthropy,* while the 400 largest American charities increased their private support by an average of 16 percent in 1999, the 15 most successful Jewish federations grew by only 4.3 percent. Observers generally attributed the poor showing to the preference of young donors to target their giving, often through the medium of private and family foundations, to specific causes that interested them rather than to a multipurpose charity such as a federation. Evidence that this was true came from the extraordinary fund-raising success of more narrowly focused Jewish organizations. The federations had for some years sought to respond to the new philanthropic mood by creating mechanisms for donors to target their money for their preferred causes under the federation aegis, and the UJC had set up a Trust for Jewish Philanthropy that was expected to do "matchmaking between the funders and doers."

Throughout the five years of negotiations that resulted in the creation of the UJC, agencies involved in relief for overseas Jewish communities—primarily the American Jewish Joint Distribution Committee (JDC)—had warned that the emerging new system, largely controlled by the federations, would tend to concentrate on domestic needs at their expense. Indeed, in 2000 the JDC complained that its allocation had been slashed and that it might be forced to curtail some of its activities, such as the provision of food to elderly Jews in the former Soviet Union.

A major selling point of the new merged entity was that it could mount a nationally coordinated strategy for motivating young Jews to rediscover Judaism: One of the UJC's four "pillars" was Jewish renaissance and renewal. In February 2000, Jonathan Woocher, president of the Jewish Educational Service of North America (JESNA), was named to head it.

A long-simmering dispute in the Jewish community over the relative priorities of Jewish and general philanthropic causes found public expression in early April at the tenth annual conference of the Jewish Funders Network, the umbrella organization for private Jewish family foundations. The theme of the keynote session, "Saving the Whales: Is it Jewish Funding?" was addressed by Dr. Jack Wertheimer, the Jewish Theological Seminary provost, and Rabbi David Saperstein, director of the Reform movement's Religious Action Center. Wertheimer bemoaned what he considered the hugely disproportionate share of the Jewish charity dollar—some two-thirds—that went to nonsectarian causes. He charged that even many who gave hefty sums to Jewish institutions gave far more to non-Jewish organizations, and calculated that if each Jewish philanthropist simply divided his or her giving equally between Jewish and general needs, the basic requirements of Jewish life could be adequately funded. Saperstein, on the other hand, asserted that Judaism gave a high priority to social justice and that Jewish philanthropy for nonsectarian causes also helped gain political allies for the Jewish community. The publicity the Wertheimer-Saperstein debate gave to the issue of Jewish funding priorities ensured that it would be noticed outside the community: journalist Michael Massing, writing in the liberal magazine *American Prospect* (November 6), complained that Jewish philanthropy had already turned far too parochial, "retreating into a narrow tribalism."

JCPA

The Jewish Council for Public Affairs (JCPA), formerly known as NJCRAC, was the umbrella organization of national Jewish bodies and local community-relations councils. In 1999 federation leaders from New York and Chicago had sharply criticized the JCPA for allegedly focusing on issues tangential to core Jewish interests. In September 2000 the JCPA reached an agreement with its funding body, the UJC, whereby the JCPA would withdraw from the realm of policy formulation and concentrate on providing services to the UJC, its member federations, and the community councils. In August, Hannah Rosenfeld was named as the new professional head of the JCPA in place of Lawrence Rubin, who had retired.

CONFERENCE OF PRESIDENTS

The criteria for membership in the Conference of Presidents of Major American Jewish Organizations, the 54-member umbrella body that served as the voice of American Jewry on issues relating to Israel and the Middle East, came up for discussion in 2000. There were, apparently, no written bylaws that defined a "major" organization, though, in response to criticism, the conference had drawn up membership criteria that included bona fide memberships, democratically elected officers and boards and "a commitment to the continuity of the Jewish faith." As the year began, Meretz USA, allied with the left-of-center Israeli party by that name, was smarting from the rejection of its membership application. In July the conference's membership committee recommended downgrading the status of three members to "associate" status: the Labor Zionist Alliance, the National Committee for Labor Israel, and the Women's League for Israel. The fact that Meretz USA and two of the three other groups were affiliated with the Israeli left led some to allege that the conference was biased toward the political right, a charge vehemently denied by conference leaders. The full conference, in any case, did not take action on the committee's recommendation.

HOLOCAUST MUSEUM

In January, President Clinton named Rabbi Irving "Yitz" Greenberg as the new chair of the U.S. Holocaust Memorial Council and its museum in Washington, D.C., replacing Miles Lerman, who had resigned. The choice of Greenberg, an Orthodox thinker who had written extensively about the theological implications of the Holocaust, was greeted with virtually unanimous approval, and it was widely hoped that the museum, under his stewardship, would successfully balance the particularistic Jewish significance of the Holocaust with its universal lessons for mankind.

CENTER FOR JEWISH HISTORY

After years of anticipation and planning, the Center for Jewish History formally opened in October 2000 in New York City. This "Jewish Library of Congress" brought together in one building five institutions that had previously operated in separate locations: the American Jewish Historical Society, the American Sephardi Federation, the Leo Baeck Institute (focusing on the history and culture of German Jewry), the Yeshiva University Museum, and the YIVO Institute for Jewish Research (dealing with Yiddish-speaking, East European Jewry). Each retained its independent board, budget, and staff. The facility, which cost $50 million to buy and renovate, was believed to contain the largest collection of Jewish archival material outside Israel.

FORWARD

In its April 28 issue, the English-language *Forward* newspaper announced that Seth Lipsky was resigning as editor. It was common knowledge that the resignation was not voluntary, and much of the rest of the staff left with him. During the ten years he had edited the weekly paper, Lipsky had made it perhaps the liveliest and certainly the most controversial Anglo-Jewish organ in the U.S., with unparalleled coverage of Jewish cultural developments, a neoconservative editorial slant, and a willingness to criticize the establishment that sometimes verged on sensationalism. These latter two qualities eventually did Lipsky in, as his *Forward* antagonized both the old-line left-of-center Jewish labor groups that still controlled the Forward Association, and the Jewish leaders that the paper pilloried. The fact that the paper lost about $2 million a year also played a role. In June, veteran journalist J.J. Goldberg, whose outlook was likely to coincide with that of the Forward Association, was named to replace Lipsky.

LAWRENCE GROSSMAN

Jewish Population in the United States, 2000

BASED ON LOCAL COMMUNITY counts—the method for identifying and enumerating Jewish population that serves as the basis of this report—the estimated size of the American Jewish community in 2000 was approximately 6.1 million, over half a million more than the 5.5 million "core" Jewish population estimated in the Council of Jewish Federations' 1990 National Jewish Population Survey (NJPS).[1] The NJPS 2000, conducted in the second half of 2000 and the first half of 2001, will provide a new national estimate (see below).

The difference between the national and aggregated local figures may be explained by the passage of time, varying definitions of "Jewishness," disparate sample sources (outdated lists, distinctive Jewish names, random digit dialing, etc.), and the lack of uniform methodology for local demographic research.

Analysis of the 1990 NJPS and other sources suggested that the population grew slightly during the late 1980s as the number of Jewish births exceeded the number of Jewish deaths. Extrapolation from the age structure, however, suggests that births and deaths were in balance by the late 1990s, creating a situation of zero population growth. It was only Jewish immigration into the U. S., particularly from the former Soviet Union, that provided growth in numbers.

The 1990 NJPS used a scientifically selected sample to project a total number for the United States as a whole, but could not provide accurate information on the state and local levels. Therefore, as in past years, this article contains local population estimates provided by knowledgeable local informants, and these serve as the basis for calculations of state and regional population counts.

Leaders at the approximately 200 Jewish federations that are part of the new philanthropic entity, United Jewish Communities (comprised of the Council of Jewish Federations, United Jewish Appeal, and United Israel Appeal), provided estimates of their communities, which are the largest Jewish population centers. However, their service areas vary in size and thus may represent quite different geographic divisions: several towns, one county, or an aggregate of several counties. In some cases we have subdivided federation areas to reflect more natural geographic boundaries or preferred U.S. Census definitions of metropolitan areas.

Local rabbis and other informed Jewish communal leaders provided estimates from small communities without federations. A form requesting the current population estimate was mailed to leaders of 67 such communities that had not pro-

---

[1]See Barry A. Kosmin et al., *Highlights of the CJF 1990 National Jewish Population Survey* (New York, Council of Jewish Federations, 1991).

vided an update in more than five years, and 32 replied. Eleven other requests were returned with indications that the synagogue whose leader had previously provided an estimate had either closed in recent years, had moved without leaving a forwarding address, or could otherwise not be found. For communities that did not provide a current estimate, figures have either been retained from past years or extrapolations were made from the older data. The estimates requested from informants were for the resident Jewish population, including those in private households and in institutional settings. Informants were asked to exclude non-Jewish family members from the total.

The state and regional totals shown in Appendix tables 1 and 2 are derived by summing the local estimates shown in table 3, including communities of less than 100, and then rounding to the nearest hundred or thousand, depending on the size of the estimate.

Because population estimation is not an exact science, the reader should be aware that in cases where a figure differs from last year's, the increase or decrease did not occur suddenly, but occurred over a period of time and has just now been substantiated. The primary sources for altering previously reported Jewish population figures in larger communities are recently completed local demographic studies. The results of such studies should be understood as either an updated calculation of gradual demographic change or the correction of faulty older estimates.

In determining Jewish population, communities count both affiliated and non-affiliated residents who are "core" Jews, as defined in NJPS 1990. This definition includes born Jews who report adherence to Judaism, Jews by choice, and born Jews without a current religion ("secular Jews"). A common method for estimating the population is to multiply the estimated number of households containing at least one self-defined Jew by the average number of self-defined Jewish persons per household. As stated above, non-Jews living in Jewish households — primarily the non-Jewish spouses and non-Jewish children — are not included in the 2000 estimates below.

Only persons residing in a community for the majority of the year are included in local counts. In many Sunbelt and resort communities, the population increases during the winter months, but these part-year residents are not included in these estimates. However, demographer Ira Sheskin notes that if we were to include residents who are present for at least three months per year, four Southeast Florida communities would increase as follows: Boca Raton-Delray Beach 30,000 (32 percent), Broward County 21,000 (10 percent), Miami-Dade County 11,000 (8 percent), and Palm Beach County (excluding Boca Raton-Delray Beach) 21,000 (20 percent). Many other Sunbelt communities, resort areas throughout the country, college towns, and communities with seasonally affected industries also become home to more Jews for part of the year, but there are no accurate data for such communities.

Local Population Changes

The community reporting the largest growth in 2000 was Las Vegas, Nevada, up 19,400 to 75,000. Though no survey has been conducted since 1995, the 35-percent increase reported by the Las Vegas Jewish Federation reflected substantial growth in the general population in recent years that is believed to include many Jews. Eight other communities experienced population increases of at least 3,000.

The suburbs east of Los Angeles showed considerable growth. The newly created Jewish Federation of Greater San Gabriel and Pomona Valleys reported a Jewish population of about 30,000. Previously, Pomona Valley itself was listed at 6,750 and towns in the San Gabriel Valley portion were either included in the Los Angeles totals or simply not counted.

As with Las Vegas, Seattle's growth of 7,900 (27 percent) reflected large increases in the general population assumed to include many Jews. Hartford's recent study showed a figure 7,000 higher than previously indicated, which was due to the inclusion of all of Hartford County and the correction of a faulty older estimate. Rockland County, New York, reported an 8-percent gain of 6,900. Finally, Atlanta posted an increase of 5,900 (7 percent) based on an extrapolation of its 1997 study and perceived continued growth. The other communities with strong growth were Denver, Colorado, which increased by 3,700; Austin, Texas, which gained 3,500; and Palm Springs, California, which grew by 3,000.

Four communities reported increases between 1,000 and 3,000: Ann Arbor, Michigan; Monmouth County, New Jersey; Syracuse, New York; and San Antonio, Texas.

Modest increases—less than 1,000—were reported in 21 areas: Chico, California; Westport, Connecticut; Fort Myers and Naples, Florida; Savannah, Georgia; Aurora, Illinois; Lexington, Kentucky; Portland-Southern Maine; Attleboro and Plymouth, Massachusetts; Grand Rapids and Kalamazoo, Michigan; Hoboken, New Jersey; Santa Fe, New Mexico; Charlotte, North Carolina; Corvallis and Eugene, Oregon; Altoona and Lancaster, Pennsylvania; Charleston, South Carolina; and Knoxville, Tennessee.

The largest decline reported for any community was 10,000 in Miami-Dade County, Florida, an 8-percent drop. This was determined in a recent survey that showed a significant decrease in Miami Beach. Buffalo's decrease of 6,000—a 23-percent decline—was also documented by recent research. The declines in other communities, all under 2,000, were nearly all in the Midwest or Northeast: Joliet, Illinois; South Bend, Indiana; Sioux City, Iowa; Flint, Michigan; Binghamton, New York; Akron and Dayton, Ohio; and Racine, Wisconsin. The one community to decline in the South was Galveston, Texas.

Regional Shifts During the 20th Century

The year 2001 is an opportune time to examine national population changes over the last century. Changes in the proportion of the U.S. Jewish population living in the New York metropolitan region are shown in figure 1, and shifts in the four U.S. Census regions from 1900 to 2000 appear in figure 2. The actual population estimates on which these figures are based appear in table 4.[2] (See pp. 278–80 below.)

Figure 1 reveals that in 1900 over half (52 percent) of the nation's nearly 1.1 million Jews lived in the New York City Consolidated Metropolitan Statistical Area (CMSA).[3] After hovering at around that level till past mid-century, the proportion began a steady decline after 1955 to its current level of 32 percent.

The proportion of U.S. Jewry in New York City's five boroughs was highest during the first few years of the 20th century, when 47 percent of American Jews lived there. The proportion gradually declined to 39 percent in 1945. After World War II it slightly increased to 42 percent in 1950, after which the decline resumed and even accelerated, falling to the current share of 17 percent. This decline has been due to movement to the suburbs, retirees relocating to Florida, and younger Jews seeking employment and educational opportunities in other regions.

In actual numbers, New York City's Jewish population grew from half a million in 1900 to two million by 1935, and remained at about that level until 1960. It has since declined to its current level of just over one million.

The share of U.S. Jewish population in New York City's suburbs located in New York State, New Jersey, and Connecticut was at 5–7 percent between 1900 and 1945. After World War II, however, it increased substantially. The suburban proportion was highest in 1980, when 18 percent of U.S. Jews lived there. Since then the New York City suburban population has declined to 15 percent of U.S. Jewry. Only about 50,000 Jews lived in these suburbs in 1900 and about one million by 1980. The figure has since fluctuated, with a current estimate of 930,000.

Figure 2 displays trends in the four U.S. census regions. It indicates that the Northeast increased its share of U.S. Jewry from 57 percent in 1900 to 70 percent by 1920. This was due primarily to massive immigration of Jews from Eastern Europe who settled mainly in New York and other port cities of the Northeast in the first part of the century. From 1920 to 1960 the Northeast share remained slightly in excess of two-thirds. After that point, however, its share steadily de-

---

[2]Sources utilized to provide historical data include various editions of the *American Jewish Year Book* from vol. 1, the 1899–1900 edition, to the present, and Jacob Rader Marcus, *To Count a People: American Jewish Population Data, 1585–1984* (Lanham, Md., 1984). Information for some years was not provided in the *Year Book* and interpolation of data was necessary.

[3]The CMSA includes the city's five boroughs, six New York State counties outside the city, 13 nearby counties in northeastern New Jersey, and one in Connecticut.

clined to its current level of 46 percent. In actual numbers, the Northeast began the century with about 600,000 Jews, increased to over three million during the 1930s, and remained above three million until the final years of the century.

The North Central states (the Midwest) began the century with about one-fourth (24 percent) of the nation's Jewish population, declined gradually to half that level (12 percent) by 1970, and is now 11 percent, their numbers overshadowed by the massive wave of Eastern European Jews immigrating to the Northeast. In the early 1900s the Midwest had a Jewish population of a quarter-million, which increased to nearly 900,000 by 1940 but has since fallen to about 700,000.

The West fluctuated between 4 and 6 percent of the U.S. Jewish population between 1900 and 1945. After World War II that region's share steadily increased to its current level of 22 percent, reflecting general population trends and economic opportunities in that region. Early in the 20th century fewer than 60,000 Jews lived in the West. Increases were modest until 1940, when approximately 224,000 Jews lived there. Since that time, the increases have been rapid and the Jewish population is now over 1.3 million.

The South declined from a 14-percent share in 1900 to 7 percent in 1940. Like the situation in the Midwest, Jewish communities in the South were demographically dwarfed by the new Jewish immigration to the Northeast. After World War II the proportion of U.S. Jews in the South grew slowly until 1970, when this growth accelerated. Today it is at 21 percent, almost equivalent to that of the West. This increase is due mainly to the migration of Jews from the Northeast and Midwest to southern Florida, Atlanta, Washington, D.C., and other areas in the South Atlantic subregion. The two other subregions that comprise the South — East South Central and West South Central — each held 3 percent of U.S. Jewry at the start of the century and are now at 1 and 2 percent, respectively. Like the West, increases in actual numbers for the South were modest earlier in the century, moving from 150,000 in 1900 to almost 500,000 in 1960. Rapid growth occurred after 1960, when Jewish population in the South more than doubled to 1.3 million by the end of the century.

NJPS 2000

Recognizing the need for current data, United Jewish Communities (UJC) is sponsoring a new National Jewish Population Survey, with interviewing taking place in 2000 and 2001. The questionnaire and overall study design were developed by the UJC's Research Department in close collaboration with its National Technical Advisory Committee (NTAC), a distinguished group of academicians and federation professionals with expertise in demography, sociology, religion, geography, economics, education, and other relevant disciplines.

In addition, the UJC Research Department worked closely with local federation planning, campaign, marketing, and other departments, as well as with the four newly formed UJC "pillars": Israel/Overseas, Human Services and Social Policy, Jewish Renaissance and Renewal, and Campaign/Financial Resource Development in preparing the NJPS questionnaire. The interviewing for NJPS 2000 was to have begun in early 2000, but was postponed till the second half of the year in order to give the four pillars sufficient opportunity for input. Meetings were held with these groups as well as with the Jewish religious denominations, other major Jewish organizations, UJC regions, and other constituencies. The NJPS Board of Trustees provided the financial resources for conducting this effort and a federation Professional Advisory Committee provided guidance on issues of relevance to the federation system. The NJPS Steering Committee, comprised of the chairs of all the committees involved in NJPS, set policy for the study. All of the aforementioned groups provided significant input toward the development of the questionnaire. Focus groups were conducted to improve the introductory part of the interview and cognitively test the phrasing of questions. The questionnaire was extensively pretested for length, the most appropriate language, and correct skip patterns.

The NJPS 2000 interviewing was conducted by telephone using random-digit-dialing techniques. The sample is approximately 5,000 adults (4,500 Jews and 500 other people with Jewish background) age 18 and older residing in the 50 United States. The sample is stratified by census region, metropolitan/non-metropolitan area, and then by zip code within each region. Areas of high density of Jewish settlement are sampled at a higher rate than other areas to increase the pace of interviewing and cut costs. Results will be weighted to ensure accurate projectability to the Jewish population at different geographic levels.

Once the findings are released in early 2002, NJPS 2000 will become the definitive source of data on the Jewish community during the first decade of the 21st century. The information will help UJC, Jewish federations, synagogues, and other Jewish organizations conduct communal planning, policy-making, resource development, Jewish education, scholarly research, and many other necessary functions.

Among the multitude of topics that are explored in NJPS 2000 are Jewish population size, socioeconomic characteristics, family structure, fertility, marital history, intermarriage, Jewish identification, religious practices, Jewish education, synagogue affiliation, philanthropic behavior, and relationship to Israel. UJC and others will underwrite a broad range of analyses based on NJPS results to help drive informed decision-making within the Jewish community. NJPS 2000 is expected to deliver the critical data and analyses necessary for strengthening Jewish life in the United States in the 21st century.

JIM SCHWARTZ
JEFFREY SCHECKNER

APPENDIX

TABLE 1. JEWISH POPULATION IN THE UNITED STATES, 2000

State	Estimated Jewish Population	Total Population*	Estimated Jewish Percent of Total
Alabama	9,100	4,447,000	0.2
Alaska	3,500	627,000	0.6
Arizona	81,500	5,131,000	1.6
Arkansas	1,600	2,673,000	0.1
California	994,000	33,872,000	2.9
Colorado	72,000	4,301,000	1.7
Connecticut	108,000	3,406,000	3.2
Delaware	13,500	784,000	1.7
Dist. of Columbia	25,500	572,000	4.5
Florida	628,000	15,982,000	3.9
Georgia	93,500	8,186,000	1.1
Hawaii	7,000	1,212,000	0.6
Idaho	1,000	1,294,000	0.1
Illinois	270,000	12,419,000	2.2
Indiana	18,000	6,080,000	0.3
Iowa	6,400	2,926,000	0.2
Kansas	14,500	2,688,000	0.5
Kentucky	11,000	4,042,000	0.3
Louisiana	16,500	4,469,000	0.4
Maine	8,000	1,275,000	0.6
Maryland	216,000	5,296,000	4.1
Massachusetts	275,000	6,349,000	4.3
Michigan	110,000	9,938,000	1.1
Minnesota	42,000	4,919,000	0.9
Mississippi	1,400	2,845,000	(z)
Missouri	62,500	5,595,000	1.1
Montana	800	902,000	0.1
Nebraska	7,000	1,711,000	0.4
Nevada	77,000	1,998,000	3.9
New Hampshire	10,000	1,236,000	0.8
New Jersey	468,000	8,414,000	5.6

State	Estimated Jewish Population	Total Population*	Estimated Jewish Percent of Total
New Mexico	10,500	1,819,000	0.6
New York	1,653,000	18,976,000	8.7
North Carolina	25,500	8,049,000	0.3
North Dakota	700	642,000	0.1
Ohio	142,000	11,353,000	1.3
Oklahoma	5,000	3,451,000	0.1
Oregon	31,000	3,421,000	0.9
Pennsylvania	283,000	12,281,000	2.3
Rhode Island	16,000	1,048,000	1.5
South Carolina	11,000	4,012,000	0.3
South Dakota	350	755,000	(z)
Tennessee	18,000	5,689,000	0.3
Texas	128,000	20,852,000	0.6
Utah	4,500	2,233,000	0.2
Vermont	5,800	609,000	1.0
Virginia	76,000	7,079,000	1.1
Washington	43,500	5,894,000	0.7
West Virginia	2,400	1,808,000	0.1
Wisconsin	28,000	5,364,000	0.5
Wyoming	400	494,000	0.1
U.S. TOTAL	**6,136,000	281,421,000	2.2

N.B. Details may not add to totals because of rounding.
* Resident population, April 1, 2000 (*Source:* U.S. Bureau of the Census, Population Division, *Census Briefs: A Short Report on the First Results of Census 2000,* April 3, 2001.)
** Exclusive of Puerto Rico and the Virgin Islands which previously reported Jewish populations of 1,500 and 350, respectively.
(z) Figure is less than 0.1 and rounds to 0.

TABLE 2. DISTRIBUTION OF U.S. JEWISH POPULATION BY REGIONS, 2000

Region	Total Population	Percent Distribution	Estimated Jewish Population	Percent Distribution
Midwest	63,393,000	22.9	701,000	11.4
East North Central ..	45,155,000	16.0	568,000	9.3
West North Central .	19,237,000	6.9	133,000	2.2
Northeast	53,594,000	18.9	2,826,000	46.1
Middle Atlantic	39,671,000	14.1	2,403,000	39.2
New England	13,923,000	4.9	423,000	6.9
South	100,237,000	35.6	1,283,000	20.9
East South Central ..	17,023,000	6.0	40,000	0.6
South Atlantic	51,768,000	18.4	1,092,000	17.8
West South Central	31,445,000	11.1	151,000	2.5
West	63,198,000	22.5	1,326,000	21.6
Mountain	18,172,000	6.5	248,000	4.0
Pacific	45,026,000	16.0	1,079,000	17.6
TOTALS	281,421,000	100.0	6,136,000	100.0

N.B. Details may not add to totals because of rounding.

TABLE 3. COMMUNITIES WITH JEWISH POPULATIONS OF 100 OR MORE, 2000
(ESTIMATED)

State and City	Jewish Population	State and City	Jewish Population	State and City	Jewish Population
ALABAMA		**CALIFORNIA**		Alameda County, under S.F. Bay Area)	
*Birmingham	5,300	***Antelope Valley	700	Ontario (incl. in San Gabriel and Pomona Valleys)	
Dothan	100	Aptos (incl. in Santa Cruz)		Orange County[N]	60,000
Huntsville	750	Bakersfield-Kern County	1,600	Oroville (incl. in Chico)	
**Mobile	1,100	Berkeley (incl. in Contra Costa County, under S.F. Bay Area)		Palmdale (incl. in Antelope Valley)	
**Montgomery	1,200	Carmel (incl. in Monterey Peninsula)		Palm Springs[N]	17,000
Tuscaloosa	300	*Chico	500	Palo Alto (incl. in South Peninsula, under S.F. Bay Area)	
Other places	350	Corona (incl. in Riverside area)		Pasadena (incl. in Chico)	
ALASKA		*Eureka	1,000	Pasadena (incl. in L.A. area)	
*Anchorage	2,300	Fairfield	800	Paso Robles (incl. in San Luis Obispo)	
*Fairbanks	540	Fontana (incl. in San Bernardino)		Petaluma (incl. in Sonoma County, under S.F. Bay Area)	
Juneau	285	*Fresno	2,300	Pomona Valley[N] (incl. in San Gabriel and Pomona Valleys)	
Kenai Peninsula	200	Lancaster (incl. in Antelope Valley)		*Redding area	150
Ketchikan (incl. in Juneau)		Long Beach[N]	15,000	Redwood Valley (incl. in Mendocino County)	
Other places	200	Los Angeles area[N]	519,000	Riverside area	2,000
ARIZONA		*Mendocino County	600	Sacramento[N]	21,300
Cochise County	350	*Merced County	190	Salinas	1,000
*Flagstaff	500	*Modesto	500	San Bernardino area	3,000
Lake Havasu City	200	Monterey Peninsula	2,300	*San Diego	70,000
*Phoenix	60,000	Moreno Valley (incl. in Riverside)			
Prescott	300	Murrieta Hot Springs	550		
Sierra Vista (incl. in Cochise County)		*Napa County	1,000		
*Tucson	20,000	Oakland (incl. in			
***Yuma	125				
Other places	200				
ARKANSAS					
***Fayetteville	150				
Hot Springs	150				
**Little Rock	1,100				
Other places	200				

[N]See Notes below. *Includes entire county. **Includes all of two counties. ***Figure not updated for at least five years.

State and City	Jewish Population
San Francisco Bay Area[N]	210,000
Alameda County	32,500
Contra Costa County	22,000
Marin County	18,500
N. Peninsula	24,500
San Francisco	49,500
San Jose	33,000
Sonoma County	9,000
S. Peninsula	21,000
San Gabriel and Pomona Valleys[N]	30,000
*San Jose (listed under S.F. Bay Area)	
*San Luis Obispo	1,700
*Santa Barbara	7,000
*Santa Cruz	6,000
Santa Maria	700
Santa Monica (incl. in Los Angeles area)	
Santa Rosa (incl. in Sonoma County, under S.F. Bay Area)	
Sonoma County (listed under S.F. Bay Area)	
*South Lake Tahoe	150
*Stockton	850
***Sun City	200
Tulare and Kings counties	300
Ukiah (incl. in Mendocino Co.)	
Vallejo area	900
*Ventura County[N]	15,000
Visalia (incl. in Tulare and Kings counties)	
Other places	200

State and City	Jewish Population
COLORADO	
Aspen	750
Boulder (incl. in Denver)	
Breckenridge (incl. in Vail)	
Colorado Springs	1,500
Denver[N]	66,700
Eagle (incl. in Vail)	
Evergreen (incl. in Denver)	
*Fort Collins	1,000
*Grand Junction	320
Greeley (incl. in Fort Collins)	
Loveland (incl. in Fort Collins)	
Pueblo[N]	425
Steamboat Springs	160
Telluride	125
**Vail	650
Other places	200
CONNECTICUT	
Bridgeport[N]	13,000
Bristol (incl. in Hartford)	
Cheshire (incl. in Waterbury)	
Colchester	300
Danbury[N]	3,200
Danielson	100
Darien (incl. in Stamford)	
Greenwich	3,900
Hartford[N]	32,200
Hebron (incl. in Colchester)	
Lebanon (incl. in Colchester)	
Lower Middlesex County[N]	1,600

State and City	Jewish Population
Manchester (incl. in Hartford)	
Meriden (incl. in New Haven)	
Middletown	1,200
New Britain (incl. in Hartford)	
New Canaan (incl. in Stamford)	
New Haven[N]	24,300
New London[N]	3,800
New Milford (incl. in Waterbury)	
Newtown (incl. in Danbury)	
Norwalk (incl. in Westport)	
Norwich (incl. in New London)	
Rockville (incl. in Hartford)	
Shelton (incl. in Bridgeport)	
Southington (incl. in Hartford)	
Stamford	9,200
Storrs (incl. in Willimantic)	
Torrington area	580
Wallingford (incl. in New Haven)	
Waterbury[N]	4,500
Westport[N]	9,500
Willimantic area	700
Other places	200
DELAWARE	
Dover (incl. in Kent and Sussex counties totals)	
Kent and Sussex counties	1,600
Newark area	4,300
Wilmington area	7,600

State and City	Jewish Population	State and City	Jewish Population	State and City	Jewish Population

DISTRICT OF COLUMBIA
Washington D.C.[N]
. . . . 25,500

FLORIDA
Arcadia (incl. in Fort
Myers)
Boca Raton-Delray
Beach (listed under
Southeast Fla.)
Brevard County. . 5,000
Broward County (listed
under Southeast Fla.)
***Crystal River . . . 100
**Daytona Beach
. . . . 2,500
Fort Lauderdale (incl.
in Broward County,
under Southeast Fla.)
**Fort Myers 8,000
Fort Pierce. 1,060
Gainesville 2,200
Hollywood-S. Broward
County (incl in
Broward County,
under Southeast Fla.)
**Jacksonville. . . . 7,300
Key West 650
***Lakeland 1,000
*Miami-Dade County
(listed under
Southeast Fla.)
Naples-Collier County
. . . . 4,200
New Port Richey (incl.
in Pasco County)
Ocala-Marion County
. . . . 500
Orlando[N] 21,000
Palm Beach County
(listed under
Southeast Fla.)
Pasco County . . . 1,000
**Pensacola 975

Pinellas County . 24,200
**Port Charlotte-Punta
Gorda (incl. in Fort
Myers
**Sarasota 17,500
Southeast Florida
. . . . 504,000
Boca Raton-Delray
Beach 93,000
Broward County
. . . . 213,000
Miami-Dade County
. . . . 124,000
Palm Beach County
(excl. Boca Raton-
Delray Beach)
. . . . 74,000
*St. Petersburg-
Clearwater (incl. in
Pinellas County)
Stuart-Port St. Lucie[N]
. . . . 4,300
Tallahassee 2,200
*Tampa 20,000
Venice (incl. in
Sarasota)
*Vero Beach. 400
Winter Haven. 300
Other places 100

GEORGIA
Albany area 200
Athens 400
Atlanta Metro Area
. . . . 85,900
Augusta[N] 1,300
Brunswick 100
**Columbus 1,100
**Dalton 125
Macon. 1,000
*Savannah. 3,000
**Valdosta 100
Other places 250

HAWAII
Hilo 280
Honolulu (incl. all of
Oahu) 6,400
Kauai. 100
Maui 210

IDAHO
**Boise 800
Lewiston (incl. in
Moscow)
Moscow 100
Other places. 150

ILLINOIS
Aurora area 750
Bloomington-Normal
. . . . 500
Carbondale (incl. in S.
Ill.)
*Champaign-Urbana
. . . . 1,400
Chicago Metro Area[N]
. . . . 261,000
**Danville 100
*Decatur 130
DeKalb 180
East St. Louis (incl. in
S. Ill.)
Elgin[N]. 500
Freeport (incl. in
Rockford)
*Joliet. 270
***Kankakee. 100
Moline (incl. in Quad
Cities)
*Peoria. 800
Quad Cities-Ill. portion
. . . . 550
Quincy 100
Rock Island (incl. in
Quad Cities)
Rockford[N] 1,100
Southern Illinois[N] . 600

State and City	Jewish Population	State and City	Jewish Population	State and City	Jewish Population
*Springfield	1,090	KENTUCKY		*Frederick	1,200
Waukegan	300	Covington-Newport		*Hagerstown	325
Other places	250	area	500	*Harford County	
		Lexington[N]	2,000		1,200
INDIANA		*Louisville	8,700	*Howard County	
Bloomington	1,000	Other places	150		10,000
Elkhart (incl. in S. Bend)				Montgomery and	
Evansville	400	LOUISIANA		Prince Georges	
**Fort Wayne	950	Alexandria[N]	350	counties	104,500
**Gary-Northwest		Baton Rouge[N]	1,600	Ocean City	100
Indiana	2,000	Lafayette (incl. in S.		Salisbury	400
**Indianapolis	10,000	Central La.)		Silver Spring (incl. in	
**Lafayette	550	Lake Charles area		Montgomery County)	
*Michigan City	300		200	Other places	250
Muncie	120	Monroe (incl. in			
South Bend[N]	1,850	Shreveport)		MASSACHUSETTS	
*Terre Haute	200	**New Orleans	13,000	Amherst area	1,300
Other places	200	**Shreveport	815	Andover[N]	2,850
		***South Central La.[N]		Athol area (incl. in N.	
IOWA			250	Worcester County)	
Ames (incl. in Des		Other places	150	Attleboro area	700
Moines)				Beverly (incl. in North	
Cedar Rapids	420	MAINE		Shore, under Boston	
Council Bluffs	150	Augusta	140	Metro Region)	
*Davenport (incl. in		***Bangor	1,000	Boston Metro Region[N]	
Quad Cities)		Biddeford-Saco (incl. in			227,300
*Des Moines	2,800	S. Maine)		Boston	21,000
*Iowa City	1,300	Brunswick-Bath (incl.		Brockton-South	
Postville	150	in S. Maine)		Central	31,500
Quad Cities-Iowa		Lewiston-Auburn	500	Brookline	20,300
portion	650	Portland (incl. in S.		Framingham	19,700
**Sioux City	400	Maine)		Near West	35,800
*Waterloo	170	Rockland area	300	Newton	27,700
Other places	300	Southern Maine[N]		North Central	22,900
			6,000	Northeast	7,700
KANSAS		*Waterville	200	North Shore	18,600
Kansas City area-		Other places	150	Northwest	13,600
Kansas portion[N]				Southeast	8,500
	12,000	MARYLAND		Brockton (listed under	
Lawrence	150	Annapolis area	3,000	Boston Metro Region)	
Manhattan	425	**Baltimore	94,500	Brookline (listed under	
*Topeka	400	Columbia (incl. in		Boston Metro Region)	
Wichita[N]	1,300	Howard County)		Cape Cod-Barnstable	
Other places	100	Cumberland	275	County	3,250

State and City	Jewish Population	State and City	Jewish Population	State and City	Jewish Population
Clinton (incl. in Worcester-Central Worcester County)		Northampton	1,200	Traverse City	200
		Peabody (incl. in N. Shore, listed under Boston Metro Region)		Other places	400
Fall River area	1,100				
Falmouth (incl. in Cape Cod)		Pittsfield-Berkshire County	3,500	MINNESOTA	
Fitchburg (incl. in N. Worcester County)		Plymouth area	1,000	**Duluth	485
		Provincetown (incl. in Cape Cod)		*Minneapolis	31,500
Framingham (listed under Boston Metro Region)				Rochester	550
		Salem (incl. in N. Shore, listed under Boston Metro Region)		**St. Paul	9,200
Gardner (incl. in N. Worcester County)				Other places	150
Gloucester (incl. N. Shore, listed under Boston Metro Region)		Southbridge (incl. in S. Worcester County)		MISSISSIPPI	
		South Worcester County	500	Biloxi-Gulfport	250
Great Barrington (incl. in Pittsfield)		Springfield[N]	10,000	**Greenville	120
*Greenfield	1,100	Taunton area	1,300	**Hattiesburg	130
Haverhill	800	Webster (incl. in S. Worcester County)		**Jackson	550
Holyoke	600			Other places	300
*Hyannis (incl. in Cape Cod)		Worcester-Central Worcester County	11,000	MISSOURI	
Lawrence (incl. in Andover)		Other places	150	Columbia	400
Leominster (incl. in N. Worcester County)				Joplin	100
		MICHIGAN		Kansas City area-Missouri portion[N]	7,100
Lowell area	2,000	*Ann Arbor	7,000	*St. Joseph	265
Lynn (incl. in N. Shore, listed under Boston Metro Region)		Bay City	150	**St. Louis	54,000
		Benton Harbor area	240	Springfield	300
*Martha's Vineyard	300	**Detroit Metro Area	94,000	Other places	150
New Bedford[N]	2,600	*Flint	1,500		
Newburyport	280	*Grand Rapids	1,800	MONTANA	
Newton (listed under Boston Metro Region)		**Jackson	200	*Billings	300
		*Kalamazoo	1,500	Butte	100
North Adams (incl. in N. Berkshire County)		Lansing area	2,100	Helena (incl. in Butte)	
		***Midland	120	*Kalispell	150
North Berkshire County	400	Mt. Clemens (incl. in Detroit)		Missoula	200
		Mt. Pleasant[N]	130	Other places	100
North Worcester County	1,500	*Muskegon	210	NEBRASKA	
		*Saginaw	115	Grand Island-Hastings (incl. in Lincoln)	
				Lincoln	700
				**Omaha	6,350
				Other places	50

State and City	Jewish Population

NEVADA
Carson City (incl. in Reno)
*Las Vegas 75,000
**Reno 2,100
Sparks (incl. in Reno)

NEW HAMPSHIRE
Bethlehem 200
Concord 500
Dover area 600
Exeter (incl. in Portsmouth)
Franconia (incl. in Bethlehem)
Hanover-Lebanon . 500
*Keene 300
**Laconia 270
Littleton (incl. in Bethlehem)
Manchester area 4,000
Nashua area 2,000
Portsmouth area 1,250
Rochester (incl. in Dover)
Salem 150
Other places 150

NEW JERSEY
Asbury Park (incl. in Monmouth County)
**Atlantic City (incl. Atlantic and Cape May counties) . 15,800
Bayonne (listed under Hudson County)
Bergen County (also incl. in Northeastern N.J.) 83,700
Bridgeton 110
Bridgewater (incl. in Somerset County)

Camden (incl. in Cherry Hill-S. N.J.)
Cherry Hill-Southern N.J.[N] 49,000
Edison (incl. in Middlesex County)
Elizabeth (incl. in Union County)
Englewood (incl. in Bergen County)
Essex County (also incl. in Northeastern N.J.)[N] 76,200
East Essex 10,800
Livingston 12,600
North Essex . . . 15,600
South Essex . . . 20,300
West Orange-Orange 16,900
*Flemington 1,500
Freehold (incl. in Monmouth County)
Gloucester (incl. in Cherry Hill-S. N.J.)
Hoboken (listed under Hudson County)
Hudson County (also incl. in Northeastern N.J.) 12,500
Bayonne 1,600
Hoboken 1,400
Jersey City 6,000
North Hudson County[N] 3,500
Jersey City (listed under Hudson County)
Lakewood (incl. in Ocean County)
Livingston (listed under Essex County)
Middlesex County (also incl. in Northeastern N.J.)[N] 45,000

Monmouth County (also incl. in Northeastern N.J.) 65,000
Morris County (also incl. in Northeastern N.J.) 33,500
Morristown (incl. in Morris County)
Mt. Holly (incl. in Cherry Hill-S. N.J.)
New Brunswick (incl. in Middlesex County)
Newark (incl. in Essex County)
Northeastern N.J.[N] 388,000
Ocean County (also incl. in Northeastern N.J.) 11,500
Passaic County (also incl. in Northeastern N.J.) 17,000
Passaic-Clifton (incl. in Passaic County)
Paterson (incl. in Passaic County)
Perth Amboy (incl. in Middlesex County)
Phillipsburg (incl. in Warren County)
Plainfield (incl. in Union County)
Princeton area . . . 3,000
Somerset County (also incl. in Northeastern N.J.) 11,000
Somerville (incl. in Somerset County)
Sussex County (also incl. in Northeastern N.J.) 4,100
Toms River (incl. in Ocean County)
Trenton[N] 6,000

State and City	Jewish Population	State and City	Jewish Population	State and City	Jewish Population
Union County (also incl. in Northeastern N.J.)	30,000	Elmira[N]	950	**Oneonta	300
Vineland[N]	1,890	Fleischmanns	100	Orange County	15,000
Warren County	400	Geneva area	300	Pawling (incl. in	
Wayne (incl. in Passaic County)		Glens Falls[N]	800	Poughkeepsie-	
Wildwood	330	*Gloversville	300	Dutchess County)	
Willingboro (incl. in Cherry Hill-S. N.J.)		*Herkimer	130	Plattsburg	250
Other places	150	Highland Falls (incl. in Orange County)		Port Jervis (incl. in Orange County)	
		*Hudson	500	Potsdam	200
NEW MEXICO		*Ithaca area	2,000	*Poughkeepsie-Dutchess County	3,600
*Albuquerque	7,500	Jamestown	100	Putnam County	1,000
Las Cruces	600	Kingston[N]	4,300	**Rochester	22,500
Los Alamos	250	Kiryas Joel (incl. in Orange County)		Rockland County	90,000
Rio Rancho (incl. in Albuquerque)		Lake George (incl. in Glens Falls)		Rome	100
Santa Fe	1,700	Liberty (incl. in Sullivan County)		Saratoga Springs	600
Taos	300	Middletown (incl. in Orange County)		**Schenectady	5,200
Other places	150	Monroe (incl. in Orange County)		Seneca Falls (incl. in Geneva)	
		Monticello (incl. in Sullivan County)		South Fallsburg (incl. in Sullivan County)	
NEW YORK		Newark (incl. in Geneva total)		***Sullivan County	7,425
*Albany	12,000	Newburgh (incl. in Orange County)		Syracuse[N]	9,000
Amenia (incl. in Poughkeepsie-Dutchess County)		New Paltz (incl. in Kingston)		Troy area	800
Amsterdam	150	New York Metro Area[N]	1,450,000	Utica[N]	1,100
*Auburn	115	Bronx	83,700	Walden (incl. in Orange County)	
Beacon (incl. in Poughkeepsie-Dutchess County)		Brooklyn	379,000	Watertown	100
*Binghamton (incl. all Broome County)	2,600	Manhattan	314,500	Woodstock (incl. in Kingston)	
Brewster (incl. in Putnam County)		Queens	238,000	Other places	490
*Buffalo	20,000	Staten Island	33,700		
Canandaigua (incl. in Geneva)		Nassau County	207,000	NORTH CAROLINA	
Catskill	200	Suffolk County	100,000	Asheville[N]	1,300
Corning (incl. in Elmira)		Westchester County	94,000	**Chapel Hill-Durham	4,000
*Cortland	150	Niagara Falls	150	Charlotte[N]	8,500
Ellenville	1,600	Olean	100	Elizabethtown (incl. in Wilmington)	
				*Fayetteville	300
				Gastonia	210
				*Greensboro	2,500

State and City	Jewish Population
Greenville	240
*Hendersonville	250
**Hickory	110
High Point (incl. in Greensboro)	
Jacksonville (incl. in Wilmington)	
Raleigh-Wake County	6,000
Whiteville (incl. in Wilmington)	
Wilmington area	1,200
Winston-Salem	485
Other places	450

NORTH DAKOTA

State and City	Jewish Population
Fargo	500
Grand Forks	130
Other places	100

OHIO

State and City	Jewish Population
**Akron	5,500
Athens	100
Bowling Green (incl. in Toledo)	
Butler County	900
**Canton	1,500
Cincinnati[N]	22,500
Cleveland[N]	81,000
*Columbus	15,600
**Dayton	5,000
Elyria	155
Fremont (incl. in Sandusky)	
Hamilton (incl. in Butler County)	
Kent (incl. in Akron)	
*Lima	180
Lorain	600
Mansfield	150
Marion[N]	125
Middletown (incl. in Butler County)	
New Philadelphia (incl. in Canton)	
Norwalk (incl. in Sandusky)	
Oberlin (incl. in Elyria)	
Oxford (incl. in Butler County)	
**Sandusky	105
Springfield	200
*Steubenville	115
Toledo[N]	5,900
Warren (incl. in Youngstown)	
Wooster	175
Youngstown[N]	3,6500
*Zanesville	100
Other places	350

OKLAHOMA

State and City	Jewish Population
Norman (incl. in Oklahoma City)	
**Oklahoma City	2,300
*Tulsa	2,650
Other places	100

OREGON

State and City	Jewish Population
Ashland (incl. in Medford)	
Bend	175
Corvallis	500
Eugene	3,250
Grants Pass (incl. in Medford)	
**Medford	1,000
Portland[N]	25,500
**Salem	1,000
Other places	200

PENNSYLVANIA

State and City	Jewish Population
Allentown (incl. in Lehigh Valley)	
*Altoona	575
Ambridge (incl. in Pittsburgh)	
Beaver Falls (incl. in Upper Beaver County)	
Bethlehem (incl. in Lehigh Valley)	
Bucks County (listed under Philadelphia area)	
*Butler	250
**Chambersburg	150
Chester (incl. in Delaware County, listed under Phila. area)	
Chester County (listed under Phila. area)	
Coatesville (incl. in Chester County, listed under Phila. area)	
Easton (incl. in Lehigh Valley)	
*Erie	850
Farrell (incl. in Sharon)	
Greensburg (incl. in Pittsburgh)	
**Harrisburg	7,000
Hazleton area	300
Honesdale (incl. in Wayne County)	
Jeannette (incl. in Pittsburgh)	
**Johnstown	275
Lancaster area	3,000
*Lebanon	350
Lehigh Valley	8,500
Lewisburg (incl. in Sunbury)	
Lock Haven (incl. in Williamsport)	
McKeesport (incl. in Pittsburgh)	
New Castle	200
Norristown (incl. in Montgomery County, listed under Phila. area)	
**Oil City	100

| | Jewish |
| State and City | Population |

Oxford-Kennett Square
(incl. in Chester
County, listed under
Phila. area)
Philadelphia area[N]
. . . . 206,000
Bucks County
. . . . 34,800
Chester County
. . . . 10,100
Delaware County
. . . . 15,700
Montgomery County
. . . . 58,900
Philadelphia . . 86,600
Phoenixville (incl. in
Chester County, listed
under Phila. area)
***Pike County 300
Pittsburgh[N] 40,000
Pottstown. 650
Pottsville 160
*Reading. 2,200
*Scranton 3,100
Shamokin (incl. in
Sunbury)
Sharon 300
State College 700
Stroudsburg 600
Sunbury[N] 200
Tamaqua (incl. in
Hazleton)
Uniontown area . . . 150
Upper Beaver County
. . . . 180
Washington (incl. in
Pittsburgh)
***Wayne County
. . . . 500
Waynesburg (incl. in
Pittsburgh)
West Chester (incl. in
Chester County, listed
under Phila. area)

| | Jewish |
| State and City | Population |

Wilkes-Barre[N] . . . 3,200
**Williamsport 225
York 1,800
Other places. 800

RHODE ISLAND
Cranston (incl. in
Providence)
Kingston (incl. in
Washington County)
Newport-Middletown
. . . . 700
Providence area . 14,200
Washington County
. . . . 1,200
Westerly (incl. in
Washington County)

SOUTH CAROLINA
*Charleston. 5,000
**Columbia 2,750
Florence area 220
Georgetown (incl. in
Myrtle Beach)
Greenville 1,200
Kingstree (incl. in
Sumter)
**Myrtle Beach 475
Rock Hill 100
*Spartanburg. 500
Sumter[N] 140
York (incl. in Rock
Hill)
Other places. 450

SOUTH DAKOTA
Sioux Falls. 180
Other places. 150

TENNESSEE
Chattanooga 1,450
Knoxville. 1,800
Memphis 8,500

| | Jewish |
| State and City | Population |

Nashville. 6,000
Oak Ridge 250
Other places. 250

TEXAS
Amarillo[N]. 200
*Austin 13,500
***Baytown. 300
Beaumont. 500
*Brownsville 450
***College Station-
Bryan 400
*Corpus Christi . . 1,400
**Dallas 45,000
El Paso 5,000
*Fort Worth 5,000
Galveston. 450
Harlingen (incl. in
Brownsville)
**Houston[N]. 42,000
Laredo 130
Longview 100
*Lubbock. 230
*McAllen[N] 500
Midland-Odessa. . . 200
Port Arthur 100
*San Antonio . . . 11,000
South Padre Island
(incl. in Brownsville)
Tyler. 400
Waco[N] 300
Wichita Falls 260
Other places. 550

UTAH
Ogden. 150
*Salt Lake City . . . 4,200
Other places. 100

VERMONT
Bennington area. . . 300
*Brattleboro. 350
**Burlington. 3,000
Manchester area. . . 325

State and City	Jewish Population	State and City	Jewish Population	State and City	Jewish Population
Montpelier-Barre	550	Northern Virginia	35,100	Clarksburg	110
Newport (incl. in St. Johnsbury)		Petersburg area	350	Huntington[N]	250
Rutland	625	Portsmouth-Suffolk (incl. in Norfolk)		Morgantown	200
**St. Johnsbury	140	Radford (incl. in Blacksburg)		Parkersburg	110
Stowe	150	Richmond[N]	15,000	**Wheeling	275
Woodstock	270	Roanoke	900	Other places	300
Other places	100	Staunton[N]	370		
		Williamsburg (incl. in Newport News)		WISCONSIN	
VIRGINIA		Winchester[N]	270	Appleton area	300
Alexandria (incl. in N. Virginia)		Other places	100	Beloit	120
Arlington (incl. in N. Virginia)				Fond du Lac (incl. in Oshkosh)	
Blacksburg	175	WASHINGTON		Green Bay	500
Charlottesville	1,500	Bellingham	500	Janesville (incl. in Beloit)	
Chesapeake (incl. in Portsmouth)		Ellensburg (incl. in Yakima)		*Kenosha	300
Colonial Heights (incl. in Petersburg)		Longview-Kelso (incl. in Vancouver)		La Crosse	100
Danville area	100	*Olympia	560	*Madison	4,500
Fairfax County (incl. in N. Virginia)		***Port Angeles	100	Milwaukee[N]	21,300
Fredericksburg[N]	500	*Seattle[N]	37,200	Oshkosh area	170
Hampton (incl. in Newport News)		Spokane	1,500	*Racine	200
Harrisonburg (incl. in Staunton)		*Tacoma	2,000	Sheboygan	140
Lexington (incl. in Staunton)		Tri Cities[N]	300	Waukesha (incl. in Milwaukee)	
Lynchburg area	275	Vancouver	600	Wausau[N]	300
**Martinsville	100	**Yakima	150	Other places	300
Newport News-Hampton[N]	2,400	Other places	350		
Norfolk-Virginia Beach	19,000			WYOMING	
		WEST VIRGINIA		Casper	100
		Bluefield-Princeton	200	Cheyenne	230
		*Charleston	975	Laramie (incl. in Cheyenne)	
				Other places	100

Notes

CALIFORNIA

Long Beach—includes in L.A. County; Long Beach, Signal Hill, Cerritos, Lakewood, Rossmoor, and Hawaiian Gardens. Also includes in Orange County, Los Alamitos, Cypress, Seal Beach, and Huntington Harbor.

Los Angeles—includes most of Los Angeles County, but excludes those places listed above that are part of the Long Beach area and also excludes the eastern portion that is listed below as part of San Gabriel and Pomona Valleys. Also includes eastern edge of Ventura County.

Orange County—includes most of Orange County, but excludes towns in northern portion that are included in Long Beach.

Palm Springs—includes Palm Springs, Desert Hot Springs, Cathedral City, Palm Desert, and Rancho Mirage.

Sacramento—includes Yolo, Placer, El Dorado, and Sacramento counties.

San Francisco Bay area—North Peninsula includes northern San Mateo County. South Peninsula includes southern San Mateo County and towns of Palo Alto and Los Altos in Santa Clara County. San Jose includes remainder of Santa Clara County.

San Gabriel and Pomona Valleys—includes in Los Angeles County: Alhambra, Altadena, Arcadia, Azusa, Baldwin Park, Bellflower, Bell Gardens, Chapman Woods, Charter Oak, Claremont, Commerce, Covina, Diamond Bar, Downey, Duarte, East Los Angeles, East Pasadena, East San Gabriel, El Monte, Glendora, Hacienda Heights, La Canada Flintridge, La Habra Heights, La Mirada, La Puente, La Verne, Los Nietos, Monrovia, Montebello, Monterey Park, Norwalk, Pico Rivera, Paramount, Pasadena, Pomona, Rosemead, Rowland Heights, San Dimas, San Gabriel, San Marino, Santa Fe Springs, Sierra Madre, South El Monte, South Pasadena, South San Gabriel, South San Jose Hills, South Whittier, Temple City, Walnut, West Covina, West Puente Valley, West Whittier, Whittier and Valinda. Also includes in San Bernardino County: Alta Loma, Chino, Chino Hills, Mira Loma, Montclair, Ontario, Rancho Cucamonga, and Upland.

COLORADO

Denver—includes Adams, Arapahoe, Boulder, Denver, and Jefferson counties.

Pueblo—includes all of Pueblo County east to Lamar, west and south to Trinidad.

CONNECTICUT

Bridgeport—includes Monroe, Easton, Trumbull, Fairfield, Bridgeport, Shelton, and Stratford.

Danbury—includes Danbury, Bethel, New Fairfield, Brookfield, Sherman, Newtown, Redding, and Ridgefield.

Hartford—includes all of Hartford County; Vernon, Rockville, Somers, and Stafford Springs in New Haven County; and Ellington and Tolland in Tolland County.

Lower Middlesex County—includes Branford, Guilford, Madison, Clinton, Westbrook, Old Saybrook, Old Lyme, Durham, and Killingworth.

New Haven—includes New Haven, East Haven, Guilford, Branford, Madison, North Haven, Hamden, West Haven, Milford, Orange, Woodbridge, Bethany, Derby, Ansonia, Quinnipiac, Meriden, Seymour, and Wallingford.

New London—includes central and southern New London County. Also includes part of Middlesex County and part of Windham County.

Waterbury—includes Bethlehem, Cheshire, Litchfield, Morris, Middlebury, Southbury, Naugatuck, Prospect, Plymouth, Roxbury, Southbury, Southington, Thomaston, Torrington, Washington, Watertown, Waterbury, Oakville, Woodbury, Wolcott, Oxford, and other towns in Litchfield County and northern New Haven County.

Westport—includes Norwalk, Weston, Westport, East Norwalk, Wilton, and Georgetown.

DISTRICT OF COLUMBIA

Washington, D.C.—For a total of the Washington, D.C., metropolitan area, include Montgomery and Prince Georges counties in Maryland, and northern Virginia.

FLORIDA

Orlando—includes all of Orange and Seminole counties, southern Volusia County, and northern Osceola County. Stuart-Port St. Lucie—includes all of Martin County and southern St. Lucie County.

GEORGIA

Augusta—includes Burke, Columbia, and Richmond counties.

ILLINOIS

Chicago—includes all of Cook and DuPage counties and a portion of Lake County. Elgin includes northern Kane County and southern McHenry County. Rockford—includes Winnebago, Boone, and Stephenson counties. Southern Illinois—includes lower portion of Illinois below Carlinville.

INDIANA

South Bend—includes St. Joseph and Elkhart counties.

KANSAS

Kansas City—includes Johnson and Wyandotte counties. For a total of the Kansas City metropolitan area, include Missouri portion.

Wichita—includes Sedgwick County and towns of Salina, Dodge City, Great Bend, Liberal, Russell, and Hays.

KENTUCKY

Lexington—includes Fayette, Bourbon, Scott, Clark, Woodford, Madison, Pulaski and Jessamine counties.

LOUSIANA

Alexandria—includes towns in Allen, Grant, Rapides and Vernon parishes.

Baton Rouge—includes E. Baton Rouge, Ascension, Livingston, St. Landry, Iberville, Pointe Coupee, and W. Baton Rouge parishes.

South Central—includes Abbeville, Lafayette, New Iberia, Crowley, Opelousas, Houma, Morgan City, Thibodaux, and Franklin.

MAINE

Southern Maine—includes York, Cumberland, and Sagadahoc counties.

MASSACHUSETTS

Andover—includes Andover, N. Andover, Boxford, Lawrence, Methuen, Tewksbury, and Dracut.

Boston Metropolitan region—Brockton-South Central includes Avon, Bridgewater, Brockton, Canton, East Bridgewater, Easton, Foxborough, Halifax, Randolph, Sharon, Stoughton, West Bridgewater, Whitman, and Wrentham. Framingham area includes Acton, Bellingham, Boxborough, Framingham, Franklin, Holliston, Hopkinton, Hudson, Marlborough, Maynard, Medfield, Medway, Milford, Millis, Southborough, and Stow. Northeast includes Chelsea, Everett, Malden, Medford, Revere, and Winthrop. North Central includes Arlington, Belmont, Cambridge, Somerville, Waltham, and Watertown. Northwest includes Bedford, Burlington, Carlisle, Concord, Lexington, Lincoln, Melrose, North Reading, Reading, Stoneham, Wakefield, Wilmington, Winchester, and Woburn. North Shore includes Lynn, Saugus, Nahant, Swampscott, Lynnfield, Peabody, Salem, Marblehead, Beverly, Danvers, Middleton, Wenham, Topsfield, Hamilton, Manchester, Ipswich, Essex, Gloucester, and Rockport. Near West includes Ashland, Dedham, Dover, Natick, Needham, Norfolk, Norwood, Sherborn, Sudbury, Walpole, Wayland, Wellesley, Weston, and Westwood. Southeast includes Abington, Braintree, Cohasset, Duxbury, Hanover, Hanson, Hingham, Holbrook, Hull, Kingston, Marshfield, Milton, Norwell, Pembroke, Quincy, Rockland, Scituate, and Weymouth.

New Bedford—includes New Bedford, Dartmouth, Fairhaven, and Mattapoisett.

Springfield—includes Springfield, Longmeadow, E. Longmeadow, Hampden, Wilbraham, Agawam and W. Springfield.

MICHIGAN
Mt. Pleasant—includes towns in Isabella, Mecosta, Gladwin. and Gratiot counties.

MISSOURI
Kansas City—For a total of the Kansas City metropolitan area, include the Kansas portion.

NEW HAMPSHIRE
Laconia—includes Laconia, Plymouth, Meredith, Conway, and Franklin.

NEW JERSEY
Cherry Hill-Southern N.J.—includes Camden, Burlington, and Gloucester counties.

Essex County-East Essex—includes Belleville, Bloomfield, East Orange, Irvington, Newark, and Nutley in Essex County, and Kearney in Hudson County. North Essex includes Caldwell, Cedar Grove, Essex Fells, Fairfield, Glen Ridge, Montclair, North Caldwell, Roseland, Verona and West Caldwell. South Essex includes Maplewood, Millburn, Short Hills, and South Orange in Essex County, and Springfield in Union County.

Middlesex County—includes in Somerset County: Kendall Park, Somerset, and Franklin; in Mercer County: Hightstown; and all of Middlesex County.

Northeastern N.J.—includes Bergen, Essex, Hudson, Middlesex, Morris, Passaic, Somerset, Union, Hunterdon, Sussex, Monmouth, and Ocean counties.

North Hudson County—includes Guttenberg, Hudson Heights, North Bergen, North Hudson, Secaucus, Union City, Weehawken, West New York, and Woodcliff.

Somerset County—includes most of Somerset County and a portion of Hunterdon County.

Trenton—includes most of Mercer County.

Union County—includes all of Union County except Springfield. Also includes a few towns in adjacent areas of Somerset and Middlesex counties.

Vineland—includes most of Cumberland County and towns in neighboring counties adjacent to Vineland.

NEW YORK
Elmira—includes Chemung, Tioga, and Schuyler counties.

Glens Falls—includes Warren and Washington counties, lower Essex County, and upper Saratoga County.

Kingston—includes eastern half of Ulster County.

New York Metropolitan area—includes the five boroughs of New York City, Westchester, Nassau and Suffolk counties. For a total Jewish population of the New

York metropolitan region, include Fairfield County, Connecticut; Rockland, Putnam and Orange counties, New York; and Northeastern New Jersey.

Syracuse—includes Onondaga County, western Madison County, and most of Oswego County.

Utica—southeastern third of Oneida County.

NORTH CAROLINA

Asheville—includes Buncombe, Haywood, and Madison counties.

Charlotte—includes Mecklenburg County. For a total of the Charlotte area, include Rock Hill, South Carolina.

OHIO

Cincinnati—includes Hamilton and Butler counties. For total of the Cincinnati area, include the Covington- Newport area of Kentucky.

Cleveland—includes all of Cuyahoga County, and portions of Lake, Geauga, Portage, and Summit counties. For metropolitan total, include Elyria, Lorain, and Akron.

Toledo—includes Fulton, Lucas, and Wood counties.

Youngstown—includes Mahoning and Trumbull counties.

PENNSYLVANIA

Philadelphia—For total Jewish population of the Philadelphia metropolitan region, include the Cherry Hill-Southern, N.J., Princeton, and Trenton areas of New Jersey, and the Wilmington and Newark areas of Delaware.

Pittsburgh—includes all of Allegheny County and adjacent portions of Washington, Westmoreland, and Beaver counties.

Sunbury—includes Shamokin, Lewisburg, Milton, Selinsgrove, and Sunbury.

Wilkes-Barre—includes all of Luzerne County except southern portion, which is included in the Hazleton total.

SOUTH CAROLINA

Sumter—includes towns in Sumter, Lee, Clarendon, and Williamsburg counties.

TEXAS

Amarillo—includes Canyon, Childress, Borger, Dumas, Memphis, Pampa, Vega, and Hereford in Texas, and Portales, New Mexico.

Houston—includes Harris, Montgomery, and Fort Bend counties, and parts of Brazoria and Galveston counties.

McAllen—includes Edinburg, Harlingen, McAllen, Mission, Pharr, Rio Grande City, San Juan, and Weslaco.

Waco   includes McLennan, Coryell, Bell, Falls, Hamilton, and Hill counties.

VIRGINIA

Fredericksburg—includes towns in Spotsylvania, Stafford, King George, and Orange counties

Newport News—includes Newport News, Hampton, Williamsburg, James City, York County, and Poquoson City.

Richmond—includes Richmond City, Henrico County, and Chesterfield County.

Staunton—includes towns in Augusta, Page, Shenandoah, Rockingham, Bath, and Highland counties.

Winchester—includes towns in Winchester, Frederick, Clarke, and Warren counties.

WASHINGTON

Seattle—includes King County and adjacent portions of Snohomish and Kitsap counties.

Tri Cities—includes Pasco, Richland, and Kennewick.

wisconsin

Milwaukee—includes Milwaukee County, eastern Waukesha County, and southern Ozaukee County.

Wausau—includes Stevens Point, Marshfield, Antigo, and Rhinelander.

TABLE 4. ESTIMATED AMERICAN JEWISH POPULATION DURING THE 20TH CENTURY

Year	Total U.S.	New York City CMSA*
1900	1,058,000	552,000
1910	2,044,000	955,000
1920	3,602,000	1,818,000
1930	4,228,000	2,070,000
1940	4,770,000	2,311,000
1950	5,000,000	2,591,000
1960	5,531,000	2,731,000
1970	5,870,000	2,742,000
1980	5,800,000	2,419,000
1990	5,981,000	2,157,000
2000	6,136,000	1,978,000

*Consolidated Metropolitan Statistical Area. The New York metropolitan region (CMSA) includes the city, six counties in New York State outside the city, 13 counties in northeastern New Jersey, and one in Connecticut.

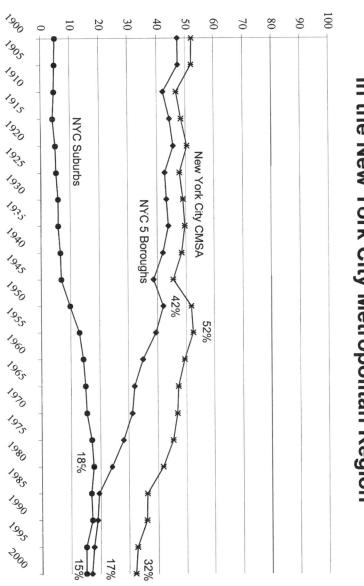

Figure 1

Share of U.S. Jewish Population 1900-2000 in the New York City Metropolitan Region

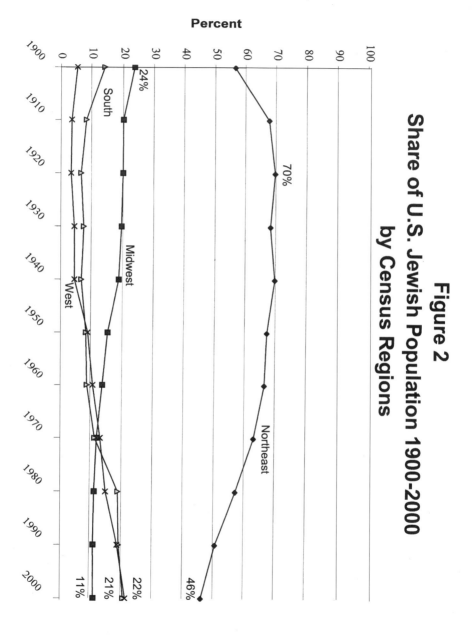

Figure 2
Share of U.S. Jewish Population 1900-2000
by Census Regions

Review
of
the
Year

OTHER COUNTRIES

Canada

National Affairs

Canada enjoyed a year of economic and political stability. Low inflation, strong economic growth, and declining unemployment produced a favorable economic environment. Substantial surpluses allowed the government to lower taxes for the first time in years. Interest rates were relatively low, especially compared to those in the United States, which contributed to another decline of the Canadian dollar to near-record lows.

Prime Minister Jean Chrétien took advantage of the favorable situation to call a federal election for November 27, over a year before the end of his normal four-year term. The risk paid off as his Liberal Party increased its majority in the House of Commons by 11, winning 172 of the 301 seats. The new Canadian Alliance (a reshaped Reform Party) came in a distant second with 66 seats, and the Bloc Québécois, Progressive Conservatives, and New Democrats trailed far behind. The comfortable majority, coupled with the divided nature of the opposition, promised smooth sailing for the Liberals for another term, barring an internal dispute over the timing of the prime minister's eventual retirement.

Six Jews were elected, all as Liberals: Anita Neville, a new MP from Manitoba, and incumbents Herb Gray and Elinor Caplan from Ontario and Irwin Cotler, Raymonde Falco, and Jacques Saada from Quebec. Gray and Caplan retained their cabinet posts.

Canadian Jews had long favored the Liberal Party, but that support was less assured than usual in 2000, for two reasons. First, the new Alliance leader, Stockwell Day, made a concerted effort to woo Jewish voters. Second, Canada's Middle East policy during the Palestinian uprising that began at the end of September angered members of the Jewish community, many of whom felt betrayed by their country's vote condemning Israel in the UN Security Council in October (see below).

Day had been courting Jews for months before the election was called. He declared in July, when he met with B'nai Brith Canada (BBC) leaders, that his Middle East stance "would be a supportive, friendly, pro-Israel policy . . . ." He continued to pursue that position through the fall campaign, by which time the issue had become much more salient. He also proposed an income tax credit for religious school tuition, a measure that would offer considerable financial relief to

Jews in Ontario, the only province that did not provide funds to Jewish day schools. Chrétien, in contrast, tried to smooth over his relationship with the Jews by reiterating his support for Israel even as his government backed UN resolutions that were widely perceived as hostile toward Israel. And on the day-school funding issue, he avoided the question by depicting it as a provincial matter for Ontario.

As a political and cultural conservative with deeply held Christian beliefs, Day was suspect in some sectors of the Jewish community. His party's roots, which contained elements of anti-Semitism, added to the anxiety. But Day went out of his way to court the Jews and seek their votes. In fact, conservative columnist David Frum characterized him as the federal party leader "who most effectively champions Jewish values and Jewish interests." In a November speech at a Thornhill synagogue he forthrightly refuted accusations of anti-Semitism, declaring that "I oppose racist and anti-Semitic views and those who propagate them, with every ounce of my being. The Canadian Alliance will have a policy of zero tolerance for these kinds of views." He continued to hammer the government for its insensitivity toward Israel, attacking its UN stance as "embarrassing and unsettling." And he stressed his determination to offer tax relief for religious school tuition. Despite his best efforts, his party proved unable to achieve any sort of a breakthrough with Jewish voters, not least because most Jews rejected its very conservative ideology. Jews generally continued to vote Liberal, with the governing party winning the districts with significant Jewish populations.

In municipal elections, also in November, Mel Lastman gained a second term as mayor of Toronto. Among city councilors elected were Erin Shapero in Markham and Mike Feldman, Howard Moscoe, and David Shiner in Toronto.

Jews joined Canadians across the country in mourning the death of former prime minister Pierre Elliott Trudeau, who died in September at the age of 81. Trudeau, who had represented a substantially Jewish district in suburban Montreal throughout his parliamentary career, was very popular with Canadian Jews despite some occasional differences over foreign policy. Jews particularly approved of his forthright stand on national unity. Barney Danson, one of his former cabinet colleagues, hailed him as "a great friend of the Jewish community." Former Canadian Jewish Congress (CJC) president Irving Abella stressed Trudeau's commitment to bringing minorities, including Jews, into high governmental positions. According to Abella, "he helped us take our proper place in Canadian society and for that we should be eternally grateful."

Israel and the Middle East

Canada's foreign policy with regard to Israel and the Palestinians was a major issue during the year. The community was outraged that Canada joined 13 other members of the UN Security Council in approving Resolution 1322 in October. Only the United States abstained. The one-sided resolution heaped all of the blame for the Palestinian uprising on Israel and condemned the Jewish state for "excessive use of force." In cities across the country Jews held rallies to protest what the *Canadian Jewish News* characterized as an "unconscionable vote." CJC president Moshe Ronen spoke about "a lot of anger" and "a feeling of betrayal" in the community.

The proximity of the vote to the election ensured that Prime Minister Chrétien would devote considerable effort to mending fences. At a late October meeting with Jewish leaders, he assigned his top foreign affairs advisor to be his liaison with the community in order to forestall a repetition of the fiasco, and there were reports that Chrétien had been insufficiently aware of the significance of the vote beforehand. Canada-Israel Committee (CIC) chair Joseph Wilder told the prime minister that there had not been "such unrest and anxiety in the Jewish community since perhaps 1973" and that Jews felt "deserted" by their government. Israeli health minister Roni Milo met separately with Chrétien to express his government's views on the recent events. In the weeks after the vote on Resolution 1322, Canada did vote against a UN Human Rights Commission resolution that labeled Israel's actions as war crimes and crimes against humanity. It also abstained on a slanted General Assembly motion.

Canada's vote on Resolution 1322 caused political difficulties for Liberal MP's with significant Jewish populations in their districts. Ministers such as Elinor Caplan, Jim Peterson, and Art Eggleton were unable to speak out on the issue because of the tradition of cabinet solidarity. But backbenchers such as Irwin Cotler, Joe Volpe, and Carolyn Bennett did speak out forcefully against their government's vote. Cotler was criticized by five members of his own caucus for his remarks, in which he denounced the Security Council resolution as "one-sided, misinformed, and prejudicial to the cause of peace in the Middle East."

The prime minister finally put out a public statement on the matter in November, a few weeks before the election. He never apologized or expressed regrets for his government's actions, though he did say that he regretted that Canada's vote had added to the Jewish community's "distress and frustration." He reiterated his commitment to Middle East peace and his assurance that "one UN vote cannot define — or redefine — the deep and long-standing friendship that exists between Canada and Israel. Our commitment to Israel is long-standing and will remain a pillar of Canada's policy in the Middle East."

Nevertheless the government antagonized the community again in December, after the election, by voting in favor of a General Assembly resolution that stated that Israel's imposition of its jurisdiction on Jerusalem was illegal. As a result, Stockwell Day, the leader of the opposition, attacked his country's policy as "incoherent and inconsistent." CIC executive director Rob Ritter expressed particular opposition to the wording of several resolutions that Canada supported. His organization also called upon the government to withhold support for unbalanced resolutions in the future. Rabbi Reuben Poupko called the vote scandalous and said that Chrétien's commitment to the community prior to the election "proved to be nothing but empty rhetoric."

On a more positive note, in May Israel was admitted to the Western European and Others Group at the UN for the first time in its history. Canada had long worked for such an outcome and was praised by CIC chair Joseph Wilder for its efforts.

In April, Jean Chrétien became the first Canadian prime minister to pay an official visit to Israel, when he received an honorary degree from the Hebrew University of Jerusalem. He met with his counterpart, Ehud Barak, as well as with a number of other leading public figures. He also visited Yad Vashem and the grave of Yitzhak Rabin. Subsequently he met with Yasir Arafat in Gaza and traveled to several Arab countries. During his time in the Middle East, Chrétien made a number of impromptu remarks that generated controversy, such as his observation to Arafat that a unilateral declaration of independence might be a useful bargaining tool. Afterwards, MP Irwin Cotler, who accompanied the prime minister, issued a statement saying that the government believed that "the issue of Palestinian statehood should be settled through negotiations between Israel and the Palestinian Authority," and that it did not favor a unilateral declaration of independence. In a June speech in Montreal, Cotler dismissed criticism of Chrétien's gaffes, explaining that the prime minister had a "folksy" way of responding to questions.

In March the Royal Canadian Mounted Police uncovered an apparent plot to bomb Israeli diplomatic offices in Ottawa and Montreal. Aymon Bondok, a Canadian of Egyptian origin, and his girlfriend were charged with possession of explosive materials, and he was charged with extortion. Tarek Khafagy, an Egyptian refugee in Montreal, was also arrested after explosive materials were found in his apartment. In October, Bondok pleaded guilty to the two charges against him and was given a suspended sentence and two years of probation. Judge Claude Parent of Quebec Court was convinced that Bondok did not intend to hurt anyone. Khafagy, the refugee, went on trial for planning to bomb the Israeli consulate, but was acquitted when the judge decided that Bondok had probably framed him.

In an April lecture in Montreal, journalist Steven Emerson charged that Islamic terrorist groups such as Hezballah were operating in Canada. He specifically pointed to a cell of Algerians in Montreal who were connected to the man picked up trying to smuggle explosives from British Columbia into the U.S. state of Washington in 1999. According to Emerson, the terrorist groups concentrated on membership drives and fund-raising, making it difficult for law enforcement agencies to file charges.

A long-standing issue between Canada and Israel that continued to fester, though with decreased intensity, was that of people coming from Israel to Canada and asking for refugee status on the grounds that they were victims of persecution in Israel. For a decade, Israel had vehemently denied the validity of such claims. According to Canada's Immigration and Refugee Board, in 1999, 29 such refugees from Israel were accepted into Canada while 305 were rejected. The acceptance rate was the highest in three years, but considerably below that of the early 1990s. Most of the claimants were former Soviet citizens. According to the Israeli government they were simply using Israel as a way station en route to Canada, and their claims of persecution in Israel had no foundation.

The case of Daniel Weiz led to some tension in Israel-Canada relations. Weiz, a 19-year-old Israeli with immigrant status in Canada who was visiting his father in Toronto, was charged with second-degree murder there in November 1999. Shortly thereafter he returned to Israel, from which Canada requested his extradition (see AJYB 2000, p. 270). In April, an Israeli judge decided that there was enough evidence to warrant a trial, and that he could therefore be extradited. Weiz's Israeli lawyer contended that the evidence against Weiz was false and that he had been framed, but the Supreme Court of Israel turned Weiz down, and he was extradited to Canada in October, where he remained in custody pending a trial in 2001. If convicted and sentenced to a prison term, Weiz would serve it in Israel.

In a talk in Toronto in November, David Bedein, bureau chief of the Israel Resource News Agency, charged that Canadian aid programs to the Palestinians, and specifically Canadian aid workers in the Palestinian refugee camps, helped organize daily school lessons promoting the Palestinian "right of return" using textbooks funded, in part, by the Canadian government. He also charged that Canada, as chair of the Refugee Working Group, supported the "right of return" even though it represented an attempt to undermine Israel as a Jewish state.

The case of the 13 Iranian Jews who faced spy charges in their homeland was taken up by Foreign Minister Lloyd Axworthy. After a meeting with MP Irwin Cotler in March, he declared that the criminal accusations were "completely unfounded." Canada made representations to Iran and put pressure on that country to release the prisoners. Later that month, addressing the CIC policy conference in Ottawa, Axworthy added, "If Iran wants to be recognized internationally, they have to show that they can live up to the international law of the land." When ten of the Iranian Jews were convicted in July, Axworthy, speaking on behalf of the government, expressed "grave concern" over the "seriously flawed" trial. He promised that Canada would continue to follow the matter closely.

Anti-Semitism and Racism

Holocaust denier and anti-Semite Ernst Zundel was tied up in legal proceedings throughout the year. The case involving his California-based Web site, which began in 1996, was still before a tribunal of the Canadian Human Rights Commission, and when proceedings resumed in December it appeared to be nearing an end. Because of the novel issues it raised, the case was regarded as having the potential to become an important precedent. In a case heard by the Federal Court of Appeal, Zundel demanded judicial review of rulings against him by the commission on the grounds that one of its members was biased against him. In June the court turned him down. In yet another case, the Supreme Court of

Canada, in July, refused to hear his appeal of an Ontario court ruling that barred him from suing members of Parliament who had refused to allow him to hold a press conference in the Parliament buildings in 1998. In December Zundel received another rebuff from the high court when it refused to hear his appeal involving his claim of Canadian citizenship, and also rejected his charges against the human-rights commission. One positive development for Zundel during the year was a bequest from the estate of Boston lawyer Richard Cotter, who died in 1999. He left Zundel $100,000 and gave over $500,000 to other anti-Semites and hate groups.

A dispute within the Parti Québécois (PQ), which governed Quebec, took on a nasty anti-Semitic dimension in December. Yves Michaud, a PQ hardliner, had announced his intention to seek his party's nomination in a Montreal district. He made a number of remarks about Jews during a radio interview, as well as in subsequent comments to the media, that the community regarded as deeply offensive, including an accusation that the Jews did not have a monopoly on suffering, and that B'nai Brith Canada and Côte St. Luc Jews deserved criticism for opposing independence for Quebec. Michaud was roundly denounced by Premier Lucien Bouchard, the leader of the PQ, and by Quebec's National Assembly, which unanimously passed a motion censuring him. The affair escalated when some separatists rose to Michaud's defense and criticized Bouchard and the National Assembly motion, thereby exposing a rift within the PQ. Meanwhile, Jewish organizations praised Bouchard for his forthright condemnation of Michaud. Michaud, for his part, claimed that he had been deliberately misinterpreted and targeted politically because of his commitment to Quebec independence. He would, he said, continue to criticize anyone who opposed independence.

The events surrounding the violence between Israel and the Palestinians in the fall sparked an upsurge in anti-Semitic incidents in various parts of the country. A number occurred in Ontario, where six synagogues were vandalized around the time of Yom Kippur. Rocks were thrown through the glass doors of Beth Shalom Synagogue in Ottawa in the early morning hours on the holy day. There was also vandalism at Beth Tefilah synagogue in London, Ontario. Three Toronto synagogues were vandalized, and anti-Israel leaflets were placed on cars parked at another Toronto synagogue. In Montreal, two Jewish boys wearing *kippot* (skullcaps) were assaulted at a subway station, and there were over a dozen incidents of graffiti and destruction of property. In mid-October, 29 headstones were knocked over at a Jewish cemetery, though officials declined to connect the incident to the Middle East situation. In November a firebomb destroyed a room at a funeral chapel, and another assault took place just outside a subway station. More serious incidents occurred in Edmonton, where two synagogues were firebombed early in November. Yousef Sandouga was charged with one count of arson for starting one of the fires, at Beth Shalom Synagogue, by throwing a Molotov cocktail inside. At the end of November, B'nai Brith Canada counted nearly 50 incidents since the beginning of October, more than double the figure for the same months in 1999. In addition, the Canadian Security Intelligence Service reported that Hamas and Hezballah were active in Canada, though no incidents had been attributed to them.

Earlier in the year, in March, a young woman in Winnipeg pleaded guilty to the desecration of over 200 monuments at a Jewish cemetery in 1999. In August a Montreal-area public school was defaced with racist graffiti that included slurs against Jews.

Bernie Farber, executive director of the Ontario Region of CJC, revealed in June the existence of a racist Web site called Anschluss Kanada, and the upgrading of the Heritage Front's Web site. He expressed concern that these developments represented an upsurge in far-right activity in Canada. The Heritage Front had planned a Canada Day rock concert in Kingston featuring four skinhead bands, but protests by antiracist groups forced its cancellation.

Caricaturist Josh Beutel appealed a 1998 court judgment against him involving one of his cartoons in which former Moncton school teacher Malcolm Ross was compared to Joseph Goebbels. Even though the court acknowledged that Beutel could legally characterize Ross as a racist and an anti-Semite, depicting him as a Nazi went too far. Beutel was ordered to pay Ross $7,500 in damages for libel. Beutel's case was argued in February in the New Brunswick Court of Appeal. Meanwhile Ross had lodged a complaint with the UN Human Rights Commission contending that Canadian courts had erred in 1995 in ruling that his anti-Semitic positions had "contributed to the creation of a poisoned environment" in the education system. But the commission rejected his contention, distinguishing between his beliefs and the "manifestation of those beliefs within a particular context."

Nazi War Criminals

In a number of instances authorities took action against war criminals who had covered up their records when applying to immigrate to Canada after World War II. Vladimir Katriuk, who was to be stripped of his citizenship after a 1999 court finding that he had fraudulently misrepresented his background, took his case to the Supreme Court, which declined to hear it. Katriuk, a voluntary participant in the activities of Battalion 118, which operated as part of the Waffen-SS in Belarus, faced eventual deportation. In a similar case, Judge Andrew MacKay of the Federal Court of Canada ruled in March that Helmut Oberlander had misrepresented his wartime activities when he had applied for immigration. He had been an interpreter with Einsatzkommando 10a of the SD during the war. The judge stated that he did not find much of Oberlander's testimony to be believable. The next step was for the government to strip him of his citizenship. Jacob Fast, an ethnic German from Ukraine accused of being an auxiliary member of the German Security Police, went before the courts in Ontario on the charge of fraudulently obtaining the right to immigrate to Canada by concealing his past.

Serge Kisluk was stripped of his citizenship in March after a court finding against him for concealing his collaboration with the Nazis when immigration authorities interviewed him. He was scheduled for a deportation hearing early in 2001.

Walter Obodzinski became the 17th man in Canada to face charges for war crimes. This native of Poland was accused of joining a Nazi unit in his homeland in 1941 that was responsible for the murder of thousands of Jews and partisans. His case was being heard by the Federal Court in Montreal, where he lived. In June his lawyers requested a permanent stay on the grounds that he was too ill to stand trial, a move opposed by prosecutors.

In the annual report of the War Crimes Program, released in June, Terry Beitner, the acting director of the war crimes section of the Justice Department, reported on the 17 cases that had been launched since 1995. He also acknowledged that the unit was far behind the target of 14 new cases in three years that it had announced in 1998, but expected several more to be launched within a year. A month before, in May, investigator Steve Rambam told a Montreal audience that there were still some 600 war criminals living in Canada. He contended that there was sufficient evidence to prosecute dozens of them, implying that the government was not pursuing matters with enough diligence.

Holocaust-Related Matters

Canada, joining 45 other countries, sent a high-level delegation to the international conference on Holocaust education, remembrance, and research held in Stockholm in January. Leaders of the delegation included Deputy Prime Minister Herb Gray and MP Irwin Cotler. By virtue of its participation, Canada undertook to recognize and commemorate the uniqueness, historicity, and magnitude of the Holocaust, to promote expanded knowledge about the events, and to observe an annual day of remembrance.

In line with those commitments, eight of the ten provinces decided to mark an annual Holocaust Memorial Day, the last being Alberta, which passed a Genocide Remembrance Act in November and adopted a Holocaust Memorial Day. In fact the day specified was the date on the Jewish calendar for Yom Hashoah, though that name was not used due to pressure from Ukrainian and Muslim groups on the provincial legislature.

The first Yom Hashoah observance in Quebec was held in May in the National Assembly. While 55 representatives of the Montreal Jewish community looked on from the gallery, the three provincial party leaders all spoke, after which all members of the legislature rose for a minute of silence. In his remarks, Premier Lucien Bouchard called on his fellow citizens to take "responsibility to make sure that such a thing will never happen again." Lawrence Bergman, a member and one of the sponsors of the bill to mark the day, termed it a "moving expression of solidarity" with Quebec's Jews.

A special ceremony was held in Ottawa in September to honor Holocaust survivors living in Canada. Part of the Zachor project, it was sponsored by several major Jewish organizations and the federal Department of Multiculturalism. Nearly 60 survivors and their representatives attended.

Two Ontario museums, the National Gallery of Canada in Ottawa and the Art Gallery of Ontario in Toronto, acknowledged in December that they owned works of art with uncertain provenances and that they would take measures to identify the proper owners. The announcement was a response to suggestions that paintings looted by the Nazis might have made their way to Canada. The museums suspected that as many as 100 paintings in the National Gallery and 20 in the Ontario museum might fall into that category.

JEWISH COMMUNITY

Demography

A new study confirmed assumptions about a substantial number of poor Jews in Canada. Allan Moscovitch, a professor of social work at Carleton University, found that about 17 percent of Canada's Jews could be classified as poor, about the same proportion as in the general community. The study found that immigrants were particularly likely to be poor, especially those who came during the early 1990s. Senior citizens also tended to be disproportionately poor, with over 21 percent of those over 65 in poverty. In both Ontario and Quebec, which together account for over 75 percent of Canada's Jews, the poverty rate exceeded that in the general population.

Communal Affairs

Steve Ain, a former top federation executive and now a consultant to UIA Federations Canada, looked back on 30 years of experience in Canadian Jewish community organizations. In an interview with the *Canadian Jewish News,* he observed that in earlier years the biggest donors to local campaigns also made the key decision on communal policy. Nowadays, in contrast, the wealthy donors were leaving the decisions to others.

Montreal's Federation CJA considered a major restructuring to try to increase efficiency and reduce overlap in the responsibilities of constituent agencies. According to the plans set out in a task-force report, agency autonomy would be reduced and there would be some mergers and more focused coordination. Another recommendation was for greater collaboration between the federation and the synagogues. After years of budget stringency, increased donations enabled the federation to increase spending for local purposes by 7.9 percent.

The recently reelected president of the Communauté Sépharade du Québec, Moïse Amselem, speaking at his organization's annual meeting in March, announced that the CSQ would move its offices to the new community campus but that it was determined to maintain its autonomy despite the centralizing pressures in Federation CJA. Acting in a spirit of "good will and solidarity," the CSQ was joining the other organizations and agencies in a physical sense, while striving to retain a separate identity. Stating that the CSQ would not be "relegated to the role of a simple agency," Amselem declared that it really represented a distinctive community whose interests had to be defended.

In Toronto, 80 employees of the Jewish Vocational Service went on strike in October, staying out about two months. The key issues were salary and time off for Jewish holidays. Compromises were reached on both issues and the employees returned to work.

The Jewish Public Library of Winnipeg, established in 1923, closed in June due to a lack of operating funds. The decision followed four years of efforts to establish a secure funding base. In the past the library had been supported by the Winnipeg Jewish Community Council, but the opening of the Asper Jewish Community Campus resulted in increased demands on the council's resources.

On a more positive note, a new Jewish home for the aged opened in September on Ottawa's community campus. The Zelikovitz Long-Term Care Facility joined a community center, day and afternoon schools, and most of the community organizations on the campus. In Toronto the UJA Federation announced plans to build a third community campus, this one in the rapidly growing suburban area of Richmond Hill, with its burgeoning Jewish population.

A two-year investigation by federal tax authorities uncovered a $60-million fraud and tax-evasion scheme that involved Tash Hassidim living in Boisbriand, Quebec, north of Montreal. A charitable organization run by these Hassidim pleaded guilty and was fined $400,000 in September. The fraud involved the issuance of inflated charitable receipts in exchange for a percentage of the amount supposedly donated.

Canadian Jews followed the incarceration, trial, and appeals of the Jews in Iran throughout the year. There were regular demonstrations and protests in a number of cities. Even after an appeals court in September reduced the length of the sentences for the ten men who were convicted, MP Irwin Cotler denounced the sentences in the House of Commons, referring to unjust charges, deprivation of rights, and "persecution of the innocent." CJC president Moshe Ronen described the judgments as "the product of a flawed judicial process that has remained biased and is not consistent with international norms of justice." He called for the prisoners to be released.

Israel-Related Matters

The community was active in supporting Israel during the last three months of the year, while the Palestinian uprising was at the center of Jewish concerns. Rallies and conferences were held, pressure was put on the Canadian government to reverse its tilt toward the Palestinians, and efforts were stepped up to communicate information about Israel's situation to the general Canadian population. In Toronto, some Jews organized protests against the *Toronto Star*, the daily with the largest circulation in Canada, for its Middle East coverage, which they contended was strongly slanted toward the Palestinian side. CJC Ontario chair Keith Landy asserted that the paper's editorials suggest "that Israel and Prime Minister Ehud Barak were largely to blame for the continuation of violence." He added that the effect of the regular columnists "is a continuous ganging up on Israel." As a result of the Jewish effort, the paper lost subscriptions and business advertising.

During a calmer period, back in March, the Canada-Israel Committee (CIC) held its parliamentary dinner in Ottawa. Over 1,000 people came from across the country to meet with members of Parliament and to hear addresses from the prime minister, representatives of the opposition parties, and Israeli elder statesman Shimon Peres. Prime Minister Chrétien pledged to do whatever was possible to help the parties in the Middle East achieve peace. He added that "the security of Israel is foremost among the concerns of Canada . . . . and we seek agreements that will allow Israel to live within secure borders."

Thomas Hecht, chair of the CIC Quebec Region, speaking at a meeting of the Canadian Institute for Jewish Research in August, urged the Israeli government to take into account the views of Diaspora Jews before making any decision on the future of Jerusalem. He proposed calling an "estates-general of the Jewish people for that purpose." Hecht added that "the potential division of Jerusalem is not only an Israeli issue; it is an issue for every Jew. Jerusalem is the indivisible capital, not only of Israel, but of the Jewish people. It belongs to all Jews, not only Israeli Jews."

In January, Israeli state comptroller Eliezer Goldberg issued a report based on an investigation of Ehud Barak's ruling party, One Israel, that castigated it for allegedly getting money from foreign sources for use in the 1999 election campaign in a "flagrant breach" of laws that prohibit raising such outside funding. His report made reference to an unnamed Canadian charity that sent 60,000 shekels to the campaign, a relatively small part of the 5.2 million shekels identified as suspect. The Kahanoff Foundation of Calgary was mentioned in an Israeli newspaper as a possible source or conduit for the funds, but James Hume, president of the foundation, denied the allegations, saying: "We don't fund political activities. We only fund charitable activities in Israel."

Religion

Montreal's most prominent and prestigious synagogue, Shaar Hashomayim, disassociated itself from the Conservative movement in October. The Shaar had long been a member of the United Synagogue of Conservative Judaism, and its rabbis through most of the 20th century had been ordained at the Jewish Theological Seminary of America. However the seminary's 1983 decision to ordain women had been opposed by Rabbi Wilfred Shuchat, the Shaar's spiritual leader and a minority member of the committee that had recommended the innovation. Moreover, the Shaar was left as the only Conservative synagogue in North America with separate seating for men and women. Since Rabbi Shuchat's retirement in the early 1990s, the rabbis of the synagogue had all had Orthodox ordination. Rabbi Barry Gelman, the current spiritual leader, ordained by Yeshiva University, announced nevertheless that the synagogue had no intention of seeking formal Orthodox affiliation, and would remain independent.

The Shaar's termination of its membership in the United Synagogue was only one indication of the Conservative movement's problems in Canada, where religious practices were somewhat more traditional than in the United States. In recent years there had also been tension between Conservative synagogues in the Toronto area and the movement's center in the United States. As Shaar vice president Jonathan Schneiderman put it, "I think that the changes in Conservative Judaism were made to meet the needs of American Jewry, which is different from our community, which is more traditional and observant." He stressed that it was the Conservative movement that had changed, not the Shaar, which had remained consistent in its practices. In contrast, another Montreal Conservative synagogue, Shaare Zion, decided to embrace the egalitarianism between men and women that was fast becoming the Conservative norm in the United States.

In a panel discussion on tradition and modernity held at an Orthodox synagogue in Toronto in March, Rabbi Reuven Bulka of Ottawa, an Orthodox rabbi, urged the audience not to deal with non-Orthodox Jews by becoming more stringent and less involved and concerned. Rather, he urged them to engage in dialogue with the non-Orthodox.

A resolution permitting same-sex commitment ceremonies, adopted by the (Reform) Central Conference of American Rabbis in March (see above, pp. 236–37), created some controversy among Canadian Reform rabbis. Rabbi Paul Golomb, executive director of the Canadian Council for Reform Judaism, regarded the resolution as "modest and balanced," allowing individual congregational rabbis to choose whether or not to officiate at the sanctification of same-sex unions. In contrast, Dow Marmur, the rabbi of Canada's most prominent Reform congregation, Toronto's Holy Blossom Temple, announced that he would not officiate at such ceremonies. "I believe in equal rights," he said, "but when it comes to holiness I find it impossible to sanctify the relationship within the framework of Judaism."

Montreal's Vaad Ha'ir, the city's main kashrut supervising agency, issued a compilation of rules in October pertaining to the granting of kashrut certification. This was the first time that such a comprehensive document had been published. What was noteworthy was the increased stringency, especially with respect to the supervision of caterers and rental companies. A rule prohibiting Vaad-certified caterers from serving functions at synagogues not on the approved list raised hackles in the Reconstructionist and Reform congregations. In addition, the rules for functions in private homes were expected to make it more difficult to hold kosher catered events in such venues.

A Montreal woman sued her ex-husband, from whom she obtained a civil divorce in 1981, in Quebec Superior Court in March. She asked for $1.35 million in damages because he had refused to issue a get (religious divorce) for 14 years, until 1995. The ex-husband countered that the provision of the Canada Divorce Act under which she was suing was unconstitutional for two reasons. First, it dealt only with problems arising from recalcitrant Jewish husbands refusing to grant gittin and not with women refusing to receive them. And second, he said, it discriminated in that it applied to Jews and not members of other religions. The man had only issued the get when a court had dismissed his contest of child-support obligations, and the court decision had cited the relevant portion of the act.

The Reform Board of Mohelim (ritual circumcisers), based in Los Angeles, appointed a physician, Dr. Harvey Lupu, as its first *mohel* in Montreal in May. Rabbi Leigh Lerner of Temple Emanu-el Beth Sholom, who trained Dr. Lupu in the relevant Jewish practices, saw the emergence of Reform *mohelim* as an indication of the movement's desire for self-sufficiency. There were already about ten other Reform *mohelim* in Canada, most of them in Ontario.

Education

Canada responded to a finding by the UN Human Rights Commission that Ontario's refusal to fund non-Catholic religious schools was discriminatory (see AJYB 2000, pp. 280–81). In a February announcement, the government reaffirmed its position that education was purely a provincial responsibility and that the federal government had no power to do anything about it, despite Canada's avowed commitment to human rights exemplified by its signature on the 1976 International Covenant on Human and Political Rights. Keith Landy, Ontario Region chair of CJC, reflected the community's long-standing outrage with the situation, describing it as a "shameful and disappointing" stance. Attorney Anne Bayefsky, who handled the case, termed it "an embarrassment for Canada." In April the day schools in Ontario decided to form a united front to pursue government funding and began to search for new strategies.

Ontario education minister Janet Ecker, in a response in May to a question in the provincial legislature, restated her government's commitment to public education as superior to private schools in terms of standards, quality, and accountability. She said: "When we were challenged by the United Nations and by the federal Liberals to back off that commitment, we stood firm and said no." Landy was quick to respond by reminding the minister that Ontario was the only Canadian jurisdiction "to publicly fund the schools of one religious denomination and not those of other religious denominations" and that it was treating those who attended non-Catholic religious schools as "second-class citizens."

In July a representative of the UN Human Rights Commission met with Canadian officials at the country's UN mission in Geneva and informed them that Canada's arguments had been rejected. Christine Chanet of the commission said: "we have asked them to find a way to end this discrimination." The problem had arisen in the first place because Catholic education in Ontario was constitutionally guaranteed. The Ontario government, obligated to fund the Catholic schools, had for decades resolutely refused to consider funding any other religious schools.

An innovative program in Montreal involving the Torah and Vocational Institute (TAV), and the Université du Québec à Montréal (UQAM) came under fire in March. TAV was established to enable Hassidim to obtain marketable skills in a familiar religious environment. The agreement with the university was designed to lead to undergraduate degrees in computer science or business administration. However during its first year of operation the professors' union of the university filed grievances because most of the courses were taught in English rather than French, and the Hassidic students, about a quarter of the total, were offered classes segregated by sex. TAV's academic coordinator, Eli Meroz, lamented the action because "it took a tremendous effort to convince 150 Hassidim to go to university. We will lose these people if we cannot have separate classes, and that would be very unfortunate." Meroz felt that UQAM was missing an opportunity to help integrate a minority group into Quebec society.

Although administrative officials of UQAM had signed the agreement in 1999, the university's senate voted in April to cancel it. In May TAV went to court, asserting that UQAM had improperly terminated the agreement and that it did so "on the basis of pure discrimination and intolerance . . . . " In August a judge of Quebec Superior Court rejected TAV's request for a permanent injunction, essentially ending the attempt to find a legal remedy.

In order to meet the needs of Jewish communities in western Canada for teachers for Jewish schools, the Western Canadian Coalition for Jewish Education joined with York University in Toronto to train local people as Jewish-studies educators. The move was in response to a lack of willingness on the part of suitable teachers to relocate to the relatively small western communities. Funding for the program was provided by New York's Covenant Foundation and by four local federations—those in Winnipeg, Calgary, Edmonton, and Vancouver.

When the University of Toronto awarded honorary doctorates to Edward Said and Noam Chomsky in June there were protests from some sectors of the Jewish community because of the recipients' anti-Israel activities. For example, university benefactor Rose Wolfe, who had endowed a chair in Holocaust studies, complained that conferring the degrees "showed real insensitivity to the Jewish community." CJC Ontario chair Landy also criticized the action.

Community officials in Montreal were concerned about the decline in the number of students graduating from Jewish elementary schools who continued on in Jewish high schools. Many appeared to be choosing expensive private high schools instead. In order to address the question of whether the Jewish high schools could be made competitive with their private counterparts, a Forum on Jewish

High Schools was set up, but it had not reported before the end of the year. Meanwhile, in November, labor problems developed in the Montreal Jewish schools. The Quebec government had given the Association of Jewish Day Schools about $1 million to pay for a retroactive salary adjustment for the teachers of secular subjects. School administrators sought to divide the money among all the teachers, including those teaching religious studies, a move that would put the compensation of secular teachers below the public-sector wage scale. Their union complained, and negotiations were still going on at the end of the year.

Community and Intergroup Relations

The issue of prayer at official government events was a matter of continuing concern. In 1999, the Ontario Court of Appeal ruled that reciting the Lord's Prayer at town and city council meetings was unconstitutional (see AJYB 2000, p. 282). In February the question was raised in the small town of Carleton Place, Ontario. In response to a complaint by a Jew who lived nearby, the mayor declared that it was "extremely offensive" not to be able to recite the prayer. The question achieved a higher profile in March when the CJC asked the provincial government to abide by the court decision and notify municipalities about it. In a letter to the municipal minister and the legislative speaker, CJC Ontario region chair Landy also asked that the prayer no longer be recited in the provincial legislature. The response was that the legislature would continue to open with the Lord's Prayer because most members wished to continue the practice despite the court ruling about municipalities.

The Quebec Human Rights Commission ruled in January, on constitutional grounds, that the Montreal Urban Community (MUC), a regional government, and two towns within the region should no longer recite nondenominational prayers to open council meetings. However, the commission declined to order the removal of religious symbols such as crucifixes from council chambers, though it suggested that their presence "poses the fundamental question about relations between the state and citizens of diverse beliefs and traditions." Public prayer, in contrast, was held to be inherently more coercive, and thus should be banned. Decisions of the commission, however, were not binding, and the prayers continued. The six Jewish members on the MUC council were split on the issue of the nondenominational prayer recited there, three voting against it, two voting to retain it, and the sixth, absent from the vote, said he would also have voted for retention. Perhaps the most prominent Jewish member to vote in favor of retaining the prayer was Saulie Zajdel, a member of the Montreal executive committee and an adherent of Chabad-Lubavitch, who explained why he did not find it offensive: "There are no Christian overtones. I showed it to rabbis and they felt the same way." In Outremont, council member Sydney Pfeiffer, an Orthodox Jew, joined the majority in voting to retain the nondenominational prayer.

Controversial far-right Austrian politician Jörg Haider paid a short visit to

Canada in February, ostensibly to attend a wedding in the Tash Hassidic community near Montreal. At the last minute the invitation was withdrawn, but he did manage to arrange a meeting with several individual members of the Montreal Jewish community to discuss compensation for Holocaust victims. CJC president Moshe Ronen dismissed the meeting: "It's a stupid move in my view." Brahm Campbell, one of those who met with Haider, responded that he did it for the good of the community because it is "better to talk." Official Jewish bodies boycotted Haider, and his request to visit the Holocaust Memorial Center was rejected. Meanwhile, Toronto Jews picketed the Austrian consulate to protest the inclusion of Haider's Freedom Party in the government. Rabbi Gunther Plaut drew an analogy between the party and an infectious disease that requires isolation to prevent the "spread of its deadly poison."

In March, however, Rabbi Lionel Moses of the Shaare Zion congregation in Montreal dissented from the community's position and regretted, in an article published in the synagogue's bulletin, that Haider had not been given a tour of the Holocaust Center. The rabbi saw the decision as "a missed opportunity" and a "public relations fiasco." CJC Quebec Region chair Dorothy Zalcman Howard demurred, claiming that she had received considerable positive feedback from both Jews and non-Jews for CJC's stand. At a panel discussion in April, two of the people who had met with Haider defended their actions, claiming that the meeting was a necessity if Jews want to understand what is happening on the far right in Europe. Leaders of the CJC and BBC countered that Haider had cynically used the publicity generated by the meeting to enhance his credibility.

The city of Outremont and adjoining areas of Montreal, home to several Hassidic groups, continued to be the site of difficult relations between Jews and the general population. Celine Forget, a member of the city council, had been carrying on a running battle with a small Hassidic congregation over the location of its synagogue. The latest event was her lawsuit against the city to rescind the granting of a building permit to remodel an existing building into a house of worship. Jack Hartstein, a spokesman for Congregation Amour pour Israel, suggested that Forget had been trying to make life difficult for the Hassidim for years. In July, in a separate matter, Forget was charged with assaulting a teenage girl from the Hassidic community. Outremont decided in October that it would not allow the construction of an *eruv* (symbolic boundary to enable carrying on the Sabbath) using wiring attached to public property. Even though other municipalities in the Montreal area had gone along with similar requests, Mayor Jerome Unterberg contended that provincial law did not allow towns to authorize religious use of public space. The CJC and BBC backed the request.

Belz Hassidim encountered difficulty when they asked to convert a house into a synagogue in Montreal. Not only was this contrary to a city policy discouraging such conversions, but neighbors also objected to having the synagogue in a residential area. The Belzers claimed that they needed additional space to accommodate their growing community. Despite the opposition, the Montreal city council approved the expansion in December in exchange for written assurances from the Belzers that there would be no further requests for additional space on that block.

In Côte St. Luc, the predominantly Jewish suburb of Montreal, the saga of the search for a location for a Chabad center continued (see AJYB 2000, p. 283). The city council rejected a request for a building permit — for a fourth time — in July, because encroachment on a snow dump raised environmental concerns. However in January 2001 that site was finally approved.

Toronto police reported that hate-motivated crimes increased 28 percent in 1999. Of the 292 reported cases, charges were filed in just 49. Of the 32 hate crimes motivated by religious hatred, most were directed against Jews. The police also concluded that an August 1999 incident in which two Toronto men were attacked on their way to Friday evening services (see AJYB 2000, p. 272) was not a hate crime.

CJC in Montreal tried to prevent the appearance of David Icke, who had a long record of Holocaust denial and promoting negative stereotypes about Jews, at a local college. The event went forward nonetheless, in May, but Icke was very circumspect in his remarks.

Quebec's highly nationalistic St. Jean Baptiste Society made an effort to reach out to the Jewish community, hosting a kosher reception to mark the launch of three French-language books on Jewish themes. Dorothy Zalcman Howard, the regional CJC chair, did not rush to grasp the symbolically outstretched hand, noting that "our community still has many old wounds that heal slowly . . . . Where there is a true spirit of rapprochement it is important to address the past in a direct way in order to move forward." Robert Libman, B'nai Brith Canada's regional director, was more blunt, charging that the initiative was part of a public-relations strategy to improve the image of the separatist movement. In contrast, Thomas Hecht, CIC regional chair, welcomed the society's new openness.

Quebec's deputy premier, Bernard Landry, speaking to a Jewish business group in May, compared Quebec to Israel and urged the Jewish community to accept Quebec's nationhood. He contended that Quebec was not a province like the other nine but rather a nation in its own right. Landry added, "I hope that no one in this room equates Quebec nationalism in any way with anti-Semitism."

The question of whether a menorah was an exclusively Jewish symbol was raised in a case in Toronto Federal Court. The Chosen People Ministries, a messianic Jewish group, had succeeded in registering the menorah as an official "mark," or symbol, of the organization. The CJC went to court to try to prevent the group from using the menorah in its logo, arguing that allowing such use would confuse people and devalue the significance of this Jewish symbol. The director of Chosen People Ministries, however, argued that "the real issue here is whether a Jewish person can believe that Jesus is the messiah." Several hearings were held on the case during the year.

Rabbi Eli Gottesman of Montreal was sentenced in February to six months of home detention by a U.S. federal judge in Binghamton, New York, after pleading guilty to one count of conspiracy to defraud the federal government by smuggling drugs and other contraband into a prison where he served as chaplain. He was placed on probation for two years and required to perform 500 hours of community service.

A coroner's report in Montreal found that physicians at Jewish General Hospital did not have informed consent when they removed Ernest Krausz from a respirator in 1998. The patient, who suffered from an incurable lung disease, died four days later. The coroner accused the doctors involved of a breach of ethics, but hospital officials interpreted the report differently. In a written statement, the hospital said that the coroner had stated "that all decisions about Mr. Krausz's care should have been his own" and the coroner had been satisfied "that Mr. Krausz repeatedly indicated that he wanted his tubes removed and that these tubes would otherwise prolong his agony."

Radio personality Dr. Laura Schlessinger, a traditional Jew, ran into problems with Canadian authorities. Gay and lesbian groups contended that remarks made on her show, which was carried in Canada, might trigger violence against homosexuals. The Canadian Broadcast Standards Council censured her in May on the grounds that her critical characterizations of homosexual behavior violated the code of ethics of the broadcasting industry.

Culture

Donald Winkler made a documentary film about Solly Levy, which premiered at the Montreal Jewish Film Festival in May. *Un Voyage Sépharade: Solly Levy . . . du Maroc à Montréal* told the story of an immigrant from Tangier who came to Montreal after the Six-Day War, and subsequently had a varied career as cantor, public-school teacher, member of a Sephardi singing group, theater director, and one-man comedy show.

Batia Bettman produced *Let Memory Speak,* a documentary featuring 27 Holocaust survivors who relate how their lives were transformed by the experience, focusing on people who were children during the war, including Elie Wiesel and Aharon Appelfeld. Another Holocaust documentary was *Timepiece,* by Valerie Weiss, which was based on her mother's experiences. The Toronto International Film Festival in September saw the premiere of *Into the Arms of Strangers: Stories from the Kindertransports,* by Mark Jonathan Harris.

Among the films exhibited at the Montreal World Film Festival in August were Zuzana Justman's *A Trial in Prague,* an account of the Slansky show trial in 1952, and *Tzomet Vulcan* by Eran Riklas. The latter, which had its Canadian premiere at the festival, told the story of a rock band in Haifa at the time of the Yom Kippur War. Three Canadian short films with Jewish themes were shown at the Toronto International Film Festival in September: Aubrey Nealon's *Abe's Manhood,* Francine Zuckerman's *Passengers,* and Elida Schogt's *The Walnut Tree.*

The world premiere of *The New Klezmorim: Voices Inside the Revival of Jewish Music,* by David Kaufman, was a highlight of the Toronto Jewish Film Festival in May, along with a number of top recent Israeli films. Kaufman's film was shot at the KlezKanada festival in 1998. The Montreal Jewish Film Festival, also in May, included *Village of Idiots,* a short film by Eugene Fedorenko and Rose Newlove based on the Chelm stories, and *Zyklon Portrait,* Elida Schogt's tribute to her grandparents who died at Auschwitz.

Montreal's Yiddish Theatre featured a production of *The Great Houdini* by Mel Shavelson in April. The Yiddish musical exposed varied aspects of the great magician's family life as well as his public career.

Tamara Gentles and Dorothy Ross won the Spertus Judaica Prize competition for their original design for a Torah mantle.

The world premiere of *Resistance,* an original dance work by Allen Kaeja, was performed at Toronto's Harbourfront Centre in February. With original music by Egardo Moreno, the work was based on Kaeja's father's life in Poland before and during World War II. It included portrayals of uprisings against the Nazis.

Nuremberg, by Yves Simoneau, had a world premiere in Montreal in August and was then shown on the CTV network in September. The compelling film not only recounted the famous trial of Nazi war criminals but also delved into important ethical and philosophical issues.

Yolande Cohen and Joseph Levy produced a CD-ROM history of Moroccan Jews entitled "Les Juifs du Maroc à travers les ages. Traditions et modernité." It covered 2000 years of Moroccan Jewish history organized in several categories, including religious life, culture, personalities, creative arts, communal and social life, and history and context.

Conductor Pinchas Zukerman led the National Arts Centre Orchestra in two concerts in Tel Aviv in October, beginning a tour that also stopped in Jordan and several European countries. This was the first tour of the Middle East by a Canadian orchestra.

Publications

Rabbi Gunther Plaut wrote an extended reflection on the process and consequences of aging in *The Price and Privilege of Growing Old.* In addition to ruminating about day-to-day problems, he offered insight on the meaning of a religious life.

James Atlas's biography, *Bellow,* delved extensively into Saul Bellow's early years growing up in the Montreal suburb of Lachine, and Atlas ascribed considerable impact to those early years: "Bellow's being Canadian had a huge influence on his writing. The shtetl-like Jewish life in Montreal, the French and English atmosphere and the lost paradise of Lachine, although part myth, shaped him. If the family had gone straight from Russia to America, Bellow would not be the writer that he is."

The late Matt Cohen left a memoir, *Typing: A Life in 26 Keys,* telling of his struggle to make it in a discouraging literary environment. Also published posthumously was *Getting Lucky,* a book of Cohen's stories.

There were several books on aspects of the Canadian Jewish past. Rabbi Wilfred Shuchat's chronicle of the distinguished congregation that he led for so many years told the story of an unusual synagogue at its 150th anniversary. *The Gate of Heaven: The Story of Congregation Shaar Hashomayim of Montreal, 1846–1996* recounted just how the clergy and the members grappled with the dilemmas of reconciling tradition and modernity, as they were admonished to do by Solomon Schechter when he visited in 1908. Guy W. Richard traced the history of Quebec City's Jews by investigating the people buried in their cemetery. Appropriately, *Le cimetière juif du Quebec: Beth Israel Ohev Sholom* focused on the dead in a once thriving but small Jewish community now severely diminished in numbers. Bryan Demchinsky and Elaine Kalman Naves wrote *Storied Streets: Montreal in the Literary Imagination,* a collection of various accounts of the city by leading writers. Joe King's *From the Ghetto to the Main: The Story of the Jews of Montreal* contained a number of previously unpublished photographs. King's focus was on how the thousands of Jewish immigrants worked their way up in a society that was often inhospitable. Pierre Anctil translated a Yiddish memoir of the Montreal experiences of Hirsch Wolofsky, founder of the Yiddish newspaper *Kanader Adler,* into French in *Mayn Lebns Rayze: Un demi-siècle de vie Yiddish à Montréal.* Anctil joined Ira Robinson and Gerard Bouchard in editing *Juifs et Canadiens Français dans la Société Québecoise.*

In *Long Shadows: Truth, Lies and History* Erna Paris tackled the problem of the historical memory of Nazism in countries such as France and Germany. Janine Stingel examined the efforts to contain a dangerous movement in *Social Discredit: Anti-Semitism, Social Credit and the Jewish Response.* Morris Biderman's account of *A Life on the Jewish Left: An Immigrant's Experience* focused on Canadian Jews who enlisted under the banner of Communism between the wars. Benjamin Freedman's posthumous *Duty and Healing: Foundations of a Jewish Bioethic* dealt with a number of perplexing issues at the intersection of Judaism and modern medicine and attempted to synthesize values derived from both perspectives. Rabbi Elyse Goldstein edited *The Women's Torah Commentary: New Insights from Women Rabbis on the 54 Weekly Torah Portions. Motion Sickness* by David Layton gave a son's view of growing up with a famous father, the noted writer Irving Layton. Other nonfiction books in 2000 included *The Nature of Economies* by Jane Jacobs; *Bloody Words: Hate and Free Speech* by David Matas; *The Perfect System* by Syd Kessler; and *La Mémoire Vivante,* edited by Sarah Arditi Ascher.

There were several books on Holocaust themes, including *Odyssey of a Survivor* by George Barta; *Dangerous Luck: A Hunted Life* by David Makow; *The Cantor's Voice* by Solomon Gisser; *Unauthorized Entry, The Truth About Nazi War Criminals in Canada, 1946–1956* by Howard Margolian; and *Delayed Impact: The Holocaust and the Canadian Jewish Community* by Frank Bialystock.

Works of fiction included Allan Levine's *Sins of the Suffragette; Rebecca* by Carol Matas; *By a Frozen River: The Short Stories of Norman Levine; L'anniversaire* by Naim Kattan; and Victor Teboul's *Que Dieu vous garde de l'homme silencieux quand il se met soudain à parler* (God Protect You from a Silent Man When He Suddenly Begins to Speak).

Georges Amsellem published a book of poetry, *Le Coeur en voyage.*

Winners of the Jewish Book Awards, presented in Toronto in June, included Nancy Huston for *The Mark of the Angel;* Arthur Schaller for *100 Cigarettes and a Bottle of Vodka;* Naomi Kramer and Ronald Headland for *The Fallacy of Race and the Shoah;* Simcha Simchovitch for *The Remnant;* Kathy Kacer for *Gabi's Dresser;* Sara Silberstein Swartz and Margie Wolfe for *From Memory to Transformation: Jewish Women's Voices;* Bruce Muirhead for *Against the Odds: The Public Life and Times of Louis Rasminsky;* Adele Reinhartz for *Why Ask My Name? Anonymity and Identity in Biblical Narrative;* Rabbi Shlomo Zalman Elazer Grafstein for *Judaism's Bible: A New and Expanded Translation;* Malca Janice Litovitz for *To Light, To Water;* and Seymour Mayne and B. Glen Rotchin for *A Rich Garland.* The J. I. Segal Awards, announced in November, went to Avner Mandelman, Benjamin Freedman, Marc-Alain Wolf, and Tzvi Eisenman.

Personalia

A number of Jews were appointed to the Order of Canada. Companions: Rabbi Gunther Plaut, Victor Goldbloom, and Raymond Klibansky. Officers: Ruth Goldbloom, Edward Bronfman, David Goltzman. Members: Irving Gerstein, Jack Hirsh, Charles Pachter, Seymour Schulich, Benjamin Shapiro, Shirley Sharzer, Morley Cohen, Sheila Leah Fischman, Jack Rabinovitch, and Jack Yazer.

Myra Freeman was named lieutenant governor of Nova Scotia. Governor General's Awards for literature went to Robert Majzels and Ghitta Caiserman-Roth. Heidi Levenson Polowin was appointed to the Superior Court of Justice of Ontario and Suzanne Handman to the Quebec Labour Court. Morris Zbar became deputy minister of correctional services in Ontario. Ben Weider was named a chevalier of the Legion of Honor by the French government. Paul Brumer won Canada's highest scientific award, the Killam Prize, while Jack Diamond won the gold medal of the Royal Architectural Institute of Canada.

Haim Divon was named Israel's ambassador to Canada while Meir Romem and Shlomo Avital became consuls general in Toronto and Montreal respectively.

The C.D. Howe Institute named Jack Mintz president, while Victor Rabinovitch was appointed president of the Canadian Museum of Civilization Corporation. Bernard Langer was elected president of the Royal College of Physicians and Surgeons of Canada. Alliance Québec elected Anthony Housefather president.

Marion Mayman was elected president of Hadassah-WIZO and Erez Anzel as copresident of Canadian Friends of Peace Now. Sheva Medjuck became the president of the Atlantic Jewish Council and Leo Adler the Canadian representative of the Simon Wiesenthal Center. Montreal's Jewish Public Library named Eva Raby executive director. Sheila Kussner was awarded the Samuel Bronfman Medal.

Members of the community who died this year included controversial rabbi and journalist Reuben Slonim, in January, aged 85; real-estate mogul Jacob Ghermezian, in January, aged 97; former judge and community leader Mayer Lerner, in January, aged 93; seniors advocate David Reinhart, in February, aged 65; Monica Bergman, founder of Montreal's Gilda's Club for cancer patients, in March, aged 52; former Canadian chess champion Abe Yanofsky, in March, aged 74; Julius Hayman, publisher and editor of the *Jewish Standard* for 63 years, in March, aged 92; social-work professor Karol Steinhouse, in March, aged 47; community leader Ralph Snow, in March, aged 78; neurobiologist Chaim Niznik, in March, aged 43; Louis Applebaum, a composer for television, films, and ballet and a leader in the arts community, in April, aged 82; real-estate executive and philanthropist Irving Zunenshine, in May, aged 73; builder Teddy Libfeld, in June, aged 72; Ben Katz, a philanthropist for the elderly, in June, aged 92; community activist Marion Vickar, in June, aged 85; author, singer and Yiddish folklorist Ruth Rubin, in June, aged 93; former Canadian welterweight champion boxer Maxie Berger, in August, aged 83; funeral director and businessman Max Paperman, in August, aged 93; advocate for women's and workers' rights Lea Roback, in August, aged 96; doctor, coroner, politician, and investment writer Morton Shulman, in August, aged 73; retailer and author Henry Henig, in September, aged 91; Yiddish journalist Sam Lipshitz, in September, aged 90; community leader Dena Wosk, in September, aged 84; champion boxer and referee Sammy Luftspring, in September, aged 84; Labor Zionist leader Josef Krystal, in October, aged 74; Yiddishist, poet, and educator Israel Hirsh Shtern, in October, aged 87; businessman and community leader Larry Rollingher, in December, aged 69; and Yiddish journalist Noach Witman, in December, aged 96.

HAROLD M. WALLER

Western Europe

Great Britain

National Affairs

T HE YEAR BEGAN BADLY FOR THE Labor government when Prime Minister Tony Blair's personal poll rating briefly fell from 62 to 49 percent, largely due to popular dissatisfaction with problems in the National Health Service, intensified by a flu epidemic. Labor's image deteriorated further when the party was unable to prevent the election of Ken Livingstone, a maverick independent left-wing MP, as the first directly elected mayor of London. Blair's warning that Livingstone's election would be "ruinous" for London did not prevent the decisive defeat of Labor's official candidate for the mayoralty. This was followed by Labor defeats in the local council elections, and in June a keynote speech by Premier Blair at a conference of the Women's Institute movement was met by a "slow handclapping." The government recovered some of its poise in July when it announced a program of public investment in transport, education, and the health service. This expenditure, it was proclaimed, was made possible by the government's prudent handling of the economy. In this way the government sought to make good what many critics considered to be its initial mistake in retaining the spending targets of the last Conservative government.

In the meantime, the Conservative opposition, led by William Hague, turned to the right, campaigning against "bogus asylum seekers," taking a hardline policy in Europe, and opposing the single EU currency. The Tories received a real boost in September when farmers and haulers blockaded a number of oil refineries in a peaceful protest of the high price of gasoline. This rapidly escalated into a nationwide protest. Panic buying by the public ensued, and 90 percent of gas stations ran out of fuel within a few days. Hospitals and emergency services were endangered before the government intervened. Public dissatisfaction with Labor's tardy response was demonstrated in a poll that, for the first time since 1992, showed the Conservatives ahead of Labor by 38 percent to 36.

This trend, however, did not last long. In November the government won three by-elections (although on a low turnout), and maintained its record—unlike any other government in the last 40 years—of not losing a single by-election. Chancellor Gordon Brown reinforced Labor's position by promising a reduction in the fuel tax, and by the end of the year Labor was again about ten points ahead in the polls. Opposition leader William Hague, however, had tasted blood, and continued to hammer away at the government's record on crime, deficiencies in the National Health Service, and education. Likewise, his skeptical line on Europe seemed to resonate with the public; a poll carried out for the European Commission in April showed that of all member countries, Britain was least supportive of the European Union, its policies, and its institutions.

Israel and the Middle East

With its historic links to the Middle East and its close relationship to all parties in the peace process, Britain could play a crucial role in ensuring the success of the negotiations, said Foreign Office minister Peter Hain in April. Lord Levy of Mill Hill, the government's special envoy, pursued this role unremittingly throughout the year. In January, Foreign Minister Robin Cook, in Amman and Cairo to discuss the peace process and bilateral ties with King Abdullah of Jordan and Egyptian president Hosni Mubarak, called on moderate Arab countries to back Palestinian leader Yasir Arafat in any far-reaching concessions he might make to clinch a final peace agreement with Israel. The same month, Levy, at the center of British efforts to revive the stalled talks between Israel and Syria, visited Damascus and Beirut. In April, Hain went on his first official visit to Israel, Jordan, and the Palestinian Authority, where he spoke with Arafat, stressing Britain's readiness to back an independent Palestinian state provided it was committed to democracy and recognized Israel's security concerns. Hain said that Britain was prepared to work with Palestinian leaders to create a national constitution that "entrenched" democratic values and "solid institutions to guarantee the rule of law, transparency and accountability." London, he said on his return, was "working with feverish energy" on both the Syrian and Palestinian fronts to assist any agreement.

Levy was back in the area in August, charged, according to Foreign Office sources, with encouraging both sides to "pursue their negotiations and redouble their efforts to reach agreement" after the failure of Camp David. Blair, in September, told a conference in Brighton, Sussex, sponsored by Labor Friends of Israel, that Arafat had to match Israeli premier Ehud Barak's risk-taking for peace. Blair held talks with both men at the United Nations millennium summit. The talks, said Hain, back in London after similar meetings in the Middle East, were part of Britain's efforts to encourage the two sides to grapple with the issue of the future of Jerusalem's holy sites. In October, Cook and Levy sought an end to violence through talks with Arafat in Gaza and Barak in Jerusalem. Britain, said Cook, was determined to persuade the leaders to "get back to the negotiating table and not let the peace process die."

Not all these efforts met with universal approval. Hain aroused protests from British Jewish organizations in September when he expressed support for Palestinian refugees' right of return to Israel. Hain explained that, in his view, a just solution to the plight of these refugees was at the heart of the search for peace. There was also an ongoing campaign to undermine the position of Lord Levy. Criticism surfaced in the House of Commons in February, when it was recalled that he had been the Labor Party's main fund-raiser in the 1997 general election. In April, Shadow Foreign Secretary Francis Maude expressed the main Tory concern that Levy was not accountable to Parliament. In June, the press carried a leaked report that millionaire Levy paid only £5,000 of income tax in 1999; in July it was reported that the Inland Revenue, the tax authority, had handed the results of investigations into the "dirty tricks" campaign against Levy to the director of public prosecutions. In December, the Islamic Human Rights Commission was purportedly behind a letter campaign targeted at Foreign Secretary Cook demanding Levy's removal from his post. He was, said the commission, an unashamed Zionist, and, accordingly, a staunch supporter of Israel.

A hiccup in Britain's generally good relationship with Israel came in May when Israeli tank fire killed BBC driver Abed Takoush on the eve of Israel's troop withdrawal from southern Lebanon, and in August the BBC presented Israel's Defense Ministry with a claim for compensation. In December Britain demanded an explanation from Israel for an attack by Jewish settlers brandishing weapons on the British consul's official car, which had been carrying official license plates and flying the Union Jack. Troops stationed nearby did not intervene, claimed an embassy official.

Solidarity missions from various sectors of the Anglo-Jewish community visited Israel in the last quarter of 2000 in response to the upsurge of violence. The United Jewish Israel Appeal (UJIA) came in November, and the Maccabi Union of Great Britain in December. In December too, Chief Rabbi Jonathan Sacks led a press mission to Israel in an attempt to rectify unsympathetic media coverage, and he also organized a three-day tour for some 50 Orthodox rabbis.

Great Britain's policy toward Iran had to take account of its arrest and trial of 13 Jews accused of espionage. In January MPs and Jewish communal leaders demonstrated outside Downing Street, where Prime Minister Blair talked with Foreign Minister Dr. Kamal Kharrazi of Iran, on behalf of the jailed Iranian Jews. MP Gillian Shepherd, chairman of Conservative Friends of Israel, castigated the government for upgrading ties with an Iranian regime that supported terrorism and violated human rights. In April a Foreign Office spokesman said that the government was maintaining pressure on the Iranian authorities to fulfill their undertaking that the trial of the 13 would be open and transparent. In May Israel's ambassador in London, Dror Zeigerman, met Foreign Office minister Hain to voice Israel's concern about Britain's expansion of trade and diplomatic ties with Iran, and Jewish leaders appealed to the government to freeze contacts with Iran until the 13 were freed. Foreign Secretary Cook's pledge to raise their plight when he visited Iran in July came to naught when his visit was first postponed and then canceled.

After ten of the Iranian Jews were found guilty, a British government statement expressed "deep concern" at the closed-door trial and the sentences, and Hain told Iran's London ambassador that he expected the appeals process against the convictions and the sentences "to be given due weight." He said, nevertheless, that isolating Iran was not the right policy. In September, when an Iranian appeals court reduced the prison sentences of the ten convicted Jews, a top-level conference was held in London aimed at boosting Britain's trade links with Iran. "I firmly believe that potentially Iran can be a major business partner for Britain," said Department of Trade and Industry minister Richard Caborn, announcing plans to visit Iran in October. In September, when a House of Commons foreign affairs select committee launched an inquiry into Britain's relations with Iran, a spokesman for the Board of Deputies of British Jews said that British Jewry found it "abhorrent" that the country was striving to boost trade when Tehran's human-rights record was under scrutiny

Anti-Semitism and Racism

Some 270 acts of anti-Semitism were reported in 1999, a rise of 16 percent over the previous year, according to Community Security Trust (CST) statistics issued in March. The 1999 total included 33 physical assaults (up 50 percent over 1998), two of them on rabbis; 31 cases of threats on community members; 8 hoax bomb threats, 5 of them against Jewish schools; and 25 incidents involving desecration of property, almost one-third of them in Manchester. The CST was particularly concerned that a number of Jewish institutions were coming under surveillance by people using cameras and videos. "There is no doubt that people are trying to collect information on the community," a CST spokesman told the *Jewish Chronicle.*

In April the Black-Jewish Forum criticized the Board of Deputies of British Jews and the Three Faith Forum for awarding its Responsible Society Award to Home Secretary Jack Straw, at a time when new regulations were making conditions more difficult for asylum-seekers. Board director-general Neville Nagler explained that Straw had done much to promote racial and religious tolerance, including introducing Holocaust Day and strengthening race-relation laws. Nevertheless, Board of Deputies president Eldred Tabachnik led an interfaith delegation to meet with Straw and voice concern at the new regulations, and also at inflammatory language being heard in the media and in Parliament regarding asylum-seekers, which, it was feared, would fuel the campaign of the extreme right-wing British National Party (BNP). A CST spokesman, in fact, pointed to a far-right demonstration in Margate, Kent, where hundreds cheered as members of the right-wing National Front chanted anti-refugee slogans. In the London mayoral elections in May, BNP treasurer and spokesman Michael Newland played openly on fears surrounding immigration and bogus asylum-seekers to take enough votes to save his deposit. In local council elections, far-right candidates won an average of 10 percent of the vote in the few seats they contested. Concern about a far-right resurgence mounted when the BNP won 26 percent of the vote in a council by-election in May in Bexley, South London, thereby pushing the Tories into third place.

Scotland Yard's intelligence activities against the far right could not be restricted to London, said Assistant Commissioner David Veness in July; cooperation was necessary with other British, European, and American law-enforcement agencies. Warning of the threat of future attacks on minority communities following the trial of former BNP member David Copeland, sentenced to life for nail-bomb attacks in London in 1999, Veness said that the police had beefed up its racial-and-violent-crime task force. It was also establishing community safety patrols as well as working with a range of voluntary agencies, such as the CST. By November fears of a far-right revival faded when its candidates attracted little support in two parliamentary by-elections: BNP chairman Nick Griffin received only 794 votes, 4 percent of the total, at West Bromwich; and BNP got 229 votes, 1 percent, at Preston.

With the outbreak of new violence in Israel at the end of September, the focus and intensity of racist outbreaks shifted sharply. Jewish institutions were placed on high alert as London-based radical Muslim groups, such as the extremist Islamist organization Al-Muhajiroun, issued fiery statements warning British Jews that backing Israel could make them "targets" for Muslims. Under the banner of the Kalifah Association, Al-Muhajiroun was also active at meetings on university campuses in London, Manchester, and Birmingham as the academic year began. During the High Holy Days, the CST's Mike Whine reported anti-Semitic incidents at some 50 synagogues, with protesters in London, Manchester, and Birmingham burning Israeli flags. In Stamford Hill, North London, a 20-year-old yeshivah student was stabbed, and fireworks were thrown at a Jewish-owned business in Stanmore, Middlesex. The Israeli government's tourist office in London protested against the Foreign Office's warning against vacation or other nonessential travel to Jerusalem. Officials of Britain's main Jewish organizations formed an emergency coordinating group, chaired by UJIA president Brian Kerner, to plan solidarity missions to Israel, to prepare briefings for the community and its institutions, and to counter slanted media coverage. Police surveillance units stepped up patrols in predominantly Jewish areas, and Home Secretary Straw assured a Jewish delegation that "the law would be vigorously enforced" to prevent violence and the dissemination of racist propaganda. "We do not want community relations poisoned by the spreading here of this conflict," Foreign Office minister Hain added.

Between October and December the number of anti-Semitic attacks, including physical assault, rose some 400–500 percent as compared to the same period in 1999, the CST reported in December. More than 100 incidents were recorded in October and November, including attacks leaving victims requiring hospitalization. Synagogues and other Jewish institutions were defaced with graffiti, Jews were subjected to verbal abuse, and anti-Jewish posters and leaflets were distributed. "We have real and valid concern that attempts are being made to transform the conflict in the Middle East into a religious war against the Jews," said a CST spokesman, but, he added, the situation in Britain was incomparably better than in some other countries, partly due to the police's efforts at protecting Jews.

In December, Home Office minister Lord Bassam told the House of Lords that the government would allocate £25m to the police over the next three years to counter the use of the Internet for racist or anti-Semitic propaganda; the money would be used to formulate a national high-tech strategy to track down and prosecute those behind the more-than 2,000 racist Web sites.

Holocaust-Related Matters

At the beginning of the year, Prime Minister Blair told the House of Commons that Britain's first Holocaust Day would be on January 27, 2001, the anniversary of the liberation of Auschwitz. This, he said, reflected Britain's continuing commitment to opposing racism, anti-Semitism, and genocide. In June it was reported that the Holocaust Education Trust would honor two people, Home Secretary Jack Straw for his leading role in instituting Holocaust Day, and American academic Deborah Lipstadt for her successful legal battle against Holocaust revisionist David Irving. Irving's libel action against Lipstadt, professor of modern Jewish and Holocaust studies at Emory University, Atlanta, and her publisher, Penguin Books, claimed that her book, *Denying the Holocaust,* falsely alleged that he deliberately distorted history. At the end of a three-month, highly publicized trial before the High Court, which heard evidence from leading historians, Mr. Justice Charles Gray found against Irving. He was, the judge concluded, an anti-Semite and Holocaust denier, who had "persistently and deliberately manipulated historical evidence," portraying Hitler favorably for ideological reasons.

In June a permanent Holocaust exhibition was officially opened at London's Imperial War Museum. Then, in July, the largest ever "Remembering for the Future" Holocaust conference was held in London and Oxford.

More than 350 works of art looted by the Nazis could be in British national collections, according to a 200-page report, "Spoilation of Works of Art during the Holocaust and World War II Period," published in February following a year-long investigation by the National Museum Directors' Conference, headed by Tate Gallery director Sir Nicholas Serota. The same month retired lord justice of appeal Sir David Hirst was named to lead an 11-person government panel to help resolve Holocaust survivors' claims to such works. Pressure by the Board of Deputies of British Jews and leading art experts for a government commitment to return the actual artworks and not just to offer financial compensation, was partially satisfied in October when a government committee on the return of illicitly traded cultural property recommended new legislation to make this possible in certain narrowly defined circumstances.

In February the government announced that more than £1.5m had been paid out to victims of Nazi persecution whose property in the United Kingdom had been confiscated during the war. The payments were instituted under a Department of Trade and Industry decision to settle outstanding claims from those whose assets were seized under legislation against trading with the enemy that came into force in 1939. Lord Archer of Sandwell had chaired a panel that assessed 948 claims from victims or their relatives.

By June "Restore UK," launched in May by the British Bankers' Association in a collaborative effort to help Holocaust victims' families reclaim assets deposited in Britain before World War II, was considering 60 claims. These had been submitted after the publication of lists of some 13,000 account-holders.

Nazi War Criminals

In January it appeared that Britain was slowing down its drive to prosecute suspected Nazi war criminals living in the country. A statement by a Crown Prosecution Service spokesman that "after careful and thorough consideration" the service believed that there was "insufficient evidence" to prosecute any of the remaining subjects in connection with murders in Nazi-occupied Europe, signaled that the investigation into some 380 people was being wound up. The operation, which had cost some £12m, was conducted by Scotland Yard's war-crimes unit, established to implement the 1991 War Crimes Act under which suspected Nazi war criminals could be tried in British courts for offences committed abroad. Some suspects had died, while the passage of time made the investigations complex, the statement explained. It was stressed, however, that if any new cases came to light they would be fully investigated.

In February, Anthony Sawoniuk, Britain's only convicted war criminal, lost his appeal against the double life sentence imposed at his Old Bailey trial in 1999 for the murder of Jews in Belarus. In June he was refused leave to appeal against the February decision. Also in February, the head of Scotland Yard's war-crimes unit attended a two-day conference in Riga, organized by the Latvian government, to discuss action against alleged war criminal Konrad Kalejs. Suspected of involvement in a Nazi death squad that killed some 30,000 Latvian Jews, Kalejs was discovered living in Britain in 1999, but allowed to leave the country in the absence of sufficient evidence to prosecute. In December Kalejs, who had become an Australian citizen, was arrested in Melbourne, the Latvian government having requested his extradition through its Australian embassy.

JEWISH COMMUNITY

Demography

The number of marriages performed under Jewish religious auspices rose from 921 in 1998 to 1,017 in 1999, for an annual average of 927 over the 1994–99 period, with all synagogue groupings showing increases, according to statistics published by the community research unit of the Board of Deputies of British Jews. Numbers of gittin (religious divorces) completed also rose, from 233 in 1998 to 259 in 1999. On the other hand, burials and cremations under Jewish religious auspices fell to 3,772 in 1999 from a revised figure of 3,938 in 1998, while birth statistics, based on figures for circumcision, showed only a small rise in 1998 to 2,673, from 2,663 in 1997. In November the Initiation Society, an organization of Orthodox *mohelim* (ritual circumcisers), launched an "audit" of religious circumcision to create a database of 1,500 cases and find out, among other things, parents' reactions to the *mohel* they engaged and the quality of his aftercare. Arguments against circumcision had appeared in the *British Medical Journal,* and the *Jewish Chronicle* had carried correspondence on the subject for seven weeks. Dr. Morris Sifman, the society's medical director, said: "We need information to defend Brit Milah [ritual circumcision] against the vehement opposition we have been experiencing." Advertisements for "medical" and "painless" circumcision not performed under Orthodox auspices had to be taken seriously, he added.

A report issued by the Reform Synagogues of Great Britain (RSGB), published in February, showed that 112 applications for conversion to Judaism were received in 1999, nearly double the 1998 figure of 67. "We are continuing our policy of welcoming genuine converts and doing all we can to facilitate their entry into our faith," said Rabbi Rodney Mariner, convenor of the RSGB Bet Din (religious court). RSGB received 208 requests for circumcision in 1999, compared with 149 in 1998.

Communal Affairs

British Jewry is too diverse for one organization or leader to speak for it, declared the report of the Commission on the Representation of the Interests of the British Jewish Community, launched by the Institute for Jewish Policy Research (JPR) in 1998. Entitled *A Community of Communities* and published in March 2000, the report found that over 100 organizations were representing British Jews in various capacities. It recommended that British Jewry regard itself as an "ethnic group" for purposes of representation to non-Jewish bodies, such as national and local government agencies, other religious faiths, and the media, and should establish "an independent, cross-communal coordinating structure" to discuss collective responses when required. Commission chairman Michael Webber, who succeeded the original chairman Clinton Silver in 1999, resigned on the eve of the report's publication. Webber made no public comment explaining his resignation, but told JPR director Barry Kosmin of his dissatisfaction with the report.

In July Jo Wagerman was elected president of the Board of Deputies of British Jews. Formerly the headmistress of London's Jewish Free School, Wagerman became the first female president in the board's 240-year history.

In February Jewish Care, Britain's largest charitable organization, announced the closure of Sarah Tunkel House, its 60-bed residential home in Highbury, North London. Occupancy had dropped below 75 percent for the previous two years and was continuing to fall. In June the Otto Schiff Housing Association (OSHA), part of the Association of Jewish Refugees (AJR), announced a merger with Jewish Care. AJR already had financial problems, said OSHA chairman Ashley Mitchell, and it would have to go out of business if it did not sell its Heinrich Stahl House. As the year ended, it remained unsold.

Religion

The plight of the *agunah*, the "chained" wife refused a religious divorce (get) by her ex-husband, continued to be an important issue. Several organizations worked on her behalf, including Chief Rabbi Jonathan Sacks's long-promised Agunah/Get Task Force, unveiled in June. Judy Nagler, wife of Board of Deputies director-general Neville Nagler, was appointed to coordinate a team of rabbis, *dayanim* (judges of Jewish religious courts), lay leaders, mediators, and legal experts, under the aegis of the Chief Rabbi's Office. But supporters of the Agunah Campaign, an already functioning group with the same aim, were disappointed when Sacks neither attended nor sent a rabbinical representative to its November forum at University College, London.

Attempts to solve the problem through legislation failed when the Divorce (Religious Marriages) Bill — inspired by yet another body, the Board of Deputies cross-communal working group — ran out of time in the House of Commons in July, despite receiving all-party support and government approval. The bill had been introduced by Jewish Liberal Democrat MP Lord Lester of Herne Hill, and received its first reading in the House of Lords in May. If passed it would have given judges the option to require that a marriage be dissolved according to Jewish law before granting a civil divorce. In December Rabbi Pini Dunner of the independent Saatchi Synagogue was naming and shaming husbands who refused their wives a get, in large advertisements in London's *Jewish Chronicle,* the main organ of British Jewry.

The United Synagogue (US), Britain's largest synagogue grouping, was in its best financial state in many years, according to president Peter Sheldon. Its projected end-of-year surplus of £87,000 partly came from the £750,000 raised by the auction, held in November in New York, of recovered books and manuscripts stolen from the London Bet Din by former *dayan* Rabbi Casriel Kaplin.

Leo Baeck College, the Progressive rabbinical training institution, purchased 45 of the 150 items offered. On the other hand, the US lost money on the first two issues of its new magazine, *People Like US,* launched in April.

In June a meeting organized by the US's community development department formed the Hertfordshire Forum for ministers and leaders of the US's five Hertfordshire synagogues to meet regularly and share ideas and information. "The forum is an opportunity for all the major synagogues to help the smaller communities in Hertfordshire to thrive and survive," said Borehamwood's rabbi, Alan Plancey. This meeting was one of a series enabling the chief rabbi to meet leaders of US congregations. In June, too, the US announced that women might hold positions as honorary officers in US constituent synagogues, though not to serve as synagogue chairmen.

In other communal news, it was reported in February that technical difficulties were delaying the North-West London *eruv* (symbolic boundary enabling carrying on the Sabbath) that was to have been operating by the end of 1999. In April the Charity Commissioners' investigation into the affairs of the L'Chaim Society revealed that its trustees failed to "exercise proper control" and that "excessive payments" had been made to its founder, Rabbi Shmuel Boteach, and his wife. In November, committal proceedings for the six men and six women charged with conspiracy to defraud in connection with irregularities at US's Waltham Abbey (Essex) cemetery in 1998, were set for late January 2001. The US allegedly lost £1.5m through their activities.

There were a number of developments in the area of kashrut. In April, after more than nine years of negotiation, the London Board for Shechita (LBS) and the Manchester Kashrut Authority signed an accord on the "mutual" certification of meat. "Fifty percent of the London Board's requirements come from the Manchester abattoir," said LBS administrator Michael Kester. "It makes sense to rationalize and streamline our overheads." In December the two groups took over Liffey Meats' idle plant in Ballyjamesduff, outside Dublin. Liffey had exported kosher meat to Israel for 15 years, till the importer switched to South American meat in 1999, leaving the plant underused. Reports that the Israeli restaurant chain El Gaucho planned to open a branch in Golders Green (North-West London) that would serve imported hindquarter meat aroused controversy. In June LBS ruled against the sale of hindquarter meat, but its vice president, Alan Kennard, said that talks would continue to investigate the possibility of introducing a centralized and uniform procedure for porging (removing the prohibited sciatic nerve) acceptable to the *dayanim.* The new restaurant opened in May, serving imported forequarter meat only, under Sephardi supervision. But in September the board of elders of the Spanish and Portuguese Congregation supported Dayan Toledano's efforts to reintroduce hindquarter meat to Britain's kosher market.

The Assembly of Masorti Synagogues (roughly equivalent to the American Conservative movement) expanded its youth involvement in October by appointing two full-time student fieldworkers and creating a department to coordinate its youth initiatives. Rabbi Louis Jacobs, whose break with the religious establishment in 1962 eventually led to the birth of the British Masorti movement, retired in July from the New London Synagogue, St. John's Wood, North-West London, that had been founded at that time. Jacobs—an eminent scholar, theologian, and author—was succeeded by Chaim Weiner, an American rabbi, who had served the Masorti synagogue in Edgware, Middlesex, from 1991 to 1998. Edgware's continuing dispute over women's role in religious services led to the formation of a breakaway egalitarian congregation. In December Dr. Harry Freedman, about to resign as director of the Assembly of Masorti Synagogues, announced that the 11 synagogues making up the organization had a total membership of 4,000.

A number of rabbis took new positions during the year: Reform rabbi Jeremy Collick was appointed to the original Edgware Masorti congregation; Rabbi Paul Glantz of Brighton and Hove Progressive Synagogue went to St. Albans Masorti; and the American-born Rabbi Neil Kraft of South London Liberal Synagogue was named director of education at Reform's West London Synagogue. The Reform movement, which, in May, launched its five-year, £4m "Living Judaism" program—a vigorous campaign to involve new members in synagogue life—ended the year with a financial deficit. Fund-raising for the "exciting projects" involved was taking "longer than expected," said Michael Frankl, deputy chief of the Reform Synagogues of Great Britain. A report issued in July by Leo Baeck College on the Reform and Liberal rabbinate found that women rabbis continued to suffer discrimination, none holding senior positions in major congregations. Also in July, Finchley Reform Synagogue (North London) restarted a selection procedure for a new minister after rejecting, amid considerable controversy, the appointment of Rabbi Melinda Carr, a lesbian, in May.

Education

The number of Jewish day schools in Britain stood at 134 in 1999–2000, up from 116 in 1998–99 and 96 in 1992–93, according to figures released by the community research unit. The number of students were 22,620 in 1999–2000, 20,580 the previous year, and 14,650 in 1992–93, with 72 percent of all current pupils going to school in Greater London. The figures included nurseries as well as primary and secondary schools, and institutions for children with special needs. The report pointed out, however, that only Greater London, Manchester, Liverpool, and Gateshead offered the full range of Jewish day-school opportunities for all ages. Illustrating the upward trend was the official opening, in June, of the £4.5m Clore Tikva primary school in Barkingside (Essex), the second school—with the Clore Shalom in Shenley (Herts)—under the pluralist umbrella of the Jewish Community Day School Advisory Board. In July the £3m state-aided Hertsmere Jewish primary school was officially opened.

In February, as part of its strategy "to develop a new educational policy," the United Jewish Israel Appeal appointed a team to work with Jewish students, mainly to ensure implementation of the recommendations of "Every Student Matters," a review commissioned in 1998. It was reported in March that the UJIA planned to spend an extra 9 percent of its 1999 budget on youth and education programs, and in June UJIA launched a five-year, £500,000 scholarship program, funded by philanthropist Stanley Cohen, to train 100 new Jewish educators.

In April the London School of Jewish Studies (LSJS, the former Jews' College) appointed Rabbi Dr. Abner Weiss as principal. Born in South Africa and based, before moving to London, in Los Angeles, Weiss would serve concurrently as minister at the Western Marble Arch Synagogue, Central London. In July Weiss introduced a new plan to train LSJS students for the Orthodox rabbinate, awarding the same rabbinic ordination as that granted by Israel's chief rabbis. "We are going to produce modern Orthodox rabbis," said Weiss, "with internationally respected qualifications."

In November the Oxford Centre for Hebrew and Jewish Studies opened a £750,000 teaching and research unit, representing, according to Peter Oppenheimer, its president, "a big step toward full membership of Oxford University." In February Leeds University's Center for Jewish Studies launched its first full-time degree course, entitled "Jewish Civilization." Also in February a Jewish music institute was established in conjunction with London University's School of Oriental and African Studies. In June it was announced that Britain's first specialist master's degree in Israeli studies would be launched at University College, London, in September. In July the Arts and Humanities Research Board announced a grant to Southampton University's Parkes Center to undertake five new research projects, mainly with Jewish themes.

Overseas Aid

In February the Jewish Emergency Aid Coalition (JEAC) launched an appeal on behalf of the victims of flood-ravaged Mozambique. Its fund-raising campaign was spearheaded by the United Kingdom Jewish Aid and International Development (UKJaid), which in 1999 raised £250,000 on the coalition's behalf. Some of the money went to the Albanian Education Development Project to help fund the first school for Kosovo refugees and local children in Albania after the crisis there. UKJaid also opened, on its own, another rebuilt school in Kosovo.

Jewish organizations continued to help communities in the former Soviet Union. In August the North-Western Reform Synagogue in London's Golders Green presented a Torah scroll to its twin congregation in Kerch, Ukraine; in September a new technology center in Dniepropetrovsk, created through a partnership between London's Lubavitch community and World ORT, was one of five Ukrainian centers opened during a six-day ORT mission; and World Jewish Relief (WJR) opened the Sunflower Center at Kiev's Solomon Jewish University, part of WJR's campaign to establish ten Jewish communal centers in the Ukraine. In June the New North London Synagogue hosted a party for Jewish children from Mogilev, Belarus, brought to Britain for medical reasons. In September London's Central Synagogue became the first United Synagogue congregation to twin with a community in Belarus, linking up with Minsk. In October the Reform Synagogues of Great Britain (RSGB) sponsored the production of a video of a Friday evening synagogue service for 90 Progressive synagogues in the former Soviet Union, as part of Exodus 2000, RSGB's support group for Progressive Jews in the region.

Publications

The 2000 *Jewish Quarterly*-Wingate award for fiction went to Howard Jacobson for *The Mighty Walzer;* and the award for nonfiction to Wladislaw Szpilman for *The Pianist*. The 1997 prize for nonfiction, given to Binjamin Wilkomirski's *Fragments, Memories of a Childhood, 1939–1948,* was now withdrawn, the book having been exposed as fictional. Jewish readers voted *The Diary of Anne Frank* the book of the century, with Primo Levi's *If This Is A Man* in second place and Chaim Potok's *The Chosen* in third.

Fiction published during the year included *Dark Inheritance* by Elaine Feinstein, whose poetic work, *Gold,* also appeared in 2000; *Faith,* a thriller by Peter James; *His Mistress's Voice* by Gillian Freeman; *When I Lived in Modern Times* by Linda Grant; *Depth of Field* by Sue Hubbard; *Only Human: A Comedy* by Jenny Diski; *The Last Survivor* by Timothy W. Ryback; *How the Dead Live* by Will Self; *Triad: The Physicists, the Analysts, the Kabbalists* by Tom Keve, a mixture of fact and fiction; and *Barcelona Plates* by Alexei Sayle, a collection of short stories. Poetry included *From Soho to Jerusalem* by Chaim Lewis; *Not Too Late for Loving* by Graham Tayar; *The Budapest File* by George Szirtes; and *Against Perfection* by Richard Burns.

Books on religion included *For the Shabbat Table* by Rabbi Chaim Wilschanski; *Celebrating Life,* short essays on such subjects as faith, happiness, and marriage, by Chief Rabbi Jonathan Sacks; *In Taking up the Timbrel,* edited by Rabbis Sylvia Rothschild and Sybil Sheridan, describing how women rabbis create rituals for Jewish women; *The Changing Face of Jesus* by Geza Vermes; *The People's Bible: Genesis,* translated by Sidney Brichto; *The David Story: A Translation with Commentary of I and II Samuel* by Robert Alter; and *The Lost Synagogues of London* by Peter Renton.

Local history was represented by Elliot Oppel's book on the history of Hull's Orthodox synagogues; *The Jews of the Channel Islands and the Rule of Law, 1940–1945* by David Fraser; *The Lost Jews of Cornwall* edited by Keith Pearce, Helen Fry, and Godfrey Simmons; and *The East End: Four Centuries of London Life* by Alan Palmer. Three books appeared on the history of institutions: *Lord*

Rothschild and the Barber: The Struggle to Establish the London Jewish Hospital by Gerry Black; *The Ajex Chronicles* by Ajex vice president Henry Morris; and the anniversary volume of the Jewish Memorial Council by Alexander Rosenzweig.

Works of history included *Zion in Africa: The Jews of Zambia* by Hugh Macmillan and Frank Shapiro; *Sunlight and Shadow,* a short history of Jews in Muslim countries, by Lucien Gubbay; *Web of Gold* by Guy Patton and Robin Mackness; *The Cliveden Set* by Norman Rose; *Motya: Unearthing a Lost Civilisation* by Gaia Servadio; *The Jewish Self-Image: American and British Perspectives, 1881–1939* by Michael Berkowitz; *One Day in September* (the day of the 1972 Olympic Games massacre) by Simon Reeve. *Whitehall and the Jews, 1933–1948* by Louise London; *Feminine Fascism: Women in Britain's Fascist Movement, 1923–1945* by Julie Gottlieb; *Hitler's Gift* (the brilliant academics from Nazi Germany who settled in Britain and the U.S.) by Jean Medawar and David Pyke; and *Pack of Thieves* by Richard Z. Chesnoff (the story of Nazi wartime art thefts) all concern the Nazi period.

Autobiographical and biographical works included *Shalom Bomb: Scenes From My Life* by poet and playwright Bernard Kops, who also published *Grandchildren and Other Poems; Fellatio, Masochism, Politics and Love* by Leo Abse; *Botchki* by David Zagier; *Paddling to Jerusalem* by David Aaronovitch; *Prince of Princes: The Life of Potemkin* by Simon Sebag Montefiore; *The Pharaoh's Shadow* by Anthony Sattin (travels in ancient and modern Egypt); *Between the Yeshivah World and Modern Orthodoxy—The Life and Works of Rabbi Jehiel Jacob Weinberg, 1884–1966* by Marc B. Shapiro; *An Unlikely Heroine* by Asher Calingold (about pioneer Zionist Esther Calingold). *Where Did It All Go Right?* by A. Alvarez was matched by a festschrift for his 70th birthday: *The Mind Has Mountains,* edited by Frank Kermode and Anthony Holden.

Holocaust studies included *Nazi Policy, Jewish Workers, German Killers* by Christopher Browning; *Making Memory: Creating Britain's First Holocaust Centre* by Stephen D. Smith; *Holocaust Literature: Schultz, Levi, Spiegelman and the Memory of the Offence* by Gillian Banner; *Shadows of the Shoah: Jewish Identity and Belonging* by Victor Seidler; *Double Jeopardy: Gender and Holocaust* edited by Judith Tydor Baumel; *Never Again: A History of the Holocaust* by Martin Gilbert; *The Past in Hiding* (the story of Marianne Strauss, who lived underground in Nazi Germany) by Mark Roseman; *When the Grey Beetles Took Over Baghdad* by Mona Yahia; and *The Nazi Officer's Wife* by Edith Hahn Ber with Susan Dworkin.

Books specifically devoted to Israel were *Israel's Wars* by Ahron Bregman; *Righteous Victims: A History of the Zionist-Arab Conflict, 1881–1999* by Benny Morris; *A Blood-Dimmed Tide* by Amos Elon; *The Jewish State: The Struggle for Israel's Soul* by Yoram Hazony; and *Fabricating Israeli History: The "New Historians"* by Efraim Karsh.

Three books gathering the writings of deceased personalities were *Chasing*

Shadows by Hugo Gryn with Naomi Gryn; *The Power of Ideas: Isaiah Berlin* edited by Henry Hardy; and *On the Other Hand* by Chaim Bermant. Other notable publications were *A Jewish Archive from Old Cairo—The History of Cambridge University's Genizah Collection* by Stefan C. Reif; *The Cricklewood Tapestry,* a collection of humorous essays by Alan Coren; *Random Harvest: The Novellas of Bialik,* translated by David Patterson and Ezra Spicehandler; and *The Jewish Year Book 2000* edited by Stephen W. Massil.

Personalia

Honors conferred on British Jews in 2000 included life peerages to Sally Greengross, Age Concern director; former European Commission vice president Sir Leon Brittan; and Oxfam chairman Joel Joffe. Labor appointments to the new list of 33 working peers included Parry Mitchell, information-technology adviser to the Labor Party; Professor Sir Leslie Turnberg, chairman of the board of the Public Health Laboratory Service; and Alex Bernstein, president of Old Vic Theatre Trust. Knighthoods went to real-estate developer Stuart Lipton, Stanhope's chief executive; to Bernard Schreier, for his contribution to developing trade between the UK and Hungary; to George Alberti in recognition of his work for medical services for diabetics; to Martin Sorrell, advertising mogul; and to Alan Sugar, computer entrepreneur. Vivien Duffield, chairperson of the Clore Foundation, was created a Dame for services to the arts; and filmmaker Steven Spielberg was named a Knight Commander of the British Empire for his contribution to the entertainment world, particularly the British movie industry.

Prominent British Jews who died in 2000 included: Judge Henry Lazarus Lachs, prominent member of Liverpool's Jewish community, in Liverpool, in January, aged 72; Norma Marion Blausten, communal worker, in London, in January, aged 75; Rabbi Dr. Ephraim Yehudah Wiesenberg, Jewish scholar, in London, in January, aged 90; Sophie Noble, WIZO stalwart, in London, in January, aged 95; Hazel Alexander, sculptress, in London, in February, aged 87; Vera Braynis, communal personality, in London, in February, aged 88; Josef Herman, artist, in London, in February, aged 89; Barry Fealdman, patron of Anglo-Jewish art, in London, in March, aged 86; Rosser Chinn, major communal leader and charity fund-raiser, in London, in March, aged 93; Edward Conway, headmaster of the Jewish Free School, 1958–76, in London, in April, aged 89; Rita Levy, active in Zionist, Jewish, and civic organizations, in London, in April, aged 85; David Spanier, journalist, in London, in April, aged 67; André Deutsch, publisher, in London, in April, aged 82; Michael Leigh, rabbi at Edgware Reform Synagogue, 1963–93, in London, in May, aged 72; Doreen Stanfield, musician, in London, in May, aged 71; Victor Dortheimer, Schindler survivor, in London, in May, aged 81; Dr. John Cohen, founder of the Association of Reform and Liberal Mohelim, in London, in June, aged 63; Rabbi Faivish Schneebalg, founder of the Vizhnitz Synagogue in Stamford Hill, North London, in London, in June, aged 71;

Harry Cohen, for 40 years headmaster of a Jewish-approved school for boys at Weybridge, Surrey, in Weybridge, in June, aged 87; Sir John Balcombe, appeals judge, in London, in June, aged 74; Harry Landy, communal activist, in London, in July, aged 89; Fred Balcombe, Manchester civic and Jewish activist, in Manchester, in July, aged 88; philosophy professor Stephan Körner in Bristol, in August, aged 86; Dayan Chanoch Padwa, principal rabbinic authority of the Union of Orthodox Hebrew Congregations (the Adath) for 45 years, in London, in August, aged 91; Michael Meyer, writer and translator, in London, in August, aged 79; Desmond Wilcox, broadcaster and filmmaker, in London, in September, aged 69; Basil Bernstein, educator, in London, in September, aged 75; Rabbi Meir Zvi Ehrentreu, outstanding scholar of Jewish law, in Manchester, in September, aged 70; Alf Bush (Abraham Isaac Shimansky), first honorary president of Cambridge's Beth Shalom Reform Synagogue, in Cambridge, in September, aged 87; Dr. Douglas Woolf, rheumatologist, in London, in October, aged 81; Rabbi Maurice Unterman, leading United Synagogue rabbi, in London, in October, aged 83; David Rubio, musical-instrument maker, in Cambridge, in October, aged 65; Mollie Brandl-Bowen, author and antiracist activist, in Brighton, in October, aged 69; Jack Lowy, scientist, in Oxford, in October, aged 78; Ruth Lowy, artist, in Oxford, in October, aged 79; Shulamith Shafir, concert pianist, in London, in November, aged 77; Carole Rosen, singer and writer, in London, in November, aged 66; Barbara Harding, stalwart of British WIZO, in London, in November, aged 57; and Simon Livingstone, photographer and philanthropist, in Birmingham, in December, aged 59.

MIRIAM & LIONEL KOCHAN

France

National Affairs

T HE YEAR 2000 WAS A YEAR of waiting, as a president of the right, Jacques Chirac, had to work with a socialist prime minister, Lionel Jospin, who was supported by a left-of-center majority in the National Assembly. Both had their sights set on the next presidential election, scheduled for 2002. Although neither had officially announced his candidacy, it seemed clear that Chirac would seek a second term and that Jospin would run against him.

Thus two potential adversaries were forced to cooperate to make the nation's institutions run smoothly as well as to conduct foreign affairs, an area traditionally managed by agreement between the president and the prime minister. The cabinet met each week in Paris at the Élysée Palace with President Chirac presiding, and adopted measures conforming to the views of Jospin.

This strange state of "cohabitation" was not without its intrigues, low blows, pointed leaks to the press, and damaging statements made with a view to destabilizing the other party. Yet each side knew that whoever initiated a major right-left confrontation would quickly feel the wrath of the public for disturbing the workings of democracy and violating the spirit of the constitution, according to which the president presides while the head-of-government governs. Thus Chirac and Jospin played out a parody of the classic final scene from an old American western movie: they moved toward one another at an agonizingly slow pace, guns in their holsters, arms by their sides, staring straight ahead. The audience knows that the confrontation will finally come. It is just a question of time.

Convinced that the center was key to winning the next election, both of the chief players were risk-averse, avoiding any initiative or statement that might alienate a segment of the electorate. In any case, the differences between the two blocs were minimal. The Rally for the Republic (RPR), Chirac's party, along with its allies (and sometimes competitors) from the Union for French Democracy (UDF), represented a moderate right that advocated both free trade and social justice, the free market and Europe, national honor and minority rights. Jospin's Socialist Party simply reversed the order of these elements: social justice and free trade, etc. The differences related to priorities, emphasis, and style.

In previous times, the absence of any real difference between the right and the left might have benefited the political extremes. But the healthy French economy throughout the year, which led to lower unemployment, quieted public discontent, weakening both the far right and the far left.

The far right had long based its policies on linking immigration with unemployment and urban violence. But unemployment and violence, while not completely eradicated, were considerably less visible in 2000. In addition, the far right still suffered from the schism that arose in 1999 between Jean-Marie Le Pen's National Front and the National Republican Movement, led by former National Front second-in-command Bruno Mégret (see AJYB 2000, p. 304). These two rival factions remained locked in a ferocious battle that had much to do with personal animosities. In by-elections, far-right candidates continued to obtain a significant share of the vote. But though many in France still worried about security and national identity—the issues of the far right—the dynamism that used to characterize Le Pen and his movement in his heyday was no longer in evidence.

Problems on the far left were different. The Communist Party, which was France's largest party for many years (in the years following World War II, one voter in four supported it), had fallen onto hard times. The fall of the Soviet Union dealt a serious blow to its prestige, and its participation in the Socialist-led government made it look like a mere appendage of the social democracy that Communist leaders had spent years denouncing. Attempts to reestablish the party's activist base proved unsuccessful. The party's daily newspaper, *L'Humanité,* continued to lose readers and frequently warned of its own impending demise.

Some proposed changing the name of the party or transforming it into a social democratic party, as occurred with its Italian counterpart, but the fact that a strong socialist party already existed in France made this unlikely. Others sought to emphasize the party's working-class orientation so as to gain recruits among the most disadvantaged sectors of the population, especially immigrant workers from North Africa. However, any such strategy had to take account of Trotskyist groups, which, though attracting few followers, were coming to represent an increasing portion of the far left.

The Green Party occupied its own segment of the left-wing landscape. This environmental party was part of the majority coalition, along with the Socialists and Communists, supporting Jospin. Its lack of an ideological tradition sometimes led it to take surprising positions on issues not directly related to the environment, and at times it was the object of infiltration efforts by neo-fascist, anti-Semitic, or rabidly anti-Israel elements. While organization on the local level has helped overcome these growing pains, some people continued to view the party with a degree of suspicion.

Israel and the Middle East

On February 23, 2000, Prime Minister Jospin arrived in Israel, hoping to demonstrate friendship toward Prime Minister Ehud Barak and help restart the Israeli-Palestinian peace process. (Employees of Israel's Ministry of Foreign Affairs had been told to display flags with France's colors—blue, white, and red—but they mistakenly reversed the colors so that Jospin was welcomed by the flag of the Netherlands. There were no hard feelings.)

The next day, Jospin inaugurated the new French cultural center in Jerusalem bearing the name of Romain Gary, a great French writer of Jewish origin who died in 1980. This center was a very important symbolic gesture since France, like many other countries, maintained a consulate in East Jerusalem that reported to the Ministry of Foreign Affairs and not to the French embassy in Tel Aviv. This consulate, widely considered a sort of embassy to the Palestinians, maintained its own cultural activities from which Israelis had felt excluded. Until 1999, a branch of the Alliance Française (a nongovernmental cultural organization linked to French authorities) operated in a Jewish neighborhood, and it was managed and frequented by Jewish Israelis. But the center had to close its doors, primarily for financial reasons. In the circumstances, the new center inaugurated by Jospin did more than just fill a cultural gap. Unlike its predecessor, this center was directly responsible to the French embassy, and thus represented an official French presence for the Jews of Jerusalem.

Jospin's next move in Israel had less predictable consequences. At a press conference, the prime minister stressed that he had found the government "available" for peace negotiations with the Arabs, while he deplored Syria's "rigidity" regarding southern Lebanon, which at that point Israel had not yet evacuated. He also condemned the Islamic militants of Hezballah for their "terrorist" actions. It was this last word that provoked strong reaction, both in the Middle East and at home. On February 26, when Jospin visited Bir Zeit University, Palestinian students threw rocks at him. Jospin met with Yasir Arafat as planned, but then cut his trip short and returned to Paris. In France, meanwhile, President Chirac publicly criticized Jospin's comments, saying that they broke France's tradition of "neutrality."

The incident quickly blossomed into a small political crisis. Chirac's inner circle had long been known to be more pro-Arab than Jospin's, and back at the Élysée Palace there was much gnashing of teeth over the prime minister's press conference in Jerusalem. All of this had at least as much to do with internal French politics as with Israel. At home, Jospin's statements represented not just a show of support for his friend Ehud Barak, but also an attempt to encroach on the president's role, further diminishing Chirac's stature as the 2002 election approached.

Chirac tried to regain the psychological advantage by calling on Jospin to explain himself. Jospin ignored the summons. As with previous clashes between them, this affair ended with newspaper articles more or less "inspired" by those close to the two antagonists. In the final analysis, Jospin appeared to have come out somewhat weakened, receiving criticism for taking the initiative on a matter of foreign affairs without appropriate consultation. Even worse, by becoming a target for rock throwers, he bore the brunt of an attack on France's image.

The Israeli-Arab conflict once again took over French politics toward the end of the year, this time in a much more dramatic way. On October 4, following the initial clashes between Israelis and Palestinians, Ehud Barak and Yasir Arafat met at the American embassy in Paris under the auspices of U.S. Secretary of State

Madeleine Albright. Apparently the two sides were very close to reaching an agreement, which was to be signed that night and then ratified the next day at Sharm el-Sheikh. At the last minute Arafat refused to sign, and as a result Barak refused to go to Sharm el-Sheikh.

Barak's people pointed an accusing finger at Jacques Chirac. According to them, the French president not only behaved badly toward the Israeli prime minister, but also encouraged Arafat to refuse to sign the document prepared by Madeleine Albright. Still according to Israeli sources, Chirac, mortified that international negotiations were taking place in Paris without his involvement, supported Arafat by calling for an international inquiry into the events of the previous days as a way to gain recognition for France's role in the process. Those who accompanied Barak also reported that the French president's manner toward the Israeli prime minister was less than diplomatic, and that he criticized the Israeli army's behavior on the basis of what he had seen "on television."

The Élysée Palace denied these accusations. The palace stated—and journalists close to the president wrote—that France had consistently encouraged an Israeli-Palestinian agreement and had called for a return to calm. But whatever role Chirac actually played, the widespread impression in Israel that France had been less than helpful was underscored by the anti-Israel position taken by most of the French media.

On September 30 a public television station, France 2, showed the killing of a 12-year-old Palestinian boy who had been caught with his father in a cross fire between Israelis and Palestinians at Netzarim junction. These images and others like them, widely broadcast, elicited strong indignation from the public, to whom no one had explained the background or the political context surrounding the clashes. On October 7 several far-left groups organized a demonstration in Paris, with participation from Arab groups. During the demonstration cries of "Jewish assassins" and "death to the Jews" could be heard. It would take several days for the organizers to issue a public condemnation of such slogans.

The degree to which France had become the battleground for an unprecedented crisis in relations between the Jews and the Arab-Muslim community was already evident earlier in the year in the treatment of the Jewish singer Enrico Macias. Following a long and brilliant career in popular music, the singer revisited the style of his youth: Judeo-Arab-Andalusian music. Accompanied by an orchestra of Muslim Algerians, Macias hoped to help bring reconciliation between the communities (see AJYB 2000, p. 312). A triumphal concert at Espace Rachi, a Jewish center in Paris, aroused great hopes, and Algerian president Abdelaziz Bouteflika invited Macias to give a series of concerts around the country in March 2000. A delegation of Algerian Jews was prepared to accompany him, many of them hoping that this would lead to a renewal of relations that would have an impact at the international (Israel-Algeria) level. But Muslim groups in Algeria orchestrated a protest against the "Zionist" Macias, and the trip was canceled (officially "put off sine die") at the last minute.

In late November, with the violent Israeli-Palestinian confrontation already in its second month, Macias was scheduled to perform in Roubaix, a city in northern France with a significant Algerian immigrant population. In an effort to have the concert canceled, some residents launched a demonstration ostensibly in defense of the Palestinian people and against the pro-Israel Macias. Journalists who were there heard protests against "the Jew who sings in Arabic." Emotions ran high, but in the end the concert did take place, with the usual Algerian orchestra, in a jam-packed hall—and under the protection of 2,000 police officers.

Anti-Semitism and Racism

MIDDLE-EAST FALLOUT

According to a nationwide poll by the BVA Institute published in October 2000 by *Télérama* (a weekly paper that reports on cultural news and belongs to a large Catholic newspaper chain), 71 percent of the French population believed that "the confrontations in the Middle East could revive anti-Semitism in France" and 77 percent believed that events in the Middle East could "lead to violent clashes between Jews and Arabs in France." The wording of the poll, however, was far from reality. There were hardly any "violent confrontations between Jews and Arabs"— the attacks were almost exclusively one-way.

Starting in early October, dozens of anti-Jewish incidents were reported. According to statistics compiled by the Ministry of the Interior, which is responsible for the national police, 43 synagogues were attacked, three cemeteries were desecrated, and in nine cases Jewish schools, teachers, students, or the buses transporting them were the targets of violence. Thirty-nine attacks were directed at people coming out of a synagogue, Jews at home, or property belonging to Jews. Eleven businesses were vandalized (in at least one case, the owner—a baker in Strasbourg named Blum who was not Jewish—was a victim of mistaken identity). Other attacks were directed at police standing guard at Jewish sites, or their vehicles. The count included 44 attempted arson attacks (carried out mostly with Molotov cocktails); 33 cases of damage in which shots were fired, rocks were thrown, or windows were broken; and 33 personal attacks, which left 11 wounded. In the most spectacular of these attacks, on October 10 three Molotov cocktails were thrown into a synagogue in Les Ulis, a Paris suburb. The synagogue suffered some fire damage, but the rabbi, who was on the scene, was unhurt. These attacks generated a feeling of insecurity in the Jewish community.

There were a couple of instances of far-right agitators trying to benefit from the situation. Members of a small neo-Nazi organization called the Union Defense Group (GUD) created a disturbance on October 11 in a Paris university, burning an Israeli flag and throwing around pamphlets entitled "Zionists, out of the faculties!" which concluded with the slogan, "In Paris as in Gaza, Intifada!" The only other anti-Semitic act claimed by the far right during this period was the attempted burning of a university building outside Paris on October 19.

Apart from these two incidents, all the attacks seemed to have come from young Muslim Arab immigrants. Living in neighborhoods rife with social problems where violence and petty crimes were part of daily life, they allowed the events in the Middle East to direct their aggression toward their Jewish neighbors. There was nothing to suggest that they belonged to any organized political or religious organizations or that their actions were coordinated. A certain amount of latent anger had been accumulating for years, sustained primarily by watching the Jewish community's steady economic success. Now it was inflamed by identification with the Palestinians, both on national (Arab) and religious (Muslim) grounds. The sensationalism and lack of balance in French media coverage of developments in the Middle East probably also played a role in encouraging these acts.

Police officials, taken by surprise, initially adopted a measured approach, in accordance with their general policy of keeping a low profile in "problem" neighborhoods. But the authorities soon realized that what had originally appeared to be local conflicts could potentially spark a larger and more dangerous movement. Jewish communal officials appealed successfully to national leaders. President Chirac declared that acts of violence against Jewish citizens were "unacceptable," and Prime Minister Jospin announced that the government would act firmly and use all necessary means to control the violence. The police began to arrest young people suspected of participating in arson attacks on Jews. These arrests had the immediate effect of reducing the number of incidents, in turn confirming the theory that they were individual and not organized actions.

Tensions decreased considerably after France's highest-ranking religious leaders—Joseph Sitruk, the chief rabbi; Dalil Boubakeur, director of the Muslim Institute of the Grand Mosque of Paris; Jean-Arnold de Clermont, president of the Protestant Federation of France; and Louis-Marie Billé, president of the Catholic Bishops' Conference—made a solemn appeal "to maintain an atmosphere of calm and peace." Local leaders worked to calm emotions within the Muslim communities. While Jewish-Muslim relations were certainly not repaired, at least the attacks and threats against Jews subsided and were no longer daily occurrences by the end of the year.

In its annual report for 2000, the National Consultative Commission on Human Rights (an advisory body under the aegis of the prime minister's office) published comments from the Ministry of the Interior about the anti-Jewish attacks that took place in the last quarter of the year. Highlighting the point that "the far right claimed responsibility for only two of these incidents," the report affirmed that "the violence that marked the last quarter of the year . . . essentially came from the immigrant population which found a target for its resentment and sense of exclusion." The 42 interrogations conducted by police showed that none of the suspects "are known for an Islamic-militant profile." Rather, "most of the individuals implicated are just involved in criminal activities and do not claim affiliation with any particular ideology. Adolescents and unemployed adults for the most part, the perpetrators nevertheless appear animated by a general hostility toward Israel, exacerbated by media reports of confrontation, leading to their projection into a conflict that in their eyes mirrors the dynamics of exclusion and failure of which they see themselves as victims in France." The incidents were, in fact, highly concentrated in specific locations, which the Ministry of the Interior delicately defined as "places containing an outpouring of urban violence."

For the year 2000 the Ministry of the Interior recorded 146 "violent racist and anti-Semitic acts," a category including acts against any minority group. Not only was this the highest figure since 1990, but it marked a whopping 265-percent jump since the year before, when there were 40 such acts. This rise was entirely attributable to anti-Semitism, as 116 of the 146 "violent racist and anti-Semitic acts" in 2000—close to 80 percent—were against Jews, and violence against members of other groups remained stable. There had already been a slight rise in anti-Semitic incidents in 1999 to nine, 22 percent of the total. Before that, only one such act was recorded in 1998, three in 1997, one in 1996 and two, including one isolated case involving a death, in 1995. Clearly, the explosion of violence did not occur in a vacuum: France experienced the crisis sparked by events in the Middle East as a catastrophe threatening intergroup relations in the country.

The chronology of anti-Semitic violence in 2000 was highly significant. Only five incidents were reported between January and September, a number corresponding to the previous year's level. There were 77 incidents between the end of September and mid-October; then the number decreased to 26 in the second half of October and to seven in November; in December, only one case of anti-Semitic violence was noted. Thus two-thirds of the recorded violent anti-Semitic acts during 2000—representing more than half of all violent racist incidents for the entire year—took place in the first half of October, the two weeks immediately following the outbreak of violence in Israel and the territories.

These statistics indicated that anti-Semitic violence in 2000 was an unprecedented phenomenon, tied to exceptional circumstances. Even calling the incidents anti-Semitic is somewhat misleading since the perpetrators did not seem to have any connection with an anti-Semitic movement in the classic sense of the term. And yet a recurrence could not be ruled out. As the Ministry of the Interior's report noted, "Rapidly settling down in the final days of the year, this blaze of concentrated attacks against Jews and their property could flare up again depending on how the situation in the Middle East evolves."

Besides the data on acts of violence, the Ministry of the Interior also reported statistics on racist, xenophobic, and anti-Semitic "threats," that is, "threatening words or gestures, graffiti, pamphlets, lesser incidents of violence." Here too, the statistics for 2000 stood out in comparison with those of previous years. Between 1997 and 1999, the ministry recorded a yearly average of 173 such "threats"—73 anti-Semitic threats and 100 other racially motivated threats, of which 70 were directed at people of North African origin. The high proportion of reported anti-Semitic threats reflected, to some extent, the fact that Jews were more likely than others to register complaints in such cases and also their greater familiarity with the process for doing so.

In the year 2000 the numbers of incidents and the proportion of the victimized groups changed radically. The Ministry of the Interior counted a total of 722 "threats," meaning that the number of threats had more than quadrupled, reaching—as with the number of violent incidents—a new record. Of the "threats," 603 were anti-Semitic and 119 were "other" racist threats (65 of which were against people of North African origin). While the number of "other" threats was similar to that of earlier years, the number of anti-Semitic threats multiplied eightfold and represented more than 80 percent of all racially motivated threats.

During the year police charged some 60 people for making anti-Semitic threats. Of this number, only five espoused the ideas of the far right; the others belonged to pro-Palestinian circles—although the Ministry of the Interior would not put it in these terms. Compared with the 603 anti-Semitic actions, the police noted 11 that were made "in retaliation" against the Arab community. Most of these "were claimed in the name of activist Jewish groups," but the claims of responsibility were not confirmed in every case.

TRACKING RACISM AND ANTI-SEMITISM

The 2000 report of the National Consultative Commission on Human Rights contained results of a public-opinion poll entitled "Xenophobia, Racism and Antiracism in France—Attitudes and Perceptions." This poll, conducted between October 2 and 14, 2000, by the Louis Harris Institute, was one in a series on this topic sponsored by the commission since the early 1990s. The clear message of the poll was that the French want minority groups to assimilate into the rest of society. This reflected the long-standing French tradition of rejecting foreigners who keep their identity of origin but accepting them once they identify with the rest of French society.

Asked which they prefer—having people of different origins (Europeans, Africans, North Africans, Asians) live in their own separate communities or integrate with the population as a whole, 68 percent chose the path of integration, while 26 percent expressed a preference for separate communities. To the question, "Do you believe that there are groups in France who live separately?" 64 percent said yes. This referred primarily to immigrants; only 3 percent of those expressing this sentiment identified "Jews" as one of the groups in question. A more "classic" form of racism persisted among a minority of respondents: the belief that "some races are inferior to others" was approved without reservation by 6 percent, and another 16 percent "somewhat" agreed. There exists, then, an irreducible core, 20–25 percent of the French population, that believes efforts to integrate are destined to fail.

Respondents were pessimistic about the evolution of French society over the next 20 years. Only 10 percent thought that people of European origin would "live together in harmony" with those from other regions of the world; 50 percent thought that they would "live together but with tensions"; 9 percent that they would "live separately but without tensions"; and 27 percent that they would "live separately but with tensions." These numbers were almost identical to those of the previous year, indicating that the anti-Jewish violence connected with events in the Middle East, taking place at the moment the poll was being taken, had no effect on the answers.

According to the poll, 62 percent of the French believed that racism in their country was "somewhat widespread," while 29 percent believed that it was "very widespread." Only 19 percent identified Jews as one of the targets of such racism, while 75 percent mentioned North Africans. In terms of their own attitudes, 43 percent said they were "a little bit racist" or "somewhat racist," compared to 54 percent who said they were not. The responses showed some contradictions: a majority (54 percent) said that France today had "too many foreigners," and 63 percent agreed with the statement that "most of the immigrants have a culture and way of life that is too different for them to integrate in France." But a similar majority (62 percent) agreed with the statement that "a democracy is also judged according to its ability to integrate foreigners," and 64 percent found the presence of people who came from non-European countries "not very disturbing."

Once the questions moved from theory to concrete practice, French attitudes were far more liberal. Racial discrimination in the workplace, for example, was strongly condemned: 81 percent considered a refusal to hire a qualified black or North African wrong (only 4 percent considered this situation "not wrong at all"). The same was true in regard to the right to housing: 66 percent of French people judged refusing to rent to a black or North African wrong. More remarkably, 57 percent considered it wrong to oppose a child's marriage to a black or a North African, while just 13 percent considered such a stance "not wrong at all."

Generally speaking, these surveys have shown a decline in prejudice since the early 1990s, which may be due to higher levels of education (there has always been a strong correlation between lower levels of education and racist beliefs) and an improvement in social and economic conditions. In 1999 and 2000, however, this trend stopped and even reversed, with the indicators of racism rising, albeit not to their previous levels. In the case of Jews, for example, 21 percent of the French felt there were "too many" of them in 1991, a figure that dropped to 14 percent by 1998, only to rise to 21 percent in 1999 and 19 percent in 2000. Similar patterns held for attitudes toward Arabs and blacks, though not for Asians, for whom the level of rejection has continued to decline.

There were also other worrisome findings in the 2000 survey. While the proportion of respondents who felt there were "too many" Jews remained under 20 percent, the statement that "Jews are French people like the rest" was affirmed by only 70 percent (23 percent rejected the statement and 7 percent did not respond). The assertion that "Jews have too much power in France" was approved by 34 percent (54 percent rejected it and 12 percent did not answer). The year before, 31 percent had approved the view that "Jews have too much power in France," with 56 percent rejecting it and 13 percent declining to answer.

Political scientists Nonna Mayer and Guy Michelat, analyzing these findings, noted that the question of the Jews' power in France ("a classic question . . . in the tradition of the famous forgery created by the tsarist police, *The Protocols of the Elders of Zion*") had been asked years earlier, in polls taken in 1988 and 1991. Then, only 20 percent of respondents agreed that "the Jews have too much power in France." Did the jump, over the course of a decade, from 20 percent to 34 percent of the French agreeing that Jews had too much power indicate a giant leap in anti-Semitism? Mayer and Michelat did not think so, pointing out that the percentage of those with "no response" had declined by 15 points during the same period. These "latent" anti-Semites, unwilling to admit their prejudices earlier, were doing so now. In other words, there were not more anti-Semites in France, just fewer embarrassed anti-Semites.

In their analysis of the 2000 sample's subgroups, Mayer and Michelat found that animosity toward Jews was most likely to be found "among the working class and those with little education, older people, those with a right-wing orientation, those who are more authoritarian and those who are more worried about their future . . . ." But they also emphasized that "this anti-Semitism is breaking all records among two groups—the Gaullist right and regularly practicing Catholics." These two minority groups—11.6 percent of respondents said they were Gaullists while 7.8 percent said they were devout Catholics—must have been strongly moved by recent events.

The Gaullists were shocked by the trial of Maurice Papon, a sub-prefect under the wartime Vichy regime and subsequently a Gaullist minister, condemned to ten years in prison for "complicity in crimes against humanity." Without a doubt, the charge against someone who had served General de Gaulle for crimes he once committed against the Jews, and the presence throughout the trial of Jewish associations and individual Jews, convinced a number of RPR supporters that the Jews had too much power in France. Furthermore, President Chirac's solemn recognition in 1995 of France's responsibility for the persecution of Jews during the German occupation was not welcomed by many of the elderly, for whom the Gaullist myth of a France in "total resistance" and innocent of the crimes of Vichy was part of their national history.

Among faithful Catholics, the event that probably played a similar role in cementing the notion of Jewish power was the "declaration of repentance" pronounced by the bishops of France in 1997 at Drancy, where Jews were interned before being deported to Auschwitz. Many Catholics protested this confession by the church, one that many Jews exerted pressure to extract. Also, as Mayer and Michelat noted, the 2000 poll was taken as the situation was deteriorating in the Middle East, and therefore "uncertainties about the status of Jerusalem could have worried the most religious of the Catholic community and brought to the surface an old well of Christian anti-Semitism."

OTHER DEVELOPMENTS

Around the edges of these broad trends, some more localized incidents in 2000 deserve mention. The first is what quickly become known as the Renaud Camus affair. Camus (no relation to Albert Camus) was not well-known to the general public, but had a strong following in certain intellectual circles. His method of writing was to keep a regular journal and then publish it in book form. It was his 1994 journal, published in early 2000 and called *La campagne de France* (*campagne* is a double entendre, meaning both "countryside" and military "campaign"), that led to scandal. In one of his journal entries, Camus mentioned a radio program he had heard called "Panorama" (no longer on the air) on France Culture, the cultural station of France's public radio. Camus noted, "Five participants, and what proportion of non-Jews among them? Infinitesimal, if not nonexistent." He then asked himself, in his personal diary, whether he was an anti-Semite. No, he answered himself. He admired the Jews' contributions to humanity and he considered the Holocaust an abomination. But he considered it wrong to have only Jews as commentators on a public radio program about subjects of general interest, and complained that the Jews had frequently brought up subjects relating specifically to Jewish culture, the Holocaust, and Israel (as in fact they had). He suggested, in conclusion, that only someone with deep French roots could really understand things touching the essence of the country's life, *la vie profonde*. A son or daughter of Jewish immigrants, in his view, would always suffer from not being completely integrated into national history and geography.

Though these thoughts appeared in Camus's journal in the context of many other remarks about a wide variety of subjects, they stood out and shocked readers. Already, Camus's regular publisher, P.O.L., had refused to publish the book because of them. At Fayard, the large publishing house that did release the book, there had been an internal debate at the highest levels, with some senior staff saying that had they been informed about the offending passages in advance they would have refused to print them. All the major French media outlets — dailies, weeklies, monthly magazines, radio, and television — covered the issue. Renaud Camus insisted that his words contained no anti-Semitism, and several of his Jewish friends agreed. But many people alarmed by the book denounced his "myth of origins" and warned that it could lead to serious consequences. In the end the book was recalled in April 2000 and then republished — without the offending passages, but with a preface by Claude Durand, director general of Fayard, in which he protested what he called a media cabal against Camus.

A quarrel of a completely different sort began with the lawsuit brought by the International League Against Racism and Anti-Semitism (LICRA) and the Union of Jewish Students of France (UEJF) against Yahoo! for giving Internet access to the auctioning of objects that are outlawed in France — Nazi insignias, anti-Semitic books, and the like. Although Yahoo!'s French affiliate obeyed French law in that its screens were free of all Nazi propaganda, access through the French Yahoo! to sites managed by the American parent company violated the law.

The judge in the case ruled that the forbidden text and images on a French computer in France were unlawful. But since the court could not force Yahoo!'s American management to censor its own sites, the only possible solution was to "filter" access by French citizens so that the outlawed contents would not be available to them. The underlying issue — freedom of expression versus antiracism — became intertwined with a technical debate about the feasibility of such a filtering system. After months of legal proceedings and testimony from experts and counter-experts, the court ordered the filtering solution. But the difference between the approaches of countries like the U.S., where free expression had priority, and countries like France, where the expression of racism, anti-Semitism, and Holocaust denial were illegal, as well as the difficulties in monitoring messages in cyberspace, made more such disputes likely.

As was the case in other European countries, there was also anti-Semitism on the soccer field. The team in Strasbourg, in the eastern part of France, lost match after match, and the local fans blamed the coach, Claude Le Roy. Soon slogans like "Le Roy, dirty Jew" appeared on the stadium benches and in the streets of the city, apparently the work of a small group. Other Strasbourg residents, concerned about the effect such slogans might have on the reputation of a city considered the capital of Europe, came to the stadium with a banner marked *"Fâchés mais pas fascistes"* ("angry, but not fascist"). Le Roy was replaced by another coach, but the performance of the team did not improve. Ironically, Claude Le Roy was not Jewish, but he declined to point this out when the anti-Semitic insults against him began, not wanting to appear, even indirectly, to justify anti-Semitism.

Holocaust-Related Matters

HOLOCAUST DENIAL

Holocaust denial was not only forbidden under French law but also severely punished by the courts. As a result, the main French deniers, or *négationnistes* (a term that has become enshrined in the French political vocabulary; only the deniers themselves continue to use the word *révisionnistes*), such as Robert Faurisson and Roger Garaudy, have had little opportunity to express themselves in their own country. There have, however, been plenty of court cases, with penalties for denial taking the form of fines or, sometimes, suspended prison sentences.

Thus, Jean Plantin appeared in court in Lyon for having published advertisements for *négationniste* books in his magazine *Akribeia;* a teacher, Jean-Louis Berger, was put on trial in Metz for having brought up *négationniste* ideas in his classroom; and a Moroccan living in Sweden, Ahmed Rami, failed to appear in court in Paris and was found guilty of disseminating an anti-Semitic denial tract on his Internet site. Henri Lewkowicz, who claimed Jewish origins through his father, called in to a radio talk show and said that the gas chambers were a fabrication; the court in Paris not only fined him but also ordered that he undergo psychiatric treatment. Finally, a sociologist, Serge Thion, was dismissed on October 4, 2000, from his position with the CNRS, the National Scientific Research Center (Centre National de la Recherche Scientifique). This came as a result of his numerous activities furthering the *négationniste* cause, in the service of which he had used his friendship with the American academic Noam Chomsky. The CNRS's decision-making bodies, made up of scholars known for their commitment to freedom of expression, determined that in this case Thion's *négationniste* activism impaired his scientific work and damaged the institution's reputation.

OTHER HOLOCAUST-RELATED MATTERS

Both houses of Parliament unanimously passed an act establishing a "national day to remember the victims of the racist and anti-Semitic crimes of the *État français* [the Vichy collaborationist regime led by Philippe Pétain between 1940 and 1944] and to honor the *'Justes'* [righteous people] of France." This law essentially repeated the substance of an order signed in 1993 by President François Mitterrand, which required authorities in every department in France to organize a commemorative event on July 16. (This was the anniversary of the roundup of 13,000 Jews in Paris, the so-called "Vél d'Hiv roundup," carried out by French police in 1942 on behalf of the Germans. Actually, the commemoration was to be on July 16 only if it was a Sunday; otherwise it would take place on the nearest Sunday.) What Parliament's action accomplished, however, was to strengthen the impact of the presidential order by giving it the force of law. In addition, Mitterand's order had not mentioned the *Justes,* who had protected or defended Jews. Finally, the law's reference to the "the racist and anti-Semitic crimes of the *État français"* was more precise and forceful than the one in the earlier presidential order: "racist and anti-Semitic persecutions committed by the de facto authority called the *'gouvernement de l'État français.'* "

At almost exactly the same time, legal proceedings were launched against 84-year-old Michel Junot, who had been sub-prefect of Pithiviers, south of Paris, during the German occupation. These were undertaken after a complaint was filed by Marc Korenbajzer, whose half-sister Aline was arrested by French police on July 16, 1942, interned in a French camp, and then deported by the Germans to Auschwitz where she was killed at the age of three. Korenbajzer maintained that he had proof Michel Junot was performing the duties of sub-prefect at the time when Jewish families—primarily women and children—were interned in camps in the Pithiviers region. He also maintained that Junot had direct authority over the camps, which made him an accomplice in crimes against humanity, something for which there was no statute of limitations under French law.

Junot, however, stated that he took up his duties only on August 26, 1942, by which time the Jews interned in Pithiviers and the surrounding region had already been transferred. In some respects, this controversy was similar to the case of Maurice Papon (see AJYB 2000, pp. 309–10). Like Papon, Junot maintained that he was a double agent working for the Gaullist resistance, and, like Papon, he became a civil servant and then a politician after the war (he was assistant to the mayor of Paris, then a member of the National Assembly representing the right). And finally, as Papon did when he was accused, Junot launched a defamation suit against his accuser. The official inquiry was still in progress as the year ended.

On the subject of Papon, who was sentenced to ten years in prison for "complicity in crimes against humanity" as a result of his activities as sub-prefect in Bordeaux under the German occupation, his lawyers made repeated requests for his freedom on grounds of poor health. Although he had launched a protest in the European Court of Human Rights against both the conduct of his trial and the conditions of his detention, Papon was still in prison at the end of 2000.

Prime Minister Jospin headed the large French delegation to the international conference on the Holocaust held in Stockholm in late January 2000. As a concrete result of French participation in this conference, a book about the Holocaust by two Swedish historians was translated and distributed free in French schools.

During a conference on the Judeo-Spanish heritage held in Thessaloniki, Greece, in mid-April, an interesting point about the Holocaust came up. Although plaques in 19 different languages had been placed at Auschwitz-Birkenau to commemorate the victims, there is no plaque in Judeo-Spanish, the mother tongue of Europe's Sephardi Jews. Professor Haïm-Vidal Sephiha, who pioneered the teaching of that language at the University of Paris and taught it there for many years, started a petition to add a plaque in Judeo-Spanish. The petition was widely distributed during 2000, but its demand had not yet been put into effect at the end of the year.

RESTITUTION

On April 17, 2000, the "study commission on the plundering of the Jews of France" submitted its final report. Established in February 1997 by then-prime minister Alain Juppé and confirmed in October of the same year by his successor, Lionel Jospin, its main task was to determine the scope of the theft of Jewish property between 1940 and 1944 by the German occupiers and the Vichy collaborationist regime for which there had been no restitution after the war. Jean Mattéoli chaired the commission, and Professor Ady Steg, president of the Alliance Israélite Universelle, was its guiding force. With the help of historians, archivists and senior civil servants placed at its disposal, it examined all the documents relating to the period.

The conclusions reached were first and foremost moral. "Plundering and pillage," it said in its 3,000-page report, which was published by the prime minister's office and was the subject of much comment in the press, "are intimately tied into the process of the destruction of the Jews of France . . . . Because we had to assess the scope of the plunder for which there had been no reparation or indemnity, we had to calculate, and sometimes to adopt the cold mathematical reasoning involved in keeping accounts. But what is irreparable in the Holocaust is the murder of men, women and children, the agony of a portion of Judaism." The report described in detail the ways in which Jewish property was plundered: bank accounts were frozen; businesses were aryanized; furniture and real estate were seized; and banknotes, jewels, and other objects were taken from Jews when they were interned in the camps from which they were subsequently deported to Auschwitz.

After the war, restitution was made for the vast majority of the goods plundered in these ways. For some goods, however, there had been neither restitution nor reimbursement, either because their owners had been killed and no heirs had come forward, or because the survivors had not wanted to undertake proceedings. Most of the Jews in France who were victims of the Holocaust (about 78,000 people, 25 percent of the Jews living in France at the time) were recent immigrants, and many were very poor. While taken individually the goods they left behind did not amount to much, in total, however, the Mattéoli Commission's experts calculated that the unclaimed goods, along with heirless bank accounts and aryanizations for which there was no restitution, had a total current value of 2.4 billion francs.

Even before it submitted its final report, the Mattéoli Commission made three recommendations, all of which were adopted by the government. The first dealt with the establishment of a special commission to examine individual restitution claims that had not yet been satisfied. This was set up in late 1999 with Pierre Drai—a Jew of Algerian origin and former president of the Court of Cassation, the highest position in the French justice system—as chair. In studying the files it has generally been favorably disposed toward claims for restitution, taking account of the fact that after more then 55 years written proof that property was plundered was often no longer available. Through an extraordinary government ruling, the Drai Commission's decisions would be binding on public authorities, and restitution would be paid out of the government's budget.

The second recommendation concerned Jewish orphans whose parents were deported. The surviving orphans, now retired, would receive special compensation in the form of a pension because, unlike other orphans who lost their parents during the war, they were themselves victims of discriminatory measures that made their reintegration into society after liberation more difficult. The government adopted this recommendation in July 2000 and began to implement it. This preferential treatment for Jewish orphans was challenged, notably by organizations representing those who were deported for acts of resistance (some of them were also Jewish). These organizations did not demand cancellation of the new measure, but that it should be extended to all categories of victims. The government rejected their demand, and early in 2001 the State Council, the highest court with authority for administrative matters, upheld the government's decision, endorsing the Mattéoli Commission's argument that the dual persecution in the case of the Jews justified unequal treatment.

The commission's third recommendation was for the creation of a Remembrance Foundation. Its initial endowment would come from the government in the amount of the plundered property that could not be restored to private individuals, a total of more than 2 billion francs. This endowment would be augmented by contributions from the major French banks, and eventually from other sources. The foundation, to be established during 2001, would be chaired by Simone Veil—a prominent Jewish political figure, former cabinet minister, and member of the Constitutional Council (the college of magistrates responsible for ensuring that the constitution is respected). She had been deported to Auschwitz as a teenager. The foundation's decision-making bodies were to be made up in large part of representatives of the major French Jewish organizations. Its main goal, as expressed by Prime Minister Jospin when he met with leaders of CRIF, the Conseil Représentatif des Institutions Juives de France (Representative Council of Jewish Institutions of France), on November 4, 2000, was "to develop research and disseminate knowledge about the anti-Semitic persecutions and attacks on the rights of the human person perpetrated during the Second World War, as well as about the victims of these persecutions." The foundation was also supposed to support initiatives taken by associations helping victims of persecution, keep track of efforts to restore goods plundered by the Nazis, and contribute to the education of French children about this period of history.

JEWISH COMMUNITY

Education

There were about 100 Jewish schools offering full-time instruction. Private schools remained a minority phenomenon in France. Most French children were educated in public schools, and the Ministry of National Education was directly responsible for all aspects of the curriculum of these schools. Only 16 percent of children attended private schools, the vast majority of which—about 80 percent—were Catholic.

Most of the Jewish schools operated under contract with the Ministry of National Education and followed the rules laid down by the 1959 act that governs "free schools," that is private schools. A small number of private schools were not under contract, and thus could determine their own curricula. However under legislation governing compulsory education to the age of 16, authorities had oversight over the content of these curricula to ensure that each student received sufficient instruction so that he or she could later transfer to a school under contract with the ministry. The "without-contract" formula existed mostly at the primary level; at higher levels of education the "under-contract" formula was more widespread. (To make things more complex, the government limited the number of new classes under contract so as not to disturb the balance of budgetary allotments between public and private education, and this meant that there could be classes under contract and classes without contracts in the same private school.)

The so-called "association" contract, the kind most frequently used in Jewish schools, distinguished between the subjects also taught in the public schools and those specific to the special mission of the private school, in this case Jewish studies. For the general subjects, a private school under contract had to follow the program and the number of hours allotted per week as determined by the ministry. The government paid the salaries of teachers of general subjects directly, and also made a lump-sum payment toward the cost of running the school. Other costs, notably salaries for Jewish-studies teachers, were the responsibility of the school, which passed them on to the parents in the form of tuition fees.

A growing number of Jewish families, eager to instill Jewish identity in their children and also aware of the declining educational level of many of the public schools, were willing to make the financial sacrifice. In 2000 there were about 24,000 students in Jewish schools that had at least some classes operating under contract with the Ministry of National Education, as compared to 16,500 students ten years earlier. A little over 80 percent studied in classes under contract, and the rest in classes without contracts. The number of students in Jewish schools operating entirely without contracts was estimated at 2,000–2,500, so that, in all, there were more than 26,000 students in Jewish day schools. On the basis of prevailing assumptions about the Jewish population of France and its demographic structure, that would represent some 20–25 percent of the relevant age group.

In a sense, the Jewish school system in France was growing too fast, without the resources to match its numerical strength. The quality of the 500–600 teachers specializing in Jewish subjects was uneven. Their training was in some cases inadequate, and their lack of real status put them at the mercy of all-powerful principals, a situation that did not encourage innovation. Furthermore, the fragmentation of the system made it hard to develop standard textbooks and other materials for Jewish education.

Communal Affairs

On June 25 Jean Kahn was reelected president of the Central Consistory of France, the organization responsible for the administration of Jewish religious affairs in the country, with 70 percent of the vote.

In Paris, the year 2000 was marked by the dedication of a number of public spaces to the memory of Jewish figures. Place Jacob Kaplan, named after the former chief rabbi of France, was inaugurated near Paris's most important synagogue, the Synagogue de la Victoire. A garden in one of the city's new green spaces was named Jardin Itzhak Rabin. And finally, those who had helped save Jews during the Holocaust were honored when a street near the Memorial to the Unknown Jewish Martyr, in central Paris near the banks of the Seine, was given the name Allée des Justes.

Kosher Slaughter

An interesting legal case concerning kosher slaughter concluded in 2000. For years, Chaaré Shalom VeTsedek, a Jewish association, had fought the French government for the authority to carry out ritual slaughter. Regulations in France, as in a number of other European countries, provide that animals have to be immobilized and stunned—that is, rendered unconscious—before being put to death. An exception is made for the Jewish religion to allow kosher slaughter, but only if the slaughterer has certification from the "intercommunity rabbinical commission" recognized by the French government (more precisely, by the Ministry of Agriculture, acting on the recommendation of the Ministry of the Interior). This commission, in turn, is under the authority of the Paris Consistory— which in legal terms is the representative of the Central Consistory, the body that, since the time of Napoleon I, has been the government's partner of choice for everything related to the Jewish religion.

In practice, the Paris Consistory allowed a number of other religious organizations to be represented on the commission, thus delegating some of its authority in this area to these organizations, which represented "strictly observant" groups, some of which had their own kashrut labels. However some certified slaughterers seceded from the consistory entirely and provided kosher meat independently. This was the origin of the Chaaré Shalom VeTsedek association, which provided meat to some 20 butcher shops and ten restaurants in the Paris region, and frozen meat to several dozen stores outside Paris, for sale to consumers. Chaaré Shalom VeTsedek was actually slaughtering animals illegally, since only the commission run by the Paris Consistory could certify ritual slaughterers. It was against this state of affairs that the association brought its complaint, claiming that the consistory's monopoly violated French law as well as international agreements to which France was a signatory.

There was more at stake here than met the eye. Jewish religious organizations in France were financially dependent on revenue from services provided to religious Jews, especially the tax levied for placing the "kosher" label on food products. The Paris Consistory charged a slaughtering tax of about eight francs per kilogram of meat ready for sale, and this alone made up half of the consistory's revenue. Chaaré Shalom VeTsedek's tax was half that, four francs per kilogram. Not surprisingly, the consistory made every effort to retain its monopoly.

The French government preferred the monopoly principle as well, for its own reasons. It has traditionally taken a dim view of the proliferation of religious groups, fearing a drift toward sectarianism that could pose a threat to public order. It wanted to abide by the Napoleonic concept of having a single interlocutor for each recognized religion, and thus the Ministry of the Interior backed the consistory's monopoly.

A more complicated problem looming behind the Jewish case was its possible implications for Islam. In 2000 there were more than three million Muslims in France, making them the second largest religious group in the country (behind the Catholics, of course, but well ahead of the roughly one million Protestants). Since a large majority of Muslims were immigrants or the children of immigrants, the mosques and Islamic schools had a distinctively foreign ambience. On the understanding that Islam would have to become culturally French before it could be integrated into French society and that some unified Muslim body was the best protection against the emergence of militant Islam, the government had already circulated proposals, in draft form, for the creation of a federation of French Muslims with its own institutions and training centers. In a word, the government would do everything it could to encourage the emergence of an Islamic interlocutor that would be the equivalent of the Jewish consistory. A first step would be to have one Muslim authority dealing with the provision of *halal* meat, the Islamic equivalent of kosher meat, instead of the several that were handling it. To accomplish this it was necessary to forestall the precedent that legal recognition of institutional pluralism in the area of kosher slaughtering would represent.

Initially, it was the consistory that had opened hostilities, accusing Chaaré Shalom VeTsedek of "misrepresenting merchandise" when it placed a kosher label on meat sold in its butcher shops. However a court decided in 1987 that separation of church and state did not allow it to intervene in this area. The same year, Chaaré Shalom VeTsedek appealed to public authorities, asking for certification to practice ritual slaughtering legally. The Ministry of the Interior opposed the request, maintaining that Chaaré Shalom VeTsedek was not a "representative religious group." The affair then went before the Paris administrative tribunal (in France cases concerning the operations of the state are brought before special courts), which decided in favor of the government in 1989 because the association did not carry out activities relating to "the public exercise of the Israelite religion." The State Council, the appeals court that hears cases from the administrative tribunal, upheld this decision in 1994.

Chaaré Shalom VeTsedek had only one legal recourse left: the European Court of Human Rights, sitting in Strasbourg, which heard complaints brought against European states. The association filed its complaint in 1995 and the hearing was held in December 1999. Chaaré Shalom VeTsedek accused the French government of violating its members' religious freedom. The 17 judges, representing a variety of European nations, rendered their decision on May 31, 2000, and made it public on June 27. A majority agreed with the French government that there had been no violation of religious freedom. However seven of the judges dissented, arguing that the principle of religious freedom implied respect for pluralism, and that the state should not grant a monopoly to an organization. That minority opinion, should it ever prevail, would threaten the entire relationship between government and religion in France, and have a profound impact on the future of Islam in the country.

Publications

Among the books of Jewish significance published in France during 2000 were: Marc Weitzmann's *Mariage mixte* (Mixed Marriage); Walter Appel's *L'histoire véridique d'Antón Fiddler et autres récits* (The True Story of Antón Fiddler and Other Stories); Michèle Hechter's *M. et M.* (M. and M.); Michèle Kahn's *La pourpre et le jasmin* (Purple and Jasmine); *La liberté n'est à personne* (Freedom Belongs to No One), poems by Jacques Givet; *Juste une petite valse* (Just a Little Waltz), short stories by Cyrille Fleischman; Alain Jomy's *Heureux comme à Monterey* (Happy as in Monterey); Jacques Lanzmann's *Imagine la Terre promise* (Imagine the Promised Land); Sylvie Weil's *Les vendanges de Rachi* (Rashi's Vintages); *Actes de présence* (Acts of Presence), poems by Alain Suied; and Marc Petit's *L'utopie du docteur Kakerlak* (Doctor Kakerlak's Utopia). In the realm of ideas: Henri Meschonnic's *Poétique du traduire* (The Poetics of Translation); Jacquot Grunewald's *Chalom, Jésus!* (Shalom, Jesus!); Gérard Bensussan's *Franz Rosenzweig, existence et philosophie* (Franz Rosenzweig, Existence and Philosophy); George-Elia Sarfati's *Le Vatican et la Shoah* (The Vatican and the Holocaust); Albert Memmi's *Le nomade immobile* (The Immobile Nomad); Shmuel Trigano's *Le monothéisme est un humanisme* (Montheism Is a Form of Humanism); Alain Finkielkraut's *Une voix vient de l'autre rive* (A Voice Comes from the Other Shore); and Bernard-Henri Lévy's *Le siècle de Sartre* (Sartre's Century).

Personalia

Jean Kahn, president of the Central Consistory of France, was named a commander of the Legion of Honor; and Serge Klarsfeld, lawyer and historian, was named an officer of the Legion of Honor.

Among prominent Jews who died in 2000 were Jacques Cypel, publisher until 1996 of the Yiddish daily *Unzer Wort,* 88, on January 5; Moshé Zalcmann, a former Communist who wrote a book about his life under Stalin that was translated from Yiddish into French, 92, on March 7; Lilly Scherr, academician and a leading figure in French Jewish cultural circles, 73, on March 30; Gisèle Freund, photographer born in Germany, 91, on March 31; Eliahu Ben-Elissar, Israel's ambassador to France, 68, on August 12; Serge Lebovici, psychoanalyst, 85, on August 12.

MEIR WAINTRATER

The Netherlands

National Affairs

THE NETHERLANDS REMAINED THE MOST densely populated country in Europe. Its population at the end of 2000 was nearly 16 million, about 140,000 more than a year before and one million more than at the end of 1990. The increase was due partly to natural increase and partly to immigration, mainly from third-world countries. The Dutch, in fact, were increasingly aware that they were living in a multicultural society.

The Netherlands, in 2000, experienced relative political stability and economic prosperity. The government coalition, made up of Labor (PvdA), the Conservative Liberals (VVD), and, as a minor partner, the Centrum-left Democrats 1966 (D'66), had come into office in August 1998 under the leadership of Premier Willem Kok (PvdA). Several public-opinion polls carried out during 2000, culminating in one taken at the very end of the year, showed that had a parliamentary election been held, the three largest parties—the PvdA, the VVD, and the opposition Christian Democrats (CDA)—would each have gained or lost only one seat. However, D'66, which had already lost half of its representation in the 1998 election, would have again lost heavily, and the two extreme left-wing parties—the Green Left, under Paul Rosenmoller, and the Socialist Party (SP) would have made striking gains. Remarkably, only 2.9 percent of the adult population belonged to any political party.

The economy grew at a rate of 3.5 percent, with low inflation. Exports increased by some 20 percent in 2000, in particular to Eastern Europe and the United States, and Dutch companies carried out some 300 takeovers of foreign firms, some in the United States. There was a boom in the building industry, with home prices rising astronomically due to the consumers' greater purchasing power, the shortage of houses for sale, and the relative ease in obtaining mortgages. Beside the full employment that characterized the building trades, hospitals, schools, cafés, and restaurants had great difficulty finding sufficient staff. There were, however, still about 190,000 registered unemployed, mostly people who were considered unemployable, among them many who could hardly speak Dutch.

For the first time in many years the government budget showed a surplus, amounting to some 2 percent, due to higher revenue from taxes and a reduction of government payments to the declining number of unemployed. A difference of opinion arose over what to do with this surplus, the VVD wanting to reduce the size of the considerable state debt, and the PvdA and D'66 preferring to use it for education and health care. A compromise was reached, and the money was divided to reflect the priorities of both political blocs.

In November, by a large majority, the Second Chamber of Parliament approved the practice of euthanasia so long as the patient has requested it, the physical suffering is unbearable and cannot be ameliorated, and the doctor's assessment is supported by a second opinion. There was severe criticism from abroad, in particular from the Vatican. In another controversial decision and with a similar strong majority, the Second Chamber legalized the official registration of marriage between two men or between two women. Such couples would also have the right to adopt a child, though contrary regulations in other countries would largely limit this to the adoption of Dutch children.

The number of applicants for political asylum rose from some 40,000 in 1999 to roughly 45,000 in 2000, or some 700 a week, and the shortage of space to house them necessitated the construction of additional special centers; there were four of these centers in Amsterdam alone. The majority of the asylum-seekers came from Iran, Iraq, Afghanistan, and Somalia, and it was often difficult to determine whether applicants were fleeing political persecution or had economic reasons for coming. As each case had to be judged individually, and as rejected applicants had the right to appeal—a process that could drag on for years—many of these centers remained full as the year ended, and some 53,000 cases remained unresolved. Further complicating matters, even applicants who lost their cases sometimes refused to return to their country of origin, were refused admission by that country, or claimed to have lost their identity papers. Another controversial group consisted of some 550 arrivals each month who were unaccompanied minors, or persons claiming to be minors, and who, according to international agreements, could not be returned to their countries of origin. In the expectation that asylum applications would rise drastically in 2001 due to the more stringent regulations for admission issued by neighboring Germany, Parliament voted, on December 11, to streamline the investigation process over a five-year period.

Immigrants from third-world countries and their children born in the Netherlands (the two largest groups were Moroccan and Turkish), were becoming an increasingly visible presence. Though the opening of the first Buddhist and Hindu temples in Amsterdam indicated the diverse origins of this migration, Muslims were far more numerous. Over half of them lived in the country's four largest cities, and it was estimated that within four years they would constitute 50 percent of the population in those cities. Already, non-Europeans made up the majority of students at many of the nation's elementary schools. The unemployment rate among these families was far higher than in the general population, and there was resentment at the strong links many of them maintained to their countries of origin.

There were some 50 Muslim elementary schools in the country, where, in addition to the standard Dutch curriculum, pupils were taught Islam and started the day with Muslim prayers. Like other denominational schools, they were largely financed by the government. In September, the first Muslim secondary school opened, in Rotterdam, with some 350 pupils, though it soon ran into difficulties enforcing its stringent dress code, and government inspectors found that the curriculum did not meet national standards. The year before, an Islamic University had opened in Rotterdam to train imams for the Dutch Muslim community. In Utrecht, performance of the play *Aysha,* about the wife of the Prophet Mohammed, was discontinued after Muslim protests. There was a common perception that an increasing number of young Muslims were fasting during the month of Ramadan, and a public-opinion poll showed that some 90 percent of Muslim young people intended to follow the religion of their parents, as compared to 27 percent for both Protestants and Roman Catholics.

Israel and the Middle East

Holland generally conformed to the European Union's Middle East policy. A nonpermanent member of the UN Security Council in the second half of 2000, the Netherlands was consistently critical of Israeli policy in the territories, and voted for the October 7 Security Council resolution (passed 14-0, with the U.S. abstaining) criticizing Israel. It abstained, though, along with six other EU states, from the October 20 General Assembly vote that blamed Israel for the upsurge in violence.

Premier Kok visited Israel and the Palestinian autonomous areas in April. He placed a wreath at Yad Vashem, met with President Weizman and Prime Minister Barak, and spoke at length with Platform Israel, an organization of Dutch-born Israeli Jews, about the restitution of Holocaust-era assets. In Bethlehem, Yasir Arafat presented Kok with a medal. A Dutch trade delegation, led by the minister of trade and industry, visited Israel in May. Throughout the year the Dutch Foreign Ministry sought to use its influence to help the Iranian Jews imprisoned in that country.

Pro-Palestinian circles in the Netherlands took steps to upgrade their public relations. In Rotterdam, the Al Aqsa Foundation was established with the aim of promoting understanding for the Palestinian cause. Another new body was the Palestinian Information Center, set up to counter the work of the pro-Israel Center for Information and Documentation on Israel (CIDI). A Palestinian tourist office was also launched to promote tourism to the Palestinian areas. Heightened Dutch sensitivity to Palestinian opinion became evident at the end of May, when the Pritzker Prize for architecture was presented to the (non-Jewish) Dutch architect Rem Koolhaas at the Western Wall in Jerusalem, with a representative of the Dutch embassy present. Palestinians immediately protested that the wall was occupied Palestinian territory. Not only did the government of the Netherlands apologize, but Koolhaas himself visited the West Bank hoping to make amends.

The outbreak of violence in Israel and the territories that broke out at the end of September received enormous attention in the Dutch news media, much of it sympathetic to the Palestinians. In addition to regular reports from Dutch correspondents in Israel, there was considerable coverage of the views of Dutch-born children of Palestinians and Dutch women or men whose Palestinian spouses were living in the Palestinian areas. Soon after the violence began, Moroccan youths demonstrated in Amsterdam against Israel and against Jews, shouting, "Hamas, Hamas, all Jews to the gas." At the annual national commemoration of Kristallnacht on November 10, where the theme was to have been opposition to racism and anti-Semitism, Abdou Menehbi, chairman of the Committee of Moroccan Workers in the Netherlands (KMAN) and of the newly established Society of Moroccans in Amsterdam, attacked Israel and advocated a Palestinian state. When some of the Jewish organizers objected, they were accused of stifling free speech. The pro-Palestinian InterChurch Broadcasting Company Netherlands (IKON) sent a group of young people to spend three weeks in Palestinian-controlled areas so that, on their return, they could inform the public of the Palestinian viewpoint. Liesbeth Cottof, after a visit to Gaza, wrote and produced a play for children, *The Day My Father Wept,* on the suffering of the Palestinians. In November, Dutch insurance companies announced that they would no longer cover travelers to Israel and the Palestinian Authority, with the exception of the southern port of Eilat.

Most disturbing, an advertisement titled "A Different Jewish Voice" appeared in Dutch newspapers on October 26 and 27. Signed by 100 Jews and persons of Jewish origin, it protested Israel's allegedly violent and arrogant behavior toward the Palestinians. The initiator of the ad was Anneke Mouthaan, an elderly woman, one of whose parents was Jewish, who had lived for a long time in the Dutch East Indies and was a leading voice in SIVMO, the Foundation for Peace in the Middle East.

Pro-Israel voices tended to be weaker. With the outbreak of the fighting, the country's Orthodox rabbis called on the Jewish community to support Israel. At the end of October, 20 Christian organizations organized a "Christians for Israel" solidarity demonstration in Amersfoort. In early November Ephraim Sneh, Israel's deputy minister of defense, visited Holland to explain the Israeli point of view, but he drew little attention. On the other hand, a meeting with Shimon Peres later that month, organized by the Center for Information and Documentation on Israel (CIDI) in The Hague, attracted a capacity audience despite the lack of advance publicity. Mr. Peres was also received by Premier Kok.

The specter of the 1992 crash of an El Al 747 cargo plane over the Bijlmer area in the southeastern tip of Amsterdam still haunted the country's relations with Israel. A parliamentary inquiry into the matter, whose proceedings were televised, gave much attention to the possibility that the cargo contained poisonous materials, perhaps of a secret military character, and that the health of the local residents and those who had helped them deal with the crash might have been damaged. The fact that the plane's voice recorder was never found added to the suspicions, as did Israel's reluctance to hand over some relevant documents.

The commission finally presented its report on April 21, 2000, and it was less unfavorable to Israel and to El Al than had been feared. It found no evidence of any conspiracy to cover up the truth, though it did give credence to some of the complaints of those who had been near the crash site that their health had been affected. The Second Chamber of Parliament discussed the report in May, and decided that the government should pay for medical examinations of all those who had physical complaints that might be related to the Bijlmer disaster. The small original number rose to 38 after a personal-injury lawyer went around collecting names, and by the end of the year there were about 5,000 people seeking the financial compensation made available to those with proof that a health problem was related to the crash. Most hospitals, arguing that too much time had passed to determine the health effects of the crash, refused to conduct examinations, so that in the end only two Amsterdam hospitals performed them. As it turned out, only a small number of those who had originally registered for the exams kept their appointments, and even so, the exams were not completed by the end of the year. Evidence of declining popular interest in the case came on October 4, when the annual commemoration of the crash drew only a few hundred people.

Anti-Semitism and Extremism

In contrast to the situation in Belgium and France, no extreme right-wing political party was represented in the Dutch Parliament. The Center Democrats (CD), who had lost their only seat in the Second Chamber of Parliament in 1998, were insignificant, and the even more extreme Nederlandse Volks Unie had dwindled down to a few diehards. There was apparently a very strong social taboo against anti-Semitism, indeed, against racism generally, which was all the more remarkable in light of the large number of immigrants from third-world countries. Indeed, such immigrants and their Dutch-born children were represented in the Second Chamber of Parliament and in several municipal councils. Despite an alarming increase in the crime rate, few incidents were of a racial or anti-Semitic nature. The theme of the annual pop festival north of Amsterdam that drew tens of thousands of young people was "Racism — Beat It," though the participants were surely more attracted by the music than by the theme.

Holocaust-Related Matters

The renovated Anne Frank House in Amsterdam was officially reopened on April 24 by Prime Minister Kok, and it sponsored an exhibit on "The Seductions of Nationalism." The Holocaust was also commemorated during the year with ceremonies at a number of other places: Schoorl, near Alkmaar, which in 1941 served for some months as a concentration camp from where the inmates were deported to Mauthausen; Rotterdam, near the former Shed 24, from which the first Jews were deported on July 24, 1942; Hollandse Schouwburg, the disused Amsterdam theater which served as the collecting point for Jews to be deported to Westerbork from 1942 till 1944; and Buitenveldert, the new southern suburb of Amsterdam, where a modest monument was unveiled depicting a Jewish child guided to a hiding place by a non-Jewish man.

The appearance of a Dutch translation of Norman Finkelstein's controversial book *The Holocaust Industry: Reflections on the Exploitation of Jewish Suffering,* which accused Jewish organizations of using the Holocaust for their own ends, received considerable publicity, and several interviews with Finkelstein appeared in the Dutch media. He delivered a lecture in Amsterdam to a capacity audience, and, in reply to a question, said that he knew nothing about the Holocaust in Holland. In May, the Amsterdam Higher Court of Justice fined the French Holocaust denier Robert Faurisson for publicly declaring that Anne Frank's diary was a forgery.

Interest grew about the postwar indifference with which non-Jewish individuals and institutions treated the Jews who emerged from hiding or returned from the camps. A new foundation, SOTO, was established, under the auspices of the Netherlands Institute for War Documentation (NIOD), to have some 40 young people interview survivors about their experiences. The plan was to publish these interviews in book form in 2001.

The determination of the amount of the "gold pool" and its first distributions were made in 2000. This was monetary gold, most of it originally held by the Netherlands State Bank (DNB), that the Germans had taken during the Nazi occupation and transferred to Switzerland, which had not returned it to the Netherlands till April 1999. This gold could not be proven to belong to the Jewish community or to individual Jews. The Kordes commission, set up by the government, had decided that Fl. 19 million should go to the Dutch Jewish community for cultural projects, and a much smaller amount for the Dutch victims of the Japanese occupation of the Dutch East Indies.

The distribution of the Jewish share was determined by a second commission, headed by Dick Dolman, a former chairman of the Second Chamber of Parliament and of the Netherlands-Israel Society, and whose other members represented the Committee of Jewish Organizations on External Matters (CJOEB). This body had been set up in 1997, before the problem of Jewish assets arose, to provide a common Jewish representation to the outside world, and to the Dutch government in particular. The six members of the CJOEB represented the three national Jewish congregations, the Federation of Dutch Zionists (FNZ), which existed mainly on paper, the Center for Information and Documentation on Israel (CIDI), and the Jewish Social Welfare Board (JMW). A considerable amount of the money was given to the newly established Crescas Foundation, which would provide popular courses on subjects of Jewish interests in communities throughout the country. Other beneficiaries were the Etz Haim Library, the weekly *Nieuw Israelitisch Weekblad* (NIW), the Bibliotheca Rosenthaliana for repair of books and manuscripts, and a project to compile a biographical lexicon of Jews or persons of Jewish origin who contributed significantly to 20th-century Dutch life.

The three other Dutch commissions appointed to investigate aspects of the restitution issue published their final reports in December 1999 and January 2000. These were the Van Kemenade Commission, which dealt with the general question of compensation, the Scholten Commission, dealing with Jewish assets held by banks and insurance companies, and the Ekkart Commission, which focused on artworks in Dutch museums that had been confiscated from Jews.

Claims of individual Dutch Jews who had lived in the Netherlands at any time between May 10, 1940 and May 8, 1945 (and their heirs) against the government, insurance companies, and banks, were coordinated for the Jewish community by the CJOEB. A key role on the Jewish side of the negotiations was also played by Awraham Roet of Tel Aviv, the Dutch-born representative of Platform Israel, an ad hoc organization representing the interests of Jews of Dutch origin in Israel. The World Jewish Congress (WJC), headquartered in New York, was involved as well, though the aggressive nature of its intervention alienated many Dutch Jews.

When the government, the banks, and the insurance companies originally balked at paying the sums demanded by the CJOEB, the American state of Minnesota threatened to block the takeover by the Dutch bank ING of Reliastar in Minneapolis, and the WJC threatened to prevent the Dutch insurance company AEGON from setting up an office in the United States. The CJOEB was eventually satisfied with the solution offered by AEGON, by which some 95 percent of all life-insurance policies taken over from defunct companies whose beneficiaries could not be traced must be paid to Jewish survivors or their "deputies." AEGON had, in fact, already honored all policies whose beneficiaries could be located. In the end, all the insurance companies together agreed to pay Fl. 50 million. Of this, Fl. 20 million would go for individual claims that might be submitted thereafter, Fl. 25 million to a foundation to be decided on by the Jewish community, and Fl. 5 million for a monument commemorating the Jews who perished.

Negotiations with the government and the banks were much more difficult. The banks pointed out that in 1953, after much litigation, they had paid back 90 percent of the value of shares confiscated from Jewish shareholders or their heirs. The CJOEB, however, wanted the remaining amount multiplied by 22 to compensate for the accrued interest. The government made a tentative offer of Fl. 250 million, later increased to Fl. 400 million, and the banks offered Fl. 314 million. Together with the insurance companies' Fl. 50 million, the total would come to Fl. 764 million. Of that amount, Fl. 639 million would go to individual Jews or their heirs—including non-Jewish spouses and children of mixed marriages who were not Jews according to Halakhah, and who, it turned out, were almost half of the recipients—and the rest to Jewish institutions. Individuals qualifying for payments would receive about Fl. 14,000 ($5,600). Children of deceased persons who qualified for payment would have to share the sum allotted to the parent. Each person could receive only one payment, including survivors who were also heirs of survivors who died after 1945. Payments were exempt from income tax, and the amount would not count in calculating old-age pensions and other government payments.

The CJOEB and Platform Israel were generally satisfied with the settlement.

Strong criticism, however, came from the Association of Victims of Persecution (VBV), which complained that the CJOEB was unrepresentative of the Jewish community since it encompassed only the religious congregations and the Zionist organization, and charged that no money should go to Jews already married to non-Jews during the war and their children, since few of them were deported. Eight VBV members asked the president of the Amsterdam Court of Justice to set aside the settlement, but were turned down. An appeal to the Higher Court of Justice was pending as the year ended.

Advertisements were placed in the local and foreign press giving information about applying for the payments. Some 8,000 applications had been made by the end of 2000, and, on the last day of the year, the first 80 payments were made, all to persons over the age of 75. This settlement created bad feeling among other victimized groups. Those interned or used for slave labor by the Japanese in the Dutch East Indies, of whom 144,000 were still alive, resented the fact that their compensation was far less per person than that received by the Jews, and some 200 Dutch-Jewish immigrants in Israel who, or whose parents had, lived in the Dutch East Indies during the war were upset that they were treated like the other victims of the Japanese and not like the Jewish victims of the Nazis.

The Ekkart Commission concluded that few objects held by Dutch museums were of dubious origin. Those that were had been acquired at auctions during the war years, and there was no way, today, of ascertaining how those who offered them for auction had acquired them. The policy already adopted by the museums was to return the items to anyone who could prove that he or she was the original owner. The case of the Goudstikker collection, housed in a number of Dutch museums, (see AJYB 1998, pp. 276–77, 1999 pp. 313–14) dragged on. A Hague court had decided in 1999 that, by accepting a cash settlement in 1952, the widow of art dealer Jacques Goudstikker had waived all further claims to the collection. Meanwhile, both she and her only son had died, and her non-Jewish daughter-in-law, Meryl Von Saher, and her two daughters, living in New York, challenged the court decision. Russia, for its part, still refused to return archives and art objects removed from Holland by the Germans and transferred to Moscow by the Soviet army.

JEWISH COMMUNITY

Demography

The results of a demographic survey of the Jews in the Netherlands, carried out by the Netherlands Interdisciplinary Demographic Institute (NIDI) at the request of the Jewish Social Welfare Board (JMV), were published in October 2000. This was the first such survey in 35 years. It found a total of 45,000 Jews living in the Netherlands, of whom 7,000 had come from Israel and another 2,000 from other countries. Of the 36,000 Jews who had Dutch citizenship, nearly half were children of mixed marriages. Though clearly a result of the trend towards assimilation, the fact that, during the German occupation, Jews married to non-Jews and their children were generally exempt from deportation, contributed to the relatively high percentage of these survivors. Only some 26 percent of Jews belonged to a Jewish congregation, 16.5 percent to the Ashkenazi Congregation (NIK), 7.5 percent to the Liberal Jewish Congregation, and 2 percent to the Sephardi Congregation. Just 7 percent of Dutch Jews said they kept kosher. Of the members of the largest religious group, the Ashkenazi Congregation, two-thirds lived in the four largest urban areas — with Amsterdam and its suburb Amstelveen having the highest number — 19 percent resided in middle-sized municipalities, and 15 percent in small towns and villages.

Communal Affairs

The NIK appointed Yehuda Vorst, a son of Rabbi Isaac Vorst of Amsterdam, as a pastoral worker in Rotterdam. Both father and son belonged to Chabad-Lubavitch. The government considerably increased the allotment of radio and television broadcasting time to the NIK.

The Sephardi Congregation, whose declining numbers were concentrated in the Amsterdam area, lacked sufficient revenues to maintain its autonomous institutions. Thus the monthly *Habinjan* of the Amsterdam Sephardi Congregation, which had existed since 1946, now shrunk to a four-page insert in *Hakehilloth,* the quarterly published by the NIK. Part of the Sephardi congregation of Amsterdam held its Sabbath services in a house in Amstelveen, as their old synagogue in the center of Amsterdam was too far to walk. The Sephardim, however, declined to amalgamate with the Amstelveen Ashkenazi synagogue since they wanted to adhere to their own liturgy. The Sephardim had no full-time rabbi, though Awraham Rosenberg, the keeper of the community's Etz Haim Library, served as rabbinical assistant, and a Sephardi rabbi from London would occasionally visit.

The restoration of the Etz Haim Library was completed with money from the government gold pool (see above, p. 346). The many old books and manuscripts that had been transferred in 1967 to the Jewish National Library in Jerusalem on loan so as to prevent their deterioration were returned to Etz Haim in the autumn of 2000, and the collection was made accessible to the public. Also restored, through the assistance of volunteers, were several tombstones in the nearly 400-year-old Sephardi burial ground, Beth Haim, at Ouderkerk-on-the-Amstel, southeast of Amsterdam.

The Liberal Jewish Congregation (LJG), which received $700,000 from the gold pool, now consisted of eight local congregations, though not all of them held a service every Sabbath. The congregation of Tilburg, in the province of Noord-Brabant, restored and took over the former Ashkenazi synagogue there. At its inauguration ceremony, a number of non-Jews who had studied for conversion were officially admitted as Jews. After many years of preparation, the LJG issued a new prayer book, compiled by the country's six Liberal rabbis. Beside the original Hebrew text, it also contained translations from American Conservative and Reform prayer books, along with translations of modern Hebrew poems. The first edition sold out even before publication.

Culture

A number of Jewish periodicals continued to appear in the Netherlands. The *Nieuw Israelitisch Weekblad* (NIW), founded in 1862, was the only Jewish weekly in the country. *Joods Journaal* was a glossy bimonthly color magazine directed at "yuppies." The Netherlands Society for Jewish Genealogy put out the quarterly *Misjpoge*. *Studia Rosenthaliana,* the biannual publication of the Bibliotheca Rosenthaliana, was taken over by a new publisher and was now entirely in English. In the fall of 2000, the first issue of *Di Grine Medine* appeared, published by the recently founded Society for the Promotion of Yiddish in the Netherlands. This was the country's first Yiddish periodical in two centuries.

Two extensive private libraries were opened to the public. One was the Yiddish library of Mira Rafalowicz, who passed away in 1998, which would now be housed in the building of the Liberal Jewish Congregation in Amsterdam. The other was the library of the late Leo Fuks, keeper of the Bibliotheca Rosenthaliana in Amsterdam, which he had willed to the provincial library of Friesland, in Leeuwarden, in gratitude for the help that many residents of this province gave Jews during the German occupation. Very few Jews now live there.

Several symposia on Jewish culture took place. The Maatschappij tot Nut der Israelieten (Society for the Benefit of the Jews), which helps support Jewish institutions, celebrated its 150th anniversary in January with a symposium on the Jewish future. On March 21 there was a symposium in Amsterdam on the subject of Turkish Jewry, arranged with the cooperation of the Turkish embassy. On May 7, a symposium was held in Amersfoort on the relations between Jews in the main cities and the provinces. This was to mark the 25-year jubilee of Rabbi Benjamin Jacobs as rabbi of the NIK for Jews outside the country's three main cities. An international Sephardi conference, attended mostly by scholars, was held in Amsterdam on October 25–27.

In other cultural news, the JMW (Jewish Social Welfare Board) held a meeting on May 22 for persons of Jewish origin who had been brought up as Christians. Half of the 34 participants had been baptized before 1940. The JMW also released "The Jewish Caravan" consisting of "cultural kits" on Jewish literature, Jewish cooking, and Jewish folk music. In August, the Amsterdam Summer University offered a course in English on the kabbalah and Jewish mysticism, which was very well attended. The lecturers and most of the students came from abroad. The annual Jewish Book Week, held in October in Amsterdam, was devoted to the work of the American novelist Philip Roth. Two important CDs appeared, one featuring the compositions of the Dutch-Jewish composer Leo Smit, who perished in 1943, and the other containing the Ashkenazi liturgy for the High Holy Days, performed by the prewar choir of the Amsterdam Great Synagogue and conducted by the late S. H. Englander.

A number of Jewish art exhibits were held. A special exhibit for children at the Jewish Historical Museum (JHM) in Amsterdam, open until the end of the year 2001, provided basic information about Jewish life and practices. There, and in the museum in Groningen, where he was born, there were simultaneous exhibitions of the work of the Dutch-Jewish painter Joseph Israels (1844–1911). The JHM also featured an exhibition of the work of the Dutch-Jewish photographer Sem Presser (1917–1986). During the summer, the Israeli embassy in The Hague exhibited 43 miniatures of buildings in Israel at the miniature village of Madurodam in Scheveningen.

Publications

Important publications included: a revised and augmented edition of *Pinkas, a Survey of the History of the Jews in the Netherlands,* by Dan Michman, Joseph Michman, and Hartog Beem, with a new chapter on recent developments by Johan Sanders; two anthologies of stories by Jewish authors—Daphne Meijer, ed., *Levi in de Lage Landen* (Levi in the Low Countries) and Maarten Verhoef and Thijs Wierema, *Aggenebbis* (Anthology); Michal Citroen, *U wordt door niemand Verwacht* (You Are Not Expected by Anybody), on the chilling reception of Jews emerging from hiding or returning from the camps in 1945; Dienke Hondius, *Terugkeer naar Nederland* (Return to The Netherlands); Peter den Hollander, *De Zaak Goudstikker* (The Goudstikker Affair); Frans Van Der Straaten, *Palestinian pioneers in Nederland,* on training centers for halutzim in the Netherlands until 1940; I.J. van Creveld, *Jewish Artists in The Hague,* with many illustrations; *Keur van Grastenen,* a reprint of D. Henriques de Castro, *op de Portuguese Begraafplaats te Ouderkerk-aan de Amstel* (Tombstones at the Sephardi Burial Ground ar Ouderkerk-on-the Amstel); J.W. Stutje, *De man die de Weg wees* (The Man Who Showed the Way), a biography of the Jewish Communist leader Paul de Groot; M. Poorthuis and Theo Salemink, *Op zoek near de Blauwe Ruiter,* a biography of Sophie (Francisca) van Leer, who converted to Catholicism and worked for better understanding between Catholics and Jews; Edith Samuel, ed., *Rose Jacobs, een roos die nooit bloeide* (A Rose that Never Flourished), the diary of the editor's sister who remained in hiding through the war and was killed by an allied bomb on the first day of the liberation of Nijmegen; and Ed van Thijn (a former mayor of Amsterdam), *Het Verhaal* (The Story), an autobiography.

Personalia

Professor Job Cohen was appointed to a six-year term as mayor of Amsterdam by a unanimous vote of the cabinet in December 2000. Cohen was the city's fourth mayor of Jewish origin within the past 35 years. A member of the Labor Party (PvdA), he was not actively engaged in Jewish life.

Author Marga Minco received the Anna Bijns Prize for feminist literature, for her entire oeuvre, including the short novel *The Bitter Herb.*

Bill Minco, chairman of the former resistance group Geuzenverzet, received an award from Germany for his efforts to enhance Dutch-German rapprochement.

Judith Frishman, wife of the Liberal rabbi Edward van Voolen, was appointed professor of the history and literature of rabbinic Judaism at the Roman Catholic University of Utrecht.

Bettina Sanders succeeded Hetty van Emden as chair of the Jewish Women's Society "Deborah."

Baruch Bar Tel was named chair of the Irgun Oleh Holland, the Society of Immigrants from Holland in Israel, succeeding Mirjam Dubi, who retired after eight years of service and was made an officer in the Dutch Order of Orange-Nassau.

Tamarah Benima retired as editor-in-chief of the *Nieuw Israelitisch Weekblad* (NIW), and was replaced by Carina Cassuto.

Tom De Swaan succeeded Mrs. Ted Musaph as chair of the board of governors of the Jewish Historical Museum in Amsterdam, a post she had held for 25 years.

Sem Dresden, professor emeritus in French and general literature at the University of Leyden, received the Joost van de Vondel Prize for his essays.

Sam Behar became chairman of the Genootschap voor de Joodse Wetenschap (Jewish Historical Society), succeeding M. S. Nihom.

Prominent Jews who died were Professor August D. Belinfante, 88, former rector of the University of Amsterdam and professor of administrative law; A.J.Z. Cohen, 90, active in the anti-Nazi resistance and initiator of many Jewish organizations in the Netherlands, in particular the ultra-Orthodox Cheider School; Professor J.W. Cohen, 77, professor of applied mathematics in Delft and then in Utrecht; Benjamin W. De Jongh, 84, in Israel, longtime secretary of the NIK and of the Ashkenazi Congregation of Amsterdam; David Goudsmit, 90, for many years a teacher at the Netherlands Rabbinical Seminary in Amsterdam and a traveling Jewish-studies instructor throughout the Netherlands; actor Lex Goudsmit, 86, known for his portrayal of Tevye; Johan Kaufman, 82, a former Dutch diplomat with the UN; Freddy Marks, 80, for many years Netherlands chair of WIZO; Jacob Parsser, 90, a leader of Amsterdam Orthodox Jewry; S. Slagter, 75, former president of the criminal court of the Amsterdam Court of Justice, who chaired the council in charge of payments on the basis of the Law on Victims of Persecution (WUV); Paula Salomon, 102, gifted singer and singing teacher; Professor Philip van Praag, 85, professor emeritus in demography at the University of Brussels; and Dr. Emanuel A. M. Speyer, 95, a leader of Revisionist Zionism in Holland.

HENRIETTE BOAS

Italy and the Vatican

National Affairs

IN APRIL, ITALIAN PRIME MINISTER Massimo D'Alema resigned after center-left candidates received a drubbing in regional elections. Giuliano Amato replaced him.

The interrelated issues of immigration and racism were major themes throughout the year. One catalyst for this was the entry of Jörg Haider's far-right Freedom Party (FPÖ) into the Austrian government in February. Upon the announcement of the inclusion of Haider's party in the ruling coalition, more than 5,000 people demonstrated outside the Austrian embassy in Rome. They included leftist politicians and Jewish leaders, among them the elderly chief rabbi of Rome, Elio Toaff. Italian Jewish leaders warmly backed the European Union's sanctions against Austria.

Haider's ascent had serious local repercussions, since he had long attempted to forge links with right-wing forces in Italy, particularly in the northeastern part of the country that borders Austria's Carinthia region, where he was governor. Indeed, he went so far as to float the idea that parts of northeastern Italy might merge with Carinthia. Italian far-right groups staged several pro-Haider demonstrations. In early February the center-right administration of the Friuli-Venezia Giulia region approved a motion of solidarity with Haider and implied that it would invite him to visit the San Sabba Nazi concentration camp outside of Trieste. Israel, in protest, canceled a diplomatic visit to Trieste. On February 9 Amos Luzzatto, president of the Union of Italian Jewish Communities (UCEI), met with Prime Minister D'Alema to express the Jewish community's concern about possible visits by Haider to Italy. On February 24 Italian president Carlo Azeglio Ciampi made a symbolically important visit to San Sabba where he stated that "nostalgia for ideologies of hate" must be rejected.

Haider did visit Italy several times during the year. In July the mayor of the northern beach resort of Jesolo, a former member of Italy's secessionist Northern League, presented Haider with the keys to the city. About 100 protesters clashed with police. After Haider visited Venice in late July, Italian foreign minister Lamberto Dini protested to Austria, saying that it was "unacceptable" for Haider to come to Italy for "purposes of political propaganda."

Haider visited Rome in mid-December to present the Vatican Christmas tree, a gift from Carinthia, to Pope John Paul II. While many of the protests against him were peaceful, riot police used tear gas and truncheons against hundreds of protesters who tried to march on St. Peter's Square while Haider was taking part in a tree-lighting ceremony. Comments by Haider before and during the visit, in which he criticized President Ciampi and accused Italy of being soft on illegal immigration, drew a sharp protest from the Italian government and threatened to trigger a diplomatic dispute.

Cardinal Giacomo Biffi of Bologna sparked a furor in September when he issued a pastoral letter warning that Muslim immigration could endanger the country and calling on Italy to "save the identity of the nation." Describing Muslims as fundamentalists who do not integrate into mainstream European society, he said that Europe would be the loser if it did not reclaim its Christian identity. Controversy over his stand intensified in October when the Northern League demonstrated against the construction of a mosque in the northern town of Lodi.

Israel and the Middle East

Throughout the year there were numerous visits and exchanges between Israel and Italy on all levels: political, commercial, cultural, scholarly, and touristic. Of particular note, many Catholic Italians traveled to Israel on pilgrimages marking the Roman Catholic Holy Year.

In February Israeli deputy defense minister Ephraim Sneh visited Italy, where, among other things, he was guest of honor at a gala event in Milan kicking off the 2000 campaign of Keren Hayesod, which raises money for Israel. That same month, Leah Rabin gave the keynote speech inaugurating the academic year at Roma Tre University. Italian opposition leader Silvio Berlusconi, head of the center-right Freedom Alliance, visited Israel in March. In May the University of Bologna awarded an honorary degree to Aharon Barak, president of Israel's Supreme Court, during a two-day "Bologna-Jerusalem" seminar on the judiciary. In July Mayor Gabriele Albertini of Milan visited Israel. When Mayor Francesco Rutelli of Rome came to Israel, he accepted a "Righteous among the Nations" award presented posthumously to his grandfather, Mario Gentili, a shopkeeper who saved a Jewish employee during the Shoah.

In August acting Israeli foreign minister Shlomo Ben-Ami visited Italy. Prime Minister Amato told him that Italy, both as a member of the European Union and as a partner of Israel and the Palestinian Authority, would continue to support the peace process and do what it could to foster a solution. Yasir Arafat also visited, meeting with Italian leaders in February.

The upsurge of violence between Israelis and Palestinians that began at the end of September prompted security to be bolstered at synagogues, embassies, Jewish and international schools, and airports. There were no instances of attacks against synagogues or other Jewish sites. A few clashes did take place in Rome, in October, between right-wing extremists demonstrating in favor of Palestinians and young Jewish militants. Italian Jewish leaders blasted what they said was one-sided media coverage that cast blame for the crisis on Israel and inflamed anti-Semitic feelings. Leone Paserman, the head of the Rome Jewish community, accused the Italian mass media of conducting "a disinformation campaign that nourishes anti-Israel and anti-Jewish hatred." In October, RAI, Italy's state-run television network, pulled out its Jerusalem correspondent, Ricardo Cristiani, after he wrote a letter, published in an Arab newspaper, apologizing to the Palestinian Authority for airing film of the lynching of two Israeli soldiers in Ramallah. The Israeli government press office had already suspended the reporter's accreditation. On the diplomatic front, Prime Minister Amato and Foreign Minister Dini met in Rome with former Israeli prime minister Shimon Peres during a trip by Peres to several European capitals in October, and offered to host a Middle East peace summit in Rome.

Elsewhere in the region, Italy expanded political and economic ties with Libya, its former colony. In August Dini met with Libyan leader Muammar Qaddafi in Tripoli and told him that Italy wanted closer political and economic relations as well as more tourism between the two countries. In December, at a meeting in Rome with Libya's foreign minister, Dini signed a series of agreements furthering such bilateral ties.

Vatican-Mideast Relations

On February 15 the Vatican and the PLO, which had established formal relations in 1994, signed a "Basic Agreement between the Holy See and the Palestine Liberation Organization," and Yasir Arafat met privately with Pope John Paul II. The new document governing relations between the two parties touched on bilateral issues, including the status of church institutions in Palestinian-ruled areas. But its preamble gave considerable attention to Jerusalem, calling for an internationally mandated "special statute" for the city. This led Israel to accuse the Vatican of interfering in its negotiations with the Palestinians.

Pope John Paul II's historic visit to the Holy Land, March 21–26, dominated relations between the Vatican and Middle East countries in the early part of the year. (Also see "Jewish-Catholic Relations" below.) The trip marked the realization of his long-held dream of making a pilgrimage to biblical sites to mark the millennium year 2000, which the Church declared a Holy Year. This pilgrimage began February 23 with a "virtual pilgrimage" to Ur, the ancient town in Iraq revered as the birthplace of Abraham. Since plans for an actual papal visit there fell through when Iraqi officials said they could not ensure security or adequately organize the event, the pope presided instead over a ceremony at the Vatican that included readings from the Bible and a film of Ur's desert ruins amid props—including torches, oak trees, and a big boulder representing the stone on which Abraham nearly sacrificed Isaac. The next day he flew to Egypt for a three-day visit. He flew around the summit of Mt. Sinai in an Egyptian military plane and prayed at the Monastery of St. Catherine at the foot of the mountain.

Then, in March, he visited Christian, Jewish, and Muslim sites in Israel, Jordan, and the Palestinian territories in what was considered the most politically and religiously sensitive trip of his pontificate. Some 18,000 Israeli police and 4,000 soldiers were mobilized to maintain order and security. On the final day of the trip, the pope prayed at the Western Wall and inserted, in a crack between the stones, a written plea for forgiveness for centuries of Christian mistreatment of Jews. The visit was hailed as a success, although the run-up to it was marked by controversy in Israel. Leading rabbis asked the pope to postpone a Saturday mass in Nazareth in deference to Shabbat, but he did not. They also voiced concern about Christian evangelical activities targeted at Jews.

Several times during the year, the pope repeated the long-held Vatican stand that Jerusalem should be placed under international guarantee. In August, for example, after the failure of the Camp David negotiations, Vatican officials reiterated this point to visiting U.S. secretary of state Madeleine Albright and Israeli acting foreign minister Shlomo Ben-Ami. And in September, the pope stressed the issue in a message welcoming the new Israeli ambassador, Yosef Lamdan, to the Holy See. "Concerning the delicate question of Jerusalem, what is important is that the way forward be the path of dialogue and agreement, not force and imposition," he said. "What is of special concern to the Holy See is that the unique religious character of the Holy City be preserved by a special, internationally guaranteed statute."

Throughout the year, too, the pope made many statements encouraging the peace process in the Middle East and also backing Palestinian rights. The day after Shimon Peres met with senior Vatican officials in October, the pope issued a strong appeal for peace in the Middle East. In November, as violence escalated there, the pope called on leaders of both sides to return to the negotiating table, saying: "the Israelis as well as the Palestinians have the right to live in their homes with dignity and security." Also in November, the Pontifical Council for Inter-Religious Dialogue issued an appeal "to the Jewish and Palestinian people to forego violence and to take up once again that dialogue which is the only way to true peace." In September the Vatican, which has diplomatic relations with both Israel and Iran, said that it had "several times, both directly and indirectly," attempted to intercede with Iranian officials on behalf of ten Jews convicted of spying for Israel.

Holocaust-Related Developments

Numerous public events were held in Rome, Milan, and elsewhere to mark the 55th anniversary of the liberation of Auschwitz, which took place January 27, 1945. In mid-January the convention of the Democratic Party of the Left dedicated a session of its meeting to a program in remembrance of the Holocaust. On July 20 a law establishing January 27 as a national "Day of Remembrance" was officially promulgated. Writer Ernesto Galli della Loggia made a widely publicized proposal that Italy adopt the famous photo of the Warsaw ghetto child with his hands raised as a symbol of man's inhumanity to man, and display it in schools and other public places.

On the eve of Passover, the city of Rome named a street after Giorgio Perlasca, an Italian businessman who masqueraded as a Spanish diplomat during World War II and saved thousands of Jews in the Budapest ghetto. In the fall, state-run Italian television began filming a two-part miniseries based on the story of an Italian police commissioner, Giovanni Palatucci, who saved Jews during the Holocaust. Palatucci, who worked in the foreigners' office in the Adriatic port of Fiume—now known as Rijeka—that was included in Yugoslavia after World War II and is now part of Croatia, is believed to have helped some 5,000 Jewish refugees leave Fiume by ship. Discovered and arrested by the Nazis, he died in Dachau in 1945.

In 2000 the choice of an essay on the Holocaust was included, for the first time, in the mandatory state high school graduation (maturity) examination, and 17 percent of those sitting for the exam chose this essay. At a news conference at the Education Ministry in July, the CD-ROM "Destinazione Auschwitz" (Destinazione Auschwitz) was officially introduced. It was to be distributed free of charge to 10,000 high schools.

On October 16 city officials, the Rome Jewish community, and an association of World War II deportees dedicated a plaque at the track at Tiburtina Station from which more than 1,000 Roman Jews were deported to Auschwitz by the Nazi occupiers on that same date in 1944. Also in October, Mayor Albertini of Milan headed a large delegation of city officials and Jewish community leaders on an official visit to Auschwitz. The guide for the trip was Marcello Pezzetti, one of Italy's leading experts on the Shoah.

In November the International Commission of Holocaust-era Insurance Claims approved a settlement resolving all such claims against the Italian insurer Generali. The settlement was based on an agreement reached in July and, according to a statement by Generali, it provided $100 million in payments for insurance claims and provision of humanitarian assistance to Holocaust survivors.

Anti-Semitism and Racism

In February Italy's ministers of interior and sports decided that those in charge of security at soccer stadiums might halt matches if fans displayed racist banners. For years, as in other countries, militant fans, sometimes linked to right-wing extremist skinhead groups, had regularly displayed racist and anti-Semitic banners directed against opposing teams. In March the presidents of Rome's two local soccer teams, Roma and Lazio, paid a joint visit to the Jewish community school and promised heightened vigilance against stadium racism. In May, in an initiative called "I am not a racist," the Napoli Junior soccer team cooperated with the Naples Jewish community and the Union of Italian Jewish Communities to erect four big photographic panels outside the San Paolo stadium. One showed the famous picture of the child in the Warsaw ghetto with his hands raised, and the caption: "In the Nazi-Fascist extermination camps 1.5 million children were tortured, killed and burned. 1.5 million children equals 30 stadiums full of children." Another panel showed a group of children at Auschwitz. The other two showed a destroyed Jewish-owned shop in Rome and a scene of refugee children in Rwanda in 1996. The latter bore the caption, "But racism still continues today."

In June, thanks to a fax and letter-writing campaign sponsored by Italian Jews, the town council of Pesche, in southern Italy, reversed a decision to name a street after Nicola Pende, an Italian scientist who backed Italy's fascist-era anti-Semitic laws. Italian Jews also began a campaign to force the southern port city of Bari to change the name of a street honoring Pende.

In September a high-school teacher in Verona claimed he was roughed up by three masked youths who shouted anti-Semitic slogans at him. The incident made headlines, but it later turned out that the teacher, a practicing Roman Catholic who came from a Jewish family, had made it all up. In November police in Pisa shut down an anti-Semitic Web site on the basis of a 1993 law against promoting racism. Following leads based on material found on the site, police searched the homes of some members of the far-right Forza Nuova and found neo-Nazi material. There were a number of incidents of anti-Semitic vandalism during the year. Among them was an attack coinciding with ceremonies marking the 55th anniversary of the liberation of Auschwitz, on January 27, when vandals spray-painted swastikas, Stars of David, and anti-Semitic slogans on the walls and shutters of some 15 Jewish-owned shops in Rome. The same thing happened in Rome again in December, the perpetrators using silicon to seal the shutters of the shops closed. In March swastikas, slogans, and other anti-Semitic graffiti were scrawled on the outer walls of the former San Sabba death camp near Trieste, the only World War II death camp on Italian soil.

JEWISH COMMUNITY

Demography

About 26,000 Jews were officially registered as members of Italian Jewish communities, but the actual number of Jews in the country was believed to be between 30,000 and 40,000. Three-quarters of Italy's Jews lived in two cities: Rome, with about 15,000, and Milan, with about 10,000. The rest were scattered in a score of other towns and cities, mostly in northern and central Italy, in communities ranging from a small handful to a thousand or so people. In a ceremony on March 21, 400 years after the Jews were expelled from the city, an organized Jewish community of about 30 people was formally reborn in Brescia, as a Jewish community center and a little synagogue were inaugurated and services held.

Communal Affairs

Italy's Jews were nominally Orthodox — Reform and Conservative streams did not officially exist. Three types of rites were celebrated: Sephardi, Ashkenazi, and Italian, the latter a local rite that evolved from the Jewish community that lived in Italy before the destruction of the Second Temple. Chabad-Lubavitch had a strong and growing presence, particularly in Rome, Milan, and Venice, where the movement ran a yeshivah. Most Italian Jews, however, were not strictly observant, and even observant Jews were highly acculturated, with a strong Italian as well as Jewish identity. Jewish leaders were concerned by what one described as a "spiral of disaffection, estrangement, and assimilation that threatens us." The rate of intermarriage was estimated at 50 percent or more. At the beginning of the year, groups of Jews in Milan and several other cities began working to form an organization of secular Jews, to be called Keshet, which would be associated with the International Federation of Secular Humanistic Jews. In December 1999 and January 2000, the Italian Zionist Federation sponsored a series of five lectures called "a journey into Judaism," explaining the various streams of Judaism, such as Reform, Conservative, Chabad, and Orthodox, as well as secular Judaism.

To combat intermarriage in Italy and neighboring countries, a number of Jewish singles events were organized. Chabad sponsored one such meeting in June. In July more than 40 Italian Jewish singles took part in an international "Jewish Love Boat" cruise through the Mediterranean. Young Italian Jews also took part in various international get-togethers and exchanges organized by the European Council of Jewish Communities and other groups.

Italian Jews had a well-organized infrastructure of schools, clubs, associations, youth organizations, and other services, including a rabbinical college. The women's organization ADEI-WIZO was particularly active nationwide, sponsoring numerous bazaars, lectures, meetings, and other social, cultural, and fundraising events. Italy was represented by 40 women at WIZO's world conference at the beginning of the year. A large Italian delegation also attended the Arachim conference on Jewish education held in Budapest in November. The conference was organized by the European Council of Jewish Communities, whose president was Cobi Benatoff, from Milan.

Italian Jewish communities retained their traditionally strong links with Israel, with many visits and exchanges. These included a Jewish Agency-sponsored family summer camp in Israel, in August, for Jewish families from Milan, Rome, and Turin. The Jewish Agency also helped organize intensive Hebrew courses in Rome, Florence, and Turin, supplying the two Israeli teachers. About 40 young Italian Jews took part in the program.

In November the board of the Union of Italian Jewish Communities approved a wide-ranging document expressing deep concern over the Italian political situation, specifically calling on Jews to fight against all forms of discrimination, not just anti-Semitism. Coming after the outbreak of renewed violence in Israel, the document reiterated the centrality of Israel to world Jewry as "one of the principal factors that guarantee our Jewish identity and its development and reinforcement," but added that Italian Jews must avoid becoming "talking crickets" for Israel. It noted strained relations with the Vatican over several matters—including the beatification of Pope Pius IX—and warned that the way the Vatican had handled its Holy Year, with "insistent" affirmations of the Catholic character of Rome and of the Italian state, gave cause for concern.

Jewish-Catholic Relations

Relations between the Vatican and Jews had their ups and downs, and ended the year on a strained note, leading some observers openly to question the state of Catholic-Jewish dialogue.

Various initiatives to promote Catholic-Jewish understanding took place throughout the year in Italy. In April the pope beatified Sister Mary Elisabeth Hesselblad, a Swedish nun who helped save Jews during World War II. In May Brooklyn-born American Jewish conductor Gilbert Levine led the London Philharmonic Orchestra and Chorus in a concert at the Vatican to mark the pope's birthday. Levine, whose mother-in-law was a Holocaust survivor, first met the pope in 1988, when Levine was the conductor of the Kraków Philharmonic. He helped organize the landmark Holocaust commemoration concert at the Vatican in 1994, and was the recipient of a Papal knighthood. In August, the Vatican Museum held an exhibition on Anne Frank, coinciding with the Church's World Youth Day, an event that brought well over a million young Catholics to Rome. The Vatican Council for Culture explained that the exhibition "ideally reinforces the dialogue between Catholics and Jews, which in recent years has made significant steps forward." There was a series of lectures on biblical themes presented jointly by priests and rabbis in Milan in November, cosponsored by the Milan Jewish community and the Office for Ecumenism and Dialogue of the Milan Roman Catholic Diocese. In December there was a seminar in Rome on Pope John XXIII and Jewish-Christian relations.

The Catholic Church designated the year 2000, marking the beginning of the third millennium of Christianity, as a Jubilee or Holy Year. In line with the pope's call to Catholics to ask forgiveness for sins as part of Holy Year observances, leading Catholic figures publicly apologized for anti-Semitism committed by Catholics. In early March the Vatican released a 92-page document, *Memory and Reconciliation: The Church and the Errors of the Past,* which reiterated previous Vatican pronouncements, including its 1998 statement of "repentance" for teachings that played a role in making the Holocaust possible (see AJYB 1999, p. 329). Then on March 12, a week before embarking on his historic visit to the Holy Land, a day officially designated the Holy Year's "day of request for forgiveness," the pope personally asked forgiveness for the many past sins of the

Church. In an unprecedented ceremony, the pope and senior cardinals listed seven categories of sins, including the treatment of Jews, heretics, women, and native peoples. In regard to the Jews, they said, "Let us pray that, in recalling the sufferings endured by the people of Israel throughout history, Christians will acknowledge the sins committed by not a few of their number against the people of the Covenant . . . ." The pope added his own words to this: "God of our fathers, you who chose Abraham and his descendants to bring your name to the nations: We are deeply saddened by the behavior of those who in the course of history have caused these children of yours [the Jews] to suffer, and asking your forgiveness we wish to commit ourselves to genuine brotherhood with the people of the Covenant." Jewish reaction, both in Italy and abroad, was mixed. Many commentators welcomed the gesture and took note of its significance but registered disappointment at the lack of any specific mention of the Holocaust.

The pope made forgiveness and reconciliation themes of his weeklong trip to Jordan, Israel, and the Palestinian territories. He met with Holocaust survivors and made a moving speech at Yad Vashem in which he expressed the sadness of the Roman Catholic Church for what he called "the hatred, acts of persecution, and displays of anti-Semitism directed against the Jews by Christians at any time and in any place." He crowned the trip with an emotional visit to the Western Wall where he prayed and left a written plea, in a crack between the stones, for forgiveness for historic Christian mistreatment of Jews. The note, later turned over to Yad Vashem, bore the words of the prayer the pope had said during the March 12 forgiveness ceremony at the Vatican.

Two developments in September deeply upset Jews. One was the beatification on September 3 of Pope Pius IX, the 19th-century pontiff who was the last to keep the Jews in a ghetto and who was behind the 1858 kidnapping of Edgardo Mortara, a young Jewish boy whose Catholic nurse claimed to have secretly baptized him as a baby. Italian Jews and international Jewish organizations had called on the pope not to go ahead with the beatification, and, at a seminar in Rome in June on Pius IX and the Jews, Italian Jewish leaders had warned that the move could have serious repercussions on Jewish-Catholic relations. Members of the Mortara family, including great-nieces and great-nephews of Edgardo, issued an open letter, published in the Italian media, condemning the move. Even so, the beatification sent mixed signals, since on the same day the pope beatified Pope John XXIII, who died in 1963 and whose five-year reign marked a positive turning point in Jewish-Catholic relations.

The second upsetting incident occurred two days after the double beatification, on September 5, when the Congregation for the Doctrine of the Faith, the Vatican's guardian of orthodoxy, released a new document, *Dominus Iesus,* "The Lord Jesus—On the Unity and Salvific Universality of Jesus Christ and the Church," which rejected the idea that other faiths were equal to Catholicism. Non-Christians, it stated, were in a "gravely deficient situation" regarding salvation, and other Christian churches had "defects." Following sharp criticism from Jews and non-Catholic Christians, the pope and other senior officials, most prominently Cardinal Edward I. Cassidy, reiterated a commitment to interfaith dialogue and acknowledged that aspects of the document may have been misinterpreted. Nonetheless, in direct response to the beatification of Pius IX and the Vatican document, two Rome rabbis pulled out of a Vatican-sponsored day of Jewish-Christian dialogue scheduled for October 3.

Another live issue was the role of Pope Pius XII during the Holocaust. In October a commission of three Jewish and three Catholic scholars set up in 1999 to examine the 11 published volumes of Vatican wartime documents issued a report posing 47 specific questions about Pius XII's role. Since, the commission noted, the already published material "does not put to rest significant questions about the Vatican during the Holocaust," and therefore "no serious historian" could accept the published, edited volumes as conclusive, it called on the Vatican to offer full access to its World War II archives. As the year drew to an end, the Vatican had not yet responded to the commission.

The pope's meeting with Jörg Haider in December, when the latter presented the Carinthian Christmas tree (see above, pp. 353–54), also rankled. The Israeli government, local Jews, and international Jewish organizations joined Italian leftists in urging the pope not to meet with Haider. The Vatican downplayed the meeting, insisting that it was purely pastoral in nature. The pope limited his private meeting with Haider to two minutes and did not mention him by name when addressing the 250-member Carinthian delegation. The Vatican also gave advance publicity to a message prepared by the pope for the upcoming January 1, 2001, World Peace Day, which strongly condemned racism and xenophobia, and distributed it to Haider and his group.

Culture

Jewish cultural organizations and communal bodies, the Israeli embassy, and non-Jewish organizations and institutions sponsored a wide range of cultural activities with Jewish themes. These included theatrical performances, concerts, film presentations, Jewish music and Jewish culture festivals, conferences, seminars, broadcasts, and publications. Many such events were cosponsored by Jewish organizations together with state or private institutions. Rome's Jewish Culture Center and Il Pitigliani JCC were especially active, sponsoring a wide range of cultural events, clubs, and classes in Rome. In February a roundtable discussion was held at the Chamber of Deputies in Rome on "Religious Minorities and European Culture: Judaism, Protestantism, Islam in the Symbolic Forms of the West." In March a major exhibition of works by the Jewish artist Emanuele Luzzati opened in Milan. Also in March the Western European premier of *Cantata for Soprano, Chorus and Orchestra* by Leopoldo Bamberini, based on the diary of Anne Frank, took place in Milan. In May a big photographic exhibition on Milan Jews opened at the city's Castello Sforzesco. Il Pitigliani organized its annual Shavuot street fair, cosponsored by the Rome city government. Work on creating a Jewish museum in Milan proceeded throughout the year, as did work on the expansion of exhibition space for the museum in Rome. On June 25–July 2 Milan was the scene of the Davar Jewish culture festival, which drew close to 1,000 people. Also in July, Ancona hosted its fifth annual klezmer music festival. In September the first European Festival of Jewish Choirs was held in Milan. On November 1 the tiny Jewish community in Padova, in collaboration with the Italian Rabbinical College, held a day-long seminar in honor of the 200th anniversary of the birth of the scholar Samuel David Luzzatto (1800–1865), known by the acronym Shadal. That same month, Italian Jewish culture was the theme of the annual Jewish Culture Week in Berlin, and numerous Italian Jews took part. Also in November, the Pitigliani JCC in Rome initiated "Rosh Hodesh," a monthly series of discussions on the role of women in the Jewish world, which was to last into 2001, and the Jewish community of Pisa held its fourth annual festival of Jewish music, which included a Jewish film series.

One of the most successful Jewish cultural endeavors was Italy's enthusiastic participation in the European Day of Jewish Culture, on September 3. More than 44,000 people visited synagogues, Jewish museums, Jewish cemeteries, and other Jewish-heritage sites in some 40 towns that were opened to the public for the day. Many of the communities involved hosted special exhibitions, concerts, and performances. The Day of Jewish Culture came under the patronage of President Ciampi, and Giovanna Melandri, the minister of culture, took part in the events in Florence, which drew 5,000 people. Other highlights included a Jewish book fair in Bologna; an open-air concert outside the newly restored synagogue in Senigallia; lectures, concerts, and guided tours in Milan; and exhibitions of modern art and ancient textiles in Urbino. Little more than two weeks later, the newly restored synagogue in Mondovi, near Turin, was inaugurated.

Publications

The main Jewish community periodicals were the *Shalom* monthly in Rome and the *Bollettino* in Milan. In addition, several smaller communities, including Turin, Florence, and Genoa, issued newsletters. There were also other publications, including the intellectual journal *Rassegna Mensile di Israel*. Italy's Jews maintained a growing presence on the Internet with a number of Web sites, and there was a regular Jewish slot on state-run television.

Scores if not hundreds of books on Jewish themes or by Jewish authors were published. These included fiction and poetry as well as all types of nonfiction — biography, history, humor, religion — both original and translations. One exceptionally important publication was the exhaustive, two-volume, 1,178-page *La comunità ebraica di Venezia e il suo cimitero antico* (The Jewish Community of Venice and its Ancient Cemetery). Several Jewish cookbooks or books about Jewish food were published, including *Mangiare alla giudia* (Eating the Jewish Way), a social history of Italian Jewish culinary traditions by Ariel Toaff. A prayer book for children, published in time for the new school year, included teaching materials about prayers. The Italian rabbinical assembly began work on a new Italian translation of the Mishnah. Many books with Jewish themes were on display at Milan's fourth annual Jewish book fair, May 21–22, which also featured lectures, public readings, and other events. Editrice La Giuntina, Italy's foremost Jewish publisher, marked 20 years of operation in 2000. There were also several other, smaller, Jewish publishers, such as Lulav and Morasha. The best-stocked Jewish bookstore in Italy was Menorah, in Rome, which also posted its catalog on its Web site. Milan's first Jewish bookstore and Judaica shop, Davar, opened in April. Three other Milan bookstores, Tikkun, Ancora, and Claudiana, had ample sections of Jewish books, and also scheduled readings, literary evenings, and presentations of books on Jewish themes. Tikkun, for example, hosted the presentation of a new Jewish cookbook, accompanied by a food-tasting and concert, and Ancona hosted presentations of a book on dance in Jewish tradition and of a new collection of Yiddish short stories, translated into Italian. Israeli authors were very popular; Aharon Appelfeld, A. B. Yehoshua, Meir Shalev, and poet Natan Zach toured and lectured in Italy during the year.

Personalia

Bruno Zevi, prominent Jewish architect, political activist and nationally known cultural figure, died in January shortly before his 82nd birthday. Author Giorgio Bassani, best known for his autobiographical novel *The Garden of the Finzi-Continis,* died in April at the age of 84. In September, the artist Paola Levi Montalcini, twin sister of Nobel Prize-winning scientist Rita Levi Montalcini, died at the age of 91. Roman Catholic Cardinal Pietro Palazzini, who was honored by Yad Vashem in 1985 as "Righteous among the Nations," died in October at the age of 88. Giorgina Arian Levi, a founder of the Turin Jewish newspaper *Ha Keillah,* turned 90 in September. In October Gad Lerner, the news director of RAI's main television channel, resigned, saying he took full responsibility for an error that led to images of child pornography being shown on the prime-time news. One of Italy's most prominent Jews, Lerner had been appointed to the post in the summer. Jewish journalist Amos Vitale, New York correspondent for the Rome Jewish monthly *Shalom,* was awarded a prize for journalism by the Province of Asti. In the autumn, Yosef Neville Lamdan took over as Israeli ambassador to the Holy See, replacing Aharon Lopez. Author and scholar Riccardo Calimani was named Switzerland's honorary consul in Venice. In November Chief Rabbi Toaff of Rome received an honorary degree from the Catholic University in Lublin, Poland. During the summer, Toaff's 85th birthday was celebrated in Rome's Campidoglio city hall, with President Ciampi and other dignitaries in attendance.

RUTH ELLEN GRUBER

Switzerland

National Affairs

SWITZERLAND WAS TORN THROUGHOUT THE YEAR between political forces favoring liberalism and internationalism, on the one hand, and elements pushing an isolationist, nationalist agenda, on the other.

Several popular referenda were held during the year. In March the voters approved a proposal for judicial reform but turned down bans on sperm donations and in-vitro fertilization, as well as quotas for women in government positions. In May over 67 percent of voters backed a package of seven bilateral agreements strengthening the country's ties with the European Union, with only the Swiss People's Party and the far-right factions opposed. This was a first step toward economic cooperation and, eventually, possible EU membership. A September referendum turned down a quota on the percentage of foreigners allowed in the country (see below). In November a proposal to cut military spending by a third was rejected.

In addition to the vote for the EU link, another important sign of growing enthusiasm for international involvement even at the cost of the nation's isolationist tradition was the filing, in March, of a petition calling for Swiss membership in the UN. It received enough signatures to require a national referendum. Also, demands were heard for English—viewed as the primary linguistic vehicle of international commerce and culture—to be taught as the primary foreign language in the schools of the German-speaking part of Switzerland.

Yet the Swiss People's Party (SVP/UDC), a nationalist and populist faction that was part of the four-party coalition that had governed Switzerland since 1954, moved in an increasingly right-wing direction, especially in its hostility toward immigration. Dramatic evidence of this came in October when Adolf Ogi, the party's representative on the seven-member Federal Council, which functioned as a cabinet, resigned from his post as minister of defense and from the Swiss presidency, which he was then holding for a one-year rotating term. Ogi stated that his Swiss People's Party had become so extreme in its views that he no longer agreed with it. While the party's guru, Christoph Blocher, sought to have a hard-liner elected to the empty Federal Council chair, the parliament instead chose another moderate member of the party, Samuel Schmid.

The forces of xenophobic nationalism were clearly in evidence when, in February, the government of neighboring Austria included the far-right Freedom Party (FPÖ), led by Jörg Haider, in the governing coalition. While the European Union strictly condemned this political alliance, Switzerland reached out to Austria and invited Chancellor Wolfgang Schüssel to Bern for an official visit. In doing so, it was following the established custom between Switzerland and Austria for new heads of state in either country to visit each other first, before any other foreign trips, a practice symbolizing their common Alpine geography and a similar sense of being small countries not fully integrated into the international community. Yet there was no sense of any embarrassment in Swiss official circles about honoring this tradition even under such unique and troubling circumstances. Left-wing parties and antiracist organizations mobilized and demonstrated in front of the parliament to express their dissatisfaction.

Israel and the Middle East

The Jewish community of Switzerland reacted to the show trial of 13 Iranian Jews accused of spying for Israel with a large demonstration, on April 13, in front of the UN headquarters in Geneva, timed to coincide with similar demonstrations in Paris and Vienna. A message of support from the Geneva government was read on this occasion. Diplomatic appeals were also made to the Ministry of Foreign Affairs, whose representatives in Iran were closely following the matter, to Mary Robinson, the UN high commissioner for human rights, and to other personalities and international nongovernmental organizations (NGOs).

The main Middle East focus in Switzerland, however, became the Palestinian riots toward the end of the year, which had serious repercussions in a country with 300,000 Muslims. There were many pro-Palestinian demonstrations, and they often included such slogans as "Israel is conducting a genocide" and "The Zionists want to kill our children," as well as outright anti-Semitism. On October 8, addressing a crowd gathered in front of the United Nations in Geneva, Hani Ramadan—grandson of the founder of the Muslim Brotherhood in Egypt and leader of the Geneva Islamic Center, which advocated fundamentalist Islam—called for jihad, holy war, for Palestine. The Jewish community reacted by holding a demonstration on the same spot, three days later, calling for an end to violence, hatred, and anti-Semitism. The call for jihad came at the beginning of the violence, at a time when many Jewish leaders and communal institutions were receiving anonymous threats. For more than two months local police provided heavily reinforced security arrangements around Swiss synagogues.

Leftist parties also supported the Palestinian cause, with anti-Zionist speeches depicting Israel as a racist and colonialist state, and even denying Israel's right to exist. Much of the media agreed. Public opinion, as far as could be determined from letters to newspapers, tended in the same direction. These letters often had anti-Semitic undertones, mixing Middle East politics with the Holocaust and Palestinian claims with Jewish class-action suits against Swiss banks. In fact the situation in the Middle East, with Israel seen as the oppressor and the Palestinians as victims, gave a welcome pretext to many Swiss to take a kind of "revenge" against the Jews after the Holocaust debate had pointed at Switzerland's shortcomings.

Even the Swiss Ministry of Foreign Affairs abandoned its neutrality at a session of the UN Commission on Human Rights in Geneva, a meeting called specially to discuss violence in the Middle East. Switzerland—which had the status of an observer, like Palestine, and not a UN member state—had its views announced by Ambassador François Nordmann, a Jew. He said that "Israeli forces, army or police, have used disproportionate repressive means and without discernment, as testified by the type of weapons and the number of casualties . . . . On both sides, hatred was expressed by shocking, barbaric scenes, lynches and destruction of houses of worship." The Swiss Federation of Jewish Communities expressed its strong disapproval to Foreign Minister Joseph Deiss, who replied by simply repeating the same arguments made at the UN. Meanwhile, the Swiss Agency for Development and Cooperation continued to fund Palestinian projects, including a film about the rigors of daily life for Palestinians under Israeli occupation. The Swiss section of Amnesty International launched a poster campaign showing a child—obviously Palestinian—holding his schoolbag while facing a soldier—obviously Israeli—aiming a gun at the child. The caption read: "Stop the killing," and listed the names and ages of dozens of Palestinian victims. Questioned about this message, Swiss Amnesty International replied that it condemned all violence in the Middle East, and paid tribute to all victims, Jewish and Arab.

Anti-Semitism and Extremism

The year 2000 saw an increase in far-right activities in Switzerland, largely the work of Holocaust deniers, skinheads, and neo-Nazis. In mainstream politics as well, which had to grapple with immigration issues, racism often surfaced.

While popular anti-Semitism, evoked by the public debate about Switzerland and the Holocaust, diminished, extremist movements heightened their activities and increased their visibility. Throughout the year hooligans associated with the Geneva Football Club shouted racist slogans and waved Nazi banners during soccer games, without once being disturbed by the police. Similar manifestations were reported in other Swiss soccer stadiums.

A striking event occurred on August 1, the Swiss National Day, during celebrations at the Grütli, the historical site where the Swiss Confederation was founded in 1291. While former president Kaspar Villiger was giving his speech, a group of skinheads displayed neo-Nazi symbols and flags, made the Nazi salute, and shouted racist slogans. The police did not react, and Villiger later said he did not know who these people were. Many felt that his reaction sent a message that he did not care very much about extremist groups interfering with the national holiday. However the incident was reported widely in the media, and it apparently made Swiss political leaders and the general public more sensitive to the growing danger posed by the far right.

According to a new report by the Federal Police, the number of skinheads had risen from 300 to 1,000 since 1998. New recruits were younger (starting as young as 13), more radical, and more inclined to use violence. In 2000, skinheads led attacks against squatters and leftists, shooting at houses and even posting a call to murder on the Internet: a Web site showed a picture of two far-left activists, with the caption: "Born to get killed." The police report stressed that skinheads were heavily armed with sophisticated and illegal equipment. What they still lacked, however was organization and a charismatic leader. Though most skinhead groups were local, two were organized nationally—the Hammerskins and Blood & Honour. The former, which considered itself an elitist white racist brotherhood, met weekly in a club in Malters (Lucerne canton), where it held concerts and other events. The latter group, the Swiss branch of a movement founded by British Nazi rocker Ian Stuart, linked itself to the traditions of the Waffen-SS. In June it published the first issue of a French-language "skinzine," *Blood & Honour Romandie.*

Skinheads had numerous ties with Holocaust deniers, who remained quite active. Several trials took place in 2000 for violation of the antiracism law, especially for Holocaust denial.

The Lausanne court sentenced veteran Nazi sympathizer and Holocaust denier Gaston-Armand Amaudruz to one year in jail and a substantial fine. While awaiting trial, Amaudruz continued to publish his 44-year-old monthly, *Courrier du Continent.* On appeal, his sentence was cut to three months and a smaller fine, the appeals court stating that Amaudruz did not play an active role in extreme-right propaganda and that his anti-Semitic prose was unlikely to sway the masses. Due to a little-known provision in the law, the Swiss Federation of Jewish Communities, antiracist organizations, and Holocaust survivors lacked standing to become parties to the suit, and a proposal to amend the law in the canton of Geneva to enable such involvement was suggested, which, if approved, might trigger similar changes in other cantons and even on the national level. Meanwhile the Amaudruz case was appealed again, this time to the Federal Court.

The Federal Court sentenced Aldo Ferraglia, convicted of distributing Holocaust-denial books, to a 20-day suspended jail sentence, leading many to believe that, like Amaudruz, Ferraglia was getting off easy. Ferraglia moved to Vuadens, near Fribourg, where he resumed selling the same books. The city said that it would not renew the lease of his bookstore in 2001.

The Federal Court also convicted two major Holocaust deniers, but neither spent a day in jail. René-Louis Berclaz was given a three-month suspended sentence. Jürgen Graf, sentenced to 15 months, disappeared from Switzerland, and was assumed to be in Iran, which had no extradition treaty with Switzerland. Seventy-nine-year-old Walter Stoll, a former Waffen-SS officer, was convicted of sending out letters containing anti-Semitic threats and sentenced to four months, but this, too, was suspended. Two employees of the federal government were fired, one for racist postings on the Internet, the other for repeated contacts with neo-Nazis.

Neo-Nazi groups continued to produce publications spreading their ideology. Vérité & Justice (Truth and Justice), an organization led by Graf, Berclaz, and

Philippe Brennenstuhl, issued a pamphlet, *The Counter-Bergier Report,* which offered a pseudohistorical "refutation" of the official Bergier report on Switzerland's role during the Holocaust. Looking for publicity, Vérité & Justice advertised a "public" lecture in the city of Sion, but denied access to reporters. The local police knew about the meeting but did not intervene. A few weeks later, their new pamphlet was sent to all members of the parliament. One of them, Patrice Mugny, the Green representative from Geneva, sued Vérité & Justice. The trial had not yet taken place as the year ended.

Other far-right publications included *Alias,* an ultraconservative leaflet from Valais that supported Amaudruz after his trial, and Max Wahl's *Eidgenoss,* sent to a "circle of friends" twice in 2000, in spite of previous convictions for fomenting hate. Ernst Indlekofer, in his leaflet *Prüfen+Handeln* (Examine and Act), available in French translation as *Examiner+Agir,* viewed the UN and the European Union as secret societies manipulated by a Jewish-Masonic conspiracy. Bernhard Schaub published a new edition of his *Rose und Adler* (Rose and Eagle), a book replete with racism and anti-Semitism, topics he lectured about as well. Erwin Kessler, a self-styled defender of animal rights, used his critique of Jewish ritual slaughter as a pretext for anti-Semitism and Holocaust denial. Geneva lawyer Pascal Junod maintained regular activities through various "New Right" circles, including Thulé, Amis de Robert Brasillac, and Cercle Proudhon. Skinheads, Holocaust deniers, and neo-Nazis attended his lectures. Avalon, a far-right club founded in 1990 by Roger Wüthrich, tried to unite skinheads, Holocaust deniers, former Waffen-SS, and neo-Nazis for lectures and parties. Wüthrich sought to become the general adviser for the entire extreme right in Switzerland.

With the outbreak of violence in Israel and the territories toward the end of the year, expressions of anti-Semitism escalated. In December hundreds of anti-Semitic stickers declaring, "Only Jews have the right to be racists," were found glued all over Geneva, echoing a similar hate campaign that took place in December 1999. A suit was filed, though no suspects could be identified.

MAINSTREAM POLITICS

The European Commission against Racism and Intolerance criticized Switzerland for restricting foreign immigration, setting up separate classes for foreign schoolchildren, not encouraging a multicultural society, and allowing political speeches that play on the population's fears. In 2000 xenophobic sentiments tended to find expression in mainstream politics during discussions about granting citizenship to foreign-born residents of the country. Switzerland's immigration laws created grave difficulties for immigrants: naturalization fees were very high, and priority was given to Europeans and Christians at a time when the bulk of potential applicants were Turkish and Balkan Muslims. Out of 1.4 million foreigners living in Switzerland, only 600,000 were even eligible to become Swiss citizens, and, in 1998, just 21,705 people were naturalized.

A national debate was set off when the town of Emmen, near Lucerne, decided that its 20,000 citizens would vote on the individual citizenship applications of foreigners living there. By March 2000, 56 people had applied, most of whom had been living in the area for over 15 years, had children born there, and spoke the local dialect. As a result of the voting, only eight of the applicants obtained Swiss citizenship, and they were all of Italian or Spanish origin. The 48 rejected applicants happened to come from Turkey, the former Yugoslavia, or Albania.

In September a popular initiative sought to restrict the foreign presence in Switzerland even further through a referendum limiting the number of foreign residents to 18 percent of the total population of the country. Supporters of the proposal—far-right groups and the Swiss People's Party (SVP/UDC)—used economic arguments to defend cutting down on the number of foreigners, but references to the threat immigrants allegedly posed to the national identity showed that xenophobia and even racism played a role in the campaign. The voters rejected the initiative, with close to 64 percent voting against it.

Earlier in the year, the media spotlighted the close relationships between certain activists in the Geneva section of the Swiss People's Party and far-right groups. Lawyer Pascal Junod, notorious for his New Right connections, maintained a quiet but significant role training young party members. Another lawyer, Pierre Schifferli, walked out of the party's national convention with his right arm raised in what looked like a Nazi salute. When challenged, he replied this was actually the original salute of Switzerland's founders. Various members of the party's Geneva section also had religious and financial ties with Islamic countries, including Iran.

Two small far-right groups remained active but had little impact. The xenophobic Union of Swiss Patriots was still unable to elect any candidate to office, and kept a very low profile. A young skinhead from Bern, David Mulas, announced the founding of a Swiss section of a German far-right party, the Nationaldemokratische Partei Deutschland (NPD), which was generally seen as neo-Nazi. After the party was sued for violation of the antiracism law, a spokesperson said that it had been dissolved. However it soon published the first issue of *Das nationale Blatt* (The National Paper), which declared itself the party's official publication, and a series of NPD stickers were spotted in the streets of Bern.

COMBATING THE EXTREMISTS

Switzerland had a Federal Commission against Racism, but it received insufficient government funding to conduct significant projects. Therefore most initiatives to combat extremism—such as educational programs, publications, lectures, and exhibits—were the work of privately funded nongovernmental organizations (NGOs). In 2000 the Ministry of Foreign Affairs announced that it would allot 10 million Swiss francs (about $6 million) to support educational projects against racism, but, after considerable consultation with the NGOs, it had not yet decided how to allocate the money as the year ended.

After the skinhead incident at the Swiss National Day (see above, p. 367), Minister of Justice and Police Ruth Metzler said: "We take far-right extremism seriously, but without dramatizing it." She denied that it was a serious security problem or a threat to public order. Her ministry commissioned a legal team to study the matter, and it suggested a number of steps: compiling a list of acts of hooliganism perpetrated in Switzerland; making far-right and racist gestures—like the Nazi salute—and symbols such as swastikas illegal and punishable; forbidding entrance into Switzerland to notorious far-right activists from abroad; monitoring the mail, phone, fax, and e-mail of the extremists; and giving up Switzerland's reservations about the International Convention for the Elimination of All Forms of Racism. None of these measures were officially implemented in 2000. A full report, expected to tackle issues related to hate on the Internet and suggest additional preventive measures, was expected in 2001.

A number of antiracist activist groups conducted demonstrations against anti-Semitism in several cities, most notably in Malters (Lucerne canton), where skinheads met regularly. CICAD (Committee against Anti-Semitism and Defamation), a Jewish organization based in Geneva, filed a complaint with the Swiss Press Council against the Lausanne daily *24 Heures* for having allowed anti-Semitic postings, with only the first names of the authors, to appear on the paper's Internet forum. The council agreed, blaming the newspaper for letting people express hate while hiding behind a cloak of anonymity and for not providing any explanatory comments that would indicate the unacceptability of the statements. DAVID (Center against Anti-Semitism and Defamation), a Zurich-based sister organization of CICAD, responded to extremist statements in the media, organized youth seminars, and published a brochure in German, *Der Antisemitismus: Historie. Fakten. Zahlen. Eine Zusammenstellung* (Anti-Semitism: History. Facts. Numbers. A Summary).

Holocaust-Related Matters

A public-opinion survey, *Swiss Attitudes towards Jews and the Holocaust,* was published in March by the American Jewish Committee. The research was conducted by the GfS Research Institute on behalf of the AJC and CICAD. The study showed that a significant minority of the population openly expressed prejudice against Jews, while a strong majority identified anti-Semitism as a problem in Switzerland and rejected Holocaust denial. Similarly mixed results prevailed concerning the reassessment of Switzerland's role during the Holocaust. A majority supported the historical findings that Switzerland's immigration policy was biased against Jews during World War II and that the Swiss banks were to blame for failing to refund dormant accounts of Holocaust victims. At the same time, however, a majority thought that Switzerland's behavior was justified by the circumstances of the war, and that therefore no apologies were necessary. And while the Swiss surveyed showed poor factual knowledge of the Holocaust, they overwhelmingly supported Holocaust education in the schools and Holocaust remembrance. The survey received tremendous media coverage both nationally and internationally. Right-wing parties and even some Swiss Jews criticized it for projecting what they felt was an overly negative image of Switzerland.

Following the global settlement reached between Jewish plaintiffs and organizations and Swiss banks in August 1998, Judge Edward Korman, of Brooklyn Federal Court in the United States, authorized to examine the claims of individual survivors of forced labor and the Holocaust — and their heirs — received about 560,000 applications. He named New York lawyer Judah Gribetz to administer the distribution of the $1.25 billion set aside for the purpose by the banks.

That many in Switzerland tended to see the restitution issue solely in terms of money, with no moral dimension, was illustrated by the case of Joseph Spring. In 1943 Spring tried to cross over from Germany into Switzerland with his cousin and a friend. A Swiss border guard arrested them, turned them over to the Germans, and identified them as Jews. They were deported to Auschwitz, and, of the three, only Spring survived. He sued Switzerland for "moral wrong" and asked for 100,000 Swiss francs in reparation. The Federal Court, which decided the case in 2000, agreed to pay Joseph Spring exactly the amount he claimed, not for moral wrong, but for his "expenses," and without acknowledging that Switzerland bore any ethical responsibility. The decision stated that "Switzerland's immigration policy, as hard as it was, was legally acceptable," and that "morality cannot influence a legal decision."

The historical commission led by Professor Jean-François Bergier that examined Switzerland's role during World War II released a report in 2000 about discriminatory immigration policy towards Gypsies. The findings contributed an important perspective to the commission's major report of December 1999 about Jewish refugees from Nazi-occupied countries who were turned back at the Swiss border (see AJYB 2000, p. 332). During 2000, some critical voices were heard in reaction to the 1999 report. Veterans' groups and other Swiss nationalists questioned the statistics and the analysis of the Bergier Commission, and argued that the number of Jewish refugees turned away was actually less than claimed. The aim of these critics was to diminish the extent of Switzerland's responsibility for the fate of those denied entry.

The Swiss Solidarity Foundation, proposed in 1997, was intended to memorialize the Holocaust by using 7 billion Swiss francs (more than $4 billion) from the national gold reserves to fight poverty and violence, both domestically and internationally, especially among young people. The plan had never been approved, and a referendum was set for 2001 to decide whether to create the foundation. Approval was considered highly unlikely since most of the political parties preferred using the money for other purposes, such as funding social security.

The Geneva canton officially admitted partial responsibility for the deportation of some Jewish refugees during World War II, and expressed its regrets to victims and their families. Geneva was one of the very few cantons whose wartime archives were still available, and they showed clear evidence of discriminatory immigration policies.

The bishops of Switzerland issued a strong statement in 2000 asking forgiveness for the Swiss Catholic Church's behavior towards Jews during the Holocaust. "Too little was done to protect and help persecuted people," it declared. "Protestations against anti-Semitic Nazi ideology were not enough." The statement was warmly greeted in Jewish circles. However the Vatican's beatification of the anti-Jewish Pope Pius IX, and its document *Dominus Iesus,* which seemed to deny the worth of other faiths, triggered opposition from the Swiss Jewish community—which considered them major setbacks to the Jewish-Christian dialogue—as well as from Protestant leaders.

The Yad Vashem Institute in Jerusalem named two more Swiss citizens "Righteous among the Nations," bringing the total number of Swiss designees to 37.

JEWISH COMMUNITY

The number of Jews in Switzerland remained about 18,000, the great majority living in urban areas. Ashkenazi families, many of which had lived in the country for several generations, tended to concentrate in the German-speaking regions, while Jews of Middle Eastern origin, relative newcomers, were the majority in the French-speaking part of Switzerland, especially Geneva.

The Swiss Federation of Jewish Communities elected a new president, Professor Alfred Donath, after the incumbent, Dr. Rolf Bloch, decided not to seek a new term. As the political organ of Swiss Jewry, the federation held regular meetings with members of the government, which were especially important in times of crisis, such as the visit of the Austrian chancellor, the trial of the Iranian Jews, and the issuance of Switzerland's statement about the Middle East. The federation also functioned as a religious body, and in that role it continued to refuse to allow the two Reform communities, one in Geneva and the other in Zurich, to join its ranks.

A number of books on Jewish issues were published in 2000: *Judenmord von Payerne* by Hans Stutz (about an anti-Semitic crime that occurred in 1940); *Couleur Espérance, mémoire du mouvement juif ouvrier* (memoirs of Jewish workers and unionists) edited by Nathan Weinstock; *J'ai oublié Maman* and *Le Mandarin givré,* two thrillers by Bertrand Weill; and a catalog accompanying an exhibit about the history of Jews in the Jura canton.

BRIGITTE SION

Central and Eastern Europe

Germany

National Affairs

HALFWAY THROUGH Chancellor Gerhard Schröder's four-year term it was clear that his Red-Green coalition—his own Social Democratic Party (SPD) together with the environmentalist Greens—had succeeded in co-opting the traditional agenda of the opposition Christian Democrats (CDU), leaving the opposition without a substantial issue. The government accomplished this by moving to the political center, primarily through a set of pro-business tax cuts that were expected to spur the economy.

The conservative opposition was also handicapped by scandal. Former chancellor Helmut Kohl shocked the nation at the end of 1999 by refusing to clarify his role in the CDU's financial irregularities, and in January 2000 he resigned as honorary chairman of the party. The affair continued to get headlines throughout 2000 as more illegal payments during the Kohl years came to light. All that Kohl himself would acknowledge was his personal receipt of some $1 million not accounted for in the party's financial records, but he refused to name the donors. Considering his "word of honor" not to divulge the source of the money more important than the German law requiring him to do so, he compared his treatment by the German mass media to the Nazi boycott of Jewish stores during the Hitler regime. Most observers believed that Kohl would end up paying a fine and would not serve any jail time.

The Kohl scandal triggered an internal party upheaval. Wolfgang Schäuble, Kohl's successor as CDU leader, admitted in February that he too had taken unreported campaign contributions, and was forced to resign. He was replaced in April by Angela Merkel, who had grown up in the former German Democratic Republic (GDR)—Communist East Germany—and considered Kohl her political mentor. She was the first woman to lead a major German party.

Charges similar to those against Kohl were also made against the local CDU in the state of Hesse, which was discovered to have its own unreported slush fund. Party officials there imaginatively attributed the money to a gift from grateful expatriate German Jews.

Strains developed in relations with the United States. The German political establishment, including parts of the conservative opposition, made little secret of its preference for Al Gore in the American presidential election, considering him by far the more experienced candidate in the area of foreign affairs. In May, Foreign Minister Joschka Fischer called for changes in the structure of the European Union that would ultimately lead to a European federal state, but he also stressed that the U.S. presence was both welcome and necessary in Germany and in Europe. German leaders criticized the plan for a U.S. national missile-defense shield supported by Republican candidate George W. Bush, criticism that increased in December when it became clear that Bush would be the next president. Many Germans also questioned the effectiveness of U.S. embargoes against Cuba and Iraq, while the U.S. government maintained serious reservations about Germany's policy of "open dialogue" with Iran.

Landmark provisions liberalizing German citizenship rules went into effect on January 1. They replaced the old principle of determining citizenship on the basis of German lineage (jus sanguinis), which went back to 1913, with the criterion of place of birth. Under the new regulations, anyone born in Germany received automatic German citizenship provided that at least one parent had been living in the country for at least eight years. Such children could also maintain their parents' nationality until age 23, when they would have to choose which passport to keep. In addition, foreigners residing in Germany gained easier access to citizenship through a reduction of the residency requirement for naturalization from fifteen years to eight. At the end of 2000 Germany was home to around 7.3 million foreigners. The largest group, the country's two-million-strong Turkish (and Kurdish) community, about 40,000 of whom held German passports, particularly welcomed the changes in the law.

Yet despite the easing of the naturalization procedures, there was only a slight upturn in the number of foreign residents applying for citizenship during 2000. It was believed that the substantial processing fees for each person — which could amount to a considerable sum for large families — acted as a deterrent, and also that a good number of the foreign residents were conflicted about whether they really wanted to take on a German identity.

As part of his pro-business thrust, Chancellor Schröder pleased German industry by making available 20,000 temporary visas to foreign computer specialists who would be allowed to stay and work in the country for from three to five years. By the end of 2000, however, only about 4,400 of these visas had been issued, perhaps because the visas were only for a limited stay in Germany and not an invitation to immigrate, or, conversely, because potential applicants feared being subjected to antiforeigner sentiment in Germany.

It was clear, though, that the issue of immigration was not going to disappear. In a report issued in November, the German Institute for Economic Research calculated that current rates of immigration from outside the European Union would have to increase drastically in order to keep the size of the labor force from shrinking as the German population aged. To examine the immigration issue in greater depth the Bundestag—the lower house of the German Parliament—set up a blue-ribbon commission led by Rita Süssmuth, a prominent CDU member. Its recommendations, due to be announced toward the middle of 2001, were expected to lead to new immigration laws.

The CDU sought to make political capital out of the immigration issue. In November, Friedrich Merz of the CDU, minority whip of the Bundestag, asserted that foreigners settling in Germany should be expected to accept *Deutsche Leitkultur,* the primacy of German culture, and other CDU leaders suggested that the chancellor's Social Democratic Party was somehow deficient in German patriotism. Many political observers saw this thrust as a conservative rejection of the increasingly multicultural nature of German society. In the wake of a number of violent incidents perpetrated by extreme right-wingers and just a few days after a large neo-Nazi demonstration in Berlin, Paul Spiegel, president of the Central Council of Jews in Germany (CCJG), responded to Merz. Speaking on November 9—the anniversary of Kristallnacht, the so-called "night of the broken glass" when synagogues and other Jewish-owned buildings in Germany had been torched and wrecked in 1938—Spiegel asked if it was also a hallmark of German *Leitkultur* to harass refugees and burn synagogues.

In February, when Jörg Haider's far-right Freedom Party (FPÖ) became part of the ruling coalition in neighboring German-speaking Austria, Andreas Nachama, president of the Berlin Jewish Community, voiced the concern of many Germans when he cautioned that this step "removes the taboo from the right-extremist position within Austrian society, encourages supporters in Germany and in other countries to present themselves more self-confidently, and influences the European right-spectrum on the whole." Germany, in fact, was one of the leading voices within the EU calling for the imposition of sanctions against Austria to protest the Freedom Party's inclusion (see below, pp. 397–98). However once the EU dropped its sanctions in the fall, the issue faded away.

Israel and the Middle East

The year began with two firsts in the history of German-Israeli relations.

On January 28 Berlin welcomed the first Israeli embassy located in the post-Bonn capital. Israeli architect Orit Willenberg-Giladi, the daughter of Holocaust survivors, was present at the topping-out ceremony for the building in the Wilmersdorf residential district, a center of Jewish life in prewar Berlin. The embassy staff had moved from Bonn into the finished building in December 1999.

On February 16 Johannes Rau, president of Germany since May 1999 and a long-time friend of Israel, became the first German president to address the Knesset—and the first person to speak before the Israeli parliament in German. He said: "In the presence of the people of Israel I bow in humility before the murdered who have no graves at which I could ask them for forgiveness. I ask for forgiveness for what Germans did, for myself and my generation, for the sake of our children and children's children, whose future I would like to see at the side of the children of Israel." The statement appeared to be in response to the words of Elie Wiesel, who, during a January 27 speech in the German Bundestag, had issued a plea to the president to ask the Jewish people directly, in the name of the Germans, for forgiveness.

Rau's Israel trip was the beginning of an 11-day diplomatic mission to the Middle East that included meetings with Israeli president Ezer Weizman, Palestinian Authority chairman Yasir Arafat, and Egyptian president Hosni Mubarak. Rau, representing Germany, was just as welcome a presence to the Arabs as he was to the Israelis. In 1994 Germany had been the first European country to open an office in the territories under Palestinian control, and since then, encouraged by Israeli officials, Germany had fortified its political support of the peace process. This included significant financial assistance to the Palestinians. Since 1996, Germany had allotted DM 140 million ($70 million) annually for cooperative projects geared toward improving the infrastructure—mainly water and sewage management—in the Palestinian areas. On a per capita basis, in fact, the Palestinians were the recipients of more German foreign aid than any other country, and Germany was the largest contributor to the region of all the EU countries.

Israel also received concrete support from Germany during the year. The third and final German-built Dolphin-class submarine was delivered to the Israeli navy in October. Once the vessels could be outfitted with Israeli-made warheads, the country would possess a formidable military deterrent, a third pillar of nuclear defense—after land and air capabilities—and the ability to strike back from the sea even after a nonconventional attack. After the Gulf War of 1991, when it was revealed that the Iraqi missiles used against Israel had been partially developed by German companies, the Kohl administration had offered to cover the costs (approximately $300 million each) for two of the three subs.

In early June, Foreign Minister Fischer spent two days in Israel and the Palestinian Autonomous Territories. To help ease tensions in the area he agreed that Germany would provide political asylum for 400 members of the SLA (South Lebanese Army), the Israel-backed militia in Lebanon that had ceased to exist with the withdrawal of Israeli forces from south Lebanon (see below, p. 482). His Israeli counterpart, David Levy, thanked Fischer for Germany's support of Israel's membership in WEOG (Western European and Others Group) at the UN, which would make Israel eligible to serve on the Security Council and other UN bodies.

During the summer, Rudolf Dressler, designated to take over the post of German ambassador to Israel, was the target of harsh criticism from across the political spectrum for comments he made favoring the placement of the city of Jerusalem under international administration. An expert on social issues, Dressler was new to the international diplomatic scene. He quickly explained that he had misspoken, and it did not appear that any lasting damage was done.

Reacting to the outbreak of violence between Israelis and Palestinians at the end of September, Chancellor Schröder travelled to the Middle East in late October for high-level talks, first with the key Arab nations—Egypt, Lebanon, Jordan, and Syria. In each country he remained unwavering in his message: the violence between Israelis and Palestinians must end, the parties must return to the negotiating table, and U.S. president Bill Clinton remained the only viable diplomatic broker. Upon Schröder's subsequent arrival in Israel, his first visit there as chancellor, Prime Minister Barak personally appealed him to take on a greater role as mediator in the conflict. Schröder declined; he felt that Germany was neither politically nor historically suited for this overwhelming task. He stressed once again that neither Germany nor the EU could replace the United States as primary facilitator. Schröder did promise Barak help in obtaining the release of three Israeli soldiers held hostage in Lebanon. In talks with the Palestinians, Schröder gave assurances of continued German financial assistance and also offered to bring 50 Palestinians injured in the conflict with Israel to Germany for medical treatment. Finally, Schröder warned both sides against unilateral measures, specifically mentioning the dangers of a Palestinian declaration of statehood.

In Germany, meanwhile, the Assembly of Representatives of the Berlin Jewish Community issued a resolution critical of the German media's "one-sided presentation" of Israel as the aggressor in the renewed Middle East conflict. Though media reporting was less aggressively pro-Arab in Germany than elsewhere in Europe, there were numerous feature articles on the plight of the Palestinians and few reports presenting the Israeli perspective. Many Jews in Germany were particularly upset that the role of the anti-Israel and sometimes anti-Semitic press in the Palestinian territories did not get sufficient coverage.

Germany had been without an Israeli ambassador since Avi Primor was recalled in the summer of 1999 (see AJYB 2000, pp. 339–40). Early in 2000, Prime Minister Barak and Foreign Minister Levy suggested the appointment of Knesset member Yossi Katz, but the nomination fell through. Mordechai Levy became Israel's chargé d'affaires in Berlin in September. The new ambassador, Shimon Stein, was to take up his post in January 2001.

Outside of the political arena, in March Germany and Israel celebrated 25 years of government-sponsored cooperative research in the sciences. According to Germany's minister of education, Edelgard Bulmahn, "Germany maintains closer scientific relations with Israel than with any other country." Later that month, the Technion in Haifa awarded President Rau an honorary doctorate for his efforts on behalf of that institution. The award ceremony was held at Berlin's Technical University.

A brand new connection between German and Israeli youth was established in 2000 at the third annual "Miza'ad Ha-ahava" (Hebrew for "Love Parade"). More than 300,000 "techno" music fans from around the world danced along Tel Aviv's beach promenade on November 10; their motto: "You Can't Stop the Love." "Dr. Motte," initiator of the tremendously successful event held annually in Berlin since 1989, called for "ravers" from Germany and the rest of Europe to attend what turned out to be—despite security concerns—a true festival of peace.

Germany made diplomatic efforts throughout the year aimed at the release of the 13 Jews jailed in Iran, efforts that Israel gratefully acknowledged. The Berlin Jewish Community protested against the visit of Iranian president Mohammed Khatami in May. In October the German economics minister traveled to Iran with a delegation of German corporate executives. Germany seemed intent on continuing its policy of cautiously improving trade and cultural relations with Iran despite the trial and imprisonment of numerous Iranian intellectuals for attending a conference in Berlin in April sponsored by the Heinrich Böll Foundation, affiliated with the Greens.

Right-Wing Extremism and Xenophobia

For the first time ever, a German president, Johannes Rau, included mention of the victims of racism and hatred in his speech on Germany's Memorial Day, November 19.

Federal Office of Criminal Investigation (FOCI) statistics registered 10,997 crimes committed by right-wing extremists in 2000—not including specifically anti-Semitic acts—as compared with 6,937 cases reported the previous year, a colossal increase of 58.2 percent, though, as explained below, much of the rise could be attributed to more accurate reporting. The number of crimes categorized as xenophobic rose from 2,283 in 1999 to 3,594 in 2000, a 57.4-percent increase. Of the year 2000 total, 641 of the incidents were of a violent nature, a 42.1-percent increase from the 451 incidents in 1999. There were an estimated 10,000 violence-prone neo-Nazis and skinheads in Germany, about a thousand more than there had been the year before. The number of German right-wing extremist home pages on the Internet jumped from 330 in 1999 to 800 in 2000.

Although the number of skinhead concerts dropped from 109 in 1999 to 76 in 2000, participants demonstrated with far greater aggressiveness when police sought to shut the concerts down than they ever had before. Interior Minister Otto Schily (SPD) announced a ban on performances by Blood & Honour Deutschland in September; this 250-member group, a mainstay of the extreme-right scene in Germany, had played a key role in the organization of skinhead concerts throughout the country.

Far-right crimes became the focus of a national debate during the summer after a bomb explosion in Düsseldorf critically injured a group of mostly Jewish immigrants, and, in a separate incident, Alberto Adriano, a father of three from Mozambique, was brutally murdered by skinheads in Dessau. In addition, allegations—later dropped—that neo-Nazis in Sebnitz had drowned six-year-old Joseph Kantelberg-Abdulla in broad daylight while bystanders stood passively nearby were also being investigated at the time. Reflecting a widespread feeling that right-wing extremism could no longer be dismissed as an isolated phenomenon confined to fringe groups, Wolfgang Thierse, president of the Bundestag, went so far as to state that such extremism had become a serious threat to "the core of [German] society."

The events of the summer triggered a closer look at the accuracy of statistics on extremist activities, and calls for "truth in crime reporting" became common. After journalists from two papers—*Tagesspiegel* and *Frankfurter Rundschau*—discovered that official statistics listed only 26 of the 93 persons murdered by right-wing extremists since German unification in 1990, Interior Minister Schily lamented bureaucratic "registration deficits" and the blurred criteria used for defining "extremist crimes" at local offices of the Federal Office of Criminal Investigation. The dramatic rise in the figures for crimes by extremists for the year 2000 was undoubtedly due, in part, to the new interest in getting the facts right, and thus the 2000 data were probably the first ever accurately to reflect the incidence of right-wing hate crimes.

As was the case in 1999, about half the crimes took place in the new federal states of the former GDR (the old East Germany), where slightly more than one-fifth of the country's population, and a much smaller proportion of foreigners, resided. "The regional emphasis of the violence is clearly East Germany, including Berlin," said Schily in an interview with *Die Woche*. He also commented that the perpetrators in the east were more militant and younger than their western counterparts: two-thirds of the culprits in the east were under 21.

A new Forsa Institute/*MAX* magazine study of attitudes toward foreigners was released in August, based on a representative sample of Germans aged 18–49. Whereas two-thirds of the respondents considered foreigners a positive addition to a modern society, 40 percent (37 percent from the west, 51 percent from the east) nonetheless believed that there were too many foreigners in Germany. Every sixth person (16 percent) thought that resident foreigners took advantage of native Germans. Three-fourths of the sample said they would not come to the aid of a foreigner under attack, though they would summon help. Every fifth person (22 percent) said that he or she would risk personal harm and assist directly; and only 2 percent would do nothing to help. The study showed that xenophobic attitudes ran highest among women, people from the former East Germany, those with low levels of education, and members of the PDS (Party of Democratic Socialism) and CDU/CSU (Christian Democratic Union/Christian Social Union). On a positive note, a large majority, 85 percent, felt that the government ought to take a significantly tougher stance against right-wing extremism.

Intellectuals and politicians concerned about the high level of extremism in the eastern part of the country debated the question of whether this had some connection to the way the memory of the Holocaust had been treated in East Germany, where the schools, under the Communist regime, had taught about the period from the perspective of a struggle between socialism and monopoly capitalism, neglecting the fate of the Jews and other minorities under Nazism. Recognizing the need to provide schools in the east with updated educational materials on the Holocaust and, in particular, on what happened to the Jews, German educational authorities approached the United States embassy for information about American programs that fostered tolerance education.

The far-right National Democratic Party (NPD) held a demonstration on January 29, the day before the anniversary of Hitler's seizure of power in 1933. Hundreds of young neo-Nazis marched toward the Brandenburg Gate for the first time since World War II, protesting the planned monument honoring the European Jews murdered by the Third Reich (see below, pp. 383–84). Though a legal injunction kept the group from marching through the gate, on March 12 the NPD held another demonstration at the gate as a sign of "national solidarity with Vienna"—March 12 was the anniversary of Hitler's invasion of Austria in 1938. Again, on November 4, a few days before Kristallnacht, 1,000 neo-Nazis and NPD members took to the streets of Berlin for a rally. Stung by voices of outrage from around the world, Chancellor Schröder supported calls for a ban on the NPD. The suggestion received considerable support in both houses of Parliament, though some believed that driving the party—whose political strength was negligible—underground would only enhance its attractiveness to fringe elements. In any case, such a ban could not be ordered by the Parliament; it would have to be issued by the Federal Constitutional Court.

Toward the end of the year, online booksellers Amazon and Barnes and Noble complied with a German Department of Justice request to halt the sale of Hitler's *Mein Kampf* to customers in Germany. Sale of "hate literature" was illegal in Germany, but orders sent over the Internet for English-language editions from the U.S. evaded the German ban, and the book was one of the most popular titles in Germany for these companies. The decision to halt the book's sale came after strong protests by the Simon Wiesenthal Center.

Some new public and private initiatives against extremism were started in Germany during 2000, including the government-funded Alliance for Democracy and Tolerance—Against Extremism and Violence (www.bmi.bund.de/demotol); Show Your Face (www.gesichtzeigen.de); and NAIIN—No Abuse in Internet (www.naiin.org). In addition, several large German Internet providers came together to create an index where sites with hate content could be registered.

Anti-Semitism

The Federal Office of Criminal Investigation (FOCI) registered a 68.7-percent increase in anti-Semitic activity during 2000, 1,378 crimes as compared with 817 in 1999. In 26 cases the crimes resulted in bodily harm, an 81.2-percent rise over the previous year's figure of 16.

Numerous Jewish cemeteries across the country were desecrated during the year, particularly in the months of February, March, July, and August. The synagogue in Erfurt was the target of an arson attack on Hitler's birthday in April. Ten immigrants (seven of them Jewish) from the former Soviet Union were seriously injured by a hand-grenade explosion in Düsseldorf in July, and in August right-wing extremists attempted to blow up a Bamberg apartment building where Jews were known to live.

Anti-Semites perpetrated a wave of attacks on and around October 3, the tenth anniversary of German reunification. Kurt Biedenkopf, Saxony's state premier, made no mention, at official "Day of German Unity" celebrations in Dresden, of two outrages that took place the evening before—a Molotov cocktail hurled at the Düsseldorf synagogue and the desecration of memorial sites at Buchenwald. Shortly thereafter, windows at Berlin's Fraenkelufer synagogue were damaged and the Jewish cemetery in Potsdam was vandalized.

Two thousand people took to the streets to protest the Düsseldorf synagogue attack. This was soon after 10,000 dog lovers—some of whom had wanted to adorn their pets with Stars of David with the word *Hund* (dog) instead of *Jude*— had marched against new measures aimed at restraining pit bulls and other dangerous fighting dogs. Michel Friedman, vice president of the CCJG, could not resist the irony, noting that Germans were more apt "to demonstrate for the rights of dogs than for the dignity of human beings."

After visiting the damaged synagogue in Düsseldorf, Chancellor Schröder called for a nationwide *Aufstand der Anständigen* (revolt of all decent people) against right-wing extremism, xenophobia, and intolerance. That same week a group of high-ranking politicians expressed solidarity with Germany's Jewish community by attending Sabbath services at Berlin's Pestalozzistrasse Synagogue. Andreas Nachama, president of the Berlin Jewish Community, received a petition against extremism and anti-Semitism signed by 1,600 pupils entitled "We've had enough!"

On November 9, the 62nd anniversary of Kristallnacht, a march against racism and for tolerance in Berlin drew some 250,000 people from across the nation. Speakers included President Rau and CCJG president Spiegel. In December German police arrested two young men and charged them with the arson attack on the Düsseldorf synagogue. The culprits, 19 and 20 years old, one a native Moroccan and the other a Palestinian from Jordan, confessed to attacking the synagogue in retaliation against Israeli policies toward the Palestinians. Anti-Semitic and extreme right-wing literature was confiscated from their apartment.

Morale in the Jewish community dropped to an all-time low over the course of the year, and Jewish leaders, fearful about the personal safety of German Jews, voiced growing consternation. Paul Spiegel, who had begun his term as president of the CCGJ on an optimistic note in January, questioned, toward the end of the year, whether Jews should have settled in postwar Germany at all. And as new bloodshed took place in Israel and the territories, the German Jewish community became increasingly concerned that hard-core racist Germans, who maintained that Germany should be free of all foreigners, might bend their principles and create an informal anti-Semitic and anti-Israel alliance together with Arabs and Muslims living in the country.

Holocaust-Related Matters

Chancellor Schröder and State Minister for Culture Michael Naumann participated in the Stockholm International Forum on the Holocaust in January.

Dani Karavan, a Paris-based Israeli, designed a memorial dedicated to the estimated 500,000 Sinti and Roma (Gypsies) murdered by the Nazi regime. The memorial will eventually be located in Berlin's Mitte district, between the Brandenburg Gate and the Reichstag building.

Ottmar Kagerer became the first recipient of the Obermayer German Jewish History Award, established by Arthur Obermayer, a native of Fürth who now lived in the U.S. Kagerer was a non-Jewish stone mason who had agreed to help repair—free of charge—the 103 gravestones at Berlin's Weissensee cemetery that had been damaged by neo-Nazis in 1999 (see AJYB 2000, p. 345). He subsequently received death threats and his workshop was ransacked, with the damage—not covered by insurance—exceeding DM 80,000 ($40,000).

In September Germany returned 80 pieces of artwork stolen by the Nazis to their rightful owners, the largest number of such items ever given back at one time.

Julius Viel, 82, likely to be one of the last German war-crimes suspects to face justice, went on trial in December. A former SS officer, retired journalist, and recipient of the German Officers Cross of Merit for his books on hiking, Viel was accused of shooting seven concentration camp inmates at Theresienstadt during the spring of 1945. A verdict was not expected until 2001.

MEMORIALIZING EUROPE'S MURDERED JEWS

A "prededication" ceremony for the $26-million Memorial to the Murdered Jews of Europe took place on a site just south of the Brandenburg Gate on January 27—the 56th anniversary of the liberation of Auschwitz and the sixth annual German Holocaust Memorial Day. Berlin mayor Eberhard Diepgen (CDU), demonstrating his continued dissent from the project, did not join Chancellor Schröder, President Rau, Bundestag president Thierse, and Elie Wiesel in attending the symbolic start of the memorial's construction. Actual construction was expected to begin in the fall of 2001 and the project was scheduled for completion sometime in 2003.

More than ten years had passed since Lea Rosh, a German journalist, began the citizen's initiative that led to the 1999 parliamentary resolution favoring construction of a national memorial commemorating the Holocaust. "The Memorial" received less public attention during 2000 than in previous years (see AJYB 2000, pp. 347–48), as the intense nationwide debate surrounding the decision of whether or not to build it subsided and was replaced by quiet, behind-the-scenes efforts to bring U.S. architect Peter Eisenman's field of some 2,700 stone pillars and an information center to fruition. The information center would house a "room of silence" where visitors might meditate and reflect. A "room of names" would provide computer access to the roughly 3.5 million recorded names of Holocaust victims, marking the first time that Yad Vashem had agreed to share its lists with another memorial site. The lives and experiences of representative families from each of the 18 countries whose Jews were murdered would be presented as exhibits in the "room of fates," and the "room of places" would provide detailed information on the Nazi death camps.

Michael Naumann, the minister for culture who had been a key figure in planning the central memorial, announced, before resigning his cabinet post later in the year, that government funding for Holocaust memorials "at authentic locations" would increase from $16 million in 2000 to $27 million by 2003.

WEHRMACHT EXHIBIT

The highly controversial exhibit, "War of Extermination: Wehrmacht Crimes 1941–1944," which had been seen by more than 82,000 people in twenty-seven German cities and six Austrian cities from 1995 through 1999, was scheduled to open in New York in late 1999. This was the first photo exhibition ever to document the participation of the German army in the murder of millions of people in Eastern Europe during World War II. However, in response to harsh criticism from those who felt that it was unfair to the Wehrmacht, the organizers finally had no recourse but to postpone its display in New York and commission an independent panel of eminent historians to investigate its content (see AJYB 2000, pp. 348–49). The panel indeed found a number of factual errors, but unanimously confirmed the accuracy of the overall presentation: "The Wehrmacht was not only peripherally involved in the murder of Jews in the Soviet Union, the crimes committed against Soviet prisoners of war, and the onslaught against the population at large." A new director was hired to overhaul the exhibit, which was expected to be ready in late 2001.

RESTITUTION

Eighteen months of strained negotiations concluded on July 17 in Berlin, with Germany signing a historic agreement to compensate nearly one million Nazi-era slave laborers and forced laborers. Months earlier, the German government and German industry had each agreed to contribute half of the required funds. Foreign Minister Fischer declared that this initiative was "above all a gesture of moral responsibility." Though hopes ran high that payments from the 10-billion-mark fund would commence before the end of the year, that turned out to be an overly optimistic expectation.

Among those at the signing in Berlin that day were the cochairs of the negotiations—Stuart Eizenstat, the U.S. deputy treasury secretary; Otto Graf Lambsdorff, the former economics minister who represented the German government; and Daimler Chrysler executive Manfred Gentz, who spoke for the industrialists. Also participating were representatives from the governments of Belarus, the Czech Republic, Poland, Russia, and the Ukraine, as well as officials and lawyers from the Conference on Material Claims Against Germany (Claims Conference).

An essential element of the complex agreement was an executive order from President Clinton recommending that federal judges dismiss pending class-action lawsuits against German firms, complemented by a German law passed in August stipulating that payments to survivors might begin once Parliament determined that a state of "legal peace"—no more class-action suits—had been achieved.

The fund provided for payments of up to 15,000 DM ($7,500) to approximately 240,000 surviving slave laborers—concentration camp prisoners, primarily Jews, whom the Nazis intended to exterminate through work. Payments of up to 5,000 DM ($2,500) per person were made available for the more than one million surviving forced laborers, those, mostly non-Jews, seized from their home countries and deported to Germany or other parts of the Nazi Reich to work under brutal conditions. Since there were far more survivors of forced labor than of slave labor, it turned out that only some 30 percent of the money was going to Jews. Seven compensation-fund partner organizations would review applicant documentation and administer payment; the Claims Conference was to do this for most of the Jewish claimants.

Money was also set aside for distribution to formerly Communist countries for payments to survivors, mostly non-Jews but also Jews, who had received no previous compensation because their Communist governments had not participated in earlier negotiations.

It was expected that once these payments were underway, public attention would turn to another provision of the agreement, the 700 million DM ($350 million) from the fund that was set aside for "Remembrance and the Future." According to a law approved by the German Parliament, this money would support projects that promote "international coexistence, social justice, youth exchange, the memory of the threat posed by totalitarian systems and tyranny, and international cooperation in areas of humanitarian projects. In the memory of and in honor of those victims of National Socialist injustice who did not survive, it should also support projects in the interests of their heirs." In December the Lawrence and Lee Ramer Center for German-Jewish Relations of the American Jewish Committee, in Berlin, sponsored a workshop bringing together more than 70 leading figures from German government, industry, and nonprofit organizations, historians, and others to discuss viable "Future Fund" concepts.

By the end of 2000 German industry had collected only 3.6 billion of the 5 billion marks it had pledged to contribute. Hundreds of German companies founded after World War II paid into the fund as a show of shared civic responsibility. Nonetheless, the majority of midsized businesses, viewing participation not as a demonstration of solidarity but as an admission of guilt, refused. As 2000 drew to a close, "legal peace" had not yet been established or declared since there were still class-action suits pending in the U.S., and therefore not one of the elderly survivors had been compensated.

JEWISH COMMUNITY

Demography

During 2000 the Jewish community in Germany continued to grow at a faster pace than any other in the world. The arrival of 6,026 Jewish newcomers, primarily from the former Soviet Union, raised the total number of Jews affiliated with the 82 communities from 81,730 to 87,756. The numbers of affiliated Jews in the largest communities, with 1999 figures as the basis for comparison, were as follows: Berlin, 11,250 (up from 11,190); Frankfurt, 6,736 (up from 6,602); Munich, 7,858 (up from 7,219); Hamburg, 4,540 (up from 4,270); and Cologne, 3,896 (up from 3,654).

Communal Affairs

Paul Spiegel, 62, a child-survivor of the Holocaust, was elected to succeed the deceased Ignatz Bubis as president of the CCJG on January 9. A journalist and founding director of a Düsseldorf talent agency, Spiegel had previously served as chairman of the Central Welfare Administration of Jews in Germany (CWA) for 11 years.

Spiegel's competitors for the CCJG's highest office, Charlotte Knobloch of Munich and Michel Friedman of Frankfurt, were elected vice presidents. Stefan Kramer, 31, was hired as the new managing director of the CCJG Berlin office on March 1. Abraham Lehrer followed in Spiegel's footsteps as the new chairman of CWA, and—celebrating 20 years of service to the CWA—Bennie Bloch continued as its managing director.

The CCJG commemorated the 50th anniversary of its founding in July. Earlier in the year, at the second annual CCJG meeting of Jewish communities from across Germany, President Spiegel described the year 2000 as the beginning of a "completely new epoch in the history of the Central Council." He said that while immigration from the former Soviet Union and the addition of Jewish communities from the former East Germany had been the hallmarks of the 1990s, a period of consolidation had now begun.

Integration of Soviet Jews and stabilization of fledgling Jewish communities remained high on the agenda. Between 1990 and 1999, the registered Jewish population had grown from 30,000 to more than 80,000. Since 1990, the federal government received more than 203,000 applications from Jews in the former Soviet

Union, and 125,000 had emigrated thus far. Approximately 30,000 immigrants were expected to continue to swell communal ranks over the next few years.

New programs implemented included a pilot leadership seminar, cosponsored by the CWA and the American Jewish Joint Distribution Committee (JDC) for 220 board members from 12 communities located in the former East Germany. A "how-to" community handbook was being developed as a guide to organizational, legal, and community-relations procedures. Another CWA initiative enabled young religious Israelis who opted to do community service instead of going into the army to teach religion and Jewish tradition to Soviet immigrants in German communities.

A study conducted by the Moses Mendelssohn Center in Potsdam demonstrated that the greatest difficulty facing Soviet Jewish immigrants in Germany were the complicated and onerous legal rulings that denied them recognition for their previous qualifications and work experience. This made it nearly impossible for older immigrants to begin their careers anew.

In happy contrast to the widespread stereotype that immigrants from the FSU did not involve themselves in Jewish life once they got to Germany, six elderly couples, all married for more than 50 years, gathered in Düsseldorf in July to affirm their commitment to Judaism and set examples for their families. Since they had not had the opportunity to marry Jewishly in the Soviet Union, together they now celebrated a belated joyous event—a traditional Jewish wedding complete with rabbi, *huppah* (wedding canopy), and *ketubot* (marriage contracts).

New centers of Jewish life were established throughout the year and old ones expanded their activities. Chemnitz's Jewish community laid the foundation stone, in March, for the first synagogue to be built in the former East Germany since the end of the Communist regime. The new synagogue in Kassel was dedicated in late May, and construction of a new synagogue in Dresden began in June. The Jewish community of Bremerhaven was officially founded in September, and Synagogue Hüttenweg, which had been part of the community chapel for the U.S. army in Berlin, was reactivated in October. Braunschweig, in June, and Hammeln, in September, welcomed the addition of sacred Torah scrolls into their houses of prayer. In August, one year after the death of Ignatz Bubis, the long-time president of the CCJG, the Jewish community center in Frankfurt am Main was renamed in his memory.

BERLIN

The passing of senior cantor Estrongo Nachama on January 13 deeply saddened the Jews of Berlin. Born in 1918 in Thessaloniki, Greece, the "singer of Auschwitz" came to Berlin after his family was killed in the Holocaust, and he served as a pillar of postwar Jewish life there for more than 50 years. Nachama was known throughout Germany for his weekly Shabbat program on RIAS (Radio in the American Sector), his support of the small Jewish community in

East Berlin during the Communist years, and his untiring efforts in the cause of interfaith understanding. Berlin's Pestalozzistrasse congregation had been his home synagogue.

To the chagrin of not a few community members, Walter Rothschild, Berlin's outspoken Liberal rabbi, was unceremoniously fired in February, more than a year before the end of his three-year contract. Rothschild, who had responsibility for four separate and highly variegated non-Orthodox congregations, had a vision of Liberal Judaism that was far more innovative than that of many of his congregants, especially those who frequented the Pestalozzistrasse Synagogue (see AJYB 2000, p. 356). An agreement was later reached that permitted him to serve in the other three synagogues, Oranienburger, Ryke, and Fraenkelufer, through December. For his part, Rabbi Rothschild lamented the damage his abrupt termination had done to Berlin's Liberal rabbinate, which had been vacant for three years before he was hired in 1998, and expressed doubt that other German-speaking rabbis would be drawn to Berlin. He planned to run for a place in the Berlin Jewish Community's Representative Assembly on a platform stressing Jewish education, in elections scheduled for March 2001.

Chaim Rozwaski, a Holocaust survivor and rabbi with Orthodox training who had become well-known in Berlin as founding director of the Lauder Jüdisches Lehrhaus, was hired to fill the Pestalozzistrasse's empty pulpit for one year.

Andreas Nachama, president of the Berlin Jewish Community, announced in February that Berlin's local government had agreed to provide DM 2.5 million for security measures for the Jewish community, including the hiring of highly trained Israeli security guards to be posted inside its buildings. Julius Schoeps, director of the Moses Mendelssohn Center in Potsdam and a member of the community's Representative Assembly, protested against the agreement on national television. He argued that the presence of Israeli guards, as opposed to the German police who guarded the exteriors of the buildings, transformed the Berlin Jewish Community into an "extraterritorial zone."

Berlin's Jüdischer Kulturverein (Jewish Culture Association) celebrated its tenth anniversary. Directed by Irene Runge, the organization had sponsored more than two thousand events aimed at the transmission of Jewish culture and tradition, and the integration of Russian immigrants within Berlin Jewish society.

Religion and Education

At a milestone event in June, Berlin's Jüdische Obershule on Grosse Hamburger Strasse awarded diplomas to the first group of young Jews since the Holocaust to graduate from the high school of a German Jewish day school. No one knew at the time, however, that this event would set the scene for an embarrassing conflict between the Berlin Jewish Community and the Lauder Foundation over the question of how to define Jewishness in postwar Germany. One of 19 graduates of the Jüdische Obershule, Jonathan Marcus, a top-notch student, became the first-ever Jewish student in postwar Germany to attend Jewish day school from kindergarten through grade 13. Marcus—whose family was respected as one of the pillars of Berlin Jewish life—then opted to study at the yearlong intensive bet-midrash program for men at the Lauder Foundation's Jüdisches Lehrhaus.

A shock wave swept the community in early autumn when Marcus was barred from being counted toward the program's prayer quorum (minyan). Josh Spinner, the young German- and Russian-speaking Canadian-born rabbi who was in charge, questioned Marcus's status as a Jew according to halakhic standards. Marcus's grandmother and mother had been converted in 1965 by the Berlin Jewish Community's rabbinical court, under the supervision of the Conference of German Rabbis. The rabbi serving at Berlin's Liberal Pestalozzistrasse Synagogue at that time was a member of that court, but it had previously been assumed—until Spinner's intervention—that his Orthodox rabbinical ordination qualified him for involvement in conversions despite his non-Orthodox synagogue affiliation.

Toward the end of the year, the Berlin Jewish Community formulated a response. While going on record in favor of continued cooperation with the Lauder Foundation, the community insisted that the foundation make all of its programs accessible to all members of the Berlin community, including not just young men like Jonathan Marcus, but also women.

The role of women in religious life was, in fact, the subject of a panel discussion in Berlin in May, on the question, "Do women really have nothing to say in the Jewish community?" One speaker, Rabbi Bea Wyler, a native of Switzerland and a graduate of the Jewish Theological Seminary in New York, was the only female rabbi in Germany. Rabbi of the Oldenburg and Delmenhorst Jewish communities, Wyler charged that her application to join the Conference of German Rabbis had been rejected "on pretense." The year 2000 saw former synagogue choir member Avital Gerstetter, 28, of Berlin, on her way to becoming the country's first German-born female cantor. Cantor Rebecca Garfein of New York had heard Gerstetter sing at Berlin's Jewish Culture Days in 1997 and 1998, and had encouraged her to prepare for the cantorate. Germany's first gathering of "Women Rabbis, Cantors, Scholars, and all Spiritually Interested Women and Men—Bet Debora" took place in May 1999. A second conference was planned for June 2001.

Rabbi Yitzhak Ehrenberg, hired by the Berlin Jewish Community in 1997 as the city's Orthodox rabbi, opened a Talmud-Torah school in April for all interested community members. Under the leadership of Yehuda Teichtal, a Brooklyn-born rabbi, Chabad-Lubavitch of Berlin offered ample opportunity for study and celebration throughout the year. Meanwhile, the flourishing egalitarian congregation at the Oranienburger Synagogue announced plans for a regular Shabbat service for children, a novelty in Germany.

Friction between the CCJG's system of *Einheitsgemeinden*—congregations of different denominations coexisting under one administrative roof in each locality—and the World Union for Progressive Judaism (WUPJ) escalated during 2000. In 1999 the WUPJ had sought to strengthen non-Orthodox communities in Germany by seeking separate funding from the government on the grounds that the existing system discriminated against progressive Judaism. Prompted by Moishe Waks, the Berlin Jewish Community retaliated by putting on its agenda the suspension of its long-standing membership in the WUPJ. There was supposed to have been a meeting on January 19, 2000, where Rabbi Richard Block, president of the WUPJ, would explain his organization's position, but Block failed to attend. Still, the Berlin Jewish Community took no action. In late spring the WUPJ and the Council of European Rabbis established an office in Berlin.

Rabbi Walter Homolka had played a prominent role in the controversy during the previous year (see AJYB 2000, pp. 355–56). In 2000 Homolka resigned as vice chairman of the Union of Progressive Jews in Germany, Austria and Switzerland (UPJGAS), an association of non-Orthodox communities affiliated with the WUPJ, that he had helped found in 1997. At the end of the year the UPJGAS consisted of 13 member communities that represented an estimated 2,000 individuals Jews. As CWA services were only available to member communities of the CCJG, the UPJGAS had, on its own, to organize and pay for the two Jewish religious retreats it held during the year. Nevertheless, an important precedent was set in the city of Hannover when the state of Lower Saxony for the first time made funding available to seven congregations that operated outside the orbit of the CCJG, six of them Liberal and one Conservative.

In 2000 the UPJGAS, in cooperation with the University of Potsdam and the Moses Mendelssohn Center, established the first rabbinical seminary in Germany since the Holocaust—Abraham Geiger College, named after the great 19th-century German Reform thinker. Opening ceremonies were held amid much festivity in Potsdam in November. Susannah Heschel, an American Jewish theologian, was honored for her book, *Abraham Geiger and the Jewish Jesus.* The seminary, as yet unaccredited, planned to train male and female rabbis, cantors, and religious educators to work in Liberal Jewish communities throughout Europe. The first class, expected to have between three and five students, was scheduled to begin its studies in the fall of 2001. Russian language studies would be a mandatory component of the curriculum.

Meanwhile, the CCJG announced plans to initiate its own rabbinical training program, also scheduled to begin in the fall of 2001, based at the University of Heidelberg.

In June a Liberal Bet Din (religious court) was established in Halberstadt, near Magdeburg, under the auspices of Rabbi Rodney Mariner of London.

Finally, a new Jewish publishing house, Jüdische Verlagsanstalt Berlin (JVB), was founded by Rabbi Walter Homolka, Julius Schoeps, and Jochen Böckler. Its goal was to issue both classic and new German Jewish publications, as well as to produce German translations of important texts of Jewish interest.

Interreligious Relations

German Jews and Christians involved in religious dialogue generally applauded Pope John Paul II's historic visit to Israel in March, but many viewed *Dominus Iesus,* the declaration issued by the Vatican in August—primarily the work of Cardinal Joseph Ratzinger—as a provocative step backward because it appeared to deny the spiritual validity of non-Christian faiths (see above, pp. 361–62). Joel Berger, spokesman for the Conference of German Rabbis and chief rabbi of the Württemberg region, deemed the document a "slap in the face." But this negative assessment was not universal in the Jewish community. Ernst Ehrlich, for example, a German-born Jew and former European director of B'nai B'rith who had taught Jewish studies in Germany and Switzerland, argued that *Dominus Iesus* was addressing religious issues relevant to Christian ecumenical activity, and had not been meant to denigrate Judaism.

The theme of the 50th annual Brotherhood Week sponsored by the Society for Christian-Jewish Cooperation (SCJC) was "The World Rests on Three Pillars: Justice, Truth, and Freedom." The organization presented President Rau its Buber-Rosenzweig medal for decades of dedication to Jewish-Christian and German-Israeli relations. The SCJC also joined, in September, with the Evangelical Academy of Berlin-Brandenburg and the Berlin office of the American Jewish Committee for a conference in Berlin on the sensitive issue of continued proselytization of Jews—many of them newcomers from the FSU—in Germany.

The Oberammergau Passion Play, enacted once every ten years since 1634, had its 40th presentation on May 21, 2000. Intensive discussions between representatives of the American Jewish Committee and the directors of this year's play—Otto Huber and Christian Stückl—led to the incorporation of a number of changes aimed at depicting the Jews of Jesus's time in less derogatory terms and providing a more accurate portrayal of the Jewish religious context in which Jesus lived. Thus the play did away with the horned costumes worn by Jewish priests, the implication that Jesus was not Jewish, and the traditional charge of eternal Jewish guilt for his death. The Last Supper was depicted, for the first time, as a Passover seder, the actor playing Jesus said the prayer over wine in Hebrew, and his disciples addressed him as "rabbi." Also, for the first time in the history of the pageant, the performance was followed by a private interfaith discussion led by the town's mayor.

Micha Brumlik, one of Germany's leading Jewish thinkers, made a plea on the front page of the *Allgemeine Jüdische Wochenzeitung* (June 8) for intensified dialogue between Germany's Jews and Muslims, referring to the Muslim community as "my brother Ishmael." Although Brumlik acknowledged the theological differences separating the two minority faiths, he also noted points of mutual interest. For example, given the predominance of Christian religious education in German public schools and state-run universities, both Jews and Muslims had a common interest in securing greater input into the development of curricula.

Culture

Some Jewish critics bemoaned the unusually meager showing of films of Jewish interest at Berlin's 50th annual international film festival, the Berlinale, in February. All three of the feature films and one of the three documentaries containing Jewish content came from the former Soviet bloc. The features were Karel Kachina's *Hanele; Glamour*, directed by Frigyes Gödrös; and Milan Cieslar's *Lebensborn*. Georgiers A. Rechwiaschwili's documentary, *The Promised Land: The Return*, explored Eastern European fascination with Zionism, using previously unpublished film from Russian archives.

Berlinale films dealing with the Holocaust included the German film *Pardon Me, I'm Alive*, and *Martin*, a documentary about Martin Zaidenstadt — the Polish survivor of Dachau who now spends his days telling visitors to the concentration camp his version of what happened there. In *Paragraph 175*, American directors Rob Epstein and Jeffrey Friedman portrayed survivors of the Nazi persecution of homosexuals.

The city of Düsseldorf initiated an annual Jewish film festival in May, offering 17 films depicting Jewish life in Europe, the United States, and Israel.

The theme of the sixth annual Berlin Jewish Film Festival in June was "Departure into the New Millennium: Visions, Utopias and Realities."

A notable television production investigated the Shoah. Guido Knopp's six-part prime-time series "Holokaust" began airing on October 17. An award-winning journalist and ZDF-television's program director for contemporary history, Knopp replaced the "c" of the word Holocaust with the Germanic "k" as a "symbolic act of owning one's own history." He explained that he was going out of his way to do this in order to show where he stood on the Walser-Bubis debate that had shaken Germany in 1998, when the writer Martin Walser had called for an end to the "incessant presentation of our disgrace." The series, produced by an international team, used new documentation that had been discovered primarily in postcommunist Eastern Europe.

Another important television series was "Juden in Deutschland nach 1945" (Jews in Germany after 1945), a three-part documentary covering postwar Jewish history, which aired for the first time in March. It was written, directed, and produced by Richard Chaim Schneider, a son of Hungarian Jews who was born in Munich in 1957.

Photo-designer Peter Liedtke produced a slide-show installation, in cooperation with the Heinrich Böll Foundation, commemorating the deportation of Germany's Jews. The presentation consisted of pictures Liedtke took at Auschwitz as well as documentation of the deportations from Postdam, Rostock, Halle, and Weimar. In each of these cities, for weeks at a time between January and April, a total of 80 slides were projected in succession onto the face of a public structure or building after the onset of twilight.

Between its opening in August 1999 and its temporary closing in June 2000, more than 300,000 visitors took architectural tours of Daniel Liebeskind's empty building that would ultimately house the Berlin Jewish Museum. Under the directorship of W. Michael Blumenthal—a German Jew who fled the Nazis and later became U.S. secretary of the treasury under President Jimmy Carter—the museum was scheduled to reopen to the public in September 2001. Its theme is the 2000-year history of the Jews in Germany, from Roman times through the reawakening of Jewish life after the Holocaust. For 12 nights in June, right before it closed, the structure's empty rooms became the backdrop for Adriana Altaras's production *Heaven's Realm,* based on stories by I.B. Singer. Tom Freudenheim, a Berlin-born American Jew, opted not to renew his contract as assistant director of the museum after June.

Chancellor Schröder attended the opening of the exhibit, "Jews in Berlin 1938–1945," on May 8 at Berlin's Centrum Judaicum. The event commemorated the 55th anniversary of the end of World War II.

Shocked by an attack against the Lübeck synagogue in 1994, a concerned group of students from Darmstadt's Technical University used CAD (Computer Aided Design) technology to bring 14 synagogues destroyed by the Nazis on Kristallnacht in 1938 "back to life." The result, six years later, was an exhibit, "Synagogues in Germany—A Virtual Reconstruction," which premiered at Bonn's Kunst-und-Austellungshalle der Bundesrepublik Deutschland for two months beginning in May.

In September, despite the rain and cold, 8,000 people visited the fourth annual Jewish Street Festival in Berlin, put on by the Jewish Students Club.

Berlin's 14th annual Jewish Culture Days in November focused on "Piazza Italia," Italian Jewry, the oldest in Europe, and on St. Petersburg, "The Venice of the North."

"Symbols of Everyday Life" were showcased in Fürth in a show entitled "x:hibit" from November 21, 1999 through early 2000. This pop-quiz-style exhibit on Jewish life challenged visitors with questions ranging from what city Germany's only female rabbi lived in, to which conventional medications were kosher, and then provided the answers.

In December, 86-year-old Heinz Berggruen permanently signed over his priceless collection of Picassos and other artwork to the city of Berlin as a sign of "reconciliation after the Holocaust." The Jewish art dealer had escaped Nazi Germany in 1936 and fled to the United States. Berggruen brought his collection to Berlin in 1995 where it became a fixture of the cultural landscape; he was awarded the National Prize in 1999.

Publications

In *Deutscher Geist und Judenhass—Das Verhältnis des philosophischen Idealismus zum Judentum* (The German Mind and anti-Semitism—The Relationship of Philosophical Idealism to the Jews), Micha Brumlik, the noted Heidelberg professor of education, explored the complex relationship to Jews and Judaism—ranging from hate to respect—of such great German minds as Kant, Fichte, Schleiermacher, Hegel, Schelling, and Marx.

In *Holokaust,* the 400-page book designed to accompany his television documentary series of the same name, Guido Knopp conveyed a precise and moving picture of the Holocaust based on years of research and investigation. Some of the material had never been published before. Simon Wiesenthal called this book "the legacy of millions of Shoah victims."

There were also numerous survivor testimonies published during the year. These included Ruth Zucker's biography, *Meine sieben Leben* (My Seven Lives); a German translation of Walter Laqueur's autobiography detailing the exodus of Jewish youth from Germany after 1933, *Geboren in Deutschland* (Born in Germany); and Herbert Z. Kesseler's *Der Weg ins Ungewisse—Von Berlin nach Holland und Belgien* (Into the Unknown—From Berlin to Holland and Belgium), a record of the author's childhood memories and refugee experiences between 1928 and 1945.

Concentrating on the country ruled by Nazi Germany's fiercest opponent, Arno Lustiger published *Rotbuch: Stalin und die Juden* (Redbook: Stalin and the Jews), an investigation of the tragic history of the Jewish Antifascist Committee during the war and the fate of Soviet Jewry until Stalin's death.

A major theme in contemporary German Jewish affairs was tackled by Julius Schoeps and W. Jasper in their collection of essays on how Jews from the former Soviet Union were faring in Germany, *Ein Neues Judentum in Deutschland?* (A New Jewry in Germany?). Richard Chaim Schneider widened the picture of postwar Jewish life in the country with *Wir sind da! Die Geschichte der Juden in Deutschland von 1945 bis heute* (We're Here! The History of the Jews in Germany from 1945 through the Present), a supplement to the three-part television documentary of the same name. The book included extensive interviews with 34 of Germany's leading Jewish figures. Adolf Diamant examined one type of anti-Semitic hate crime in *Geschändete jüdische Friedhöfe in Deutschland 1945 bis 1999* (Desecrated Jewish Cemeteries in Germany, 1945 to 1999). Diamant found that approximately 1,000 Jewish cemeteries in Germany had been desecrated since the end of World War II, with a disproportionate increase in such incidents since German unification.

The new *Metzler Lexikon der deutsch-jüdischen Literatur* (Metzler Dictionary of German-Jewish Literature) gave detailed information about German-language Jewish literature from the Enlightenment of the 18th century to the present, with 270 entries arranged alphabetically, "from Adler to Zuckerman."

New releases by contemporary Jewish authors from Germany included Maxim Biller's *Die Tochter* (The Daughter); Barbara Honigmann's *Alles, Alles Liebe* (All My Love); and Ralph Giordano's *Morris. Die Fischmanns* (The Fischmanns) and *Schlossgasse 21* (Schloss Street 21) were two long-awaited rereleases, in paperback, of books by H.W. Katz. Popular Israeli novels published in German translation included Zaruya Shalev's *LiebesLeben* (LoveLife) and Dorit Rabinyan's *Unsere Hochzeiten* (Our Weddings).

The need for updated and authoritative German-language material on Jewish religion, culture, history, and customs was met by two new books, Julius Schoeps's *Neues Lexikon des Judentums* (The New Jewish Lexicon), and *Das Judentum hat viele Gesichter* (The Many Faces of Judaism) by Rabbis Walter Homolka and Gilbert S. Rosenthal. The new publishing house Jüdische Verlagsanstalt Berlin (JVB) rereleased *Liberales Judentum* (Liberal Judaism), Max Dienemann's classic work of the 1930s, as well as *Die Tora*, a careful adaptation into modern German of the first Jewish translation of the Torah into High German, done by Moses Mendelssohn more than 200 years before.

The Munich-based publisher Piper-Verlag came under strong criticism during the fall for its plans to publish, in February 2001, a German-language edition of Norman Finkelstein's controversial book *The Holocaust Industry: Reflections on the Exploitation of Jewish Suffering,* which accused Jewish organizations and the State of Israel of using the Holocaust for their own aggrandizement. Some German observers, Jewish and non-Jewish, feared that the book would be used to justify anti-Semitism and, in the words of Frankfurt Jewish community leader and CCJG member Solomon Korn, "garner applause from the wrong side" (for evidence that these fears were justified, see above, pp. 18–20). Piper, however, insisted on the "necessity of publishing a German-language edition as a basis for political discussion" and said it would invite Finkelstein to Germany in 2001.

Personalia

In August, one year after the death of Ignatz Bubis, the former president of the CCGJ, the city of Frankfurt am Main renamed its Obermain Bridge, built in 1872, in his honor.

Else and Berthold Beitz, both octogenarians, received the CCJG's 1999 Leo Baeck Prize, awarded on February 10, 2000. Ignatz Bubis had nominated them before his death. As manager of a German oil company in occupied Poland, Mr. Beitz, with the help of his wife, had saved Jews — among them Bubis's brother-in-law and his wife — from deportation to extermination camps by having them work for his company or hiding them in his home. Friede Springer, wife of deceased German publisher Axel Springer, received the 2000 Leo Baeck Prize in November.

On the order of French president Jacques Chirac, the Officer's Insignia of the Legion of Honor, the highest French honor, was presented to CCJG president Paul Spiegel (in September) and CCJG vice president Michel Friedman (in November), in recognition of their efforts to promote understanding between Jews and non-Jews.

The New York German-language newspaper *Aufbau* awarded Frankfurt author Arno Lustiger its Aufbau Cultural Prize on February 29, for his work on the history of Jewish resistance against the Nazis. Barbara Honigmann, a Strasbourg resident born and raised in East Berlin, received the Kleist Prize in Berlin.

American Jews decorated in Germany included Israel Singer, secretary general of the World Jewish Congress, recipient of the Heinz Galinski Prize, and W. Michael Blumenthal, director of the Berlin Jewish Museum, named honorary citizen of his hometown, Oranienburg. Robert B. Goldmann, journalist and European representative of the Anti-Defamation League, had an academic scholarship named after him by the city of Reinheim, his childhood home.

Among the prominent Jews who passed away during 2000 were Cantor Estrongo Nachama, 82 (see above, pp. 387–88); Alphons Silbermann, 90, renowned sociologist, musicologist, and author; Gisele Freund, 82, photographer and Berlin native; and Rabbi Benjamin Gelles, 84, one of the last representatives of the prewar German-Jewish rabbinate, and most recently rabbi of the Cologne Jewish community, 1984–1992.

WENDY KLOKE

EDITOR'S NOTE

The reference to Prof. Dr. Michael Wolffsohn that appeared in the 1997 AJYB stated that he was "labeled positively" as "nationally oriented" by the neo-Nazi publication *Wer ist wer im Judentum?* In fact the neo-Nazi publication says that Prof. Dr. Wolfssohn is "hostile to the National Right in Germany."

Austria

National Affairs

THE NATIONAL ELECTIONS OF October 3, 1999, dramatically shifted the country's balance of political power. The far-right Freedom Party (FPÖ), which had, until then, been excluded from sharing power at the national level, emerged as a major force, winning an unprecedented 27.2 percent of the vote and edging out the People's Party (ÖVP) for second place. The latter, which for 13 years had shared power as the junior partner in coalition with the dominant left-of-center Social Democratic Party (SPÖ), was now relegated to third place with 26.9 percent.

After the election, President Thomas Klestil ignored the electoral gains of the FPÖ and invited Chancellor Viktor Klima, the leaders of the Social Democrats, and Foreign Minister Wolfgang Schüssel, head of the People's Party, to form a new government and reconstitute their long-standing coalition. In pursuing this course, President Klestil sought to prevent the Freedom Party and its charismatic leader, Jörg Haider, from attaining political power at the federal level. Haider, who had taken control of the FPÖ in 1986, had made it a major party by playing on racism and xenophobia. However the president's political maneuvering did not succeed because the leaders of the Social Democrats and the People's Party could not agree on a joint program for ruling the country. Left with no other alternative, President Klestil called on the ÖVP's Schüssel to form a coalition government with the Freedom Party. Under the agreement they reached, the Freedom Party would have three important cabinet portfolios: finance, defense, and interior. Haider himself would not enter the cabinet, but would stay on in his post as governor of the province of Carinthia, where his party had attained power the previous year. Despite his apparent withdrawal from the national political scene, there was little doubt that Haider's views would determine the actions and positions of his party.

The response, both at home and abroad, came quickly. A huge crowd of about 150,000 crammed a historic Vienna square to protest the inclusion of the Freedom Party in the government. No sooner had the government taken office than it found itself on a collision course with the other 14 members of the European Union. Within days, these countries—acting individually, since Austria had broken no EU rules—announced measures to isolate Austria diplomatically. They scaled back diplomatic ties to Vienna, refused to endorse Austrians for European Union and other international posts, and adopted other, largely symbolic, measures to show their displeasure.

This sudden, unprecedented action by the other EU members appeared to be motivated by several factors. One was genuine concern about the racist and xenophobic views of Haider and many of his supporters, which were viewed as incompatible with European values. In speech after speech, the leader of the Freedom Party had virulently attacked foreigners, charging them with causing much of the crime in Austria. In several speeches he singled out Africans for drug trafficking. Immigrants, he darkly warned, were a threat to the nation's economy, taking jobs away from native Austrians and forcing many onto the welfare rolls. The Europeans were also deeply troubled by past statements of Haider expressing admiration for certain aspects of Nazism. For example, he once praised Hitler's "orderly labor policy," though he later apologized. There was, in addition, a pragmatic political reason, never explicitly articulated, for the actions against Austria. This was the fear that the presence of the Freedom Party in the Austrian national government might boost the political prospects of similar right-wing extremist parties in other countries. France and Belgium, two countries with strong far-right parties, were the most vociferous supporters of the EU sanctions.

In an apparent effort to bring an end to the sanctions, Haider announced in May that he was giving up the leadership of the party, which would pass into the hands of Vice Chancellor Susanne Riess-Passer. Few doubted, however, that Haider continued to pull the strings. Soon there was growing uneasiness about the sanctions among some of the EU states, notably Denmark, Finland, and other small countries, which feared the appearance of being dominated by such larger powers as France and Germany. Enthusiasm for the sanctions also cooled when it became clear that Austria's coalition government was not about to impair the rights of foreigners or adopt other undemocratic measures. For their part, Austrians were becoming increasingly resentful toward the EU, which they accused of meddling in their country's internal affairs. Nothing in the EU constitution, critics said, barred members from including extreme nationalists in their governments, so long as they remained democratic and acted within the law. These views found an increasingly receptive audience in the other EU countries.

To escape from an embarrassing situation, the EU appointed a panel of three "wise men" to review the political situation in Austria and determine whether sanctions should be lifted. In a report submitted in September, the panel recommended an end to the sanctions, which, it stated, had become "counterproductive." The report found that Austria was "respectful of common European values" and had continued to uphold the rights of immigrants, refugees, and minorities. A week after receiving the report, the EU members agreed to lift the sanctions and resume normal diplomatic ties with Austria. Israel, however, roundly condemned the decision and refused to return its ambassador to Vienna.

Despite the EU's favorable action, many Austrians, unhappy over the diplomatic sanctions, had second thoughts about remaining in the union. More than 100,000 Austrians signed a petition calling for a referendum on whether to quit the European Union, and this obliged Parliament to discuss the issue within six months. The petition charged the EU with stripping Austria of its sovereignty, undermining its agriculture, and threatening its neutrality. Austria had joined the European Union in 1995 after 75 percent of the voters favored it in a referendum, but recent polls had shown a drastic decline of support for continued Austrian membership.

In its first test of strength since entering the national coalition, the Freedom Party suffered a stunning defeat in the October 15 election in the southeastern province of Styria, winning only 12.7 percent of the vote. This was down 4.7 points from the party's performance in the Styrian election of 1995, and less than half of the 27 percent the party had racked up there in the 1999 general election. The Freedom Party continued on a downward spiral, finishing a distant third in the provincial election in Burgenland, Austria's poorest province, with only 12.6 percent of the vote. This showing was nearly two percentage points lower than in the previous provincial election four years earlier, and, more significantly, a drop of 9 percent from what the party received in the province in the federal election of 1999. In fact, the results in Styria and Burgenland confirmed the findings of public-opinion polls that showed a fall in the party's popularity since it joined the ruling coalition.

Many observers viewed the downturn in Freedom Party fortunes as the inevitable price it had to pay for transforming itself from a party of protesting "outsiders" into a party of government "insiders." As the junior partner in the coalition, and hampered, furthermore, by the charismatic Haider's absence from the national scene, the party alienated its natural constituency by supporting painful spending cuts, tax increases, and public-sector job losses, unpopular fiscal measures instituted by the government in the hope of balancing the budget by 2002. The party's image as defender of the interests of the "ordinary man" was seriously tarnished.

The FPÖ was also hurt by allegations that Haider's allies in the Austrian national police had illegally given the party confidential information about politicians, journalists, artists, and others from classified police intelligence files. In addition, Freedom Party ministers in the government attacked official investigations into the conduct of Haider and some party associates. Justice Minister Dieter Böhmdorfer, for example, who had been Haider's personal lawyer until his appointment to the cabinet, seemingly prejudged the outcome of an independent investigation when he stated that Haider was "above all suspicion." It was in this context that 1,300 judges and public prosecutors issued an open letter in December addressed to President Klestil and members of the governing coalition urging politicians to respect the rule of law and not to try to use the judicial system for political purposes. The judiciary's "independence" as well as "the separation of powers," the letter said, "are in danger if blatant political pressure is applied to influence current investigations." The letter did not mention the Freedom Party or any of its officials by name, but was quite clearly aimed at them.

In an apparent effort to stem his party's declining fortunes, Haider returned to his familiar xenophobic theme, denouncing the presence of immigrants in Austria. In a rabble-rousing speech to party faithful in Vienna on October 22, he said: "There are too many illegals, far too many drug dealers . . . and it must be our job to bring about a thorough getting rid of [them]." Controversy swirled around Haider again in December over his trip to the Vatican, where he presented a Christmas tree from Carinthia, where he was governor, to Pope John Paul II. World War II resistance fighters, the secretary of the Italian Communist Party, and the president of Rome's Jewish community signed a protest statement against the Haider visit, while Israel condemned it as a cause of "considerable disappointment and displeasure to the government of Israel." In response, Vatican secretary of state Cardinal Angelo Sodano said: "The Holy See is open to everyone—no one should be surprised by that."

Israel and the Middle East

Relations between Israel and Austria were frozen following the formation of the new coalition on February 4. Jerusalem made good on its threat to withdraw its ambassador in the event the Freedom Party became part of the new government. The Austrian government, in contrast, kept its ambassador, Wolfgang Paul, in Tel Aviv. Significantly, Israel's withdrawal of its ambassador provoked no reaction in the Austrian media nor did it lead to a political debate in the country. High government officials stated on several occasions that the door remained open for the resumption of normal ties between the two countries. Ilan Ben Dov, the chargé d'affaires ad interim, represented Israeli interests in Austria and maintained contact with government ministries. Similarly, Ambassador Paul was afforded full access to Israeli government offices. High-level political contacts between the two countries, however, remained suspended. Despite the political constraints, trade between the two countries grew, with Austrian exports to Israel rising 13.8 percent. The mayor of Vienna, Michael Häupl, visited Jerusalem in September and was received by Prime Minister Ehud Barak and Minister of Justice Yossi Beilin. Three groups of teachers and educators visited Israel in August and November as part of the Austrian-Israel exchange program.

On the international scene, the European Union nations split over a United Nations General Assembly resolution, on October 20, condemning Israel for using excessive force in its attempt to put down the violence in the West Bank and Gaza. Austria was one of the eight EU members supporting the resolution (the other seven abstained).

Austria was reported, in December, to be involved in secret efforts to facilitate a prisoner exchange between Israel and the Lebanese Hezballah militia. An Austrian defense official confirmed Austrian and Israeli press reports that Defense Minister Herbert Scheibner, a member of the far-right Freedom Party, had been in the Middle East where he met with representatives of the two sides. According to the Vienna daily *Die Presse,* Scheibner met with Israeli deputy defense minister Ephraim Sneh in early November as part of an effort to secure the release of three Israeli soldiers abducted by Hezballah in October. In exchange, the Lebanese wanted the release of 19 Lebanese men imprisoned in Israel.

Holocaust-Related Developments

WAR CRIMINALS

Dr. Heinrich Gross, an 84-year-old former Nazi doctor, had been put on trial in March 1999 for acting as an accessory to the murder of nine disabled children at Vienna's Spiegelgrund clinic in 1944. He denied the charges. The trial was suspended when the court heard from an Austrian psychiatrist that Gross was suffering from dementia. Gross had became a leading neurologist in postwar Austria despite several attempts to bring him to trial (see AJYB 2000, pp. 367–68). In 2000 the state prosecutor asked for a new medical evaluation after Gross gave a television interview in which he appeared normal and alert. However, a new medical report, this time by a Swiss psychiatrist, stated that Gross would be unable to follow court proceedings. An official of the Vienna district court announced that the trial would be suspended for another six months while the prosecutor decided whether to order yet another medical examination.

COMPENSATION

Under the skillful negotiating hand of Stuart Eizenstat, deputy treasury secretary of the United States, the signing of a wide-ranging deal to compensate Austrian Holocaust victims was close at hand at year's end. The Austrian negotiators, headed by Ambassador Ernst Sucharipa, director of the Austrian Diplomatic Academy, made a detailed offer on December 21 in what appeared to be a final bid to settle outstanding Jewish claims. The proposals were complex and covered several different areas. Total payments offered came to $950 million, with an additional amount to be paid in settlement of claims for looted assets.

Included in the sum were $150 million in "immediate compensation" for survivors originating from or living in Austria, to cover the loss of apartment and office leases, household property, and personal valuables. Such payment had been recommended by the Historiker Kommission (Historical Commission), created in September 1998 to examine instances of property confiscation during the Nazi period and to determine what had been done after the war to restore such property to rightful owners or heirs or to compensate them (see AJYB 2000, p. 368). The commission issued a report in October 2000 stating that Austria had failed to compensate Jewish survivors of the Holocaust for being thrown out of their homes. Austria never passed legislation enabling Jews to return to their homes after World War II, according to the panel of historians, mainly because lawmakers knew that doing so would have angered former Nazis who made up a large segment of the country's voters. Clemens Jabloner, the commission chairman, declined to say what sum would be appropriate to compensate the 23,000 tenants alive today. Some 60,000 rented homes occupied by Jewish families in Vienna were cleared of their inhabitants shortly after Austria was annexed to Hitler's Third Reich in 1938. The "clearances" were initially spontaneous acts by armed members of the Nazi party. Susan Kowarc, one of the historians who wrote the report, said at a news conference: "This happened in part with the collaboration of the Austrian public."

The proposed sum also included $45 million which Bank Austria, the largest bank in the country, agreed to pay for its role in confiscating Jewish assets. Austria also said it would pass legislation to pay about $65 million over a period of ten years for health benefits to Holocaust survivors living outside Austria. The government had already, in May, signed an agreement to compensate wartime victims of Nazi forced and slave labor. Under this accord, Austria would set up a $415-million fund to compensate the estimated 150,000 survivors who were obliged by the Nazis to toil under horrendous conditions in industry and agriculture. Most of them were non-Jews from many different European countries. While Jewish groups endorsed the Bank Austria settlement and expressed satisfaction with the payment to slave laborers, they noted that a number of issues were still outstanding, such as how unpaid claims against Austrian insurers should be settled and how funds should be distributed among needy survivors. Further negotiations to finalize the agreement were planned for January 2001 in Vienna and Washington.

The Nationalfond, established by the Austrian government in June 1995, was the special fund "for the victims of national socialism." It was to help compensate anyone, Jew or non-Jew, who had been persecuted because of political beliefs, religion, nationality, sexual orientation, physical or mental disability, or whom the Nazis considered "asocial," as well as anyone forced to flee Austria to escape persecution. By 2000, the fund—headed by Hannah Lessing, who was also a member of the Austrian team negotiating terms of compensation to Jewish Holocaust survivors—had contacted over 31,000 persons it considered eligible to receive payment. By the end of 2000, payments had been made to over 28,000 people in 65 countries. The country with the largest number of recipients was the United States, followed by Austria, Israel, and Australia. The amount paid to each beneficiary was fixed at 70,000 shillings ($4,800), though in special cases this could be as much as tripled.

As Austria accelerated the pace of negotiations to settle outstanding compensation issues for Jewish survivors, the Nationalfond was increasingly assigned administrative and other responsibilities for handling looted, heirless Jewish assets and using them to fund projects. At the London meeting of the Tripartite Gold Commission in December 1997, which dealt with monetary gold looted by the

Nazis, Austria had agreed to relinquish its rights to the 860 kilograms of gold owed to it and hand over the monetary value of this gold—then valued at approximately $8.5 million—to the Nationalfond for distribution to needy Holocaust survivors and to other worthwhile causes (AJYB 1999, p. 360). Only a few payments were subsequently made to individuals, as most of the money was earmarked for projects in Eastern European countries. Two examples in 2000 were the updating of the X-ray facilities of the Jewish Hospital in Budapest and the funding of the Vilnius International Forum on Holocaust-Era Looted Cultural Assets, held in the Lithuanian capital October 3–5.

Building on a 1999 initiative by the Federation of Jewish Communities in Austria, on September 15 four organizations—the federation, the Committee for Jewish Claims on Austria, the Council of Jews from Austria in Israel, and the American Council for Equal Compensation of Nazi Victims from Austria, Inc. (ACOA)—joined to form an international steering committee to promote the interests of Jewish Holocaust victims in and from Austria. The committee established a Holocaust Victims' Information and Support Center (HVISC, "Anlaufstelle") with a ten-person staff, which would register the names and assets of the Jewish victims, along with archival and other relevant material, and thereby create a continually updated database for claims to possible restitution or compensation in the future. Cases were organized both by names of individuals and by types of loss: business assets, real estate, capital assets, insurance policies, moveable assets (personal effects, household furnishings, artworks, jewelry), as well as compensation for the termination of tenant rights, dismissal from a profession or academic institution and the resultant loss of legal and/or pension rights, and compensation for discriminatory taxes and charges ("Reich Flight Tax," "Jewish Atonement Payment"). The HVISC sent out a questionnaire to approximately 12,000 Holocaust survivors in different countries to gather information. At regular intervals the data, in the form of "dossiers," was to be submitted to the parent body, the international steering committee.

LOOTED JEWISH ARTWORK

A federal judge in New York ruled in December that the U.S. government could renew its effort to force an Austrian museum to forfeit an Egon Schiele painting stolen by the Nazis from a Jewish family during World War II (see AJYB 2000, pp. 370–71). U.S. District Judge Michael Mukasey, who dismissed the government's original case in July, now ruled that federal prosecutors could file an amended lawsuit setting forth new arguments. The government was seeking the surrender of the painting *Portrait of Wally,* which had been loaned to New York's Museum of Modern Art by Austria's Leopold Museum Privatstiftung. The portrait had been in the possession of a Viennese Jewish art-gallery owner in Vienna before the war. After the Nazis came to power they forced the owner, Lea Bondi

Jaray, to surrender *Wally,* which was part of her private collection. After the war, the painting was erroneously placed in the collection of a private person, who eventually sold it to the Leopold. Jaray's heirs were now seeking its return.

The judge had found in July that the Leopold could not be considered the holder of stolen property because the painting had been recovered by the U.S. armed forces before the museum bought it. This recovery, he ruled, ". . . purged the painting of the taint it had." In the December decision, however, the judge recognized that the government now wanted to argue that paintings seized during and after the war were not held by the armed forces for the purpose of returning them to their true owners, and therefore the "taint" may not have been removed. In allowing the amendment to the original suit, Judge Mukasey said: "This case involves substantial issues of public policy relating to property stolen during World War Two as part of a program implemented by the German government."

COMMEMORATION AND EDUCATION

To mark the liberation of the Mauthausen concentration camp, the Vienna Philharmonic Orchestra performed a concert at the site of the camp on May 5. Several years earlier the Austrian Parliament had proclaimed this day as the nation's "Memorial Day Against Violence and Racism in Memory of the Victims of National Socialism."

A special exhibition, held in the Depot of Movables in Vienna's seventh district on September 7–19, was about "The Looting of Furniture from Jewish Households." It showed examples of the various household objects, such as furniture, cutlery, and photographs, which were aryanized, seized by the Nazis, after the German annexation of Austria in March 1938. The starting point of the exhibition showed a file listing the "Judenmobil" — Jewish moveable property — of eight Viennese Jewish families that was confiscated and stored in the state-owned Depot of Movables, a huge storage facility built in the reign of Maria Theresa. Attached to the file was a receipt stating: "Seized for the benefit of the Austrian state." In 1938 a total of about 5,000 looted objects were listed, and of these about 600 were inventoried, thereby becoming state property. Furniture and other household objects were lent to Nazi government offices and other borrowers. Few of the objects were restored to their owners after the war, and, until recently, they were still being used in government offices or Austrian embassies abroad, with the users generally unaware of their origins. Recent research on the original ownership of these objects had led to the return of items when the families were traceable.

On October 25 (the eve of the Austrian National Day), President Klestil formally dedicated Vienna's memorial for the 65,000 Austrian victims of the Shoah, the idea for which had been first proposed by famed Nazi-hunter Simon Wiesenthal. The memorial itself, based on a design by the British architect Rachel

Whiteread, was a reinforced concrete cube standing 32 feet by 23 feet, and 12 feet high. The outer sides were in the form of shelves of books with their spines turned inward, enclosing an area made inaccessible by a locked door. "It's about not being able to enter," said Whiteread. "It is an abstract library because you obviously can't read the books and have no idea what the spines of the books might be," and the empty space inside symbolized the many readers of the library who did not live. The names of the concentration camps to which Austrian Jews were sent are engraved around the base of the monument, and the names of the murdered Jews and other information are available nearby. Located on the Judenplatz (old Jewish street), the memorial was at the site of an underground medieval synagogue, excavated by archeologists, and an adjoining Museum on Medieval Jewish Life, which featured, as a permanent exhibit, a multimedia presentation on the religious, cultural, and social life of the Viennese Jewish community in the Middle Ages until its end in the persecutions of 1420–21.

Austria applied in December for membership in the nine-nation Task Force for International Cooperation in Holocaust Education, Remembrance and Research. Interest in the Holocaust and compensation issues prompted the University of Vienna to organize a series of symposia, from October 9, 2000 to January 15, 2001, on "The Political Economy of the Holocaust."

JEWISH COMMUNITY

Demography

About 6,600 Jews were registered with the Israelitische Kultusgemeinde (IKG), but knowledgeable observers claimed that the actual number of Jews was at least twice as large. One hundred new members were signed up during the year as a result of an IKG campaign offering financial incentives to parents to register newborn children with the community. Continuing a long-established pattern, the overwhelming majority of Jews were concentrated in Vienna, with only about 500–600 making their homes elsewhere, primarily in the large provincial cities of Salzburg, Innsbruck, Graz, and Linz.

The Jewish community—heavily dependent on an influx of immigrants—has continued to shrink in numbers, due to a small but steady trickle of emigration and the virtual absence of new immigrants. Several hundred Jews, many of whom had come from the former Soviet republic of Georgia, emigrated in search of better economic opportunities, mainly in Eastern Europe. These Georgians, and other Sephardi Jews as well, were concentrated in the garment and shoe trades, which were undergoing a severe depression. To offset this outflow, the IKG has requested the government to waive certain provisions of the country's highly restrictive immigration laws so as to allow in the same number of Jews who had left. The government had yet to act on the request.

Communal Affairs

On November 9, the 62nd anniversary of Kristallnacht, a new synagogue was dedicated in Graz on the same site as the old one, constructed in 1892, that went up in flames during the Kristallnacht pogrom. Among those present at the inaugural ceremony were President Klestil, Alfred Stingl, the mayor of Graz, Ilan Ben Dov, Israeli chargé d'affaires, Paul Chaim Eisenberg, the chief rabbi of Austria, Ariel Muzicant, president of the Austrian Jewish community, and Kurt David Bruhl, president of the Graz Jewish community. The initiative and financial support for constructing the new synagogue came from the Graz municipal government and the provincial government of Styria, which said they wanted to right the historical wrong committed against the Jewish community of Graz. At the time of Kristallnacht, there were 1,700 Jews living in the city; now, the mostly elderly Jewish populace numbered 120. For years following the war, the local government took no action to invite the city's Holocaust survivors back, and few returned on their own.

The European regional office of the Anti-Defamation League (ADL), which opened in Vienna in August 1997 under the direction of journalist Marta Halpert, expanded its effort to combat prejudice and xenophobia in schools and in government ministries. In response to a request from the Austrian federal government to develop an antibias project for the ministries of Education, Interior, and Foreign Affairs, the ADL office prepared three-year contracts with each of these ministries to train people to train others to combat prejudice. The programs were based on the principles and techniques of the ADL's New York-based "A World of Difference" project. Officials of these ministries were invited to attend the training seminars. The first phase of the project was completed in August, when a group of eight trainers participated in an eight-day "train the trainer" workshop in Chicago and New York, cosponsored by the ADL, the United States embassy in Vienna, and AUA, the Austrian national airline. This was followed by a series of workshops attended by officials from government ministries, nongovernmental organizations (NGOs), and opinion leaders.

The Third International Theodor Herzl Symposium was held March 13–15 at the Vienna City Hall. The lectures and panel discussions focused mainly on the Middle East peace process. Austrian president Thomas Klestil opened the symposium with an address to the delegates. Other well-known speakers were Helmut Zilk, the former mayor of Vienna, and Cardinal Franz König.

The Jewish Cultural Weeks festival, running from October 26 through November 29, provided a wide array of cultural events, including cantorial concerts, films, and plays. A special feature of the festival was a two-day symposium at the Jewish Museum on the topic, "Walled Cities and the Building of Communities: The European Ghetto as an Urban Space."

Among the exhibitions mounted by the Jewish Museum of Vienna in 2000, one attracted special attention. This was "Between East and West: The Jews of Galicia and Vienna," which opened on November 7. The exhibition, scheduled to run through February 18, 2001, presented the works of different artists depicting the life of Jews in Vienna who had come from Galicia, the most northerly crown land of the Habsburg Empire. More than 10 percent of the population of turn-of-the-century Galicia, which today is divided between Poland and Ukraine, was Jewish, and a great many Galician Jews, popularly called Ostjuden (Eastern Jews), fled to Vienna during World War I as the ravages of the war spread to this Hapsburg province. The exhibition looked at the multifaceted relationship between Galicia and Vienna and the fundamental conflict it embodied, that between western and eastern forms of Judaism, which was manifested in the contrasting images and myths on the two sides.

MURRAY GORDON

East-Central Europe

CONTINUING THE PATTERN SET over the preceding decade, postcommunist countries developed and integrated into Europe at different rates, based largely on their economic progress. Concern persisted over ongoing manifestations of racism—directed primarily against Roma (Gypsies)—and anti-Semitism. These issues became more acute after the far-right Freedom Party (FPÖ) entered the Austrian government in February. Skinhead groups operated in various countries, and xenophobic and/or nationalist parties or political figures were outspoken in some places. The publication of Hitler's *Mein Kampf* in several countries caused alarm. At the same time, however, liberal political forces also achieved electoral successes, and the ouster of Slobodan Milosevic in Yugoslavia gave rise to hopes for improved stability in the Balkans.

In much the same way as the nations of which they were part, Jewish communities, institutions, and individuals also continued the process of integration and cooperation on regional and international levels at various rates of speed. Many communities and institutions set up or enlarged Web sites and Internet links. Several countries in the region took part in the European Day of Jewish Culture on September 3, a continent-wide initiative that saw hundreds of Jewish heritage sites in 16 countries opened to the public. Arachim, a seminar on Jewish education organized by the European Council of Jewish Communities and held in Budapest in November, drew more than 200 Jewish educators from all over Europe.

Internally, many Jewish communities confronted a crisis of leadership, both lay and rabbinic. Also, Jewish communities divided over the questions of "Who is a Jew?" and "How can one become a Jew?"—that is, whether criteria for conversion and membership in the Jewish community should be according to Halakhah or according to the Israeli Law of Return. The rift over these matters tended to coincide with the split between the Orthodox, on the one hand, and liberal and secular Jews, on the other. In August the American Jewish Joint Distribution Committee (JDC) appointed Rabbi Menachem Hacohen, an Israel-based rabbi also serving as chief rabbi in Romania, as its adviser on rabbinical affairs for worldwide programs, to assess these issues, particularly in Eastern and Central Europe.

Bosnia-Herzegovina

In February Muslim leader Alija Izetbegovic assumed the rotating chair of Bosnia's joint presidency, replacing the Croat Ante Jelavic. Nationalist parties made strong showings in the November elections. The estimated GDP growth in 2000 was 15 percent, but this still left the GDP at a level one-third of what it was before the Bosnian war of the 1990s. Unemployment was estimated at about 45 percent, and there was an enormous trade deficit, with exports covering only about 30 percent of imports. Inflation, however, was low, about 3 percent over the year.

Some 700 Jews lived in Bosnia-Herzegovina, most of them in the capital, Sarajevo. Jews in Bosnia were active in both local and international interfaith initiatives. Jakob Finci, president of the Jewish community, was a member of the Bosnian Interfaith Council, whose members also included the head of the local Muslim clerics, the Roman Catholic archbishop, and the Serbian Orthodox metropolitan. A Women's European Interfaith Conference was held in Sarajevo in mid-September. Cosponsored by the International Council of Jewish Women, the meeting drew Jewish, Muslim, and Christian women from several countries. The aim was to see how both sisterhood and common religious values could be used to foster peace initiatives and international understanding.

La Benevolencija, the Jewish cultural, educational, and humanitarian aid organization of Sarajevo, carried out a nonsectarian home-care program serving 540 needy, elderly residents of the city. All the beneficiaries were over 65, had a monthly income of less than $100, were chronically ill, and lived alone, with no children in Sarajevo to help them. More than 180 were Jews—all Holocaust survivors—but the majority consisted of Muslims, Serbs, Croats, Roma (Gypsies), and others.

On the eve of Bosnian elections in November, vandals overturned about 30 tombstones in Sarajevo's historic Jewish cemetery. Local officials and representatives of the UN went to the cemetery as a demonstration of solidarity with the Jewish community. Police detained four teenagers who confessed to the desecration. The cemetery, founded in the 16th century, had been heavily damaged during the 1992–95 Bosnian war, and just a few weeks before the desecration, in October, the U.S. Commission for the Preservation of America's Heritage Abroad presented $40,000 to officials in Sarajevo—matching funds raised by the city and canton of Sarajevo—to aid in its restoration. This was the first installment of a total of $100,000 appropriated by the U.S. government for this purpose.

Bulgaria

In January President Petar Stoyanov made a four-day official visit to Israel. He met with Prime Minister Barak and told Israeli businessmen that Bulgaria wanted to develop mutually beneficial cooperation with Israel, matching Bulgaria's supply of cheap labor with Israeli know-how in agriculture, technology, and the defense industry. Bulgarian and Israeli officials signed agreements on avoiding double taxation and on agricultural cooperation. Stoyanov dedicated a "Bulgaria Square" in Jerusalem honoring Bulgaria's refusal to deport its 50,000 Jews during the Holocaust. He visited Yad Vashem and paid "deep respect" to Jewish Holocaust victims, including the 14,000 Jews who were deported from Thrace and

Macedonia, Bulgarian-occupied parts of Greece. Stoyanov also met in Bethlehem with Palestinian Authority chairman Yasir Arafat, who thanked him for Bulgaria's "long-standing support for the Palestinian cause and of the Palestinian people."

Bulgaria's role during the Shoah remained a touchy issue. Less than two weeks after his trip to Israel, Stoyanov told delegates to a high-level international conference on the Holocaust in Stockholm that Bulgaria was proud that it had saved its 50,000 Jews from deportation. But protests from leaders of the Greek Jewish community, who noted that the Bulgarians had deported the 14,000 Jews from the parts of Greece it had occupied, convinced the conference to omit any special recognition of Bulgaria from its final declaration. Nevertheless in March, Bulgarian foreign minister Nadia Michaelova was honored in Washington by B'nai B'rith International for Bulgaria's "rescuing its Jewish population during the Holocaust and for its continuing display of tolerance and ethnic coexistence in the Balkans." At least two documentary films on Bulgaria's wartime role were in preparation.

Israeli investors maintained a high-profile presence in Bulgaria. Israeli Gad Zeevi owned a 75-percent share in Bulgaria's Balkan Airlines, whose pilots went on strike in May. Zeevi threatened to pull his money out if the government could not end the strike. In December three Israeli investors announced that they were buying Mobitel, Bulgaria's only mobile telephone company.

About 5,000 Jews lived in Bulgaria, mainly in the capital, Sofia, and in Plovdiv. In March a Jewish nursing home opened in Sofia. The $600,000 facility, designed to serve 40 patients, was a joint venture involving the American Jewish Joint Distribution Committee, the Claims Conference, and Shalom, the umbrella organization of Bulgarian Jewry. In the summer, Esperansa, a festival of Ladino culture, took place for the second time, near Sofia. In August Hashomer Hatzair sponsored an international seminar for more than 100 European Jewish teenagers at Batak, about 120 miles from Sofia. In December Bulgaria's Jewish community protested against the publication of what was advertised as "the first unabridged Bulgarian version" of *Mein Kampf,* and called for a ban on its sale.

Croatia

Croatia entered a new era following the death, in December 1999, of the longtime strongman, President Franjo Tudjman. The first few weeks of the year 2000 saw what amounted to a political revolution. In parliamentary elections on January 3, the center-left parties defeated Tudjman's Croatian Democratic Union (HDZ). Ivica Racan, a 55-year-old former Communist, became prime minister at the head of a six-party coalition. On February 7 populist Stipe Mesic, 65, was elected Croatian president and vowed to overturn Tudjman's nationalistic policies. Though Croatia's 2,000-strong Jewish community did not take an official stand on the elections, Croatian Jews warmly welcomed the changes and expressed the hope that they would facilitate the nation's integration into Europe.

That is indeed what ensued. In May Croatia was invited to join NATO's Partnership for Peace program. In July the EU's commissioner for foreign affairs announced that talks would soon begin over the terms of a stabilization and association agreement. Then in November, Parliament voted to amend the constitution so as to reduce the powers of the presidency, moving Croatia further in the direction of parliamentary democracy.

Ties with Israel and the United States became closer under the new government. Deputy Prime Minister Goran Granic visited Israel during the summer and signed agreements on trade and economic cooperation, including an end to the visa requirements for Croatians visiting Israel. Israel and Croatia also set up a joint committee to explore possible arms deals. A top Croatian delegation, including President Mesic and Prime Minster Racan, met with B'nai B'rith and American Jewish Committee leaders during a visit to Washington in August. Mesic said he wanted to correct injustices concerning Holocaust-era restitution claims.

In October Croatia's supreme court rejected an appeal from Dinko Sakic, the commander of the Jasenovac World War II concentration camp, who, in 1999, was sentenced to 20 years in jail for wartime crimes. In December the Zagreb city council voted to change the name of the Square of Croatian Heroes back to the Square of the Victims of Fascism. The name had been changed in the early 1990s as part of Tudjman's nationalist policy.

In the spring, the Zagreb Jewish community announced plans to build a cultural and religious center, including a Holocaust memorial and Jewish museum, on the site of the city's main synagogue, which had been destroyed in World War II. In late summer plans were also announced for a museum to be established next to the medieval synagogue in Dubrovnik that would house precious items of Judaica. In September so-called "middle-generation," or adult, Jews from all over the former Yugoslavia met at Brac, on the Croatian Adriatic coast. In November a plaque commemorating 165 Jewish youths killed in Croatia during World War II was unveiled at the offices of the Jewish community in Zagreb.

Czech Republic

On January 24 the cabinet approved a draft law on Jewish property restitution covering land and other property confiscated from individuals and organizations during World War II and subsequently not returned because of the Communist takeover in 1948. Parliament passed the law in June. The government set aside the equivalent of more than $8 million—the money going into a fund established by the Czech Jewish community—to compensate owners for property that could not be returned. The commission set up by the government for compensating Holocaust victims announced that about 2,500 items currently in Czech state museums had been confiscated from Czech Jews by the Nazis.

When Israeli foreign minister David Levy visited Prague in late January, he praised the Czech government's decision to go ahead with the restitution law and also its efforts to counter anti-Semitism. Levy and President Václav Havel met at

Prague Castle with Holocaust survivors on January 27 to mark the 55th anniversary of the liberation of Auschwitz. Havel voiced support for recognizing January 27 as a "day for victims of Nazism . . . and the fight against racism." In February a gala celebration was held in Prague to mark the tenth anniversary of the restoration of diplomatic relations with Israel, which followed the fall of Communism. Czech foreign minister Jan Kavan, whose father was Jewish, visited Israel in July. At Yad Vashem, Kavan discovered his grandmother's name in a database of Czech Jews who died in the Shoah, and learned that she had perished in Buchenwald. In May Israeli ambassador Erella Hadar honored four families in the village of Trsice for helping Jews during World War II. In the fall, Olga Fierz, a Swiss-born woman who helped Czech Jews during World War II and who died in 1990, was honored posthumously by President Havel. In December Czech officials presented the Dutch state archives with newly discovered Jewish documents that the Nazis had stolen from Amsterdam and transported to Prague.

Xenophobia, racism, and hate crimes, particularly against Roma (Gypsies), continued to raise concern throughout the year. There were also manifestations of anti-Semitism from the far right, and an estimated 5,000 skinheads were active around the country. Results of a poll conducted among 1,124 respondents and released in January showed that only 17 percent could be described as "tolerant." During the year several international organizations—including the Anti-Defamation League (ADL), Amnesty International, and the Council of Europe—issued reports criticizing or raising alarm about discrimination and violence against Roma and others.

Attempts to take legal steps against extremists accomplished little. In January a court in the town of Jesenik sentenced Jiri Tuma to ten months in prison for fostering a pro-Nazi movement. But also in January, a Prague district prosecutor dropped charges against Vladimir Skoupy, leader of the far-right National Alliance, who had been accused of defamation of a people and inciting racial hatred for publicly questioning whether the Holocaust had taken place. In the wake of this, Czech Jewish leader Tomas Kraus called for Holocaust denial to be made a crime. In February, despite a police ban, Skoupy led a demonstration on Prague's Wenceslas Square in support of Austrian far-right leader Jörg Haider. About 120 demonstrators, mostly skinheads, shouted slogans against "U.S.-Israel dictates" and against President Havel. Separated from the skinheads by police, about 50 left-wing youths staged a counterdemonstration against Haider and against racism. Skoupy, rearrested later in February after another illegal demonstration, was released in June, less than a month after being sentenced to one year in jail for propagating Nazism and inciting racial hatred. At the end of March the Czech interior minister issued an order disbanding the National Alliance.

The release of a Czech translation of *Mein Kampf* by the Prague-based Otakar II publishing house provoked controversy. Jewish and Romany groups, nongovernmental organizations (NGOs), and others protested the publication, which ran without footnotes or explanatory introduction, unlike a 1993 Czech edition of the book, which included explanatory notes. The new edition's first print run of 4,000 sold out in three days. In May a survey reported that 39 percent of Czechs opposed the sale of a Czech-language edition of Hitler's book, while 30 percent did not mind. Among those who approved the sale, 49 percent said they opposed any form of censorship, 28 percent believed that the book provided a lesson about the dangers of Nazism, and 12 percent said it was "part of history." At the beginning of June police charged Michal Zitko, owner of the publishing house, with supporting a movement aimed at suppressing minorities, and, in a police raid on June 5, 300 copies of the book were confiscated. This move was criticized on June 14 by two groups, the Committee for the Protection of Freedom of Speech and the Syndicate of Czech Journalists. In December Zitko received a three-year suspended sentence for promoting Nazism, and was ordered to pay a $50,000 fine. He appealed the verdict. Also in December, Czech state prosecutors brought charges against Vit Varak, owner of an Internet site selling Czech translations of *Mein Kampf* on-line. Varak was accused of promoting movements that seek to suppress human rights.

In March Jan Kasl, the mayor of Prague, unveiled three bronze plaques in Czech, English, and Hebrew on a 17th-century statue of Christ on Prague's Charles Bridge. The statue has a gilded Hebrew inscription, "kadosh kadosh kadosh" (holy holy holy), put there in 1696 and paid for from a fine imposed on a Prague Jew who allegedly mocked the cross. The new plaques explained this historical background. Members of the Czech Jewish community, the U.S. ambassador, and representatives of the Roman Catholic Church attended the unveiling. In April the Prague city council renamed a square in Prague's Old Town after the great Jewish writer Franz Kafka. The square, located just off the Old Town Square, is where Kafka was born in 1883. A Kafka museum already stands on the site of the house where he was born. In October an 11-member panel chose a massive statue designed by sculptor Jaroslav Ron to serve as a monument to Kafka. The statue—of a suit walking without a body in it—was to be placed near the Spanish synagogue.

JEWISH COMMUNITY

There were approximately 3,000 registered members of Jewish communities in the Czech Republic. About half lived in Prague, but Jewish leaders estimated that there were 10,000–15,000, or even more unaffiliated Jews in the country. The officially recognized Jewish communities and a number of secular Jewish institutions came under the aegis of the Federation of Jewish Communities. Among these organizations were Bejt Praha, a non-Orthodox congregation in Prague that attracted expatriate Americans and other foreigners as well as Czechs, the Union of Jewish Youth, the Maccabi and Hakoach sports clubs, the Women's Zionist Organization (WIZO), and the Terezin Initiative, a group of Czech Holocaust survivors. Jewish organizations functioning outside the federation umbrella included Bejt Simcha, an independent group that maintained links with Progressive Judaism and attracted people who were not Jewish according to Halakhah, and Chabad-Lubavitch. The Web site www.chaverim.sk provided extensive information about the Jewish communities in both the Czech Republic and Slovakia.

While the official community was Orthodox, only a few dozen Czech Jews were believed to be strict observers of kashrut. Some smaller communities in provincial cities were increasingly aligning themselves with non-Orthodox forms of Judaism, and a new Liberal Union was established in 2000. On February 13 about 200 Czech and Slovak Jews attended a seminar in Brno on the status of Orthodoxy and Liberal Judaism in the Czech and Slovak Republics. One of the speakers, Czech chief rabbi Karol Sidon, himself Orthodox, said that adopting a liberal communal orientation not only threatened "the Jewish character" of the communities, but also portended disunity. Income from restituted property enabled the Jewish communities in the Czech Republic to finance the welfare needs of their members as well as to handle other costs. Among other institutions, the community maintained a summer camp for Czech Jewish youngsters and a home for the aged. A new Jewish club opened in September in the spa town of Karlovy Vary, where about 90 Jews lived.

Controversy continued to rage over the medieval Jewish cemetery discovered in 1999 during construction of an insurance building in downtown Prague, pitting Czech Jews against Orthodox groups from abroad and also against the Czech government (see AJYB 2000, pp. 379–80). Dating to the 13th century and voluntarily relinquished by Prague's Jewish community in the 15th century, the cemetery had been built over ever since. It came to light in 1999, when a Czech insurance company began preparations for the construction of a high-rise apartment block and underground garage on the site. In November 1999 Rabbi Sidon had reached a compromise with the insurance company, Pojistovna, that called for excavating the ground beneath the existing level of burial remains, encasing the existing remains in concrete, and then sinking these remains to a deeper level, which would remain undisturbed by any future development on the site. This solution, however, was decisively rejected by many Orthodox groups around the world, which issued statements, held street protests in Prague and outside Czech consulates abroad, and carried on an e-mail campaign. In January 2000 the chief rabbinate of Israel issued an opinion that the site should remain sacred with no further construction on it, and Prague's Jewish community withdrew its assent to the November agreement with Pojistovna. In March the Czech cabinet reached an agreement with the Prague Jewish community and the insurance company for a compromise, mediated by the U.S. embassy, whereby the foundations of the office block would be built around the cemetery site, which itself would be encased in concrete, preserving the remains. The Czech government agreed to contribute more than $1 million to enable the plan to be carried out.

Though the agreement was praised by a number of Jewish leaders at home and abroad, some Orthodox Jews outside the country continued to protest, much to the chagrin of local Jews. In June police broke up several protests by Orthodox Jews who physically attempted to halt construction. In August an Orthodox group called the Committee for the Preservation of Jewish Cemeteries filed a complaint against the Czech government at the European Court of Human Rights, and various foreign representatives cautioned the Czech government on the matter. Czech culture minister Pavel Dostal, meanwhile, sparked outrage with a sarcastic newspaper editorial that was bitterly scornful of certain Jewish individuals involved in the affair and the positions they took. In September the Jewish community reburied the remains of some 160 people found at the medieval site in another Prague Jewish cemetery, "where all related religious rules can be complied with without problems."

There were numerous cultural, educational, and scholarly events throughout the year. Prague's Spanish Synagogue hosted a series of concerts. In February a memorial evening was held in Prague in memory of Charles Jordan, vice chairman of the JDC, who died under mysterious circumstances in Prague in 1967 (see AJYB 1968, p. 510). In March the Jewish Museum of Prague hosted the annual meeting of the Association of European Jewish Museums, with 40 representatives of Jewish museums from a dozen countries attending. In May a concert was held at Terezin of music composed by Jewish musicians who were held prisoner at the Terezin ghetto during the Holocaust and died in Nazi death camps. A plaque was unveiled at the concert dedicated to these musicians, and a Japanese pianist performed on a $25,000 grand piano donated to the town of Terezin by nearly 900 Japanese citizens. In June a Polish klezmer group, Kroke, headlined a festival of ethnic music at Prague Castle. In October the town of Jihlava held a three-day festival celebrating the 140th anniversary of the birth of composer Gustav Mahler. December saw the opening of "Jewish Moravia, Jewish Brno," a festival to last several months featuring concerts, films, theater productions, and exhibitions, organized by the Czech-based Association for Culture and Dialogue. Relaying a message from Pope John Paul II at the start of the festival, Cardinal Edward I. Cassidy, president of the Pontifical Commission for Religious Dialogue with the Jews, said the pope wanted to encourage Jews, Christians, and all others to work together for the good of the world.

The Prague Jewish Museum issued a number of publications and other material, including a CD-ROM on the history of Jews in Bohemia and Moravia. Early in the year the Prague Jewish Museum Education Center, in cooperation with the Terezin Memorial, the Museum of Roma Culture in Brno, and the Czech Ministry of Education, launched a seminar for primary- and secondary-school teachers on how to teach about the Holocaust. More than 500 teachers applied to take part. The museum center also sponsored various other education projects, including "Workshop 2000," aimed at promoting cultural tolerance among primary-school pupils. The Office of the President of the Czech Republic was among the sponsors of the "Lost Neighbors" project, aimed at making teenagers aware of the fate of those from their own neighborhoods who were killed or deported during World War II. In November a three-day international conference on the Nazis' seizure of the property of Czech Jews during the war was held in Prague. In December a number of events were held in Prague to mark the 100th anniversary of the birth of the Czech Jewish actor Hugo Haas, who died in 1969.

There were many initiatives taken to preserve Jewish heritage sites. In the late summer, the Czech Ministry of Culture nominated the former Jewish quarter in the Moravian town of Trebic for inclusion in UNESCO's list of world heritage sites. On September 5, after three years of reconstruction, the synagogue in the town of Polna opened as a regional Jewish museum. It included an exhibit on the so-called Hilsner affair, a blood-libel case that took place in Polna in 1899, when a 22-year-old Jew, Leopold Hilsner, was sentenced to death for the murder of a young woman amid accusations that he had killed her to use her blood for Jewish ritual purposes. He was pardoned in 1918 and died in Vienna. In June 2000 his newly restored grave was unveiled. In September Israeli ambassador Erella Hadar unveiled a memorial plaque to local Holocaust victims in the newly restored synagogue in Breclav. In October, after years of restoration work, the synagogue in Ledec opened as a Jewish museum, exhibition center, and memorial to the town's Jews. In November a new synagogue was dedicated within a Jewish cultural complex built on the site of the prewar synagogue in Liberec, which was destroyed in 1938 on Kristallnacht.

The writer Eduard Goldstücker, who also served as the first Czechoslovak ambassador to Israel, died in Prague in the autumn at the age of 87. Goldstücker was a prominent intellectual and champion of the work of Franz Kafka.

Hungary

Jews were concerned throughout the year about what they perceived as far-right influence on the government, and a creeping, if ambiguous, form of political anti-Semitism. There was a perception among some observers that Prime Minister Viktor Orban welcomed parliamentary support from the notorious right-wing nationalist István Csurka and his Hungarian Justice and Life Party (MIEP), which had entered parliament in 1998 with about 5 percent of the vote and 14 seats in the 386-seat body. MIEP's newspaper, *Magyar Forum,* frequently ran articles that were patently anti-Semitic, even if they used code words and indirect references in place of the word "Jew."

On January 16 Budapest's St. Stephen's Basilica was almost filled for a mass organized by MIEP in memory of Laszlo Bardossy, the World War II prime minister who declared war on the Allies, instituted tough anti-Semitic legislation, and was executed for war crimes in 1946. Csurka and MIEP welcomed the entry of Jörg Haider's Freedom Party into the Austrian government and predicted that it would boost the far right in Hungary. On February 13 about 1,000 people demonstrated in support of Haider outside the Austrian embassy in a rally organized by MIEP's youth section. On the same day, however, President Arpád Goncz and former Prime Minister Gyula Horn of the opposition Socialist Party joined an estimated 10,000 people at a rally denouncing fascism and hate-mongering. (Upon completion of his second term in August, the popular Goncz was succeeded as president by Ferenc Madl, a conservative legal scholar). Although Prime Minister Orban and his government reacted coolly to Haider's success, Austrian foreign minister Benita Ferrero-Waldner visited Hungary soon after the new Austrian coalition came to power in February, and Orban gave a warm welcome to Austrian prime minister Wolfgang Schüssel in Budapest in April.

In March the Council of Europe's Commission against Racism and Intolerance criticized "latent anti-Semitism" in Hungarian society and some of its media, as well as the situation of Hungary's Roma population. It said that "elements in the parliament" were using overtly nationalist slogans, including some "coded" anti-Semitic and xenophobic statements. At a meeting of the executive committee of the European Jewish Congress held in Strasbourg in March, the executive director of the Federation of Hungarian Jewish Communities, Gusztav Zoltai, accused the Hungarian cabinet of not distancing itself from anti-Semitic groups. His implication, that anti-Semitism was becoming institutionalized in Hungary, was rejected by Prime Minister Orban. In May a conference on the future of Jewry in Europe and promoting Christian-Jewish dialogue was held in Debrecen. Jozsef Torgyan, the minister of agriculture and development, told the conference that "there can be no Europe without Hungarians, and there can be no Hungarians without Jews," adding that incitement to hatred must be "stifled at [its] source" no matter whom it is directed against. In August Orban sent a letter to Jewish leaders on the occasion of ceremonies marking Hungary's 1,000th anniversary. The letter said that Hungary needed "the contribution, the belief, and the spiritual and emotional strength of Hungarian Jewry." Still, Jewish leaders voiced their concern about the rise of far-right forces in Hungary to U.S. secretary of state Madeleine Albright when they met with her during her one-day trip to Hungary in December. Albright also visited the main Dohany Street Synagogue and paid tribute to the hundreds of thousands of Hungarian Jews who were killed in the Holocaust.

As in other countries, there was concern over anti-Semitism and racism at soccer matches. Anti-Semitic taunts were aimed particularly at the soccer club MTK, which in the past had been owned by Jews. In the spring Foreign Ministry state secretary Zsolt Nemeth met with the Israeli ambassador and pledged to deal with the issue, and after the meeting the Foreign Ministry publicly called for a crackdown. Later, in May, the Central and East European office of the ADL sent a letter to Orban urging the government to take strong legal measures against the offenders, saying that existing legislation had been applied "ineffectively or too leniently."

On April 16, the anniversary of the beginning of the deportation of the country's Jews in 1944, Hungary held its first Holocaust Remembrance Day. It was low-key, and one Hungarian Jewish journalist said it was "barely noticed" in the media. In May the American Jewish Committee released its analysis of how Hungarian high-school textbooks dealt with Jewish-related issues. There were, it turned out, scant references to Jews except as the forebears of Christianity and victims of the Holocaust. Even in regard to the Holocaust, none of the texts portrayed the magnitude of the slaughter, let alone the importance of Jews in prewar Hungarian intellectual life, and some of the references to Jews were highly negative. In July UN secretary general Kofi Annan and his wife joined Budapest's mayor, diplomats, other dignitaries, and local Jews at a ceremony paying tribute to Raoul Wallenberg, the Swedish diplomat who saved thousands of Hungarian Jews from deportation in the last year of the war.

There were a number of reports of cemetery desecrations. In March the cemeteries in Tiszatured and Nagyatad were vandalized. In September vandals toppled more than a dozen tombstones in the Jewish cemetery in Szombathely. On November 2 some 30 tombstones were vandalized in Budapest's main Jewish cemetery. The damage was reportedly put at the equivalent of $16,000. Christian groups expressed solidarity with Jews for the damage. At the same time, initiatives were begun to restore several synagogues, including the baroque synagogue in Mad, northern Hungary, which received financial support from the Hungarian government and from the World Monuments Fund's Jewish heritage program. In the fall the Hungarian and Israeli post offices collaborated in issuing stamps showing the Dohany Street Synagogue, with the Israeli stamp showing the interior and the Hungarian stamp the exterior. The government's recognition of the importance of Jewish heritage figured in an agreement regulating relations between the state and the Jewish community that was signed in December by Culture Minister Zoltan Rockenbauer and representatives of the Hungarian Federation of Jewish Communities. In this document, the government said it "highly appreciates" the traditions of the Jewish faith and the community's contribution to "the moral and intellectual progress" of Hungary, as well as its participation in Hungarian "freedom struggles," and promised to support efforts for the dissemination of knowledge about the Holocaust in educational institutions and to provide assistance for the preservation of Jewish memorial sites. The agreement was similar to accords concluded with the Calvinist, Lutheran, Baptist, and Serbian Orthodox communities in Hungary.

In February 48-year-old Yehudit Varnai-Sorer became the first woman and the first sabra (native-born Israeli) to serve as Israel's ambassador to Hungary. All three previous ambassadors were born in Hungary. Ms. Varnai-Sorer, the child of Hungarian parents, was fluent in Hungarian.

JEWISH COMMUNITY

Estimates of the number of Jews in Hungary ranged from 54,000 to 130,000, or even more. About 90 percent of Hungary's Jews lived in Budapest, the vast majority of them nonobservant, secular, disaffected, or totally unaffiliated. Only 6,000 or so were formally registered with the Jewish community, and about 20,000 had some sort of affiliation with Jewish organizations or institutions. Throughout the year the independent Jewish monthly *Szombat* wrote critically about the operation of Jewish communal bodies, reporting particularly on charges of autocratic leadership and suspected financial irregularities. Reports about personal and political feuding among both the lay and the religious leadership also circulated within the community.

The dominant religious affiliation was Neolog, similar to Conservative Judaism in the United States. There was a very small Orthodox community made up of both modern Orthodox and Hassidim. Neolog communities were grouped in the Federation of Jewish Communities in Hungary, while the Orthodox operated as the Autonomous Orthodox Community. Rabbi Jozsef Schweitzer, who was in his 80s, resigned as the Neolog chief rabbi in the fall. Sim Shalom, a 50-family Reform congregation established in Budapest in 1992, which functioned outside these official umbrella structures, associated with the World Union for Progressive Judaism and was led by a female rabbi. There was also an active Chabad-Lubavitch presence. Chabad ran a yeshivah and other educational programs, held Friday-night dinners for worshipers after services in its synagogue, and its newsletter went to what was reputed to be the largest Hungarian Jewish mailing list. Chabad rabbi Baruch Oberlander oversaw publication of a detailed Passover Haggadah with Hungarian translation, which included a "who's who" of the personalities quoted or mentioned in the Passover seder.

Three Jewish day schools and several kindergartens operated in Budapest. The city also had a rabbinical seminary and a teacher-training college, which together were called the Jewish University. Total enrollment in all these educational institutions was about 1,800. In late August some 350 young Jews from 32 countries took part in the annual summer university held by the European Union of Jewish Students, a weeklong program that took place in Budapest and at the JDC/Lauder Foundation Jewish camp at Szarvas, in southern Hungary. In November Budapest was the site of Arachim, a conference on Jewish education sponsored by the European Council of Jewish Communities, which drew more than 200 Jewish educators from all over Europe.

In the spring, the first results of an in-depth survey of Hungary's Jewish community, carried out in 1999, were made public. The survey, the first such study in any postcommunist state, was directed by Budapest sociologist Andras Kovács, and it aimed to provide the first full-scale postwar demographic portrait of the community, probing social, political, and religious attitudes, as well as lifestyle, identity, and behavioral patterns. The survey found that Hungary's Jews were well-educated, well-off, and well-integrated into the social mainstream, but highly ambivalent about their Jewish identity and rather detached from Jewish communal life. Though young Jews were trying to reconnect with Jewish traditions, memory of the Holocaust and anti-Semitic persecution appeared to be the most important factors, overall, in Hungarian Jews' sense of what it meant to be a Jew.

In June, Keren Hayesod had its 80th-anniversary convention in Budapest and announced that it was reopening its offices there after a 60-year hiatus. Hungarian foreign minister Janos Martonyi, addressing the convention, said the government was "deeply ashamed" of Hungary's role in the Holocaust. He pledged to fight against "all sorts of anti-Semitism in whatever form it might appear." Jews, meanwhile, expressed anger at Hungary's Holocaust compensation law and demanded it be changed. The 1997 law mandated a payment of about $100 for each parent killed in the Holocaust, and about $16 for each sibling. This was in contrast to a 1992 law that provided about $3,300 in compensation for relatives killed in the Stalinist show trials of the 1950s. By October more than 360 people had returned their payments in protest, and Jozsef Schweitzer, the Neolog chief rabbi, told a government representative that the Holocaust compensation law was "unlawful and discriminatory."

Also in October, after a trial lasting almost a year, Martha Nierenberg of Armonk, New York, was recognized as the rightful owner of artworks looted by Nazi SS commander Adolf Eichmann in 1944 from her grandfather, a wealthy Jewish baron and art collector. A Budapest court ruled that all but two of the 12 disputed paintings, which for decades had been displayed in Hungarian museums, should be returned to Nierenberg. In November the government said it would appeal the ruling.

There were numerous cultural events with Jewish themes throughout the year. An exhibition of paintings of Laszlo Feher, a Jewish painter, took place in March, and the third annual festival of Jewish culture, at the end of August, drew thousands of people to concerts, exhibitions, performances, and other events in Budapest and several other cities. Festival sponsors included the Budapest municipality, the Cultural Heritage Ministry, and an Israeli investor. Various local klezmer groups performed concerts and issued CDs, and in December there was a "klezmer and literature" concert in Budapest that combined music and readings, with Laszlo Fekete, the chief cantor at the Dohany Street Synagogue, performing with one of the local Budapest klezmer bands. The Balint Jewish Community Center sponsored a full roster of events, including lectures, concerts, classes, clubs, and performances.

Two major motion pictures addressed the theme of Hungarian Jewish identity. One, *Sunshine*, was directed by István Szabo and starred Ralph Fiennes. The film was an epic family saga showing how a Jewish family assimilates into Hungarian society over the course of a century. Fiennes himself portrayed three generations of the family: a Jewishly observant lawyer during the waning days of the Austro-Hungarian Empire; his son, an Olympic fencing champion who converts to Catholicism but is killed by the Nazis; and his politically active grandson. *Sunshine* sparked a debate over the validity of assimilation and over Jewish/Hungarian identity. The other film, *Glamour*, recounted the story of the family of the director, Frigyes Gödrös. Meanwhile, filming began in Hungary on a documentary about the life of Carl Lutz, a Swiss diplomat instrumental in saving thousands of Hungarian Jews during World War II.

Macedonia

Macedonia's government was weak, plagued by corruption and internal conflict. Local elections in September were marred by ballot-stuffing, intimidation, and shoot-outs in which one person was killed and several injured. The voting was so chaotic that official results had not been released as the year ended. Simmering tensions between the large ethnic Albanian minority and the Slav majority also created problems. Ethnic Albanians made up 25–30 percent of the 2.5-million population.

About 200 Jews lived in Macedonia, virtually all of them in the capital, Skopje. In March Prime Minister Ljupco Georgievski, other senior officials, religious leaders, and diplomats joined Macedonia's Jews for commemorative events marking the 57th anniversary of the deportation of more than 7,000 Macedonian Jews to Treblinka. Featured on the program were a gala concert by Cantor Joseph Malovany of New York and a Holocaust commemoration and Jewish history exhibition in the town of Bitola. The occasion also saw the inauguration of what was apparently the first new synagogue to be built in the Balkans since the end of World War II, called Bet Yaakov, located on the top floor of the Jewish community center in Skopje. Construction was funded primarily by the members of Congregation Beth Israel of Phoenix, Arizona. Rabbi Yitzhak Asiel, the chief rabbi of Yugoslavia, traveled from Belgrade to conduct the first synagogue services to be held in Skopje in half a century, and to affix a mezuzah to the door. Jews from neighboring Balkan countries and from Israel, the United States, and Canada also attended, as did U.S. ambassador Michael Einik and his Israeli-born wife. Two Torah scrolls, one donated by the Jewish community of Bulgaria and the other by the Pasadena Jewish Center and Temple in California, were placed in the new ark. Local television filmed the start of services.

Visiting Jewish representatives from a half-dozen Balkan countries took advantage of the Skopje events to meet together and discuss the possibility of founding a Southeastern Europe regional Jewish association. There were several key areas of common interest, including fighting assimilation, gaining access to resources through restitution and compensation, promoting cultural and religious education among a Jewish population that is mostly secular, and facilitating conversion—a vital problem in communities whose members were overwhelmingly partners in, or children of, mixed marriages.

Prime Minister Georgievski, in meetings with Macedonian Jewish leaders and visiting representatives of the JDC and the American Jewish Committee, renewed his pledge to finance construction of a Holocaust museum and educational center on the site of Skopje's former Jewish quarter. Macedonian Jews continued the work of the aid organization Dobre Volje (Good Will), founded in 1999. Closely coordinated with the JDC, it was dedicated to channeling nonsectarian humanitarian aid to Albanian, Serbian, and Romany (Gypsy) refugees who fled to Macedonia during and after the Kosovo conflict. In September young Jews from Macedonia, Yugoslavia, Croatia, and Israel met in Bitola where, during a weeklong seminar called David 2000, they did restoration work on the Jewish cemetery.

Poland

Aleksander Kwasniewski was decisively reelected president of Poland in October. During the campaign, several marginal candidates tried to exploit anti-Semitism, but they won little support. Still, events through the year demonstrated a continuing ambiguity in Polish attitudes toward Jews. There were many positive developments, including events commemorating the Holocaust and its victims, but there were also incidents that were, or were at least perceived to be, anti-Semitic, that also tended to focus on Holocaust memory.

Relations with Israel continued to expand. Israel's overall annual investment in the Polish market economy amounted to at least $1 billion, and economic relations between the two countries grew, especially in the high-tech and agricultural sectors. In January the Israeli son of Polish Holocaust survivors opened an Israeli-Jewish restaurant, Warszawa-Jerozolima (Warsaw-Jerusalem), in the neighborhood that had been Warsaw's prewar Jewish quarter and the wartime Warsaw Ghetto. Israeli ambassador Yigal Antebi completed his tour of duty in the fall and was replaced by Shevach Weiss, a Holocaust survivor from Poland and former speaker of the Knesset. President Kwasniewski visited Israel in May. He held meetings with President Ezer Weizman and Prime Minister Ehud Barak, where the topics included how to increase Poland's exports to Israel—then estimated at $40 million—and to encourage more Israeli investment in Poland. He also discussed cooperation between the Polish and Israeli arms industries.

In June Wladyslaw Bartoszewksi, 78, was appointed foreign minister. An Auschwitz survivor, designated "Righteous among the Nations" by Yad Vashem for saving Jews during the Holocaust, and chairman of the Poland-Israel Friendship Association, Bartoszewksi replaced the highly respected Bronislaw Geremek (who was of Jewish origin) after members of Geremek's Freedom Union party pulled out of the ruling coalition. The next month Bartoszewski appointed Wojciech Adamiecki, a journalist and former Polish ambassador to Israel, to be the new ambassador to the Jewish Diaspora in the Ministry of Foreign Affairs. Accompanied by some of Poland's Jewish leaders, Bartoszewski visited Israel in early December to mark the tenth anniversary of the restoration of full diplomatic relations between Israel and Poland.

In January Marek Edelman, the only surviving leader of the Warsaw Ghetto uprising and a longtime human rights activist, was named 1999 Man of the Year in the central Polish city Lodz, where he lives. In March, however, vandals scrawled anti-Semitic slogans on the walls of Edelman's home there and also on the local synagogue. Prime Minister Jerzy Buzek and President Kwasniewski sent strong letters of support and apology to Edelman, and the Polish media expressed indignation. The vandalism occurred just after thousands of volunteers in Lodz, in a day-long initiative dubbed "Action Colorful Tolerance," cleaned up city walls that had long been defaced by racist and anti-Semitic graffiti. Cosponsored by the newspaper *Gazeta Wyborcza,* the cleanup involved thousands of volunteers, including city authorities, the Union of Jewish Students, the Catholic Youth Association, and other groups. Lodz was, in fact, infamous for its anti-Semitic graffiti, much of it, as in several other countries, scrawled by fanatical local soccer fans, sometimes linked to skinhead groups, and directed against opposing teams. In April Prime Minster Buzek marked the 57th anniversary of the Warsaw Ghetto uprising by paying public tribute to the "heroic struggle."

In April leaders of the Open Republic Association Against Anti-Semitism and Xenophobia met with Buzek, who promised to crack down on anti-Semitic publications that were being sold openly at Polish newsstands. These included the periodical *Teraz Polska,* edited by Leszek Bubel, who was well known for his anti-Semitic views and was an associate of Kazimierz Switon, the anti-Semitic extremist who was behind the movement to set up crosses at the site of the Auschwitz-Birkenau death camp in 1998–99. An opinion poll published in the daily *Gazeta Wyborcza* in July showed that three-quarters of Polish citizens favored some sort of punishment for anti-Semitic activities.

A number of such cases came up during the year. In January a court in Oswięcim (Auschwitz) fined Switon the equivalent of $98 and gave him a six-month suspended sentence—provided that he committed no other similar crime over the next two years—for inciting hatred toward Jews and others by rallying supporters to erect the hundreds of crosses. In June an appeals court upheld the conviction but reduced the six-month suspended term to a fine of $313, and then forgave the fine. In February the senate of the Catholic University in Lublin initiated disciplinary procedures against Professor Ryszard Bender, who, in January, had said, on the radical Catholic station Radio Maryja, that Auschwitz was not a death camp but a labor camp for Jews and others. In April the state-run University of Opole fired Dariusz Ratajczak, a professor who was tried but not punished in 1999 for spreading Holocaust revisionism, and he was banned from teaching elsewhere in Poland for three years. The university said that Ratajczak had violated ethical standards with the publication of his book *Dangerous Topics,* which took a sympathetic approach toward published material that denied the Holocaust. Ratajczak, 37, said he would appeal the decision. On November 11 about 400 extremists, including many skinheads, staged a demonstration in Katowice during which they chanted anti-Semitic slogans and burned the EU and Israeli flags.

On the other hand, there were many attempts to promote dialogue between Catholics and Jews. In January Poland's Roman Catholic Church marked its third annual Day of Judaism. Leaders of the Polish Jewish community joined Catholic priests and scholars for discussions, lectures, conferences, and other activities in several major cities. In June the Polish Council of Christians and Jews presented its Figure of Reconciliation award to a German priest, Rev. Manfred Deselaers, who lived for the previous decade near Auschwitz, where he fostered programs aimed at dialogue among Jews, Christian Poles, and Germans. At an outdoor Mass in Warsaw, in May, celebrating two millennia of Christianity, the Polish Roman Catholic primate, Cardinal Jozef Glemp, apologized for lingering anti-Semitism among Polish priests. Then in August, Polish bishops issued a sweeping letter, read out in parishes around the country, asking forgiveness for the Catholic Church's toleration of anti-Semitism and other forms of religious discrimination. The bishops' letter acknowledged that some Poles were guilty of indifference and even enmity toward Jews during the Holocaust. This series of apologies was part of the Catholic Church's millennium-year agenda of self-examination, apology, and penitence, and the bishops' letter in particular was seen as going further than a similar letter they had issued in 1991. There had apparently been intense debate within the hierarchy over the new letter, with some viewing it as unnecessary and others feeling that it did not go far enough. In August, for example, Father Stanislaw Musial, a leading Polish Jesuit, wrote a series of articles in *Gazeta Wyborcza* urging the removal of eight 18th-century paintings from churches in Sandomierz that portrayed the blood-libel accusation.

The official apologies were followed by a number of public events. At an interfaith ceremony in Lublin in September, Jews—some of them Holocaust survivors—and Catholics planted grapevines in shared soil. Lublin was also the site of an interfaith conference in November, at which the city's Catholic University granted an honorary degree to Rome's chief rabbi, Elio Toaff. An impressive commemoration ceremony was held at the site of the Majdanek death camp, near Lublin. Guests included 5,000 local schoolchildren and representatives of five religious denominations—Jews, Catholics, Eastern Orthodox, Protestants, and Muslims—who offered prayers. As part of the ceremony, all participants left fingertip marks on clay that was mixed with soil from the camp. In the fall, the influential daily *Gazeta Wyborcza* published a Polish translation of "Dabru Emet," a statement by leading Jewish thinkers on Christians and Christianity, along with a commentary by Stanislaw Krajewski, a Polish Jewish leader involved in interfaith activities.

A new and very emotional debate over Poland's role in the Holocaust was sparked by the publication, in Polish, of *Neighbors,* by Jan T. Gross, a Polish-born American scholar with Jewish roots. The book described the massacre of 1,600 Jews in the village of Jedwabne by local Poles on June 10, 1941. According to Gross's reconstruction of the events, the Jews were first clubbed and stoned, and those still alive were forced into a barn that was set on fire. At the time, the town was under German occupation, but the Germans did not take part in the massacre. During the period of Communist rule in Poland, the massacre was blamed on Nazi collaborators, and a plaque to that effect was erected. The book had an immediate impact. On July 10, 2000, the anniversary of the massacre, local authorities in Jedwabne for the first time laid wreaths at the site of the massacre.

There was considerable public debate and much media attention, and production was underway on a film about the Jedwabne affair.

In November, in the first such case in more than 25 years, a Polish man identified only as 77-year-old Henry M. was charged in Poznan of collaborating with the Nazis in carrying out genocide at the Chelmno death camp.

Auschwitz was in the news throughout the year. In early January the German government pledged $5 million for the upkeep of the Auschwitz-Birkenau memorial museum. On January 27 President Kwasniewski took part in official ceremonies marking the 55th anniversary of the liberation of Auschwitz, and prayers were recited by representatives of Catholicism, Eastern Orthodoxy, Protestantism, Judaism, Islam, and Buddhism. Afterwards, Kwasniewski and a Buddhist teacher from New York who initiated the project, Bernard Glassman, inaugurated a hospice for the terminally ill in Oswięcim. There was also a concert in an Oswięcim church by a 100-person choir from a Catholic school in Berlin.

In May Kwasniewski and Israeli president Weizman led 6,000 participants in the annual March of the Living in their walk from Auschwitz to Birkenau. The next day some of the teenagers from around the world participating in the march were taunted by youths when they visited Majdanek. Prime Minister Buzek apologized for the incident and for the fact that anti-Semitic graffiti were visible near Majdanek. This year there was an effort to broaden the scope of the March of the Living and show the positive developments that had occurred in Poland since the fall of Communism, including the revival of Jewish life. For the first time, there were non-Jewish participants—some 800, including about 750 Poles.

During the summer, a furor erupted over the establishment of a discotheque in a building about a mile from the Auschwitz death camp, on the site of a former tannery where slave laborers from Auschwitz worked and died. Protests came from Jewish and survivor groups, as well as from the Polish government, which urged the disco to relocate even though it was not situated within an officially "protected" zone where activities that could be offensive to the memory of victims are prohibited. This disco controversy was just the latest of several similar conflicts over the commercial use of sites associated with Holocaust suffering. In August Poland's Ministry of Internal Affairs lifted a ban on building a controversial shopping center across the street from the Auschwitz camp. The president of the company developing the project was quoted as saying that plans for the center would be changed so that it would now serve the needs of the hundreds of thousands of people who visited Auschwitz each year.

The Auschwitz Jewish Center—a place for prayer and study honoring Jewish life—opened in the reconstructed synagogue of Oswięcim in September. Prince Hassan of Jordan joined Polish, U.S., and Israeli officials, Roman Catholic clergy, Holocaust survivors, and local Jews in an emotional dedication ceremony. Besides facilities for prayer and study, the $10-million complex included educational and exhibition facilities. Encompassing Chevra Lomdei Mishnayot, the only surviving synagogue in the town, the center would be the only active Jewish institution in the Auschwitz area. The project was conceived and sponsored by the New York-based Auschwitz Jewish Center Foundation, established in 1995 by philanthropist and businessman Fred Schwartz. Participants in the inaugural ceremony paid tribute to Shimshon Kluger, the last Jew living in Oswięcim, who died in the spring at the age of 72. Kluger was given a halakhic funeral and was buried in Oswięcim's Jewish cemetery by Rabbi Sasha Pecaric, the Lauder Foundation director in Kraków, aided by 34 high-school students from the Ramaz School in New York City who happened to be in Poland on a Holocaust-and-Jewish-heritage educational tour.

In September President Kwasniewski awarded the Commander's Cross with the Star of the Order of Merit of the Republic of Poland, the highest honor the nation could give to a noncitizen, to Michael Lewan, chairman of the U.S. Commission for the Preservation of America's Heritage Abroad, for his contributions to cultural understanding among Poles, Jews, and Americans. Lewan was a Roman Catholic with Polish roots, and the commission he chaired played a major role in documenting, restoring, and preserving sites in Eastern and Central Europe that were important to Americans, including old Jewish cemeteries. Kwasniewski said: "The Jewish people for many long centuries found hospitality on Polish land. It is our wish that material proof of the centuries-old community of our history be maintained. We desire that places of the martyrdom of the Jews be the subject of care and respect, that the memory of the tragedy they encountered be a warning to all."

JEWISH COMMUNITY

Estimates of the number of Jews in Poland ranged widely, from the 7,000–8,000 officially registered with the community or receiving aid from the JDC, to the 10,000–15,000 people of Jewish ancestry who showed interest in rediscovering their heritage, to as many as 30,000–40,000 people thought to have some Jewish ancestry. The Web site www.jewish.org.pl provided extensive information on the Jewish community in Poland. The Lauder Foundation ran the country's most extensive Jewish educational programs, and the JDC, which provided social welfare aid, continued to refocus its activities on education and leadership training. Rabbi Michael Schudrich, an American who had directed the Lauder Foundation's activities in Poland for nearly a decade before returning to the United States in 1998, was hired as rabbi of the Warsaw Jewish community in the summer. He divided his time between New York and Warsaw, and provided his own funding. The fact that he spent only part of his time in Warsaw was regarded by some as a potential problem.

Internal divisions continued to plague the reviving Jewish community. Beside the religious/secular and Orthodox/liberal tensions, there was also competition among the numerous Jewish organizations, some of which did not belong to the community's umbrella body, the Union of Jewish Congregations in Poland. The status of the Jewish community in Gdansk continued to be a source of problems. Jakub Szadaj, the former chairman, had been accused of financial irregularities by the Union of Polish Jewish Communities and stripped of his position in 1999. In 2000 he broke away and, after obtaining the requisite 100+ signatures, registered his own rival Independent Union of Jewish Communities, based in Gdansk. Szadaj also remained president of the local chapter of the Social-Cultural Association of Jews in Poland (TSKZ), a nationwide secular body. Some speculated that Szadaj had set up his own organization in order to obtain restituted properties, which, by law, can only be returned to Polish Jewish communal bodies. At the end of the year the influential daily *Gazeta Wyborcza* published an article highly critical of Szadaj's methods.

During the summer and early fall a group of Polish and American expatriate Jews in Warsaw formed a liberal group, Beit Warszawa, outside the established Jewish structures. Composed mainly of businesspeople and professionals, the group held monthly Friday evening services in private homes. For the High Holy Days the group brought over Rabbi Cynthia Culpepper from the United States to lead services in a rented theater and to conduct study sessions. This was believed to be the first time that a woman rabbi had ever led High Holy Day services in Poland. Also, for the first High Holy Day season in decades, Jews in Warsaw had a choice of services to attend — the liberal Beit Warszawa services, which drew more than 100 people, or Orthodox services in the Nozyk synagogue, led by Rabbi Schudrich, where the 200-seat sanctuary was filled for evening prayers. The formation of Beit Warszawa caused some initial friction with the established religious community, but the two groups soon began working together on some matters. Beit Warszawa also established contacts with Beit Praha, a similar group in Prague that had been founded several years earlier.

Several milestones of both a communal and personal nature took place during the year. In February a Polish chapter of the International Association of Jewish Lawyers and Jurists was launched in Warsaw. The sons of two pioneers of the Jewish revival in Poland each became bar mitzvah in the Nozyk synagogue in Warsaw — Gabriel Krajewski, son of mathematician Stanislaw Krajewski, in January — and Szymek Gebert, son of journalist Konstanty Gebert, in November. These lifecycle events symbolized the continuity of the renewed Jewish community, since the two fathers were among the first Jews of the postwar generation to rediscover their Jewish identity. In the late 1970s and early 1980s they were part of the so-called Flying Jewish University, a group of young people who essentially taught themselves Judaism. Since then they have become respected leaders of Poland's Jewish community. At the end of October the daughter of Yale Reisner and Helise Lieberman was bat mitzvah in Warsaw. Both parents worked for the Lauder Foundation, Reisner running its genealogy project and Lieberman serving as principal of the Jewish school in Warsaw, which has an enrollment of over 160. Two Jewish weddings were celebrated during the winter educational retreat sponsored by the Lauder Foundation near Warsaw.

Then in July, the first wedding in a quarter-century took place in the partly restored White Stork synagogue in Wroclaw, when two Americans got married there. With about 750 Jews, Wroclaw was the second largest Jewish community in Poland, after Warsaw, and it saw the event as a symbol of renewed Jewish life. The couple getting married, journalists who made a documentary film about the Jewish revival in Poland, brought their own Conservative rabbi from New Jersey to perform the ceremony. Local media gave the story extensive coverage.

As in previous years, a great variety of cultural events with Jewish themes took place—scholarly and educational sessions, conferences, performances, and exhibitions. Not only did the annual summer festival of Jewish culture take place in July, but the Jewish Culture Center in Warsaw also sponsored a full roster of events each month, including concerts, readings, and exhibits. Among the most notable were a conference on "The Polish Church and Battling Anti-Semitism: An Exchange of American and Polish Experiences" in June, and an exhibit, in September, of monotype prints of Jewish cemeteries and abandoned synagogues by the American artist Shirley Moskowitz. The annual month-long Bajit Chadasz series of events, organized in cooperation with the Italian Culture Institute and the Goethe Institute in Kraków, was held in October. On September 14 city authorities in Kielce, site of an infamous postwar pogrom, sponsored a conference on the event, with members of the Kielce *landsmanschaft* (organization of Jews hailing from Kielce) in Israel participating, along with local journalists and academics. About 500 people attended. Also in September, at a ceremony in Warsaw attended by several high-ranking political figures, Professor Moshe Rosman of Israel's Bar-Ilan University was awarded the Milewski Prize by Poland's Jerzy Milewski Foundation in recognition of his scholarly work on Polish Jewish history. The foundation, which backs liberal social and political initiatives, was also to cosponsor the Polish translation and publication of Rosman's book, *The Lord's Jews*. That same month the Ringelblum Archives—the underground archives of the wartime Warsaw Ghetto—were sent to Germany to be exhibited at the Frankfurt Jewish Museum. Warsaw held its third annual Jewish book fair in October. In November the Lauder Foundation organized what it said was Warsaw's first postwar Jewish women's seminar, featuring lectures, workshops, meetings, panel discussions, and study sessions. The city hosted a scholarly conference on the Jews of Warsaw in December.

There were a number of developments regarding the interrelated issues of property restitution and preservation of Jewish heritage sites. After many months of sometimes bitter negotiations between the Polish Jewish community and the World Jewish Restitution Organization as to how to divide up reclaimed property and/or compensation payments, an agreement was reached in June to establish a joint foundation to submit the formal applications to the Polish government for restitution of Jewish communal property and for the authority to manage returned property and proceeds. Estimates of the number of properties that might be subject to restitution ranged from 2,000 to 6,000. The deadline for submitting claims was May 2002.

In July, at the close of the annual Kraków festival of Jewish culture, the Israeli embassy honored seven Polish gentiles for their volunteer work in caring for and preserving the Polish Jewish heritage. This was the third year that such awards were presented. Also in Kraków, after nearly a decade, work was completed on the full-scale restoration of the 19th-century Tempel Synagogue. During the summer, a priest in the village of Krasiczyn organized young people to clean up the abandoned Jewish cemetery. When the work was done, Catholic and Orthodox clergy attended a memorial ceremony at the site where a rabbi recited kaddish. Jan Karski—the World War II resistance hero who risked his life to bring eyewitness accounts of the Holocaust to the West and remained a powerful moral voice for postwar Poles—died in Washington on July 13, at the age of 86. In Warsaw, Polish Jews held a memorial ceremony in the Nozyk Synagogue attended by some 200 people, including representatives of the government and the Roman Catholic Church. Rabbi Chaskiel Besser, the New York-based director of Central European programs for the Lauder Foundation, praised Karski's courage and moral integrity, and recounted their decades of friendship. Karski had requested in his will that Rabbi Besser say kaddish over his grave.

Scholar Maurycy Horn, a former director of the Jewish Historical Institute, died in Warsaw in November, aged 83.

Romania

Romania began accession talks with the EU in 2000, but was the poorest of the 12 candidates. Some 44 percent of the population lived on an average of $4.30 a day, with many subsisting on much less. The annual inflation rate was over 40 percent, the highest in East-Central Europe.

President Emil Constantinescu visited Israel at the beginning of January, where he publicly suggested that Romania, Israel, and Turkey set up a "strategic partnership." Constantinescu raised with Israeli authorities the complaints he had received from some of the 50,000 Romanians working in Israel about discrimination and poor living conditions. He also met with Israeli businessmen. During a visit to Yad Vashem, the Romanian president expressed "profound regret" for Jewish suffering in Romania during World War II under the regime of Ion Antonescu. He denied, however, that anti-Semitism played any significant role in contemporary Romania, saying it was an "isolated and marginalized" phenomenon. He admitted, though, that certain Romanian factions, such as Corneliu Vadim Tudor's Greater Romania Party, had adopted anti-Semitic positions, and that other political groups "openly or covertly collaborate with [such parties] out of electoral considerations or considerations linked with the struggle for power." During his visit Constantinescu also met in Bethlehem with Yasir Arafat, invited him to visit Romania, and agreed to examine ways of increasing cooperation with the Palestinian Authority. In Jericho he met with Patriarch Teoctist of the Orthodox Church. Together they laid the cornerstone of a Romanian religious establishment and joined representatives from 14 Orthodox churches for celebrations marking the 2,000th anniversary of Christianity. Defense Minister Victor Babiuc, who accompanied the president, met with Ephraim Sneh, Israel's deputy defense minister, and the two agreed to boost military cooperation between their countries.

Despite Constantinescu's disavowal of anti-Semitism and of the Antonescu regime there were a number of attempts during the year to honor or rehabilitate Antonescu and other wartime leaders, and these caused great concern. In January the Supreme Court of Justice rehabilitated Netta Gheron, who had served as finance minister in Antonescu's government and was jailed by the postwar Communist regime for "crimes against peace." Municipal authorities in Cluj began construction in March for a planned statue of Antonescu. In April Romanian Jewish leaders called on the government to act against the revival by extremists of the wartime fascist movement known as the Legionaires. In June the Iasi branch of the Union of War Veterans unveiled a statue of Antonescu in the town's military cemetery.

There were several reported episodes of anti-Semitism. In February vandals daubed swastikas and anti-Semitic graffiti on city walls and trams in Timisoara, apparently in connection with the entry of the Freedom Party into the Austrian government. In May a Bucharest court gave journalist Mihai Bogdan Antonescu nothing more than a two-year suspended prison sentence for "nationalist propaganda," including anti-Semitic articles. Matters came to a head in the fall elections. Economic and social instability as well as widespread corruption and political bickering led to the stunning defeat of the centrist government that had held power since 1996. In the first round of the presidential election, the extreme nationalist Corneliu Vadim Tudor, leader of the Greater Romania Party, came in second to Ion Iliescu, a former Communist who had served as Romania's president in 1990–96. Before the two faced each other in a run-off, the Romanian Jewish Federation issued a statement saying that Tudor had been "a staunch enemy of the Jews" in Romania for many years and had repeatedly expressed anti-Semitism. The statement also condemned Tudor's "aggressive stance" against other minorities, the Hungarian and Roma ethnic groups. Though Iliescu scored a two-to-one victory over Tudor in the second round, the strength of support for Tudor and the Greater Romania Party caused widespread alarm: that party, having garnered about 20 percent of the vote, was now the second largest in Parliament.

A serious anti-Semitic incident took place at the end of December when two men smashed windows, threw objects, and punched and choked a guard at the Jewish Museum in Bucharest. The intruders demanded to know where there was "soap made of human fat." To dramatize the seriousness of anti-Jewish feeling in the country, Canadian-Israeli documentary filmmaker Simcha Jacobovici, in

December, placed an unauthorized plaque commemorating Holocaust victims on a wall at the police station in Iasi. He charged that Holocaust denial in Romania had come to represent mainstream opinion.

JEWISH COMMUNITY

Between 11,000 and 16,000 Jews were believed to be living in Romania, about half of them in the capital, Bucharest. Most Romanian Jews were elderly. Only about 800 were between the ages of 15 and 35. Educational, religious, and welfare programs were carried out by the Federation of Romanian Jewish Communities (FEDROM), which was funded by the JDC. The Lauder Foundation ran the Lauder Reut Kindergarten and Lower School in Bucharest. The Jewish publishing house HaSefer issued books on Jewish themes, and a biweekly Jewish newspaper, *Realitatea Evreiasca,* included pages in Hebrew and English as well as Romanian. In October the Moshe Carmilly Institute for Hebrew and Jewish History at Babes-Bolyai University in Cluj held its annual conference on Jewish studies. The director of the institute, Ladislau Gyemant, was also serving as coordinator for a comprehensive inventory of Jewish cemeteries in Romania, being carried out under the auspices of the U.S. Commission for the Preservation of America's Heritage Abroad.

The year 2000 brought the implementation of an ambitious and unprecedented program of Jewish outreach and leadership development, a dramatic change in communal policy. Approved by FEDROM at the end of 1999, the program entailed revamping the educational system, developing a network of youth clubs and activities for children, and reaching out to unaffiliated adults, particularly those of the so-called "middle generation." For decades the pattern of Jewish life in Romania had been to encourage young people to immigrate to Israel and, with the support of the JDC, to make sure that the elderly who stayed behind lived out their lives in dignity. Even after the fall of Communism, little had been done to break this pattern.

By August youth clubs had been established in seven Romanian cities, and, in October, 81 young people from 25 Jewish communities took part in the first seminar to train youth-club leaders and activists so that they might plan and execute programs. In the fall members of the newly created Jewish Youth Organization (OTER) published their own siddur in Hebrew, Hebrew transliterated, and Romanian, also including annotations and teaching instructions for prayers and holiday observances. OTER also began the publication of a newspaper for youth. Jewish Education through the Mail (JEM) courses also proved popular, as more than 400 Jews, mostly young people, in 37 cities and towns signed up for long-distance study. Yosef Hirsch, a young American serving as a JDC volunteer in Romania, designed the courses, and Hirsch also compiled a database of names and contact numbers of young Romanian Jews. In addition, Jodi Guralnick, the JDC Ralph Goldman Fellow in Romania for 1999–2000, carried out an unprecedented survey of the "missing middle generation" of Romanian Jews to ascertain numbers, attitudes, and potential for community involvement and leadership training.

Slovakia

At the International Conference on the Holocaust held in Stockholm in January, President Rudolf Schuster of Slovakia condemned the pro-Nazi government of the wartime independent Slovak state, led by Father Jozef Tiso. In February Schuster became the first Slovak head-of-state ever to visit Israel, going on a four-day trip. Emerging from Yad Vashem, he apologized for Slovakia's role during the Holocaust and called for changes in the Slovak school curriculum so that young people might learn about that "dark chapter" of their country's history. He called for September 9—the anniversary of the date on which the wartime Slovak government introduced anti-Semitic legislation—to be declared the annual Holocaust memorial day in Slovakia. This was approved later in the year. While in Israel Schuster praised the Jewish state's decision to withdraw its ambassador from Vienna in protest of the Freedom Party's entry into the Austrian government, and urged Israel to relocate its regional embassy to the Slovak capital. In Bratislava, however, the extremist Slovak National Party congratulated Freedom Party leader Jörg Haider and Austrian chancellor Wolfgang Schüssel. The mainstream Christian Democratic Party congratulated only Schüssel.

In February and early March controversy erupted over a decision by the municipal council of the town of Zilina to erect a plaque honoring Tiso. Zilina's plan to unveil the plaque on March 14, the 61st anniversary of the establishment of the wartime puppet state, was spearheaded by Mayor Jan Slota, leader of the Slovak National Party, which supported the rehabilitation of Tiso and regarded him as a national hero. Following protests by Slovak government leaders and Jewish groups at home and abroad, plans for the plaque were canceled. Still, about 200 pro-Tiso demonstrators gathered outside the presidential palace in Bratislava on March 14 to mark the anniversary. In August the Slovak National Bank reversed an earlier decision to issue a commemorative coin honoring children's author Ludo Ondrejov. The reversal was due to Ondrejov's "aryanization" activities during World War II. In the autumn Jews protested the Vatican's plan to canonize an anticommunist Slovak bishop, Jan Vojtassak, who died in 1965. Vojtassak was jailed for 13 years after a Communist purge of church officials in 1950. But five Israeli historians said, in October, that they had found evidence that Vojtassak had been vice chairman of the pro-Nazi Slovak State Council in 1942, when the council agreed to deport thousands of Slovak Jews. In December the first Slovak translation of *Mein Kampf* went on sale. Some 5,000 copies were printed. The translation included a 30-page commentary stressing the book's racism, anti-Semitism, and violent nature. Even so, the Slovak Jewish community and the deputy premier in charge of human rights criticized the publication.

JEWISH COMMUNITY

Fewer than 4,000 Jews were believed to be living in Slovakia. The main communities were the capital city of Bratislava and Košice, in eastern Slovakia, each with about 500 Jews. As in other postcommunist states, Jewish life had flowered after the fall of communism, with regular classes and clubs, seminars, cultural events, and other activities, including a kindergarten and an annual two-week summer camp in Bratislava cosponsored by the Lauder Foundation and Chabad. The Federation of Jewish Communities ran a kosher restaurant and a pension, Chez David, in Bratislava, plus the Jewish old-age home Ohel David, and a Holocaust-documentation center. There were Jewish museums in Bratislava and Presov and an Institute of Jewish Studies in Bratislava. Košice also had a kosher restaurant, Jewish clubs, and other activities. In October, there was a weeklong series of cultural events in Bratislava devoted to Prague-born Jewish writer Franz Kafka, organized by the Czech Center, the Goethe Institute, the Austrian Culture Center, and the Museum of Jewish Culture in Slovakia.

The Ester Association, a local affiliate of the International Council of Jewish Women, was active in Košice. In September it organized a three-day meeting of women from the postcommunist nations of Europe. After a memorial service at the Jewish cemetery, there was a solemn Holocaust commemoration in Košice's state theater, held under the auspices of President Schuster, a former mayor of the city. There was a concert as well as personal testimony by Jews from several countries. The event coincided with the European Day of Jewish Culture, September 3, when hundreds of Jewish-heritage sites in 16 countries across the continent were opened to the public in order to promote knowledge of Jewish culture and tradition, and it reflected President Schuster's desire to make September 9 Holocaust memorial day in Slovakia.

Jewish community headquarters in Bratislava inaugurated a new kosher kitchen and dining room in 2000 that served hot lunches every day and provided meals-on-wheels to homebound members. Rabbi Baruch Myers, an American-born adherent of Chabad, served the religious needs of Bratislava Jews. Jewish holidays were celebrated with communal events, some of which drew well over 100 people. On the holiday of Lag b'Omer, in May, some 75 people joined Myers on an hour-long boat ride on the Danube with refreshments, some teaching, and entertainment. During the year, *mohelim* were brought in from abroad to perform circumcisions. In January a spacious new Jewish-education center opened in Bratislava, under Chabad auspices. It was not officially inaugurated, however, till December, with a ceremony attended by local Jews, government figures, and representatives of international Jewish organizations.

Rabbi Myers's strict Orthodoxy was not in tune with large sectors of this primarily secular, liberal community. Also, the implicit contradiction between his position as rabbi of the entire community and his role as *shaliah* (representative) of the Chabad movement raised concern. A key issue was Myers's insistence on the Halakhah as the standard for Jewish identity, and his reluctance to facilitate conversions to Judaism. His stand on this matter evoked complaints in a community whose members included many mixed-married families as well as children of mixed marriages who had long considered themselves Jewish. Children of non-Jewish mothers, for example, were excluded from the kindergarten, so that the kindergarten had only nine pupils.

In mid-March the 22nd annual International Conference of European Rabbis took place in Bratislava. It was originally to have taken place in Vienna, but the venue was changed to protest the entry of the Freedom Party into the Austrian government. President Schuster and Prime Minister Mikuláš Dzurinda attended the opening reception.

In June unidentified vandals desecrated the Jewish cemetery in the town of Dunajska Streda. During the summer 40 young people from Slovakia, the Czech Republic, and Israel went to work restoring one of Slovakia's oldest Jewish cemeteries, in Nitrianske Rudno. The project was part of the annual summer camp run by the Slovak Union of Jewish Youth. In October Slovak Jews sued Germany for the return of funds paid by Slovakia's wartime fascist government to cover the costs of deporting nearly 58,000 Slovakian Jews in 1942. The Slovak regime, the only Nazi puppet state to have made such payments, gave Germany 500 marks for each Jew deported.

Yugoslavia

The ouster of strongman Slobodan Milosevic marked a political revolution in Yugoslavia. Milosevic lost the September 24 election to opposition leader Vojislav Kostunica, but refused to accept the results. Only after hundreds of thousands of opposition supporters marched on Belgrade and stormed parliament on October 5 did Milosevic finally concede defeat. Kostunica initiated democratic changes aimed at ending Yugoslavia's isolation and dire economic situation. In December Kostunica's supporters crushed Milosevic forces in elections for the Serbian parliament.

Yugoslavia's 3,000 Jews, about half of whom lived in Belgrade, were highly integrated into the broader society, mostly secular, and, often, intermarried. Jews welcomed the ouster of Milosevic, and many took part—as individuals—in the street demonstrations. However the Federation of Jewish Communities, the Jewish umbrella organization, had maintained an official policy of political neutrality throughout the Milosevic regime. Although this neutrality was intended to prevent political manipulation or exploitation and to stress the federation's nonpolitical nature, some Jews feared that neutrality in the face of Milosevic's policies might be interpreted as de facto acquiescence. In fact the 200-member Jewish community in Subotica, the country's third largest Jewish community, attempted to demonstrate opposition to Milosevic through nonpolitical means, contributing to the nonsectarian humanitarian organization La Benevolencija, which was modeled on the organization of the same name in Sarajevo, and aiding Roma (Gypsies) and other refugees, particularly in Montenegro.

The JDC distributed medication and aid packages, and opened soup kitchens in Belgrade and six other Jewish communities which served a total of more than 700 hot lunches a day, five days a week. The economic crisis jeopardized the community's social-welfare programs. In October suppliers for soup kitchens in several towns said that without financial assistance they could no longer provide meals at prices low enough to be covered by local Jewish-community budgets, and Jewish leaders said the communities might need emergency financial aid on a long-term basis.

A crisis of leadership marked by personal and political infighting affected the Jewish community. The unexpected death from cancer in May of Misha David, vice president of the Federation of Jewish Communities, was a particularly hard blow. David, who was in his late 50s and was regarded as one of the few members of the "younger" generation capable of taking on the job, had been expected to replace 78-year-old Aca Singer as president of the federation. Meanwhile, the Jewish community was hit by a general Yugoslav brain drain: an estimated 300–400 Jews left Yugoslavia in 1999–2000 in the wake of the Kosovo conflict and the NATO bombing, including many, if not most, of the student-age and young-adult generation.

Religious observance was important to only a minority of Yugoslav Jews, and, indeed, the federation officially defined itself as an "ethnic-religious" organization. Rabbi Yitzhak Asiel, who was Orthodox, focused his attention on strengthening religious involvement. He attempted to raise private funds to build a *mikveh* (ritual bath) and a kosher kitchen, and to publish Jewish religious texts.

The federation and local Jewish communities maintained a wide program of cultural and communal activities, which were reported in the monthly *Bilten* newsletter. Jews from Yugoslavia took part in the meeting of Jews from all parts of former Yugoslavia that was held in Brac, Croatia, during the summer.

RUTH ELLEN GRUBER

Former Soviet Union

National Affairs

WHEN BORIS YELTSIN resigned as president of Russia on December 31, 1999, Prime Minister Vladimir Putin became acting president, pending a new election scheduled for March 26, 2000. Yeltsin left the country almost immediately for a vacation in Israel and the Palestinian territories. The visit was described as private, but Israelis and Palestinians treated Yeltsin as a head of state. Putin, meanwhile, as acting president, immediately began replacing the presidential staff, including Pavel Borodin, chief of the Kremlin property management office, and Yuri Skuratov, who, as prosecutor-general, had investigated corruption in the Kremlin.

The presidential campaign began early in the year, with Putin the heavy favorite in an 11-candidate field. Putin won with 53 percent of the vote, averting the need for a run-off with the second-place candidate, the Communist Gennady Zyuganov, who got 29 percent. Grigory Yavlinsky of the Yabloko party won 6 percent, and no other candidate registered more than 3 percent. Whereas Yeltsin, in the previous election, had carried only 57 of the 89 Russian regions, Putin won a majority in all but six regions. Twice during the campaign, state television (ORT) intervened in ways that cast Jews in a negative light. First, it broadcast the charge that Yavlinsky, the leading liberal candidate, was backed by Jews, homosexuals, and foreigners. Then, it showed Vladimir Gusinsky, a wealthy Russian Jewish "oligarch" during the Yeltsin years and now a supporter of Moscow mayor Yuri Luzhkov for the presidency, attending a banquet with Hassidim who were dressed in their traditional garb.

On May 7 Vladimir Putin was inaugurated as president. He appointed Mikhail Kasyanov, a liberal economist and former deputy prime minister under Putin, as his prime minister. Over the course of the year Putin's plans for Russia's future remained unclear. Some of the government's statements gave the impression of wanting to raise Russia's international visibility and enhance its role in world affairs. Prime examples of this were the announcement that Russia would consider first use of nuclear weapons if attacked by large-scale conventional forces, and a declaration that Russia would increase spending for weapons procurement by 50 percent. However there seemed to be no program to deal with the nation's enormous economic problems.

Putin did appear determined to control the mass media more tightly than had been done during the Yeltsin regime. On January 5, 2000, Putin signed a decree granting the FSB (the federal security service, successor to the KGB) authority

436

to monitor e-mail and Internet usage. Andrei Babitsky, a reporter for Radio Liberty working in Chechnya, was arrested by Russian forces and then handed over to unidentified Chechen forces. When Babitsky was finally released in March, Putin sharply rebuked him for having reported on alleged Russian atrocities in Chechnya. In June the Federal Security Council approved a new "information doctrine" which warned the media not to "pose a threat to national security." The Duma (lower house of parliament) also approved a law granting the head of state the right to introduce a state of emergency at will. This included the power to close down political parties and censor the media, with approval by the Duma.

The new president moved vigorously to establish central authority in Russia's 89 regions. Putin's followers in the Duma could have formed a coalition without backing from the Communists, who constituted the largest single party in that body. Putin, however, masterminded a deal with the Communists whereby his supporters backed Gennady Seleznyov, a Communist, for reelection as speaker of the Duma, and divided the important committee chairmanships with the Communists. As a result, there was little opposition to the new regime's centralization program.

Under Yeltsin, the autonomous powers of the 89 regional governments had often made it difficult to run the country. Putin now, by presidential decree, consolidated the 89 regions into seven new administrative districts to be overseen by people chosen by him. It did not pass unnoticed that five of the seven new chief administrators turned out to have had military, police, or intelligence backgrounds. (Putin himself, of course, had been a career KGB officer.) The new administrators were charged with overseeing the implementation of federal legislation and ensuring that local laws complied with federal rules. Next, Putin induced the Duma to pass legislation removing the governors of the 89 regions from their seats in the Federation Council, the upper house of the parliament; instead, the regions would be represented there by lower-level officials elected by the voters of each region.

What these changes signified was that the governors would lose their independent authority and immunity from prosecution, and federal appointees would control not only the federal funds flowing into the regions, but also the patronage and control over law enforcement. Boris Berezovsky, one of the most powerful "oligarchs" closely tied to the Yeltsin regime, who, together with Roman Abramovich, the chief owner of Sibneft, a major oil company, had acquired a major share of the Russian aluminum industry at a very favorable price, criticized Putin's administrative changes for reintroducing the dependence of the citizen on the state and its central authorities that had characterized the Soviet era.

Putin moved to curb the power of the "oligarchs" Berezovsky and Gusinsky, both known as Jews. On May 11 FSB agents raided the offices of Media-Most, the large media conglomerate owned by Vladimir Gusinsky. Among Media-Most's holdings were NTV, the major independent television station; Ekho Moskvy, a radio station; the daily newspaper *Sevodnya;* and the popular magazine *Itogi*. Gusinsky, who was also president of the Russian Jewish Congress, had opposed Putin's candidacy for president, as had the media under his control. While Putin had not commented about Gusinsky, Kremlin chief-of-staff Alexander Voloshin had severely criticized Media-Most. The FSB justified the raid and the seizure of records, saying that it could provide evidence of illegalities in connection with Gusinsky's acquisitions. Gusinsky himself was arrested on June 13 on suspicion of embezzling $10 million or more in federal property when he acquired a government-owned television station in 1996. He was held in a Moscow prison with a reputation for harsh conditions.

President Putin, on a trip to Germany at the time, professed surprise at Gusinsky's arrest. He pointed out that Media-Most owed huge sums to Gazprom, Russia's largest gas company, but said that the jailing was "excessive." Mayor Luzhkov of Moscow offered himself as a replacement in jail. Gusinsky's rival, Berezovsky, criticized the jailing, but said that Gusinsky had brought the problem on himself. After four days Gusinsky was released, but Gazprom began to press for repayment of a $211-million loan. In November Gusinsky left Russia for Spain to avoid arrest. In December authorities raided the offices of ORT television, in which Boris Berezovsky held a 49-percent stake. He too fled the country.

The war in the breakaway region of Chechnya continued to rage. Prime Minister Kasyanov estimated in January that, since the reentry of Russian troops into the region in October 1999, the war had cost Russia $178 million. With presidential elections scheduled for March, Putin moved in January to crush the Chechens. In February Russian forces captured what remained of the devastated Chechen capital, Grozny, but Chechens mounted guerilla actions south of the city. Committing more troops and munitions, the Russian forces attempted to suppress rebel attacks. Russian television showed troops pillaging and killing civilians, but the Russian public seemed generally to support harsh measures against the Muslim Chechen forces. In June Putin appointed Mufti Akhmed Kadyrov, a Chechen, as governor of Chechnya in a political attempt to blunt renewed Chechen attacks, but in the following month at least 37 Russian soldiers were killed in bombings.

An upturn in the world petroleum market helped the Russian economy. The GDP at the end of September was up 7.3 percent from the same point in 1999, and unemployment steadily declined. Inflation was half of what it had been the year before, and the standard of living rose perceptibly. But corruption was rampant, with an estimated 25 percent of the economy consisting of unreported "shadow" transactions. Two Russian Jewish émigrés pleaded guilty in the United States to laundering billions of dollars from Russia through the Bank of New York, where one of them was employed. The International Monetary Fund said in March that the Ukrainian Central Bank and its Russian counterpart had overstated the amount of currency reserves they held. Ukrainian prime minister Viktor Yushchenko, previously the head of the Ukrainian Central Bank, canceled a visit to the United States, and a former Ukrainian prime minister, Petro Lazarenko, was living in the U.S. while Ukraine and other countries tried to extradite him for absconding with Ukrainian state funds.

On August 12 one of Russia's newest and most formidable submarines, the Kursk, sank in Arctic waters after an explosion. Russian divers and navy personnel were unable to open the submarine, and for four days the government rejected help offered by NATO as unnecessary. President Putin did not interrupt his vacation until it became obvious that this was a major disaster. Norwegian divers finally opened the ship, but there were no survivors. Russian officials tried to blame the disaster on foreign submarines, which were said to have collided with the Kursk. But months later an investigative commission determined that exploding torpedoes had caused the tragedy. Though President Putin was severely criticized in the immediate aftermath of the accident, he soon regained his very high ratings in the opinion polls.

Israel and the Middle East

Israeli foreign minister David Levy visited Russia in December 1999 and expressed understanding for Russia's "fight against terrorism" in Chechnya. He later amplified his statement to express regret over the loss of life and state his hopes for a peaceful solution. Nine months later, in September 2000, Natan Sharansky, who had resigned as Israel's minister of the interior in July, was received by President Putin. The former political prisoner who served a long sentence in a Russian jail when he was known as Anatoly Shcharansky, and the former KGB officer now Russian president, exchanged views on Russian-Israeli relations. Sharansky also visited Uzbekistan and met with President Islam Karimov, who stressed the common Israeli-Uzbekistan interest in fighting Islamic terrorism.

The Russian Duma ratified a Russian-Israeli convention on avoiding dual taxation, something previous Dumas had failed to accomplish over six years.

About ten Israelis with roots in the former Soviet Union were said to be detained for ransom by Chechen rebels. During Sharansky's visit, a teenage Israeli held by the Chechens was released.

Anti-Semitism

Vytautas Sustauskas, the new mayor of Lithuania's second largest city, Kaunas, made a number of public anti-Semitic remarks during the year and accused a "Jewish mafia" of controlling the city. Kaunas's Jewish population was estimated at less than 300. In May a "national-socialist" party, claiming 700 members, was founded in Lithuania that advocated restrictions on immigration and on the importation of foreign goods. It remained unclear, however, whether the authorities would register the party.

In September the Lithuanian Seimas (parliament) resolved to treat as an "act of state" the declaration issued by the "provisional Lithuanian government" on June 23, 1941, which restored Lithuanian independence after its annexation to the USSR the previous year. It was that independent Lithuanian regime that had sent a telegram to Adolf Hitler assuring him that "his genius had spurred the

Lithuanian people to join the victorious crusade to exterminate Judaism." The Seimas's legitimization of the "provisional government" aroused protests, and President Valdas Adamkus criticized the legislators opposed to the act for not having blocked it earlier in the legislative process.

Anti-Semitic acts occurred in several Russian cities. On September 17 a Jewish Sunday school in Ryazan was invaded by 15 neo-Nazis armed with chains, who vandalized the school and terrorized the students, ages six to thirteen, and their teachers. Shouting "Death to the Jews!" and other threats, the gang did not physically injure anyone, but the children were traumatized. Some accused the local media and the Chabad-dominated Federation of Jewish Communities of Russia of ignoring the incident in order not to cast a shadow on the dedication of a new Chabad-Lubavitch community center taking place in Moscow at the same time.

In Nizhni Novgorod vandals destroyed 40 Jewish gravestones. In 1996, 140 had been destroyed in the same cemetery and the perpetrators had never been apprehended. In the Latvian city of Daugavpils two men were charged with desecrating the Jewish cemetery. An anti-Semitic book that included material from the infamous *Protocols of the Elders of Zion* was published in Minsk, the capital of Belarus, and a district court there rejected a libel suit against the publisher. Jewish activists in Belarus pointed out that, though for several years the press had not featured anti-Semitic articles, it was now publishing quite a few, and that people who had published "anti-Zionist" propaganda in the Soviet period were now publishing anti-Jewish material in several newspapers. In Russia, President Putin invited Alexander Prokhanov, editor of the nationalist and anti-Semitic newspaper *Zavtra,* to a meeting he convened of leading editors to discuss his general policy directions. The head of the Department of History at St. Petersburg University, Igor Froyanov, was accused by some students and faculty of spreading anti-Semitic ideas in the classroom and in the department.

Holocaust-Related Developments

Toward the end of World War II, Nazi SS troops drove about 7,000 Jews, mostly women, into the icy Baltic Sea. This atrocity went unmarked until January 2000 when it was acknowledged publicly in the town of Yantarny, Kaliningrad region, and a monument was erected in memory of the victims. In July a Holocaust memorial was dedicated in a public ceremony in Minsk attended by Belarussian president Aleksandr Lukashenko.

Konrad Kalejs, accused of executing Jews and others while a member of the Latvian Arajs Commando during the war, left Great Britain for Australia, where he held citizenship. About 13,000 Latvians had been accused by the Soviet government of "war crimes," and some were pardoned by the post-Soviet Latvian government in the early 1990s. In February Israel honored nine Latvians who had saved Jews as "Righteous among the Nations." With this designation, 71 of the approximately 15,000 people so honored were Latvian.

U.S. Congressman Tom Lantos, a Holocaust survivor, met in January with Lithuanian officials and urged more vigorous prosecution of war criminals. Afterwards, he expressed disappointment with the meetings. However, at an international conference on the Holocaust in Stockholm, Sweden, Lithuanian prime minister Andrius Kubilius and Latvian president Vaira Vike-Fraiberga pledged to seek justice in their respective countries and prosecute war criminals. In June a medical commission said the trial in Lithuania of Aleksandras Lileikis, police chief of Vilnius during the Nazi occupation, could resume despite his advanced age (93) and poor health. The trial was indeed resumed, but was halted after a few minutes, and, in July, the case was suspended indefinitely. On September 28 Lileikis died of a heart attack.

Lithuanian officials accused several Jews residing in Israel of participating, as members of the Soviet secret police, in deportations of Lithuanians in the 1940s. Israeli officials refused to assist the Lithuanians in investigating these cases, or the case of Nachman Dushansky, accused of having taken part in the Soviet campaign against Lithuanian nationalists after World War II.

JEWISH COMMUNITY

Emigration

After rising in 1999—probably due to economic difficulties and some manifestations of anti-Semitism—Jewish emigration from the former Soviet Union declined somewhat in 2000. Whereas a total of 72,372 Jews had emigrated in 1999, 56,647 did so in 2000, 50,859 of them (nearly 90 percent) going to Israel. Immigration to the United States continued to decline, with only 5,787 immigrants from the FSU. Israeli officials announced that in 1999 a slight majority of the immigrants were not Jews according to Halakhah (Jewish law), but relatives or descendants of Jews; 10 percent of the immigrants had no Jewish spouse or parent, but only a Jewish grandparent. High rates of intermarriage and the shrinking number of Jews in the FSU led Israeli officials to expect a continuing rise in the proportion of non-Jews in the immigration.

Communal Affairs

The 16th seminar of the Association of Jewish Schools and Principals of the CIS (Commonwealth of Independent States) and Baltic States took place in October, and 50 schools were represented. The chairman of the group is Grigory Lipman, who heads one of Moscow's largest Jewish schools.

There were now 26 Hillel organizations in the former Soviet Union. Serving mostly university-age Jews, Hillel claimed to reach 10,000 people through its Lehrhaus program, in which teachers commit to six weeks of intensive study in Israel followed by a year of Judaica teaching in their FSU localities.

The American Jewish Joint Distribution Committee (JDC) continued its wide-ranging philanthropic and communal work. In Belarus it was said to be aiding some 18,000–20,000 Jews (30,135 people declared themselves Jews in the 1999 Belarussian census) mainly through local welfare societies (*hasadim*) and the distribution of 70,000 food parcels per year around holiday times. The JDC was criticized by Yuri Dorn, head of the Union of Religious Jewish Congregations in Belarus, for supporting Chabad-Lubavitch, Aish HaTorah, and the Movement for Progressive Judaism, all affiliated with the Union of Jewish Organizations and Communities, while not aiding the Union of Religious Jewish Congregations. The JDC responded that it had provided 17 percent of the latter's budget in 1999.

The biggest conflict in the Jewish communities of the FSU emerged when Vladimir Gusinsky, president of the Russian Jewish Congress, was arrested in June (see above). The very day before Gusinsky's arrest Putin had received in the Kremlin members of the Federation of Jewish Communities of Russia, a Chabad-Lubavitch organization. The next day, as Gusinsky was arrested, the federation announced that it had elected Berel Lazar, the chief Chabad emissary in Russia, to the post of chief rabbi. However, Adolf Shaevich was already chief rabbi of Russia, and Pinchas Goldschmidt chief rabbi of Moscow. But they, along with Zinovy Kogan, head of the Reform movement, as well as many secular Jewish leaders, were on the governing board of the Russian Jewish Congress, presided over by Gusinsky. On June 19 Mikhail Shvydkoi, the Russian minister of culture, signed an agreement of cooperation with the Federation of Jewish Communities of Russia, whose representatives were Mikhail Gluz, formerly a Jewish theater director, and Rabbi Berel Lazar. It seemed to many observers, domestic and foreign, that Putin was using a willing Chabad to demonstrate that though he was after Gusinsky, he was not anti-Semitic, since he had his own "court Jews."

The September groundbreaking of a Jewish community center in Moscow, sponsored by the Russian Jewish Congress, was postponed indefinitely after invitations had been issued (and Putin was listed as attending). At the very same time the groundbreaking was supposed to take place, Putin instead delivered a speech at the opening of a seven-story, 50-room Chabad community center said to cost $10 million, most of it contributed by diamond merchant and Chabad supporter Levi Levayev, a Bukharan Jew. The grateful Hassidim gave Putin a shofar. Rabbi Shaevich did not attend but Rabbi Goldschmidt did, praising Chabad's work in the FSU but criticizing its federation for being too close to the Kremlin. Apparently spurred by Chabad's successes, Rabbi Shaevich and his supporters made a five-day, five-city tour of smaller Jewish communities in Russia just before Rosh Hashanah. In October armed police spent ten hours searching Moscow's main Choral Synagogue, presided over by Rabbis Shaevich and Goldschmidt, claiming they were looking for Gusinsky's financial records. On November 13 a warrant was issued for the arrest of Gusinsky, who fled to Spain. In December the World Jewish Congress asked Interpol not to arrest Gusinsky because he was being prosecuted on political, not criminal, grounds. Gusinsky was nevertheless placed under house arrest.

Earlier in the year a Restitution Agency had been formed to channel an expected $2.5 million in German restitution payments that was to be divided up among about 2,000 Holocaust survivors. Vladimir Gusinsky was appointed chairman of the new body, which included representatives of the JDC, local Jewish organizations, and survivors' groups. Since about 20 percent of the funds were earmarked for educational and communal development, Chabad demanded representation in the agency.

The aggressiveness of the new Chabad-controlled federation and its challenges to the Russian Jewish Congress gave rise to two theories. Some felt that this was nothing more than war over turf. Others thought Chabad was trying to establish a monopoly on Jewish life in the territory it considered its historical home grounds and that it had, in fact, put more effort into building Jewish life in Russia over the years than any other Jewish body, with the exception of the JDC.

Religion

In March Kiev's Great Synagogue, also known as the Brodsky Synagogue, was rededicated in a ceremony attended by Ukrainian president Leonid Kuchma. Built in 1898 and financed by Lazar Brodsky, a sugar merchant, the centrally located synagogue was seized by the Soviet government in 1926 and had recently served as a puppet theater. The efforts of Vadim Rabinovich, a controversial Ukrainian Jewish businessman with close ties to the government, facilitated the return of the structure. Because most Ukrainian Jewish organizations and Ukrainian chief rabbi Yaakov Bleich had distanced themselves from Rabinovich, Rabbi Moshe Asman, the Chabad-Lubavitch representative who called himself "chief rabbi" of the country, was installed as the synagogue's leader.

As in Ukraine and Moscow, there were tensions in the Urals city of Ekaterinburg between local Jewish activists, operating as the Jewish Cultural Society, and the local Chabad-Lubavitch. The latter succeeded where the local activists had failed, and obtained land from the city for a synagogue. Rabbi Zelig Ashkenazi of Chabad headed a high school there with some 200 students. Not to be outdone, the Russian Jewish Congress imported a Ukrainian-born rabbi, Moshe Steinberg, from Israel to serve as its Ekaterinburg rabbi. A similar conflict broke out in Novosibirsk, but in the Urals city of Chelyabinsk the local cultural activists and Chabad worked together.

ZVI GITELMAN

Australia

National Affairs

THE MAJOR POLITICAL ISSUE Australians confronted in 2000 was the implementation of an administratively complicated 10-percent goods-and-services tax. This was expected eventually to cause major problems for the Liberal-National coalition government led by John Howard, but on the whole criticism was less than anticipated, though it grew toward the end of the year as the law was implemented. Through most of the year the governing coalition trailed the opposition Australian Labor Party (ALP) in the polls as the Australian dollar fell to its lowest value ever against the U.S. dollar, oil prices soared, and the economy slowed toward year's end. The next election was due at the end of 2001, with the opposition needing a very small electoral swing to win the few seats it would require to gain power.

Pauline Hanson's far-right One Nation Party continued to confront problems. It had received a grant of $500,000 from the Queensland Electoral Commission for having 11 members elected in the 1998 state elections. However the courts subsequently found that the party was fraudulently registered for funding and it had to give the money back. Responsibility for the payment fell to Pauline Hanson, and she spent most of the year raising the money. Hanson also had a major falling-out with the party's two top functionaries, David Oldfield and David Ettridge. Hanson attempted to expel the "two Davids" from the party for registering two new parties, which, she said, breached the One Nation constitution. They responded that, as directors of the party, they could not be expelled, and a round of recriminations and lockouts followed. Despite Hanson's setbacks the resentment that fueled her popularity still simmered, and she was by no means politically finished.

Mainstream nonindigenous Australians embraced reconciliation with Aboriginals to a greater extent in 2000 than ever before. Reconciliation marches throughout the country during the year drew over a million people, with the largest marches in Sydney in May and in Melbourne in December. A new body, Reconciliation Australia, was formed to further the work of Aboriginal reconciliation. One board member of the new group was Mark Leibler, chairman of AIJAC (Australia/Israel and Jewish Affairs Council). In addition, the federal government appointed Dr. Colin Rubenstein, AIJAC executive director, to the Council for

Multicultural Australia. This body was established to help the government implement its "new agenda for multicultural Australia" announced in December 1999 (see AJYB 2000, p. 406).

The government of the state of Victoria released a discussion paper on the subject of legislation against racial hatred. Victoria remained the only state without such legislation, the national government and all other states having laws of one kind or another in this area.

The September 2000 Olympic Games, which took place in Sydney, were a great success, generating an outpouring of Australian national pride unparalleled since World War II. The community torch relay, which included several Jewish torch carriers, unified the nation behind the games. The events themselves went without a hitch, and at the closing ceremony Juan Antonio Samaranch, president of the International Olympic Committee (IOC), described the games as the best ever (see below, pp. 453–54).

Australian army personnel continued their participation in the international peacekeeping force in East Timor, while relations with Indonesia slightly improved. Australia also played a major role in negotiating a resolution to the ethnic-based civil war in the Solomon Islands. Partly as a response to this new role as regional peacekeeper, the government released and held public hearings on a new white paper on defense, which recommended a $24-billion boost in defense spending.

In a move that sparked controversy, the government withdrew from the UN Human Rights Commission system after the UN condemned Australian mandatory sentencing laws while remaining silent on serious human-rights violations by other, nondemocratic regimes. Australia also confronted some of the international problems it had previously been spared, with the expulsion of suspected terrorists in the lead-up to the Olympics and the violent Seattle-like "S11" protests at the World Economic Forum in Melbourne in September.

An area of continuing controversy was the treatment of asylum-seeking illegal immigrants, most of whom arrive by boat and have come, in recent years, mainly from the Middle East and Afghanistan. This year there were riots at and escapes from the isolated detention centers used to house these people, including one mass breakout. There were allegations of abuse at the Woomera Detention Center in South Australia, which critics described as a "hellhole." Australian policy on allowing immigrants into the country came under increasing fire for being too harsh, while the government responded that considerations of security, health, and equity necessitated a thorough and at times lengthy scrutiny of applicants. There were indications that procedures might be liberalized in 2001.

Israel and the Middle East

The Australian government continued to maintain warm relations with Israel, expressing full support for a continuation of the Middle East peace process. Australia maintained this posture even after the onset of the new surge of violence in late September, with Foreign Minister Alexander Downer stating that security cooperation between Israelis and the Palestinians must recommence and that the peace process could not be abandoned.

Prime Minister John Howard paid a highly successful state visit to Israel on April 29–May 2, only the third time that an Australian prime minister had visited Israel. Howard's discussions with Israeli prime minister Ehud Barak ranged over the Middle East peace process, Nazi war criminals, and compensation for the victims of the Maccabiah bridge tragedy (see below). Howard had briefings with leading Israeli industrialists and with high-tech companies that focused on the encouragement of Israeli-Australian joint ventures as well as the establishment of a Binational Industrial Research and Development Fund (BIRD). Howard also met with Palestinian leader Yasir Arafat, whom he described as "a fascinating person to meet . . . a man who is searching for peace, who is conscious of the extremist elements that seek to overthrow him."

More than just a diplomatic journey, the visit to Israel was also personally meaningful to Prime Minister Howard, who had maintained close ties to the Jewish community and had been a strong supporter of Israel throughout his political career. In his acceptance speech upon receiving an honorary doctorate from Bar-Ilan University he said: "The personal affection I have for the State of Israel, the personal regard I have for the Jewish people of the world, will never be diminished. It is something I hold dearly, something I value as part of my being and as part of what I have tried to do with my life."

Howard, back in Australia, further reflected on his trip to Israel when he addressed an AIJAC and United Israel Appeal dinner in his honor on November 22. He said, "I don't believe any prime minister of Israel could have offered more than did Ehud Barak at Camp David in July. It was an offer that should have been accepted and it is tragic in the extreme that it was not accepted."

There were other high-profile Australian visitors to Israel in 2000. In January an Australian Young Political Leaders Tour, involving eight young and rising political leaders, visited Israel in a program run in cooperation with AIJAC. Various successful trade missions took place, one in August led by Federal Education Minister David Kemp, and another in November led by Communications Minister Richard Alston, his second such trip in two years. As a direct outcome of the November mission, Telstra, Australia's largest telecommunications carrier, made its first venture-capital investment in Israel.

Foreign Minister Downer visited Iran at the end of July and, as on many previous occasions, he spoke to Iranian ministers and officials about the ten Iranian Jews convicted and imprisoned on espionage charges. In September he stated that "while the reduction in their sentences is a step in the right direction, I am disappointed that the prison sentences remain in place and were not overturned. I call upon the Iranian authorities to extend clemency to each of the ten Jews." Downer's counterpart in the political opposition, Laurie Brereton, stated on July 3 that "as a long-standing trading partner of Iran, Australia should make it absolutely clear to the Iranian government that persecution of people as a consequence of their religious beliefs can only damage Iran's international standing and further delay normalization of Iran's relations with much of the world."

Nevertheless, in May the Australian government voted in favor of two loans from the World Bank to Iran totaling $232 million, the first loans the World Bank had made to Iran in more than seven years. The U.S., France, and Canada sought to postpone the loans, but were outvoted.

In April a joint committee of the Federal Parliament conducted the first comprehensive review of Australia's policies in the Middle East in many years. Responding to the committee's request for the submission of testimony, a number of Jewish communal organizations—including AIJAC, the Executive Council of Australian Jewry (ECAJ), and the Australia-Israel Chamber of Commerce—and several Christian-based groups prepared testimony arguing for a strong Australia-Israel relationship. Among the topics covered were the benefits of trade relations with Israel, Australia's role in the peace process and the importance of its continuing pro-Israel stance, Australia's defense relationship with the region, how the UN might promote regional stability, sanctions against Iraq, the dangers inherent in the production and dissemination of weapons of mass destruction, human-rights priorities, and social and cultural links.

In the UN, Australia was one of Israel's earliest supporters in its bid to join WEOG (Western European and Others Group), which would enable Israel to gain membership on the Security Council and other specialized UN bodies, a campaign that succeeded in May, albeit with limitations. With Palestinian violence raging in December, however, Australia voted for resolutions slanted against Israel in the UN General Assembly on "Jerusalem," "peaceful settlement of the question of Palestine," and the "Special Information Programme on Palestine of the Department of Public Information of the Secretariat." It abstained from voting on anti-Israel resolutions regarding "Syrian Golan," the "Division for Palestinian Rights of the Secretariat," and the "Committee on the Exercise of the Inalienable Rights of the Palestinian People."

Despite this mixed voting record in the General Assembly, Penny Wensley, Australia's ambassador to the UN, said that unbalanced criticism and the singling out of one side only for blame was unhelpful. She strongly supported the call of the International Red Cross for both sides to respect, and to ensure respect for, international humanitarian law, and to protect civilians, medical personnel and the activities of ambulances and hospitals. She further urged all states in the region to become parties to all relevant international arms-control instruments.

In December a delegation of Australian Jews led by Colin Rubenstein, executive director of AIJAC, Nina Bassat, president of the Executive Council of Australian Jewry, and Ron Weiser, president of the Zionist Federation of Australia, went to Canberra to meet with influential parliamentarians, party officials, and ministerial advisers about matters of concern to the Jewish community, particularly Australian reaction to the new Palestinian war of attrition against Israel. The Jewish leaders reported that senior government and opposition figures expressed understanding and support.

MEDIA BIAS

Media coverage of issues relating to the Australian Jewish community, extensive and out of proportion to the community's size, was generally responsible. On some subjects, particularly the unresolved issues emanating from the Nazi Holocaust such as war criminals and compensation, coverage tended to be sympathetic to the Jewish community. However that was not the case with regard to Israel and the Middle East.

A prime example was the Australian version of "Sixty Minutes," which treated the upsurge of Palestinian violence toward the end of the year as a simple story of Palestinians with rocks and stones confronting Israeli guns and tanks. The entire context of Palestinian incitement against Israel was ignored, as was the fact that Israel had been ready to accept a Palestinian state. The tragic shooting of the young Muhammad al-Dura in a cross fire between Israeli troops and Palestinian fighters was made to seem a simple act of execution; reporter Richard Carleton declared that the "overwhelming evidence is that the boy was targeted, murdered by Israeli soldiers." He made no mention of any shooting by Palestinians and sought no explanation from the Israeli side.

For some years the government-funded ethnic SBS (Special Broadcasting Service) television had shown bias against Israel. It aired a documentary in June, "Children of Shatilla," which blamed Israeli policies of expulsion and land seizure for the plight of the Palestinian refugees. In October, with the upcoming American presidential election in the news, SBS screened a BBC report about an American Jewish "lobby," allegedly "one of the most powerful in the country," and suggested that Jews control American policy through their donations to political parties. The reporter attributed to Muslims the view that American Jews "are responsible for ensuring that the Palestinians don't stand a chance." Despite complaints from viewers, SBS stood by its story. There was, in fact, only one SBS program, "Dateline," that regularly presented both sides of the Middle East conflict.

On radio, Neil Mitchell, Melbourne's leading talk-show host, commented on children being shot in the Gaza Strip: "I'd love to hear the Jewish community shouting about it in this country. I'd love to hear the Jewish community, which is so willing to pass judgement on others, telling the Israeli government that perhaps shooting kids isn't a great idea. Perhaps shooting children isn't a great way to win friends." Once again, provocations and context were ignored.

The Australian print media also ran reports, editorials, and opinion pieces with an anti-Israel slant, some by their own journalists and others taken from overseas publications. Often, sensationalist headlines, photographs, and stories seemed to be of more importance than a balanced review of events. The worst offender was the *Canberra Times,* the major paper in the national capital.

Not surprisingly, some of the Arabic-language media in Australia combined anti-Zionism with anti-Semitism. The Internet magazine *al-Moharrer al-Austrui* claimed that "the will of the United States is being controlled and manipulated by Zionist interests. Taxpayers' money is being siphoned to 'Israel,' the illegitimate state in Palestine." *Nida'ul Islam,* available both on the Internet and as a magazine, published such comments as "the Jews are extremely arrogant towards Allah" and that they have succeeded in their "infiltration into Hollywood, the Media and Congress."

Anti-Semitism and Extremism

Three unique circumstances influenced extremist and anti-Semitic manifestations in 2000.

The first of these was the commencement of "Y2K," the year 2000. A number of millenarian and other extremist organizations received more than their usual share of media limelight, as did the terrorist organizations, which, it was believed in some circles, would seek to capitalize on any disruption of normal life caused by the change of calendar.

Second, the Sydney Olympics in September activated the largest peacetime security operation ever seen in Australia. As a consequence of pre-Olympics investigations, a number of situations came to light that might otherwise have created problems for the Jewish community. For example, careful scrutiny of foreigners entering the country undoubtedly kept out terrorists from the Middle East. And the arrest of a self-styled neo-Nazi white supremacist in possession of weapons and hate literature surely would not have occurred if not for the heightened state of alert connected to the Olympics.

Third, the acceleration of violence in Israel and the territories beginning at the end of September triggered a spate of high-profile incidents across Australia. Among them were the firebombing of a Canberra synagogue; the repeated firebombing of a Sydney rabbi's sukkah and home; and pro-Palestinian demonstrations in Melbourne and Sydney where Israeli and American flags were burned along with posters of Israeli prime minister Ehud Barak, and with the protestors in Sydney trying to storm the American consulate. Such incidents received widespread media coverage and led to the establishment of a special police investigative task force in Sydney. This sad state of affairs culminated in the cancellation of a public Hanukkah candle-lighting ceremony in Sydney, for fear of further anti-Semitic incidents.

For all of 2000, the database of anti-Semitic incidents compiled by the Executive Council of Australian Jewry (ECAJ) recorded 327 reports of violence, vandalism, intimidation, and harassment directed at Australian Jews and Jewish communal institutions. This was 47 percent higher than the number for 1999 and 62 percent higher than the average for the previous ten years. The incidence of attacks involving physical assault, face-to-face harassment, property damage, and graffiti was 6 percent higher than the ten-year average, and the number of threats—primarily via electronic hate mail—was almost 50 percent higher.

EXTREMIST GROUPS

Extremist and anti-Semitic groups in Australia varied greatly in their memberships, activities, and target audiences. Most of the better-known Australian groups maintained links with foreign extremists such as militia movements in the U.S., Christian Identity churches, the Lyndon LaRouche organization, various groups of conspiracy theorists, the Australian League of Rights, and others that promoted anti-Jewish mythology.

In October the Human Rights and Equal Opportunity Commission ordered one group, the Adelaide Institute—a small organization run by Dr. Frederick Toben devoted to Holocaust denial—to remove offensive material from its Internet Web site. The commission found that this material breached the Racial Discrimination Act by being "vilificatory, bullying, insulting and offensive" to the Jewish population. Dr. Toben was also ordered to prepare a written apology to the Jewish community of Australia, to appear on the Web site's home page, for "having published materials inciting hatred against the Jewish people."

The Australian League of Rights, described by the Human Rights and Equal Opportunity Commission as "undoubtedly the most influential and effective, as well as the best organized and most substantially financed, racist organization in Australia," continued to hold meetings, conduct action campaigns, and seek publicity for its anti-Semitic assessments of domestic and international affairs. Under new director Betty Luks, the league published weekly newsletters, monthly magazines, and a quarterly journal. It has also begun advertising its meetings and publications, and has its own Web site.

The Citizens Electoral Councils (CEC) continued to distribute large quantities of literature reflecting the views of their mentor, Lyndon LaRouche. These included bizarre and offensive anti-Semitic conspiracy theories targeting Jewish and other antiracist organizations in Australia. Beside mass mailings, another common tactic was handing out pamphlets and magazines to unsuspecting citizens in shopping areas commonly frequented by Jews. CEC was particularly active in campaigning against the proposal, in Victoria, to outlaw racial hatred (see above, p. 445). Throughout the year, Jews in Victoria, Western Australia, and New South Wales complained about CEC activities.

Small neo-Nazi groups, such as the Sydney-based Southern Cross Hammer Skinheads and their Melbourne counterpart, Blood and Honour, made their presence felt primarily through the Internet. The largest neo-Nazi group was the Adelaide-based National Action, whose leader claimed on its Web site that he was being persecuted "because he states that he does not think that the plan to exterminate Europe's Jews in the Second World War is proven." National Action sued a journalist who called it racist for defamation, but the court ruled that "denial of the Holocaust and failure to condemn the principles espoused by Adolf Hitler and the Nazi party" were proof of racism. In December it became known that at least two members of a neo-Nazi band called Blood Oath had been, until recently, members of the Australian army's parachute battalion, 3RAR.

The deceptively named Australian Civil Liberties Union (ACLU) continued to advocate Holocaust denial, with most of the group's public announcements aimed at protecting the "rights" of Holocaust deniers and other extremists. *Your Rights 2000* was the 26th annual edition of the ACLU's handbook. Advertised on the front cover were references to such heroes of the organization as Holocaust deniers David Irving and Frederick Toben and war criminal Konrad Kalejs. Irving was promoted as if it were he whose free speech was threatened, rather than that of Professor Deborah Lipstadt, whom he was suing for libel in London (see above, p. 310). The book presented Toben as a "scholar and educator" persecuted for "historical accuracy" and Kalejs as a casualty of "vengeful hunts" while the world ignores "far bigger Holocausts than the Holocaust of the Jews."

In November AIJAC and the Freilich Foundation — based at the Australian National University — sponsored a two-day conference in Sydney on "Cyberhate: Bigotry and Prejudice on the Internet." Three of the world's leading experts in on-line bigotry — David Goldman from the U.S., who established hatewatch.org; Ken McVay from Canada, who set up the Nizkor Holocaust Education Project; and Michael Whine from Great Britain, who wrote and lectured extensively on Internet abuse — discussed how the Internet is used as an unregulated conduit for extremist ideas, how to attack on-line bigotry, and the pros and cons of government regulation.

Nazi War Criminals

Major developments took place in the case of 87-year-old Konrad Kalejs. After being deported from the U.S. and Canada for his involvement in Nazi crimes against humanity in his native Latvia, Kalejs lived in England until he was exposed by the media there late in 1999. Rather than face deportation, Kalejs, who had received Australian citizenship in 1957 by hiding his past, returned to Australia in January 2000. But in August Australia and Latvia signed an extradition treaty, and in December Latvia charged Kalejs with genocide and war crimes, and served a formal request for his extradition. Kalejs was arrested and released on bail, with extradition proceedings to commence in 2001.

Others charged with war crimes — Heinrich Wagner, Karlis Ozols, and Antanas

Gudelis—continued to attract attention. Wagner died late in the year, a free man, eight years after his 1992 trial was aborted following a heart attack and medical testimony indicating that he would not recover if the trial continued. Ozols, another Latvian, was reportedly suffering the effects of old age, but there was a possibility that, with the extradition treaty and the Kalejs precedent, Latvia might also seek to extradite him. Gudelis, a Lithuanian, had been officially under investigation in his home country since 1999. Australia was in the process of negotiating an extradition treaty with Lithuania.

JEWISH COMMUNITY

Demography

The Australian Jewish community continued to grow through immigration, particularly from South Africa and the former Soviet Union. The total number of Jews was between 110,000 and 125,000 out of a total population of some 19 million. There were probably hundreds of thousands of other Australians who had some ancestral relationship with the Jewish community, largely due to the predominantly male Jewish immigration in the first century of European colonization. Of the Jews born overseas, South African Jews were the largest group, followed by natives of Poland, Russia, Hungary, and Germany. Losses attributable to aliyah and a low birthrate were more than compensated for by immigration. The Jewish community was still heavily concentrated in Melbourne and Sydney, with the Brisbane-Gold Coast area showing the fastest growth.

Census figures—which were approximate, since answering questions on religion was not compulsory—indicated that 15–20 percent of married Jewish men and women had non-Jewish partners in 2000, though anecdotal evidence suggested a considerably higher figure. Compared to members of other religions, Jewish Australians were more likely to marry and to do so at a later age, and they were less likely to cohabit without marriage. The Jewish community included an exceptionally high percentage of elderly members, placing a considerable burden on the community's welfare and service agencies.

There were 14,000–20,000 Jews from the former Soviet Union in Australia, most of them living in Sydney and Melbourne. Australia's Jewish community had received, per capita, more immigrants from the FSU than even Israel, at least double the proportion received by the U.S., and seven times the number that went to Canada. Integrating this community continued to be a major challenge, especially since many of the new arrivals lacked Jewish literacy. Despite the assistance provided by local communities, particularly on the arrival of these Jews in the country, communal leadership remained concerned that these newcomers were finding it easier to assimilate into Australian society than to integrate into its Jewish community.

Communal Affairs

Nina Bassat entered her third and final year as president of the Executive Council of Australian Jewry (ECAJ), while Ron Weiser served his final year as president of the Zionist Federation of Australia (ZFA). Mark Leibler remained national chairman of the Australia/Israel and Jewish Affairs Council (AIJAC) and also federal president of the United Israel Appeal, and Dr. Colin Rubenstein continued as AIJAC's executive director. AIJAC continued its close association with the American Jewish Committee.

The year 2000 saw a successful merger in the state of Victoria between the Montefiore Homes, which provided care for the aged, and Jewish Community Services, which offered counseling, assistance to migrants, and community-welfare services. The new combined entity, to be called Jewish Care, would be responsible for all these services combined.

JEWS AND THE SYDNEY OLYMPICS

Jewish members of the Australian team were synchronized swimmer Irena Olevsky, wrestler Igor Praporshchikov, softball reserve Natalie Shapiro, wrestling coach Alex Sher, and handball manager Tom York, as well as chief physiotherapist Ross Smith. In addition, two Australian Jewish composers—Elena Katz-Chernin and John Foreman—had songs they had written performed at the opening ceremony, while many other Jews held prominent positions on the organizing committee. Israel sent its largest team ever, 39 athletes; Michael Kalganov won bronze in the 500-meter kayaking competition and Eitan Orbach became the first Israeli to make a swimming final. The star Jewish athlete of the games was United States backstroker Lenny Krayzelberg, who won three gold medals. Another notable Jewish athlete from the U.S. was Anthony Ervin, who tied for gold in the 50-meters freestyle. Ervin, Jason Lezak, and Scott Goldblatt won silver as members of U.S. relay teams. South African breaststroker Sarah Poewe and American shot-putter Andy Bloom both came in fourth in their events.

Two weeks after the Olympics, Sydney hosted the equally successful Paralympic Games. Israel won six medals, including three golds for swimmer Keren Leibovitch.

Sydney became the first Olympic city to honor the memory of the 11 Israeli athletes killed at the 1972 Munich Olympics when, in October 1999, memorials were unveiled at the Olympic village by Shane Gould, the Australian swimming gold medalist at the Munich Olympics, the Honorable Jim Spigelman, chief justice of New South Wales, and Brian Sherman, a board member of SOCOG (Sydney Organizing Committee for the Olympic Games). This was a privately funded initiative begun by Sherman and fellow Sydney businessman Geoff Levy, assisted by David Gonski, Fred Sweet, and Peter Ivany, and supported by SOCOG and the Olympic Coordinating Committee.

A second memorial was unveiled on September 26, 2000—the exact anniversary of the killings—at Moriah College, Sydney's largest Jewish day school. It was attended by the entire Israeli team; Matan Vilnai, Israel's sports minister; Walter Tröger, mayor of the Munich Olympic Village; Zvi Yarshaviak, president of the Israeli Olympic Committee; Yoram Oberkovich, secretary general of the International Olympic Committee (IOC); Peter Ryan, police commissioner of New South Wales; members of Australia's 1972 Olympic team; and diplomatic representatives from several countries. The memorial and ceremony were funded by the Jewish National Fund, the Israeli Olympic team, the New South Wales Board of Deputies, the Hakoah Club, the State Zionist Council, and New South Wales Maccabi.

In October Matan Vilnai unveiled yet a third memorial, this one at the Chevra Kadisha Cemetery in Melbourne, consisting of a plaque and an avenue of pines, funded by the Jewish National Fund and the Israeli Olympic Committee.

MACCABIAH TRAGEDY

There were further developments in relation to the tragedy that occurred in 1997, when a bridge collapsed at the Maccabiah games in Israel killing four Australian athletes and injuring more than 70 others. A criminal trial of those responsible concluded in Israel in May, with all five defendants found guilty. Four were sentenced to prison terms while the other, the sole Maccabi World Union (MWU) official charged, was sentenced to community service. All five appealed the verdicts. MWU chairman Uzi Netanel resigned immediately, and its president, Ronald Bakalarz, stepped down in August after the Knesset inquiry into the tragedy recommended that he do so.

Maccabi Australia Inc. (MAI), which suspended its membership in the MWU in May, resumed membership in November. By the end of the year adequate safety procedures for future games were in place and 41 of the approximately 60 compensation claims had been settled. But despite ongoing efforts by leaders of the Australian Jewish community, the major compensation claims were unresolved and the MAI still had not reversed its decision to stay away from the 2001 games.

Education

More than half of all Jewish children aged 4–18—including almost 70 percent of those aged 4–12—received full-time Jewish education in the 19 Jewish day schools in Australia. Spanning the religious spectrum, these schools continued to rank at the highest level for academic achievement. This reflected the community's major investment in the schools as a means of preserving Jewish continuity. Day-school enrollments continued to grow, despite ongoing concerns over high costs and the challenge to the community to find new sources of funding. In Melbourne alone there were over 5,500 children in Jewish day schools, and in Sydney one school had a waiting list of over 300.

In 2000 the federal government established a new funding system for non-government schools that was based on socioeconomic status (SES). Funding would be calculated by estimating the needs and socioeconomic status of the parents, determined by where the families lived, as opposed to the old system that geared funding to the cost of attending the school. The government argued that the new system was more accurate, transparent, objective, and fair than its predecessor. When the measure passed toward the end of the year, it received support from the main opposition Labor Party, which also promised to keep the new system if it won power at the next election.

The government promised that no school would lose funding under the arrangement, and the Australian Coordinating Committee of Jewish Day Schools supported the new law. But the coordinating committee did produce evidence that many families sending their children to Jewish schools from wealthy neighborhoods were above average size, and that the formula for establishing the SES in these areas, based on average family size, would shortchange several Jewish day schools. The committee requested rectification of this anomaly, and the government pledged to deal with it early in 2001.

There was an increased emphasis on adult education, largely under the influence of the Melton Program, which had nearly 500 students in Sydney and Melbourne. Short-term courses utilizing guest lecturers also proved popular. Top priorities for the future, according to Australian Jewish educators, were expanded Jewish studies on the university level and teacher education to provide quality faculty for the day schools.

Interfaith Dialogue

The Australian Jewish community maintained interfaith dialogue on a number of levels. The ECAJ continued its formal, high-level dialogues with the Uniting Church in Australia (biannually), and with the Catholic Bishops' Conference (annually). The ECAJ and its state affiliates also participated in the activities of the World Conference on Religion and Peace and the Councils of Christians and Jews, bringing Jewish leaders into regular contact with leading representatives of many different faith groups.

Despite positive and constructive interreligious relationships on many issues, significant areas of tension remained, such as the sympathetic attitude of the Anglican Church in New South Wales to the targeted evangelization of Jews, and the pro-Palestinian position taken by a number of Christian bodies.

Culture

Australian Jews played a significant role in the artistic and cultural life of the country. Examples in 2000 included Esther Erlich's painting *Never Been Better,* voted most popular by the public who came to view the portraits entered for the Archibald Prize; Alanah Zitserman's romantic comedy *Russian Doll,* named best original screenplay at the Australian Film Institute (AFI) annual awards; David Barda and Stephen Jenner's *If* magazine, which won a $10,000 award for innovative contribution to the Australian film industry; Jonathan Teplitzsky's film *Better than Sex,* nominated for eight awards, including best film; and comedienne Rachel Berger's performance, *Not Kosher,* at the Melbourne Comedy Festival. In addition, Sam Lipski, the former editor of the *Jewish News,* was appointed head of the State Library Board of Victoria.

Apart from the extremely valuable contributions to Jewish cultural life made by the Jewish Museum of Australia, the refurbished Holocaust Museum in Melbourne, and the Sydney Jewish Museum—all of which were world-class institutions—the various Australian Jewish film festivals and Jewish theater groups added immeasurably to the cultural life of the community. The Melbourne International Festival of the Arts in 2000 was opened by Israel's Batsheva dance company.

Personalia

The following members of the Jewish community received national honors: Jim Spigelman, eminent achievement and merit in the service of the nation, AC, Australia's highest honor; Sam Fiszman, service to the tourism industry, AO; Geoffrey Cohen, service to business and commerce, AM; Flora Erna Davis, Ursula Flicker, Catherine Gluck, and Zelda Rosenbaum, communal service, OAM; Ervin Graf, builder and property developer, OAM; Sam Moshinsky and David Smorgon, communal service, OAM.

Australia and the wider Jewish community mourned the death of Rabbi Ronald Lubofsky AM, rabbi emeritus of St. Kilda Synagogue in Melbourne.

COLIN L. RUBENSTEIN

South Africa

DESPITE THE FURTHER CONSOLIDATION of South Africa's six-year-old democracy and growing international respect for the country's macroeconomic and monetary policies, foreign investment declined, the rand—the unit of South African currency—depreciated to over 7.50 to the dollar, and unemployment remained at about 30 percent. Even some encouraging economic reforms, including deregulation, the relaxation of trade barriers, and privatization, failed to boost confidence in the face of the strong dollar and high oil prices, which pushed inflation up toward the end of the year to about 8 percent. On the positive side, South Africa did record a growth rate of nearly 3 percent.

In the local government elections held across the country in November, the African National Congress (ANC) won comfortably, although it ran 5 percent behind the electoral support it had in the 1999 general election, apparently due to ANC supporters staying home on election day. The opposition Democratic Alliance (DA), created through a merger in July of the Democratic Party (DP), the New National Party (NNP), and the Federal Alliance (FA), gained 23 percent of the vote, with a comfortable majority in the new Cape Town "unicity," or metropolitan council, an amalgamation of six municipalities. Support for the DA came largely from the white population, with substantial backing, as well, from "mixed-race" Coloreds and Indians.

Issues of race and the legacy of apartheid remained. This came to the fore in August during a conference in Johannesburg on "Racism in South Africa," organized by the South African Human Rights Commission. Crime continued to be a major source of concern, although the Community Crime Coalition in Johannesburg, a group of community organizations brought together by the South African Jewish Board of Deputies (SAJBOD), reported substantial success. From August to November a series of bomb blasts occurred in Cape Town. Speculation was rife that PAGAD (People Against Gangsterism and Drugs) was responsible, and a number of its members were arrested and charged.

The government was criticized over its handling of the crisis in Zimbabwe, instances where the rule of law was ignored, inefficiency in the delivery of essential services, and President Mbeki's insistence that there was no link between HIV and AIDS. South Africa had 10 percent of the world's HIV carriers, and Dr.

Ruben Sher, director of HIVCARE International and head of the HIV/AIDS Clinic at the Johannesburg Hospital, said that South Africa was destined for a biological Holocaust unless it declared war on the AIDS virus. After criticism both at home and abroad, Mbeki announced his withdrawal from the AIDS debate.

Former president Nelson Mandela reacted lukewarmly to requests to intervene with the Iranian government to save 13 Jews arrested on spy charges. He pledged to use his influence to avert death sentences, but felt that interference in Iranian affairs would be counterproductive. In May the New York-based American Jewish Committee canceled, on short notice, an award ceremony honoring Mandela, in apparent reaction to his comments on the Iranian spy charges.

In his Rosh Hashanah message to South African Jews, President Mbeki expressed his belief that the nation's Jews had every reason to feel positive about the coming year. And he was "optimistic about the future of South Africa—a country which embraces the rich heritage of all its peoples."

Israel-Related Activity

In January Motti Talmor was appointed the new aliyah director of the South African Zionist Federation (SAZF).

Stephen Danziger, the chief executive officer of the South African/Israel Chamber of Commerce, reported that the chamber had extended its infrastructure and teamed up with the Department of Trade and Industry to foster increased trade with Israel and the surrounding territories—primarily the Palestinian Authority, but also Jordan and Egypt. Trade between South Africa and Israel had been steadily increasing. According to Joseph Abraham, Israel's first secretary for economic affairs in Johannesburg, in 1998 exports from Israel to South Africa were 245 percent higher than 1985's $64 million, while South African exports to Israel had increased from $175 million in 1985 to $274 million in 1998 (*Business Day,* January 17).

A select group of black South African professionals attended a monthlong leadership seminar under the auspices of the He'atid program at the International Institute in Kfar Saba, Israel. Most were from private companies, with some coming from government and nonprofit organizations. The program was initiated by the Mizrachi Organization of South Africa and Krok Vision, set up by two wealthy Jewish industrialists, the brothers Abe and Solly Krok. He'atid centers in a number of South African cities helped train black leaders.

South African born Yona-Ann Goldberg, past chairman of the women's campaign of the United Jewish Appeal of America, was the guest speaker at the 98th annual meeting of the B'noth Zion Association in Johannesburg. Her address focused on the international role of the American Jewish Joint Distribution Committee (JDC).

Addressing the 87th Women's International Zionist Organization (WIZO) annual meeting in April, Malcolm Ferguson, chief director of the Department of

Foreign Affairs' Middle Eastern section, reported that South Africa enjoyed warm relations with Israel. Ferguson, a former South African ambassador to Israel, praised Prime Minister Ehud Barak for his peace efforts.

But positive sentiment weakened in the wake of the failed Camp David talks in July between the Palestinian Authority and Israel. Shortly after the breakdown, Yasir Arafat visited South Africa to request former president Mandela to mediate the Middle East crisis. Mandela turned down the request but indicated that he was willing to play a role as part of a larger team. He called on the United States, the United Kingdom, France, and Arab countries such as Saudi Arabia and Egypt to work together to achieve peace in the region. Palestinian ambassador Salman El Herfi stressed the Palestinian Authority's support for a negotiating team with Mandela in a primary position. Speaking in his personal capacity, Abe Abrahamson, honorary president of the South African Zionist Federation (SAZF), said that other countries should not get involved in the peace process because they had their own vested interests. In his view, Mandela was not an acceptable mediator.

President Thabo Mbeki indicated that South Africa would maintain its policy of supporting negotiations, and urged both parties to intensify their peace efforts. However, he added that those who had previously advised the Palestinian Authority to delay a declaration of statehood now had an obligation to recognize Palestinian independence. "Everybody who advised postponement, creating all manner of pressures and risks, now has the moral and political obligation to respond like the Palestinian Authority has responded" (*Sowetan,* August 4).

Israel's ambassador to South Africa, Uri Oren, issued a statement noting that Arafat's intention unilaterally to declare an independent state negated the basic principles of the peace process, which insisted on mutual agreement between the parties. The SAJBOD urged President Mbeki "to maintain his usual fair and even-handed approach to Middle East peace." The Jewish community was somewhat relieved when Deputy Minister of Foreign Affairs Aziz Pahad said the government would not take any new steps to resolve the Israel-Palestine crisis.

In early October, shortly after the outbreak of violence in Jerusalem, a number of South African Jewish leaders called for a just peace between Israelis and Palestinians at a special service at the Oxford Synagogue in Johannesburg. The service, led by Chief Rabbi Cyril Harris, was held under the auspices of the SAJBOD and the SAZF.

The violence generated substantial anti-Israel feeling in South Africa, where the Muslim population numbered 850,000. The ANC, the ruling party, organized a Palestinian solidarity demonstration in Cape Town, where about 80 protesters carried placards proclaiming "Free Palestine," "Stop the Killings," and "Sharon, you have blood on your hands." Events nearly turned ugly when a kaffiyeh-clad demonstrator shouting "Stop the Zionist killers, stop the Jews" tried to join the protest. He was ordered to leave, while another demonstrator circled the area in a vehicle, shouting "Death to Israel."

Discussing the demonstration, ANC Western Cape spokesperson Cameron

Dugmore said it was meant to send a clear message that the ANC was "shocked and horrified at the ongoing violence in the Middle East and in particular at the killing of a large number of Palestinians and other people. We believe that, as South Africans who also struggled to achieve self-determination, we should give support to the peace process and to the Palestinian people, in particular, in terms of their right to self-determination." Dugmore added that this was only fair, since the Arabs recognized Israel's right to exist. "We have a large number of Jewish people within the ANC and within South Africa who have made a huge contribution to the liberation struggle," he added, "so it's nothing against the Israeli people. We are critical of the Israeli government and particular people in the opposition" (*SA Jewish Report,* November 20).

Michael Bagraim, chairman of the Cape Council of the SAJBOD, criticized the ANC's one-sided approach, arguing that the Palestinians had played a major role in fomenting the violence. Bagraim called for calm and expressed regret at the loss of life on both sides. Marlene Bethlehem, national president of the SAJBOD, added her voice, criticizing the "cheap political game" played by the ANC, which clearly wanted to curry favor with Muslim voters in the upcoming local elections. Tony Leon, the leader of the DA opposition party, similarly castigated the ANC's behavior as opportunistic.

In addition to the Cape Town protest, approximately 1,000 Muslims, including many women and children, marched on the U.S. and Israeli embassies in Pretoria. This self-styled "Free Palestine Campaign" demanded that the South African government sever ties with Israel and that the United States end its support for the Jewish state. Protestors carried placards calling for an end to Israeli "apartheid," and urged "Stop the Holocaust and genocide of the people of Palestine" (*Citizen,* October 14). Three people were arrested when the march turned violent after a protester chanted, "One bullet, one Israeli settler," while trying to break a police barrier outside the United States embassy.

Demonstrations also took place at the University of the Witwatersrand, and, in Cape Town, Muslim students marched on the Kaplan Centre for Jewish Studies and Research at the University of Cape Town. A McDonald's store, which apparently symbolized American influence, was attacked in Cape Town (*Business Day,* October 16). Further solidarity protests were held outside the Israel Trade Center and the El Al Airline office in Johannesburg.

Mounting tension was exacerbated by a bomb blast outside the Kenilworth offices of the DA opposition party in Cape Town. Initial speculation related the bomb to the fact that Tony Leon, the leader of the DA, was Jewish. Leon criticized the "grossly irresponsible behavior of the ANC recently in whipping up emotions among extremist elements, such as Qibla [a radical Muslim group founded in 1980 and inspired by the Iranian revolution] and PAGAD [People Against Gangsterism and Drugs] who were nothing more than missionaries of hatred and revenge" (*SA Jewish Report,* November 20).

At the SAJBOD's request, a meeting of the SAJBOD and the Department of

Foreign Affairs took place, where it was agreed to maintain daily contact. "We were given a wonderfully warm reception and left with a feeling of reassurance," explained Russell Gaddin, national chairman of the SAJBOD. Gaddin was confident that the government wanted to remain evenhanded in its Middle East policy. A joint statement after the meeting urged that the conflict be resolved by negotiations, and appealed "to both the Muslim and Jewish communities in South Africa not to let the Middle East conflict lead to disturbances of the public peace in South Africa" (*SA Jewish Report,* October 27). The sentiment was similar to an earlier public statement issued by the South African chapter of the World Conference on Religion and Peace. Shortly after the meeting between the SAJBOD and the government, Jewish leaders held public meetings in Cape Town and Pretoria expressing solidarity with Israel.

Despite the encouraging meeting between the government and the SAJBOD, the ANC organized a special parliamentary debate on the Middle East during which Israel was identified as the villain. The chief whip, Tony Yengeni, introduced the debate, arguing that the ANC had always "supported the right of the Palestinian people to reside in the land they call home as they supported our struggle against apartheid. Israeli settlement policies and the failure to deal with the Palestinian refugees had provoked this reaction," according to Yengeni. He condemned what he described as the Israelis' use of excessive force as well as their "refusal to abide by UN resolutions." Despite this, Yengeni warned that the conflict would not be allowed to play out on South African soil.

In his response to Yengeni, DA leader Tony Leon asked why the ANC-led South African government had sold Israel arms worth 42 million rand (about $5.5 million) in 1997 if "Israel was the sole human rights violator in the Middle East." Leon accused Yengeni of inflaming passions. Another Jewish member, the ANC's Ben Turok, entered the debate, making comparisons between the Israelis and the old apartheid government in how they dealt with stone throwers. Speaking for the government, Deputy Minister of Foreign Affairs Aziz Pahad called for a just and lasting solution to the conflict.

Prior to the local elections, a poster appeared in Cape Town declaring: "A vote for the DA is a vote for Israel." In response to complaints from the DA, the ANC denied any knowledge of who printed or put up the poster. However, an anonymous caller who claimed to own a printing company said he was approached by the ANC to print the poster, and had refused. DA spokesperson Ryan Coetzee claimed that his party had information that ANC officials were waging an anti-Semitic campaign in some Cape Town mosques, directed against Tony Leon, the DA leader, who was not only a Jew but had an Israeli fiancée.

South African Jewish leaders expressed dismay at President Mbeki's harsh condemnation of Israel at the ninth session of the Organization of the Islamic Conference summit in Doha, Qatar. Speaking in his capacity as chairman of the "nonaligned movement," Mbeki told the meeting that the "Palestinian people have a right to return to their homeland and to have their own independent state with Jerusalem as its capital." Commenting on the speech, Chief Rabbi Harris said the president had merely attempted to gain the support of the Arab countries. Nonetheless, he considered the speech unacceptable from the standpoint of the Jewish community, "especially given the generosity of Prime Minister Barak's offer to the Palestinians." SAJBOD national chairman Russell Gaddin believed Mbeki was simply expressing long-held ANC views. "It is nevertheless sad for us," he added, "as loyal South Africans and Jews loyal to our brothers and sisters in Israel, that we should continue to see our government ignoring the historical truths of Israel's position in the Middle East and its ongoing failure to acknowledge the refusal of the Arab nations to guarantee Israel's security." In an editorial, the *SA Jewish Report* (October 17) expressed the hope "that our President takes the trouble to further acquaint himself with the Middle East situation, its history, the fact that the Palestinian refugee problem was not one of Israel's creation—rather largely that of the Arab states themselves—and that he endeavor to learn about the concept 'jihad' and what it means to Muslims to die in a holy war; or to sacrifice their children's lives for it."

As the crisis intensified the South African government called on Israel to withdraw its forces as a means of restoring stability. "We urge the United Nations to deploy its peacekeeping forces to stop the carnage in the Middle East and restore peace," said Dumisani Rasheleng, spokesman for the Department of Foreign Affairs (*Sowetan,* November 23).

Anti-Semitism

There were a number of troubling incidents during 2000, including offensive comments on radio talk shows, anti-Semitic letters to the press, incidents of vandalism of Jewish property, the desecration of Jewish graves, the sale, at an Islamic conference in Pretoria, of books denying the Holocaust, and accusations of Jewish conspiratorial power. Often, anti-Zionist rhetoric blurred with traditional anti-Semitic motifs, especially with the upsurge of violence in Israel and the territories.

In January the SAJBOD invited Dani Olesker of the Jerusalem Center for Communication and Advocacy Training to come to South Africa and discuss strategies for coping with anti-Semitic propaganda. In February representatives of the SAJBOD met with the South African Human Rights Commission to discuss strategies to combat racism in the media and to explore ways in which the Jewish community could help build a human-rights culture in South Africa. In June several PAGAD members suspected of bombing the Wynberg Synagogue in Cape Town in December 1998 went on trial. The proceedings were expected to be lengthy. Jews in Johannesburg reported a number of incidents of verbal abuse and threats by Muslims in August, after the breakdown of the Camp David peace negotiations.

The SAJBOD maintained a vigilant posture and took action against anti-Semitism when it was able. For example, it wrote to a bookstore selling the *Pro-*

tocols of the Elders of Zion, pointing out that the book was banned and requesting—unsuccessfully—the names of those who had purchased it. The SAJBOD also intervened when students from King David schools confronted anti-Semitism on the sports field from pupils of opposing schools. It also challenged comments made by Barney Pityana, chair of the South African Human Rights Commission, who tastelessly minimized the significance of the Holocaust in a discussion on reparations, slavery, colonialism, and the Holocaust.

Holocaust-Related Matters

The London trial in which David Irving sued Deborah Lipstadt for libel for calling him a Holocaust denier received substantial media attention. The *SA Jewish Report* (April 28) applauded the defeat of Irving in an editorial, "After the Irving Verdict": "The defeat of David Irving in court is gratifying, but we should not let ourselves believe that the battle against those who would deny the Holocaust has been won."

Irene Steinfeld, coordinator of educational programs at Yad Vashem in Israel, was guest speaker at the Yom Hashoah ceremony in Johannesburg in May.

In June the ANC successfully proposed a motion in parliament to adopt the Stockholm Declaration, in which, at an international gathering in Stockholm in January 2000, 46 countries committed themselves to Holocaust education and remembrance The debate in parliament was led by a Jewish ANC member, Andrew Feinstein. This was the first time the Holocaust had been a subject of debate in the South African parliament. In his emotional address, Feinstein told a subdued parliament that at "a time when racism and xenophobia are rearing their heads close to home and in faraway lands, let us ensure that the Holocaust will always hold universal meaning which transcends race, religion, and nationality."

Speaking to the *SA Jewish Report* (June 2), Feinstein explained that he had been shocked at the paucity of knowledge among his parliamentary colleagues about the Holocaust. "With the help of the Holocaust Centre, we've designed a format for getting information to members." Indeed, the Cape Town Holocaust Centre, which opened in August 1999 (see AJYB 2000, p. 425), made a huge impression on South African society with its programs for school children and other interested parties, including civil servants. In its first year of operation, 10,000 visitors passed through its doors, including 2,500 tourists from other parts of South Africa and from 30 countries. The Holocaust Centre's first anniversary lecture was delivered by Professor Hubert Locke, dean and professor emeritus of the Graduate School for Public Affairs at the University of Washington. In August the Holocaust Centre hosted an exhibition of children's drawings from Theresienstadt, courtesy of the Czech embassy and the Jewish Museum in Prague.

An editorial in the *SA Jewish Report* (June 23) supported the decision of a commission set up by the British Jewish community not to seek the outlawing of Holocaust denial.

In November the Johannesburg High Court opened proceedings on a case originating in 1998. At that time, the SAJBOD registered a complaint with the Independent Broadcasting Authority (IBA) following the broadcast of an anti-Semitic interview on Radio 786 with Dr. Yaqub Zaki. The interview was riddled with notions of Jewish conspiracies, and Dr. Zaki disputed the idea that Jews were murdered or gassed during the Holocaust. He claimed that "about a million Jews had died, like other people in the camps, of typhus and other infectious diseases" (*Cape Jewish Chronicle,* February 2001). In response to the SAJBOD's complaint, Radio 786 gave notice that it intended to apply for an order from the Johannesburg High Court setting aside the IBA code of conduct for community radio stations. The code stated that material broadcast should not be "offensive to the religious convictions or feelings of any section of the population . . . or likely to prejudice relations between sections of the population." The radio station claimed that this went against the freedom of speech guaranteed by the nation's constitution. As the year ended, the court had not yet handed down its judgement.

JEWISH COMMUNITY

Demography

At the conference of the Gauteng Council of the SAJBOD in Johannesburg in August, David Saks, senior researcher of the SAJBOD, estimated that there were 80,000 Jews in South Africa. Johannesburg had 57,000; Cape Town 19,000; Durban 3,000; Pretoria 1,500; and the remainder were spread across the country. Saks noted that deaths exceeded births, with 500–550 births and 600–650 deaths per annum. There were no exact figures for emigration, but, according to Saks, enrollment at Jewish day schools was declining 2–3 percent a year, which meant that some 1,800 Jews emigrated each year. Assessing these trends, Saks contended that "South African Jewry is not in a state of collapse. Many feel positive and are staying to make a contribution. Even if trends continue in such a way, in 20 years there will still be about 40,000 Jews left." Acknowledging physical dangers in South Africa, Saks highlighted the absence of spiritual danger: the intermarriage rate was only 7 percent (*SA Jewish Report,* August 18).

Business Day (February 23) carried an article by Chief Rabbi Cyril Harris asking Jews to stay in South Africa. Acknowledging that all transitional situations are difficult, he nevertheless called on Jews to foster a spirit of optimism.

Despite urbanization and emigration, there were indications, according to Rabbi Moshe Silberhaft, spiritual leader of the country communities department of the SAJBOD, that Jews were returning to live in small towns. Examples cited by the rabbi were Hermanus, George, and even very small towns like Ficksburg, Clarens, Nelspruit, Knysna, and Plettenberg Bay.

Communal Affairs

Rabbi Jonathan Sacks, chief rabbi of the British Commonwealth, visited South Africa in January and publicly referred to South African Jewry as a "model community." It was, however, a community facing serious challenges: anti-Semitism emanating from extremist elements among the Muslim population (noted above), financial problems, and crime. All were highlighted by Yehuda Kay, the incoming national director of the SAJBOD, in an interview in the *SA Jewish Report* (February 4). He noted that anti-Semitism was being dealt with and that the SAJBOD had formed a Community Crime Coalition.

As the youngest person ever to take up the position of SAJBOD national director, the 24-year-old Kay hoped that his youthfulness would enable him to bring fresh ideas to the job, without "huge emotional baggage." "The Board must continue to build better relationships with government in terms of both civic and non-governmental matters. We will continue to make these overtures and be an integral part of the South African community," said Kay. He believed the SAJBOD was highly regarded by the government. He said: "We have positioned ourselves very nicely and are known as the organization it talks to. It is important that when government talks to the community on political matters, it knows it is talking to one body."

As the year began, the *SA Jewish Report* reported that "an organized Israeli crime syndicate, involved in 'deals' worth hundreds of thousands of rands, is active in the Johannesburg suburbs of Norwood and Sandringham." Superintendent Anton van Jaarsveld, commander of the Norwood police station, said it was difficult to determine the exact number of those involved. "We suspect the group consists of between 20 and 30 people. All of those we know of are Israelis. It is important to note that this is a syndicate and not an Israeli mafia. Although those involved work as debt collectors, they are doing much more. They are intimidating people across the spectrum. They are not targeting Jewish people per se and have even targeted Israelis. Several people have been shot at. All the people they harass are themselves busy with illegal stuff and can't pay these guys. Therefore they do not want to lay charges" (*SA Jewish Report,* January 1).

Commenting on the allegations, Ze'ev Luria, political counselor to the Israeli embassy, said he was aware of and concerned about violence being perpetrated "by some Israelis" in South Africa. The matter also attracted the attention of the Afrikaans daily, *Beeld.* Its headline, "Mafia terroreer SA Jode" (Mafia terrorizes South African Jews), upset the SAJBOD, which complained of misrepresentation and fabrication in the article. Two months later, Superintendent Chris Wilkin, spokesperson for the South African Police Services, claimed that the so-called "Israeli mafia" was not a major threat to the Jewish community or to other South African citizens.

The need for financial rationalization was taken up in Johannesburg by the creation of the Johannesburg United Jewish Organizations structure, known as Beyachad ("Together" in Hebrew). In February Errol Goodman, national director of the Israel United Appeal-United Communal Fund (IUA-UCF), and incoming CEO of Beyachad, warned of bankruptcy if major Jewish organizations failed to come together. "Many of our beneficiary organizations no longer have government subsidies, particularly the schools and homes for the aged." In addition, Goodman explained that the emigration of many potential donors had put a financial strain on communal organizations. Therefore, he concluded, "restructuring and rationalization" were necessary (*SA Jewish Report,* February 11).

Financial hardship among the elderly led the Union of Jewish Women (UJW) to provide kosher meals for more than 120 Jews in Johannesburg. Our Parents' Home, a residence for senior citizens founded in the 1930s for German-Jewish refugees in Johannesburg, was in danger of closing due to the withdrawal of state subsidies.

In line with the new imperatives, Jewish Communal Services (JCS), after 52 years of autonomy, merged with the Johannesburg Jewish Helping Hand and Burial Society (Hevrah Kadisha). According to the director of JCS, Brenda Solarsh, the merger was not the product of a shrinking community; rather, it was driven by opportunities for access to resources and expertise. JCS would continue to offer a full range of services.

In June, under the guidance of Beyachad, the SAJBOD, the SAZF (South African Zionist Federation), and the UCF (United Communal Fund) signed an administrative cooperation agreement. Marlene Bethlehem, national president of the SAJBOD, described the event as "one of the most important days in the history of the community." Errol Goodman explained that the agreement was precipitated by a financial "crisis" driven by emigration. All three organizations would be housed under one roof in Raedene, Johannesburg. Under the new setup, each organization would maintain its autonomy while Beyachad (the organization responsible for the agreement) would control the administration, library facilities, and marketing and accounting departments of the three. A number of satellite organizations would also be housed in the new premises, which would include a library, archives, a small synagogue, a museum and exhibition area, boardrooms, and youth facilities.

An editorial in the *SA Jewish Report* (June 30) applauded the agreement, which, the paper believed, provided an opportunity for democratic governance. "On a more subtle level, the agreement marks the beginning of a new, more democratic communal structure, a stronger, more broadly based leadership and hopefully, the end of the 'edifice complex' to which Jewish organizations were prone. This 'complex' — largely a phenomenon of the '60s, '70s and '80s — caused splits and divisiveness, a 'let's form our own organization in our own set up' attitude in efforts to retain perceived power bases and hang onto obsolete leadership positions."

Minister of Trade and Industry Alec Erwin was keynote speaker at the Gauteng 2000 conference of the SAJBOD held in Johannesburg in August. Erwin was upbeat about the economy, arguing that South Africa was "turning around the economic ship." The country, he maintained, was no longer plagued with "an inefficient, uncompetitive economy."

Max Strous, executive director of Our Parents' Home, told the Gauteng 2000 conference that longevity and changing demographics were causing a huge strain on communal services for the aged. "At no time in history has our community been so taxed. The demographic changes have caused people living in Hillbrow, Berea, and Yeoville to leave their homes. The wealthier aged, living in more affluent areas, suffer from loneliness and ill health and many have children who have emigrated. Ours is an aging community and therefore the demand for homes for the aged is growing. Our financial position is in dire straits and our deficit is growing, especially since government grants have disappeared."

In the wake of the Gauteng conference, the *SA Jewish Report* (August 18) called for courageous leadership. The weekly referred to the speech of Russell Gaddin, who said that the community now faced the most serious issues in his 30 years of communal work. A profound despondency had overtaken the community, said Gaddin, due to emigration, crime, economic hardship, and a diminishing donor base for essential welfare and educational institutions. "Many Jews had withdrawn inwards," said Gaddin, "and a resounding 'silence' pervaded the community." Notwithstanding these somber observations, the editorial reminded readers that "despite the diminishing numbers," the South African Jewish community "still remains a vibrant one with an abundant resource of competent, energetic and dedicated people. It is in times like these that courageous leadership, willing to take radical new initiatives, is crucial if the process of corrective adaptations to the new situation in South Africa is to genuinely take hold." The *SA Jewish Report* was confident that the community was seriously addressing its problems.

This did not appear to be the view of Gail Goldberg, outgoing national president of the Union of Jewish Women (UJW). Speaking at the opening of the UJWs 26th national triennial conference in Johannesburg in August, she railed against what she saw as Jewish apathy. "People seem to be deliberately avoiding commitment to their Jewish communal organizations and to their obligations to the general community. . . . A laager [circle-the-wagons] mentality prevails," she said. Nearly all the Jewish communal organizations, Goldberg contended, were experiencing difficulties and a lack of "people power." Goldberg highlighted AIDS and tuberculosis, a weak currency, violence, and emigration as the problems not being addressed.

At the same conference, Chief Rabbi Harris warned of communal "hemorrhaging in the middle," by which he meant the 25–45-year-old generation, portending problems in the long term. But he believed there was much to be positive about, including a low rate of intermarriage, a high percentage of Jewish children studying at Jewish day schools, and extensive Jewish involvement in the wider society. Nonetheless, he said that crime remained a major problem.

In her Rosh Hashanah editorial, Suzanne Belling, editor of the *SA Jewish Report,* lamented that even the rationalization of communal resources effected by the merger of Jewish organizations had not "translated into true togetherness. It does not mean unity or a united community for which we should strive in word, intent, deed and thought. For, while South African Jewry has an international reputation for vibrancy, commitment, observance, *Yiddishkeit* and identification with Israel, these praiseworthy attributes cannot compensate for the fragmentation, splinter groups, fringe organizations, personal agendas, 'edifice complexes,' internal squabbling in the community as a whole and within specific structures. . . . What we need for the year 5761 is to resolve to do likewise in our own community and to aim for recognition of our own diversity of views and beliefs, yet be a people united through the lofty wisdom of our own sacred teachings" (September 22).

The Great Park Synagogue, Johannesburg, established a new community center on the site of its new building in November. The director, Max Katz, explained that the center would have a coffee shop, a cinema, an Internet café, and a restaurant. "We're going to try to create a center where people can do activities outside normal activities," said Katz.

Community Relations

In February, Tikkun, a Jewish program to help the underprivileged, announced that former president Nelson Mandela had agreed to become the organization's patron-in-chief. Also, Tikkun was now incorporated and registered in the United States, enabling American donors to obtain federal tax exemptions for their gifts.

Tikkun involved itself in a massive effort to alleviate the plight of hundreds of flood victims in Alexandra Township, Johannesburg, Also, in combination with the Oxford Synagogue Skills and Adult Center (OSSAC), Tikkun ran an adult literacy program for women so that they would not be totally dependent on men. On an ongoing basis, Tikkun ran a crèche for 70 children in Hillbrow, Johannesburg, to enable mothers to seek work. In addition, it set up a rural project at Orange Farm, outside Johannesburg, where women baked, planted, and made preserves as a way of earning a living.

At the Gauteng conference of the SAJBOD, Craig Hummel, chairman of the youth sector of Tikkun, appealed for greater Jewish involvement in the wider society. "We can only ensure our future if we involve ourselves with the economic, social and educational development of the majority of the people of this land," he declared (*SA Jewish Report,* August 18).

In September a new series of efforts were initiated, and existing programs expanded, to help the unfortunate both locally and internationally. Herby Rosenberg, Tikkun's CEO, accompanied Nelson Mandela to Sydney, Australia, on a fund-raising drive. But, as Tikkun stalwart Ann Harris pointed out, the organization did not "simply collect money." Tikkun announced the launching of a Web site for Tikkun and for the Nelson Mandela Children's Fund. Jewish awareness of economic deprivation in the country was raised through partnerships with organizations in Cape Town. An example was the Intra-Communal Development Program, a community-development outreach project initiated by the Cape Council of the SAJBOD and the United Herzlia Schools in association with Tikkun. The program included two after-school programs in underprivileged "black" areas. A number of Jewish primary schools had relations with disadvantaged schools, including a joint program to teach reading initiated by Rhona Dubow.

The Cape Council of the SAJBOD promoted initiatives to bring the Muslim and Jewish communities together, with the encouragement and participation of two ANC parliamentarians, Andrew Feinstein and Salie Manie. The plan was for joint social activities for the elderly and sports for the young. It was expected that these efforts would complement the work of the long-standing Cape Town Interfaith Initiative.

In March South African Jewish communal organizations joined L'Atet, an Israeli humanitarian voluntary organization, to coordinate a relief-and-rescue project for flood victims in neighboring Mozambique. Yehuda Kay, national director of the SAJBOD, said it was important for the Jewish community to get involved. "From a Jewish perspective, we are always involved in Africa and South Africa" (*SA Jewish Report,* March 24). Mervyn Smith, chairman of the African Jewish Congress (AJC), pledged support for the victims when he met with Joaquim Chissano, the Mozambican president, in the wake of the devastating flood. This meeting preceded the AJC conference held in Maputo, Mozambique.

In February Temple Emanuel, as part of its outreach program, established a recreation center for people who were HIV positive, under the aegis of the United Sisterhood. In September Jewish day schools embarked on an outreach program by collecting educational toys for preschool children.

Religion

The year 2000 saw the emergence of significant tensions between those embracing an inclusive view of Judaism and the Jewish community, and those seeking clearer borders, especially between Orthodox and Reform Judaism. Reform, according to Simon Jocum, president of the South African Union of Progressive Judaism, numbered 7,000 people, or 14 percent of affiliated Jews in South Africa. There were eight Reform temples and five rabbis, as well as several others preparing to be rabbis. Notwithstanding its relatively small numbers, Reform's voice and those of others critical of the Orthodox and lay establishment were given substantial coverage in the pages of the *SA Jewish Report,* much to the chagrin of the communal leadership.

The tensions were evident early in the year when David Saks, senior researcher for the SAJBOD, referred to the resilience of Orthodox Judaism, despite predictions of its demise in the face of modernity. Saks noted an increase in anti-Orthodox propaganda, which, he believed, had to be seriously engaged. It was widely assumed that what he had in mind in the reference to critics of Orthodoxy was the editorial team of the *SA Jewish Report.* In April, after the paper had reported on the (Reform) Central Conference of American Rabbis' approval of same-sex marriages, Geoff Sifrin, editor of the "Opinion and Features" section of the *Report,* wrote of pressure being exerted on the newspaper by a senior Jewish figure not even to hint at support for the move or even to take a "neutral" stand. Sifrin used the opportunity to express the need for healthy debate and open engagement on all issues concerning Jews.

One month later the newspaper took a swipe at lay leaders, advocating a more important role in policy formation for Jewish communal professionals. "Often," it editorialized, "top portfolios are given to voluntary people because of their wealth or prominence in the business world. They present the face of their organizations to the public, while the professionals, trained in the field, are relegated to the back room." Even congregational rabbis, the editorial contended, "are, on occasion, subjected to the whims of their committees and are brought to book if they overstep the 'acceptable' in their sermons or public statements" (*SA Jewish Report,* May 19).

This call came in the immediate wake of a religious controversy in Cape Town. Rabbi David Hoffman of the Cape Town Progressive Jewish Congregation gave the guest lecture at the Holocaust Day ceremony. It was rumored that Orthodox rabbis had boycotted the event, a charge denied by the SAJBOD and the United Orthodox Synagogues (UOS). It appeared to be true, however, that the Orthodox rabbis had been told not to sit on the platform for the occasion. The issue evoked such anger that the Cape Council of the SAJBOD issued the following statement:

> Considerable concern has been expressed by members of the Cape Town Jewish community following the non-attendance by certain members of the Jewish community at this year's Yom Hashoah Vehagevura [Holocaust Day] commemoration in Cape Town because the main speaker was a Reform rabbi.
>
> As we come out of the Omer period, a time of reflection, we are reminded once again that we Jews are one people, irrevocably linked by destiny and history to each other. We have celebrated the accomplishments of the Jewish people and mourned with her when tragedies occurred.
>
> All the more reason why we are deeply concerned about the events surrounding Yom Hashoah, which have left many in the Cape Town Jewish community feeling deeply alienated, hurt and angered.
>
> While the South African Jewish Board of Deputies (Cape Council) respects the religious beliefs of those concerned, we call on religious streams to deal with disagreements in a constructive communal manner so as not to harm and divide the Jewish community.
>
> We furthermore call upon all responsible leaders to speak in the spirit of *ahavat Yisrael,* love of all Jews, that despite the issues on which we differ, we remain united (*SA Jewish Report,* June 8).

Further evidence of dissatisfaction with the UOS emerged in August when a motion for the Green and Sea Point Hebrew Congregation to break away from the UOS was made at the synagogue's annual general meeting. According to the man who proposed the motion, Dr. Clive Rabinowitz, the relationship between the congregation and the UOS had deteriorated because the UOS and its Bet Din (religious court) had "moved considerably to the right and became more hardline." Problems had been manifest in 1999 when the congregation's rabbi, E. J. Steinhorn, had been declared persona non grata (see AJYB 2000, p. 424). Although that matter had been resolved, many congregants sympathized with the proposal to break away. The majority, however, opposed the move in the belief that negotiation rather than withdrawal was the best strategy. Commenting on the outcome, Jack Friedman, Cape chair of the UOS, said he was pleased that the congregation was staying in the fold. For his part, Rabbi Steinhorn said that the large turnout for the synagogue meeting was a positive indication that people were concerned about the interpretation of Judaism (*SA Jewish Report,* September 1).

There was another storm brewing, this time around one of the *Report*'s columnists, Steven Friedman. The first public indication of the problem emerged in the *Mail & Guardian,* a national weekly, which reported (September 15–21) that, under pressure from Chief Rabbi Harris, the board of the *Report* had unanimously voted to stop running Friedman's column, since "Friedman's liberal views on Judaism and Zionist politics have raised the hackles of the paper's readership since the column's inception."

Friedman, director of the highly regarded Centre for Policy Studies in Johannesburg, had indeed used his column to criticize the conformity of the Jewish establishment and its inability to accept what he termed the "deviant" Jew. In his view this was because "most do not conform to the community and its leadership's stereotype of the 'good Jew'—a person who leads a middle class suburban lifestyle, a shul member (if not goer) and, preferably a business person. . . . Jews not conforming to that stereotype," maintained Friedman, "face a thick wall of prejudice which prevents them contributing even if they wanted to. . . ." He believed that the result was the loss of talented potential leaders and a "leadership which might be good at making things happen, but is very bad at working out what should happen if the community is to fulfill its potential" (*SA Jewish Report,* May 19).

Friedman's harsh attacks on the lay establishment and the Orthodox way of life generated a predictable response, especially after he criticized what he termed "mumbo-jumbo" customs performed by Orthodox Jews in South Africa, which, he claimed, were devoid of halakhic basis (*SA Jewish Report,* June 2). "Arrogant and ill informed" was how Chief Rabbi Harris referred to Friedman, and the rabbi called for a more "positive" view to be expressed in a Jewish newspaper (*SA Jewish Report,* June 16). His colleague, Rabbi Norman Bernhard of Johannesburg, was even harsher, claiming that if "there were a Pulitzer Prize for impudence, arrogance and ignorance," Friedman would win it (*SA Jewish Report,* June 23).

Undeterred, Friedman further challenged the establishment by calling for the inclusion in the community of the Lemba, a black group claiming Jewish ancestry. The question of the status of the Lemba had surfaced periodically, but the rabbinate had always maintained that the Lemba were not Jewish according to

Halakhah (see AJYB 2000, p. 424). In Friedman's opinion, this was not a sufficient reason for their exclusion (*SA Jewish Report,* June 30).

It was shortly after the Lemba broadside that the story of Friedman's dismissal broke in the *Mail & Guardian.* A flood of angry letters to both the *Mail & Guardian* and the *SA Jewish Report* condemned the actions of the board as a form of censorship, and Friedman himself berated "fundamentalists," who, he said, "are not the only 'real Jews.'" Friedman urged the community not to allow "a small minority to decide for the rest of us who and what is really Jewish" (*SA Jewish Report,* October 6). In response, Chief Rabbi Harris denied that the *SA Jewish Report* had "stifled all dissenting voices." Friedman, he argued, had been intemperate and had not contributed to sound debate. "It is ludicrous to suggest," argued the rabbi, "in the name of press independence, that the Jewish community newspaper should allow a regular columnist to trample in an offensive manner on the deeply held beliefs and cherished practices of the majority of its readers." In the end, Friedman's establishment detractors won the battle and his column was terminated.

Another problem for the UOS was the proliferation of *shtieblach* (small Orthodox prayer groups) in Johannesburg. Many of these mushrooming houses of prayer did not support the UOS financially, a matter raised by Chief Rabbi Harris at the Gauteng 2000 conference of the SAJBOD. While he acknowledged that the growth of *shtieblach* demonstrated that the younger generation was religiously vibrant and concerned with Jewish study and observance, and expressed pleasure at some examples of cooperation with mainstream congregations, Rabbi Harris regretted the insistence of the *shtieblach* on maintaining their independence and not affiliating with larger synagogues.

Responding to Rabbi Harris, Shawn Zagnoev said the *shtieblach* would continue to thrive and that the large synagogues would have to accept the new reality. Zagnoev pointed out that *shtieblach* were increasingly in demand because of the *ba'al teshuvah* (return to tradition) movement. He said there were about 20 *shtieblach* in Johannesburg, most of which did not exist 15 years before, with an estimated 1,300 families. Zagnoev warned of the danger of a wedge being driven between the synagogues and the *shtieblach*. "We cannot allow for two different streams of Orthodox Judaism to emerge which are hostile to one another. The reason why the South African Jewish community has remained homogeneous is because all streams of Orthodoxy have been accepting of each other. Any attempt to marginalize the *shtieblach* will have, in my opinion, unfortunate and unnecessary repercussions" (*SA Jewish Report,* August 18).

Notwithstanding these challenges to its hegemony from the left and the right, the UOS continued to maintain a successful Bet Din, including a kashrut department, and Chief Rabbi Harris continued to enjoy a fine reputation, within and outside the Jewish community. Indeed, in September he was invited to deliver the 16th annual Desmond Tutu Peace Lecture in Durban, jointly hosted by the South African chapter of the World Conference on Religion and Peace, and the Council for KwaZulu-Natal Jewry. Rabbi Harris used the occasion to make a passionate plea for the return of morality in South Africa and for the "haves" to assist the "have-nots."

Demographic shifts had predictable effects on synagogues and other religious institutions. In May the Berea Synagogue in Johannesburg held its valedictory service, after long-standing financial problems coupled with demographic changes took their toll, and in August the Potchefstroom synagogue was closed. Another synagogue, Adath Yeshurun in Percelia, Johannesburg, had to shut down after neighbors (most of them Jewish) objected to having a large synagogue complex, with its attendant traffic and security problems, in their midst. The synagogue had moved there from Yeoville in 1998. In Pretoria, meanwhile, it was announced that the Adath Israel Synagogue would be relocated from its Crawford College premises to Groenkloof, Pretoria. In March the foundation stone of the new Park Road Synagogue was laid in Johannesburg; the synagogue was modeled on the old Great Synagogue in Wolmarans Street in the Johannesburg inner city. In April Johannesburg's newest *mikveh* (ritual bath), the Chaya Esther Mikveh, in Fairmount, was officially opened. It was named in memory of Adele Taback, who died in a car accident in 1998. In May a plaque marking the site of the first South African synagogue was unveiled in Cape Town by Rabbi Simon Harris of the Cape Town Hebrew Congregation. The Pretoria Progressive Congregation, Beth Menorah, celebrated its jubilee in 2000.

Rabbi Norman Bernhard retired from the Oxford Synagogue Center in Johannesburg after 35 years of service. The synagogue had experienced substantial dissension and waning membership. According to a report in the *SA Jewish Report* (January 14), its problems had been solved and a new strategic management plan was in place.

In June Russell Gaddin, national chairman of the SAJBOD, expressed concern at Christian proselytizing in South Africa, particularly on the campus of the University of the Witwatersrand in Johannesburg. In October the anticult organization Jews for Judaism held a seminar on how to deal with various aspects of Christian missionizing in South Africa, focusing on the "Jews for Jesus" phenomenon, which tried to persuade Jews that they could remain Jewish while accepting Jesus as their messiah.

Education

In March the minister of education, Professor Kadar Asmal, addressed the biennial conference of the Association of Principals of Jewish Schools of South Africa, meeting in Cape Town. Asmal appealed to the Jewish community to contribute to the development of the country, particularly in the field of education. "The Jewish dynamic has been a dynamic of enormous intellectual discourse and the triumph of ideas. And you who have faced adversity will more than anybody else, be able to communicate with those who have been despised" (*SA Jewish Report,* March 17).

A gloomy picture of the plight of Jewish day schools was presented at the Gauteng 2000 conference of the SAJBOD in Johannesburg in August. Frank Samuels, principal of Yeshivah College, Johannesburg, told the conference that the day schools faced a huge challenge from private schools, which attracted a high number of Jewish pupils. The withdrawal of state subsidies for independent schools also created financial problems for Jewish schools. According to Samuels, the King David schools in Johannesburg had received 6.7 million rand (approximately $1 million) in 1995, 3.4 million rand in 1999, and nothing in 2000. Even though tuition fees had not been raised to offset the loss, many parents were still unable to afford to send their children to King David. Another factor adding to the difficulties of the day schools, said Samuels, was the emigration of Jews who had previously contributed money to the community. Plans to raise funds for Jewish education were set in motion against the somber backdrop of a cut in subsidies from the United Communal Fund (UCF).

A new Tzeirei Tzion synagogue was opened on the Yeshivah College campus in Glenhazel, Johannesburg. Jack Kersh, executive director of the Yeshivah complex, referred to the synagogue as "a demonstration of our belief in the country's future."

Culture

The Israeli film *Kadosh* was the premier feature at the Israeli film festival in Johannesburg in February. The Orthodox community was offended at the way it portrayed the treatment of women in Jerusalem's Haredi community of Meah She'arim. Chief Rabbi Harris protested to Israel's consul general, noting that the film had caused a great deal of confusion and harm. Israeli ambassador Uri Oren acknowledged that the embassy had received many complaints.

The South African Jewish Arts and Culture Trust (SAJACT) reported that, since its inception in 1993, it had made a substantial contribution to Jewish culture, especially in the fields of music, art, and theater. SAJACT provided a platform for Jewish artists, offered scholarships and grants, and nurtured and promoted new talent.

A Marc Chagall exhibition opened in Johannesburg in October.

In December the new South African Jewish Museum was officially opened in Cape Town by former president Mandela. The museum was the brainchild of Mendel Kaplan, international Jewish leader and industrialist, and was supported by the Kaplan Kushlick Foundation. Vivienne Anstey was named director.

Publications

Some noteworthy new publications of Jewish interest were *To Reach for the Moon: The South African Rabbinate of Rabbi Dr. L. I. Rabinowitz* by Rabbi Dr. Gerald Mazabow; *Riteve: A Jewish Shtetl in Lithuania* edited by Dina Porat and Roni Stauber and based on *A Yizkor Book to Riteve: A Jewish Shtetl in Lithua-*

nia edited by Alter Levite; *For Heaven's Sake: The Chief Rabbi's Diary* by Chief Rabbi Cyril Harris; *For Humanity: Reflections of a War Crimes Investigator* by Richard Goldstone; and *Israel: Culture, Religion and Society, 1948–1998* edited by Stuart A. Cohen and Milton Shain.

Personalia

Professor Valerie Mizrachi, University of the Witwatersrand, awarded the UNESCO Woman in Science (Africa) Award for her work on HIV/AIDS and tuberculosis; Dr Sheila Aronstam named "Bloemfonteiner of the Year" for her involvement in crime prevention, service to the blind, and Jewish communal work; Julius Feinstein, cofounder and senior partner of Grant Thornton, Kessel Feinstein, honored by the Johannesburg Jewish Helping Hand and Burial Society (Hevrah Kadisha) for 65 years of honorary service; Leon Wilder, distinguished Cape Town communal leader, received Keren Hayesod's "Yakir" award; Geoffrey Neiman granted a special award, the *Cruz de Oficial de la Orden de Isabel la Catolica,* from King Juan Carlos of Spain, for Spanish dancing; Gershon Hurwitz appointed national chairman of the South African Union of Jewish Students; Ray Wolder, elected president of the Union of Jewish Women of South Africa; Sylvia Berzack awarded honorary life presidency of the WZO; Maria Parness and Anette Price each awarded honorary life vice presidency of the WZO; Chief Rabbi Cyril Harris and Ann Harris received the Commonwealth Jewish Council Year 2000, given by the British Commonwealth Jewish Council, for service to South African Jewry.

Among prominent South African Jews who died in 2000 were Frank Bradlow, communal leader and art historian; Professor Sam Kleinot, public health specialist; Jean Kluk, Durban Jewish leader; Cecil Margo, jurist, Jewish communal leader, and one-time advisor on aviation to David Ben-Gurion; Aaron Mendelow, advocate and Jewish communal leader; Rachiel Rapoport, Women's Zionist leader; Morris Rutstein, Jewish leader and founding member of Histadruth Ivrith in South Africa; Gaby Shapiro, antiapartheid activist; and Leon Traub, businessman and founder of Metro Cash and Carry.

MILTON SHAIN

Israel

In Israel during 2000 all eyes were focused on the complex interplay of diplomacy, politics, and violence. The government of Prime Minister Ehud Barak, who defeated incumbent Benjamin Netanyahu by a convincing 12-percentage-point margin in May 1999, began the year still optimistic about reaching a settlement with the Syrians over the Golan Heights as a first step toward a comprehensive Middle East peace. By year's end not only was peace with Syria as far away as ever, but, despite the far-reaching, unprecedented concessions offered by Barak, American-sponsored negotiations during the summer at Camp David with the Palestinians had broken down in recriminations, destruction, and death. And in December, after a year-and-a-half in power, Prime Minister Barak, deserted by erstwhile political allies and coalition partners and bereft of a majority in the Knesset, was forced to resign and call for a new election.

DIPLOMACY AND SECURITY

Syrian Talks

Prime Minister Ehud Barak's attempt to revive the broken-off peace talks with Syria fizzled in early 2000, largely because of Syrian insistence that the final border between the two countries be based on the lines that were in effect prior to June 4, 1967, before the Six-Day War in which Israel won the Golan Heights from Syria. Those lines would have given Syria territory along the northeastern coast of the Sea of Galilee (Lake Kinneret), Israel's main water reservoir.

The last round of Israel-Syrian talks was held at Shepherdstown, West Virginia, January 3–10, following up on a previous round of negotiations in December 1999. The delegations at Shepherdstown were headed by Israeli prime minister Barak and Syrian foreign minister Farouq a-Shara. Both sides were given a U.S. working paper which defined areas of agreement and differences between them, though the actual talks did not proceed much beyond procedural matters.

On the question of borders, the U.S. paper noted that Syria insisted on a return to the de facto border that existed on June 4, 1967, the eve of the 1967 Arab-Israeli war, while Israel demanded modifications based on security considerations and on the fact that the border at that time included territory that Syria had seized by force during the 1948 Arab-Israeli war. As to security arrangements, Israel sought the establishment of a demilitarized zone in all of the territory from which it would withdraw, in addition to the existing demilitarized zone established in the 1974 disengagement agreement after the 1973 Arab-Israeli war. Syria, however, insisted that any demilitarized zone be of equal size on both sides of the border. Israel also called for retention of its early-warning capability on Mount Hermon, the highest point on the Golan plateau, but Syria wanted these facilities to be under the auspices of the United States and France. Israel wanted security arrangements to be monitored by both sides in cooperation with a multinational force, while Syria preferred an international peacekeeping force. As to the issue of water, since most of the Golan's waters drain into the Sea of Galilee — Israel's largest reservoir, which furnished roughly 30 percent of the country's water — Israel sought continued access to this water at its current level of use, with measures to prevent contamination, pollution, or depletion of water supplies. Syria maintained that such arrangements would have to be negotiated.

In addition to these procedural and substantive differences, the Israelis found that the Syrians were unwilling to build confidence through any public display of warmth towards their opposite numbers. Shara, for example, refused the shake hands with Barak, and would not talk to the Israelis unless President Clinton was in the room. This Syrian attitude reportedly prompted one unidentified Israeli negotiator to say that if peace were ever reached between the two countries, it would be the "mother of cold peaces."

At Shepherdstown, Israel also presented American officials with a formula to upgrade its relations with the United States. This reportedly included commitments by Washington to long-term military assistance for Israel, an emergency aid package to defray the costs of a redeployment of the Jewish state's forces once the Golan Heights returned to Syrian hands, U.S. guarantees that Israel would maintain its deterrent capacity against any possible attack from Arab countries, an intensified antiterror campaign combined with removal of the terrorist threat from Syria itself, and American guarantees of a continued flow of crude oil to meet Israel's energy needs. According to one report, Israel was also seeking at least $17 billion in direct military aid to finance the purchase of a new arsenal of weapons including state-of-the-art Apache helicopters and Tomahawk cruise missiles, as well as a ground station to collect information from U.S. spy satellites overflying the region.

Top U.S. leaders attended the Shepherdstown talks, including President Clinton, who visited Shepherdstown on five separate occasions, and Secretary of State Madeleine Albright. On January 9, in fact, Clinton prevailed on an angry Barak not to leave the talks. But the meeting broke up the following day without any formal conclusion. Barak — who had reportedly expressed willingness, in a final agreement, to give Syria sovereignty over all of the Golan up to the international border determined in the Sykes-Picot agreement at the end of World War I — returned home to mounting opposition over a Golan move. On January 10 an estimated 150,000 people, many of them bused in from the Golan itself and from settlements in the West Bank and Gaza, demonstrated in Tel Aviv's

Rabin Square against a withdrawal. And both Natan Sharansky, leader of the Russian immigrant party Yisrael ba'Aliya, who was interior minister, and Yitzhak Levy, leader of the National Religious Party and housing minister, said they would resign from the government if Israel agreed to give up the Golan.

The talks were to have resumed on January 19. But two days before, Syria said that it would not come back to the negotiating table without a firm Israeli commitment to a full withdrawal from the Golan Heights to the pre-June-4 line that had represented Israeli and Syrian positions before the start of the 1967 war. Secretary of State Albright said that the postponement came because each side "wants to have its needs decided first. And what we are trying to do is to develop some simultaneously, and try to move the whole package forward."

U.S. efforts to get the talks back on track included an hour-long phone conversation on January 18 between Clinton and President Hafez al-Assad of Syria. But the Americans did not succeed, and the following day Shara announced that Syria would not rejoin the talks until the United States obtained a firm and unequivocal Israeli commitment for the return of the Golan to Syria.

The Americans continued their efforts—and the Syrians continued to rebuff them—for several months after the collapse of the Shepherdstown talks. Hopes were briefly raised when Clinton announced, during an Asian tour, that he would stop in Geneva on March 26 for new talks with Assad. Assad's consent to make a rare trip abroad was certainly cause for optimism. But the three-hour meeting failed to achieve any tangible results, as both sides conceded afterward. Following the meeting, a White House spokesman said that the U.S. no longer believed it would be productive to resume the talks, as the gaps between the Israeli and Syrian positions had not narrowed. Syria tried to shift the blame onto Israel, claiming that Jerusalem had not given the U.S. president any new proposals, particularly concerning the northeastern shore of the Sea of Galilee. At their meeting in Geneva, Assad told Clinton: "[Lake Kinneret] is the place I know as the border between Syria and Israel. Until 1967, I would swim in Lake Kinneret, I had barbecues there and ate fish."

Prospects for progress receded further when the Knesset approved a bill requiring that any return of the Golan be approved by 50 percent of all eligible voters (not actual voters) in a referendum, raising the number of votes needed to approve such an agreement to nearly 60 percent of those likely to vote in such a referendum. Even worse for Barak's government, that bill was passed with the votes of three members of his already-shaky coalition—Shas, Yisrael ba'Aliya, and the National Religious Party.

In April, with peace prospects apparently left for dead by both sides, Barak lifted the freeze on the building of Israeli housing units on the Golan, which had been imposed when the Syrian talks resumed in December 1999. "As long as the Syrians continue to express their positions the way they have for the past few days," Jerusalem Affairs Minister Haim Ramon said, explaining the move, "there is no point to negotiation." Work began almost immediately on 200 new homes in Katzrin, the informal Israeli "capital" of the Golan, which had a population of about 7,000.

During the period of negotiations, many Israelis had theorized that Hafez al-Assad had returned to the peace table in the hope of obtaining the Golan as part of a legacy that would stablize the regime of his chosen successor, his 37-year-old son Bashai, who had been groomed for the presidency since the death of his oldest brother, Basil, in a 1994 automobile accident. Those hopes evaporated when the Syrian president died, at the age of 69, on June 10.

Early Israeli assessments were that Syria's new president, who was formally elected to succeed his father on July 10, might be more modern and moderate, but would have neither the political muscle nor the solid support necessary to show any more flexibility than his father had on the Golan, at least in the short term. These predictions proved correct during the early months of the new Assad administration, as the successor son seemed to maintain a hard-line position similar to that of his late father.

Out of Lebanon

During the 1999 election campaign, Ehud Barak had promised to withdraw Israeli forces from Lebanon, in conjunction with reaching a peace agreement with Syria, within one year of taking office. But the fighting escalated in late January and early February, after a Hezballah bomb killed Col. Aqel Hashem, second in command to Gen. Antoine Lahad, the leader of the South Lebanon Army (SLA), the pro-Israel Lebanese militia that Israel had set up in its "security zone." Hashem's death, at his home village of Dabel, near Tyre in the western part of South Lebanon, was followed by the killing of three Israeli soldiers—Tidhar Tempelhof, Lior Niv, and Tzachi Malcha—in a Hezballah missile attack on the Galgalit outpost in South Lebanon. After these and other attacks, Barak vowed retaliation and said talks with Syria would not resume until Damascus reined in the Hezballah, the Iranian-supported Shi'ite Muslim fundamentalist militia. Knesset opposition members railed against what they said was Barak's policy of restraint. The time had come, said Ariel Sharon, leader of Likud, the main opposition party, "to leave Lebanon without an infrastructure."

As Hezballah kept on attacking, an Israeli helicopter, on February 4, rocketed the vehicle of Ibrahim Aql, Hezballah's military chief. On February 7, Israeli planes bombed several power-relay stations in Lebanon (at Baalbek in the Syrian-controlled Biq'a valley, near the Syrian border, and near Beirut) hoping to pressure the government in Beirut into acting against Hezballah. The next day, with the attacks against their troops continuing, Israeli planes hit a TV-relay station, Hezballah bases, and a radar station located on the top floor of a building in the South Lebanese coastal city of Tyre. Lebanese sources estimated the damage from Israeli raids at about $200 million. Hezballah retaliated with a Katyusha rocket attack on the security zone in which another soldier was killed, and Israel ordered residents of the northern border area into shelters, fearing that the Katyushas would be launched on Israel proper. As tensions mounted on the border, Foreign Minister David Levy told the Knesset that if Katyushas rained down on Israel, Lebanese "soil will burn." (A fortnight later, Levy spoke even more strongly, saying that Lebanon would pay "soul for soul, blood for blood, child for child" for any Hezballah attack on northern Israel.)

Hezballah attacks, and Israeli retaliation against suspected Hezballah targets, continued. On February 16, in response to an appeal by Chief-of-Staff Shaul Mofaz for authorization to respond more quickly to Hezballah attacks on populated areas, the security cabinet appointed a subcommittee consisting of Barak, who was both the prime minister and defense minister, Transport Minister Yitzhak Mordechai, and Foreign Minister Levy to authorize immediate retaliation. And, as anti-Israel and anti-U.S. demonstrations took place in Beirut, the Hezballah leader, Sheikh Hassan Nasrallah, said that his forces had the capacity to launch heavy missile attacks on northern Israel.

On March 5, 2000, the Israeli cabinet unanimously voted to withdraw from Lebanon unilaterally, even without a Syrian deal, by July 7. The cabinet announcement stated that after the pullout the army would deploy on the northern border and secure the safety of Israeli towns and villages from new positions there. "It's the end of the tragedy," said Barak, speaking on Israel TV after the vote, "the return of the boys home and the end of the bleeding."

But even after the announcement, Hezballah attacks on Israeli and SLA positions inside the security zone continued virtually unabated, and, in response, Israeli planes struck at some new targets. On March 13 they bombed two camps of hard-line "rejectionist" Palestinian factions that opposed Yasir Arafat's peace process with Israel, in the eastern part of Lebanon, which was under Syrian control. Some Lebanese sources viewed these raids as an Israeli response to an Arab League communiqué on March 11, following a meeting in Beirut, which warned that a unilateral Israeli pullout from Lebanon could trigger armed Palestinian attacks across the border. The Arab League said that this could happen if Israel did not agree to negotiations, at the time of the pullback, on the repatriation of well over 600,000 Palestinian refugees living in camps in Lebanon.

On April 17 Israel formally told the United Nations that it would withdraw its troops, "in one phase," by July 7. And, Israeli ambassador Yehuda Lancry announced, Israel would take in about 4,000 SLA fighters and their families after the pullback. Prime Minister Selim al-Hoss of Lebanon hailed Israel's statement as "a resounding victory" for Lebanon, and said his county would accept UN peacekeeping forces into the area to fill the power vacuum left by the withdrawing Israelis. At the same time, Syria quickly dissociated itself from a threat made by Lebanon's defense minister, Ghazi Zuytar, who said that his country might ask Damascus to place its forces in the newly vacated border zone. That, Zuytar said, would "put Tel Aviv in the range of Syrian rockets." (Israeli intelligence estimated that most of northern Israel, including the suburbs of Haifa, came within the range of Katyushas possessed by Hezballah. Prior to the pullback, the "Katyusha line" ran only as far south as the coastal resort town of Nahariya.)

In early May Israel began handing over some installations to members of the SLA, and Hezballah responded by stepping up its attacks. Desertions from the pro-Israel militia increased as the Israeli withdrawal drew closer, and after several senior SLA commanders were killed in Hezballah attacks. Israel responded, again, with more aerial bombings. After a chain of events triggered by the killing of seven Lebanese civilians in SLA-controlled territory and Israeli bombardments of two South Lebanese villages, Hezballah fired Katyushas on Kiryat Shmona, the northern Israeli border city, and other Israeli villages. One soldier was killed in the attack. Almost immediately Israeli planes hit two more power-relay stations, at Deir Ammar and Besalim, on May 5, causing what the Lebanese said was $50 million in damage just as work was getting under way to repair the other power substations hit by Israel. Israeli planes also took out tanks belonging to the Popular Front for the Liberation of Palestine, which had been deployed in the Syrian-controlled Biq'a valley of eastern Lebanon.

It was still not clear when Israel would carry out its withdrawal, though signs that it would do so before the self-declared July 7 deadline were accumulating. In mid-May Israel began moving more and more troops in the direction of the international border, handing over fortified positions in the security zone to the SLA. With morale declining, the SLA found itself unable to hold many of these positions. On May 21, for example, members of the Shi'ite battalion of the Lebanese militia abandoned the key Taibeh outpost. After that, other outposts were stormed by unarmed civilians and overrun, as SLA fighters lay down their arms and fled. As the central sector collapsed, the security zone was divided into two halves, and became virtually indefensible. The eastern sector, manned largely by Christian fighters, collapsed on May 23; Hezballah took over the SLA command center in the Christian town of Marjayoun and overran the al-Khiam prison, freeing almost 150 prisoners.

With the security zone in total collapse, it became clear that Israel had days, perhaps only hours, to effect its own withdrawal. With so little time left to move materiel and munitions across the border into Israel in an orderly fashion, Israeli troops began destroying them. Meanwhile, many SLA men and their families were gathering at various border crossings, seeking refuge. On the night of May 23–24, Israel moved all of its troops back into Israel. Opposition politicians criticized the government for staging a hasty, disorganized withdrawal, but army sources noted with obvious satisfaction that though the operation had been rushed because of the SLA's implosion, there had been no Israeli casualties on the final day.

The last Israeli soldier left Lebanon on the morning of May 24, 2000, about six weeks before the declared July 7 deadline and two weeks short of 18 years since Israel invaded the country. Thus ended an Israeli presence in South Lebanon that began in 1982, when Israeli troops moved all the way to the outskirts of Beirut in Operation Peace for Galilee, an attempt to set up a new order in Lebanon and wipe out the PLO "state within a state" that had blossomed there since the start of the Lebanese civil war in 1975. Israeli troops had besieged Beirut, the PLO headquarters at the time, forcing Arafat and his operatives to withdraw from the Lebanese capital and to set up new headquarters in Tunis. Israel troops remained in the southern part of Lebanon for more than two years after that, until mounting international pressure — and a guerrilla war conducted by the Shi'ite al-Amal organization, later joined by the more fundamentalist Hezballah — prompted a withdrawal to the South Lebanese security zone in 1985. A guerrilla war against the Hezballah, which vowed to get Israel off Lebanese soil, was waged for much of the intervening 15 years, punctuated by larger outbreaks of violence. Israel responded to what it saw as continued Hezballah provocations in July 1993 by launching the weeklong bombing campaign known as Operation Accountability, and in 1996, in Operation Grapes of Wrath, conducting a prolonged air, sea, and artillery bombardment of most of South Lebanon, in addition to hitting targets near Baalbek, in the Syrian-controlled Biq'a Valley, and in Beirut and the South Lebanese port city of Tyre.

In all, Israel lost more than 900 soldiers killed during its occupation of parts of Lebanon, including the security zone that it established in 1984 in a partial withdrawal from territory taken during the 1982 Lebanese offensive. Hundreds of members of the pro-Israel South Lebanese Army were also killed over the years, as were more than 1,000 fighters for Hezballah.

After the pullback, Barak said that Israel was leaving every inch of Lebanese territory, and warned that any attack on Israeli territory would be considered an act of war. Within hours after the Israeli departure about 250,000 Lebanese civilians, together with Hezballah fighters, marched into the zone. Despite predictions of anarchy, the takeover was orderly, with Hezballah maintaining a low profile although it was the strongest force there at the time. The government in Beirut proclaimed May 25 as National Liberation Day. In the south, civilians began to gather at the former "Good Fence" crossing point opposite the Israeli town of Metulla, hurling insults, and sometimes stones or firebombs, at Israeli troops on the other side of the fence. The Israelis followed strict orders not to respond.

About 6,000 members of the former SLA and their families managed to make their way into Israel in the final few days of the Israeli presence, leaving all of their worldly possessions, including homes and cars, on the other side of the fence. Most were processed at Israeli transit camps, including a former vacation resort village on the northern shore of Lake Kinneret. Although the Lebanese government rejected SLA leader Gen. Antoine Lahad's call for a general amnesty for SLA members and SLA-linked civilians, about 1,500 of them remained in Lebanon and gave themselves up to government troops. The day after the pullback was completed Barak, addressing the Knesset, called on Lebanon to "exploit the moment and talk peace." Barak said that Israel "extends its hand toward peace out of a vision of a joint future, which will be better for the children of both peoples."

Not long after, UN teams, responding to a statement by the government in Beirut that Lebanon would not assume responsibility for the area until the Israeli pullback was complete, began a careful examination of the frontier. Lebanon continued to demand that Israel pull back from an area known as the Shebba farms, on the slopes of Mt. Hermon, which Israel had taken during its conquest of the Golan Heights in 1967. On June 18 the UN Security Council agreed to endorse Secretary General Kofi Annan's verification that Israel had, in fact, complied with Security Council Resolution 425, which called for its withdrawal from Lebanon. The Lebanese government, however, claimed that Israel held six positions on Lebanese land, and Hezballah accused the international body of condoning Israel's continued violation of Lebanese territory.

In July UN peacekeeping troops from Ireland and Ghana were deployed in areas of the security zone vacated by Israel. Two of the disputed areas still remained unresolved. In August a combined unit of about 1,000 Lebanese army troops and Lebanese gendarmes deployed in the area, and took over the former SLA barracks at Marjayoun and Bint Jbail in the south-central part of the former zone. These troops were the first security personnel of the central government in Beirut to be present in the area since 1975, when the Lebanese civil war broke out. The Lebanese troops were charged with maintaining general security there, while leaving control of the border areas to the peacekeeping forces of UNIFIL (the UN Interim Force in Lebanon). Timur Göksel, spokesman for the UN and the 600-man UNIFIL, called the Lebanese deployment an important step towards stabilization. "It is a victory for Lebanon and for the UN," he said.

In the ensuing months, the Lebanese border was largely quiet. But while there were no major incidents except for the kidnapping of three Israeli soldiers in early October (see below), Lebanese and Palestinian civilians continued to gather at the former Metulla crossing point to toss stones and insults—and occasionally a firebomb as well—at Israeli soldiers across the border. And the Israeli army—as well as most of the border zone's residents—were in a waiting mode, since it would not take much for the frontier to heat up once again.

Prisoner Release and Kidnap Victims

Israel released 13 Lebanese prisoners who had been taken into custody in the 1980s and held between 11 and 13 years as bargaining chips against the possible release of Israeli navigator Ron Arad, missing since his plane went down over South Lebanon in 1986, and three soldiers missing since the 1982 battle of Sultan Yaakub, in the Biq'a valley of eastern Lebanon. Israel kept two other prisoners in custody—Sheikh Abdul Karam Obeid, taken from his home in the South Lebanese village of Jibshit in 1989, and Mustafa Dirani, abducted in 1994.

The release took place on April 19, a week after the Supreme Court, in a historic 6-3 ruling, said that the continued holding of the men was not justified since

Israeli law did not give the Defense Ministry the right to detain individuals who did not pose a threat to state security. Obeid and Dirani had been convicted in Israel of membership in Hezballah and sentenced to jail for one-to-three years. When their jail terms had ended, however, they were kept in Israel under administrative detention, without charge. In convincing the court that Obeid and Dirani should be held, the government successfully argued that the pair — who, unlike the freed prisoners, were high-ranking members of the Hezballah infrastructure — did pose such a threat. The court turned down appeals to free Obeid and Dirani, although there were rumors late in the year that they might be freed as part of an exchange for Adi Avitan, Benny Avraham, and Omar Sueid, kidnapped by Hezballah near Har Dov (Jebel Ros) in the foothills of Mt. Hermon on October 7, and businessman Elhanan Tannenbaum, lured into Lebanon by Hezballah and taken into captivity little more than a week after the three soldiers were captured.

On December 10, rumors surfaced that German mediators had been in contact with Sheikh Hassan Nasrallah, the leader of Hezballah, about a possible exchange involving the four kidnapped Israelis. But after the initial reports — including one that acting foreign minister Shlomo Ben-Ami had flown to Europe for consultations on a possible prisoner exchange — hopes faded. On December 19 the daily *Ha'aretz* reported that Israel had offered bodies of Hezballah men killed in action during the occupation of the security zone in exchange for information about the kidnap victims. But Nasrallah, while admitting that there had been contacts through third parties, insisted that a deal was a long way off. Israel, the Hezballah leader repeated on numerous occasions, would have to pay a high price for the prisoners, or even for information about them. Nasrallah would not confirm reports that one or more of the soldiers had been wounded in the kidnap operation, and would not allow the Red Cross or other international bodies to visit them.

An independent Israeli committee, headed by former general Yossi Peled, was appointed in November to investigate the circumstances of the kidnapping. The committee reported, in early January 2001, that serious operational shortcomings were evident both prior to the kidnapping and in the army's failure to mount an immediate rescue operation. The report also rejected suggestions that the three soldiers had been involved in illegal activities, possibly including drug smuggling, at the time they were kidnapped.

On December 28 the International Committee of the Red Cross confirmed, in a report to the UN, that it was "acting as a neutral intermediary between the Israeli authorities and Hezballah, with a view to facilitating a solution based on humanitarian considerations. To this end, the ICRC is in regular contact with the parties involved." But an official of the Austrian Ministry of Defense said that his country was also involved in secret mediation efforts. According to these reports, Defense Minister Herbert Scheibner, a member of Jörg Haider's far-right Freedom Party, had been in the Middle East to meet representatives of the two sides. Scheibner reportedly met with Ephraim Sneh, Israel's deputy defense minister, in November as well—despite the fact that Israel had no ambassador in Vienna, having frozen relations following the entry of the Freedom Party into the Austrian coalition. Peter Sichrovsky, a Jew serving as a deputy in the European Parliament for Haider's party, said that mediation began in both Israel and Syria on November 3.

In late December Hezballah's deputy secretary general, Sheikh Na'eem Kassem, said that the Germans were "still involved in the mediation" and denied that there were any other mediators. "The German mediators are working to meet our demands, but as we said before, for every piece of information, there is a price," Kassem said. Nasrallah's previous public demands had included the release of all Lebanese and Arab prisoners from Israeli jails and the provision of maps of mines planted across southern Lebanon.

This was not the first time that Hezballah had been involved in kidnapping. In the 1980s, operating under a different name but backed—as now—by Iran, it had kidnapped Westerners in Lebanon. But as *Ha'aretz* military commentator Ze'ev Schiff pointed out shortly after the October kidnappings, "Hezballah excels in surprise operations, the majority of which have not been met with an Israeli response. The organization, with the help of Iranian intelligence agents, bombed Israeli and Jewish targets in Buenos Aires in the early 1990s. Hezballah also surprised Israel and the South Lebanon Army when it used unarmed civilians to head military columns [in May, just before Israel pulled out of South Lebanon]. This move resulted in the rapid collapse of outposts in the security zone in southern Lebanon, since Israel did not fire at civilians." The Israeli army, Schiff wrote, "believes that Hezballah will not cease its operations after the recent kidnappings. Iran is backing the organization's actions and Damascus is also not free from blame: It has failed to condemn these actions, and perhaps even indirectly encouraged them."

On May 14 the Palestinian Authority said it had arrested Hamas bomb expert Muhammad Dief. The successor to Hamas "engineer" Yihya Ayash, killed in an Israeli booby trap in early 1996, Dief had been the target of a five-year manhunt. Although Israel sought the extradition of Dief, who was involved in the 1996 suicide bus bombings that cost more than 50 Israeli lives, he was placed under house arrest in Gaza. His arrest left Muhammad Abu Hanud as the most wanted Hamas terrorist still at large. More than three months later, on August 26, Abu Hanoud would walk out of an ambush by the elite Duvdevan antiterror army unit, in which three soldiers were shot and killed by their own comrades as they encircled Abu Hanoud's hideout in his home village, Assira al-Shamaliya. The wanted man then made his way into PA territory, where he gave himself up to Palestinian security forces. Later in the year, Palestinian sources denied that either Dief or Abu Hanoud was among the Hamas activists they released in mid-October, after Israeli retaliatory raids hit at key police and Fatah installations in the West Bank and Gaza.

Bumpy Road to Camp David

Israel and the Palestinian Authority began 2000 with efforts to implement the agreement they had signed at Sharm el-Sheikh, in Egyptian Sinai, in September 1999. That agreement provided for implementation of a transfer of land in the West Bank, the conclusion by February 2000 of a framework for a final-status agreement between the two parties, and the conclusion in September 2000 of the final-status agreement itself. At Sharm el-Sheikh, Prime Minister Barak and Chairman Arafat had agreed to implement an earlier agreement signed by Arafat and then prime minister Benjamin Netanyahu in October 1998, under which Israel would redeploy from 13 percent of the West Bank, transferring that land to Palestinian Authority control.

In early January, Israeli and Palestinian negotiators ended months of dead-locked talks by agreeing to a formula for the implementation of a 6.1-percent re-deployment, actually a withdrawal. (Israel had completed an earlier redeployment, including a substantial "upgrade" of land designated as Area C, under full Israeli control, to Area B, under Palestinian civil control and Israeli military authority, in November 1999. The rest of the land was not transferred because the two sides found it impossible to agree on the details of the redeployment.) Under terms of the agreement, Israel implemented, on January 6–7, a redeployment from 2 percent of the area from Area B status to full Palestinian Authority control, as Area A. Also, an additional 3 percent was upgraded from Area C status to Area B.

Additional land, amounting to about 6 percent of the West Bank (5.1 percent from Area B to Area A status, and 1 percent from Area B to Area A status) was due to be transferred on January 16. But a few days before, Barak announced that he was delaying the transfer due to what he said was Palestinian "foot-dragging" in the final-status negotiations. Two days later, on January 17, at the Erez check-point on the northern end of the Gaza strip, the Israeli prime minister asked Arafat's agreement to delay the February 13 deadline for the "framework" pact. Arafat rejected the military map presented by Barak, because, unlike previous maps, it failed to include the town of Abu Dis, northeast of Jerusalem, on the eastern slopes of the Mount of Olives. The Palestinian response to Barak's uni-lateral decision was to denounce both the move and what they said was the Is-raeli leader's "deliberate attitude of supremacy."

On January 20 Arafat traveled to Washington for meetings with President Clin-ton; a few days later Foreign Ministry official Oded Eran, the former ambassador to Jordan who, at the time, headed the Israeli team for the final-status talks, ex-pressed doubt that the February 13 deadline could be met, because of the wide differences between the parties on all major aspects of final-status—Jerusalem, water, refugees, borders and security arrangements, and the status of Israeli set-tlements in the West Bank and Gaza after a final-status agreement had been reached.

At about the same time, reports began to surface of warnings by Israeli security agencies about the possibility of new violence in the territories, which was likely to break out in late March, after the planned visit to Israel and the Palestinian Authority by Pope John Paul II. According to one report in the daily *Ha'aretz* newspaper, intelligence sources said that "the handwriting is already on the wall." The anonymous sources compared the situation to late 1987, before the start of the so-called Palestinian intifada, when Israel saw signs of what was brewing but did not react in time. The security sources said that Arafat, by accusing Israel of systematically violating agreements that had been reached between the two sides, including the unimplemented withdrawal agreements of Sharm el-Sheikh, was preparing his people for a crisis. In addition, they said that Arafat, through his operatives inside the PA, was accusing Israel of showing disdain for him and, through him, for the Palestinian people, and of creating unfounded disputes over lands that, in his view, were rightfully Palestinian.

As the February 13 deadline drew closer, it became more and more apparent that no agreement was going to be reached. A meeting between Barak and Arafat at the Erez checkpoint on February 3 ended with both sides leaving in anger. Three days later, on February 6, the Palestinians announced that contacts with Israel had been frozen. Negotiations remained in a state of suspension even after a visit to the region by U.S. peace envoy Dennis Ross, who met with both sides but failed to achieve a breakthrough.

On March 2 security forces acted to prevent what appeared to be a large-scale terrorist attack in central Israel. Acting on a tip, police and army units surrounded a dwelling in the Israeli Arab town of Taibeh, in the Sharon area, which had been rented a few days earlier by members of a Hamas terror squad who had slipped into the country. The police antiterror unit killed four terrorists—including two who came out of the building carrying an explosives-filled suitcase—and captured a fifth. PA security forces captured a sixth member of the team a few days later in the West Bank town of Tul Karm. One member of the police unit was injured in the shoot-out.

In early March, Ross arranged and attended two meetings between Barak and Arafat in the Palestinian town of Ramallah, north of Jerusalem, and on March 8 Ross announced that Israel and the Palestinians would resume the broken-off final-status talks in Washington later in the month. About a week afterward Oded Eran and Sa'eb Erakat, the Palestinian negotiator, announced that they had reached agreement on the transfer of the "remaining" 6.1 percent of West Bank land to PA control. Barak's inner cabinet approved the transfer plan on March 15, so that 6.1 percent of West Bank land was moved to full or partial Palestinian control on March 21. This transfer meant that almost 43 percent of the territory of the West Bank was under either full or partial PA control, as Area A or B. That included villages in the Hebron district, and others near Ramallah, Jericho, and the northern West Bank city of Jenin. But it did not include the Jerusalem suburb of Anata; Prime Minister Barak was forced to revise the transfer map after right-wing members of his coalition, including the National Religious Party and Sharansky's Yisrael ba'Aliya, the Russian immigrant party, threatened to resign if Anata were included in the pull-out.

In mid-March Arafat, speaking to the PA Legislative Council in Ramallah, raised fears that, if final-status negotiations were not completed by the September 13 deadline set at Sharm el-Sheikh, he would assert Palestinian independence. "I declare," he told the Palestinian lawmakers, "that the year 2000 is the year of the Palestinian state, with al-Quds [Jerusalem] as its capital."

With the transfer of territory, Israeli-Palestinian talks resumed in late March at Bolling Air Force Base outside Washington, D.C. Just before the talks opened, an Egyptian official said that Israel could not expect a warm peace unless it consented to a Palestinian state and "dealt with Jerusalem." Speaking in Washington, Egyptian ambassador to the U.S. Nabil Fahmy said that Israelis "do not understand the frustration Arabs feel that there is still occupation." Two sessions of the talks were held between delegations headed by the Palestinians' Yasir Abd Rabbo and Israel's Oded Eran. Although the atmosphere was considered to be positive, U.S. national security adviser Samuel Berger said after the talks that progress had not been rapid. "Time is not the friend of peace in the Middle East," said Berger. "Any sense of urgency comes from [the Israeli and Palestinian] clocks and not our clocks."

Barak and Clinton met on April 11 in Washington, after which American officials said that Israel had agreed to an increased U.S. presence in future negotiations. According to a report in the daily Ha'aretz, however, there were several specific points of agreement reached at the Clinton-Barak summit: Barak agreed to accelerated talks on the Palestinian track, in the hope of finalizing a framework agreement by May and including the third pullback in it; American representatives would sit in on future talks between Israel and the Palestinians, which would continue outside Washington; Israel would ensure that the Palestinians would get contiguous territory in the West Bank in return for territories annexed to Israel; Israel would withdraw from Lebanon to the line set by the UN in 1978 and would not leave any outposts or security fences on the Lebanese side of the border, and the U.S. would muster international support for the implementation of UN resolution 425 calling for Israeli withdrawal from Lebanon and the posting of international security forces on the Lebanese side of the frontier; and the U.S. would suspend mediation efforts on the Syrian track and "wait for developments."

A few days after Barak's return to Israel, the prime minister reportedly raised with his ministers the probability of the establishment of a Palestinian state. Barak's office issued a statement saying that the prime minister had told the cabinet that "no serious person could imagine any future entity would be a protectorate or autonomous area not comprising contiguous territories, or would prevent the free movement of people." But Barak continued to insist that such a Palestinian entity must be demilitarized, and that an "absolute majority" of Jewish settlers in the West Bank and Gaza would remain under Israeli sovereignty.

Arafat and Barak met again in Ramallah on May 7, the first time they had met since March. At the Ramallah talks, the Palestinians agreed on the lapse of the revised May 13 "target date" for reaching a framework agreement, which had been set after the Palestinians and Israelis had failed to reach such an agreement by the original deadline of February 13.

On May 15, in a 16-6 vote, Barak's cabinet approved a plan to hand over the towns of Abu Dis, al-Azariya (Bethany), and Sawhara to the Palestinian Authority, a plan he said would avoid "stalemate and deterioration" in the peace process. He also said that the transfer of Abu Dis, which some Israelis thought at the time would satisfy the Palestinian demand for making Jerusalem the capital of their state-to-be, would assure the future of Jerusalem itself. (This assessment, widely held at the time, failed to recognize the adamant insistence of Arafat that he would accept no less than "a Palestinian state whose capital is al-Quds [Jerusalem].")

The Knesset approved the Abu Dis transfer, 56-48. After the vote the National Religious Party, led by Housing and Construction Minister Yitzhak Levy, threatened to resign from the government and the coalition if Abu Dis were actually handed over. But Barak delayed the transfer anyway because of rioting in the Palestinian territories on the 52nd anniversary of Israeli statehood, which Palestinians called al-Naqba (the disaster), by which they meant the displacement of hundreds of thousands of refugees during Israel's War of Independence. The violence, including shooting incidents, was the bloodiest seen in the territories since the tunnel riots of September 1996 when 15 Israelis and some 70 Palestinians were killed (see AJYB 1998, pp. 414–15). Israeli soldiers, usually responding with rubber bullets, were said to have killed seven Palestinians and wounded 1,000 in street fighting, which one observer said made the West Bank resemble "a huge battlefield."

Israel said that some Palestinian police officers and other members of Arafat's security forces had taken part in the fighting, using guns that had been provided to them under the Oslo agreements against Israeli troops. The Palestinians, who said that one of their police officers had been shot dead during the four days of fighting, claimed that officers had only used their weapons in self-defense, and only to return Israeli fire. There were no Israeli deaths, evidence of Israeli policies, adopted after the 1996 tunnel riots, which reduced the exposure of IDF troops.

The Israel Defense Force Central Command, which was responsible for the West Bank, said on May 16 that the events of al-Naqba had been "planned by the Palestinian Authority, which wanted to 'heat up' the populace and then lost control of events. The Palestinian police," it charged, "made no effort to calm the disturbances, while IDF soldiers used crowd-dispersal means in a calm and responsible manner, and live fire was used only after" fire was opened on Israeli troops. Some of those who had opened fire on Israeli soldiers at the Ayosh junction near Ramallah, said the IDF, were members of Tanzim, the Palestinian militia affiliated with Arafat's mainstream Fatah movement. "The PA," an army officer told a press briefing, "used the prisoner issue [of Palestinian terrorists held in Israeli jails] and al-Naqba day to incite the 'street.' But the PA did not control the strength of the flames."

A fire bomb was tossed into an Israeli car traveling through the Palestinian town of Jericho on May 21 and an Israeli girl was seriously hurt, prompting Prime Minister Barak to suspend a "secret track" of Israeli-Palestinian peace talks in Stockholm between Internal Security Minister Shlomo Ben-Ami and Abu Ala, speaker of the Palestinian Legislative Assembly, who had been the main Palestinian negotiator during the 1993 secret talks in Norway that led to the Oslo agreements. Disclosure that the talks had been going on irked both Foreign Minister David Levy and Yasir Abd Rabbo, the head of the PA team for final-status talks. Abd al-Rabbo called the Stockholm negotiations "an Israeli conspiracy aimed at extracting fundamental concessions" from the Palestinians.

The Americans again tried to revive the broken-off talks. Barak met with Clinton in Portugal on June 1, and the U.S. president subsequently dispatched Secretary of State Albright to the Middle East. During her visit to Israel and the Palestinian areas, Albright attempted to lay the groundwork for a tripartite summit between Clinton, Arafat, and Barak. In Cairo for meetings with Egyptian president Hosni Mubarak, Albright said that she and Clinton were ready "to roll up our sleeves and do everything to facilitate the process." Arafat later flew to Washington for additional talks with Clinton on June 15, but there was no firm plan, as yet, for a summit meeting.

Camp David

It was not till July 5, after weeks of uncertainty about the next step in the peace process, that Clinton announced he would host a make-or-break summit beginning July 11 at the Camp David presidential retreat in the Maryland hills. The PLO central committee, meeting in Gaza, had previously empowered Arafat to declare a Palestinian state on September 13, the deadline set at the 1999 Sharm el-Sheikh summit for concluding a final-status agreement. This empowering resolution was passed unanimously by the PLO delegates without a strong reaction from Hamas, the Islamic resistance movement in the territories, which had been responsible, over the years, for many of the suicide bomb attacks on Israeli soldiers and civilians.

But if Arafat had a relatively strong mandate going into Camp David, Barak's position was shaky. His governing coalition effectively collapsed on July 9 when Shas, the ultra-Orthodox party of Sephardi (Middle Eastern) Jews, the National Religious Party (NRP), and Yisrael ba'Aliya, the Russian immigrant party led by Natan Sharansky, withdrew their support for the government because Barak had refused to consult them on the Camp David summit. Eli Yishai, the Shas leader, said he had not been informed what "red lines," if any, Barak had set for himself at Camp David. At the same time the six ministers from these parties —

Shas's Yishai (labor and social affairs), Yitzhak Cohen (religious affairs), Shlomo Benizri (health), and Eliyahu Suissa (national infrastructure), the settler-supported NRP's Yitzhak Levy (housing and construction), and Interior Minister Sharansky — resigned. Barak was forced to delay his departure for Washington until a no-confidence vote was conducted in the Knesset on two motions by the opposition Likud. Barak lost the vote 54-52, but the opposition failed to get the 61-vote absolute majority necessary in the 120-member Knesset to bring down the government.

Barak suffered an additional blow when David Levy, his foreign minister and deputy prime minister, refused to accompany him to the summit. Levy, who had bolted the Likud to take his Gesher (Bridge) party into Barak's One Israel before the 1999 elections, said he was upset about positions Barak might take at the summit. In addition, Levy was thought to be peeved that Ben-Ami, and not he, had been given a senior role in peace negotiations with the Palestinians.

The Israeli prime minister, leaving for the summit with a political crisis behind him, said that he was facing an historic task. "The time has come," he said in his departure statement, "to take decisions and to bequeath a better future to our children, a different reality from that known by our and our parents' generations. This is the time to devote our best resources to education, to reducing unemployment, to bridging social gaps, to equal opportunity, and to taking advantage of the enormous talents of our young generation . . . . This is the meaning of peace and security," Barak said, providing a hint of the far-reaching concessions he was about to offer the Palestinians: "There is no peace without a price, just as there is no peace at all costs."

The Camp David talks focused on five key areas that had been set aside for determination in final-status talks: the future status of Jerusalem, including the holy places in the Old City and on the Temple Mount (known to Muslims as Haram al-Sharif); delineation of final borders between the Palestinian and Israeli entities and security arrangements between them; the future of Israeli settlements in the West Bank and the Gaza Strip; the question of refugees and the Palestinian claim of the "right of return" to their homes, some of them in Israel proper, for people displaced in both the 1948 War of Independence and the 1967 Six-Day War; and the resolution of disputes over the division of water supplies. Even if no final agreement could be reached on these thorny issues, it was hoped that at least the two sides could agree on some kind of framework for the continuation of negotiations after Camp David.

In a move unprecedented in the history of Israeli diplomacy, Barak opted to strike out for a complete and final settlement of all issues, in exchange for a Palestinian agreement to the "end of the conflict." In doing so, he was willing to discuss not only the creation of a Palestinian state — an almost unthinkable notion a year earlier — but also the possibility of ceding much more territory to the Palestinians than had ever been mooted before, as much as 95 percent of the West Bank. Furthermore, Barak stepped back from the traditional Israeli position that Jerusalem must remain the undivided and united capital of Israel, raising the possibility that Israel might recognize PA sovereignty over Palestinian neighborhoods in Jerusalem, including parts of the Old City.

Despite an official news blackout during the July 11–19 talks, reports leaked out about arguments between the two sides. Clinton, who was due to leave the summit for the three-day G-8 summit meetings in Okinawa on July 19 (when the talks were due to end), delayed his departure for 24 hours to keep the parties at the bargaining table. After some effort, both sides agreed to stay on, with Albright conducting the negotiations until Clinton's return from Okinawa. But the optimism generated by the continuation of talks evaporated after Clinton came back to Camp David on July 25, and two days later the summit collapsed. Both Barak and Arafat left the United States for home on July 26.

At the end of the summit, the parties released the following joint statement:

> Between July 11 and 24, under the auspices of President Clinton, Prime Minister Barak and Chairman Arafat met at Camp David in an effort to reach an agreement on permanent status. While they were not able to bridge the gaps and reach an agreement, their negotiations were unprecedented in both scope and detail. Building on the progress achieved at Camp David, the two leaders agreed on the following principles to guide their negotiations:
> 1) The two sides agreed that the aim of their negotiations is to put an end to decades of conflict and achieve a just and lasting peace.
> 2) The two sides commit themselves to continue their efforts to conclude an agreement on all permanent status issues as soon as possible.
> 3) Both sides agree that negotiations based on UN Security Council Resolutions 242 and 338 are the only way to achieve such an agreement and they undertake to create an environment for negotiations free from pressure, intimidation and threats of violence.
> 4) The two sides understand the importance of avoiding unilateral actions that prejudge the outcome of negotiations and that their differences will be resolved only by good faith negotiations.
> 5) Both sides agree that the United States remains a vital partner in the search for peace and will continue to consult closely with President Clinton and Secretary Albright in the period ahead.

In the aftermath of Camp David, Clinton praised "the courageous actions that the prime minister and the Israeli team took at the summit," and pledged a "comprehensive review of the U.S.-Israeli strategic relationship, with a view towards what we can do to ensure that Israel maintains its qualitative edge, modernizes the army and meets the new threats that Israel and the other countries will face in the 21st century." He also promised that a memorandum of understanding on bilateral assistance would be formulated. While he gave most of the credit to Israel, Clinton added that "the Palestinians did make some moves at these talks that have never been made before. And while I made it clear in my statement, I thought that the prime minister [Barak] was more creative and more courageous. They did make some moves, and . . . the negotiating teams, for the first time in a formal setting where it counted, actually discussed these issues."

In an extraordinary interview with Israel TV's Ehud Ya'ari, Clinton stated that Barak "in no way ever compromised the vital interests of the security of the State of Israel." He added that most of the progress in the talks were made in the area of security, and that, in his view, there was "a clear willingness to try to come to grips with what were very different positions on this issue when they met, and come together." On the issue of Jerusalem, Clinton said that he had kept on telling the Palestinians "that you cannot make an agreement over something as important as a city that is the holiest place in the world—to the Jews, to the Christians, and one of the holiest places in the world to the Muslims—if it is required of one side to say, 'I completely defeated the interest of the other side.' If either side gets to say that at the end, there won't be an agreement. There can't be . . . there are legitimate interests on both sides, in Jerusalem, in such a way that they are met and honored and that the sanctity of the Holy City is uplifted. There has to be a way to do that."

Barak spoke of his own efforts "to do everything possible to bring about an end to the conflict—but not at any price—while at the same time strengthening the State of Israel, and Jerusalem its capital. In the course of the negotiations," he said, "we touched the most sensitive nerves, ours and the Palestinians, but regretfully—with no result." Israel, he concluded, "was prepared to pay a painful price to bring about an end to the conflict, but not any price. . . . In the past year, we have exhausted every possibility to bring an end to the 100-year-old conflict between us and the Palestinians, but regrettably the conditions were not yet ripe."

After the summit, Arafat returned to a hero's welcome in Gaza, and almost immediately departed on an international tour—including visits to France, South Africa, China, Egypt, Japan, Malaysia, Vietnam, and other countries—in an attempt to secure diplomatic support for his position and to fix the blame for the summit's failure on Jerusalem. With Israeli officials following him on most of these stops and explaining their government's views, he was largely unsuccessful. Many of the world leaders reportedly cautioned Arafat against unilaterally declaring Palestinian statehood on the September 13 deadline. Even the Jerusalem committee of the Organization of Islamic Conference, meeting on August 28, fell short of backing unilateral Palestinian statehood. Israel said that a unilateral Palestinian declaration of statehood would violate existing Israeli-PLO agreements, and would specifically break commitments enshrined in the trilateral Arafat-Barak-Clinton statement at the end of the unsuccessful Camp David summit. Clinton, for his part, sought to maintain the peace momentum by holding separate talks with the Israeli and Palestinian leaders in advance of the September 13 deadline.

Barak, back home, had to deal with David Levy, who on August 2 announced his resignation as foreign minister in protest over the far-reaching concessions Barak had offered at Camp David. Within a few days Barak named Ben-Ami, who had been deeply involved in peace negotiations with the Palestinians, as acting foreign minister. At about the same time he began allocating the portfolios of the six ministers who had resigned earlier in the summer to other members of his cabinet on an "acting" basis: Communications Minister Binyamin Ben-Eliezer took charge of housing and construction as well, also assuming the vacated post of deputy prime minister; Minister for Jerusalem Affairs Haim Ramon took on responsibility for the interior; and Justice Minister Yossi Beilin added the religious affairs portfolio to his duties. (Somewhat later, Tourism Minister Amnon Lipkin-Shahak took over the transport post vacated by Yitzhak Mordechai, and former Tel Aviv mayor Roni Milo became the acting health minister.)

U.S. efforts to bring the two parties together continued, and Clinton met with both Barak and Arafat at the UN Millennium Summit in New York in early September. In his speech to the summit, Clinton repeated the theme his representatives and emissaries had been stressing—that both Israel and the Palestinians should take the "hard risks for peace." Pressure mounted on the Palestinians, who were generally viewed as principally responsible for the failure to reach agreement, but both sides failed to budge on the key issue of Jerusalem.

Talks between the parties did renew, briefly, in the United States on September 11, between delegations headed by Ben-Ami for Israel and Abu Ala for the Palestinians. But those negotiations broke off on September 19. A week later Arafat came to Barak's home at Kochav Yair, northeast of Tel Aviv, for the first meeting between them since Camp David. This get-together was described as "the best ever" between the two leaders, and both sides stressed the positive atmosphere of the meeting.

Nevertheless, the two sides remained at odds on the key issue of sovereignty over the Temple Mount, sacred to Jews as the site of both Solomon's and Herod's temples, and the third holiest site for Islam. Israel had made several proposals, but Arafat remained steadfast in his rejection of anything less than absolute Palestinian sovereignty over it and over the other non-Jewish holy places in the Old City. In late September Barak said that he saw no reason why, in the future, Jerusalem could not contain both a Palestinian and an Israeli entity, indicating that he thought the Temple Mount could be "dealt with under a time frame and a mutually agreed procedure." On September 27, Sgt. David Biri, 19, was killed near Netzarim, in Gaza. The next day, September 28, Ariel Sharon visited the Temple Mount.

The Explosion

Outside Israel, at least, it was assumed that Likud leader Ariel Sharon's visit to the Temple Mount triggered the armed Israeli-Palestinian conflict that raged throughout the West Bank and Gaza and spilled over into Israel proper during the last three months of 2000. However Sharon and his supporters—and other Israeli observers as well—insisted that the Sharon visit was no more than an excuse for the outburst of violence, which would have been set off even had the controversial Sharon not made his politically charged inspection of the site.

Accompanied by Likud Knesset members and hundreds of armed police who were deployed all over the Western Wall plaza and around him, Sharon arrived at the mount at 7:30 A.M. on Thursday, September 28. He entered the compound through the Moghrabi gate, and visited the area near Al-Aqsa and the underground area called Solomon Stables that, some years before, had been converted into a mosque. During the visit, an Israeli Arab member of the Knesset who was present, but not part of the delegation, called out to Sharon and accused him of being a "murderer." Members of Sharon's Likud entourage replied by charging that the heckler was inciting to violence. As the Likud group departed, police escorts prevented Palestinian youths shouting "Allahu akbar" from getting close to the politicians. The youths then began to throw stones and other objects at the police, but nothing further happened that day.

After Israel captured the Old City of Jerusalem in the 1967 Six-Day War, it left both the Al-Aqsa Mosque and the Dome of the Rock, located on the Temple Mount, under the control of the Wakf, the Muslim religious trust, which generally allowed Jews to visit there, but not to pray or do anything else that might suggest Jewish ownership. Commenting on the incident after he had left the scene, Sharon said that "the Temple Mount is under Israeli sovereignty and it is the right of every Jewish person to visit the site. There cannot exist a situation in which Jews cannot visit the holiest site in the world for Judaism."

After Friday Muslim prayers on September 29—the eve of the Jewish holiday of Rosh Hashanah—Palestinians rioted on the Temple Mount, throwing stones on Jewish worshipers at the Western Wall plaza below and clashing with police. Four Palestinians were killed and a reported 200 were wounded, as police fired both rubber bullets (rubber-coated steel pellets designed for use in riot control) and live ammunition at the mob.

In the ensuing days, demonstrations and violent clashes—with Palestinians firing automatic weapons at Israeli positions—erupted throughout the West Bank and Gaza to protest the killings on the Temple Mount. Israeli authorities claimed that the violence had been planned and orchestrated in advance of the Sharon incident. The clashes escalated over the weekend, particularly after TV broadcasts of the death of 12-year-old Muhammad al-Dura, who was caught in a cross fire between Israeli troops and Palestinian gunmen at the Netzarim junction in Gaza. Israeli investigations cast doubt on the generally accepted thesis that IDF bullets killed the boy, and suggested that the fatal shots may have come from Palestinian fire. But the impact of the case was beyond doubt: To the Palestinians and to much of the world, Muhammad al-Dura was a victim of "Israeli brutality."

Palestinians declared a "day of rage" following the death of nine Palestinians in Gaza, the West Bank, and Jerusalem. On October 7 Palestinians—apparently including armed members of the Tanzim, the militia aligned with Arafat's mainstream Fatah movement—stormed the army outpost at Joseph's Tomb in Nablus. Yusuf Madhat, 19, a border police sergeant from the Israeli Druse town of Beit Jann, bled to death when a rescue force was unable to enter the besieged site. (Israeli troops were careful about entering the site where, in the 1996 Hasmonean tunnel riots, a rescue force had been ambushed and six soldiers killed.) Among those who attempted to bring the injured Madhat out was Jibril Rajoub, head of the Palestinian Preventive Security Force in the West Bank. The tomb area, which served as a yeshivah, was later evacuated by Israeli forces. Noting that it was a recognized Jewish holy site, the Israeli army announced that the PA had violated provisions of the Oslo agreements, which required it to protect the tomb. According to the IDF, the PA had agreed to protect the site after its voluntary evacuation. "This pledge was brazenly violated," an IDF statement said, "about two hours after the evacuation, when a Palestinian mob entered the tomb compound and began to systematically destroy everything in sight, including all remnants of the yeshivah, furniture, and [holy] books that were left behind."

As the violence escalated, there were efforts to bring it under control. Arafat and Barak attended an October 4 meeting with Secretary Albright at the residence of the U.S. ambassador in Paris. Arafat, in sessions with the two others and in one-on-one talks with Albright, insisted that Israel agree to an international inquiry into the outbreak of the violence; Barak categorically rejected the effort to internationalize the conflict. At one point during the meeting Arafat walked out, and Albright, wearing high heels, had to chase the Palestinian leader across the cobblestoned courtyard and order embassy guards to close the gates so his car could not leave. No agreement was reached at the talks, but Albright said they constituted progress towards a cease-fire. According to some reports, Arafat then spoke to President Jacques Chirac at the Élysée Palace, who advised him not to close a cease-fire deal as long as the Israelis did not agree to an international inquiry. Albright, Arafat, and Barak were due to meet on the following day, October 5, with Egyptian president Hosni Mubarak at Sharm el-Sheikh. Barak, however, said there was no point in the meeting and returned home; following a session with Albright and Arafat, Mubarak called an emergency summit of Arab heads of state for October 21 in Cairo.

As fighting continued, Barak warned Arafat on October 7 that peace negotiations would be suspended if violence did not stop within 48 hours. That same day, the UN Security Council (with the United States abstaining rather than exercising its veto power to kill the proposal) voted to condemn "the excessive use of force against the Palestinians." Israel's ambassador to the UN, Yehuda Lancry, told the council: "We are not faced with peaceful demonstrators, but rather a coordinated escalation of the violent confrontation throughout the West Bank and Gaza. There have been numerous instances of live fire emanating from within rioting crowds. In all these cases, Israeli security forces returned fire only when absolutely necessary, and only when faced with an imminent threat to life and limb." His assertion that Israelis only shot as a last resort was meant to answer Palestinian claims that Israeli troops had been given shoot-to-kill orders. (Other Israeli spokesmen would explain, in ensuing weeks, that the army had changed its tactics after the September 1996 tunnel riots, so that soldiers would not be exposed to Palestinian fire. These changes apparently included the use of specially reinforced vehicles and the employment of snipers who had orders to fire at Palestinians about to use weapons against Israelis.)

Clashes and diplomatic efforts to end them continued, and it was unclear whether Arafat tacitly approved of the violence or whether the activities on the ground, including the actions of his own Tanzim militia, had spun out of his control. Then, on October 12, army reservists Vadim Nozich and Yosef Avrahami, on their way back from home leave to their base in the Ramallah area, mistakenly passed through Israeli checkpoints and ended up at a Palestinian roadblock. The two men were taken to the PA police station in Ramallah, where word of their presence reached a group of Palestinians dispersing from the funeral of two people killed the previous day. The mob besieged the police station, broke in, and beat both men severely, to death or the verge of death. One was tossed out of a window, where pictures taken by an Italian TV crew showed him being hit repeatedly by a man with a heavy metal window frame. The body of one man was dragged through the streets of the town. The Italian TV crew managed to get the videotape it had taken of the incident out of the West Bank, and the horrifying pictures were passed on to other networks as well and seen around the world. The two bodies were returned to Israel a few hours later.

Israel responded with selective bombing—using helicopter gunships—of Arafat's Fatah offices in Gaza and Ramallah, and the police station itself. Arafat condemned the attacks as a "declaration of war," acting Israeli foreign minister Ben-Ami said the peace process was "at an end," and Barak, announcing that he no longer considered Arafat a peace partner, began talks to bring the Likud and its leader, Ariel Sharon, into a national unity or emergency government. An ashen-faced Amnon Lipkin-Shahak, speaking for the Israeli government soon after the killings, said Israel would leave no stone unturned to bring the killers to justice. Identifying some of those responsible from the TV pictures, Israeli security forces acted within weeks, arresting about a dozen members of the lynch mob, including the man pictured standing in the second-floor window of the Ramallah police station displaying his bloody hands to the mob below. The arrests—or at least most of them—were made in Area B, under Israeli security control, and in Area C, under Israeli security and civil jurisdiction, under the terms of Oslo. On December 7 Muhammad Daoud Hamdan, of Arora, north of Ramallah, a village under full Palestinian Authority control, was indicted for his role in the gruesome killings.

Later in October, Ricardo Cristiani, the correspondent of RAI, the Italian government TV network, published an open letter in a Palestinian newspaper apologizing to the Palestinian Authority for the release of the lynch videotape—which had been taken, in fact, by a rival station owned by media mogul Silvio Berlusconi. In his letter, Cristiani said that he and his colleagues would "follow the rules" about the broadcast of sensitive material. As a result, the Israeli government press office lifted the credentials of the RAI broadcaster and his network recalled him to Rome. After death threats were made against them, other Italian broadcasters also returned home.

As fighting escalated, Kofi Annan, King Abdullah of Jordan, and other foreign leaders again tried to broker a deal that would cool things down. After some jockeying, it was agreed that Mubarak would host an emergency summit at Sharm el-Sheikh on October 16–17, to be attended by Clinton, Barak, Arafat, King Abdullah, and Annan. The Sharm summit ended with a modicum of success. Barak and Arafat did not shake hands nor could they agree to a signed written statement at the conclusion of the meeting. Instead, President Clinton issued an oral statement at the end of the summit. He noted that both sides had agreed to call publicly and unequivocally for an end to the violence, and that they would take immediate concrete measures to end the confrontation, eliminate points of friction, and ensure an end to violence and incitement. Both sides also promised to act immediately to return the situation to the way it was prior to the current crisis. In addition, the president said, the United States, together with the Israelis and the Palestinians, and in consultation with Secretary General Annan, would set up a fact-finding committee to investigate the violence, its causes, and means to prevent its recurrence. Finally, the Clinton statement spoke of the need to find a pathway back to negotiations and the resumption of final-status talks, with both Israel and the PA agreeing to consult with the United States over the following two weeks on new ways to move the stalled process forward.

The Sharm meeting contained positive points for both leaders. For his part, Barak had gained a vague promise that Arafat would try to lower the level of violence, while the latter had secured Israel's agreement to begin pulling back its forces from the advanced positions they had taken during the fighting, and to lift the state of siege which Israel had placed over much of the Palestinian territory. Particularly important for Arafat was Israel's agreement to allow the reopening of the Gaza airport at Dehaniya. At the same time, Arafat managed to avoid being pushed into a public commitment to take back into custody several dozen key figures in the fundamentalist Islamic Jihad and Hamas movements, who had been released from PA jails after Israeli helicopter attacks a few weeks earlier.

Israel did pull back its forces—as it would do several more times during the period as quid pro quo for vague assurances from Arafat that he would rein in attacks against Israelis—but Arafat's promised public call for an end to violence did not materialize. Instead, more violence flared. Over the next weeks there were heavy shooting attacks on the settlement of Psagot, near Ramallah, and on the south Jerusalem neighborhood of Gilo from the Christian town of Beit Jala, in the Palestinian Authority's Area A, and from a nearby refugee camp. Israelis were horrified and shocked by the intermittent attacks on part of their capital, and public calls mounted to "let the army do its job" and launch heavy attacks on the Palestinians. Barak, however, followed a policy of restraint, fearing that massive retaliation would escalate and widen the crisis.

In late October, with the situation getting no better, Barak appointed a team to work on a blueprint for unilateral separation of Israel from the Palestinian-controlled territories. The plans, never formally put on the table, sought to minimize contact between the two populations by restricting the movement of Palestinians into Israel (as had happened, de facto, during the extended closure of the territories enforced during much of this period). In the short run, it was clearly impossible for Israel to cut many of the economic and infrastructure links between the two entities, which had been tightened as part of a deliberate Israeli policy after the 1967 Six-Day War. While it would not have been difficult to break apart the telephone networks (though the PA had its own 970 international calling code, calls still passed through Israeli switching stations), the electricity and water grids were completely interlinked, and, for security reasons, Israel would not give up control of the entry points between the PA and Jordan in the east, and Egypt in the south. While many Israelis were highly skeptical about the practicability of separation, the Palestinians were adamant in their opposition. It was, Sa'eb Erakat said, "a plan of occupation and suffocation."

The Arab summit took place in Cairo on October 21–22. It was the first meeting of Arab heads-of-state since June 1996, when they convened to discuss the impact of Benjamin Netanyahu's election as Israel's prime minister. While some of the more radical Arab states called for strong measures against Israel, President Mubarak of Egypt kept them at bay. The summit's communiqué did, of course, condemn Israeli actions in the West Bank and Gaza, called for a downgrading of relations with Israel, and affirmed the leaders' commitment to a just, lasting, and comprehensive peace in the region. It also recommended the establishment of an international tribunal to judge Israeli "war crimes." But the only tangible measure taken was to set up two funds, totaling $1 billion, one to preserve the Arab identity of Jerusalem and the other to provide support to families of Palestinians killed in the violence. (In the wake of the summit, Oman, Morocco, and Tunisia downgraded the level of their diplomatic contacts with Israel; on November 21, Egypt recalled its ambassador to Israel, Mohammed Bassiouny, from Tel Aviv, but fell short of breaking diplomatic relations.)

The Prime Minister's Office in Israel issued a statement "utterly rejecting" the conclusions of the Cairo summit and the "strong language" the communiqué contained. Israel, it said, "calls on the Palestinians to honor their commitments to halt the violence and incitement and immediately to restore calm and order before there is—Heaven forbid—an additional escalation." It said that Israel would "uncompromisingly" defend its vital security interests and "continue to act to foster reconciliation between it and the Arab world, but not at any price and not under pressure of violence." Barak announced that Israel would take a time-out from the peace process; Arafat's response was to say, at a press conference, that anyone who sought to block the establishment of an independent Palestinian state in the West Bank and Gaza, with Jerusalem as its capital, "can go to hell."

After yet another surge of Palestinian-initiated violence in late October, Israeli gunships attacked a number of Palestinian targets in the West Bank and Gaza, particularly the headquarters of the Tanzim militia, whose members had been involved in many of the shooting incidents. The attacks were part of a new Israeli policy of taking the initiative and striking out against those it deemed responsible for the terror. Over the next few months that policy appeared to be behind the killings, in separate shooting incidents, of a number of leaders linked to Fatah and Tanzim in the territories, including the local boss thought to have been responsible for the firing on Gilo from Beit Jala, and Thabet Thabet, 49, the Fatah leader in the West Bank town of Tul Karm. Arafat's response was a threat that the uprising would not cease until "a Palestinian boy or girl raises the flag of Palestine over Jerusalem, the capital of our Palestinian state."

On November 7 Clinton announced the formation of the fact-finding committee that had been agreed on at Sharm el-Sheikh three weeks earlier. The committee, headed by former U.S. senator George Mitchell, had as members another former U.S. senator, Warren Rudman, former Turkish president Suleyman Demirel, the European Union's security representative, Javier Solana, and Foreign Minister Thorbjörn Jagland of Norway. The committee began its work with a visit to the Middle East in late December; Roni Milo, the acting health minister, was liaison for the panel until the end of the year.

November saw several serious terrorist attacks inside Israel proper and on Israelis in the territories. On November 2 a car bomb exploded on a side street near Jerusalem's busy Mahane Yehuda outdoor produce market, killing two passersby: Ayelet Hashahar Levy, the 28-year-old adopted daughter of NRP leader Yitzhak Levy, and Hanan Levi, a 33-year-old lawyer who was on his way back to his office after eating lunch in a restaurant in the market area. Police said that the explosive device—which the Islamic Jihad later said it had placed—was probably planned to go off closer to the market, where the damage and loss of life and limb would have been much greater.

On November 20 a roadside bomb exploded at 7:30 in the morning alongside a bus carrying children from Kfar Darom to school in Gush Katif, in the southern Gaza Strip. Two adults accompanying the children were killed, and nine others, including five children, were injured. The five seriously injured included three members of the Cohen family of Kfar Darom, each of whom lost parts of their legs. Defense officials told the emergency security cabinet meeting that the Palestinian Authority was completely responsible for the terror attack, which was carried out by the Fatah's Tanzim forces.

At 5:30 P.M. on November 22, a car bomb was detonated just as a bus was passing it on the main street of the coastal town of Hadera, about 40 kilometers (25 miles) north of Tel Aviv. At the time of the blast the area was full of shoppers and people driving home from work. Shoshana Reis, 21, of Hadera, and Meir Bahrame, 35, of Givat Olga, were killed, and 60 Israelis were wounded in the blast—one of them critically and five seriously. Among those seriously injured was Thara Abu-Hussein, an 18-month-old Arab Israeli girl, who suffered burns over 15 percent of her body. Barak said that responsibility rested with the Palestinian Authority, which had released terrorists, members of Hamas and Islamic Jihad, "and encourages and directs its people to carry out attacks. The State of Israel will settle accounts with the perpetrators and those who sent them."

The atmosphere remained bleak. In late November, speaking to a Finance Ministry budgeting session, former Shin Bet security service head Ami Ayalon said that at least some Palestinians had reverted to the old pre-Oslo assessment that they could gain statehood by violent means. The PLO's 1993 decision at Oslo to take the path of negotiation, he observed, was based on the assumption that a Palestinian state could be attained only through negotiations. "Now some Palestinians think that there is another alternative, and that what we are offering them is not honorable," Ayalon said. "As they see it, we . . . halted the process, and returned to it only under threat of violence." Ayalon recalled the 1996 Hasmonean tunnel incident, after which the prime minister at the time, Benjamin Netanyahu, "ran to Washington and gave them Hebron." The former Shin Bet chief also discussed the option of separation, which, he said, had profound implications for the future character of Israel as a state. He asked rhetorically, "Is the option of a Jewish democracy with apartheid acceptable?" And he answered: "In my view it is not."

As the year drew to an end, Israeli and Palestinian negotiating teams met in Washington on December 19–23. After the sessions concluded, President Clinton presented a series of bridging proposals to both sides that were subsequently accepted, with numerous reservations, by the Israelis and the Palestinians. These were to be discussed at future negotiations. According to the Hebrew daily *Ha'aretz,* the Clinton proposals included the following points:

Jerusalem: Arab neighborhoods will become part of Palestine, Jewish neighborhoods will remain part of Israel. On the Temple Mount, the Al-Aqsa Mosque, the Dome of the Rock, and the plaza between them will be under Palestinian sovereignty, but the Palestinians will be forbidden to conduct archaeological digs there and will have to acknowledge the Jewish connection to the site. The Western Wall, the Jewish Quarter of the Old City, and most of the Armenian Quarter will remain Israeli. The entire Old City will be open, with no border controls. Jerusalem will be the capital of both countries.

Refugees: Palestinian refugees will be granted the right to return to their "homeland," which will be defined in the agreement as the Palestinian state. There will be no right of return to Israel, but Israel will absorb tens of thousands of refugees on a humanitarian basis. An international framework, with Israel participating, will be set up for compensating and resettling the refugees. The agreement will recognize Israel as the historic homeland of the Jewish people.

Borders: The lines of June 4, 1967, will mark the borders between the two states, with minor adjustments for which Israel will compensate the Palestinians with territory in the Negev, around the Halutza dunes located on the Egyptian border south of the Gaza Strip. The Palestinians will control some 95 percent of the West Bank; about 80 percent of the settlers will be annexed to Israel, with territorial contiguity between Israel and the annexed settlements. Israel will guarantee safe passage between Gaza and the West Bank, as had been provided in the earlier Oslo agreements.

Settlements: The Washington talks did not discuss evacuating settlements, but *Ha'aretz* said that, according to sources in Prime Minister Barak's office, all settlements not annexed will be evacuated.

Finality: Upon signing the agreement, both sides will declare "an end to the conflict." The agreement will be implemented in two stages, the first lasting three years and the second six years. When implementation is complete, the Palestinians will announce that they have no further claims against Israel.

A few days later, on December 28, Clinton told a Washington press conference: "I think that if it can be resolved at all, it can be resolved in the next three weeks. . . . I don't think the circumstances are going to get better. I think, that in all probability, they'll get more difficult."

Israeli Soldiers and Jewish Civilians Killed, September 27 – December 31, 2000

September 27 — Sgt. David Biri, 19, of Jerusalem, fatally wounded in a bombing near Netzarim in Gaza.

September 29 — Border Police Supt. Yossi Tabaja, 27, of Ramle, shot to death by his Palestinian counterpart on a joint patrol near Kalkilya.

October 1 — Border Police Cpl. Yusuf Madhat, 19, of Beit Jann, at Joseph's Tomb in Nablus.

October 2 — Wichlav Zalsevsky, 24, of Ashdod, shot in the head when he went to a West Bank village to get his car fixed; Sgt. Max Hazan, 20, of Dimona, shot in a gunfight near Beit Sahur, in the vicinity of Bethlehem.

October 8 — Hillel Lieberman, 36, of Elon Moreh, found dead near Nablus after he had walked into the Palestinian areas to protest the desecration of Joseph's Tomb by a Palestinian mob.

October 10 — Alon Zargari, 28, of Eli, north of Nablus, run over by a car driven by a Palestinian while he was standing at a hitchhiking station near the settlement.

October 12 — Prc. Sgt. Yosef Avrahami and Sgt. Vadim Nozich, 33, reserve IDF soldiers, lynched by a Palestinian mob at the Ramallah police station.

October 19 — Rabbi Binyamin Herling, 64, of Kedumim, killed in a gun battle after a group of settlers went on a tour to Mount Ebal near Nablus, and moved down the slopes of the mountain to vantage points where they could view Joseph's Tomb.

October 28 — The bullet-riddled body of Marik Gavrilov, 25, of Bene Ayish in the central part of the country, was found inside his burned-out car, between Bituniya and Ramallah on the West Bank. Apparently taken to Ramallah by a Palestinian friend, he was spotted by Palestinian gunmen and killed.

October 30 — Esh-Kodesh Gilmore, 25, of Mevo Modi'in, the village in Israel largely populated by followers of the late Rabbi Shlomo Carlebach, shot to death by an anonymous gunman while he was working as a security guard at the National Insurance Institute branch on busy Salah al-Din Street, in East Jerusalem; Amos Machlouf, 30, of the Gilo neighborhood in Jerusalem, found murdered in a ravine near Beit Jala.

November 1 — Lt. David-Hen Cohen, 21, of Karmiel, and Sgt. Shlomo Adshina, 20, of Kibbutz Tze'elim in the Negev, killed in a gun battle with Palestinians in the Al-Hader area, near Bethlehem; Maj. (res.) Amir Zohar, 34, of Jerusalem, killed in the Nahal Elisha settlement in the Jordan Valley while on active reserve duty.

November 2 — Ayelet Hashahar Levy, 28, and Hanan Levi, 33, killed in a car-bomb explosion near the Mahane Yehuda market in Jerusalem. The Islamic Jihad claimed responsibility.

November 8 — Noa Dahan, 25, of Moshav Mivtahim in the south, shot to death while driving to her job at the Rafah border crossing in Gaza.

November 10 — Sgt. Shahar Vekret, 20, of Lod, fatally shot by a Palestinian sniper near Rachel's Tomb at the entrance to Bethlehem.

November 12 — Sgt. Avner Shalom, 28, of Eilat, shot at the Gush Katif junction in the Gaza Strip.

November 13 — Sarah Leisha, 42, of the Neveh Tzuf settlement, killed by gunfire from a passing car while travelling near Ofra, north of Ramallah. Ariel Sarel, who was driving, described the incident: "We were driving in the car and talking about how we're like sitting ducks at the funfair, that every day people are being injured here, and the army doesn't react. And then a light [colored] Fiat Uno approached us and the shots were fired that killed Sarah"; Cpl. Elad Wallenstein, 18, of Ashkelon, and Cpl. Amit Zanna, 19, of Netanya, killed by shots from a passing car as they were traveling in an unarmored military bus taking them to guard duty at settlements in the Ofra area, not far from Ramallah; Gabi Zaghouri, 36, of Netivot, killed by gunfire directed at the truck he was driving near the Kissufim junction in the southern part of Gaza.

November 18 — Sgt. Baruch (Snir) Flum, 21, of Tel Aviv, shot by a Palestinian Preventive Security Service officer at the Kfar Darom greenhouses in southern Gaza. (Sgt. Sharon Shitoubi, 21, of Ramle, wounded in the same attack, died of his wounds on November 20. Shitoubi was one of the last soldiers to leave Lebanon in May, and was a central figure in a famous photograph of soldiers rejoicing at the end of the occupation of southern Lebanon.)

November 20 — Miriam Amitai, 35, and Gavriel Biton, 34, both of Kfar Darom, killed by a roadside bomb attack on a bus carrying children from Kfar Darom to school in another part of the Gush Katif settlement bloc, in Gaza.

November 21 — Itamar Yefet, 18, of Netzer Hazani, shot in the head by Palestinian sniper fire at the Gush Katif junction.

November 22 — Shoshana Reis, 21, of Hadera, and Meir Bahrame, 35, of Givat Olga, killed by a powerful car bomb detonated alongside a passing bus on Hadera's main street, when the area was packed with shoppers and people were driving home from work. Sixty people were wounded in the attack.

November 23—Sgt. Samar Hussein, 19, of Hurfeish, killed by Palestinian sniper fire at a patrol near the Erez crossing point, at the northern end of the Gaza Strip; Lt. Edward Matchnik, 21, of Beersheba, killed in an explosion at the district coordination office near Gush Katif in Gaza. (The joint Israeli-Palestinian DCOs, responsible for security coordination, had been established at the borders of Palestinian-ruled areas under the Oslo interim peace accords.)

November 24—Maj. Sharon Arameh, 25, of Ashkelon, killed by Palestinian sniper fire near Neve Dekalim in northern Gaza; Ariel Jeraffi, 40, of Petah Tikvah, a civilian employed by the IDF, killed by Palestinian fire in the West Bank.

December 8—Rina Didovsky, 39, a Beit Hagai school teacher on her way to work, and Eliyahu Ben-Ami, 41, of Otniel, the driver of the van, killed by fire from a passing car near Kiryat Arba, in the Hebron sector of the West Bank; Sgt. Tal Gordon, 19, killed as he headed home on a Tiberias-Jerusalem bus, by fire from a passing car on the Jericho bypass road.

December 21—Driving teacher Eliyahu Cohen, 29, of Modi'in, shot and killed by fire from an ambush a few kilometers west of Givat Ze'ev on Road 443, the secondary highway between Jerusalem and the coastal plain. After the incident and another shooting a week later, Israeli motorists stopped using the road, and the resulting increased traffic on the main Jerusalem-Tel Aviv highway caused massive traffic jams. Use of Road 443 remained low even after the army stationed tanks along the route.

December 28—Capt. Gad Marasha, 30, of Kiryat Arba, and Border Police Sgt.-Maj. Yonatan Vermullen, 29, of Ben-Shemen, killed when called to dismantle a roadside bomb near the Sufa crossing in Gaza. The Islamic Jihad claimed responsibility.

December 31—Binyamin Ze'ev Kahane, 34, son of the late right-wing leader Meir Kahane, and his wife, Talia, 31, killed by snipers on the Ramallah bypass road. Five of their children, aged two months to 10 years, were injured.

Investigation into Arab Deaths

During early October, Israeli Arabs in several northern towns blocked roads, threw stones, and burned tires to demonstrate solidarity with the actions of the Palestinians and to draw attention to what they viewed as Israel's discrimination against the country's Arab population. The protests came as a great shock to many Israeli Jews who had previously taken the loyalty of Israel's one million Arab citizens for granted. Police dealt with the situation by quickly resorting to their guns—in many instances eschewing the standard crowd-control responses of tear gas and water cannon—and killed 13 demonstrators. One of them was a young man from the town of Arabeh, who had been an activist in the "Seeds of Peace" youth movement that involved Israeli Arab and Jewish teenagers.

Almost immediately the families of the victims, Arab Knesset members, and some Israeli Jews as well charged the police with being too quick on the trigger. They pointed out that this was the first time that Israeli police had ever used large-scale firing of live ammunition against a protest by Israeli citizens, and, rather than reducing the violence, the police had caused it to escalate. Police officials, for their part, noted that the officers had been seriously outnumbered and, feeling that their lives were being threatened, they fired in self-defense.

The government initially launched a low-level probe of the killings. But it soon came to light that the police in the Northern District and their commander, Alik Ron, had previously been charged with excessive brutality against Israeli Arabs. Also, the performance of the police contrasted markedly with what happened in other locations where similar protests took place in October. In the Negev, there were major demonstrations by Bedouin in Rahat, Tel Sheva, and other towns. Although banks and other institutions were attacked and burned, no one was killed because the Southern District police commander worked with the local leadership of the towns in order to calm the demonstrators and restore order. In Haifa, Mayor Amram Mitzna went out into the streets beside the demonstrators, addressing the crowd and calling on the police not to use firearms.

The riots and the killings threatened to undermine the delicate fabric of Arab-Jewish coexistence in the Galilee, and, indeed, Arab-Jewish relations in the country as a whole. On November 8 the Barak government agreed to establish a formal commission of inquiry, to be chaired by Justice Theodor Or of the Supreme Court.

Other Developments

PHALCON DEAL CANCELED

The government of Israel announced on July 12 that it had canceled — under U.S. pressure — the sale of a $250-million AWACS-type aerial command post and reconnaissance plane to China. The U.S. government, and, most importantly, members of key congressional committees, had threatened to block U.S. aid to Israel if the sale of the aircraft, known as the Phalcon, was completed. The Americans claimed that the presence of such an advanced aircraft in Chinese hands would upset the balance of power in the China Straits, and might endanger U.S. forces involved in some future conflict between Taiwan and Beijing. Work on the aircraft had already been completed, and the plane — with sophisticated avionics from government-owned Israel Aircraft Industries (IAI), mounted on an Ilyushin airliner the Chinese had purchased from Russia — was parked in a corner of IAI's facilities at Ben-Gurion International Airport, waiting for a go-ahead. Also lost was the possible sale of another Phalcon to China, which would have represented an additional $250-million sale for IAI.

Barak had been under pressure for several months to cancel the Phalcon deal. But inside Israel there were sharp divisions over whether the delivery should go ahead. Those in favor said that the Americans had known about it for years, and were only raising objections now, when delivery was near, more for reasons of commercial rivalry than because of the plane's strategic importance. Those favoring cancellation said that important as it might be to IAI or Israeli economic interests, the sale could do irreparable damage to Israeli-American relations.

The Chinese demanded a refund of the $250 million they had paid for the plane, but sources at IAI said there had been no decision on where the money would come from. IAI subsequently lost out — to American contractors — on contracts for Phalcon-type aircraft for Australia and Turkey; some sources suggested that the cancellation of the Phalcon deal had been a factor in the decisions by Ankara and Canberra to purchase American planes.

MULTILATERALS RESUME

For the first time since they broke off in 1995, multilateral Middle East peace talks resumed in Moscow on February 1, with a meeting of the multinational steering committee. Members of the committee pledged to work for regional cooperation and to relaunch the four working groups dealing with development, the environment, Palestinian refugees, and water issues (only the water group had met, informally, during the more-than four years the talks had been suspended). There was no agreement, however, on whether to reconvene the fifth working group, the one on arms control.

Addressing the foreign ministers assembled at the session, U.S. secretary of state Albright said that world leaders "can sit on the sidelines and wait while opportunity after opportunity passes by the Middle East without stopping. We can watch this region of promise fall further behind and grow further apart. Or we can come together and do our part to assist the parties in building a comprehensive and lasting peace for the benefit of all." President Clinton, Albright went on to say, "has made clear that the choice of the United States is to help build peace and bring opportunity."

RAU'S DECLARATION

"I bow in humility before those murdered, before those who do not have graves where I can ask for forgiveness. I am asking for forgiveness for what Germans have done, for myself and my generation, for the sake of our children and grandchildren whose future I would like to see alongside the children of Israel." With those words German president Johannes Rau addressed the Knesset on February 16, as part of a historic visit to Israel. The German leader spent five days in Israel, touring holy sites and meeting government leaders.

POLITICS

The Road to Early Elections

Ehud Barak, elected prime minister by a comfortable margin in May 1999, had based his peace plans on building a broad coalition, including traditionally right-wing and Orthodox elements, in the Knesset. Over the course of 2000, however, he saw his government slowly crumble. This gradual process of dissolution culminated on December 10 with the calling of early elections for prime minister.

Often during the year Barak displayed what was generally seen as weakness, making a series of contradictory moves that his opponents—and some of his colleagues and staunch supporters as well—saw as a path of zigs and zags. At the same time, Barak reinforced his reputation as an autocrat, an army commander who gave orders and expected them to be carried out, unable, either due to his military background or perhaps because of a temperamental impatience, to engage in the give-and-take of the political process.

In early May, for example, after several months of debate, Barak's cabinet approved the recommendations of a committee headed by Avi Ben-Bassat, the director general of the Finance Ministry, for a major overhaul of the tax system. The goal was to ease the tax burden on the ordinary citizen while imposing levies on previously untaxed sources of income, such as earnings from the trading of shares on the stock market and gifts and inheritances, and closing the tax loopholes afforded by so-called "training funds" for employees, in which the employer deposits money allegedly for professional-advancement courses, but which can be withdrawn tax-free by the employee after seven years. Barak and Finance Minister Avraham Shochat enthusiastically backed the reform, launching a vigorous advertising campaign intended to convince the public that the changed tax rules would increase the average citizen's monthly income while marginally increasing the burden on better-off Israelis.

The plan failed to gain public support. Under pressure from the Histadrut trade union federation, which sought to preserve the untaxed status of the training funds, and business and commercial groups opposed to the gift and capital-gains taxes, Barak and Shochat—who at one stage said he would resign if the tax plan were not adopted in toto—decided in early August to "suspend" efforts to implement it. The tax plan was to be the final item on the agenda of the Knesset summer session, but Shochat, who had also declined to present the draft budget to the Knesset, said that it would not be presented. The Finance Committee chairman, MK Eli Goldschmidt (One Israel) said there was no reason to bring laws for a first reading until there was a stable government, because otherwise there was no chance of passage in committee. In November another bid to get a diluted form of tax reform through the Knesset failed when Shas threatened to make the measure a vote of no confidence in the government, and Shochat was forced to withdraw the proposal.

Over the first half of 2000—as had been the case for almost all of the first six months of his term in 1999—Barak was forced to mediate between two of his coalition partners. On the one hand was the left-leaning Meretz Party, led by Minister of Education Yossi Sarid, who insisted that funding for the Sephardi Orthodox Shas schools comply with all the standard requirements for governmental funding and allocation. Shas, on the other hand, wanted its deputy minister of education to have full authority over ultra-Orthodox education, a demand that Sarid refused.

On June 11 a bill to disband the Knesset and call early elections passed the Knesset. Among those voting for the bill were Shas, the National Religious Party and Yisrael ba'Aliya, all members of Barak's coalition. Barak declined to fire the four Shas ministers who violated coalition discipline by voting against the government (or, for that matter, the single ministers from each of the other two parties). Two days later, on June 13, the Shas Council of Sages, its governing body of rabbis, brought the simmering crisis to a head by deciding that the movement's ministers would tender their resignations at the cabinet meeting the following Sunday. The council's secretary, former MK Rabbi Rafael Pinhasi, said that his party did not feel it was a full partner in social and foreign policy, and expressed reservations over the financial recovery plan for the Shas education network, which needed 100 million shekels to cover accumulated debts. The Shas leader, Minister of Labor and Social Affairs Eli Yishai, took an even harder line, saying, "Shas has reached the end of the road in the coalition."

A little over a week later Barak made it clear that he would accede to Shas's demands even if it meant that Meretz—One Israel's natural ideological partner and ally in the election campaign—would leave the government. The difference, of course, was that unlike Shas, which was not ideologically committed to the government's peace policies, even if Meretz ministers Yossi Sarid (education), Haim Oron (agriculture), and Ran Cohen (industry and trade) would no longer hold portfolios, the party would have no choice but to continue to support the government in Knesset votes.

In late June, a few hours before their letters of resignation were due to take effect, the Shas ministers withdrew them under an agreement whereby Barak and Yossi Kucik, director general of the Prime Minister's Office, would supervise the Shas school network. Yishai said that Shas was not gloating over Meretz's departure from the cabinet. "The education of Jewish children is important to us. Security for the State of Israel is important to us. Social affairs are important to us. The fact that Sarid is not in the Ministry of Education is important for the Israeli nation and for the Jewish people," he said. Finance Minister Shochat justified the abandonment of Meretz. "In political life," he said, "there are moments when decisions must be taken. This is a difficult decision, that Meretz members are not to be in the government."

The breather, though, was short-lived. On July 8 Natan Sharansky resigned from the cabinet and took Yisrael ba'Aliya out of the coalition. Sharansky said he could no longer support Barak's diplomatic efforts. From the very start of the Barak government in the summer of 1999, the immigrant leader said, he had not felt he was part of the diplomatic process. Immediately after his resignation Sharansky told a rally against Camp David that Barak was going to Washington without broad backing from the coalition, let alone from the nation. For this reason, Sharansky added, there was a danger of a rift in the nation. "I tried to use my influence from the inside to promote the establishment of a national unity government. Having exhausted all means at my disposal, I'm planning to fight for this cause from the outside," Sharansky said.

On July 9, the next day, Shas and the National Religious Party left the coalition, with the five ministers of these two religious parties all handing in their resignations (see above, pp. 490–91). The NRP left because of Barak's negotiating stance, while Shas said it did not feel part of the current diplomatic process. However Shas leader Eli Yishai said that though in opposition, Shas would back the government if a "good" agreement were reached at Camp David. At the last minute Barak sent Communications Minister Binyamin Ben-Eliezer as an emissary to Rabbi Ovadia Yosef, the Shas spiritual leader. Ben-Eliezer sought, unsuccessfully, to persuade Rabbi Yosef to wait until after the Camp David summit before ordering the ministers to quit.

Meanwhile, Minister of Foreign Affairs Levy—who for some months had been advocating the forging of a national unity government encompassing the Likud, the party he and his Gesher movement left to join Barak's One Israel in 1999—said he would stay in Israel rather than accompany Barak to Camp David. Levy's announcement was construed as an expression of no confidence in Barak's handling of diplomatic matters. Thus when Barak left for Camp David on July 10 only a third of the 120-member Knesset supported his government. There was considerable talk of the possibility of a national unity government in the event that the summit failed.

On his return, Barak was hit by two serious political blows. First, the Knesset, in a surprise vote, defeated favored Labor/One Israel candidate Shimon Peres and elected the Likud's Moshe Katzav as president to succeed Ezer Weizman, who had resigned (see below). And on August 2 Levy resigned from the cabinet and the coalition, and voted for a bill that, on preliminary reading, called for early elections. This was one of the last bills passed before the end of the Knesset's summer session, and no further action could be taken on it until the parliament returned in October, after the High Holy Days.

On August 19 Barak drew the wrath of the already alienated religious and ultra-Orthodox parties by unveiling his blueprint for "civil reform" in Israel. The plan called for completion of Israel's constitution by passing four "basic laws," which, in the Israeli system, are equivalent to constitutional provisions. One spelled out the courts' powers of judicial review, and the three others specified individual rights, including the options of civil marriage and divorce, which would upset the status quo whereby matters of personal status were the domain of religious courts. Civil reform was also to include dismantling the Ministry of Religious Affairs, a stronghold of Shas in recent years and a vehicle for funding many projects of the Orthodox parties; universal national service for all Israelis, including both Israeli Arabs and ultra-Orthodox men and women; and requiring the teaching of English, mathematics, and civics in all government-funded schools, even the ultra-Orthodox ones where these subjects were not taught; and the operation of public transport—including El Al, the national air carrier—on the Sabbath and Jewish holidays.

Political observers saw these proposals as calculated to attract the support of the secular Russian voters of Sharansky's Yisrael ba'Aliya, an essential element in any possible coalition Barak might form in the absence of a peace breakthrough with the Palestinians. Ultra-Orthodox parties roundly condemned the initiative, seeing it as a threat to Israel's Jewishness. On September 25 Arye Deri, the former Shas leader, demonstrated the depth of ultra-Orthodox feeling against Barak's civil reform: "Barak is spreading hatred among the Israeli people. He is creating an atmosphere of hatred by secular Jews against us. He has broken all the rules that past prime ministers followed. We've never had a creature like this in Israel."

After beginning to dismantle the Religious Affairs Ministry, which was then under the jurisdiction of acting minister Haim Ramon, Barak backed down on his civil-reform plans in November as part of a deal in which Shas gave him a parliamentary "safety net" of support. The opposition painted the move as yet another of Barak's zigs and zags, and the public largely accepted this interpretation, which would gain even more credence at year's end when Barak resurrected civil reform to attract the Russian immigrant vote for the 2001 prime ministerial campaign.

Nor was Barak's cause helped by the resignations of two members of his inner circle. On August 21 Haim Mendel-Shaked, the prime minister's chief-of-staff, quit, just a few days after his deputy, Shimon Battat, left. Both men, longtime Barak associates from their army days, gave interviews to the press in which they criticized Barak for making too many decisions on his own, without consultation.

During the course of the three months of violence that began after Sharon's visit to the Temple Mount, Barak drew sharp criticism for his alleged inconsistency—announcing that Israel would not negotiate with the Palestinians as long as there was widespread violence in the territories while maintaining diplomatic contacts with them, and pulling back troops from advanced positions before the violence had really subsided. As terror mounted and more Israelis were killed in the territories, he was also criticized by settlers and members of the political right wing who claimed that the army was being unnecessarily and unwisely restrained from taking forceful action.

Almost immediately after the outbreak, Barak called on the Likud to join a government of national unity, or a limited-time emergency government. He launched talks with Likud opposition leader Sharon, which continued intermittently until early December. But while agreement seemed close on a number of issues, Barak steadfastly refused to give Sharon a veto over the government's negotiating positions. At the same time, most of the 19 Likud MKs were sharply critical of Sharon's participation in unity talks.

On November 29 Barak announced that he favored early elections but said that he would not resign. In reaction, Sharon voiced the view of many opposition members when he said: "We are witnessing an enormous effort by Barak, which will continue, to conclude a diplomatic document that he can flush out during the election campaign. The danger is that he may try to reach an agreement at all costs, and this will also affect the government's willingness to fight terrorism." Other Likud politicians, including former communications minister Limor Livnat, voiced a similar theme: Barak, they said, had no right to negotiate with the Palestinians because of his precarious political position and because his government was backed by little more than a quarter of the members of the Knesset. At a meeting of opposition MKs, Yosef (Tommy) Lapid, head of the anticlerical party Shinui (Change), who had often been courted by Barak for a "secular" coalition, suggested that the Knesset be dissolved before the December holiday of Hanukkah so that new elections could be held for both the Knesset and for prime minister. Referring to the raft of special-interest bills on the Knesset's agenda, Lapid declared that an election was needed "in order to put an end to the wasteful and populist legislation, which will only worsen in the coming weeks."

As opposition members sought to muster the 61 votes necessary to dissolve the Knesset, pressure for elections mounted. On Saturday night, December 9, Barak called a dramatic press conference to announce that he was resigning as prime minister. In such a case, under election law, a special election must be held for prime minister only, and not for the Knesset, within 60 days—and only sitting members of the Knesset were eligible to run. This would presumably exclude the candidacy of Benjamin Netanyahu, the former prime minister who had resigned his Knesset seat after losing the May 1999 election to Barak. Netanyahu, on a speaking tour in San Francisco, headed home to announce that he was a candidate anyway. "I am presenting my candidacy for the leadership of the Likud movement and for the leadership of the State of Israel," Netanyahu told a press conference at Jerusalem's King David Hotel a few hours after his plane had landed. He accused Barak of practicing "a transparent trick" by resigning. "When someone is afraid of a challenge, apparently he has a reason," said Netanyahu. At the time, opinion polls showed Barak running slightly ahead of Sharon, the Likud leader, but far behind Netanyahu. Netanyahu declared, though, that he would enter the race only on condition that there were elections for both the Knesset and the prime minister, and that would require the parliament to vote to dissolve itself. He noted the fractured state of the sitting Knesset, in which neither the Labor-led bloc nor the Likud could create an effective majority coalition.

Under those conditions, he said, no one elected in a special vote for prime minister only could hope to govern.

In response to Netanyahu's initiative, political moves were launched in the Knesset to help him. Yair Peretz, the Knesset whip of Shas, initiated what was called the "Netanyahu law," an amendment to Basic Law: Government, that would allow nonmembers of the Knesset to run in a special prime ministerial election. The bill was quickly pushed forward through parliamentary committee so that it could come up for a vote on December 18. At the same time Netanyahu supporters pressed the Knesset dissolution bill to meet Netanyahu's condition for running. The Likud scheduled its primaries to choose a prime ministerial candidate—only Sharon, the sitting party leader, and Netanyahu were running—for December 19, the day after the Knesset vote. On the night of December 18, the two bills came up for a final vote. The "Netanyahu law" passed 65-40, with four abstentions. But, with the support of Shas and Labor, the Knesset voted down the bill to dissolve itself, 69-49. With only the prime minister's position at stake in the election, Netanyahu, true to his promise, withdrew from the Likud leadership ballot, leaving Sharon as the sole candidate. At the same time, the former prime minister vowed to return to the political wars.

On December 21, after polls suggested that he could defeat Sharon in a race for prime minister, Shimon Peres sought to become a third candidate in the race, representing the left-wing Meretz party. Meretz, though, declined to sponsor a Peres candidacy. With only Barak and Sharon left in the running, public-opinion polls showed a widening gap in favor of the Likud challenger. At year's end, most surveys showed Sharon leading Barak by around 20 percentage points.

A New President

Fifty-five-year-old Moshe Katzav was installed as Israel's eighth president on August 1 after winning a surprise victory over former prime minister Shimon Peres in a special election by the Knesset. Born in Mashhad, Iran, Katzav became the first head of state from "the second Israel," the immigrants from Middle Eastern countries who came to Israel in the early years of the state and who, by and large, had occupied the lower end of the socioeconomic scale through the country's 52 years of statehood.

Katzav replaced Ezer Weizman, who resigned under pressure after it had been disclosed that he accepted illegal contributions from French Jewish businessman Edouard Saroussi. The Weizman affair came to light in early January, when investigative journalist Yoav Yitzhak, a gadfly known for his clashes with members of the Israeli establishment, called an unusual press conference. Yitzhak disclosed that between 1988 and 1993, when Weizman had been a member of the Knesset and a cabinet minister, he had received a total of about $450,000 in regular cash payments from Saroussi, who lived in France but was of Sudanese origin. Weizman responded that the payments were legitimate gifts from a personal friend, unconnected to any business interests in Israel. It subsequently emerged, however, that Saroussi and Weizman had been partners in some lucrative arms deals, mainly in Latin America, in the early 1980s.

On January 20 the attorney general, Elyakim Rubinstein, ordered a full criminal inquiry into the Weizman affair, saying his office had found evidence of the business relationship between the two men. Weizman, in response, said he would "fight for the truth to the end" and would never resign the presidency. A police report released in early April concluded that Weizman had committed fraud and breach of trust by accepting unauthorized funds from both Saroussi and Israeli businessman Rami Ungar and not reporting them to the tax authorities. But it said that the president could not be indicted for the crimes because there was insufficient evidence to prove criminality and because the statute of limitations on some of the offenses had expired.

As public pressure continued to mount—including charges that Weizman, an Ashkenazi Jew, was being treated lightly for ethnic reasons, while the state had pushed forward with the prosecution and conviction of Arye Deri, the former leader of the ultra-Orthodox Sephardi Shas party—the president continued to insist that he would stay in office until the end of his term. But on May 28 Weizman said that he would step down as head of state on July 10. He explained that, because of the state of his health, he had long intended to leave office before his term was due to expire in 2003.

The Knesset scheduled an election for August 1 to name Weizman's successor. In the interim between Weizman's departure from office on July 10 and the installation of the new president, Knesset speaker Avraham Burg—who, under law, would have been in line to succeed the president—served as interim president. After some internal jockeying, the Likud's Moshe Katzav and Shimon Peres, of Prime Minister Barak's One Israel/Labor Party, emerged as the main candidates for the vacated presidency. At one stage there were efforts to convince Meir Shamgar, the retired president of Israel's Supreme Court, to stand for the traditionally nonpartisan office, largely because both Katzav and Peres were long-time political figures with clear partisan records. But the Shamgar candidacy fizzled as the former judge insisted that he would only put his hat into the ring if he were already assured a majority of the votes in the 120-member legislature.

Throughout the campaign Peres and his supporters maintained that they had been assured the support of more than 61 members of the 120-seat Knesset, and were therefore certain that the former prime minister and Nobel Peace Prize laureate, then serving as minister for regional cooperation in the Barak government, would be elected. But when the ballots were counted it was Katzav who emerged victorious, 63-57. After the surprise vote, angry Peres supporters and the press suggested that Peres, who had allegedly been promised at least five Shas votes, had been deliberately deceived by the 17-member Shas delegation in the Knesset, which had been given the freedom to vote for the candidate of their choice by both Rabbi Ovadia Yosef, the Shas spiritual leader, and by the movement's

Council of Torah Sages. Shas spokesmen insisted that their people had kept all of their promises in the secret ballot and suggested that Peres's defeat was due to defectors from Barak's ruling coalition, including the core Labor Party, who had voted for Katzav. Credit for Katzav's surprise victory was generally given to the new president himself, a veteran political figure who had launched his career in his early twenties as mayor of his hometown, Kiryat Malachi, and had served as a cabinet minister in successive Likud governments—most recently as tourism minister in Benjamin Netanyahu's 1996–99 cabinet. Meanwhile, Likud leader Ariel Sharon led members of his party in presenting the Katzav victory as an unofficial no-confidence vote against the Barak government.

During the election campaign Katzav had promised to be a nonpartisan president. But in the months after he took office the new president drew criticism from members of the Israeli left for statements they saw as having a partisan nature, including expressions of support for the continuation of the controversial Jewish settlement in the heart of the West Bank city of Hebron.

ECONOMIC DEVELOPMENTS

Rapid Growth, then Slowdown

Despite a downturn in the fourth quarter, when the security situation began to deteriorate, 2000 was one of the best years in Israel's economic history. But as the year drew to an end, it became clear that the emergence from the 1997–99 recession was going to be short-lived, and that the country's economy was on the verge of slipping back into yet another recession.

In economic terms, 2000 consisted of two distinctive "years"—the nine-month period from January to September, which saw stunning growth rates averaging around 8 percent of the GDP (gross domestic product), and the three months October through December, which saw a sharp decline in almost all economic indicators. Third-quarter growth was 9 percent, the highest in the history of the Israeli economy, following growth rates of 6.5 percent in the first quarter and 8 percent in the second. In the fourth quarter, however, GDP declined by 8 percent, the largest decline, in percentage terms, since the Gulf War in 1991.

According to most estimates, the ongoing violence cost the economy as much as $750 million during the last three months of the year. When looked at as a whole, however, the statistics were deceptively positive. GDP for the year, according to the Central Bureau of Statistics, amounted to 448 billion shekels, or slightly more than $110 billion. Annual GDP stood at 5.9 percent, up from 1999's 2.3 percent. (The latter figure, it should be noted, probably represented negative economic growth, since Israel's population increased by 2–2.5 percent.) Even more impressive was the growth of the GDP of the business sector, which rose by 7 percent in 2000 after increasing by only 2 percent in 1999. The acceleration in the business product, though, was due largely to the sale of Israeli companies to foreign companies, mainly in the high-tech sector, which contributed about 3 percent to business product growth.

Per capita GDP rose to a record $17,700, an increase of 3.4 percent, following two years of stagnation or worse in this key indicator. (In 1999 per capita GDP declined by 0.2 percent, after registering no change in 1998.)

The value of exports increased over 25 percent to about $28 billion. Some 40 percent of all exports came from the growing high-tech sector, with diamonds and agriculture also figuring prominently. Export figures included the proceeds of several sales of Israeli start-up companies to foreign buyers. The biggest of such sales was that of Chromatis, a maker of optical networking equipment, to international giant Lucent, in a share deal valued, at the time of the transaction in July, at $4.8 billion. The valuation of that deal declined sharply as the year progressed, as the price of Lucent shares went down.

Industrial product increased by 10.3 percent in 2000, after rising by only 1.2 percent in 1999. The continued stunning growth of the high-tech sector caused a 12-percent rise in the trade-and-commodities statistic, slightly better than the 10-percent increase for this indicator in the preceding year. The number of employed grew by 4.1 percent, amounting to nearly 100,000 new jobs. More importantly, this figure was higher than the rate of population increase for the year, which was 2.4 percent. As a consequence, the proportion of the total population in the work force grew from 53.8 percent in 1999 to 54.6 percent in 2000. But unemployment was 8.8 percent for the year, down only 0.1 percent from 1999.

According to the Finance Ministry's original projections, unemployment—a so-called "lagging indicator" that traditionally falls as much as a year after the economy begins to improve—should have begun dropping in the middle of 2000. Yet even though the economy, as noted above, produced new jobs at a higher rate than that of population increase, the sharp drop in unemployment failed to materialize because an increasing number of women, new immigrants, and non-Jews (Arabs and Druze) joined the labor force, attracted by the positive atmosphere of the first three quarters, and because of increases in productivity.

Declining Deficit

The government's deficit for 2000 was far lower than expected, due largely to unexpectedly large tax collections during the first three quarters, when there was a great deal of economic activity. (The tax burden for the country, including various levies and duties, rose to 41.5 percent of GDP in 2000, compared to 39 percent in 1999. This increase of 2.5 percent of GDP represented about 11 billion shekels [$2.2 billion] more in tax revenue.) The deficit amounted to 2.8 billion shekels (about $680 million), compared to original projections of 10.9 billion shekels ($2.7 billion). Thus the deficit amounted to 0.6 percent of GDP, as compared to the 2.5 percent target set when the budget was passed early in 2000. The total government deficit was even lower than the 2.25 percent posted in 1999, and put the government well ahead of the European Union's recommendations for gradual budget reduction, as enshrined in the EU's Maastricht agreement of the mid-1990s.

But the government deficit rose during the months of November and December as the economy showed increasing signs of slowing down, tax collections became smaller, and outlays for defense and security increased. The deficit for that two-month period was 3.25 billion shekels, and this prevented the government from enjoying a budget surplus for the year.

The unrest in the territories caused defense expenditures to rise by 3 billion shekels (about $750 million), of which 2 billion were spent to finance the withdrawal from Lebanon and the construction of a new security fence and other defenses along the northern border.

Zero Inflation, Lower Interest

Israel had zero inflation in 2000. The Consumer Price Index (CPI) declined by 0.1 percent in December, culminating a moderate decline that saw the CPI fall, in nominal terms, by 2 percent in the last four months of 2000. But despite the zero inflation—second lowest in the world after Japan, which had -7 percent as its consumer price index—it was not the lowest inflation in Israeli history. That distinction went to 1950, two years after the establishment of the state, when the CPI fell by 6.6 percent. The year with the highest inflation was 1984, when the CPI soared by 444.9 percent; in 1979–85, the hyperinflationary period before extensive economic reforms began the process of shaping Israel into a modern, Western-style, free-market economy, inflation reached a cumulative 1,298 percent.

The Bank of Israel continued to reduce the interest rate on its monetary loans during 2000. The rate went from 13.5 percent in December 1998 to 11.2 percent in December 1999 and to 8.2 percent in December 2000. Some industrialists and political figures said the reductions were too conservative and that more rapid lowering of interest rates would stimulate the slowing economy, but the central bank defended its incremental approach on the grounds that it was consistent with the achievement of the government's multiyear inflation target, which was 2–3 percent annually. The representative rate of the shekel on the last trading day of 2000 was 4.1726 against the currency basket, denoting an appreciation of 5.5 percent during the year, and 4.041 against the dollar, an annual appreciation of 2.7 percent, 9.8 percent against the euro, and 13.5 percent against the Japanese yen. Conversion of dollars, drawn by relatively high interest rates over the year, were a major reason for the currency's strength. Israel's foreign exchange reserves totaled $22.9 billion at the end of December, $1.2 billion more than at the end of

November, mainly due to the receipt of civilian aid from the U.S. government. Civilian aid, which was being phased out at the rate of $120 million a year, had been granted to Israel since the mid-1970s to service debts incurred during the period when the United States made foreign-aid loans to Israel, rather than direct grants, to finance the purchase of military equipment.

Exports Up, Investment High

Total exports reached the $28-billion level, with industrial exports (excluding diamonds) increasing by 32 percent to $20.9 billion in 2000. The growth rate of high-tech exports fell from 16 percent in the second quarter to 6 percent in the third quarter and 3.5 percent in the fourth quarter.

According to Bank of Israel figures, foreign residents' investments in shares of Israeli companies totaled a record $7 billion in 2000, continuing 1999's rapid growth. After the surge in overseas-share issues by Israeli companies in the first four months of 2000, particularly on U.S. stock exchanges, the volume of new issues declined in the United States as more Israeli companies sought to have their shares traded on one of the new European exchanges devoted to technology.

High-tech companies raised a record $3.1 billion for the whole of 2000, which was 207 percent higher than in 1999, when just over $1 billion was invested. But venture-capital investment in Israel fell in the last quarter of the year. From October through December investment was 18 percent lower than in the previous quarter, although it still totaled $845 million, invested in 193 companies. One worrying sign was that Israeli funds invested $343 million, or 41 percent of the total, in the fourth quarter, up from 30 percent in the third quarter. This signified a decline in foreign interest in Israeli companies. While one key factor was a change in investor attitude in the aftermath of several major declines in the value of all shares on NASDAQ, the New York exchange that had emerged as the main market for technology shares, it also reflected, albeit to a lesser extent, investor concern over the security situation in Israel.

The average amount of capital raised by an Israeli high-tech company in 2000 was $6 million, double the figure raised, on average, in 1999. Most remarkable in terms of investment in 2000 was the communications sector, which accounted for 40 percent of all capital raised, up from 29 percent in 1999. No less than 137 communications companies raised a total of $1.248 billion in 2000, at an average of $9.1 million per company, as compared to $4.6 million in 1999.

Another sector registering sharp growth was biotechnology, which many investors had ignored during the Internet investment boom years. A survey published by the Business Data Israel (BDI) research firm showed Israel in third place in the world in the number of biotechnology start-ups. The number of such start-ups reached a record 96 in 2000, while the total number of biotechnology companies in Israel grew from 135 in 1999 to 160 in 2000. In 1988 there had been only 25 such firms in Israel.

Tourism's Woes

The good news for tourism in 2000, like that for the entire Israeli economy, was mixed with a very large dose of bad news. A record of 2.67 million visitors entered, 4 percent higher than 1999 when 2.4 million came. But this number was significantly lower than the 3–3.5 million tourists expected for what was, to the Christian world, the millennium year.

According to the Central Bureau of Statistics, there was a 25-percent increase in tourism from January to the end of September. But the final three months of the year brought only 314,000 tourists, down 54 percent from the 523,000 arrivals in the corresponding period in 1999. Tourist-nights in hotels showed a similar trend, rising by 7 percent for the year for a total of 9.7 million. However, average room occupancy declined 2 percent, according to figures released by the Israel Hotel Association's economics department, because of an increase in the number of rooms available. The figures for 2000 also showed that prior to the outbreak of disturbances, tourist-nights at hotels rose sharply, by 32 percent, but that fourth-quarter figures were 51 percent below the figures for 1999. The declines were felt through most of the country, with the exceptions of the Dead Sea and Eilat, which posted more moderate declines.

At the same time, tourism by Israelis grew. Israeli tourist-nights increased by 13 percent for the year. The biggest rise was in Tel Aviv (30 percent), followed by Eilat (24 percent), Herzliya (17 percent), and the Dead Sea and Haifa (10 percent each). The Israel Hotel Association attributed the increase to sales campaigns and large discounts offered to Israelis.

But prospects for the tourism industry were not good. Preliminary Ministry of Tourism estimates projected that there would be only 1.8 million tourists in 2001, the lowest figure in a decade. As one indicator of the trend, industry sources noted that tourist-nights fell by 45 percent to only 336,000 in December. The sharpest decreases came in Tiberias, which had long been a popular northern winter tourist spot (-68 percent), followed by Jerusalem (-61 percent), and Nazareth (-58 percent). There were also reports of closings and staff cutbacks at as much as a third of the hotels in the country, and of employees working short workweeks in order to preserve some jobs. It was generally accepted, in late December, that even more layoffs could be expected and that some hotels would be forced to close down even if there were a dramatic improvement in the security situation. Industry sources pointed out that it takes several months, or even more, for tourist bookings to pick up, noting that the slump after the end of the 1991 Gulf War lasted more than a year.

Particularly hard hit were the hotels in East Jerusalem, run by Palestinians. The Israel Hotel Association reported in late December that 29 of the 31 hotels that were in the eastern part of town at the beginning of 2000 had closed down.

A relatively new form of tourism, Birthright Israel, was granted support by the government of Israel. Devised in 1998 by American Jewish philanthropists

Charles Bronfman and Michael Steinhardt, it brought North American Jewish teenagers on an all-expense-paid ten-day trip to Israel with the hope that these young people would return as more committed Jews and dedicated advocates for Israel. In a ceremony at the Knesset building on June 29, a five-year funding plan was announced: The main contributors—the government of Israel, American Jewish fund-raising organizations, and private donors headed by Bronfman and Steinhardt—would each contribute $70 million to the landmark project. More than 10,000 young Jews had already visited through Birthright Israel.

The Klein Appointment

David Klein was appointed governor of the Bank of Israel on January 9, 2000, a post carrying with it the responsibility of economic adviser to the government. Klein replaced Jacob Frenkel, the head of Israel's central bank since the early 1990s. Frenkel had come under sharp criticism from industrialists and economists who complained about his restrictive monetary policies and refusal to make significant reductions in the interest rate. Nevertheless, Prime Minister Barak and Finance Minister Shochat chose Klein, also known as a strict monetarist, to the governorship.

Klein surprised many observers by cutting the interest rate by 3.2 percent over the course of 2000, culminating in a 0.2-percent reduction at the end of January, the sixth consecutive month in which interest was cut. The reduction was possible, central bank sources emphasized, because inflationary expectations for 2001 remained low. But those same inflationary expectations meant that the real interest rate—the gap between basic interest, 8 percent in December, and the expectations for inflation—was still about 6.5 percent.

Assessing the state of the economy in a report to the Knesset at year's end, Klein indicated that a further fall in the world's capital markets could upset Israel's market and financial stability, and that therefore he would continue a cautious interest-rate policy. This went against recommendations from his critics to speed up the lowering of interest rates for either economic or political reasons, such as shocks in the world financial markets (particularly NASDAQ), the disturbances in the territories, domestic political instability, and early elections. "The gradual process of reducing the interest rate stems from the need to examine market response following each reduction, and prevent as much as possible sharp changes in the interest rate that could harm the functioning of the markets," he stated in the report.

One of the reasons Klein was able to persist in his moderate interest policy over the course of the year appears to have been the long-term stability of the risk premium for the country on international markets. The ten-year risk premium increased from 1.8 percent in September, before the outbreak of the disturbances in the West Bank and Gaza, to a very high 3.2 percent in October. But then it began to fall, reaching 1.9 percent in December. According to a Bank of Israel review, "It is important to closely follow Israel's risk premium, since a sudden rise indicates a problem. A rise in the risk premium is likely to lead foreign investors to change the Israeli assets-and-components mix in their portfolios, which would immediately affect the exchange rate and price levels" in Israel itself.

RELIGION

Religion and State

The perennial questions revolving around the relationship between religion and state in Israel declined in relative importance in 2000 as attention focused on the Barak government's peace-process diplomacy, the outbreak of a new cycle of violence, and the call for new elections. The primary issue of religious interest during the year was the controversy over the Barak coalition's proposed civil reform program (see above), but other matters involving religion also made news.

In mid-July a Jerusalem rabbinical court accepted as converts to Judaism the first three graduates of a joint Orthodox-Reform-Conservative conversion institute. Many considered the willingness of the Orthodox court to recognize the Jewishness of converts not trained under strict Orthodox supervision to be a major breakthrough in the direction of loosening the Orthodox monopoly over the determination of Jewish identity in Israel. Prof. Benjamin Ish-Shalom, head of the institute, himself an Orthodox Jew, said: "We have proved that the rabbinic courts will convert our graduates. . . . because for them the issue is the individual they are converting and not where the individual studied." In 1998 the Chief Rabbinate had rejected a package of proposals, including such a conversion institute, put forward by a committee headed by former finance minister Ya'akov Ne'eman. The proposals were designed to solve the problem of about 250,000 non-Jewish immigrants, mostly from the former Soviet Union and many of them married to Jews, who were living in Israel (see AJYB 1999, p. 469). Despite the cold shoulder from the Chief Rabbinate and doubts harbored by the non-Orthodox movements about whether the graduates would have their conversions accepted, the government had gone ahead anyway and established the institute to conduct conversion classes around the country.

As the year ended, the Supreme Court had not yet ruled on an appeal by Attorney General Elyakim Rubinstein to review a landmark ruling, handed down in May, allowing a group called the Women of the Wall to hold full prayer services, complete with Torah readings and the wearing of tallitot (prayer shawls), at the Western Wall plaza in Jerusalem's Old City. Over the years attempts by women to conduct such services there had triggered verbal and physical attacks by Orthodox Jews who considered these activities by women to be against Jewish law.

Another longstanding matter of controversy was the exemption of yeshivah students from military service. On July 3 the Knesset voted on the first reading of a bill that would set up procedures for drafting yeshivah students into the army. This legislation was based on the recommendations of the Tal Commission, which had been formed to devise a response to a Supreme Court decision declaring that the existing blanket exemptions of yeshivah students had no basis in law. Ultra-Orthodox elements were furious that the Likud and its leader, Ariel Sharon, allowed the party's Knesset members freedom to vote as they pleased on the bill, and pledged revenge. Despite heavy pressure from the Orthodox and ultra-Orthodox, Prime Minister Ehud Barak's One Israel voted for the bill, which passed on first reading by 52-43, with seven abstentions. But the law did not achieve final passage. On December 20 the Knesset voted simply to extend the existing system of draft deferments for yeshivah students, with Sharon voting to extend the exemption and Barak voting to end it.

The Ultra-Orthodox

Early in the year, Minister of Education Yossi Sarid antagonized the ultra-Orthodox by refusing to give his Shas deputy significant duties in the ministry and by insisting that schools in the Shas network follow the same financial and academic standards — including class size and teacher qualifications — as the rest of the state-funded schools, including those of the "state religious" Zionist Orthodox (see above). In his pre-Purim sermon in March, Shas spiritual mentor Rabbi Ovadia Yosef verbally attacked Sarid, the leader of the secular, left-leaning Meretz. Yosef declared: "Yossi Sarid is evil. The Holy One blessed be He will obliterate his name from the world. Yossi Sarid is Haman, may his name and memory be wiped out. . . . He is Satan. . . . God will destroy him as He destroyed Amalek." After several months of investigation, Attorney General Rubinstein decided in September not to bring criminal charges against the rabbi for incitement to do bodily harm.

Even so, the very fact that the attorney general, himself a modern Orthodox Jew, had launched the investigation evoked strong criticism from Shas. "Rubinstein is a dangerous Jew who stabbed his rabbi and sold his religion for a seat on the Supreme Court," charged Rabbi Moshe Maya, a member of Shas's Council of Torah Sages. Despite the investigation and in the face of widespread criticism from those outside ultra-Orthodox circles, Rabbi Yosef continued making controversial statements, suggesting that those who died in the Holocaust had had to pay for sins committed by their souls in previous incarnations, and commenting, on Barak's concessions to the Palestinians at Camp David: "He doesn't have any sense, this person. He is going to give them a part of the Old City. . . . The Ishmaelites are all cursed evildoers, Israel-haters. The Holy One, blessed be He, regrets having made these Ishmaelites."

Three ultra-Orthodox men were arrested on July 27 in connection with the June arson at the Ya'ar Ramot Masorti (Conservative) congregation in the Ramot neighborhood of Jerusalem. Windows at the synagogue were broken and burning rags were thrown into the sanctuary, setting several chairs on fire. The blaze had been spotted and put out before it reached the Torah ark. A few days after the attack, Minister for Diaspora Affairs Michael Melchior visited the synagogue and rabbis of all the movements, including the Orthodox, denounced the attack. The arrested men had not yet gone to trial as the year ended.

Papal Visit

Pope John Paul II expressed his profound sorrow and apologized to Jews for "acts of persecution and anti-Semitism" against the Jews by Christians "at any time in any place," during a stop at the Yad Vashem Holocaust memorial on March 23. The visit was part of a six-day trip by the ailing pontiff to Israel and the Palestinian territories on March 20–26. Prime Minister Barak called the visit to Yad Vashem a "climax to this historic journey of healing."

The pontiff also prayed at the Western Wall and conducted a Mass for the thousands of pilgrims who came to the Holy Land from around the world to be there during his historic visit. He met with Yasir Arafat in Bethlehem, the traditional city of Jesus's birth, where the pontiff referred to the suffering of the Palestinians and told his audience that they had "a natural right to a homeland . . . " and that their "torment" had gone on too long.

There was little that was new in anything the Pope said about Jews and about Christianity's historical record. Nevertheless, the visits to the Western Wall and Yad Vashem served to communicate his message to millions of the Catholic faithful around the world and to the Jews of Israel. The pope drove home the Vatican's positive view of the Jewish people, referring to Jews as "the dearly beloved elder brothers of the original covenant, never revoked by God." Perhaps the most moving message was the one the pontiff left on a piece of paper he placed between the stones of the Western Wall on March 26: "God of our fathers. You chose Abraham and his descendants to bring Your name to the nations. We are deeply saddened by those who in the course of history have caused these children of Yours to suffer. And asking Your forgiveness, we wish to commit ourselves to genuine brotherhood with the people of the Covenant. Signed: John Paul II."

Even though almost a decade had passed since the establishment of diplomatic relations between Israel and the Vatican, many Israeli Jews had been unaware, before the visit, that the Roman Catholic Church had dropped its attitude of hostility towards Jews and Israel. Proof of the visit's impact came with the distribution of a Ministry of Education circular to all schools encouraging discussion of the changes that had taken place in the Roman Catholic-Jewish dialogue, particularly since John Paul II assumed the papacy.

OTHER DOMESTIC MATTERS

Demography

At the end of 2000 Israel had a population of 6,364,000, according to Central Bureau of Statistics estimates. Of these, 4,952,200, over 80 percent, were Jews. During the year there were 136,251 births—92,021 Jews, 35,626 Muslims, 2,777 Christians, and 2,705 Druze. There were 37,596 deaths—33,364 Jews, 4,232 Muslims, 2,661 Christians, and 732 Druze. The immigration figure for 2000, the lowest in 11 years, was 60,130, a 22-percent decrease from the 76,766 people who came in 1999. The drop was attributed to a decline in immigration from the former Soviet Union both because of a perception that the situation there was stabilizing and also because of the violence in Israel at the end of the year.

The number of road accidents fell from over 22,000 in 1999 to 19,925 in 2000. The number of fatal accidents, however, rose slightly from 1999's 414 to 421 in 2000. Even so, the number of fatalities in those accidents (461) and the number of seriously injured (2,896), were down sharply from 1999, when the figures were, respectively, 471 and 3,111. The drop was even more impressive when compared to the peak year of 1998, when there were 548 dead and 3,374 seriously hurt.

Violence on the Rise

President Moshe Katzav said on December 14 that he would "never even discuss" the pardon of a man who had killed his wife or children. Katzav said that "this type of crime is so serious that it never deserves a pardon, under any circumstances." He made the statement at the end of a week when three women were brutally murdered by the men in their lives: Tzahala Gelfand of Bene Beraq, strangled to death by her husband Roni, who in 1994 had been given a suspended sentence for beating her; Natalya Psimanyuk, stabbed to death with a shoemaker's knife; and Shoshana Huta, battered to death in front of her three-year-old son.

Though horrifying, the week's incidents were not exceptional, as both violent crime and domestic violence had been on the rise for a decade. From 1990 to late 2000, over 200 husbands had killed their wives or children. Violent domestic crime in 1999, the last year for which statistics were available, had reached some 4,000 reported cases, up from 3,000 for 1998 and 1,600 in both 1996 and 1997.

There were also other signs that Israel was becoming a more violent society. In 1999 police received reports of 35,465 violent crimes of all kinds—including murder and robbery—a figure that had been steadily increasing since 1990, when 13,300 violent crimes were reported. Some observers felt that much of the increase, particularly in domestic violence, was due to the new immigrant populations. However others suggested that a high level of violence in the family had been present for decades, but that greater awareness and more publicity of earlier cases made the reporting of such incidents more likely now.

Knesset member Yael Dayan, long a leader in the fight for Israeli women's rights, argued that the outbreak of Palestinian violence was no reason to turn a blind eye to increased domestic violence. "The political situation," Dayan said, "is not reason to give murderers, rapists, and sex criminals a break." President Katzav, for his part, called on the entire legal and law enforcement system "to think hard and concentrate efforts to deal with this horrible phenomenon." He conceded the need for stiffer penalties for men who kill their wives or children, but declined to recommend capital punishment. At the end of the year, Na'amat, the women's organization affiliated with the Histadrut trade union federation, pressed forward with a bill that would increase the penalty for stalking a woman or threatening her privacy, income, property, or reputation to a maximum of ten years in prison.

Torture Report

The Shin Bet internal security service had systematically tortured Palestinian prisoners and lied about the use of such extreme force from 1987 to 1993, according to the summary of a report by former state comptroller Miriam Ben-Porat. The report, presented to the Knesset in 1995, had been kept secret until February 9, 2000, when the Knesset subcommittee on intelligence released a nine-page summary.

One important specific determination was that in the Gaza Strip, then under Israeli control, the Shin Bet had carried out "severe and systematic violations" of the rules set up in 1987 by a commission headed by former Supreme Court justice Moshe Landau that allowed the use of only "moderate physical pressure," and even that only against people suspected of being involved in imminent terror attacks against Israeli targets. The Supreme Court banned the use of even such moderate force in September 1999, when it ruled that the Landau standard was a violation of human rights.

Land Sales to Arabs

The Supreme Court ruled on March 8 that the state could not allocate land strictly to Jews on the basis of religion, or act to prevent the sale of land to Arab citizens because they were Arabs. The decision came in response to a petition by Adel Kadan and his wife Iman, who had applied for a building plot in the town of Katzir, in northern Israel, but were turned down by the Jewish Agency, the town's developer. Kadan and his wife, both professionals, said that the standard of living and lifestyle of Jewish Katzir was closer to their own than what was available in the Arab town of Baka al-Gharbiya, where they lived. But the Jewish Agency rejected them, saying the town was only for Jews. Civil rights activists hailed the decision as a landmark, an important step towards achieving equality for Israel's Arab citizens.

Nuclear Debate

The Knesset held its first-ever debate on Israel's nuclear-weapons program on February 2, after Issam Mahlul, a member from the mixed Arab-Jewish Hadash Party (Democratic Front for Peace and Equality), threatened to petition the Supreme Court. Twenty right-wing members walked out of the Knesset plenum in protest after Speaker Avraham Burg authorized the debate to take place.

Mahlul, speaking to the Knesset, charged that Israel — with the help of South Africa — had stockpiled as many as 300 nuclear bombs, planned to adapt some of its submarines to carry nuclear materials, and had exported nuclear waste to Mauritania. Israel, according to Mahlul, had established nuclear missile sites near Kfar Zecharia, a town not far from Jerusalem, and in the Galilee. He also accused Israel of producing biological weapons.

NPO Inquiry

On January 27 State Comptroller Eliezer Goldberg issued a strongly worded report accusing Ehud Barak's One Israel, and, to a lesser extent, other parties, of violating campaign-financing laws. According to the report — which in fact substantiated allegations made by Likud Knesset members, particularly former science minister Michael Eitan, since shortly after the May 1999 elections — Barak's campaign had funneled illegal foreign campaign donations through a number of nonprofit organizations (NPOs), which then used the funds for campaign purposes. Attorney General Elyakim Rubinstein ordered a police inquiry into the allegations, which involved several figures very close to Barak himself, including lawyer Yitzhak Herzog, the cabinet secretary during the Barak administration, and Barak's brother-in-law, Doron Cohen.

Barak said that he did not know NPOs had been involved in raising funds for his campaign, and that he was not involved, during the 1999 campaign, in the activities of any such organizations. Cohen refused to answer police questions during his interrogation, citing the right against self-incrimination. The state comptroller said that in January 1999 Cohen registered a not-for-profit organization, Our Israel-Our One Israel, which later became the basis for Barak to form his One Israel bloc out of the old Labor Party and other political elements, including David Levy's Gesher, and Meimad, a moderate modern Orthodox party whose main figures included both Barak's minister for diaspora affairs, Michael Melchior, and Hebrew University professor Avi Ravitzky.

Police also questioned Herzog under warning on two occasions, and he too refused to answer questions. In late December the police gave the results of their investigation to Attorney General Rubinstein and subsequently to Shmuel Hollander, the civil service commissioner, to determine whether criminal charges could be filed against Herzog and whether he should be suspended from his post until the investigation was completed. According to press reports not officially confirmed, there was sufficient evidence to support allegations that Herzog raised millions of dollars from overseas donors prior to the 1999 campaign.

Deri Goes to Jail

About 10,000 demonstrators and supporters accompanied former Shas leader Arye Deri to Ma'siyahu prison in the town of Ramle in central Israel on September 3 as Deri began his three-year sentence for bribery and fraud (see AJYB 2000, pp. 476–77). Speaking to the assembled multitude, Deri asked for forgiveness. But other Shas leaders who were there pressed the line that their party's former strongman had been the victim of ethnic discrimination against Jews of Sephardi or Middle Eastern origin, pointing out that Deri was serving three years for allegedly accepting about $100,000, while former president Ezer Weizman, who had admitted to taking much more, had gone to his home in Caesarea rather than to prison.

The protests continued after Deri's jailing as his supporters set up an impromptu yeshivah, Sha'agat Arye (the Lion's Roar, a play on Deri's first name), outside the prison. And in the political arena, calls for Deri's pardon continued. In the Knesset, a private bill—which passed its preliminary reading—called for prisoners to become eligible for parole after completing half of their sentence, rather than the two-thirds previously required. This suggested change in the law, as understood in the political establishment and by the public, was aimed at obtaining Deri's early release for good behavior, even though it would also make possible the early freedom of many other criminal offenders.

In July the Supreme Court had upheld the conviction of Deri, but reduced his original sentence, imposed by a Jerusalem district court in 1999, from four years to three.

Mordechai Case

Yitzhak Mordechai, the former leader of the Center Party and transport minister in the Barak government, was indicted in July on three charges of performing indecent acts against three different women. According to the charge sheet, Mordechai, while serving as head of the IDF's Northern Command in the early 1990s, committed indecent acts against a female soldier including touching her, putting his outgoing mail in a lower desk drawer so that she would have to bend over next to him to get it, and forcing her to leave his car in a deserted area, at night, when she refused his sexual advances. Under the second count, as minister of defense in the Netanyahu government, Mordechai invited a woman to his home in Motza, outside Jerusalem, to discuss possible government employment, and made sexual advances. And in the third count, it was alleged that in February 2000, while he was transport minister, Mordechai, alone in his Tel Aviv office with a 23-year-old female worker, forced her to lie down on a sofa and placed his hand under her blouse.

The last of these cases was the first to come to light, and members of the minister's staff allegedly attempted to dissuade the woman involved from formally complaining to the police. She decided to go public after consulting with Knesset speaker Avraham Burg and Zehava Gal-On, a female member of the Knesset from the Meretz Party. Mordechai denied the charge and, at one stage, reportedly suggested to police that the complainant had been planted in his office by former Tel Aviv mayor Roni Milo, a fellow member of Mordechai's Center Party. The female soldier and the would-be Defense Ministry employee came forward with their charges after the story about Mordechai's conduct in the Transport Ministry made the headlines, and he denied their allegations as well.

Mordechai resigned as leader of the Center Party and as transport minister. He was succeeded in both posts by Amnon Lipkin-Shahak, the former chief-of-staff, who also retained his previous post as tourism minister. But Mordechai retained his seat as one of the Center Party's five Knesset members. In October the Knesset House Committee scheduled hearings on lifting Mordechai's parliamentary immunity so that he could stand trial. Mordechai first obtained a month's delay in order to prepare his defense before the committee, and then, in November, on the eve of the rescheduled hearing, he lifted his objections to the removal of immunity, enabling court proceedings to go forward. They began on November 21.

Netanyahu Case

On September 27 Attorney General Rubinstein announced that there was insufficient evidence to indict former prime minister Benjamin Netanyahu and his wife, Sara, for bribery and unauthorized taking of state gifts. The decision came even though both the police and State's Attorney Edna Arbel had recommended prosecution. Moving contractor Avner Amedi, a central figure in the case, had disclosed that he had performed unpaid services for the Netanyahus—and it had been alleged that these were given in exchange for expected business favors from the prime minister. Amedi said he might still sue the Netanyahus for payment.

Even though Rubinstein failed to recommend criminal charges, his report was severely critical of Netanyahu's conduct in accepting services without paying. That prompted prominent journalist Matti Golan to write, in the *Globes* business daily: "For years Netanyahu employed a contractor without paying him. This is a fact, and he himself has admitted it. The attorney general has reached the conclusion that there is insufficient evidence of bribery, and that no criminal intent can be established." But that, Golan added, "does not mean that the man is fit for public office."

More Investigations of Prominent People

On March 16, police recommended the criminal indictment of Avigdor Kahalani, the public security minister in the 1996–99 Netanyahu administration, for interfering in the 1999 investigation of Ofer Nimrodi, the former publisher of the *Ma'ariv* Hebrew daily. Kahalani, head of the Third Way, a party that lost all of its seats and disappeared in the 1999 election, was suspected of passing on information about the then-secret investigation that eventually resulted in charges against Nimrodi for conspiring to murder two of his competitors, *Yediot Aharonot* publisher Arnon Mozes and *Ha'aretz* publisher Amos Schocken, and a key witness in Nimrodi's previous conviction on wiretap charges (see AJYB 2000, p. 478). Police also recommended that Yossi Levi, the director of operations of the Public Security Ministry when Kahalani was minister, be charged with breach of trust for relaying information about the probe to the minister.

Later that month two top police officers, Jerusalem police commander Yair Yitzhaki and Ya'akov Raz, head of the community police and the civil guard, were cleared by an internal police inquiry of criminal responsibility for failing to report a 1999 meeting with Nimrodi—who was then "under investigation"—to their superior officers. But while exonerating them the police judges decried the practice of "shoulder rubbing" between top police officers and prominent or wealthy people. Police later placed Ofer Nimrodi's father, Ya'akov—a businessman who had past links with the Mossad (secret service) and was engaged in the arms trade—under house arrest on suspicion that he attempted to tamper with witnesses in his son's trial.

In January Attorney General Rubinstein reportedly decided to file criminal charges against Tsachi Hanegbi, the justice minister in the Netanyahu administration, for putting to personal use funds donated to Derech Tzleha (Bon Voyage), a nonprofit group dedicated to the war on traffic accidents, that he headed in the mid-1990s, when he chaired the Knesset Economics Committee. In 1994 Derech Tzleha received contributions from fuel companies. The recommendation to charge Hanegbi with fraud and breach of trust—and possibly bribery as well—was reportedly based on evidence gathered by the police that Derech Tzleha raised 375,000 shekels and distributed 288,000 to Hanegbi, mostly in reimbursement for ordinary and automobile expenses, and allegations that the Likud politician, in his role as committee chairman, acted in favor of the fuel companies. As the year ended the Knesset had not yet acted to lift Hanegbi's parliamentary immunity, a necessary precondition to any criminal proceeding.

Shimon Sheves, director-general of the Prime Minister's Office under Yitzhak Rabin, was convicted by a Tel Aviv District Court on one charge of breach of trust. Details of the case, in which Sheves, acting as a middleman for an undisclosed foreign country, concealed his own personal interest in the matter from Rabin, remained secret, but they were rumored to involve Taiwan. On December 1 Sheves was sentenced to two years in jail.

On March 28 the Knesset House Committee refused to lift the parliamentary immunity of Knesset member Avigdor Lieberman, leader of the Yisrael Beitenu right-leaning immigrant party. Lieberman faced criminal prosecution for insulting and threatening a public official, having allegedly called top police investigator Moshe Mizrachi a "racist" and an "anti-Semite."

Other Developments

Shlomo Aharonishki, the Tel Aviv District chief of police, was appointed Israel's national police chief on September 28 to succeed Yehuda Wilk. Public Security Minister Shlomo Ben-Ami originally wanted to appoint Ami Ayalon, the former Shin Bet security service head, but top members of the force publicly voiced their opposition to Ben-Ami's intention of "parachuting" someone who was "inorganic to the force" into the job. Former Jerusalem police chief Yair Yitzhaki, who had long been considered the front-runner to succeed Wilk, was eliminated from consideration when he was accused of illegally associating with former *Ma'ariv* publisher Ofer Nimrodi at the same time that a secret police investigation was being conducted of Nimrodi for conspiracy to commit murder. Yitzhaki, however, as noted above, was cleared of the charges.

Israel temporarily grounded all of its American-made F-16 warplanes after the third crash of this advanced aircraft, which had become the workhorse of the Israel Air Force, on August 1. A crash of the same model plane on March 27 had claimed the life of Yonatan Begin, son of former science minister Ze'ev B. (Benny) Begin and grandson of the late former prime minister, Menachem Begin.

Israelis got their first chance to see the new gardens at the Bahai Temple on Haifa's Mt. Carmel on July 17, though the gardens, which many observers considered the Eighth Wonder of the World, were not scheduled for formal opening to the public until May 2001. The two square kilometers of greenery, planted flowers, and landscaped paths surrounding the Bahai Temple were part of a $20-million renovation of the site that had been carried out over several years.

Four-year-old David Hadad of Pardes Daka, a very poor neighborhood in Tel Aviv-Jaffa, slipped from his mother's arms and drowned in floodwaters that covered large sections of Tel Aviv on October 25. The flooding—which had occurred on several past occasions after especially heavy rainfalls—followed a four-inch downpour that day, which represented about one-fifth of the city's annual precipitation. Hundreds of residents were evacuated and spent several days, at the expense of city hall, in shelters set up in hotels. The municipality of Tel Aviv said it did not have the funds to build proper drains in the affected neighborhoods.

Israeli skiers, whose numbers had increased during the prosperous mid-1990s, had to travel abroad to visit the slopes in the winter of 2000–2001. This was because, in mid-November, the army said that Neve Ativ, Israel's home-grown ski resort on the slopes of Mt. Hermon in the Golan Heights, would not be allowed to open since it was too easy for Hezballah infiltrators to attack the site. Menachem Baruch, the resort's manager, objected strongly. "There have never been security problems at the site, and we have never been affected by any of the tensions of the northern border," Baruch said, even though Neve Ativ was only about six miles from the spot on the Lebanese border where Hezballah abducted three Israeli soldiers on October 7. The resort, which had previously attracted about 300,000 visitors during ski season, was the major source of income for the 32 families living in Neve Ativ, and they had spent about $1 million to upgrade the site during the summer of 2000.

Personalia

HONORS AND AWARDS

Profs. Hillel Daleski of the Hebrew University of Jerusalem and Harel (Harold) Fisch of Bar-Ilan University, the Israel Prize for Literature; Emeritus Prof. Jonah Fraenkel of the Hebrew University, the Israel Prize in Talmud; Raymond David of the University of Pennsylvania and Masatoshi Koshiba of Tokyo, the Wolf Prize for Physics, for their research into neutrinos; Prince Hassan of Jordan, former crown prince under his late brother King Hussein, an honorary Haifa University doctorate in recognition of his contributions to Middle East peace; David Hartman, Jerusalem philosopher-scholar, the Avichai Prize for promoting understanding among Jews; Kirk Douglas, born Issur Danelovich, a Jerusalem Film Festival prize for lifetime achievement; Wladyslaw Bartoszewski, Auschwitz survivor and Yad Vashem "Righteous among the Nations," made an honorary Israeli citizen; Prof. Moshe Rosman, expert on Hassidism and winner of the U.S. National Jewish Book Award for his *Founder of Hasidism: A Quest for the Historical Ba'al Shem Tov,* the Zalman Shazar Prize for Jewish history.

APPOINTMENTS

David Ivri, former Israel Air Force commander and former director general of the Defense Ministry, named Israel's ambassador to Washington, replacing Likud appointee Zalman Shoval; Avraham (Avi) Dichter, named head of the Shin Bet, Israel's internal security service, replacing the retired Ami Ayalon; Maj.-Gen. Dan Halutz, the new commander of the Israel Air Force, replacing Eitan Ben-Eliyahu, who, after his retirement, became a high-tech businessman; career diplomat David Dadon, named Israel's third ambassador to the Hashemite Kingdom of Jordan, replacing Oded Eran; Prof. David Bankier of the Hebrew University, made head of Yad Vashem's Holocaust Research Institute, succeeding Yehuda Bauer; Brig.-Gen. Orit Adato, former head of the Chen Women's Army Corps, appointed to head Israel's Prisons Service, the first woman to hold the position.

MEDALS

Jerusalemite Mickey Halika, a bronze medal in the 400-meter medley at the short-course swimming world championships in Athens; the dance troupe of the Beit Halohem army rehabilitation center in Tel Aviv, a bronze medal at the wheelchair ballroom dancing world championships in Amsterdam; backstroker Yoav Gat, a bronze medal in the 200 meters at the European championships in Helsinki, only the third European swim medal won by an Israeli.

NECROLOGY

Czech native Peter Friestadt, 69, film actor and producer in his native land and in Israel, in January; international singing star Ofra Haza, 42, in February; former *Jerusalem Post* publisher Yehuda Levy, 64, in February; Cela Netanyahu, 97, mother of ex-prime minister Benjamin Netanyahu and wife of historian Benzion Netanyahu, in February; Jerusalem graphic artist, writer, and raconteur Alex Berlyne, 75, in February; Kariel Gardosh (Dosh), a cartoonist who created the *kova-tembel*-hatted character Srulik, for many years the popular symbol of Israel, 79, in February; Lily Sharon, 62, wife of Likud leader Ariel Sharon, in March; Israeli-born Raphael de Rothschild, 23, son of Natanel and Nili de Rothschild and grandson of Mordechai Limon, a former Israel Air Force commander and ambassador, in New York, in April; Avraham (Munya) Shapira, 79, the all-powerful chairman of the Knesset Finance Committee as an Agudat Yisrael MK in the 1970s and 1980s, in July; Uri Gordon, 65, former head of the Jewish Agency's Department of Immigration and Absorption, in July; Eliahu Ben-Elissar, 68, Israeli ambassador to France, in Paris, after prime minister Barak had ordered his replacement, in August; Akiva Lewinsky, 82, former Bank Hapoalim managing director and Jewish Agency treasurer, who was one of the first to address the problem of unclaimed Holocaust-era accounts in Swiss banks, in August; David Shallon, 49, former musical director of the Jerusalem Symphony Orchestra, while on a trip to Japan to conduct the Tokyo Symphony Orchestra, in September; Israel Prize Laureate Prof. David Flusser, noted authority on the Dead Sea Scrolls and early Christianity, on his 83rd birthday, in September; Yehuda Amichai, renowned and beloved Hebrew poet, 76, in September; Leah Rabin, widow of the assassinated prime minister Yitzhak Rabin, 72, in November.

HANAN SHER

World Jewish Population, 2001

THE WORLD'S JEWISH POPULATION was estimated at 13.25 million at the beginning of 2001 — an increase of about 40,000 over the previous year's revised estimate.[1]

Figures on population size, characteristics, and trends constitute a primary tool in the assessment of Jewish community needs and prospects at the local level and worldwide. The estimates for major regions and individual countries reported in this article reflect a prolonged and ongoing effort to study scientifically the demography of contemporary world Jewry.[2] Data collection and comparative research have benefited from the collaboration of scholars and institutions in many countries, including replies to direct inquiries regarding current estimates. It should be emphasized, however, that the elaboration of a worldwide set of estimates for the Jewish populations of the various countries is beset with difficulties and uncertainties.[3] Users of Jewish population estimates should be aware of these difficulties and of the inherent limitations of our estimates.

Major geopolitical changes have affected the world scene since the end of the 1980s, particularly the political breakup of the Soviet Union into 15 independent states, Germany's political reunion, and the volatile political process along with significant socioeconomic change in Israel and the Middle East. Jewish population trends were most sensitive to these developments, large-scale emigration from the former USSR (FSU) and rapid population growth in Israel being the most visible effects. Geographical mobility and the increased fragmentation of the global system of nations notwithstanding, over 80 percent of world Jewry live in two countries, the United States and Israel, and 95 percent are concentrated

---

[1]The previous estimates, as of January 1, 2000, were published in AJYB 2000, vol. 100, pp. 484–95. See also Sergio DellaPergola, Uzi Rebhun, and Mark Tolts, "Prospecting the Jewish Future: Population Projections 2000–2080," ibid, pp. 103–146; and previous AJYB volumes for further details on previous estimates.

[2]Many of these activities are carried out by, or in coordination with, the Division of Jewish Demography and Statistics at the A. Harman Institute of Contemporary Jewry (ICJ), the Hebrew University of Jerusalem. The collaboration of the many institutions and individuals in the different countries who have supplied information for this update is acknowledged with thanks.

[3]For overviews of the subject matter and technical issues see Paul Ritterband, Barry A. Kosmin, and Jeffrey Scheckner, "Counting Jewish Populations: Methods and Problems," AJYB 1988, vol. 88, pp. 204–21; Sergio DellaPergola, "Modern Jewish Demography," in Jack Wertheimer, ed., *The Modern Jewish Experience* (New York, 1993), pp. 275–90.

in ten countries. The aggregate of these major Jewish population centers virtually determines the assessment of world Jewry's total size.

Main Problems in Jewish Population Research

DETERMINANTS OF JEWISH POPULATION CHANGE

One fundamental aspect of population in general and of Jewish population in particular is its perpetual change. Population size and composition continuously change reflecting a well-known array of determinants. Two of these are shared by all populations: (a) the balance of vital events (births and deaths); (b) the balance of international migration (immigration and emigration). Both of these factors affect increases or decreases in the physical presence of individuals in a given place. The third determinant consists of identificational changes (accessions and secessions) and only applies to populations defined by some cultural or symbolic peculiarity, as is the case with Jews. The latter type of change does not affect people's physical presence but rather their willingness to identify with a specific religious, ethnic or otherwise culturally defined group.

The country figures presented here for 2001 were updated from those for 2000 in accordance with the known or estimated changes in the interval—vital events, migrations, and identificational changes. In our updating procedure, whether or not exact data on intervening changes are available, we consistently point to the known or assumed direction of change, and, accordingly, add to or subtract from previous Jewish population estimates unless there is evidence that intervening changes balanced each other off and total size remained unchanged. This procedure proved highly efficient in the past when a new improved Jewish population figure became available reflecting a new census or survey, and our annually updated estimates generally proved on target.

The most recent findings basically confirmed the estimates we had reported in previous AJYB volumes and, perhaps more importantly, our interpretation of the trends now prevailing in the demography of world Jewry.[4] Concisely stated, these involve a positive balance of vital events in Israel and a negative one in nearly all other Jewish communities; a positive migration balance for Israel, the United States and a few other western countries, and a negative one in Latin America, Eastern Europe, Muslim countries, and some western countries as well; a positive balance of accessions and secessions in Israel, and an often negative, or in

---

[4]See Roberto Bachi, *Population Trends of World Jewry* (Jerusalem, 1976); U.O. Schmelz, "Jewish Survival: The Demographic Factors," AJYB 1981, vol. 81, pp. 61–117; U.O. Schmelz, *Aging of World Jewry* (Jerusalem, 1984); Sergio DellaPergola, "Changing Cores and Peripheries: Fifty Years in Socio-demographic Perspective," in Robert S. Wistrich, ed., *Terms of Survival: The Jewish World since 1945* (London, 1995), pp. 13–43; Sergio DellaPergola, *World Jewry Beyond 2000: Demographic Prospects* (Oxford, 1999).

any event rather mixed one elsewhere. While allowing for improvements and corrections, the 2001 population estimates highlight the increasing complexity of the
sociodemographic and identificational processes underlying the definition of
Jewish populations, and hence the estimates of their sizes. This complexity is
heightened at a time of enhanced international migration, often implying double counts of people on the move. Consequently, as will be clarified below, the
analyst has to come to terms with the paradox of the *permanently provisional* character of Jewish population estimates.

SOURCES OF DATA

In general, the amount and quality of documentation on Jewish population size
and characteristics is far from satisfactory. In recent years, however, important
new data and estimates became available for several countries through official
population censuses and Jewish-sponsored sociodemographic surveys. National
censuses yielded results on Jewish populations in the Soviet Union (1989),
Switzerland (1990), Canada, South Africa, Australia, and New Zealand (both
1991 and 1996), Brazil, Ireland, the Czech Republic, and India (1991), Romania
and Bulgaria (1992), the Russian Republic and Macedonia (1994), Israel (1995),
Belarus, Azerbaijan, Kazakhstan, and Kyrgyzstan (1999), and Latvia (2000).
Permanent national population registers, including information on the Jewish religious or national group, exist in several European countries (Switzerland, Norway, Finland, Estonia, Latvia, Lithuania), and in Israel.

Where official sources on Jewish population are not available, independent sociodemographic studies have provided most valuable information on Jewish demography and socioeconomic stratification, as well as on Jewish identification.
The largest of such studies so far have been the National Jewish Population Survey (NJPS) in the United States (1970–71 and 1990). Similar surveys were conducted over the last decade in South Africa (1991 and 1998), Mexico (1991),
Lithuania (1993), the United Kingdom and Chile (1995), Venezuela (1998–99),
Hungary, the Netherlands, Guatemala, and Moldova (1999), and Sweden (2000).
Several further Jewish population studies were separately conducted in major
cities in the United States and in other countries. Additional evidence on Jewish
population trends can be obtained from the systematic monitoring of membership registers, vital statistics, and migration records available from Jewish communities and other Jewish organizations in many countries or cities, notably in
the United Kingdom, Germany, and Buenos Aires. Detailed data on Jewish immigration routinely collected in Israel help to assess changing Jewish population
sizes in other countries. Some of this ongoing research is part of a coordinated
effort to constantly update the profile of world Jewry.[5] A new round of official

---

[5]Following the International Conference on Jewish Population Problems held in
Jerusalem in 1987, initiated by the late Dr. Roberto Bachi of the Hebrew University and

censuses and Jewish surveys is expected to highlight the demographic profile of large Jewish communities at the dawn of the new millennium, primarily the new U.S. National Jewish Population Survey (2000–01), the 2001 Canadian census, and censuses of several of the republics of the FSU planned for 2001 and subsequent years. The U.K. 2001 census will include a new optional question on religion.

DEFINITIONS

A major problem in Jewish population estimates periodically circulated by individual scholars or Jewish organizations is a lack of coherence and uniformity in the definition criteria followed—when the issue of defining the Jewish population is addressed at all. The following estimates of Jewish population distribution in each continent (table 1 below), country (tables 2–9), and metropolitan area (table 10) consistently aim at the concept of core Jewish population.[6]

The *core Jewish population* includes all those who, when asked, identify themselves as Jews; or, if the respondent is a different person in the same household, are identified by him/her as Jews. This is an intentionally comprehensive and pragmatic approach. Such definition of a person as a Jew, reflecting subjective feelings, broadly overlaps but does not necessarily coincide with Halakhah (rabbinic law) or other normatively binding definitions. It does not depend on any measure of that person's Jewish commitment or behavior—in terms of religiosity, beliefs, knowledge, communal affiliation, or otherwise. Included in the core Jewish population are all those who converted to Judaism by any procedure, or joined the Jewish group informally and declare themselves to be Jewish. Persons of Jewish descent who adopted another religion are excluded, as are other individuals who did not convert out but currently refuse to acknowledge their Jewish identification. In Israel personal status is subject to the ruling of the Minister of Interior, which relies on rabbinical authorities.

Two additional operative concepts must be considered in the study of Jewish demography. The *extended Jewish population* includes the sum of (a) the *core* Jewish population and (b) all other persons of Jewish parentage who are not Jews currently (or at the time of investigation). These non-Jews with Jewish background, as far as they can be ascertained, include: (a) persons who have them-

---

sponsored by major Jewish organizations worldwide, an International Scientific Advisory Committee (ISAC) was established. Currently chaired by Dr. Sidney Goldstein of Brown University, ISAC aims to coordinate and monitor Jewish population data collection internationally. See Sergio DellaPergola and Leah Cohen, eds., *World Jewish Population: Trends and Policies* (Jerusalem, 1992).

[6]The term *core Jewish population* was initially suggested by Barry A. Kosmin, Sidney Goldstein, Joseph Waksberg, Nava Lerer, Ariella Keysar, and Jeffrey Scheckner, *Highlights of the CJF 1990 National Jewish Population Survey* (New York, 1991).

selves adopted another religion, even though they may claim still to be Jews ethnically; (b) other persons with Jewish parentage who say they are not Jews. It is customary in sociodemographic surveys to consider the religio-ethnic identification of parents. Some censuses, however, do ask about more distant ancestry. The *enlarged Jewish population*[7]—in addition to all those who belong in the *extended* Jewish population—also includes all of the respective further non-Jewish household members (spouses, children, etc.). For both conceptual and practical reasons, this definition does not include any other non-Jewish relatives living elsewhere in exclusively non-Jewish households.

The Law of Return, Israel's distinctive legal framework for the acceptance and absorption of new immigrants, awards Jewish new immigrants immediate citizenship and other civil rights. According to the current, amended version of the Law of Return, a Jew is any person born to a Jewish mother, or converted to Judaism (regardless of denomination—Orthodox, Conservative, or Reform), who does not have another religious identity. By ruling of Israel's Supreme Court, conversion from Judaism, as in the case of some ethnic Jews who currently identify with another religion, entails loss of eligibility for Law of Return purposes. The law per se does not affect a person's Jewish status, which, as noted, is adjudicated by Israel's Ministry of Interior and rabbinical authorities. The law extends its provisions to all current Jews and to their Jewish or non-Jewish spouses, children, and grandchildren, as well as to the spouses of such children and grandchildren. As a result of its three-generation time perspective and lateral extension, the Law of Return applies to a sizeable population, one of significantly wider scope than *core, extended,* and *enlarged* Jewish populations defined above.[8] It is actually quite difficult to estimate what the total size of the *Law of Return* population could be. These higher estimates are not discussed below systematically, but some notion of their possible extent is given for the major countries.

Presentation of Data

While Jewish population estimates presented in volumes of the *American Jewish Year Book* until 1999 referred to December 31 of the year preceding by two the date of publication, since 2000 our estimates refer to January 1 of the current year of publication. This attempt to present the most recent possible picture

---

[7]The term *enlarged Jewish population* was initially suggested in Sergio DellaPergola, "The Italian Jewish Population Study: Demographic Characteristics and Trends," in U.O. Schmelz, P. Glikson, and S.J. Gould, eds., *Studies in Jewish Demography; Survey for 1969–1971* (Jerusalem-London, 1975), pp. 60–97.

[8]For a concise review of the rules of attribution of Jewish personal status in rabbinic and Israeli law, including reference to Jewish sects, isolated communities, and apostates, see Michael Corinaldi, "Jewish Identity," chap. 2 of his *Jewish Identity: The Case of Ethiopian Jewry* (Jerusalem, 1998).

entails a shorter span of time for evaluation and correction of the available information, thus somewhat increasing the margin of inaccuracy. Indeed, where appropriate, we revised our previous estimates in the light of newly accrued information on Jewish populations (see tables 1 and 2). Corrections were also applied retrospectively to the 2000 figures for major geographical regions so as to ensure a better base for comparisons with the 2001 estimates. Corrections of the latest estimates, if needed, will be presented in future volumes of the AJYB.

ACCURACY RATING

We provide separate figures for each country with approximately 100 or more resident *core* Jews. Residual estimates of Jews living in other smaller communities supplement some of the continental totals. For each of the reported countries, the four columns in tables 3–7 provide an estimate of midyear 2000 total population,[9] the estimated 1/1/2001 Jewish population, the proportion of Jews per 1,000 of total population, and a rating of the accuracy of the Jewish population estimate.

There is wide variation in the quality of the Jewish population estimates for different countries. For many Diaspora countries it would be best to indicate a range (minimum-maximum) rather than a definite figure for the number of Jews. It would be confusing, however, for the reader to be confronted with a long list of ranges; this would also complicate the regional and world totals. Therefore figures actually indicated for most of the Diaspora communities should be understood as being the central value of the plausible range of the respective core Jewish populations. The relative magnitude of this range varies inversely to the accuracy of the estimate.

The three main elements that affect the accuracy of each estimate are the nature and quality of the base data, how recent the base data are, and the method of updating. A simple code combining these elements is used to provide a general evaluation of the reliability of the Jewish population figures reported in the detailed tables below. The code indicates different quality levels of the reported estimates: (A) Base figure derived from countrywide census or relatively reliable Jewish population survey; updated on the basis of full or partial information on Jewish population movements in the country during the intervening period. (B) Base figure derived from less accurate but recent countrywide Jewish population data; partial information on population movements in the intervening period. (C) Base figure derived from less recent sources, and/or unsatisfactory or partial coverage of a country's Jewish population; updating according to demographic information illustrative of regional demographic trends. (D) Base figure essentially

---

[9]Data and estimates derived from the United Nations Population Division, *World Population Prospects, The 2000 Revision, Highlights* (New York, 2001).

speculative; no reliable updating procedure. In categories (A), (B), and (C), the year in which the country's base figure or important partial updates were obtained are also stated. For countries whose Jewish population estimate for 2001 was not only updated but also revised in the light of improved information, the sign "X" is appended to the accuracy rating.

One additional tool for updating Jewish population estimates is provided by a new set of demographic projections recently developed at the Hebrew University of Jerusalem.[10] Such projections extrapolate the most likely observed or expected trends out of a Jewish population baseline assessed by sex and detailed age groups as of end-year 1995. Even where detailed information on the dynamics of Jewish population change is not immediately available, the powerful connection that generally exists between age composition of a population and the respective vital and migration movements helps provide plausible scenarios of the developments bound to occur in the short term. Where better data was lacking we used indications from these projections to refine the 2001 estimates as against previous years. On the other hand, projections are clearly shaped by a definite and comparatively limited set of assumptions and need to be periodically updated in the light of actual demographic developments.

Global Overview

WORLD JEWISH POPULATION SIZE

The size of world Jewry at the beginning of 2001 is assessed at 13,254,100. World Jewry constituted about 2.19 per 1,000 of the world's total population in 2000. One in about 457 people in the world is a Jew. According to the revised figures, between 2000 and 2001 the Jewish population grew by an estimated 41,300 people, or about 0.3 percent. The world's total annual rate of population growth is 1.4 percent (0.1 percent in more developed countries, 1.7 percent in less developed countries). Despite all the imperfections in the estimates, world Jewry continued to be close to "zero population growth," with the natural increase in Israel slightly overcoming the decline in the Diaspora.

Table 1 gives an overall picture of Jewish population for the beginning of 2001 as compared to 2000. For 2000 the originally published estimates are presented along with somewhat revised figures that take into account, retrospectively, the corrections made in certain country estimates in the light of improved information. These corrections resulted in a net increase of the 2000 world Jewry's estimated size by 21,300. This change resulted from upward corrections for Ukraine (+27,000), Latvia (+1,800), the Netherlands (+2,000), Portugal (+200), Azerbaijan (+2,000), Uzbekistan (+1,000), and New Zealand (+300), and downward cor-

---

[10]See DellaPergola, Rebhun, and Tolts, "Prospecting the Jewish Future."

rections for Israel (–9,200), Venezuela (–2,000), Guatemala (–100), Kazakhstan (–1,000), Kyrgyzstan (–600), and Tajikistan (–100). Explanations are given below of the reasons for these corrections.

The number of Jews in Israel rose from a revised figure of 4,872,800 in 2000 to 4,952,200 at the beginning of 2001, an increase of 79,400 people, or 1.6 percent. In contrast, the estimated Jewish population in the Diaspora declined from 8,340,000 (according to the revised figures) to 8,301,900—a decrease of 38,100 people, or –0.5 percent. These changes primarily reflect the continuing Jewish emigration from the FSU. In 2000, the estimated Israel-Diaspora net migratory balance amounted to a gain of about 20,000 Jews for Israel.[11] Internal demographic evolution (including vital events and conversions) produced a further growth of about 59,000 among the Jewish population in Israel, and a further loss of about 18,000 in the Diaspora. Recently, instances of accession or "return" to Judaism can be observed in connection with the emigration process from Eastern Europe and Ethiopia, and the comprehensive provisions of the Israeli Law of Return (see above). The return or first-time access to Judaism of some of such previously unincluded or unidentified individuals has contributed to slowing down the pace of decline of the relevant Diaspora Jewish populations and some further gains for the Jewish population in Israel.

As noted, it is customary to introduce corrections in previously published Jewish population estimates in the light of improved information that became available at a later date. Table 2 provides a synopsis of the world Jewish population estimates relating to the period 1945–2001, as first published each year in the *American Jewish Year Book* and as corrected retroactively, incorporating all subsequent revisions. These revised data correct, sometimes significantly, the figures published until 1980 by other authors, and since 1981 by ourselves. Thanks to the development over the years of an improved data base, these new revisions are not necessarily the same revised estimates as those published year by year in the AJYB based on the information that was available at each date; nor is it unlikely that further retrospective revisions will become necessary as a product of future research.

The revised figures in table 2 clearly portray the slowing down of Jewish population growth globally since World War II. Based on a post-Holocaust world Jewish population estimate of 11,000,000, a growth of 1,079,000 occurred between 1945 and 1960, followed by growths of 506,000 in the 1960s, 234,000 in the 1970s, 49,000 in the 1980s, and 344,000 in the 1990s. While it took 13 years to add one million to world Jewry's postwar size, it took 38 years to add another million. The modest recovery of the 1990s mostly reflects the already noted cases of individuals, especially from Eastern Europe, first entering or returning to Judaism, as well as a short-lived "echo effect" of the postwar baby boom (see below).

---

[11]Israel Central Bureau of Statistics, *Population and Vital Statistics 1997* (Jerusalem, 1998), pp. 2–8.

TABLE 1. ESTIMATED JEWISH POPULATION, BY CONTINENTS AND MAJOR GEOGRAPHICAL REGIONS, 2000 AND 2001[a]

Region	2000			2001		Yearly % Change 2000–2001
	Original	Revised				
	Abs. N.	Abs. N.	Percent[b]	Abs. N.	Percent[b]	
World	13,191,500	13,212,800	100.0	13,254,100	100.0	0.3
Diaspora	8,309,500	8,340,000	63.1	8,301,900	62.6	−0.5
Israel	4,882,000	4,872,800	36.9	4,952,200	37.4	1.6
America, Total	6,483,900	6,481,800	49.1	6,479,300	48.9	−0.0
North[c]	6,062,000	6,062,000	45.9	6,064,000	45.8	0.0
Central	52,800	52,700	0.4	52,600	0.4	−0.2
South	369,100	367,100	2.8	362,700	2.7	−1.2
Europe, Total	1,583,000	1,614,000	12.2	1,582,800	11.9	−1.9
European Union	1,026,700	1,028,900	7.8	1,032,100	7.8	0.3
Other West	19,900	19,900	0.2	19,700	0.1	−1.0
Former USSR[d]	438,100	466,900	3.5	434,000	3.3	−7.0
Other East and Balkans[d]	98,300	98,300	0.7	97,000	0.7	−1.3
Asia, Total	4,932,900	4,925,000	37.3	5,000,500	37.7	1.5
Israel	4,882,000	4,872,800	36.9	4,952,200	37.4	1.6
Former USSR[d]	30,000	31,300	0.2	28,000	0.2	−10.5
Other[f]	20,900	20,900	0.2	20,300	0.2	−2.9
Africa, Total	89,800	89,800	0.7	88,300	0.7	−1.7
North[e]	7,700	7,700	0.1	7,500	0.1	−2.6
South[f]	82,100	82,100	0.6	80,800	0.6	−1.6
Oceania[g]	101,900	102,200	0.8	103,200	0.8	1.0

[a]January 1.
[b]Minor discrepancies due to rounding.
[c]U.S.A. and Canada.
[d]The Asian parts of Russia and Turkey are included in Europe.
[e]Including Ethiopia.
[f]South Africa, Zimbabwe, and other sub-Saharan countries.
[g]Australia, New Zealand.

TABLE 2.   WORLD JEWISH POPULATION ESTIMATES: ORIGINAL AND CORRECTED,
1945-2001

Year	Original Estimate[a]	Corrected Estimate[b]	Yearly % Change[c]
1945, May 1	11,000,000	11,000,000	
1950, Jan. 1	11,303,400	11,297,000	0.57
1960, Jan. 1	12,792,800	12,079,000	0.67
1970, Jan. 1	13,950,900	12,585,000	0.41
1980, Jan. 1	14,527,100	12,819,000	0.18
1990, Jan. 1	12,810,300	12,868,000	0.04
2000, Jan. 1	13,191,500	13,212,500	0.26
2001, Jan. 1	13,254,100	=	0.31

[a]As published in AJYB, various years. Estimates reported here as of Jan. 1 were originally published as of end of previous year.
[b]Based on updated, revised, or otherwise improved information. Original estimates for 1990 and after, and all corrected estimates: The A. Harman Institute of Contemporary Jewry, The Hebrew University of Jerusalem.
[c]Based on corrected estimates, besides latest year.

DISTRIBUTION BY MAJOR REGIONS

Just about half of the world's Jews reside in the Americas, with about 46 percent in North America. Over 37 percent live in Asia, including the Asian republics of the former USSR (but not the Asian parts of the Russian Republic and Turkey)—most of them in Israel. Europe, including the Asian territories of the Russian Republic and Turkey, accounts for about 12 percent of the total. Fewer than 2 percent of the world's Jews live in Africa and Oceania. Among the major geographical regions listed in table 1, the number of Jews in Israel—and, consequently, in total Asia—increased in 2000. Moderate Jewish population gains were also estimated for North America, the European Union (including 15 member countries), and Oceania. Central and South America, Eastern Europe, Asian countries outside of Israel, and Africa sustained decreases in Jewish population size.

Individual Countries

THE AMERICAS

In 2001 the total number of Jews in the American continents was estimated at close to 6.5 million. The overwhelming majority (94 percent) resided in the United States and Canada, fewer than 1 percent lived in Central America including Mexico, and about 6 percent lived in South America—with Argentina and Brazil the largest Jewish communities.

TABLE 3.   ESTIMATED JEWISH POPULATION DISTRIBUTION IN THE AMERICAS, 1/1/2001

Country	Total Population	Jewish Population	Jews per 1,000 Population	Accuracy Rating	
Canada	30,757,000	364,000	11.8	B 1996	
United States	283,230,000	5,700,000	20.1	B 1990	
Total North America[a]	314,114,000	6,064,000	19.3		
Bahamas	304,000	300	1.0	D	
Costa Rica	4,024,000	2,500	0.6	C 1993	
Cuba	11,199,000	600	0.1	C 1990	
Dominican Republic	8,373,000	100	0.0	D	
El Salvador	6,278,000	100	0.0	C 1993	
Guatemala	11,385,000	900	0.1	A 1999	X
Jamaica	2,576,000	300	0.1	A 1995	
Mexico	98,872,000	40,500	0.4	B 1991	
Netherlands Antilles	215,000	200	0.9	B 1998	
Panama	2,856,000	5,000	1.8	C 1990	
Puerto Rico	3,915,000	1,500	0.4	C 1990	
Virgin Islands	114,000	300	2.6	C 1986	
Other	23,051,000	300	0.0	D	
Total Central America	173,162,000	52,600	0.3		
Argentina	37,032,000	197,000	5.3	C 1990	
Bolivia	8,239,000	500	0.1	C 1999	
Brazil	170,406,000	97,500	0.6	B 1991	
Chile	15,211,000	21,000	1.4	B 1995	
Colombia	42,105,000	3,500	0.1	C 1996	
Ecuador	12,646,000	900	0.1	C 1985	
Paraguay	5,496,000	900	0.2	B 1997	
Peru	25,662,000	2,700	0.1	C 1993	
Suriname	417,000	200	0.5	B 1986	
Uruguay	3,337,000	22,500	6.7	C 1993	
Venezuela	24,170,000	16,000	0.7	A 1999	X
Total South America[a]	345,647,000	362,700	1.0		
Total	832,923,000	6,479,300	7.8		

[a]Including countries not listed separately.

United States. The 1989–1990 National Jewish Population Survey (NJPS), sponsored by the Council of Jewish Federations and the North American Jewish Data Bank (NAJDB), provided new benchmark information about the size and characteristics of U.S. Jewry—the largest Jewish population in the world—and the basis for subsequent updates.[12] According to the official report of the results of this important national sample study, the core Jewish population in the United States comprised 5,515,000 persons in the summer of 1990. Of these, 185,000 were not born or raised as Jews but identified with Judaism at the time of the survey. An estimated 210,000 persons, not included in the previous figures, were born or raised as Jews but in 1990 identified with another religion. A further 1,115,000 people—415,000 adults and 700,000 children below age 18—were of Jewish parentage but had not themselves been raised as Jews, and declared a religion other than Judaism at the time of the survey. All together, these various groups formed an extended Jewish population of 6,840,000. NJPS also covered 1,350,000 non-Jewish-born members of eligible (Jewish or mixed) households. The study's enlarged Jewish population thus consisted of about 8,200,000 persons. The 1990 Jewish population estimates are within the range of a sampling error of plus or minus 3.5 percent.[13] This means a range between 5.3 and 5.7 millions for the core Jewish population in 1990.

Since 1990, the international migration balance of U.S. Jewry should have generated an actual increase of Jewish population size. According to HIAS (Hebrew Immigrant Aid Society), the main agency involved in assisting Jewish migration from the FSU to the United States, over 250,000 migrants were assisted over the period 1991–2000.[14] These figures refer to the *enlarged* Jewish population concept, incorporating the non-Jewish members of mixed households. The actual number of FSU Jews settling in the U.S. was therefore somewhat smaller than 250,000, still substantial though steadily declining since 1992. More migrants arrived from Israel, Latin America, South Africa, Iran, and other countries. At the same time Israeli statistics continue to show moderate but steady numbers of immigrants from the United States. Between 1990 and 2000, a total of about 20,000 American Jews went on aliyah, and larger numbers of Israelis left the United

---

[12]The 1989–1990 National Jewish Population Survey was conducted under the auspices of the Council of Jewish Federations with the supervision of a National Technical Advisory Committee chaired by Dr. Sidney Goldstein of Brown University. Dr. Barry Kosmin of the North American Jewish Data Bank and City University of New York Graduate School directed the study. See: Kosmin et al., *Highlights;* and Sidney Goldstein, "Profile of American Jewry: Insights from the 1990 National Jewish Population Survey," *AJYB* 1992, vol. 92, pp. 77–173.

[13]See Kosmin et al., *Highlights,* p. 39.

[14]HIAS, *Annual Report 1997* (New York, 1998). See also: Barry R. Chiswick, "Soviet Jews in the United States: An Analysis of Their Linguistic and Economic Adjustment," *Economic Quarterly,* July 1991, no. 148, pp. 188–211 (Hebrew), and *International Migration Review,* 1993 (English).

States after a prolonged stay and returned to Israel, bringing with them their U.S.-born children.[15]

Detailed analyses of the 1990 NJPS data provide evidence of a variety of factors contributing to slow Jewish population growth in the U.S.: low levels of "effectively Jewish" fertility, aging of the Jewish population, increasing rates of outmarriage, declining rates of conversion to Judaism (or "choosing" Judaism), rather low proportions of children of mixed marriages being identified as Jews, and a growing tendency to adopt non-Jewish rituals.[16] A temporary increase in the Jewish birthrate occurred during the late 1980s, because the large cohorts born during the baby boom of the 1950s and early 1960s were in the prime procreative ages. However, by the mid-1990s this echo effect had faded away, as the much smaller cohorts born since the late 1960s reached the stage of parenthood. A surplus of Jewish deaths over Jewish births probably prevailed among U.S. Jewry.

Our estimate starts from the NJPS benchmark core Jewish population of 5,515,000, accounts for a positive balance of immigration net of emigration, and assumes some quantitative erosion in the light of recent marriage, fertility, and age-composition trends. After reaching a level of 5,700,000 at the end of 1996, we have assumed a stable population total for the U.S. core Jewish population.

The research team of the NAJDB that was responsible for the primary handling of NJPS data also continued its yearly compilation of local Jewish population estimates. These are reported elsewhere in this volume.[17] NAJDB estimated the U.S. Jewish population in 1986 at 5,814,000, including "under 2 percent" non-Jewish household members. This closely matched our own pre-NJPS 1990 estimate of 5,700,000. The NAJDB estimates were later updated up to 6,061,000 in 2000. Besides a significant downward revision in 1991, following NJPS, changes in NAJDB estimates reflected corrections and adaptations made in the figures for several local communities — some of them in the light of new community studies. Clearly, compilations of local estimates, even if done as painstakingly as in the case of the NAJDB, are subject to a great many local biases, and tend to fall behind the actual pace of national trends. This is especially true in a context of

---

[15]*Statistical Abstract of Israel,* vol. 49, 1998, pp. 4-3, 4-5, 5-7; Yinon Cohen and Yitzchak Haberfeld, "The Number of Israeli Immigrants in the United States in 1990," *Demography* 34, no. 2, 1997, pp. 199–212.

[16]See Goldstein, "Profile"; U.O. Schmelz and Sergio DellaPergola, *Basic Trends in U.S. Jewish Demography* (American Jewish Committee, New York, 1988); and Sergio DellaPergola, "New Data on Demography and Identification among Jews in the U.S.: Trends, Inconsistencies and Disagreements," *Contemporary Jewry* 12, 1991, pp. 67–97.

[17]The first in a new series of yearly compilations of local U.S. Jewish population estimates appeared in Barry A. Kosmin, Paul Ritterband, and Jeffrey Scheckner, "Jewish Population in the United States, 1987," AJYB 1987, vol. 87, pp. 164–91. For 1999 see Jim Schwartz and Jeffrey Scheckner, "Jewish Population in the United States, 1999," AJYB 2000, vol. 100, pp. 242–264. The 2000 update appears elsewhere in the present volume.

vigorous internal migration, as in the United States.[18] In our view, NJPS figures, in spite of sample-survey biases, offer a more reliable baseline for assessing national Jewish population than the sum of local estimates.[19] A corrected baseline will be provided by the new NJPS to be completed in the course of 2001.

Canada. The 1996 Canadian census provided new evidence for the estimate of the local Jewish population. As customary in Canada, this mid-decade census provided information on ethnic origins whereas the 1991 census included questions on both religion and ethnic origin, besides information on year of immigration of the foreign-born, and languages. In 1996, 351,705 Canadians reported a Jewish ethnic origin—195,810 as a single response, and 155,900 as one selection in a multiple response with up to four options.[20] To interpret these data it is necessary to make reference to the previous census and to the special processing by a joint team of researchers from McGill University's Consortium for Ethnicity and Strategic Social Planning, Statistics Canada, and Council of Jewish Federations Canada.[21]

The 1991 census enumerated 318,070 Jews according to religion; of these, 281,680 also reported to be Jewish by ethnicity (as one of up to four options to the latter question), while 36,390 reported one or more other ethnic origins. Another 38,245 persons reported no religion and a Jewish ethnic origin, again as one of up to four options.[22] After due allowance is made for the latter group, a total core Jewish population of 356,315 was estimated for 1991. A further 49,640 Canadians, who reported being Jewish by ethnic origin but identified with another religion (such as Catholic, Anglican, etc.), were not included in the 1991 core estimate. Including them would produce an extended Jewish population of 405,955 in 1991.

The 1991 census equivalent of the 1996 census figure of 351,705 ethnic Jews (including those not Jewish by religion, but excluding those Jews who did not re-

---

[18]See Uzi Rebhun, "Changing Patterns of Internal Migration 1970–1990: A Comparative Analysis of Jews and Whites in the United States," *Demography* 34, no. 2, 1997, pp. 213–223.

[19]The NAJDB estimate for the total U.S. Jewry in 2000 exceeds ours by over 360,000 (a difference of 6.3 percent). Over the years 1990–2000 we have estimated a Jewish population increase of 185,000 as against 546,000 according to NAJDB.

[20]The sum inconsistency appears in the original report: Statistics Canada, *Top 25 Ethnic Origins in Canada, Showing Single and Multiple Responses, for Canada, 1996 Census (20% Sample Data)* (Ottawa, 1998).

[21]Jim L. Torczyner, Shari L. Brotman, Kathy Viragh, and Gustave J. Goldmann, *Demographic Challenges Facing Canadian Jewry; Initial Findings from the 1991 Census* (Montreal, 1993); Jim L. Torczyner and Shari L. Brotman, "The Jews of Canada: A Profile from the Census," AJYB 1995, vol. 95, pp. 227–260.

[22]Statistics Canada, *Religions in Canada—1991 Census* (Ottawa, 1993). See also Leo Davids, "The Jewish Population of Canada, 1991" in Sergio DellaPergola and Judith Even, eds., *Papers in Jewish Demography 1993 in Memory of U.O. Schmelz* (Jerusalem, 1997) pp. 311–323.

port a Jewish ethnic origin), was 349,565. Based on a similar criterion of ethnic origin, Canadian Jewry thus increased by 2,140 people over the 1991–1996 period. Though it should be stressed that the ethnic origin definition is not consistent with our concept of a core Jewish population, the evidence was of very slow Jewish population increase—notwithstanding continuing immigration. Taking into account the increasingly aged Jewish population structure, we suggest that in years following the 1991 census the continuing migratory surplus would have generated a modest surplus over the probably negative balance of internal evolution. For the beginning of 2001 we updated the 1991 baseline of 356,300 to 364,000, making the Canadian Jewish population the world's fourth largest.

Central America. Results of the 1991 population survey of the Jews in the Mexico City metropolitan area[23] pointed to a community less affected than others in the Diaspora by the common trends of low fertility, intermarriage, and aging. Some comparatively traditional sectors in the Jewish community still contributed a surplus of births over deaths, and overall—thanks also to some immigration—the Jewish population was stable or moderately increasing. The new medium Jewish population estimate for 1991 was put at 37,500 in the Mexico City metropolitan area, and at 40,000 nationally. Official Mexican censuses over the years provided rather erratic and unreliable Jewish population figures. This was the case with the 1990 census, which came up with a national total of 57,918 (aged five and over). As in the past, most of the problem derived from unacceptably high figures for peripheral states. The new census figures for the Mexico City metropolitan area (33,932 Jews aged five and over in the Federal District and State of Mexico) came quite close—in fact were slightly below—our survey's estimates. Taking into account a modest residual potential for natural increase, as shown by the 1991 survey, but also some emigration, we estimated the Jewish population at 40,500 in 2001.

The Jewish population was estimated at about 5,000 in Panama, 2,500 in Costa Rica, 1,500 in Puerto Rico, and 900 in Guatemala.[24]

South America.[25] The Jewish population of Argentina, the largest in Latin

---

[23]Sergio DellaPergola and Susana Lerner, *La población judía de México: Perfil demográfico, social y cultural* (México-Jerusalén, 1995). The project, conducted in cooperation between the Centro de Estudios Urbanos y de Desarrollo Urbano (CEUDU), El Colegio de Mexico, and the Division of Jewish Demography and Statistics of the A. Harman Institute of Contemporary Jewry, The Hebrew University, was sponsored by the Asociación Mexicana de Amigos de la Universidad Hebrea de Jerusalén.

[24]Carlos Tapiero, "The Jewish Community of Guatemala: Sociodemographic Profile and Cultural and Religious Identity" (Hebrew and Spanish), unpublished M.A. thesis, Jerusalem, 2001.

[25]For a more detailed discussion of the region's Jewish population trends, see U.O. Schmelz and Sergio DellaPergola, "The Demography of Latin American Jewry," AJYB 1985, vol. 85, pp. 51–102; Sergio DellaPergola, "Demographic Trends of Latin American Jewry," in J. Laikin Elkin and G.W. Merks, eds., *The Jewish Presence in Latin America* (Boston, 1987), pp. 85–133.

America and seventh largest in the world, was marked by a negative balance of internal evolution. Various surveys conducted in some central sections of Buenos Aires at the initiative of the Asociación Mutualista Israelita Argentina (AMIA), as well as in several provincial cities, pointed to growing aging and intermarriage.[26] In the absence of a major new survey in the Greater Buenos Aires area, quality of national estimates remained inadequate. Since the early 1960s, when the Jewish population was estimated at 310,000, the pace of emigration and return migration has been significantly affected by the variable nature of economic and political trends in the country, generating a negative balance of external migrations. Most Jews lived in the Greater Buenos Aires area, with about 25,000–30,000 left in provincial cities and minor centers. The predominantly middle-class Jewish community confronted serious economic difficulties, to the point that the problem of a "new Jewish poverty" was noted.[27] This in turn negatively affected the Jewish institutional network, including Jewish education. Between 1990 and 2000, over 10,000 persons migrated to Israel, while unspecified numbers moved to other countries. Steady decline in the number of burials performed by Jewish funeral societies was another symptom of population decline, though the high cost of Jewish funerals might have induced some Jewish families to prefer a non-Jewish ceremony. Accordingly, the estimate for Argentinean Jewry was reduced to 197,000 in 2001.

In Brazil, the population census of 1991 indicated a Jewish population of 86,816, a decline of 4,979 against the previous 1980 census. In 1991, 42,871 Jews lived in the state of São Paulo (44,569 in 1980), 26,190 in the state of Rio de Janeiro (29,157), 8,091 in Rio Grande do Sul (8,330), and 9,264 in other states (9,739).[28] Since some otherwise identifying Jews might have failed to declare themselves as such in that census, we had adopted a corrected estimate of 100,000 since 1980, assuming that the overall balance of Jewish vital events, identificational changes, and external migrations was close to zero. The 1991 census figures pointed to Jewish population decline countrywide, most of it in Rio de Janeiro where Jewish population was decreasing since 1960. On the other hand, in São Paulo—Brazil's major Jewish community—all previous census returns since 1940 and various other Jewish survey and register data supported the widely held perception of a growing community, but the 1991 census figure contradicted that assumption.[29] A 1992 study in the state of Rio Grande do Sul and its capi-

---

[26]Rosa N. Geldstein, *Censo de la Poblacion Judia de la ciudad de Salta, 1986; Informe final* (Buenos Aires, 1988); Yacov Rubel, *Los Judios de Villa Crespo y Almagro: Perfil Sociodemográfico* (Buenos Aires, 1989); Yacov Rubel and Mario Toer, *Censo de la Población Judía de Rosario, 1990* (Buenos Aires, 1992); Centro Union Israelita de Cordoba, *First Sociodemographic Study of Jewish Population; Cordoba 1993* (Cordoba, 1995).

[27]See a brief overview of the problems in Laura Golbert, Norma Lew, and Alejandro Rofman, *La nueva pobreza judía* (Buenos Aires, 1997).

[28]IBGE, *Censo demográfico do Brazil* (Rio de Janeiro, 1997).

[29]Henrique Rattner, "Recenseamento e pesquisa sociológica da comunidade judaica de São

tal Porto Alegre — Brazil's third largest community — unveiled an enlarged Jewish population of about 11,000.[30] Excluding the non-Jewish household members, the core Jewish population could be estimated at about 9,000, some 10 percent above the 1991 census figure. In the light of this and other evidence of a substantially stable Jewish population — though one confronting high rates of intermarriage and a definite erosion in the younger age groups[31] — we estimated the Jewish population at 97,500 in 2001, making Brazil the 11th largest Jewish community in the world.

In Chile, a sociodemographic survey conducted in the Santiago metropolitan area in 1995 indicated an enlarged Jewish population of 21,450, 19,700 of them Jews and 1,750 non-Jewish relatives, including persons not affiliated with any Jewish organization.[32] Assuming another 1,300 Jews living in smaller provincial communities, a new countrywide estimate of 21,000 Jews was obtained. Previous lower estimates, reflecting results of the 1970 population census and a 1982–83 community survey, possibly overestimated the net effects of Jewish emigration. The new survey portrayed a rather stable community, with incipient signs of aging and assimilation.

In Venezuela, a new sociodemographic survey was carried out in 1998.[33] Based on a comprehensive list of affiliated households and an indicative sample of the unaffiliated, and supplemented by a compilation of Jewish death records, the survey suggested a downward revision of the Jewish population estimate to 16,000.

On the strength of fragmentary information available, our estimates for Uruguay, Colombia, and Peru[34] were slightly reduced to 22,500, 3,500, and 2,700 respectively.

Paulo, 1968," in Henrique Rattner, ed., *Nos caminhos da diáspora* (São Paulo, 1972); Claudia Milnitzky, ed., *Apendice estatistico da comunidade judaica do estado de São Paulo* (São Paulo, 1980); Egon and Frieda Wolff, *Documentos V; Os recenseamentos demograficos oficiais do seculo XX* (Rio de Janeiro, 1993–1994).

[30]Anita Brumer, *Identidade em mudança; Pesquisa sociológica sobre os judeus do Rio Grande do Sul* (Porto Alegre, 1994).

[31]Rene D. Decol "Imigrações urbanas para o Brasil: o caso dos Judeus," unpublished Ph.D. diss., Campinas, 1999; Daniel Sasson, *A comunidade judaica do Rio de Janeiro; Metodologia da pesquisa* (Rio de Janeiro, 1997).

[32]Gabriel Berger et al., *Estudio Socio-Demográfico de la Comunidad Judía de Chile* (Santiago-Buenos Aires, 1995).

[33]Sergio DellaPergola, Salomon Benzaquen, and Tony Beker de Weinraub, *Perfil sociodemográfico y cutural de la comunidad judía de Caracas* (Caracas, 2000). The survey was sponsored by the two main local Jewish community organizations, the Asociación Israelita de Venezuela and the Union Israelita de Caracas, and by the Asociación de Amigos de la Universidad Hebrea de Jerusalén.

[34]Local observers had expected quicker reduction of Jewish population size. See Leon Trahtemberg Siederer, *Demografia judía del Peru* (Lima, 1988).

EUROPE

About 1.6 million Jews lived in Europe at the beginning of 2001; 66 percent lived in Western Europe and 34 percent in Eastern Europe and the Balkan countries—including the Asian territories of the Russian Republic and Turkey (see table 4). In 2000 Europe lost 1.9 percent of its Jewish population, mainly through the continuing emigration from the European republics of the FSU.

European Union. Incorporating 15 countries since the 1995 accession of Austria, Finland, and Sweden, the European Union (EU) had an estimated combined Jewish population of 1,032,100—an increase of 0.3 percent over the previous year. Different trends affected the Jewish populations in each member country.[35]

With the breakup of the USSR, France had the third largest Jewish population in the world, after the United States and Israel. The size of French Jewry was estimated at 530,000 when a major survey was taken in the 1970s.[36] Over the following 20 years, the plausible trends of both the internal evolution and external migrations of Jews in France suggest little net change in Jewish population size. A study conducted in 1988 at the initiative of the Fonds Social Juif Unifié (FSJU) confirmed the basic demographic stability of French Jewry.[37] The French Jewish community continued to absorb a small inflow of Jews from North Africa, and its age composition was younger than in other European countries. However, migration to Israel amounted to 7,500 in 1980–1989 and over 15,000 in 1990–2000. Since the 1990s, aging tended to determine a moderate surplus of deaths over births. In view of these trends, our French Jewish population estimate was revised to 525,000 in 1995 and 520,000 at the beginning of 2001.

A significant revision of the size of Jewish population in the United Kingdom was released in 1998 by the Community Research Unit (CRU) of the Board of Deputies of British Jews.[38] Current evaluation of Jewish birth and death records confirmed the downward trend that had emerged from previous research and generated a new estimate of 285,000 for 1995. The vital statistical records regularly compiled by the CRU showed an excess of deaths over births in the range of about 1,000–1,500 a year.[39] An attitudinal survey of British Jews conducted in 1995 in-

[35]Sergio DellaPergola, "Jews in the European Community: Sociodemographic Trends and Challenges," AJYB 1993, vol. 93, pp. 25–82.

[36]Doris Bensimon and Sergio DellaPergola, *La population juive de France: sociodémographie et identité* (Jerusalem-Paris, 1984).

[37]Erik H. Cohen, *L'Etude et l'éducation juive en France ou l'avenir d'une communauté* (Paris, 1991).

[38]Marlena Schmool, Frances Cohen, *A Profile of British Jewry: Patterns and Trends at the Turn of the Century* (London, 1998)

[39]Steven Haberman, Barry A. Kosmin, Caren Levy, "Mortality Patterns of British Jews 1975–79: Insights and Applications for the Size and Structure of British Jewry," *Journal of the Royal Statistical Society,* A, 146, pt. 3, 1983, pp. 294–310; Steven Haberman and Marlena Schmool, "Estimates of British Jewish Population 1984–88," *Journal of the Royal Statistical Society,* A, 158, pt. 3, 1995, pp. 547–62; Stanley Waterman and Barry Kosmin,

dicated a significant rise in intermarriage (38 percent of all married men, 50 percent of married men under 30), implying increasing assimilatory losses.[40] Further attrition derived from emigration (over 7,000 emigrants to Israel in 1980–1989 and about 6,000 in 1990–2000). Allowing for a continuation of these well-established trends, we adopted an estimate of 275,000 for 2001 (fifth largest worldwide).

In 1990, Germany was politically reunited. In the former (West) German Federal Republic, the 1987 population census reported 32,319 Jews.[41] Immigration compensated for the surplus of deaths over births in this aging Jewish population. Estimates about the small Jewish population in the former (East) German Democratic Republic ranged between 500 and 2,000. According to available reports, over 100,000 immigrants from the FSU settled in united Germany since the end of 1989, including non-Jewish family members.[42] Detailed estimates are available for Jews affiliated with the Zentralwohlfahrtstelle der Juden in Deutschland (ZDJ).[43] The total of Jews registered in German Jewish communities increased from 27,711 at the beginning of 1990 to 87,756 at the beginning of 2001. It should be noted that by the same community registers, the number of Jews would have declined from about 28,000 in 1990 to 19,000 in 2001 due to the continuing excess of Jewish deaths over Jewish births, were it not for steady immigration from the FSU. Our own population estimates assume there are enough incentives for most newcomers to be willing to affiliate with the Jewish community, but allow for some time lag between immigration and registration with the organized Jewish community, and take into account a certain amount of permanent nonaffiliation. Assuming the latter at about 10,000, an estimate of 98,000 core Jews (not including non-Jewish members of households) obtained for 2001, bringing Germany to the position of ninth largest Jewish community worldwide.

Belgium, Italy, and the Netherlands each had Jewish populations ranging around 30,000. There was a tendency toward internal shrinkage of all these Jewries, but in some instances this was offset by immigration. In Belgium, the size of the Jewish population, estimated at 31,500, was probably quite stable owing to

---

British Jewry in the Eighties: A Statistical and Geographical Guide (London, 1986); Marlena Schmool, Report of Community Statistics (London, yearly publication).

[40]Marlena Schmool and Frances Cohen, British Synagogue Membership in 1990 (London, 1991); Stephen Miller, Marlena Schmool, and Antony Lerman, Social and Political Attitudes of British Jews: Some Key Findings of the JPR Survey (London, 1996).

[41]Statistisches Bundesamt, Bevölkerung und Erwerbstätigkeit, Volkszählung vom 25 Mai 1987, Heft 6 (Stuttgart, 1990).

[42]See Madeleine Tress, "Welfare State Type, Labour Markets and Refugees: A Comparison of Jews from the Former Soviet Union in the United States and the Federal Republic of Germany," Ethnic and Racial Studies 21, no. 1, 1998, 116–137.

[43]Zentralwohlfartsstelle der Juden in Deutschland, Mitgliederstatistik; Der Einzelnen Jüdischen Gemeinden und Landesverbände in Deutschland (Frankfurt, yearly publication).

the comparatively strong Orthodox sector in that community. In Italy, membership in Jewish communities became voluntary in 1987, a change from the long-standing system of compulsory affiliation. Although most Jews reaffiliated, the new, looser legal framework facilitated the ongoing attrition of the Jewish population. Recent Jewish community records for Milan indicated an affiliated Jewish population of 6,500, in contrast to over 8,000 in the 1960s, despite substantial immigration from other countries in the intervening period. This evidence, and data on declining birthrates in most other cities, prompted a reduction in our national estimate for Italy to 29,500.[44] In the Netherlands, a recent study indicated a growing number of residents of Israeli origin, substantially offsetting the declining trends among veteran Jews.[45] In the light of a new Jewish population survey that covered an enlarged Jewish population of 43,000–45,000, including Israeli and Russian new immigrants, we revised the core Jewish population estimate to 28,000 in 2001.[46]

Other EU member countries had smaller and, overall, slowly declining Jewish populations. Possible exceptions are Sweden and Spain, whose Jewish populations were very tentatively estimated at 15,000 and 12,000, respectively, based on figures on affiliation in the major cities. Austria's permanent Jewish population was estimated at 9,000. While a negative balance of births and deaths has long prevailed, connected with great aging and frequent outmarriage, immigration from the FSU tended to offset internal losses. The small Jewish populations in other Nordic countries were, on the whole, numerically stable. In Ireland, the 1991 census indicated 1,581 Jews. Since 1961 the Jewish population has regularly declined by 500–600 every ten years. We put the 2001 estimate at 1,000.

Other West Europe. Few countries remain in Western Europe which have not joined the EU. In 2001 they accounted for a combined Jewish population of 19,700. The estimate of Switzerland's Jewish population was based on the results of the 1990 census. The official count indicated 17,577 Jews as against 18,330 in 1980 — a decline of 4 percent.[47] Allowing for undeclared Jews, and also for about 1,000 emigrants to Israel during the 1990s, we put the estimate at 17,800.

---

[44]For an overview see Sergio DellaPergola, "La popolazione ebraica in Italia nel contesto ebraico globale" in *Storia d'Italia, Ebrei in Italia,* ed. Corrado Vivanti (Torino, 1997), vol. 2, pp. 895–936.

[45]C. Kooyman and J. Almagor, *Israelis in Holland: A Sociodemographic Study of Israelis and Former Israelis in Holland* (Amsterdam, 1996); Philip van Praag, "Between Speculation and Reality," *Studia Rosenthaliana,* special issue published together with vol. 23, no. 2, 1989, pp. 175–179.

[46]Personal communication from Dr. Chris Kooyman, Stichting Joods Maatschappelijk Werk, Amsterdam.

[47]Bundesamt für Statistik, *Wohnbevölkerung nach Konfession und Geschlecht, 1980 und 1990* (Bern, 1993).

TABLE 4. ESTIMATED JEWISH POPULATION DISTRIBUTION IN EUROPE,
1/1/2001

Country	Total Population	Jewish Population	Jews per 1,000 Population	Accuracy Rating
Austria	8,080,000	9,000	1.1	C 1995
Belgium	10,249,000	31,500	3.1	C 1987
Denmark	5,320,000	6,400	1.2	C 1990
Finland	5,172,000	1,100	0.2	B 1999
France[a]	59,268,000	520,000	8.8	C 1990
Germany	82,017,000	98,000	1.2	B 2001
Greece	10,610,000	4,500	0.4	B 1995
Ireland	3,803,000	1,000	0.3	B 1993
Italy	57,530,000	29,500	0.5	B 1995
Luxembourg	437,000	600	1.4	B 2000
Netherlands	15,864,000	28,000	1.8	B 1999 X
Portugal	10,016,000	500	0.0	C 1999 X
Spain	39,910,000	12,000	0.3	D
Sweden	8,842,000	15,000	1.7	C 1990
United Kingdom	59,415,000	275,000	4.6	B 1995
Total European Union	376,533,000	1,032,100	2.7	
Gibraltar	25,000	600	24.0	B 1991
Norway	4,469,000	1,200	0.3	B 1995
Switzerland	7,170,000	17,800	2.5	B 1990
Other	829,000	100	0.1	D
Total other West Europe	12,493,000	19,700	1.6	
Belarus	10,187,000	25,000	2.5	B 1999
Estonia	1,393,000	2,000	1.4	B 2000
Latvia	2,421,000	10,000	4.1	B 2000 X
Lithuania	3,696,000	4,000	1.1	B 2000
Moldova	4,295,000	6,000	1.4	B 2000
Russia[b]	145,491,000	275,000	1.9	B 2000
Ukraine	49,568,000	112,000	2.3	C 1997 X
Total former USSR in Europe	217,051,000	434,000	2.0	

TABLE 4.—*(Continued)*

Country	Total Population	Jewish Population	Jews per 1,000 Population	Accuracy Rating
Bosnia-Herzegovina	3,977,000	300	0.1	C 1996
Bulgaria	7,949,000	2,500	0.3	B 1992
Croatia	4,654,000	1,300	0.3	C 1996
Czech Republic	10,272,000	2,800	0.3	B 1998
Hungary	9,968,000	51,500	5.2	C 1999
Macedonia (FYR)	2,034,000	100	0.0	C 1996
Poland	38,605,000	3,500	0.1	D
Romania	22,438,000	11,000	0.5	B 1997
Slovakia	5,399,000	3,300	0.6	D
Slovenia	1,988,000	100	0.1	C 1996
Turkey[b]	66,668,000	18,900	0.3	C 1996
Yugoslavia[c]	10,552,000	1,700	0.2	C 1996
Total other East Europe and Balkans[d]	187,638,000	97,000	0.5	
Total	793,715,000	1,582,800	2.0	

[a]Including Monaco.
[b]Including Asian regions.
[c]Serbia and Montenegro.
[d]Including Albania.

Former USSR (European parts). Since 1989, the demographic situation of East European Jewry has been radically transformed by the dramatic geopolitical changes in the region.[48] Official governmental sources provide the fundamental basis for information on the number of Jews in the FSU.[49] The Soviet Union's and subsequent data distinguish the Jews as one recognized "nationality" (ethnic group). In a society that, until recently, left little or no space for re-

[48]For the historical demographic background see U.O. Schmelz, "New Evidence on Basic Issues in the Demography of Soviet Jews," *Jewish Journal of Sociology* 16, no. 2, 1974, pp. 209–23; Mordechai Altshuler, *Soviet Jewry Since the Second World War: Population and Social Structure* (Westport, 1987); Mordechai Altshuler, *Soviet Jewry on the Eve of the Holocaust: A Social and Demographic Profile* (Jerusalem, 1998).
[49]Dr. Mark Tolts of the A. Harman Institute of Contemporary Jewry at the Hebrew University actively contributed to the preparation of FSU Jewish population estimates. See Mark Tolts, *Main Demographic Trends of the Jews in Russia and the FSU* (Jerusalem, 2001).

ligions, the ethnic definition criterion could be considered comprehensive and valid. Data from the last all-Soviet population census, carried out in January 1989, revealed a total of 1,450,500 Jews,[50] confirming the declining trend shown by the previous three USSR censuses: 2,267,800 in 1959, 2,150,700 in 1970, and 1,810,900 in 1979.

Our reservation about USSR Jewish census figures in previous AJYB volumes bears repeating: some underreporting is not impossible, but it cannot be easily quantified and should not be exaggerated. The prolonged existence of a totalitarian regime produced conflicting effects on census declarations: on the one hand, it stimulated a preference for other than Jewish nationalities in the various parts of the FSU, especially in connection with mixed marriages; on the other hand, it preserved a formal Jewish identification by coercion, through the mandatory registration of nationality on official documents such as internal passports. Viewed conceptually, the census figures represent the core Jewish population in the USSR. They actually constitute a good example of a large and empirically measured core Jewish population in the Diaspora, consisting of the aggregate of self-identifying Jews. The figures of successive censuses were remarkably consistent with one another, and with the known patterns of emigration and internal demographic evolution of the Jewish population in recent decades.

Jewish emigration played the major role among demographic changes intervening since 1989.[51] The economic and political crisis that culminated in the disintegration of the Soviet Union as a state in 1991 generated a major emigration upsurge in 1990 and 1991. Emigration continued at lower but significant levels throughout 2000. Over the whole 1990–2000 period, over 1.4 million people emigrated from the FSU who were Jewish according to the enlarged Law of Return definition. Of these, nearly 900,000 went to Israel, about 300,000 to the United States, and over 200,000 chose other countries, mainly Germany. Out of the total number, about 980,000 were Jewish by the core definition. Periodic declines in the volume of emigration should not be misconstrued: when compared to the fast declining Jewish population figures in the FSU, the emigration trend remained remarkably stable.

---

[50]Goskomstat SSSR, *Vestnik Statistiki* 10, 1990, pp. 69–71. This figure does not include about 30,000 Tats who were in fact Mountain Jews—a group mostly concentrated in the Caucasus area that enjoys fully Jewish status and the prerogatives granted by Israel's Law of Return.

[51]Yearly migration estimates can be compiled using (ex-)Soviet, Israeli, American, German, and other sources, especially Israel Central Bureau of Statistics and HIAS yearly reports. See also Mark Tolts, "Demography of the Jews in the Former Soviet Union: Yesterday and Today," in *Jewish Life After the USSR: A Community in Transition* (Cambridge, 1999); Yoel Florsheim, "Emigration of Jews from the Soviet Union in 1989," *Jews and Jewish Topics in the Soviet Union and Eastern Europe*, 2, no. 12, 1990, pp. 22–31; Sidney Heitman, "Soviet Emigration in 1990," *Berichte des Bundesinstitut fur Ostwissenschaftliche und internationale studien,* vol. 33, 1991; Tress, "Welfare State Type, Labour Markets and Refugees"; and Zentralwohlfahrtsstelle.

While mass emigration was an obvious factor in Jewish population decrease, a heavy deficit of internal population dynamics developed and even intensified due to the great aging that prevailed for many decades among FSU Jewry. For example, in 1993–1994 the balance of recorded vital events in Russia included 2.8 Jewish births versus 30.0 deaths per 1,000 Jewish population; in Ukraine, the respective figures were 4.2 and 35.9 per 1,000; in Belarus, 5.2 and 32.6 per 1,000; in Latvia, 3.1 and 24.5 per 1,000; in Moldova 5.9 and 34.6 per 1,000.[52] These figures imply yearly losses of many thousands to the respective Jewish populations. Frequencies of outmarriage were close to 70 percent of Jewish spouses who married in Russia in 1988, and close to 80 percent in Ukraine and Latvia in 1996; furthermore a non-Jewish nationality was generally preferred for the children of the outmarried.[53] Aging in the countries of origin was exacerbated by the significantly younger age composition of Jewish emigrants.[54] As a result, the Jewish population rapidly shrank.[55]

On the strength of these considerations, our estimate of the core Jewish population in the USSR (including the Asian regions) was reduced from the census figure of 1,480,000 at the beginning of 1989 (including Tats) to 890,000 in 1993.

---

[52]Mark Tolts, "The Jewish Population of Russia, 1989–1995," *Jews in Eastern Europe* 3, no. 31, 1996; idem., "Demography of the Jews in the Former Soviet Union: Yesterday and Today."

[53]Mark Tolts, "Some Basic Trends in Soviet Jewish Demography," in U.O. Schmelz and S. DellaPergola, eds., *Papers in Jewish Demography 1989* (Jerusalem, 1993), pp. 237–243; Viacheslav Konstantinov, "Jewish Population of the USSR on the Eve of the Great Exodus," *Jews and Jewish Topics in the Soviet Union and Eastern Europe* 3, no. 16, 1991, pp. 5–23; Mordechai Altshuler, "Socio-demographic Profile of Moscow Jews," ibid., pp. 24–40; Mark Tolts, "The Balance of Births and Deaths Among Soviet Jewry," *Jews and Jewish Topics in the Soviet Union and Eastern Europe* 2, no. 18, 1992, pp. 13–26; Leonid E. Darsky, "Fertility in the USSR; Basic Trends" (paper presented at European Population Conference, Paris, 1991); Mark Tolts, "Jewish Marriages in the USSR: A Demographic Analysis," *East European Jewish Affairs* 22, no. 2, 1992; Sidney and Alice Goldstein, *Lithuanian Jewry 1993: A Demographic and Sociocultural Profile* (Jerusalem, 1997).

[54]Age structures of the Jewish population in the Russian Federal Republic were reported in: Goskomstat SSSR, *Itogi vsesoiuznoi perepisi naseleniia 1970 goda,* vol. 4, table 33 (Moscow, 1973); Goskomstat SSSR, *Itogi vsesoiuznoi perepisi naseleniia 1979 goda,* vol. 4, part 2, table 2 (Moscow, 1989); Goskomstat SSSR, *Itogi vsesoiuznoi perepisi naseleniia 1989 goda* (Moscow, 1991). Age structures of recent Jewish migrants from the USSR to the United States and to Israel appear, respectively, in HIAS, *Statistical Report* (New York, yearly publication) and unpublished annual data kindly communicated to the author; Israel Central Bureau of Statistics, *Immigration to Israel*, Special Series (Jerusalem, yearly publication); Yoel Florsheim, "Immigration to Israel and the United States from the former Soviet Union, 1992," *Jews in Eastern Europe* 3, no. 22, 1993, pp. 31–39; Mark Tolts, "Trends in Soviet Jewish Demography since the Second World War," in Ya'acov Ro'i , ed., *Jews and Jewish Life in Russia and the Soviet Union* (London, 1995), pp. 365–82; and Mark Tolts, "Demography of the Jews in the Former Soviet Union: Yesterday and Today."

[55]Mark Tolts, "Demographic Trends of the Jews in the Three Slavic Republics of the Former USSR: A Comparative Analysis," in S. DellaPergola and J. Even, eds., *Papers in Jewish Demography 1993* (Jerusalem, 1997), pp. 147–175; Mark Tolts, "The Interrelationship

The February 1994 national Microcensus of the Russian republic confirmed the known trends.[56] The data, based on a 5-percent sample, revealed a Jewish population of about 400,000 plus approximately 8,000 Tats, for a total of 408,000, with a range of variation between 401,000 and 415,000 allowing for sampling errors. Our subsequent estimates, as usual, reflect for each FSU republic separately all available data and estimates concerning Jewish emigration, births, deaths, and geographical mobility between republics.

The total Jewish population for the FSU was estimated at 462,000 at the beginning of 2001. Of this total, 434,000 lived in the European republics and 28,000 in the Asian republics (see below). Russia kept the largest Jewish population in any of the FSU republics—currently the fifth largest in the world. Our 2001 estimate for Russia was 275,000 (as against census-based estimates of 570,000 [including Tats] for 1989 and 410,000 for 1994). In spite of decline, Russia's share of the total Jewish population of the FSU significantly increased over time due to lower emigration frequencies. Jews in the Ukraine were estimated at 112,000 (reflecting an upward correction, but also the large-scale emigration of recent years), making the Jewish community the eighth largest worldwide (487,300 in 1989). In Belarus, the 1999 census[57] indicated a Jewish population of 27,798 (112,000 in 1989). For 2001 we estimated 25,000 Jews there. In the Republic of Moldova a survey initiated by the American Joint Distribution Committee (JDC) in 1999 confirmed the declining trends and sustained a 6,000 estimate for 2001 (65,800 in 1989). Based on updated figures from the local national population registers, a combined total of 16,000 were estimated for the three Baltic states of Latvia, Lithuania, and Estonia (versus 39,900 in 1989). The figure for Latvia includes a 1,800 upward correction based on the 2000 census.[58]

It should be reiterated that the new population censuses conducted in parts of the FSU produced figures only barely higher than our estimates obtained through a ten-year accountancy of known or expected vital events and international migration. Some of these inconsistencies can be explained by any combination of the following five factors: (a) migration of several thousands of Jews between the various FSU republics since 1991, especially to the Russian repub-

---

between Emigration and the Sociodemographic Trends of Russian Jewry," in Noah Lewin-Epstein, Yaakov Ro'i , and Paul Ritterband, eds., *Russian Jews on Three Continents* (London, 1997), pp. 147–176.

[56]See V. Aleksandrova, "Mikroperepisis' naseleniia Rossiiskoi Federatsii," *Voprosy Statistiki*, 1994 (1), p. 37 (Moscow, 1994). See also Mark Tolts, "The Interrelationship between Emigration and the Socio-Demographic Profile of Russian Jewry."

[57]Ministry of Statistics and Analysis of the Republic of Belarus, *Population of the Republic of Belarus: Results of the 1999 Population Census Conducted in the Republic of Belarus* (Minsk, 2000).

[58]Goldstein, *Lithuanian Jewry 1993*; Lithuanian Department of Statistics, *Demographic Yearbook 1996* (Vilnius, 1997); Central Statistical Bureau of Latvia, *Demographic Yearbook of Latvia 1997* (Riga, 1997); Anna Stroi, "Latvia v chelovecheskom izmerenii: etnicheskii aspekt," *Diena* (Riga, 1997).

lic; (b) a higher proportion of non-Jews than previously assumed among the enlarged pool of Jewish emigrants from the FSU, resulting in excessively lowered estimates of the number of core Jews remaining there; (c) a Jewish identification in the most recent sources by people who declared a different national (ethnic) identification in previous censuses; (d) counting in the republics' national censuses and population registers some people as residents—according to the legal criteria of the country of origin—who have actually emigrated to the State of Israel or other countries; (e) some returns to Russia and other republics from Israel[59] and other countries by migrants who are still registered as residents of the latter. While it is difficult to establish the respective weight of each of these factors, their overall impact has so far been quite secondary in the assessment of Jewish population changes. Factors (d) and (e) above point to likely double counts of FSU Jews in the respective countries of origin and of emigration. Consequently our world synopsis of core Jewish populations may be overestimated by several thousands.

The respective figures for the enlarged Jewish population—including all current Jews as well as other persons of Jewish parentage and their non-Jewish household members—are substantially higher in the FSU, where high intermarriage rates have prevailed for decades. While a definitive estimate for the total USSR cannot be provided for lack of appropriate data, evidence for Russia and the other Slavic republics indicated a high ratio of non-Jews to Jews in the enlarged Jewish population. In 1989, 570,000 Jews in Russia, together with 340,000 non-Jewish household members, formed an enlarged Jewish population of 910,000; in 2001, the 275,000 core Jews and their 245,000 non-Jewish household members produced an enlarged population of 520,000.[60] The ratio of enlarged to core therefore increased from 1.6 in 1989 to 1.9 in 2001. Due to the highly self-selective character of aliyah, non-Jews constituted a relatively smaller share of all new immigrants from the FSU than their share among the Jewish population in the countries of origin, but such share was rapidly increasing.[61]

It is obvious that the wide provisions of Israel's Law of Return apply to virtually the maximum emigration pool of self-declared Jews and close non-Jewish relatives. Any of the large figures attributed in recent years to the size of Soviet Jewry, insofar as they were based on demographic reasoning, did not relate to the

[59]Council of Europe, *Recent Demographic Developments in Europe, 2000* (Strasbourg, 2000).

[60]Mark Tolts, "Jews in the Russian Republic since the Second World War: The Dynamics of Demographic Erosion," in International Union for the Scientific Study of Population, *International Population Conference* (Montreal, 1993), vol. 3, pp. 99–111; Evgeni Andreev, "Jews in the Households in Russia," forthcoming in S. DellaPergola and J. Even, eds., *Papers in Jewish Demography 1997* (Jerusalem); Tolts, *Main Demographic Trends and Characteristics*.

[61]Israel's Ministry of Interior records the religion-nationality of each person, including new immigrants. Such attribution is made on the basis of documentary evidence supplied by the immigrants themselves, and is checked by competent authorities in Israel. Accord-

core but to various (unspecified) measures of an enlarged Jewish population. The evidence also suggests that in the FSU core Jews constitute a smaller share (and the non-Jewish fringe a larger share) of the enlarged Jewish population than in some Western countries, such as the United States. Just as the number of declared Jews evolved consistently between censuses, the number of persons of Jewish descent who preferred not to be identified as Jews was rather consistent too. However, the recent political developments, and especially the current emigration urge, probably led to greater readiness to acknowledge a Jewish self-identification by persons who did not describe themselves as such in past censuses. These "returnees" imply an actual net increment to the core Jewish population of the FSU, Israel, and world Jewry.

Other East Europe and Balkans. A new survey of Hungarian Jewry provided new evidence on the size and characteristics of the largest community in Eastern Europe outside the FSU.[62] As against an overall membership in local Jewish organizations estimated at about 20,000–25,000, the new data revealed a wide gap between core and enlarged Jewish population figures. The broader definition including all persons of Jewish ancestry referred to 150,000–200,000 persons. On the other hand a detailed assessment of Jewish migrations and vital statistics based on an end-1945 estimate of about 144,000 Holocaust survivors produced a total of 50,000–55,000 for end-2000. Our core Jewish population estimate of 51,500 attempts to reflect the significant excess of deaths over births that prevails in Hungary according to available indications.

The January 1992 census of Romania reported a Jewish population of 9,107. Based on the detailed Jewish community records available with the Federatia Comunitatilor Evreiesi, our estimate for the beginning of 2001 was 11,000. The Czech census of 1991 reported 1,292 Jews, but according to the Federation of Jewish Communities there were at least twice as many, reflected in our estimate of 2,800. The number of Jews in Poland and Slovakia was very tentatively estimated at 3,500 and 3,300 respectively. In Bulgaria, the December 4, 1992, census reported 3,461 Jews;[63] our 2001 estimate, reflecting emigration, was 2,500. Crisis continued in the former Yugoslavia, spurring Jewish population decline. The core Jewish population for the total of the five successor republics, reduced through emigration, was assessed at about 3,500 at the beginning of 2001. Of these, fewer

---

ing to data available from the Interior Ministry's Central Population Register, 90.3 percent of all new immigrants from the USSR during the period October 1989–August 1992 were recorded as Jewish. In 1994, the percent had declined to 71.6, in 1998 it was below 60 percent, and in 2000 below 50 percent. Israel Central Bureau of Statistics, *Immigration to Israel 1998* (Jerusalem, 2000), and unpublished data. See also Sergio DellaPergola, "The Demographic Context of the Soviet Aliya," in *Jews and Jewish Topics in the Soviet Union and Eastern Europe* 3, no. 16, 1991, pp. 41–56.

[62]The survey was directed by Prof. Andras Kovács of the Central European University in Budapest. Publication is forthcoming.

[63]*Statistical Yearbook* (Sofia, 1992).

than 2,000 lived in the territorially shrunken Yugoslavia (Serbia with Montenegro), and 1,300 in Croatia.[64] The Jewish population of Turkey, where a significant surplus of deaths over births has been reported for several years,[65] was estimated at about 19,000.

ASIA

Israel. At the beginning of 2001, Israel's Jewish population was 4,952,200.[66] This was half a million more than the 4,459,696 Jews enumerated in the November 1995 census. Adding the roughly 250,000 non-Jewish members of immigrant families, mostly from the FSU but also from Ethiopia and other countries, an enlarged Jewish population of 5.2 million obtained,[67] out of a total population of 6,363,800.

Israel accounted for 99 percent of the 5 million Jews in Asia, including the Asian republics of the former USSR but excluding the Asian territories of the Russian Republic and Turkey (see table 5). By the beginning of 2001, Israel Jews constituted 37.4 percent of total world Jewry.[68] Israel's Jewish population grew in 2001 by 79,400, or 1.6 percent. The pace of growth was slowing down after reaching growth rates of 6.2 percent in 1990, 5 percent in 1991, and 2–2.5 percent between 1992 and 1996. The number of new immigrants in 2000 (60,130) declined by 21.7 percent from 1999 (76,766) which in turn represented a 35-percent increase over 1998 (56,730). About 25 percent of Jewish population growth in 2000 derived from the net migration balance, as against 42 percent in 2000; most Jewish population growth derived from natural increase. Moreover, 4,000 persons underwent Orthodox conversion in Israel in 1999, and 4,600 were attending conversion classes in 2000—most of them immigrants from Ethiopia and the FSU and their children, who were previously listed as non-Jews.[69] More than half of all new candidates for conversion to Judaism attended the Institute for Judaism

---

[64]For an overview see Melita Svob, *Jews in Croatia: Migration and Changes in Jewish Population* (Zagreb, 1997).

[65]Shaul Tuval, "The Jewish Community of Istanbul, 1948-1992: A Study in Cultural, Economic and Social Processes," unpublished Ph.D. diss., Jerusalem, 1999.

[66]Israel Central Bureau of Statistics, *Population and Vital Statistics 1999* (Jerusalem, 2000); *Monthly Bulletin of Statistics* (Jerusalem, 2001).

[67]The Israel Central Bureau of Statistics refers to such enlarged population as "Jews and others."

[68]Thanks to the staff of Israel's Central Bureau of Statistics for facilitating compilation of published and unpublished data. For a comprehensive review of sociodemographic changes in Israel, see U.O. Schmelz, Sergio DellaPergola, and Uri Avner, "Ethnic Differences among Israeli Jews: A New Look," AJYB 1990, vol. 90, pp. 3–204. See also Sergio DellaPergola, "Demographic Changes in Israel in the Early 1990s," in Y. Kop, ed., *Israel's Social Services 1992–93* (Jerusalem, 1993), pp. 57–115.

[69]Data released by rabbinical courts and special conversion courts. See *Ha'aretz*, December 24, 2000.

Studies conducted jointly in Israel by the Orthodox, Conservative, and Reform movements.

TABLE 5. ESTIMATED JEWISH POPULATION DISTRIBUTION IN ASIA, 1/1/2001

Country	Total Population	Jewish Population	Jews per 1,000 Population	Accuracy Rating
Israel[a]	6,363,800	4,952,200	778.2	A 2001 X
Azerbaijan	8,041,000	7,500	0.9	C 1999 X
Georgia	5,262,000	5,500	1.0	C 2000
Kazakhstan	16,172,000	5,200	0.3	B 1999 X
Kyrgyzstan	4,921,000	1,100	0.2	B 1999 X
Tajikistan	6,087,000	1,000	0.2	C 1999 X
Turkmenistan	4,737,000	700	0.1	C 1999
Uzbekistan	24,881,000	7,000	0.3	C 1999 X
Total former USSR in Asia[b]	73,888,000	28,000	0.4	
China[c]	1,282,437,000	1,000	0.0	D
India	1,008,937,000	5,400	0.0	B 1996
Iran	70,330,000	11,500	0.2	C 1986
Iraq	22,946,000	100	0.0	C 1997
Japan	127,096,000	1,000	0.0	C 1993
Korea, South	46,740,000	100	0.0	C 1998
Philippines	75,653,000	100	0.0	C
Singapore	4,018,000	300	0.1	B 1990
Syria	16,189,000	100	0.0	C 1995
Thailand	62,806,000	200	0.0	C 1988
Yemen	18,349,000	200	0.0	B 1995
Other	789,579,200	300	0.0	D
Total other Asia	3,525,080,200	20,300	0.0	
Total	3,605,332,000	5,000,500	1.4	

[a]Total population of Israel 1/1/2001. Jewish population includes residents within Palestinian Autonomy.
[b]Including Armenia. Not including Asian regions of Russian Republic.
[c]Including Hong Kong.

Former USSR (Asian parts). The total Jewish population in the Asian republics of the former USSR was estimated at 28,000 at the beginning of 2001. Ethnic conflicts in the Caucasus area and the fear of Muslim fundamentalism in Central Asia continued to cause concern and stimulated Jewish emigration.[70] At the beginning of the 1990s, minimal rates of natural increase still existed among the more traditional sections of these Jewish communities, but conditions were rapidly eroding this residual surplus.[71] Reflecting these trends, the largest community remained in Azerbaijan (8,900 according to the 1999 census and 7,500 in 2001[72] versus 30,800 in 1989), followed by Uzbekistan (7,000 in 2001 vs. 94,900), Georgia (5,500 vs. 24,800), Kazakhstan (6,800 according to the 1999 census[73] and 5,200 in 2001, vs. 19,900 in 1989), and the remaining republics (2,800, thereof 1,600 in Kyrgyzstan according to the 1999 Kyrgyzstan census, vs. 24,000 in 1989).

Other countries. It is difficult to estimate the Jewish population of Iran, last counted in the 1986 national census.[74] Based on evidence of continuing decline, the 2001 estimate was reduced to 11,500. In other Asian countries with small, old communities the Jewish population tended to decline, even to the point of disappearance. The recent reduction was more notable in Syria and Yemen after Jews were officially allowed to emigrate.

In India, the 1991 census provided a figure of 5,271 Jews, 63 percent of whom lived in the state of Maharashtra, including the main community of Mumbai.[75] Another 1,067 persons, belonging to such religious groups as Messianic Judaism and Enoka Israel, all from Mizoram, were also counted. A survey conducted in 1995–96 by ORT India covered 3,330 individuals, fairly well educated and experiencing the customary patterns of postponed marriage, declining fertility, and aging.

Very small Jewish communities, partially of a transient character, exist in several countries of Southeast Asia. After the reunion in 1997 of Hong Kong with mainland China, China's permanent Jewish population was estimated at roughly 1,000, the same as Japan's.

---

[70]Israel Central Bureau of Statistics, *Immigration to Israel 1998* (Jerusalem, 2000); Ministry of Immigrants Absorption, Division of Data Systems, *Selected Data on Aliyah, 2000* (Jerusalem, 2001); Jewish Agency for Israel, Division of Aliyah and Absorption, *Data on Aliyah by Continents and Selected Countries* (Jerusalem, 2001).

[71]Tolts, "The Balance of Births and Deaths."

[72]Not including the Jewish portion of the Tat group.

[73]Statistical Agency of the Republic of Kazakhstan, *Natsionaln'nyi sostav naseleniia Respubliki Kazakhstan: Itogi perepisi naseleniia 1999 goda v Respublike Kazakhstan*, vol. 1 (Almaty, 2000).

[74]Data kindly provided by Dr. Mehdi Bozorgmehr, Von Grunebaum Center for Near Eastern Studies, University of California-UCLA, Los Angeles.

[75]Asha A. Bhende, Ralphy E. Jhirad, Prakash Fulpagare, *Demographic and Socio-Economic Characteristics of the Jews in India* (Mumbai, 1997).

AFRICA

About 88,000 Jews were estimated to remain in Africa at the beginning of 2001, of which about 90 percent lived in the Republic of South Africa (see table 6). According to the 1980 national census, there were about 118,000 Jews among South Africa's white population.[76] Substantial Jewish emigration since then was partially compensated for by Jewish immigration and the return migration of former emigrants, but an incipient negative balance of internal changes produced some further attrition. The 1991 population census did not provide a reliable new national figure on Jewish population size since the question on religion was optional and only 65,406 white people declared themselves to be Jewish. The results of a Jewish-sponsored survey of the Jewish population in the five major South African urban centers, completed—like the census—in 1991, confirmed the ongoing demographic decline.[77] Based on that evidence, the most likely range of Jewish population size was estimated at 92,000 to 106,000 for 1991, with a central value of 100,000. According to the 1996 census there were 55,734 white Jews, 10,449 black Jews, 1,058 "coloured" (mixed-race) Jews, and 359 Indian Jews. Continuing Jewish emigration from South Africa to Israel and other Western countries (especially Australia) stimulated by personal insecurity and other fears about the future was reflected in a new survey carried out in 1998.[78] A new estimate was suggested of 80,000 for 2000, lowered to 79,000 in 2001, making South Africa the 12th largest Jewish population worldwide.

In recent years, the Jewish community of Ethiopia was at the center of an international rescue effort. In the course of 1991, the overwhelming majority of Ethiopian Jews—about 20,000 people—were brought to Israel, most of them in a dramatic one-day airlift. Some of these migrants were non-Jewish members of mixed households. It was assumed that few Jews had remained in Ethiopia, but in subsequent years the small remaining core Jewish population appeared to be larger than previously estimated. Between 1992 and 2000, 17,700 immigrants from Ethiopia arrived in Israel—mostly non-Jewish immigrants seeking reunification with their Jewish relatives. Although it is possible that more Jews may appear asking to emigrate to Israel, and that more Christian relatives of Jews already in Israel will press for emigration before Israel terminates the family reunification program for such relatives, a conservative estimate of 100 Jews was

---

[76]Sergio DellaPergola and Allie A. Dubb, "South African Jewry: A Sociodemographic Profile," AJYB 1988, vol. 88, pp. 59–140.

[77]The study was directed by Dr. Allie A. Dubb and supported by the Kaplan Centre for Jewish Studies, University of Cape Town. See Allie A. Dubb, *The Jewish Population of South Africa; The 1991 Sociodemographic Survey* (Cape Town, 1994).

[78]Barry A. Kosmin, Jaqueline Goldberg, Milton Shain, and Shirley Bruk, *Jews of the New South Africa: Highlights of the 1998 National Survey of South African Jews* (London, 1999).

tentatively suggested for 2001. Small Jewish populations remained in various other African countries south of the Sahara.

The remnant of Moroccan and Tunisian Jewry tended to shrink slowly through emigration, mostly to Israel, France, and Canada. The 2001 estimate was 5,700 for Morocco and 1,500 for Tunisia.[79] As some Jews had a foothold both in Morocco or Tunisia and also in France or other Western countries, their geographical attribution was uncertain.

TABLE 6. ESTIMATED JEWISH POPULATION DISTRIBUTION IN AFRICA, 1/1/2001

Country	Total Population	Jewish Population	Jews per 1,000 Population	Accuracy Rating
Egypt	67,884,000	100	0.0	C 1993
Ethiopia	62,908,000	100	0.0	C 1998
Morocco	29,878,000	5,700	0.2	B 1995
Tunisia	9,459,000	1,500	0.2	B 1995
Other	69,593,000	100	0.0	D
Total North Africa	239,722,000	7,500	0.0	
Botswana	1,541,000	100	0.1	B 1993
Congo D.R.	50,948,000	100	0.0	B 1993
Kenya	30,669,000	400	0.0	B 1990
Namibia	1,757,000	100	0.1	B 1993
Nigeria	113,862,000	100	0.0	D
South Africa	43,309,000	79,000	1.8	B 1999
Zimbabwe	12,627,000	700	0.1	B 1993
Other	299,565,000	300	0.0	D
Total other Africa	554,278,000	80,800	0.1	
Total	794,000,000	88,300	0.1	

[79]See George E. Gruen, "Jews in the Middle East and North Africa," AJYB 1994, vol. 94, pp. 438–464; and data communicated by Jewish organizations.

OCEANIA

The major country of Jewish residence in Oceania (Australasia) is Australia, where 95 percent of the estimated total of 103,000 Jews live (see table 7). A total of 79,805 people in Australia described their religion as Jewish in the 1996 national census.[80] This represented an increase of 5,419 (7.3 percent) over the 1991 census figure of 74,186 declared Jews.[81] In Australia the question on religion is optional. In 1996, over 25 percent (and in 1991, over 23 percent) of the country's whole population either did not specify their religion or stated explicitly that they had none. This large group must be assumed to contain persons who identify in other ways as Jews, though there is no way to know whether Jews in Australia are more or less likely to state their religion than are other Australians.

TABLE 7. ESTIMATED JEWISH POPULATION DISTRIBUTION IN OCEANIA, 1/1/200

Country	Total Population	Jewish Population	Jews per 1,000 Population	Accuracy Rating
Australia	19,138,000	98,000	5.1	B 1996
New Zealand	3,778,000	5,100	1.3	B 1996 X
Other	7,645,000	100	0.0	D
Total	30,561,000	103,200	3.4	

In a 1991 survey in Melbourne, where roughly half of all Australia's Jews live, less than 7 percent of the Jewish respondents stated they had not identified as Jews in the census.[82] The Melbourne survey actually depicted a very stable community, one that combined growing acculturation with moderate levels of intermarriage. Australian Jewry has received migratory reinforcements during the last decade, especially from South Africa, the FSU, and Israel. At the same time, there were demographic patterns with negative effects on Jewish population size, such as declining birth cohorts and strong aging.[83] Taking into account these various factors, our 2001 estimate was 98,000—ninth largest community worldwide—

---

[80]William D. Rubinstein, "Jews in the 1996 Australian Census," *Australian Jewish Historical Society Journal* 14, no. 3, 1998, pp. 495–507.

[81]Bill Rubinstein, "Census Total for Jews Up by 7.7 Percent; Big Gains in Smaller States," unpublished report (Geelong, Victoria, 1993).

[82]John Goldlust, *The Jews of Melbourne; A Report of the Findings of the Jewish Community Survey, 1991* (Melbourne, 1993).

[83]Sol Encel and Nathan Moss, *Sydney Jewish Community: Demographic Profile* (Sydney, 1995).

substantially more than official census returns, but less than would obtain by adding the full proportion of those who did not report any religion in the census.

In New Zealand, according to the 1996 census, 4,821 people indicated a Jewish religious affiliation; a total of 1,545 indicated an Israeli/Jewish/Hebrew ethnicity, of which 633 were also Jewish by religion, 609 had another religion, and 303 reported no religion. Adding the latter to those who reported a Jewish religion, a core Jewish population estimate of 5,124 obtained.[84]

Dispersion and Concentration

COUNTRY PATTERNS

While Jews are widely dispersed throughout the world, they are also concentrated to a large extent (see table 8). In 2001, over 97 percent of world Jewry lived in the 15 countries with the largest Jewish populations; and over 80 percent lived in the two largest communities—the United States and Israel. Similarly, ten leading Diaspora countries together comprised over 93 percent of the Diaspora Jewish population; three countries (United States, France, and Canada) accounted for 79 percent, and the United States alone for nearly 69 percent of total Diaspora Jewry.

TABLE 8.   COUNTRIES WITH LARGEST JEWISH POPULATIONS, 1/1/2001

| | | | % of Total Jewish Population | | | |
| | | Jewish | In the World | | In the Diaspora | |
Rank	Country	Population	%	Cumulative %	%	Cumulative %
1	United States	5,700,000	43.0	43.0	68.7	68.7
2	Israel	4,952,200	37.4	80.4	=	=
3	France	520,000	3.9	84.3	6.3	74.9
4	Canada	364,000	2.7	87.0	4.4	79.3
5	United Kingdom	275,000	2.1	89.1	3.3	82.6
	Russia	275,000	2.1	91.2	3.3	85.9
7	Argentina	197,000	1.5	92.7	2.4	88.3
8	Ukraine	112,000	0.8	93.5	1.3	89.7
9	Germany	98,000	0.7	94.3	1.2	90.8
	Australia	98,000	0.7	95.0	1.2	92.0
11	Brazil	97,500	0.7	95.7	1.2	93.2
12	South Africa	79,000	0.6	96.3	1.0	94.1
13	Hungary	51,500	0.4	96.7	0.6	94.8
14	Mexico	40,500	0.3	97.0	0.5	95.2
15	Belgium	31,500	0.2	97.3	0.4	95.6

---

[84]Statistics New Zealand, *1996 Census of Population and Dwellings, Ethnic Groups* (Wellington, 1997).

Table 9 demonstrates the magnitude of Jewish dispersion. The 94 individual countries listed above as each having at least 100 Jews are scattered over six continents. In 2001, 8 countries had a Jewish population of 100,000 or more; another 5 countries had 50,000 or more; 15 countries had 10,000−50,000; 11 countries had 5,000−10,000; and 55 countries had fewer than 5,000 Jews each. In relative terms, too, the Jews were thinly scattered nearly everywhere in the Diaspora. There is not a single Diaspora country where Jews amounted to 25 per 1,000 (2.5 percent) of the total population. In most countries they constituted a far smaller fraction. Only 3 Diaspora countries had more than 10 per 1,000 (1 percent) Jews in their total population; and only 5 countries had more than 5 Jews per 1,000 (0.5 percent) of population. The respective 8 countries were, in descending order of the proportion, but regardless of the absolute number of their Jews: Gibraltar (24.0 per 1,000), United States (20.1), Canada (11.8), France (8.8), Uruguay (6.7), Argentina (5.3), Hungary (5.2), and Australia (5.1). Other major Diaspora communities having lower proportions of Jews per 1,000 of total population were the United Kingdom (4.6 per 1,000), Russia (1.9), Ukraine (2.3), Germany (1.2), Brazil (0.6), South Africa (1.8), Mexico (0.4), and Belgium (3.1).

In the State of Israel, by contrast, the Jewish majority amounted to 778 per 1,000 (77.8 percent) in 2001 — not including the Arab population of the Palestinian Autonomy and administered areas.

CONCENTRATION IN MAJOR CITIES

Intensive international and internal migrations led to the concentration of an overwhelming majority of the Jews into large urban areas. Table 10 ranks the cities where the largest Jewish populations were found in 2001.[85] These 20 central places and their suburban and satellite areas altogether comprised over 70 percent of the whole world Jewish population. Ten of these cities were in the U.S., four in Israel, two in Canada, and one each in France, the United Kingdom, Argentina, and Russia. The ten metropolitan areas in the United States included 78 percent of total U.S. Jewry, and the four Israeli major urban areas included 80 percent of Israel's Jewish population.

---

[85]Definitions of metropolitan statistical areas vary across countries. Estimates reported here reflect the criteria adopted in each place. For U.S. estimates see Schwartz and Scheckner, "Jewish Population," AJYB 1998; for Canadian estimates see Torczyner and Brotman, "Jews of Canada"; for other Diaspora estimates see A. Harman Institute of Contemporary Jewry; for Israeli estimates see Israel Central Bureau of Statistics, *Population and Vital Statistics 1999*; and *Monthly Bulletin of Statistics*. Following the 1995 population census in Israel, major metropolitan urban areas were redefined. The two cities of Netanya and Ashdod, each with a Jewish population exceeding 100,000, were included in the outer ring of the expanded greater Tel Aviv area.

TABLE 9. DISTRIBUTION OF THE WORLD'S JEWS, BY NUMBER, AND PROPORTION
(PER 1,000 POPULATION) IN EACH COUNTRY, 1/1/2001

Number of Jews in Country	Jews per 1,000 Population					
	Total	0.0-0.9	1.0-4.9	5.0-9.9	10.0-24.9	25.0+
Number of Countries						
Total[a]	94	62	23	5	3	1
100–900	34	30	3	-	1	-
1,000–4,900	21	19	2	-	-	-
5,000–9,900	11	5	6	-	-	-
10,000–49,900	15	7	7	1	-	-
50,000–99,900	5	1	2	2	-	-
100,000–999,900	6	-	3	2	1	-
1,000,000 or more	2	-	-	-	1	1
Jewish Population Distribution (Absolute Numbers)						
Total	13,254,100	315,600	1,031,500	889,000	6,064,600	4,952,200
100–900	11,000	9,200	1,200	0	600	0
1,000–4,900	44,700	38,700	6,000	0	0	0
5,000–9,900	67,800	30,800	37,000	0	0	0
10,000–49,900	310,200	139,400	148,300	22,500	0	0
50,000–99,900	424,000	97,500	177,000	149,500	0	0
100,000–999,900	1,743,000	0	662,000	717,000	364,000	0
1,000,000 or more	10,652,200	0	0	0	5,700,000	4,952,200
Jewish Population Distribution (Percent of World's Jews)						
Total	100.0	2.4	7.8	6.7	45.8	37.4
100–900	0.1	0.1	0.0	-	0.0	-
1,000–4,900	0.3	0.3	0.0	-	-	-
5,000–9,900	0.5	0.2	0.3	-	-	-
10,000–49,900	2.3	1.1	1.1	0.2	-	-
50,000–99,900	3.2	0.7	1.3	1.1	-	-
100,000–999,900	13.2	-	5.0	5.4	2.7	-
1,000,000 or more	80.4	-	-	-	43.0	37.4

[a]Excluding countries with fewer than 100 Jews, with a total of 1,200 Jews. Minor discrepancies due to rounding.

TABLE 10.   METROPOLITAN AREAS WITH LARGEST JEWISH POPULATIONS,
1/1/2001

Rank	Metro Area[a]	Country	Jewish Population	Share of World's Jews %	Cumulative %
1	Tel Aviv[b,c]	Israel	2,560,000	19.3	19.3
2	New York[d]	U.S.	1,970,000	14.9	34.2
3	Haifa[b]	Israel	655,000	4.9	39.1
4	Los Angeles[e]	U.S.	621,000	4.7	43.8
5	Jerusalem[f]	Israel	570,000	4.3	48.1
6	Southeast Florida[g]	U.S.	514,000	3.9	52.0
7	Paris[h]	France	310,000	2.3	54.3
8	Philadelphia[i]	U.S.	276,000	2.1	56.4
9	Chicago[j]	U.S.	261,000	2.0	58.4
10	Boston	U.S.	227,000	1.7	60.1
11	San Francisco[k]	U.S.	210,000	1.6	61.7
12	London[l]	United Kingdom	195,000	1.5	63.1
13	Buenos Aires	Argentina	175,000	1.3	64.5
14	Toronto	Canada	175,000	1.3	65.8
15	Washington[m]	U.S.	165,000	1.2	67.0
16	Be'er Sheva[n]	Israel	165,000	1.2	68.3
17	Moscow[o]	Russia	108,000	0.8	69.1
18	Baltimore	U.S.	95,000	0.7	69.8
19	Montreal	Canada	95,000	0.7	70.5
20	Detroit	U.S.	94,000	0.7	71.2

[a]Most metropolitan areas include extended inhabited territory and several municipal authorities around central city. Definitions vary by country.
[b]As newly defined in the 1995 Census.
[c]Includes Ramat Gan, Bene Beraq, Petach Tikwa, Bat Yam, Holon, Rishon LeZiyon, Netanya and Ashdod, all with a Jewish population above 100,000.
[d]Includes Orange, Putnam, and Rockland counties, Northeastern New Jersey, and Fairfield County in Connecticut.
[e]Includes Orange, Riverside, San Bernardino, Ventura counties.
[f]Adapted from data supplied by Jerusalem Municipality, Division of Strategic Planning and Research.
[g]Dade, Broward, Palm Beach counties.
[h]Departments 75, 77, 78, 91, 92, 93, 94, 95.
[i]Includes Cherry Hill-Southern N.J., Princeton and Trenton areas in New Jersey, and Wilmington and Newark areas in Delaware.
[j]Includes Cook and DuPage counties and part of Lake County.
[k]Includes Alameda, Contra Costa, Marin, Sonoma, San Mateo, Santa Clara counties.
[l]Greater London and contiguous postcode areas.
[m]Includes Montgomery and Prince Georges counties in Maryland, and northern Virginia.
[n]Central city only. Our estimate from total population data.
[o]Territory administered by city council.

Even more striking evidence of the extraordinary urbanization of the Jews is the fact that over one-third of all world Jewry live in the metropolitan areas of Tel Aviv and New York, and 52 percent live in only six large metropolitan areas: in and around New York (including areas in New Jersey and Connecticut), Los Angeles (including neighboring counties), and Southeastern Florida in the U.S.; and Greater Tel Aviv, Haifa, and Jerusalem in Israel.

SERGIO DELLAPERGOLA

Directories
Lists
Obituaries

National Jewish Organizations*

UNITED STATES

Organizations are listed according to functions as follows:

COMMUNITY RELATIONS

AMERICAN COUNCIL FOR JUDAISM (1943). PO Box 9009, Alexandria, VA 22304. (703)836-2546. Pres. Alan V. Stone; Exec. Dir. Allan C. Brownfeld. Seeks to advance the universal principles of a Judaism free of nationalism, and the national, civic, cultural, and social integration into American institutions of Americans of Jewish faith. *Issues of the American Council for Judaism; Special Interest Report.* (WWW.ACJNA.ORG)

AMERICAN JEWISH COMMITTEE (1906). The Jacob Blaustein Building, 165 E. 56 St., NYC 10022. (212)751-4000. FAX: (212) 750-0326. Pres. Harold Tanner; Exec. Dir. David A. Harris. Protects the rights and freedoms of Jews the world over; combats bigotry and anti-Semitism and promotes democracy and human rights for all; works for the security of Israel and deepened understanding between Americans and Israelis; advocates public-policy positions rooted in American democratic values and the perspectives of Jewish her-

---

*The information in this directory is based on replies to questionnaires circulated by the editors. Web site addresses, where provided, appear at end of entries.

itage; and enhances the creative vitality of the Jewish people. Includes Jacob and Hilda Blaustein Center for Human Relations, Project Interchange, William Petschek National Jewish Family Center, Jacob Blaustein Institute for the Advancement of Human Rights, Institute on American Jewish-Israeli Relations. *American Jewish Year Book; Commentary; AJC Journal.* (WWW.AJC.ORG)

AMERICAN JEWISH CONGRESS (1918). Stephen Wise Congress House, 15 E. 84 St., NYC 10028. (212)879-4500. FAX: (212)249-3672. E-mail: pr@ajcongress. org. Pres. Jack Rosen; Exec. Dir. Phil Baum. Works to foster the creative survival of the Jewish people; to help Israel develop in peace, freedom, and security; to eliminate all forms of racial and religious bigotry; to advance civil rights, protect civil liberties, defend religious freedom, and safeguard the separation of church and state; "The Attorney General for the Jewish Community." *Congress Monthly; Judaism; Inside Israel; Radical Islamic Fundamentalism Update.* (www. AJCONGRESS.ORG)

AMERICAN JEWISH PUBLIC RELATIONS SOCIETY (1957). 575 Lexington Ave., Suite 600, NYC 10022. (212)644-2663. FAX: (212)644-3887. Pres. Diane J. Ehrlich; V-Pres., membership, Lauren R. Marcus. Advances professional status of public-relations practitioners employed by Jewish organizations and institutions or who represent Jewish-related clients, services, or products; upholds a professional code of ethics and standards; provides continuing education and networking opportunities at monthly meetings; serves as a clearinghouse for employment opportunities. *AJPRS Reporter; AJPRS Membership Directory.*

ANTI-DEFAMATION LEAGUE OF B'NAI B'RITH (1913). 823 United Nations Plaza, NYC 10017. (212)885-7700. FAX: (212) 867-0779. E-mail: webmaster@adl.org. Natl. Chmn. Glen A. Tobias; Natl. Dir. Abraham H. Foxman. Seeks to combat anti-Semitism and to secure justice and fair treatment for all citizens through law, education, and community relations. *ADL on the Frontline; Law Enforcement Bulletin; Dimensions: A Journal of Holocaust Studies; Hidden Child Newsletter; International Reports; Civil Rights Reports.* (WWW.ADL.ORG)

ASSOCIATION OF JEWISH COMMUNITY RELATIONS WORKERS (1950). 7800 Northaven Road, Dallas, TX 75230. (214)369-3313. FAX: (214)373-3186. Pres. Marlene Gorin. Aims to stimulate higher standards of professional practice in Jewish community relations; encourages research and training toward that end; conducts educational programs and seminars; aims to encourage cooperation between community-relations workers and those working in other areas of Jewish communal service.

CENTER FOR JEWISH COMMUNITY STUDIES (1970). Temple University, Center City Campus, 1515 Locust St., Suite 703, Philadelphia, PA 19102. (215)772-0564. FAX: (215)772-0566. E-mail: jcpa@ netvision.net or cjcs@worldnet.att.net. Jerusalem office:Jerusalem Center for Public Affairs. Pres. Amb. Dore Gold; Dir. Gen. Zvi Marom; Chmn. Bd. of Overseers Michael Rukin. Worldwide policy-studies institute devoted to the study of Jewish community organization, political thought, and public affairs, past and present, in Israel and throughout the world. Publishes original articles, essays, and monographs; maintains library, archives, and reprint series. *Jerusalem Letter/Viewpoints; Jewish Political Studies Review.* (WWW.JCPA.ORG).

CENTER FOR RUSSIAN JEWRY WITH STUDENT STRUGGLE FOR SOVIET JEWRY/SSSJ (1964). 240 Cabrini Blvd., #5B, NYC 10033. (212)928-7451. FAX: (212)795-8867. Dir./Founder Jacob Birnbaum; Chmn. Dr. Ernest Bloch; Student Coord. Glenn Richter. Campaigns for the human rights of the Jews of the former USSR, with emphasis on emigration and Jewish identity; supports programs for needy Jews there and for newcomers in Israel and USA, stressing employment and Jewish education. As the originator of the grassroots movement for Soviet Jewry in the early 1960s, possesses unique archives.

COALITION ON THE ENVIRONMENT & JEWISH LIFE (1993). 443 Park Ave. S., 11th fl., NYC 10016-7322. (212)684-6950, ext. 210. FAX: (212)686-1353. E-mail: info@ coejl.org. Dir. Mark X. Jacobs. Promotes environmental education, advocacy, and action in the American Jewish community. Sponsored by a broad coalition of Jewish organizations; member of the National Religious Partnership for the Environment. *Bi-annual newsletter.* (WWW. COEJL.ORG)

COMMISSION ON SOCIAL ACTION OF RE-FORM JUDAISM (1953, joint instrumentality of the Union of American Hebrew Congregations and the Central Conference of American Rabbis). 633 Third Ave., 7th fl., NYC 10017. (212)650-4160. FAX: (212)650-4229. E-mail: csarj@ uahc.org. Wash. Office:2027 Massachusetts Ave., NW, Washington, DC 20036. Chmn. Judge David Davidson; Dir. Rabbi Daniel Polish; Dir. Religious Action Center of Reform Judaism, Rabbi David Saperstein. Policy-making body that relates ethical and spiritual principles of Judaism to social-justice issues; implements resolutions through the Religious Action Center in Washington, DC, via advocacy, development of educational materials, and congregational programs. *Tzedek V'Shalom (social action newsletter), Chai Impact (legislative update).*

CONFERENCE OF PRESIDENTS OF MAJOR AMERICAN JEWISH ORGANIZATIONS (1955). 633 Third Ave., NYC 10017. (212)318-6111. FAX: (212)644-4135. Chmn. Mortimer B. Zuckerman; Exec. V.-Chmn. Malcolm Hoenlein. Seeks to strengthen the U.S.-Israel alliance and to protect and enhance the security and dignity of Jews abroad. Toward this end, the Conference of Presidents speaks and acts on the basis of consensus of its 54 member agencies on issues of national and international Jewish concern.

CONSULTATIVE COUNCIL OF JEWISH ORGANIZATIONS-CCJO (1946). 420 Lexington Ave., Suite 1731, NYC 10170. (212)808-5437. Chmn. Ady Steg & Clemens N. Nathan; Sec.-Gen. Warren Green. A nongovernmental organization in consultative status with the UN, UN-ESCO, ILO, UNICEF, and the Council of Europe; cooperates and consults with, advises, and renders assistance to the Economic and Social Council of the UN on all problems relating to human rights and economic, social, cultural, educational, and related matters pertaining to Jews.

COORDINATING BOARD OF JEWISH ORGANIZATIONS (1947). 823 United Nations Plaza, NYC 10017. (212)557-9008. FAX: (212)687-3429. Ch. Cheryl Halpern; Exec. Dir. Dr. Harris O. Schoenberg. To promote the purposes and principles for which the UN was created.

COUNCIL OF JEWISH ORGANIZATIONS IN CIVIL SERVICE, INC. (1948). 45 E. 33 St., Rm. 310, NYC 10016. (212)689-2015. FAX: (212)684-7694. Pres. Louis Weiser; 1st V.-Pres. Melvyn Birnbaum. Supports merit system; encourages recruitment of Jewish youth to government service; member of Coalition to Free Soviet Jews, NY Jewish Community Relations Council, NY Metropolitan Coordinating Council on Jewish Poverty, Jewish Labor Committee, America-Israel Friendship League. *Council Digest.*

INSTITUTE FOR PUBLIC AFFAIRS (*see* UNION OF ORTHODOX JEWISH CONGREGATIONS OF AMERICA)

INTERNATIONAL LEAGUE FOR THE REPATRIATION OF RUSSIAN JEWS, INC. (1963). 2 Fountain Lane, Suite 2J, Scarsdale, NY 10583. (914)683-3225. FAX: (914)683-3221. Pres. Morris Brafman; Chmn. James H. Rapp. Helped to bring the situation of Soviet Jews to world attention; catalyst for advocacy efforts, educational projects, and programs on behalf of Russian Jews in the former USSR, Israel, and U.S. Provides funds to help Russian Jewry in Israel and the former Soviet Union.

JEWISH COUNCIL FOR PUBLIC AFFAIRS (formerly NATIONAL JEWISH COMMUNITY RELATIONS ADVISORY COUNCIL) (1944). 443 Park Ave. S., 11th fl., NYC 10016-7322. (212)684-6950. FAX: (212)686-1353. E-mail: contactus@jcpa.org. Chmn. Dr. Leonard A. Cole; Exec. V.-Chmn. Hannah Rosenthal. National coordinating body for the field of Jewish community relations, comprising 13 national and 122 local Jewish community-relations agencies. Promotes understanding of Israel and the Middle East; supports Jewish communities around the world; advocates for equality and pluralism, and against discrimination, in American society. Through the Council's work, its constituent organizations seek agreement on policies, strategies, and programs for effective utilization of their resources for common ends. *JCPA Agenda for Public Affairs.* (WWW.JEWISHPUBLICAFFAIRS.ORG)

JEWISH LABOR COMMITTEE (1934). Atran Center for Jewish Culture, 25 E. 21 St., NYC 10010. (212)477-0707. FAX: (212)477-1918. Pres. Morton Bahr; Exec.

Dir. Avram B. Lyon. Serves as liaison between the Jewish community and the trade union movement; works with the U.S. and international labor movement to combat anti-Semitism, promote intergroup relations, and engender support for the State of Israel and Jews in and from the former Soviet Union; promotes teaching in public schools about the Holocaust and Jewish resistance; strengthens support within the Jewish community for the social goals and programs of the labor movement; supports Yiddish-language and cultural institutions. *Jewish Labor Committee Review; Issues Alert; Alumni Newsletter.*

———, NATIONAL TRADE UNION COUNCIL FOR HUMAN RIGHTS (1956). Atran Center for Jewish Culture, 25 E. 21 St., NYC 10010. (212)477-0707. FAX: (212)477-1918. Exec. Dir. Avram Lyon. Works with the American labor movement in advancing the struggle for social justice and equal opportunity, and assists unions in every issue affecting human rights. Fights discrimination on all levels and helps to promote labor's broad social and economic goals.

JEWISH PEACE FELLOWSHIP (1941). Box 271, Nyack, NY 10960. (914)358-4601. FAX: (914)358-4924. E-mail: jpf@forusa. org. Hon. Pres. Rabbi Philip Bentley; Ch. Murray Polner. Unites those who believe that Jewish ideals and experience provide inspiration for a nonviolent philosophy and way of life; offers draft counseling, especially for conscientious objection based on Jewish "religious training and belief"; encourages Jewish community to become more knowledgeable, concerned, and active in regard to the war/peace problem. *Shalom/Jewish Peace Letter.* (WWW.JEWISHPEACEFELLOWSHIP.ORG)

JEWISH WAR VETERANS OF THE UNITED STATES OF AMERICA (1896). 1811 R St., NW, Washington, DC 20009. (202)265-6280. FAX: (202)234-5662. E-mail: jwv@erols.com. Natl. Exec. Dir. Herb Rosenbleeth; Natl. Commander Ronald Ziegler. Seeks to foster true allegiance to the United States; to combat bigotry and prevent defamation of Jews; to encourage the doctrine of universal liberty, equal rights, and full justice for all; to cooperate with and support existing educational institutions and establish new ones; to foster the education of ex-servicemen, ex-service-women, and members in the ideals and principles of Americanism. *Jewish Veteran.*

———, NATIONAL MUSEUM OF AMERICAN JEWISH MILITARY HISTORY (1958). 1811 R St., NW, Washington, DC 20009. E-mail: jwv@jwv.com. (202)265-6280. FAX: (202)234-5662. Pres. Neil Goldman; Asst. Dir./Archivist Sandor B. Cohen; Curator, Ramela Feltus. Documents and preserves the contributions of Jewish Americans to the peace and freedom of the United States; educates the public concerning the courage, heroism, and sacrifices made by Jewish Americans who served in the armed forces; and works to combat anti-Semitism. *The Jewish War Veterans).*

NATIONAL ASSOCIATION OF JEWISH LEGISLATORS (1976). 65 Oakwood St., Albany, NY 12208. (518)527-3353. FAX: (518) 458-8512. E-mail: najl01@aol.com. Exec. Dir. Marc Hiller; Pres. Sen. Richard Cohen, Minn. state senator. A nonpartisan Jewish state legislative network focusing on domestic issues and publishing newsletters. Maintains close ties with the Knesset and Israeli leaders.

NCSJ: ADVOCATES ON BEHALF OF JEWS IN RUSSIA, UKRAINE, THE BALTIC STATES AND EURASIA (formerly AMERICAN JEWISH CONFERENCE ON SOVIET JEWRY) (1964; reorg. 1971). 1640 Rhode Island Ave., NW, Suite 501, Washington, DC 20036-3278. (202)898-2500. FAX: (202) 898-0822. E-mail: ncsj@ncsj.org. N.Y. office:823 United Nations Plaza, NYC 10017. (212)808-0295. Chmn. Harold Paulluks; Pres. Dr. Robert J. Meth. Coordinating agency for major national Jewish organizations and local community groups in the U.S., acting on behalf of Jews in the former Soviet Union (FSU); provides information about Jews in the FSU through public education and social action; reports and special pamphlets, special programs and projects, public meetings and forums. *Newswatch; annual report; action and program kits; Tekuma.* (WWW.NCSJ.ORG)

———, SOVIET JEWRY RESEARCH BUREAU. Chmn. Denis C. Braham; Pres. Howard E. Sachs. Organized by NCSJ to monitor emigration trends. Primary task is the accumulation, evaluation, and processing of information regarding Jews in the FSU, especially those who apply for emigration.

NATIONAL JEWISH COMMISSION ON LAW AND PUBLIC AFFAIRS (COLPA) (1965). 135 W. 50 St., 6th fl., NYC 10020. (212)641-8992. FAX: (212)641-8197. Pres. Allen L. Rothenberg; Exec. Dir. Dennis Rapps. Voluntary association of attorneys whose purpose is to represent the observant Jewish community on legal, legislative, and public-affairs matters.

NATIONAL JEWISH COMMUNITY RELATIONS ADVISORY COUNCIL (see JEWISH COUNCIL FOR PUBLIC AFFAIRS)

NATIONAL JEWISH DEMOCRATIC COUNCIL (1990). 777 N. Capital St., NE, Suite 305, Washington, DC 20002. (202)216-9060. FAX: (202)216-9061. E-mail: njdconline@aol.com. Chmn. Monte Friedkin; Founding Chmn. Morton Mandel; Exec. Dir. Ira N. Forman. NJDC is the national voice of Jewish Democrats. Committed to those values shared by the Democratic Party and the vast majority of American Jews – including the separation of church and state, a strong US-Israel relationship, and reproductive freedom – NJDC educates Jewish voters, informs candidates about Jewish issues and advocates on behalf of Jewish and Democratic ideals. *NJDC In Action, Capital Communiqué, and Periodic Special Reports.* (WWW.NJDC.ORG)

REPUBLICAN JEWISH COALITION (1985). 415 2nd St., NE, Suite 100, Washington, DC 20002. (202)216-9060. FAX: (202)216-9061. E-mail: rjc@rjchq.org. Natl. Chmn. Sam Fox; Hon. Chmn. Max M. Fisher, Richard J. Fox, Cheryl Halpern, Lawrence Kadish, George Klein, and Amb. Mel Sembler; Exec. Dir. Matt Brooks. Promotes involvement in Republican politics among its members; sensitizes Republican leaders to the concerns of the American Jewish community; promotes principles of free enterprise, a strong national defense, and an internationalist foreign policy. *RJC Bulletin.* (WWW.RJCHQ.ORG)

SHALEM CENTER (1994). 5505 Connecticut Avenue, NW, No. 1140, Washington, DC 20015. (877)298-7300. FAX: (888)766-1506. E-mail: shalem@shalem.org.il. Pres. Yoram Hazony (Israel); Academic Director, Daniel Polisar (Israel). The purposes and activities of the Shalem Center are to increase public understanding and conduct educational and research activities on the improvement of Jewish national public life, and to develop a community of intellectual leaders to shape the state of Israel into a secure, free, and prosperous society. *Azure.* (WWW.SHALEMCENTER.ORG)

SHALOM CENTER (1983). 6711 Lincoln Dr., Philadelphia, PA 19119. (215)844-8494. E-mail: shalomctr@aol.com. (Part of Aleph Alliance for Jewish Renewal.) Exec. Dir. Rabbi Arthur Waskow. National resource and organizing center for Jewish perspectives on dealing with overwork in American society, environmental dangers, unrestrained technology, and corporate irresponsibility. Initiated A.J. Heschel 25th Yahrzeit observance. Trains next generation of *tikkun olam* activists. Holds colloquia on issues like environmental causes of cancer. *New Menorah.* (WWW.SHALOMCTR.ORG)

STUDENT STRUGGLE FOR SOVIET JEWRY (see CENTER FOR RUSSIAN JEWRY)

UN WATCH (1993). 1, rue de Varembé, PO Box 191, 1211 Geneva 20, Switzerland. (41-22)734.14.72/3. FAX: (41-22)734.16.13. E-mail: unwatch@unwatch.org. Assoc. Exec. Dir. Andrew Srulevitch. An affiliate of the American Jewish Committee, UN Watch measures UN performance by the yardstick of the UN's Charter; advocates the non-discriminatory application of the Charter; opposes the use of UN fora to attack Israel and promote anti-Semitism; and seeks to institutionalize at the UN the fight against worldwide anti-Semitism. *The Wednesday Watch.* (WWW.UNWATCH.ORG)

UNION OF COUNCILS (formerly UNION OF COUNCILS FOR SOVIET JEWS) (1970). 1819 H St., NW, Suite 230, Washington, DC 20005. (202)775-9770. FAX: (202)775-9776. E-mail: ucsj@ucsj.com. Pres. Yosef I. Abramowitz; Natl. Dir. Micah H. Naftalin. Devoted to promoting religious liberty, freedom of emigration, and security for Jews in the FSU (former Soviet Union) through advocacy and monitoring of anti-Semitism, neo-facism, human rights, rule of law, and democracy. Offers educational, cultural, medical, and humanitarian aid through the Yad L'Yad partnership program pairing Jewish communities in the US and the FSU; advocates for refuseniks and political prisoner. (WWW.FSUMONITOR.COM)

WORLD CONGRESS OF GAY, LESBIAN, BISEXUAL & TRANSGENDER JEWS (1980). 8 Letitia St., Philadelphia, PA 19106-3050. (609)396-1972. FAX: (215)873-0108. E-mail: president@wcgljo.org. Pres. Scott R. Gansl (Philadelphia, PA); V.-Pres. Francois Spiero (Paris, France). Supports, strengthens, and represents over 67 Jewish gay and lesbian organizations across the globe and the needs of gay and lesbian Jews generally. Challenges homophobia and sexism within the Jewish community and responds to anti-Semitism at large. Sponsors regional and international conferences. *The Digest.* (WWW.WCGLJO.ORG/WCGLJO/)

WORLD JEWISH CONGRESS (1936; org. in U.S. 1939). 501 Madison Ave., 17th fl., NYC 10022. (212) 755-5770. FAX: (212)755-5883. Pres. Edgar M. Bronfman; Co-Chmn. N. Amer. Branch Prof. Irwin Cotler (Montreal) & Evelyn Sommer; Sec.-Gen. Israel Singer; Exec. Dir. Elan Steinberg. Seeks to intensify bonds of world Jewry with Israel; to strengthen solidarity among Jews everywhere and secure their rights, status, and interests as individuals and communities; to encourage Jewish social, religious, and cultural life throughout the world and coordinate efforts by Jewish communities and organizations to cope with any Jewish problem; to work for human rights generally. Represents its affiliated organizations-most representative bodies of Jewish communities in more than 80 countries and 35 national organizations in American section-at UN, OAS, UNESCO, Council of Europe, ILO, UNICEF, and other governmental, intergovernmental, and international authorities. *WJC Report; Bolet'n Informativo OJI; Christian-Jewish Relations; Dateline: World Jewry; Coloquio; Batfutsot; Gesher.*

CULTURAL

AMERICAN ACADEMY FOR JEWISH RESEARCH (1929). 420 Walnut Street, Philadelphia, PA 19106. (215)238-1290. FAX: (215)238-1540. Pres. Robert Chazan. Encourages Jewish learning and research; holds annual or semiannual meeting; awards grants for publication of scholarly works. *Proceedings of the American Academy for Jewish Research; Texts and Studies; Monograph Series.*

AMERICAN GATHERING OF JEWISH HOLOCAUST SURVIVORS. 122 W. 30 St., #205.

NYC 10001. (212)239-4230. FAX: (212)279-2926. E-mail: mail@american-gathering.org. Pres. Benjamin Meed. Dedicated to documenting the past and passing on a legacy of remembrance. Compiles the National Registry of Jewish Holocaust Survivors-to date, the records of more than 165,000 survivors and their families-housed at the U.S. Holocaust Memorial Museum in Washington, DC; holds an annual Yom Hashoah commemoration and occasional international gatherings; sponsors an intensive summer program for U.S. teachers in Poland and Israel to prepare them to teach about the Holocaust. *Together (newspaper).* (www.AMERICANGATHERING.ORG)

AMERICAN GUILD OF JUDAIC ART (1991). 15 Greenspring Valley Rd., Owings Mills, MD 21117. (410)902-0411. FAX: (410)581-0108. E-mail: lbarch@erols. com. Pres. Mark D. Levin; 1st V.-Pres. Richard McBee. A not-for-profit membership organization for those with interests in the Judaic arts, including artists, galleries, collectors & retailers of Judaica, writers, educators, appraisers, museum curators, conservators, lecturers, and others personally or professionally involved in the field. Helps to promote members' art. *Hiddur (quarterly); Update (members' networking newsletter).*

AMERICAN JEWISH HISTORICAL SOCIETY (1892). Center for Jewish History, 15 W. 16 St., NYC 10011-6301. (212)294-6160. FAX: (212)294-6161. E-mail: ajhs@ajhs. org. Pres. Kenneth J. Bialkin; Dir. Dr. Michael Feldberg. Collects, catalogues, publishes, and displays material on the history of the Jews in America; serves as an information center for inquiries on American Jewish history; maintains archives of original source material on American Jewish history; sponsors lectures and exhibitions; makes available audiovisual material. *American Jewish History; Heritage.* (WWW.AJHS.ORG)

AMERICAN JEWISH PRESS ASSOCIATION (1944). Natl. Admin. Off.: 1828 L St. NW, Suite 720, Washington, DC 20036. (202)785-2282. FAX: (202)785-2307. E-mail: toby@dershowitz.com. Pres. Marc Klein; Exec. Dir. Toby Dershowitz. Seeks the advancement of Jewish journalism and the maintenance of a strong Jewish press in the U.S. and Canada; encourages the attainment of the highest editorial and business standards; sponsors workshops, services for members; sponsors annual competition for Simon Rockower Awards for excellence in Jewish journalism. *Membership bulletin newsletter.*

AMERICAN SEPHARDI FEDERATION (1973). Center for Jewish History, 15 W. 16 St., NYC 10011-6301. (212)294-8350. FAX: (212)294-8348. E-mail: vroumani@asf. cjh.org. Natl. Pres. Leon Levy; Exec. Dir. Vivienne Roumani-Denn. The central voice of the American Sephardic community, representing a broad spectrum of Sephardic organizations, congregations, and educational institutions. Seeks to strengthen and unify the community through education, communication, advocacy, and leadership development, creating greater awareness and appreciation of its rich and unique history and culture. *Sephardic Today.* (WWW.AMSEPHFED.ORG)

AMERICAN SOCIETY FOR JEWISH MUSIC (1974). c/o The Center for Jewish History, 15 W. 16 St., NYC 10011. (212)294-8328. FAX: (212)294-6161. Pres. Hadassah B. Markson; V.-Pres. Judith Tischler & Martha Novick; Sec. Fortuna Calvo Roth; Bd. Chmn. Rabbi Henry D. Michelman; Treas. Michael Leavitt. Promotes the knowledge, appreciation, and development of Jewish music, past and present, for professional and lay audiences; seeks to raise the standards of composition and performance in Jewish music, to encourage research, and to sponsor performances of new and rarely heard works. *Musica Judaica Journal.*

ASSOCIATION OF JEWISH BOOK PUBLISHERS (1962). c/o Jewish Book Council, 15 East 26th Street, 10th Floor, New York, NY 10010. (212)532-4949. FAX: (212)481-4174. Email: arjhill@jewishbooks.com. Pres. Ellen Frankel. As a nonprofit group, provides a forum for discussion of mutual areas of interest among Jewish publishers, and promotes cooperative exhibits and promotional opportunities for members. Membership fee is $85 annually per publishing house.

ASSOCIATION OF JEWISH LIBRARIES (1965). 15 E. 26 St.,10th fl, NYC 10010. (212)725-5359. FAX: (212)481-4174. E-mail: ajl@jewishbooks.org. Pres. David T. Gilner; V.-Pres. Toby Rossner. Seeks to promote and improve services and professional standards in Jewish libraries; disseminates Jewish library information and guidance; promotes publication of literature in the field; encourages the establishment of Jewish libraries and collections of Judaica and the choice of Judaica librarianship as a profession; cocertifies Jewish libraries (with Jewish Book Council). *AJL Newsletter, Judaica Librarianship.*

B'NAI B'RITH KLUTZNICK NATIONAL JEWISH MUSEUM (1957). 1640 Rhode Island Ave., NW, Washington, DC 20036. (202)857-6583. FAX: (202)857-1099. A center of Jewish art and history in the nation's capital, maintains temporary and permanent exhibition galleries, permanent collection of Jewish ceremonial objects, folk art, and contemporary fine art, outdoor sculpture garden and museum shop, as well as the American Jewish Sports Hall of Fame. Provides exhibitions, tours, educational programs, research assistance, and tourist information. *Permanent collection catalogue; temporary exhibit catalogues.*

CENTRAL YIDDISH CULTURE ORGANIZATION (CYCO), INC. (1943). 25 E. 21 St., 3rd fl., NYC 10010. (212)505-8305. FAX: (212) 505-8044. Mng. David Kirszencwejg. Promotes, publishes, and distributes Yiddish books; publishes catalogues.

CONFERENCE ON JEWISH SOCIAL STUDIES, INC. (formerly CONFERENCE ON JEWISH RELATIONS, INC.) (1939). Bldg. 240, Rm. 103. Program in Jewish Studies, Stanford University, Stanford, CA 94305-2190. (650)725-0829. FAX:(650)725-2920. E-mail: jss@leland.stanford.edu. Pres. Steven J. Zipperstein; V.-Pres. Aron Rodrigue. *Jewish Social Studies.*

CONGREGATION BINA (1981). 600 W. End Ave., Suite 1-C, NYC 10024. (212)873-4261. E-mail: ernasam@dellnet.com. Pres. Joseph Moses; Exec. V. Pres. Moses Samson; Hon. Pres. Samuel M. Daniel; Sec. Gen. Elijah E. Jhirad. Serves the religious, cultural, charitable, and philanthropic needs of the Children of Israel who originated in India and now reside in the U.S. Works to foster and preserve the ancient traditions, customs, liturgy, music, and folklore of Indian Jewry and to maintain needed institutions. *Kol Bina.*

CONGRESS FOR JEWISH CULTURE (1948). 25 E. 21 St., NYC 10010. (212)505-8040. FAX: (212)505-8044. Co-Pres. Prof.

Yonia Fain & Dr. Barnett Zumoff. Congress for Jewish Culture administers the book store CYCO and publishes the world's oldest Yiddish journal, *The Zukunft*. Currently producing a two volume anthology of Yiddish literature in America. Activities include yearly memorials for the Warsaw ghetto uprising and the murdered Soviet Yiddish writers, also readings and literary afternoons. *The Zukunft; Bulletin: In the World of Yiddish.*

ELAINE KAUFMAN CULTURAL CENTER (1952). 129 W. 67 St., NYC 10023. (212)501-3303. FAX: (212)874-7865. Email: lhard@ekcc.org. Hon. Chmn. Leonard Goodman; Chmn. Elaine Kaufman; Pres. Phyllis Feder; Exec. Dir. Lydia Kontos. Offers instruction in its Lucy Moses School for Music and Dance in music, dance, art, and theater to children and adults, in Western culture and Jewish traditions. Presents frequent performances of Jewish and general music by leading artists and ensembles in its Merkin Concert Hall and Ann Goodman Recital Hall. The Birnbaum Music Library houses Jewish music scores and reference books. *In Harmony (quarterly newsletter); EKCC Events (bimonthly calendar); Bimonthly concert calendars; catalogues and brochures.* (WWW.EKCC.ORG)

HISTADRUTH IVRITH OF AMERICA (1916; reorg. 1922). 426 W. 58 St., NYC 10019. (212)957-6659. Fax: (212)957-5811. E-mail: general@hist-ivrit.org. Pres. Miriam Ostow. Emphasizes the primacy of Hebrew in Jewish life, culture, and education; aims to disseminate knowledge of written and spoken Hebrew in N. America, thus building a cultural bridge between the State of Israel and Jewish communities throughout N. America. *Hadoar; Lamishpacha; Tov Lichtov; Sulam Yaakov; Hebrew Week; Ulpan.* (WWW.HIST-IVRIT.ORG)

HOLOCAUST CENTER OF THE UNITED JEWISH FEDERATION OF GREATER PITTSBURGH (1980). 5738 Darlington Rd., Pittsburgh, PA 15217. (412)421-1500. FAX: (412) 422-1996. E-mail: lhurwitz@ujf.net. Pres. Holocaust Comm. Edgar Snyder; Bd. Ch. Karen Shapira; Dir. Linda F. Hurwitz. Develops programs and provides resources to further understanding of the Holocaust and its impact on civilization. Maintains a library, archive; provides speakers, educational materials; organizes community programs. Published collection of survivor and liberator stories. (WWW.UJFHC.NET)

HOLOCAUST MEMORIAL CENTER (1984). 6602 West Maple Rd., West Bloomfield, MI 48322. (248)661-0840. FAX: (248) 661-4204. E-mail: info@holocaustcenter.org. Founder & Exec. V.-Pres. Rabbi Charles Rosenzveig. America's first freestanding Holocaust center comprising a museum, library-archive, oral history collection, garden of the righteous, research institute and academic advisory committee. Provides tours, lecture series, teacher training, Yom Hashoah commemorations, exhibits, educational outreach programs, speakers' bureau, computer database on 1,200 destroyed Jewish communities, guided travel tours to concentration camps and Israel, and museum shop. Published *World Reacts to the Holocaust; Newsletter.*

HOLOCAUST MEMORIAL RESOURCE & EDUCATION CENTER OF CENTRAL FLORIDA (1982). 851 N. Maitland Ave., Maitland, FL 32751. (407)628-0555. FAX: (407)628-1079. E-mail: execdir@holocaustedu.org. Pres. Stan Sujka, MD; Bd. Chmn. Tess Wise. An interfaith educational center devoted to teaching the lessons of the Holocaust. Houses permanent multimedia educational exhibit; maintains library of books, videotapes, films, and other visuals to serve the entire educational establishment; offers lectures, teacher training, and other activities. *Newsletter; Bibliography; "Holocaust-Lessons for Tomorrow"; elementary and middle school curriculum.*

THE HOLOCAUST MUSEUM AND LEARNING CENTER IN MEMORY OF GLORIA GOLDSTEIN (1995) (formerly St. Louis Center for Holocaust Studies) (1977). 12 Millstone Campus Dr., St. Louis, MO 63146. (314)432-0020. FAX: (314)432-1277. E-mail: dreich@jfedstl.org. Chmn. Richard W. Stein; Dir. Dan A. Reich; Asst. Dir. Brian Bray. Develops programs and provides resources and educational materials to further an understanding of the Holocaust and its impact on civilization; has a 5,000 sq. ft. museum containing photographs, artifacts, and audiovisual displays. *Newsletter.*

INTERNATIONAL ASSOCIATION OF JEWISH GENEALOGICAL SOCIETIES (1988). 4430

Mt. Paran Pkwy NW, Atlanta, GA 30327-3747. (404)261-8662. Fax: (404) 228-7125. E-mail: homargol@aol.com. Pres. Howard Margol. Umbrella organization of more than 70 Jewish Genealogical Societies (JGS) worldwide. Represents organized Jewish genealogy, encourages Jews to research their family history, promotes new JGSs, supports existing societies, implements projects of interest to individuals researching their Jewish family histories. Holds annual conference where members learn and exchange ideas. (WWW.IAJGS.ORG)

INTERNATIONAL JEWISH MEDIA ASSOCIATION (1987). U.S.: c/o St. Louis Jewish Light, 12 Millstone Campus Dr., St. Louis, MO 63146. (314)432-3353. FAX: (314)432-0515. E-mail: stlouislgt@aol.com and ajpamr@aol.com. Israel:PO Box 92, Jerusalem 91920. 02-202-222. FAX: 02-513-642. Pres. Robert A. Cohn (c/o St. Louis Jewish Light); Exec. Dir. Toby Dershowitz. 1828 L St. NW, Suite 402, Washington, DC 20036. (202)785-2282. FAX: (202)785-2307. E-mail: toby@dershowitz.com. Israel Liaisons Jacob Gispan & Lifsha Ben-Shach, WZO Dept. of Info. A worldwide network of Jewish journalists, publications and other media in the Jewish and general media, which seeks to provide a forum for the exchange of materials and ideas and to enhance the status of Jewish media and journalists throughout the world. *IJMA Newsletter; Proceedings of the International Conference on Jewish Media.*

INTERNATIONAL NETWORK OF CHILDREN OF JEWISH HOLOCAUST SURVIVORS, INC. (1981). 3000 NE 151 St., N. Miami, FL 33181. (305)919-5690. FAX: (305)919-5691. E-mail: xholocau@fiu.edu. Pres. Rositta E. Kenigsberg; Founding Chmn. Menachem Z. Rosensaft. Links Second Generation groups and individuals throughout the world. Represents the shared interests of children of Holocaust survivors; aims to perpetuate the authentic memory of the Holocaust and prevent its recurrence; to strengthen and preserve the Jewish spiritual, ideological, and cultural heritage, to fight anti-Semitism and all forms of discrimination, persecution, and oppression anywhere in the world.

JACOB RADER MARCUS CENTER OF THE AMERICAN JEWISH ARCHIVES (1947). 3101 Clifton Ave., Cincinnati, OH 45220. (513)221-1875 ext. 403. FAX: (513)221-7812. E-mail: aja@cn.huc.edu. Dir. Dr. Gary P. Zola. Promotes the study and preservation of the Western Hemisphere Jewish experience through research, publications, collection of important source materials, and a vigorous public-outreach program. *American Jewish Archives Journal (biannual).*

JEWISH BOOK COUNCIL (1946; reorg. 1993). 15 E. 26 St., NYC 10010. (212)532-4949, ext. 297. E-mail: jbc@jewishbooks.org. Pres. Rabbi Maurice S. Corson; Bd. Chmn. Henry Everett; Exec. Dir. Carolyn Starman Hessel. Serves as literary arm of the American Jewish community and clearinghouse for Jewish-content literature; assists readers, writers, publishers, and those who market and sell products. Provides bibliographies, list of publishers, bookstores, book fairs. Sponsors National Jewish Book Awards, Jewish Book Month, Jewish Book Fair Network. *Jewish Book Annual; Jewish Book World.* (WWW.JEWISHBOOKCOUNCIL.ORG)

THE JEWISH FEDERATION'S LOS ANGELES MUSEUM OF THE HOLOCAUST (MARTYRS MEMORIAL) (org. mid-1960s; opened 1978). 6006 Wilshire Blvd., Los Angeles, CA 90036. (323)761-8170. FAX: (323) 761-8174. E-mail: museumgroup@ jewishla.org. Chmn. Gary John Schiller, M.D.; Dir./Curator Marcia Reines Josephy. A photo-narrative museum and resource center dedicated to Holocaust history, issues of genocide and prejudice, curriculum development, teacher training, research and exhibitions. *PAGES, a newsletter; Those Who Dared; Rescuers and Rescued; Guide to Schindler's List; Anne Frank: A Teaching.*

JEWISH HERITAGE PROJECT (1981). 150 Franklin St., #1W, NYC 10013. (212)925-9067. E-mail: jhpffh@jps.net. Exec. Dir. Alan Adelson. Strives to bring to the broadest possible audience authentic works of literary and historical value relating to Jewish history and culture. With funding from the National Endowment of the Arts, Jewish Heritage runs the National Initiative in the Literature of the Holocaust. Not a grant giving organization. Distributor of the film *Lodz Ghetto,* which it developed, as well as its companion volume *Lodz Ghetto: Inside a Community Under Siege; Better Than Gold: An Immigrant Family's First Years in Brooklyn.*

JEWISH MUSEUM (1904, under auspices of Jewish Theological Seminary). 1109 Fifth Ave., NYC 10128. (212)423-3200. FAX: (212)423-3232. Dir. Joan H. Rosenbaum; Bd. Chmn. Robert J. Hurst. Expanded museum features permanent exhibition on the Jewish experience. Repository of the largest collection of Jewish related paintings, prints, photographs, sculpture, coins, medals, antiquities, textiles, and other decorative arts in the Western Hemisphere. Includes the National Jewish Archive of Broadcasting. Tours, lectures, film showings, and concerts; special programs for children; cafe; shop. *Special exhibition catalogues; annual report.* (www. THEJEWISHMUSEUM.ORG)

JEWISH PUBLICATION SOCIETY (1888). 2100 Arch St., 2nd fl., Philadelphia, PA 19103. (215)832-0600. FAX: (215)568-2017. E-mail: jewishbook@jewishpub.org. Pres. Judge Norma L. Shapiro; CEO/Ed.-in-Chief Dr. Ellen Frankel. Publishes and disseminates books of Jewish interest for adults and children; titles include TANAKH, religious studies and practices, life cycle, folklore, classics, art, history, belles-lettres. *The Bookmark; JPS Catalogue.* (WWW.JEWISHPUB.ORG)

JUDAH L. MAGNES MUSEUM-JEWISH MUSEUM OF THE WEST (1962). 2911 Russell St., Berkeley, CA 94705. (510)549-6950. FAX: (510)849-3673. E-mail: pfpr@magnesmuseum.org. Pres. Fred Weiss; Dir. Susan Morris. Collects, preserves, and makes available Jewish art, culture, history, and literature from throughout the world. Permanent collections of fine and ceremonial art; rare Judaica library, Western Jewish History Center (archives), Jewish-American Hall of Fame. Changing exhibits, traveling exhibits, docent tours, lectures, numismatics series, poetry and video awards, museum shop. *Magnes News; special exhibition catalogues; scholarly books.*

JUDAICA CAPTIONED FILM CENTER, INC. (1983). PO Box 21439, Baltimore, MD 21208-0439. Voice Relay Service (1-800)735-2258; TDD (410)655-6767. E-mail: lweiner@jhucep.org. Pres. Lois Lilienfeld Weiner. Developing a comprehensive library of captioned and subtitled films and tapes on Jewish subjects; distributes them to organizations serving the hearing-impaired, including mainstream classes and senior adult groups, on a free-loan, handling/shipping-charge-only basis. *Newsletter.*

LEAGUE FOR YIDDISH, INC. (1979). 200 W. 72 St., Suite 40, NYC 10023. (212)787-6675. E-mail: mschaecht@aol.com. Pres. Dr. Zuni Zelitch; Exec. Dir. Dr. Mordkhe Schaechter. Encourages the development and use of Yiddish as a living language; promotes its modernization and standardization; publisher of Yiddish textbooks and English-Yiddish dictionaries; most recent book *The Standardized Yiddish Orthography (New York, 2000); Afn Shvel (quarterly).*

LEO BAECK INSTITUTE, INC. (1955). Center for Jewish History, 15 W. 16 St., NYC 10011-6301. (212)744-6400. FAX: (212) 988-1305. E-mail: lbi1@lbi.com. Pres. Ismar Schorsch; Exec. Dir. Carol Kahn Strauss. A research, study, and lecture center, museum, library, and archive relating to the history of German-speaking Jewry. Offers lectures, exhibits, faculty seminars; publishes a series of monographs, yearbooks, and journals. *LBI News; LBI Yearbook; LBI Memorial Lecture; occasional papers.*

LIVING TRADITIONS (1994), (c/o WORKMAN'S CIRLE) 45 East 33rd Street, New York, NY 10016. (212)532-8202. E-mail: henry@livingtraditions.org. Pres. Henry Sapoznik; V.-Pres. Sherry Mayrent. Nonprofit membership organization dedicated to the study, preservation, and innovative continuity of traditional folk and popular culture through workshops, concerts, recordings, radio and film documentaries; clearinghouse for research in klezmer and other traditional music; sponsors yearly weeklong international cultural event, "Yiddish Folk Arts Program/'KlezKamp.'" *Living Traditions (newsletter)* (WWW.LIVINGTRADITIONS. ORG)

THE MARTIN BUBER FORUM (1990), PMB #2212 101 W. 23 St., NYC (10011). (212)242-5637. Hon. Chmn. Prof. Maurice Friedman; Pres. Martin Warmbrand. Conducts discussion groups on the life and thought of Buber. *Martin Buber Review (annual).*

MEMORIAL FOUNDATION FOR JEWISH CULTURE, INC. (1964). 15 E. 26 St., Suite 1703, NYC 10010. (212)679-4074. FAX: (212)889-9080. Exec. V.-Pres. Jerry Hochbaum. Through the grants that it awards, encourages Jewish scholarship, culture, and education; supports communities that are struggling to maintain Jewish life; assists professional training for careers in communal service in Jewishly deprived communities; and stimulates the documentation, commemoration, and teaching of the Holocaust.

MUSEUM OF JEWISH HERITAGE—A LIVING MEMORIAL TO THE HOLOCAUST (1984). One Battery Park Plaza, NYC 10004-1484. (212)968-1800. FAX: (212)968-1368. Bd. Chmn. Robert M. Morgenthau; Museum Pres. Dr. Alfred Gottschalk; Museum Dir. David Marwell. New York tri-state's principal institution for educating people of all ages and backgrounds about 20th-century Jewish history and the Holocaust. Repository of Steven Spielberg's Survivors of the Shoah Visual History Foundation videotaped testimonies. Core and special exhibitions. *18 First Place (newsletter); Holocaust bibliography; educational materials.* (WWW.MJH-NYC.ORG)

MUSEUM OF TOLERANCE OF THE SIMON WIESENTHAL CENTER (1993). 9786 W. Pico Blvd., Los Angeles, CA 90035-4792. (310)553-8403. FAX: (310)553-4521. E-mail: avra@wiesenthal.com. Dean-Founder Rabbi Marvin Hier; Assoc. Dean Rabbi Abraham Cooper; Exec. Dir. Rabbi Meyer May. A unique experiential museum focusing on personal prejudice, group intolerance, struggle for civil rights, and 20th-century genocides, culminating in a major exhibition on the Holocaust. Archives, Multimedia Learning Center designed for individualized research, 6,700-square-foot temporary exhibit space, 324-seat theater, 150-seat auditorium, and outdoor memorial plaza. *Response Magazine.* (WWW.WIESENTHAL. COM)

NATIONAL CENTER FOR THE HEBREW LANGUAGE (1996). 633 Third Ave., 21st Fl., NYC 10017. (212)339-6023. FAX: (212) 318-6193. E-mail: ivritnow@aol.com. Pres. Dr. Alvin I. Schiff; Exec. Dir. Dr. Joseph Lowin. The NCHL advocates for Hebrew language and culture; serves as a Hebrew resource center; and is a catalyst for networking in Hebrew language and culture. It coordinates a Mini-Ulpan at the GA, publishes "Directory of Hebrew Classes," organizes "Lunch & Hebrew Lit" nationwide, and runs a Conference of Hebrew Teacher Trainers. *IvritNow/Ivrit-Akhshav.* (WWW.IVRIT.ORG)

NATIONAL FOUNDATION FOR JEWISH CULTURE (1960). 330 Seventh Ave., 21st fl., NYC 10001. (212)629-0500. FAX: (212) 629-0508. E-mail: nfjc@jewishculture. org. Pres. Lynn Korda Kroll; Exec. Dir. Richard A. Siegel. The leading Jewish organization devoted to promoting Jewish culture in the U.S. Manages the Jewish Endowment for the Arts and Humanities; administers the Council of American Jewish Museums and Council of Archives and Research Libraries in Jewish Studies; offers doctoral dissertation fellowships, new play commissions, and grants for documentary films, recording of Jewish music, contemporary choreography, fiction and non-fiction writing, and cultural preservation; coordinates community cultural residencies, local cultural councils, and national cultural consortia; sponsors conferences, symposia, and festivals in the arts and humanities. *Jewish Culture News; Culture Currents (electronic).*

NATIONAL MUSEUM OF AMERICAN JEWISH MILITARY HISTORY (*see* JEWISH WAR VETERANS OF THE U.S.A.)

NATIONAL YIDDISH BOOK CENTER (1980). 1021 West St., Amherst, MA 01002. (413)256-4900. FAX: (413)256-4700. E-mail: yiddish@bikher.org. Pres. Aaron Lansky; V.-Pres. Nancy Sherman. Since 1980 the center has collected 1.5 million Yiddish books for distribution to libraries and readers worldwide; offers innovative English-language programs and produces a magazine. New permanent home in Amherst, open to the public, features a book repository, exhibits, a bookstore, and a theater. *The Pakn Treger (English language magazine).*

ORTHODOX JEWISH ARCHIVES (1978). 42 Broadway, New York, NY 10004. (212)797-9000, ext. 73. FAX: (212)269-2843. Exec. V-Pres. Rabbi Shmuel Bloom & Shlomo Gertzullin; Dir. Rabbi Moshe Kolodny. Founded by Agudath Israel of America; houses historical documents, photographs, periodicals, and other publications relating to the growth of Orthodox Jewry in the U.S. and related communities in Europe, Israel, and elsewhere. Particularly noteworthy are its holdings relating to rescue activities organized during the Holocaust and its traveling exhibits available to schools and other institutions.

RESEARCH FOUNDATION FOR JEWISH IMMIGRATION, INC. (1971). 570 Seventh Ave., NYC 10018. (212)921-3871. FAX: (212)575-1918. Pres. Curt C. Silberman; Sec./Coord. of Research Herbert A. Strauss; Archivist Dennis E. Rohrbaugh. Studies and records the history of the migration and acculturation of Central European German-speaking Jewish and non-Jewish Nazi persecutees in various resettlement countries worldwide, with special emphasis on the American experience. *International Biographical Dictionary of Central European Emigrés, 1933-1945; Jewish Immigrants of the Nazi Period in the USA.*

SEPHARDIC EDUCATIONAL CENTER (1979). 10808 Santa Monica Blvd., Los Angeles, CA 90025. (310)441-9361. FAX: (310) 441-9561. E-mail: secforever@aol.com. Founder & Chmn. Jose A. Nessim, M.D. Has chapters in the U.S., North, Central, and South America, Europe, and Asia, a spiritual and educational center in the Old City of Jerusalem, and executive office in Los Angeles. Serves as a meeting ground for Sephardim from many nations; sponsors the first worldwide movement for Sephardic youth and young adults. Disseminates information about Sephardic Jewry in the form of motion pictures, pamphlets, and books, which it produces. *Hamerkaz (quarterly bulletin in English).* (WWW.SECWORLDWIDE.ORG)

SEPHARDIC HOUSE (1978). 15 West 16th Street, NYC 10011. (212)294-6170. FAX: (212)294-6149. E-mail: sephardichouse@cjs.org. Pres. Morrie R.Yohai; Exec. Dir. Dr. Janice E. Ovadiah. A cultural organization dedicated to fostering Sephardic history and culture; sponsors a wide variety of classes and public programs, film festivals, including summer program in France for high-school students; publication program disseminates materials of Sephardic value; outreach program to communities outside of the New York area; program bureau provides program ideas, speakers, and entertainers; International Sephardic Film Festival every two years. *Sephardic House Newsletter; Publication Catalogue.* (WWW. SEPHARDICHOUSE.ORG)

SIMON WIESENTHAL CENTER (1977). 1399 South Roxbury Drive., Los Angeles, CA

90035-4701. (310)553-9036. FAX: (310) 553-4521. Email: mhmay@wiesenthal. com. Dean-Founder Rabbi Marvin Hier; Assoc. Dean Rabbi Abraham Cooper; Exec. Dir. Rabbi Meyer May. Regional offices in New York, Miami, Baltimore, Toronto, Paris, Jerusalem, Buenos Aires. The largest institution of its kind in N. America, dedicated to the study of the Holocaust, its contemporary implications, and related human-rights issues through education and awareness. Incorporates 185,000-sq.-ft. Museum of Tolerance, library, media department, archives, "Testimony to the Truth" oral histories, educational outreach, research department, international social action, "Page One" (syndicated weekly radio news magazine presenting contemporary Jewish issues). *Response Magazine.* (WWW.WIESENTHAL.COM)

SKIRBALL CULTURAL CENTER (1996), an affiliate of Hebrew Union College. 2701 N. Sepulveda Blvd., Los Angeles, CA 90049. (310)440-4500. FAX: (310)440-4595. Pres. & CEO Uri D. Herscher; Bd. Chmn. Howard Friedman. Seeks to interpret the Jewish experience and to strengthen American society through a range of cultural programs, including museum exhibitions, children's Discovery Center, concerts, lectures, performances, readings, symposia, film, and educational offerings for adults and children of all ages and backgrounds, through interpretive museum exhibits and programming; museum shop and café. *Oasis magazine; catalogues of exhibits and collections.* (WWW.SKIRBALL.ORG)

SOCIETY FOR THE HISTORY OF CZECHOSLOVAK JEWS, INC. (1961). 760 Pompton Ave., Cedar Grove, NJ 07009. (973)239-2333. FAX: (973)239-7935. Pres. Rabbi Norman Patz; V.-Pres. Prof. Fred Hahn; Sec. Anita Grosz. Studies the history of Czechoslovak Jews; collects material and disseminates information through the publication of books and pamphlets; conducts annual memorial service for Czech Holocaust victims. *The Jews of Czechoslovakia (3 vols.); Review I-VI.*

THE SOCIETY OF FRIENDS OF TOURO SYNAGOGUE NATIONAL HISTORIC SITE, INC. (1948). 85 Touro St., Newport, RI 02840. (401)847-4794. FAX: (401)845-6790. E-mail: sof@tourosynagogue.org. Pres. Andrew M. Teitz; Exec. Dir. B. Schlessinger Ross. Helps maintain Touro Synagogue as a national historic site, opening and interpreting it for visitors; promotes public awareness of its preeminent role in the tradition of American religious liberty; annually commemorates George Washington's letter of 1790 to the Hebrew Congregation of Newport. *Society Update.*

————, TOURO NATIONAL HERITAGE TRUST (1984). 85 Touro St., Newport, RI 02840. (401)847-0810. FAX (401)847-8121. Pres. Bernard Bell; Chmn. Benjamin D. Holloway. Works to establish national education center within Touro compound; sponsors Touro Fellow through John Carter Brown Library; presents seminars and other educational programs; promotes knowledge of the early Jewish experience in this country.

SPERTUS MUSEUM, SPERTUS INSTITUTE OF JEWISH STUDIES (1968). 618 S. Michigan Ave., Chicago, IL 60605. (312)322-1747. FAX: (312)922-6406. Pres. Spertus Institute of Jewish Studies, Dr. Howard A. Sulkin. The largest, most comprehensive Judaic museum in the Midwest with 12,000 square feet of exhibit space and a permanent collection of some 10,000 works reflecting 5,000 years of Jewish history and culture. Also includes the redesigned Zell Holocaust Memorial, permanent collection, changing visual arts and special exhibits, and the children's ARTIFACT Center for a hands-on archaeological adventure. Plus, traveling exhibits for Jewish educators, life-cycle workshops, ADA accessible. *Exhibition catalogues; educational pamphlets.*

————, ASHER LIBRARY, SPERTUS INSTITUTE OF JEWISH STUDIES, (approx. 1930), 618 S. Michigan Ave., Chicago, IL 60605. (312) 322-1749, FAX (312) 922-6406. Pres. Spertus Institute of Jewish Studeis, Dr. Howard A. Sulkin; Director, Asher Library, Glenn Ferdman. Asher Library is the largest public Jewish Library in the Midwest, with over 100, 000 books and 550 periodicals; extensive collections of music, art, rare books, maps and electronic resources; nearly 1,000 feature and documentary films available on video cassette. Online catalogue access available. Also, the Chicago Jewish Archives collects historical material of Chicago individuals, families, synagogues and organizations. ADA accessible.

SURVIVORS OF THE SHOAH VISUAL HISTORY FOUNDATION (1994). PO Box 3168, Los Angeles, CA 90078-3168. (818)777-7802. FAX: (818)866-0312. Exec. Dir. Ari C. Zev. A nonprofit organization, founded and chaired by Steven Spielberg, dedicated to videotaping and preserving interviews with Holocaust survivors throughout the world. The archive of testimonies will be used as a tool for global education about the Holocaust and to teach racial, ethnic, and cultural tolerance.

UNITED STATES HOLOCAUST MEMORIAL MUSEUM (1980; opened Apr. 1993). 100 Raoul Wallenberg Place, SW, Washington, DC 20024. (202)488-0400. FAX: (202)488-2690. Chmn. Rabbi Irving Greenberg; Dir. Sara J. Bloomfield. Federally chartered and privately built, its mission is to teach about the Nazi persecution and murder of six million Jews and millions of others from 1933 to 1945 and to inspire visitors to contemplate their moral responsibilities as citizens of a democratic nation. Opened in April 1993 near the national Mall in Washington, DC, the museum's permanent exhibition tells the story of the Holocaust through authentic artifacts, videotaped oral testimonies, documentary film, and historical photographs. Offers educational programs for students and adults, an interactive computerized learning center, and special exhibitions and community programs. *United States Holocaust Memorial Museum Update (bimonthly); Directory of Holocaust Institutions; Journal of Holocaust and Genocide Studies (quarterly).* (WWW.USHMM.ORG)

THE WILSTEIN (SUSAN & DAVID) INSTITUTE OF JEWISH POLICY STUDIES (1988). 43 Hawes St., Brookline, MA 02146. (617) 278-4974. FAX: (617)264-9264. E-mail: wilstein@hebrewcollege.edu. Dir. Dr. David M. Gordis; Assoc. Dir. Rabbi Zachary I. Heller; Chmn. Howard I. Friedman. The Wilstein Institute's West Coast Center in Los Angeles and East Coast Center at Hebrew College in Boston provide a bridge between academics, community leaders, professionals, and the organizations and institutions of Jewish life. The institute serves as an international research and development resource for American Jewry. *Bulletins, various newsletters, monographs, research reports, and books.*

YESHIVA UNIVERSITY MUSEUM (1973). Center for Jewish History, 15 W. 16 St.,

NYC 10011-6301. (212)294-8330. E-mail: rglickberg@yum.cjh.org. Dir. Sylvia A. Herskowitz; Chmn. Erica Jesselson. Collects, preserves, and interprets Jewish life and culture through changing exhibitions of ceremonial objects, paintings, rare books and documents, synagogue architecture, textiles, contemporary art, and photographs. Oral history archive. Special events, holiday workshops, live performances, lectures, etc. for adults and children. Guided tours and workshops are offered. Exhibitions and children's art education programs also at branch galleries on Yeshiva University's Main Campus, 2520 Amsterdam Ave., NYC 10033-3201. *Seasonal calendars; special exhibition catalogues; newsletters.*

YIDDISHER KULTUR FARBAND-YKUF (1937). 1133 Broadway, Rm. 820, NYC 10010. (212)243-1304. FAX: (212) 243-1305. E-mail: mahosu@amc.one. Pres./Ed. Itche Goldberg. Publishes a bimonthly magazine and books by contemporary and classical Jewish writers; conducts cultural forums; exhibits works by contemporary Jewish artists and materials of Jewish historical value; organizes reading circles. *Yiddishe Kultur.*

YIVO INSTITUTE FOR JEWISH RESEARCH (1925). Center for Jewish History, 15 W. 16 St., NYC 10011-6301. (212)246-6080. FAX: (212)292-1892. E-mail: yivomail@yivo.cjh.org. Chmn. Bruce Slovin; Exec. Dir. Dr. Carl J. Rheins. Engages in historical research and education pertaining to East European Jewish life; maintains library and archives which provide a major international, national and New York resource used by institutions, individual scholars, and the public; provides graduate fellowships in East European and American Jewish studies; offers Yiddish language classes at all levels, exhibits, conferences, public programs; publishes books. *Yedies-YIVO News; YIVO Bleter.*

———, MAX WEINREICH CENTER FOR ADVANCED JEWISH STUDIES/YIVO INSTITUTE (1968). 15 W. 16 St., NYC 10011. (212)246-6080. FAX: (212)292-1892. E-mail: mweinreich@yivo.cjh.org. Provides advanced-level training in Yiddish language and literature, ethnography, folklore, linguistics, and history; offers guidance on dissertation or independent research; post-doctoral fellowships available.

YUGNTRUF-YOUTH FOR YIDDISH (1964). 200 W. 72 St., Suite 40, NYC 10023. (212)787-6675. FAX: (212)799-1517. E-mail: ruvn@aol.com. Chmn. Dr. Paul Glasser; V.-Chmn. Marc Caplan; Coord. Brukhe Lang Caplan. A worldwide, nonpolitical organization for young people with a knowledge of, or interest in, Yiddish; fosters Yiddish as a living language and culture. Sponsors all activities in Yiddish:reading, conversation, and creative writing groups; annual weeklong retreat in Berkshires; children's Yiddish play group; sale of shirts. *Yugntruf Journal.*

ISRAEL-RELATED

THE ABRAHAM FUND (1989). 477 Madison Ave., 4th fl., NYC 10022. (212)303-9421. FAX: (212)935-1834. E-mail: INFO@AbrahamFund.org. Chmn. & Co-founder Alan B. Slifka; Co-founder Dr. Eugene Weiner. Seeks to enhance coexistence between Israel's Jewish and Arab citizens. Since 1993, has granted $6 million to grassroots coexistence projects in a wide array of fields, including education, social services, economic development, and arts and culture. Publishes *The Handbook of Interethnic Coexistence. Coexistence Newsletter.* (WWW.COEXISTENCE.ORG)

AMERICA-ISRAEL CULTURAL FOUNDATION, INC. (1939). 51 E. 42nd St., Suite 400, NYC 10017. (212)557-1600. FAX: (212)557-1611. E-mail: USA AICF@aol.com. Chmn. Emer. Isaac Stern; Pres. Vera Stern. Supports and encourages the growth of cultural excellence in Israel through grants to cultural institutions; scholarships to gifted young artists and musicians. *Newsletter.*

AMERICA-ISRAEL FRIENDSHIP LEAGUE, INC. (1971). 134 E. 39 St., NYC 10016. (212) 213-8630. FAX: (212)683-3475. E-mail: aifl@nyworld.com. Hon. Chmn. Mortimer B. Zuckerman; Bd. Chmn. Kenneth J. Bialkin; Exec.V.-Pres. Ilana Artman. A nonsectarian, nonpartisan organization which seeks to broaden the base of support for Israel among Americans of all faiths and backgrounds. Activities include educational exchanges, tours of Israel for American leadership groups, symposia and public-education activities, and the dissemination of printed information. *Newsletter.*

AMERICAN ASSOCIATES, BEN-GURION UNIVERSITY OF THE NEGEV (1973). 342 Madison Ave., Suite 1224, NYC 10173.

(212)687-7721. FAX: (212)370-0686. E-mail: info@aabgu.org. Pres. Zvi Alov; Exec. V-Pres. Seth Moscovitz. Raises funds for Israel's youngest university, an institution dedicated to providing a world-class higher education and fulfilling David Ben-Gurion's vision to develop the Negev and make Israel a 'light unto the nations' through education, research, and projects that fight hunger, disease, and poverty in nearly 50 countries worldwide. *IMPACT Newsletter; videos and brochures.*

AMERICAN COMMITTEE FOR SHAARE ZEDEK JERUSALEM MEDICAL CENTER (1949). 49 W. 45 St., Suite 1100, NYC 10036. (212) 354-8801. FAX: (212)391-2674. E-mail: pr@szmc.org.il. Natl. Pres. & Chmn. Intl. Bd. of Gov. Menno Ratzker; Chair Erica Jesselson. Increases awareness and raises funds for the various needs of this 100-year old hospital, including new medical centers of excellence, equipment, medical supplies, school of nursing and research; supports exchange program between Shaare Zedek Jerusalem Medical Center and Albert Einstein College of Medicine, NY. *Heartbeat Magazine.*

AMERICAN COMMITTEE FOR SHENKAR COLLEGE IN ISRAEL, INC. (1971). 855 Ave. of the Americas, #531, NYC 10001. (212) 947-1597. FAX: (212)643-9887. E-mail: acfsc@worldnet.att.net. Pres. Nahum G. (Sonny) Shar; Exec. Dir. Charlotte A. Fainblatt. Raises funds for capital improvement, research and development projects, laboratory equipment, scholarships, lectureships, fellowships, and library/archives of fashion and textile design at Shenkar College in Israel, Israel's only fashion and textile technology college. New departments of computer science and jewelry design. Accredited by the Council of Higher Education, the college is the chief source of personnel for Israel's fashion and apparel industry. *Shenkar News.*

AMERICAN COMMITTEE FOR THE BEER-SHEVA FOUNDATION (1988). PO Box 179, NYC 10028. (212)534-3715. FAX: (973) 992-8651. Pres. Ronald Slevin; Sr. V.-Pres. Joanna Slevin; Bd. Chmn. Sidney Cooperman. U.S. fundraising arm of the Beer-Sheva Foundation, which funds vital projects to improve the quality of life in the city of Beer-Sheva: nursery schools for pre-K toddlers, residential and day centers for needy seniors, educational programs, facilities and scholarships (especially for new olim, the physically and mentally challenged), parks, playgrounds, and other important projects. Also offers special services for immigrants—such as heaters, blankets, clothing, school supplies, etc. *Brochures.*

AMERICAN COMMITTEE FOR THE WEIZMANN INSTITUTE OF SCIENCE (1944). 130 E. 59 St., NYC 10022. (212)895-7900. FAX: (212)8957999. E-mail: info@acwis. org. Chmn. Robert Asher; Pres. Albert Willner, M.D.; Exec. V.-Pres. Martin Kraar. Through 13 regional offices in the U.S. raises funds, disseminates information, and does American purchasing for the Weizmann Institute in Rehovot, Israel, a world-renowned center of scientific research and graduate study. The institute conducts research in disease, energy, the environment, and other areas; runs an international summer science program for gifted high-school students. *Interface; Weizmann Now; annual report.* (WWW.WEIZMANN-USA.ORG)

AMERICAN FRIENDS OF ALYN HOSPITAL (1932). 19 W. 44 St., Suite 1418, NYC 10036. (212)869-8085. FAX: (212)768-0979. E-mail: friendsofalyn@mindspring. com. Pres. Minette Halpern Brown; Exec. Dir. Cathy M Lanyard. Supports the Woldenberg Family Orthopedic Hospital and Pediatric Rehabilitation Center in Jerusalem. Treats children suffering from birth defects (such as muscular dystrophy and spina bifida) and traumas (car accidents, cancer, and fire), enables patients and their families to achieve independence and a better quality of life. (www. ALYN.ORG)

AMERICAN FRIENDS OF ASSAF HAROFEH MEDICAL CENTER (1975). PO Box 21051, NYC 10129. (212)481-5653. FAX: (212)481-5672. Chmn. Kenneth Kronen; Exec. Dir. Rhoda Levental; Treas. Robert Kastin. Support group for Assaf Harofeh, Israel's third-largest government hospital, serving a poor population of over 400,000 in the area between Tel Aviv and Jerusalem. Raises funds for medical equipment, medical training for immigrants, hospital expansion, school of nursing, and school of physiotherapy. *Newsletter.*

AMERICAN FRIENDS OF BAR-ILAN UNIVERSITY (1955). 235 Park Ave. So., NYC 10003. (212)673-3460. FAX: (212)673-

4856. Email: nationaladmin@biuny.com. beverlyf@biuny.com. Chancellor Rabbi Emanuel Rackman; Chmn. Global Bd. Aharon Dahan; Pres. Amer. Bd. Melvin Stein; Exec. V.-Pres. Gen. Yehuda Halevy. Supports Bar-Ilan University, an institution that integrates the highest standards of contemporary scholarship in liberal arts and sciences with a Judaic studies program as a requirement. Located in Ramat-Gan, Israel, and chartered by the Board of Regents of the State of NY. *Bar-Ilan News; Bar-Ilan University Scholar; Heritage Newsletter.*

AMERICAN FRIENDS OF BETH HATEFUTSOTH (1976). 633 Third Ave., 21st fl., NYC 10017. (212)339-6034. FAX: (212)318-6176. E-mail: afbhusa@aol.com. Pres. Stephen Greenberg; Chmn. Sam E. Bloch; Exec. Dir. Gloria Golan. Supports the maintenance and development of Beth Hatefutsoth, the Nahum Goldmann Museum of the Jewish Diaspora in Tel Aviv, and its cultural and educational programs for youth and adults. Circulates its traveling exhibitions and provides various cultural programs to local Jewish communities. Includes Jewish genealogy center (DOROT), the center for Jewish music, and photodocumentation center. *Beth Hatefutsoth (quarterly newsletter).*

AMERICAN FRIENDS OF HAIFA UNIVERSITY (*see* AMERICAN SOCIETY OF THE UNIVERSITY OF HAIFA)

AMERICAN FRIENDS OF HERZOG HOSPITAL/EZRATH NASHIM-JERUSALEM (1895). 800 Second Ave., 8th fl., NYC 10017. (212)499-9092. FAX:(212)499-9085. E-mail: herzogpr@hotmail.com. info@herzoghospital.org. Co-Pres. Dr. Joy Zagoren, Amir Sternhell; Exec. Dir. Stephen Schwartz. Israel's foremost center for geriatric and psychiatric health care. It is Jerusalem's third largest hospital with 330 beds. It is a major teaching hospital and maintains a leading research center in the fields of genetics, alzheimer's and schizophrenia. Geriatric specialization in neurogeriatrics; physical rehabilitation; and complex nursing care. Community Mental Health Center treats 25,000 people annually with expertise in treating children with ADHD. *Update newsletter.*

AMERICAN FRIENDS OF LIKUD. P.O.Box 8711, JAF Station, NYC 10116. (212)308-5595. FAX: (212)688-1327. E-mail: Thelikud@aol.com. Natl. Chmn. J. Phillip Rosen, Esq; Pres. Julio Messer, M.D; Exec. Dir. Salomon L. Vaz Dias. Devoted to promoting public education on the situation in the Middle East, particularly in Israel, as well as advancing a general awareness of Zionism. American Friends of Likud provides a solid partnership of public support for the State of Israel, its citizens and its democratically-elected governments. Members receive opportunities to meet with Likud leaders at exclusive seminars; regular information on Israel and Zionism, including the most accurate, reliable, and up-to-date news, official briefings and behind-the-lines journalism from Israel; opportunities to make views known to American, Israeli and other politicians, as well as members of the media; invitations to members-only briefings by senior Israeli and U.S. government officials. American Friends of Likud is an active member of Conference of Presidents of Major American Jewish Organizations; American Zionist Movement; World Zionist Organization; Jewish Agency for Israel; Jewish National Fund.

AMERICAN FRIENDS OF NEVE SHALOM/ WAHAT AL-SALAM (1988). 121 Sixth Ave., Suite #507, NYC 10013. (212) 226-9246. FAX: (212) 226-6817. E-mail: afnswas@compuserve.com. Pres. Adeeb Fadil; V.-Pres. Deborah First; Exec. Dir. Deanna Armbruster. Supports and publicizes the projects of the community of Neve Shalom/Wahat Al-Salam, the "Oasis of Peace," where, for more than 20 years, Jewish and Palestinian citizens of Israel have lived and worked together as equals. The community teaches tolerance, understanding and mutual respect well beyond its own borders by being a model for peace and reaching out through its educational institutions. A bilingual, bicultural primary school serves the village and the surrounding communities. Encounter workshops conducted by the school, both in the community and beyond, have reached tens of thousands of Jewish and Palestinian youth and adults.

AMERICAN FRIENDS OF RABIN MEDICAL CENTER (1994). 220 Fifth Avenue, Suite 1301, NYC 10001-2121. (212) 279-2522. Fax: (212)279-0179. E-mail: afrmc826@aol.com. Pres. Woody Goldberg; Exec.

Dir. Burton Lazarow. Supports the maintenance and development of this medical, research, and teaching institution in central Israel, which unites the Golda and Beilinson hospitals, providing 12% of all hospitalization in Israel. Department of Organ Transplantation performs 80% of all kidney and 60% of all liver transplants in Israel. Affiliated with Tel Aviv University's Sackler School of Medicine. *New Directions Quarterly.*

AMERICAN FRIENDS OF RAMBAM MEDICAL CENTER (1969). 226 West 26th Street, NYC 10001. (212)644-1049. FAX: (212) 644-8939. E-mail: rambam@earthlink. net. michaelstoler@princetoncommercial. com. Pres/CEO. Michael R. Stoler. Represents and raises funds for Rambam Medical Center (Haifa), an 887-bed hospital serving approx. one-third of Israel's population, incl. the entire population of northern Israel (and south Lebanon), the U.S. Sixth Fleet, and the UN Peacekeeping Forces in the region. Rambam is the teaching hospital for the Technion's medical school.

AMERICAN FRIENDS OF TEL AVIV UNIVERSITY, INC. (1955). 39 Broadway, 15th Floor., NYC 10006. (212)742-9070. FAX: (212)742-9071. Email: info@aftau.org. Bd. Chmn. Alan L. Aufzien; Pres. Robert J. Topchik; Exec. V.-Pres. Sam Witkin. Promotes higher education at Tel Aviv University, Israel's largest and most comprehensive institution of higher learning. Included in its nine faculties are the Sackler School of Medicine with its fully accredited NY State English-language program, the Rubin Academy of Music, and 70 research institutes, including the Moshe Dayan Center for Middle East & African Studies and the Jaffe Center for Strategic Studies. *Tel Aviv University News; FAX Flash.*

AMERICAN FRIENDS OF THE HEBREW UNIVERSITY (1925; inc. 1931). 11 E. 69 St., NYC 10021. (212)472-9800. FAX: (212) 744-2324. E-mail: info@afhu.org. Pres. Ira Lee Sorkin; Bd. Chmn. Keith L. Sachs; Exec. V.-Pres. Adam Kahan. Fosters the growth, development, and maintenance of the Hebrew University of Jerusalem; collects funds and conducts informational programs throughout the U.S., highlighting the university's achievements and its significance. *Wisdom; Scopus Magazine.* (WWW.AFHU.ORG)

AMERICAN FRIENDS OF THE ISRAEL MUSEUM (1972). 500 Fifth Ave., Suite 2540, NYC 10110. (212)997-5611. FAX: (212) 997-5536. Pres. Barbara Lane; Exec. Dir. Carolyn Cohen. Raises funds for special projects of the Israel Museum in Jerusalem; solicits works of art for permanent collection, exhibitions, and educational purposes. *Newsletter.*

AMERICAN FRIENDS OF THE ISRAEL PHILHARMONIC ORCHESTRA (AFIPO) (1972). 122 E. 42 St., Suite 4507, NYC 10168. (212)697-2949. FAX: (212)697-2943. Pres. Herman Sandler; Exec. Dir. Suzanne K. Ponsot. Works to secure the financial future of the orchestra so that it may continue to travel throughout the world bringing its message of peace and cultural understanding through music. Supports the orchestra's international touring program, educational projects, and a wide array of musical activities in Israel. *Passport to Music (newsletter).*

AMERICAN FRIENDS OF THE OPEN UNIVERSITY OF ISRAEL. 180 W. 80 St., NYC 10024. (212)712-1800. FAX: (212)496-3296. E-mail: afoui@aol.com. Natl. Chmn. Irving M. Rosenbaum; Exec.V.-Pres. Eric G. Heffler. *Open Letter.* (WWW. OPENU.AC.IL).

AMERICAN FRIENDS OF THE SHALOM HARTMAN INSTITUTE (1976). 42 E. 69 St., Suite 401, NYC 10021. (212)772-9711. FAX: (212)772-9720. E-mail: afshi@banet.net. Pres. Richard F. Kaufman; Exec. V.-Pres. Fred Lafer; Admin. Dorothy Minchin. Supports the Shalom Hartman Institute in Jerusalem, an international center for pluralist Jewish education and research, serving Israel and world Jewry. Founded in 1976 by David Hartman, the Institute includes:the Institute for Advanced Judaic Studies, with research centers for contemporary halakha, religious pluralism, political thought and peace and reconciliation; the Institute for Teacher and Leadership Training, educating Israeli principals, teachers, graduate students and leaders; and the Institute for Diaspora Education, which offers seminars and sabbaticals to rabbis, educators and lay leaders of diverse ideological commitments. (WWW.HARTMANINSTITUTE.COM)

AMERICAN FRIENDS OF THE TEL AVIV MUSEUM OF ART (1974). 545 Madison Ave. (55 St.), NYC 10022. (212)319-0555.

FAX: (212)754-2987. Email: dnaftam@ aol.com. Chmn. Stanley I. Batkin; Exec. Dir. Dorey Neilinger. Raises funds for the Tel Aviv Museum of Art for special projects, art acquisitions, and exhibitions; seeks contributions of art to expand the museum's collection; encourages art loans and traveling exhibitions; creates an awareness of the museum in the USA; makes available exhibition catalogues, monthly calendars, and posters published by the museum.

AMERICAN-ISRAEL ENVIRONMENTAL COUNCIL (formerly COUNCIL FOR A BEAUTIFUL ISRAEL ENVIRONMENTAL EDUCATION FOUNDATION) (1973). c/o Perry Davis Assoc., 25 W. 45 St., Suite 1405, NYC 10036. (212)575-7530. Fax: (212)840-1514. Co-Pres. Mel Atlas & Edythe Roland Grodnick. A support group for the Israeli body, whose activities include education, town planning, lobbying for legislation to protect and enhance the environment, preservation of historical sites, the improvement and beautification of industrial and commercial areas, and sponsoring the CBI Center for Environmental Studies located in Yarkon Park, Tel Aviv. *Yearly newsletter; yearly theme oriented calendars in color.*

AMERICAN ISRAEL PUBLIC AFFAIRS COMMITTEE (AIPAC) (1954). 440 First St., NW, Washington, DC 20001. (202)639-5200. FAX: (202)347-4889. Pres. Lonny Kaplan; Exec. Dir. Howard A. Kohr. Registered to lobby on behalf of legislation affecting U.S.-Israel relations; represents Americans who believe support for a secure Israel is in U.S. interest. Works for a strong U.S.-Israel relationship. *Near East Report.* (WWW.AIPAC.ORG)

AMERICAN-ISRAELI LIGHTHOUSE, INC. (1928; reorg. 1955). 276 Fifth Ave., Suite 713, NYC 10001. (212)686-7110. Pres. Mrs. Leonard F. Dank; Sec. Mrs. Ida Rhein. Provides a vast network for blind and physically handicapped persons throughout Israel, to effect their social and vocational integration into the mainstream of their communities. Center of Services for the blind; built and maintains Rehabilitation Center for blind and handicapped persons (Migdal Or) in Haifa.

AMERICAN JEWISH LEAGUE FOR ISRAEL (1957). 130 E. 59 St., NYC 10022. (212)371-1583. FAX: (212)371-3265. E-

mail: AJLImlk@aol.com. Pres. Dr. Martin L. Kalmanson. Seeks to unite all those who, notwithstanding differing philosophies of Jewish life, are committed to the historical ideals of Zionism; works independently of class, party, or religious affiliation for the welfare of Israel as a whole. Not identified with any political parties in Israel. Member of World Jewish Congress, World Zionist Organization, American Zionist Movement. *Newsletter.*

AMERICAN PHYSICIANS FELLOWSHIP FOR MEDICINE IN ISRAEL (1950). 2001 Beacon St., Suite 210, Boston, MA 02135-7771. (617)232-5382. FAX: (617) 739-2616. E-mail: apf@apfmed.org. Pres. Sherwood L. Gorbach, M.D.; Exec. Dir. Ellen-Ann Lacey. Supports projects that advance medical education, research, and care in Israel and builds links between the medical communities of Israel and N. Amer.; provides fellowships for Israeli physicians training in N. Amer. and arranges lectureships in Israel by prominent N. Amer. physicians; sponsors CME seminars in Israel and N. Amer.; coordinates U.S./Canadian medical emergency volunteers for Israel. *APF News.*

AMERICAN RED MAGEN DAVID FOR ISRAEL, INC. (1940) (a/k/a ARMDI & RED MAGEN DAVID). 888 Seventh Ave., Suite 403, NYC 10106. (212)757-1627. FAX: (212)757-4662. E-mail: armdi@att.net. Natl. Pres. Robert L. Sadoff, M.D.; Exec. V.-Pres. Benjamin Saxe. An authorized tax-exempt organization; the sole support arm in the U.S. of Magen David Adom (MDA), Israel's equivalent to a Red Cross Society; raises funds for the MDA emergency medical, ambulance, blood, and disaster relief services which help Israel's defense forces and civilian population. Helps to supply and equip ambulances, bloodmobiles, and cardiac rescue ambulances as well as 45 pre-hospital MDA Emergency Medical Clinics and the MDA National Blood Service Center and MDA Fractionation Institute in Ramat Gan, Israel. *Lifeline.*

AMERICAN SOCIETY FOR TECHNION-ISRAEL INSTITUTE OF TECHNOLOGY (1940). 810 Seventh Ave., 24th fl., NYC 10019. (212) 262-6200. FAX: (212)262-6155. Pres. Lawrence Jackier; Chmn. Irving A. Shepard; Exec. V.-Pres. Melvyn H. Bloom. The American Technion Society (ATS), with more than 20,000 supporters and 19 satellite offices around the country, is driven by the belief that the economic future of Israel is in high technology and the future of high technology in Israel is at the Technion. *Technion USA.*

AMERICAN SOCIETY FOR THE PROTECTION OF NATURE IN ISRAEL, INC. (1986). 28 Arrandale Ave., Great Neck, NY 11024. (212) 398-6750. FAX: (212) 398-1665. E-mail: aspni@aol.com. Co-Chmn. Edward I. Geffner & Russell Rothman. A non-profit organization supporting the work of SPNI, an Israeli organization devoted to environmental protection and nature education. SPNI runs 26 Field Study Centers and has 45 municipal offices throughout Israel; offers education programs, organized hikes, and other activities; seeks ways to address the needs of an expanding society while preserving precious natural resources. *SPNI News.*

AMERICAN SOCIETY FOR YAD VASHEM (1981). 500 Fifth Ave., Suite 1600, NYC 10110-1699. (212)220-4304. FAX: (212)220-4308. E-mail: yadvashem@aol.com. Chmn. Eli Zborowski; Exec. Dir. Rochel U. Berman; Dev. Dir. Shraga Y. Mekel; Ed. Dir. Marlene Warshawski Yahalom, Ph.D. Development arm of Yad Vashem, Jerusalem, the central international authority created by the Knesset in 1953 for the purposes of commemoration and education in connection with the Holocaust. *Martyrdom and Resistance (newsletter).* (WWW.YADVASHEM.ORG)

AMERICAN SOCIETY OF THE UNIVERSITY OF HAIFA (formerly AMERICAN FRIENDS OF HAIFA UNIVERSITY) (1972). 220 Fifth Ave., Suite 1301, NYC 10001. (212) 685-7880. FAX: (212)267-5916. Pres. Paul Amir; Sec./Treas. Robert Jay Benowitz. Promotes, encourages, and aids higher and secondary education, research, and training in all branches of knowledge in Israel and elsewhere; aids in the maintenance and development of Haifa University; raises and allocates funds for the above purposes; provides scholarships; promotes exchanges of teachers and students.

AMERICAN ZIONIST MOVEMENT (formerly AMERICAN ZIONIST FEDERATION) (1939; reorg. 1949, 1970, 1993). 110 E. 59 St., NYC 10022. (212)318-6100. FAX: (212) 935-3578. E-mail: info@azm.com. Pres.

Melvin Salberg; Exec. Dir. Karen J. Rubinstein. Umbrella organization for 20 American Zionist organizations and the voice of unified Zionism in the U.S. Conducts advocacy for Israel; strengthens Jewish identity; promotes the Israel experience; prepares the next generation of Zionist leadership. Regional offices in Chicago and Dallas. Groups in Detroit, Pittsburgh, Washington, DC. *The Zionist Advocate.* (WWW.AZM.ORG)

AMERICANS FOR A SAFE ISRAEL (AFSI) (1971). 1623 Third Ave., Suite 205, NYC 10128. (212)828-2424. FAX: (212)828-1717. E-mail: afsi@rcn.com. Chmn. Herbert Zweibon; Exec. Dir. Helen Freedman. Seeks to educate Americans in Congress, the media, and the public about Israel's role as a strategic asset for the West; through meetings with legislators and the media, in press releases and publications AFSI promotes Jewish rights to Judea and Samaria, the Golan, Gaza, an indivisible Jerusalem, and to all of Israel. AFSI believes in the concept of "peace for peace" and rejects the concept of "territory for peace." *The Outpost (monthly).* (WWW.AFSI.ORG.AFSI)

AMERICANS FOR PEACE NOW (1984). 1815 H St., NW, 9th fl., Washington, DC 20006. (212)728-1893. FAX: (212)728-1895. E-mail: apndc@peacenow.org. Pres. & CEO Debra DeLee; Chmn. Pat Barr. Conducts educational programs and raises funds to support the Israeli peace movement, Shalom Achshav (Peace Now), and coordinates U.S. advocacy efforts through APN's Washington-based Center for Israeli Peace and Security. *Jerusalem Watch; Peace Now News; Settlement Watch; Fax Facts; Middle East Update (on-line); Benefits of Peace.* (WWW.PEACENOW.ORG)

AMIT (1925). 817 Broadway, NYC 10003. (212)477-4720. FAX: (212)353-2312. E-mail: info@amitchildren.org. Pres. Sondra Sokal; Exec. Dir. Marvin Leff. The State of Israel's official reshet (network) for religious secondary technological education; maintains innovative children's homes and youth villages in Israel in an environment of traditional Judaism; promotes cultural activities for the purpose of disseminating Zionist ideals and strengthening traditional Judaism in America. *AMIT Magazine.*

AMPAL-AMERICAN ISRAEL CORPORATION (1942). 1177 Avenue of the Americas, NYC 10036. (212)782-2100. FAX: (212) 782-2114. E-mail: ampal@aol.com. Bd. Chmn. Daniel Steinmetz; CEO Shuki Gleitman. Acquires interests in businesses located in the State of Israel or that are Israel-related. Interests include leisure-time, real estate, finance, energy distribution, basic industry, high technology, and communications. *Annual report; quarterly reports.*

ARZA/WORLD UNION, NORTH AMERICA (1977). 633 Third Ave., 6th fl., NYC 10017-6778. (212)650-4280. FAX: (212)650-4289. E-mail: arza/wupjna@ uahc.org. Pres. Philip Meltzer; Exec. Dir. Rabbi Ammiel Hirsch. Membership organization dedicated to furthering the development of Progressive Judaism in Israel, the FSU, and throughout the world. Encourages Jewish solidarity, promoting religious pluralism and furthering Zionism. Works to strengthen the relationship of N. American Reform Jews with Progressive Jewish communities worldwide and to educate and inform them on relevant issues. *Quarterly newsletter.* (WWW.RJ. ORG/ARZAWUNA)

BETAR EDUCATIONAL YOUTH ORGANIZATION (1935). 4 East 34th Street, NYC, 10016. (646)742-9364. FAX: (646)742-9366. E-mail: betarorg@idt.net. Pres. Shav Rubinstein. Betar is a Zionist active college students' movement, which dedicates itself to promoting Israeli issues in the American media. Betar was founded in 1923 by Zeev Jabotinsky, among its' famous alumni are Nenachem Begin and Itzhak Shamir. Betar's goal is the gathering of all Jewish people in their ancient land.

BOYS TOWN JERUSALEM FOUNDATION OF AMERICA INC. (1948). 12 W. 31 St., Suite 300, NYC 10001. (212)244-2766. (800) 469-2697. FAX: (212)244-2052. E-mail: btjny@compuserve.com. Raphael Benaroya, Pres. Michael J. Scharf; Chmn. Josh S. Weston; V.-Chmn. Moshe Linchner; Exec. V.-Pres. Rabbi Ronald L. Gray. Raises funds for Boys Town Jerusalem, which was established in 1948 to offer a comprehensive academic, religious, and technological education to disadvantaged Israeli and immigrant boys from over 45 different countries, including Ethiopia, the former Soviet Union, and Iran. Enrollment:over 1,000 students in jr. high school, academic and technical high school, and a college of applied engineering. Boys Town was recently designated as the "CISCO Regional Academy," the first center in Jerusalem for the instruction of the CISCO Networking Management Program. *BTJ Newsbrief.*

CAMERA-COMMITTEE FOR ACCURACY IN MIDDLE EAST REPORTING IN AMERICA (1983). PO Box 428, Boston, MA 02456. (617)789-3672. FAX: (617)787-7853. E-mail: media@camera.org. Pres./Exec. Dir. Andrea Levin; Chmn. Leonard Wisse. Monitors and responds to media distortion in order to promote better understanding of Middle East; urges members to alert the public and the media to errors, omissions, and distortions. *CAMERA Media Report (quarterly); CAMERA on Campus; Action Alerts; Media Directories; Monographs.*(WWW.CAMERA.ORG)

COUNCIL FOR A BEAUTIFUL ISRAEL ENVIRONMENTAL EDUCATION FOUNDATION (*see* AMERICAN-ISRAEL ENVIRONMENTAL COUNCIL)

EMUNAH OF AMERICA (formerly HAPOEL HAMIZRACHI WOMEN'S ORGANIZATION) (1948). 7 Penn Plaza, NYC 10001. (212)564-9045, (800)368-6440. FAX: (212)643-9731. E-mail: info@emunah. org. Natl. Pres. Dr. Marcia Genuth; Exec. V.-Pres. Carol Sufian. Maintains and supports 200 educational and social-welfare institutions in Israel within a religious framework, including day-care centers, kindergartens, children's residential homes, vocational schools for the underprivileged, senior-citizen centers, a college complex, and Holocaust study center. Also involved in absorption of Soviet and Ethiopian immigrants (recognized by Israeli government as an official absorption agency). *Emunah Magazine; Lest We Forget.* (WWW.EMUNAH.ORG)

FEDERATED COUNCIL OF ISRAEL INSTITUTIONS—FCII (1940). 4702 15th Ave., Brooklyn, NY 11219. (718)972-5530. Bd. Chmn. Z. Shapiro; Exec. V.-Pres. Rabbi Julius Novack. Central fund-raising organization for over 100 affiliated institutions; handles and executes estates, wills, and bequests for the traditional institutions in Israel; clearinghouse for information on budget, size, functions, etc. of traditional educational, welfare, and philanthropic institutions in Israel, working cooperatively with the Israeli government and the overseas department of the Council of Jewish Federations. *Annual financial reports and statistics on affiliates.*

FRIENDS OF THE ISRAEL DEFENSE FORCES (1981). 298 5th Avenue, NYC 10001. (212)244-3118. FAX: (212)244-3119. E-mail: fidf@fidf.com. Chmn. Marvin Josephson; Pres. Jay Zises; Natl. Dir. Brig. Gen. Eliezer Hemeli. Supports the Agudah Lema'an Hahayal, Israel's Assoc. for the Well-Being of Soldiers, founded in the early 1940s, which provides social, recreational, and educational programs for soldiers, special services for the sick and wounded, and summer programs for widows and children of fallen soldiers. (WWW.FIDF.COM)

GESHER FOUNDATION (1969). 25 W. 45 St. Suite 1405, NYC 10036. (212)840-1166. FAX: (212)840-1514. E-mail: gesherfoundation@aol.com. Pres./Founder Daniel Tropper; Chmn. Philip Schatten. Seeks to bridge the gap between Jews of various backgrounds in Israel by stressing the interdependence of all Jews. Runs encounter seminars for Israeli youth; distributes curricular materials in public schools; offers Jewish identity classes for Russian youth, and a video series in Russian and English on famous Jewish personalities.

GIVAT HAVIVA EDUCATIONAL FOUNDATION, INC. (1966). 114 W. 26 St., Suite 1001, NYC 10001. (212)989-9272. FAX: (212) 989-9840. E-mail: mail@givathaviva.org. Chmn. Yvonne Baum Silverman. Supports programs at the Givat Haviva Institute, Israel's leading organization dedicated to promoting coexistence between Arabs and Jews, with 40,000 people participating each year in programs teaching conflict resolution, Middle East studies and languages, and Holocaust studies. Publishes research papers on Arab-Jewish relations, Holocaust studies, kibbutz life. In the U.S., GHEF sponsors public-education programs and lectures by Israeli speakers. *Givat Haviva News; special reports.*(WWW.DIALOGATE.ORG.IL)

HABONIM-DROR NORTH AMERICA (1935). 114 W. 26 St., Suite 1004, NYC 10001-6812. (212)255-1796. FAX: (212)929-3459. E-mail: programs@habonimdror. org. (Mazkir Tnua) Jamie Levin. Fosters

identification with progressive, cooperative living in Israel; stimulates study of Jewish and Zionist culture, history, and contemporary society. Sponsors summer and year programs in Israel and on kibbutz, 7 summer camps in N. America modeled after kibbutzim, and aliyah frameworks. *B'Tnua (on-line and print newsletter).* (WWW.HABONIMDROR.ORG)

HADASSAH, THE WOMEN'S ZIONIST ORGANIZATION OF AMERICA, INC. (1912). 50 W. 58 St., NYC 10019. (212)355-7900. FAX: (212)303-8282. Pres. Bonnie Lipton; Exec. Dir. Ellen Marson. Largest women's, largest Jewish, and largest Zionist membership organization in U.S. In Israel: Founded and funds Hadassah Medical Organization, Hadassah College of Technology, Hadassah Career Counseling Institute, Young Judea summer and year-course programs, as well as providing support for Youth Aliyah and JNF. U.S. programs: Jewish and women's health education; advocacy on Israel, Zionism and women's issues; Young Judaea youth movement, including six camps; Hadassah Leadership Academy; Hadassah Research Institute on Jewish Women; Hadassah Foundation. *Hadassah Magazine; Heart & Soul; Update; Hadassah International Newsletter; Medical Update; American Scene.* (www. HADASSAH.ORG)

————, YOUNG JUDAEA (1909; reorg. 1967). 50 W. 58 St., NYC 10019. (212)303-8014. FAX: (212)303-4572. E-mail: info@young judaea.org. Natl. Dir. Doron Krakow. Religiously pluralist, politically nonpartisan Zionist youth movement sponsored by Hadassah; seeks to educate Jewish youth aged 8-25 toward Jewish and Zionist values, active commitment to and participation in the American and Israeli Jewish communities; maintains six summer camps in the U.S.; runs both summer and year programs in Israel, and a jr. year program in connection with both Hebrew University in Jerusalem. College-age arm, Hamagshimim, supports Zionist activity on campuses. *Kol Hat'nua; The Young Judaean; Ad Kahn.* (WWW.YOUNGJUDAEA. ORG)

HASHOMER HATZAIR, SOCIALIST ZIONIST YOUTH MOVEMENT (1923). 114 W. 26 St., Suite 1001, NYC 10001. (212)627-2830. FAX: (212)989-9840. E-mail: mail@ hashomerhatzair.org. Dir. Giora Salz;

Natl. Sec. Ben Zviti & Minna Dubin. Seeks to educate Jewish youth to an understanding of Zionism as the national liberation movement of the Jewish people. Promotes aliyah to kibbutzim. Affiliated with Kibbutz Artzi Federation. Espouses socialist-Zionist ideals of peace, justice, democracy, and intergroup harmony. *Young Guard.* (WWW.HASHOMER HAZAIR.ORG)

INTERNS FOR PEACE (1976). 475 Riverside Dr., Room 204., NYC 10115. (212)870-2226. FAX: (212)870-2119. Intl. Dir. Rabbi Bruce M. Cohen; Intl. Coord. Karen Wald Cohen. An independent, nonprofit, nonpolitical educational program training professional community peace workers. In Israel, initiated and operated jointly by Jews and Arabs; over 190 interns trained in 35 cities; over 80,000 Israeli citizens participating in joint programs in education, sports, culture, business, women's affairs, and community development; since the peace accord, Palestinians from West Bank and Gaza training as interns. Martin Luther King Project for Black/Jewish relations. *IFP Reports Quarterly; Guidebooks for Ethnic Conflict Resolution.* (WWW.INTERNSFOR PEACE.ORG)

ISRAEL CANCER RESEARCH FUND (1975). 1290 Avenue of the Americas, NYC 10104. (212)969-9800. FAX: (212)969-9822. E-mail: icrf-hq-ny@worldnet.att.net. Pres. Yashar Hirshaut, M.D.; Chmn. Leah Susskind. The largest single source of private funds for cancer research in Israel. Has a threefold mission:To encourage innovative cancer research by Israeli scientists; to harness Israel's vast intellectual and creative resources to establish a world-class center for cancer study; to broaden research opportunities within Israel to stop the exodus of talented Israeli cancer researchers. *Annual Report; Research Awards; ICRF Brochure; Newsletter.*

ISRAEL HISTADRUT FOUNDATION (*see* ISRAEL HUMANITARIAN FOUNDATION)

ISRAEL HUMANITARIAN FOUNDATION (IHF) (1960). 276 Fifth Ave., Suite 901, NYC 10001. (212)683-5676, (800)434-5IHF. FAX: (212)213-9233. E-mail: info@ihf.net. Pres. Marvin M. Sirota; Exec.V.-Pres. Stanley J. Abrams. Nonprofit American philanthropic organization that supports humanitarian needs in Israel; strives to improve the standard of living of Israel's population in need through its support of education, general health and neonatal care, medical and cancer research, the elderly, disabled and youth-in-need. *Impact.*

ISRAEL POLICY FORUM (1993). 165 East 56th Street, 2nd Floor, NYC 10022. (212)245-4227. FAX: (212)245-0517. E-mail: ipf@ipforum.org. 1030 15 St., NW, Suite 850, Washington, DC 20005. (202)842-1700. FAX:(202)842-1722. E-mail: ipf@ipforum.org. Chmn. Jack Bendheim; Pres. Judy Stern Peck; Exec. Dir. Debra Wasserman. An independent leadership institution whose mission is to encourage an active U.S. role in resolving the Arab-Israeli conflict. IPF generates this support by involving leaders from the business, political, entertainment, academic, and philanthropic communitites in the peace effort, and by fostering a deeper understanding of the peace process among the American public. *Forum Fax, Washington Bulletin, Security Watch.* (WWW.IPFORUM.ORG)

THE JERUSALEM FOUNDATION, INC. (1966). 60 E. 42 St., Suite 1936, NYC 10165. (212) 697-4188. FAX: (212) 697-4022. E-mail: info@jfoundation.com. Chmn. William Ackman; Exec. Dir. Sandra Rubin. A nonprofit organization devoted to improving the quality of life for all Jerusalemites, regardless of ethnic, religious, or socioeconomic background; has initiated and implemented more than 1,500 projects that span education, culture, community services, beautification, and preservation of the city's historic heritage and religious sites.

JEWISH INSTITUTE FOR NATIONAL SECURITY AFFAIRS (JINSA) (1976). 1717 K St., NW, Suite 800, Washington, DC 20006. (202)833-0020. FAX: (202)296-6452. E-mail: info@jinsa.org. Pres. Norman Hascoe; Exec. Dir. Tom Neumann. A nonprofit, nonpartisan educational organization working within the American Jewish community to explain the link between American defense policy and the security of the State of Israel; and within the national security establishment to explain the key role Israel plays in bolstering American interests. (WWW.JINSA.ORG)

JEWISH INSTITUTE FOR THE BLIND-JERUSALEM, INC. (1902, Jerusalem). 15 E. 26 St., NYC 10010. (212) 532-4155. FAX: (212) 447-7683. Pres. Rabbi David E.

Lapp; Admin. Eric L. Loeb. Supports a dormitory and school for the Israeli blind and handicapped in Jerusalem. *INsight.*

JEWISH NATIONAL FUND OF AMERICA (1901). 42 E. 69 St., NYC 10021. (212)879-9300. (1-800-542-TREE). FAX: (212)517-3293. E-mail: communications @jnf.com. Pres. Ronald S. Lauder; Exec. V.-Pres. Russell F. Robinson. The American fund-raising arm of Keren Kayemeth LeYisrael, the official land agency in Israel; supports KKL in reclamation of land for planting and forestry; environmental concerns; water conservation; recreation and agriculture; employment of new immigrants; tourism; and research and development. (WWW.JNF.ORG)

JEWISH PEACE LOBBY (1989). 8604 Second Avnue, PMB 317, Silver Spring, MD 20910. (301)589-8764. FAX: (301)589-2722. Email: peacelobby@msn.com. Pres. Jerome M. Segal. A legally registered lobby promoting changes in U.S. policy vis-a-vis the Israeli-Palestinian conflict. Supports Israel's right to peace within secure borders; a political settlement based on mutual recognition of the right of self-determination of both peoples; a two-state solution as the most likely means to a stable peace. *Annual Report.*

KEREN OR, INC. JERUSALEM CENTER FOR MULTI-HANDICAPPED BLIND CHILDREN (1956). 350 Seventh Ave., Suite 200, NYC 10001. (212)279-4070. FAX: (212)279-4043. E-mail: kerenorinc@aol.com. Chmn. Dr. Edward L. Steinberg; Pres. Dr. Albert Hornblass; Exec. Dir. Rochelle B. Silberman. Funds the Keren-Or Center for Multi-Handicapped Blind Children at 3 Abba Hillel Silver St., Ramot, Jerusalem, housing and caring for over 70 resident and day students who in addition to blindness or very low vision suffer from other severe physical and/or mental disabilities. Students range in age from 1 1/2 through young adulthood. Provides training in daily living skills, as well as therapy, rehabilitation, and education to the optimum level of the individual. *Insights Newsletter.*

LABOR ZIONIST ALLIANCE (formerly FARBAND LABOR ZIONIST ORDER) (1913). 275 Seventh Ave., NYC 10001. (212)366-1194. FAX: (212)675-7685. E-mail: labzionA@ aol.com. Pres. Jeffry Mallow; Exec. Dir. Stephane Acel. Seeks to enhance Jewish life, culture, and education in U.S.; aids in building State of Israel as a cooperative commonwealth and its Labor movement organized in the Histadrut; supports efforts toward a more democratic society throughout the world; furthers the democratization of the Jewish community in America and the welfare of Jews everywhere; works with labor and liberal forces in America; sponsors Habonim-Dror labor Zionist youth movement. *Jewish Frontier; Yiddisher Kempfer.* (WWW. JEWISHFRONTIER.ORG)

MACCABI USA/SPORTS FOR ISRAEL (formerly UNITED STATES COMMITTEE SPORTS FOR ISRAEL) (1948). 1926 Arch St., 4R, Philadelphia, PA 19103. (215)561-6900. Fax: (215)561-5470. E-mail: maccabi @maccabiusa.com. Pres. Robert E. Spivak; Exec. Dir. Barbara G. Lissy. Sponsors U.S. team for World Maccabiah Games in Israel every four years; seeks to enrich the lives of Jewish youth in the U.S., Israel, and the Diaspora through athletic, cultural, and educational programs; develops, promotes, and supports international, national, and regional athletic-based activities and facilities. *Sportscene Newsletter; Commemorative Maccabiah Games Journal; financial report.* (WWW.MACCABIUSA.COM)

MERCAZ USA (1979). 155 Fifth Ave., NYC 10010. (212)533-7800, ext. 2016. FAX: (212)533-2601. E-mail: mercaz@ compuserve.com. Pres. Evelyn Seelig; Exec. Dir. Rabbi Robert R. Golub. The U.S. Zionist organization for Conservative/Masorti Judaism; works for religious pluralism in Israel, defending and promoting Conservative/Masorti institutions and individuals; fosters Zionist education and *aliyah* and develops young leadership. *Mercaz USA Quarterly Newsletter.* (WWW. MERCAZUSA.ORG)

MERETZ USA FOR ISRAELI CIVIL RIGHTS AND PEACE (1991). 114 W. 26 St., Suite 1002, NYC 10001. (212)242-4500. FAX: (212)242-5718. E-mail: meretzusa@aol. com. Pres. Harold M. Shapiro; Exec. Dir. Charney V. Bromberg. A forum for addressing the issues of social justice and peace in Israel. Educates about issues related to democracy, human and civil rights, religious pluralism, and equality for women and ethnic minorities; promotes the resolution of Israel's conflict with the Palestinians on the basis of mutual recognition, self-determination, and peaceful coexistence. *Israel Horizons.*

NA'AMAT USA, THE WOMEN'S LABOR ZION-
IST ORGANIZATION OF AMERICA, INC.
(formerly PIONEER WOMEN/NA'AMAT)
(1925). 350 Fifth Ave., Suite 4700, NYC
10118-4799. (212)563-5222. FAX: (212)
563-5710. E-mail: naamat@naamat.org.
Natl. Pres. Dina Spector. Part of the
World Movement of Na'amat (movement
of working women and volunteers), the
largest Jewish women's organization in
the world, Na'amat USA helps provide
social, educational, and legal services for
women, teenagers, and children in Israel.
It also advocates legislation for women's
rights and child welfare in Israel and the
U.S., furthers Jewish education, and supports Habonim Dror, the Labor Zionist
youth movement. *Na'amat Woman magazine.* (WWW.NAAMAT.ORG)

NATIONAL COMMITTEE FOR LABOR ISRAEL
(1923). 275 Seventh Ave., NYC 10001.
(212)647-0300. FAX: (212)647-0308. E-
mail: ncli@laborisrael.org. Pres. Jay
Mazur; Exec. Dir. Jerry Goodman;
Chmn. Trade Union Council Morton
Bahr. Serves as a bridge among Israel's
labor sector, including its General Federation of Labor, Histadrut, the American
labor movement, the Jewish community
and the general public. Brings together
Jews and non-Jews to build support for Israel and advance closer Israel-Arab ties.
Cooperates with Israels labor sector. National in scope, it conducts education in
the Jewish community and among labor
groups to promote better relations with
labor Israel. Raises funds for youth, educational, health, social and cultural projects in Israel from a constituency which
includes labor unions, foundations, government agencies and individual donors
and supporters. *Occasional background
papers* (WWW.LABORISRAEL.ORG)

NEW ISRAEL FUND (1979). 1101 14th St.,
NW, 6th fl., Washington, DC 20005-5639.
(202)842-0900. FAX: (202)842-0991. E-
mail: info@nif.org. New York office:165
E. 56 St., NYC 10022. (212)750-2333.
FAX: (212)750-8043. Pres. Yoram Peri;
Exec. Dir. Norman S. Rosenberg. A partnership of Israelis and North Americans
dedicated to promoting social justice, coexistence, and pluralism in Israel, the New
Israel Fund helps strengthen Israeli
democracy by providing grants and technical assistance to the public-interest sector, cultivating a new generation of social
activists, and educating citizens in Israel
and the Diaspora about the challenges to
Israeli democracy. *Quarterly newsletter;
annual report; other reports.* (WWW.NIF.
ORG)

PEF ISRAEL ENDOWMENT FUNDS, INC.
(1922). 317 Madison Ave., Suite 607,
NYC 10017. (212)599-1260. Chmn. Sidney A. Luria; Pres. B. Harrison Frankel;
Sec. Mark Bane. A totally volunteer organization that makes grants to educational, scientific, social, religious, health,
and other philanthropic institutions in Israel. *Annual report.*

PIONEER WOMEN/NA'AMAT (*see* NA'AMAT
USA)

POALE AGUDATH ISRAEL OF AMERICA, INC.
(1948). 2920 Avenue J, Brooklyn, NY
11210. (718)258-2228. FAX: (718)258-
2288. Pres. Rabbi Fabian Schonfeld. Aims
to educate American Jews to the values of
Orthodoxy and aliyah; supports kibbutzim, trade schools, yeshivot,
moshavim, kollelim, research centers, and
children's homes in Israel. *PAI News;
She'arim; Hamayan.*

———, WOMEN'S DIVISION OF (1948). Pres.
Miriam Lubling; Presidium: Sarah
Ivanisky, Tili Stark, Peppi Petzenbaum.
Assists Poale Agudath Israel to build and
support children's homes, kindergartens,
and trade schools in Israel. *Yediot PAI.*

PRO ISRAEL (1990). 1328 Broadway, Suite
435, NYC. (212)594-8996. FAX: (212)
594-8986. E-mail: proisrael@aol.com.
Pres. Dr. Ernest Bloch; Exec. Dir. Rabbi
Julian M. White. Educates the public
about Israel and the Middle East; provides support for community development throughout the Land of Israel, particularly in Judea, Samaria, Gaza, and the
Golan Heights. Projects include the Ariel
Center for Policy Research and Professors for a Strong Israel.

PROJECT NISHMA (*see* ISRAEL POLICY
FORUM)

RELIGIOUS ZIONISTS OF AMERICA. 25 W. 26
St., NYC 10010. (212)689-1414. FAX:
(212)779-3043.

———, BNEI AKIVA OF THE U.S. & CANADA
(1934). 25 W. 26 St., NYC 10010.
(212)889-5260. FAX: (212)213-3053.
Exec. Dir. Judi Srebro; Natl. Dir. Steve
Frankel. The only religious Zionist youth

movement in North America, serving over 10,000 young people from grade school through graduate school in 16 active regions across the United States and Canada, six summer camps, seven established summer, winter, and year programs in Israel. Stresses communal involvement, social activism, leadership training, and substantive programming to educate young people toward a commitment to Judaism and Israel. *Akivon; Pinkas Lamadrich; Daf Rayonot; Me'OhalaiTorah;Zraim.* (WWW.BNEIAKIVA. ORG)

———, MIZRACHI-HAPOEL HAMIZRACHI (1909; merged 1957). 25 W. 26 St., NYC 10010. (212)689-1414. FAX: (212)779-3043. Pres.Rabbi Simcha Krauss; Exec. V.-Pres. Dr. Mandell I. Ganchrow. Disseminates ideals of religious Zionism; conducts cultural work, educational program, public relations; raises funds for religious educational institutions in Israel, including yeshivot hesder and Bnei Akiva. *Newsletters; Kolenu.*

———, NATIONAL COUNCIL FOR TORAH EDUCATION OF MIZRACHI-HAPOEL HAMIZRACHI (1939). 25 W. 26 St., NYC 10010. Pres. Rabbi Israel Schorr. Organizes and supervises yeshivot and Talmud Torahs; prepares and trains teachers; publishes textbooks and educational materials; organizes summer seminars for Hebrew educators in cooperation with Torah Department of Jewish Agency; conducts ulpan. *Hazarkor, Chemed.*

SCHNEIDER CHILDREN'S MEDICAL CENTER OF ISRAEL (1982). 130 E. 59 St., Suite 1203, NYC 10022. (212)759-3370. FAX: (212)759-0120. E-mail: mdiscmci@aol. com. Bd. Chmn. H. Irwin Levy; Exec. Dir. Shlomit Manson. Its primary goal is to provide the best medical care to children in the Middle East. *UPDATE Newsletter*

SOCIETY OF ISRAEL PHILATELISTS (1949). 24355 Tunbridge Lane, Beachwood, OH 44122. (216)292-3843. Pres Henry B. Stern; Exec. Secry. Howard S. Chapman; Journal Ed. Dr. Oscar Stadtler. Promotes interest in, and knowledge of, all phases of Israel philately through sponsorship of chapters and research groups, maintenance of a philatelic library, and support of public and private exhibitions. *The Israel Philatelist; monographs; books.*

STATE OF ISRAEL BONDS (1951). 575 Lexington Ave., Suite 600, NYC 10022. (212)644-2663; (800)229-9650. FAX: (212)644-3887. E-mail: raphaelrothstein @israelbonds.com. Bd. Chmn. Burton P. Resnick; Pres./CEO Gideon Patt. An international organization offering securities issued by the government of Israel. Since its inception in 1951 has secured $20 billion in investment capital for the development of every aspect of Israel's economic infrastructure, including agriculture, commerce, and industry, and for absorption of immigrants. *Israel "Hadashot-News."* (WWW.ISRAELBONDS. COM)

THEODOR HERZL FOUNDATION (1954). 633 Third Ave., 21st fl., NYC 10017. (212)339-6040. FAX: (212)318-6176. Email: info@ midstream.org. Chmn. Kalman Sultanik; Sec. Sam E. Bloch. Offers cultural activities, lectures, conferences, courses in modern Hebrew and Jewish subjects, Israel, Zionism, and Jewish history. *Midstream.*

———, HERZL PRESS. Chmn. Kalman Sultanik; Dir. of Pub. Sam E. Bloch. Serves as "the Zionist Press of record," publishing books that are important for the light they shed on Zionist philosophy, Israeli history, contemporary Israel and the Diaspora and the relationship between them. They are important as contributions to Zionist letters and history. *Midstream.*

TSOMET-TECHIYA USA (1978). 185 Montague St., 3rd fl., Brooklyn, NY 11201. (718)596-2119. FAX: (718)858-4074. E-mail: eliahu@aol.com. Chmn. Howard B. Weber. Supports the activities of the Israeli Tsomet party, which advocates Israeli control over the entire Land of Israel.

UNITED CHARITY INSTITUTIONS OF JERUSALEM, INC. (1903). 1467 48 St., Brooklyn, NY 11219. (718)633-8469. FAX: (718)633-8478. Chmn. Rabbi Charlop; Exec. Dir. Rabbi Pollak. Raises funds for the maintenance of schools, kitchens, clinics, and dispensaries in Israel; free loan foundations in Israel.

UNITED ISRAEL APPEAL, INC. (1925). 111 Eighth Ave., Suite 11E, NYC 10011. (212)284-6900. FAX: (212)284-6988. Chmn. Bennett L. Aaron; Exec. V.-Chmn. Daniel R. Allen. Provides funds raised by UJA/

Federation campaigns in the U.S. to aid the people of Israel through the programs of the Jewish Agency for Israel, UIA's operating agent. Serves as link between American Jewish community and Jewish Agency for Israel; assists in resettlement and absorption of refugees in Israel, and supervises flow and expenditure of funds for this purpose. *Annual report; newsletters; brochures.*

UNITED STATES COMMITTEE SPORTS FOR ISRAEL (*see* MACCABI USA/SPORTS FOR ISRAEL)

US/ISRAEL WOMEN TO WOMEN (1979). 275 Seventh Ave., 8th fl., NYC 10001. (212) 206-8057. FAX: (212) 206-7031. E-mail: usisrw2w@aol.com. Ch. Jewel Bellush; Exec. Dir. Joan Gordon. Provides critical seed money for grassroots efforts advocating equal status and fair treatment for women in all spheres of Israeli life; targets small, innovative, Israeli-run programs that seek to bring about social change in health, education, civil rights, domestic violence, family planning, and other spheres of Israeli life. *Newsletters.*

VOLUNTEERS FOR ISRAEL (1982). 330 W. 42 St., Suite 1618, NYC 10036-6902. (212) 643-4848. FAX: (212)643-4855. E-mail: vol4israel@aol.com. Pres. Rickey Cherner; Exec. Dir. Edie Silberstein. Provides aid to Israel through volunteer work, building lasting relationships between Israelis and Americans. Affords persons aged 18 and over the opportunity to participate in various duties currently performed by overburdened Israelis on IDF bases and in other settings, enabling them to meet and work closely with Israelis and to gain an inside view of Israeli life and culture. *Quarterly newsletter; information documents.*

WOMEN'S LEAGUE FOR ISRAEL, INC. (1928). 160 E. 56 St., NYC 10022. (212)838-1997. FAX: (212)888-5972. Pres. Harriet Lainer; Exec. Dir. Dorothy Leffler. Maintains centers in Haifa, Tel Aviv, Jerusalem, Natanya. Projects include Family Therapy and Training Center, Centers for the Prevention of Domestic Violence, Meeting Places (supervised centers for noncustodial parents and their children), DROR (supporting families at risk), Yachdav-"Together" (long-term therapy for parents and children), Central School for Training Social Service Counselors, the National Library for Social Work, and the Hebrew University Blind Students' Unit.

WORLD CONFEDERATION OF UNITED ZIONISTS (1946; reorg.1958). 130 E. 59 St., NYC 10022. (212)371-1452. FAX: (212) 371-3265. Co-Pres. Marlene Post & Kalman Sultanik. Promotes Zionist education, sponsors nonparty youth movements in the Diaspora, and strives for an Israel-oriented creative Jewish survival in the Diaspora. *Zionist Information Views (in English and Spanish).*

WORLD ZIONIST ORGANIZATION-AMERICAN SECTION (1971). 633 Third Ave., 21st fl., NYC 10017. (212)688-3197. Chmn. Kalman Sultanik. As the American section of the overall Zionist body throughout the world, it operates primarily in the field of aliyah from the free countries, education in the Diaspora, youth and Hechalutz, organization and information, cultural institutions, publications; conducts a worldwide Hebrew cultural program including special seminars and pedagogic manuals; disperses information and assists in research projects concerning Israel; promotes, publishes, and distributes books, periodicals, and pamphlets concerning developments in Israel, Zionism, and Jewish history. *Midstream.*

———, DEPARTMENT OF EDUCATION AND CULTURE (1948). 633 Third Ave., 21st fl., NYC 10017. (212)339-6001. FAX: (212) 826-8959. Renders educational services to boards and schools: study programs, books, AV aids, instruction, teacher-in-training service. Judaic and Hebrew subjects. Annual National Bible Contest; Israel summer and winter programs for teachers and students.

———, ISRAEL ALIYAH CENTER (1993). 633 Third Ave., 21st fl., NYC 10017. (212)339-6060. FAX: (212)832-2597. Exec. Dir. N. Amer. Aliyah Delegation, Kalman Grossman. Through 26 offices throughout N. Amer., staffed by *shlichim* (emissaries), works with potential immigrants to plan their future in Israel and processes immigration documents. Through Israel Aliyah Program Center provides support, information, and programming for olim and their families; promotes long-term programs and fact-finding trips to Israel. Cooperates with Tnuat Aliyah in Jerusalem and serves as American contact with Association of Americans and Canadians in Israel.

YOUTH RENEWAL FUND (1989). 488 Madison Ave., 10ᵗʰ fl., NYC 10022. (212)207-3195. FAX: (212)207-8379. E-mail: info@ youthrenewalfund.org. Pres. Samuel L. Katz; Exec. Dir. Judith Margolis. Provides underprivileged Israeli youth with supplemental educational programs in core subjects including math, science, English, Hebrew, and computers. Since 1989, YRF has raised over $6 million, which has benefited more than 12,500 Israeli children. *YRF Review*. (www. YOUTHRENEWALFUND.ORG)

ZIONA (2000). 641 Lexington Avenu, 24ᵗʰ Floor, NYC 10022. (212) 688-2890. FAX: (212) 688-1327. E-mail: thezionist@ aol.com. Pres. Arnie T. Goldfarb; Ex. Vice Pres. Rev. Salomon L. Vaz Dias. In Israel, ZIONA initiates and supports pace-setting health care, educational, and youth institutions, as well as land development to meet the country's changing needs. ZIONA helps restore the ancient cemetery on the Mount of Olives in Jerusalem. ZIONA's Medical Organization (H.M.O.), is dedicated to quality and excellence in care and service. Patients from all over Israel and beyond its borders are treated annually, without distinction of race, religion or nationality. In the United States, ZIONA enhances the quality of American and Jewish life through its education and Zionist youth programs, promotes health awareness, and provides personal enrichment and growth for its members. *The Zionist Update* (www.ZIONA.ORG)

ZIONIST ORGANIZATION OF AMERICA (1897). ZOA House, 4 E. 34 St., NYC 10016. (212)481-1500. FAX: (212)481-1515. E-mail: email@zoa.com. Natl. Pres. Morton A. Klein; Exec. Dir. Dr. Janice J. Sokolovsky. Strengthens the relationship between Israel and the U.S. through Zionist educational activities that explain Israel's importance to the U.S. and the dangers that Israel faces. Works on behalf of pro-Israel legislation; combats anti-Israel bias in the media, textbooks, travel guides, and on campuses; promotes *aliyah*. Maintains the ZOA House in Tel Aviv, a cultural center, and the Kfar Silver Agricultural and Technical High School in Ashkelon, which provides vocational training for new immigrants.

ZOA Report; Israel and the Middle East:Behind the Headlines. (www.ZOA. ORG)

OVERSEAS AID

AMERICAN FRIENDS OF THE ALLIANCE ISRAÉLITE UNIVERSELLE, INC. (1946). 420 Lexington Ave., Suite 1731, NYC 10170. (212)808-5437. FAX: (212)983-0094. E-mail: afaiu@onsiteaccess.com. Pres. Albert Sibony; Exec. Dir. Warren Green. Participates in educational and human-rights activities of the AIU and supports the Alliance system of Jewish schools, teachers' colleges, and remedial programs in Israel, North Africa, the Middle East, Europe, and Canada. *Alliance Review.*

AMERICAN JEWISH JOINT DISTRIBUTION COMMITTEE, INC.—JDC (1914). 711 Third Ave., NYC 10017-4014. (212)687-6200. FAX: (212)370-5467. E-mail: new york@jdcny.org. Pres. Eugene J. Ribakoff; Exec. V.-Pres. Michael Schneider. Provides assistance to Jewish communities in Europe, Asia, Africa, and the Mideast, including welfare programs for Jews in need. Current concerns include:Rescuing Jews from areas of distress, facilitating community development in the former Soviet Union; helping to meet Israel's social service needs by developing innovative programs that create new opportunities for the country's most vulnerable populations; youth activities in Eastern Europe and nonsectarian development and disaster assistance. *Annual Report; Snapshots: JDC's Activities in the Former Soviet Union; JDC: One People, One Heart.* (www.JDC.ORG).

AMERICAN JEWISH PHILANTHROPIC FUND (1955). 122 E. 42 St., 12th fl., NYC 10168-1289. (212)755-5640. FAX: (212)644-0979. Pres. Charles J. Tanenbaum. Provides college scholarship assistance to Jewish refugees through pilot programs being administered by the Jewish Family Service in Los Angeles and NYANA in New York.

AMERICAN JEWISH WORLD SERVICE (1985). 989 Sixth Ave., 10th Fl., NYC 10018. (212)736-2597. FAX: (212)736-3463. E-mail:jws@jws.org. Chmn. Don Abramson; Pres. Ruth W. Messinger. Provides nonsectarian, humanitarian assistance and emergency relief to people in need in Africa, Asia, Latin America, Russia, Ukraine, and the Middle East; works in partnership with local nongovernmental organizations to support and implement self-sustaining grassroots development projects; serves as a vehicle through which the Jewish community can act as global citizens. *AJWS Reports (newsletter).* (WWW.AJWS.ORG)

AMERICAN ORT, INC. (1922). 817 Broadway, NYC 10003. (212)353-5800/(800)364-9678. FAX: (212)353-5888. E-mail: info @aort.org. Pres. Robert L. Sill; Exec. V.-Pres. Brian J. Strum. American ORT coordinates all ORT operations in the U.S., in cooperation with Women's American ORT; promotes and raises funds for ORT, the world's largest non-governmental education and training organization, with a global network teaching over 300,000 students in more than 60 countries. In Israel, 100,000 students attend 140 schools and training centers; there are 22 ORT schools and centers in the former Soviet Union; and in the U.S., over 15,000 students are served by ORT's Technical Institutes in Chicago, Los Angeles, and New York, and in Jewish day school programs in Atlanta, Chicago, Cleveland, Detroit, Florida, Los Angeles, and the National Capital Area (Washington, D.C.). *American ORT News; American ORT Annual Report; Monthly Report to the Board of Directors; American ORT Planned Giving Annual Report; American ORT Planned Giving News.* (WWW.AORT. ORG)

————, WOMEN'S AMERICAN ORT (1927). 315 Park Ave. S., NYC 10010-3677. (212)505-7700; (800)51-WAORT. FAX: (212)674-3057. E-mail: waort@waort. org. Pres. Pepi Dunay; Natl. Exec. Dir. Alice Herman. Strengthens the worldwide Jewish community by empowering people to achieve economic self-sufficiency through technological and vocational training; educates 280,000 students in 60 countries including the United States, Israel and the former Soviet Union; supports ORT programs through membership, fundraising and leadership development; domestic agenda promotes quality public education, women's rights and literacy. *Women's American ORT Reporter; Women's American ORT Annual Report.* (WWW.WAORT.ORG)

CONFERENCE ON JEWISH MATERIAL CLAIMS AGAINST GERMANY, INC. (1951). 15 E. 26 St., Rm. 906, NYC 10010. (212)696-4944. FAX: (212)679-2126. E-mail: info@

claimscon.org. Pres. Dr. Israel Miller; Exec. V.-Pres. Gideon Taylor. Represents Jewish survivors in negotiations for compensation from the German government and other entities once controlled by the Nazis. Also an operating agency that administers compensation funds, recovers Jewish property and allocates funds to institutions that serve Holocaust survivors. The Claims Conference—made up of the conference on Jewish Material Claims Against Germany and the Committee for Jewish Claims on Austria—is one of the founders of the World Jewish Restitution Organization, Memorial Foundation for Jewish Culture and the United Restitution Organization. *Newsletter; Annual Report; Guide to Restitution and Compensation; Special Update.* (WWW.CLAIMSCON. ORG)

HIAS, INC. (HEBREW IMMIGRANT AID SOCIETY) (1880; reorg. 1954). 333 Seventh Ave., NYC 10001-5004. (212)967-4100. FAX: (212)967-4442. E-mail:info@hias. org. Pres. Neil Greenbaum; Exec. V.-Pres. Leonard Glickman. The oldest international migration and refugee resettlement agency in the United States, dedicated to assisting persecuted and oppressed people worldwide and delivering them to countries of safe haven. As the migration arm of the American Jewish community, it also advocates for fair and just policies affecting refugees and immigrants. Since its founding in 1880, the agency has rescued more than four and a half million people. *Annual report.*

THE JEWISH FOUNDATION FOR THE RIGHTEOUS (1986). 305 Seventh Ave., 19th fl., NYC 10001. (212)727-9955. FAX: (212) 727-9956. E-mail: jfr@jfr.org. Chmn. Harvey Schulweis; Exec. Dir. Stanlee J. Stahl. Provides monthly support to 1,700 aged and needy Righteous Gentiles living in 30 countries who risked their lives to save Jews during the Holocaust. The Foundation's education program focuses on educating teachers and their students about the history of the Holocaust and the significance of altruistic behavior for our society. *Newsletter (3 times a year).* (WWW.JFR.ORG)

NORTH AMERICAN CONFERENCE ON ETHIOPIAN JEWRY (NACOEJ) (1982). 132 Nassau St., Suite 412, NYC 10038. (212)233-5200. FAX: (212)233-5243. E-mail: nacoej@aol.com. Pres. Kenneth Kaiserman; Exec. Dir. Barbara Ribakove

Gordon. Provides programming for Ethiopian Jews in Israel in the areas of education (elementary school, high school and college) and cultural preservation. Assists Ethiopian Jews remaining in Ethiopia. National speakers bureau offers programs to synagogues, schools, and Jewish and non-Jewish organizations. Exhibits of Ethiopian Jewish artifacts, photos, handicrafts, etc. available. *Lifeline (newsletter)*. (WWW.CIRCUS.ORG/NACOEJ)

RE'UTH WOMEN'S SOCIAL SERVICE, INC. (1937). 130 E. 59 St., Suite 1200, NYC 10022. (212)836-1570. FAX: (212)836-1114. Chmn. Ursula Merkin; Pres. Rosa Strygler. Maintains, in Israel, subsidized housing for self-reliant elderly; old-age homes for more dependent elderly; Lichtenstadter Hospital for chronically ill and young accident victims not accepted by other hospitals; subsidized meals; Golden Age clubs. Recently opened a wing for chronically ill children. *Annual dinner journal.*

THANKS TO SCANDINAVIA, INC. (1963). The American Jewish Committee, 165 East 56th Street, 8th Fl., NYC 10022. (212)751-4000 ext. 403. FAX: (212)838-2120. Email: tts@ajc.org. Pres. Richard Netter; Exec. Dir. Rebecca Neuwirth. Provides scholarships and fellowships at American universities and medical centers to students and doctors from Denmark, Finland, Norway, and Sweden in appreciation of the rescue of Jews from the Holocaust. Informs Americans and Scandinavians of these singular examples of humanity and bravery. Speakers available on rescue in Scandinavia; also books, videos, and tapes. *Annual report.*

UJA FEDERATION OF NORTH AMERICA. (1939). (*see* UNITED JEWISH COMMUNITIES)

UNITED JEWISH COMMUNITIES (1999). 111 Eighth Ave., 11th fl., NYC 10011-5201. (212)284-6500. FAX: (212)284-6822. Chmn. Charles R. Bronfman; Pres./CEO. Stephen D. Solender. Formed from the recent merger of the United Jewish Appeal, the Council of Jewish Federations and United Israel Appeal, is the dominant fundraising arm for North American Jewry, and represents 189 Jewish Federations and 400 independent communities across the continent. It reflects the values and traditions of education, leadership,

advocacy and social justice, and continuity of community that define the Jewish people.

RELIGIOUS AND EDUCATIONAL ORGANIZATIONS

AGUDATH ISRAEL OF AMERICA (1922). 42 Broadway, NYC, 10004. (212)797-9000. FAX: (212)269-2843. Exec. V.-Pres. Rabbi Samuel Bloom; Exec. Dir. Rabbi Boruch B. Borchardt. Mobilizes Orthodox Jews to cope with Jewish problems in the spirit of the Torah; speaks out on contemporary issues from an Orthodox viewpoint; sponsors a broad range of projects aimed at enhancing religious living, education, children's welfare, protection of Jewish religious rights, outreach to the assimilated and to arrivals from the former Soviet Union, and social services. *Jewish Observer; Dos Yiddishe Vort; Coalition.*

————, AGUDAH WOMEN OF AMERICA-N'SHEI AGUDATH ISRAEL (1940). 42 Broadway, NYC 10004. (212)363-8940. FAX: (212)747-8763. Presidium Aliza Grund & Rose Isbee; Dir. Hannah Kalish, Esq. Organizes Jewish women for philanthropic work in the U.S. and Israel and for intensive Torah education. Its new division, N'shei C.A.R.E.S., (Community, Awareness, Responsibility, Education, & Support), conducts seminars and support groups promoting the health and well-being of Jewish women and their families.

————, BOYS' DIVISION-PIRCHEI AGUDATH ISRAEL (1925) 42 Broadway, NYC 10004 (212)797-9000. Natl. Coord. Rabbi Shimon Grama. Educates Orthodox Jewish children in Torah; encourages sense of communal responsibility. Branches sponsor weekly youth groups and Jewish welfare projects. National Mishnah contests, rallies, and conventions foster unity on a national level. *Leaders Guides.*

————, GIRLS' DIVISION—BNOS AGUDATH ISRAEL (1921). 42 Broadway, NYC 10004. (212)797-9000. Natl. Dir. Leah Zagelbaum. Sponsors regular weekly programs on the local level and unites girls from throughout the Torah world with extensive regional and national activities. *Kol Bnos.*

————, YOUNG MEN'S DIVISION—ZEIREI AGUDATH ISRAEL (1921). 42 Broadway, NYC 10004. (212)797-9000, ext. 57. Dir. Rabbi Labish Becker. Educates youth to see Torah as source of guidance for all issues facing Jews as individuals and as a people. Inculcates a spirit of activism through projects in religious, Torah-educational, and community-welfare fields. *Am Hatorah; Daf Chizuk.*

AGUDATH ISRAEL WORLD ORGANIZATION (1912) 42 Broadway, NYC 10004. (212) 797-9000. FAX: (212)269-2843. Chmn. Rabbi Yehudah Meir Abramowitz; U.N. Rep. Prof. Harry Reicher, Esq. Represents the interests of Orthodox Jewry on the national and international scenes. Sponsors projects to strengthen Torah life worldwide.

ALEPH: ALLIANCE FOR JEWISH RENEWAL (1963; reorg. 1993). 7318 Germantown Ave., Philadelphia, PA 19119-1720. (215) 247-9700. FAX: (215)247-9703. Bd. Chmn. Dr. Martin Kantrowitz; Rabbinic Dir. R. Daniel Siegel. Serving the worldwide grassroots movement for Jewish spiritual renewal, ALEPH organizes and nurtures communities, trains lay and rabbinic leaders, creates new liturgy and adult learning resources, sponsors conferences, retreats and seminars and works for social and environmental justice. *New Menorah/Or Hador combined quarterly journal and newletter of the Network of Jewish Renewal Communities (NJRC).* (WWW.ALEPH.ORG)

AM KOLEL JUDAIC RESOURCE CENTER (1990). 15 W. Montgomery Ave., Rockville, MD 20850. (301)309-2310. FAX: (301)309-2328. E-mail: amkolel@aol.com. Pres. David Shneyer. An independent Jewish resource center, providing a progressive Jewish voice in the community. Activities include:religion, educational and cultural programs; classes, workshops and seminars; interfaith workshops and programs; tikkun olam (social action) opportunities. The staff provides training and resources to emerging and independent communities throughout N. America. Am Kolel sponsors Jews United for Justice, the Center for Inclusiveness in Jewish Life (CIJL) and Yedid DC. *Directory of Independent Jewish Communities and Havurot in Maryland, DC and Virginia; Rock Creek Haggadah.*

AMERICAN ASSOCIATION OF RABBIS (1978). 350 Fifth Ave., Suite 3304, NYC 10118. (212)244-3350, (516)244-7113. FAX: (516) 344-0779. E-mail: tefu@aol.com. Pres.

Rabbi Jeffrey Wartenberg; Exec. Dir. Rabbi David L. Dunn. An organization of rabbis serving in pulpits, in areas of education, and in social work. *Quarterly bulletin; monthly newsletter.*

AMERICAN STUDENTS TO ACTIVATE PRIDE (ASAP/OU College Affairs) (1993). 11 Broadway, 14th fl., NYC 10004. (212) 563-4000. FAX: (212)564-9058. E-mail: davidfel@ix.netcom.com. Pres. Zelda Goldsmith; Natl. Dir. Rabbi David Felsenthal; Chmn. Bernard Falk. A spiritual fitness movement of Jewish college students promoting Torah learning and discussion. Supports 100 learning groups at over 65 campuses as well as regional and national seminars and shabbatonim. *Good Shabbos (weekly); Rimon Discussion Guide (monthly); Jewish Student College Survival Guide (yearly).*

ASSOCIATION FOR JEWISH STUDIES (1969). MB 0001, Brandeis University, PO Box 549110, Waltham, MA 02454-9110. (781) 736-2981. FAX: (781)736-2982. E-mail: ajs@brandeis.edu. Pres. Lawrence H. Schiffman; Exec. Dir. Aaron L. Katchen. Seeks to promote, maintain, and improve the teaching of Jewish studies in colleges and universities by sponsoring meetings and conferences, publishing a newsletter and other scholarly materials, aiding in the placement of teachers, coordinating research, and cooperating with other scholarly organizations. *AJS Review;AJS Perspectives.* (WWW.BRANDEIS.EDU/AJS)

ASSOCIATION FOR THE SOCIAL SCIENTIFIC STUDY OF JEWRY (1971). c/o Prof. Carmel U. Chiswick, Department of Economics (m/c 144), University of Illinois at Chicago, 601 S. Morgan Street, Chicago, Il 60607-7121 (312)996-2683. FAX: (312) 996-3344. E-mail: cchis@uic.edu, Israel@brandeis.edu. Pres. Sherry Israel; V.-Pres. Riv-Ellen Prell; Sec.-Treas. Carmel Chiswick. Journal Ed. Rela Geffen; Mng. Ed. Egon Mayer; Newsletter Ed. Gail Glicksman. Arranges academic sessions and facilitates communication among social scientists studying Jewry through meetings, journal, newsletter and related materials and activities. *Contemporary Jewry; ASSJ Newsletter.*

ASSOCIATION OF HILLEL/JEWISH CAMPUS PROFESSIONALS (*see* TEKIAH: ASSOCIATION OF HILLEL/JEWISH CAMPUS PROFESSIONALS)

ASSOCIATION OF ORTHODOX JEWISH SCIEN-TISTS (1948). 25 W. 45ᵗˢᵗ·, Suite 1405, NYC 10036. (212)840-1166. FAX: (212)840-1514. E-mail: aojs@jerusalemail.com. Pres. Allen J. Bennett, M.D.; Bd. Chmn. Rabbi Nachman Cohen. Seeks to con-tribute to the development of science within the framework of Orthodox Jew-ish tradition; to obtain and disseminate information relating to the interaction be-tween the Jewish traditional way of life and scientific developments—on both an ideological and practical level; to assist in the solution of problems pertaining to Orthodox Jews engaged in scientific teaching or research. Two main conven-tions are held each year. *Intercom; Pro-ceedings; Halacha Bulletin; newsletter.*

B'NAI B'RITH HILLEL FOUNDATIONS (*see* HILLEL)

B'NAI B'RITH YOUTH ORGANIZATION (1924). 1640 Rhode Island Ave., NW, Washing-ton, DC 20036. (202)857-6633. FAX: (212)857-6568. Chmn. Youth Comm. Au-drey Y. Brooks; Dir. Sam Fisher. Helps Jewish teenagers achieve self-fulfillment and make a maximum contribution to the Jewish community and their country's culture; helps members acquire a greater knowledge and appreciation of Jewish re-ligion and culture. *Shofar; Monday Morn-ing; BBYO Parents' Line; Hakol; Kesher; The Connector.*

CANTORS ASSEMBLY (1947). 3080 Broadway, Suite 613, NYC 10027. (212)678-8834. FAX: (212)662-8989. E-mail: caoffice@ jtsa.edu. Pres. Chaim Najman; Exec. V.-Pres. Stephen J. Stein. Seeks to unite all cantors who adhere to traditional Ju-daism and who serve as full-time cantors in bona fide congregations to conserve and promote the musical traditions of the Jews and to elevate the status of the can-torial profession. *Annual Proceedings, Journal of Synagogue Music.* (WWW.JTSA. EDU/ORG/CANTOR)

CENTER FOR CHRISTIAN-JEWISH UNDER-STANDING OF SACRED HEART UNIVERSITY (1992). 5151 Park Ave., Fairfield, CT 06432. (203)365-7592. FAX: (203)365-4815. Pres. Dr. Anthony J. Cernera; Exec. Dir. Rabbi Joseph H. Ehrenkranz. An ed-ucational and research division of Sacred Heart University; brings together clergy, laity, scholars, theologians, and educators with the purpose of promoting interreli-gious research, education, and dialogue, with particular focus on current religious thinking within Christianity and Judaism. *CCJU Perspective.*

CENTRAL CONFERENCE OF AMERICAN RAB-BIS (1889). 355 Lexington Ave., NYC 10017. (212)972-3636. FAX: (212)692-0819. E-mail: info@ccarnet.org. Pres. Rabbi Charles A. Kroloff; Exec. V.-Pres. Rabbi Paul J. Menitoff. Seeks to conserve and promote Judaism and to disseminate its teachings in a liberal spirit. The CCAR Press provides liturgy and prayerbooks to the worldwide Reform Jewish community. *CCAR Journal: A Reform Jewish Quar-terly; CCAR Yearbook.* (WWW.CCARNET. ORG)

CLAL—NATIONAL JEWISH CENTER FOR LEARNING AND LEADERSHIP (1974). 440 Park Ave. S., 4th fl., NYC 10016-8012. (212)779-3300. FAX: (212)779-1009. E-mail: info@clal.org. Pres. Rabbi Irwin Kula; Chmn. Barbara B. Friedman; Exec. V.-Chmn. Donna M. Rosenthal. Provides leadership training for lay leaders, rabbis, educators, and communal professionals. A faculty of rabbis and scholars repre-senting all the denominations of Judaism make Judaism come alive, applying the wisdom of the Jewish heritage to help shape tomorrow's Jewish communities. Offers seminars and courses, retreats, symposia and conferences, lecture bureau and the latest on-line information through CLAL web site. *Sacred Days cal-endar; monographs; holiday brochures; CLAL Update.* (WWW.CLAL.ORG)

COALITION FOR THE ADVANCEMENT OF JEW-ISH EDUCATION (CAJE) (1977). 261 W. 35 St., #12A, NYC 10001. (212)268-4210. FAX: (212)268-4214. E-mail: cajeny@ caje.org. Chmn. Sylvia Abrams; Exec. Dir. Dr. Eliot G. Spack. Brings together Jews from all ideologies who are involved in every facet of Jewish education and are committed to transmitting the Jewish her-itage. Sponsors annual Conference on Al-ternatives in Jewish Education and Cur-riculum Bank; publishes a wide variety of publications; organizes shared-interest networks; offers mini-grants for special projects; sponsors Mini-CAJEs (one- or two-day in-service programs) around the country; maintains a website for Jewish educators. *Jewish Education News; CAJE Page; timely curricular publications; Hanukat CAJE series.* (WWW.CAJE.ORG)

CONGRESS OF SECULAR JEWISH ORGANIZATIONS (1970). 19657 Villa Dr. N., Southfield, MI 48076. (248)569-8127. FAX: (248)569-5222. E-mail: rifke@mediaone. net. Chmn. Alan J. Wiener; V.-Chmn. Karen Knecht; Exec. Dir. Dr. Eliot G. Spack. An umbrella organization of schools and adult clubs; facilitates exchange of curricula and educational programs for children and adults stressing the Jewish historical and cultural heritage and the continuity of the Jewish people. *New Yorkish (Yiddish literature translations); Haggadah; The Hanuka Festival; Mame-Loshn.*

CONVERSION TO JUDAISM RESOURCE CENTER (1997). 74 Hauppauge Rd., Rm. 53, Commack, NY 11725. (631) 462-5826. E-mail: inform@convert.org. Pres. Dr. Lawrence J. Epstein; Exec. Dir. Susan Lustig. Provides information and advice for people who wish to convert to Judaism or who have converted. Puts potential converts in touch with rabbis from all branches of Judaism.

COUNCIL FOR JEWISH EDUCATION (1926) 426 W. 58 St., NYC 10019. (914)368-8657. Pres. Dr. Morton J. Summer; Journal Ed. Dr. Bernard Ducoff. Fellowship of Jewish education professionals-administrators, supervisors, and teachers in Hebrew high schools and Jewish teachers colleges-of all ideological groupings; conducts national and regional conferences; represents the Jewish education profession before the Jewish community; co-sponsors, with the Jewish Education Service of North America, a personnel committee and other projects; cooperates with Jewish Agency Department of Education in promoting Hebrew culture and studies. *Journal of Jewish Education.*

EDAH (1996) 47 W. 34 St., Suite 700, NYC 10001. (212) 244-7501. FAX: (212)244-7855. Pres. Dr. Michael Hammer; Dir. Rabbi Saul J. Berman. Gives voice to the ideology and values of modern Orthodoxy, valuing open intellectual inquiry and expression in both secular and religious arenas, engagement with the social, political, and technological realities of the modern world, the religious significance of the State of Israel, and the unity of Clal Yisrael. (WWW.EDAH.ORG)

FEDERATION OF JEWISH MEN'S CLUBS (1929). 475 Riverside Dr., Suite 450, NYC 10115. (212)749-8100; (800)288-FJMC. FAX: (212)316-4271. E-mail: fjmc@jtsa. edu. Intl. Pres. Leonard Gimb; Exec. Dir. Rabbi Charles E. Simon. Promotes principles of Conservative Judaism; develops family education and leadership training programs; offers the Art of Jewish Living series and Yom HaShoah Home Commemoration; sponsors Hebrew literacy adult-education program; presents awards for service to American Jewry. Latest innovation-"The Ties that Bind," a motivational and instructional video about Tefillin. *Torchlight; Hearing Men's Voices.* (WWW.FJMC.ORG)

FEDERATION OF RECONSTRUCTIONIST CONGREGATIONS AND HAVUROT (*see* JEWISH RECONSTRUCTIONIST FEDERATION)

HILLEL: THE FOUNDATION FOR JEWISH CAMPUS LIFE (formerly B'NAI B'RITH HILLEL FOUNDATIONS) (1923). 1640 Rhode Island Ave., NW, Washington, DC 20036. (202)857-6560. FAX: (202)857-6693. E-mail: info@hillel.org. Chmn. Intl. Bd. Govs. Edgar M. Bronfman; Chmn. Foundation for Jewish Campus Life Chuck Newman; Pres. & Intl. Dir. Richard M. Joel. The largest Jewish campus organization in the world, its network of 500 regional centers, campus-based foundations, and affiliates serves as a catalyst for creating a celebratory community and a rich, diverse Jewish life on the campus. *The Hillel Annual Report; On Campus newsletter; Hillel Now newsletter; The Hillel Guide to Jewish Life on Campus (published with Princeton Review).* (www. HILLEL.ORG)

INSTITUTE FOR COMPUTERS IN JEWISH LIFE (1978). 7074 N. Western Ave., Chicago, IL 60645. (773)262-9200. FAX: (773) 262-9298. E-mail: rosirv@aol.com. Pres. Thomas Klutznick; Exec. V.-Pres. Dr. Irving J. Rosenbaum. Explores, develops, and disseminates applications of computer technology to appropriate areas of Jewish life, with special emphasis on Jewish education; creates educational software for use in Jewish schools; provides consulting service and assistance for national Jewish organizations, seminaries, and synagogues.

INTERNATIONAL FEDERATION OF SECULAR HUMANISTIC JEWS (1983). 224 West 35th Street, Suite 410, NYC 10001. (212)564-6711. FAX: (212)564-6721. E-mail: info@

ifshj.org. Co-Ch. Felix Posen (Europe), Yair Tzaban (Israel) & Sherwin Wine (USA). The International Federation of Secular Humanistic Jews provides a voice for secular Jews worldwide in their common goal to foster Secular Humanistic Judaism as an option for modern Jewish identity. The IFSHJ develops awareness of Secular and Humanistic Judaism by serving as a resource and for general information, and developing literature, conferences, and communications that promote philosophy of Secular and Humanistic Judaism in the world community. *Newsletter (Hofesh); Digest (Contemplate) available spring 2001.*

INTERNATIONAL INSTITUTE FOR SECULAR HUMANISTIC JUDAISM (1985). 28611 West Twelve Mile Rd., Farmington Hills, MI 48334. (248)476-9532. FAX: (248)476-8509. E-mail: iishj@iishj.net. Chmn. Rabbi Sherwin T. Wine. Established in 1985 in Jerusalem to serve the needs of a growing movement, its two primary purposes are to commission and publish educational materials and to train rabbis, leaders, teachers, and spokespersons for the movement. The Institute has two offices—one in Israel (Jerusalem) and one in N. America and offers educational and training programs in Israel, N. America, and the countries of the former Soviet Union. The N. American office, located in a suburb of Detroit, offers the Rabbinic Program, the Leadership Program, and the Adult Education Program. *Brochure, educational papers, and projects.*

JEWISH CHAUTAUQUA SOCIETY, INC. (sponsored by NORTH AMERICAN FEDERATION OF TEMPLE BROTHERHOODS) (1893). 633 Third Ave., NYC 10017. (212)650-4100/(800)765-6200. FAX: (212)650-4189. E-mail: jcs@uahc.org. Pres. Irving B. Shnaider; Chancellor Stuart J. Aaronson; Exec. Dir. Douglas E. Barden. Works to promote interfaith understanding by sponsoring accredited college courses and one-day lectures on Judaic topics, providing book grants to educational institutions, producing educational videotapes on interfaith topics, and convening interfaith institutes. A founding sponsor of the National Black/Jewish Relations Center at Dillard University. *ACHIM Magazine.*

JEWISH EDUCATION IN MEDIA (1978). PO Box 180, Riverdale Sta., NYC 10471. (212)362-7633. FAX: (203)359-1381. Pres.

Ken Asher; Exec. Dir. Rabbi Mark S. Golub. Devoted to producing television, film, and video-cassettes for a popular Jewish audience, in order to inform, entertain, and inspire a greater sense of Jewish identity and Jewish commitment. "L'Chayim," JEM's weekly half-hour program, which is seen nationally on NJT/National Jewish Television, features outstanding figures in the Jewish world addressing issues and events of importance to the Jewish community. (www.LCHAYIM.COM)

JEWISH EDUCATION SERVICE OF NORTH AMERICA (JESNA) (1981). 111 Eighth Ave., 11th fl., NYC 10011. (212)284-6950. FAX: (212)284-6951. E-mail: info@jesna. org. Pres. Jonathan S. Woocher; Bd. Ch. Joseph Kanfer. The Jewish Federation system's educational coordinating, planning, and development agency. Promotes excellence in Jewish education by initiating exchange of ideas, programs, and materials; providing information, consultation, educational resources, and policy guidance; and collaborating with partners in N. America and Israel to develop educational programs. *Agenda:Jewish Education; planning guides on Jewish Renaissance; research reports; Jewish Educators Electronic Toolkit.* (WWW.JESNA.ORG)

JEWISH RECONSTRUCTIONIST FEDERATION (formerly FEDERATION OF RECONSTRUCTIONIST CONGREGATIONS AND HAVUROT) (1954). 7804 Montgomery Ave., Suite 9, Elkins Park, PA 19027-2649. (215)782-8500. Fax: (215)782-8805. E-mail: info@jrf.org. Pres. Richard Haimowitz; Exec. V.-Pres. Mark Seal. Provides educational and consulting services to affiliated congregations and havurot; fosters the establishment of new Reconstructionist communities. Publishes *Kol Haneshamah*, an innovative series of prayer books, including a new mahzor and haggadah; provides programmatic materials. Regional offices in New York, Los Angeles, Chicago, Philadelphia, and Washington DC. *Reconstructionism Today.* (WWW.JRF.ORG)

———, RECONSTRUCTIONIST RABBINICAL ASSOCIATION (1974). 1299 Church Rd., Wyncote, PA 19095. (215)576-5210. FAX: (215)576-8051. E-mail: rraassoc@aol. com. Pres. Rabbi Dan Ehrenkrantz; Exec. Dir. Rabbi Richard Hirsh. Professional organization for graduates of the Reconstructionist Rabbinical College and other rabbis who identify with Reconstructionist Judaism; cooperates with Jewish Reconstructionist Federation in furthering Reconstructionism in the world. *Newsletters; position papers.*

———, RECONSTRUCTIONIST RABBINICAL COLLEGE (*see* p. 620)

JEWISH TEACHERS ASSOCIATION—MORIM (1931). 45 E. 33 St., Suite 310, NYC 10016-5336. (212)684-0556. Pres. Phyllis L. Pullman; V.-Pres. Ronni David; Sec. Helen Parnes; Treas. Mildred Safar. Protects teachers from abuse of seniority rights; fights the encroachment of anti-Semitism in education; offers scholarships to qualified students; encourages teachers to assume active roles in Jewish communal and religious affairs. *Morim JTA Newsletter.*

KULANU, INC. (formerly AMISHAV USA) (1993). 11603 Gilsan St., Silver Spring, MD 20902. (301)681-5679. FAX: (301)681-1587. Email: jdzeller@umich. edu. Pres. Jack Zeller; Sec. Karen Primack. Engages in outreach to dispersed Jewish communities around the world who wish to return to their Jewish roots. Current projects include the formal conversion of Shinlung-Menashe tribesmen in India currently practicing Judaism, and supplying materials and rabbis for conversos/marranos in Mexico and Brazil. *Newsletter.*

NATIONAL COMMITTEE FOR FURTHERANCE OF JEWISH EDUCATION (1941). 824 Eastern Pkwy., Brooklyn, NY 11213. (718)735-0200; (800)33-NCFJE. FAX: (718)735-4455. Pres. Dr. Steven Rubel; Bd. Chmn. Rabbi Shea Hecht; Chmn. Exec. Com. Rabbi Sholem Ber Hecht. Seeks to disseminate the ideals of Torah-true education among the youth of America; provides education and compassionate care for the poor, sick, and needy in U.S. and Israel; provides aid to Iranian Jewish youth; sponsors camps and educational functions, family and vocational counseling services, family and early intervention, after-school and preschool programs, drug and alcohol education and prevention; maintains schools in Brooklyn and Queens. *Panorama; Cultbusters; Intermarriage; Brimstone & Fire; Focus; A Life Full of Giving.*

NATIONAL COUNCIL OF YOUNG ISRAEL (1912). 3 W. 16 St., NYC 10011. (212)929-1525. FAX: (212)727-9526. E-mail: ncyi@youngisrael.org. Pres. Shlomo Mostofsky; Exec. V.-Pres. Rabbi Pesach Lerner. Through its network of member synagogues in N. America and Israel maintains a program of spiritual, cultural, social, and communal activity aimed at the advancement and perpetuation of traditional, Torah-true Judaism; seeks to instill in American youth an understanding and appreciation of the ethical and spiritual values of Judaism. Sponsors rabbinic and lay leadership conferences, synagogue services, rabbinic services, rabbinic and lay leader training, rabbinic placement, women's division, kosher dining clubs, and youth programs. *Viewpoint Magazine; Divrei Torah Bulletin; NCYI Suggestion Box; The Rabbi's Letter.* (www. YOUNGISRAEL.ORG)

———, AMERICAN FRIENDS OF YOUNG ISRAEL IN ISRAEL—YISRAEL HATZA'IR (1926). 3 W. 16 St., NYC 10011. (212)929-1525. FAX: (212)727-9526. E-mail: ncyi@youngisrael.org. Pres. Meir Mishkoff. Promotes Young Israel synagogues and youth work in Israel; works to help absorb Russian and Ethiopian immigrants.

———, YOUNG ISRAEL DEPARTMENT OF YOUTH AND YOUNG ADULTS ACTIVITIES (reorg. 1981). 3 W. 16 St., NYC 10011. (212)929-1525; (800)617-NCYI. FAX: (212)243-1222. Email: youth@yiyouth. org. Chmn. Kenneth Block; Dir. Richard Stareshefsky. Fosters varied program of activities for the advancement and perpetuation of traditional Torah-true Judaism; instills ethical and spiritual values and appreciation for compatibility of ancient faith of Israel with good Americanism. Runs leadership training programs and youth shabbatonim; support programs for synagogue youth programs; annual national conference of youth directors; ACHVA summer programs for teens IN Israel and U.S.; Nachala summer program in Israel for Yeshiva H.S. girls and Natzach summer program for Yeshiva H.S. boys. *Torah Kidbits; Shabbat Youth Manual; Y.I. Can Assist You; Synagogue Youth Director Handbook.* (www.YIYOUTH.ORG)

NATIONAL HAVURAH COMMITTEE (1979). 7135 Germantown Ave., Philadelphia, PA 19119-1720. (215)248-1335. FAX: (215)248-9760. E-mail: institute@havurah.org. Ch. Solomon Mowshowitz. A center for

Jewish renewal devoted to spreading Jewish ideas, ethics, and religious practices through havurot, participatory and inclusive religious mini-communities. Maintains a directory of N. American havurot and sponsors a weeklong summer institute, regional weekend retreats. *Havurah!* *(newsletter).* (WWW.HAVURAH.ORG)

NATIONAL JEWISH CENTER FOR LEARNING AND LEADERSHIP (*see* CLAL)

NATIONAL JEWISH COMMITTEE ON SCOUTING (Boy Scouts of America) (1926). 1325 West Walnut Hill Lane, PO Box 152079, Irving, TX 75015-2079. (972)580-2000. FAX: (972)580-7870. Chmn. Jerrold Lockshin. Assists Jewish institutions in meeting their needs and concerns through use of the resources of scouting. Works through local Jewish committees on scouting to establish Tiger Cub groups (1st grade), Cub Scout packs, Boy Scout troops, and coed Explorer posts in synagogues, Jewish community centers, day schools, and other Jewish organizations wishing to draw Jewish youth. Support materials and resources on request.

NATIONAL JEWISH GIRL SCOUT COMMITTEE (1972). 33 Central Dr., Bronxville, NY 10708. (914)738-3986, (718)252-6072. FAX: (914)738-6752. E-mail: njgsc@aol.com. Chmn. Rabbi Herbert W. Bomzer; Field Chmn. Adele Wasko. Serves to further Jewish education by promoting Jewish award programs, encouraging religious services, promoting cultural exchanges with the Israel Boy and Girl Scouts Federation, and extending membership in the Jewish community by assisting councils in organizing Girl Scout troops and local Jewish Girl Scout committees. *Newsletter.*

NATIONAL JEWISH HOSPITALITY COMMITTEE (1973; reorg. 1993). PO Box 53691, Philadelphia, PA 19105. (800)745-0301. Pres. Rabbi Allen S. Maller; Exec. Dir. Steven S. Jacobs. Assists persons interested in Judaism-for intermarriage, conversion, general information, or to respond to missionaries. *Special reports.*

NORTH AMERICAN ALLIANCE FOR JEWISH YOUTH (1996). 16 Pearl Street, Suite 201, Metuchen, NJ 08840 (732)494-1023. FAX: (732)906-9371. E-mail: hpkibel@earthlink.net. Chmn. Joseph E. Brown; Dir. Heather Kibel. Serves the cause of informal Jewish and Zionist education in America; provides a forum for the professional leaders of the major N. American youth movements, camps, Israel programs, and university programs to address common issues and concerns, and to represent those issues with a single voice to the wider Jewish and Zionist community. Sponsors annual Conference on Informal Jewish Education for Jewish youth professionals from across the continent.

OZAR HATORAH, INC. (1946). 1350 Sixth Ave., 32nd fl., NYC 10019. (212)582-2050. FAX: (212) 307-0044. Pres. Joseph Shalom; Sec. Sam Sutton; Exec. Dir. Rabbi Biniamine Amoyelle. An international educational network which builds Sephardic communities worldwide through Jewish education.

PARDES PROGRESSIVE ASSOCIATION OF REFORM DAY SCHOOLS (1990). 633 Third Ave., NYC 10017-6778. (212)650-4000. FAX: (480)951-0829. E-mail: educate@uahc.org. Pres. Zita Gardner; Chmn. Carol Nemo. An affiliate of the Union of American Hebrew Congregations; brings together day schools and professional and lay leaders committed to advancing the cause of full-time Reform Jewish education; advocates for the continuing development of day schools within the Reform movement as a means to foster Jewish identity, literacy, and continuity; promotes cooperation among our member schools and with other Jewish organizations that share similar goals. *Visions of Excellence (manual).*

P'EYLIM-LEV L'ACHIM (1951). 1034 E. 12 St. Brooklyn, NY 11230. (718)258-7760. FAX: (718)258-4672. E-mail: joskarmel @aol.com. Natl. Dir. Rabbi Joseph C. Karmel; Exec. V.-Pres. Rabbi Nachum Barnetsky. Seeks to bring irreligious Jews in Israel back to their heritage. Conducts outreach through 12 major divisions consisting of thousands of volunteers and hundreds of professionals across the country; conducts anti-missionary and assimilation programs; operates shelters for abused women and children; recruits children for Torah schools.

RABBINICAL ALLIANCE OF AMERICA (Igud Harabonim) (1942). 3 W. 16 St., 4th fl., NYC 10011. (212)242-6420. FAX: (212) 255-8313. Pres. Rabbi Abraham B. Hecht; Admin. Judge of Beth Din (Rabbinical

Court) Rabbi Herschel Kurzrock. Seeks to promulgate the cause of Torah-true Judaism through an organized rabbinate that is consistently Orthodox; seeks to elevate the position of Orthodox rabbis nationally and to defend the welfare of Jews the world over. Also has Beth Din Rabbinical Court for Jewish divorces, litigation, marriage counseling, and family problems. *Perspective; Nahalim; Torah Message of the Week; Registry.*

RABBINICAL ASSEMBLY (1901). 3080 Broadway, NYC 10027. (212)280-6000. FAX: (212)749-9166. Pres. Rabbi Vernon H. Kurtz; Exec. V.-Pres. Rabbi Joel H. Meyers. The international association of Conservative rabbis; actively promotes the cause of Conservative Judaism and works to benefit *klal yisrael*; publishes learned texts, prayer books, and works of Jewish interest; administers the work of the Committee on Jewish Law and Standards for the Conservative movement; serves the professional and personal needs of its members through publications, conferences, and benefit programs and administers the movement's Joint Placement Commission. *Conservative Judaism; Proceedings of the Rabbinical Assembly; Rabbinical Assembly Newsletter.*

RABBINICAL COUNCIL OF AMERICA, INC. (1923; reorg. 1935). 305 Seventh Ave., Suite 1200, NYC 10001. (212)807-7888. FAX: (212)727-8452. Pres. Rabbi Hershel Billet; Exec. V.-Pres. Rabbi Steven M. Dworken. Promotes Orthodox Judaism in the community; supports institutions for study of Torah; stimulates creation of new traditional agencies. *Hadorom; RCA Record; Sermon Manual; Tradition; Resource Magazine.* (WWW.RABBIS.ORG)

SOCIETY FOR HUMANISTIC JUDAISM (1969). 28611 W. Twelve Mile Rd., Farmington Hills, MI 48334. (248)478-7610. FAX: (248)478-3159. E-mail: info@shj.org. Pres. Ron Hirsch; Exec. Dir. M. Bonnie Cousens. Serves as a voice for Jews who value their Jewish identity and who seek an alternative to conventional Judaism, who reject supernatural authority and affirm the right of individuals to be the masters of their own lives. Publishes educational and ceremonial materials; organizes congregations and groups. *Humanistic Judaism (quarterly journal); Humanorah (quarterly newsletter).* (www. SHJ.ORG)

TEKIAH: ASSOCIATION OF HILLEL/JEWISH CAMPUS PROFESSIONALS (1949). c/o Hillel Foundation of New Orleans, 912 Broadway, New Orleans, LA 70118. (504)866-7060. FAX: (504)861-8909. E-mail: president@tekiah.org. Pres. Rabbi Jeffrey Kurtz-Lendner. Seeks to promote professional relationships and exchanges of experience, develop personnel standards and qualifications, safeguard integrity of Hillel profession; represents and advocates before the Foundation for Jewish Campus Life, Council of Jewish Federations. *Handbook for Hillel Professionals; Guide to Hillel Personnel Practices.* (www. TEKIAH.ORG)

TEVA LEARNING CENTER/SHOMREI ADAMAH (1988). 307 Seventh Ave., #900, NYC 10001. (212)807-6376. FAX: (212)924-5112. E-mail: tevacenter@aol.com. Co-Dir. Nili Simhai (Dir. of Ed. & Prog.) & Amy Bram (Dir. of Admin.) Exists to renew the ecological wisdom inherent in Judaism. Runs Jewish environmental education programs for Jewish day schools, synagogues, community centers, camps, university groups and other organized groups. *A Garden of Choice Fruit; Let the Earth Teach You Torah.*

TORAH SCHOOLS FOR ISRAEL–CHINUCH ATZMAI (1953). 40 Exchange Pl., NYC 10005. (212)248-6200. FAX: (212)248-6202. Pres. Rabbi Abraham Pam; Exec. Dir. Rabbi Henach Cohen. Conducts information programs for the American Jewish community on activities of the independent Torah schools educational network in Israel; coordinates role of American members of international board of governors; funds special programs of Mercaz Hachinuch Ha-Atzmai B'Eretz Yisroel; funds religous education programs in America and abroad.

TORAH UMESORAH–NATIONAL SOCIETY FOR HEBREW DAY SCHOOLS (1944). 160 Broadway, NYC 10038. (212)227-1000. FAX: (212)406-6934. E-mail: umesorah @aol.com. Chmn. David Singer; Pres. Yaakov Rajchenbach; Exec. V.-Pres. Rabbi Joshua Fishman. Establishes Hebrew day schools and Yeshivas in U.S. and Canada and provides a full gamut of services, including placement, curriculum guidance, and teacher training. Parent Enrichment Program provides enhanced educational experience for students from less Jewishly educated and marginally affiliated homes through parent-education programs and Partners in Torah, a one-on-one learning program. Publishes textbooks; runs shabbatonim, extracurricular activities; national PTA groups; national and regional teacher conventions. *Olomeinu-Our World.*

———, NATIONAL ASSOCIATION OF HEBREW DAY SCHOOL PARENT-TEACHER ASSOCIATIONS (1948). 160 Broadway, NYC 10038. (212)227-1000. FAX: (212)406-6934. Natl. PTA Coord. Bernice Brand. Acts as a clearinghouse and service agency to PTAs of Hebrew day schools; organizes parent education courses and sets up programs for individual PTAs. *Fundraising with a Flair; PTA with a Purpose for the Hebrew Day School.*

———, NATIONAL CONFERENCE OF YESHIVA PRINCIPALS (1956). 160 Broadway, NYC 10038. (212)227-1000. FAX: (212)406-6934. E-mail: umesorah@aol.com. Pres. Rabbi Rabbi Schneur Aisenstark; Bd. Chmn. Rabbi Dov Leibenstein; Exec. V.-Pres. Rabbi A. Moshe Possick. Professional organization of elementary and secondary yeshivah/day school principals providing yeshivah/day schools with school evaluation and guidance, teacher and principal conferences-including a Mid-Winter Conference and a National Educators Convention; offers placement service for principals and teachers in yeshivah/day schools. *Directory of Elementary Schools and High Schools.*

———, NATIONAL YESHIVA TEACHERS BOARD OF LICENSE (1953). 160 Broadway, NYC 10038. (212)227-1000. Exec. V.-Pres. Rabbi Joshua Fishman; Dir. Rabbi Yitzchock Merkin. Issues licenses to qualified instructors for all grades of the Hebrew day school and the general field of Torah education.

UNION FOR TRADITIONAL JUDAISM (1984). 241 Cedar Lane, Teaneck, NJ 07666. (201)801-0707. FAX: (201)801-0449. Pres. Burton G. Greenblatt; Exec. V.-Pres. Rabbi Ronald D. Price. Through innovative outreach programs, seeks to bring the greatest possible number of Jews closer to an open-minded observant Jewish lifestyle. Activities include Kashrut Initiative, Operation Pesah, the Panel of Halakhic Inquiry, Speakers Bureau, adult and youth conferences, and congrega-

tional services. Includes, since 1992, the MORASHAH rabbinic fellowship. *Hagahelet (quarterly newsletter); Cornerstone (journal); Tomeikh Kahalakhah (Jewish legal responsa).*

UNION OF AMERICAN HEBREW CONGREGATIONS (1873). 633 Third Ave., NYC 10017-6778. (212)650-4000. FAX: (212) 650-4169. E-mail: uahc@uahc.org. Pres. Rabbi Eric H. Yoffie; V.-Pres. Rabbi Lennard R. Thal; Bd. Chmn. Russell Silverman. Serves as the central congregational body of Reform Judaism in the Western Hemisphere; serves its approximately 900 affiliated temples and membership with religious, educational, cultural, and administrative programs. *Reform Judaism.* (WWW.UAHC.ORG)

———, AMERICAN CONFERENCE OF CANTORS (1953). 5591 Chamblee Dunwoody Rd. Bldg. 1360, Ste. 200, Atlanta, GA 30338. (770)390-0006. FAX: (770)390-0020. E-mail: accantors@aol.com. Pres. Richard Cohen, Judith K. Rowland (interim until April 15); Exec. V.-Pres. Scott E. Colbert EVP; Dir. of Placement Ida Rae Cohana; Admin. Asst. Jacqueline A. Maron. Members receive investiture and commissioning as cantors at recognized seminaries, i.e., Hebrew Union College-Jewish Institute of Religion, School of Sacred Music, as well as full certification through HUC-JIR-SSM. Through the Joint Cantorial Placement Commission, the ACC serves Reform congregations seeking cantors. Dedicated to creative Judaism, preserving the best of the past, and encouraging new and vital approaches to religious ritual, music, and ceremonies. *Koleinu.*

———, COMMISSION ON SOCIAL ACTION OF REFORM JUDAISM (*see* p. 575)

———, COMMISSION ON SYNAGOGUE MANAGEMENT (UAHC-CCAR) (1962). 633 Third Ave., NYC 10017-6778. (212)650-4040. FAX: (212)650-4239. Chmn. Marshall Krolick; Dir. Dale A. Glasser. Assists congregations in management, finance, building maintenance, design, construction, and art aspects of synagogues; maintains the Synagogue Architectural Library.

———, NATA (NATIONAL ASSOCIATION OF TEMPLE ADMINISTRATORS) (1941). 6114 La Salle Ave., Box 731, Oakland, CA 94611. (800)966-6282. FAX: (925)283-

7713. E-mail: nataorg@hotmail.com. Pres. Fern M. Kamen. Professional organization for UAHC synagogue administrators. Sponsors graduate training in synagogue management with Hebrew Union College; offers in-service training, workshops, and conferences leading to certification; provides NATA Consulting Service, NATA Placement Service for synagogues seeking advice or professional administrators; establishes professional standards. *NATA Journal; Temple Management Manual.*

———, NATIONAL ASSOCIATION OF TEMPLE EDUCATORS (NATE) (1955). 633 Third Ave., 7th fl., NYC 10017-6778. (212)452-6510. FAX: (212)452-6512. E-mail: nateoff@aol.com. Pres. Julie A. Vanek; Exec. Dir. Rabbi Stanley T. Schickler. Represents the temple educator within the general body of Reform Judaism; fosters the full-time profession of the temple educator; encourages the growth and development of Jewish religious education consistent with the aims of Reform Judaism; stimulates communal interest in and responsibility for Jewish religious education. *NATE NEWS.* (WWW.RJ.ORG/NATE)

———, NORTH AMERICAN FEDERATION OF TEMPLE BROTHERHOODS (1923). 633 Third Ave., NYC 10017. (212)650-4100. FAX: (212)650-4189. E-mail: nftb@uahc. org. Pres.Irving B. Shnaider; JCS Chancellor Stuart J. Aaronson; Exec. Dir. Douglas Barden. Dedicated to enhancing the world through the ideal of brotherhood, NFTB and its 300 affiliated clubs are actively involved in education, social action, youth activities, and other programs that contribute to temple and community life. Supports the Jewish Chautauqua Society, an interfaith educational project. *ACHIM (formerly Brotherhood magazine)* (www. RJ.ORG/NFTB)

———, UAHC DEPARTMENT OF JEWISH EDUCATION (1923). 633 Third Ave., 7th fl., NYC 10017. (212)650-4112. FAX: (212)650-4229. E-mail: jkatzew@uahc. org. Chmn. Dr. Rabbi Jan Katzew, Robert Heller; Dir. Dr. Rabbi Jan Katzew. Long-range planning and policy development for congregational programs of lifelong education; materials concerning Reform Jewish Outreach, Teacher Development and Reform Day Schools; activities administered by the UAHC Department of Education. *V'Shinantam; Torah at the*

Center, Family Shabbat Table Talk, Galilee Diary, Jewish Parent Page.

———, WOMEN OF REFORM JUDAISM— THE FEDERATION OF TEMPLE SISTERHOODS (1913). 633 Third Ave., NYC 10017. (212)650-4050. FAX: (212)650-4059. E-mail: wrj@uahc.org. Pres. Judith Silverman; Exec. Dir. Ellen Y. Rosenberg. Serves more than 600 sisterhoods of Reform Judaism; promotes interreligious understanding and social justice; provides funding for scholarships for rabbinic students; founded the Jewish Braille Institute, which provides braille and large-type Judaic materials for Jewish blind; supports projects for Israel; is the women's agency of Reform Judaism, an affiliate of the UAHC; works in behalf of the Hebrew Union College-Jewish Institute of Religion and the World Union for Progressive Judaism. *Notes for Now; Art Calendar; Windows on WRJ.* (WWW.RJ.ORG/WRJ)

———, YOUTH DIVISION AND NORTH AMERICAN FEDERATION OF TEMPLE YOUTH (1939). 633 Third Ave, NYC 10017-6778. (212)650-4070. FAX: (212)650-4199. E-mail: youthdivision@ uahc.org. Dir. UAHC Youth Div. Rabbi Allan L. Smith; Assoc. Dir. UAHC Youth Div. Rabbi Andrew Davids. Dedicated to Jewishly enhancing the lives of the young people of North America's Reform congregations through a program of informal education carried out in UAHC Camp-Institutes (11 camps for grades 2 and up), UAHC/NFTY Israel Programs (summer and semester), European and domestic teen travel, NFTY/Junior & Senior High School Programs (youth groups), and Kesher/College Education Department (Reform havurot on campuses).

UNION OF ORTHODOX JEWISH CONGREGATIONS OF AMERICA (1898). 11 Broadway, 14th fl., NYC 10004. (212)563-4000. FAX: (212)564-9058. E-mail: ou@ou.org. Pres. Harvey Blitz. Serves as the national central body of Orthodox synagogues; national OU kashrut supervision and certification service; sponsors Institute for Public Affairs; National Conference of Synagogue Youth; National Jewish Council for the Disabled; Israel Center in Jerusalem; Torah Center in the Ukraine; New Young Leadership Division; Pardes; provides educational, religious, and organization programs, events, and guidance to synagogues and groups; represents the Orthodox Jewish community to governmental and civic bodies and the general Jewish community. *Jewish Action magazine; OU Kosher Directory; OU Passover Directory; OU News Reporter; Synagogue Trends; Our Way magazine; Yachad magazine; Luach & Limud Personal Torah Study.*(WWW.OU.ORG)

————, INSTITUTE FOR PUBLIC AFFAIRS (1989). 11 Broadway, 14th fl., NYC 10004. (212)613-8123. FAX: (212)613-0724. E-mail: ipa@ou.org. Chmn. Richard Stone; Dir. Nathan Diament; Dir. Intl. Affairs & Comm. Rel. Betty Ehrenberg. Serves as the policy analysis, advocacy, mobilization, and programming department responsible for representing Orthodox/traditional American Jewry. *IPA Currents (quarterly newsletter).*

————, NATIONAL CONFERENCE OF SYNAGOGUE YOUTH (1954). 11 Broadway, 14th fl., NYC 10004. (212)563-4000. E-mail: ncsy@ou.org. Dir. Rabbi David Kaminetsky. Central body for youth groups of Orthodox congregations; provides educational guidance, Torah study groups, community service, program consultation, Torah library, Torah fund scholarships, Ben Zakkai Honor Society, Friends of NCSY, weeklong seminars, Israel Summer Experience for teens and Camp NCSY East Summer Kollel & Michlelet, Teen Torah Center. Divisions include Senior NCSY, Junior NCSY for preteens, Our Way for the Jewish deaf, Yachad for the developmentally disabled, Israel Center in Jerusalem, and NCSY in Israel. *Keeping Posted with NCSY; Darchei Da'at.*

————, WOMEN'S BRANCH OF THE ORTHODOX UNION (1923). 156 Fifth Ave., NYC 10010. (212)929-8857. Pres. Sophic Ebert. Umbrella organization of Orthodox sisterhoods in U.S. and Canada, educating women in Jewish learning and observance; provides programming, leadership, and organizational guidance, conferences, conventions, Marriage Committee and projects concerning mikvah, Shalom Task Force, and Welcoming Guests. Works with Orthodox Union Commissions and outreach; supports Stern and Touro College scholarships and Jewish braille publications; supplies Shabbat candelabra for hospital patients; NGO representative at UN. *Hachodesh; Hakol.*

UNION OF ORTHODOX RABBIS OF THE UNITED STATES AND CANADA (1902). 235 E. Broadway, NYC 10002. (212)964-6337(8). Dir. Rabbi Hersh M. Ginsberg. Seeks to foster and promote Torah-true Judaism in the U.S. and Canada; assists in the establishment and maintenance of yeshivot in the U.S.; maintains committee on marriage and divorce and aids individuals with marital difficulties; disseminates knowledge of traditional Jewish rites and practices and publishes regulations on synagogal structure; maintains rabbinical court for resolving individual and communal conflicts. *Ha-Pardes.*

UNION OF SEPHARDIC CONGREGATIONS, INC. (1929). 8 W. 70 St., NYC 10023. (212)873-0300. FAX: (212)724-6165. Pres. Rabbi Marc D. Angel; Bd. Chmn. Alvin Deutsch. Promotes the religious interests of Sephardic Jews; prints and distributes Sephardic prayer books. *Annual International Directory of Sephardic Congregations.*

UNITED LUBAVITCHER YESHIVOTH (1940). 841-853 Ocean Pkwy., Brooklyn, NY 11230. (718)859-7600. FAX: (718)434-1519. Supports and organizes Jewish day schools and rabbinical seminaries in the U.S. and abroad.

UNITED SYNAGOGUE OF CONSERVATIVE JUDAISM (1913). 155 Fifth Ave., NYC 10010-6802. (212)533-7800. FAX: (212) 353-9439. E-mail: info@uscj.org. Pres. Stephen S. Wolnek; Exec. V.-Pres. Rabbi Jerome M. Epstein. International organization of 760 Conservative congregations. Maintains 12 departments and 19 regional offices to assist its affiliates with religious, educational, youth, community, and administrative programming and guidance; aims to enhance the cause of Conservative Judaism, further religious observance, encourage establishment of Jewish religious schools, draw youth closer to Jewish tradition. Extensive Israel programs. *United Synagogue Review; Art/Engagement Calendar; Program Suggestions; Directory & Resource Guide; Book Service Catalogue of Publications.* (WWW.USCJ.ORG)

————, COMMISSION ON JEWISH EDUCATION (1930). 155 Fifth Ave., NYC 10010. (212)533-7800. FAX: (212)353-9439. E-mail: education@uscj.org. Chmn. Temma

Kingsley; Dir. Rabbi Robert Abramson. Develops educational policy for the United Synagogue of Conservative Judaism and sets the educational direction for Conservative congregations, their schools, and the Solomon Schechter Day Schools. Seeks to enhance the educational effectiveness of congregations through the publication of materials and in-service programs. *Tov L'Horot; Your Child; Shiboley Schechter; Advisories.*

———, COMMISSION ON SOCIAL ACTION AND PUBLIC POLICY (1958). 155 Fifth Ave., NYC 10010. (212)533-7800. FAX: (212)353-9439. Chmn. Hon. Jerry Wagner; Dir. Sarrae G. Crane. Develops and implements positions and programs on issues of social action and public policy for the United Synagogue of Conservative Judaism; represents these positions to other Jewish and civic organizations, the media, and government; and provides guidance, both informational and programmatic, to its affiliated congregations in these areas. *HaMa'aseh.*

———, JEWISH EDUCATORS ASSEMBLY (1951). 426 W. 58 St., NYC 10019. (212)765-3303. FAX: (212)765-3310. Pres. Dr. Mark S. Silk; Exec. Dir. Susan Mitrani Knapp. The Jewish Educators Assembly is the professional organization for the Jewish educators within the Conservative movement. The JEA provides a forum to discuss the trends and challenges within Conservative Jewish education as well as provides professional development and a sense of community for educational directors. Services offered: annual conference, placement service, career services, research grants, personal benefits and *V'Aleh Ha-Chadashot* newsletter.

———, KADIMA (formerly PRE-USY; reorg. 1968). 155 Fifth Ave., NYC 10010-6802. (212)533-7800. FAX: (212)353-9439. E-mail: kadima@uscj.org. Dir. Karen L. Stein; Dir. of Youth Activities Jules A Gutin. Involves Jewish preteens in a meaningful religious, educational, and social environment; fosters a sense of identity and commitment to the Jewish community and the Conservative movement; conducts synagogue-based chapter programs and regional Kadima days and weekends. *Mitzvah of the Month; Kadima Kesher; Chagim; Advisors Aid; Games; quarterly Kol Kadima magazine.*

———, NORTH AMERICAN ASSOCIATION OF SYNAGOGUE EXECUTIVES (1948). 155 Fifth Ave., NYC 10010. (212)533-7800, ext 2609. FAX: (631)732-9461. E-mail: office@naase.org. Pres. Judith Kranz, FSA, ATz; Hon. Pres. Amir Pilch, FSA; Exec. Dir. Harry Hauser. Aids congregations affiliated with the United Synagogue of Conservative Judaism to further the aims of Conservative Judaism through more effective administration (Program for Assistance by Liaisons to Synagogues—PALS); advances professional standards and promotes new methods in administration; cooperates in United Synagogue placement services and administrative surveys. *NAASE Connections Newsletter; NAASE Journal.*

———, UNITED SYNAGOGUE YOUTH (1951). 155 Fifth Ave., NYC 10010. (212)533-7800. FAX: (212)353-9439. E-mail: youth@uscj.org. Pres. Eitan Hersh; Exec. Dir. Jules A. Gutin. Seeks to strengthen identification with Conservative Judaism, based on the personality, development, needs, and interests of the adolescent, in a mitzvah framework. *Achshav; Tikun Olam; A.J. Heschel Honor Society Newsletter; SATO Newsletter; USY Program Bank; Hakesher Newsletter for Advisors.*

VAAD MISHMERETH STAM (1976). 4907 16th Ave., Brooklyn, NYC 11204. (718) 438-4980. FAX: (718)438-9343. Pres. Rabbi David L. Greenfield. A nonprofit consumer-protection agency dedicated to preserving and protecting the halakhic integrity of Torah scrolls, tefillin, phylacteries, and mezuzoth. Publishes material for laymen and scholars in the field of scribal arts; makes presentations and conducts examination campaigns in schools and synagogues; created an optical software system to detect possible textual errors in stam. Teaching and certifying sofrim worldwide. Offices in Israel, Strasbourg, Chicago, London, Manchester, Montreal, and Zurich. Publishes *Guide to Mezuzah* and *Encyclopedia of the Secret Aleph Beth. The Jewish Quill; and many other publications.*

WASHINGTON INSTITUTE FOR JEWISH LEADERSHIP & VALUES (1988). 6101 Montrose Road, Suite 200, Rockville, MD 20852. (301) 770-5070. FAX: (301) 770-6365. E-mail: wijlv@wijlv.org. Founder/Pres. Rabbi Sidney Schwarz; Bd. Chmn. Ellen

Kagen Waghelstein. An educational organization dedicated to the renewal of American Jewish life through the integration of Jewish learning, tikkun olam, and spirituality. Flagship program is *Panim el Panim*:High School in Washington, which promotes activism and civiv engagement among Jewish teens, grounded in Jewish learning and values. Also sponsors the Jewish Civics Iniative, combining Judaic study and community service; *E Pluribus Unum*, an interfaith project on religion, social justice and the common good; pre and post Israelexperience programs; leadership training, and a synagogue transformation project. *Jewish Civics: A Tikkun Olam/World Repair Manual; Jews, Judaism and Civic Responsibility.*

WOMEN'S LEAGUE FOR CONSERVATIVE JUDAISM (1918). 48 E. 74 St., NYC 10021. (212)628-1600. FAX: (212)772-3507. Email: wleague@aol.com Pres. Janet Tobin; Exec. Dir. Bernice Balter. Parent body of Conservative (Masorti) women's synagogue groups in U.S., Canada, Puerto Rico, Mexico, and Israel; provides programs and resources in Jewish education, social action, Israel affairs, American and Canadian public affairs, leadership training, community service programs for persons with disabilities, conferences on world affairs, study institutes, publicity techniques; publishes books of Jewish interest; contributes to support of Jewish Theological Seminary of America. *Women's League Outlook* magazine; *Ba'Olam world affairs newsletter.*

WORLD COUNCIL OF CONSERVATIVE/ MASORTI SYNAGOGUES (1957). 155 Fifth Ave., NYC 10010. (212)533-7800, ext. 2014, 2018. FAX: (212)533-9439. E-mail: worldcouncil@compuserve.com. Pres. Rabbi Alan Silverstein; Rabbi of Council, Rabbi Benjamin Z. Kreitman. Organizes and supports Conservative/Masorti congregations in Latin America, Europe, Australia and South Africa. *World Spectrum.*

WORLD UNION FOR PROGRESSIVE JUDAISM (1926). 633 Third Ave., NYC 10017. (212) 650-4280. FAX: (212)650-4289. E-mail: arzawupjna@uahc.org. Pres. Ruth Cohen; Exec. Dir. Rabbi Dow Marmur. International umbrella organization of Liberal Judaism; prmotes and coordi-nates efforts of Liberal congregations throughout the world; starts new congregations, recruits rabbis and rabbinical students for all countries; organizes international conferences of Liberal Jews. *World News.*

SCHOOLS, INSTITUTIONS

ACADEMY FOR JEWISH RELIGION (1956). 15 W. 86 St., NYC 10024. (212)875-0540. FAX: (212)875-0541. E-mail: admin@ ajrsem.org. Acting Pres. Rabbi David Greenstein; Acting Dean Rabbi Dr. Ora Horn Prouser. The only rabbinic and cantorial seminary in the U.S. at which students explore the full range of Jewish spiritual learning and practice. Graduates serve in Conservative, Reform, Reconstructionist, and Orthodox congregations, chaplaincies, and educational institutions. Programs include rabbinic and cantorial studies in NYC and LA, and on/off-campus nonmatriculated studies. Evening classes open to the public.

ANNENBERG RESEARCH INSTITUTE (*see* CENTER FOR JUDAIC STUDIES)

BALTIMORE HEBREW UNIVERSITY (1919). 5800 Park Heights Ave., Baltimore, MD 21215. (410)578-6900; (888)248-7420. FAX: (410)578-6940. E-mail: bhu@bhu. edu. Pres. Dr. Rella Mintz Geffen; Bd. Chmn. Rabbi Mark G. Loeb. Offers PhD, MA, BA, and AA programs in Jewish studies, Jewish education, biblical and Near Eastern archaeology, philosophy, literature, history, Hebrew language, literature, and contemporary Jewish civilization; School of Continuing Education; Joseph Meyerhoff Library; community lectures, film series, seminars. *BHU Today.* (WWW.BHU.EDU)

——, BALTIMORE INSTITUTE FOR JEWISH COMMUNAL SERVICE. (410)578-6932. FAX: (410)578-1803. Dir. Karen S. Bernstein; Co-Dir. Cindy Goldstein. Trains Jewish communal professionals; offers a joint degree program: an MA from BHU and an MAJE from BHU, an MSW from U. of Maryland School of Social Work, or an MPS in policy sciences from UMBC; MA with Meyerhoff Graduate School and Johns Hopkins U. in non-profit management.

——, BERNARD MANEKIN SCHOOL OF UNDERGRADUATE STUDIES. Dean Dr. George Berlin. BA program; interinstitutional program with Johns Hopkins University; interdisciplinary concentrations: contemporary Middle East, American Jewish culture, and the humanities; Russian/English program for new Americans; assoc. of arts (AA) in Jewish studies.

————, LEONARD AND HELEN R. STULMAN SCHOOL OF CONTINUING EDUCATION. Dean Dr. George Berlin. Noncredit program open to the community, offering a variety of courses, trips, and events covering a range of Jewish subjects. *Elderhostel, Ulpan Modern Hebrew Department.*

————, PEGGY MEYERHOFF PEARLSTONE SCHOOL OF GRADUATE STUDIES. Dean Dr. Barry M. Gittlen. PhD and MA programs; MA in Jewish studies; MAJE in Jewish education; PhD in Jewish studies; a double master's degree with an MA from BHU and an MAJE from BHU, an MSW from the University of Maryland School of Social Work, or an MPS in policy sciences from UMBC; MA with Baltimore Institute and Johns Hopkins U. in nonprofit management.

BRAMSON ORT COLLEGE (1977). 69-30 Austin St., Forest Hills, NY 11375. (718)261-5800. Dean of Academic Services Barry Glotzer. A two-year Jewish technical college offering certificates and associate degrees in technology and business fields, including accounting, computer programming, electronics technology, business management, office technology. Additional locations in Brooklyn.

BRANDEIS-BARDIN INSTITUTE (1941). 1101 Peppertree Lane, Brandeis, CA 93064. (805)582-4450. FAX: (805)526-1398. E-mail: info@thebbi.org. Pres. Dr. Lee T. Bycel; Chair, Bd. Of Dir. Helen Zukin. A Jewish pluralistic, nondenominational educational institution providing programs for people of all ages:BCI (Brandeis Collegiate Institute), a summer leadership program for college-age adults from around the world; Camp Alonim, a summer Jewish experience for children 8-16; Gan Alonim Day Camp for children in kindergarten to 6th grade; weekend retreats for adults with leading contemporary Jewish scholars-in-residence; Jewish music concerts; Family Days and Weekends, Grandparents Weekends, Elderhostel, Young Adult programs, dance week-

ends, institute for newly marrieds. *Monthly Updates; BBI Newsletter.*

BRANDEIS UNIVERSITY (1948). 415 South St., Waltham, MA 02454. (781)736-2000. Pres. Jehuda Reinharz; Provost Irving Epstein; Exec. V.-Pres./CEO Peter B. French; Sr. V.-Pres. of Devel. Nancy Winship. Founded under Jewish sponsorship as a nonsectarian institution offering undergraduate and graduate education. The Lown School is the center for all programs of teaching and research in Judaic studies, ancient Near Eastern studies, and Islamic and modern Middle Eastern studies. The school includes the Department of Near Eastern and Judaic Studies; the Hornstein Program in Jewish Communal Service, a professional training program; the Cohen Center for Modern Jewish Studies, which conducts research and teaching in contemporary Jewish studies, primarily in American Jewish studies; and the Tauber Institute for the study of European Jewry. *Various newsletters, scholarly publications.*

————, NATIONAL WOMEN'S COMMITTEE (1948). MS 132, Waltham, MA 02454-9110. (781) 736-4160. FAX: (781)736-4183. E-mail: bunwc@brandeis.edu. Pres. Marcia F. Levy; Exec. Dir. Joan C. Bowen. Provides support for Brandeis University and its libraries. It connects Brandeis, a non-sectarian university founded by the American Jewish community, to its members and their communities through programs that reflect the ideals of social justice and academic excellence. In addition to its fundraising activities, NWC offers its members opportunity for intellectual pursuit, continuing education, community service, social interaction, personal enrichment and leadership development. Open to all, regardless of race, religion, nationality or gender. *Connecting.*

CENTER FOR JUDAIC STUDIES, School of Arts and Sciences, University of Pennsylvania. 420 Walnut St., Philadelphia, PA 19106. (215)238-1290. FAX: (215) 238-1540. Dir. David B. Ruderman. *Jewish Quarterly Review.*

CLEVELAND COLLEGE OF JEWISH STUDIES (1964). 26500 Shaker Blvd., Beachwood, OH 44122. (216)464-4050. FAX: (216) 464-5827. Pres. David S. Ariel; Dir. of Student Services Diane M. Kleinman.

Provides courses in all areas of Judaic and Hebrew studies to adults and college-age students; offers continuing education for Jewish educators and administrators; serves as a center for Jewish life and culture; expands the availability of courses in Judaic studies by exchanging faculty, students, and credits with neighboring academic institutions; grants bachelor's and master's degrees.

DROPSIE COLLEGE FOR HEBREW AND COGNATE LEARNING (see CENTER FOR JUDAIC STUDIES)

GRATZ COLLEGE (1895). 7605 Old York Rd., Melrose Park, PA 19027. (215)635-7300. FAX: (215)635-7320. Bd. Chmn. Alan Gordon, Esq.; Pres. Dr. Jonathan Rosenbaum. Offers a wide variety of undergraduate and graduate degrees and continuing education programs in Judaic, Hebraic, and Middle Eastern studies. Grants BA and MA in Jewish studies, MA in Jewish education (joint program in special needs education with La Salle U.), MA in Jewish music, MA in Jewish liberal studies, MA in Jewish communal studies, certificates in Jewish communal studies (joint program with U. of Penna. School of Social Work), Jewish education, Israel studies, Judaica librarianship (joint program with Drexel U.), and Jewish music. Joint graduate program with Reconstructionist Rabbinical College in Jewish education and Jewish music. Netzky Division of Continuing Education and Jewish Community High School. *Various newsletters, annual academic bulletin, scholarly publications, centennial volume, and occasional papers.*

HEBREW COLLEGE (1921). 43 Hawes St., Brookline, MA 02446. (617)232-8710. FAX: (617)264-9264. Pres. Dr. David M. Gordis; Ch. Bd. Dir. Mickey Cail; Ch. Bd. Trustees Ted Benard-Cutler. Through training in Jewish texts, history, literature, ethics, and Hebrew language, prepares students to become literate participants in the global Jewish community. Offers graduate and undergraduate degrees and certificates in all aspects of Jewish education, Jewish studies, and Jewish music; serves students of all ages through its Prozdor High School, Camp Yavneh, Ulpan Center for Adult Jewish Learning, and *Me'ah*–One Hundred Hours of Adult Jewish Learning. *Hebrew College Today; Likut.* (WWW.HEBREWCOLLEGE.EDU)

HEBREW SEMINARY OF THE DEAF (1992). 4435 W. Oakton, Skokie, IL 60076. (847) 677-3330. FAX: (847)677-7945. E-mail: hebrewsemdeaf@juno.com. Pres. Rabbi Douglas Goldhamer; Bd. Co-Chmn. Rabbi William Frankel & Alan Crane. Trains deaf and hearing men and women to become rabbis and teachers for Jewish deaf communities across America. All classes in the 5-year program are interpreted in Sign Language. Rabbis teaching in the seminary are Reform, Conservative, and Reconstructionist.

HEBREW THEOLOGICAL COLLEGE (1922). 7135 N. Carpenter Rd., Skokie, IL 60077. (847)982-2500. FAX: (847)674-6381. E-mail: htc@htcnet.edu. Chancellor Rabbi Dr. Jerold Isenberg; Rosh Hayeshiva Rabbi Shlomo Morgenstern. Hebrew Theological College, a fully accredited institution, includes the Bet Midrash for Men, Blitstein Institute for Women, Kanter School of Liberal Arts and Sciences, Fasman Yeshiva High School, Community Service Devision, Silber Memorial Library, Bellows Kollel, Israel Experience Program and Yeshivas HaKayitz summer camp. *Likutei Pshatim, Or Shmuel, Academic Journal.* (WWW.HTCNET.EDU)

HEBREW UNION COLLEGE–JEWISH INSTITUTE OF RELIGION (1875). 3101 Clifton Ave., Cincinnati, OH 45220. (513)221-1875. FAX: (513)221-1847. Acting Pres. Dr. Norman J. Cohen; Chancellor Emeritus; V.-Pres. Admin. & Finance Arthur R. Grant; V.-Pres. Devel. Erica S. Frederick; Chmn. Bd. Govs. Burton Lehman; Provost Dr. Norman J. Cohen. Academic centers: 3101 Clifton Ave., Cincinnati, OH 45220 (1875), Dean Rabbi Kenneth Ehrlich. 1 W. 4 St., NYC 10012 (1922), Dean Rabbi Aaron Panken. FAX: (212) 388-1720. 3077 University Ave., Los Angeles, CA 90007 (1954), Dean Rabbi Lewis Barth; FAX: (213)747-6128. 13 King David St., Jerusalem, Israel 94101 (1963), Dean Rabbi Michael Marmur; FAX: (972-2)6251478. Prepares students for Reform rabbinate, cantorate, Jewish education and educational administration, communal service, academic careers; promotes Jewish studies; maintains libraries, archives, and museums; offers master's and doctoral degrees; engages in archaeological excavations; publishes scholarly works through Hebrew Union College Press. *American Jewish Archives;*

Bibliographica Judaica; HUC-JIR Catalogue; Hebrew Union College Annual; Studies in Bibliography and Booklore; The Chronicle; Kesher. (WWW.HUC.EDU)

——, AMERICAN JEWISH PERIODICAL CENTER (1957). 3101 Clifton Ave., Cincinnati, OH 45220. (513)221-1875, ext. 396. FAX: (513)221-0519. Dir. Herbert C. Zafren. Maintains microfilms of all American Jewish periodicals 1823-1925, selected periodicals since 1925. *Jewish Periodicals and Newspapers on Microfilm (1957); First Supplement (1960); Augmented Edition (1984).*

——, BLAUSTEIN CENTER FOR PASTORAL COUNSELING (2000). 1 West 4th Street, NYC 10012. (212)824-2238. FAX: (212)388-1720. E-mail: nwiener@huc. edu. Dir. Nancy Wiener. In partnership with CCAR, prepares spiritual leaders to sensitively and capably help congregants deal with the critical issues they face throughout their lives; enables rabbinical students to complete a variety of supervised clinical experiences, including a year of congregational work as well as pastoral counseling internships, and an academic grounding in psychodynamics and pastoral counseling; and develops new approaches to teaching counseling skills, grounding reflections on practical field work experiences in the teachings of Jewish texts.

——, CENTER FOR HOLOCAUST AND HUMANITY EDUCATION (2000). 3101 Clifton Ave., Cincinnati, OH 45220. (513)221-1875, ext. 355. FAX: (513)221-1842. E-mail: holocaustandhumanity@huc.edu. Dir. Dr. Racelle R. Weiman. Cosponsored by Hebrew Union College-Jewish Institute of Religion and Combined Generations of the Holocaust of Greater Cincinnati; offers graduate level courses for educational professionals and clergy; surveys and assesses Holocaust education needs in public and private sectors; innovates curriculum development and evaluation; provides teacher training, pedagogic resources, and programming for general public of all ages and faiths; convenes conferences and symposia; cooperates with university consortium on outreach initiatives; creates traveling exhibits; fosters tolerance education and prejudice reduction in the school system.

——, EDGAR F. MAGNIN SCHOOL OF GRADUATE STUDIES (1956). 3077 University Ave., Los Angeles, CA 90007. (213) 749-3424. FAX: (213)747-6128. E-mail: magnin@huc.edu. Dir. Dr. Reuven Firestone. Supervises programs leading to DHS, DHL, and MA degrees; participates in cooperative PhD programs with U. of S. Calif.

——, GRADUATE STUDIES PROGRAM. 1 W. 4 St. NYC 10012. (212)824-2252. FAX: (212)388-1720. E-mail: nysgrad@huc. edu. Dir. Dr. Carol Ochs. Offers the DHL (doctor of Hebrew letters) degree in a variety of fields; the MAJS (master of arts in Judaic studies), a multidisciplinary degree; and is the only Jewish seminary to offer the DMin (doctor of ministry) degree in pastoral care and counseling.

——, HUC-UC CENTER FOR THE STUDY OF ETHICS AND CONTEMPORARY MORAL PROBLEMS (1986). 3101 Clifton Ave., Cincinnati, OH 45220. (513)221-1875, ext. 367. FAX: (5130221-1842. E-mail: ethics@huc.edu. Dir. Dr. Jonathan Cohen. Cosponsored by Hebrew Unon College-Jewish Institute of Religion and the University of Cincinnati; dedicated to the study of contemporary moral problems on the basis of values that are at the heart of Judeo-Christian and secular ethical traditions; provides forum for open discussion and reflection on important moral dilemmas that arise in modern life; promotes the incorporation of ethical values in personal life, professional practice, and community development; launching MA and PhD programs in Jewish and Comparative Law and Applied Ethics; offering development programs for legal, medical, and social work professionals; promoting cooperative research among academic institutions, social service, and not-for-profit organizations in Greater Cincinnati.

——, IRWIN DANIELS SCHOOL OF JEWISH COMMUNAL SERVICE (1968). 3077 University Ave., Los Angeles, CA 90007. (800)899-0925. FAX: (213)747-6128. E-mail: swindmueller@huc.edu. Dir. Dr. Steven F. Windmueller. Offers certificate and master's degree to those employed in Jewish communal services, or preparing for such work; offers joint MA in Jewish education and communal service with Rhea Hirsch School; offers dual degrees with the School of Social Work, the School of Public Administration, the Annenberg School for Communication,

Marshall School of Business and the School of Gerontology of the U. of S. Calif. and with other institutions. Single master's degrees can be completed in 15 months and certificates are awarded for the completion of two full-time summer sessions. (WWW.HUC.EDU)

———, JACOB RADER MARCUS CENTER OF THE AMERICAN JEWISH ARCHIVES (see p. 581)

———, JEROME H. LOUCHHEIM SCHOOL OF JUDAIC STUDIES (1969). 3077 University Ave., Los Angeles, CA 90007. (213)749-3424. FAX: (213)747-6128. Dir. Dr. Reuven Firestone. Offers programs leading to MA, BS, BA, and AA degrees; offers courses as part of the undergraduate program of the U. of S. Calif.

———, NELSON GLUECK SCHOOL OF BIBLICAL ARCHAEOLOGY (1963). 13 King David St., Jerusalem, Israel 94101. (972)2-6203333. FAX: (972)2-6251478. Dir. Avraham Biran. Offers graduate-level research programs in Bible and archaeology. Summer excavations are carried out by scholars and students. University credit may be earned by participants in excavations. Consortium of colleges, universities, and seminaries is affiliated with the school. Skirball Museum of Biblical Archaeology (artifacts from Tel Dan, Tel Gezer, and Aroer).

———, RHEA HIRSCH SCHOOL OF EDUCATION (1967). 3077 University Ave., Los Angeles, CA 90007. (213)749-3424. FAX: (213)747-6128. Dir. Sara Lee. Offers PhD and MA programs in Jewish and Hebrew education; conducts joint degree programs with U. of S. Calif.; offers courses for Jewish teachers, librarians, and early educators on a nonmatriculating basis; conducts summer institutes for professional Jewish educators.

———, SCHOOL OF EDUCATION (1947). 1 W. 4 St., NYC 10012. (212)824-2213. FAX: (212)388-1720. E-mail: nysed@huc.edu. Dir. Jo Kay. Trains teachers and principals for Reform religious schools; offers MA degree with specialization in religious education.

———, SCHOOL OF GRADUATE STUDIES (1949). 3101 Clifton Ave., Cincinnati, OH 45220. (513)221-1875, ext. 230. FAX: (513)221-0321. E-mail: gradschool@huc.edu. Dir. Dr. Adam Kamesar. Offers pro-

grams leading to MA and PhD degrees; offers program leading to DHL degree for rabbinic graduates of the college.

———, SCHOOL OF JEWISH STUDIES (1963). 13 King David St., Jerusalem, Israel 94101. (972)2-6203333. FAX: (972)2-6251478. E-mail: jerusalem@huc.edu. Acting Pres. Dr. Norman J. Cohen; Dean Rabbi Michael Marmur; Assoc. Dean Rabbi Shaul R. Feinberg. Offers first year of graduate rabbinic, cantorial, and Jewish education studies (required) for North American students; graduate program leading to ordination for Israeli rabbinic students; non-degree Beit Midrash/Liberal Yeshivah program of Jewish studies (English language); in-service educational programming for teachers and educators (Hebrew language); Hebrew Ulpan for immigrants and visitors; Abramov Library of Judaica, Hebraica, Ancient Near East and American Jewish Experience; Skirball Museum of Biblical Archaeology; public outreach programs (lectures, courses, concerts, exhibits).

———, SCHOOL OF SACRED MUSIC (1947). 1 W. 4 St., NYC 10012. (212)824-2225. FAX: (212)388-1720. Dir. Cantor Israel Goldstein. Trains cantors for congregations; offers MSM degree. Sacred Music Press.

———, SKIRBALL CULTURAL CENTER (see p. 584)

INSTITUTE OF TRADITIONAL JUDAISM (1990). 811 Palisade Ave., Teaneck, NJ 07666. (201)801-0707. FAX: (201)801-0449. Rector (Reish Metivta) Rabbi David Weiss Halivni; Dean Rabbi Ronald D. Price. A nondenominational halakhic rabbinical school dedicated to genuine faith combined with intellectual honesty and the love of Israel. Graduates receive "yoreh yoreh" smikhah.

JEWISH THEOLOGICAL SEMINARY (1886; reorg. 1902). 3080 Broadway, NYC 10027-4649. (212)678-8000. FAX: (212) 678-8947. Chancellor Dr. Ismar Schorsch; Bd. Chmn. Gershon Kekst. Operates undergraduate and graduate programs in Judaic studies; professional schools for training Conservative rabbis, educators and cantors; the JTS Library; the Ratner Center for the Study of Conservative Judaism; Melton Research Center for Jewish Education; the Jewish Museum; Ramah Camps and the Ivry

Prozdor high-school honors program. Other outreach activities include the Distance Learning Project, the Finkelstein Institute for Religious and Social Studies, the Havruta Program, and the Wagner Institute lay leadership program. *Academic Bulletin; JTS Magazine; Gleanings; JTS News.* (WWW.JTSA.EDU)

————, ALBERT A. LIST COLLEGE OF JEWISH STUDIES (formerly SEMINARY COLLEGE OF JEWISH STUDIES—TEACHERS INSTITUTE) (1909). 3080 Broadway, NYC 10027. (212)678-8826. Dean Dr. Shuly Rubin Schwartz. Offers complete undergraduate program in Judaica leading to BA degree; conducts joint programs with Columbia University and Barnard College enabling students to receive two BA degrees.

————, GRADUATE SCHOOL OF JTS (formerly INSTITUTE FOR ADVANCED STUDY IN THE HUMANITIES) (1968). 3080 Broadway, NYC 10027-4649. (212)678-8024. FAX: (212)678-8947. E-mail: gradschool @jtsa.edu. Dean Dr. Stephen P. Garfinkel; Asst. Dean Dr. Bruce E. Nielsen. Programs leading to MA, DHL, and PhD degrees in Judaic studies; specializations include Ancient Judaism, Bible and Ancient Semitic Languages, Interdepartmental Studies, Jewish Art and Material Culture, Jewish Education, Jewish History, Jewish Literature, Jewish Philosophy, Jewish Women's Studies, Liturgy, Medieval Jewish Studies, Midrash, Modern Jewish Studies, Talmud and Rabbinics, and Dual Degree Program with Columbia University School of Social Work.

————, H.L. MILLER CANTORIAL SCHOOL AND COLLEGE OF JEWISH MUSIC (1952). 3080 Broadway, NYC 10027. (212)678-8036. FAX: (212)678-8947. Dean Cantor Henry Rosenblum. Trains cantors, music teachers, and choral directors for congregations. Offers full-time programs in sacred music leading to degree of MSM, and diploma of *Hazzan.*

————, JEWISH MUSEUM (*see* p. 582)

————, LIBRARY OF THE JEWISH THEOLOGICAL SEMINARY. 3080 Broadway, NYC 10027. (212)678-8075. FAX: (212)678-8998. E-mail: library@jtsa.edu. Librarian Dr. Mayer E. Rabinowitz. Contains one of the largest collections of Hebraica and Judaica in the world, including manuscripts, incunabula, rare books, and Cairo Geniza material. The 320,000-item collection includes books, manuscripts, periodicals, sound recordings, prints, broadsides, photographs, postcards, microform, videos and CD-ROM. Exhibition of items from the collection are ongoing. Exhibition catalogs are available for sale. The Library is open to the public for on-site use (photo identification required). *Between the Lines.* (WWW.JTSA. EDU/LIBRARY)

————, LOUIS FINKELSTEIN INSTITUTE FOR RELIGIOUS AND SOCIAL STUDIES (1938). 3080 Broadway, NYC 10027. (212)870-3180. FAX: (212)678-8947. E-mail: finkelstein@jtsa.edu. Dir. Rabbi Gerald Wolpe. Since 1938 has maintained an innovative interfaith and intergroup relations program, pioneering new approaches to dialogue across religious lines. Through scholarly and practical fellowship, highlights the relevance of Judaism and other contemporary religions to current theological, ethical, and scientific issues, including the emerging challenge of bioethics.

————, MELTON RESEARCH CENTER FOR JEWISH EDUCATION (1960). 3080 Broadway, NYC 10027. (212)678-8031. E-mail: stbrown@jtsa.edu. Dir. Dr. Steven M. Brown; Admin. Lisa Siberstein-Weber. Develops new curricula and materials for Jewish education; prepares educators through seminars and in-service programs; maintains consultant and supervisory relationships with a limited number of pilot schools; develops and implements research initiatives; sponsors "renewal" retreats. *Gleanings; Courtyard: A Journal of Research and Reflection on Jewish Education.*

————, NATIONAL RAMAH COMMISSION (1947). 3080 Broadway, NYC 10027. (212)678-8881. FAX: (212)749-8251. Pres. Alan H. Silberman; Natl. Dir. Sheldon Dorph. Sponsors an international network of 16 summer camps located in the US, Canada, S. America, Russia, and Israel, emphasizing Jewish education, living, and culture; offers opportunities for qualified college students and older to serve as counselors, administrators, specialists, etc., and programs for children with special needs (Tikvah program); offers special programs in U.S. and Israel, including National Ramah Staff Training

Institute, Ramah Israel Seminar, Ulpan Ramah Plus, and Tichon Ramah Yerushalayim. Family and synagogue tours to Israel and summer day camp in Israel for Americans.

———, PROJECT JUDAICA (1992). 3080 Broadway, NYC 10027. (212)678-8983. Dir. Dr. David Fishman. Students in this intensive, five year program sponsored with YIVO and the Russian State University for the Humanities in Moscow pursue the university's general curriculum while majoring in Jewish history and culture taught by JTS faculty and advanced students. Graduates receive a diploma (the equivalent of an MA) or a candidate of sciences degree (the equivalent of a PhD) from RSUH.

———, RABBINICAL SCHOOL (1886). 3080 Broadway, NYC 10027. (212)678-8817. Dean Allan Kensky. Offers a program of graduate and professional studies leading to the degree of Master of Arts and ordination; includes one year of study in Jerusalem and an extensive field-work program.

———, RADIO AND TELEVISION (1944). 3080 Broadway, NYC 10027. (212)678-8020. Produces radio and TV programs expressing the Jewish tradition in its broadest sense, including hour-long documentaries on NBC and ABC. Distributes cassettes of programs at minimum charge.

———, REBECCA AND ISRAEL IVRY PROZDOR (1951). 3080 Broadway, NYC 10027. (212)678-8824. E-mail: prozdor@jtsa.edu. Principal Rhonda Rosenheck; Community Advisory Board Chmn. Michael Katz. The Hebrew high school of JTS, offers a program of Jewish studies for day school and congregational school graduates in classical texts, Hebrew, interdisciplinary seminars, training in educational leadership, and classes for college credit. Classes meet one evening a week and on Sundays in Manhattan and at affiliated programs. *High School Curricula*.

———, SAUL LIEBERMAN INSTITUTE FOR TALMUDIC RESEARCH (1985). 3080 Broadway, NYC 10027. (212)678-8994. FAX: (212)678D8947. E-mail: liebinst@jtsa.edu. Dir. Shamma Friedman; Coord. Jonathan Milgram. Engaged in preparing for publication a series of scholarly editions of selected chapters of the Talmud.

The following projects support and help disseminate the research:Talmud Text Database; Bibliography of Talmudic Literature; Catalogue of Geniza Fragments.

———, SCHOCKEN INSTITUTE FOR JEWISH RESEARCH (1961). 6 Balfour St., Jerusalem, Israel 92102. (972)2-5631288. FAX: (972)2-5636857. E-mail: sjssg@vms.huji.ac.il. Dir. Dr. Shmuel Glick. Comprises the Schocken collection of rare books and manuscripts and a research institute dedicated to the exploration of Hebrew religious poetry (*piyyut*). *Schocken Institute Yearbook (P'raqim)*.

———, WILLIAM DAVIDSON GRADUATE SCHOOL OF JEWISH EDUCATION (1996). 3080 Broadway, NYC 10027. (212) 678-8030. E-mail: edschool@jtsa.edu. Dean Dr. Aryeh Davidson. Offers master's and doctoral degrees in Jewish education; continuing education courses for Jewish educators and Jewish communal professionals; and programs that take advantage of the latest technology, including distance learning and interactive video classrooms.

MAALOT—A SEMINARY FOR CANTORS AND JUDAISTS (1987). 15 W. Montgomery Ave., Suite 204, Rockville, MD 20850. (301)309-2310. FAX: (301)309-2328. Pres./Exec. Off. David Shneyer. An educational program established to train individuals in Jewish music, the liturgical arts, and the use, design, and application of Jewish customs and ceremonies. Offers classes, seminars, and an independent study program.

MESIVTA YESHIVA RABBI CHAIM BERLIN RABBINICAL ACADEMY (1905). 1605 Coney Island Ave., Brooklyn, NY 11230. (718)377-0777. Exec. Dir. Y. Mayer Lasker. Maintains fully accredited elementary and high schools; collegiate and postgraduate school for advanced Jewish studies, both in America and Israel; Camp Morris, a summer study retreat; Prof. Nathan Isaacs Memorial Library; Gur Aryeh Publications.

NER ISRAEL RABBINICAL COLLEGE (1933). 400 Mt. Wilson Lane, Baltimore, MD 21208. (410)484-7200. FAX: (410)484-3060. Pres. Rabbi Herman N. Neuberger. Trains rabbis and educators for Jewish communities in America and worldwide. Offers bachelor's, master's, and doctoral degrees in talmudic law, as well as teacher's diploma. College has four divisions: Israel Henry Beren High School, Rabbinical College, Teachers Training Institute, Graduate School. Maintains an active community-service division. Operates special programs for Iranian and Russian Jewish students. *Ner Israel Update; Alumni Bulletin; Ohr Hanair Talmudic Journal; Iranian B'nei Torah Bulletin.*

RABBINICAL COLLEGE OF TELSHE, INC. (1941). 28400 Euclid Ave., Wickliffe, OH 44092. (216)943-5300. Roshei Hayeshiva and Pres. Rabbi Zalman Gifter and Rabbi Yitzchok Sorotzkin ; V.-Pres. Rabbi Abba Zalka Gewirtz. College for higher Jewish learning specializing in talmudic studies and rabbinics; maintains a preparatory academy including a secular high school, postgraduate department, teacher-training school, and teachers' seminary for women. *Pri Etz Chaim; Peer Mordechai; Alumni Bulletin.*

RECONSTRUCTIONIST RABBINICAL COLLEGE (1968). 1299 Church Rd., Wyncote, PA 19095. (215)576-0800. FAX: (215)576-6143. E-mail: rrcinfo@rrc.edu. Pres. David Teutsch; Bd. Chmn. Donald L. Shapiro; Genl. Chmn. Aaron Ziegelman. Coeducational. Trains rabbis and cantors for all areas of Jewish communal life:synagogues, academic and educational positions, Hillel centers, federation agencies, and chaplaincy for hospitals, hospices, and geriatric centers; confers title of rabbi and cantor and grants degrees of Master and Doctor of Hebrew Letters and Master of Arts in Jewish Studies. *RRC Report; Reconstructionist.*

SPERTUS INSTITUTE OF JEWISH STUDIES (1924). 618 S. Michigan Ave., Chicago, IL 60605. (312)922-9012. FAX: (312)922-6406. Pres. Howard A. Sulkin; Bd. Chmn. Franklin Nitikman; V.-Pres. for Academic Affairs Byron L. Sherwin. An accredited institution of higher learning offering one doctor of Jewish studies degree; master's degree programs in Jewish studies, Jewish education, Jewish communal service, and human-services administration; plus an extensive program of continuing education. Major resources of the college encompass Spertus Museum, Asher Library, Chicago Jewish Archives, and Spertus College of Judaica Press.

———, SPERTUS MUSEUM (*see* p. 585)

TOURO COLLEGE (1970). Executive Offices: 50 W. 23 St., NYC 10010. (212)643-0700. FAX: (212)714-9048. Pres. Dr. Bernard Lander; Bd. Chmn. Mark Hasten. Chartered by NY State Board of Regents as a nonprofit four-year college with Judaic studies, health sciences, business, and liberal arts programs leading to BA, BS, and MA, MS degrees; emphasizes relevance of Jewish heritage to general culture of Western civilization. Also offers JD degree and a biomedical program leading to the MD degree from Technion-Israel Institute of Technology, Haifa.

———, COLLEGE OF LIBERAL ARTS AND SCIENCES. 27-33 W. 23 St., NYC 10010. (212)463-0400. FAX: (212)627-9144. Exec. Dean Stanley Boylan. Offers comprehensive Jewish studies along with studies in the arts, sciences, humanities, and preprofessional studies in health sciences, law, accounting, business, computer science, education, and finance. Women's Division, 160 Lexington Ave., NYC 10016. (212)213-2230. FAX: (212)683-3281. Dean Sara E. Freifeld.

———, INSTITUTE OF JEWISH LAW. (631) 421-2244, ext. 335. A constituent of Touro College Jacob D. Fuchsberg Law Center, the Institute of Jewish Law provides an intellectual framework for the study and teaching of Jewish law. Coedits *Dinei Israel* (Jewish Law Journal) with Tel Aviv University Law School.

———, JACOB D. FUCHSBERG LAW CENTER (1980). Long Island Campus, 300 Nassau Rd., Huntington, NY 11743. (516) 421-2244. Dean Howard A. Glickstein. Offers studies leading to JD degree.

———, MOSCOW BRANCH. Oztozhenka #38, Moscow, Russia 119837. Offers BS program in business and BA program in Jewish studies.

———, SCHOOL OF GENERAL STUDIES. Midtown Main Campus, 27 W. 23 St., NYC 10010. (212)463-0400; Harlem Main Campus, 240 E. 123 St., NYC 10035; Sunset Park extension, 475 53rd St., Brooklyn, NY 11220; Flushing Extension, 133-35 Roosevelt Ave., Queens, NY 11374. Dean Stephen Adolphus. Associate and bachelor degree programs in human services, education N-6, computing, business and liberal arts; special emphasis on service to non-traditional students.

———, TOURO COLLEGE FLATBUSH CENTER (1979). 1602 Ave. J, Brooklyn, NY 11230. (718)252-7800. Dean Robert Goldschmidt. A division of the College of Liberal Arts and Sciences; options offered in accounting and business, education, mathematics, political science, psychology, special education and speech. Classes are given on weeknights and during the day on Sunday.

———, TOURO COLLEGE ISRAEL. 20 Pierre Koenig St., Jerusalem, Israel. (02) 6796666. FAX: (02)6796688. V-Pres., Israel, Matityahu Adler; Dean of Faculty, Israel, Prof. Moshe Lieberman. Touro College Israel offers both undergraduate and graduate degrees in management, marketing, economics, finance, and accounting. Touro College also offers a graduate degree in Jewish Studies. Courses in both these programs are given in Hebrew. In addition undergraduate courses in our one year program are offered in English. (WWW.TOURO. AC.IL)

———, TOURO COLLEGE SCHOOL OF HEALTH SCIENCES (1986). 1700 Union Blvd, Bay Shore, NY 11706. (516)665-1600. FAX: (516)665-6902. E-mail: edwarda@touro.edu. Pres. Dr. Bernard Lander; Dean Dr. Joseph Weisberg. Offers the following programs:MS/MD with Faculty of Medicine, Technion Institute, Israel; BS/MS Occupational Therapy; BS/MS Physical Therapy; MS Public Health; Advanced MS Orthopedic Physical Therapy; MS Forensic Examination; MS Clinical Engineering; MS Early Intervention; MS Gerontology; BS Physician Assistant; AAS Occupational Therapy Assistant; AAS Physical Therapists Assistant.

———, TOURO GRADUATE SCHOOL OF JEWISH STUDIES (1981). 160 Lexington Ave., NYC 10016. (212)213-2230. FAX: (212)683-3281. E-mail: moshesh@touro. edu. Pres. Bernard Lander; Dean Michael A. Shmidman. Offers courses leading to an MA in Jewish studies, with concentrations in Jewish history or Jewish education. Students may complete part of their program in Israel through MA courses offered by Touro faculty at Touro's Jerusalem center.

UNIVERSITY OF JUDAISM (1947). 15600 Mulholland Dr., Los Angeles, CA 90077. (310)440-1210. FAX: (310)476-0347. E-mail: gleuenthal@uj.edu. Pres. Dr. Robert D. Wexler; Acting Provost John R. Lutzker. The College of Arts and Sciences is an accredited liberal arts college for undergraduates offering a core curriculum of Jewish, Western, and non-Western studies, with majors including bioethics (a premedical track in partnership with Cedars-Sinai Medical Center), business, English, Jewish studies, journalism, literature & politics, political science, psychology, and U.S. public policy. Accredited graduate programs in nonprofit business administration (MBA), Jewish education, and psychology with an emphasis on developmental disabilities. The Ziegler School of Rabbinic Studies provides an intensive four-year program with Conservative ordination. Home of the Center for Policy Options, conducting public policy research in areas of concern to the Jewish community, and the Whizin Center for the Jewish Future, a research and programming institute. Offers the largest adult Jewish education program in the U.S., cultural-arts programs, and a variety of outreach services for West Coast Jewish communities. *The Vision.*

WEST COAST TALMUDICAL SEMINARY (Yeshiva Ohr Elchonon Chabad) (1953). 7215 Waring Ave., Los Angeles, CA 90046. (323)937-3763. FAX: (323)937-9456. Dean Rabbi Ezra Schochet. Provides facilities for intensive Torah education as well as Orthodox rabbinical training on the West Coast; conducts an accredited college preparatory high school combined with a full program of Torah-talmudic training and a graduate talmudical division on the college level. *Torah Quiz; Kovetz Migdal Ohr; Kovetz Ohr HaMigdal.*

YESHIVA TORAH VODAATH AND MESIVTA TORAH VODAATH RABBINICAL SEMINARY (1918). 425 E. 9 St., Brooklyn, NY 11218. (718)941-8000. Bd. Chmn. Chaim Leshkowitz. Offers Hebrew and secular education from elementary level through rabbinical ordination and postgraduate work; maintains a teachers institute and community-service bureau; maintains a dormitory and a nonprofit camp program for boys. *Chronicle; Mesivta Vanguard; Thought of the Week; Torah Vodaath News; Ha'Mesifta.*

————, YESHIVA TORAH VODAATH ALUMNI ASSOCIATION (1941). 425 E. 9 St., Brooklyn, NY 11218. (718)941-8000. Pres. George Weinberger. Promotes social and cultural ties between the alumni and the schools through classes and lectures and fund-raising; offers vocational guidance to students; operates Camp Ohr Shraga; sponsors research fellowship program for boys. *Annual Journal; Hamesivta Torah periodical.*

YESHIVA UNIVERSITY (1886). Main Campus, 500 W. 185 St., NYC 10033-3201. (212)960-5400. FAX: (212)960-0055. Pres. Dr. Norman Lamm; Chmn. Bd. of Trustees Robert M. Beren;. In its second century, the nation's oldest and most comprehensive independent university founded under Jewish auspices, with 18 undergraduate and graduate schools, divisions, and affiliates; widespread programs of research and community outreach; publications; and a museum. A broad range of curricula lead to bachelor's, master's, doctoral, and professional degrees. Undergraduate schools provide general studies curricula supplemented by courses in Jewish learning; graduate schools prepare for careers in medicine, law, social work, Jewish education, psychology, Jewish studies, and other fields. It has seven undergraduate schools, seven graduate and professional schools, and four affiliates. *Yeshiva University Review; Yeshiva University Today.* (WWW.YU.EDU)

Yeshiva University has four campuses in Manhattan and the Bronx: Main Campus, 500 W. 185 St., NYC 10033-3201; Midtown Campus, 245 Lexington Ave., NYC 10016-4699; Brookdale Center, 55 Fifth Ave., NYC 10003-4391; Jack and Pearl Resnick Campus, Eastchester Rd. & Morris Pk. Ave., Bronx, NY 10461-1602.

Undergraduate schools for men at Main Campus (212)960-5400: Yeshiva College (Bd. Chmn. Jay Schottenstein; Dean Dr. Norman T. Adler) provides liberal arts and sciences curricula; grants BA degree. Isaac Breuer College of Hebraic Studies (Dean Dr. Michael D. Shmidman) awards Hebrew teacher's diploma, AA, BA, and BS. James Striar School of General Jewish Studies (Dean Dr. Michael D. Shmidman) grants AA degree. Yeshiva Program/Mazer School of Talmudic Studies (Max and Marion Grill Dean Rabbi Zevulun Charlop) offers advanced course of study in Talmudic texts

and commentaries. Irving I. Stone Beit Midrash Program (Dean Dr. Michael D. Shmidman) offers diversified curriculum combining Talmud with Jewish studies.

Undergraduate school for women at Midtown Campus (212)340-7700: Stern College for Women (Bd. Chmn. Marjorie Diener Blenden; Dr. Monique C. Katz; Dean Dr. Karen Bacon) offers liberal arts and sciences curricula supplemented by Jewish studies programs; awards BA, AA, and Hebrew teacher's diploma.

Sy Syms School of Business at Main Campus and Midtown Campus (Bd. Chmn. Bernard L. Madoff; Dean Dr. Charles Snow) offers undergraduate business curricula in conjunction with study at Yeshiva College or Stern College; grants BS degree.

Universitywide programs include the S. Daniel Abraham Israel Program; Joseph Alexander Foundation Program for Enhancemant of Science Education; Samuel H. and Rachel Golding Center for Judaic Studies; Samuel H. and Rachel Golding Institute for Biomedical Education; Carl C. Icahn Foundation Institutes for Child Protection; Irving and Hanni Rosenbaum Aliyah Incentive Fund; Holocaust Studies Program; Yeshiva University Press; Yeshiva University Museum.

————, ALBERT EINSTEIN COLLEGE OF MEDICINE (1955). Eastchester Rd. & Morris Pk. Ave., Bronx, NY 10461-1602. (718)430-2000. Pres. Dr. Norman Lamm; Chpers. Bd. of Overseers Robert A. Belfer; Marilyn and Stanley M. Katz Dean Dr. Dominick P. Purpura. Prepares physicians and conducts research in the health sciences; awards MD degree; includes Sue Golding Graduate Division of Medical Sciences (Dir. Dr. Anne M. Etgen), which grants PhD degree. Einstein's clinical facilities and affiliates encompass Jack D. Weiler Hospital of Albert Einstein College of Medicine, Jacobi Medical Center, Montefiore Medical Center, Long Island Jewish Medical Center, Beth Israel Medical Center, Bronx-Lebanon Hospital Center, and Rose F. Kennedy Center for Research in Mental Retardation and Developmental Disabilities. *Einstein; Einstein Today; Einstein Quarterly Journal of Biology and Medicine.*

————, ALUMNI OFFICE, 500 W. 185 St., NYC 10033-3201. (212)960-5373. FAX:

(212)960-5336. E-mail: alumdesk@ymail. yu.edu. University Dir. Alumni Affairs Robert R. Saltzman; Dir. Undergraduate Alumni Affairs Toby Hilsenrad Weiss. Seeks to foster a close allegiance of alumni to their alma mater by maintaining ties with all alumni and servicing the following associations.Yeshiva College Alumni (Pres. Stuart Verstandig); Stern College for Women Alumnae (Pres. Yonina Langer); Sy Syms School of Business Alumni (Pres. Chaim Haas); Albert Einstein College of Medicine Alumni (Pres. Dr. Harriette Mogul); Ferkauf Graduate School of Psychology Alumni (Pres. Dr. Nancy Dallek); Wurzweiler School of Social Work Alumni (Co-Pres. Joel Katz & Annette Prager); Rabbinic Alumni (Pres. Rabbi Shmuel Goldin); Benjamin N. Cardozo School of Law Alumni (Pres. Joshua Sohn). *Yeshiva University Review; AECOM Alumni News; Ferkauf Progress Notes; Wurzweiler Update; Jewish Social Work Forum.*

————, AZRIELI GRADUATE SCHOOL OF JEWISH EDUCATION AND ADMINISTRATION (1945). 245 Lexington Ave., NYC 10016-4699. (212)340-7705. FAX: (212) 340-7787. Pres. Dr. Norman Lamm; Chmn. Bd. Of Directors Moshael J. Straus; Dir. Dr. Yitzchak S. Handel. Offers MS degree in Jewish elementary and secondary education; specialist's certificate and EdD in administration and supervision of Jewish education. Block Education Program, subsidized by a grant from the Jewish Agency's Joint Program for Jewish Education, provides summer course work to complement year-round field instruction in local communities.

————, BELFER INSTITUTE FOR ADVANCED BIOMEDICAL STUDIES (1978). Eastchester Rd. & Morris Pk. Ave., Bronx, NY 10461-1602. (718)430-2801. Dir. Dr. Dennis Shields. Integrates and coordinates the Albert Einstein College of Medicine's postdoctoral research and training-grant programs in the basic and clinical biomedical sciences. Awards certificate as research fellow or research associate on completion of training.

————, BENJAMIN N. CARDOZO SCHOOL OF LAW (1976). 55 Fifth Ave., NYC 10003-4391. (212)790-0200. E-mail:lawinfo@ymail.yu.edu. Pres. Dr. Norman Lamm; Chmn. Bd. Of Directors Earle I. Mack; Dean Paul R. Verkuil. Offers a rigorous and enriched legal education leading to juris doctor (JD) degree and two LLM programs—in intellectual property and in general law—for those interested in specialized training and for international students. Programs and services include Jacob Burns Institute for Advanced Legal Studies; Jacob Burns Center for Ethics in the Practice of Law; Bet Tzedek Legal Services Clinic, including the Herman J. Stich Program for the Aged and Disabled; Cardozo International Institute/Uri and Caroline Bauer Israel Program; Leonard and Bea Diener Institute of Jewish Law; Floersheimer Center for Constitutional Democracy; Ford Foundation Program in International Law and Human Rights; Samuel and Ronnie Heyman Center on Corporate Governance; Kukin Program for Conflict Resolution; Romie Shapiro Program in International Law and Human Rights; Stephen B. Siegel Program in Real Estate Law; Sol S. Singer Research Program in Real Property Law; Howard M. Squadron Program in Law, Media, and Society; Center for Professional Development. *Cardozo Life; Cardozo Law Review; Cardozo Arts and Entertainment Law Journal; Cardozo Women's Law Journal; Cardozo Journal of International and Comparative Law; Cardozo Studies in Law and Literature; Post-Soviet Media Law and Policy Newsletter; New York Real Estate Reporter.*

————, BERNARD REVEL GRADUATE SCHOOL OF JEWISH STUDIES (1935). 500 W. 185 St., NYC 10033-3201. (212)960-5253. Pres. Dr. Norman Lamm; Chmn. Bd. Of Directors Mordecai D. Katz; Dean Dr. Arthur Hyman. Offers graduate programs in Bible, Talmudic studies, Jewish history, and Jewish philosophy; confers MA and PhD degrees. Harry Fischel Summer Program offers the Revel program during the summer.

————, FERKAUF GRADUATE SCHOOL OF PSYCHOLOGY (1957). Eastchester Rd. & Morris Pk. Ave., Bronx, NY 10461-1602. (718)430-3941. FAX: (718)430-3960. E-mail: gill@aecom.yu.edu. Pres. Dr. Norman Lamm; Chair Bd. of Governors. Dr. Jayne G. Beker; Dean Dr. Lawrence J. Siegel. Offers MA in applied psychology; PsyD in clinical and school-clinical child psychology; and PhD in developmental and clinical health psychology. Programs and services include the Leonard and

Muriel Marcus Family Project for the Study of the Disturbed Adolescent; Max and Celia Parnes Family Psychological and Psychoeducational Services Clinic.

———, (affiliate) PHILIP AND SARAH BELZ SCHOOL OF JEWISH MUSIC (1954). 560 W. 185 St., NYC 10033-3201. (212)960-5353. FAX: (212)960-5359. Dir. Cantor Bernard Beer. Provides professional training of cantors and courses in Jewish liturgical music; conducts outreach; publishes *Journal of Jewish Music and Literature;* awards associate cantor's certificate and cantorial diploma.

———, (affiliate) RABBI ISAAC ELCHANAN THEOLOGICAL SEMINARY (1896). 2540 Amsterdam Ave., NYC 10033-9986. (212)960-5344. FAX: (212)960-0061. Chmn. Bd. of Trustees Julius Berman; Max and Marion Grill Dean Rabbi Zevulun Charlop. Leading center in the Western Hemisphere for Torah study and rabbinic training. RIETS complex encompasses 15 educational entities and a major service and outreach center with some 20 programs. Grants semikhah (ordination) and the degrees of master of religious education, master of Hebrew literature, doctor of religious education, and doctor of Hebrew literature. Includes Rabbi Joseph B. Soloveitchik Center of Rabbinic Studies; Gabriel Levine Post-Graduate School for Rabbinic Studies; Morris and Nellie L. Kawaler Rabbinic Training Program; Irving I. Stone Rabbinic Internship Program; Aaron, Martha, Isidore N., and Blanche Rosansky Foundation Contemporary Halakhah Program.

Kollelim include Marcos and Adina Katz Kollel (Institute for Advanced Research in Rabbinics); Kollel l'Horaah (Yadin Yadin) and External Yadin Yadin; Israel Henry Beren Institute for Higher Talmudic Studies (HaMachon HaGavohah L'Talmud); Bella and Harry Wexner Kollel Elyon and Semikhah Honors Program; Ludwig Jesselson Kollel Chaverim; Caroline and Joseph S. Gruss Institute in Jerusalem.

RIETS sponsors one high school for boys (Manhattan) and one for girls (Queens).

The Max Stern Division of Communal Services (Acting Dir. Rabbi David A. Israel), provides personal and professional service to the rabbinate and related fields, as well as educational, consultative, organizational, and placement services to congregations, schools, and communal organizations around the world; coordinates a broad spectrum of outreach programs, including Association of Modern Orthodox Day Schools and Yeshiva High Schools, Stone-Sapirstein Center for Jewish Education, Gertrude and Morris Bienenfeld Department of Rabbinic Services, Gindi Program for the Enhancement of Professional Rabbinics, Continuing Rabbinic Education Initiatives, Leadership Education and Development Program (LEAD), Kiruv College Outreach Program, Community Kollel and Beit Midrash and Boardroom Learning Programs, Project Kehillah, Myer and Pauline Senders Off-Campus Lecture Series, Jewish Medical Ethics Consultation Service, National Commission on Torah Education. The Torah U-Madda Project, supported by the Joseph J. and Bertha K. Green Memorial Fund, includes the Orthodox Forum and publishes the *The Torah U-Madda Journal* and *Ten Da'at.*

Sephardic components are Jacob E. Safra Institute of Sephardic Studies and the Institute of Yemenite Studies; Sephardic Community Program; Dr. Joseph and Rachel Ades Sephardic Outreach Program; Maybaum Sephardic Fellowship Program.

———, SIMON WIESENTHAL CENTER (*see* p. 584)

———, WOMEN'S ORGANIZATION (1928). 500 W. 185 St., NYC 10033-3201. (212) 960-0855. Chmn. Natl. Bd. Dinah Pinczower. Supports Yeshiva University's national scholarship program for students training in education, community service, law, medicine, and other professions. Its Torah Chesed Fund provides monthly stipends to needy undergraduate students.

———, WURZWEILER SCHOOL OF SOCIAL WORK (1957). 500 W. 185 St., NYC 10033-3201. (212)960-0800. FAX: (212) 960-0822. Pres. Dr. Norman Lamm; Chair Bd. of Governors David I. Schachne; Dorothy and David I. Schachne Dean Dr. Sheldon R. Gelman. Offers graduate programs in social work and Jewish communal service; grants MSW and PhD degrees and certificate in Jewish communal service. MSW programs are: Concurrent Plan, 2-year, full-time track, combining classroom study and supervised field instruction; Plan for Employed Persons (PEP), for people working in social agencies; Block Education Plan (Dir. Dr. Adele Weiner), which combines summer course work with regular-year field placement in local agencies; Clergy Plan, training in counseling for clergy of all denominations; Silvia and Irwin Leiferman Center for Professional Training in the Care of the Elderly. *Jewish Social Work Forum.*

———, (affiliate) YESHIVA OF LOS ANGELES (1977). 9760 W. Pico Blvd., Los Angeles, CA 90035-4701. (310)772-2424. FAX: (310)772-7661. E-mail: mhmay@ wiesenthal.com. Dean Rabbi Marvin Hier; Bd. Chmn. Samuel Belzberg; Dir. Academic Programs Rabbi Sholom Tendler. Affiliates are Yeshiva University High Schools of Los Angeles, Jewish Studies Institute and Kollel Torah MiTzion.

———, YESHIVA UNIVERSITY MUSEUM (*see* p. 585)

SOCIAL, MUTUAL BENEFIT

ALPHA EPSILON PI FRATERNITY (1913). 8815 Wesleyan Rd., Indianapolis, IN 46268-1171. (317)876-1913. FAX: (317) 876-1057. E-mail: office@aepi.org. Internatl. Pres. Andrew P. Fradkin; Exec. V.-Pres. Sidney N. Dunn. International Jewish fraternity active on over 100 campuses in the U.S. and Canada; encourages Jewish students to remain loyal to their heritage and to assume leadership roles in the community; active in behalf of Soviet Jewry, the State of Israel, the United States Holocaust Memorial Museum, Tay Sachs Disease, Mazon:A Jewish Response to Hunger, and other causes. *The Lion of Alpha Epsilon Pi (quarterly magazine).*

AMERICAN ASSOCIATION OF JEWS FROM THE FORMER USSR, INC. (AAJFSU) (1989). 119 Fulton St., 5th fl., rm.3, NYC 10038. (212) (212) 964-1946. FAX: (212)964-1946. E-mail: AAJFSU@yahoo.com. Pres. Yury Zilberman; Bd. Chmn. Mark Gurevich. National not-for-profit, grassroots mutual assistance and refugee advocacy organization, which unites and represents interests of over 600,000 Russian speaking Jewish refugees and legal immigrants from the former Soviet Union. Has chapters and independent associations in 7 states, including New York, Ohio, Colorado, New Jersey, Massachu-

setts, Wisconsin and Maryland. The national organization is a member of the National Immigration Forum and it is affiliated with the United Jewish Communities, Washington Action Office. New York Chapter is a member of the Jewish Community Relations Council of New York and the New York Immigration Coalition. Local Chapters work in cooperation with Jewish Federation of New York. The AAJFSU assists newcomers in their resettlement and vocational and cultural adjustment, fosters their Jewish identity and involvement in civic and social affairs, fights anti-Semitism and violation of human rights in the FSU and the U.S. through cooperation with other human rights organizations and advocacy, supports struggle of Israeli Jews for sustainable peace, provides advocacy in cases of political asylum for victims of anti-Semitism in the FSU and naturalization, provides assistance in social safety net and naturalization of the elderly and disabled. *Chronicles of Anti-Semitism and Nationalism in Republics of the Former USSR (in English, annually); Information Bulletin (in Russian, bimonthly).*

AMERICAN FEDERATION OF JEWS FROM CENTRAL EUROPE, INC. (1938). 570 Seventh Ave., NYC 10018. (212)921-3871. FAX: (212) 575-1918. Pres. Fritz Weinschenk; Bd. Chmn. Curt C. Silberman; Exec. Asst. Dennis E. Rohrbaugh. Seeks to safeguard the rights and interests of American Jews of German-speaking Central European descent, especially in reference to restitution and indemnification; through its affiliate Research Foundation for Jewish Immigration sponsors research and publications on the history, immigration, and acculturation of Central European émigrés in the U.S. and worldwide; through its affiliate Jewish Philanthropic Fund of 1933 supports social programs for needy Nazi victims in the U.S.; undertakes cultural activities, annual conferences, publications; member, Council of Jews from Germany, London.

AMERICAN VETERANS OF ISRAEL (1951). 136 E. 39 St., NYC 10016. E-mail: spielgelsi@aol.com. Pres. Samuel Z. Klausner; V-Pres. David Kaplan. Maintains contact with American and Canadian volunteers who served in Aliyah Bet and/or Israel's

War of Independence; promotes Israel's welfare; holds memorial services at grave of Col. David Marcus; is affiliated with World Mahal. *Newsletter.*

ASSOCIATION OF YUGOSLAV JEWS IN THE UNITED STATES, INC. (1941). 130 E. 59 St., Suite 1202, NYC 10022. (212)371-6891. V.-Pres. & Chmn. Emanuel Salom; Sec. Dr. Joseph Stock. Assistance to all Jews originally from Yugoslavia—Bosnia, Serbia, Croatia—and new settlers in Israel. *Bulletins.*

BNAI ZION–THE AMERICAN FRATERNAL ZIONIST ORGANIZATION (1908). 136 E. 39 St., NYC 10016. (212)725-1211. FAX: (212)684-6327. Pres. Hon. Alan G. Hevesi; Exec. V.-Pres. Mel Parness. Fosters principles of Americanism, fraternalism, and Zionism. The Bnai Zion Foundation supports various humanitarian projects in Israel and the USA, chiefly the Bnai Zion Medical Center in Haifa and homes for retarded children-Maon Bnai Zion in Rosh Ha'ayin and the Herman Z. Quittman Center in Jerusalem. Also supports building of new central library in Ma'aleh Adumim. In U.S. sponsors program of awards for excellence in Hebrew for high school and college students. Chapters all over U.S. *Bnai Zion Voice (quarterly).*

BRITH ABRAHAM (1859; reorg. 1887). 136 E. 39 St., NYC 10016. (212)725-1211. FAX: (212)684-6327. Grand Master Robert Freeman. Protects Jewish rights and combats anti-Semitism; supports Soviet and Ethiopian emigration and the safety and dignity of Jews worldwide; helps to support Bnai Zion Medical Center in Haifa and other Israeli institutions; aids and supports various programs and projects in the U.S.: Hebrew Excellence Program-Gold Medal presentation in high schools and colleges; Camp Loyaltown; Brith Abraham and Bnai Zion Foundations. *Voice.*

BRITH SHOLOM (1905). 3939 Conshohocken Ave., Philadelphia, PA 19131. (215)878-5696. FAX: (215) 878-5699. Pres. Seymour Rose; Exec. Dir. Louis Mason. Fraternal organization devoted to community welfare, protection of rights of Jewish people, and activities that foster Jewish identity and provide support for Israel. Through its philanthropic arm, the Brith Sholom Foundation (1962), sponsors Brith Sholom House in Philadelphia, nonprofit senior-citizen apartments; and Brith Sholom Beit Halochem in Haifa, Israel, rehabilitation, social, and sports center for disabled Israeli veterans, operated by Zahal. Chmn. Bennett Goldstein; Exec. Dir. Saundra Laub. *Brith Sholom Digest; monthly news bulletin.*

FREE SONS OF ISRAEL (1849). 250 Fifth Ave., Suite 201, NYC 10001. (212)725-3690. FAX: (212)725-5874. Grand Master Arlene Hoberman Kyler; Grand Sec. Ronald J. Laszlo. Oldest Jewish fraternal-benefit society in U.S. Affordable membership men & women (18+). Supports Israel, UJA projects, non-sectarian toy drives/philanthropies. Social Action fights anti-Semitism, supports human rights. Member benefits-IBM Metro Credit Union, scholarships, cemetery, discounted Long Term Care Insurance, educational and social functions, Free Model Seder. *Free Sons Reporter.* (WWW.FREESONS.ORG)

JEWISH LABOR BUND (Directed by World Coordinating Committee of the Bund) (1897; reorg. 1947). 25 E. 21 St., NYC 10010. (212)475-0059. FAX: (212) 473-5102. Acting Pres. Motl Zelmanowics; Sec. Gen. Benjamin Nades. Coordinates activities of Bund organizations throughout the world and represents them in the Socialist International; spreads the ideas of socialism as formulated by the Jewish Labor Bund; publishes books and periodicals on world problems, Jewish life, socialist theory and policy, and on the history, activities, and ideology of the Jewish Labor Bund. *Unser Tsait* (U.S.); *Lebns-Fragn* (Israel); *Unser Gedank* (Australia).

SEPHARDIC JEWISH BROTHERHOOD OF AMERICA, INC. (1915). 97-45 Queens Blvd., Rm. 610, Rego Park, NY 11374. (718)459-1600. Pres. Bernard Ouziel; Sec. Irving Barocas. A benevolent fraternal organization seeking to promote the industrial, social, educational, and religious welfare of its members. *Sephardic Brother.*

THE WORKMEN'S CIRCLE/ARBETER RING (1900). 45 E. 33 St., NYC 10016. (212) 889-6800. FAX: (212)532-7518. E-mail: member@circle.org. Pres. Martin Krupnick; Exec. Dir. Robert Kestenbaum. Fosters Jewish identity and participation in Jewish life through Jewish, especially Yiddish, culture and education, friendship, mutual aid, and the pursuit of social and economic justice. Offices are located throughout the U.S. and Canada. Member services include:Jewish cultural seminars, concerts, theater, Jewish schools, children's camp and adult resort, fraternal and singles activities, a Jewish Book Center, public affairs/social action, health insurance plans, medical/dental/legal services, life insurance plans, cemetery/funeral benefits, social services, geriatric homes and centers, and travel services. *The Call.* (WWW.CIRCLE.ORG)

ZETA BETA TAU FRATERNITY (1898). 3905 Vincennes Rd., Suite 101, Indianapolis, IN 46268. (317)334-1898. FAX: (317)334-1899. E-mail: zbt@zbtnational.org. Pres. Ronald J. Taylor, M.D.; Exec. Dir. Jonathan I. Yulish. Oldest and historically largest Jewish fraternity; promotes intellectual awareness, social responsibility, integrity, and brotherhood among over 5,000 undergrads and 110,000 alumni in the U.S. and Canada. Encourages leadership and diversity through mutual respect of all heritages; nonsectarian since 1954. A brotherhood of Kappa Nu, Phi Alpha, Phi Epsilon Pi, Phi Sigma Delta, Zeta Beta Tau. *The Deltan (quarterly).* (WWW.ZBT.ORG)

SOCIAL WELFARE

AMC CANCER RESEARCH CENTER (formerly JEWISH CONSUMPTIVES' RELIEF SOCIETY, 1904; incorporated as American Medical Center at Denver, 1954). 1600 Pierce St., Denver, CO 80214. (303) 233-6501. FAX: (303)239-3400. E-mail: edelmanj@amc.org. Pres./CEO Bob R. Baker; Exec. V-Pres. Research Dr. Tom Slaga. A nationally recognized leader in the fight against cancer; employs a three-pronged, interdisciplinary approach that combines laboratory, clinical, and community cancer-control research to advance the prevention, early detection, diagnosis, and treatment of the disease. The exclusive scientific focus of our work is the prevention and control of cancer and other major diseases. *The Quest for Answers; Annual Report. (*WWW.AMC.ORG*)*

AMCHA FOR TSEDAKAH (1990). 9800 Cherry Hill Rd., College Park, MD 20740. (301)937-2600. Pres. Rabbi Bruce E. Kahn. Solicits and distributes contributions to Jewish charitable organizations in the U.S. and Israel; accredits organizations which serve an important tsedakah purpose, demonstrate efficiency and fiscal integrity, and also support pluralism. Contributions are encouraged to earmark contributions for specific organizations; all contributions to General Fund are forwarded to the charitable institutions, as operating expenses are covered by a separate fund. *Newspaper supplement.*

AMERICAN JEWISH CORRECTIONAL CHAPLAINS ASSOCIATION, INC. (formerly NATIONAL COUNCIL OF JEWISH PRISON CHAPLAINS) (1937). 10 E. 73 St., NYC 10021-4194. (212)879-8415. FAX: (212) 772-3977. (Cooperates with the New York Board of Rabbis.) Supports spiritual, moral, and social services for Jewish men and women in corrections; stimulates support of correctional chaplaincy; provides spiritual and professional fellowship for Jewish correctional chaplains; promotes sound standards for correctional chaplaincy, schedules workshops and research to aid chaplains in counseling and with religious services for Jewish inmates. Constituent, American Correctional Chaplains Association. *Chaplains Manual.*

AMERICAN JEWISH SOCIETY FOR SERVICE, INC. (1950). 15 E. 26 St., Rm. 1029, NYC 10010. (212)683-6178. Email: aud1750@aol.com. Founder/Chmn. Henry Kohn; Pres. Lawrence G. Green; Exec. Dirs. Carl & Audrey Brenner. Conducts voluntary work-service camps each summer to enable high school juniors and seniors to perform humanitarian service.

ASSOCIATION OF JEWISH AGING SERVICES (formerly NORTH AMERICAN ASSOCIATION OF JEWISH HOMES AND HOUSING FOR THE AGING) (1960). 316 Pennsylvania Ave., SE, Suite 402, Washington, DC 20003. (202) 543-7500. FAX: (202) 543-4090. E-mail: ajas@ajas.org. Pres. Lawrence M. Zippin; Chmn. Ms. Nita Corré. Represents nearly all the not-for-profit charitable homes and housing for the Jewish aging; promotes excellence in performance and quality of service through fostering communication and education and encouraging advocacy for the aging; conducts annual conferences and institutes. *Directory; The Scribe (quarterly newsletter).*

ASSOCIATION OF JEWISH CENTER PROFESSIONALS (1918). 15 E. 26 St., NYC 10010-1579. (212)532-4949. FAX: (212) 481-4174. E-mail: ajcp@jcca.org. Pres. Jodi L.

Lyons; V.-Pres. Susan Bender & David Jacobs; Chmn. Michael J. Ellentuck; Exec. Dir. Joe Harris. Seeks to enhance the standards, techniques, practices, scope, and public understanding of Jewish community center professionals and kindred agency work. *Kesher.*

ASSOCIATION OF JEWISH COMMUNITY ORGANIZATION PERSONNEL (AJCOP) (1969). 14619 Horseshoe Trace, Wellington, FL 33414. (561)795-4853. FAX: (561)798-0358. E-mail: marlene@ajcop.org. Pres. Richard Jacobs; Exec. Dir. Louis B. Solomon. An organization of professionals engaged in areas of fund-raising, endowments, budgeting, social planning, financing, administration, and coordination of services. Objectives are to develop and enhance professional practices in Jewish communal work; to maintain and improve standards, practices, scope, and public understanding of the field of community organization, as practiced through local federations, national agencies, other organizations, settings, and private practitioners. *Prolog (quarterly newspaper); Proceedings (annual record of papers and speeches).* (WWW.AJCOP.ORG)

ASSOCIATION OF JEWISH FAMILY AND CHILDREN'S AGENCIES (1972). 557 Cranbury Rd., Suite 2, E. Brunswick, NJ 08816-5419. (800) 634-7346. FAX: (732)432-7127. E-mail: ajfca@ajfca.org. Pres. Richard K. Blankstein; Exec. V.-Pres. Bert J. Goldberg. The national service organization for Jewish family and children's agencies in the U.S. and Canada. Reinforces member agencies in their efforts to sustain and enhance the quality of Jewish family and communal life. Operates the Elder Support Network for the national Jewish community. *Tachlis (quarterly); Professional Opportunities Bulletin; Executive Digest (monthly).* (WWW.AJFCA.ORG)

BARON DE HIRSCH FUND (1891). 130 E. 59 St., 12th fl., NYC 10022. (212)836-1358. FAX: (212)453-6512. Pres. Joan Morgenthal; Mng. Dir. Lauren Katzowitz. Aids Jewish immigrants in the U.S. and Israel by giving grants to agencies active in educational, community, and vocational fields.

B'NAI B'RITH (1843). 1640 Rhode Island Ave., NW, Washington, DC 20036.

(202)857-6600. FAX: (202)857-1099. Pres. Richard D. Heideman; Exec. V.-Pres. Daniel S. Mariaschin. International Jewish organization, with affiliates in 58 countries. Offers programs designed to ensure the preservation of Jewry and Judaism: Jewish education, community volunteer service, expansion of human rights, assistance to Israel, housing for the elderly, leadership training, rights of Jews in all countries to study their heritage. *International Jewish Monthly; B'nai B'rith Today.*

———, ANTI-DEFAMATION LEAGUE OF (*see* p. 574)

———, HILLEL (*see* p. 604)

———, KLUTZNICK MUSEUM (*see* p. 579)

———, YOUTH ORGANIZATION (*see* p. 693)

CITY OF HOPE NATIONAL MEDICAL CENTER AND BECKMAN RESEARCH INSTITUTE (1913). 1500 E. Duarte Rd., Duarte, CA 91010. (626)359-8111. FAX: (626) 301-8115. E-mail: dhalper@coh.org. Pres./CEO Gil N. Schwartzberg. Offers care to those with cancer and other catastrophic diseases, medical consultation service for second opinions, and research programs in genetics, immunology, and the basic life process. *City of Hope Cancer Research Center Report.*

CONFERENCE OF JEWISH COMMUNAL SERVICE (*see* JEWISH COMMUNAL SERVICE ASSOCIATION OF N. AMERICA)

COUNCIL OF JEWISH FEDERATIONS (*see* UNITED JEWISH COMMUNITIES)

INTERNATIONAL ASSOCIATION OF JEWISH VOCATIONAL SERVICES (formerly JEWISH OCCUPATIONAL COUNCIL) (1939). 1845 Walnut St., Suite 640, Philadelphia, PA 19103. (215) 854-0233. FAX: (215)854-0212. E-mail: coheng@iajus.org. Exec. Dir. Genie Cohen. Not-for-profit trade association of Jewish-sponsored social service agencies in the U.S., Canada, and Israel. Provides member agencies with technical, informational, and communications support; researches funding opportunities, develops collaborative program models, and represents Jewish vocational network nationally and internationally. Sponsors annual conference for members. Member agencies provide a wide range of educational, vocational, and rehabilitation services to both the

Jewish and non-Jewish communities. *Executive quarterly newsletter.* (WWW.IAJVS.ORG)

INTERNATIONAL COUNCIL ON JEWISH SOCIAL AND WELFARE SERVICES (1961). c/o American Jewish Joint Distribution Committee, 711 Third Ave., NYC 10017. (NY liaison office with UN headquarters.) (212)687-6200. FAX: (212)370-5467. E-mail: steve@jdcny.org. Chmn. David Cope-Thompson; Exec. Sec. Eli Benson. Provides for exchange of views and information among member agencies on problems of Jewish social and welfare services, including medical care, old age, welfare, child care, rehabilitation, technical assistance, vocational training, agricultural and other resettlement, economic assistance, refugees, migration, integration, and related problems; representation of views to governments and international organizations. Members:six national and international organizations.

JEWISH BRAILLE INSTITUTE OF AMERICA, INC. (1931). 110 E. 30 St., NYC 10016. (212)889-2525. FAX: (212)689-3692. Pres. Barbara B. Friedman; Exec. V.-Pres. Gerald M. Kass. Provides Judaic materials in braille, talking books, and large print for blind, visually impaired, and reading-disabled; offers counseling for full integration into the life of the Jewish community. International program serves clients in more than 50 countries; sponsors special programs in Israel and Eastern Europe to assist the elderly as well as students. *Jewish Braille Review; JBI Voice; Likutim, Hebrew-language magazine on blindness issues.* (WWW.JEWISHBRAILLE.ORG)

JEWISH CHILDREN'S ADOPTION NETWORK (1990). PO Box 16544, Denver, CO 80216-0544. (303)573-8113. FAX: (303) 893-1447. E-mail: jcan@qwest.net. Pres. Stephen Krausz; Exec. Dir. Vicki Krausz. An adoption exchange founded for the primary purpose of locating adoptive families for Jewish infants and children. Works with some 200 children a year, throughout N. Amer., 85-90% of whom have special needs. No fees charged for services, which include birth-parent and adoptive-parent counseling. *Quarterly newsletter.* (WWW.USERS.QWEST.NET/JCAN)

JEWISH COMMUNAL SERVICE ASSOCIATION OF N. AMERICA (1899; formerly Conference of Jewish Communal Service). 3084 State Hwy. 27, Suite 9, Kendall Park, NJ 08824-1657. (732)821-1871. FAX: (732) 821-5335. E-mail: jcsana@aol.com. Pres. Dr. Ron B. Meier; Exec. Dir. Joel Ollander. Serves as forum for all professional philosophies in community service, for testing new experiences, proposing new ideas, and questioning or reaffirming old concepts; umbrella organization for 7 major Jewish communal service groups. Concerned with advancement of professional personnel practices and standards. *Journal of Jewish Communal Service; Concurrents.*

JEWISH COMMUNITY CENTERS ASSOCIATION OF NORTH AMERICA (formerly JWB) (1917). 15 E. 26 St., NYC 10010-1579. (212)532-4949. FAX: (212)481-4174. E-mail: info@jcca.org. Pres. Allan Finkelstein; Chmn. Jerome B. Makowsky. The leadership network of, and central agency for, the Jewish Community Center movement, comprising more than 275 JCCs, YM-YWHAs, and camps in the U.S. and Canada, which annually serve more than one million members and an additional million non-member users. The JCC Association offers a wide range of services and resources to strengthen the capacity of its affiliates to provide educational, cultural, social, Jewish identity-building, and recreational programs to enhance the lives of North American Jews of all ages and backgrounds. Additionally, the movement fosters and strengthens connections between North American Jews and Israel as well as with world Jewry. JCC Association is also the U.S. government-accredited agency for serving the religious and social needs of Jewish military personnel, their families, and patients in VA hospitals through JWB Chaplains Council. *JCC Circle; Chaplines; other newsletters for JCC professionals.* (WWW.JCCA.ORG)

———, JEWISH WELFARE BOARD JEWISH CHAPLAINS COUNCIL (formerly COMMISSION ON JEWISH CHAPLAINCY) (1940). 15 E. 26 St., NYC 10010-1579. (212) 532-4949. FAX: (212)481-4174. E-mail: nathanlandman@jcca.com. Chmn. Rabbi Jacob J. Greenberg; Dir. Rabbi David Lapp; Dep. Dir. Rabbi Nathan M. Landman. Recruits, endorses, and serves Jewish military and Veterans Administration chaplains on behalf of the American Jewish community and the major rabbinic bodies; trains and assists Jewish lay leaders where there are no chaplains, for service to Jewish military personnel, their families, and hospitalized veterans. *CHAPLINES newsletter.*

JEWISH FAMILY AND CHILDREN'S PROFESSIONALS ASSOCIATION (*see* JEWISH SOCIAL SERVICES PROFESSIONALS ASSOCIATION)

JEWISH FUND FOR JUSTICE (1984). 260 Fifth Ave., Suite 701, NYC 10001. (212)213-2113. FAX: (212)213-2233. E-mail: jfjustice@jfjustice.org. Bd. Chmn. John Levy; Exec. Dir. Marlene Provizer. A national grant-making foundation supporting efforts to combat the causes and consequences of poverty in the U.S. Provides diverse opportunities for giving, including family and youth endowment funds and the Purim Fund for Women in Poverty; develops educational materials linking Jewish teachings and rituals with contemporary social justice issues; supports Jewish involvement in community-based anti-poverty efforts; and works cooperatively with other denominational and social change philanthropies. *Annual report, newsletter.* (WWW.JFJUSTICE.ORG)

JEWISH FUNDERS NETWORK (1990). 15 E. 26 St., Suite 1038, NYC 10010. (212) 726-0177. FAX: (212) 726-0195. E-mail: jfn@jfunders.org. Exec. Dir. Evan Mendelson. A national membership organization dedicated to advancing the growth and quality of Jewish philanthropy through more effective grant making to Jewish and secular causes. Individual philanthropists, foundation trustees, and foundation staff discuss emerging issues, gain expertise in operational aspects of grant making, explore intergenerational/family dynamics of family foundations, and exchange information among peers. *Quarterly Newsletter; Special Reports on Philanthropy.* (WWW.JFUNDERS. ORG)

JEWISH SOCIAL SERVICES PROFESSIONALS ASSOCIATION (JSSPA) (1965). c/o AJFCA, 557 Cranbury Rd., Suite 2, E. Brunswick, NJ 08816-0549. (800) 634-7346. FAX: (732)432-7127. E-mail: ajfca@ajfca.org. Chmn. Linda Kislowicz. Brings together executives, supervisors, managers, caseworkers, and related professionals in Jewish Family Service and related agencies. Seeks to enhance pro-

fessional skills, improve personnel standards, further Jewish continuity and identity, and strengthen Jewish family life. Provides a national and regional forum for professional discussion and learning; functions under the auspices of the Association of Jewish Family and Children's Agencies. *Newsletter.* (WWW.AJFCA.ORG)

JEWISH WOMEN INTERNATIONAL (1897). 1828 L St., NW, Suite 250, Washington, DC 20036. (202)857-1300. FAX: (202) 857-1380. E-mail: jwi@jwi.org. Pres. Barbara Rabkin; Exec. Dir. Gail Rubinson. Jewish Women International breaks the cycle of violence by developing emotionally healthy adults, empowering women and strengthening families. Jewish Women International accomplishes its goals through direct service programs, education, advocacy and the promotion of "best practice" models. Offers programs in the United States, Canada, and Israel. *Jewish Woman Magazine (quarterly).* (WWW.JEWISHWOMEN.ORG)

JWB (*see* JEWISH COMMUNITY CENTERS ASSOCIATION OF NORTH AMERICA)

LEVI HOSPITAL (sponsored by B'nai B'rith) (1914). 300 Prospect Ave., Hot Springs, AR 71901. (501)624-1281. FAX: (501) 622-3500. E-mail: levihospital @hsnp.com. Pres. Philip M. Clay; Admin. Patrick G. McCabe. Offers outpatient rehab, including therapy sessions in large thermal heated pool. Other programs: adult/geriatric inpatient and outpatient psychiatric program, child/adolescent psychiatric clinic, hospice care, home health care, osteoporosis clinic, Levi Rehabilitation Unit, a cooperative effort of Levi and St. Joseph's hospitals (inpatient rehab). *The Progress Chart; The Legacy.*

MAZON: A JEWISH RESPONSE TO HUNGER (1985). 12401 Wilshire Blvd., Suite 303, Los Angeles, CA 90025. (310)442-0020. FAX: (310)442-0030. E-mail: mazonmail @aol.com. Bd. Chmn. Daniel Levenson; Exec. Dir. H. Eric Schockman, PhD. A grant-making and fund-raising organization that raises funds in the Jewish community and provides grants to nonprofit 501(c)(3) organizations which aim to prevent and alleviate hunger in the United States and abroad. Grantees include food pantries, food banks, multi-service organizations, advocacy, education and research projects, and international relief and development organizations. 1998 grants totaled $2.3 million. *Mazon Newsletter.*

NATIONAL ASSOCIATION OF JEWISH CHAPLAINS (1988). 901 Route 10, Whippany, NJ 07981. (973)884-4800 ext. 287. FAX: (973) 736-9193. E-mail: cecille3@juno. com. Pres. Rabbi Solomon Schiff; Natl. Coord. Cecille Allman Asekoff. A professional organization for people functioning as Jewish chaplains in hospitals, nursing homes, geriatric, psychiatric, correctional, and military facilities. Provides collegial support, continuing education, professional certification, and resources for the Jewish community on issues of pastoral and spiritual care. *The Jewish Chaplain.*

NATIONAL COUNCIL OF JEWISH PRISON CHAPLAINS, INC. (*see* AMERICAN JEWISH CORRECTIONAL CHAPLAINS ASSOCIATION, INC.)

NATIONAL COUNCIL OF JEWISH WOMEN (1893). 53 W. 23 St., NYC 10010. (212)645-4048. FAX: (212)645-7466. E-mail: actionline@ncjw.org. Pres. Jan Schneiderman; Exec. Dir. Susan Katz. Works to improve the lives of women, children, and families in the United States and Israel; strives to insure individual rights and freedoms for all. NCJW volunteers deliver vital services in 500 U.S. communities and carry out NCJW's advocacy agenda through a powerful grassroots network. *NCJW Journal; Washington Newsletter.* (WWW.NCJW.ORG)

NATIONAL INSTITUTE FOR JEWISH HOSPICE (1985). PO Box 48025, Los Angeles, CA 90048. (800)446-4448. 330 Broad Ave., Englewood, NJ 07631. (201)816-7324. FAX: (201)816-7321. Pres. Rabbi Maurice Lamm; Exec. Dir. Shirley Lamm. Serves as a national Jewish hospice resource center. Through conferences, research, publications, referrals, and counseling services offers guidance, training, and information to patients, family members, clergy of all faiths, professional caregivers, and volunteers who work with the Jewish terminally ill. *Jewish Hospice Times.*

NATIONAL JEWISH CHILDREN'S LEUKEMIA FOUNDATION (1990). 172 Madison Avenue, NYC 10016. (212)686-2722. FAX: (212)686-2750. E-mail: leukemia@erols. com. Pres./Founder Zvi Shor. Dedicated to saving the lives of children. Programs:Bone Marrow Donor Search, Stem Cell Banking-freezing cells from babies' umbilical cords for long-term storage, in case of need for bone marrow; Make-A-Dream-Come True-granting wishes for terminally ill children; Referral Service; Patient Advocacy. (WWW.LEUKEMIAFOUNDATION.ORG)

NATIONAL JEWISH MEDICAL AND RESEARCH CENTER (formerly NATIONAL JEWISH HOSPITAL/NATIONAL ASTHMA CENTER) (1899). 1400 Jackson St., Denver, CO 80206. (800)222-LUNG. E-mail: lungline@njc.org. Pres./CEO Lynn M. Taussig, MD; Bd. Chmn. Lawrence Gelfond. The only medical and research center in the United States devoted entirely to respiratory, allergic, and immune system diseases, including asthma, tuberculosis, emphysema, severe allergies, AIDS, and cancer, and autoimmune diseases such as lupus. Dedicated to enhancing prevention, treatment, and cures through research, and to developing and providing innovative clinical programs for treating patients regardless of age, religion, race, or ability to pay. *New Directions; Medical Scientific Update.*(WWW.NATIONALJEWISH. ORG)

NORTH AMERICAN ASSOCIATION OF JEWISH HOMES AND HOUSING FOR THE AGING (*see* ASSOCIATION OF JEWISH AGING SERVICES)

UNITED JEWISH COMMUNITIES (see p. 000)

UNITED ORDER TRUE SISTERS, INC. (UOTS) (1846). 100 State St., Albany, NY 12207. (518)436-1670. Pres. Kathleen Fugazzi; Fin. Sec. Betty Peyser; Treas. Rose Goldberg. Charitable, community service, especially home supplies, etc., for indigent cancer victims; supports camps for children with cancer. *Inside UotS.*

WORLD COUNCIL OF JEWISH COMMUNAL SERVICE (1966; reorg. 1994). 711 Third Ave., 10th fl., NYC 10017. (212)687-6200. FAX: (212)370-5467. Pres. Howard Charish; Assoc. Pres. Dr. Jack Habib; Exec. V.-Pres. Theodore Comet. Seeks to build Jewish community worldwide by enhancing professional-to-professional connections, improving professional practice through interchange of experience and sharing of expertise, fostering professional training programs, and stimulating research. Conducts quadrennial conferences in Jerusalem and periodic regional meetings. *Proceedings of international conferences; newsletters.*

PROFESSIONAL ASSOCIATIONS*

AMERICAN ASSOCIATION OF RABBIS (Religious, Educational)

AMERICAN CONFERENCE OF CANTORS, UNION OF AMERICAN HEBREW CONGREGATIONS (Religious, Educational)

AMERICAN JEWISH CORRECTIONAL CHAPLAINS ASSOCIATION, INC. (Social Welfare)

AMERICAN JEWISH PRESS ASSOCIATION (Cultural)

AMERICAN JEWISH PUBLIC RELATIONS SOCIETY (Community Relations)

ASSOCIATION OF HILLEL/JEWISH CAMPUS PROFESSIONALS (Religious, Educational)

ASSOCIATION OF JEWISH CENTER PROFESSIONALS (Social Welfare)

ASSOCIATION OF JEWISH COMMUNITY ORGANIZATION PERSONNEL (Social Welfare)

ASSOCIATION OF JEWISH COMMUNITY RELATIONS WORKERS (Community Relations)

CANTORS ASSEMBLY (RELIGIOUS, EDUCATIONAL)

CENTRAL CONFERENCE OF AMERICAN RABBIS (Religious, Educational)

COUNCIL OF JEWISH ORGANIZATIONS IN CIVIL SERVICE (Community Relations)

INTERNATIONAL JEWISH MEDIA ASSOCIATION (Cultural)

JEWISH CHAPLAINS COUNCIL, JWB (Social Welfare)

JEWISH COMMUNAL SERVICE ASSOCIATION OF N. AMERICA (Social Welfare)

JEWISH EDUCATORS ASSEMBLY, UNITED SYNAGOGUE OF CONSERVATIVE JUDAISM (Religious, Educational)

JEWISH SOCIAL SERVICES PROFESSIONALS ASSOCIATION (Social Welfare)

JEWISH TEACHERS ASSOCIATION–MORIM (Religious, Educational)

NATIONAL ASSOCIATION OF HEBREW DAY SCHOOL ADMINISTRATORS, TORAH UMESORAH (Religious, Educational)

NATIONAL ASSOCIATION OF JEWISH CHAPLAINS (Social Welfare)

NATIONAL ASSOCIATION OF TEMPLE ADMINISTRATORS, UNION OF AMERICAN HEBREW CONGREGATIONS (Religious, Educational)

NATIONAL ASSOCIATION OF TEMPLE EDUCATORS, UNION OF AMERICAN HEBREW CONGREGATIONS (Religious, Educational)

NATIONAL CONFERENCE OF YESHIVA PRINCIPALS, TORAH UMESORAH (Religious, Educational)

NORTH AMERICAN ASSOCIATION OF SYNAGOGUE EXECUTIVES, UNITED SYNAGOGUE OF CONSERVATIVE JUDAISM (Religious, Educational)

RABBINICAL ALLIANCE OF AMERICA (Religious, Educational)

RABBINICAL ASSEMBLY (Religious, Educational)

RABBINICAL COUNCIL OF AMERICA (Religious, Educational)

RECONSTRUCTIONIST RABBINICAL ASSOCIATION (Religious, Educational)

UNION OF ORTHODOX RABBIS OF THE U.S. AND CANADA (Religious, Educational)

WORLD CONFERENCE OF JEWISH COMMUNAL SERVICE (Community Relations)

WOMEN'S ORGANIZATIONS*

AMIT WOMEN (Israel-Related)

BRANDEIS UNIVERSITY NATIONAL WOMEN'S COMMITTEE (Educational)

EMUNAH WOMEN OF AMERICA (Israel-Related)

HADASSAH, THE WOMEN'S ZIONIST ORGANIZATION OF AMERICA (Israel-Related)

JEWISH WOMEN INTERNATIONAL (Social Welfare)

NA'AMAT USA, THE WOMEN'S LABOR ZIONIST ORGANIZATION OF AMERICA (Israel-Related)

NATIONAL COUNCIL OF JEWISH WOMEN (Social Welfare)

UOTS (SOCIAL WELFARE)

---

*For fuller listings see under categories in parentheses.

WOMEN OF REFORM JUDAISM—FEDERATION OF TEMPLE SISTERHOODS, UNION OF AMERICAN HEBREW CONGREGATIONS (Religious, Educational)

WOMEN'S AMERICAN ORT, AMERICAN ORT FEDERATION (Overseas Aid)

WOMEN'S BRANCH OF THE UNION OF ORTHODOX JEWISH CONGREGATIONS OF AMERICA (Religious, Educational)

WOMEN'S DIVISION OF POALE AGUDATH ISRAEL OF AMERICA (Israel-Related)

WOMEN'S LEAGUE FOR CONSERVATIVE JUDAISM (Religious, Educational)

WOMEN'S LEAGUE FOR ISRAEL, INC. (Israel-Related)

WOMEN'S ORGANIZATION, YESHIVA UNIVERSITY (Religious, Educational)

YOUTH AND STUDENT ORGANIZATIONS*

AGUDATH ISRAEL OF AMERICA (Religious, Educational)

B'NAI B'RITH YOUTH ORGANIZATION (Religious, Educational)

BNEI AKIVA OF NORTH AMERICA, RELIGIOUS ZIONISTS OF AMERICA (Israel-Related)

HABONIM—DROR NORTH AMERICA (Israel-Related)

HASHOMER HATZAIR, SOCIALIST ZIONIST YOUTH MOVEMENT (Israel-Related)

HILLEL (Religious, Educational)

KADIMA, UNITED SYNAGOGUE OF CONSERVATIVE JUDAISM (Religious, Educational)

NATIONAL CONFERENCE OF SYNAGOGUE YOUTH, UNION OF ORTHODOX JEWISH CONGREGATIONS OF AMERICA (Religious, Educational)

NATIONAL JEWISH COMMITTEE ON SCOUTING (Religious, Educational)

NATIONAL JEWISH GIRL SCOUT COMMITTEE (Religious, Educational)

NORTH AMERICAN ALLIANCE FOR JEWISH YOUTH (Religious, Educational)

NORTH AMERICAN FEDERATION OF TEMPLE YOUTH, UNION OF AMERICAN HEBREW CONGREGATIONS (Religious, Educational)

STUDENT STRUGGLE FOR SOVIET JEWRY— see CENTER FOR RUSSIAN JEWRY (Community Relations)

YOUNG JUDAEA/HASHACHAR, HADASSAH (Israel-Related)

YUGNTRUF–YOUTH FOR YIDDISH (Cultural)

CANADA

AISH HATORAH (1981). 949 Clark Ave., W., Thornhill, ONT L4J8G6. (905)764-1818. FAX: (905)764-1606. E-mail: toronto@aish.com. Pres. Harold Nashman; Edu. Dir. Rabbi Ahron Hoch. An educational center, a community center, and a network of synagogues throughout Toronto; seeks to reawaken Jewish values, ignite Jewish pride and promote Jewish unity through education; reaches out to Jews from all backgrounds in a friendly, warm and non-judgmental environment. *Shabbat Shalom Fax.* (www. AISH.EDU).

B'NAI BRITH CANADA (1875). 15 Hove St., Downsview, ONT M3H 4Y8. (416) 633-6224. FAX: (416)630-2159. E-mail: faimant@bnaibrith.ca. Pres. Dr. Allan Seidenfeld; Exec. V.-Pres. Frank Dimant. Canadian Jewry's major advocacy and service organization; maintains an office of Government Relations in Ottawa and co-sponsors the Canada Israel Committee; makes representations to all levels of government on matters of Jewish concern; promotes humanitarian causes and educational programs, community projects, adult Jewish education, and leadership development; dedicated to the preservation and unity of the Jewish community in Canada and to human rights. *The Jewish Tribune.*

———, INSTITUTE FOR INTERNATIONAL AFFAIRS (1987). E-mail: institute@bnaibrith.ca. Ch. Rochelle Wilner; Natl. Dir. Ruth Klein. Identifies and protests the abuse of human rights worldwide. Advocates on behalf of Israel and Jewish communities in distress. Monitors national and international legislation dealing with war crimes. Activities include briefs and consultations with governmental and non-governmental organizations, research and public education, advocacy and community mobilization, media monitoring, and international confer-

---

*For fuller listings see under categories in parentheses.

ences and fact-finding missions. *Ad hoc publications on human rights issues.*

————, LEAGUE FOR HUMAN RIGHTS (1964). Co-Chmn. Marvin Kurz & Dr Harriet Morris. National volunteer association dedicated to combating racism, bigotry, and anti-Semitism. Educational programs include multicultural antiracist workshops, public speakers, Holocaust education, Media Human Rights Awards; legal and legislative activity includes government submissions, court interventions, monitoring hate-group activity, responding to incidents of racism and anti-Semitism; community liaison includes intergroup dialogue and support for aggrieved vulnerable communities and groups. Canadian distributor of ADL material. *Heritage Front Report: 1994; Anti-Semitism on Campus; Skinheads in Canada; Annual Audit of Anti-Semitic Incidents; Holocaust and Hope Educators' Newsletter; Combatting Hate: Guidelines for Community Action.*

————, NATIONAL FIELD SERVICES DEPARTMENT. Natl. Dir. Pearl Gladman. Services community affordable housing projects, sports leagues, food baskets for the needy; coordinates hands-on national volunteer programming, Tel-Aide Distress Line; responsible for lodge membership; direct-mail campaigns, annual convention and foundation dinners.

CANADIAN FRIENDS OF CALI & AMAL (1944). 7005 Kildare Rd., Suite 14, Côte St. Luc, Quebec, H4W 1C1. (514)484-9430. FAX: (514)484-0968. Pres. Harry J.F. Bloomfield, QC; Exec. Dir. Fran Kula. Incorporates Canadian Association for Labour Israel (Histadrut) and Canadian Friends of Amal; supports comprehensive health care and education in Israel. Helps to provide modern medical and surgical facilities and the finest vocational, technical education to the Israeli people of all ages.

CANADIAN FRIENDS OF THE HEBREW UNIVERSITY OF JERUSALEM (1944). 3080 Yonge St., Suite 5024, Toronto, ONT M4N 3N1. (416) 485-8000. FAX: (416) 485-8565. E-mail: inquiry@cfhu.org. Pres. Dr. Charles C. Gold; Natl. Dir. Charles S. Diamond. Represents the Hebrew University of Jerusalem in Canada; serves as fund-raising arm for the university in Canada; recruits Canadian students and promotes study programs for foreign students at the university; sponsors social and educational events across Canada.

CANADIAN JEWISH CONGRESS (1919; reorg. 1934). 100 Sparks Street, Ottawa, Ontario K1P 5B7. (613)233-8703. FAX: (613)233-8748. E-mail: canadianjewishcongress @cjc.ca. Pres. Moshe Ronen; Exec. V. Pres. Jack Silverstone; Natl. Exec. Dir./Genl. Counsel Jack Silverstone. The community's national voice on public affairs, Canadian Jewish Congress works with governments, community organizations and other partners to fight anti-semitism and racism, to promote positive links to Israel and to other Jewish communities, and to support humanitarian and human rights efforts. *National Small Communities Newsletter; DAIS; National Archives Newsletter; regional newsletters.*

CANADIAN YOUNG JUDAEA (1917). 788 Marlee Ave., Suite 205, Toronto, ONT M6B 3K1. (416)781-5156. FAX: (416) 787-3100. E-mail: cyj@idirect.com Natl. Shaliach Ryan Hass; Eastern Region Shaliach Yossi Cadan; Natl. Exec. Dir. Risa Epstein. Strives to attract Jewish youth to Zionism, with goal of aliyah; educates youth about Jewish history and Zionism; prepares them to provide leadership in Young Judaea camps in Canada and Israel and to be concerned Jews. *Judaean L'Madrich; Young Judaean.*

CANADIAN ZIONIST FEDERATION (1967). 5151 Côte St. Catherine Rd., #206, Montreal, PQ H3W 1M6. (514)739-7300. FAX: (514)739-9412. Pres. Kurt Rothschild; Natl. Sec. Florence Simon. Umbrella organization of distinct constituent member Zionist organizations in Canada; carries on major activities in all areas of Jewish life through its departments of education and culture, aliyah, youth and students, public affairs, and small Jewish communities, for the purpose of strengthening the State of Israel and the Canadian Jewish community. *Canadian Zionist.*

————, BUREAU OF EDUCATION AND CULTURE (1972). Pres. Kurt Rothschild. Provides counseling by pedagogic experts, in-service teacher-training courses and seminars in Canada and Israel; national pedagogic council and research center; distributes educational material and teaching aids; supports annual Bible contest and Hebrew-language courses for adults; awards scholarships to Canadian high-school graduates studying for one year in Israel.

FRIENDS OF PIONEERING ISRAEL (1950s). 1111 Finch Ave. W., Suite 456, Downsview, ONT M3J 2E5. (416)736-1339. FAX: (416)736-1405. Pres. Joseph Podemski. Acts as a voice of Socialist-Democratic and Zionist points of view within the Jewish community and a focal point for progressive Zionist elements in Canada; Canadian representative of Meretz; affiliated with Hashomer Hatzair and the Givat Haviva Educational Center.

HADASSAH–WIZO ORGANIZATION OF CANADA (1917). 1310 Greene Ave., Suite 900, Montreal, PQ H3Z 2B8. (514)937-9431. FAX: (514)933-6483. E-mail: natoff@canadian-hadassah-wizo.org. Natl. Pres. Marion Mayman; Natl. Exec. V.-Pres. Lily Frank. Largest women's volunteer Zionist organization in Canada, located in 43 Canadian cities; dedicated to advancing the quality of life of the women and children in Israel through financial assistance and support of its many projects, day-care centers, schools, institutions, and hospitals. In Canada, the organization promotes Canadian ideals of democracy and is a stalwart advocate of women's issues. *Orah Magazine.*

HASHOMER HATZAIR (1913). 1111 Finch Ave. W., #456, Downsview, ONT M3J 2E5. (416)736-1339. FAX: (416)736-1405. E-mail: mail@givathaviva.com. Shaliach Noam Massad; Exec. Off. Mintzy Clement. Zionist youth movement associated with the Kibbutz Artzi Federation in Israel. Educational activities emphasize Jewish culture and identity as well as the kibbutz lifestyle and values; runs winter and summer camps as well as programs in Israel.

INTERNATIONAL JEWISH CORRESPONDENCE (IJC) (1978). c/o Canadian Jewish Congress, 1590 Dr. Penfield Ave., Montreal, PQ H3G 1C5.9 (514)931-7531. FAX: (514)931-0548. E-mail: barrys@cjc.ca. Founder/Dir. Barry Simon. Aims to encourage contact between Jews of all ages and backgrounds, in all countries, through pen-pal correspondence. Send autobiographical data and stamped self-addressed envelope or its equivalent (to cover cost of Canadian postage) to receive addresses.

JEWISH IMMIGRANT AID SERVICES OF MONTREAL (JIAS) (1922). Decarie Square, 6900 Decarie, Suite 217A, Côte St Luc, Quebec, H3X 2T8. (514)342-9351. FAX: (514)342-8452. E-mail: jiasmail@aol.com. Pres. Barry Silverman; Exec. Dir. Bob Luck; Coord. Edna Mendelson. JIAS is a national organization assisting the lawful entry of Jews into Canada, as well as their settlement and integration. *JIAS News for Clients.*

JEWISH NATIONAL FUND OF CANADA (Keren Kayemeth Le'Israel, Inc.) (1901). 1980 Sherbrooke St. W., Suite 500, Montreal, PQ H3H 1E8. (514)934-0313. FAX: (514)934-0382. Natl. Pres. Naomi Frankenburg; Exec. V.-Pres. Avner Regev. Fundraising organization affiliated with the World Zionist Organization; involved in afforestation, soil reclamation, and development of the land of Israel, including the construction of roads and preparation of sites for new settlements; provides educational materials and programs to Jewish schools across Canada.

LABOUR ZIONIST ALLIANCE OF CANADA (1909). 272 Codsell Ave., Downsview, ONT M3H 3X2. (416)630-9444. FAX: (416)630-9451. Pres. Josef Krystal; City Committee Chmn. Montreal-Harry Froimovitch. Associated with the World Labor Zionist movement and allied with the Israel Labor party. Provides recreational and cultural programs, mutual aid, and fraternal care to enhance the social welfare of its membership; actively promotes Zionist education, cultural projects, and forums on aspects of Jewish and Canadian concern.

MIZRACHI ORGANIZATION OF CANADA (1941). 296 Wilson Ave., North York, ONT M3H 1S8. (416)630-9266. FAX: (416)630-2305. Pres. Jack Kahn. Promotes religious Zionism, aimed at making Israel a state based on Torah; maintains Bnei Akiva, a summer camp, adult education program, and touring department; supports Mizrachi-Hapoel Hamizrachi and other religious Zionist institutions in Israel which strengthen traditional Judaism. *Mizrachi Newsletter.*

NATIONAL COMMUNITY RELATIONS COMMITTEE OF CANADIAN JEWISH CONGRESS

(1936). 4600 Bathurst St., Willowdale, Toronto, ONT M2R 3V2. (416)631-5673. FAX: (416)635-1408. E-mail: mprutschi @ujafed.org. Chmn. Mark S. Weintraub; Pres. Moshe Ronen; Dir. Manuel Prutschi. Seeks to safeguard the status, rights, and welfare of Jews in Canada; to combat anti-Semitism, and promote understanding and goodwill among all ethnic and religious groups.

NATIONAL COUNCIL OF JEWISH WOMEN OF CANADA (1897). 118-1588 Main St., Winnipeg, MAN R2V 1Y3. (204)339-9700. FAX: (204)334-3779. E-mail: info@ ncjwc.org. Chmn. Carol Slater; Natl. V.-Pres. Roz Fine & Brenlee Gurvey Gales. Dedicated to furthering human welfare in the Jewish and general communities, locally, nationally, and internationally; through an integrated program of education, service, and social action seeks to fulfill unmet needs and to serve the individual and the community. *National By-Lines.*

ORT CANADA (1948). 3101 Bathurst St., Suite 604, Toronto, ONT M6A 2A6. (416)787-0339. FAX: (416) 787-9420. E-mail: ortcan@pathcom.com. Pres. Dr. Roger Korman; Exec. Dir. Joel Shapiro; Admin. Beverley Schneider. Chapters in 11 Canadian cities raise funds for ORT's nonprofit global network of schools where Jewish students learn a wide range of marketable skills, including the most advanced high-tech professions. *Focus Magazine.*

STATE OF ISRAEL BONDS (CANADA-ISRAEL SECURITIES, LTD.) (1953). 970 Lawrence Ave. W., Suite 502, Toronto, ONT M6A 3B6. (416)789-3351. FAX: (416)789-9436. Pres. Norman Spector; Bd. Chmn. George A. Cohon. An international securities organization offering interest-bearing instruments issued by the government of Israel. Invests in every aspect of Israel's economy, including agriculture, commerce, and industry. Israel Bonds are RRSP-approved.

Jewish Federations, Welfare Funds, Community Councils

ALABAMA

BIRMINGHAM

BIRMINGHAM JEWISH FEDERATION (1936; reorg. 1971); PO Box 130219. (35213-0219); (205)879-0416. FAX: (205)803-1526. E-mail: federation@bjf.org.

MOBILE

MOBILE JEWISH WELFARE FUND, INC. (inc. 1966); One Office Park, Suite 219 (36609); (334)343-7197. FAX: (334)343-7197. E-mail: mjwf123@aol.com. Pres. Eileen Susman.

MONTGOMERY

JEWISH FEDERATION OF MONTGOMERY, INC. (1930); 2820 Fairlane Dr. (36120-0058); (334)277-5820. FAX: (334)277-8383. E-mail: jfedmgm@aol.com. Pres. Alan Weil; Admin. Dir. Susan Mayer Bruchis.

ARIZONA

PHOENIX

JEWISH FEDERATION OF GREATER PHOENIX (1940); 32 W. Coolidge, Suite 200 (85013); (602)274-1800. FAX: (602)266-7875. E-mail: info@jewishphoenix.org. Pres. Neil Hiller; Exec. Dir. Arthur Paikowsky.

TUCSON

JEWISH FEDERATION OF SOUTHERN ARIZONA (1946); 3822 East River Rd., Suite 100 (85718); (520)577-9393. FAX: (520)577-0734. E-mail: jfink@jfsa.org. Pres. Linda Tumarkin; Exec. Dir. Stuart Mellan.

ARKANSAS

LITTLE ROCK

JEWISH FEDERATION OF ARKANSAS (1911); 425 N. University (72205); (501)663-3571. FAX: (501)663-7286. E-mail: jflar@aristotle.net. Pres. Doris Krain; Exec. Dir. Ziva Starr.

CALIFORNIA

EAST BAY

JEWISH FEDERATION OF THE GREATER EAST BAY (INCLUDING ALAMEDA & CONTRA COSTA COUNTIES) (1917); 401 Grand Ave., Oakland (94610-5022); (510)839-2900. FAX: (510)839-3996. E-mail: admin@jfed. org. Pres. Jerry Yanowitz; Exec. V.-Pres. Ami Nahshon.

FRESNO

JEWISH FEDERATION OF FRESNO; 295 W. CROMWELL AVE., SUITE 111 (93711-6161); (559)432-2162. FAX: (559)432-0425.

LONG BEACH

JEWISH FEDERATION OF GREATER LONG BEACH AND W. ORANGE COUNTY (1937; inc. 1946); 3801 E. Willow St. (90815); (562)426-7601. FAX: (562)424-3915. E-mail: kgibbs@ jewishlongbeach.org. Pres. Richard Lipeles; Exec. Dir. Michael S. Rassler.

LOS ANGELES

JEWISH FEDERATION COUNCIL OF GREATER LOS ANGELES (1912; reorg. 1959); 6505 Wilshire Blvd., 8th fl. (90048); (323)761-

8000. FAX: (323)761-8235. E-mail: webco-ordinator@jewishla.org. Pres. Lionel Bell; Exec. V.-Pres. John Fishel.

ORANGE COUNTY

JEWISH FEDERATION OF ORANGE COUNTY (1964; inc. 1965); 250 Baker St., Suite A, Costa Mesa (92626); (714)755-5555. FAX: (714)755-0307. E-mail: info@jfoc.org. Pres. Charles Karp; Exec. Dir. Bunnie Mauldin.

PALM SPRINGS

JEWISH FEDERATION OF PALM SPRINGS AND DESERT AREA (1971); 255 N. El Cielo, Suite 430 (92262-6990); (760)325-7281. FAX: (760)325-2188. E-mail: msjfedps@gte.net. Pres. Larry Pitts; Exec. Dir. Mitzi Schafer.

SACRAMENTO

JEWISH FEDERATION OF THE SACRAMENTO REGION (1948); 2351 Wyda Way (95825); (916)486-0906. FAX: (916)486-0816. E-mail: jfed2@juno.com. Pres. Skip Rosenbloom; Exec. Dir. Phillis Helene Cohen.

SAN DIEGO

UNITED JEWISH FEDERATION OF SAN DIEGO COUNTY (1936); 4797 Mercury St. (92111-2102); (858)571-3444. FAX: (858)571-0701. E-mail: fedujf@ujfsd.org. Pres. Mary Ann Scher; Exec. V.-Pres. Stephen M. Abramson.

SAN FRANCISCO

JEWISH COMMUNITY FEDERATION OF SAN FRANCISCO, THE PENINSULA, MARIN, AND SONOMA COUNTIES (1910; reorg. 1955); 121 Steuart St. (94105); (415)777-0411. FAX: (415)495-6635. Pres. John Goldman; Exec. V.-Pres. Phyllis Cook.

SAN GABRIEL AND POMONA VALLEYS

JEWISH FEDERATION OF THE GREATER SAN GABRIEL AND POMONA VALLEYS; 258 W. Badillo St. (91723-1906); (626)967-3656. FAX: (626)967-5135. E-mail: sgpvfed@aol. com.

SAN JOSE

JEWISH FEDERATION OF GREATER SAN JOSE (incl. Santa Clara County except Palo Alto and Los Altos) (1930; reorg. 1950); 14855 Oka Rd., Suite 2, Los Gatos (95030); (408)358-3033. FAX: (408)356-0733. E-mail: federation@jfgsj.org. Pres. Howard May; Exec. Dir. Jon Friedenberg.

SANTA BARBARA

SANTA BARBARA JEWISH FEDERATION (1974); 524 Chapala St. (93190); (805)957-1115. FAX: (805)957-9230. E-mail: sb-jfed@silcom.com. Pres. Jeri Eigner; Exec. Dir. Shelly Katz.

VENTURA COUNTY

JEWISH FEDERATION OF VENTURA COUNTY; 7620 Foothill Rd. (93004); (805)647-7800. FAX: (805)647-0482. E-mail: ujavtacty@ worldnet.att.net.

COLORADO

DENVER/BOULDER

ALLIED JEWISH FEDERATION OF COLORADO (1936); 300 S. Dahlia St., Denver (80222); (303)321-3399. FAX: (303)322-8328. E-mail: ajfcolo@aol.com. Chmn. Edward A. Robinson; Pres. & CEO:Steve Gelfand.

CONNECTICUT

BRIDGEPORT

JEWISH FEDERATION OF EASTERN FAIR-FIELD COUNTY. (1936; reorg. 1981); 4200 Park Ave. (06604-1092); (203)372-6567. FAX: (203)374-0770. E-mail: jccs@snet.net. Chmn. Stanley Strouch; Pres. & CEO Daniel P. Baker.

DANBURY

THE JEWISH FEDERATION OF GREATER DANBURY, INC. (1945); 105 Newton Rd. (06810); (203)792-6353. FAX: (203)748-5099. Pres. Daniel Wolinsky; Exec. Dir. Judy Prager.

EASTERN CONNECTICUT

JEWISH FEDERATION OF EASTERN CON-NECTICUT, INC. (1950; inc. 1970); 28 Channing St., New London (06320); (860)442-8062. FAX: (860)443-4175. E-mail: jfec@ worldnet.att.net. Pres. Myron Hendel; Exec. Dir. Jerome E. Fischer.

GREENWICH

GREENWICH JEWISH FEDERATION (1956); One Holly Hill Lane (06830-6080); (203)622-1434. FAX: (203)622-1237. E-mail: pezmom3@aol.com. Pres. Jonathan Nelson; Exec. Dir. Pam Zur.

HARTFORD

JEWISH FEDERATION OF GREATER HART-FORD (1945); 333 Bloomfield Ave., W. Hartford (06117); (860)232-4483. FAX:

(860)232-5221. E-mail: aperrault@jewish-hartford.org. Pres. Henry M. Zachs; Acting Exec. Dir. Steven Bayer.

NEW HAVEN

JEWISH FEDERATION OF GREATER NEW HAVEN (1928); 360 Amity Rd., Woodbridge (06525); (203)387-2424. FAX: (203)387-1818. E-mail: marinak@megahits.com Pres. David Schaefer; Exec. Dir. Neil Berro.

NORWALK
(See Westport)

STAMFORD

UNITED JEWISH FEDERATION (inc. 1973); 1035 Newfield Ave., PO Box 3038 (06905); (203)321-1373. FAX: (203)322-3277. E-mail: office@ujf.org. Pres. Corrine Lotstein; Dir. of Dev. Edith Samers.

WATERBURY

JEWISH FEDERATION OF WESTERN CONNECTICUT (1938); 73 Main St. S., Box F, Woodbury (06798-3404); (203)263-5121. FAX: (203)263-5143. E-mail: jfedwtby@aol.com. Pres. Dan Goodman; Exec. Dir. Rob Zwang.

WESTPORT-WESTON-WILTON-NORWALK

UJA/FEDERATION OF WESTPORT—WESTON—WILTON—NORWALK (inc. 1980); 431 Post Road E., Suite 22, Westport (06880); (203)226-8197. FAX: (203)226-5051. E-mail: rkessler@optonline.net. Pres. Sandra Lefkowitz; Exec. Dir. Robert Kessler.

DELAWARE

WILMINGTON

JEWISH FEDERATION OF DELAWARE, INC. (1934); 100 W. 10th St., Suite 301 (19801-1628); (302)427-2100. FAX: (302)427-2438. E-mail: delawarejfd@jon.cjfny.org. Pres. Barbara H. Schoenberg; Exec. V. Pres. Judy Wortman.

DISTRICT OF COLUMBIA

WASHINGTON

THE JEWISH FEDERATION OF GREATER WASHINGTON, INC. (1935); 6101 Montrose Rd., Rockville, MD (20852); (301)230-7200. FAX: (301)230-7265. E-mail: info@jewishfedwash.org. Pres. Dede Feinberg; Exec. V.-Pres. Misha Galperin.

FLORIDA

BREVARD COUNTY

JEWISH FEDERATION OF BREVARD (1974); 108-A Barton Ave., Rockledge (32955); (407)636-1824. FAX: (407)636-0614. E-mail: jfbrevard@aol.com. Pres. Gary Singer; Exec. Dir. Joanne Bishins.

BROWARD COUNTY

JEWISH FEDERATION OF BROWARD COUNTY (1943; 1968); 5890 S. Pine Island Rd., Davie (33351-7319); (954)748-8400. FAX: (954) 748-6332. E-mail: info@jewishfedbroward.org. Pres. David B. Schulman; Exec. Dir. Gary N. Rubin.

COLLIER COUNTY

JEWISH FEDERATION OF COLLIER COUNTY (1974); 1250 Tamiami Trail N., Suite 202, Naples (33940); (941) 263-4205. FAX: (941) 263-3813. E-mail: jfccfl@aol.com. Pres. Ann Jacobson.

DAYTONA BEACH
(See Volusia & Flagler Counties)

FT. LAUDERDALE
(See Broward County)

GAINESVILLE

GAINESVILLE JEWISH APPEAL, INC.; 1816 NW 21 Street (32604); (352)371-3846. E-mail: oberger@gnv.fdt.net.

JACKSONVILLE

JACKSONVILLE JEWISH FEDERATION, INC. (1935); 8505 San Jose Blvd. (32217); (904)448-5000. FAX: (904)448-5715. E-mail: jaxjewishfed@jon.cjfny.org. Pres. Dr. Kenneth Sekine; Exec. V.-Pres. Alan Margolies.

LEE COUNTY

JEWISH FEDERATION OF LEE AND CHARLOTTE COUNTIES (1974); 6237-E Presidential Court, Ft. Myers (33919-3568); (941)481-4449. FAX: (941)481-0139. E-mail: jfedswfl@aol.com. Pres. Rozzi Osterman; Exec. Dir. Annette Goodman.

MIAMI

GREATER MIAMI JEWISH FEDERATION, INC. (1938); 4200 Biscayne Blvd. (33137); (305)576-4000. FAX: (305)573-4584. Pres. Michael Scheck; Exec. V.-Pres. Jacob Solomon.

ORLANDO

JEWISH FEDERATION OF GREATER ORLANDO (1949); 851 N. Maitland Ave.; PO Box 941508, Maitland (32794-1508); (407)645-5933. FAX: (407)645-1172. Pres. James S. Grodin; Exec. Dir. Eric Geboff.

PALM BEACH COUNTY

JEWISH FEDERATION OF PALM BEACH COUNTY, INC. (1962); 4601 Community Dr., W. Palm Beach (33417-2760); (561)478-0700. FAX: (561)478-9696. E-mail: info@jfedpbco.org. Pres. Eugene J. Ribakoff; Exec. V.-Pres. Jeffrey L. Klein.

JEWISH FEDERATION OF SOUTH PALM BEACH COUNTY, INC. (1979); 9901 Donna Klein Blvd. Boca Raton (33428-1788); (561)852-3105. FAX: (561)852-3136. E-mail: dstern@jewishboca.org.

PENSACOLA

PENSACOLA JEWISH FEDERATION; 800 No. Palafox (32501); (850)434-7992.

PINELLAS COUNTY

JEWISH FEDERATION OF PINELLAS COUNTY, INC. (incl. Clearwater and St. Petersburg) (1950; reincorp. 1974); 13191 Starkey Rd., #8, Largo (33773-1438); (727) 530-3223. FAX: (727)531-0221. E-mail: pinellas@jfedpinellas.org. Pres. David Abelson; Interim Exec. Dir. Bonnie Friedman.

SARASOTA-MANATEE

SARASOTA-MANATEE JEWISH FEDERATION (1959); 580 S. McIntosh Rd. (34232-1959); (941)371-4546. FAX: (941)378-2947. E-mail: jlederman@smjf.org. Pres. Scott Gordon; Exec. Dir. Jan C. Lederman.

TALLAHASSEE

APALACHEE FEDERATION OF JEWISH CHARITIES; PO Box 14825 (32317-4825); (850)877-3989; FAX: (850)877-7989. E-mail: mdlevy@pol.net.

TAMPA

TAMPA JEWISH FEDERATION (1941); 13009 Community Campus Dr. (33625-4000); (813)264-9000. FAX: (813)265-8450. E-mail: jfjcc@aol.com. Pres. Lili Kaufman; Exec. V.-Pres. Howard Borer.

VOLUSIA & FLAGLER COUNTIES

JEWISH FEDERATION OF VOLUSIA & FLAGLER COUNTIES, INC. (1980); 733 S. Nova Rd., Ormond Beach (32174); (904)672-0294. FAX: (904)673-1316. Pres. Steven I. Unatin; Exec. Dir. Gloria Max.

GEORGIA

ATLANTA

JEWISH FEDERATION OF GREATER ATLANTA, INC. (1905; reorg. 1967); 1440 Spring St., NW (30309-2837); (404)873-1661. FAX: (404)874-7043/881-4027. E-mail: kkaplan @jfga.org. Pres. Dr. Arnold Rubenstein; Exec. Dir. David I. Sarnat.

AUGUSTA

AUGUSTA JEWISH FEDERATION (1937); 898 Weinberger Way, Evans (30809-3636); (706)228-3636. FAX: (706)868-1660/823-3960. E-mail: mpousman@hotmail.com. Pres. Dr. Louis Scharff; Exec. Dir. Michael Pousman.

COLUMBUS

JEWISH FEDERATION OF COLUMBUS, INC. (1944); PO Box 6313 (31906); (706)568-6668. Pres. Murray Solomon; Sec. Irene Rainbow.

SAVANNAH

SAVANNAH JEWISH FEDERATION (1943); 5111 Abercorn St. (31403); (912)355-8111. FAX: (912)355-8116. E-mail: jrgreen4@juno.com. Pres. Dr. Paul Kulbersh; Exec. Dir. Sharon Gal.

ILLINOIS

CHAMPAIGN-URBANA

CHAMPAIGN-URBANA JEWISH FEDERATION (1929); 503 E. John St., Champaign (61820); (217)367-9872. FAX: (217)367-0077. E-mail: cujf@shalomcu.org. Pres. Anthony E. Novak; Exec. Dir. Lee Melhado.

CHICAGO

JEWISH FEDERATION OF METROPOLITAN CHICAGO/JEWISH UNITED FUND OF METROPOLITAN CHICAGO (1900); Ben Gurion Way, 1 S. Franklin St. (60606-4694); (312) 444-2800. FAX: (312)444-2806. E-mail: webinfo@juf.org. Chmn. Fred Bondy; Pres. Steven B. Nasatir.

JOLIET

JOLIET JEWISH WELFARE CHEST (1938); 250 N. Midland Ave. at Campbell St. (60435); (815)741-4600.

PEORIA

JEWISH FEDERATION OF PEORIA (1933; inc. 1947); 2000 W. Pioneer Pwky., Suite 10B (61615-1835); (309)689-0063. FAX: (309) 689-0575. Pres. Jennifer Dolin; Exec. Dir. Eunice Galsky.

QUAD CITIES

JEWISH FEDERATION OF QUAD CITIES (1938; comb. 1973); 1705 2nd Ave., Suite 405, Rock Island (61201); (309)793-1300. FAX: (309)793-1345. E-mail: qcfederation@juno.com. Pres. Paul Light; Exec. Dir. Ida Kramer.

ROCKFORD

JEWISH FEDERATION OF GREATER ROCKFORD (1937); 1500 Parkview Ave. (61107); (815)399-5497. FAX: (815)399-9835. E-mail: rockfordfederation@juno.com. Pres. Sterne Roufa; Exec. Dir. Marilyn Youman.

SOUTHERN ILLINOIS

JEWISH FEDERATION OF SOUTHERN ILLINOIS, SOUTHEASTERN MISSOURI, AND WESTERN KENTUCKY (1941); 6464 W. Main, Suite 7A, Belleville (62223); (618)398-6100. FAX: (618)398-0539. E-mail: silfed@aol.com. Co-Pres. Harvey Cohen & Carol Rudman; Exec. Dir. Steven C. Low.

SPRINGFIELD

SPRINGFIELD JEWISH FEDERATION (1941); 2815 Old Jacksonville Rd., Ste 103A (62704); (217)787-7263. FAX: (217)787-7470. E-mail: sjf@springnet1.com. Pres. Rita Victor; Exec. Dir. Gloria Schwartz.

INDIANA

FORT WAYNE

FORT WAYNE JEWISH FEDERATION (1921); 227 E. Washington Blvd. (46802-3121); (219)422-8566. FAX: (219)422-8567. E-mail: fwjewfed@aol.com. Pres. Scott Salon; Exec. Dir. Jeff Gubitz.

INDIANAPOLIS

JEWISH FEDERATION OF GREATER INDIANAPOLIS, INC. (1905); 6705 Hoover Rd. (46260-4120); (317)726-5450. FAX: (317) 205-0307. E-mail controljfg@aol.com. Pres. Claudette Einhorn; Exec. V.-Pres. Harry Nadler.

LAFAYETTE

JEWISH FEDERATION OF GREATER LAFAYETTE (1924); PO Box 3802, W. Lafayette (47906); (765)426-4724. E-mail: jfgl1@aol.com. Pres.Earl Prohofsky; Finan. Sec. Laura Starr; Admin. Judy Upton.

NORTHWEST INDIANA

JEWISH FEDERATION OF NORTHWEST INDIANA (1941; reorg. 1959); 2939 Jewett St., Highland (46322); (219)972-2250. FAX:

(219)972-4779. E-mail: defwej@aol.com. Pres. Carol Karol; Exec. Dir. David Tein.

ST. JOSEPH VALLEY

JEWISH FEDERATION OF ST. JOSEPH VALLEY (1946); 3202 Shalom Way, South Bend (46615); (219)233-1164. FAX: (219)288-4103. E-mail: mgardncr@fcdsjv.org. Pres. Dr. Douglas H. Barton; Exec. V.-Pres. Marilyn Gardner.

IOWA

DES MOINES

JEWISH FEDERATION OF GREATER DES MOINES (1914); 910 Polk Blvd. (50312); (515)277-6321. FAX: (515)277-4069. E-mail: jcrcia@aol.com. Pres. Robert M. Pomerantz; Exec. Dir. Elaine Steinger.

SIOUX CITY

JEWISH FEDERATION OF SIOUX CITY (1921); 815 38th St. (51104-1417); (712)258-0618. FAX: (712)258-0619. Pres. Michele Ivener; Admin. Dir. Doris Rosenthal.

KANSAS

KANSAS CITY

See listing under Missouri

WICHITA

MID-KANSAS JEWISH FEDERATION, INC. (serving South Central Kansas) (1935); 400 N. Woodlawn, Suite 8 (67208); (316)686-4741. FAX: (316)686-6008. Pres. Marie Levy; Exec. Dir. Judy Press.

KENTUCKY

CENTRAL KENTUCKY

CENTRAL KENTUCKY JEWISH FEDERATION (1976); 340 Romany Rd., Lexington (40502-2400); (606)268-0672. FAX: (606)268-0775. Pres.Martin Barr; Exec. Dir. Daniel Chejfec.

LOUISVILLE

JEWISH COMMUNITY FEDERATION OF LOUISVILLE, INC. (1934); 3630 Dutchmans Lane (40205); (502)451-8840. FAX: (502) 458-0702. E-mail: jfed@iglou.com. Pres. Gerald D. Temes MD; Exec. Dir. Alan S. Engel.

LOUISIANA

BATON ROUGE

JEWISH FEDERATION OF GREATER BATON ROUGE (1971); 3354 Kleinert Ave. (70806); (504) 387-9744. FAX: (504)387-9487. E-mail: jfedofbr@postoffice.att.net. Pres. Harvey Hoffman.

NEW ORLEANS

JEWISH FEDERATION OF GREATER NEW ORLEANS (1913; reorg. 1977); 3500 N. Causeway Blvd., Suite 1240, Metairie (70002-3524); (504)828-2125. FAX: (504)828-2827. E-mail: jewishnews@jewishnola.com. Pres. Hugo Kahn; Exec. Dir. Eli Skora.

SHREVEPORT

NORTHERN LOUISIANA JEWISH FEDERATION (1941; inc. 1967); 4700 Line Ave., Suite 117 (71106-1533); (318)868-1200. FAX: (318) 868-1272. E-mail: sjfed@juno.com. Pres. Rick Murov; Exec. Dir. Howard L. Ross.

MAINE

LEWISTON-AUBURN

LEWISTON-AUBURN JEWISH FEDERATION (1947); 74 Bradman St., Auburn (04210); (207)786-4201. FAX: (207)783-1000. Pres. Scott Nussinow.

PORTLAND

JEWISH COMMUNITY ALLIANCE OF SOUTHERN MAINE (1942); 57 Ashmont St. (04103); (207)773-7254. FAX: (207)772-2234. E-mail: info@mainejewish.org. Pres. Michael Peisner; Exec. Dir. David Unger.

MARYLAND

BALTIMORE

THE ASSOCIATED: JEWISH COMMUNITY FEDERATION OF BALTIMORE (1920; reorg. 1969); 101 W. Mt. Royal Ave. (21201-5728); (410) 727-4828. FAX: (410)752-1177. E-mail: information@associated.org. Chmn. Barbara L. Himmelrich; Pres. Darrell D. Friedman.

COLUMBIA

JEWISH FEDERATION OF HOWARD COUNTY; 8950 Rte. 108, Suite 115, Columbia (21045); (410)730-4976; FAX: (410)730-9393. E-mail: jfohc@starpower.net. Pres. Toby Knopf; Exec. Dir. Roberta Greenstein.

MASSACHUSETTS

BERKSHIRE COUNTY

JEWISH FEDERATION OF THE BERKSHIRES (1940); 235 East St., Pittsfield (01201); (413)442-4360. FAX: (413)443-6070. E-mail: jreichbaum@berkshire.net. Pres. Stephen Rudin; Exec. Dir. Jaquelynne Reichbaum.

BOSTON

COMBINED JEWISH PHILANTHROPIES OF GREATER BOSTON, INC. (1895; inc. 1961); 126 High St. (02110-2700); (617)457-8500. FAX: (617)988-6262. E-mail: info@cjp.org. Chmn. Cynthia B. Shulman; Pres. Barry Shrage.

MERRIMACK VALLEY

MERRIMACK VALLEY JEWISH FEDERATION (Serves Andover, Haverhill, Lawrence, Lowell, Newburyport, and 22 surrounding communities) (1988); 805 Turnpike St., N. Andover (01845-6182); (978)688-0466. FAX: (978)688-1097. E-mail: jan@mvjf.org. Pres. James H. Shainker; Exec. Dir. Jan Steven Brodie.

NEW BEDFORD

JEWISH FEDERATION OF GREATER NEW BEDFORD, INC. (1938; inc. 1954); 467 Hawthorn St., N. Dartmouth (02747); (508) 997-7471. FAX: (508)997-7730. Co-Pres. Harriet Philips, Patricia Rosenfield; Exec. Dir. Wil Herrup.

NORTH SHORE

JEWISH FEDERATION OF THE NORTH SHORE, INC. (1938); 21 Front St., Salem (01970-3707); (978)598-1810. FAX: (978)741-7507. E-mail: mail@jfns.org. Pres. Shepard M. Remis; Exec. Dir. Neil A. Cooper.

SPRINGFIELD

JEWISH FEDERATION OF GREATER SPRINGFIELD, INC. (1925); 1160 Dickinson St. (01108); (413)737-4313. FAX: (413)737-4348. E-mail: cfschwartz@jewishspringfield.org. Pres. Jeffrey Mandell; Exec. Dir. Joel Weiss.

WORCESTER

JEWISH FEDERATION OF CENTRAL MASSACHUSETTS (1947; inc. 1957); 633 Salisbury St. (01609); (508)756-1543. FAX: (508)798-0962. E-mail: meyerb@aol.com. Pres. Dr. Robert Honig; Exec. Dir. Meyer L. Bodoff.

MICHIGAN

ANN ARBOR

JEWISH FEDERATION OF WASHTENAW COUNTY/UJA (1986); 2939 Birch Hollow Dr. (48108); (734)677-0100. FAX: (734)677-0109. E-mail: jccfed@aol.com. Pres. Morley Witus; Exec. Dir. Nancy N. Margolis.

DETROIT

JEWISH FEDERATION OF METROPOLITAN DE-

TROIT (1899); 6735 Telegraph Rd., Suite 30, PO Box 2030, Bloomfield Hills (48301-2030); (248)642-4260. FAX: (248)642-4985. E-mail: jfmd@jfmd.org. Pres. Penny Blumenstein; Exec. V.-Pres. Robert P. Aronson.

FLINT

FLINT JEWISH FEDERATION (1936); 619 Wallenberg St. (48502); (810)767-5922. FAX: (810)767-9024. E-mail: fjf@tm.net. Pres. Dr. Steve Burton; Exec. Dir. Joel B. Kaplan.

GRAND RAPIDS

JEWISH COMMUNITY FUND OF GRAND RAPIDS (1930); 330 Fuller NE (49503); (616)456-5553. FAX: (616)456-5780. E-mail: jcfgr@iserv.net. Pres. Richard Stevens; Admin. Dir. Rosalie Stein; V.P. Maxine Shapiro.

MINNESOTA

DULUTH-SUPERIOR

NORTHLAND JEWISH FUND (1937); 1602 E. Second St., Duluth (55812); (218)724-8857. FAX: (218)724-2560. E-mail: sstevens@ computerpro.com. Pres. Neil Glazman.

MINNEAPOLIS

MINNEAPOLIS JEWISH FEDERATION (1929; inc. 1930); 13100 Wayzota Blvd. (55305); (612)593-2600. FAX: (612)593-2544. E-mail: sfreeman@mplsfed.org. Pres. Michael Horovitz; Exec. Dir. Joshua Fogelson.

ST. PAUL

UNITED JEWISH FUND AND COUNCIL (1935); 790 S. Cleveland, Suite 201 (55116); (651)690-1707. FAX: (651)690-0228. Pres. James Stein; Exec. Dir. Samuel Asher.

MISSOURI

KANSAS CITY

JEWISH FEDERATION OF GREATER KANSAS CITY MO/KS (1933); 5801 W. 115 St., Overland Park, KS (66211-1824); (913)327-8100. FAX: (913)327-8110. E-mail: cherylm@jewishkc.org. Pres. John Uhlmann; Exec. Dir. Todd Stettner.

ST. JOSEPH

UNITED JEWISH FUND OF ST. JOSEPH (1915); 1816 Walnut (64503); (816)233-1186. FAX: (816)233-9399. Elliot Zidell; Exec. Sec. Sherri Ott.

ST. LOUIS

JEWISH FEDERATION OF ST. LOUIS (incl. St. Louis County) (1901); 12 Millstone Campus

Dr. (63146-9812); (314)432-0020. FAX: (314)432-1277. Pres. Mont S. Levy; Exec. V.-Pres. Barry Rosenberg.

NEBRASKA

LINCOLN

JEWISH FEDERATION OF LINCOLN, INC. (1931; inc. 1961); PO Box 67218 (68506); (402)489-1015. FAX: (402)476-8364. Pres. Herb Friedman; Exec. Dir. Karen Sommer.

OMAHA

JEWISH FEDERATION OF OMAHA (1903); 333 S. 132nd St. (68154-2198); (402)334-8200. FAX: (402)334-1330. E-mail: pmonsk@top. net. Pres. Howard Kooper; Exec. Dir. Jan Perelman.

NEVADA

LAS VEGAS

JEWISH FEDERATION OF LAS VEGAS (1973); 3909 S. Maryland Pkwy. (89119-7520); (702)732-0556. FAX: (702)732-3228. Pres. David Dahan; Exec. Dir. Ronni Epstein.

NEW HAMPSHIRE

MANCHESTER

JEWISH FEDERATION OF GREATER MANCHESTER (1974); 698 Beech St. (03104-3626); (603)627-7679. FAX: (603) 627-7963.

NEW JERSEY

ATLANTIC AND CAPE MAY COUNTIES

JEWISH FEDERATION OF ATLANTIC AND CAPE MAY COUNTIES (1924); 3393 Bargaintown Rd., Box 617, Northfield (08225-0196); (609)653-3030. FAX: (609)653-8881. E-mail: jfedacm@cyberenet.net. Pres. Joseph Rodgers; Exec. V.-Pres. Bernard Cohen.

BERGEN COUNTY

UJA FEDERATION OF BERGEN COUNTY AND NORTH HUDSON (inc. 1978); 111 Kinderkamack Rd., River Edge (07661); (201)488-6800. FAX: (201)488-1507. E-mail: contact@jewishbergen.org. Pres. Edward Dauber; Exec. V.-Pres. Ron B. Meier.

CENTRAL NEW JERSEY

JEWISH FEDERATION OF CENTRAL NEW JERSEY (1940; merged 1973); 1391 Martine Ave., Scotch Plains (07076); (908)889-5335. FAX: (908)889-5370. E-mail: community @jfedcnj.org. Pres. Alfred A. Gelfand; Exec. V.-Pres. Stanley Stone.

CLIFTON-PASSAIC

JEWISH FEDERATION OF GREATER CLIFTON-PASSAIC (1933); 199 Scoles Ave., Clifton (07012-1125). (973)777-7031. FAX: (973) 777-6701. E-mail: yymuskin@jfedclifton-passaic.com. Pres. George Kramer; Exec. V.-Pres. Yosef Y. Muskin.

CUMBERLAND COUNTY

JEWISH FEDERATION OF CUMBERLAND COUNTY (inc. 1971); 1063 E. Landis Ave. Suite B, Vineland (08360-3752); (609)696-4445. FAX: (609)696-3428. E-mail: jfedcc@aol.com. Pres. James Potter; Exec. Dir. Ann Lynn Lipton.

METROWEST NEW JERSEY

UNITED JEWISH FEDERATION OF METRO-WEST (1923); 901 Route 10, Whippany (07981-1156); (973)884-4800. FAX: (973) 884-7361. E-mail: webmail@ujfmetrowest.org. Pres. Steven Klinghoffer; Exec. V.-Pres. Max L. Kleinman.

MIDDLESEX COUNTY

JEWISH FEDERATION OF GREATER MIDDLESEX COUNTY (org. 1948; reorg. 1985); 230 Old Bridge Tpk., S. River (08882-2000); (732)432-7711. FAX: (732)432-0292. E-mail: jfednj@aol.com. Pres. Roy Tanzman; Exec. Dir. Gerrie Bamira.

MONMOUTH COUNTY

JEWISH FEDERATION OF GREATER MONMOUTH COUNTY (1971); 100 Grant Ave., PO Box 210, Deal (07723-0210); (732)531-6200-1. FAX: (732)531-9518. E-mail: pfdnuss@msn.com. Pres. David Portman; Chmn. William A. Schwartz; Exec. Dir. David A. Nussbaum.

NORTH JERSEY

JEWISH FEDERATION OF NORTH JERSEY (1933); One Pike Dr., Wayne (07470-2498); (973)595-0555. FAX: (973)595-1532. Branch Office: 17-10 River Rd., Fair Lawn (07410-1250); (973)794-1111. E-mail: jfnj@aol.com. Pres. George Liss; Exec. Dir. Martin Greenberg.

OCEAN COUNTY

OCEAN COUNTY JEWISH FEDERATION (1977); 301 Madison Ave., Lakewood (08701); (732)363-0530. FAX: (732)363-2097. Pres. David Rosen; Exec. Dir. Alan Nydick.

PRINCETON MERCER BUCKS

UNITED JEWISH FEDERATION OF PRINCETON MERCER BUCKS (merged 1996); 3131 Princeton Pike, Bldg. 2A, Lawrenceville (08648-2207); (609)219-0555. FAX: (609)219-9040. E-mail: ujfpmb@bellatlantic.net. Pres. Eliot Freeman; Exec. Dir. Andrew Frank.

SOMERSET COUNTY

JEWISH FEDERATION OF SOMERSET, HUNTERDON & WARREN COUNTIES (1960); 775 Talamini Rd., Bridgewater (08807); (908)725-6994. FAX: (908)725-9753. E-mail: somerset@mindpulse.com. Pres. Martin Siegal; Exec. Dir. Daniel A. Nadelman.

SOUTHERN NEW JERSEY

JEWISH FEDERATION OF SOUTHERN NEW JERSEY (incl. Camden, Burlington, and Gloucester counties) (1922); 1301 Springdale Rd., Suite 200, Cherry Hill (08003-2769); (856)751-9500. FAX: (856)751-1697. Pres. Dr. Robert Belafsky; Exec. V.-Pres. Stuart Alperin.

NEW MEXICO

ALBUQUERQUE

JEWISH FEDERATION OF GREATER ALBUQUERQUE (1938); 5520 Wyoming Blvd., NE (87109-3167); (505)821-3214. FAX: (505)821-3351. E-mail: nmjfga@nmjfga.org. Pres. Dr. Larry Lubar; Exec. Dir. Andrew Lipman.

NEW YORK

ALBANY

(See Northeastern New York)

BROOME COUNTY

JEWISH FEDERATION OF BROOME COUNTY; 500 Clubhouse Rd., Vestal (13850); (607)724-2332; FAX: (607)724-2311.

BUFFALO (INCL. NIAGARA FALLS)

JEWISH FEDERATION OF GREATER BUFFALO, INC. (1903); 787 Delaware Ave. (14209); (716)886-7750. FAX: (716)886-1367. Pres. Irving M. Shuman; Exec. Dir. James M. Lodge.

DUTCHESS COUNTY

JEWISH FEDERATION OF DUTCHESS COUNTY; 110 Grand Ave., Poughkeepsie (12603); (914)471-9811. FAX: (914) 471-0659. E-mail: jfeddutchess@mindspring.com. Pres. Tomasina Schneider; Exec. Dir. Bonnie Meadow.

ELMIRA-CORNING

JEWISH CENTER AND FEDERATION OF THE

TWIN TIERS (1942); PO Box 3087, Elmira (14905-0087); (607)734-8122. FAX: (607) 734-8123. Pres. John Spiegler; Admin. Diane Huglies.

NEW YORK

UJA-FEDERATION OF JEWISH PHILANTHROPIES OF NEW YORK, INC. (incl. Greater NY, Westchester, Nassau, and Suffolk counties) (Fed. org. 1917; UJA 1939; merged 1986); 130 E. 59 St. (10022-1302); (212)980-1000. FAX: (212)888-7538. E-mail: contact@ujafedny.org. Pres. James S. Tisch; Exec. V.-Pres. & CEO John Ruskay.

NORTHEASTERN NEW YORK

UNITED JEWISH FEDERATION OF NORTHEASTERN NEW YORK (1986); Latham Circle Mall, 800 New Loudon Rd., Latham (12110); (518)783-7800. FAX: (518)783-1557. E-mail: info@jewishfedny.org. Pres. Dr. Lewis Morrison; Exec. Dir. Jerry S. Neimand.

ORANGE COUNTY

JEWISH FEDERATION OF GREATER ORANGE COUNTY (1977); 68 Stewart Ave., Newburgh (12550); (845)562-7860. FAX: (914)562-5114. E-mail: jfogoc@aol.com. Pres. Mona Rieger; Admin. Dir. Joyce Waschitz.

ROCHESTER

JEWISH COMMUNITY FEDERATION OF GREATER ROCHESTER, NY, INC. (1939); 441 East Ave. (14607-1932); (716)461-0490. FAX: (716)461-0912. E-mail: info@jewishrochester.org. Pres. Jay Birnbaum; Exec. Dir. Lawrence W. Fine.

ROCKLAND COUNTY

JEWISH FEDERATION OF ROCKLAND COUNTY (1985); 900 Route 45, Suite 1, New City (10956-1140); (914)362-4200. Fax: (914)362-4282.

SCHENECTADY

(See Northeastern New York)

SYRACUSE

SYRACUSE JEWISH FEDERATION, INC. (1918); 5655 Thompson Rd. So., DeWitt (13214-0511); (315)445-2040. FAX: (315)445-1559. Pres. Linda Alexander; Exec. V.-Pres. Richard Friedman.

TROY

(See Northeastern New York)

ULSTER COUNTY

JEWISH FEDERATION OF ULSTER COUNTY (1951); 159 Green St., Kingston (12401); (845)338-8131. FAX: (845)338-8131. E-mail: ucjf@ulster.net. Pres. Michelle Tuchman; Exec. Dir. Joan Plotsky.

UTICA

JEWISH COMMUNITY FEDERATION AND CENTER OF UTICA (1950; reorg. 1994); 2310 Oneida St. (13501-6009); (315)733-2343. FAX: (315)733-2346. Pres. Ann Siegel; Exec. Dir. Barbara Ratner-gantshar.

NORTH CAROLINA

ASHEVILLE

WESTERN NORTH CAROLINA JEWISH FEDERATION (1935); 236 Charlotte St. (28801-1434); (828)253-0701. FAX: (828)254-7666. Pres. Stan Greenberg; Exec. Dir. Marlene Berger-Joyce.

CHARLOTTE

THE JEWISH FEDERATION OF GREATER CHARLOTTE (1938); 5007 Providence Rd. (28226-5849); (704)366-5007. FAX: (704) 944-6766. E-mail: magman@shalom charlotte.org. Pres. Sarah Schreibman; Exec. Dir. Marvin Goldberg.

DURHAM-CHAPEL HILL

DURHAM-CHAPEL HILL JEWISH FEDERATION & COMMUNITY COUNCIL (1979); 3700 Lyckan Pkwy., Suite B, Durham (27707-2541); (919)489-5335. FAX: (919)489-5788. E-mail: federation@shalomdch.org. Pres. Elaine Marcus; Exec. Dir. Lew Borman.

GREENSBORO

GREENSBORO JEWISH FEDERATION (1940); 5509C W. Friendly Ave. (27410-4211); (336)852-5433. FAX: (336)852-4346. Pres. Ronald Green; Exec. Dir. Marilyn Forman-Chandler.

RALEIGH

RALEIGH-CARY JEWISH FEDERATION (1987); 8210 Creedmoor Rd., Suite 104 (27613); (919)676-2200. FAX: (919)676-2122. E-mail: info@rcjf.org. Pres. Jim Maass; Exec. Dir. Judah Segal.

OHIO

AKRON

AKRON JEWISH COMMUNITY FEDERATION (1935); 750 White Pond Dr. (44320-1128); (330)869-CHAI (2424). FAX: (330)867-8498. Pres. David Kock; Exec. Dir. Michael Wise.

CANTON

CANTON JEWISH COMMUNITY FEDERATION (1935; reorg. 1955); 2631 Harvard Ave., NW (44709-3147); (330)452-6444. FAX: (330) 452-4487. E-mail: cantonjcf@aol.com. Pres. Edward Buxbaum.

CINCINNATI

JEWISH FEDERATION OF CINCINNATI (1896; reorg. 1967); 4380 Malsbary Rd., Suite 200 (45242-5644); (513) 985-1500. FAX: (513)985-1503. E-mail: jfed@jfedcin.org. Pres. Harry B. Davidow; Chief Exec. Officer Rabbi Michael R. Zedek.

CLEVELAND

JEWISH COMMUNITY FEDERATION OF CLEVELAND (1903); 1750 Euclid Ave. (44115-2106); (216)566-9200. FAX: (216) 861-1230. E-mail: info@jcfcleve.org. Pres. Stephen H. Hoffman; Exec. V.-Pres. & CEO Joel Fox.

COLUMBUS

COLUMBUS JEWISH FEDERATION (1926); 1175 College Ave. (43209); (614)237-7686. FAX: (614)237-2221. E-mail: cjf@tcjf.org. Pres. Gordon Zacks; Exec. Dir. Mitchel Orlik.

DAYTON

JEWISH FEDERATION OF GREATER DAYTON (1910); 4501 Denlinger Rd. (45426-2395); (937)854-4150. FAX: (937)854-2850. Pres. Joseph Bettman; Exec. V.-Pres. Peter H. Wells.

STEUBENVILLE

JEWISH COMMUNITY COUNCIL (1938); 300 Lovers Lane (43952); (614)264-5514. FAX:: (740)264-7190. Pres. Curtis L. Greenberg; Exec. Sec. Jennie Bernstein.

TOLEDO

JEWISH FEDERATION OF GREATER TOLEDO (1907; reorg. 1960); 6505 Sylvania Ave., Sylvania (43560-3918); (419)885-4461. FAX: (419)885-3207. E-mail: jftoledo@cjfny.org. Pres. Joel Beren; Exec. Dir. Alix Greenblatt.

YOUNGSTOWN

YOUNGSTOWN AREA JEWISH FEDERATION (1935); 505 Gypsy Lane (44504-1314); (330)746-3251. FAX: (330)746-7926. E-mail: samkoopl@juno.com. Pres. Dr. Ronald Roth; Exec. V.-Pres. Sam Kooperman.

OKLAHOMA

OKLAHOMA CITY

JEWISH FEDERATION OF GREATER OKLAHOMA CITY (1941); 710 W. Wilshire, Suite C (73116-7736). (405)848-3132. FAX: (405) 848-3180. E-mail: okcfed@flash.net. Pres. Harriet Carson; Exec. Dir. Edie S. Roodman.

TULSA

JEWISH FEDERATION OF TULSA (1938); 2021 E. 71 St. (74136); (918)495-1100. FAX: (918)495-1220. Pres. Andrew M. Wolov; Exec. Dir. David Bernstein.

OREGON

PORTLAND

JEWISH FEDERATION OF PORTLAND (incl. Northwest Oregon and Southwest Washington communities) (1920; reorg. 1956); 6651 SW Capitol Hwy. (97219); (503) 245-6219. FAX: (503)245-6603. E-mail: charlie@jewishportland.org. Pres. Priscilla Kostiner; Exec. Dir. Charles Schiffman.

PENNSYLVANIA

BUCKS COUNTY

(See Jewish Federation of Greater Philadelphia)

ERIE

JEWISH COMMUNITY COUNCIL OF ERIE (1946); 1611 Peach St., Suite 405 (16501-2123); (814)455-4474. FAX: (814)455-4475. E-mail: jcceri@erie.net. Pres. Robert Cohen; Admin. Dir. Cynthia Penman; Dir. of Soc. Srvcs. Barbara Singer.

HARRISBURG

UNITED JEWISH COMMUNITY OF GREATER HARRISBURG (1941); 3301 N. Front St. (17110-1436); (717)236-9555. FAX: (717)236-8104. E-mail: communityreview@ desupernet.net. Pres. Raphael Aronson; Exec. Dir. David Weisberg.

LEHIGH VALLEY

JEWISH FEDERATION OF THE LEHIGH VALLEY (1948); 702 N. 22nd St., Allentown (18104); (610)821-5500. FAX: (610)821-8946. E-mail: ivfed@enter.net.

PHILADELPHIA

JEWISH FEDERATION OF GREATER PHILADELPHIA (incl. Bucks, Chester, Delaware, Montgomery, and Philadelphia counties) (1901; reorg. 1956); 2100 Arch St. (19103); (215)832-0500. FAX: (215)832-1510. E-mail: lyouman@philjnet.org. Pres. Michael R. Belman; Exec. V.-Pres. Howard E. Charish.

PITTSBURGH

UNITED JEWISH FEDERATION OF GREATER PITTSBURGH (1912; reorg. 1955); 234 McKee Pl. (15213-3916); (412)681-8000. FAX: (412) 681-3980. E-mail: information@ujf.net. Chmn. David Burstin; Pres. Howard M. Rieger.

READING

JEWISH FEDERATION OF READING, PA., INC. (1935; reorg. 1972); 1700 City Line St. (19604); (610)921-2766. FAX: (610)929-0886. E-mail: stanr@epix.net. Pres. Sheila Lattin; Exec. Dir. Stanley Ramati.

SCRANTON

JEWISH FEDERATION OF NORTHEASTERN PENNSYLVANIA (1945); 601 Jefferson Ave. (18510); (570)961-2300. FAX: (570)346-6147. E-mail: jfednepa@epix.net. Pres. Louis Nivert; Exec. Dir. Seymour Brotman.

WILKES-BARRE

JEWISH FEDERATION OF GREATER WILKES-BARRE (1950); 60 S. River St. (18702-2493); (717)822-4146. FAX: (717)824-5966. E-mail: wbreport@aol.com. Pres. Murray Ufberg; Exec. Dir. Don Cooper.

RHODE ISLAND

PROVIDENCE

JEWISH FEDERATION OF RHODE ISLAND (1945); 130 Sessions St. (02906); (401)421-4111. FAX: (401)331-7961. E-mail: shalom @jfri.org. Pres. Edward D. Feldstein; Exec. Dir. Steven A. Rakitt.

SOUTH CAROLINA

CHARLESTON

CHARLESTON JEWISH FEDERATION (1949); 1645 Raoul Wallenberg Blvd., PO Box 31298 (29407); (843)571-6565. FAX: (843)852-3547. E-mail: ejkatzman@aol.com. Pres. Anita Zucker; Exec. Dir. Ellen J. Katzman.

COLUMBIA

COLUMBIA JEWISH FEDERATION (1960); 4540 Trenholm Rd., PO Box 6968 (29206-4462); (803)787-2023. FAX: (803)787-0475.

E-mail: ternercjf@hotmail.com. Pres. Stephen Serbin; Exec. Dir. Steven Terner.

SOUTH DAKOTA

SIOUX FALLS

JEWISH WELFARE FUND (1938); 510 S. First Ave. (57102-1003); (605)332-3335. FAX: (605)334-2298. E-mail: asnh94@prodigy. com. Pres. Laurence Bierman; Exec. Sec. Stephen Rosenthal.

TENNESSEE

CHATTANOOGA

JEWISH COMMUNITY FEDERATION OF GREATER CHATTANOOGA (1931); 3601 Ringgold Rd. (37412); PO Box 8947 (37412); (423)493-0270. FAX: (423)493-9997. E-mail: dlevine@jcfgc.com. Pres. Claire Binder; Exec. Dir. Debra Levine.

KNOXVILLE

KNOXVILLE JEWISH FEDERATION, INC. (1939); 7800 Deane Hill Dr. (37919); (423)693-5837. FAX: (423)694-4861. E-mail: ajcckjf@aol.com. Pres. Pace Robinson; Exec. Dir. Dr. Bernard Rosenblatt.

MEMPHIS

MEMPHIS JEWISH FEDERATION (incl. Shelby County) (1935); 6560 Poplar Ave. (38138-3614); (901)767-7100. FAX: (901)767-7128. E-mail: jfeld@memjfed.org. Pres. Louise Sklar; Exec. Dir. Jeffrey Feld.

NASHVILLE

NASHVILLE JEWISH FEDERATION (1936); 801 Percy Warner Blvd. (37205-4009); (615) 356-3242. FAX: (615)352-0056. E-mail: jnashjfed@aol.com. Pres. Peter Haas.

TEXAS

AUSTIN

JEWISH COMMUNTY ASSOCIATION OF AUSTIN (1939; reorg. 1956); 7300 Hart Lane (78731); (512)735-8000. FAX: (512)735-8001. E-mail: austinjfed@jfaustin.org. Pres. Linda Millstone; Exec. Dir. Sandy Sack.

BEAUMONT

BEAUMONT JEWISH FEDERATION; PO Box 1891 (77704-1981); (409)832-2881.

CORPUS CHRISTI

COMBINED JEWISH APPEAL OF CORPUS CHRISTI; 750 Everhart Rd. (78411-1906; (512)855-6239. FAX: (512)853-9040.

DALLAS

JEWISH FEDERATION OF GREATER DALLAS (1911); 7800 Northaven Rd. (75230-3226); (214)369-3313. FAX: (214)369-8943. Pres. Donald Schaffer; Exec. Dir. Gary Weinstein.

EL PASO

JEWISH FEDERATION OF EL PASO, INC. (1937); 405 Wallenberg Dr. (79912-5605); (915)584-4437. FAX: (915)584-0243. Pres. Gary Weiser; Exec. Dir. Larry Harris.

FORT WORTH

JEWISH FEDERATION OF FORT WORTH AND TARRANT COUNTY (1936); 4801-B Briarhaven Rd. (76109); (817)569-0892. FAX: (817)569-0896. E-mail: jfedfwtc@aol.com. Pres. Harold Gernsbacher; Exec. Dir. Naomi Rosenfield.

HOUSTON

JEWISH FEDERATION OF GREATER HOUSTON (1936); 5603 S. Braeswood Blvd. (77096-3907); (713)729-7000. FAX: (713)721-6232. E-mail: lwunsch@houstonjewish.org. Pres. Marvin Woskow; Exec. V.-Pres. Lee Wunsch.

SAN ANTONIO

JEWISH FEDERATION OF SAN ANTONIO (incl. Bexar County) (1922); 12500 NW Military Hwy., Suite 200 (78231); (210)302-6960. FAX: (210)408-2332. E-mail: markjfsa@aol.com. Pres. Elaine Cohen; Exec. Dir. Mark Freedman.

WACO

JEWISH FEDERATION OF WACO & CENTRAL TEXAS (1949); PO Box 8031 (76714-8031); (817)776-3740. E-mail: debhersh@aol.com. Pres. Abbye M. Silver; Exec. Sec. Debbie Hersh-Levy.

UTAH

SALT LAKE CITY

UNITED JEWISH FEDERATION OF UTAH (1936); 2416 E. 1700 South (84108); (801)581-0102. FAX: (801) 581-1334. Pres. Robert Wolff; Exec. Dir. Donald Gartman.

VIRGINIA

RICHMOND

JEWISH COMMUNITY FEDERATION OF RICHMOND (1935); 5403 Monument Ave., PO Box 17128 (23226-7128); (804)288-0045. FAX: (804)282-7507. E-mail: executivedirector@jewishrich.com. Pres. Stewart Kasen; Exec. Dir. Marsha F. Hurwitz.

TIDEWATER

UNITED JEWISH FEDERATION OF TIDEWATER (incl. Norfolk, Portsmouth, and Virginia Beach) (1937); 5029 Corporate Woods Dr., Suite 225, Virginia Beach (23462-4370); (757)671-1600. FAX: (757)671-7613. E-mail: ujft@ujft.org. Pres. David Brand; Exec. V.-Pres. Mark L. Goldstein.

VIRGINIA PENINSULA

UNITED JEWISH COMMUNITY OF THE VIRGINIA PENINSULA, INC. (1942); 2700 Spring Rd., Newport News (23606); (757)930-1422. FAX: (757)930-3762. E-mail: unitedjc@erols.com. Pres. Roy H. Lasris; Exec. Dir. Rodney J. Margolis.

WASHINGTON

SEATTLE

JEWISH FEDERATION OF GREATER SEATTLE (incl. King County, Everett, and Bremerton) (1926); 2031 Third Ave. (98121); (206)443-5400. FAX: (206)443-0306. E-mail: wnedyj@jewishinseattle.org. Pres. Dr. Michael Spektor; Exec. V.-Pres. Barry M. Goren.

WEST VIRGINIA

CHARLESTON

FEDERATED JEWISH CHARITIES OF CHARLESTON, INC. (1937); PO Box 1613 (25326); (304)345-2320. FAX: (304)345-2325. E-mail: mzltov@aol.com. Pres. Stuart May; Exec. Sec. Lee Diznoff.

WISCONSIN

MADISON

MADISON JEWISH COMMUNITY COUNCIL, INC. (1940); 6434 Enterprise Lane (53719-1117); (608)278-1808. FAX:(608)278-7814. E-mail: morrison@mjcc.net. Pres. Joel Minkoff; Exec. Dir. Steven H. Morrison.

MILWAUKEE

MILWAUKEE JEWISH FEDERATION, INC. (1902); 1360 N. Prospect Ave. (53202); (414)390-5700. FAX: (414)390-5782. E-mail: info@milwaukeejewish.org. Pres. Stephen L. Chernof; Exec. V.-Pres. Richard H. Meyer.

CANADA

ALBERTA

CALGARY

CALGARY JEWISH COMMUNITY COUNCIL (1962); 1607 90th Ave. SW (T2V 4V7); (403)253-8600. FAX: (403)253-7915. E-mail: cjcc@jewish-calgary.com. Pres. Nate Feldman; Exec. Dir. Myrna Linder.

EDMONTON

JEWISH FEDERATION OF EDMONTON (1954; reorg. 1982); 7200-156th St. (T5R 1X3); (780)487-5120. FAX: (780)481-1854. E-mail: edjfed@net.com.ca. Pres. Stephen Mandel; Exec. Dir. Lesley A. Jacobson.

BRITISH COLUMBIA

VANCOUVER

JEWISH FEDERATION OF GREATER VANCOUVER (1932; reorg. 1987); 950 W. 41st Ave., Suite 200 (V5Z 2N7); (604)257-5100. FAX: (604)257-5110. E-mail: jfed@jfgv.com. Pres. Sondra Ritter.

MANITOBA

WINNIPEG

JEWISH FEDERATION OF WINNIPEG/COMBINED JEWISH APPEAL (1938; reorg. 1973); 123 Doncaster St., Suite C300 (R3N 2B2); (204)477-7400. FAX: (204)477-7405. E-mail: bfreedman@aspercampus.mb.ca. Pres. Howard Morry; Exec. V.-Pres. Robert Freedman.

ONTARIO

HAMILTON

UJA/JEWISH FEDERATION OF HAMILTON/WENTWORTH & AREA (1932; merged 1971); PO Box 7258, 1030 Lower Lions Club Rd., Ancaster (L9G 3N6); (905)648-0605 #305. FAX: (905)648-8350. E-mail: hamujajf@interlynx.net. Pres. Cheryl Greenbaum; Exec. Dir. Patricia Tolkin Eppel.

LONDON

LONDON JEWISH FEDERATION (1932); 536 Huron St. (N5Y 4J5); (519)673-3310. FAX: (519)673-1161. Pres. Ron Wolf; Off. Mgr. Debra Chatterley.

OTTAWA

UNITED JEWISH APPEAL OF OTTAWA (1934); 21 Nadolny Sachs Private (K2A 1R9); (613)798-4696. FAX: (613)798-4695. E-mail: uja@jccottawa.com. Pres. Barbara Farber; Exec. Dir. Mitchell Bellman.

TORONTO

UJA FEDERATION OF GREATER TORONTO (1917); 4600 Bathurst St. (M2R 3V2); (416)635-2883. FAX: (416)631-5715. E-mail: webmaven@feduja.org. Pres. Joseph Steiner; Exec. V.-Pres. Allan Reitzes.

WINDSOR

JEWISH COMMUNITY FEDERATION (1938); 1641 Ouellette Ave. (N8X 1K9); (519)973-1772. FAX: (519)973-1774. Pres. Dr. Michael Malowitz; Exec. Dir. Steven Brownstein.

QUEBEC

MONTREAL

FEDERATION CJA (formerly Allied Jewish Community Services) (1965); 1 Carrie Cummings Square (H3W 1M6); (514)735-3541. FAX: (514)735-8972. E-mail: dcantor@federationcja.org. Pres. Stanley Plotnick; Exec. V.-Pres. Danyael Cantor.

Jewish Periodicals*

UNITED STATES

ALABAMA

DEEP SOUTH JEWISH VOICE (1990) (formerly THE SOUTHERN SHOFAR). PO Box 130052, Birmingham, 35213. (205) 595-9255. FAX: (205)595-9256. E-mail: dsjvoice@aol.com. Lawrence M. Brook. Monthly. (WWW.DEEPSOUTHJEWISHVOICE.COM)

ARIZONA

ARIZONA JEWISH POST (1946). 2601 N. Campbell Ave., #205, Tucson, 85719. (520)319-1112. FAX: (520)319-1118. E-mail: posteds@aol.com. Sandra R. Heiman. Fortnightly. Jewish Federation of Southern Arizona.

JEWISH NEWS OF GREATER PHOENIX (1948). 1625 E. Northern Ave., Suite 106, Phoenix, 85020. (602)870-9470. FAX: (602)870-0426. E-mail: editor@jewishaz.com. Ed./Pub. Florence Eckstein. Weekly. (WWW.JEWISHAZ.COM)

CALIFORNIA

THE AMERICAN RABBI (1968). 22711 Cass Ave., Woodland Hills, 91364. (818)225-9631. FAX: (818)225-8354. E-mail: david@inpubco.com. Ed.-in-Ch./Pub. David Epstein; Ed. Harry Essrig. Quarterly.

CENTRAL CALIFORNIA JEWISH HERITAGE (1914). 20201 Sherman Way, Winnetka, 91306. (818) 576-9000. FAX: (818) 576-9910. E-mail: heritagepub@earthlink.net. Dan Brin. Six times a year. Heritage Group.

HERITAGE-SOUTHWEST JEWISH PRESS (1914). 20201 Sherman Way, Suite 204, Winnetka, 91306. (818) 576-9000. FAX: (818) 576-9910. E-mail: heritagepub @earthlink.net. Dan Brin. Weekly. Heritage Group.

JEWISH BULLETIN OF NORTHERN CALIFORNIA (1896). 225 Bush St., Suite 1480, San Francisco, 94104-4281. (415)263-7200. FAX: (415)263-7223. E-mail: sanfranbul @aol.com. Marc S. Klein. Weekly. San Francisco Jewish Community Publications, Inc.

JEWISH COMMUNITY CHRONICLE (1947). 3801 E. Willow St., Long Beach, 90815. (562)426-7601, ext. 1021. FAX: (562)595-5543. E-mail: jchron@surfside.net. Harriette Ellis; Bus. Mng./Prod. Chris Berry. Fortnightly. Jewish Federation of Greater Long Beach & West Orange County.

JEWISH COMMUNITY NEWS (1976). 14855 Oka Rd., Suite 2, Los Gatos, 95030. (408)358-3033, ext. 31. FAX: (408)356-0733. E-mail: jcn@jfgsj.org. Eileen Goss; Adv. Lindsay Greensweig (408)286-6669. Monthly. Jewish Federation of Greater San Jose.

JEWISH JOURNAL OF GREATER LOS ANGELES (1986). 3660 Wilshire Blvd., Suite 204, Los Angeles, 90010. (213)368-1661. FAX: (213)368-1684. E-mail:jjla@aol.com. Gene Lichtenstein. Weekly.

JEWISH NEWS (1973). 11071 Ventura Blvd., Studio City, 91604. (818)786-4000. FAX: (818)760-4648. Phil Blazer. Monthly.

---

*The information in this directory is based on replies to questionnaires circulated by the editors. For organization bulletins, see the directory of Jewish organizations.

(Also weekly Sunday TV and radio broadcasts in LA, NY, and Miami.)

JEWISH SOCIAL STUDIES: HISTORY, CULTURE, AND SOCIETY (1939). c/o Program in Jewish Studies, Bldg. 240, Rm. 103, Stanford University, Stanford, 94305-2190. (650)725-0829. FAX: (650)725-2920. E-mail: jss@leland.stanford.edu. Steven J. Zipperstein, Aron Rodrigue. Three times a year. Conference on Jewish Social Studies, Inc.

JEWISH SPORTS REVIEW. 1800 S. Robertson Blvd., #174, Los Angeles, 90035. (800)510-9003. E-mail: shel@jewish sportsreview.com. Shel Wallman/ Ephraim Moxson. Bimonthly. (www. JEWISHSPORTSREVIEW.COM)

LOS ANGELES JEWISH TIMES (formerly B'NAI B'RITH MESSENGER) (1897). 5455 Wilshire Blvd., Suite 903, Los Angeles, 90036. (323)933 0131. FAX: (323)933-7928. E-mail: lajtart@aol.com. Ed.-in-Chief Joe Bobker; Mng. Ed. Jane Fried. Weekly.

ORANGE COUNTY JEWISH HERITAGE. 24331 Muirlands Blvd., Suite D-347, Lake Forest, 92630. Phone/FAX: (949)362-4446. E-mail: ocnews@hotmail.com. Stan Brin. Bi-weekly.

SAN DIEGO JEWISH PRESS HERITAGE (1914). 3615 Kearny Villa Rd., #111, San Diego, 92123. (858)560-0992. FAX: (858) 560-0993. E-mail: sdheritage@aol.com. Aaron Hoskins. Weekly.

SAN DIEGO JEWISH TIMES (1979). 4731 Palm Ave., La Mesa, 91941. (619)463-5515. FAX: (619) 463-1309. E-mail: jewish times@msn.com. Colleen Silea. Fortnightly.

SHALOM L.A. (1988). 16027 Ventura Blvd., #400, Encino, 91436. (818)783-3090. FAX: (818)783-1104. Gal Shor. Weekly. Hebrew.

TIKKUN MAGAZINE (1986). 2107 Van Ness Ave., Suite 302, San Francisco, 94109. (415)575-1200. FAX: (415)575-1434. E-mail: magazine@tikkun.org. Michael Lerner. Bimonthly. Institute for Labor & Mental Health. (WWW.TIKKUN.ORG)

WESTERN STATES JEWISH HISTORY (1968). 22711 Cass Ave., Woodland Hills, 91364. (818)225-9631. FAX: (818)225-8354. E-mail: david@inpubco.com. Ed.-in-Ch. Gladys Sturman; Ed. David Epstein.

Quarterly. Western States Jewish History Association.

COLORADO

INTERMOUNTAIN JEWISH NEWS (1913). 1275 Sherman St., Suite 214, Denver, 80203-2299. (303)861-2234. FAX: (303)832-6942. E-mail: ijn@rmii.com. Exec. Ed. Rabbi Hillel Goldberg; Pub. Miriam Goldberg. Weekly.

CONNECTICUT

CONNECTICUT JEWISH LEDGER (1929). 740 N. Main St., W. Hartford, 06117. (860)231-2424. FAX: (860)231-2428. E-mail: editorial@jewishledger.com. Lisa Lenkiewicz. Weekly.

JEWISH LEADER (1974). 28 Channing St., PO Box 1468, New London, 06320. (860)442-7395. FAX: (860)443-4175. E-mailjfccmim@aol.com. Ed. Mimi Perl; Mng. Henry Savin. Biweekly. Jewish Federation of Eastern Connecticut.

DELAWARE

JEWISH VOICE. 100 W. 10th St., Suite 301, Wilmington, 19801. (302) 427-2100. FAX: (302) 427-2438. E-mail: jewishvoic @aol.com. Lynn Edelman. 22 times per year. Jewish Federation of Delaware.

DISTRICT OF COLUMBIA

AZURE (1996). 1140 Connecticut Ave., NW, Suite 801, Washington, 20036. (202)887-1270. FAX: (202)887-1277. E-mail: patrick@shalemcenter.org. Dan Polisar. Quarterly. Hebrew/English. The Shalem Center.

B'NAI B'RITH INTERNATIONAL JEWISH MONTHLY (1886, under the name Menorah). 1640 Rhode Island Ave., NW, Washington, 20036. (202)857-6646. FAX: (202)296-1092. E-mail: erozenman@ bnaibrith.org. Eric Rozenman. Bimonthly. B'nai B'rith International.

CAPITAL COMMUNIQUÉ (1991). 777 N. Capital St., NE, Suite 305, Washington, 20002. (202)216-9060. FAX: (202)216-9061. Jason Silberberg. Bi-annually. National Jewish Democratic Council.

THE JEWISH VETERAN (1896). 1811 R St., NW, Washington, 20009-1659. (202)265-6280. FAX: (202)234-5662. E-mail: jwv@ jwv.org. Seymour Brody. 5 times per year. Jewish War Veterans of the U.S.A.

MOMENT (1975). 4710 41 St., NW, Washington, 20016. (202)364-3300. FAX: (202)364-2636. E-mail: editor@moment mag.com. Hershel Shanks. Bimonthly. Jewish Educational Ventures, Inc.

FSU MONITOR (1990). 1819 H Street, NW, Suite 230, Washington, 20006. (202)775-9770. FAX: (202)775-9776. E-mail: ucsj @ucsj.com. Nickolai Butkevich. Quarterly. Union of Councils for Soviet Jews. (WWW.FSUMONITOR.COM)

NEAR EAST REPORT (1957). 440 First St., NW, Suite 607, Washington, 20001. (202)639-5254. FAX: (202) 347-4916. Dr. Raphael Danziger. Fortnightly. Near East Research, Inc.

SECURITY AFFAIRS (1976). 1717 K St., NW, Suite 800, Washington, 20006. (202)833-0020. FAX: (202)296-6452. E-mail: info@jinsa.org. Jim Colbert. Quarterly. Jewish Institute for National Security Affairs.

WASHINGTON JEWISH WEEK. *See under* MARYLAND

FLORIDA

THE CHRONICLE (1971). 580 S. McIntosh Rd., Sarasota, 34232. (941)371-4546. FAX: (941)378-2947. Barry Millman. Fortnightly. Sarasota-Manatee Jewish Federation.

HERITAGE FLORIDA JEWISH NEWS (1976). PO Box 300742, Fern Park, 32730. (407)834-8787. FAX: (407)831-0507. E-mail: heritagefl@aol.com. Pub. Jeffrey Gaeser; Asst. Ed. Shari Lee Beymon. Weekly.

JACKSONVILLE JEWISH NEWS (1988). 8505 San Jose Blvd., Jacksonville, 32217. (904)448-5000, (904)262-1971. FAX: (904)448-5715. E-mail: srgnews@aol. com. Susan R. Goetz. Monthly. Jacksonville Jewish Federation.

JEWISH JOURNAL (PALM BEACH-BROWARD-DADE) (1977). 601 Fairway Dr., Deerfield Beach, 33441. (954)698-6397. FAX: (954) 429-1207. Alan Gosh. Weekly. South Florida Newspaper Network.

JEWISH PRESS OF PINELLAS COUNTY (Clearwater-St.Petersburg) (1985). PO Box 6970, Clearwater, 33758-6970; 13191 Starkey Rd., Crownpointe #8, Largo, 33773-1438. (727)535-4400. FAX: (727) 530-3039. E-mail: jptb@aol.com. Karen

Wolfson Dawkins. Biweekly. Jewish Press Group of Tampa Bay (FL), Inc. in cooperation with the Jewish Federation of Pinellas County.

JEWISH PRESS OF TAMPA (1987). PO Box 6970, Clearwater 33758-6970; 13191 Starkey Rd., Crownpointe #8, Largo 33773-1438. (727)535-4400. FAX: (727) 530-3039. E-mail: jptb@aol.com. Karen Wolfson Dawkins. Biweekly. Jewish Press Group of Tampa Bay (FL), Inc.

SHALOM (1994). 8358 W. Oakland Park Blvd., Suite 305, Ft. Lauderdale, 33351. (954)748-8400. FAX: (954) 748-4509. Ed.-in-Chief Rhonda Roseman-Seriani; Mng. Ed. Elliot Goldenberg. Biweekly. Jewish Federation of Broward County.

GEORGIA

JEWISH CIVIC PRESS (1972). 500 Sugar Mill Rd., Suite B-210, Atlanta, 30350. (404) 231-2194. Abner L. Tritt. Monthly.

ILLINOIS

CHICAGO JEWISH NEWS (1994). 5301 W. Dempster, Skokie, Ill 60077. (847)966-0606. FAX: (847)966-1656. E-mail: info@ chicagojewishnews.com. Joseph Aaron. Weekly.

CHICAGO JEWISH STAR (1991). PO Box 268, Skokie, 60076-0268. (847)674-7827. FAX: (847)674-0014. E-mail: chicago-jewish-star@mcimail.com. Ed. Douglas Wertheimer; Assoc. Ed. Gila Wertheimer. Fortnightly.

JEWISH COMMUNITY NEWS (1941). 6464 W. Main, Suite 7A, Belleville, 62223. (618) 398-6100/(314)567-6955. FAX: (618)398-0539. Steve Low. Quarterly. Jewish Federation of Southern Illinois.

JUF NEWS & GUIDE TO JEWISH LIVING IN CHICAGO (1972). One S. Franklin St., Rm. 701G, Chicago, 60606. (312)357-4848. FAX: (312)855-2470. E-mail: jufnews@ juf.org. Aaron B. Cohen. Monthly (Guide, annually). Jewish United Fund/ Jewish Federation of Metropolitan Chicago.

INDIANA

ILLIANA NEWS (1976). 2939 Jewett St., Highland, 46322. (219)972-2250. FAX: (219)972-4779. E-mail: jfedofnwi@aol. com. Monthly (except July/Aug.). Jewish Federation of Northwest Indiana, Inc.

INDIANA JEWISH POST AND OPINION (1935). 238 S. Meridian St., #502, Indianapolis, 46225. (317)972-7800. FAX: (317)972-7807. E-mail: jpost@surf-ici.com. Ed Stattmann. Weekly.

NATIONAL JEWISH POST AND OPINION (1932). 238 S. Meridian St., Indianapolis, 46225. (317)972-7800. FAX: (317)972-7807. Gabriel Cohen. Weekly.

PROOFTEXTS: A JOURNAL OF JEWISH LITERARY HISTORY (1980). Indiana University Press, 601 N. Morton St., Bloomington, 47404. (812)855-9449. FAX: (812)855-8507. E-mail: journals@indiana.edu. Editorial address (for contributors):NEJS Dept., Brandeis U., Waltham, MA 02254. Alan Mintz, David G. Roskies. Three times a year.

KANSAS

KANSAS CITY JEWISH CHRONICLE (1920) 7373 W. 107 St., Overland Park, 66212. (913)648-4620. FAX: (913)381-1402. E-mail: chronicle@sunpublications.com. Rick Hellman. Weekly. Sun Publications.

KENTUCKY

COMMUNITY (1975). 3630 Dutchmans Lane, Louisville, 40205-3200. (502) 451-8840. FAX: (502) 458-0702. E-mail: jfed@iglou.com. Shiela Steinman Wallace. Biweekly. Jewish Community Federation of Louisville.

KENTUCKY JEWISH POST AND OPINION (1931). 1701 Bardstown Rd., Louisville, 40205. (502)459-1914. Ed Stattman. Weekly.

LOUISIANA

JEWISH CIVIC PRESS (1965). 924 Valmont St., New Orleans, 70115. (504)895-8784. Claire & Abner Tritt, eds. and pubs. Monthly.

JEWISH NEWS (1995). 3500 N. Causeway Blvd., Suite 1240, Metairie, 70002. (504) 828-2125. FAX: (504)828-2827. E-mail: jewishnews@jewishnola.com. Gail Naron Chalew. Fortnightly. Jewish Federation of Greater New Orleans.

MARYLAND

BALTIMORE JEWISH TIMES (1919). 2104 N. Charles St., Baltimore, 21218. (410)752-3504. FAX: (410)752-2375. Phil Jacobs. Weekly.

WASHINGTON JEWISH WEEK (1930, as the National Jewish Ledger). 1500 East Jefferson St., Rockville, 20852. (301)230-2222. FAX: (301)881-6362. E-mail: wjweek@aol.com. Debra Rubin. Weekly.

MASSACHUSETTS

AMERICAN JEWISH HISTORY (1893). Two Thornton Rd., Waltham, 02453. (781) 891-8110. FAX: (781)899-9208. E-mail: ajhs@ajhs.org. Marc Lee Raphael. Quarterly. American Jewish Historical Society.

JEWISH ADVOCATE (1902). 15 School St., Boston, 02108. (617)367-9100. FAX: (617)367-9310. E-mail: thejewadv@aol.com. Steven Rosenberg. Weekly.

THE JEWISH CHRONICLE (1927). 131 Lincoln St., Worcester, 01605. (508)752-2512. E-mail: jchronicle@aol.com. Pub. Sondra Shapiro; Ed. Ellen Weingart. Bimonthly.

JEWISH GUIDE TO BOSTON & NEW ENGLAND (1972). 15 School St., Boston, 02108. (617)367-9100. FAX: (617)367-9310. Rosie Rosenzweig. Irregularly. The Jewish Advocate.

THE JEWISH JOURNAL/NORTH OF BOSTON (1976). 201 Washington St., PO Box 555, Salem, 01970. (978)745-4111. FAX: (978) 745-5333. E-mail: editorial@jewishjournal.org. Judith Klein. Biweekly. Russian section. North Shore Jewish Press Ltd.

THE JEWISH NEWS OF WESTERN MASSACHUSETTS (see Jewish Advocate)

METROWEST JEWISH REPORTER (1970). 76 Salem End Rd., Framingham, 01702. (508)872-4808. FAX: (508)879-5856. Marcia T. Rivin. Monthly. Combined Jewish Philanthropies of Greater Boston.

PAKN-TREGER (1980). 1021 West St., Amherst, 01002. (413)256-4900. FAX: (413) 256-4700. E-mail: pt@bikher.org. Nancy Sherman. Three times a year. National Yiddish Book Center.

SH'MA (1970). 90 Oak Street, 4th Floor, Newton MA 02464. (877)568-SHMA. FAX: (617)965-7772. E-mail: susanb@jfl-media.com. Susan Berrin. Monthly. Jewish Family & Life. (WWW.SHMA.COM)

MICHIGAN

DETROIT JEWISH NEWS (1942). 27676 Franklin Rd., Southfield, 48034. (248) 354-6060. FAX: (248)354-6069. E-mail: smanello@thejewishnews.com. Robert Sklar. Weekly.

HUMANISTIC JUDAISM (1968). 28611 W. Twelve Mile Rd., Farmington Hills, 48334. (248)478-7610. FAX: (248)478-3159. E-mail: info@shj.org. M. Bonnie Cousens, Ruth D. Feldman. Quarterly. Society for Humanistic Judaism.

WASHTENAW JEWISH NEWS (1978). 2935 Birch Hollow Dr., Ann Arbor, 48108. (734)971-1800. FAX: (734)971-1801. E-mail: wjna2@aol.com. Susan Kravitz Ayer. Monthly.

MINNESOTA

AMERICAN JEWISH WORLD (1912). 4509 Minnetonka Blvd., Minneapolis, MN 55416. (952)259-5280. FAX: (952)920-6205. E-mail: amjewish@isd.net. Mordecai Specktor. Weekly.

MISSISSIPPI

DEEP SOUTH JEWISH VOICE (see Alabama)

MISSOURI

KANSAS CITY JEWISH CHRONICLE. See under KANSAS

ST. LOUIS JEWISH LIGHT (1947; reorg. 1963). 12 Millstone Campus Dr., St. Louis, 63146. (314)432-3353. FAX: (314)432-0515. E-mail: stlouislgt@aol.com. Robert A. Cohn. Weekly. St. Louis Jewish Light.

NEBRASKA

JEWISH PRESS (1920). 333 S. 132 St., Omaha, 68154. (402)334-6450. FAX: (402)334-5422. E-mail: ckatzman@jewishomaha. org. Carol Katzman. Weekly. Jewish Federation of Omaha.

NEVADA

JEWISH REPORTER (1976). 3909 S. Maryland Pkwy., Suite 400, Las Vegas, 89119-7520. (702)948-5129. FAX: (702)967-1082. E-mail: lvjewishreporter@aol.com. Terri Herman. Bimonthly. Jewish Federation of Las Vegas. (JEWISHLASVEGAS.COM)

LAS VEGAS ISRAELITE (1965). PO Box 14096, Las Vegas, 89114. (702)876-1255. FAX: (702)364-1009. Michael Tell. Bimonthly.

NEW HAMPSHIRE

JEWISH SPECATOR (1935). P.O. Box 267, New London, 03257. (603)526-2513. FAX: (603)526-2514. E-mail: jsisrael@ netmedia.net.il. Rabbi Mark Bleiweiss.

Quarterly. Friends of Jewish Spectator, Inc.

NEW JERSEY

AVOTAYNU (1985). 155 N. Washington Ave., Bergenfield, 07621. (201)387-7200. FAX: (201)387-2855. E-mail: info@avotaynu. com. Sallyann Amdur Sack. Quarterly.

JEWISH CHRONICLE (1982). 1063 East Landis Ave.,Suite B, Vineland, 08360. (856)696-4445. FAX: (856)696-3428. E-mail: jfedcc@aol.com. Ann Lynn Lipton. Bimonthly. The Jewish Federation of Cumberland County.

JEWISH COMMUNITY NEWS. 1086 Teaneck Rd., Teaneck, 07666. (201) 837-8818. FAX: (201) 833-4959. E-mail: jewish-std2@aol.com. Rebecca Kaplan Boroson. Fortnightly. Jewish Federation of North Jersey and Jewish Federation of Greater Clifton-Passaic.

JEWISH COMMUNITY VOICE (1941). 1301 Springdale Rd., Suite 250, Cherry Hill, 08003-2762. (856)751-9500, ext. 217. FAX: (856)489-8253. E-mail: jvchedi-tor@aol.com. Harriet Kessler. Biweekly. Jewish Federation of Southern NJ.

THE JEWISH JOURNAL (1999). 320 Raritan Ave., Suite 203, Highland Park, 08904. (732)393-0023. FAX: (732)393-0026. E-mail: jewish@castle.net. Ron Ostroff. Monthly. Published in cooperation with the Ocean County Jewish Federation.

JEWISH STANDARD (1931). 1086 Teaneck Rd., Teaneck, 07666. (201)837-8818. FAX: (201)833-4959. Rebecca Kaplan Boroson. Weekly.

JEWISH STAR (1985). 230 Old Bridge Turnpike, South River, 08882-2000. (732)432-7711. FAX: (732)432-0292. E-mail: jfgmc @aol.com. Marlene A. Heller. Fortnightly. Jewish Federation of Greater Middlesex County.

THE JEWISH STATE (1996). 320 Raritan Ave., Suite 203, Highland Park, 08904. (732)393-0023. FAX: (732)393-0026. E-mail: jewish@castle.net. Ron Ostroff. Weekly.

JEWISH VOICE & OPINION (1987). 73 Dana Place, Englewood, 07631. (201) 569-2845. FAX: (201)569-1739. Susan L. Rosenbluth. Monthly.

JEWISH VOICE OF GREATER MONMOUTH COUNTY (1971). 100 Grant Ave., Deal

Park, 07723. (732)531-6200. FAX: (732)531-9518. E-mail: pfdnuss@msn. com. Lauren Silver. Monthly. Jewish Federation of Greater Monmouth County and Ocean County Jewish Federation.

JOURNAL OF JEWISH COMMUNAL SERVICE (1899). 3084 State Hwy. 27, Suite 9, Kendall Pk., 08824-1657. (732)821-1871. FAX: (732)821-5335. E-mail: jcsana@aol. com. Gail Naron Chalew. Quarterly. Jewish Communal Service Association of North America.

NEW JERSEY JEWISH NEWS (1947). 901 Route 10, Whippany, 07981-1157. (973) 887-3900. FAX: (973)887-5999. E-mail: 6853202@mcimail.com. David Twersky. Weekly. United Jewish Federation of MetroWest.

THE SPEAKER (1999). 320 Raritan Ave., Suite 203, Highland Park, 08904. (732) 393-0023. FAX: (732)393-0026. E-mail: jewish@castle.net. Ron Ostroff. Monthly. Published in cooperation with the Jewish Federation of Somerset, Hunterdon & Warren Counties.

NEW MEXICO

NEW MEXICO JEWISH LINK (1971). 5520 Wyoming NE, Albuquerque, 87109. (505) 821-3214. FAX: (505)821-3351. E-mail: nmjlink@aol.com. Tema Milstein. Monthly. Jewish Federation of Greater Albuquerque.

NEW YORK

AFN SHVEL (1941). 200 W. 72 St., Suite 40, NYC, 10023. (212)787-6675. E-mail: yid league@aol.com. Mordkhe Schaechter. Quarterly. Yiddish. League for Yiddish, Inc.

AGENDA: JEWISH EDUCATION (1949; formerly PEDAGOGIC REPORTER). JESNA, 111 Eighth Ave., Suite 11E, NYC, 10011-5201. (212)284-6950. FAX: (212)284-6951. E-mail: info@jesna.org. Rabbi Arthur Vernon. Twice a year. Jewish Education Service of North America, Inc.

ALGEMEINER JOURNAL (1972). 225 E. Broadway, NYC, 10002. (212)267-5561. FAX: (212)267-5624. E-mail: Algemeiner @aol.com. Gershon Jacobson. Weekly. Yiddish-English.

AMERICAN JEWISH YEAR BOOK (1899). 165 E. 56 St., NYC, 10022. (212)751-4000. FAX: (212)751-4017. E-mail: research @ajc.org. David Singer, Lawrence Grossman. Annually. American Jewish Committee.

AMIT (1925). 817 Broadway, NYC, 10003. (212)477-4720. FAX: (212)353-2312. E-mail: amitmag@aol.com. Rita Schwalb. Quarterly. AMIT (formerly AMERICAN MIZRACHI WOMEN).

AUFBAU (1934). 2121 Broadway, NYC, 10023. (212)873-7400. Voice mail: (212) 579-6578. FAX: (212)496-5736. E-mail: aufbau2000@aol.com. Monika Ziegler/ Andreas Mink/Irene Armbruster. Fortnightly. German-English. New World Club, Inc.

BUFFALO JEWISH REVIEW (1918). 15 E. Mohawk St., Buffalo, 14203. (716)854-2192. FAX: (716)854-2198. E-mail: buffjewrev @aoc.com. Harlan C. Abbey. Weekly. Kahaal Nahalot Israel.

THE CALL (1933). 45 E. 33 St., NYC, 10016. (212)889-6800, ext. 225. FAX: (212)532-7518. E-mail: socolove@circle.org. Emily Socolov. Three times a year. The Workmen's Circle/Arbeter Ring.

CCAR JOURNAL: A REFORM JEWISH QUARTERLY (formerly JOURNAL OF REFORM JUDAISM) (1953). 355 Lexington Ave., NYC, 10017. (212)972-3636. FAX: (212)692-0819. Ed. Stephen Pearce. Mng. Ed. Elliot Stevens. Quarterly. Central Conference of American Rabbis.

CIRCLE (1943). 15 E. 26 St., NYC, 10010-1579. (212)532-4949. FAX: (212)481-4174. E-mail: info@jcca.org. Jason Black. Quarterly. Jewish Community Centers Association of North America (formerly JWB).

COMMENTARY (1945). 165 E. 56 St., NYC, 10022. (212)751-4000. FAX: (212)751-1174. E-mail: commentary@compuserve. com. Ed. Neal Kozodoy, Ed.-at-Large Norman Podhoretz. Monthly. American Jewish Committee.

CONGRESS MONTHLY (1933). 15 E. 84 St., NYC, 10028. (212)879-4500. Jack Fischel. Six times a year. American Jewish Congress.

CONSERVATIVE JUDAISM (1945). 3080 Broadway, NYC, 10027. (212)280-6065. FAX: (212)749-9166. E-mail: rapubs@jtsa.edu. Rabbi Martin S. Cohen. Quarterly. Rabbinical Assembly and Jewish Theological Seminary of America.

FORVERTS (Yiddish Forward) (1897). 45 E. 33 St., NYC, 10016. (212)889-8200. FAX: (212)684-3949. Boris Sandler. Weekly. Yiddish. Forward Association, Inc.

FORWARD (1897). 45 E. 33 St., NYC, 10016. (212)889-8200. FAX: (212)447-6406. E-mail: newsdesk@forward.com. J. J. Goldberg. Weekly. Forward Newspaper, L.L.C.

HADAROM (1957). 305 Seventh Ave., NYC, 10001. (212)807-7888. FAX: (212)727-8452. Rabbi Gedalia Dov Schwartz. Annual. Hebrew. Rabbinical Council of America.

HADASSAH MAGAZINE (1914). 50 W. 58 St., NYC, 10019. (212)688-0227. FAX: (212)446-9521. Alan M. Tigay. Monthly (except for combined issues of June-July and Aug.-Sept.). Hadassah, the Women's Zionist Organization of America.

HADOAR (1921). 426 W. 58 St., NYC, 10019. (212)957-6659. FAX: (212)957-5811. E-mail: general@hist-ivrit.org. Ed. Shlomo Shamir; Lit. Ed. Dr. Yael Feldman. Biweekly. Hebrew. Hadoar Association, Inc., Organ of the Histadruth of America.

I.A.J.E. NEWSLETTER (1999). (718)339-0337. E-mail: sanuav@stjohns.edu. Victor D. Sanua. International Association of Jews from Egypt.

JBI VOICE (1978). 110 E. 30 St., NYC, 10016. (212)889-2525, (800)433-1531. Dr. Reuven Kimelman. Ten times a year in U.S. (audiocassettes). English. Jewish Braille Institute of America.

JEWISH ACTION (1950). 11 Broadway, NYC, 10004. (212)613-8146. FAX: (212)613-0646. E-mail: ja@ou.org. Nechama Carmel. Quarterly. Orthodox Union.

JEWISH BOOK ANNUAL (1942). 15 E. 26 St., 10th fl., NYC, 10010. (212)532-4949, ext. 297. E-mail: jbc@jewishbooks.org. Dr. Stephen H. Garrin. Hebrew & English with bibliography in Yiddish. Jewish Book Council.

JEWISH BOOK WORLD (1945). 15 E. 26 St., NYC, 10010. (212)532-4949, ext. 297. FAX: (212)481-4174. E-mail: jbc@jewish books.org. Esther Nussbaum. Three times annually. Jewish Book Council.

JEWISH BRAILLE REVIEW (1931). 110 E. 30 St., NYC, 10016. (212)889-2525, (800) 433-1531. Dr. Reuven Kimelman. 10 times a year in U.S. (braille). English. Jewish Braille Institute of America.

JEWISH CURRENTS (1946). 22 E. 17 St., Suite 601, NYC, 10003-1919. (212)924-5740. FAX: (212)414-2227. Monthly (July/Aug. combined). Association for Promotion of Jewish Secularism, Inc.

JEWISH EDUCATION NEWS (1980). 261 W. 35 St., Fl. 12A, NYC 10001. (212) 268-4210. FAX: (212)268-4214. E-mail: publications @caje.org. Mng. Ed. Judi Resnick. Triannually. Coalition for the Advancement of Jewish Education.

JEWISH FRONTIER (1934). 275 Seventh Ave., 17th fl., NYC, 10001. (212)229-2280. FAX: (212)675-7685. Nahum Guttman. Bimonthly. Labor Zionist Letters, Inc.

JEWISH HERALD (1984). 1689 46 St., Brooklyn, 11204. (718)972-4000. E-mail: jewish herald@aol.com. Leon J. Sternheim. Weekly.

JEWISH JOURNAL (1969). 11 Sunrise Plaza, Valley Stream, 11580. (516)561-6900. FAX: (516)561-6971. Ed. Paul Rubens; Pub. Harold Singer. Weekly.

JEWISH LEDGER (1924). 2535 Brighton-Henrietta Town Line Rd., Rochester, 14623. (716)427-2434. FAX: (716)427-8521. Barbara Morgenstern. Weekly.

JEWISH OBSERVER (1963). 84 William St., NYC, 10038. (212)797-9000. FAX: (212)269-2843. E-mail: aiamail@aol.com. Rabbi Nisson Wolpin. Monthly (except July and Aug.). Agudath Israel of America.

JEWISH OBSERVER OF CENTRAL NEW YORK (1978). PO Box 510, DeWitt, 13214. (315) 445-2040. FAX: (315)445-1559. E-mail: jocny@aol.com. Judith Huober. Biweekly. Syracuse Jewish Federation, Inc.

JEWISH POST OF NY (1993). 130 W. 29 St., 10th fl., NYC, 10001-5312. (212)967-7313. FAX: (212)967-8321. E-mail: jpost @nais.com. Ed. Gad Nahshon; Pub. & Ed.-in-Chief Henry J. Levy. Monthly. Link Marketing & Promotion, Inc.

JEWISH PRESS (1950). 338 Third Ave., Brooklyn, 11215. (718)330-1100. FAX: (718)935-1215. E-mail: jpeditor@aol. com. Jerry Greenwald. Weekly.

JEWISH TELEGRAPHIC AGENCY COMMUNITY NEWS REPORTER (1962). 330 Seventh

Ave., 11th fl., NYC, 10001-5010. (212) 643-1890. FAX: (212)643-8498. Lisa Hostein. Monthly. (WWW.JTA.ORG)

JEWISH TELEGRAPHIC AGENCY DAILY NEWS BULLETIN (1917). 330 Seventh Ave., 11th fl., NYC, 10001-5010. (212)643-1890. FAX: (212)643-8498. Exec. Ed. Mark Joffe; Ed. Lisa Hostein. Daily. (WWW.JTA. ORG)

JEWISH TELEGRAPHIC AGENCY WEEKLY NEWS DIGEST (1933). 330 Seventh Ave., 11th fl., NYC, 10001-5010. (212)643-1890. FAX: (212)643-8498. Exec. Ed. Mark Joffe; Ed. Lisa Hostein. Weekly. (WWW.JTA.ORG)

JEWISH TRIBUNE. PMB #372, 169 South Main St., New City, 10956; Exec. off. (mailing address): 115 Middle Neck Rd., Great Neck, 11021. (845)352-5151. FAX: (516)829-4776. E-mail: lijeworld@ aol.com. Jerome W. Lippman. Weekly. Jewish Tribune; Long Island Jewish World; Manhattan Jewish Sentinel.

JEWISH WEEK (1876; reorg. 1970). 1501 Broadway, NYC, 10036-5503. (212) 921-7822. FAX: (212)921-8420. E-mail: editor@jewishweek.org. Gary Rosenblatt. Weekly.

JEWISH WORLD (1965). 1104 Central Ave., Albany, 12205. (518)459-8455. FAX: (518)459-5289. E-mail: 6859675@mcimail. com. Laurie J. Clevenson. Weekly.

JOURNAL OF JEWISH EDUCATION-CJE (formerly Jewish EDUCATION) (1929). 426 W. 58 St., Suite 329, NYC, 10019. (914)368-8657. FAX: (212)284-6951. Dr. Bernard Ducoff. Three times a year. Council for Jewish Education.

JOURNAL OF REFORM JUDAISM. *See* CCAR Journal

JTS MAGAZINE (formerly MASORET) (1991). 3080 Broadway, NYC, 10027. (212)678-8950. FAX: (212)864-0109. E-mail: joginsberg@jtsa.edu. Johanna R. Ginsberg. Three times a year. Jewish Theological Seminary. (WWW.JTSA.EDU)

JUDAISM (1952). 15 E. 84 St., NYC, 10028. (212)360-1500. FAX: (212)249-3672. Editor's address: Kresge Col., U. of California, Santa Cruz, CA, 95064. (408) 459-2566. FAX: (408)459-4872. Subscription address: 15 E. 84 St., NYC 10028. (212)360-1500. E-mail: judaism @cats.ucsc.edu. Prof. Murray Baum-

garten. Quarterly. American Jewish Congress.

KASHRUS MONTHLY-YOUR UPDATE ON KOSHER (1990). PO Box 204, Brooklyn, 11204. (718)336-8544. Rabbi Yosef Wikler. Monthly. Kashrus Institute. (www. KOSHERMAGAZINE.COM)

KASHRUS MAGAZINE-THE PERIODICAL FOR THE KOSHER CONSUMER (1980). PO BOX 204, Brooklyn, 11204. (718)336-8544. Rabbi Yosef Wikler. Five times per year (February, April, June, September, December). Kashrus Institute. (WWW.KOSHER MAGAZINE.COM)

KOL HAT'NUA (Voice of the Movement) (1975). c/o Young Judaea, 50 W. 58 St., NYC, 10019. (212)303-4576. FAX: (212)303-4572. E-mail: meat345@aol. com. Dov Wilker. Quarterly. Hadassah Zionist Youth Commission-Young Judaea.

KULTUR UN LEBN-CULTURE AND LIFE (1960). 45 E. 33 St., NYC, 10016. (212)889-6800. FAX: (212)532-7518. E-mail: wcfriends@aol.com. Joseph Mlotek. Quarterly. Yiddish. The Workmen's Circle.

LAMISHPAHA (1963). 426 W. 58 St., NYC, 10019. (212)957-6659. FAX: (212)957-5811. E-mail: general@hist-ivrit.org. Dr. Vered Cohen-Raphaeli. Illustrated. Monthly (except July and Aug.). Hebrew. Histadruth Ivrith of America.

LIKUTIM (1981). 110 E. 30 St., NYC, 10016. (212)889-2525. Joanne Jahr. Two times a year in Israel (print and audiocassettes). Hebrew. Jewish Braille Institute of America.

LILITH-THE INDEPENDENT JEWISH WOMEN'S MAGAZINE (1976). 250 W. 57 St., #2432, NYC, 10107. (212)757-0818. FAX: (212) 757-5705. E-mail: lilithmag@aol.com. Susan Weidman Schneider. Quarterly. (WWW.LILITHMAG.COM)

LONG ISLAND JEWISH WORLD (1971). 115 Middle Neck Rd., Great Neck, 11021. (516)829-4000. FAX: (516)829-4776. E-mail: lijeworld@aol.com. Jerome W. Lippman. Weekly.

MANHATTAN JEWISH SENTINEL (1993). 115 Middle Neck Rd., Great Neck, 11021. (212)244-4949. FAX: (212)244-2257. E-mail: lijeworld@aol.com. Jerome W. Lippman. Weekly.

MARTYRDOM AND RESISTANCE (1974). 500 Fifth Ave., Suite 1600, NYC, 10110-1699. (212)220-4304. FAX: (212)220-4308. E-mail: yadvashem@aol.com. Ed. Dr. Harvey Rosenfeld; Ed.-in-Chief Eli Zborowski. Bimonthly. International Society for Yad Vashem.

MIDSTREAM (1954). 633 Third Ave., 21st fl., NYC, 10017. (212)339-6020. FAX: (212)318-6176. E-mail: info@midstream.org. Joel Carmichael. Eight times a year. Theodor Herzl Foundation, Inc.

NA'AMAT WOMAN (1925). 350 Fifth Ave., Suite 4700, NYC, 10118-4799. (212)563-5222. FAX: (212)563-5710. Judith A. Sokoloff. Quarterly. English-Yiddish-Hebrew. NA'AMAT USA, the Women's Labor Zionist Organization of America. (WWW.NAAMAT.ORG)

OLOMEINU-OUR WORLD (1945). 5723 18th Ave., Brooklyn, 11204. (718)259-1223. FAX: (718)259-1795. E-mail: torahumesorah@torahworld.net. Rabbi Yaakov Fruchter. Monthly. English-Hebrew. Torah Umesorah-National Society for Hebrew Day Schools.

PASSOVER DIRECTORY (1923). 11 Broadway, NYC, 10004. (212)613-8135. FAX: (212)613-0772. Email: lieberd@ou.org Deborah Lieber. Annually. Union of Orthodox Jewish Congregations of America.

PROCEEDINGS OF THE AMERICAN ACADEMY FOR JEWISH RESEARCH (1920). 51 Washington Sq. South, NYC, 10012-1075. (212)998-3550. FAX: (212)995-4178. Dr. Nahum Sarna. Annually. English-Hebrew - French - Arabic - Persian - Greek. American Academy for Jewish Research.

RCA RECORD (1953). 305 Seventh Ave. NYC, 10001. (212)807-7888. FAX: (212) 727-8452. Rabbi Mark Dratch. Quarterly. Rabbinical Council of America.

REFORM JUDAISM (1972; formerly Dimensions in American Judaism). 633 Third Ave., 6th fl., NYC, 10017. (212)650-4240. Aron Hirt-Manheimer. Quarterly. Union of American Hebrew Congregations. (WWW.UAHC.ORG/RJMAG)

THE REPORTER (1971). 500 Clubhouse Rd., Vestal, 13850. (607)724-2360. FAX: (607)724-2311. E-mail: TReporter@aol.com. Judith S. Huober. Weekly. Jewish Federation of Broome County, Inc.

THE REPORTER (1966). 315 Park Ave. S., NYC 10010. (212)505-7700, ext. 265. FAX: (212)674-3057. E-mail; mheller@waort.org. Marlene A. Heller. Quarterly. Women's American ORT, Inc. (www.WAORT.ORG)

RESPONSE: A CONTEMPORARY JEWISH REVIEW (1967). Columbia University Post Office, PO Box 250892, NYC, 10025. E-mail: response@panix.com. Chanita Baumhaft. Annual.

RUSSIAN FORWARD (1995). 45 E. 33 St., NYC, 10016. (212)576-0868. FAX: (212)448-9124. E-mail: rforward99@yahoo.com. Leonid Shkolnik. Weekly. Russian.

SYNAGOGUE LIGHT AND KOSHER LIFE (1933). 47 Beekman St., NYC, 10038. (212)227-7800. Rabbi Meyer Hager. Quarterly. The Kosher Food Institute.

TRADITION (1958). 305 Seventh Ave., NYC, 10001. (212)807-7888. FAX: (212)727-8452. Rabbi Emanuel Feldman. Quarterly. Rabbinical Council of America.

UNITED SYNAGOGUE REVIEW (1943). 155 Fifth Ave., NYC, 10010. (212)533-7800. FAX: (212)353-9439. E-mail: info@uscj.org. Lois Goldrich. Semiannually. United Synagogue of Conservative Judaism.

UNSER TSAIT (1941). 25 E. 21 St., 3rd fl., NYC, 10010. (212)475-0055. Bimonthly. Yiddish. Jewish Labor Bund.

VIEWPOINT MAGAZINE (1952). 3 W. 16 St., NYC, 10011. (212)929-1525, ext. 131. E-mail: ncyi@youngisrael.org. Esther Altman. Quarterly. National Council of Young Israel.

VOICE OF THE DUTCHESS JEWISH COMMUNITY (1989). 110 Grand Ave., Poughkeepsie, 12603. (914)471-9811. FAX: (914)471-0659. E-mail: jfeddutchess@mindspring.com. Business off.:500 Clubhouse Rd., Vestal, 13850. (607)724-2360. FAX: (607)724-2311. Marc S. Goldberg, Sandy Gardner. Monthly. Jewish Federation of Dutchess County, Inc.

WOMEN'S LEAGUE OUTLOOK MAGAZINE (1930). 48 E. 74 St., New York, 10021. (212)628-1600. FAX: (212)772-3507. E-mail: wleague74@aol.com. Marjorie Saulson. Quarterly. Women's League for Conservative Judaism.

WORKMEN'S CIRCLE CALL. See The Call

WYOMING VALLEY JEWISH REPORTER (formerly WE ARE ONE) (1995). 500 Clubhouse Rd., Vestal, 13850. (607)724-2360. FAX: (607)724-2311. E-mail: TReporter @aol.com. Judith S. Huober. Every other week. Wilkes-Barre Jewish Community Board.

YEARBOOK OF THE CENTRAL CONFERENCE OF AMERICAN RABBIS (1890). 355 Lexington Ave., NYC, 10017. (212)972-3636. FAX: (212)692-0819. Rabbi Elliot L. Stevens. Annually. Central Conference of American Rabbis.

YIDDISH (1973). Queens College, NSF 350, 65-30 Kissena Blvd., Flushing, 11367. (718)997-3622. Joseph C. Landis. Quarterly. Queens College Press.

DI YIDDISHE HEIM (1958). 770 Eastern Pkwy., Brooklyn, 11213. (718)735-0458. Rachel Altein, Tema Gurary. Twice a year. English-Yiddish. Neshei Ub'nos Chabad-Lubavitch Women's Organization.

YIDDISHE KULTUR (1938). 1133 Broadway, Rm. 820, NYC, 10010. (212)243-1304. FAX: (212)243-1305. E-mail:mahosu@ aol.com. Itche Goldberg. Bimonthly. Yiddish. Yiddisher Kultur Farband, Inc.—YKUF.

DOS YIDDISHE VORT (1953). 84 William St., NYC, 10038. (212)797-9000. Joseph Friedenson. Bimonthly, (November-December monthly). Yiddish. Agudath Israel of America.

YIDDISHER KEMFER (1900). 275 Seventh Ave., NYC, 10001. (212)675-7808. FAX: (212) 675-7685. Dr. Jacob Weitzney. Bimonthly. Yiddish. Labor Zionist Alliance.

YIDISHE SHPRAKH (1941). 15 W. 16 St., NYC, 10011. (212)246-6080, ext. 6139. FAX: (212) 292-1892. Dr. Mordkhe Schaechter. Irregularly. Yiddish. YIVO Institute for Jewish Research.

YIVO BLETER (1931). 15 W. 16 St., NYC, 10011. (212)246-6080. FAX: (212)292-1892.E-mail: yivomail@yivo.cjh.org. Dr. David E. Fishman. Biannually. Yiddish. YIVO Institute for Jewish Research.

THE YOUNG JUDEAN (1909). 50 W. 58 St., NYC, 10019. (212)303-4588. FAX: (212)303-4572. Email: ugoldflam@ youngjudaea.org. Uri Goldflam. Quarterly. Young Judaea Zionist Youth Movement/Hadassah. (WWW.YOUNG JUDAEA.ORG)

YUGNTRUF: YIDDISH YOUTH MAGAZINE (1964). 200 W. 72 St., Suite 40, NYC, 10023. (212)787-6675. FAX: (212)799-1517. E-mail: mschaecht@aol.com. Elinor Robinson. Two to four times a year. Yiddish. Yugntruf Youth for Yiddish.

ZUKUNFT (The Future) (1892). 25 E. 21 St., NYC, 10010. (212)505-8040. FAX: (212) 505-8044. Chaim Beider & Yonia Fain. Quarterly. Yiddish. Congress for Jewish Culture.

NORTH CAROLINA

AMERICAN JEWISH TIMES OUTLOOK (1934; reorg. 1950). PO Box 33218, Charlotte, 28233-3218. (704)372-3296. FAX: (704) 377-9237. E-mail: geri@pop.vnet.net. Geri Zhiss. Monthly. The Blumenthal Foundation.

CHARLOTTE JEWISH NEWS (1978). 5007 Providence Rd., Charlotte, 28226. (704) 944-6765. FAX: (704) 365-4507. E-mail: amontoni@shalomcharlotte.org. Amy Krakovitz. Monthly (except July). Jewish Federation of Greater Charlotte.

JEWISH FEDERATION NEWS (1986). 8210 Creedmoor Rd., Suite 104, Raleigh, 27613. (919)676-2200. FAX: (919)676-2122. Sarah Falk. Monthly. Wake County Jewish Federation.

MODERN JUDAISM (1980). Oxford University Press, 2001 Evans Rd., Cary, 27513. (919)677-0977. FAX: (919)677-1714. E-mail: jnlorders@oup-usa.org. (Editorial address:Center for Judaic Studies, Boston University, 745 Commonwealth Ave., Boston, 02215. (617)353-8096. FAX: (617)353-5441.) Steven T. Katz. Three times a year.

OHIO

AKRON JEWISH NEWS (1929). 750 White Pond Drive, Akron, 44320. (330)869-2424. FAX: (330)867-8498. E-mail: TobyLiberman@jewishakron.org. Toby Liberman. Fortnightly. Jewish Community Board of Akron.

AMERICAN ISRAELITE (1854). 906 Main St., Rm. 508, Cincinnati, 45202-1371. (513) 621-3145. FAX: (513)621-3744. E-mail: amisralite@aol.com. John Guip. Weekly.

AMERICAN JEWISH ARCHIVES JOURNAL (1948). 3101 Clifton Ave., Cincinnati, 45220-2488. (513)221-1875. FAX: (513) 221-7812. E-mail: aja@cn.huc.edu. Ed.

Dr. Gary P. Zola; Mng. Ed. Dr. Frederic Krome. Twice a year. Jacob Rader Marcus Center, American Jewish Archives, HUC-JIR.

CLEVELAND JEWISH NEWS (1964). 3645 Warrensville Center Rd., Suite 230, Cleveland, 44122. (216)991-8300. FAX: (216)991-2088. E-mail: editorial@cjn.org. Cynthia Dettelbach. Weekly. Cleveland Jewish News Publication Co. (www.CLEVELANDJEWISHNEWS.COM)

DAYTON JEWISH OBSERVER (1996), 4501 Denlinger Rd., Dayton, 45426. (937)854-4150. E-mail: mweiss@jfgd.net. Marshall Weiss. Monthly. Jewish Federation of Greater Dayton.

INDEX TO JEWISH PERIODICALS (1963). PO Box 18525, Cleveland Hts., 44118. (216)381-4846. FAX: (216)381-4321. E-mail: index@jewishperiodicals.com. Lenore Pfeffer Koppel. Annually. Available in book and CD-ROM form. (www.JEWISHPERIODICALS.COM)

JEWISH JOURNAL (1987). 505 Gypsy Lane, Youngstown, 44504-1314. (330)744-7902. FAX: (330)746-7926. Email: yojjournal@aol.com Sherry Weinblatt. Biweekly (except July/Aug.). Youngstown Area Jewish Federation.

OHIO JEWISH CHRONICLE (1922). 2862 Johnstown Rd., Columbus, 43219. (614)337-2055. FAX: (614)337-2059. Email: ojc@iwaynet.net. Roberta Keck. Weekly.

STARK JEWISH NEWS (1920). 2631 Harvard Ave. NW, Canton, 44709. (330)452-6444. FAX: (330)452-4487. E-mail: canton jcf@aol.com. Linda Sirak. Monthly. Canton Jewish Community Federation; United Jewish Council of Greater Toledo.

STUDIES IN BIBLIOGRAPHY AND BOOKLORE (1953). 3101 Clifton Ave., Cincinnati, 45220. (513)221-1875. FAX: (513)221-0519. E-mail: lwolfson@huc.edu. Herbert C. Zafren. Irregularly. English-Hebrew-etc. Library of Hebrew Union College-Jewish Institute of Religion.

TOLEDO JEWISH NEWS (1951). 6505 Sylvania Ave., Sylvania, 43560. (419)885-4461. FAX: (419)724-0423. E-mail: Toljewnew @aol.com. Laurie Cohen. Monthly. Jewish Federation of Greater Toledo.

OKLAHOMA

TULSA JEWISH REVIEW (1930). 2021 E. 71 St., Tulsa, 74136. (918)495-1100. FAX: (918)495-1220. Ed Ulrich. Monthly. Jewish Federation of Tulsa.

OREGON

BRIDGES: A JOURNAL FOR JEWISH FEMINISTS AND OUR FRIENDS (1990). PO Box 24839, Eugene, 97402. (541)343-7617. FAX: (541)343-7617. E-mail: ckinberg @pond.net. Mng. Ed. Clare Kinberg. Semiannually.

JEWISH REVIEW (1959). 506 SW Sixth Ave., Suite 606, Portland, 97204. Edit.:(503) 227-7464. FAX: (503) 227-7438. Adv.: 503) 670-2883. FAX: (503) 620-3433. E-mail: editorial@jewishreview.org. Paul Haist. Regular column in Russian. Fortnightly. Jewish Federation of Portland. (WWW.JEWISHREVIEW.ORG)

PENNSYLVANIA

COMMUNITY REVIEW (1925). 3301 N. Front St. Annex, Harrisburg, 17110. (717)236-9555, ext.3402. FAX:(717)236-2552. E-mail: communityreview@desupernet.net. Carol L. Cohen. Fortnightly. United Jewish Community of Greater Harrisburg.

CONTEMPORARY JEWRY (1974, under the name JEWISH SOCIOLOGY AND SOCIAL RESEARCH). Gratz College, 7605 Old York Rd., Melrose Park, 19027. (215)635-7300. FAX:(215)635-7320. E-mail:rela1@aol.com. Ed. Rela Mintz Geffen; Mng. Ed. Egon Mayer. Annually. Association for the Social Scientific Study of Jewry.

JERUSALEM LETTER/VIEWPOINTS (1978). 1515 Locust St., Suite 703, Philadelphia, 19102. (215)772-0564. FAX: (215)772-0566. Zvi R. Marom. Fortnightly. Jerusalem Center for Public Affairs.

JEWISH CHRONICLE OF PITTSBURGH (1962). 5600 Baum Blvd., Pittsburgh, 15206. (412)687-1000. FAX: (412)687-5119. E-mail: pittjewchr@aol.com. Joel Roteman. Weekly. Pittsburgh Jewish Publication and Education Foundation.

JEWISH EXPONENT (1887). 2100 Arch St., Philadelphia, 19103. (215)832-0740. FAX: (215)569-3389. E-mail: jexponent @aol.com. Jonathan S. Tobin. Weekly. Jewish Federation of Greater Philadelphia.

JEWISH POLITICAL STUDIES REVIEW (1989). 1515 Locust St., Suite 703, Philadelphia, 19102. (215)772-0564. FAX: (215)772-0566. Mark Ami-El. Twice a year. Jerusalem Center for Public Affairs.

JEWISH QUARTERLY REVIEW (1910). 420 Walnut St., Philadelphia, 19106. (215) 238-1290. FAX: (215)238-1540. E-mail: jqroffice@sas.upenn.edu. Ed. David M. Goldenberg; Mng. Ed. Bonnie L. Blankenship. Quarterly. Center for Advanced Jewish Studies, University of Pennsylvania.

NEW MENORAH (1978). 7318 Germantown Ave., Philadelphia, 19119-1793. (215)247-9700. FAX: (215)247-9703. Rabbi Arthur Waskow, PhD. Quarterly. Aleph: Alliance for Jewish Renewal.

RECONSTRUCTIONISM TODAY (1993). Beit Devora, 7804 Montgomery Ave., Suite 9, Elkins Park, 19027-2649. (215)782-8500. FAX: (215)782-8805. E-mail: jrfnatl@aol.com. Lawrence Bush. Quarterly. Jewish Reconstructionist Federation.

THE RECONSTRUCTIONIST (1935). 1299 Church Rd., Wyncote, 19095 1898. (215)576-5210. FAX: (215)576-8051. E-mail: rraassoc@aol.com. Rabbi Richard Hirsh. Semiannually. Reconstructionist Rabbinical College.

SCRANTON FEDERATION REPORTER (1994). 500 Clubhouse Rd., Vestal, NY, 13850. (607)724-2360. FAX: (607)724-2311. E-mail: TReporter@aol.com. Marc S. Goldberg. Biweekly. Scranton-Lackawanna Jewish Federation.

RHODE ISLAND

JEWISH VOICE OF RHODE ISLAND (1973). 130 Sessions St., Providence, 02906. (401)421-4111. FAX: (401)331-7961. E-mail: jvoice@aol.com. Jane S. Sprague. Monthly. Jewish Federation of Rhode Island.

RHODE ISLAND JEWISH HERALD (1930). 99 Webster St., Pawtucket, 02860. (401)724-0200. FAX: (401)726-5820. Luke O'Neill. Weekly. Herald Press Publishing Company.

RHODE ISLAND JEWISH HISTORICAL NOTES (1951). 130 Sessions St., Providence, 02906. (401)331-1360. FAX: (401)272-6729. E-mail: rjhist@aol.com. Leonard Moss. Annually. Rhode Island Jewish Historical Association.

SOUTH CAROLINA

CHARLESTON JEWISH JOURNAL. 1645 Wallenberg Blvd., Charleston, 29407. (843)571-6565. FAX: (843)556-6206. Ellen Katman. Monthly. Charleston Jewish Federation.

TENNESSEE

HEBREW WATCHMAN (1925). 4646 Poplar Ave., Suite 232, Memphis, 38117. (901)763-2215. FAX: (901)763-2216. Herman I. Goldberger. Weekly.

OBSERVER (1934). 801 Percy Warner Blvd., Suite 102, Nashville, 37205. (615)354-1637, ext. 237. FAX: (615)352-0056. E-mail: judy@jewishnashville.org. Judith A. Saks. Biweekly (except July). Jewish Federation of Nashville.

SHOFAR. PO Box 8947, Chattanooga, 37414. (423)493-0270, Ext. 12. FAX: (423) 493-9997. E-mail: shofar@jcfgc.com. Rachel Schulson. Ten times a year. Jewish Federation of Greater Chattanooga.

TEXAS

JEWISH HERALD-VOICE (1908). 3403 Audley Street, Houston, 77098-1923. (713)630-0391. FAX: (713)630-0404. E-mail: joexhk@aol.com. Jeanne Samuels. Weekly. Four special issues:Rosh Hashanah; Passover; Wedding Planner; Bar/Bat Mitzvah Planner.

JEWISH JOURNAL OF SAN ANTONIO (1973). 8434 Ahern, San Antonio, 78213. (210) 828-9511. FAX: (210)342-8098. Barbara Richmond. Monthly (11 issues). Jewish Federation of San Antonio.

TEXAS JEWISH POST (1947). 3120 S. Freeway, Fort Worth, 76110. (817)927-2831. FAX: (817)429-0840. 11333 N. Central Expressway, Suite 213, Dallas, 75243. (214)692-7283. FAX: (214)692-7285. Weekly.

VIRGINIA

RENEWAL MAGAZINE (1984). 5029 Corporate World Dr., Suite 225, Virginia Beach, 23462. (757)671-1600. FAX: (757)671-7613. E-mail: news@ujft.org. Reba Karp. Quarterly. United Jewish Federation of Tidewater.

SOUTHEASTERN VIRGINIA JEWISH NEWS (1959). 5029 Corporate World Dr., Suite 225, Virginia Beach, 23462. (757)671-1600. FAX: (757)671-7613. E-mail: news@ujft.org. Reba Karp. 22 issues yearly. United Jewish Federation of Tidewater.

WASHINGTON

JEWISH TRANSCRIPT (1924). 2041 Third Ave., Seattle, 98121. (206)441-4553. FAX: (206)441-2736. E-mail: jewishtran@aol.

com. Donna Gordon Blankinship. Fortnightly. Jewish Federation of Greater Seattle.

WISCONSIN

WISCONSIN JEWISH CHRONICLE (1921). 1360 N. Prospect Ave., Milwaukee, 53202. (414)390-5888. FAX: (414)271-0487. E-mail: milwaukeej@aol.com. Vivian M. Rothschild. Weekly. Milwaukee Jewish Federation.

INDEXES

INDEX TO JEWISH PERIODICALS (1963). PO Box 18525, Cleveland Hts., OH 44118. (216)381-4846. FAX: (216)381-4321. E-mail: index@jewishperiodicals.com. Lenore Pfeffer Koppel. Annually. Available in book and CD-ROM form. (WWW.JEWISHPERIODICALS.COM)

NEWS SYNDICATES

JEWISH TELEGRAPHIC AGENCY, INC. (1917). 330 Seventh Ave., 11th fl., NYC., 10001-5010. (212)643-1890. FAX: (212)643-8498. Mark J. Joffe, Lisa Hostein. Daily. (WWW.JTA.ORG)

CANADA

CANADIAN JEWISH HERALD (1977). 17 Anselme Lavigne, Dollard des Ormeaux, PQ H9A 1N3. (514)684-7667. FAX: (514) 684-7667. Ed./Pub. Dan Nimrod. Irregularly. Dawn Publishing Co., Ltd.

THE CANADIAN JEWISH NEWS (1971). 1500 Don Mills Rd., Suite 205, North York, ONT M3B 3K4. (416)391-1836. FAX: (416)391-0829 (Adv.); (416)391-1836. FAX: (416)391-0829. Mordechai Ben-Dat. 50 issues a year. Some French.

CANADIAN JEWISH OUTLOOK (1963). #3-6184 Ash St., Vancouver, BC V5Z 3G9. (604)324-5101. FAX: (604)325-2470. E-mail: hjberson@axionet.com. Carl Rosenberg. Six times per year. Canadian Jewish Outlook Society.

DAIS (1985) (formerly INTERCOM). 100 Sparks St., #650, Ottawa, ONT KIP 5B7. (613)233-8703. FAX: (613)233-8748. E-mail: canadianjewishcongress@cjc.ca.

Jack Silverstone. Three times a year. Canadian Jewish Congress.

DIRECTIONS (1998) (formerly DIALOGUE (1988)). 1 Carré Cummings, Suite 202, Montreal, Quebec H3W 1M6. (514)345-64111. FAX: (514)345-6412. E-mail: etay @cjc.ca. Eta Yudin. Quarterly. French-English. Canadian Jewish Congress, Quebec Region.

JEWISH FREE PRESS (1990). 8411 Elbow Dr., SW Calgary, AB. T2V 1K8. (403)252-9423. FAX: (403)255-5640. E-mail: jewishfp@cadvision.com. Judy Shapiro. Fortnightly.

JEWISH POST & NEWS (1987). 113 Hutchings St., Winnipeg, MAN R2X 2V4. (204)694-3332. FAX: (204)694-3916. E-mail: jewishp@pangea.ca. Matt Bellan. Weekly.

JEWISH STANDARD (1928). 77 Mowat Ave., Suite 016, Toronto, ONT M6K 3E3. (416)537-2696. FAX: (416)789-3872. Email: thejewishstandardasympatico.ca. Ed./Pub. Michael Hayman. Fortnightly.

THE JEWISH TRIBUNE (1950). 15 Hove St., Toronto, ONT M3H 4Y8. (416)633-6224. FAX: (416)633-6299. E-mail: dantrib @interlog.com. Daniel Horowitz. Biweekly.

JEWISH WESTERN BULLETIN (1930). 301, 68 E. Second Ave., Vancouver, BC V5T 1B1. (604)689-1520. FAX: (604)689-1525. E-mail: jbeditor@istar.ca. Baila Lazarus. Weekly. 57786 BC Ltd.

JOURNAL OF PSYCHOLOGY AND JUDAISM (1976). 1747 Featherston Dr., Ottawa, ONT K1H 6P4. (613)731-9119. Reuven P. Bulka. Quarterly. Center for the Study of Psychology and Judaism.

OTTAWA JEWISH BULLETIN (1954). 1780 Kerr Ave., Ottawa, ONT K2A 1R9. (613)798-4696. FAX: (613)798-4730. E-mail: bulletin@jccottawa.com. Myra Aronson. Nineteen times a year. Ottawa Jewish Bulletin Publishing Co. Ltd.

SHALOM (1975). 5670 Spring Garden Rd., Suite 508, Halifax, NS, B3J 1H1. (902)422-7491. FAX: (902)425-3722. E-mail: jgoldberg@theajc.ns.ca. Jon M. Goldberg. Quarterly. Atlantic Jewish Council.

LA VOIX SÉPHARADE (1966). 1 Carré Cummings, Montreal, PQ H3W 1M6. (514)

733-4998, (514)733-8696. FAX: (514)733-3158. E-mail: csq@csq.qc.ca. Ed. James Dahan; Pub. Elie Benchitrit. Bimonthly (five times a year). French and occasional Spanish and English. Communauté Sépharade du Québec.

NEWS AND VIEWS (1942) (formerly WINDSOR JEWISH FEDERATION). 1641 Ouellette Ave., Windsor, ONT N8X 1K9. (519)973-1772. FAX: (519)973-1774. Exec. Dir. Harvey Kessler. Quarterly. Windsor Jewish Federation.

THE WORLD OF LUBAVITCH (1980). 770 Chabad Gate, Thornhill, ONT L4J 3V9. (905)731-7000. FAX: (905)731-7005. Rabbi Moshe Spalter. Bimonthly. English-Hebrew. Chabad Lubavitch of Southern Ont.

Obituaries: United States*

ABRAM, MORRIS B., diplomat, communal leader; b. Fitzgerald, Ga., June 19, 1918; d. Geneva, Switzerland, Mar. 16, 2000. Educ.: U. Georgia (BA); Rhodes Scholar Oxford U., England (BA, MA); U. Chicago (JD). Served U.S. Army Air Force, WWII. Staff of prosecution, Nuremberg trials of Nazi war criminals, 1946; private law practice, 1940s–1961; genl. counsel, Peace Corps, 1961; partner, Paul, Weiss, Rifkind. Wharton & Garrison, NYC, 1962–68, 1970–89, of counsel, 1989–; pres., Amer. Jewish Com., 1963–68; cochmn., White House Conference on Civil Rights, 1965; U.S. rep., UN Comm. on Human Rights, 1965–68; pres., Brandeis U., 1968–70; chmn., United Negro Coll. Fund, 1970–79; chmn., (N.Y. State) Moreland Act Comm. on Nursing Homes and Residential Facilities, 1975–76; chmn., Pres.'s Comm. for Study of Ethics in Medicine and Biomedical and Behavioral Research, 1979–83; chmn., Natl. Conf. on Soviet Jewry, 1983–88; v.-chmn., U.S. Comm. on Human Rights, 1984–86; chmn., Conf. of Pres. of Major Amer. Jewish Orgs., 1986–88; U.S. permanent ambassador to UN, Geneva, 1989–93; founder and chmn., UN Watch (now part of Amer. Jewish Com.), 1993–. Played major role in civil rights for blacks, one-man-one-vote Supreme Court ruling (1963), mass demonstration for Soviet Jews in Wash-ington, D.C. (1987); opposition to racial quotas. Au.: *The Day Is Short* (1982), an autobiography. Recipient: Legion of Merit; Amer. Jewish Com. Natl. Distinguished Leadership Award.

ABRAMOWICZ, DINA, librarian; b. Vilna, Russia, May 8, 1909; d. NYC, Apr. 3, 2000; in U.S. since 1946. Educ.: Stefan Batory U. (masters in humanities); Columbia U. (MLS). Librarian, Jewish Central Children's Library, Vilna, 1936–39, Vilna Ghetto Library, 1939–43; with liquidation of the ghetto escaped and joined partisan fighters, 1943–45; librarian, Smith Coll., 1946–47; librarian, YIVO Inst. for Jewish Research, NYC, 1947–62, head librarian, 1962–87, reference librarian, 1987–. Oversaw YIVO's acquisition of hundreds of thousands of volumes. Ed.: *Profiles of a Lost World* (1999), English translation of Yiddish work by her father. Recipient: Berl Frimer Prize for Cultural Achievement, Congress for Jewish Culture; Leonard Wertheimer Multicultural Public Library Service Award, Public Library Assoc.

ABROMOVITZ, MOSES, economist; b. NYC (Brooklyn), Jan. 1, 1912; d. Stanford, Cal., Dec. 1, 2000. Educ.: Harvard U. (BA); Columbia U. (PhD). Served U.S. Army, WWII. Instr., economics, Harvard U., 1936–38; research staff, Natl. Bureau of Economic Research, 1938–69; lect.,

---

*Including American Jews who died between January 1 and December 31, 2000.

Columbia U., 1940–42, 1946–48; prof., economics, Stanford U., 1948–78, Coe prof. of Amer. economic hist., 1963–74; prin. economist, War Production Bd., 1942; Office of Strategic Services, 1943–44; economic advisor, U.S. rep. to Allied Comm. on Reparations, 1944–46. Au.: *Price Theory for a Changing Economy* (1939), *Inventories and Business Cycles* (1950), *The Growth of Public Employment in Great Britain* (1957), *Thinking About Growth* (1989). Managing ed., *Journal of Economic Literature,* 1981–85. Pres., Amer. Economic Assoc., Amer. Economic Hist. Assoc., Western Economic Assoc.

BASKIN, LEONARD, sculptor, graphic artist; b. New Brunswick, N.J., Aug. 15, 1922; d. Northampton, Mass., June 3, 2000. Educ.: NYU School of Architecture and Applied Arts; Yale U.; New School for Social Research (AB); Académie de la Grade Chaumière (Paris); Accadèmia di Belle Arti (Florence). Served U.S. Navy, WWII. Founded Gehenna Press, 1942; prof., graphics, Smith Coll., 1953–74; visiting prof., art, Hampshire Coll., 1984–94. First solo show in NYC, 1953, many subsequent solo shows in NYC, Boston, London, Rotterdam, Paris; represented in permanent collections of leading U.S. museums; best known for wood, limestone, and bronze sculptures, large-scale wood-block prints; created bas relief of funeral cortège for Franklin D. Roosevelt Memorial in Washington, D.C., and seven-foot-high bronze figure for Ann Arbor (Mich.) Holocaust Memorial. Recipient: Tiffany Fellowship, Guggenheim Fellowship; Natl. Inst. of Arts and Letters grant; Amer. Inst. of Graphic Arts medal.

BORGE, VICTOR (Borge Rosenbaum), entertainer; b. Copenhagen, Denmark, Jan. 3, 1909; d. Greenwich, Conn., Dec. 23, 2000; in U.S. since 1940. Educ.: Copenhagen Music Conservatory; private music study, Vienna and Berlin. Concert performances, 1922–34; first musical comedy performance, 1934, becoming popular entertainer in Scandinavia; acted in first motion picture, 1937; in U.S., after escaping Nazis, developed comedy routines in English mixed with serious classical music, performing live and on radio as regular cast member, "Kraft Music Hall," 1941–43, and other programs; first

Carnegie Hall performance, 1945, followed by performances as soloist or guest conductor with major orchestras, as well as numerous nightclub and television appearances; his show "Comedy of Music" ran on Broadway for 849 performances, nearly three years, 1953–56, still a record for one-man engagement, numerous internat'l tours, 1970s–80s. Founder, natl. chmn., Thanks to Scandinavia Foundation (now part of Amer. Jewish Com.), 1963–; active in CARE and Multiple Sclerosis Soc. Recipient: Royal Order Daneborg, Absalom (Denmark); Knight First Class Order St. Olav (Norway); Order of Vasa (Sweden); CARE Public Service Award; awards from U.S. Cong., UN.

BULLATY, SONJA, photographer; b. Prague, Czechoslovakia, Oct. 17, 1923; d. NYC, Oct. 5, 2000; in U.S. since 1947. Deported to Lodz ghetto, 1941, and subsequently to Auschwitz and Gross Rosen, escaped death march and returned to Prague, 1945, where she worked for well-known Czech photographer Josef Sudek; in U.S. married and worked together with Angelo Lomeo, their photographs, first in black and white and then in color, appearing in magazines, major museum exhibitions, and books: *Provence* (1993), *Tuscany* (1995), *Venice and the Veneto* (1998), *Circle of Seasons: Central Park Celebrated* (1984), and *America, America* (1999).

CHRZANOWSKI, GERARD, psychoanalyst; b. Gleiwitz, Germany (now Poland), June 13, 1913; d. NYC, Nov. 1, 2000; in U.S. since 1940. Educ.: Medical degree and psychiatric training, Zurich, Switzerland. On arrival in U.S. worked at several mental hospitals; founder and medical director, Bleuler Psychotherapy Center, Queens, N.Y., providing low-cost mental treatment, 1949–82. Advocate of interpersonal theory that broke with strict Freudianism, a founder of Internat'l Fed. of Psychoanalytic Societies (1962); pioneered use of psychoanalysis for schizophrenia instead of shock treatments and drugs; model for the caring psychiatrist in Mary Jane Ward's 1946 autobiographical novel *The Snake Pit,* made into a film in 1948.

COHEN, ALEXANDER H., producer; b. NYC, July 24, 1920; d. NYC, Apr. 22, 2000. Educ.: NYU, Columbia U. Served U.S.

Army, WWII. Produced first show, "Angel Street," (1941) while working as publicity dir. for Bulova Watch Co. Among his 100 shows were "At the Drop of a Hat" (1954), "The Homecoming" (1967)—which won a Tony—"Anna Christie" (1977), "I Remember Mama" (1979); also produced numerous plays in London's West End; responsible for many television specials, including annual Tony Award show, 1967–86, and "Night of 100 Stars" and "Parade of Stars" to raise money for Actors' Fund; opened and managed O'Keefe Center theater, Toronto; Rich Forum at the Stamford (Conn.) Center for the Arts; and other theaters.

COHEN, HASKELL, publicist; b. Worcester, Mass., Mar. 12, 1914; d. Fort Lee, N.J, June 28, 2000. Educ.: Boston U. School of Journalism. Contributing ed., *Parade* magazine, for which he created high school all-American sports teams; sports editor, Jewish Telegraphic Agency; war correspondent in Italy, WWII; ghostwriter of autobiography of heavyweight boxing champion Joe Louis (1947); founder (1948) and president, Maccabi USA/ Sports for Israel, sponsor of U.S. participation in World Maccabiah Games; publicity director, Natl. Basketball Assoc., 1951–69, pioneering the 24-second clock and the NBA all-star game.

EPSTEIN, JULIUS J., screenwriter; b. NYC, Aug. 22, 1909; d. Los Angeles, Cal., Dec. 30, 2000. Educ.: Pennsylvania State U. (BA). Hollywood scriptwriter, mostly for Warner Brothers, (with twin brother Philip till the latter's death in 1952), 1934–84, writing over 50 movies, including Oscar nominee *Four Daughters* (1938), Oscar-winning classic *Casablanca* (1943), *Mr. Skeffington* (1944), and Oscar nominees *Pete 'n' Tillie* (1972) and *Reuben, Reuben* (1984). Recipient: Laurel Award, Screen Writers Guild; Career Achievement Award, Los Angeles Film Critics Assn.

FESHBACH, HERMAN, physicist; b. NYC, June 2, 1917; d. Cambridge, Mass., Dec. 21, 2000. Educ.: CCNY (BS); Mass. Inst. of Technology (PhD). Instr., physics, Mass. Inst. of Technology, 1941–45, asst. prof., 1945–47, assoc. prof., 1947–55, prof., 1955–87, emer., 1987–, dir., Center for Theoretical Physics, 1967–73, chmn., dept. of physics, 1973–83. Discovered "Feshbach resonance" effect in collision of atoms; opposed development of nuclear weapons; supported human rights. Au.: *Methods of Theoretical Physics*, with P.M. Morse (1953); *Theoretical Nuclear Physics: Nuclear Reactions* (1992); ed., *Annals of Physics* journal. Pres., Amer. Physical Soc., 1980–81. Recipient: Guggenheim Fellowship, Ford Fellowship, Natl. Medal of Science

FORTUNOFF, ALAN, businessman and philanthropist; b. NYC (Brooklyn), Sept. 19, 1932; d. Old Westbury, N.Y., July 5, 2000. Educ.: NYU (BS, LLB, LLM). Worked for Fortunoff housewares store in Brooklyn, founded by his parents in 1922; instrumental in moving store to Westbury, Long Island, 1964, where he was in charge of jewelry division and his sister handled home furnishings; opened branches in Wayne, Paramus, and Woodbridge, N.J., and, in 1979, on Fifth Avenue in Manhattan; named pres. and chmn., 1983; built The Mall at the Source, large retail shopping mall next to the Westbury store, 1997; one of earliest store chains to launch an Internet Web site. Sponsored Fortunoff Video Archives of Holocaust Testimonies, Yale U.; trustee, NYU Law Center Found.; mem., Dean's Adv. Council, Stern School of Business, NYU; trustee, Nature Conservancy; major supporter of N.Y. UJA-Fed., Parker Jewish Inst. for Health Care and Rehabilitation, Solomon Schechter School of Nassau County. Recipient: Champion of Liberty Award, Anti-Defamation League.

GURALNIK, DAVID B., lexicographer; b. Cleveland, Ohio, June 17, 1920; d. Shaker Heights, Ohio, May 19, 2000. Educ.: Western Reserve U. (BA, MA). Translator for U.S. Army, WWII. Ed., World Publishing Co., 1941–43, 1945–48; ed.-in-chief, Webster's New World dictionaries, 1948–85, best known for influential and widely used "college edition," first appearing in 1953. These dictionaries emphasized how English was actually spoken, included up-to-date terms and definitions in line with social and technological changes, and removed anti-Semitic and other ethnic slurs. Guralnik eventually convinced the publisher of the Oxford English Dictionary to include an etymological explanation of the pejorative use of the word "Jew." Pres., Cleveland Jewish Community Center; v.-pres.,

Cleveland Jewish News; trustee, Jewish Community Fed. of Cleveland; broadcast weekly radio segments on origins of Yiddish words.

HALBERSTAM, SHLOMO, rabbi and Hassidic leader; b. Bobov, Galicia (now Poland), Nov. 7, 1908; d. NYC (Brooklyn), Aug. 2, 2000; in U.S. since 1946. Descended from long line of Hassidic masters. Escaped with his eldest son after Nazis killed his first wife, his other children, and his father, who was rabbi of Bobov; settled on West Side of Manhattan, then Borough Park, Brooklyn; revived the sect through the creation of a yeshivah, the power of his charismatic personality, and the avoidance of disputes, attracting many Holocaust survivors not previously affiliated with his group; made Bobov third largest Hassidic sect in U.S.

HERMELIN, DAVID, diplomat, philanthropist; b. Detroit, Mich., Dec. 27, 1936; d. Detroit, Mich., Nov. 22, 2000. Educ.: U. Mich. (BA). After working in his father's insurance business, became real estate developer, specializing in apartment houses and shopping centers around the country; developed Palace of Auburn Hills, home court of Detroit Pistons of Natl. Basketball Assoc., and Pine Knob Entertainment Center and Meadow Brook Music Center, both in Detroit. As U.S. ambassador to Norway, 1997–2000, helped negotiate several joint business projects and arranged first visit by U.S. pres. to Norway. Internat'l chmn., State of Israel Bonds; chmn., Israel 50th Anniversary Com.; natl. v.-chmn., UJA; pres., World ORT Union, American ORT Fed.; v.-pres. Jewish Fed. of Metropolitan Detroit; board member and major contributor, Jewish educational and social-welfare orgs.

ISRAEL, RICHARD J., rabbi; b. Chicago, Ill, Nov. 5, 1929; d. hiking in New Hampshire, July 12, 2000. Educ.: U. Chicago (BA); HUC-JIR (BHL, MA, ordination). Dir., Jewish Religious Union, 1955–56; assoc. dir., Hillel Council, UCLA, 1957–59; dir., Hillel Found., chaplain to Jewish students, Yale U., 1959–71. Also advised Jewish students at Brandeis U., Duke U., Princeton U., U. Mass., and U. Winnipeg. Pres., Natl. Assoc. of Hillel Dirs. Au.: *Jewish Identity Games: A How-To-Do-It Book* (1993); *The Kosher Pig and Other Curiosities of Modern Jewish Life* (1995).

KLASS, SHOLOM, publisher; b. NYC (Brooklyn), Mar. 8, 1916; d. NYC (Brooklyn), January 17, 2000. Educ.: Yeshiva Torah Vodaath (ordination). Cofounder, with his father-in-law, of the weekly *Jewish Press* (1949), originally a local Brooklyn paper, that Klass, as sole publisher beginning in 1960, made into the nation's largest Anglo-Jewish newspaper, with a circulation of some 100,000. Oriented toward the Orthodox community, Klass's paper published columns by Rabbi Meir Kahane and supported Kahane's Jewish Defense League, opposed territorial compromise by Israel, and responded to questions on Halakhah. Recipient: Lifetime Achievement Award in Journalism, Rabbi Isaac Elchanan Theological Seminary (Yeshiva University).

KLEMPERER, WERNER, actor; b. Cologne, Germany, Mar. 22, 1920; d. NYC, Dec. 6, 2000; in U.S. since 1933. Served U.S. Army, WWII. Opera performer, orchestra narrator, actor in theater, films, and television; best known for his role on the successful CBS television sitcom "Hogan's Heroes" (1965–71) as Col. Klink, the bumbling Nazi guard of a POW camp during World War II, for which he received Emmy nominations each year and won in 1968 and 1969.

KOSLOWE, IRVING, rabbi; b. White Plains, N.Y., Jan. 16, 1920; d. NYC, Dec. 6, 2000. Educ.: Yeshiva U. (BA, DHL, ordination); NYU (MA). Rabbi, Westchester Jewish Center, Mamaroneck, N.Y., 1943–87; adj. prof., pastoral counseling, Westchester Community Coll., Mercy Coll., Pace U.; Jewish chaplain, Sing Sing Prison, 1949–99, where he conducted services for Jewish inmates and counseled 17 who were executed, including atomic spies Julius and Ethel Rosenberg in 1953. Pres., Amer. Correctional Chaplains Assn., 1955–56, Natl. Council of Jewish Penal Chaplains, 1958–59; Westchester Council of Rabbis, 1956–59; consultant, N.Y. State Dept. of Correctional Services, for dealing with various prison disturbances, including Attica riots of 1971.

KRENTS, MILTON, broadcast executive; b. Springfield, Mass., Dec. 22, 1911; d. NYC, Jan. 8, 2000. Educ.: NYU (BS). NBC radio, 1935–38; dir., radio and television, Amer. Jewish Com., 1937–44; dir., radio activities, Council for Democracy, WWII; producer, Jewish Theol. Seminary's "The Eternal Light" series on Jewish themes, first on radio and then on television, 1944–89, that pioneered serious religious programming and by 1979 was the longest-running continuous drama series on radio; dir., William E. Wiener Oral History Library of the Amer. Jewish Com., 1969–77, amassing interviews with 2,500 Amer. Jews, collection now housed at N.Y. Public Library. Recipient: Lifetime Achievement Award, Natl. Acad. of Television Arts and Sciences; Media Arts Award, Natl. Found. for Jewish Culture.

LEVI, EDWARD H., legal scholar, govt. official; b. Chicago, Ill., June 26, 1911; d. Chicago, Ill., Mar. 7, 2000. Educ.: U. Chicago (BA, JD); Yale U. (JSD). Asst. prof., U. Chicago Law School, 1936–40; special asst. to U.S. attorney genl., 1940–45; prof., U. Chicago Law School, 1945–75, dean, 1950–62; provost, U. Chicago, 1962–68, pres., 1968–75 (first Jewish pres. of a major American university not under Jewish auspices), pres. emer., 1975–; U.S. attorney genl., 1975–77, credited with restoring faith in nation's legal system in aftermath of Watergate. Pioneered "law and economics" approach to legal analysis, founding *Journal of Law and Economics*. Au: *Introduction to Legal Reasoning* (1949), *Four Talks on Legal Education* (1952), *Point of View* (1969). Recipient of numerous awards.

LIEBOWITZ, JACK, publisher; b. Proskurov, Ukraine, Oct. 10, 1900; d. Great Neck, N.Y., Dec. 11, 2000; in U.S. since 1910. After working as a magazine distributor, went into partnership with Harry Donenfeld to create Detective Comics (1937), which introduced the character of Batman, Action Comics (1938), which introduced Superman—whose first print run was 200,000 copies, but quickly approached one million copies a month—and All American Comics, which featured The Flash, Wonder Woman, and Green Lantern. Liebowitz moved "Superman" into radio (1940) and television (1951). Founding trustee, Long Island Jewish Hosp. (now North Shore-Long Island Jewish Health System), 1949–, pres. 1956–68; board mem., N.Y. Fed. of Jewish Philanthropies.

MATTHAU, WALTER, actor; b. NYC, Oct. 1, 1920; d. Santa Monica, Cal., July 1, 2000. Served U.S. Army Air Corps, WWII. Studied acting at New School Dramatic Workshop, first appearing on Broadway in 1948; won first Tony for performance in "A Shot in the Dark" (1962); won another Tony in Neil Simon's "The Odd Couple" (1965), in which he played the slovenly Oscar Madison, a role he played in the movie version as well, opposite Jack Lemmon, who played the fussy roommate, Felix Unger (1968). Among Matthau's other films were *Hello Dolly* (1969), *Plaza Suite* (1971), *The Taking of Pelham One Two Three* (1974), *The Sunshine Boys* (1975), *Dennis the Menace* (1993), *Grumpy Old Men* (1993), and *I'm Not Rappaport* (1996).

MERRICK, DAVID (David Margulois), theatrical producer; b. St. Louis, Mo., Nov. 27, 1911; d. London, England, Apr. 26, 2000. Educ.: Washington U. (BA), St. Louis U. (LLB). Entered the business in 1940s with the use of aggressive publicity techniques; generally acknowledged as the dominant Broadway producer of the 1960s. "Fanny" (1954), his first hit, ran for two years and was the most profitable show, on weekly basis, up to that time; among his many other hits were Tony winners "Becket" (1960), "Luther" (1963), "Hello Dolly" (1964), "The Persecution and Assassination of of Jean Paul Marat as Performed by the Inmates of the Asylum of Charenton Under the Direction of the Marquis de Sade" (1965), "Rosencrantz and Guildenstern Are Dead" (1967), "Travesties" (1968), and "42nd Street" (1980).

MILTON, SYBIL, historian; b. NYC, Oct. 6, 1941; d. Bethesda, Md., Oct. 16, 2000. Educ.: Barnard Coll. (BA); Stanford U. (MA, PhD). Dir. of archives, Leo Baeck Inst., NYC, 1974–84; consultant, sr. resident historian, U.S. Holocaust Memorial Museum, 1989–97; sr. v.-pres., Independent Comm. of Experts on Switzerland during WWII, 1996–; archival consultant, U.S. Justice Dept., Amer. Jewish Joint Distrib. Com., Agudath Israel of Amer.; curator and consultant, "Art and Exile: Felix Nussbaum," Jewish Museum, 1985. Au.: *Art of the Holocaust*, with J. Blatter (1982), winner of Natl. Jewish Book Award.

MLOTEK, JOSEPH, Yiddish expert; b. Proszowice, Poland, July 25, 1918; d. NYC, July 2, 2000; in U.S. since 1949. Educ: secular Yiddish schools (Warsaw); YIVO Inst. for Jewish Research (Vilna); Jewish

Teachers Seminary (NYC); New School for Social Research (NYC). Active in Jewish Labor Bund and wrote for its *Naye Folks Tseitung,* Warsaw (1936–39); fled Poland in 1939 to Lithuania, Shanghai, and Calgary before arrival in U.S; teacher, Workmen's Circle schools, 1949–51; exec. sec., Youth Dept., Cong. for Jewish Culture, 1950–1966; educ. dir., Workmen's Circle Arbeiter Ring, 1966–; pres., Forward Association; managing ed., coed., *Forward* newspaper (Yiddish); hosted Workmen's Circle radio program on WEVD and arranged free Yiddish music concerts in Central Park. Au.: Yiddish textbooks; anthologies and recordings of Yiddish songs (together with his wife, Chana). Recipient: Manger Prize (Israel); Jewish Cultural Achievement Award, Natl. Found. for Jewish Culture.

PAIS, ABRAHAM, physicist; b. Amsterdam, Holland, May 19, 1918; d. Copenhagen, Denmark, July 28, 2000; in U.S. since 1946. Educ.: U. Amsterdam (BS), U. Utrecht (MS, PhD). Research fellow, Inst. for Theoretical Physics, Copenhagen, Denmark, 1946; prof., physics, Inst. for Advanced Sudies, Princeton, N.J., 1950–63; prof., physics, Rockefeller Inst., 1963–81, Detlev W. Bronk prof., 1981–88, emer., 1988–. Known for path-breaking work in theory of elementary particles and as historian of science. Au.: "*Subtle is the Lord": The Science and Life of Albert Einstein* (1983), which won the Amer. Book Award and the Amer. Inst. of Physics Award; *Inward Bound: Of Matter and Forces in the Physical World* (1986), *Niels Bohr's Times: In Physics, Philosophy, and Polity* (1991); *Einstein Lived Here: Essays for the Layman* (1994); *A Tale of Two Continents: A Physicist's Life in a Turbulent World* (1997); and *The Genius of Science: A Portrait Gallery of Twentieth-Century Physicists* (2000).

RUBIN, RUTH, Yiddish folklorist; b. Montreal, Canada, Sept. 1, 1906; d. Mamaroneck, N.Y., June 11, 2000; in U.S. since 1929. Educ.: YIVO Inst. for Jewish Research; Union Graduate School, Cleveland (PhD). Beginning in 1930s recorded Yiddish songs of immigrants in Canada and U.S., many of them women, amassing a collection of 2,000 items; gave live performances at Carnegie Hall and elsewhere, and produced recordings of the songs. Au.: *A Treasury of Jewish Folksong* (1950); and *The Story of Yiddish Folksong* (1963), works considered a bridge between the immigrant generation and the current revival of interest in Yiddish culture. Recipient: Lifetime Achievement Award, YIVO.

SCHINDLER, ALEXANDER M., rabbi, communal leader; b. Munich, Germany, Oct. 4, 1925; d. Westport, Conn., Nov. 15, 2000; in U.S. since 1937. Educ.: CCNY (BSS); HUC-JIR (BHL, MHL, ordination). Served U.S. Army, WWII. Asst.-assoc. rabbi, Temple Emanuel, Worcester, Mass., 1953–59; dir., Fed. of New England Reform Temples, 1959–63; dir. of education, Union of Amer. Hebrew Congs. 1963–67, v.-pres., 1967–73, pres., 1973–96; pres., Conf. of Pres. of Major Amer. Jewish Orgs., 1976–78; pres., Natl. Found. for Jewish Culture, 1996–. Led Reform movement in outreach to intermarried, patrilineal descent, ordaining women as rabbis, acceptance of homosexuals, greater attention to religious ritual; as head of Conf. of Pres. subordinated personal views to establish united backing for Begin govt. in Israel.

SCHUSTERMAN, CHARLES, philanthropist; b. Tulsa, Okla., Sept. 21, 1935; d. Tulsa, Okla., Dec. 30, 2000. Educ.: U. Okla. (BS). Served U.S. Army. After work in oilfield salvage, moved into acquiring and operating marginal oil properties, 1961; founder, pres., ceo, Samson Resources Co., later Samson Properties and Samson Investment Co., 1971–2000, second largest independent gas producing company in the state. With wife, founded Charles and Lynn Schusterman Family Foundation, 1987, which gives 75 percent of funds to Jewish causes, such as Amer. Jewish Joint Distrib. Com., Hillel, AIPAC, World Union for Progressive Judaism, Partnership for Excellence in Jewish Educ.; founder of Birthright Israel (gave $5 million) to provide free trips to Israel for Jewish teenagers; major force behind Synagogue Transformation and Renewal (STAR), to revitalize the synagogue (gave $11.25 million); proponent and supporter of outreach programs to intermarried families; gave $10 million to U. Okla. for Schusterman Center. Member: Okla. Hall of Fame; Tulsa Hall of Fame. Recipient: Humanitarian Award, Natl. Jewish Center for Immunology and Respiratory Medicine; Maimonides Award, Jewish Fed. of Tulsa.

SEGAL, GEORGE, sculptor; b. NYC, Nov. 26, 1924; d. South Brunswick, N.J., June 9, 2000. Educ.: NYU (BS), Rutgers U. (MFA). After training in abstract expressionist painting, rejected that school in favor of realism; considered among the founders of "pop art"; known for his distinctive use of full-body plaster cast method of portraying "real" people and situations; also influenced by social causes of the time. After solo shows at Hansa Gallery and Green Gallery, achieved fame by inclusion in "New Realists" show at Sidney Janis Gallery (1962), which represented him from 1965 on. Among his works were three tableaus for the Franklin Delano Roosevelt Memorial in Washington, D.C.: "Depression Breadline," "Appalachian Farm Couple," and "Fireside Chat." Recipient: Premium Imperiale (Japan); National Medal of the Arts.

SHAPIRO, KARL, poet; b. Baltimore, Md., Nov. 10, 1913; d. NYC, May 14, 2000. Educ.: Johns Hopkins U.; Served U.S. Army, WWII. Poetry consultant, Library of Cong., 1946–47; assoc. prof., writing, Johns Hopkins U., 1947–50; ed., *Poetry: A Magazine of Verse,* 1950–56; prof., English, U. Neb., 1956–66, U. Ill., Chicago Circle, 1966–68, U. Cal. at Davis, 1968–85. First achieved recognition for poems written while stationed in the South Pacific, winning Pulitzer Prize for the collection *V-Letter and Other Poems* (1945). Among his other works: *English Prosody and Modern Poetry* (1947), *Poems of a Jew* (1958), and *The Bourgeois Poet* (1964). Cast dissenting vote and publicly disassociated himself from award of 1949 Bollingen Prize for Poetry to Ezra Pound, on grounds of Pound's pro-Fascist radio broadcasts. Recipient: Shelley Memorial Prize, Poetry Soc. of Amer.; Oscar Blumenthal Prize; Bollingen Prize for Poetry; Guggenheim Fellowship (twice).

SLAIMAN, DONALD S., labor leader; b. NYC, Mar. 18, 1919; d. Alexandria, Va., Oct. 24, 2000. Educ.: CCNY (BA); U. Mich. Served U.S. Army, WWII. Worked for Bell Aircraft (Buffalo, N.Y.) where he organized workers and was blacklisted as the result of a strike (1949); active in United Automobile Workers union, Detroit; dir., Jewish Labor Com. Detroit office, 1957–59; asst. dir., AFL-CIO civil rights dept., 1959–64, dir., 1964–74; deputy dir., AFL-CIO organization and field services, 1974–89; pres., Jewish Labor Com., 1979–83; pres. and chmn., Social Democrats USA, 1989–. Instrumental in gaining equality for minority members in unions, involvement of organized labor in civil-rights movement, passage of Civil Rights Act of 1964, and creation of Labor Council for Latin Amer. Advancement.

SNITOW, VIRGINIA, communal leader; b. NYC (Brooklyn), Apr. 9, 1911; d. Scarsdale, N.Y., Oct. 16, 2000. Educ.: Hunter Coll. (BA). Teacher, Wadleigh High School (Harlem), 1932–47; natl. v.-pres., Amer. Jewish Cong., 1964–, pres., women's div., 1964–72; chwmn., Leadership Conf. of Natl. Jewish Women's Orgs., 1970–73; founder and chwmn., US/Israel Women to Women, 1977–90. Active in labor, peace, civil rights, feminist, antinuclear, and Israeli leftist causes: participant in Montgomery, Ala., civil-rights march (1965); influential in getting AJCong. to become first national Jewish organization publicly to oppose Vietnam War; organized funding for shelters for battered women in Israel. Recipient: Louise Waterman Prize; Woman of our Time Award.

SOKOLOW, ANNA, choreographer; b. Hartford, Conn., (?), 1910; d. NYC, Mar. 29, 2000. Studied dance with Martha Graham at Neighborhood Playhouse (NYC); danced with Graham Dance Co. and then organized WPA Dance Unit in 1930s which toured USSR in 1934; founded La Paloma Azul, modern-dance company in Mexico, 1940, returning there often and helping create National Academy of Dance; artistic advisor to Inbal, Yemenite dance troupe in Israel, 1954, returning to Israel many times thereafter to advise Batsheva, Kibbutz Dance Company, and Lyric Theater; teacher of dance and theater, Julliard School, HB Studio, and at several universities; director of her own company, Player's Project, that premiered her choreography. Known for pieces depicting loneliness, alienation, and youthful defiance, such as *Lyric Suite* (1953), *Rooms* (1955)—later presented on national television—and *Opus 65* (1965). Recipient: Dance Magazine Award; Fulbright Fellowship (in Japan); Choreographic Fellowship, National Foundation for the Arts; Lifetime Achievement Award, American/Israeli Cultural Foundation.

STONE, IRVING, businessman, philanthropist; b. Cleveland, Ohio, Apr. 5, 1909; d. Cleveland, Ohio, Jan. 17, 2000. Educ.: Case Western Reserve U.; Cleveland Inst. of Art. Cofounder, with his father, American Greetings Corp. (world's largest privately owned greeting-card company), 1923, pres., 1960–78, chmn., 1978–. One of first Jewish leaders to press for communal support of Jewish day schools; funded the popular Stone Chumash published by Artscroll (1993); endowed four programs in rabbinical training and Jewish educ. at Yeshiva U. Chmn., Hebrew Acad. of Cleveland; v.-pres., Boys Town Jerusalem; bd. mem., Yeshiva U., Bar-Ilan U.; founder, Kiryat Telshe Stone, neighborhood outside Jerusalem.

THURSZ, DANIEL, communal professional; b. Casablanca, Morocco, Jan. 25, 1929; d. Bethesda, Md., Jan. 18, 2000; in U.S. since 1941. Educ.: Queens Coll., City U. of N.Y. (BA); Catholic U. (MSW, DSW). Served U.S. Army, Korean War. Dir., leadership programs, B'nai B'rith Youth Org., 1954–77; assoc. prof., social work, Catholic U., 1961–63; assoc. prof., U. Md., 1963–65; assoc. natl. dir., Volunteers in Service to Amer., 1965–66; dean, U. Md. School of Social Work and Community Planning, 1967–77; exec. v.-pres., B'nai B'rith Internat'l, 1977–87.

VLOCK, LAUREL F., archivist; b. New Haven, Conn., Aug. 5, 1926; d. New Haven, Conn., July 8, 2000. Educ.: Cornell U. (BA); Queens Coll., City U. of N.Y. (MA). Founder and head, WHAI, local Connecticut television station, 1978–; cofounder, Holocaust Survivor Film Project to videotape and archive interviews with survivors, 1979; co-founder, Fortunoff Archive of Holocaust Testimonies at Yale U., 1982 (now containing well over 4,000 interviews), remaining advisor to the project. Recipient: Emmy Award for "Forever Yesterday," television documentary based on interviews with survivors, 1981.

WECHSLER, HERBERT, legal scholar; b. NYC, Dec. 4, 1909; d. NYC, Apr. 26, 2000. Educ.: CCNY (BA); Columbia U. Law School (LLB). Ed.-in-chief, Columbia U. Law Review, 1930–31; law sec. to Justice Harlan F. Stone, U.S. Supreme Court, 1932–33; instr., Columbia U. Law School, 1931–32, asst. prof., 1933–38, assoc. prof., 1938–45, prof., 1945–, Harlan Fiske Stone prof. of constitutional law, 1957–78, emeritus, 1978–; asst. U.S. attorney genl., war division, 1944–46; chief technical advisor to U.S. judges, Nuremberg trials of Nazi war criminals, 1945–46; dir., Amer. Law Inst., 1963–84. Best known for successful defense of press freedom before U.S. Supreme Court in N.Y. Times v. Sullivan, 1964, and compilation of Model Penal Code, 1952–62. Au.: The Federal Courts and the Federal System, with H.M. Hart (first ed. 1953, now in fourth ed.); Principles, Politics, and Fundamental Law (1961); The Nationalization of Civil Liberties and Civil Rights (1969). Recipient: Medal, Assoc. of the Bar of City of N.Y.; Townsend Harris Medal; Learned Hand Award.

WOLKE, MARSHALL, communal leader; b. Poland, Jan. 2, 1920; d. en route to Israel, Aug. 15, 2000; in U.S. since 1937. Educ.: Northwestern U.; U. Chicago. Served U.S. Army, WWII. Worked at uncle's dept. store, Wolke & Kotler, Chicago, now Wolke's Inc., pres. 1967–86. Pres., West Suburban Temple Har Zion, River Forest, 1957–76; Midwest regional pres., United Synagogue of Amer., 1975–76, natl. pres., 1981–85; pres., World Council of Synagogues, 1985–89; consultant, adult-education lect., Spertus Coll. of Judaica, 1986–98.

YARMOLINSKY, ADAM, govt. official; b. NYC, Nov. 17, 1922; d. Washington, D.C., Jan. 5, 2000. Harvard U. (BA); Yale U. (LLB). Served U.S. Army Air Corps, WWII. Law clerk, U.S. Court of Appeals, second circuit,1948–49; assoc., Root, Ballantine, Harlan, Bushby & Palmer, 1949–50; law clerk to Justice Stanley Reed, U.S. Supreme Court, 1950 51; assoc., Cleary, Gottlieb, Friendly & Ball, 1951–55; dir., Washington office, Fund for the Republic, 1955–56, sec., 1956–57; public affairs ed., Doubleday & Co., 1957–59; consultant to private founds., 1959–60; special asst. to sec. of defense, 1961–64; deputy dir., pres.'s anti-poverty task force, 1964; deputy asst. sec. of defense for internat'l security affairs, 1965–66; prof., law, Harvard U., 1966–72; university prof., U. Mass., 1972–77; counselor, U.S. Arms Control and Disarmament Agcy., 1977–79; of counsel, Fort &

Schlefer, 1979–. Au.: *Recognition of Excellence* (1960), *The Military Establishment* (1971), *Paradoxes of Power* (1983). Recipient: Distinguished Public Service Medal, Dept of Defense.

YATES, SIDNEY R., legislator; b. Chicago, Ill., Aug. 27, 1909; d. Washington, D.C., Oct. 5, 2000. Educ.: U. Chicago (PhB, JD). Served U.S. Navy, WWII. Private legal practice, 1933–35, 1945–49; asst. attorney, Ill. State Bank Receiver, 1935–37; asst. attorney genl., Illinois Commerce Comm., 1937–40; mem., U.S. House of Representatives, Ill., 1949–62, 1965–98, serving on appropriations, interior, foreign operations coms. Known for support for federal funding of the arts and opposition to age discrimination.

Calendars

SUMMARY JEWISH CALENDAR, 5761–5765 (Sept. 2000–Aug. 2005)

HOLIDAY	5761	5762	5763	5764	5765
	2000	2001	2002		
Rosh Ha-shanah, 1st day	Sa Sept. 30	T Sept. 18	Sa Sept. 7	Sa Sept. 27	Th Sept. 16
Rosh Ha-shanah, 2nd day	S Oct. 1	W Sept. 19	S Sept. 8	S Sept. 28	F Sept. 17
Fast of Gedaliah	M Oct. 2	Th Sept. 20	M Sept. 9	M Sept. 29	S Sept. 19
Yom Kippur	M Oct. 9	Th Sept. 27	M Sept. 16	M Oct. 6	Sa Sept. 25
Sukkot, 1st day	Sa Oct. 14	T Oct. 2	Sa Sept. 21	Sa Oct. 11	Th Sept. 30
Sukkot, 2nd day	S Oct. 15	W Oct. 3	S Sept. 22	S Oct. 12	F Oct. 1
Hosha'na' Rabbah	F Oct. 20	M Oct. 8	F Sept. 27	F Oct. 17	W Oct. 6
Shemini 'Azeret	Sa Oct. 21	T Oct. 9	Sa Sept. 28	Sa Oct. 18	Th Oct. 7
Simhat Torah	S Oct. 22	W Oct. 10	S Sept. 29	S Oct. 19	F Oct. 8
New Moon, Heshwan, 1st day	S Oct. 29	W Oct. 17	S Oct. 6	S Oct. 26	F Oct. 15
New Moon, Heshwan, 2nd day	M Oct. 30	Th Oct. 18	M Oct. 7	M Oct. 27	Sa Oct. 16
New Moon, Kislew, 1st day	T Nov. 28	F Nov. 16	T Nov. 5	T Nov. 25	S Nov. 14
New Moon, Kislew, 2nd day			W Nov. 6	W Nov. 26	
Hanukkah, 1st day	F Dec. 22	M Dec. 10	Sa Nov. 30	Sa Dec. 20	W Dec. 8
New Moon, Tevet, 1st day	W Dec. 27	Sa Dec. 15	Th Dec. 5	Th Dec. 25	M Dec. 13
New Moon, Tevet, 2nd day		S Dec. 16	F Dec. 6	F Dec. 26	
	2001			2004	
Fast of 10th of Tevet	F Jan. 5	T Dec. 25	S Dec. 15	S Jan. 4	W Dec. 22

Holiday	2001			2002			2003			2004			2005		
New Moon, Shevat	Th	Jan.	25	M	Jan.	14	Sa	Jan.	4	Sa	Jan.	24	T	Jan.	11
Hamishshah-ʿasar bi-Shevat	Th	Feb.	8	M	Jan.	28	Sa	Jan.	18	Sa	Feb.	7	T	Jan.	25
New Moon, Adar I, 1st day	F	Feb.	23	T	Feb.	12	S	Feb.	2	S	Feb.	22	W	Feb.	9
New Moon, Adar I, 2nd day	Sa	Feb.	24	W	Feb.	13	M	Feb.	3	M	Feb.	23	Th	Feb.	10
New Moon, Adar II, 1st day							T	Mar.	4				F	Mar.	11
New Moon, Adar II, 2nd day							W	Mar.	5				Sa	Mar.	12
Fast of Esther	Th	Mar.	8	M	Feb.	25	M	Mar.	17	Th	Mar.	4	Th	Mar.	24
Purim	F	Mar.	9	T	Feb.	26	T	Mar.	18	S	Mar.	7	F	Mar.	25
Shushan Purim	Sa	Mar.	10	W	Feb.	27	W	Mar.	19	M	Mar.	8	Sa	Mar.	26
New Moon, Nisan	S	Mar.	25	Th	Mar.	14	Th	Apr.	3	T	Mar.	23	S	Apr.	10
Passover, 1st day	S	Apr.	8	Th	Mar.	28	Th	Apr.	17	T	Apr.	6	S	Apr.	24
Passover, 2nd day	M	Apr.	9	F	Mar.	29	F	Apr.	18	W	Apr.	7	M	Apr.	25
Passover, 7th day	Sa	Apr.	14	W	Apr.	3	W	Apr.	23	M	Apr.	12	Sa	Apr.	30
Passover, 8th day	S	Apr.	15	Th	Apr.	4	Th	Apr.	24	T	Apr.	13	S	May	1
Holocaust Memorial Day	F	Apr.	20*	T	Apr.	9	Tu	Apr.	29	S	Apr.	18	F	May	6*
New Moon, Iyar, 1st day	M	Apr.	23	F	Apr.	12	F	May	2	W	Apr.	21	M	May	9
New Moon, Iyar, 2nd day	T	Apr.	24	Sa	Apr.	13	Sa	May	3	Th	Apr.	22	T	May	10
Israel Independence Day	Sa	Apr.	28†	W	Apr.	17	W	May	7	M	Apr.	26	Sa	May	14†
Lag Baʿomer	F	May	11	T	Apr.	30*	T	May	20	S	May	9	F	May	27
Jerusalem Day	M	May	21	F	May	10*	F	May	30*	W	May	19	M	June	6
New Moon, Siwan	W	May	23	S	May	12	S	June	1	F	May	21	W	June	8
Shavuʿot, 1st day	M	May	28	F	May	17	F	June	6	W	May	26	M	June	13
Shavuʿot, 2nd day	T	May	29	Sa	May	18	Sa	June	7	Th	May	27	T	June	14
New Moon, Tammuz, 1st day	Th	June	21	M	June	10	M	June	30	Sa	June	19	Th	July	7
New Moon, Tammuz, 2nd day	F	June	22	T	June	11	T	July	1	S	June	20	F	July	8
Fast of 17th of Tammuz	S	July	8	Th	June	27	Th	July	17	T	July	6	S	July	24
New Moon, Av	Sa	July	21	W	July	10	W	July	30	M	July	19	Sa	Aug.	6
Fast of 9th of Av	S	July	29	Th	July	18	Th	Aug.	7	T	July	27	S	Aug.	14
New Moon, Elul, 1st day	S	Aug.	19	Th	Aug.	8	Th	Aug.	28	T	Aug.	17	S	Sept.	4
New Moon, Elul, 2nd day	M	Aug.	20	F	Aug.	9	F	Aug.	29	W	Aug.	18	M	Sept.	5

*Observed Thursday, a day earlier, to avoid conflict with the Sabbath.
†Observed Thursday, two days earlier, to avoid conflict with the Sabbath.

CONDENSED MONTHLY CALENDAR
(2000–2003)

2000, Jan. 8–Feb. 6] SHEVAṬ (30 DAYS) [5760

Civil Date	Day of the Week	Jewish Date	SABBATHS, FESTIVALS, FASTS	PENTATEUCHAL READING	PROPHETICAL READING
Jan. 8	Sa	Shevaṭ 1	Wa-'era'; New Moon	Exod. 6:2–9:35 Num. 28:9–15	Isaiah 66:1–24
15	Sa	8	Bo'	Exod. 10:1–13:16	Jeremiah 46:13–28
22	Sa	15	Be-shallaḥ (Shabbat Shirah); Ḥamishah 'asar bi-Shevaṭ	Exod. 13:17–17:16	Judges 4:4–5:31 *Judges 5:1–31*
29	Sa	22	Yitro	Exod. 18:1–20:23	Isaiah 6:1–7:6; 9:5–6 *Isaiah 6:1–13*
Feb. 5	Sa	29	Mishpaṭim	Exod. 21:1–24:18	I Samuel 20:18–42
6	S	30	New Moon, first day	Num. 28:1–15	

Italics are for Sephardi Minhag.

2000, Feb. 7 – Mar. 7]   ADAR I (30 DAYS)   [5760

Civil Date	Day of the Week	Jewish Date	SABBATHS, FESTIVALS, FASTS	PENTATEUCHAL READING	PROPHETICAL READING
Feb. 7	M	Adar I 1	New Moon, second day	Num. 28:1–15	
12	Sa	6	Terumah	Exod. 25:1–27:19	I Kings 5:26–6:13
19	Sa	13	Teẓawweh	Exod. 27:20–30:10	Ezekiel 43:10–27
26	Sa	20	Ki tissa'	Exod. 30:11–34:35	I Kings 18:1–39 *I Kings 18:20–39*
Mar. 4	Sa	27	Wa-yakhel (Shabbat Sheḳalim)	Exod. 35:1–38:20 Exod. 30:11–16	II Kings 12:1–17 *II Kings 11:17–12:17*
7	T	30	New Moon, first day	Num. 28:1–15	

Italics are for Sephardi Minhag.

2000, Mar. 8–Apr. 5]   ADAR II (29 DAYS)   [5760

Civil Date	Day of the Week	Jewish Date	SABBATHS, FESTIVALS, FASTS	PENTATEUCHAL READING	PROPHETICAL READING
Mar. 8	W	Adar II 1	New Moon, second day	Num. 28:1–15	
11	Sa	4	Peḳude	Exod. 38:21–40:38	I Kings 7:51–8:21 *I Kings 7:40–50*
18	Sa	11	Wa-yiḳra' (Shabbat Zakhor)	Levit. 1:1–5:26 Deut. 25:17–19	I Samuel 15:2–34 *I Samuel 15:1–34*
20	M	13	Fast of Esther	Exod. 32:11–14 Exod. 34:1–10 (morning and afternoon)	Isaiah 55:6–56:8 (afternoon only)
21	T	14	Purim	Exod. 17:8–16	Book of Esther (night before and in the morning)
22	W	15	Shushan Purim		
25	Sa	18	Ẓaw (Shabbat Parah)	Levit. 6:1–8:36 Num. 19:1–22	Ezekiel 36:16–38 *Ezekiel 36:16–36*
Apr. 1	Sa	25	Shemini (Shabbat Ha-ḥodesh)	Levit. 9:1–11:47 Exod. 12:1–20	Ezekiel 45:16–46:18 *Ezekiel 45:18–46:15*

Italics are for
Sephardi Minhag.

2000, Apr. 6–May 5]   NISAN (30 DAYS)   [5760

Civil Date	Day of the Week	Jewish Date	SABBATHS, FESTIVALS, FASTS	PENTATEUCHAL READING	PROPHETICAL READING
Apr. 6	Th	Nisan 1	New Moon	Num. 28:1–15	
8	Sa	3	Tazria'	Levit. 12:1–13:59	II Kings 4:42–5:19
15	Sa	10	Mezora' (Shabbat Ha-gadol)	Levit. 14:1–15:33	Malachi 3:4–24
19	W	14	Fast of Firstborn		
20	Th	15	Passover, first day	Exod. 12:21–51 Num. 28:16–25	Joshua 5:2–6:1, 27
21	F	16	Passover, second day	Levit. 22:26–23:44 Num. 28:16–25	II Kings 23:1–9, 21–25
22	Sa	17	Hol Ha-mo'ed, first day	Exod. 33:12–34:26 Num. 28:19–25	Ezekiel 37:1–14
23	S	18	Hol Ha-mo'ed, second day	Exod. 13:1–16 Num. 28:19–25	
24	M	19	Hol Ha-mo'ed, third day	Exod. 22:24–23:19 Num. 28:19–25	
25	T	20	Hol Ha-mo'ed, fourth day	Num. 9:1–14 Num. 28:19–25	
26	W	21	Passover, seventh day	Exod. 13:17–15:26 Num. 28:19–25	II Samuel 22:1–51
27	Th	22	Passover, eighth day	Deut. 15:19–16:17 Num. 28:19–25	Isaiah 10:32–12:6
29	Sa	24	Aḥare mot	Levit 16:1–18:30	Amos 9:7–15 *Ezekiel 22:1–16*
May 2	T	27	Holocaust Memorial Day		
5	F	30	New Moon, first day	Num. 28:1–15	

Italics are for Sephardi Minhag.

2000, May 6–June 3]   IYAR (29 DAYS)   [5760

Civil Date	Day of the Week	Jewish Date	SABBATHS, FESTIVALS, FASTS	PENTATEUCHAL READING	PROPHETICAL READING
May 6	Sa	Iyar 1	Ḳedoshim; New Moon, second day	Levit. 19:1–20:27 Num. 28:9–15	Isaiah 66:1–24
10	W	5	Israel Independence Day		
13	Sa	8	Emor	Levit. 21:1–24:23	Ezekiel 44:15–31
20	Sa	15	Be-har	Levit 25:1–26:2	Jeremiah 32:6–27
23	T	18	Lag Ba-'omer		
27	Sa	22	Be-ḥukḳotai	Levit. 26:3–27:34	Jeremiah 16:19–17:14
June 2	F	28	Jerusalem Day*		
3	Sa	29	Be-midbar	Num. 1:1–4:20	I Samuel 20:18–42

*Observed June 1, to avoid conflict with the Sabbath.

Italics are for Sephardi Minhag.

2000, June 4–July 3] SIWAN (30 DAYS) [5760

Civil Date	Day of the Week	Jewish Date	SABBATHS, FESTIVALS, FASTS	PENTATEUCHAL READING	PROPHETICAL READING
June 4	S	Siwan 1	New Moon	Num. 28:1–15	
9	F	6	Shavu'ot, first day	Exod. 19:1–20:23 Num. 28:26–31	Ezekiel 1:1–28, 3:12
10	Sa	7	Shavu'ot, second day	Deut. 15:19–16:17 Num. 28:26–31	Habbakuk 3:1–19 *Habbakuk 2:20–3:19*
17	Sa	14	Naso'	Num. 4:21–7:89	Judges 13:2–25
24	Sa	21	Be-ha'alotekha	Num. 8:1–12:16	Zechariah 2:14–4:7
July 1	Sa	28	Shelaḥ lekha	Num. 13:1–15:41	Joshua 2:1–24
3	M	30	New Moon, first day	Num. 28:1–15	

Italics are for Sephardi Minhag.

2000, July 4–Aug. 1]   TAMMUZ (29 DAYS)   [5760

Civil Date	Day of the Week	Jewish Date	SABBATHS, FESTIVALS, FASTS	PENTATEUCHAL READING	PROPHETICAL READING
July 4	T	Tammuz 1	New Moon, second day	Num. 28:1–15	
8	Sa	5	Ķoraḥ	Num. 16:1–18:32	I Samuel 11:14–12:22
15	Sa	12	Ḥuķķat, Balaķ	Num. 19:1–25:9	Micah 5:6–6:8
20	Th	17	Fast of 17th of Tammuz	Exod. 32:11–14 Exod. 34:1–10 (morning and afternoon)	Isaiah 55:6–56:8 (afternoon only)
22	Sa	19	Pineḥas	Num. 25:10–30:1	Jeremiah 1:1–2:3
29	Sa	26	Maṭṭot, Mas'e	Num. 30:2–36:13	Jeremiah 2:4–28 Jeremiah 3:4 *Jeremiah 2:4–28* *Jeremiah 4:1–2*

Italics are for
Sephardi Minhag.

2000, Aug. 2 – Aug. 31]   AV (30 DAYS)   [5760

Civil Date	Day of the Week	Jewish Date	SABBATHS, FESTIVALS, FASTS	PENTATEUCHAL READING	PROPHETICAL READING
Aug. 2	W	Av 1	New Moon	Num. 28:1–15	
5	Sa	4	Devarim (Shabbat Ḥazon)	Deut. 1:1–3:22	Isaiah 1:1–27
10	Th	9	Fast of 9th of Av	Morning: Deut. 4:25–40 Afternoon: Exod. 32:11–14 Exod. 34:1–10	(Lamentations is read the night before) Jeremiah 8:13–9:23 (morning) Isaiah 55:6–56:8 (afternoon)
12	Sa	11	Wa-etḥannan (Shabbat Naḥamu)	Deut. 3:23–7:11	Isaiah 40:1–26
19	Sa	18	'Eḳev	Deut. 7:12–11:25	Isaiah 49:14–51:3
26	Sa	25	Re'eh	Deut. 11:26–16:17	Isaiah 54:11–55:5
31	Th	30	New Moon, first day	Num. 28:1–15	

Italics are for Sephardi Minhag.

2000, Sept. 1 – Sept. 29]   ELUL (29 DAYS)   [5760

Civil Date	Day of the Week	Jewish Date	SABBATHS, FESTIVALS, FASTS	PENTATEUCHAL READING	PROPHETICAL READING
Sept. 1	F	Elul 1	New Moon, second day	Num. 28:1–15	
2	Sa	2	Shofeṭim	Deut. 16:18–21:9	Isaiah 51:12–52:12
9	Sa	9	Ki teẓe'	Deut. 21:10–25:19	Isaiah 54:1–10
16	Sa	16	Ki tavo'	Deut. 26:1–29:8	Isaiah 60:1–22
23	Sa	23	Niẓẓavim, Wa-yelekh	Deut. 29:9–30:20	Isaiah 61:10–63:9

*Italics are for
Sephardi Minhag.*

2000, Sept. 30–Oct. 29] TISHRI (30 DAYS) [5761

Civil Date	Day of the Week	Jewish Date	SABBATHS, FESTIVALS, FASTS	PENTATEUCHAL READING	PROPHETICAL READING
Sept. 30	Sa	Tishri 1	Rosh Ha-shanah, first day	Gen. 21:1–34 Num. 29:1–6	I Samuel 1:1–2:10
Oct. 1	S	2	Rosh Ha-shanah, second day	Gen. 22:1–24 Num. 29:1–6	Jeremiah 31:2–20
2	M	3	Fast of Gedaliah	Exod. 32:11–14 Exod. 34:1–10 (morning and afternoon)	Isaiah 55:6–56:8 (afternoon only)
7	Sa	8	Ha'azinu (Shabbat Shuvah)	Deut. 32:1–52	Hosea 14:2–10 Micah 7:18–20 Joel 2:15–27 *Hosea 14:2 10* *Micah 7:18–20*
9	M	10	Yom Kippur	Morning: Levit. 16:1–34 Num. 29:7–11 Afternoon: Levit. 18:1–30	Isaiah 57:14–58:14 Jonah: 1:1–4:11 Micah 7:18–20
14	Sa	15	Sukkot, first day	Levit. 22:26–23:44 Num. 29:12–16	Zechariah 14:1–21
15	S	16	Sukkot, second day	Levit. 22:26–23:44 Num. 29:12–16	I Kings 8:2–21
16–19	M–Th	17–20	Ḥol Ha-mo‘ed	M: Num. 29:17–25 T: Num. 29:20–28 W: Num. 29:23–31 Th: Num. 29:26–34	
20	F	21	Hosha‘na' Rabbah	Num. 29:26–34	
21	Sa	22	Shemini 'Azeret	Deut. 14:22 16:17 Num. 29:35–30:1	I Kings 8:54–66
22	S	23	Simḥat Torah	Deut. 33:1–34:12 Gen. 1:1–2:3 Num. 29:35–30:1	Joshua 1:1–18 *Joshua 1:1–9*
28	Sa	29	Be-re'shit	Gen. 1:1–6:8	I Samuel 20:18–42
29	S	30	New Moon, first day	Num. 28:1–15	

Italics are for
Sephardi Minhag.

2000, Oct. 30 – Nov. 27]   ḤESHWAN (29 DAYS)   [5761

Civil Date	Day of the Week	Jewish Date	SABBATHS, FESTIVALS, FASTS	PENTATEUCHAL READING	PROPHETICAL READING
Oct. 30	M	Heshwan 1	New Moon, second day	Num. 28:1 – 15	
Nov. 4	Sa	6	Noaḥ	Gen. 6:9 – 11:32	Isaiah 54:1 – 55:5 *Isaiah 54:1 – 10*
11	Sa	13	Lekh lekha	Gen. 12:1 – 17:27	Isaiah 40:27 – 41:16
18	Sa	20	Wa-yera'	Gen. 18:1 – 22:24	II Kings 4:1 – 37 *II Kings 4:1 – 23*
25	Sa	27	Ḥayye Sarah	Gen. 23:1 – 25:18	I Kings 1:1 – 31

*Italics are for
Sephardi Minhag.*

2000, Nov. 28 – Dec. 26]   KISLEW (29 DAYS)   [5761

Civil Date	Day of the Week	Jewish Date	SABBATHS, FESTIVALS, FASTS	PENTATEUCHAL READING	PROPHETICAL READING
Nov. 28	T	Kislew 1	New Moon	Num. 28:1–15	
Dec. 2	Sa	5	Toledot	Gen. 25:19–28:9	Malachi 1:1–2:7
9	Sa	12	Wa-yeẓe'	Gen. 28:10–32:3	Hosea 12:13–14:10 *Hosea 11:7–12:12*
16	Sa	19	Wa-yishlaḥ	Gen. 32:4–36:43	Hosea 11:7–12:12 *Obadiah 1:1–21*
22	F	25	Hanukkah, first day	Num. 7:1–17	
23	Sa	26	Wa-yeshev; Hanukkah, second day	Gen. 37:1–40:23 Num. 7:18–23	Zechariah 2:14–4:7
24–26	S–T	27–29	Hanukkah, third to fifth days	S Num. 7:24–35 M Num. 7:30–41 T Num. 7:36–47	

Italics are for Sephardi Minhag.

2000, Dec. 27–Jan. 24, 2001] ṬEVET (29 DAYS) [5761

Civil Date	Day of the Week	Jewish Date	SABBATHS, FESTIVALS, FASTS	PENTATEUCHAL READING	PROPHETICAL READING
Dec. 27	W	Ṭevet 1	New Moon; Hanukkah, sixth day	Num. 28:1–15 Num. 7:42–47	
28	Th	2	Hanukkah, seventh day	Num. 7:48–53	
29	F	3	Hanukkah, eighth day	Num. 7:54–8:4	
30	Sa	4	Mi-keẓ	Gen. 41:1–44:17	I Kings 3:15–4:1
2001 Jan. 5	F	10	Fast of 10th of Ṭevet	Exod. 32:11–14 Exod. 34:1–10 (morning and afternoon)	Isaiah 55:6–56:8 (afternoon only)
6	Sa	11	Wa-yiggash	Gen. 44:18–47:27	Ezekiel 37:15–28
13	Sa	18	Wa-yeḥi	Gen. 47:28–50:26	I Kings 2:1–12
20	Sa	25	Shemot	Exod. 1:1–6:1	Isaiah 27:6–28:13 Isaiah 29:22–23 *Jeremiah 1:1–2:3*

*Italics are for
Sephardi Minhag.*

2001, Jan. 25 – Feb. 23]   SHEVAṬ (30 DAYS)   [5761

Civil Date	Day of the Week	Jewish Date	SABBATHS, FESTIVALS, FASTS	PENTATEUCHAL READING	PROPHETICAL READING
Jan. 25	Th	Shevaṭ 1	New Moon	Num. 28: 1 – 15	
27	Sa	3	Wa-'era'	Exod. 6:2 – 9:35	Ezekiel 28:25 – 29:21
Feb. 3	Sa	10	Bo'	Exod. 10:1 – 13:16	Jeremiah 46:13 – 28
8	Th	15	Ḥamishah 'asar Bi-Shevaṭ		
10	Sa	17	Be-shallaḥ (Shabbat Shirah)	Exod. 13:17 – 17:16	Judges 4:4 – 5:31 *Judges 5:1 – 31*
17	Sa	24	Yitro	Exod. 18:1 – 20:23	Isaiah 6:1 – 7:6; 9:5 – 6 *Isaiah 6:1 – 13*
23	F	30	New Moon, first day	Num. 28:1 – 15	

Italics are for Sephardi Minhag.

2001, Feb. 24 – Mar. 24] ADAR (29 DAYS) [5761

Civil Date	Day of the Week	Jewish Date	SABBATHS, FESTIVALS, FASTS	PENTATEUCHAL READING	PROPHETICAL READING
Feb. 24	Sa	Adar 1	Mishpaṭim, New Moon, second day (Shabbat Sheḳalim)	Exod. 21:1–24:18 Num. 28:9–15 Exod. 30:11–16	II Kings 12:1–17 *II Kings 11:17–12:17*
Mar. 3	Sa	8	Terumah (Shabbat Zakhor)	Exod. 25:1–27:19 Deut. 25:17–19	I Samuel 15:2–34 *I Samuel 15:1–34*
8	Th	13	Fast of Esther	Exod. 32:11–14 Exod. 34:1–10 (morning and afternoon)	Isaiah 55:6–56:8 (afternoon only)
9	F	14	Purim	Exod. 17:8–16	Book of Esther (night before and in the morning)
10	Sa	15	Teẓawweh Shúshan Purim	Exod. 27:20–30:10	Ezekiel 43:10–27
17	Sa	22	Ki tissa' (Shabbat Parah)	Exod. 30:11–34:35 Num. 19:1–22	Ezekiel 36:16–38 *Ezekiel 36:16–36*
24	Sa	29	Wa-yaḳhel-Peḳude (Shabbat Ha-ḥodesh)	Exod. 35:1–40:38 Exod. 12:1–20	Ezekiel 45:16–46:18 *Ezekiel 45:18–46:15*

Italics are for Sephardi Minhag.

2001, Mar. 25 – Apr. 23]   NISAN (30 DAYS)   [5761

Civil Date	Day of the Week	Jewish Date	SABBATHS, FESTIVALS, FASTS	PENTATEUCHAL READING	PROPHETICAL READING
Mar. 25	S	Nisan 1	New Moon	Num. 28:1–15	
31	Sa	7	Wa-yikra'	Levit. 1:1–5:26	Isaiah 43:21–44:24
Apr. 5	Th	12	Fast of Firstborn		
7	Sa	14	Ẓaw (Shabbat Ha-gadol)	Levit. 6:1–8:36	Malachi 3:4–24
8	S	15	Passover, first day	Exod. 12:21–51 Num. 28:16–25	Joshua 5:2–6:1,27
9	M	16	Passover, second day	Levit. 22:26–23:44 Num. 28:16–25	II Kings 23:1–9, 21–25
10	T	17	Ḥol Ha–mo 'ed, first day	Exod. 13:1–16 Num. 28:19–25	
11	W	18	Ḥol Ha–mo'ed second day	Exod. 22:24–23:19, Num. 28:19–25	
12	Th	19	Ḥol Ha–mo'ed, third day	Exod. 34:1–26 Num. 28:19–25	
13	F	20	Ḥol Ha–mo'ed, fourth day	Num. 9:1–14 Num. 28:19–25	
14	Sa	21	Passover, seventh day	Exod. 13:17–15:26 Num. 28:19–25	II Samuel 22:1–51
15	S	22	Passover, eighth day	Deut. 15:19–16:17 Num. 28:19–25	Isaiah 10:32–12:6
20	F	27*	Holocaust Memorial Day		
21	Sa	28	Shemini	Levit. 9:1–11:47	II Samuel 6:1–7:17 *II Samuel 6:1–19*
23	M	30	New Moon, first day	Num. 28:1–15	

*Observed April 19, to avoid conflict with the Sabbath.

Italics are for Sephardi Minhag.

2001, Apr. 24–May 22] IYAR (29 DAYS) [5761

Civil Date	Day of the Week	Jewish Date	SABBATHS, FESTIVALS, FASTS	PENTATEUCHAL READING	PROPHETICAL READING
Apr. 24	T	Iyar 1	New Moon, second day	Num. 28:1–15	
28	Sa	5**	Tazria', Mezora'	Levit. 12:1–15:33	II Kings 7:3–20
May 5	Sa	12	Aḥare mot, Ḳedoshim	Levit.16:1–20:27	Amos 9:7–15 *Ezekiel 20:2–20*
11	F	18	Lag Ba-'omer		
12	Sa	19	Emor	Levit. 21:1–24:23	Ezekiel 44:15–31
19	Sa	26	Be-har, Be-ḥuḳḳotai	Levit. 25:1–27:34	Jeremiah 16:19–17:14
21	M	28	Jerusalem Day		

** Also Israel Independence Day, observed April 26 to avoid conflict with the Sabbath.

*Italics are for
Sephardi Minhag.*

2001 May 23–Jun. 21] SIWAN (30 DAYS) [5761

Civil Date	Day of the Week	Jewish Date	SABBATHS, FESTIVALS, FASTS	PENTATEUCHAL READING	PROPHETICAL READING
May 23	W	Siwan 1	New Moon	Num. 28:1–15	
26	Sa	4	Be-midbar	Num. 1:1–4:20	Hosea 2:1–22
28	M	6	Shavu'ot, first day	Exod. 19:1–20:23 Num. 28:26–31	Ezekiel 1:1–28; 3:12
29	T	7	Shavu'ot, second day	Deut. 15:19–16:17 Num. 28:26–31	Habbakuk 3:1–19 *Habbakuk 2:20–3:19*
June 2	Sa	11	Naso'	Num. 4:21–7:89	Judges 13:2–25
9	Sa	18	Be-ha'alotekha	Num. 8:1–12:16	Zechariah 2:14–4:7
16	Sa	25	Shelah lekha	Num. 13:1–15:41	Joshua 2:1–24
21	Th	30	New Moon, first day	Num. 28:1–15	

Italics are for Sephardi Minhag.

2001, June 22 – July 20]   TAMMUZ (29 Days)   [5761

Civil Date	Day of the Week	Jewish Date	SABBATHS, FESTIVALS, FASTS	PENTATEUCHAL READING	PROPHETICAL READING
June 22	F	Tammuz 1	New Moon, second day	Num. 28:1–15	
23	Sa	2	Ḳoraḥ	Num. 16:1–18:32	I Samuel 11:14–12:22
30	Sa	9	Ḥuḳḳat	Num. 19:1–22:1	Judges 11:1–33
July 7	Sa	16	Balaḳ	Num. 22:2–25:9	Micah 5:6–6:8
8	S	17	Fast of 17th of Tammuz	Exod. 32:11–14 Exod. 34:1–10 (morning and afternoon)	Isaiah 55:6–56:8 (afternoon only)
14	Sa	23	Pineḥas	Num. 25:10–30:1	Jeremiah 1:1–2:3

Italics are for
Sephardi Minhag.

2001, July 21–Aug. 19]   AV (30 DAYS)   [5761

Civil Date	Day of the Week	Jewish Date	SABBATHS, FESTIVALS, FASTS	PENTATEUCHAL READING	PROPHETICAL READING
July 21	Sa	Av 1	Maṭṭot, Masʿe New Moon	Num. 30:2–36:13 Num. 28:9–15	Jeremiah 2:4–28; 3:4 *Jeremiah 2:4–28; 4:1–2*
28	Sa	8	Devarim (Shabbat Hazon)	Deut. 1:1–3:22	Isaiah 1:1–27
29	S	9	Fast of 9th of Av	Morning: Deut. 4:25–40 Afternoon: Exod. 32:11–14 34:1–10	(Lamentations is read the night before) Jeremiah 8:13–9:23 (morning) Isaiah 55:6–56:8 (afternoon)
Aug. 4	Sa	15	Wa-etḥannan (Shabbat Naḥamu)	Deut. 3:23–7:11	Isaiah 40:1–26
11	Sa	22	ʿEḳev	Deut. 7:12–11:25	Isaiah 49:14–51:3
18	Sa	29	Reʾeh	Deut. 11:26–16:17	I Samuel 20:18–42
19	S	30	New Moon, first day	Num. 28:1–15	

Italics are for Sephardi Minhag.

2001, Aug. 20 – Sept. 17]   ELUL (29 DAYS)   [5761

Civil Date	Day of the Week	Jewish Date	SABBATHS, FESTIVALS, FASTS	PENTATEUCHAL READING	PROPHETICAL READING
Aug 20	M	Elul 1	New Moon, second day	Num. 28:1–15	
25	Sa	6	Shofeṭim	Deut. 16:18–21:9	Isaiah 51:12–52:12
Sept 1	Sa	13	Ki Teẓe'	Deut. 21:10–25:19	Isaiah 54:1–55:5
8	Sa	20	Ki Tavo'	Deut. 26:1–29:8	Isaiah 60:1–22
15	Sa	27	Niẓẓavim	Deut. 29:9–30:20	Isaiah 61:10–63:9

Italics are for
Sephardi Minhag.

2001, Sept. 18–Oct. 17] TISHRI (30 DAYS) [5762

Civil Date	Day of the Week	Jewish Date	SABBATHS, FESTIVALS, FASTS	PENTATEUCHAL READING	PROPHETICAL READING
Sept. 18	T	Tishri 1	Rosh Ha-shanah, first day	Gen. 21:1–34 Num. 29:1–6	1 Sam. 1:1–2:10
19	W	2	Rosh Ha-shanah second day	Gen. 22:1–24 Num. 29:1–6	Jeremiah 3:2–20
20	Th	3	Fast of Gedaliah	Exod. 32:11–14 34:1–10 (morning & afternoon)	Isaiah 55:6–56:8 (afternoon only)
22	Sa	5	Wa-yelekh (Shabbat Shuvah)	Deut. 31:1–30	Hosea 14:2–10 Micah 7:18–20 Joel 2:15–27 *Hosea 14:2 10* *Micah 7:18–20*
27	Th	10	Yom Kippur	Morning: Levit. 16:1–34 Num. 29:7–11 Afternoon: Levit. 18:1–30	Isaiah 57:14–58:14 Jonah 1:1–4:11 Micah 7:18–20
29	Sa	12	Ha'azinu	Deut. 32:1–52	II Samuel 22:1–51
Oct 2	T	15	Sukkot, first day	Levit. 22:26–23:44 Num. 29:12–16	Zechariah 14:1–21
3	W	16	Sukkot, second day	Levit. 22:26–23:44 Num. 29:12–16	I Kings 8:2–21
4–7	Th–S	17–20	Ḥol Ha-mo'ed	Th Num. 29:17–25 F Num. 29: 20–28 Sa Exod. 33:12–34:26, Num. 29:26–34 S Num. 29:26–34	Ezekiel 38:18–39:16
8	M	21	Hosha'na' Rabbah	Num. 29:26–34	
9	T	22	Shemini 'Azeret	Deut. 14:22–16:17 Num. 29:35–30:1	I Kings 8:54–66
10	W	23	Simḥat Torah	Deut. 33:1–34:12 Gen. 1:1–2:3 Num. 29:35–30:1	Joshua 1:1–18 *Joshua 1:1–9*
13	Sa	26	Be-re'shit	Gen. 1:1–6:8	Isaiah 42:5–43:10 *Isaiah 42:5–21*
17	W	30	New Moon first day	Num. 28:1–15	

Italics are for
Sephardi Minhag.

2001, Oct. 18 – Nov. 15]   ḤESHWAN (29 DAYS)   [5762

Civil Date	Day of the Week	Jewish Date	SABBATHS, FESTIVALS, FASTS	PENTATEUCHAL READING	PROPHETICAL READING
Oct. 18	Th	Ḥeshwan 1	New Moon, second day	Num. 28:1–15	
20	Sa	3	Noaḥ	Gen. 6:9–11:32	Isaiah 54:1–55:5 *Isaiah 54:1–10*
27	Sa	10	Lekh lekha	Gen. 12:1–17:27	Isaiah 40:27–41:16
Nov. 3	Sa	17	Wa-yera'	Gen. 18:1–22:24	II Kings 4:1–37 *II Kings 4:1–23*
10	Sa	24	Ḥayye Sarah	Gen. 23:1–25:18	I Kings 1:1–31

Italics are for
Sephardi Minhag.

2001, Nov. 16–Dec. 15]   KISLEW (30 DAYS)   [5762

Civil Date	Day of the Week	Jewish Date	SABBATHS, FESTIVALS, FASTS	PENTATEUCHAL READING	PROPHETICAL READING
Nov. 16	F	Kislew 1	New Moon	Num. 28:1–15	
17	Sa	2	Toledot	Gen. 25:19–28:9	Malachi 1:1–2:7
24	Sa	9	Wa-yeze'	Gen. 28:10–32:3	Hosea 12:13–14:10 *Hosea 11:7–12:12*
Dec. 1	Sa	16	Wa-yishlah	Gen. 32:4–36:43	Hosea 11:7–12:12 *Obadiah 1:1–21*
8	Sa	23	Wa-yeshev	Gen. 37:1–40:23	Amos 2:6–3:8
10–14	M–F	25–29	Ḥanukkah, first to fifth days	M Num. 7:1–17 T Num. 7:18–29 W Num. 7:24–35 Th Num. 7:30–41 F Num. 7:36–47	
15	Sa	30	Miḳeẓ; New Moon, first day; Ḥanukkah, sixth day	Gen. 41:1–44:17 Num. 28:9–15 Num. 7:42–47	Zechariah 2:14–4:7 *Zechariah 2:14–4:7* *Isaiah 66:1, 24* *Isaiah 20:18,42*

Italics are for
Sephardi Minhag.

2001, Dec. 16–Jan. 13, 2002]   ṬEVET (29 DAYS)   [5762

Civil Date	Day of the Week	Jewish Date	SABBATHS, FESTIVALS, FASTS	PENTATEUCHAL READING	PROPHETICAL READING
Dec. 16	S	Ṭevet 1	New Moon, second day; Ḥanukkah, seventh day	Num. 28:1–15 Num. 7:48–53	
17	M	2	Ḥanukkah, eighth day	Num. 7:54–8:4	
22	Sa	7	Wa-yiggash	Gen. 44:18–47:27	Ezekiel 37:15–28
25	T	10	Fast of 10th of Ṭevet	Exod. 32:11–14; 34:1–10 (morning and afternoon)	Isaiah 55:6–56:8 (afternoon only)
29	Sa	14	Wa-yeḥi	Gen. 47:28–50:26	I Kings 2:1–12
2002 Jan. 5	Sa	21	Shemot	Exod. 1:1–6:1	Isaiah 27:6–28:13; 29:22–23 *Jeremiah 1:1–2:3*
12	Sa	28	Wa-'era'	Exod. 6:2–9:35	Ezekiel 28:25–29:21

Italics are for Sephardi Minhag.

2002, Jan. 14–Feb. 12]   SHEVAṬ (30 DAYS)   [5762

Civil Date	Day of the Week	Jewish Date	SABBATHS, FESTIVALS, FASTS	PENTATEUCHAL READING	PROPHETICAL READING
Jan. 14	M	Shevaṭ 1	New Moon	Num. 28:1–15	
19	Sa	6	Bo'	Exod. 10:1–13:16	Jeremiah 46:13–28
26	Sa	13	Be-shallaḥ (Shabbat Shirah)	Exod. 13:17–17:16	Judges 4:4–5:31 *Judges 5:1–31*
28	M	15	Ḥamishah 'asar bi-Shevaṭ		
Feb. 2	Sa	20	Yitro	Exod. 18:1–20:23	Isaiah 6:1–7:6; 9:5–6 Isaiah 6: 1–13
9	Sa	27	Mishpaṭim (Shabbat Sheḳalim)	Exod. 21:1–24:18 Exod. 30:11–16	II Kings 12:1–17 *II Kings 11:17–12:17*
12	T	30	New Moon, first day	Num. 28: 1–15	

Italics are for Sephardi Minhag.

2002, Feb. 13–Mar. 13]   ADAR (29 DAYS)   [5762

Civil Date	Day of the Week	Jewish Date	SABBATHS, FESTIVALS, FASTS	PENTATEUCHAL READING	PROPHETICAL READING
Feb. 13	W	Adar 1	New Moon, second day	Num. 28:1–15	
16	Sa	4	Terumah	Exod. 25:1–27:19	I Kings 5:26–6:13
23	Sa	11	Teẓawweh (Shabbat Zakhor)	Exod. 27:20–30:10 Deut. 25:17–19	I Samuel 15:2–34 *I Samuel 15:1–34*
25	M	13	Fast of Esther	Exod. 32:11–14 Exod. 34:1–10 (morning and afternoon)	Isaiah 55:6–56:8 (afternoon only)
26	T	14	Purim	Exod. 17:8–16	Book of Esther (night before and in the morning)
27	W	15	Shushan Purim		
Mar. 2	Sa	18	Ki tissa' (Shabbat Parah)	Exod. 30:11–34:35 Num. 19: 1–22	Ezekiel 36:16–38 *Ezekiel 36:16–36*
9	Sa	25	Wa-yaḵhel, Peḵude (Shabbat Ha-ḥodesh)	Exod. 35:1–40:38 Exod. 12:1–20	Ezekiel 45:16–46:18 *Ezekiel 45:18–46:15*

Italics are for Sephardi Minhag.

2002, Mar. 14–Apr. 12]   NISAN (30 DAYS)   [5762

Civil Date	Day of the Week	Jewish Date	SABBATHS, FESTIVALS, FASTS	PENTATEUCHAL READING	PROPHETICAL READING
Mar. 14	Th	Nisan 1	New Moon	Num. 28:1–15	
16	Sa	3	Wa—yiḳra'	Levit. 1:1–5: 26	Isaiah 43:21–44:24
23	Sa	10	Ẓaw (Shabbat Ha-gadol)	Levit. 6:1–8: 36	Malachi 3:4–24
27	W	14	Fast of Firstborn		
28	Th	15	Passover, first day	Exod. 12:21–51 Num. 28:16–25	Joshua 5:2–6:1, 27
29	F	16	Passover, second day	Levit. 22:26–23:44 Num. 28:16–25	II Kings 23:1–9, 21–25
30	Sa	17	Ḥol Ha-mo'ed, first day	Exod. 33:12–34:26 Num. 28:16–25	Ezekiel 37:1–14
31	S	18	Ḥol Ha-mo'ed, second day	Exod. 33:12–34:26 Num. 28:19–25	
Apr. 1	M	19	Ḥol Ha-mo'ed, third day	Exod. 22:24–23:19 Num. 28:19–25	
2	T	20	Ḥol Ha-mo'ed, fourth day	Num. 28: 19–25	
3	W	21	Passover, seventh day	Exod. 13:17–15:26 Num. 28:19–25	II Samuel 22:1—51
4	Th	22	Passover, eight day	Deut. 15:1–16:17 Num. 28:19 –25	Isaiah 10:32–12:6
6	Sa	24	Shemini	Levit. 9:1–11:47	II Samuel 6:1 –7:17 *II Samuel 6:1–19*
9	T	27	Holocaust Memorial Day		
12	F	30	New Moon, first day	Num. 28:1–15	

Italics are for Sephardi Minhag.

2002, Apr. 13–May 11]   IYAR (29 DAYS)   [5762

Civil Date	Day of the Week	Jewish Date	SABBATHS, FESTIVALS, FASTS	PENTATEUCHAL READING	PROPHETICAL READING
Apr. 13	Sa	Iyar 1	Tazria', Mezora'; New Moon, second day	Levit. 12:1–15:33 Num. 28:9–15	Isaiah 66:1–24
17	W	5	Israel Independence Day		
20	Sa	8	Ahare mot, Kedoshim	Levit. 16:1–20:27	Amos 9:7–15 *Ezekiel 20:2–20*
27	Sa	15	Emor	Levit. 21:1–24:23	Ezekiel 44:15–31
30	T	18	Lag Ba-'omer		
May 4	Sa	22	Be-har, Be-hukkotai	Levit. 25:1–27:34	Jeremiah 16:19–17:14
10	F	28	Jerusalem Day*		
11	Sa	29	Be-midbar	Num 1:1–4:20	I Samuel 20:18–42

*Observed May 9, to avoid conflict with the Sabbath.

Italics are for Sephardi Minhag.

2002, May 12– June 10] SIWAN (30 DAYS) [5762

Civil Date	Day of the Week	Jewish Date	SABBATHS, FESTIVALS, FASTS	PENTATEUCHAL READING	PROPHETICAL READING
May 12	S	Siwan 1	New Moon	Num. 28:1–15	
17	F	6	Shavu'ot, first day	Exod. 19:1–20:23 Num. 28:26–31	Ezekiel 1:1–28, Ezekiel 3:12
18	Sa	7	Shavu'ot, second day	Deut. 15:19–16: 17 Num. 28:26–31	Habbakuk 3:1–19 *Habbakuk 2:20–3:19*
25	Sa	14	Naso'	Num. 4:21–7:89	Judges 13:2–25
June 1	Sa	21	Be-ha'alotekha	Num. 8:1–12:16	Zechariah 2:14–4: 7
8	Sa	28	Shelaḥ lekha	Num. 13:1–15:41	Joshua 2:1–24
10	M	30	New Moon, first day	Num. 28:1–15	

Italics are for Sephardi Minhag.

2002, June 11–July 9]   TAMMUZ (29 DAYS)   [5762

Civil Date	Day of the Week	Jewish Date	SABBATHS, FESTIVALS, FASTS	PENTATEUCHAL READING	PROPHETICAL READING
Jun 11	T	Tammuz 1	New Moon, second day	Num. 28:1–15	
15	Sa	5	Ķoraḥ	Num. 16:1–18:32	I Samuel 11:14–12:22
22	Sa	12	Ḥuķķat, Balaķ	Num. 19:1–25:9	Micah 5:6–6:8
27	Th	17	Fast of 17th of Tammuz	Exod. 32:11–14 Exod. 34: 1–10 (morning and afternoon)	Isaiah 55:6–56:8 (afternoon only)
29	Sa	19	Pineḥas	Num. 25:10–30:1	Jeremiah 1:1–2:3
July 6	Sa	26	Maṭṭot Mas‘e	Num. 30:2–36:13	Jeremiah 2:4–28 Jeremiah 3:4 *Jeremiah 2:4–28* *Jeremiah 4:1–2*

Italics are for
Sephardi Minhag.

2002, July 10–Aug. 8]   AV (30 DAYS)   [5762

Civil Date	Day of the Week	Jewish Date	SABBATHS, FESTIVALS, FASTS	PENTATEUCHAL READING	PROPHETICAL READING
July 10	W	Av 1	New Moon	Num. 28:1–15	
13	Sa	4	Devarim (Shabbat Ḥazon)	Deut. 1:1–3:22	Isaiah 1:1–27
18	Th	9	Fast of 9th of Av	Morning: Deut. 4:25–40 Afternoon: Exod. 32:1–14 Exod. 34:1–10	(Lamentations is read the night before) Jeremiah 8:13–9:23 (morning) Isaiah 55:6–56:8 (afternoon)
20	Sa	11	Wa-etḥannan (Shabbat Nahamu)	Deut. 3:23–7:11	Isaiah 40:1–26
27	Sa	18	'Eḳev	Deut. 7:12–11:25	Isaiah 49:14–51:3
Aug. 3	Sa	25	Re'eh	Deut. 11:26–16:17	Isaiah 54:11–55:5
8	Th	30	New Moon, first day	Numbers 28:1– 15	

Italics are for
Sephardi Minhag.

2002, Aug. 9–Sept. 6] ELUL (29 DAYS) [5762

Civil Date	Day of the Week	Jewish Date	SABBATHS, FESTIVALS, FASTS	PENTATEUCHAL READING	PROPHETICAL READING
Aug. 9	F	Elul 1	New Moon, second day	Num. 28:1–15	
10	Sa	2	Shofeṭim	Deut. 16:18–21:9	Isaiah 51:12–52:12
17	Sa	9	Ki teze'	Deut. 21:10–25:19	Isaiah 54:1–10
24	Sa	16	Ki tavo'	Deut. 26: 1–29:8	Isaiah 60:1–22
31	Sa	23	Niẓẓavim, Wa-yelekh	Deut. 29:9–31:30	Isaiah 61:10–63:9

Italics are for
Sephardi Minhag.

2002, Sept. 7–Oct. 6]　　　TISHRI (30 DAYS)　　　[5763

Civil Date	Day of the Week	Jewish Date	SABBATHS, FESTIVALS, FASTS	PENTATEUCHAL READING	PROPHETICAL READING
Sept. 7	Sa	Tishri 1	Rosh Ha-shanah, first day	Gen. 21:1–34 Num. 29:1–6	I Samuel 1:1–2:10
8	S	2	Rosh Ha-shana, second day	Gen. 22:1–24 Num. 29:1–6	Jeremiah 31:2–20
9	M	3	Fast of Gedaliah	Exod. 32:11–14 Exod. 34:1–10 (morning and afternoon)	Isaiah 55: 6–56:8 (afternoon only)
14	Sa	8	Ha'azinu (Shabbat Shuvah)	Deut. 32:1–52	Hosea 14:2–10 Micah 7:18–20 Joel 2:15–27 *Hosea 14:2–10* *Micah 7:18–20*
16	M	10	Yom Kippur	Morning: Levit. 16:1–34 Num. 29:7–11 Afternoon: Levit. 18:1–30	Isaiah 57:14–58:14 Jonah 1:1–4:11 Micah 7:18–20
21	Sa	15	Sukkot, first day	Levit. 22:26–23:44 Num. 29:12–16	Zechariah 14:1–21
22	S	16	Sukkot, second day	Levit. 22:26–23:44 Num. 29:12–16	I Kings 8:2–21
23–26	M-Th	17-20	Ḥol Ha'mo'ed	M: Num. 29:17–25 T: Num. 29:20–28 W: Num. 29:23–31 Th: Num. 29:26–34	
27	F	21	Hosha'na' Rabbah	Num. 29:26–34	
28	Sa	22	Shemini 'Aẓeret	Deut. 14:22–16:17 Num. 29:35–30:1	I Kings 8:54–66
29	S	23	Simḥat Torah	Deut. 33:1–34:12 Gen. 1:1–2:3 Num. 29:35–30:1	Joshua 1:1–18 *Joshua 1:1–9*
Oct. 5	Sa	29	Be-re'shit	Gen. 1:1–6:8	I Samuel 20:18–42
6	S	30	New Moon, first day	Num. 28: 1–15	

Italics are for Sephardi Minhag.

2002, Oct. 7–Nov. 5]   ḤESHWAN(30 DAYS)   [5763

Civil Date	Day of the Week	Jewish Date	SABBATHS, FESTIVALS, FASTS	PENTATEUCHAL READING	PROPHETICAL READING
Oct. 7	M	Ḥeshwan 1	New Moon, second day	Num. 28:1–15	
12	Sa	6	Noaḥ	Gen. 6:9–11:32	Isaiah 54:1–55:5 *Isaiah 54:1–10*
19	Sa	13	Lekh lekha	Gen. 12:1–17:27	Isaiah 40:27–41:16
26	Sa	20	Wa-yera'	Gen. 18:11–22:24	II Kings 4:1–37 *II Kings 4:1–23*
Nov. 2	Sa	27	Ḥayye Sarah	Gen. 23:1–25:18	I Kings 1:1–31
5	T	30	New Moon, first day	Num. 28:1–15	

Italics are for
Sephardi Minhag.

2002, Nov. 6–Dec. 5] KISLEW(30 DAYS) [5763

Civil Date	Day of the Week	Jewish Date	SABBATHS, FESTIVALS, FASTS	PENTATEUCHAL READING	PROPHETICAL READING
Nov. 6	W	Kislew 1	New Moon, second day	Num. 28:1–15	
9	Sa	4	Toledot	Gen. 25:19–28:9	Malachi 1:1–2:7
16	Sa	11	Wa-yeze'	Gen. 28:10–32:3	Hosea 12:13–14:10 *Hosea 11:7–12:12*
23	Sa	18	Wa-yishlah	Gen. 32:4–36:43	Hosea 11:7–12:12 *Obadiah 1:1–21*
30	Sa	25	Wa-yeshev; Hanukkah, first day	Gen. 37:1–40:23 Num. 7:1–17	Zechariah 2:14–4:7
Dec. 1-4	S–W	26–29	Hanukkah, second to fifth days	S Num. 7:18–29 M Num. 7:24–35 T Num. 7:30–41 W Num. 7:36–41	
5	Th	30	New Moon, first day; Hanukkah, sixth day	Num. 28:1–15 Num. 7:42–47	

*Italics are for
Sephardi Minhag.*

2002, Dec. 6–Jan. 3, 2003]   ṬEVET(29 DAYS)   [5763

Civil Date	Day of the Week	Jewish Date	SABBATHS, FESTIVALS, FASTS	PENTATEUCHAL READING	PROPHETICAL READING
Dec. 6	F	Ṭevet 1	New Moon, second day; Ḥanukkah, seventh day	Num. 28:1–15 Num. 7:48–59	
7	Sa	2	Mi-ḳeẓ; Ḥanukkah, eight day	Gen. 41:1–44:17 Num. 7:54–8:4	I Kings 7:40–50
14	Sa	9	Wa-yiggash	Gen. 44:18–47:27	Ezekiel 37:15–28
15	S	10	Fast of 10th of Ṭevet	Exod. 32:11–14 Exod. 34:1–10 (morning and afternoon)	Isaiah 55:6–56:8 (afternoon only)
21	Sa	16	Wa-yeḥi	Gen. 47:28–50:26	I Kings 2:1–12
28	Sa	23	Shemot	Exod. 1:1–6:1	Isaiah 27:6–28:13 Isaiah 29:22–23 *Jeremiah 1:1–2:3*

Italics are for Sephardi Minhag.

Index